Further Mathematics
for the IB Diploma
Standard Level

CAMBRIDGE
UNIVERSITY PRESS

CAMBRIDGE UNIVERSITY PRESS
Cambridge, New York, Melbourne, Madrid, Cape Town, Singapore, São Paulo, Delhi

Cambridge University Press
The Edinburgh Building, Cambridge CB2 8RU, UK

www.cambridge.org
Information on this title: www.cambridge.org/9780521714662

First published 2008

A catalogue record for this publication is available from the British Library

ISBN   978-0-521-71466-2 paperback

The authors and the publishers are grateful to the following examination boards for permission to reproduce
questions from past examination papers, identified in the text as follows.
OCR   Oxford, Cambridge and RSA Examinations
IBO   International Baccalaureate Organization
The authors, and not the examination boards, are responsible for the method and accuracy of the answers
to examination questions given; these may not necessarily constitute the only possible solutions.

This material has been developed independently of the International Baccalaureate Organization (IBO).
This text is in no way connected with, nor endorsed by, the IBO.

Contents

Topic 1 – Geometry

Topic 2 – Statistics and probability

Topic 3 – Sets, relations and groups

Topic 4 – Series and differential equations

Topic 5 – Discrete mathematics

Topic 1
Geometry

Hugh Neill and Douglas Quadling

Series Editor Hugh Neill

 CAMBRIDGE
UNIVERSITY PRESS

Contents

Introduction   v

1   Preliminaries   1

2   Some properties of triangles   15

3   Triangles and circles   27

4   Concyclic points   39

5   The orthocentre of a triangle   49

6   Internal and external bisectors   58

7   The theorems of Ceva and Menelaus   69

8   Analytical methods   87

9   Finding loci by analytical methods   96

10   More properties of circles   107

11   Vector methods   116

Review exercise   129

Answers   132

Index   136

Introduction

Geometry has been written especially for the International Baccalaureate Further Mathematics SL examination. This section covers the syllabus for Topic 1.

Each topic is developed initially using purely geometrical arguments, but towards the end of the book there are chapters which demonstrate how coordinates or vectors can be used to provide alternative approaches to some topics. It is assumed that students are familiar with basic ideas of Euclidean geometry such as congruence and properties of special triangles and quadrilaterals, and also with straight line coordinate geometry and right-angle trigonometry. Knowledge of the contents of the chapters in Mathematics Higher Level Books 1 and 2 dealing with trigonometry (including identities and the sine and cosine rules) and vectors (including scalar and vector products) is also assumed.

There is a small amount of material which extends a topic beyond the syllabus as printed, with the aim of enhancing students' appreciation of the subject. This is indicated by an asterisk (*) at the appropriate place in the text.

Occasionally within the text paragraphs appear in *this type style*. These paragraphs are usually outside the main stream of the mathematical argument, but may help to give insight, or suggest extra work or different approaches.

There are plenty of exercises throughout. At the end of the book there is a Review exercise which includes some questions from past International Baccalaureate examinations, but on a different syllabus. At the time of writing there is no backlog of examination questions on the current syllabus.

The authors thank IBO for permission to use some examination questions and Cambridge University Press for their help in producing this book. Particular thanks are due to Sharon Dunkley, for her help and advice. However, the responsibility for the text, and for any errors, remains with the authors.

1 Preliminaries

This chapter reviews some basic geometric ideas. When you have completed it, you should

- understand what is meant by a theorem and its converse, and be familiar with various methods of proof
- know what is meant by a locus, and how to construct figures by using the intersection of two loci
- be able to carry out proportion calculations and apply them to geometrical figures
- know the basic properties of circles and the associated vocabulary.

1.1 Points and lines

The study of geometry began because people wanted to understand and control the physical environment. To do this, mathematicians simplified their observations, describing objects such as planets as single points and stretched ropes as straight lines, so as to create a **mathematical model** of their surroundings.

In this way a number of different kinds of geometry were created. This course is about **plane geometry**, in which everything is supposed to take place on a flat surface, taking no account of the fact that the earth is curved. You could also study 'solid geometry', which deals with objects in three-dimensional space, or 'spherical geometry', in which the objects all lie on the surface of a sphere. More recently mathematicians have invented other, more theoretical kinds of geometry such as non-Euclidean, projective and finite geometries, some of which have enlarged our understanding of the physical environment or have useful applications in other branches of mathematics.

The two most important objects in plane geometry are **points** and **straight lines** (often simply called 'lines'). You will be used to denoting points by capital letters A, B, C, ... ; it is sometimes helpful to use single letters to denote lines, in which case small letters l, m, n, ... will be used.

Fig. 1.1 is a geometrical construction made up entirely of points and lines. It begins with two lines, labelled l and m. There are three points on each line, labelled A, B, C and D, E, F respectively. There are then lines joining B to F and C to E, which meet at a point X; lines joining C to D and A to F, meeting at Y; and lines joining A to E and B to D, meeting at Z. Do you notice anything interesting about the points X, Y and Z?

Make a construction like Fig. 1.1 for yourself. You can use anything straight to draw the lines, such as the edge of a ruler, a set square or a book. Do the points X, Y and Z on your figure have the same property as you noticed in Fig. 1.1?

You probably noticed that the points X, Y and Z all lie on the same straight line. If you set your straight edge against the points X and Y, you should find that it also lies against Z. This property is described by saying that the points X, Y, Z are **collinear**.

The fact that X, Y, Z in Fig. 1.1 are collinear is called the 'Pappus property'.

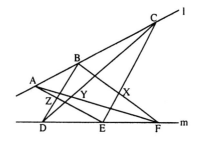

Fig. 1.1

Pappus didn't only describe his property, or justify it from a drawing as in Fig. 1.1. He also showed how it could be deduced logically from simpler properties which were already known. (It is surprisingly difficult!) So he gave a **proof** of the property. The statement of the property and its proof make it into a **theorem**. It is always known as 'Pappus's theorem'.

In Fig. 1.1 it is only necessary to use the straight edge to draw the part of each line between the two points. This is called the **line segment** joining the points. It is denoted by putting the letters for the two points in square brackets. For example, in Fig. 1.1 the line segment joining C to E is denoted by [CE].

But now go back to your own drawing, and change the order of the points on the line m from D, E, F to F, E, D. If you carry out the construction again, you will find that none of the pairs of line segments defining the points X, Y, Z meet each other. To get intersections you will need to extend each line segment in one direction or the other; the line segment is then said to be 'produced' in that direction. When you do this, are the points X, Y, Z still collinear?

When you state a geometrical property, you want to describe it in such a way that it applies however the figure is drawn. In this example, it is therefore better to say that X is the point where the complete lines (lines produced in both directions) through B and F, C and E meet – not just the line segments. The notation for this is to put the letters for the two points in round brackets. For example, the complete line through C and E is denoted by (CE).

All this can now be put together to give a statement of Pappus's theorem:

> **Pappus's theorem**   Two lines l, m lie in a plane. A, B, C are three points on l, and D, E, F are three points on m. The lines (BF) and (CE) meet at X, (CD) and (AF) meet at Y, (AE) and (BD) meet at Z. Then X, Y, Z are collinear.

In statements like this, 'two lines l, m' means any two lines, and 'A, B, C are three points' means any three points, unless something more is said about them. For example, the lines may or may not be parallel, and A, B, C may be placed in any order on the line. But it is usually understood that l, m are two different lines, and A, B, C are three different points. And the pairs of lines such as (BF) and (CE) can't be parallel, since if they were they wouldn't meet, so the point X would not exist.

You may be surprised at the way in which the points X, Y, Z are labelled, but there is a good reason for this. The definition of the point X depends on the points B, C, E, F but not A or D. Since A and D are the first points of the triples A, B, C and D, E, F, you label this point as the first of the triple X, Y, Z. (This is rather like the convention for labelling the lengths of the sides of a triangle ABC, where the length of the side [BC] is denoted by a.)

1.2   Introducing lengths and angles

You will have noticed that Pappus's theorem says nothing about lengths or angles. The construction in Fig. 1.1 involves only joining pairs of points with lines, and finding the points in which pairs of lines intersect. Properties like this are called 'incidence properties', and you will meet some more in Chapter 7.

But many geometrical properties do involve the length of lines or the size of angles. One that you will certainly know is the Pythagoras property, that in a right-angled triangle the square of the length of the hypotenuse is equal to the sum of the squares of the lengths of the other two sides.

To make a statement of the property it is useful to introduce some more notation. If A and B are two points, then the symbol AB (with no brackets round it) is used to denote the length of the line segment [AB]. And if A, B, C are three points, then $B\hat{A}C$ denotes the angle bechords (Notice that the middle letter A indicates the point common to the two line segments.) You can then write:

> **Pythagoras's theorem**   In a triangle ABC, if $B\hat{A}C$ is a right angle, then
>
> $$AB^2 + AC^2 = BC^2.$$

Notice the form of this statement. 'In a triangle ABC' could mean 'in *any* triangle', but 'if ..., then ...' indicates that the theorem only tells you something if the triangle is right-angled.

1.3 Converses

By looking at ancient structures, such as pyramids and temples, it is obvious that the builders knew how to mark out right angles. It is known that one of the methods they used was to make a rope triangle with sides of length 3 units, 4 units and 5 units; the angle between the two shortest sides is then a right angle. (In practice there will be a small error, because the mathematical model does not exactly correspond to physical reality.)

The reason for this is that $3^2 + 4^2 = 9 + 16 = 25 = 5^2$, so that if $AB = 3$, $AC = 4$ and $BC = 5$, then $AB^2 + AC^2 = BC^2$. It follows that angle $B\hat{A}C$ is a right angle. People often say that this is 'because of Pythagoras's theorem', but this is not correct. The property used here is that

if $AB^2 + AC^2 = BC^2$, then $B\hat{A}C$ is a right angle.

And if you compare this with the statement of Pythagoras's theorem given above, you will see that the 'if' and the 'then' statements have been reversed. This produces a new property which is called the **converse** of the original property.

In fact the converse of Pythagoras's theorem is true, so that the conclusion that $B\hat{A}C$ is a right angle is correct. A proof of this can be constructed, based on two theorems which are taken as known:

1   Pythagoras's theorem as stated in Section 1.2.
2   The 'three sides' condition for two triangles to be congruent: that, for two triangles XYZ and ABC, if $XY = AB$, $XZ = AC$ and $YZ = BC$, then $Y\hat{X}Z = B\hat{A}C$.

It is important to be clear what you are taking as given, and what you are aiming to prove. In this theorem you are *given* a triangle ABC with $AB^2 + AC^2 = BC^2$, and you have to *prove* that $B\hat{A}C$ is a right angle.

The method of proof is to construct a second triangle XYZ alongside triangle ABC which has $XY = AB$, $XZ = AC$ and the angle $Y\hat{X}Z$ a right angle. This is shown in Fig. 1.2. Marks have been placed on the sides XY, AB, XZ and AC of the triangles and on the angle $Y\hat{X}Z$ to remind you what you know about the figure; the fact there are no marks on other parts of the figure also reminds you what you *don't* know.

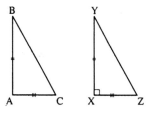

Fig. 1.2

The strategy is to show, from this construction and what is given, that the other sides BC and YZ in the two triangles are equal, and that therefore the triangles are congruent. It will then follow that $\hat{BAC} = \hat{YXZ}$, so that $\hat{BAC}$ is a right angle. This argument can now be set out formally, with reasons given in brackets beside the important steps.

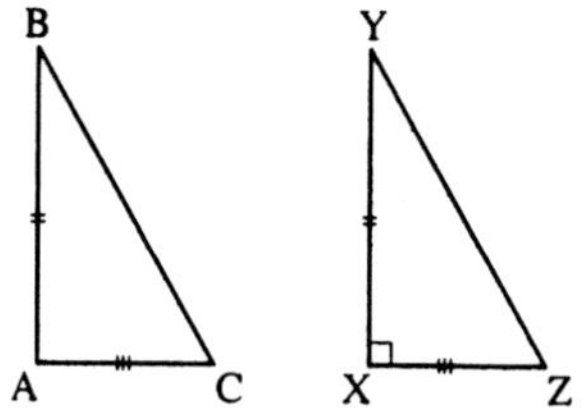

Proof

Since $\hat{YXZ}$ is a right angle,

$$XY^2 + XZ^2 = YZ^2.$$ (Pythagoras's theorem)

Therefore, since $XY = AB$ and $XZ = AC$ (by the construction),

$$YZ^2 = AB^2 + AC^2.$$

But you are given that $AB^2 + AC^2 = BC^2$. So $YZ^2 = BC^2$, and therefore

$$YZ = BC.$$

Therefore, since $XY = AB$, $XZ = AC$ and $YZ = BC$,

$$\hat{YXZ} = \hat{BAC}.$$ (congruent triangles theorem, 3 sides equal)

But $\hat{YXZ}$ is a right angle.   (construction)

Therefore $\hat{BAC}$ is a right angle.

Fig. 1.2

This completes the proof, and establishes the converse property as a theorem:

Converse of Pythagoras's theorem   In a triangle ABC, if $AB^2 + AC^2 = BC^2$, then $\hat{BAC}$ is a right angle.

1.4 Methods of proof

The kind of proof used in the last section goes back to Euclid, whose famous book, the *Elements*, established it as the standard form of geometrical argument. Proofs like this are described as **Euclidean**, even when the actual properties being proved were not known until long after his time.

Euclidean methods are not the only ways of proving geometrical properties. Another method is to associate points of the plane with coordinates (x, y), and to express the properties in the form of algebraic equations. The word **analytical** is used to describe this kind of proof.

A third, more modern method is to use vectors. For some properties vector algebra provides a very powerful and economical form of argument.

In this book Euclidean proofs are given of all the theorems, but alternative proofs of some of them by analytical or vector methods are given in Chapters 8 to 11. There are cross-references which will enable you to compare proofs by different methods.

Yet another method of proving geometrical properties (not covered in this book) is to use complex numbers. Each complex number can be associated with a point in the Argand diagram, and many geometrical properties correspond to an algebraic relationship between complex numbers.

1.5   The idea of a locus

'If a point has a certain property, what can we say about its position?' Questions of this type often occur when you solve geometrical problems.

For example, you might have a figure which includes two points A and B whose positions are known, as in Fig. 1.3. You are then told that there is another point P which is the same distance from A as B is from A; that is, AP = AB. What can you say about the position of P?

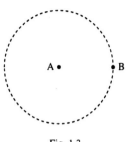

Obviously this information is not enough to be able to locate P precisely. On the other hand, P cannot be everywhere in the plane; the given information restricts the possible positions of the point. In this example P has to lie on a circle with centre A and radius equal to AB; this is the circle drawn with a dotted line in Fig. 1.3.

Fig. 1.3

The geometrical word for this is 'locus'. But you already have a more general word for it in mathematics, which is 'set'.

> The **locus** of a point with a given geometrical property is the set of points which have the property.

So you can say

'the locus of points P such that AP = AB is the circle with centre A and radius AB'

or

'the set of points P such that AP = AB is the circle with centre A and radius AB'.

Both have exactly the same meaning. (The Latin word *locus* means 'place'. Its plural is *loci*, and this is also used in English.)

In this example it is possible that there is some reason why P cannot coincide with B. In that case you would have to modify the statement, and say that 'the locus of points P (other than B) such that AP = AB is the circle with centre A and radius AB excluding the point B'.

Example 1.5.1
You are given a line l and a point A which is not on l. Find the locus of points whose perpendicular distance from l is equal to the distance of A from l.

Draw a line through A parallel to l. Any point P on this line has the same perpendicular distance from l as A.

But this is not the complete locus. There are also points with the given property below l. If A is reflected in l to give a point B, then the distances of A and B from l are the same. So any point on the line through B parallel to l also has the same perpendicular distance from l as A.

Apart from these two lines there are no other points with the given property.

The locus is therefore a pair of lines (shown dotted in the figure) parallel to l through A and B.

Example 1.5.1 makes an important point about loci. The locus of points which have a certain property has to contain all the points which have the property, but no points which don't have the property. So, if a particular geometrical property is denoted by π, the statement that

'the locus of points with the property π is $\mathcal{L}$'

means both that

- if P has the property π, then P belongs to $\mathcal{L}$, and
- if P belongs to $\mathcal{L}$, then P has the property π.

So to prove a locus statement, you have to prove a theorem and its converse.

This is similar to proving that two sets are equal, as in Sets, Relations and Groups, Section 1.6.

Example 1.5.2
A and B are two points. Find the locus of points P such that PA = PB.

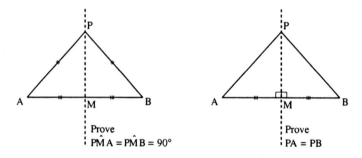

You will easily guess that the locus is the perpendicular bisector of [AB]: that is, the line through the mid-point M of [AB] which is perpendicular to [AB]. So you have to prove that

- if PA = PB, then [PM] is perpendicular to [AB] (that is, $\stackrel{\wedge}{\text{PMA}} = \stackrel{\wedge}{\text{PMB}} = 90°$), and
- if [PM] is perpendicular to [AB], then PA = PB.

Both of these are easy to prove by showing that the triangles PMA and PMB are congruent. The markings on the two figures indicate what you are given for each of the two theorems. For the first result you know that the three pairs of corresponding sides are equal; for the second two pairs of corresponding sides are equal, and the angles included between them are equal.

The two theorems together establish that the locus of points P such that PA = PB is the perpendicular bisector of [AB].

Notice where both the 'theorem' and the 'converse' are used in this argument.

The idea of a locus is the basis of many geometrical constructions. For example, suppose that you want to draw a triangle ABC with BC = 7 cm, CA = 4 cm and AB = 6 cm. You begin by marking two points B, C on the paper 7 cm apart. The problem is now to locate the point A. You know that this has to be 6 cm from B, and the locus of points which are 6 cm from B is a circle with centre B and radius 6 cm. It also has to be 4 cm from C, and the locus of points which are 4 cm from C is a circle with centre C and radius 4 cm. The required point A has to have both these properties, so A can only be at one of the two points where these circles intersect.

Example 1.5.3
A point A is 1 cm from a line l. Find all the points which are 2 cm from l and 3 cm from A.

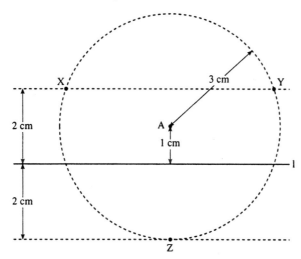

The locus of points which are 2 cm from l is a pair of lines parallel to l. The locus of points which are 3 cm from A is a circle with centre A and radius 3 cm. You can see from the figure that there are three points, marked X, Y and Z, which are common to both loci.

All the loci in this section have been made up of lines or circles, but locus problems often lead to new kinds of geometrical figures. For example, if you are given a point A and a line l, the locus of points whose distances from A and l are equal is the curve drawn in Fig. 1.4. It is called a 'parabola'.

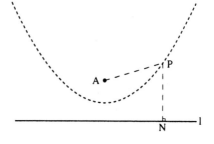

Fig. 1.4

1.6   Proportional division of a line segment

Geometrical properties often involve the idea of proportion. You may, for example, have three points A, P and B on a straight line as in Fig. 1.5, and be told that 'P divides the line segment [AB] in the proportion (or 'ratio') $m:n$'. This means that, measured in some unit, the length AP is m units, and the

length PB is n units. You can also write this as an equation involving fractions, $\dfrac{AP}{PB} = \dfrac{m}{n}$.

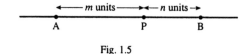

Fig. 1.5

If AP = m units and PB = n units, then AB = $(m + n)$ units, so that you can also write

$$\frac{AP}{AB} = \frac{m}{m+n} \quad \text{and} \quad \frac{PB}{AB} = \frac{n}{m+n}.$$

The numbers m and n are often integers with no common factor, but they may also be surds, with proportions such as $1:\sqrt{2}$. But you would not usually write a proportion such as 6:9 (since 6 and 9 have a common factor 3, so the proportion is better written as 2:3), or with fractions such as $\frac{2}{3}:\frac{1}{4}$ (since $\frac{2}{3} = \frac{8}{12}$ and $\frac{1}{4} = \frac{3}{12}$, so the proportion would be better written as 8:3).

If $m = n = 1$, P is the mid-point of [AB]; if $m = 1$ and $n = 2$, or $m = 2$ and $n = 1$, P is said to be a **point of trisection** of [AB].

Example 1.6.1

If AB = 20 cm and P divides [AB] in the proportion 7:3, find the distance AP.

$$AP = \frac{m}{m+n} AB = \frac{7}{10} \times 20 \text{ cm} = 14 \text{ cm.}$$

If you extend the line segment [AB] to the whole line (AB), there is another point Q such that $\dfrac{AQ}{QB} = \dfrac{m}{n}$

(unless $m = n$). In Fig. 1.6, for which $m > n$, AQ = m units, QB = n units and AB = $(m - n)$ units, so

that $\dfrac{AQ}{AB} = \dfrac{m}{m-n}$ and $\dfrac{QB}{AB} = \dfrac{n}{m-n}$.

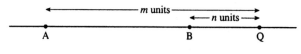

Fig. 1.6

If $m > n$, Q lies on [AB] produced beyond B; if $m < n$, Q lies on [BA] produced beyond A.

You need a form of words to distinguish between Fig. 1.5 and Fig. 1.6. In Fig. 1.5 P is said to divide [AB] **internally** in the proportion $m:n$. In Fig. 1.6 Q is said to divide [AB] **externally** in the proportion $m:n$.

Example 1.6.2

If AB = 20 cm and Q divides [AB] externally in the proportion 7:3, find the distances AQ and QB.

$$AQ = \frac{m}{m-n} AB = \frac{7}{4} \times 20 \text{ cm} = 35 \text{ cm,}$$

$$QB = \frac{n}{n-m} AB = \frac{3}{4} \times 20 \text{ cm} = 15 \text{ cm}.$$

As a check, $AQ - QB = (35 - 15) \text{ cm} = 20 \text{ cm}.$

When you get to Chapter 7, you will find that for some applications it is helpful to allow lengths to be positive or negative, according to the direction in which they are measured along the line. But for the time being lengths will always be positive numbers of units, and both QB *and* BQ *will stand for the distance from* B *to* Q.

You will sometimes come across a diagram like Fig. 1.7, in which two lines k, l are cut by three parallel lines (AC), (PQ) and (BD). Then P divides $[AB]$ in the same proportion as Q divides $[CD]$; that is, $\frac{AP}{PB} = \frac{CQ}{QD}$. This is true whether P divides $[AB]$ internally (as in the figure) or externally. It is called the **intercept theorem**.

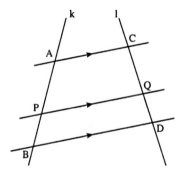

Fig. 1.7

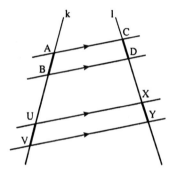

Fig. 1.8

Now you know that, if $\frac{AP}{PB} = \frac{m}{n}$, then $\frac{AP}{AB} = \frac{m}{m+n}$, and similarly for $\frac{CQ}{QD}$. So you can also write the equality of proportions in the form $\frac{AP}{AB} = \frac{CQ}{CD}$. More generally, you can take any two lengths AB, UV on the line k and corresponding lengths CD, XY on l such that the lines (AC), (BD), (UX) and (VY) are parallel, as in Fig. 1.8, and then $\frac{AB}{UV} = \frac{CD}{XY}$.

Fig. 1.9 is a special case of Fig. 1.7 in which the points A and C coincide where the lines k and l meet, so that $\frac{AP}{PB} = \frac{AQ}{QD}$. This figure can be adapted to give a way of constructing the point P which divides a line segment $[AB]$ in a given proportion. A typical application is described in Example 1.6.3.

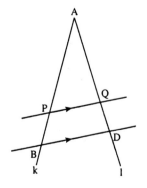

Fig. 1.9

Example 1.6.3

A and B are two given points. Use a geometrical construction to find the point P which divides [AB] internally in the proportion 5:2.

Draw any line m through A, and mark along m seven points R, S, T, U, V, W, X such that AR = RS = ST = TU = UV = VW = WX. (You can choose AR to have any convenient length.) Join [XB], and join V to a point P on [AB] so that [VP] is parallel to [XB]. Then P is the point required.

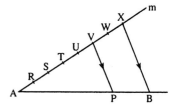

Proof

The construction of the points on m ensures that $AV = 5AR$ and $VX = 2AR$, so that $\dfrac{AV}{VX} = \dfrac{5}{2}$. As [VP] is parallel to [XB], $\dfrac{AP}{PB} = \dfrac{AV}{VX}$. Therefore $\dfrac{AP}{PB} = \dfrac{5}{2}$. So P divides [AB] in the ratio 5:2.

1.7   Some properties of circles

Circles will feature prominently in this course, and the purpose of this section is to make sure that you are familiar with the technical terms and some of the basic properties of circles, which will be assumed in the following chapters. You may find that you only need to read it through quickly to check that there is nothing that you don't know already.

The term 'circle' means just the circumference, that is, the locus of a point which is at a given distance (the radius) from a fixed point (the centre O). If A and B are two points on the circle, they separate the circle into two **arcs**. Unless [AB] is a diameter of the circle, the arcs will be of different sizes; the larger is the **major arc**, the smaller the **minor arc** (see Fig. 1.10). The line segment [AB] is a **chord**, and many properties of circles are based on the fact that the chord [AB] together with the radii [OA] and [OB] form an isosceles triangle. The complete line (AB) is called a **secant**.

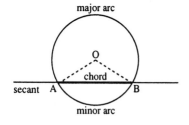

Fig. 1.10

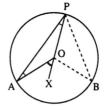

Fig. 1.11

In Fig. 1.11 P is a point on the major arc AB of a circle. The radius [PO] is produced to X. Then the triangle OAP is isosceles, so that $O\hat{A}P = O\hat{P}A$. Also the exterior angle $A\hat{O}X$ of the triangle, is given by $A\hat{O}X = O\hat{A}P + O\hat{P}A$. Therefore $A\hat{O}X = 2 \times O\hat{P}A$. An exactly similar argument can be used with the triangle OBP, giving $B\hat{O}X = 2 \times O\hat{P}B$.

There are several possible figures, two of which are drawn in Fig. 1.11, depending on where P is on the arc AB. (Try drawing another for yourself.) On the left, you can add the angles $A\hat{O}X$ and $B\hat{O}X$ to get

$$A\hat{O}B = A\hat{O}X + B\hat{O}X = 2 \times O\hat{P}A + 2 \times O\hat{P}B = 2 \times \left(O\hat{P}A + O\hat{P}B\right) = 2 \times A\hat{P}B.$$

On the right, you can subtract to get

$$A\hat{O}B = A\hat{O}X - B\hat{O}X = 2 \times O\hat{P}A - 2 \times O\hat{P}B = 2 \times \left(O\hat{P}A - O\hat{P}B\right) = 2 \times A\hat{P}B.$$

Either way, the conclusion that $A\hat{O}B = 2 \times A\hat{P}B$ is the same. This is illustrated in Fig. 1.12, and can be stated as a theorem. You can refer to it as the 'angle at the centre' theorem.

Theorem   If P is any point on an arc AB of a circle with centre O, then $A\hat{O}B = 2 \times A\hat{P}B$.

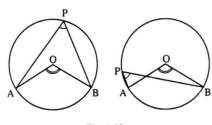

Fig. 1.12

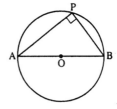

Fig. 1.13

Fig. 1.13 illustrates the theorem when P is on the minor arc AB. The proof is just the same, but now the sum of the angles $A\hat{O}X$ and $B\hat{O}X$ is the angle $A\hat{O}B$ which is greater than $180°$. This is called the **reflex angle** $A\hat{O}B$.

An important special case is when AB is a diameter of the circle, as in Fig. 1.14. Then $A\hat{O}B = 180°$, so that $A\hat{P}B = \frac{1}{2} \times 180° = 90°$. This occurs so often that it is worth listing as a separate theorem known as the 'angle in a semicircle' theorem.

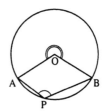

Theorem   If AB is a diameter of a circle and P is any other point on the circle, then $A\hat{P}B$ is a right angle.

Fig. 1.14

A convenient shorthand is to say that 'the angle in a semicircle is a right angle'.

The converse of this theorem is also true.

Converse of 'angle in a semicircle'   If $A\hat{P}B$ is a right angle, then P lies on the circle with diameter AB.

Proof
Fig. 1.15 shows a triangle ABP with $A\hat{P}B = 90°$. The perpendicular bisector of the side [AP] (shown as a dotted line) meets [AB] at Z, and Z is joined to P.

You know from Example 1.5.2 that, since Z is on the perpendicular bisector of [AP], $ZA = ZP$. The triangle AZP is isosceles, so that $P\hat{A}Z = A\hat{P}Z$.

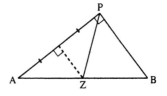

Fig. 1.15

In triangle APB, since $A\hat{P}B = 90°$, $P\hat{A}Z + Z\hat{B}P = 90°$. Also $A\hat{P}Z + Z\hat{P}B = A\hat{P}B = 90°$. Therefore, since $P\hat{A}Z = A\hat{P}Z$, $Z\hat{B}P = Z\hat{P}B$. The triangle ZBP is isosceles, so that $ZB = ZP$.

Therefore $ZA = ZB = ZP$. That is, A, B and P lie on a circle with centre Z. And since [AB] contains the point Z, [AB] is a diameter of the circle.

The key to this proof is to define Z as a point on the perpendicular bisector of [AP]. If you begin by defining M as the mid-point of [AB], it is harder to prove that the triangles AMP and MBP are isosceles. Notice that the proof uses both the isosceles triangle theorem (that if the sides are equal, the opposite angles are equal) and its converse.

To summarise:

> If P is any point on an arc AB of a circle with centre O, then $A\hat{O}B = 2 \times A\hat{P}B$.
>
> If AB is a diameter of a circle and P is any other point on the circle, then $A\hat{P}B$ is a right angle.
>
> If $A\hat{P}B$ is a right angle, then P lies on the circle with diameter AB.

Other important properties of a circle depend on the idea of the tangent at a point. If A and B are two points on a circle, then $O\hat{A}B$ is less than 90°. So if you draw a line through A perpendicular to the radius [OA], as in Fig. 1.16, there can't be any point other than A which is on both the line and the circle. This line is the **tangent** to the circle at A, and the line is said to **touch** the circle. The point A is called the **point of contact** of the tangent with the circle.

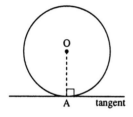

Fig. 1.16

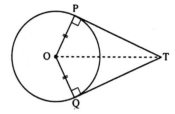

Fig. 1.17

In Fig. 1.17 the tangents to the circle at two points P and Q meet at T. The triangles TOP and TOQ have a common side [TO], a pair of equal sides [OP] and [OQ], and a pair of equal right angles $T\hat{P}O$ and $T\hat{Q}O$, so the triangles are congruent. This has two important consequences, which are stated as theorems.

> **Theorem**   The tangents to a circle from a point outside it have equal lengths.
>
> **Theorem**   The angle between the tangents to a circle with centre O from a point T outside the circle is bisected by [TO].

Two other words which you should know describe regions inside a circle. A region bounded by a chord and an arc is called a **segment**, and a region bounded by two radii and an arc is called a **sector**. Thus in Fig. 1.18 the chord [AB] separates the interior of the circle into two segments, the **major segment** and **minor segment**. In Fig. 1.19 the radii [OA] and [OB] together separate it into two sectors; the sector containing a reflex angle is known as the **reflex sector**.

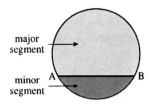

Fig. 1.18

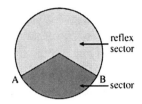

Fig. 1.19

1.8   A note on history

Many of the properties of triangles and circles in the early chapters of this book were developed by Greek scholars between the time of Thales and Pythagoras (6th century BC) and Euclid (about 300 BC). These were collected and systematised by Euclid in a set of books known as the *Elements.*

Euclid himself taught in Alexandria, on the Mediterranean coast of present-day Egypt, and this remained the most important centre for the study of geometry over the next 600 years. In this book you will find theorems attributed to Apollonius (late 2nd century BC), Menelaus (late 1st century AD), Ptolemy (early 2nd century AD) and Pappus (late 3rd century AD), all of whom worked in the city.

Most ideas in mathematics emerge gradually, and often begin as special cases which later take a more general form. In Greek geometry it is especially difficult to know who actually 'discovered' a particular result, because the contents of many of the texts are lost and are known only through references to them in the writings of later mathematicians. So you should not assume that a name attached to a theorem is evidence that this person was the first to know it, or that he published it in exactly the form in which it is stated nowadays.

There was a revival of interest in Greek geometry in Europe in the 17th and 18th centuries. You will meet the names of the Swiss mathematician Leonhard Euler, who worked in Prussia and Russia, and of a group of Scots: Robert Simson, professor at the University of Glasgow for nearly 50 years, and his pupils Matthew Stewart and William Wallace, both professors at the University of Edinburgh. The editions of works by Euclid and Apollonius produced by Simson had an important influence on the modern study of geometry.

Exercise 1

1   Use a straight edge to make an accurate drawing of the following figure.

[OA], [OB], [OC] are three line segments with a common point O. Points X, Y, Z are marked on [OA], [OB], [OC] respectively. The lines (BC) and (YZ) meet at L, (CA) and (ZX) meet at M, (AB) and (XY) meet at N.

What does your figure suggest about the points L, M, N? (This is called the *Désargues property.*)

Now imagine the figure in three dimensions, so that the line segments are the legs of a tripod standing on the floor. What can you now say about the points L, M, N?

2   Here are three theorems about figures formed from four points A, B, C, D. State their converses, and say whether the converses are true or false. If false, say how they could be amended to give a true statement.

(a) If a quadrilateral ABCD is a rhombus, then [AC] is perpendicular to [BD].

(b) If the diagonals of a parallelogram meet at M, then AM = MC.

(c) If [AB] is parallel to [CD], then the triangles ABC and ABD have equal areas.

3   Two part lines l, m terminate in a common point A, as shown in the figure. Find the locus of points whose distances from l and m are equal. Prove your answer.

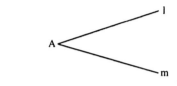

4   Two lines l, m intersect at a point A, as shown in the figure. Find the locus of points whose distances from l and m are equal.

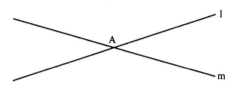

5   Draw a triangle XYZ. Then find as many points P as you can such that YP = YZ and XP is parallel to YZ.

What condition must be satisfied for such points to exist?

6   Two points A, B are given. State the locus of points P such that

(a) $A\hat{P}B = 90°$,   (b) $A\hat{P}B = 45°$.

Remember to mention any excluded points.

7   On a line A, B, C, D are four points, and AB = 24 cm. Points C and D divide AB internally and externally in the proportion 1:5. Calculate the lengths BC and BD, and show that

(a) $\dfrac{1}{BA} = \dfrac{1}{2}\left(\dfrac{1}{BC} + \dfrac{1}{BD}\right)$,

(b) if M is the mid-point of AB, then $MC \times MD = MA^2$.

Investigate whether the results in (a) and (b) still hold if the proportion is changed to 1:3 and 1:7.

8   A point T is outside a circle whose centre is O. If P is a point on the circle such that TP is a tangent, what can you say about the angle $T\hat{P}O$? Use your answer to describe how to find the points of contact of the tangents to the circle which pass through T.

9   State the converse of the property illustrated by Fig. 1.9, and prove it.

Three line segments [OA], [OB], [OC] have a common point O. Points X, Y, Z are marked on the line segments such that [XY] and [AB] are parallel, and [XZ] and [AC] are parallel. Prove that [YZ] and [BC] are parallel, giving a reason for each step.

2 Some properties of triangles

The triangle is the most basic figure made up of straight lines, and it has many special properties. When you have completed this chapter, you should

- know what is meant by similar figures, and the conditions for triangles to be similar
- be able to perform calculations using similar triangles
- know that the medians of a triangle are concurrent at the centroid
- know Euclid's theorem for proportional segments in a right-angled triangle
- know Apollonius's theorem for the length of a median and Stewart's generalisation.

2.1 Similar triangles

Many interesting properties of triangles depend on the idea of similarity.

Two geometrical figures are said to be similar if one can be regarded as an enlargement of the other. That is, you can set up a correspondence between their points, lines, etc. such that the angles at all the corresponding points are equal, and all corresponding lengths are in the same proportion. For example, the two pentagons ABCDE and VWXYZ in Fig. 2.1 are similar because the angles at A, B, C, D, E are equal to the angles at V, W, X, Y, Z respectively, and also $\dfrac{AB}{VW} = \dfrac{BC}{WX} = \dfrac{CD}{XY} = \dfrac{DE}{YZ} = \dfrac{EA}{ZV}$.

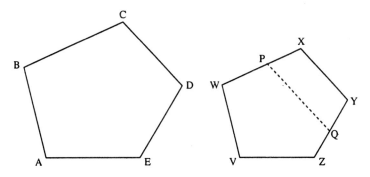

Fig. 2.1

Notice that it is not enough just to say that the angles have to be equal; you also need to check the proportions of the lengths of the sides. To see this, make a new pentagon VWPQZ by taking points P and Q on the sides [WX] and [YZ] of VWXYZ so that [PQ] is parallel to [XY]. This doesn't change the angles, so that the pentagons ABCDE and VWPQZ also have equal angles at corresponding points. But, since the lengths VW and ZV are unchanged and WP < WX and QZ < YZ, corresponding lengths in the two pentagons are certainly not in the same proportion. The pentagons ABCDE and VWPQZ are therefore not similar.

But triangles are special: for two triangles to be similar, it is sufficient for them to have corresponding angles equal. Corresponding sides are then automatically proportional.

You can easily see that the two triangles in Fig. 2.2, with $\hat{A} = \hat{X}$, $\hat{B} = \hat{Y}$ and $\hat{C} = \hat{Z}$, are similar to each other. If you imagine triangle XYZ to be enlarged so that YZ becomes equal to BC, then ZX would become equal to CA, and XY to AB, so that the enlarged $\triangle$XYZ would be congruent to $\triangle$ABC. The two triangles are said to be **directly similar**.

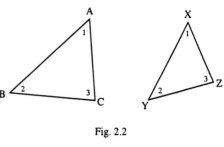

Fig. 2.2

It is not quite so easy to see that the two triangles in Fig. 2.3 are similar. If you imagine triangle XYZ to be enlarged as before, then you would still get two congruent triangles, but you would need to flip one of them over before it would fit on the other. The two triangles are said to be **indirectly similar**.

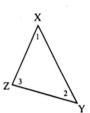

What is the minimum information you need to be sure that two triangles $\triangle$ABC, $\triangle$XYZ are similar?

Fig. 2.3

There are four possible answers to this question, one corresponding to each of the four sets of conditions which you know for two triangles to be congruent: one side and two angles equal (sometimes denoted by ASA), three sides equal (SSS), two sides and the angle included between them equal (SAS), two sides and a non-included right angle equal (SSR).

Four sets of conditions which ensure that two triangles ABC, XYZ are similar are:

- two angles of one triangle are equal to two corresponding angles of the other: if $\hat{A} = \hat{X}$ and $\hat{B} = \hat{Y}$ (and therefore also $\hat{C} = \hat{Z}$, since the angles of a triangle total 180°), then $\dfrac{BC}{YZ} = \dfrac{CA}{ZX} = \dfrac{AB}{XY}$.

- the lengths of corresponding sides are in the same proportion: if $\dfrac{BC}{YZ} = \dfrac{CA}{ZX} = \dfrac{AB}{XY}$, then $\hat{A} = \hat{X}$, $\hat{B} = \hat{Y}$ and $\hat{C} = \hat{Z}$. This is the converse of the first condition.

- the lengths of two corresponding sides are in the same proportion, and the angles between them are equal: if $\dfrac{CA}{ZX} = \dfrac{AB}{XY}$ and $\hat{A} = \hat{X}$, then also $\dfrac{BC}{YZ} = \dfrac{CA}{ZX}$, $\hat{B} = \hat{Y}$ and $\hat{C} = \hat{Z}$.

- the lengths of two corresponding sides are in the same proportion, and one pair of corresponding angles not included between them are right angles: if $\dfrac{CA}{ZX} = \dfrac{AB}{XY}$ and $\hat{C} = \hat{Z} = 90°$, then also $\dfrac{BC}{YZ} = \dfrac{CA}{ZX}$, $\hat{A} = \hat{X}$ and $\hat{B} = \hat{Y}$.

The last condition is the basis of many calculations in trigonometry (see Fig. 2.4). The equation $\dfrac{CA}{ZX} = \dfrac{AB}{XY}$ can also be written in the form $\dfrac{CA}{AB} = \dfrac{ZX}{XY}$, that is $\cos \hat{A} = \cos \hat{X}$; and it follows that $\hat{A} = \hat{X}$.

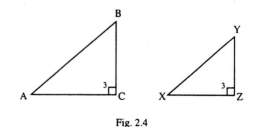

Fig. 2.4

You will often apply these properties in situations where the triangles are not separated as in Fig. 2.2 or Fig. 2.3, but have some sides along the same lines. Figs. 2.5 to 2.10 show some examples in which the triangles have one common vertex A, and the other vertices lie on one or other of two lines through A.

In Fig. 2.5 and Fig. 2.6 the line segments [BC] and [DE] are parallel, so that the corresponding angles of triangles ABC and ADE are equal. In both figures the triangles are directly similar, and it follows that

$$\frac{BC}{DE} = \frac{CA}{EA} = \frac{AB}{AD}.$$

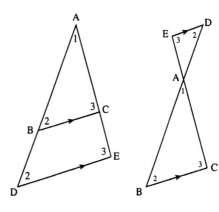

Fig. 2.5   Fig. 2.6

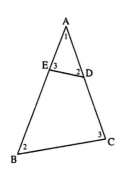

Fig. 2.7

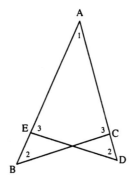

Fig. 2.8

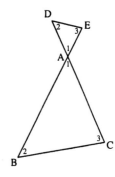

Fig. 2.9

In Fig. 2.7, Fig. 2.8 and Fig. 2.9 the triangles are indirectly similar. It is still true that the angle at B in △ABC is equal to the angle at D in △ADE, but now D lies on the line (AC) and E lies on (AB). It again follows that $\frac{BC}{DE} = \frac{CA}{EA} = \frac{AB}{AD}$.

You can think of Fig. 2.10 as a halfway stage between Fig. 2.7 and Fig. 2.8 in which the points C and D coalesce at the point marked C, so that the triangles have two vertices in common. However, the common side [AC] is opposite to the angle marked 2 in △ABC, but opposite to the angle marked 3 in △ACE, so this side does not correspond to itself. The corresponding vertices are A and A, B and C, and C and E, so the equal fractions are

$$\frac{BC}{CE} = \frac{CA}{EA} = \frac{AB}{AC}.$$

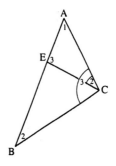

Fig. 2.10

When you name a pair of similar triangles, always order the letters so that corresponding vertices are written in corresponding positions. The vertices in △ACE corresponding to A, B, C in △ABC are A, C, E, so call the triangles △ABC and △ACE, not △ABC and △AEC. You can then write down the equal fractions directly from the way in which you have named the triangles.

2.2 Medians and the centroid

A line segment joining a vertex of a triangle to the
mid-point of the opposite side is called a **median**.

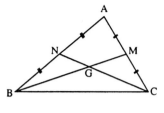

Fig. 2.11 shows a triangle ABC with two of its
medians, [BM] and [CN]. The markings on the
sides show that M and N are mid-points of the
sides [AC] and [AB] respectively.

Fig. 2.11

If you join M and N, you get a figure in which you should be able to recognise examples of both Fig. 2.5
and Fig. 2.6; these are shown by the heavy black lines in Fig. 2.12 and Fig. 2.13. You can then use the
properties of similar triangles to find the position of the point G where the two medians meet.

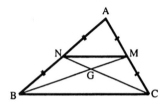

Fig. 2.12

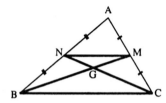

Fig. 2.13

Mini-theorem   If the medians BM, CN of a triangle ABC meet at G, then $BG = \frac{2}{3}BM$ and
$CG = \frac{2}{3}CN$.

That is, G is a point of trisection of the medians [BM] and [CN].

Proof

Fig. 2.12 shows the triangles ABC and ANM. Since $AN = NB$ and $AM = MC$, $\dfrac{AB}{AN} = \dfrac{AC}{AM} = 2$.
Also the triangles have a common angle at A, so $B\hat{A}C = N\hat{A}M$. Therefore (by the third of the four
conditions listed in Section 2.1) the triangles are similar. It follows that

(i) $\dfrac{BC}{NM} = 2$, and

(ii) $A\hat{B}C = A\hat{N}M$, so that the line segments [BC], [NM] are parallel.

Fig. 2.13 shows the triangles GBC and GMN. Since [BC], [NM] are parallel, $G\hat{B}C = G\hat{M}N$
(these are called 'alternate angles' or 'Z angles') and $B\hat{G}C = M\hat{G}N$ ('vertically opposite angles' or
'X angles'). Therefore (by the first of the four conditions in Section 2.1) the triangles are similar. It
follows that $\dfrac{GB}{GM} = \dfrac{GC}{GN} = \dfrac{BC}{MN}$.

But it has already been proved that $\dfrac{BC}{MN} = 2$. Therefore $\dfrac{GB}{GM} = \dfrac{GC}{GN} = 2$, so $BG = 2GM$ and
$CG = 2GN$. That is, $BG = \frac{2}{3}BM$ and $CG = \frac{2}{3}CN$.

What about the third median of the triangle joining A to L, the mid-point of BC?

Fig. 2.14   Fig. 2.15

Fig. 2.14 shows the medians $[AL]$, $[CN]$ meeting at a point H. This is in fact just like Fig. 2.11, but with different letters. You can therefore apply the mini-theorem to this figure, and deduce that $AH = \frac{2}{3}AL$ and $CH = \frac{2}{3}CN$.

But you already know that $CG = \frac{2}{3}CN$, so that $CG = CH$. That is, G and H are the same point. It follows that the median $[AL]$ also passes through G.

The argument can be summed up in the statement of a theorem, which is illustrated in Fig. 2.15.

> **Theorem**   The three medians of a triangle all pass through a common point, which is the point of trisection of each median further from the corresponding vertex.

Lines which pass through a common point are said to be **concurrent**. The point of concurrence of the medians is called the **centroid** of the triangle.

Notice the strategy used in proving this theorem. You don't draw all three medians straight away, but begin with just two medians, which certainly pass through a common point. You then find some property of this common point which ensures that the third median passes through it. This is a strategy which you will use again in proving that other sets of lines are concurrent.

Exercise 2A

1   In figures (a) to (d) the arrows indicate parallel lines and the arcs indicate equal angles. The numbers show the lengths of the line segments in suitable units. Find the lengths marked x and y.

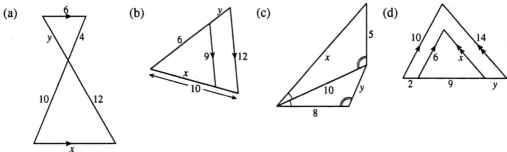

2   In figures (a) to (c) the arcs indicate equal angles. The numbers show the lengths of the line segments in suitable units. Find the lengths marked x and y.

(a)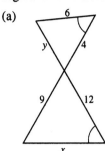

(b)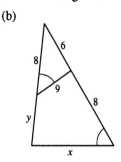

(c)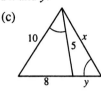

3   (a) In the figure $A\hat{C}E = A\hat{B}C$. Prove that
$AC^2 = AB \times AE$.

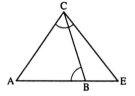

(b) In the figure $A\hat{C}B = A\hat{D}E$. Prove that
$AB \times AD = AC \times AE$.

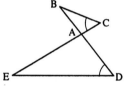

4   E is a point on the side $[AB]$ of a triangle ABC. If $AC^2 = AB \times AE$, prove that
$BC \times AE = AC \times CE$.

5   In a triangle ABC, X and Y are points on the sides $[AC]$ and $[AB]$ such that $AX = \frac{1}{3}AC$ and
$AY = \frac{1}{3}AB$. The line segments $[BX]$ and $[CY]$ intersect at Z. Express the length BZ as a fraction of BX.

6   E is a point on the side $[AB]$ of a triangle ABC. Given that both $\triangle ACE$ and $\triangle CBE$ are similar to $\triangle ABC$, what can you say about the angles in the figure?

7   In Fig. 2.15, prove that G is the centroid of $\triangle LMN$.

8   ABCD and WXYZ are two quadrilaterals. You are given that $\dfrac{AB}{WX} = \dfrac{BC}{XY} = \dfrac{CD}{YZ} = \dfrac{DA}{ZW}$ and that
$A\hat{B}C = W\hat{X}Y$. Prove that the quadrilaterals are similar. (You should state carefully which of the four conditions for similar triangles you are using at each step.)

9   ABCD and WXYZ are quadrilaterals such that their corresponding angles are equal.

(a) Prove that, if also $\dfrac{AB}{WX} = \dfrac{BC}{XY}$, then the quadrilaterals are similar.

(b) Find a counterexample to show that, if also $\dfrac{AB}{WX} = \dfrac{CD}{YZ}$, then the quadrilaterals may not be similar.

10   Carry out the following construction.

On a line k mark three points A, B, C in that order. Draw parallel lines l, m through A, B in any direction, and a line n through C in another direction. The lines l, n meet in X, and m, n in Y. Draw lines (AY), (BX) meeting in Z. Draw a line through Z parallel to l and m to intersect k at D.

(a) By considering pairs of similar triangles, prove that $\dfrac{CA}{CB} = \dfrac{AZ}{ZY}$, and deduce that $\dfrac{CA}{CB} = \dfrac{AD}{DB}$.

(b) Show that, whatever the directions in which you draw the lines l and n, your construction always leads to the same point D. Verify this by repeating your construction with different lines l, m and n.

2.3   An application to right-angled triangles

Fig. 2.10, at the end of Section 2.1, showed two similar triangles ABC and ACE having a non-corresponding side in common. The special case in which the equal angles $A\hat{C}B$ and $A\hat{E}C$ are right angles is drawn in Fig. 2.16.

The lengths of the various lines in Fig. 2.16 have been denoted by single letters. In the large triangle ABC the lengths of the sides opposite A, B, C are denoted as usual by a, b, c. The length of [CE], which is the perpendicular from C to [AB], is h; and the lengths of [AE] and [BE] are q and p respectively.

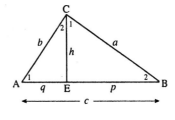

Fig. 2.16

Because the common side [AC] is not a corresponding side in the two triangles, its length comes into two of the fractions, $\dfrac{AC}{AE} = \dfrac{AB}{AC}$. This can then be written as $\dfrac{b}{q} = \dfrac{c}{b}$, so that $b^2 = qc$.

One new feature of Fig. 2.16 compared with Fig. 2.10 is that the triangle ABC is also similar to triangle CBE, because the angle $C\hat{E}B$ is also a right angle. So you can write another equation, $\dfrac{BC}{BE} = \dfrac{BA}{BC}$. This can be written as $\dfrac{a}{p} = \dfrac{c}{a}$, so that $a^2 = pc$.

*The line segments [AE] and [BE] are called the **projections** of [AC] and [BC] on the base [AB]. If [AC] and [BC] were paths up a hill from A and B to the summit C, these would be shown on a map by the line segments [AE] and [BE]. So the two equations $b^2 = qc$ and $a^2 = pc$ could be expressed in words by saying that 'in a right-angled triangle the square of the length of one of the shorter sides is equal to the product of the lengths of the hypotenuse and the projection of that side on the hypotenuse'.*

From the two equations $a^2 = pc$ and $b^2 = qc$ you can obtain

$$a^2 + b^2 = pc + qc = (p+q)c = c \times c = c^2,$$

which is a simple way of proving Pythagoras's theorem.

You can get another useful equation from Fig. 2.16. Since $\triangle ABC$ is similar to both $\triangle ACE$ and $\triangle CBE$ (note the order of the letters), these last two triangles are also similar to each other. They also have a common side $[CE]$, whose length will appear in two of the fractions $\dfrac{CE}{BE} = \dfrac{AE}{CE}$.

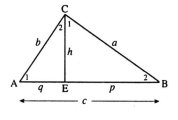

This can be written as $\dfrac{h}{p} = \dfrac{q}{h}$, so that $h^2 = pq$.

Fig. 2.16

The equations in this section were proved as mini-theorems (or 'lemmas') in Euclid's *Elements*. They are sometimes referred to as **Euclid's theorem for proportional segments** in a right-angled triangle.

Exercise 2B

1   This question uses the notation of Fig. 2.16.

(a) If $a = 6$ and $p = 4$, find q, h and b.   (b) If $p = 20$ and $q = 5$, find h, a and b.

(c) If $a = 5$ and $b = 12$, find p, q and h.

(d) If $h = 12$ and $c = 26$, and if $p > q$, find p, q, a and b.

(e) If $p = 4q$, prove that $a = 2b$.

2.4   The theorems of Apollonius and Stewart

You can use Pythagoras's theorem to find expressions for the lengths of the medians in terms of the sides of the triangle. This was known to the Greek mathematicians, and is attributed to Apollonius.

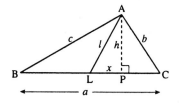

You will find it easiest to use modern algebraic notation, which was not available in Apollonius's time. In Fig. 2.17 $[AL]$ is the median of $\triangle ABC$ through the vertex A, and $[AP]$ is drawn perpendicular to $[BC]$. Denote the lengths of the sides of the triangle as usual by a, b and c, and let the lengths AL, AP and LP be l, h and x respectively.

Fig. 2.17

You should be able to recognise three right-angled triangles in the figure, so you can use Pythagoras's theorem to write three equations. Notice that, since $BL = LC = \frac{1}{2}a$, $BP = \frac{1}{2}a + x$ and $PC = \frac{1}{2}a - x$.

In $\triangle ALP$: $x^2 + h^2 = l^2$.

In $\triangle ABP$: $\left(\frac{1}{2}a + x\right)^2 + h^2 = c^2$,   that is $\frac{1}{4}a^2 + ax + x^2 + h^2 = c^2$.

In $\triangle ACP$: $\left(\frac{1}{2}a - x\right)^2 + h^2 = b^2$,   that is $\frac{1}{4}a^2 - ax + x^2 + h^2 = b^2$.

Now to get l in terms of a, b and c, you want an equation which does not involve either x or l. This is easy to arrange. Notice first that, by adding the last two equations, you get rid of the term ax; and you can use the first equation to replace the terms $x^2 + h^2$ by l^2. This gives

$$\frac{1}{2}a^2 + 2l^2 = c^2 + b^2 \quad \text{so that} \quad l^2 = \frac{1}{2}b^2 + \frac{1}{2}c^2 - \frac{1}{4}a^2.$$

This is the expression you want to calculate l in terms of a, b and c.

There is just one snag. This argument is based on the assumption that P is between L and C, as in Fig. 2.17. But it is possible that P might be between L and B, as in Fig. 2.18, in which case BP and PC would be given by $BP = \frac{1}{2}a - x$ and $PC = \frac{1}{2}a + x$. Or one of the angles $\hat{B}$ or $\hat{C}$ might be obtuse, in which case P would lie outside the line segment $[BC]$; for example, in Fig. 2.19, $BP = \frac{1}{2}a + x$ but $PC = x - \frac{1}{2}a$. You need to check that the conclusion still holds for these figures as well, even if some of the details of the proof are different.

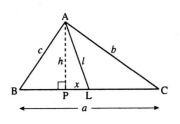

Fig. 2.18

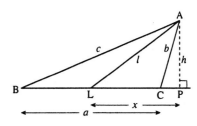

Fig. 2.19

Check that the equation $\frac{1}{2}a^2 + 2l^2 = c^2 + b^2$ is true for Fig. 2.18 and Fig. 2.19.

This result is called Apollonius's theorem. It is often stated in a slightly different form from that given above, using the fact that $\frac{1}{2}a^2$ can be written as $2\left(\frac{1}{2}a\right)^2$, which is $2BL^2$. You then get:

> **Apollonius's theorem** In a triangle ABC, if L is the mid-point of $[BC]$, then
> $AB^2 + AC^2 = 2\left(AL^2 + BL^2\right)$.

Example 2.4.1

A point D is taken on the side $[BC]$ of a triangle ABC such that $\dfrac{BD}{DC} = \dfrac{1}{3}$. If $AD = d$ find an equation connecting a, b, c and d.

Since $DC = 3BD$, $BC = BD + DC = 4BD$, so $BD = \frac{1}{4}BC = \frac{1}{4}a$. But $BL = \frac{1}{2}a$, so AD is a median of $\triangle ABL$, You can therefore apply Apollonius's theorem to $\triangle ABL$ (remembering that the length of the base BL is $\frac{1}{2}a$, not a). This gives

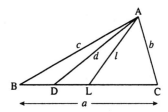

$$\frac{1}{2}\left(\frac{1}{2}a\right)^2 + 2d^2 = c^2 + l^2.$$

But you know that $l^2 = \frac{1}{2}b^2 + \frac{1}{2}c^2 - \frac{1}{4}a^2$, so

$$\frac{1}{8}a^2 + 2d^2 = c^2 + \frac{1}{2}b^2 + \frac{1}{2}c^2 - \frac{1}{4}a^2.$$

Multiplying by 8 to clear all the fractions, and rearranging,

$$3a^2 + 16d^2 = 4b^2 + 12c^2.$$

You might think that the statement of Appolonius's theorem in the shaded box is slightly unsatisfactory, because the right side is not symmetrical; it involves BL but not CL as well. It would be better (but rather fussy) to replace $2BL^2$ by $BL^2 + CL^2$, and to write the equation in the form
$AB^2 + AC^2 = 2AL^2 + BL^2 + CL^2$.

The point of this comment is that it leads to a generalisation of Apollonius's theorem which is known as Stewart's theorem. In Apollonius's theorem L is the point which divides the line segment [BC] in the ratio 1:1. Stewart gave an equation for calculating the length of [AD], where D divides [BC] in any ratio $m:n$.

> **Stewart's theorem**   If D is the point on the side [BC] of a triangle ABC such that $\dfrac{BD}{DC} = \dfrac{m}{n}$, then $nAB^2 + mAC^2 = (m+n)AD^2 + nBD^2 + mCD^2$.

Proof
The method is essentially the same as that used to prove Apollonius's theorem. In Fig. 2.20 draw [AP], of length h, perpendicular to [BC] and let the length DP be x. This creates three right-angled triangles, and Pythagoras's theorem is applied in each of these.

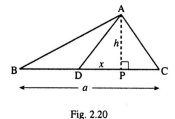

Fig. 2.20

In $\triangle ADP$: $x^2 + h^2 = AD^2$.

In $\triangle ABP$: $(BD + x)^2 + h^2 = AB^2$.

In $\triangle ACP$: $(CD - x)^2 + h^2 = AC^2$.

Slightly different equations are needed for different figures, for example if D is between P and C, or if one of the angles $\hat{B}$ or $\hat{C}$ is obtuse. You should investigate these for yourself.

Multiplying out the brackets in the last two equations, and then using the first equation to replace $x^2 + h^2$ by AD^2, gives

$$BD^2 + 2BD \times x + AD^2 = AB^2$$

and $CD^2 - 2CD \times x + AD^2 = AC^2$.

Now $\dfrac{BD}{DC} = \dfrac{m}{n}$, so $nBD = mCD$. So if you add n times the first equation to m times the second equation, the second terms give $2(nBD - mCD)x = 0$. Therefore

$$nBD^2 + mCD^2 + (n+m)AD^2 = nAB^2 + mAC^2,$$

which can be rearranged as

$$nAB^2 + mAC^2 = (m+n)AD^2 + nBD^2 + mCD^2.$$

Example 2.4.2

Use Stewart's theorem to obtain the equation in Example 2.4.1.

With $m = 1$ and $n = 3$, and writing AB, AC and AD as c, b and d, Stewart's theorem gives

$$3c^2 + b^2 = 4d^2 + 3\text{BD}^2 + \text{CD}^2.$$

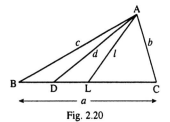

Fig. 2.20

Also $\text{BD} = \tfrac{1}{4}a$ and $\text{CD} = \tfrac{3}{4}a$, so

$$3\text{BD}^2 + \text{CD}^2 = 3 \times \tfrac{1}{16}a^2 + \tfrac{9}{16}a^2 = \tfrac{12}{16}a^2 = \tfrac{3}{4}a^2.$$

So, multiplying by 4 to clear all the fractions,

$$12c^2 + 4b^2 = 16d^2 + 3a^2,$$

which is a rearrangement of the equation in Example 2.4.1.

Example 2.4.2 suggests a slightly different presentation of the equation in Stewart's theorem.

Since $n\text{BD} = m\text{CD}$, and $\text{CD} = \text{BC} - \text{BD}$,

$$(m+n)\text{BD} = m\text{BC},$$

so that $\text{BD} = \dfrac{m}{m+n}\text{BC}$ and $\text{CD} = \dfrac{n}{m+n}\text{BC}$. It follows that

$$n\text{BD}^2 + m\text{CD}^2 = \frac{nm^2 + mn^2}{(m+n)^2}\text{BC}^2 = \frac{mn(m+n)}{(m+n)^2}\text{BC}^2 = \frac{mn}{m+n}\text{BC}^2.$$

Using single letters to represent the lengths (see Fig. 2.21), the equation in Stewart's theorem then becomes

$$mb^2 + nc^2 = (m+n)d^2 + \frac{mn}{m+n}a^2.$$

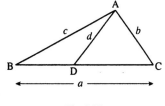

Fig. 2.21

As a check, putting $m = n = 1$ and replacing d by l brings you back to Apollonius's theorem,

$$b^2 + c^2 = 2l^2 + \tfrac{1}{2}a^2.$$

Exercise 2C

1   A triangle has sides of length 10 cm, 12 cm and 14 cm. Find the lengths of the medians.

2   A triangle has sides of length a, b, c and medians of length l, m, n. Prove that
$$l^2 + m^2 + n^2 = \tfrac{3}{4}\left(a^2 + b^2 + c^2\right).$$

3   Prove that in a parallelogram the sum of the squares of the lengths of the two diagonals is equal to the sum of the squares of the lengths of the four sides.

4   Prove that if, in a triangle ABC, $AC > BC$, then the median through B is shorter than the median through A.

5   In a triangle ABC, P and Q are the points of trisection of $[BC]$, and $AP = p$, $AQ = q$. Write equations connecting p, q, a, b, c for Apollonius's theorem in $\triangle ABQ$ and $\triangle APC$. By eliminating q between these equations, find an equation connecting p, a, b, c, and show that this is the equation given by Stewart's theorem with $m = 1$ and $n = 2$.

6   A train runs 20 km along a straight track, from which a radio mast is continuously in view. At the beginning of the journey the mast is 30 km away, and at the end it is 25 km away. How far away is the mast when the train has gone 4 km?

7   The median $[AL]$ of $\triangle ABC$ has length l. P is a point on the median such that $PL = kl$, where $0 < k < 1$. Show that the value of $PA^2 + PB^2 + PC^2$ is least when P is at the centroid of the triangle, and find an expression for this least value in terms of a, b and c.

8 ABC is a triangle with sides $a = 77$, $b = 40$, $c = 51$. D is a point on $[BC]$ such that $\dfrac{BD}{DC} = m$. If the length $AD = 30$, find two possible values for the length BD.

9 B and C are two points 10 cm apart.
   (a) Use Apollonius's theorem to find the locus of points P such that $PB^2 + PC^2 = 250$.
   (b) Use Stewart's theorem to find the locus of points P such that $2PB^2 + 3PC^2 = 1100$.

10 Prove Stewart's theorem trigonometrically by applying the cosine rule to triangles ABC and ABD and then eliminating $\cos \hat{B}$.

11 (a) ABC is a triangle and R is the foot of the perpendicular from A to (BC). Prove that
        $$AB^2 + AC^2 = 2AR^2 + BR^2 + CR^2.$$
   (b) Prove that, if D is a point on (BC) such that $AB^2 + AC^2 = 2AD^2 + BD^2 + CD^2$, then D is either the mid-point of $[BC]$ or the foot of the perpendicular from A to (BC).

12 (a) ABC is a triangle such that $A\hat{C}B$ is *not* a right angle. L is the mid-point of $[BC]$ and N is the mid-point of $[AB]$. K is the other point on (BC) such that $NK = NL$.
        Use Apollonius's theorem to prove that $KA^2 + KB^2 = LA^2 + LB^2$.
   (b) One way of stating Apollonius's theorem is:
        ABC is a triangle and L is a point on (BC).
        If L is the mid-point of $[BC]$, then $AB^2 + AC^2 = 2AL^2 + 2BL^2$.
        Show that, stated in this form, the converse is false.

3 Triangles and circles

There are several circles associated with a triangle, and this chapter introduces the two most important of these. When you have completed it, you should

- know how to construct the circumcircle and the incircle of a triangle
- be familiar with properties of quadrilaterals circumscribed to a circle.

3.1 The circumcircle of a triangle

In Fig. 3.1 you are given two points A and B. How would you draw a circle which passes through A and B?

When you are asked to 'draw a circle' you need to know two things: where is its centre, and what is its radius? In practical terms, where must you put the point of the compass, and how wide must you open it out?

The trouble in this case is that the question is not precise enough. You could draw any number of circles through A and B. But they all have something in common, so that is a good place to start.

If P is the centre of any one of these circles, then [PA] and [PB] must both be radii, so the distance PA must equal PB. Now it was shown in Example 1.5.2 that the locus of points such that PA = PB is the perpendicular bisector of [AB]. So the centre of any circle through A and B must lie on the perpendicular bisector of [AB].

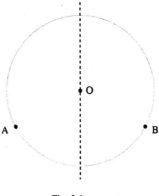

Fig. 3.1

What is more, you know the converse, that if P is any point on the perpendicular bisector then PA = PB. So any point O on the perpendicular bisector can be chosen as the centre. This is shown in Fig. 3.1.

Once you have chosen the centre, you must choose the radius so that the circle passes through A. This means that the radius is the length OA. And because O is on the perpendicular bisector, you can be sure that the circle will then also pass through B.

But because there are infinitely many possible circles, you can also make some other condition that you want the circle to satisfy. For example, in Example 3.1.1 the circle is required to have a given radius.

Example 3.1.1

A and B are points 3 cm apart. Draw a circle of radius 2 cm to pass through A and B.

You know that O, the centre of the circle, has to be on the perpendicular bisector of [AB]. But also the length OA has to be 2 cm.

Now A is a known point, so to locate O you have to find a point which is 2 cm from A. But the locus of points which are 2 cm from A is a circle with centre A and radius 2 cm. This is shown as a dotted circle in the figure.

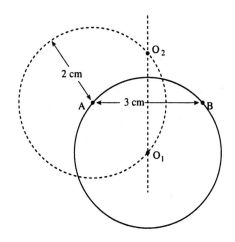

So O has to lie on two loci, the perpendicular bisector and the dotted circle. You can see that there are two possible positions for O, labelled O_1 and O_2.

The figure shows one answer to the problem, the circle with centre O_1 and radius 2 cm. There is another possible answer, the circle with centre O_2 and radius 2 cm.

One possible extra condition that you could make is to require that the circle through A and B should also pass through a third point C. How could you draw that?

You already know that, since the circle has to pass through A and B, its centre lies on the perpendicular bisector of [AB]. But you could use exactly the same argument, replacing B by C. The circle has to pass through A and C, so its centre lies on the perpendicular bisector of [AC]. This is shown in Fig. 3.2.

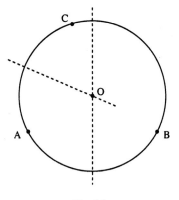

Fig. 3.2

The only possible position for the centre is therefore the point where the two perpendicular bisectors meet, marked O in Fig. 3.2. Since this point is on both loci, you know that OA = OB and that OA = OC. So the circle with centre O and radius OA passes through A, B and C; and it is the only circle that can do so.

Strictly you have to dispose of one special case. If A, B and C were all in the same straight line, then the perpendicular bisectors of [AB] and [AC] would be parallel, so they wouldn't meet, and there would be no solution to the problem. You can't draw a circle through three collinear points. That is, put another way, a circle and a straight line can't have more than two points in common.

This can be summarised as a theorem. But before doing this, it is worth noticing that, because $OA = OB$ and $OA = OC$, it is also true that $OB = OC$, so that O also lies on the perpendicular bisector of $[BC]$. That is, all three perpendicular bisectors are concurrent at the point O.

> **Theorem**   The perpendicular bisectors of the three sides of a triangle have a common point, which is the centre of the unique circle which passes through the three vertices of the triangle.

This theorem is illustrated in Fig. 3.3.

The circle which passes through the vertices of the triangle is called the **circumcircle** of the triangle (from the Latin word *circum*, meaning 'around'). Its centre is the **circumcentre**, usually denoted by the letter O. Its radius is sometimes called the **circumradius**, usually denoted by R.

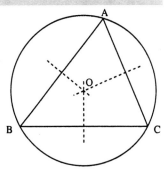

Fig. 3.3

3.2   Some properties of the circumcircle

Fig. 3.4 shows a triangle ABC with its circumcircle, and the vertices B and C joined to the circumcentre O. You will recognise the figure for the 'angle at the centre' theorem, so that $\hat{BOC} = 2 \times \hat{BAC}$.

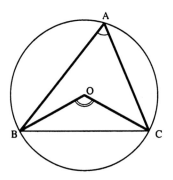

Fig. 3.4

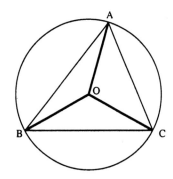

Fig. 3.5

You have often used the notation a, b, c for the lengths of the sides $[BC]$, $[CA]$, $[AB]$ of a triangle ABC, and $\hat{A}$, $\hat{B}$, $\hat{C}$ for the sizes of the angles at A, B, C. With this notation you can write $\hat{BOC} = 2\hat{A}$.

Repeating this argument round the triangle in Fig. 3.5, you get the equations

$$\hat{BOC} = 2\hat{A}, \quad \hat{COA} = 2\hat{B}, \quad \hat{AOB} = 2\hat{C}.$$

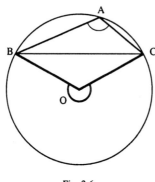

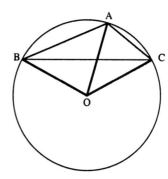

Fig. 3.6   Fig. 3.7

In Fig. 3.6 and Fig. 3.7 the triangle is drawn with an obtuse angle at A. The equations are still true, but with one important modification, that it is now the *reflex* angle $B\hat{O}C$ that has size $2\hat{A}$. The internal angle $B\hat{O}C$ in the triangle OBC has size $360° - 2\hat{A}$.

What Fig. 3.5 and Fig. 3.7 show is that if all the angles of $\triangle ABC$ are acute, then the circumcentre is inside the triangle. But if one of the angles of the triangle is obtuse, then the circumcentre is outside the triangle.

Where is the circumcentre of a right-angled triangle?

Now look at the triangle OBC. Fig. 3.8 shows this for the cases when the angle at A is (a) acute and (b) obtuse. The mid-point of $[BC]$ is L. Since the triangle is isosceles, $[OL]$ is perpendicular to $[BC]$ and $[OL]$ bisects $B\hat{O}C$.

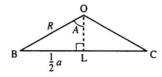

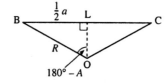

Fig. 3.8a   Fig. 3.8b

In Fig. 3.8a $B\hat{O}C = 2\hat{A}$, so $B\hat{O}L = \frac{1}{2} \times (2\hat{A}) = \hat{A}$. Also $BL = \frac{1}{2}a$. Therefore, from the right-angled triangle OBL, $\frac{1}{2}a = R\sin\hat{A}$. That is, $a = 2R\sin\hat{A}$.

In Fig. 3.8b, $B\hat{O}C = 360° - 2\hat{A}$, so $B\hat{O}L = \frac{1}{2} \times (360° - 2\hat{A}) = 180° - \hat{A}$. In this case $\frac{1}{2}a = R\sin(180° - \hat{A})$. But since $\sin(180° - \hat{A}) = \sin\hat{A}$, this again gives $a = 2R\sin\hat{A}$.

You can use a similar argument to show that $b = 2R\sin\hat{B}$ and $c = 2R\sin\hat{C}$. It follows that

$$\frac{a}{\sin\hat{A}} = \frac{b}{\sin\hat{B}} = \frac{c}{\sin\hat{C}} = 2R.$$

You will recognise the first two equations as the sine rule, which you have used to find the lengths of sides and the sizes of angles in triangles. What is new is that each of these fractions is also equal to the diameter of the circumcircle.

1 Draw a triangle ABC with $a = 5$ cm, $\hat{B} = 50°$ and $\hat{C} = 85°$. Add the perpendicular bisectors of the three sides to your figure, and draw the circumcircle. Measure the circumradius, and compare your answer with that given by the equation $a = 2R \sin \hat{A}$.

2 Repeat Question 1 with $a = 6$, $\hat{B} = 20°$ and $\hat{C} = 45°$.

3 For the triangle in Question 1 construct a circle which passes through B and C and which touches [AB] at B. Measure the radius of the circle.

Prove that the radius r of the circle satisfies the equation $2r \sin \hat{B} = a$. Calculate this radius, and compare the answer with your measured value.

4 For the triangle in Question 2 construct two circles which pass through B and C and whose centres are at a distance from A equal to c. Measure their radii.

5 If Δ denotes the area of the triangle ABC, prove that $abc = 4\Delta R$.

6 A is the apex of an isosceles triangle with circumradius R. Show that the distance between the centroid and the circumcentre is $R \times \left| \frac{4}{3} \cos^2 \frac{1}{2} \hat{A} - 1 \right|$.

7 (a) X is a point on the side [BC] of a triangle ABC. If P and Q are the circumcentres of the triangles XAB and XAC, prove that PQ is perpendicular to AX.

(b) ABCD is a quadrilateral whose diagonals [AC] and [BD] meet at X. P, Q, R, S are the circumcentres of triangles XAB, XBC, XCD, XDA. What sort of quadrilateral is PQRS?

3.3 The incircle of a triangle

It is also possible to draw a circle which touches all three sides of a triangle. To do this, you can use a strategy very similar to that described in Section 3.1 for the circumcircle.

Begin by taking just two sides of the triangle, [AB] and [AC]. You can avoid some complication if you imagine these sides produced indefinitely beyond B and C, as in Fig. 3.9. For a circle to touch each of these two lines, the perpendicular distances from the centre to each line must be equal. So begin by asking the question 'What is the locus of points which are equidistant from the two lines?'

Some people like to use the notation [AB) *for the part-line which begins at A but is produced indefinitely beyond* B.

In Fig. 3.9, let P be a point on the locus, and draw [PQ], [PR] perpendicular to [AB], [AC] so that PQ = PR. Then the triangles AQP and ARP are congruent (having a common side, a pair of equal sides and a non-included right angle). From this you can deduce that $\hat{PAQ} = \hat{PAR}$; which is the same as $\hat{PAB} = \hat{PAC}$. That is, [AP] bisects the angle $\hat{BAC}$.

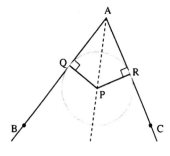

Fig. 3.9

The converse is equally easy to prove. If P is a point on the line which bisects the angle $\hat{BAC}$, so that $\hat{PAB} = \hat{PAC}$, and if PQ, PR are drawn perpendicular to [AB], [AC], then the triangles are again congruent (having a common side and two angles equal), so that PQ = PR.

You can sum this up in a single statement:

> The locus of points which are equidistant from [AB] and [AC] (produced indefinitely beyond B and C) is the bisector of the angle $\hat{BAC}$.

Now take another pair of sides, for example [BA] and [BC]. The locus of points equidistant from these is the bisector of the angle $\hat{CBA}$. Then the point common to these two loci is equidistant from all three sides of the triangle.

And you can remark that, since this point is equidistant from [CB] and [CA], it also lies on the bisector of the angle $\hat{ACB}$. So you get, as a bonus, the information that the bisectors of the three angles of the triangle have a point in common.

> **Theorem**   The bisectors of the three angles of a triangle have a common point, which is the centre of the unique circle which touches the three sides of the triangle.

This theorem is illustrated in Fig. 3.10.

The circle which touches the sides of a triangle is called the **incircle** of the triangle. Its centre is the **incentre**, usually denoted by I. Its radius is sometimes called the **inradius**, usually denoted by r.

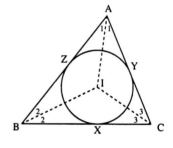

Fig. 3.10

3.4   Some properties of the incircle

Unlike the circumcentre, the incentre of a triangle is always inside the triangle, and there is no need to consider acute-angled and obtuse-angled triangles separately.

Another difference is that the triangle IBC is not isosceles, since $\hat{IBC} = \frac{1}{2}\hat{B}$ and $\hat{ICB} = \frac{1}{2}\hat{C}$ So

$$\hat{BIC} = 180° - \tfrac{1}{2}\hat{B} - \tfrac{1}{2}\hat{C}$$
$$= 180° - \tfrac{1}{2}\left(\hat{B} + \hat{C}\right)$$
$$= 180° - \tfrac{1}{2}\left(180° - \hat{A}\right) = 90° + \tfrac{1}{2}\hat{A}.$$

Similarly $\hat{CIA} = 90° + \frac{1}{2}\hat{B}$ and $\hat{AIB} = 90° + \frac{1}{2}\hat{C}$.

The points of contact of the incircle with the sides of the triangle are denoted in Fig. 3.10 by X, Y and Z. The positions of these points can be found by using the fact proved in Section 1.7 that the tangents from a point to a circle have equal lengths. So let $AY = AZ = x$, $BZ = BX = y$ and $CX = CY = z$. Then you can write three equations to find x, y and z:

$$y + z = a,$$
$$x \quad + z = b,$$
$$x + y \quad = c.$$

To solve these, add the three equations to get

$$2x + 2y + 2z = a + b + c, \quad \text{so} \quad x + y + z = \tfrac{1}{2}(a + b + c).$$

You can now find x, y and z by subtracting each of the original equations from this.

$$x = (x + y + z) - (y + z)$$
$$= \tfrac{1}{2}(a + b + c) - a$$
$$= \tfrac{1}{2}(-a + b + c),$$

and similarly $y = \tfrac{1}{2}(a - b + c)$ and $z = \tfrac{1}{2}(a + b - c)$.

The quantity $\tfrac{1}{2}(a + b + c)$ is one-half of the perimeter of the triangle ABC. It is often denoted by the letter s (standing for semi-perimeter). The lengths x, y, z can then be written simply as

$$x = s - a, \quad y = s - b, \quad z = s - c.$$

Example 3.4.1
A right-angled triangle ABC has sides of length $BC = 5$ cm, $CA = 4$ cm and $AB = 3$ cm. The incircle touches the sides at X, Y and Z. Find

(a) the length YZ,   (b) the inradius r,   (c) the angle $Y\hat{X}Z$.

(a)   The perimeter of triangle ABC is 12 cm, so that $s = 6$ cm and $AY = AZ = (6 - 5)$ cm = 1 cm. Since $Y\hat{A}Z$ is a right angle,

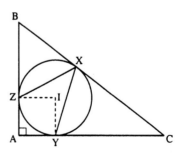

$$YZ = \sqrt{AY^2 + AZ^2}$$
$$= \sqrt{1^2 + 1^2} \text{ cm} = \sqrt{2} \text{ cm}.$$

(b)   Since $Z\hat{A}Y$, $A\hat{Y}I$ and $A\hat{Z}I$ are right angles and $AY = AZ$, the quadrilateral AYIZ is a square. Therefore

$$r = IY = AY = 1 \text{ cm}.$$

(c)   Since AYIZ is a square, $Y\hat{I}Z = 90°$. Therefore, by the angle at the centre theorem,

$$Y\hat{X}Z = \tfrac{1}{2} \times Y\hat{I}Z = \tfrac{1}{2} \times 90° = 45°.$$

3.5 Circumscribed polygons

Two words which you will come across in geometry are 'circumscribe' and 'inscribe'. Since 'scribe' means to draw, to 'circumscribe' simply means to draw round, and to 'inscribe' means to draw inside.

Thus if you have a triangle, the circumcircle is circumscribed to it, and the incircle is inscribed in it.

So far, so good. But now look at it from the point of view of the circle. Suppose that it is the incircle of a triangle ABC, and that it is the circumcircle of a triangle PQR, as in Fig. 3.11. Then you would say that ΔABC is circumscribed to the circle, and that ΔPQR is inscribed in it. Which is rather confusing!

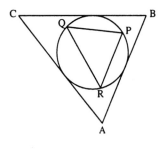

Fig. 3.11

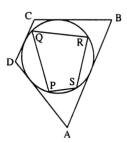

Fig. 3.12

These words can be used to describe the relation of any polygon to a circle, not just a triangle. For example, in Fig. 3.12, the quadrilateral ABCD is circumscribed to the circle, and the quadrilateral PQRS is inscribed in it.

The properties of quadrilaterals inscribed in a circle will be investigated in Chapter 4, so this section will deal only with quadrilaterals circumscribed to a circle. Some of the properties still hold for polygons with more than four sides.

Fig. 3.13 shows a quadrilateral ABCD circumscribed to a circle whose centre is I and radius r. The perpendicular distances from I to the sides are all equal to r, so the lines $[IA]$, $[IB]$, $[IC]$, $[ID]$ must bisect the angles $D\hat{A}B$, $A\hat{B}C$, $B\hat{C}D$, $C\hat{D}A$ respectively.

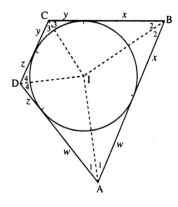

Fig. 3.13

If the sizes of the angles at A, B, C, D are denoted by $\hat{A}$, $\hat{B}$, $\hat{C}$, $\hat{D}$ then $B\hat{I}C = 180° - \frac{1}{2}(\hat{B} + \hat{C})$ just as for the triangle (Section 3.4). But you can no longer write this as $90° + \frac{1}{2}\hat{A}$, since it is no longer true that $\hat{A} + \hat{B} + \hat{C} = 180°$. However, you do know that, for any quadrilateral ABCD, $\hat{A} + \hat{B} + \hat{C} + \hat{D} = 360°$.

So you can combine the equation $B\hat{I}C = 180° - \frac{1}{2}(\hat{B} + \hat{C})$ with a similar equation $D\hat{I}A = 180° - \frac{1}{2}(\hat{D} + \hat{A})$ to get

$$B\hat{I}C + D\hat{I}A = 360° - \frac{1}{2}(\hat{B} + \hat{C} + \hat{D} + \hat{A})$$
$$= 360° - \frac{1}{2} \times 360° = 180°.$$

Two angles whose sum makes 180° are said to be **supplementary**. So, in Fig. 3.13, the angles $B\hat{I}C$ and $D\hat{I}A$ are supplementary.

A useful addition to geometrical vocabulary is to describe the angle $B\hat{I}C$ as the angle **subtended** by the chord [BC] at the point I. (Think of yourself positioned at I and looking at the chord; $B\hat{I}C$ is the angle your eye has to turn through to look along the chord from B to C.) The property can then be summarised in a general statement.

> If a quadrilateral is circumscribed to a circle, then the angles subtended at the centre of the circle by the opposite sides of the quadrilateral are supplementary.

What about the distances w, x, y, z from the vertices of the quadrilateral to the points of contact? Are there expressions for these in terms of the lengths of the sides of the quadrilateral, as there were for the triangle?

Denote the lengths of the sides [AB], [BC], [CD], [DA] by a, b, c, d respectively.

Unfortunately there is no perfectly symmetrical way of labelling the sides of a quadrilateral, like the convention $BC = a$, $CA = b$, $AB = c$ for a triangle.

Then you can write down four equations for w, x, y, z.

$$
\begin{aligned}
w + x \qquad\quad &= a, \\
x + y \quad\; &= b, \\
y + z &= c, \\
w \qquad + z &= d.
\end{aligned}
$$

Try to solve these for yourself. What's the problem?

You probably found that, when you tried to solve these equations, you kept going round in circles. The reason for this is that, if you add together the first and third equations, and the second and fourth equations, you get

$$w + x + y + z = a + c \quad \text{and} \quad w + x + y + z = b + d.$$

So the equations don't have any solutions unless $a + c = b + d$. But if $a + c$ does equal $b + d$, then the result of adding the first and third equations is the same as the result of adding the second and fourth; so by adding the first and third equations and subtracting the second you can deduce the fourth. In effect, although it looks as if you have four equations, you really only have three. And you can't expect to find four unknowns from three equations!

But although the problem hasn't been solved, you have found one important fact:

> If a quadrilateral ABCD is circumscribed to a circle, then $AB + CD = BC + AD$.

Is the converse true? That is, if $AB + CD = BC + AD$, can you always inscribe a circle in the quadrilateral?

The straight answer to this question is 'no'. Fig. 3.14 shows a quadrilateral ABCD in which you certainly can't inscribe a circle. A quadrilateral like this, one of whose angles is a reflex angle, is said to be **re-entrant**. It is obvious from Fig. 3.12 above that a quadrilateral circumscribed to a circle can't be re-entrant. (But see Exercise 2C Question 10).

Fig. 3.14

So you must restrict the problem to quadrilaterals whose angles are all less than 180°. These are called **convex** quadrilaterals.

Another property which distinguishes convex from re-entrant polygons is that all the diagonals lie inside the polygon. In a re-entrant polygon one of the diagonals lies outside the polygon.

So the question has to be rephrased. If a *convex* quadrilateral has $AB + CD = BC + AD$, can you always inscribe a circle in it?

One way of answering this is to note that if you take just three sides of this quadrilateral, they form a triangle, and you know that you can inscribe a circle in a triangle. Will the fourth side then also be a tangent to the circle?

The statement that there are three sides which form a triangle needs to be justified. To form a triangle, the angles must add up to 180°; so two angles must add up to less than 180°. So calculate $\hat{A} + \hat{B}$. If this is less then 180°, then [AB] together with [AD] produced and [BC] produced form a triangle (see Fig. 3.15). If $\hat{A} + \hat{B} > 180°$, then $\hat{C} + \hat{D} < 180°$ (since all the angles of the quadrilateral add up to 360°), so you can use a triangle based on [CD] rather than [AB]. And if $\hat{A} + \hat{B} = 180°$, then [AD] is parallel to [BC] so that ABCD is a trapezium; in that case, use a triangle based on either [BC] or [DA], whichever gives you a sum less than 180°.

The only quadrilaterals which are left out in this argument are parallelograms, which have every pair of adjacent angles adding to 180°. But if ABCD is a parallelogram and $AB + CD = BC + AD$, then all four sides must be equal in length, so the quadrilateral is a rhombus; and you can certainly inscribe a circle in a rhombus.

So suppose that $\hat{A} + \hat{B} < 180°$, and draw the incircle of the triangle formed by [AB], [AD] produced and [BC] produced. There are then three possibilities: the side [CD] may meet the circle in two points (Fig. 3.16), one point (Fig. 3.17) or no points (Fig. 3.18).

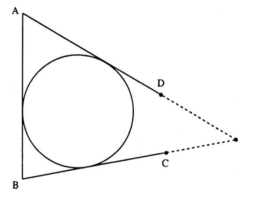

Fig. 3.15

Take Fig. 3.16 first, and draw a line segment [PQ] parallel to [CD] which touches the circle. Then you are given that $AB + CD = BC + AD$, and you know that $AB + PQ = BP + AQ$ (because the quadrilateral ABPQ circumscribes the circle). So, eliminating AB from these equations, you get

$$BC + AD - CD = BP + AQ - PQ,$$

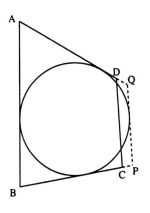

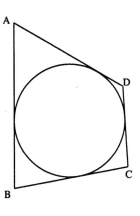

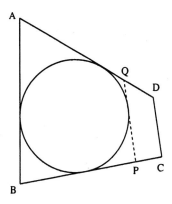

Fig. 3.16   Fig. 3.17   Fig. 3.18

that is

$$PQ = (BP - BC) + CD + (AQ - AD)$$
$$= PC + CD + DQ.$$

This is obviously impossible: to get from P to Q it is certainly shorter to go directly along the line segment [PQ] than to go through C and D.

So try Fig. 3.18. Drawing the line segment [PQ] parallel to [CD] as before, you now get

$$CD = (BC - BP) + PQ + (AD - AQ)$$
$$= CP + PQ + QD,$$

which is also impossible. (Check the details for yourself.)

So the only possibility is Fig. 3.17. That is, if $AB + CD = BC + AD$, then the quadrilateral ABCD circumscribes the circle.

The complete argument can be summed up as a theorem:

> **Theorem**   A circle can be inscribed in a convex quadrilateral if, and only if, the sums of the lengths of the pairs of opposite sides are equal.

This is an extraordinary property. Suppose you made a quadrilateral out of four rods, hinged together at their ends. Then if the sums of the lengths of pairs of opposite rods are equal, the rods will touch a circle whatever quadrilateral shape they form, provided that it is convex . But if not, they cannot touch a circle.

And if they do touch a circle, then of course the bisectors of the angles at the four corners have a common point. You could check this for yourself by accurate drawing.

Exercise 3B

1   Prove that in an equilateral triangle the radius of the circumcircle is twice the radius of the incircle.

2   In Fig. 3.10 prove that $Y\hat{X}Z = 90° - \frac{1}{2}\hat{A}$. Hence show that $YZ = 2r\cos\frac{1}{2}\hat{A}$.

3 Prove that $r = (s - a)\tan\frac{1}{2}\hat{A}$, where s is the semi-perimeter $\frac{1}{2}(a + b + c)$.

4 Use Fig. 3.10 to prove that the area of $\triangle ABC$ is rs. Does a similar result hold for a quadrilateral circumscribed to a circle?

5 A pentagon ABCDE is circumscribed to a circle, and the side AB touches the circle at V. Prove that $AV = \frac{1}{2}(AB - BC + CD - DE + EA)$.

6 A hexagon ABCDEF is circumscribed to a circle with centre O.

   (a) Prove that $AB + CD + EF = BC + DE + FA$.

   (b) Is the converse true? If so, prove it. If not, give a counterexample.

   (c) Prove that $A\hat{O}B + C\hat{O}D + E\hat{O}F = 180°$.

7 In the figure A, B, C are the centres of three circles which touch each other in pairs. Show that the common tangents to the circles at their points of contact meet at the incentre of $\triangle ABC$.

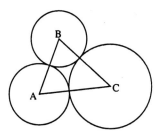

8 In the figure A, B, C, D are the centres of four circles which touch each other in turn.

   (a) Prove that the quadrilateral ABCD is circumscribed to a circle.

   (b) Do the common tangents to the circles at their points of contact meet at a point?

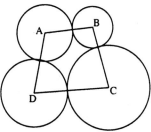

9 Draw an acute-angled triangle ABC. On your figure show the lines needed to find the circumcentres O, P, Q, R of the triangles ABC, OBC, OCA, OAB.

   (a) Prove that $O\hat{P}Q = O\hat{P}R = 90° - \hat{A}$.

   (b) Prove that O is the incentre of $\triangle PQR$.

10 A re-entrant quadrilateral ABCD has a reflex interior angle at C. Show that, if a circle can be drawn to touch [AB], [AD] and [BC] and [CD] produced, as in the figure, then

$$AB + CD = BC + AD.$$

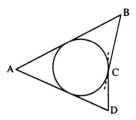

4 Concyclic points

This chapter introduces some properties of circles and two remarkable results which follow from these. When you have completed it, you should

- know that angles on the same arc are equal and that angles on opposite arcs are supplementary
- be able to use the converse theorems to prove that sets of points are concyclic
- be familiar with Ptolemy's theorem and the Simson line property.

4.1 Angle properties of a circle

Of all geometrical figures, circles are the easiest to construct. They are also the most symmetrical: you can rotate a circle through any angle about its centre, or reflect it in any diameter, without changing it. This partly explains why circles feature so largely in the natural world (the eye, the shape of the full moon, the trunk of a tree, ...) and in the man-made world (wheels, coins, cans, ...).

The circles which featured in Chapter 3 owed their existence to these symmetrical properties. But what is more surprising is that circles also have a number of unsymmetrical properties. These are the subject of this chapter.

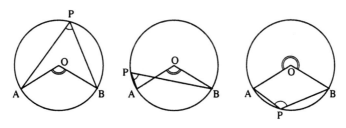

Fig. 4.1

The starting point is the 'angle at the centre' theorem which was proved in Section 1.7. It is illustrated in Fig. 4.1 (which has already appeared as Figs. 1.12 and 1.13). In each of these diagrams the marked angle $A\hat{O}B$ is twice the marked angle $A\hat{P}B$. Using the language introduced in Section 3.5 you can say that the angle subtended by [AB] at the centre of the circle is twice the angle subtended at a point on the arc AB.

Now, with A and B in any position on the circle, suppose that P and Q are two other points on the circle. These may be either on the same arc AB (major or minor) as in Fig. 4.2, or on opposite arcs (one major and the other minor) as in Fig. 4.3.

In Fig. 4.2 the angles $A\hat{P}B$ and $A\hat{Q}B$ are each half of the same angle $A\hat{O}B$, so that $A\hat{P}B = A\hat{Q}B$. These are traditionally described as 'angles in the same segment', but it would be more correct to call them 'angles on the same arc'. (Remember that a segment is the whole region bounded by the chord and the arc; see Section 1.7, Fig. 1.18.)

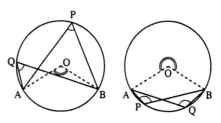

Fig. 4.2

Theorem   If P and Q are two points on the same arc AB of a circle, then
$A\hat{P}B = A\hat{Q}B$.

In Fig. 4.3 $A\hat{P}B$ is half of the lower angle $A\hat{O}B$,
but $A\hat{Q}B$ is half of the upper (reflex) angle $A\hat{O}B$.
The two angles $A\hat{O}B$ together add up to 360°, so
$A\hat{P}B$ and $A\hat{Q}B$ add up to 180°.

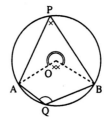

Fig. 4.3

Theorem   If P and Q are two points on opposite arcs AB of a circle, then
$A\hat{P}B + A\hat{Q}B = 180°$.

The figure APBQ whose vertices all lie on the same circle is called a **cyclic quadrilateral**. So the theorem could be summed up in words as
    'the opposite angles of a cyclic quadrilateral are supplementary'.

It is sometimes convenient to make a small
modification to this theorem by producing the side
[BQ] of the quadrilateral to a point X beyond Q,
as in Fig. 4.4. This then makes another angle $A\hat{Q}X$
which is also supplementary to $A\hat{Q}B$, so that the
angles $A\hat{Q}X$ and $A\hat{P}B$ are equal.

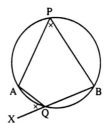

Fig. 4.4

The angle $A\hat{Q}X$ is called the **exterior angle** of the quadrilateral APBQ at Q, to distinguish it from the interior angle $A\hat{P}B$ at P. It is worth recognising this as a separate theorem.

Theorem   In a cyclic quadrilateral the exterior angle at one vertex is equal to
the interior angle at the opposite vertex.

Example 4.1.1
Two circles intersect each other at A and B. Lines l, m are drawn through A, B respectively. The line l cuts the circles again at C and D, and m cuts them at E and F. What can you say about the lines (CE) and (DF)?

Two possible figures are shown. On the left l and m intersect each other outside the circles, on the right they intersect each other inside one of the circles. In each figure the points A and B have been joined by a line segment [AB].

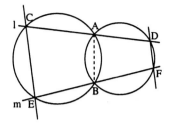 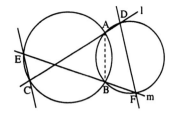

Look at the left figure. Here you have two cyclic quadrilaterals, ABEC and ABFD. Angle $A\hat{B}E$ is the exterior angle of the quadrilateral ABFD at B, so it is equal to the interior angle at D, which is $A\hat{D}F$. But $A\hat{B}E$ is also the interior angle of the quadrilateral ABEC at B, so it is supplementary to the opposite interior angle, which is $A\hat{C}E$. So $A\hat{D}F$ and $A\hat{C}E$ are supplementary.

But these angles could also be labelled as $C\hat{D}F$ and $D\hat{C}E$, which are the angles which the line (CD) makes with (DF) and (CE) respectively. Since these angles are supplementary, the lines (CE) and (DF) are parallel.

Is this still true in the figure on the right? The first step of the proof, that $A\hat{B}E$ is equal to $A\hat{D}F$, holds for the same reason as before. But in the circle on the left you now have the figure for the 'angles on the same arc' theorem, which gives $A\hat{B}E = A\hat{C}E$. So $A\hat{D}F = A\hat{C}E$, or (re-labelling) $C\hat{D}F = D\hat{C}E$. The final conclusion, that (CE) and (DF) are parallel, remains true, but for a different reason.

4.2 Ptolemy's theorem

In Fig. 4.5 a cyclic quadrilateral ABCD is drawn, together with its diagonals [AC] and [BD]. You should be able to see several instances of 'angles on the same arc' in the figure. One of these, based on the arc AB, shows that $A\hat{C}B = A\hat{D}B$.

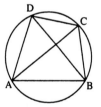

Fig. 4.5

This suggests that you might be able to find a point E on [BD] which makes the triangle AED similar to triangle ABC. To do this, choose E so that $D\hat{A}E = C\hat{A}B$. The corresponding angles of the two triangles will then be equal. The similar triangles are picked out with heavy lines in Fig. 4.6. You can then deduce that

$$\frac{AD}{AC} = \frac{DE}{CB}.$$

(You could of course add '$= \dfrac{AE}{AB}$', but the line AE is not relevant to the argument.)

Now the third angles of these triangles, which are also equal, are $A\hat{E}D$ and $A\hat{B}C$. And if you look at the figure, you will find that you know angles which are supplementary to each of these: $A\hat{E}B$ (because DEB is a straight line) and $A\hat{D}C$ (because ABCD is a cyclic quadrilateral).

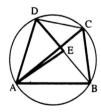

Fig. 4.6

So if you consider the triangles AEB and ADC, which are shown with heavy lines in Fig. 4.7, they also have their corresponding angles equal: $A\hat{E}B = A\hat{D}C$ because they are supplementary to $A\hat{E}D$ and $A\hat{B}C$, and $A\hat{B}E = A\hat{C}D$ because they are angles on the same arc AD. So

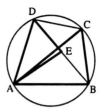

Fig. 4.6

$$\frac{AB}{AC} = \frac{EB}{DC}.$$

(Again, leave out the fraction which includes AE.)

From the two pairs of equal fractions you can derive the equations

$$AD \times CB = AC \times DE$$

and

$$AB \times DC = AC \times EB.$$

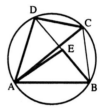

Fig. 4.7

Adding these, you get

$$AD \times CB + AB \times DC = AC \times DE + AC \times EB$$
$$= AC \times (DE + EB)$$
$$= AC \times DB.$$

Look back now at Fig. 4.5 to interpret this result, which is known as Ptolemy's theorem. On the left side you have the lengths of all four sides of the quadrilateral: [AD] and [CB] are one pair of opposite sides, [AB] and [DC] are the other pair. On the right side you have the lengths of the diagonals.

> **Ptolemy's theorem**   In a cyclic quadrilateral the sum of the products of the lengths of the pairs of opposite sides is equal to the product of the diagonals.

Example 4.2.1

The figure shows a design for roof timbers in the shape of an isosceles trapezium. The horizontal beams have lengths a and b, and the oblique beams have length c. The structure is made rigid by diagonal beams of length d. Find d in terms of a, b and c.

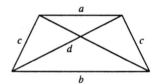

There is no mention of a circle, but an isosceles trapezium can certainly be inscribed in a circle, with its centre at the intersection of the perpendicular bisectors of the oblique and the horizontal beams. So, by Ptolemy's theorem, $ab + c^2 = d^2$.

The length of the diagonal beams is therefore $\sqrt{ab + c^2}$.

Exercise 4A

1   ABCD is a cyclic quadrilateral with $AB = BC$. If $A\hat{B}D = 30°$ and $B\hat{D}C = 45°$, calculate $D\hat{A}C$.

2   ABCDE is a pentagon inscribed in a circle with AD perpendicular to CE. If $E\hat{A}D = 25°$ and $A\hat{C}D = 60°$, calculate $D\hat{B}C$.

3   ABCDE is a pentagon inscribed in a circle. If $A\hat{B}C = 120°$ and $C\hat{D}E = 100°$, calculate $A\hat{C}E$.

4   The diagonals of a cyclic quadrilateral ABCD meet at X. Prove that the triangles ABX, DCX are similar.

5   What can you say about a parallelogram inscribed in a circle?

6   A and B are two points on a circle. [AX] and [BY] are parallel chords through A and B. Another circle through X and Y cuts these chords at P and Q respectively. Prove that APQB is a parallelogram.

7   ABC is an acute-angled triangle. D is the foot of the perpendicular from B to [AC], and X is the point on the circumcircle diametrically opposite to B. Prove that triangles ABD and XBC are similar, and deduce that $BD = \dfrac{ac}{2R}$.

8   O is the centre of a circle, and a second circle passes through O. The two circles intersect at A and B. A line through A cuts the first circle at P and the second circle at Q. Prove that $\triangle QPB$ is isosceles.

9   In the figure prove that $Q\hat{B}R = P\hat{X}S$.

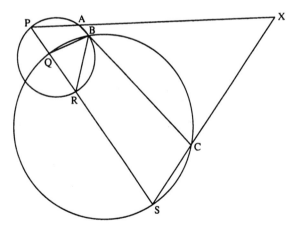

10   AB is a diameter of a circle of length 50 cm. X and Y are points of the circle on opposite sides of AB. If $AX = 40$ cm, $AY = 48$ cm, calculate the length XY.

11   Draw a regular pentagon inscribed in a circle and join all the diagonals.

   (a) Show that all the angles in the figure are multiples of $36°$.

   (b) Use Ptolemy's theorem to prove that, if the sides of the pentagon have length 1 unit and the diagonals have length x units, then $x^2 = x + 1$. (The ratio $x:1$ defines the *golden section*.)

   (c) Deduce that $\cos 36° = \frac{1}{4}\left(1 + \sqrt{5}\right)$.

12   A regular heptagon (7 sides) has sides of length 1 unit and diagonals of two different lengths x units and y units, where $x < y$. Prove that $x^2 = 1 + y$ and $xy = x + y$, and deduce that $(x^2 - 1)(x - 1) = x$.

13   The semicircle in the figure has diameter $PQ = 1$ unit.

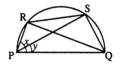

   (a)   Show that $RS = \sin(x - y)$ units.

   (b)   What result do you get by applying Ptolemy's theorem to the cyclic quadrilateral PQSR?

14   ABCDEF is a hexagon inscribed in a circle. Prove that $\hat{A} + \hat{C} + \hat{E} = 2\pi$ radians. Find a comparable result for an octagon ABCDEFGH inscribed in a circle.

4.3   The converse theorems

You know from Section 3.1 that you can draw any number of circles through two given points A, B. But if you are given three points A, B, C, then there is only one circle which passes through them. And if you have four points A, B, C, D, it is very unlikely that you can draw a circle through them all.

But, of course, it is sometimes possible to do so, if the points are suitably chosen. Which suggests the question 'given four points A, B, C, D, how can you tell whether or not they all lie on the same circle?'

> If four or more points A, B, C, D, … are situated so that a circle can be drawn to pass through all of them, the points are said to be **concyclic**.

The question above can be partially answered by the converses of the three theorems in Section 4.1.

These can be stated as follows.

> **Converse of 'angles on the same arc'**   If P and Q are two points on the same side of the line (AB) such that $A\hat{P}B = A\hat{Q}B$, then they lie on the same arc AB of a circle.

Why do you need the extra condition that P and Q have to be on the same side of AB? Fig. 4.8 suggests the answer.

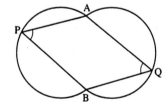

Fig. 4.8

> **Converse of 'opposite angles of a cyclic quadrilateral'**   If a convex quadrilateral APBQ has the internal angles $A\hat{P}B + A\hat{Q}B = 180°$, then the points A, P, B, Q are concyclic.

Converse of 'exterior angle of a cyclic quadrilateral'   If a convex quadrilateral APQB has the exterior angle at Q equal to the interior angle at the opposite vertex P, then the points A, P, B, Q are concyclic.

The proofs of all these converses are very similar to each other. Only the last will be given here. You should then be able to make up proofs of the others for yourself.

The method used is 'proof by contradiction'. Assume that the points are not concyclic, and show that this leads to a false conclusion. It must then follow that the points are concyclic.

Proof of converse of 'exterior angle of a cyclic quadrilateral'

Suppose that the points A, P, B, Q are not concyclic. Draw the circle through A, B and Q. Then P is not on this circle, so it must be either inside or outside it. (See Fig. 4.9).

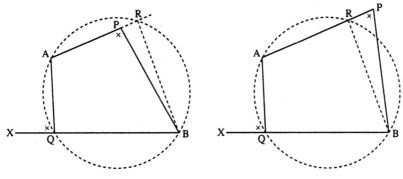

Fig. 4.9

Let the line (AP) meet the circle again at R. Then ARBQ is a cyclic quadrilateral. Therefore, by the exterior angle theorem, $A\hat{Q}X = A\hat{R}B$. But it is given that $A\hat{Q}X = A\hat{P}B$. Therefore $A\hat{P}B = A\hat{R}B$. It follows that [PB] and [RB] are parallel.

But these line segments have a point B in common, so they are not parallel.

This is a contradiction. It follows that the points A, P, B, Q are concyclic.

Example 4.3.1

Two part-lines l, m are drawn from A. Points B and D are taken on l, and C and E on m, such that $AB = 4$ cm, $BD = 5$ cm, $AC = 3$ cm, $CE = 9$ cm. Prove that the quadrilateral BDEC is cyclic.

Calculate $AD = 9$ cm and $AE = 12$ cm, so that

$\dfrac{AE}{AB} = \dfrac{12}{4} = 3$ and $\dfrac{AD}{AC} = \dfrac{9}{3} = 3$. So the triangles AED, ABC have a common angle at A and the sides enclosing that angle are in the same proportion. They are therefore similar, so that $A\hat{B}C = A\hat{E}D$. But $A\hat{B}C$ is the exterior angle at B of the quadrilateral BDEC, and $A\hat{E}D$ is the interior angle at E. Since these are equal, the quadrilateral BDEC is cyclic.

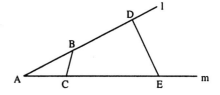

It is interesting that the result of this example is true whatever the size of the angle at $\hat{A}$.

4.4   Simson's line

If two lines meet at a point A, and you draw perpendiculars PM, PN to each of these lines from a point P, then you get one of the diagrams in Fig. 4.10. You will recognise that in the upper diagram you have the opposite angles $P\hat{M}A$ and $P\hat{N}A$ supplementary (because $90° + 90° = 180°$), while in the lower diagram these angles are equal. In both cases it follows that P, M, A, N are concyclic.

In fact, since $P\hat{M}A = P\hat{N}A = 90°$ you could deduce that M and N are points on the circle with diameter PA, by the converse of the 'angle in a semicircle' theorem. But here it is the concyclic property that is important.

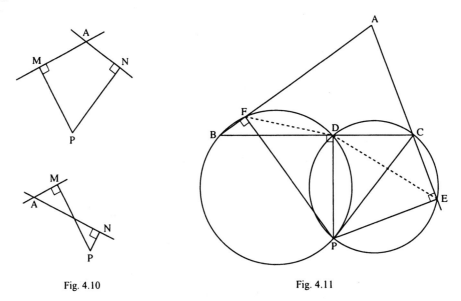

Fig. 4.10   Fig. 4.11

In Fig. 4.11 there is a triangle ABC with lines drawn perpendicular to each side from a point P outside the triangle. You should be able to identify three examples of Fig. 4.10: the quadrilaterals PECD and PEAF are cyclic because opposite angles are supplementary, and B, P, D, F are concyclic because of the equal angles on the arc BP. For the first and last cases the circles have been included in the figure.

There are two other lines in the figure, [DE] and [DF], which are drawn dotted. The property known as 'Simson's line' is that, if P is a point on the circumcircle of triangle ABC, then the points D, E, F are collinear.

Fig. 4.11, in which P is not on the circumcircle, suggests how you might go about proving this. The angle $F\hat{D}E$ is made up of the sum of two angles $F\hat{D}P$ and $P\hat{D}E$. If you could prove that these two angles are supplementary, then the points F, D, E would be in a straight line. And each of these angles is formed from points on one of the circles drawn in Fig. 4.11.

> **Simson's line**   Perpendiculars are drawn from a point to the three sides of a triangle. If the point lies on the circumcircle of the triangle, then the feet of the perpendiculars are collinear; the line is called Simson's line.

Proof

Since the diagram is rather complicated, three copies of it have been drawn with the relevant lines and circles for each step emphasised.

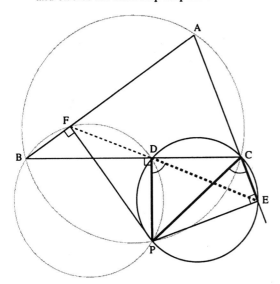

Fig. 4.12

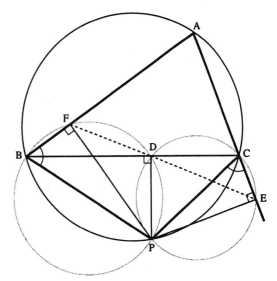

Fig. 4.13

Since $\hat{PDC} + \hat{PEC} = 90° + 90° = 180°$, the points P, D, C, E are concyclic (see Fig. 4.12). Therefore $\hat{PDE} = \hat{PCE}$ (angles on the same arc PE).

The points A, B, C, P all lie on the circumcircle of $\triangle ABC$ (see Fig. 4.13). Therefore, in the quadrilateral ABPC, the exterior angle $\hat{PCE}$ is equal to the interior opposite angle $\hat{PBA}$.

Notice that this is the step which would be missing in Fig. 4.11 where P is not on the circumcircle.

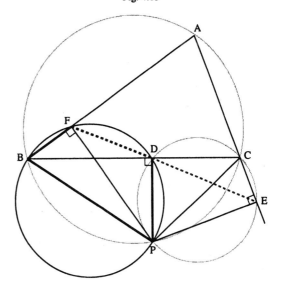

Fig. 4.14

Since $\hat{BFP} = \hat{BDP} = 90°$, the points B, P, D, F are concyclic (see Fig. 4.14). Therefore the opposite angles of the quadrilateral BPDF, $\hat{PBF}$ (which is the same as $\hat{PBA}$) and $\hat{FDP}$ are supplementary.

Therefore $\hat{PDE}$ and $\hat{FDP}$ are supplementary, so that $\hat{FDE} = 180°$. That is, the points F, D, E are collinear.

There is some doubt whether this property is correctly named, since its first appearance in print was due to Wallace 11 years after Simson died. So perhaps the line FDE should really be called 'Wallace's line'.

Exercise 4B

1 X and Y are points on parallel chords [AP] and [BQ] of a circle such that $AX = BY$. Prove that the points X, Y, P, Q are concyclic.

2 X is a point on the side [BC] of $\triangle ABC$ and O is a point inside the triangle. The circumcircles of triangles BXO and CXO cut [AB] and [AC] respectively at P and Q. Prove that the points A, P, O, Q are concyclic.

3 A figure contains three circles c_1, c_2, c_3. The circles c_1, c_2 intersect at P and Q, and c_2, c_3 intersect at R and S. The line (PR) meets c_1 and c_3 again at E and F, and (QS) meets c_1 and c_3 again at G and H. Prove that E, F, G, H are concyclic. (There are many possible figures. Try drawing more than one, and investigate whether the same proof holds for each, or whether it needs to be modified.)

4 For a triangle ABC, identify the Simson lines of

(a) the vertex A,

(b) the point A$'$ diametrically opposite to A on the circumcircle.

5 Four lines intersect in six points as shown in the figure. The circumcircles of $\triangle AFE$ and $\triangle CDE$ intersect at O.

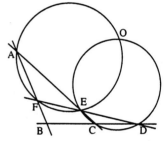

(a) Prove that O also lies on the circumcircles of $\triangle ABC$ and $\triangle FBD$.

(b) Prove that the feet of the perpendiculars from O to the four lines are collinear.

6 P is a point on the circumcircle of $\triangle ABC$. The feet of the perpendiculars from P to (BC) and (AC) are D and E. The line (PD) meets the circumcircle again at X.

(a) From the set $\{A,C,D,E,P,X\}$ identify two concyclic sets of four points. Use these to prove that the Simson line of P is parallel to (AX).

(b) Q is another point on the circumcircle of $\triangle ABC$. Prove that the angle between the Simson lines of P and Q is one half of $P\hat{O}Q$, where O is the circumcentre of $\triangle ABC$.

(c) If the Simson lines of P and Q are perpendicular, what can you say about P and Q?

5 The orthocentre of a triangle

This chapter shows another set of concurrent lines in a triangle. When you have completed it, you should

- know what is meant by an altitude, and that the altitudes of a triangle are concurrent at the orthocentre
- know that in any triangle the centroid, circumcentre and the orthocentre are collinear on Euler's line
- know the Euler circle property
- understand how these properties can be interpreted in terms of an orthocentric quadrangle.

In Section 11.4 there is an alternative treatment using vectors of many of the properties in this chapter.

5.1 Altitudes

You have often used the idea of the height of a triangle, especially when calculating its area. The line drawn from a vertex of a triangle perpendicular to the opposite side is called an **altitude**. In Fig. 5.1 the line segment [AR] is an altitude of the triangle ABC. Notice that when the triangle has an obtuse angle at C, as in the diagram on the right, the side [BC] has to be produced to show the point R, the foot of the altitude.

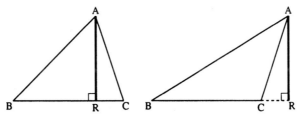

Fig. 5.1

In ordinary usage words like 'height' and 'altitude' are used only for vertical lines, but in geometry they can be used to describe perpendiculars in any direction. Fig. 5.2 and Fig. 5.3 show the other two altitudes [BS] and [CT] of the triangle ABC, meeting at a point H. You will see that in Fig. 5.3, with an obtuse angle at C, these altitudes have to be produced to show the point of intersection.

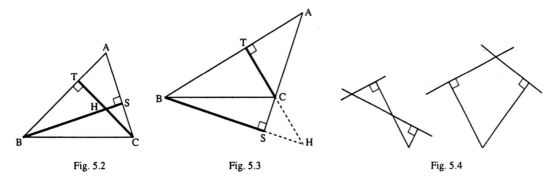

Fig. 5.2   Fig. 5.3   Fig. 5.4

In both figures you will recognise examples of the 'two perpendiculars' patterns (Fig. 5.4) which indicate the existence of concyclic points (compare Fig. 4.10). Using the converses of the 'angles on the same arc' and 'opposite angles of a cyclic quadrilateral' theorems, it follows that the sets of points B, C, S, T and A, S, T, H are concyclic. These circles have been inserted in Fig. 5.5 and Fig. 5.6.

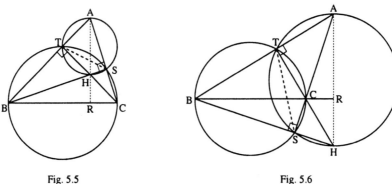

Fig. 5.5   Fig. 5.6

The most important property of the altitudes is that they meet at a common point. The strategy used to show this is the same as you used for the medians in Section 2.2. Rather than drawing all three altitudes, begin with just two of them, join their point of intersection to the third vertex, and then show that this line is also an altitude.

> **Theorem**   The three altitudes of a triangle are concurrent.

Proof
Let the altitudes [BS] and [CT] meet at H. Join [AH], and let it meet [BC] at R (producing the line segments if necessary). Join [ST].

The points A, S, T, H are concyclic (opposite angles at S and T are supplementary in Fig. 5.5, angles at S and T on the same arc AH are equal in Fig. 5.6). So $H\hat{A}S = H\hat{T}S$ (on the same arc HS).

The points B, C, S, T are concyclic (angles at S and T on the same arc BC are equal in Fig. 5.5, opposite angles at S and T are supplementary in Fig. 5.6). So $C\hat{T}S = C\hat{B}S$ (on the same arc CS).

But $H\hat{T}S$ and $C\hat{T}S$ are different labels for the same angle. So $H\hat{A}S = C\hat{B}S$; that is, $R\hat{A}C = C\hat{B}S$.

These are angles in the triangles ACR and BCS respectively. The angles at C are also equal (the same angle in Fig. 5.5, vertically opposite angles in Fig. 5.6). So the third angles are equal, $A\hat{R}C = B\hat{S}C = 90°$.

Therefore [AR] is an altitude. So the three altitudes are concurrent at the point H.

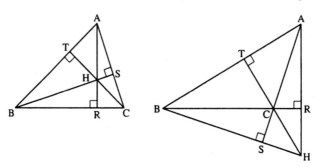

Fig. 5.7

The theorem is illustrated in Fig. 5.7. Both for the acute-angled and the obtuse-angled triangle, the figure is full of similar triangles and cyclic quadrilaterals – see how many you can find.

The point at which the three altitudes of a triangle meet is called the **orthocentre**. For an acute-angled triangle it is inside the triangle, for an obtuse-angled triangle it is outside.

Although called a 'centre', the orthocentre is not the centre of any particular circle associated with the triangle.

The prefix 'ortho-' in Greek means 'right'; you meet it in words such as 'orthodox', which means 'having the right opinion'. In mathematics it indicates that right angles are involved in the definition.

Example 5.1.1
In Fig. 5.7, prove that   (a) $HA \times HR = HB \times HS$,   (b) $CR \times CB = CH \times CT$.

(a)   Triangles HAS, HBR have corresponding angles equal. So $\dfrac{HA}{HB} = \dfrac{HS}{HR}$, and
$HA \times HR = HB \times HS$.

(b)   Triangles CRH, CTB have corresponding angles equal. So $\dfrac{CR}{CT} = \dfrac{CH}{CB}$, and
$CR \times CB = CH \times CT$.

Exercise 5A

1   Prove that, in both diagrams of Fig. 5.7,
(a) $HA \times HR = HB \times HS = HC \times HT$,   (b) $AR \times AH = AS \times AC = AT \times AB$.

2   Prove that, in an acute-angled triangle ABC,
(a) $AH = 2R \cos \hat{A}$,   (b) $O\hat{A}H = \left| \hat{C} - \hat{B} \right|$.
Deduce that $OH^2 = R^2 \left(1 - 8 \cos \hat{A} \cos \hat{B} \cos \hat{C} \right)$.
Investigate any changes in these results which are necessary if either $\hat{A}$ or $\hat{C}$ is obtuse.

3   What lengths in Fig. 5.7 are equal to
(a) $2R \sin \hat{B} \sin \hat{C}$,   (b) $2R \cos \hat{B} \cos \hat{C}$?

5.2   Euler's line

You now know several different sets of concurrent lines associated with a triangle ABC:

- the medians $[AL]$, $[BM]$, $[CN]$ joining the vertices to the mid-points of opposite sides, which meet at the centroid G;
- the perpendicular bisectors of the sides, which meet at the circumcentre O;
- the bisectors of the angles at the vertices, which meet at the incentre I;
- the altitudes $[AR]$, $[BS]$, $[CT]$ through the vertices perpendicular to the opposite sides, which meet at the orthocentre H.

The next step is to explore the connections between these various centres.

Let B′ be the point on the
circumcircle diametrically opposite
to B. This is shown in Fig. 5.8 for
both the acute-angled and obtuse-
angled triangle, but the argument is
just the same for both.

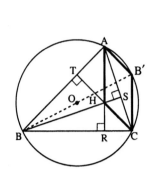
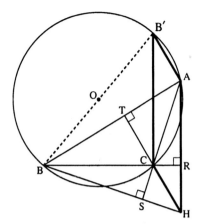

Then, by the angle in a semicircle
property, [B′A] is perpendicular to
[BA] and [B′C] is perpendicular
to [BC]. It follows that [B′A] is
parallel to the altitude [CH], and
[B′C] is parallel to [AH].
Therefore AHCB′ is a
parallelogram, so that $AH = B′C$.

Fig. 5.8

Now concentrate on the triangles
BB′C and BOL, where L is the
mid-point of [BC] (see Fig. 5.9).
These triangles are similar, so that
$OL = \frac{1}{2}B′C$. So $OL = \frac{1}{2}AH$.

This proves:

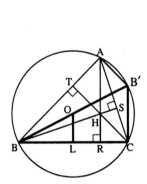
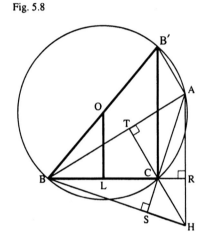

Fig. 5.9

Mini-theorem   If O is the circumcentre and H the orthocentre of a triangle ABC, and if L is
the mid-point of [BC], then $OL = \frac{1}{2}AH$.

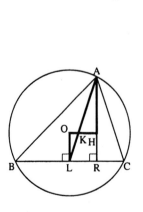
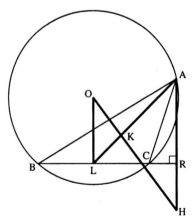

Fig. 5.10

Now join the line segment [OH], and denote its point of intersection with the median [AL] by K (see Fig. 5.10). The line segments [OL] and [AH] are both perpendicular to [BC] so they are parallel. The triangles KAH and KLO are therefore similar. It follows that

$$\frac{AK}{LK} = \frac{KH}{KO} = \frac{AH}{LO}.$$

And since $AH = 2LO$, you can deduce that $AK = 2LK$ and $KH = 2KO$. That is, K divides [HO] in the proportion 2:1, and K divides [AL] in the proportion 2:1.

But you know, from Section 2.2, that the point which divides the median [AL] in the proportion 2:1 is the centroid of the triangle. So the point labelled K is in fact the centroid G of the triangle. This means that O, G and H all lie on the same line; it is called 'Euler's line'.

Although Fig. 5.10 shows only the altitude [AR] and the mid-point of [BC], you would reach the same conclusion by taking a different altitude and side, such as [BS] and [CA]. There is nothing to be gained by repeating the argument with these. The final result gives no clue as to which altitude and side you chose for the proof.

> **Euler's line**   The circumcentre O, the centroid G and the orthocentre H of a triangle are collinear, and G divides HO in the proportion 2:1.

Exercise 5B

1   In $\triangle ABC$ the mid-points of the sides are L, M, N and the points on the circumcircle opposite to A, B, C are A′, B′, C′. Prove that the lines (A′L), (B′M), (C′N) are concurrent, and state the point of concurrence.

2   In the left diagram of Fig. 5.8, if the line (HR) meets the circumcircle again at J, prove that $HR = RJ$.

3   F and G are two points on the same arc of a circle through B and C. H and I are the orthocentres of $\triangle FBC$ and $\triangle GBC$. Prove that [HI] is parallel to [FG].

4   If L, M, N are the mid-points of the sides of $\triangle ABC$, and O is the circumcentre, how is O related to $\triangle LMN$?

   You proved in Exercise 2A Question 7 that G is the centroid of $\triangle LMN$. Use this to show that $\triangle ABC$ and $\triangle LMN$ have a common Euler line. Where is the circumcentre of $\triangle LMN$?

5   Show that if, in triangle $\triangle ABC$, $\hat{B}$ and $\hat{C}$ are acute, then the angles subtended by [BC] at A and H, the orthocentre, are supplementary. What is the corresponding result if either of $\hat{B}$ or $\hat{C}$ is obtuse? Deduce that, in either case, the circumradii of $\triangle ABC$, $\triangle HBC$, $\triangle HCA$, $\triangle HAB$ are equal. If the circumcentres of $\triangle HBC$, $\triangle HCA$, $\triangle HAB$ are X, Y, Z, how is H related to $\triangle XYZ$?

5.3   Euler's circle

There is more yet to be found out about a triangle and its altitudes, but before taking the next step it will be useful to prove a property of quadrilaterals.

Mini-theorem   The mid-points of the sides of a quadrilateral are vertices of a parallelogram, with sides parallel to the diagonals of the quadrilateral.

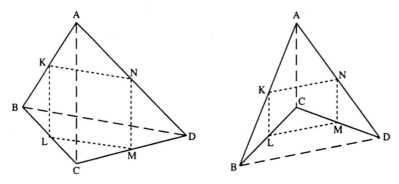

Fig. 5.11

Proof

Two diagrams are shown in Fig. 5.11, one with a convex and one with a re-entrant quadrilateral. The result is true for both, and the proof is just the same. The quadrilateral ABCD has sides with mid-points K, L, M, N.

Look first at the triangles ABC and KBL. These have a common angle at B, and BA = 2BK, BC = 2BL. So the triangles are similar. It follows that [KL] is parallel to [AC].

In just the same way, from triangles ADC and NDM, [NM] is parallel to [AC]. Therefore [NM] is parallel to [KL].

The same argument, using triangles ABD and AKN, and CBD and CLM, shows that [KN] and [LM] are both parallel to [BD], and therefore parallel to each other.

So KLMN is a parallelogram, with sides parallel to [AC] and [BD].

This mini-theorem can now be applied to Fig. 5.12. Besides the triangle ABC with its altitudes and the mid-points of the sides, this also shows the mid-points of [AH], [BH] and [CH], which are labelled U, V and W respectively. (It is left to you to draw the corresponding figure with the angle at C obtuse; the argument applies word-for-word to this figure, though in the final result some of the points will appear in a different order.)

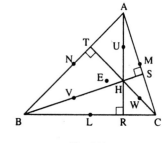

Fig. 5.12

You should be able to see several examples of the re-entrant version of Fig. 5.11 in Fig. 5.12. For example, from the quadrilateral ABHC it follows that the mid-points N, V, W, M are the vertices of a parallelogram, with sides parallel to the diagonals [AH] and [BC]. And since [AH] is perpendicular to [BC], this parallelogram is a rectangle.

In the same way, from the quadrilaterals BCHA and CAHB, you can deduce that L, W, U, N and M, U, V, L are vertices of rectangles. These last two rectangles are shown in Fig. 5.13, with their diagonals shown as broken lines. (The other rectangle has been left out to avoid complicating the diagram unnecessarily; you can prove all you need with just two rectangles.)

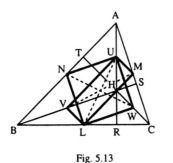

Fig. 5.13

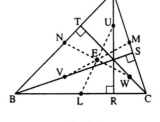

Fig. 5.14

Now what you know about the diagonals of a rectangle is that they meet at their mid-points and have equal lengths. Since the two rectangles have a common diagonal [LU], it follows that all three diagonals meet at a point (labelled E) and have equal lengths. This is shown in Fig. 5.14.

So the six points L, M, N, U, V, W lie on a circle with centre E. This is called **Euler's circle**.

Can you find the radius of this circle? Since it is the circumcircle of the triangle LMN, whose sides have lengths which are half those of the sides of triangle ABC, the radius must be $\frac{1}{2}R$.

And you should be able to see three more points on the circle. Since [LU] is a diameter, and $L\hat{R}U$ is a right angle, you can use the converse of the 'angle in a semicircle' to prove that R lies on the circle. And using the other diameters [MV] and [NW], it follows in the same way that S and T are on the circle.

This can all be summed up as a theorem:

> **Euler's circle**   In a triangle, the feet of the altitudes, the mid-points of the sides and the mid-points of the line segments joining the vertices to the orthocentre lie on a circle whose radius is one-half of the radius of the circumcircle.

Euler's circle is illustrated in Fig. 5.15. Because it passes through nine known points, it is often called the **nine-point circle**, and in some books the theorem is called the nine-point circle theorem.

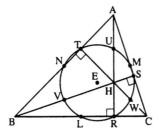

Fig. 5.15

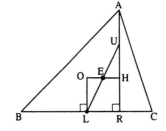

Fig. 5.16

Where is its centre? This can be answered from Fig. 5.16. The mini-theorem in Section 5.2 showed that $OL = \frac{1}{2}AH$. So, since U is the mid-point of [AH], OL = UH. Also [UH] is parallel to [OL], since both are perpendicular to [BC]. Therefore UHLO is a parallelogram. And since E is the mid-point of [UL], it is also the mid-point of [OH], which is Euler's line.

> **Theorem**   The centre of Euler's circle lies on Euler's line, and is the mid-point of the line segment joining the circumcentre to the orthocentre.

Amongst other properties of Euler's circle is that it touches the incircle of the triangle. This is known as 'Feuerbach's theorem'. It is too difficult to prove here, but you might find it interesting to check it by making an accurate drawing.

5.4* A change of perspective

The purpose of this section is not to extend further the theory of the altitudes, Euler's line and Euler's circle, but to look at what has already been proved from a different point of view. You can treat it as optional, and leave it out or come back to it later if you wish.

In Fig. 5.15, where is the orthocentre of the triangle BCH, and which points are on its Euler circle?

Because $\hat{B}HC$ is an obtuse angle, the sides [BH] and [CH] have to be produced in order to find the altitudes, which are [BT], [CS] and [HR]. These line segments, when produced, intersect at A. So the orthocentre of ΔBCH is A. Similarly, the orthocentre of ΔCAH is B, and the orthocentre of ΔABH is C.

The points on Euler's circle of ΔBCH are the mid-points of the sides, which are W, V and L; the mid-points of the lines between the vertices and the orthocentre, which are N, M and U; and the feet of the altitudes, which are S, T and R. These are just the same points as before, though differently organised.

You could express this new interpretation by stating that 'the points A, B, C, H are such that each is the orthocentre of the triangle formed by the other three, and these triangles all have the same Euler circle'. So it would perhaps be better to think of Fig. 5.15 as showing four points having equal status, rather than of a triangle ABC and a separate point H. From this point of view it would be more sensible to re-label the point H as D.

A set of four points is called a quadrangle; the four points can be placed anywhere in the plane, provided that no three are collinear, and (unlike the quadrilateral) the points are not visited in any particular order. Fig. 5.17 shows a typical quadrangle. The points A, B, C, D can be joined by six lines: (BC), (CA), (AB), (AD), (BD), (CD). Call these lines 'joins'.

In a quadrilateral four of the joins would be called 'sides' and the other two would be called 'diagonals'. But in a quadrangle, where no order is specified, there is no way of distinguishing one kind of join from another. However,

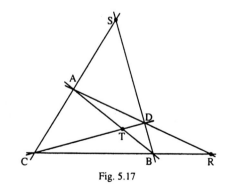

Fig. 5.17

the joins do separate out into three pairs: (BC) with (AD), (CA) with (BD), (AB) with (CD). All the pairs involve each vertex just once; they can be called pairs of 'opposite' joins. Unless they happen to be parallel, each pair of opposite joins intersect in a point. These are the points R, S, T marked with a small dot in Fig. 5.17; they are called the 'diagonal points' of the quadrangle.

Now look back at the theorem that the altitudes are concurrent in Section 5.1. The proof began by taking the two altitudes through B and C perpendicular to [CA] and [AB], which met at the point H (which is now D in Fig. 5.18.) That is, for the quadrangle A, B, C, D two pairs of joins (BD), (CA) and (CD), (AB) consist of lines at right angles: the technical word is 'orthogonal'. It was then proved that [AD] is perpendicular to [BC], so that the third pair of joins (AD), (BC) is orthogonal. So you could state the orthocentre theorem in Section 5.1 as:

> If two pairs of opposite joins of a quadrangle are orthogonal, the third pair is also orthogonal.

This is illustrated in Fig. 5.18. The quadrangle is then called an 'orthocentric quadrangle'.

Now look at the Euler circle in the figure. The six mid-points L, M, N, U, V, W are the mid-points of [BC], [CA], [AB], [AD], [BD], [CD], the six joins. The feet R, S, T of the altitudes are the diagonal points of the quadrangle. So the Euler's circle property can be stated as:

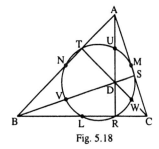

Fig. 5.18

> In an orthocentric quadrangle, the mid-points of the six joins and the three diagonal points are concyclic.

This defines the Euler circle as a property of the complete quadrangle rather than of the separate triangles. Note that each triangle has a different Euler line, with a different orthocentre, circumcentre and centroid, even though all the Euler lines pass through E, the centre of the Euler circle which they all share.

Exercise 5C

1   In Fig. 5.16 prove that the radius [EL] of the Euler circle is parallel to the radius [OA] of the circumcircle. Also, if J is the point defined in Exercise 5B Question 2, prove that the radius [ER] of the Euler circle is parallel to the radius [OJ] of the circumcircle.

2   If $\hat{A}$ is a right angle, how many of the nine points on the Euler circle can be distinguished? What is the radius of the Euler circle in this case?

3   In Exercise 5B Question 5 prove that the figure formed by O, X, Y, Z is congruent to the figure formed by H, A, B, C. What can you say about its Euler circle?

4   B and C are fixed points on a circle of radius R, and P is a variable point on the circle. Describe the locus of

(a) the orthocentre of $\triangle PBC$,   (b) the centre of the Euler circle of $\triangle PBC$.

6 Internal and external bisectors

In Chapter 3 only the internal bisectors of an angle were used. Taking the internal and external bisectors together generates more geometrical properties. When you have completed this chapter, you should

- know the angle bisector theorem for a triangle in both internal and external forms
- know that a triangle has three escribed circles, and how to construct them
- understand Apollonius's circle as a locus.

6.1 The angle bisector theorem

In Section 3.3 you made use of the angle bisectors at the vertices of a triangle to find the centre of the incircle. This chapter asks questions about angle bisectors as lines in their own right. For example, in Fig. 6.1, if the bisector of angle $\hat{A}$ meets the opposite side $[BC]$ at D, in what proportion does D divide $[BC]$? What is the length of $[AD]$?

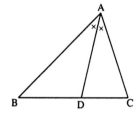

Fig. 6.1

The answer to the first question is provided by the following theorem.

> **The angle bisector theorem**   The proportion in which the bisector of the angle at a vertex of a triangle divides the opposite side is equal to the proportion of the lengths of the sides which meet at the vertex.

That is, in Fig. 6.1, $\dfrac{BD}{DC} = \dfrac{AB}{AC}$.

To decide how to prove this, look back to Section 1.6, Fig. 1.9, where a pair of parallel lines cuts two intersecting lines in equal proportions. You could create a figure like this by producing the side $[BA]$ and drawing a line $[CX]$ parallel to $[DA]$, as in Fig. 6.2.

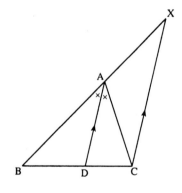

Fig. 6.2

Proof

Since $[CX]$ is parallel to $[DA]$, $\dfrac{BD}{DC} = \dfrac{BA}{AX}$.

Three of the lengths in the equation that you want to prove are already in this equation. All that remains is to prove that $AC = AX$; that is, that triangle ACX is isosceles.

From the parallel lines, $\hat{BAD} = \hat{AXC}$ (corresponding, or F angles) and $\hat{DAC} = \hat{ACX}$ (alternate, or Z angles). Also, since $[AD]$ bisects $\hat{BAC}$, $\hat{BAD} = \hat{DAC}$. Therefore $\hat{AXC} = \hat{ACX}$.

It follows that $AC = AX$, so $\dfrac{BD}{DC} = \dfrac{BA}{AC}$.

Example 6.1.1

The lengths of the sides of $\triangle ABC$ are $AB = 4$ cm, $BC = 5$ cm, $CA = 6$ cm. The bisector of $\hat{A}$ meets $[BC]$ at D. Find the lengths BD, DC and AD.

By the angle bisector theorem, $\dfrac{BD}{DC} = \dfrac{AB}{AC} = \dfrac{4}{6} = \dfrac{2}{3}$.

This gives $\dfrac{BD}{BC} = \dfrac{2}{5}$, so $BD = \frac{2}{5} \times 5$ cm $= 2$ cm, and similarly $DC = \frac{3}{5} \times 5$ cm $= 3$ cm.

To find AD, you can use Stewart's theorem (see Section 2.4). It is simplest to use it in the alternative form

$$mb^2 + nc^2 = (m+n)d^2 + \frac{mn}{m+n} a^2,$$

where D divides $[BC]$ in the proportion $m:n$, and d denotes the length AD. In this example, $a = 5$, $b = 6$, $c = 4$, and you can take $m = 2$ and $n = 3$. So

$$2 \times 6^2 + 3 \times 4^2 = 5 \times d^2 + \tfrac{6}{5} \times 5^2.$$

This gives $d^2 = 18$, so the length AD is $\sqrt{18}$ cm, or more simply $3\sqrt{2}$ cm.

The converse of the angle bisector theorem is also true.

Converse of the angle bisector theorem   If a point on one side of a triangle divides that side in the same proportion as that of the lengths of the adjacent sides, then the line joining that point to the opposite vertex bisects the angle at that vertex.

That is, in Fig. 6.1, if $\dfrac{BD}{DC} = \dfrac{AB}{AC}$, then $[AD]$ bisects $\hat{A}$.

The proof is simply a reversal of the steps in the proof of the theorem itself.

Proof

Construct $[CX]$ parallel to $[DA]$ as in Fig. 6.2. Then $\dfrac{BD}{DC} = \dfrac{BA}{AX}$. But you are given that $\dfrac{BD}{DC} = \dfrac{AB}{AC}$. Therefore $AC = AX$, so $\triangle ACX$ is isosceles and $\hat{AXC} = \hat{ACX}$.

Also, since $[CX]$ and $[DA]$ are parallel, $\hat{BAD} = \hat{AXC}$ and $\hat{DAC} = \hat{ACX}$. Therefore $\hat{BAD} = \hat{DAC}$, that is $[AD]$ bisects $\hat{A}$.

6.2   Escribed circles

Fig. 6.3 shows triangle ABC with the sides [AB], [AC] produced to U, V. You know that all the circles which touch both the lines (AU) and (AV) have their centres on the bisector of Â. Suppose you start at A and move along the bisector, drawing circles which touch both lines. When you reach I the circle will also touch the third side [BC]. Carrying on down the bisector, you will get circles for which [BC] is a secant, until you reach J, when the circle again touches [BC]. This circle is called an 'escribed circle' of the triangle ABC; it touches two of the sides produced, and one side internally.

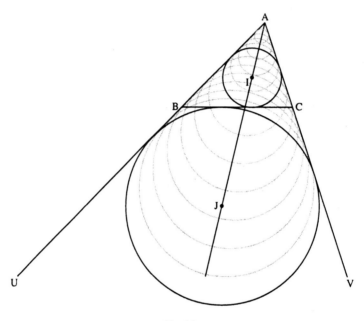

Fig. 6.3

Because the circle touches both [BC] and [BU], the centre J is also on the bisector of $C\hat{B}U$. The point where the two bisectors meet is at the same distance (the radius) from all three sides, so it is also on the bisector of $B\hat{C}V$. The angles $C\hat{B}U$ and $B\hat{C}V$ are exterior angles of the triangle ABC at B and C respectively. The words **internal bisector** and **external bisector** are used to describe the bisectors of the interior and exterior angles at the vertex of a triangle.

> In a triangle the internal bisector at one vertex and the external bisectors at the other two vertices are concurrent. Their common point is the centre of a circle which touches the first side internally and the other two sides produced. This circle is called an **escribed circle** of the triangle (often shortened to **e-circle**), and its centre is an **e-centre**.

A triangle has three e-circles in all, one corresponding to each vertex. These are illustrated in Fig. 6.4.

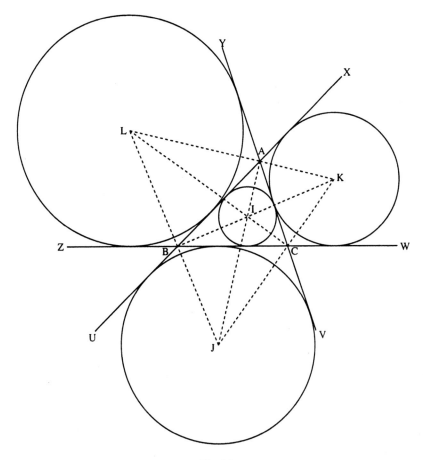

Fig. 6.4

Example 6.2.1

A right-angled triangle ABC has BC = 5 cm, CA = 4 cm, AB = 3 cm. The e-circle opposite A touches the sides (produced where necessary) at X, Y, Z, and the e-circle opposite B touches the sides at U, V, W. Find

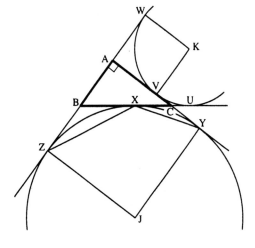

(a) AZ,

(b) the radius of the e-circle opposite A,

(c) the angle $Z\hat{X}Y$,

(d) the radius of the e-circle opposite B.

(Compare Example 3.4.1.)

    (a)   The tangents from B and C to the e-circle are equal, so BZ = BX and CX = CY. Therefore

$$AZ + AY = AB + BZ + AC + CY = AB + AC + (BX + CX) = AB + AC + BC = 12 \text{ cm}.$$

But also AZ = AY. Therefore AZ = 6 cm.

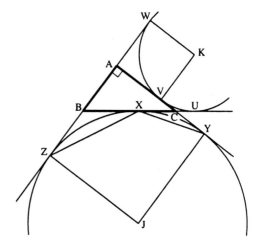

(b)   Since $Z\hat{A}Y = A\hat{Z}J = A\hat{Y}J = 90°$ and $JY = JZ$, the quadrilateral $AZJY$ is a square. Therefore $JZ = AZ$, and the e-circle has radius $JZ = 6$ cm.

(c)   By the 'angle at the centre' theorem, $Z\hat{X}Y$ is half of the reflex angle $Z\hat{J}Y$, which is $270°$. Therefore $Z\hat{X}Y = 135°$.

(d)   By the same reasoning as in part (a), $BW = BU = 6$ cm, and $AVKW$ is a square. (Work through the details for yourself.) Therefore $KW = AW = 3$ cm.

You will need to know a small but important property of internal and external bisectors.

> **Theorem**   The internal and external bisectors at a vertex of a triangle are at right angles to each other.

Proof
In Fig. 6.5 BI and BJ are the internal and external bisectors at a vertex B of a triangle ABC. Then $I\hat{B}C = \frac{1}{2} \times A\hat{B}C$ and $C\hat{B}J = \frac{1}{2} \times C\hat{B}U$, so

$$I\hat{B}J = I\hat{B}C + C\hat{B}J$$
$$= \frac{1}{2} \times \left(A\hat{B}C + C\hat{B}U\right)$$
$$= \frac{1}{2} \times 180° = 90°.$$

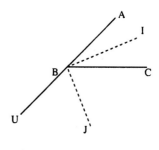

Fig. 6.5

There is also a property of external bisectors like the internal angle bisector theorem proved in Section 6.1.

> **The external angle bisector theorem**   The proportion in which the external bisector of the angle at the vertex of a triangle divides the opposite side externally is equal to the proportion of the lengths of the sides which meet at the vertex.

That is, in Fig. 6.6, $\dfrac{BE}{EC} = \dfrac{AB}{AC}$.

The proof follows very closely the proof for the internal angle bisector theorem. The figure is drawn with $AB > AC$, but the proof is easily adapted to a triangle with $AB < AC$.

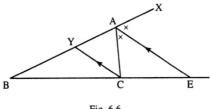

Fig. 6.6

Proof
Draw a line through C parallel to [EA] to meet [AB] at Y.

Since [CY] is parallel to [EA], $\dfrac{BE}{EC} = \dfrac{BA}{AY}$. Also $C\hat{Y}A = E\hat{A}X$ (corresponding angles) and $A\hat{C}Y = C\hat{A}E$ (alternate angles). But [AE] bisects $C\hat{A}X$, so $C\hat{A}E = E\hat{A}X$. Therefore $A\hat{C}Y = C\hat{Y}A$, so $AY = AC$. It follows that $\dfrac{BE}{EC} = \dfrac{AB}{AC}$.

Example 6.2.2
For the triangle in Example 6.1.1, with AB = 4 cm, BC = 5 cm and CA = 6 cm, the external bisector of $\hat{A}$ meets the side [BC] produced at E. Find the lengths BE, EC and AE.

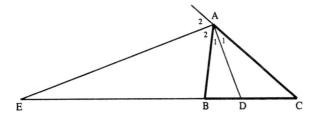

Because AB < AC, the point E is on the side [CB] produced to the left beyond B. By the external angle bisector theorem, $\dfrac{BE}{EC} = \dfrac{AB}{AC} = \dfrac{4}{6} = \dfrac{2}{3}$. So if BE = 2 units, EC = 3 units, and therefore BC is 1 unit. A unit is therefore 5 cm, so that BE = 10 cm and EC = 15 cm.

As in Example 6.1.1, Stewart's theorem, in the form $mb^2 + nc^2 = (m+n)d^2 + \dfrac{mn}{m+n}a^2$ can be used to find AE. There are two methods that you might try.

Method 1   You could apply Stewart's theorem using the triangle AEC rather than ABC, with B dividing [EC] in the proportion 2:1. The equation would take the form

$$mAC^2 + nAE^2 = (m+n)AB^2 + \frac{mn}{m+n}EC^2.$$

With $m = 2$, $n = 1$, this gives

$$2 \times 6^2 + 1 \times AE^2 = 3 \times 4^2 + \tfrac{2}{3} \times 15^2,$$

$$AE^2 = 48 + 150 - 72 = 126.$$

So $AE = \sqrt{126}$ cm $= 3\sqrt{14}$ cm.

You could check this answer by using Pythagoras's theorem, since $[AE]$ is at right angles to $[AD]$, and you found in Example 6.1.1 that $AD = \sqrt{18}$ cm. This would give $ED^2 = 126 + 18 = 144$, so that $ED = 12$ cm. This agrees with the other lengths you have found, $EB = 10$ cm and (from Example 6.1.1) $BD = 2$ cm.

Method 2   This is somewhat experimental. Would it be possible to apply Stewart's theorem to triangle ABC, as you did in Example 6.1.1, but taking m to be -2 rather than 2, because BE is measured in the opposite direction to EC? With $m = -2$, $n = 3$, and a, b, c having their usual meanings, this would give

$$-2 \times 6^2 + 3 \times 4^2 = (-2 + 3)AE^2 + \frac{-2 \times 3}{-2 + 3} \times 5^2,$$

$$AE^2 = -72 + 48 + 150 = 126.$$

So, as with the first method, $AE = \sqrt{126}$ cm $= 3\sqrt{14}$ cm.

The method seems to work! The idea of negative proportions will be developed further in Chapter 7, but this first success looks promising.

Exercise 6A

1   This question uses the notation of Fig. 6.4.

   (a) Find an expression for $K\hat{J}L$ in terms of the angles of $\triangle ABC$.

   (b) Show that $\triangle JKL$ is always acute-angled.

   (c) State how the point I is related to $\triangle JKL$.

   (d) Identify the Euler circle of $\triangle JKL$.

   (e) Show that the circumradius of $\triangle JKL$ is $2R$.

2   In a triangle ABC the incircle touches $[BC]$ at X, and the e-circle opposite A touches $[BC]$ at X_1 and the sides $[AC]$ and $[AB]$ produced at Y_1 and Z_1.

   (a) Prove that $AY_1 = AZ_1 = s$, where $s = \frac{1}{2}(a + b + c)$.

   (b) Prove that $BX_1 = CX = s - c$.

   (c) If the radius of the e-circle is r_1, prove that $r_1 = s \tan \frac{1}{2}\hat{A} = (s - c) \cot \frac{1}{2}\hat{B} = (s - b) \cot \frac{1}{2}\hat{C}$.

   (d) Express the sides and angles of $\triangle X_1 Y_1 Z_1$ in terms of the sides and angles of $\triangle ABC$.

3   A triangle ABC has sides of length $a = 6$ cm, $b = 5$ cm, $c = 7$ cm. The internal and external bisectors of $\hat{A}$ meet (BC) at D and E. Calculate the lengths

   (a) CD,   (b) CE,   (c) AD,   (d) AE.

4   Repeat Question 3 for a general triangle ABC for which $c > b$, giving your answers in terms of a, b, c.

5   M is the mid-point of the side $[BC]$ of $\triangle ABC$. The bisector of $A\hat{M}B$ meets $[AB]$ at D, and E is a point on $[AC]$ such that $[DE]$ is parallel to $[BC]$. Prove that ME bisects $A\hat{M}C$.

6.3   Apollonius's locus problem

When mathematicians have solved one problem, they often go on to ask a more general question, of which the previous problem is a special case.

In Section 1.5 you found that the locus of a point P with the property that PA = PB is the perpendicular bisector of [AB]. Now suppose that the equation PA = PB is replaced by the more general equation PA = $k \times$ PB, where k is some constant number other than 1. What would the locus of P be then?

To simplify the argument, suppose that the constant k is greater than 1. This is not really a restriction, since if k were less than 1 you could write k as $\frac{1}{k'}$ where $k' > 1$, and then PB = $k' \times$ PA – which is just the same question as before with different letters. With $k > 1$, the point P is closer to B than to A.

The clue to the solution is to write PA = $k \times$ PB as $\frac{PA}{PB} = k$, which suggests using the angle bisector theorems. So take any point P on the locus and draw the internal and external bisectors of $A\hat{P}B$, as in Fig. 6.7. Suppose that these meet the line (AB) at points D and E. Then you know that $\frac{AD}{DB} = \frac{PA}{PB} = k$, and that $\frac{AE}{EB} = \frac{PA}{PB} = k$. That is, D and E are the points which divide [AB] internally and externally in the proportion $k:1$. And the important point is that these are *fixed* points; they don't depend on which particular point on the locus P is.

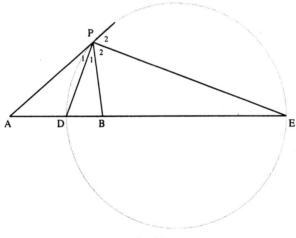

Fig. 6.7

But you also know another property of the figure, that the internal and external bisectors are at right angles to each other, so $D\hat{P}E = 90°$.

You are now on familiar ground. The converse of the 'angle in a semicircle' theorem states that, if $D\hat{P}E = 90°$, then P lies on the circle with diameter [DE].

So what has been proved so far is:

> On the line (AB), D and E are the points which divide [AB] internally and externally in the proportion $k:1$. If $\frac{PA}{PB} = k$, then P lies on the circle with diameter [DE].

Now, as in all locus problems, you have to prove the converse:

On the line (AB), D and E are the points which divide [AB] internally and externally in the proportion $k:1$. If P lies on the circle with diameter [DE], then $\dfrac{PA}{PB} = k$.

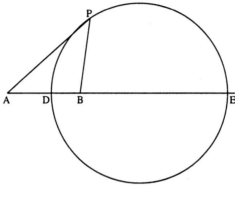

Fig. 6.8

This is illustrated in Fig. 6.8. You now know that P lies on the circle and that $\dfrac{AD}{DB} = \dfrac{AE}{EB} = k$, but you don't know that [PD] and [PE] are the bisectors of angle $A\hat{P}B$.

The proof of the converse is in three stages; the first uses the equation $\dfrac{AD}{DB} = \dfrac{AE}{EB}$, the second brings in the fact that P lies on the circle, and the two are then put together to show that $\dfrac{PA}{PB}$ is constant.

The clue is to introduce two new lines to the figure like the lines [CX] in Fig. 6.2 and [CY] in Fig. 6.6. This has been done in Fig. 6.9, where [BQ] and [BR] are drawn parallel to [DP] and [EP] respectively. You can then use the intercept theorem (Section 1.6) to deduce that

$$\frac{AD}{DB} = \frac{AP}{PQ} \quad \text{and} \quad \frac{AE}{EB} = \frac{AP}{PR}.$$

And since you are given that $\dfrac{AD}{DB} = \dfrac{AE}{EB}$, it follows that

$$\frac{AP}{PQ} = \frac{AP}{PR}.$$

That is, $PQ = PR$.

Now look at the part of the figure involving the points B, P, Q, R, shown with heavy lines in Fig. 6.10. You have seen a figure like this before, in Section 1.7, Fig. 1.15 (with points P, Z, A, B respectively corresponding to B, P, Q, R).

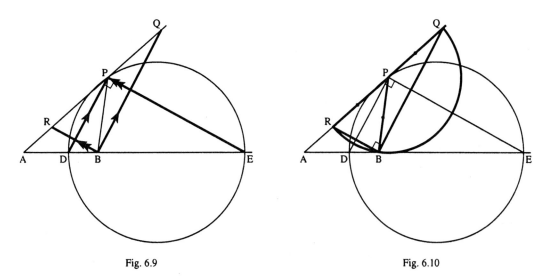

Fig. 6.9   Fig. 6.10

Since P is on the circle with diameter [DE], [DP] is perpendicular to [EP]. And since [BQ] is parallel to [DP] and [BR] is parallel to [EP], [BQ] is perpendicular to [BR]. So, by the converse of the angle in a semicircle theorem, B is a point on the circle with diameter [QR]. And since PQ = PR, P is the centre of this circle. It follows that PB = PQ.

This is the key fact that you need to complete the proof. You already know that $\dfrac{AP}{PQ} = \dfrac{AD}{DB}$. Replacing PQ by PB in this equation,

$$\frac{PA}{PB} = \frac{AD}{DB} = k.$$

There is just one more tiny point to clear up. The converse was proved for a point P which was not on the line (AB). This is because, if P is at D or E, then it is meaningless to make any statement about $D\hat{P}E$. But you are given that $\dfrac{AD}{DB} = \dfrac{AE}{EB} = k$, which means that D and E are certainly points on the locus such that $\dfrac{PA}{PB} = k$. So the locus consists of the whole circle with diameter [DE], including D and E.

The final conclusion can now be stated as a theorem:

> **Apollonius's circle theorem**   Given two fixed points A and B, the locus of points P such that $\dfrac{PA}{PB} = k$ is the circle with diameter [DE], where D and E are the points on the line (AB) such that $\dfrac{AD}{DB} = \dfrac{AE}{EB} = k$.

Other proofs of this property using coordinates or vectors are given in Section 9.2 and Section 11.5.

Exercise 6B

1 Mark two points A, B on a line 6 cm apart. By finding points D, E on the line such that $\dfrac{AD}{DB} = \dfrac{AE}{EB} = k$, draw the Apollonius circles for $k = 5, 4, 3, 2, \frac{1}{2}, \frac{1}{3}, \frac{1}{4}, \frac{1}{5}$.

2 Explain why, for two fixed points A, B, none of the Apollonius circles for different values of k can intersect each other.

3 Draw a triangle ABC with $\hat{A} = 90°$, $b = 8$ cm, $c = 6$ cm. Find two points P with the property that $PA:PB:PC = 1:2:3$. For each point, measure the length PA.

4 A, B, C are three points on a line on that order. What is the locus of points P such that $A\hat{P}B = B\hat{P}C$?

5 A, B are two fixed points, and c is an Apollonius circle with constant $k > 1$. If a chord [PQ] of c passes through B, prove that [AB] bisects $P\hat{A}Q$.

7 The theorems of Ceva and Menelaus

This chapter introduces two general theorems about concurrent lines through the vertices of a triangle and collinear points on the sides. When you have completed the chapter, you should

- know and be able to apply Ceva's theorem and its converse
- know how the theorem can be extended using the idea of sensed length
- know and be able to apply Menelaus's theorem and its converse
- recognise the harmonic construction.

Alternative proofs of these theorems by vector methods will be found in Sections 11.1 and 11.2.

7.1 Ceva's theorem

In Chapters 2, 3 and 5 you have met three examples in which lines through the vertices of a triangle – the medians, the angle bisectors and the altitudes – meet in a single point. Ceva's theorem (or, more precisely, its converse) sums up all these properties by means of a single equation.

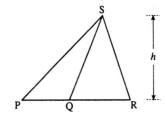

Fig. 7.1

The key diagram which you need to recognise to prove Ceva's theorem is shown in Fig. 7.1, which shows collinear points P, Q, R and two triangles SPQ and SQR with a common vertex S.

These triangles have the same height (call it h), so

$$\frac{\text{area}(\triangle SPQ)}{\text{area}(\triangle SQR)} = \frac{\frac{1}{2}PQ \times h}{\frac{1}{2}QR \times h} = \frac{PQ}{QR}.$$

Ceva's theorem is about a triangle ABC with points D on the side [BC], E on [CA] and F on [AB] such that the line segments [AD], [BE] and [CF] have a common point O (see Fig. 7.2).

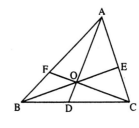

Fig. 7.2

Taking [BC] as the base, you should be able to see the key diagram (Fig. 7.1) twice in Fig. 7.2: with triangles ABD and ADC, and with triangles OBD and ODC. They are emphasised in Fig. 7.3. From them you can write down two equations,

$$\frac{\text{area}(\triangle ABD)}{\text{area}(\triangle ADC)} = \frac{BD}{DC} \quad \text{and} \quad \frac{\text{area}(\triangle OBD)}{\text{area}(\triangle ODC)} = \frac{BD}{DC}.$$

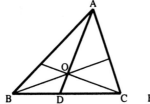
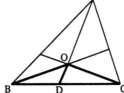

Fig. 7.3

Now you can use a very useful result in algebra, that if you have two fractions $\frac{p}{q}$ and $\frac{r}{s}$ which are both

equal to x, then $\frac{p-r}{q-s}$ is also equal to x. This is easy to prove. If $\frac{p}{q} = x$ and $\frac{r}{s} = x$, then $p = xq$ and

$r = xs$. So $p - r = xq - xs = x(q-s)$, and therefore $\frac{p-r}{q-s} = x$.

Now, going back to Fig. 7.2, $\dfrac{\text{area}(\triangle ABD)}{\text{area}(\triangle ADC)}$ and $\dfrac{\text{area}(\triangle OBD)}{\text{area}(\triangle ODC)}$ are two fractions both equal to $\dfrac{BD}{DC}$, and it

follows that $\dfrac{\text{area}(\triangle ABD) - \text{area}(\triangle OBD)}{\text{area}(\triangle ADC) - \text{area}(\triangle ODC)}$ is also equal to $\dfrac{BD}{DC}$. That is,

$$\frac{\text{area}(\triangle OAB)}{\text{area}(\triangle OCA)} = \frac{BD}{DC}.$$

This is the equation you get by looking at the triangle ABC with [BC] as its base. But by turning Fig. 7.2 round you could also see the same figure with [CA] or [AB] as base. You would then deduce that

$$\frac{\text{area}(\triangle OBC)}{\text{area}(\triangle OAB)} = \frac{CE}{EA} \quad \text{and} \quad \frac{\text{area}(\triangle OCA)}{\text{area}(\triangle OBC)} = \frac{AF}{FB}.$$

By labelling the figure sensibly, with the point D on the side opposite A, E opposite B and F opposite C, you can get these two equations from the first by simply making the letter transformations $A \to B \to C \to A$ and $D \to E \to F \to D$. So OAB becomes OBC, BD becomes CE and so on.

Notice that only three triangles – $\triangle OAB$, $\triangle OCA$ and $\triangle OBC$ – appear in these equations; they are illustrated in Fig. 7.4. Also, the area of each triangle occurs once in the numerator of a fraction and once in the denominator. So if you multiply the three fractions together, the product is 1. That is,

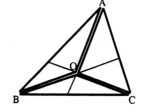

Fig. 7.4

$$\frac{BD}{DC} \times \frac{CE}{EA} \times \frac{AF}{FB} = \frac{\text{area}(\triangle OAB)}{\text{area}(\triangle OCA)} \times \frac{\text{area}(\triangle OBC)}{\text{area}(\triangle OAB)} \times \frac{\text{area}(\triangle OCA)}{\text{area}(\triangle OBC)}$$

$$= 1.$$

This is Ceva's theorem.

Ceva's theorem   ABC is a triangle and D, E, F are points on [BC], [CA], [AB] respectively.

If [AD], [BE] and [CF] are concurrent, then $\dfrac{BD}{DC} \times \dfrac{CE}{EA} \times \dfrac{AF}{FB} = 1.$

Example 7.1.1

The sides of a triangle ABC have lengths BC = 14 cm, CA = 12 cm, AB = 18 cm. The points D on [BC] and E on [CA] are both 4 cm from C. The line segments [AD] and [BE] intersect at O, and the line segment [CO] is produced to meet [AB] at F. Show that AF = AE and BF = BD.

You can use a diagram like Fig. 7.2 to illustrate this example, and calculate

$$BD = (14 - 4)\text{ cm} = 10\text{ cm} \quad \text{and} \quad EA = (12 - 4)\text{ cm} = 8\text{ cm}.$$

So, by Ceva's theorem,

$$\frac{10}{4} \times \frac{4}{8} \times \frac{AF}{FB} = 1, \quad \text{which gives} \quad \frac{AF}{FB} = \frac{4}{5}.$$

Therefore $AF = \frac{4}{9} \times 18\text{ cm} = 8\text{ cm}$ and $FB = \frac{5}{9} \times 18\text{ cm} = 10\text{ cm}.$

That is, AF = AE and BF = BD.

7.2 The converse theorem

To get the converse of Ceva's theorem you simply interchange the 'if' and 'then' statements.

> **Converse of Ceva's theorem** ABC is a triangle and D, E, F are points on [BC], [CA], [AB] respectively.
>
> If $\frac{BD}{DC} \times \frac{CE}{EA} \times \frac{AF}{FB} = 1$, then [AD], [BE] and [CF] are concurrent.

The proof will be deferred until Section 7.5, where it can be given in a form that also applies to the extended version of the theorem.

The converse theorem can be used to prove some of the results in Chapters 2, 3 and 5 about concurrent lines in a triangle.

For example, if [AD], [BE] and [CF] are the medians, then BD = DC, CE = EA and AF = FB. So $\frac{BD}{DC} \times \frac{CE}{EA} \times \frac{AF}{FB} = 1 \times 1 \times 1 = 1$. Therefore, by the converse of Ceva's theorem, the medians of the triangle are concurrent.

If [AD], [BE] and [CF] are the angle bisectors, then the angle bisector theorem (Section 6.1) states that $\frac{BD}{DC} = \frac{AB}{AC} = \frac{c}{b}$, and similarly $\frac{CE}{EA} = \frac{a}{c}$ and $\frac{AF}{FB} = \frac{b}{a}$. So $\frac{BD}{DC} \times \frac{CE}{EA} \times \frac{AF}{FB} = \frac{c}{b} \times \frac{a}{c} \times \frac{b}{a} = 1$. Therefore, by the converse of Ceva's theorem, the angle bisectors are concurrent.

If [AD], [BE] and [CF] are the altitudes, then you can see from Fig. 7.5 that $AD = BD \tan \hat{B} = DC \tan \hat{C}$ (where $\hat{B}, \hat{C}$ denote the angles at B, C respectively). Therefore $\dfrac{BD}{DC} = \dfrac{\tan \hat{C}}{\tan \hat{B}}$. By similar reasoning, $\dfrac{CE}{EA} = \dfrac{\tan \hat{A}}{\tan \hat{C}}$ and $\dfrac{AF}{FB} = \dfrac{\tan \hat{B}}{\tan \hat{A}}$, so that

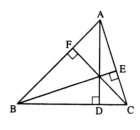

Fig. 7.5

$$\frac{BD}{DC} \times \frac{CE}{EA} \times \frac{AF}{FB} = \frac{\tan \hat{C}}{\tan \hat{B}} \times \frac{\tan \hat{A}}{\tan \hat{C}} \times \frac{\tan \hat{B}}{\tan \hat{A}} = 1.$$

Therefore, by the converse of Ceva's theorem, the altitudes are concurrent.

But notice that this argument only holds if all the angles of the triangle ABC are acute. If, for example, $\hat{C}$ is obtuse, then the point D lies outside the line segment [BC]. To deal with the situation where one of the angles is obtuse, you need the extended form of Ceva's theorem discussed in the following sections.

Exercise 7A

1 A triangle ABC has $a = 12$ cm, $b = 10$ cm, $c = 9$ cm. Points X, Y, Z on [BC], [CA], [AB] are such that [AX], [BY], [CZ] are concurrent. If CX = 3 cm, CY = 4 cm, find AZ.

2 In $\triangle ABC$, D is the point of trisection of the side [BC] nearer to B, and E is the point of trisection of the side [CA] nearer to C. The line segments [AD], [BE] meet at X, and [CX] is produced to meet the side [BC] at F. In what proportion does F divide [AB]?

3 With the notation of Fig. 7.2, BD = 1 cm, DC = 6 cm, CE = 4 cm, EA = 2 cm and AB = 4 cm.

   (a) Prove that $\dfrac{AF}{AC} = \dfrac{AE}{AB}$.

   (b) Prove that BFEC is a cyclic quadrilateral.

   (c) Calculate EF.

4 The incircle of $\triangle ABC$ touches the sides [BC], [CA], [AB] at P, Q, R. Prove that [AP], [BQ], [CR] are concurrent.

5 X, Y are points on the sides [AB], [AC] of $\triangle ABC$. L is the mid-point of [BC]. If [BY] and [CX] meet on the median [AL], prove that [XY] is parallel to [BC].

6 X, Y, Z are points on the sides [BC], [CA], [AB] of a triangle ABC such that [AX], [BY], [CZ] are concurrent. P, Q, R are points on these sides such that BP = CX, CQ = AY, AR = BZ. Prove that [AP], [BQ], [CR] are concurrent.

7.3 Extending Ceva's theorem

If you are asked to draw a triangle ABC, you will usually draw simply the line segments [BC], [CA] and [AB]. But sometimes you need to show the triangle with the complete lines (BC), (CA) and (AB), as in Fig. 7.6. The effect of this is to split the plane into seven regions., which are of three different types:

- the interior of the triangle, labelled I, whose boundary consists of the three sides of the triangle;
- three regions labelled J, whose boundary consists of one of the sides of the triangle and two unbounded part-lines;
- three regions labelled K, whose boundary consists of just two unbounded part-lines.

In Section 7.1 the point of concurrence O of the line segments [AD], [BE], [CF] is in the interior I of the triangle. What happens if you replace the line segments by complete lines (AD), (BE), (CF) which meet in a point O in one of the other regions?

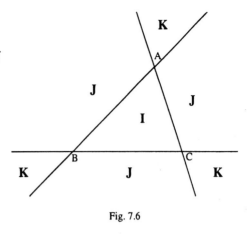

Fig. 7.6

Fig. 7.7 and Fig. 7.8 show how Fig. 7.2 has to be modified if O lies in the J-region opposite A or the K-region whose boundary includes A. You will see that in each case the point D is still on the line segment [BC], but the points E and F are on the lines (CA) and (AB) obtained by producing [CA] and [AB] in one direction or the other.

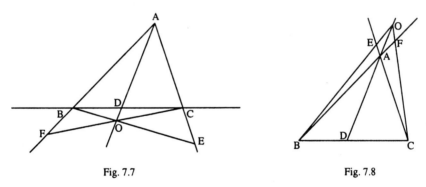

Fig. 7.7   Fig. 7.8

So if you want to extend Ceva's theorem so that it applies to these figures, you will have to interpret the expressions $\dfrac{CE}{EA}$ and $\dfrac{AF}{FB}$ in cases where the points E and F lie on the lines (CA) and (AB) but outside the line segments [CA] and [AB]. To do this, it is useful to introduce the idea of 'sensed length'.

7.4 Sensed length and sensed area

In Fig. 7.2, Fig. 7.7 and Fig. 7.8 the points A, B, F on the line (AB) appear in three different orders: with F between A and B, on the line produced beyond B, and on the line produced beyond A. These orders are reproduced in Fig. 7.9.

You have been used to thinking of length as a positive number. But by introducing the idea of sensed length on a line, which can be either positive or negative, you can use the same equations whatever the order of the points on the line. (Sensed length is sometimes called 'directed length'.)

Begin by choosing a 'positive direction' on the line; it doesn't matter which direction you choose, so take the direction from A towards B to be positive. Then lengths are defined to be positive if the displacement from the first point to the second is in the positive direction, and negative if the displacement is in the negative direction.

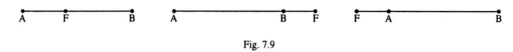

Fig. 7.9

In Fig. 7.9 the positive direction is from right to left. The diagram on the left has both AF and FB positive, so that $\frac{AF}{FB}$ is positive. In the middle, AF is positive and FB is negative, so that $\frac{AF}{FB}$ is negative. And on the right, AF is negative and FB is positive, so that $\frac{AF}{FB}$ is again negative.

Notice that, if you had chosen the positive direction in Fig. 7.9 to be from right to left, the signs of AF and FB would be changed in all the diagrams, but this would not affect the value of $\frac{AF}{FB}$. So the fraction is positive if F lies in the line segment [AB], and negative if F lies on the line (AB) outside the line segment.

Example 7.4.1
A line contains three points X, Y, Z, with sensed lengths $XY = 3$ cm, $YZ = 5$ cm.

(a) State the sensed lengths XZ, ZY, ZX, YX.

(b) Calculate $XZ + ZX$, $XZ + ZY$, $YZ - YX$, $XY + YZ + ZX$.

(c) Calculate $\dfrac{XZ}{ZY}$, $\dfrac{YZ}{ZX}$, $\dfrac{XY}{YZ}$, $\dfrac{ZY}{YX}$.

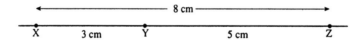

(a)   On the figure, the positive direction is from left to right.

So $XZ = 8$ cm, $ZY = -5$ cm, $ZX = -8$ cm, $YX = -3$ cm.

(b) $XZ + ZX = (8 + (-8))$ cm $= 0$, $XZ + ZY = (8 + (-5))$ cm $= 3$ cm,

$YZ - YX = (5 - (-3))$ cm $= 8$ cm, $XY + YZ + ZX = (3 + 5 + (-8))$ cm $= 0$.

(c) $\dfrac{XZ}{ZY} = \dfrac{8}{-5} = -\dfrac{8}{5}$, $\dfrac{YZ}{ZX} = \dfrac{5}{-8} = -\dfrac{5}{8}$, $\dfrac{XY}{YZ} = \dfrac{3}{5}$, $\dfrac{ZY}{YX} = \dfrac{-5}{-3} = \dfrac{5}{3}$.

It is worthwhile looking back at the figure to interpret these answers geometrically.

From Example 7.4.1 you will guess that there are algebraic rules which hold for sensed lengths, which do not depend on the particular order of points on the line. The basic rule is that, if X, Y, Z are any three points on a line, then $XY + YZ = XZ$. From this you can deduce that, for example,

$XY + YX = XX = 0$, $XY + YZ + ZX = XZ + ZX = 0$,   and $YZ = XZ - XY$.

Check the rule $XY + YZ = XZ$ for yourself by drawing figures with the points X, Y, Z in all possible orders on the line.

Now in Section 7.1 Ceva's theorem was obtained by applying the equation $\dfrac{\text{area}(\Delta SPQ)}{\text{area}(\Delta SQR)} = \dfrac{PQ}{QR}$ in Fig. 7.1 to various parts of Fig. 7.2. For the extension of Ceva's theorem you need to consider whether this equation still holds when the order of the letters P, Q, R is changed. To do this, you can introduce the idea of sensed area.

The triangle in Fig. 7.10 could be labelled in six different ways: as ΔABC, ΔBCA, ΔCAB, ΔCBA, ΔBAC, or ΔACB. If you follow the triangle round in the order of the letters, you will notice that the first three take you round anticlockwise, and the last three take you round clockwise. These are distinguished by taking the sensed area of the first three to be positive, and the sensed area of the last three to be negative.

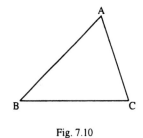

Fig. 7.10

For example, if the triangle has base of length 4 cm and height 3 cm, you would write, for the sensed areas,

$$\text{area}(\Delta ABC) = \text{area}(\Delta BCA) = \text{area}(\Delta CAB) = +\,6 \text{ cm}^2,$$

and

$$\text{area}(\Delta CBA) = \text{area}(\Delta BAC) = \text{area}(\Delta ACB) = -\,6 \text{ cm}^2.$$

With this convention you can then establish the following mini-theorem, which will be used to prove Ceva's theorem in its extended form.

Mini-theorem   P, Q, R are three points on a line, and S is a point not on the line. Then

(a) $\dfrac{\text{area}(\Delta SPQ)}{\text{area}(\Delta SQR)} = \dfrac{PQ}{QR}$,

(b)   (i) $\text{area}(\Delta PRS) - \text{area}(\Delta PQS) = \text{area}(\Delta QRS)$,

      (ii) $\text{area}(\Delta SQP) - \text{area}(\Delta SRP) = \text{area}(\Delta QRS)$.

You can see parts (a) and (b)(i) directly if the points are in the order P, Q, R as in Fig. 7.1, since all the lengths and areas are then positive; but in part (b) (ii) all the areas are negative. The proof will be given for the arrangement R, P, Q shown in Fig. 7.11, taking the positive direction on the line (RQ) from left to right.

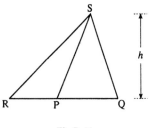

Fig.7.11

You should investigate other possible orders of the points for yourself.

Proof   Suppose that the unsigned areas of triangles ΔPSR, ΔPQS and ΔRQS are x, y and z, where $z = x + y$. Then

$$x = \tfrac{1}{2}RP \times h, \quad y = \tfrac{1}{2}PQ \times h \quad \text{and} \quad z = \tfrac{1}{2}RQ \times h.$$

(a)   ΔSPQ is labelled anticlockwise, but ΔSQR is labelled clockwise. So area(ΔSPQ) = y and area(ΔSQR) = $-z$. Also RQ = $-$QR. Therefore

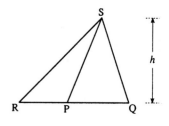

Fig. 7.11

$$\frac{\text{area}(\Delta SPQ)}{\text{area}(\Delta SQR)} = \frac{\frac{1}{2}PQ \times h}{-\frac{1}{2}RQ \times h} = \frac{PQ}{-RQ} = \frac{PQ}{QR}.$$

(b)   (i)   ΔPQS is labelled anticlockwise, but ΔPRS and ΔQRS are labelled clockwise.

So area(ΔPRS) = $-$area(ΔPSR) = $-x$, area(ΔPQS) = y and

area(ΔQRS) = $-$area(ΔRQS) = $-z$.

Since $z = x + y$,

$-$area(ΔQRS) = $-$area(ΔPRS) + area(ΔPQS).

That is,

area(ΔPRS) $-$ area(ΔPQS) = area(ΔQRS).

(ii)   This follows from part (i) by noting that

area(ΔPRS) = $-$area(ΔSRP),   and   area(ΔSQP) = $-$area(ΔPQS),

so

area(ΔSQP) $-$ area(ΔSRP) = area(ΔQRS).

The reason for giving two forms for (b) is that sometimes you want to eliminate the first letter (P in (i)) on the left side, sometimes the last letter (P in (ii)).

7.5 Proof of the extended theorems

The mini-theorem in Section 7.4 makes it possible to give a proof of Ceva's theorem which applies equally to Fig. 7.2, Fig. 7.7 and Fig. 7.8. This follows exactly the same lines as the proof in Section 7.1, in which all the triangles are labelled anticlockwise and all sensed lengths have the same sign. But by using sensed lengths and sensed areas it works also for figures in which the point O lies outside the triangle.

> **Ceva's theorem (extended version)**   ABC is a triangle and D, E, F are points on (BC), (CA), (AB) respectively.
>
> If (AD), (BE) and (CF) are concurrent, then $\dfrac{BD}{DC} \times \dfrac{CE}{EA} \times \dfrac{AF}{FB} = 1$, where the lengths in each fraction are sensed lengths along their respective lines.

Try to follow this proof using each of the figures 7.2, 7.7 and 7.8 in turn. You should be able to recognise the mini-theorem diagram at each step, and then carefully follow the order of the letters in the equations.

Proof

$$\frac{\text{area}\,(\Delta ABD)}{\text{area}\,(\Delta ADC)} = \frac{BD}{DC} \qquad ((a),\ \text{with P, Q, R, S = B, D, C, A})$$

$$\text{and}\quad \frac{\text{area}\,(\Delta OBD)}{\text{area}\,(\Delta ODC)} = \frac{BD}{DC}, \qquad ((a),\ \text{with P, Q, R, S = B, D, C, O})$$

$$\text{so}\quad \frac{BD}{DC} = \frac{\text{area}\,(\Delta ABD) - \text{area}\,(\Delta OBD)}{\text{area}\,(\Delta ADC) - \text{area}\,(\Delta ODC)} \qquad (\text{as shown in Section 7.1})$$

$$= \frac{\text{area}\,(\Delta DAB) - \text{area}\,(\Delta DOB)}{\text{area}\,(\Delta CAD) - \text{area}\,(\Delta COD)} \qquad (\text{changing letter order without changing sense})$$

$$= \frac{\text{area}\,(\Delta OAB)}{\text{area}\,(\Delta AOC)} \qquad ((b)(i)\ \text{in the top line, (b)(ii) in the bottom})^{\dagger}$$

$$= \frac{\text{area}\,(\Delta OAB)}{\text{area}\,(\Delta OCA)}.$$

† *The algebra at this step is slightly tricky. You should keep in mind that the aim is to end up with an expression involving only* O, A, B, C *and not* D. *So in the top line of the fraction use (b)(i) with* P, Q, R, S = D, O, A, B; *and in the bottom line use (b)(ii) with* P, Q, R, S = D, A, O, C. *Then in the next line of the equation change the order of the letters (without changing the sense) so as to get* O *in the same position as in the top line.*

You now carry out the same steps taking CA and then AB as base rather than BC. This gives

$$\frac{CE}{EA} = \frac{\text{area}\,(\Delta OBC)}{\text{area}\,(\Delta OAB)} \qquad \text{and} \qquad \frac{AF}{FB} = \frac{\text{area}\,(\Delta OCA)}{\text{area}\,(\Delta OBC)}.$$

Try writing out the details for yourself, and check them against the figures.

$$\text{So}\quad \frac{BD}{DC} \times \frac{CE}{EA} \times \frac{AF}{FB} = \frac{\text{area}\,(\Delta OAB)}{\text{area}\,(\Delta OCA)} \times \frac{\text{area}\,(\Delta OBC)}{\text{area}\,(\Delta OAB)} \times \frac{\text{area}\,(\Delta OCA)}{\text{area}\,(\Delta OBC)} = 1.$$

Example 7.5.1

In a triangle ABC, the side [BC] is produced to D such that BC = CD, and the side [CA] is produced to E such that CA = AE. The lines (AD) and (BE) meet at O, and the line (CO) meets the side [AB] at F. If the side [AB] has length c, how far is F from A?

The length BD is twice the length CD, and the sensed lengths

BD and DC have opposite signs, so $\dfrac{BD}{DC} = -2$. Similarly

$\dfrac{CE}{EA} = -2$. Since the lines (AD), (BE) and (CF) all pass through

O, by Ceva's theorem $(-2) \times (-2) \times \dfrac{AF}{FB} = 1$. So $4AF = FB$.

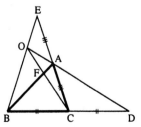

You are given that the length of the side [AB] is c, and want to find AF. So use the rules for sensed lengths to write FB = AB − AF. Then $4AF = AB - AF$, so that $AF = \frac{1}{5} AB$. Therefore the distance from A to F is $\frac{1}{5} c$.

To complete the theory of Ceva's theorem, you also need a proof of the converse. This also holds, with sensed lengths, whether the point of concurrence is inside or outside the triangle.

> **Converse of Ceva's theorem (extended version)**   ABC is a triangle and D, E, F are points on (BC), (CA), (AB) respectively.
>
> If $\dfrac{BD}{DC} \times \dfrac{CE}{EA} \times \dfrac{AF}{FB} = 1$, where the lengths in each fraction are sensed lengths along their respective lines, then (AD), (BE) and (CF) are concurrent.

The method used is proof by contradiction. That is, you suppose that (AD), (BE), (CF) *are not concurrent, and show that this leads to a false conclusion. The proof is the same whether the point of concurrence is inside or outside the triangle.*

Proof
Suppose that (AD), (BE), (CF) are not concurrent (see Fig. 7.12). Denote the point of intersection of (AD) and (BE) by O, and let (CO) meet the side (AB) in G. Then F and G are different points. Also (AD), (BE), (CG) are concurrent, so by Ceva's theorem $\dfrac{BD}{DC} \times \dfrac{CE}{EA} \times \dfrac{AG}{GB} = 1$.

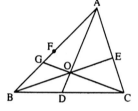

Fig. 7.12

But you are given that $\dfrac{BD}{DC} \times \dfrac{CE}{EA} \times \dfrac{AF}{FB} = 1$, so it follows that $\dfrac{AG}{GB} = \dfrac{AF}{FB}$.

Now use the algebraic result stated in Section 7.1, from which you can deduce that each of these fractions is also equal to $\dfrac{AG - AF}{GB - FB}$. Using the rules for sensed lengths given in Section 7.4,

$AG - AF = FG$, and $GB - FB = BF - BG = GF = -FG$. It follows that $\dfrac{AG - AF}{GB - FB} = \dfrac{FG}{-FG} = -1$.

Notice that, by the assumption that F *and* G *are different points, the length* $FG \neq 0$.

So $\dfrac{AF}{FB} = -1$, from which it follows that $AF = -FB$, $AF + FB = 0$, so $AB = 0$. But $[AB]$ is a side of the triangle, so its length is certainly not 0. The supposition that F and G are different points is therefore false. That is, (AD), (BE) and (CF) are concurrent.

The extension of the converse theorem to include points of concurrence outside the triangle makes it possible to complete the proof that the altitudes are concurrent, which was given for acute-angled triangles in Section 7.2.

Fig. 7.13 shows a triangle ABC with the angle at C obtuse, so that the altitudes (AD) and (BE) lie outside the triangle. Then, from triangle ABD, it is still true that $AD = BD \tan \hat{B}$. But, from triangle ACD, you now have $AD = CD \tan(180° - \hat{C})$. However, since $CD = -DC$ and $\tan(180° - \hat{C}) = -\tan \hat{C}$, this can also be written as $AD = DC \tan \hat{C}$. So just as for the acute-angled triangle, $BD \tan \hat{B} = DC \tan \hat{C}$.

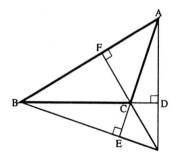

Fig. 7.13

In the same way, by equating expressions for BE from triangles BEA and BEC, you can show that $BE = CE \tan(180° - \hat{C}) = -CE \tan\hat{C}$ and $BE = AE \tan\hat{A} = -EA \tan\hat{A}$, so $CE \tan\hat{C} = EA \tan\hat{A}$. The proof that $AF \tan\hat{A} = FB \tan\hat{B}$ is the same as in the acute-angled case. It follows that, as before,

$$\frac{BD}{DC} \times \frac{CE}{EA} \times \frac{AF}{FB} = \frac{\tan\hat{C}}{\tan\hat{B}} \times \frac{\tan\hat{A}}{\tan\hat{C}} \times \frac{\tan\hat{B}}{\tan\hat{A}} = 1.$$

Therefore, by the converse of Ceva's theorem, the altitudes are concurrent.

Exercise 7B

1 W, X, Y, Z are four points on a line in any order. Write as single lengths

(a) $WY + YZ$,   (b) $XZ - WZ$,   (c) $XZ - XY$,

(d) $WZ - WY - XZ$,   (e) $WY - WZ + XZ$.

2 A, B, C, D are four points on a line in that order, with $AB = 3$ cm, $AC = 5$ cm, $AD = 15$ cm. Using the notation of sensed lengths, prove that

(a) $\dfrac{AB}{BC} = -\dfrac{AD}{DC}$,   (b) $\dfrac{BA}{AD} = -\dfrac{BC}{CD}$,   (c) $\dfrac{1}{AC} = \dfrac{1}{2}\left(\dfrac{1}{AB} + \dfrac{1}{AD}\right)$,

(d) $\dfrac{1}{BD} = \dfrac{1}{2}\left(\dfrac{1}{BA} + \dfrac{1}{BC}\right)$,   (e) $\dfrac{1}{CA} = \dfrac{1}{2}\left(\dfrac{1}{CB} + \dfrac{1}{CD}\right)$.

3 A, B, C, D are four points on a line such that $\dfrac{AB}{BC} = -\dfrac{AD}{DC}$. By expressing BC and DC in the form $Ax - Ay$ (where x and y each stand for one of B, C or D), prove that $\dfrac{1}{AC} = \dfrac{1}{2}\left(\dfrac{1}{AB} + \dfrac{1}{AD}\right)$. Prove also that $\dfrac{1}{BD} = \dfrac{1}{2}\left(\dfrac{1}{BA} + \dfrac{1}{BC}\right)$.

4 The sides of $\triangle ABC$ have lengths $a = 10$ cm, $b = 13$ cm, $c = 8$ cm. P is a point on the side $[BC]$ such that $BP = 6$ cm.

(a) Q is a point on the side $[AB]$ produced beyond B such that $BQ = 2$ cm. The lines (AP) and (CQ) meet at X, and the lines (BX) and (AC) meet at S. Find the distance CS.

(b) R is a point on the side $[AB]$ produced beyond A such that $AR = 2$ cm. The lines (AP) and (CR) meet at Y, and the lines (BY) and (AC) meet at T. Find the distance AT.

5 The e-circle of $\triangle ABC$ opposite A touches the side $[BC]$ at X, and the sides $[AC]$ and $[AB]$ produced at Y and Z. Prove that (AX), (BY), (CZ) are concurrent.

6 P and D are points on (BC) such that, in the notation of sensed lengths, $CP = -BD$. Prove that $BP = -CD$.

O is a point outside a triangle ABC. The line (AO) meets (BC) at D, (BO) meets (CA) at E, (CO) meets (AB) at F. Points P, Q, R are defined on (BC), (CA), (AB) such that $CP = -BD$, $AQ = -CE$, $BR = -AF$. Prove that (AP), (BQ), (CR) are concurrent.

7.6   Menelaus's theorem

There is a second theorem which looks rather like Ceva's theorem, but in which a straight line (often called a 'transversal') cuts all three sides of a triangle, produced where necessary, as in the diagrams in Fig. 7.14.

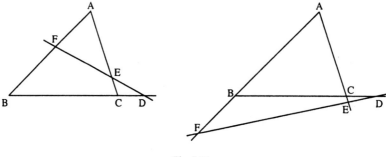

Fig. 7.14

The proof depends on the intercept theorem (see Section 1.6). In Fig. 7.15, in which a pair of lines l, m which intersect at X are cut by a pair of lines at S, U and T, V respectively,

if ST is parallel to UV, then $\dfrac{XS}{SU} = \dfrac{XT}{TV}$.

There is also a converse theorem, that

if $\dfrac{XS}{SU} = \dfrac{XT}{TV}$, then ST is parallel to UV.

As in Ceva's theorem, signs are associated with the lengths to indicate the directions of the displacements along the lines l, m. With this convention, you can also write other equations such as $\dfrac{XU}{US} = \dfrac{XV}{VT}$ or $\dfrac{SX}{XU} = \dfrac{TX}{XV}$.

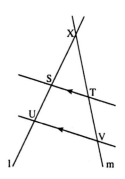

Fig. 7.15

Using this you can easily deduce the following property in Fig. 7.14.

> **Menelaus's theorem**   A transversal intersects the sides (BC), (CA), (AB) of a triangle (produced if necessary) in points D, E, F. Then $\dfrac{BD}{DC} \times \dfrac{CE}{EA} \times \dfrac{AF}{FB} = -1$.

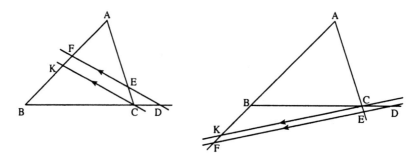

Fig. 7.16

Proof
In Fig. 7.14 draw a line (CK) parallel to the transversal (DF), to get Fig. 7.16. You should then be able to recognise some examples of Fig. 7.15 in Fig. 7.16.

Taking for l, m the lines (BC) and (BA), $\dfrac{BD}{DC} = \dfrac{BF}{FK}$.

Taking for l, m the lines (AB) and (AC), $\dfrac{CE}{EA} = \dfrac{KF}{FA}$.

Check that these equations hold for both diagrams in Fig. 7.16.

Therefore

$$\frac{BD}{DC} \times \frac{CE}{EA} \times \frac{AF}{FB} = \frac{BF}{FK} \times \frac{KF}{FA} \times \frac{AF}{FB}$$
$$= \frac{BF}{FK} \times \frac{-FK}{-AF} \times \frac{AF}{-BF} = -1.$$

Example 7.6.1
For the triangle in Example 7.5.1, the side [BA] is produced to meet the line (DE) at H. Find the distance of H from A.

As in Example 7.5.1, $\dfrac{BD}{DC} = -2$ and $\dfrac{CE}{EA} = -2$.

By Menelaus's theorem,

$$(-2) \times (-2) \times \frac{AH}{HB} = -1,$$

so that $4AH = -HB$.

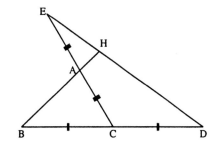

You are given that the side [AB] has length c, and you want to find AH. So use the rules for sensed lengths to write $HB = AB - AH$. Then $4AH = -AB + AH$, so $AH = -\frac{1}{3}AB$. The distance of H from A is therefore $\frac{1}{3}c$.

To prove the converse of Menelaus's theorem you can use the same method as was used for the converse of Ceva's theorem in Section 7.5.

Converse of Menelaus's theorem   ABC is a triangle and D, E, F are points on (BC), (CA), (AB).

If $\dfrac{BD}{DC} \times \dfrac{CE}{EA} \times \dfrac{AF}{FB} = -1$, then D, E, F are collinear.

Proof

Suppose that D, E, F are not collinear (see Fig. 7.17). Let the line (DE) meet the side (AB) in G. Then F and G are different points. Also D, E, G are collinear, so by Menelaus's theorem

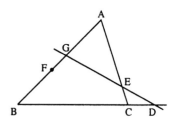

$$\frac{BD}{DC} \times \frac{CE}{EA} \times \frac{AG}{GB} = -1.$$

But you are given that $\frac{BD}{DC} \times \frac{CE}{EA} \times \frac{AF}{FB} = -1$, so it follows that

$$\frac{AG}{GB} = \frac{AF}{FB}.$$

Fig. 7.17

This is exactly the same equation as you reached for the converse of Ceva's theorem. The rest of the argument is exactly the same as in the earlier proof, and it follows that $AB = 0$, which is not true.

The supposition that F and G are different points is therefore false, That is, D, E, F are collinear.

7.7 The harmonic property

Look at Fig. 7.18. Can you recognise in it both the Ceva figure and the Menelaus figure?

You have seen a diagram very much like this before. See Section 5.4, Fig. 5.18. In Fig. 7.18, B, C, E, F form a quadrangle, and A, O, G are the diagonal points.

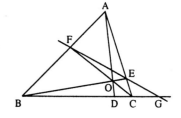

The lines (AD), (BE), (CF) are concurrent at O, so that $\frac{BD}{DC} \times \frac{CE}{EA} \times \frac{AF}{FB} = 1$. Also the transversal (GF) meets the sides (BC), (CA), (AB) of triangle ABC in G, E, F, so that

Fig. 7.18

$$\frac{BG}{GC} \times \frac{CE}{EA} \times \frac{AF}{FB} = -1.$$

It follows that $\frac{BG}{GC} \times \frac{CE}{EA} \times \frac{AF}{FB} = -\frac{BD}{DC} \times \frac{CE}{EA} \times \frac{AF}{FB}$, so $\frac{BG}{GC} = -\frac{BD}{DC}$.

Writing GC as $-CG$ (so that all the displacements have the same sense),

$$\frac{BG}{CG} = \frac{BD}{DC}.$$

The interpretation of this equation is that the ratio in which the point G divides the line segment [BC] externally is equal to the ratio in which D divides it internally. Points which are related in this way are said to form a **harmonic range**, or to be in **harmonic ratio**. The points D and G are said to be **harmonic conjugates** with respect to B and C.

You met an example of this property in Chapter 6. If the internal and external bisectors of $\hat{A}$ in $\triangle ABC$ meet (BC) at D and E, then the points B, C, D, E form a harmonic range.

Example 7.7.1

Given two points B and C on a line, use Fig. 7.18 to divide the line segment [BC] into three equal parts.

If DC is $\frac{1}{3}$ of BC, BD is $\frac{2}{3}$ of BC, so that $\frac{BD}{DC} = 2$. It is not easy to locate D directly, but it is easy to find the point G such that $\frac{BG}{GC} = -2$; that is, BG = 2CG, so that CG = BC.

So begin by producing the line segment [BC], and taking a point G on the line such that CG = BC (for example by drawing arcs of a circle with centre C and radius BC).

Then draw lines (BA), (CA) through B, C to meet at A and a line through G to meet (BA), (CA) at F, E. Next draw lines (BE), (CF) to meet at O. Finally draw (AO) to meet BC at D. Then D is one of the points of trisection required.

The second point of trisection can be constructed in the same way by interchanging B and C, and beginning with a point H such that BH = CB.

The remarkable feature about this example is that you can draw *any* lines (BA), (CA) through B and C, and *any* line through G (provided that it doesn't go through A) meeting these at F and E. Then if (BE) and (CF) meet at O, and (BF) and (CE) meet at A, (OA) always meets (BC) at the same point D. This is called the **harmonic construction**.

Try this for yourself as an experiment. Draw a figure above a line segment [BC], *like Fig. 7.18, then repeat the construction below* [BC] *with any lines you like through* B, C *and* G. *Do both your constructions end up at the same point* D?

Notice that this is another example of an incidence property, like Pappus's theorem which you met in Chapter 1. Although lengths are used in the proof, you can draw the figure using any straight edge that you like – it doesn't have to be marked out in centimetres like a ruler.

The harmonic relationship has some important properties. Notice first that if, in the equation $\frac{BG}{GC} = -\frac{BD}{DC}$, you replace BG by $-GB$ and DC $= -CD$, the equation becomes

$$-\frac{GB}{GC} = \frac{BD}{CD},$$

which can also be written as

$$\frac{GC}{CD} = -\frac{GB}{BD}.$$

What does this mean? The original equation states that the points G and D divide the line segment [BC] internally and externally in the same proportion. The last equation states that the points C and B divide the line segment [GD] internally and externally in the same proportion. So there is a symmetry between the pairs B, C and G, D:

Given two pairs of points on a line such that one pair divides the other internally and externally in the same proportion, then the second pair also divides the first pair internally and externally in the same proportion.

Example 7.7.2

In Fig. 7.18 denote the intersection of (AD) and (GF) by H. Join (DE) and (GO) and let them meet at J. Prove that H, J, C are collinear.

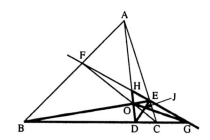

You can recognise the figure picked out with heavy lines as another example of the harmonic construction. (DH), (GH) are lines through D and G, meeting at H. The transversal (BE) cuts these lines at O and E. The lines (DE), (GO) meet at J. Then the line (HJ) meets (GD) in the point which is the harmonic conjugate of B with respect to G and D.

But since D and G divide [BC] internally and externally in the same proportion, C and B divide [GD] internally and externally in the same proportion. That is, C is the harmonic conjugate of B with respect to G and D. So (HJ) meets (GD) at C.

That is, H, J, C are collinear.

You proved another important property of harmonic ranges in Exercise 7B Question 3. You were given that $\dfrac{AB}{BC} = -\dfrac{AD}{DC}$, and proved that $\dfrac{1}{AC} = \tfrac{1}{2}\left(\dfrac{1}{AB} + \dfrac{1}{AD}\right)$ and that $\dfrac{1}{BD} = \tfrac{1}{2}\left(\dfrac{1}{BA} + \dfrac{1}{BC}\right)$.

A number h such that $\dfrac{1}{h} = \tfrac{1}{2}\left(\dfrac{1}{p} + \dfrac{1}{q}\right)$ is called the **harmonic mean** of p and q. So what you proved was that, if B, D are harmonic conjugates with respect to A, C, then AC is the harmonic mean of AB and AD, and BD is the harmonic mean of BA and BC, provided that sensed lengths are used. This can be summed up in a general statement.

If two pairs of points on a line form a harmonic range, then the (sensed) distance of any one of the points from its partner is the harmonic mean of the (sensed) distances of the point from the other pair of points.

The idea of a harmonic mean has an application in music. The chords which sound most pleasant are those in which the frequencies of the notes are in simple proportions to each other. For example, in an ideal major chord, if the frequency of the lowest note is f_1, then the frequency of the middle note would be $f_2 = \tfrac{5}{4} f_1$ and the frequency of the top note would be $f_3 = \tfrac{3}{2} f_1$, so that f_2 is the arithmetic mean of f_1 and f_3. But if you make the note with a pipe, the frequency of the note is proportional to the reciprocal of its length. So the length of the pipe for the middle note is the harmonic mean of the lengths for the outer notes. It is possible that this is how the musical term 'harmonic' came to be used in geometry.

Exercise 7C

1 An equilateral triangle ABC has sides of length 12 cm. P, Q, R are points on the sides [BC], [CA], [AB] such that BP = 2 cm, CQ = 3 cm, AR = 4 cm. The lines (QR), (RP), (PQ) meet the sides of the triangle produced at U, V, W. Calculate the lengths CU, AV, BW.

2 $\triangle ABC$ has sides of length $a = 9$ cm, $b = 6$ cm, $c = 12$ cm. A circle with centre A and radius 4 cm meets [AC], [AB] at E, F. The secant (EF) meets (BC) at D. Calculate the length CD.

3 An equilateral triangle ABC has sides of length 3 cm. P and Q are points of trisection of [AB], and M is the mid-point of [AC]. The line (MP) meets (BC) at R, and (QR) meets (AC) at N. Calculate the length MN.

4 O is a point inside a triangle ABC, and (AO), (BO), (CO) meet the sides at D, E, F. If $BD = \frac{2}{5}BC$ and $CE = \frac{1}{5}CA$, calculate

(a) $\dfrac{AF}{FB}$,   (b) $\dfrac{AO}{OD}$.

5 The sides [BC], [AC] of $\triangle ABC$ are produced to D, E so that BC = 2CD and AC = 3CE. The lines (BE), (AD) meet at O. Calculate $\dfrac{BO}{OE}$.

6 The figure shows three parallel lines l, m, n. Points A and X are marked on l, B and Y on m, and C and Z on n. Corresponding sides of $\triangle ABC$, $\triangle XYZ$, produced if necessary, meet at P, Q, R. Prove that P, Q, R are collinear.

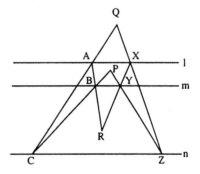

7 Check that the figure in Example 7.7.2 can be described as follows.

> (AF), (DG), (EO) are three lines with a common point B. Points F, G, O are on (BA), (BD), (BE) respectively. The lines (DE) and (GO) meet at J, (EA) and (OF) meet at C, (AD) and (FG) meet at H.

Compare this with the description of the figure that you drew in Exercise 1 Question 1. Do the conclusions correspond?

8 In a triangle ABC the escribed circle opposite A touches the sides [AB], [AC] produced at X_1, Y_1. Points X_2, Y_2 and X_3, Y_3 are defined similarly for the escribed circles opposite B and C. The lines (X_1Y_1), (BC) meet at D, (X_2Y_2), (CA) meet at E, (X_3Y_3), (AB) meet at F. Prove that D, E, F are collinear.

9 Points B, D on a line are harmonic conjugates with respect to A, C. O is the mid-point of [AC]. By writing each of the sensed lengths in the harmonic equation in the form $Ox - Oy$, where x and y each stand for one of the points A, B, C, D, prove that $OA^2 = OB \times OD$.

10   A, B, C, D are points on a line, and O is a point not on the line. Prove that

$$\frac{AB}{BC} = \frac{OA\sin A\hat{O}B}{OC\sin B\hat{O}C}.$$

Prove that the pairs A, C and B, D form a harmonic range if and only if

$$\frac{\sin A\hat{O}B}{\sin B\hat{O}C} = -\frac{\sin A\hat{O}D}{\sin D\hat{O}C},$$

where the angles are 'sensed angles'.

Hence show that, if a transversal meets the lines (OA), (OB), (OC), (OD) in E, F, G, H, then the pairs E, G and F, H form a harmonic range.

8 Analytical methods

This chapter introduces a different way of doing geometry, using coordinates. When you have completed the chapter, you should

- be able to use coordinates to prove results about figures composed of straight lines
- know how to find, recognise and use the equation of a circle.

8.1 Basics

You sometimes need imagination, ingenuity and even a bit of luck when tackling geometry problems. It is not always easy to spot a suitable construction, or to decide which technique will lead to a solution. When coordinates were invented, they opened up a completely new approach to geometry, by converting geometrical relationships into algebraic equations. In algebra procedures tend to be more automatic, and they can sometimes lead more directly to a desired conclusion than purely geometrical arguments.

You are probably already familiar with the idea of Cartesian coordinates (x, y) and their use in writing equations of straight lines. If not, you will find the most important results and procedures in Chapter 8 of Higher Level Book 1. Here is a summary of the properties which you need to know.

Formulae relating to a pair of points (see Fig. 8.1)

- The distance P_1P_2 is $\sqrt{(x_2 - x_1)^2 + (y_2 - y_1)^2}$.
- The mid-point M of the line segment $[P_1P_2]$ has coordinates $\left(\dfrac{x_1 + x_2}{2}, \dfrac{y_1 + y_2}{2} \right)$.

- The line (P_1P_2) has gradient $\dfrac{y_2 - y_1}{x_2 - x_1}$ (provided that $x_1 \neq x_2$; the gradient is not defined if $x_1 = x_2$).

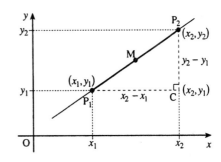

Fig. 8.1

Parallel and perpendicular lines (see Fig. 8.2)

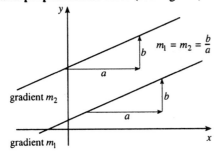
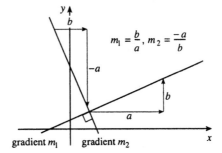

Fig. 8.2

- If two lines have gradients m_1 and m_2, the lines are

    parallel if $m_1 = m_2$,

    perpendicular if $m_1 m_2 = -1$.

- The equation for perpendicular lines cannot be used if either m_1 or m_2 is 0; that is, if one of the lines is parallel to the x-axis. In that case the perpendicular line is parallel to the y-axis, so that its gradient is not defined. (As stated above, the formula for the gradient of a line is not valid if $x_1 = x_2$.)

Equations of lines

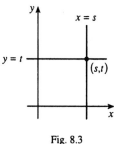

Fig. 8.3

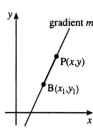

Fig. 8.4

- The equation $x = s$ represents a line parallel to the y-axis, and $y = t$ represents a line parallel to the x-axis (see Fig. 8.3).
- The equation of a line with gradient m and y-intercept k is $y = mx + k$.
- The equation of the line through the point (x_1, y_1) with gradient m is $y - y_1 = m(x - x_1)$ (see Fig. 8.4).
- Every line has an equation of the form $ax + by + c = 0$, where a and b are not both 0.

The questions in Exercise 8A use analytical methods to investigate some of the geometrical properties you have met in earlier chapters.

Exercise 8A

1 Points P_1, P_2 have coordinates (x_1, y_1), (x_2, y_2). M is the mid-point of $[P_1P_2]$, and P_3 is the point on $[P_1P_2]$ produced so that $MP_2 = P_2P_3$.

(a) Use the fact that P_2 is the mid-point of $[MP_3]$ to find the coordinates (x_3, y_3) of P_3.

(b) Express the coordinates of P_2 and M in terms of the coordinates of P_1 and P_3.

You are given that the coordinates of the point L such that $\dfrac{P_1L}{LP_2} = \lambda$ are given by

$\left(\dfrac{x_1 + \lambda x_2}{1 + \lambda}, \dfrac{y_1 + \lambda y_2}{1 + \lambda}\right)$. Verify this from your answers to parts (a) and (b).

2 The vertices A, B, C of a triangle have coordinates $(3, 15)$, $(-12, 0)$, $(12, 0)$.

(a) Find the equations of the altitudes, show that they are concurrent and find the coordinates of the orthocentre H.

(b) Find the equations of the medians, show that they are concurrent and find the coordinates of the centroid G.

(c) Use the answer to part (a) of Question 1 to find the coordinates of the point S on $[HG]$ produced such that $GS = \frac{1}{2}HG$.

(d) Find the distances of S from A, B, and C. What can you deduce about the point S?

(e) Use a similar method to find the circumcentres of $\triangle HBC$ and $\triangle HCA$. Show that for both triangles the radius of the circumcircle is equal to that of $\triangle ABC$.

3   By a suitable choice of axes the coordinates of the vertices of any triangle ABC can be taken to be (j,k), $(-i,0)$, $(i,0)$.

  (a) Find the coordinates of the orthocentre H.

  (b) Find the coordinates of the centroid G.

  (c) Find the coordinates of the point S on [HG] produced such that $GS = \frac{1}{2}HG$.

  (d) Prove that the distance of each vertex of the triangle from S is

$$\frac{1}{2k}\sqrt{i^4 + j^4 + k^4 + 2k^2 i^2 + 2k^2 j^2 - 2i^2 j^2}\,.$$

4   (a) Show that the points $A(0,5)$, $B(-3,-4)$, $C(5,0)$, $D(4,3)$, $E(3,-4)$ all lie on a circle centre O with radius 5.

  (b) Find the coordinates of the feet of the perpendiculars from the point D to the sides of the triangle ABC, produced if necessary. Prove that these are collinear, and give the equation of the Simson line.

  (c) Repeat part (b) for the point E and the triangle ABC.

  (d) Use the formula for $\tan(\theta - \phi)$ to find the angle between the two Simson lines, and show that this is one-half of $D\hat{O}E$.

5   Points $A(2,4)$, $B(1,2)$, $C(3,6)$ lie on the line $y = 2x$, and points $D(2,0)$, $E(5,0)$, $F(1,0)$ lie on the x-axis. The lines (BF), (CE) meet at X, the lines (CD), (AF) meet at Y, the lines (AE), (BD) meet at Z. Prove that X, Y, Z lie on a line, and find its equation.

8.2 Equations of circles

To prove that the equation of the line through the point (x_1, y_1) with gradient m is $y - y_1 = m(x - x_1)$, you begin by looking for a property which is satisfied by every point (x,y) on the line, but by no other points. This property is that the gradient of the line joining (x,y) to (x_1, y_1) has gradient m. You then express

this property in the form of an equation, $\dfrac{y - y_1}{x - x_1} = m$, which is more conveniently written as

$$y - y_1 = m(x - x_1).$$

In fact, it is not only 'more convenient'. The first equation is meaningless if you put (x,y) equal to (x_1, y_1), but in the form $y - y_1 = m(x - x_1)$ the equation is also satisfied by (x_1, y_1), as of course it should be.

You begin in the same way when you want to find the equation of a circle, and look for a property that is satisfied by every point on the circle, but by no other point.

This is, of course, that a circle is the set of points which are at a known distance (the radius) from a known point (the centre). If you are given the centre and radius, the circle is completely determined. All you have to do is to turn this definition into an equation.

Example 8.2.1

Find the equation of the circle with centre $(3,2)$ and radius 5.

If P is a point with coordinates (x,y), the distance from $(3,2)$ to P is $\sqrt{(x-3)^2 + (y-2)^2}$. So the equation of the circle is

$$\sqrt{(x-3)^2 + (y-2)^2} = 5.$$

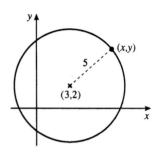

You should understand that there are really two statements here. If (x,y) lies on the circle, then x and y satisfy this equation; and if x and y are two numbers which satisfy this equation, then the point with coordinates (x,y) lies on the circle. You have met this 'theorem and converse' situation before in connection with loci.

This is not a very neat equation. It is better to tidy it up by squaring and then multiplying out the brackets.

$$(x-3)^2 + (y-2)^2 = 25,$$
$$x^2 - 6x + 9 + y^2 - 4y + 4 - 25 = 0,$$
$$x^2 + y^2 - 6x - 4y - 12 = 0.$$

This is the usual form used to write the equation of a circle.

Notice again that this argument works both backwards and forwards. Each step in the algebra could be reversed. (The first step involves squaring both sides of the equation, but this is reversible because $\sqrt{}$ always stands for the positive square root.). So if x and y satisfy the final equation, they satisfy the first equation, and the point (x,y) is on the circle.

The method used in Example 8.2.1 is perfectly general. If you want the equation of the circle with centre (h,k) and radius r, then you write an equation stating that the distance from (x,y) to (h,k) is equal to r. That is,

$$\sqrt{(x-h)^2 + (y-k)^2} = r.$$

It is neater to square both sides, and to write the equation as

$$(x-h)^2 + (y-k)^2 = r^2.$$

> The circle with centre (h,k) and radius r has equation $(x-h)^2 + (y-k)^2 = r^2$.

If you multiply out the brackets, this equation becomes

$$x^2 - 2hx + h^2 + y^2 - 2ky + k^2 = r^2,$$
$$x^2 + y^2 - 2hx - 2ky + \left(h^2 + k^2 - r^2\right) = 0.$$

Notice the form of this equation. It begins with the terms $x^2 + y^2$, then there are terms with a constant times x and a constant times y (where the constants depend on the coordinates of the centre but not the radius), and finally a constant term. You could say that it is typically of the form

$x^2 + y^2 + ax + by + c = 0,$ where a, b and c are constants.

Is any equation of this form the equation of a circle?

Example 8.2.2

What geometrical figures are represented by the equations

(a) $x^2 + y^2 + 4x - 6y - 3 = 0$, (b) $x^2 + y^2 + 4x - 6y + 13 = 0$, (c) $x^2 + y^2 + 4x - 6y + 23 = 0$?

(a)   You want to get the equation back into the form $(x - ...)^2 + (y - ...)^2 = ...^2$, so begin by collecting the x-terms together, then the y-terms, and put the constant on the right side, as

$$\left(x^2 + 4x \quad \right) + \left(y^2 - 6y \quad \right) = 3.$$

Space has been left inside the brackets to insert a number so as to make a square expression.

The square which begins $x^2 + 4x$ is $(x + 2)^2$, which is $x^2 + 4x + 4$; and the square which begins $y^2 - 6y$ is $(y - 3)^2$, which is $y^2 - 6y + 9$. So insert extra terms $+4$, $+9$ in the brackets, and also on the other side, to give

$$\left(x^2 + 4x + 4\right) + \left(y^2 - 6y + 9\right) = 3 + 4 + 9.$$

That is, $(x + 2)^2 + (y - 3)^2 = 16$,

$$\sqrt{(x + 2)^2 + (y - 3)^2} = 4.$$

This expresses the fact that the distance from the point (x, y) to $(-2, 3)$ is 4. So the equation represents a circle with centre $(-2, 3)$ and radius 4.

You will recognise this procedure as 'completing the square', which you have used in graphing quadratic functions and solving quadratic equations. The only difference here is that you use it twice.

(b)   If you carry out the same procedure, you get

$$\left(x^2 + 4x + 4\right) + \left(y^2 - 6y + 9\right) = -13 + 4 + 9,$$

so $(x + 2)^2 + (y - 3)^2 = 0$.

What does this mean? The left side is the sum of two squares, which can't be negative. The only way that they can add up to 0 is for both squares separately to be 0. The equation is satisfied only if $x = -2$ and $y = 3$, so P can only be the single point $(-2, 3)$. It is sometimes called a 'point circle'.

(c)   This equation is

$$\left(x^2 + 4x + 4\right) + \left(y^2 - 6y + 9\right) = -23 + 4 + 9,$$

which is

$$(x + 2)^2 + (y - 3)^2 = -10.$$

This is impossible! The squares on the left side can't be negative, so they can't add up to a negative number. There are no points whose coordinates satisfy the equation.

The method used in Example 8.2.2 could be applied to any equation of the form

$$x^2 + y^2 + ax + by + c = 0.$$

Begin by writing this as

$$\left(x^2 + ax \quad\right) + \left(y^2 + by \quad\right) = -c.$$

The squares which begin with the terms in the brackets are $\left(x + \tfrac{1}{2}a\right)^2$ and $\left(y + \tfrac{1}{2}b\right)^2$, so add the constants $\left(\tfrac{1}{2}a\right)^2$ and $\left(\tfrac{1}{2}b\right)^2$ to both sides of the equation. It then becomes

$$\left(x + \tfrac{1}{2}a\right)^2 + \left(y + \tfrac{1}{2}b\right)^2 = \tfrac{1}{4}a^2 + \tfrac{1}{4}b^2 - c.$$

There are then three possibilities.

- If $a^2 + b^2 - 4c > 0$, you can take the square root of both sides of the equation to get

$$\sqrt{\left(x + \tfrac{1}{2}a\right)^2 + \left(y + \tfrac{1}{2}b\right)^2} = \sqrt{\tfrac{1}{4}a^2 + \tfrac{1}{4}b^2 - c}.$$

  Since $x + \tfrac{1}{2}a = x - \left(-\tfrac{1}{2}a\right)$ and $y + \tfrac{1}{2}b = y - \left(-\tfrac{1}{2}b\right)$, this means that the distance of the point (x, y) from $\left(-\tfrac{1}{2}a, -\tfrac{1}{2}b\right)$ has the constant value $\sqrt{\tfrac{1}{4}a^2 + \tfrac{1}{4}b^2 - c}$. That is, the point lies on a circle with centre $\left(-\tfrac{1}{2}a, -\tfrac{1}{2}b\right)$ and radius $\sqrt{\tfrac{1}{4}a^2 + \tfrac{1}{4}b^2 - c}$.

- If $a^2 + b^2 - 4c = 0$, the equation is satisfied only by $x = -\tfrac{1}{2}a$ and $y = -\tfrac{1}{2}b$. It then represents the point circle $\left(-\tfrac{1}{2}a, -\tfrac{1}{2}b\right)$.

- If $a^2 + b^2 - 4c < 0$, there are no points whose coordinates satisfy the equation.

> If $a^2 + b^2 - 4c > 0$, the equation $x^2 + y^2 + ax + by + c = 0$ represents a circle with centre $\left(-\tfrac{1}{2}a, -\tfrac{1}{2}b\right)$ and radius $\sqrt{\tfrac{1}{4}a^2 + \tfrac{1}{4}b^2 - c}$.

There is no need to try to remember the formulae for the centre and radius, but it is important to understand the method and to be able to apply it.

Example 8.2.3

A circle has equation $x^2 + y^2 - 20x - 40y + 450 = 0$.

(a) Show that the point $(11, 13)$ lies on the circle, and find the equation of the tangent at this point.

(b) Find the equations of the two tangents to the circle which pass through the origin.

  (a) If $x = 11$ and $y = 13$, then

$$x^2 + y^2 - 20x - 40y + 450 = 121 + 169 - 220 - 520 + 450 = 0.$$

These values satisfy the equation, so the point $(11, 13)$ lies on the circle.

To find the equation of the tangent, use the fact that it is perpendicular to the radius from the centre to the point. The circle has centre $\left(-\tfrac{1}{2} \times (-20), -\tfrac{1}{2} \times (-40)\right)$, which is $(10, 20)$. The gradient of the radius is $\dfrac{13 - 20}{11 - 10} = \dfrac{-7}{1} = -7$, so the gradient of the tangent is $-\dfrac{1}{-7} = \dfrac{1}{7}$.

The tangent is the line through $(11,13)$ with gradient $\frac{1}{7}$, so its equation is

$$y - 13 = \tfrac{1}{7}(x - 11),$$

or more simply

$$7y - 91 = x - 11, \quad \text{which is} \quad x - 7y + 80 = 0.$$

(b) Two methods are suggested. The first begins by using your geometrical knowledge to find a way of constructing the tangents, and then turns this into an algebraic form. The second is a more purely algebraic approach.

Method 1 In the figure C is the centre of the circle with coordinates $(10, 20)$, and (OS) and (OT) are the tangents which pass through the origin O. Since $O\hat{S}C = O\hat{T}C = 90°$, the points S and T lie on a circle with diameter [OC]. The method is to find the equation of this circle, and then to use algebra to find where it meets the given circle.

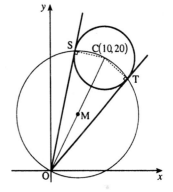

The centre of the circle with diameter [OC] is at M, the mid-point of [OC], which has coordinates $(5,10)$. The radius is equal to OM, which is $\sqrt{5^2 + 10^2} = \sqrt{125}$. So its equation is

$$(x - 5)^2 + (y - 10)^2 = \left(\sqrt{125}\right)^2$$

which can be written more simply as

$$x^2 + y^2 - 10x - 20y = 0.$$

So you need to find the values of x and y which satisfy the two equations

$$x^2 + y^2 - 20x - 40y + 450 = 0 \quad \text{and} \quad x^2 + y^2 - 10x - 20y = 0.$$

A useful first step would be to remove the terms $x^2 + y^2$ by subtracting, to give

$$(-20 - (-10))x + (-40 - (-20))y + 450 = 0,$$

which is

$$x + 2y = 45.$$

Notice that this is the equation of a straight line, and it is satisfied by the coordinates of S and T. So it must be the equation of the line (ST).

You can now replace x by $45 - 2y$ in one of the circle equations – preferably the second, since it is slightly simpler. This leads to an equation for y,

$$(45 - 2y)^2 + y^2 - 10(45 - 2y) - 20y = 0,$$

which can be simplified as

$$y^2 - 36y + 315 = 0.$$

This can be factorised as

$$(y-21)(y-15) = 0,$$

so that $y = 21$ or $y = 15$. The corresponding values of x are $45 - 2 \times 21 = 3$ and $45 - 2 \times 15 = 15$. So S and T have coordinates $(3,21)$ and $(15,15)$.

The equations of the tangents (OS) and (OT) are therefore $y = 7x$ and $y = x$.

Method 2   This uses the definition of a tangent as a line which meets the circle in only one point (or, as some people like to say, in 'two coincident points'). You want the tangents through O, which will have equations of the form $y = mx$ for some values of m. So begin by writing an equation to find where such a line meets the circle.

Substituting mx for y in the equation $x^2 + y^2 - 20x - 40y + 450 = 0$ gives a quadratic equation for x,

$$x^2 + m^2 x^2 - 20x - 40mx + 450 = 0,$$

that is

$$\left(1 + m^2\right)x^2 - 20(1 + 2m)x + 450 = 0.$$

If the line is to be a tangent this equation must have a repeated root, so the discriminant (that is '$b^2 - 4ac$' in the standard notation for quadratics) must be 0.

This gives

$$400(1 + 2m)^2 - 4\left(1 + m^2\right) \times 450 = 0,$$

which can be simplified to

$$m^2 - 8m + 7 = 0.$$

This factorises as

$$(m - 7)(m - 1) = 0,$$

giving $m = 7$ and $m = 1$.

So the tangents from O to the circle are $y = 7x$ and $y = x$.

Exercise 8B

1   Give the equations of the following circles, in the form $x^2 + y^2 + ax + by + c = 0$.

(a) Centre $(2,-5)$, radius 7   (b) Centre $(0,-3)$, radius 2   (c) Centre $(4,3)$, radius 5

2   What is represented by the following equations?

(a) $x^2 + y^2 + 6x + 4y - 3 = 0$ (b) $x^2 + y^2 - 3x + y = 0$

(c) $x^2 + y^2 - 2x + 6y + 10 = 0$ (d) $x^2 + y^2 + 5x + y + 7 = 0$

3 (a) Tangents PT, PU are drawn from $P(3,1)$ to the circle with equation
$x^2 + y^2 - 10x + 8y + 28 = 0$. Find the length PT.

(b) Tangents PT, PU are drawn from $P(p,q)$ to the circle with equation
$x^2 + y^2 + ax + by + c = 0$. Find the length PT.

4 The centres and the points of intersection of the circles with equations $x^2 + y^2 - 8y = 0$ and
$x^2 + y^2 - 6x - 4y + 5 = 0$ form a quadrilateral. Find the equations of the diagonals.

5 Consider the following pairs of circles.

(a) $x^2 + y^2 + 10x = 0$, $\quad x^2 + y^2 - 2x - 6y = 0$

(b) $x^2 + y^2 + 6x + 14y + 22 = 0$, $\quad x^2 + y^2 - 4x - 10y + 20 = 0$

(c) $x^2 + y^2 + 2x - 6y + 1 = 0$, $\quad x^2 + y^2 - 6x + 5 = 0$

(d) $x^2 + y^2 - 4x - 2y + 1 = 0$, $\quad x^2 + y^2 - 6y - 11 = 0$

(e) $x^2 + y^2 - 10x - 4y + 25 = 0$, $\quad x^2 + y^2 - 10x - 6y + 18 = 0$

If the circles intersect, give the coordinates of the points of intersection.

If the circles touch each other, find the coordinates of the point of contact and the equation of the tangent at this point.

If the circles have no points in common, find the shortest distance between them.

6 (a) Find the equation of the tangent, t, to $x^2 + y^2 + 8x - 4y - 17 = 0$ at the point $(2,1)$.

(b) Find the equation of the tangent parallel to t.

(c) Find the equations of the tangents perpendicular to t.

7 Find the equations of the tangents to the circle $x^2 + y^2 - 4x - 10y + 13 = 0$ from

(a) $(2,0)$, $\qquad\qquad$ (b) $(-2,0)$.

8 A triangle has vertices at $(3,0)$ and $(-3,0)$, and the equation of its incircle is
$x^2 + y^2 - 2x - 4y + 1 = 0$. Find

(a) the coordinates of the third vertex,

(b) the equation of the circumcircle,

(c) the equation of the Euler circle.

Prove that the Euler circle touches the incircle.

9* The sides (BC), (CA), (AB) of a triangle $\triangle ABC$ have equations $x - y = 16$, $7x + y = 80$,
$x + 7y = 80$.

(a) Find the coordinates of the vertices.

(b) Find the perpendicular distances from the origin O to the three sides, possibly produced.
Hence show that a circle with centre O touches all three sides of the triangle. With the help of
a sketch, determine how this circle is related to the triangle.

(c) Find the centre and radius of the Euler circle of the triangle.

(d) Prove that the Euler circle touches the circle in part (b).

9 Finding loci by analytical methods

This chapter builds on the methods of Chapter 8. When you have completed it, you should

- know how to formulate equations to express geometrical conditions
- be able to choose axes and scales to facilitate geometrical interpretation
- be able to investigate the reversibility of the argument in algebraic terms.

9.1 Matching equations to data

When you found the equation of a straight line in the form

$$\frac{y - y_1}{x - x_1} = m,$$

or the equation of a circle as

$$\sqrt{(x - h)^2 + (y - k)^2} = r,$$

you were using the idea of a locus. The straight line is

the locus of points (x, y) which, when joined to (x_1, y_1), form a line segment of gradient m;

and the circle is

the locus of points (x, y) whose distance from (h, k) is equal to r.

But sometimes you want to find the equation of a line or a circle from other kinds of data. You could begin by trying to find the gradient and a point on the line, or the centre and radius of the circle. But it is often easier to find it directly from a locus property. This section gives two examples where this is especially effective.

The perpendicular bisector

Example 9.1.1
Find the perpendicular bisector of $[AB]$, where A and B have coordinates $(5, 7)$ and $(9, -2)$.

Here are two ways of doing it for you to compare.

Method 1   The mid-point of $[AB]$ has coordinates $\left(\frac{5+9}{2}, \frac{7+(-2)}{2}\right)$, that is $\left(7, \frac{5}{2}\right)$.

The line segment has gradient $\frac{(-2)-7}{9-5} = -\frac{9}{4}$, so the perpendicular has gradient $-\frac{1}{-\frac{9}{4}} = \frac{4}{9}$.

You therefore want the equation of a line with gradient $\frac{4}{9}$ through $\left(7, \frac{5}{2}\right)$, which is

$$y - \frac{5}{2} = \frac{4}{9}(x - 7).$$

Multiplying by 18 to clear all fractions,

$$18y - 45 = 8x - 56, \quad \text{which is} \quad 8x - 18y - 11 = 0.$$

Method 2   Use the fact that the perpendicular bisector is the locus of points P such that PA = PB, and express this algebraically. If (x, y) is a point on the locus,

$$\sqrt{(x-5)^2 + (y-7)^2} = \sqrt{(x-9)^2 + (y-(-2))^2}.$$

Squaring and multiplying out the brackets gives

$$x^2 - 10x + 25 + y^2 - 14y + 49 = x^2 - 18x + 81 + y^2 + 4y + 4.$$

The terms involving x^2 and y^2 disappear when you simplify this, giving

$$8x - 18y - 11 = 0.$$

In this example the second method not only involves less calculation, it also avoids the tiresome fractions.

It would be easy to adapt the second method to produce a general expression for the perpendicular bisector of the line segment with ends (a, c) and (b, d). Since PA = PB,

$$\sqrt{(x-a)^2 + (y-c)^2} = \sqrt{(x-b)^2 + (y-d)^2}.$$

So $x^2 - 2ax + a^2 + y^2 - 2cy + c^2 = x^2 - 2bx + b^2 + y^2 - 2dy + d^2$

$$2(b-a)x + 2(d-c)y + (a^2 - b^2 + c^2 - d^2) = 0.$$

Check for yourself that this line contains the mid-point $\left(\dfrac{a+b}{2}, \dfrac{c+d}{2}\right)$ of [AB] and that the product of the gradients of the line and of [AB] is -1.

The circle with a given diameter

Example 9.1.2
Find the equation of the circle whose diameter is [AB], where (as in Example 9.1.1) A and B have coordinates $(5,7)$ and $(9,-2)$.

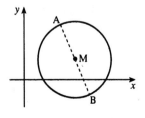

Again, two methods are presented for comparison.

Method 1   The centre of the circle is at the mid-point M of [AB], which was found in Example 9.1.1 to be $\left(7, \frac{5}{2}\right)$. The radius is the distance MA, which is

$$\sqrt{(5-7)^2 + \left(7 - \tfrac{5}{2}\right)^2} = \sqrt{(-2)^2 + \left(\tfrac{9}{2}\right)^2} = \sqrt{4 + \tfrac{81}{4}} = \sqrt{\tfrac{97}{4}}.$$

So the equation of the circle is

$$(x-7)^2 + \left(y - \tfrac{5}{2}\right)^2 = \left(\sqrt{\tfrac{97}{4}}\right)^2,$$

which can be simplified as

$$x^2 - 14x + 49 + y^2 - 5y + \tfrac{25}{4} = \tfrac{97}{4}, \quad \text{or} \quad x^2 + y^2 - 14x - 5y + 31 = 0.$$

Method 2   If P is a point on the circle, then [AP] is perpendicular to [BP]. The gradients of [AP] and [BP] are $\dfrac{y-7}{x-5}$ and $\dfrac{y-(-2)}{x-9}$. The product of these is -1, so

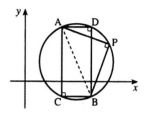

$$\frac{y-7}{x-5} \times \frac{y+2}{x-9} = -1.$$

Then

$$(y-7)(y+2) = -(x-5)(x-9),$$
$$y^2 - 5y - 14 = -\left(x^2 - 14x + 45\right),$$
$$x^2 + y^2 - 14x - 5y + 31 = 0.$$

There are two small glitches in this solution.

- *If P is at A or B then you can't say that [AP] is perpendicular to [BP]. So the solution should begin 'If P is a point on the circle other than A or B'.*

- *There are two other points C and D, with coordinates $(5,-2)$ and $(9,7)$, at which one or other of the expressions for the gradient is meaningless. At these points it is true that [AP] is perpendicular to [BP], but one of these lines is parallel to the y-axis and has no gradient.*

When you get to the equation $(y-7)(y+2) = -(x-5)(x-9)$, it is easy to check that this is also satisfied by the coordinates of A, B, C and D. But a really careful solution would deal with these four points separately.

Again, this argument is easily generalised to the case when A is (a,c) and B is (b,d). If P is any point other than A or B on the circle, then $A\hat{P}B = 90°$. And if P is any point other than A, B, C and D on the circle (where C and D have coordinates (a,d) and (b,c)) the gradients of [AP] and [BP] are $\dfrac{y-c}{x-a}$ and $\dfrac{y-d}{x-b}$. So, except at these points,

$$\frac{y-c}{x-a} \times \frac{y-d}{x-b} = -1.$$

That is,

$$(y-c)(y-d) = -(x-a)(x-b).$$

This equation is also satisfied by the coordinates of A, B, C and D. It therefore holds for any point (x,y) on the circle.

The argument can also be reversed. Suppose that $(y-c)(y-d) = -(x-a)(x-b)$.

- *If $x \neq a$ or b, then $\dfrac{y-c}{x-a} \times \dfrac{y-d}{x-b} = -1$, so [AP] is perpendicular to [BP], and P lies on the circle with diameter [AB].*

- *If $x = a$, then $y = c$ (with P at A, which is certainly on the circle) or $y = d$ (with P at C); and at (a,d), (AP) has equation $x = a$ and (BP) has equation $y = d$, so [AP] is perpendicular to [BP].*

- If $x = b$, then $y = c$ (with P at D) or $y = d$ (with P at B, which is certainly on the circle); and at (b,c), (AP) has equation $y = c$ and (BP) has equation $x = b$, so [AP] is perpendicular to [BP].

This completes the proof that the equation of the circle with diameter [AB] is

$$(x - a)(x - b) + (y - c)(y - d) = 0.$$

You could avoid the awkward discussion about the exceptional points by expressing the fact that $A\hat{P}B = 90°$ using Pythagoras's theorem:

$$A\hat{P}B = 90° \Leftrightarrow PA^2 + PB^2 = AB^2$$
$$\Leftrightarrow \left((x - a)^2 + (y - c)^2\right) + \left((x - b)^2 + (y - d)^2\right) = (b - a)^2 + (d - c)^2.$$

If you multiply this out you will find that you reach the same conclusion as before. But this doesn't produce the equation in its neat factorised form.

9.2 Finding loci from given conditions

The examples in Section 9.1 were both of a type in which you used a locus that you already knew to find an equation. But you can also use analytical methods to find new loci, for points having some given property.

One advantage of doing this is that you can choose the coordinates of any fixed points so as to make the algebra simple. For example, if you have two fixed points you might choose one to be at the origin and the other to be on the x-axis; or you might find it better to place them on the y-axis at equal distances above and below the origin. If you have a hunch what the locus might be, then it is a good idea to choose the origin and axes so that it will be easy to interpret the equation of the locus.

Example 9.2.1

Find the locus of points P such that $PA^2 - PB^2 = k^2$, where A and B are fixed points a distance a apart, and k is a constant.

There is no reason to regard A as more or less important than B, so it would probably be best to place them on one of the axes at equal distances from the origin. Since they are a distance a apart, let A and B have coordinates $\left(-\tfrac{1}{2}a, 0\right)$ and $\left(\tfrac{1}{2}a, 0\right)$ respectively, as shown in the figure. Since $PA > PB$, the locus should then be on the positive side of the y-axis, which would be convenient.

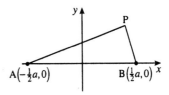

Let a point P on the locus have coordinates (x, y). Then $PA^2 = \left(x + \tfrac{1}{2}a\right)^2 + y^2$ and $PB^2 = \left(x - \tfrac{1}{2}a\right)^2 + y^2$, so that

$$PA^2 - PB^2 = \left(x + \tfrac{1}{2}a\right)^2 - \left(x - \tfrac{1}{2}a\right)^2$$
$$= \left(x^2 + ax + \tfrac{1}{4}a^2\right) - \left(x^2 - ax + \tfrac{1}{4}a^2\right)$$
$$= 2ax.$$

The condition $PA^2 - PB^2 = k^2$ can therefore be written as $2ax = k^2$, or

$$x = \frac{k^2}{2a}.$$

This is the equation of a line parallel to the y-axis.

Notice that this argument also works backwards. If $x = \frac{k^2}{2a}$, then

$$PA^2 - PB^2 = 2a \times \frac{k^2}{2a} = k^2.$$

So if P satisfies the condition, then it lies on the line; and if it lies on the line, it satisfies the condition. You need both to be true before you can assert that the locus of P is the line.

Finally, you have to interpret the equation of the locus. There is no mention in the question of the y-axis, so you have to say what it means in relation to A and B. Since these points were chosen symmetrically, the y-axis is in fact the perpendicular bisector of $[AB]$. So you could describe the locus as being the line perpendicular to $[AB]$ at a distance $\frac{k^2}{2a}$ from the mid-point of $[AB]$, on the same side of the mid-point as B.

Example 9.2.2
A square ABCD has sides of length a. Find the locus of points P such that

$$PA^2 + PB^2 + PC^2 + PD^2 = 4a^2.$$

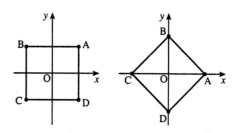

The symmetry of the condition suggests that the origin should be chosen at the centre of the square. You could then set the square either with its sides parallel to the axes and vertices at $\left(\pm\frac{1}{2}a, \pm\frac{1}{2}a\right)$, or with its diagonals along the axes and vertices at $\left(\pm\frac{a}{\sqrt{2}}, 0\right)$ and $\left(0, \pm\frac{a}{\sqrt{2}}\right)$. Both possibilities are shown in the figure. The example will be worked with the diagram on the right; you may like to try it for yourself with the diagram on the left.

If a point P on the locus has coordinates (x, y), it has to satisfy the equation

$$\left(\left(x - \frac{a}{\sqrt{2}}\right)^2 + y^2\right) + \left(x^2 + \left(y - \frac{a}{\sqrt{2}}\right)^2\right) + \left(\left(x + \frac{a}{\sqrt{2}}\right)^2 + y^2\right) + \left(x^2 + \left(y + \frac{a}{\sqrt{2}}\right)^2\right) = 4a^2.$$

This can be simplified as

$$4x^2 + 4y^2 + 2a^2 = 4a^2,$$

or

$$x^2 + y^2 = \tfrac{1}{2}a^2.$$

The argument can obviously be reversed:

$$\text{if } x^2 + y^2 = \tfrac{1}{2}a^2, \text{ then } PA^2 + PB^2 + PC^2 + PD^2 = 4a^2.$$

You will recognise $x^2 + y^2 = \tfrac{1}{2}a^2$ as the equation of a circle with its centre at the origin and radius $\dfrac{a}{\sqrt{2}}$. Since this radius is equal to OA, the circle passes through the vertices of the square.

The locus of P is the circumcircle of the square.

Example 9.2.3

A line l contains a fixed point A. Find the locus of points P which are twice as far from A as they are from l.

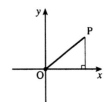

Before launching into the algebra, can you guess what the locus is?

An obvious choice is to take the line l to be the x-axis, and the fixed point A to be the origin O, as shown in the figure.

If a point on the locus has coordinates (x, y), its distance from the origin is $\sqrt{x^2 + y^2}$, and its distance from the line is $|y|$. (Remember that the point may be on either side of the line.) So the condition is expressed by the equation

$$\sqrt{x^2 + y^2} = 2|y|.$$

Squaring this, using the fact that $|y|^2 = y^2$,

$$x^2 + y^2 = 4y^2,$$

so

$$x^2 = 3y^2.$$

This also works backwards. If $x^2 = 3y^2$, then $x^2 + y^2 = 4y^2$, and therefore $\sqrt{x^2 + y^2} = 2|y|$.

You might have thought that the last step should be $\sqrt{x^2 + y^2} = 2|y|$ or $\sqrt{x^2 + y^2} = -2|y|$; but the second equation is impossible, since the left side is positive and the right side is negative.

From $x^2 = 3y^2$ it follows that $x = \sqrt{3}y$ or $x = -\sqrt{3}y$.

That is, P lies on one of two lines through the origin with gradients $\dfrac{1}{\sqrt{3}}$ or $-\dfrac{1}{\sqrt{3}}$. Since $\dfrac{1}{\sqrt{3}} = \tan 30°$, these lines make angles of $30°$ with the x-axis.

The locus of P is a pair of lines through the fixed point at $30°$ to the line l.

Example 9.2.4

If A and B are fixed points, find the locus of points P such that $\dfrac{PA}{PB} = k$, where k is a constant greater than 1.

This is Apollonius's locus problem. See Section 6.3.

It would be convenient to place A and B symmetrically about the y-axis, as in Example 9.2.1. To avoid fractions, let A be $(-a,0)$ and B be $(a,0)$, so that the distance AB is $2a$. If the coordinates of any point P on the locus are (x,y), then

$$\frac{\sqrt{(x+a)^2 + y^2}}{\sqrt{(x-a)^2 + y^2}} = k, \quad \text{so} \quad (x+a)^2 + y^2 = k^2\big((x-a)^2 + y^2\big).$$

Notice that this step is reversible, since both k and the square roots are positive.

The equation can be rearranged as

$$x^2(k^2 - 1) - 2ax(k^2 + 1) + a^2(k^2 - 1) + y^2(k^2 - 1) = 0,$$

or

$$x^2 - 2ax\left(\frac{k^2 + 1}{k^2 - 1}\right) + a^2 + y^2 = 0.$$

You will recognise this as the equation of a circle. To find its centre and radius, write it in the form

$$\left(x - \frac{k^2 + 1}{k^2 - 1}a\right)^2 + y^2 = -a^2 + \left(\frac{k^2 + 1}{k^2 - 1}\right)^2 a^2,$$

and simplify the right side as

$$\frac{(k^2 + 1)^2 - (k^2 - 1)^2}{(k^2 - 1)^2}a^2 = \frac{4k^2}{(k^2 - 1)^2}a^2 = \left(\frac{2k}{k^2 - 1}a\right)^2.$$

The equation is therefore

$$\left(x - \frac{k^2 + 1}{k^2 - 1}a\right)^2 + y^2 = \left(\frac{2k}{k^2 - 1}a\right)^2,$$

which represents a circle with its centre at $\left(\dfrac{k^2 + 1}{k^2 - 1}a, 0\right)$ and radius $\dfrac{2k}{k^2 - 1}a$.

You can easily check that each step of the algebra can be reversed. So it is also true that, if P lies on the circle, then $\dfrac{PA}{PB} = k$.

If you compare this proof of the Apollonius's circle property with the proof in Section 6.3, there are two significant differences. First, the method shown here is completely standard; you don't need to begin by spotting a particular construction (in this example, drawing the internal and external bisectors of $A\hat{P}B$). Secondly, you can see directly from the algebra that the argument reads equally well backwards as forwards; in the proof by pure geometry the proof of the converse was quite tricky.

On the other hand, the analytical method doesn't give as much insight into the geometry of the figure, since it doesn't reveal the important property that (in the notation of Fig. 6.7) [PD] and [PE] are the internal and external bisectors of $A\hat{P}B$. The example is a good illustration of the strengths and weaknesses of the two different approaches.

Example 9.2.5*

Given a line l and a fixed point A not on the line, find the locus of points which are twice as far from A as they are from l.

This looks almost the same as Example 9.2.3, except that A is not now a point on l. So take the line l to be the x-axis as before, and take A to be a point on the y-axis as shown in the figure. It is worth noticing that, if you take the coordinates of A to be $(0, 3a)$, then the points of the locus which are on the y-axis will be $(0, a)$ and $(0, -3a)$, which don't involve fractions.

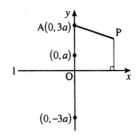

If (x, y) is a point of the locus, then its distance from A is $\sqrt{x^2 + (y - 3a)^2}$ and its distance from the x-axis is $|y|$ so

$$\sqrt{x^2 + (y - 3a)^2} = 2|y|.$$

Squaring this gives

$$x^2 + (y - 3a)^2 = 4y^2,$$

which can be simplified as

$$x^2 = 3y^2 + 6ay - 9a^2, \quad \text{or} \quad 3(y + a)^2 - x^2 = 12a^2.$$

This is an equation you probably won't recognise. It certainly isn't the equation of a straight line or a circle. But when that happens you have one great advantage that was not available to Euclid, Apollonius, Descartes, Simson or Euler – you can key in the equation to a computer program or a graphic display calculator (having chosen a suitable numerical value for the constant a) and the locus will be drawn for you.

With this equation, the result is the pair of curves shown in the figure. It is called a 'hyperbola'.

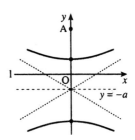

You will notice some interesting features of the graph. It's not surprising that it is symmetrical about the y-axis, but it is also symmetrical about the line $y = -a$, which is the perpendicular bisector of the line segment joining the points $(0, a)$ and $(0, -3a)$ where the graph cuts the y-axis. There are two asymptotes (drawn as dotted lines) which are parallel to the lines in Example 9.2.3, but passing through the centre of symmetry $(0, -a)$.

9.3   A non-reversible example

In most examples of Section 9.2 there is a mention of the fact that the argument is reversible: that not only does every point of the locus lie on the curve with the equation you found, but also every point on the curve has the property which defines the locus. You may have thought that this was just a formality, so this section gives an example where the situation is more complicated.

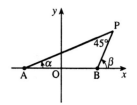

Suppose that you have two fixed points A and B, and want to find the locus of points P such that $\hat{APB} = 45°$. Take the coordinates of A and B to be $(-a,0)$ and $(a,0)$, as in Example 9.2.4, and let a general point P on the locus have coordinates (x,y). Then, if α and β denote the angles measured from the direction of the positive x-axis to the directed lines from A and B to P (see Fig. 9.1), the gradients of the line segments $[AP]$ and $[BP]$ are

Fig. 9.1

$$\tan\alpha = \frac{y}{x-(-a)} = \frac{y}{x+a} \quad \text{and} \quad \tan\beta = \frac{y}{x-a}.$$

If P is on the locus, then the exterior angle theorem for a triangle gives $\beta - \alpha = 45°$, so that $\tan(\beta - \alpha) = 1$. Substituting the expressions for $\tan\alpha$ and $\tan\beta$ from the equations above in the identity

$$\tan(\beta - \alpha) \equiv \frac{\tan\beta - \tan\alpha}{1 + \tan\beta\tan\alpha}$$

gives

$$\frac{\dfrac{y}{x-a} - \dfrac{y}{x+a}}{1 + \dfrac{y}{x-a} \times \dfrac{y}{x+a}} = 1, \quad \text{so} \quad \frac{y}{x-a} - \frac{y}{x+a} = 1 + \frac{y^2}{(x-a)(x+a)}.$$

Multiplying both sides by $(x-a)(x+a)$,

$$y(x+a) - y(x-a) = (x-a)(x+a) + y^2,$$

so

$$2ay = x^2 - a^2 + y^2, \quad \text{or} \quad x^2 + y^2 - 2ay = a^2.$$

This should be the equation of the locus.

Unfortunately it isn't!

To see why, notice that the equation can be written as

$$x^2 + (y-a)^2 = 2a^2,$$

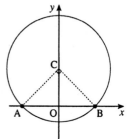

which represents a circle with centre at C, with coordinates $(0,a)$, and radius $\sqrt{2}a$. This is drawn in Fig. 9.2.

It is easy to see that, since OAC and OCB are isosceles right-angled triangles, $\hat{ACB}$ is a right angle. Therefore, if P is any point on the major arc AB, $\hat{APB} = \frac{1}{2} \times 90° = 45°$. But if P is a point on the minor arc AB, for which $y < 0$, $\hat{APB} = \frac{1}{2} \times 270° = 135°$, and P is not on the locus.

Fig. 9.2

The reason why points on the minor arc appear in the equation can be seen from Fig. 9.3, which shows a point P on the circle for which $y < 0$. The angles α and β, defined as before, are now reflex angles, and the exterior angle theorem for triangle APB can be used in the form

$$(\alpha - 180°) - (\beta - 180)° = 135°, \quad \text{so} \quad \beta - \alpha = -135°.$$

And since $\tan(-135°) = 1$, this again produces the equation $\tan(\beta - \alpha) = 1$.

So although all the algebraic steps involving x and y are reversible (except where $x = \pm a$; see the note at the end of this section), the first step

$$\beta - \alpha = 45° \quad \Rightarrow \quad \tan(\beta - \alpha) = 1$$

is not. And the effect of this is to produce some points which satisfy the equation of the circle but which are not on the locus.

But the major arc AB of the circle in Fig. 9.2 is not the complete locus, and you need to examine more closely what happens if y is negative. Fig. 9.4 shows a point P of the locus with $y < 0$. The exterior angle theorem for triangle APB now takes the form

$$(\alpha - 180°) - (\beta - 180)° = 45°,$$

so $\alpha - \beta = 45°$ and $\tan(\beta - \alpha) = -1$.

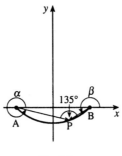

Fig. 9.3

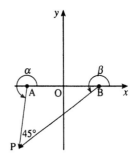

Fig. 9.4

The expressions for the gradients of $[AP]$ and $[BP]$ are unchanged. You can then work through the algebra just as before, and you will find that (x, y) satisfies the equation

$$x^2 + (y + a)^2 = 2a^2.$$

This represents a circle with centre at D, with coordinates $(0, -a)$, and radius $\sqrt{2}a$. And by the same argument as before, only the major arc of this circle is part of the locus.

So the complete locus consists of the pair of major arcs AB of circles with centres C and D. This is drawn in Fig. 9.5.

Notice that the points A and B are not part of the locus, since you can't give a meaning to $A\hat{P}B$ if P is at A or B. A common convention is to indicate this by drawing very small circles round these points.

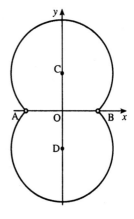

Fig. 9.5

A really careful proof would consider separately the points at which x is equal to $-a$ or a, since at these points one or other of the expressions $\dfrac{y}{x+a}$ and $\dfrac{y}{x-a}$ for the gradients of $[AP]$, $[BP]$ cannot be used. It is easy to see that the coordinates of these points are $(\pm a, \pm 2a)$, and that these points are on the locus as described.

Exercise 9

1   A quadrilateral has vertices $A(-1,5)$, $B(4,7)$, $C(7,-1)$, $D(-2,1)$. Find the coordinates of the point P such that $PA = PC$ and $PB = PD$.

2   A quadrilateral has vertices $A(-2,4)$, $B(5,11)$, $C(12,7)$, $D(6,-2)$. Find the coordinates of the points P such that $A\hat{P}C = B\hat{P}D = 90°$.

3   A triangle has vertices $A(-7,2)$, $B(2,3)$, $C(4,-1)$. Find the coordinates of the points P such that $A\hat{P}B = 90°$ and $PB = PC$.

4   B and C are two points 10 units apart.

   (a) Find the locus of points P such that $PB^2 + PC^2 = 250$.

   (b) Find the locus of points P such that $2PB^2 + 3PC^2 = 1100$.

   (See Exercise 2C Question 9.)

5   A triangle has vertices $A(0,0)$, $B(10,0)$, $C(8,12)$. Find the locus of points P such that $PA^2 + PB^2 + PC^2 = k$. Hence find the point in the plane of the triangle for which $PA^2 + PB^2 + PC^2$ has its smallest value.

6   A and B are two points a distance a apart. A circle c_1 has centre A and radius r, and a circle c_2 has centre B and radius s. Find the locus of points P such that the tangents from P to c_1 and c_2 are equal in length.

7   ABCD is a square. Find the locus of points such that

   (a) $PA \times PC = PB \times PD$,   (b) $PA \times PB = PC \times PD$.

8*   A is a fixed point and l is a line not passing through A. Find the locus of points whose distance from A is equal to its distance from l, and interpret your answer geometrically.

10 More properties of circles

This chapter introduces another set of theorems about circles. When you have completed it, you should

- know the intersecting chords and secant-secant theorems
- know the tangent and chord theorem and be able to use it to extend the secant-secant theorem
- know what is meant by the power of a point with respect to a circle
- be familiar with analytical expressions for the power of a point.

There is an alternative treatment of these topics using vectors in Section 11.6.

10.1 Intersecting chords and secants

Fig. 10.1 and Fig. 10.2 are copies of figures which were used in Section 2.1 to illustrate triangles which are indirectly similar.

These figures also have similarities with Fig. 4.4 and Fig. 4.2 in the chapter on concyclic points. In Fig. 10.1 the angles marked 2 are the exterior angle at D and the interior angle at B of the quadrilateral BEDC. In Fig. 10.2 the angles marked 2 are the angles subtended at B and D by the line segment [EC]. It follows in both cases that the points B, E, D, C are concyclic. Fig. 10.3 and Fig. 10.4 are copies of Fig. 10.1 and Fig. 10.2 with the circles added.

Since in both figures $\triangle ABC$ is similar to $\triangle ADE$, you can equate proportions of corresponding sides to give

$$\frac{AB}{AD} = \frac{AC}{AE},$$

that is

$$AE \times AB = AD \times AC.$$

For the present purpose the third sides, [BC] and [DE], are not needed. Fig. 10.5 and Fig. 10.6 show Fig. 10.3 and Fig. 10.4 with these sides removed. You will see that in each figure you have two chords of a circle, [BE] and [CD]. The only difference is that in Fig. 10.6 the chords meet at a point A inside the circle, whereas in Fig. 10.5 the chords are produced to form secants meeting at a point A outside the circle.

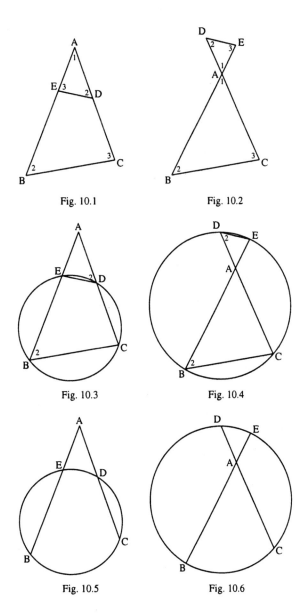

Fig. 10.1

Fig. 10.2

Fig. 10.3

Fig. 10.4

Fig. 10.5

Fig. 10.6

> **The intersecting chords theorem**   If chords [BE] and [CD] of a circle intersect at a point A inside the circle, then $AE \times AB = AD \times AC$.
>
> **The secant-secant theorem**   If secants (BE) and (CD) of a circle intersect at a point A outside the circle, then $AE \times AB = AD \times AC$.

The term 'intersecting chords' is often used to describe both theorems.

Example 10.1.1

A vertical cross-section of a skateboarding area is an arc of a circle with a horizontal width of 20 metres. It is designed so that the surface at the boundary is 2 metres higher than at the lowest point. Find the radius of the circular arc.

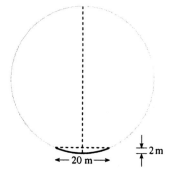

The figure shows a simplified model of the skateboarding area. Let the radius be r metres. Then the vertical diameter is split by the horizontal chord into two parts, of lengths 2 metres and $(2r-2)$ metres; and the chord is split into two parts by the diameter, each of length 10 metres. So, by the intersecting chords theorem,

$$2 \times (2r-2) = 10 \times 10.$$

This gives

$$r - 1 = 25, \quad \text{so} \quad r = 26.$$

The radius of the circular arc is 26 metres.

10.2 The tangent and chord theorem

So far the only property of tangents that you have used is that the tangent is perpendicular to the radius through the point of contact. This section introduces a more general property about the angle between the tangent and any chord through the point of contact.

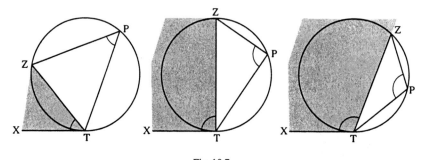

Fig. 10.7

Fig. 10.7 illustrates three possibilities. The angle between the tangent TX and the chord TZ may be acute, a right angle or obtuse. The region enclosed within this angle is shaded grey. At a point P on the unshaded arc of the circle the chord subtends an angle $\hat{TPZ}$. This angle may also be acute, a right angle or obtuse. The result to be proved is that the two angles, $\hat{XTZ}$ and $\hat{TPZ}$, are in fact equal.

The tangent and chord theorem   The angle between a tangent to a circle and a chord through the point of contact is equal to the angle subtended by the chord at a point of the circumference on the other side of the chord.

This theorem is often referred to as the 'alternate segment theorem'.

The proof is in three parts, one for each of the figures in Fig. 10.7.

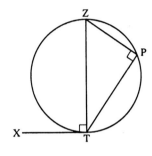

Fig. 10.8

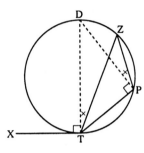

Fig. 10.9

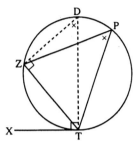

Fig. 10.10

Proof

(i)   XT̂Z is a right angle (Fig. 10.8)

This case is almost obvious. If $X\hat{T}Z = 90°$, [TZ] is a diameter of the circle. So, by the angle in a semicircle theorem, $T\hat{P}Z = 90°$. Therefore $X\hat{T}Z = T\hat{P}Z$.

(ii)   XT̂Z is an obtuse angle (Fig. 10.9)

To use what you already know about tangents, you must begin by drawing the diameter [TD] through T. Then join [DP].

You will see that Fig. 10.9 contains the figure for case (i), but with the letter Z replaced by D. So $X\hat{T}D = T\hat{P}D$. Also $D\hat{T}Z = D\hat{P}Z$ (angles on the same arc DZ).

So $X\hat{T}Z = X\hat{T}D + D\hat{T}Z$

$= T\hat{P}D + D\hat{P}Z = T\hat{P}Z.$

(iii)   XT̂Z is an acute angle (Fig. 10.10)

Again draw the diameter [TD], but now it is better to join [DZ].

As $T\hat{Z}D = 90°$ (angle in a semicircle) and the angles of $\triangle TZD$ add up to $180°$, $T\hat{D}Z + Z\hat{T}D = 90°$. But also $X\hat{T}Z + Z\hat{T}D = 90°$. So

$X\hat{T}Z = T\hat{D}Z.$

Also $T\hat{D}Z = T\hat{P}Z$ (angles on the same arc TZ).

Therefore $X\hat{T}Z = T\hat{P}Z$.

Example 10.2.1

Two circles c_1 and c_2 intersect at A and B. The tangent at A to c_1 meets c_2 again at C, and the tangent at A to c_2 meets c_1 again at D. Prove that the common chord $[BA]$ bisects $C\hat{B}D$.

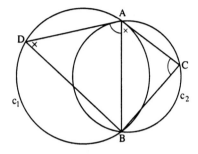

The tangent and chord theorem for c_1 states that $C\hat{A}B = A\hat{D}B$.

Similarly, for c_2, $D\hat{A}B = A\hat{C}B$.

The triangles ABC and ABD therefore have two pairs of angles equal, so the third angles are equal. That is, $A\hat{B}C = A\hat{B}D$. Therefore $[BA]$ bisects $C\hat{B}D$.

10.3 The tangent-secant theorem

You can use the tangent and chord theorem to extend the secant-secant theorem to include the length of the tangent from a point outside the circle.

Fig. 10.11 shows a circle with the tangent $[AC]$ from a point A and a secant (EB) passing through A. You will recognise in this a figure which you have already seen as Fig. 2.10 in Section 2.1, reproduced here as Fig. 10.12.

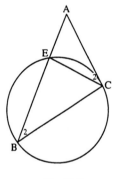

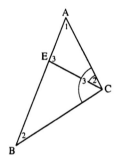

Fig. 10.11   Fig. 10.12

In Fig. 10.11 $A\hat{C}E$ is the angle between the tangent $[AC]$ and the chord $[CE]$, and $C\hat{B}E$ is the angle subtended by the chord $[CE]$ at a point B of the arc on the other side of the chord. These are the angles marked 2 in Fig. 10.12.

Since the triangles ABC and ACE are similar,

$$\frac{AC}{AE} = \frac{AB}{AC},$$

so $AC^2 = AE \times AB$.

> **The tangent-secant theorem**   If A is a point outside a circle, $[AC]$ is a tangent and (BE) is a secant passing through A, then $AC^2 = AE \times AB$.

Exercise 10A

1   This question uses the notation of Fig. 10.5.

   (a) If $AD = 4$ cm, $AC = 6$ cm and $AB = 8$ cm, find AE.

   (b) If $AE = 5$ cm, $EB = 3$ cm and $AD = 4$ cm, find DC.

   (c) If $AD = 8$ cm, $DC = 10$ cm and $EB = 18$ cm, find AE.

2   This question uses the notation of Fig. 10.6.

   (a) If $AB = 12$ cm, $AC = 10$ cm and $AD = 6$ cm, find AE.

   (b) If $BE = 21$ cm, $CD = 23$ cm and $AE = 6$ cm, find AC.

3   This question uses the notation of Fig. 10.11.

   (a) If $AE = 4$ cm and $EB = 5$ cm, find AC.

   (b) If $AC = 12$ cm, $EB = 7$ cm and $BC = 8$ cm, find AE and EC.

4   Two circles intersect at A and B. A common tangent touches the circles at S and T. Prove that the secant (AB) bisects [ST].

5   Two circles c_1 and c_2 have centres A and B. The tangent [AS] from A to c_2 intersects the tangent [BT] from B to c_1 at X. Prove that $AX \times XS = BX \times XT$.

6   Prove the following for the figure in Example 10.2.1.

   (a) $BA^2 = BC \times BD$.

   (b) If [CD] cuts c_1 at X and c_2 at Y, then $AX = AY$.

7   A quadrilateral ABCD is circumscribed to a circle. The sides [AB], [BC], [CD], [DA] touch the circle at P, Q, R, S. The chords [PR] and [QS] intersect at X. Find, in terms of the angles of the quadrilateral ABCD,

   (a) $P\hat{Q}R$,   (b) $P\hat{X}Q$.

8   Two circles touch each other at A. Two lines l, m through A cut the first circle at P, Q and the second circle at R, S. Prove that the lines (PQ), (RS) are parallel. (Consider two cases, with the circles external to each other and with one circle inside the other.)

9   [BC] is a diameter of a circle, and A is a point on (BC) outside the circle. [AT] is a tangent to the circle, and N is the point on [BC] such that [TN] is perpendicular to [BC]. Prove that [TB] bisects $A\hat{T}N$.

10   The earth is approximately a sphere of radius 6400 km. The sun deck of a cruise liner is 20 metres above sea level. By making sensible approximations, show that the distance to the horizon is about 16 km.

10.4   The power of a point with respect to a circle

Fig. 10.13 shows a point A outside a circle, with the two tangents from A and a number of secants through A. If a typical secant cuts the circle at P and Q, then the product AP × AQ has the same value for every one of the secants, and it is equal to the square of the length of the tangents. If AP and AQ are sensed lengths (see Section 7.4), then these are either both positive or both negative, depending on which direction on the line you take to be positive. It follows that the product of the lengths is positive.

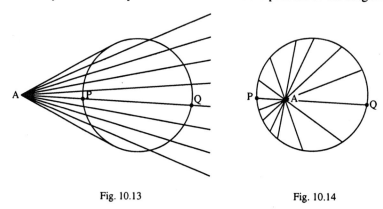

Fig. 10.13   Fig. 10.14

In Fig. 10.14 the point A is inside the circle, and the figure shows a number of chords through A. If [PQ] is a typical chord, the product AP × AQ has the same value for every one of the chords. But if AP and AQ are interpreted as sensed lengths, then one is positive and one is negative, so the product is negative.

In either case the product of the sensed lengths AP × AQ is called the **power** of the point with respect to the circle. Its value depends on the radius of the circle and the distance of the point from the centre, as the following theorem shows.

> **Theorem**   The power of the point A with respect to a circle with centre O and radius r is equal to $d^2 - r^2$, where d is the distance AO. If a circle has equation

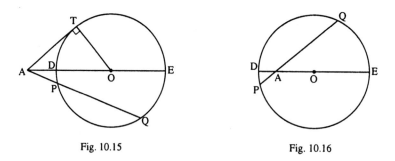

Fig. 10.15   Fig. 10.16

Proof

The result is the same whether A is outside or inside the circle, but the details are slightly different, so the two cases are taken separately.

Point outside the circle

Fig. 10.15 shows a typical secant (PQ) through A, the diameter (DE) through A and a tangent [AT] from A to the circle.

Method 1   Since $DO = OE = r$, $AD = d - r$ and $AE = d + r$.

By the secant-secant theorem,

$$AP \times AQ = AD \times AE$$
$$= (d - r) \times (d + r) = d^2 - r^2.$$

Method 2   By the tangent-secant theorem, $AP \times AQ = AT^2$.

Since $A\hat{T}O = 90°$, Pythagoras's theorem gives

$$AT^2 = AO^2 - OT^2 = d^2 - r^2.$$

Therefore

$$AP \times AQ = d^2 - r^2.$$

Point inside the circle

Fig. 10.16 shows a typical chord [PQ] through A and the diameter [DE] through A.

Only Method 1 can now be used. Take the positive direction on the diameter to be from D to E. Then $AE = d + r$ and $DA = r - d$, so $AD = -(r - d) = d - r$.

By the intersecting chords theorem,

$$AP \times AQ = AD \times AE$$
$$= (d - r) \times (d + r) = d^2 - r^2.$$

Notice that, for a point inside the circle, $r > d$, so $d^2 - r^2$, the power of the point with respect to the circle is always negative. If the point is on the circle, $r = d$, so the power of the point is 0.

10.5   A proof using coordinates

If the centre O of the circle has coordinates (h, k), and the coordinates of A are (x_0, y_0), then the distance $d = OA$ is given by

$$d^2 = (x_0 - h)^2 + (y_0 - k)^2.$$

So by the theorem in Section 10.4, the power of A with respect to the circle is

$$d^2 - r^2 = (x_0 - h)^2 + (y_0 - k)^2 - r^2.$$

It is also possible to find this expression by using an analytical method to prove the intersecting chords theorem, the secant-secant theorem and the tangent-secant theorem directly. In the proof which follows it makes no difference whether A is outside, inside or on the circle.

In Fig. 10.17 a secant (PQ) passes through
$A(x_0, y_0)$. A positive direction is chosen on the
secant, and this makes an angle θ with the
x-direction. Z is a point on the secant such that the
sensed length AZ is equal to z. Then in moving
from A to Z the x- and y-coordinates increase by
$z \cos \theta$ and $z \sin \theta$ respectively. So the coordinates
of Z are

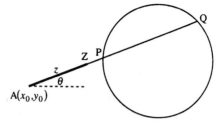

Fig. 10.17

$$\left(x_0 + z \cos \theta, y_0 + z \sin \theta\right).$$

Let the equation of the circle be $x^2 + y^2 + ax + by + c = 0$. Then the sensed lengths AP and AQ are the
values of z for which the point Z lies on the circle. That is, they are the roots for z of the equation

$$\left(x_0 + z \cos \theta\right)^2 + \left(y_0 + z \sin \theta\right)^2 + a\left(x_0 + z \cos \theta\right) + b\left(y_0 + z \sin \theta\right) + c = 0.$$

Collecting together the terms with the same degree in z, this is

$$z^2\left(\cos^2 \theta + \sin^2 \theta\right) + z\left(2x_0 \cos \theta + 2y_0 \sin \theta + a \cos \theta + b \sin \theta\right) + \left(x_0^2 + y_0^2 + ax_0 + by_0 + c\right) = 0.$$

Since $\cos^2 \theta + \sin^2 \theta \equiv 1$, this can be simplified as

$$z^2 + z\left(2x_0 \cos \theta + 2y_0 \sin \theta + a \cos \theta + b \sin \theta\right) + \left(x_0^2 + y_0^2 + ax_0 + by_0 + c\right) = 0.$$

This is a quadratic equation which may have two real roots, a repeated root or no real roots depending on
the value of θ. If the roots are real, they will be the lengths AP and AQ (or, in the case of a repeated
root, the length AT of the tangent).

So suppose the lengths AP, AQ are z_1, z_2. Then the equation must be equivalent to

$$\left(z - z_1\right)\left(z - z_2\right) = 0,$$

that is

$$z^2 - z\left(z_1 + z_2\right) + z_1 z_2 = 0.$$

You are interested in the product $AP \times AQ = z_1 \times z_2$, so compare the constant terms in the two equations.
This gives

$$z_1 z_2 = x_0^2 + y_0^2 + ax_0 + by_0 + c.$$

So there is a simple rule for finding the power of a point in coordinate form:

> If a circle has equation $x^2 + y^2 + ax + by + c = 0$, the power of a point with
> respect to the circle is found by substituting the coordinates (x_0, y_0) of the point
> in place of (x, y) in the expression on the left side of the equation.

You will recall from Section 8.2 that this form of the equation of the circle was obtained by multiplying
out the brackets in the equation

$$(x - h)^2 + (y - k)^2 - r^2 = 0.$$

So the power of (x_0, y_0) can also be found by substituting (x_0, y_0) in place of (x, y) in the left side of this equation, which gives $(x_0 - h)^2 + (y_0 - k)^2 - r^2$. This is the expression given at the beginning of this section, using the form $d^2 - r^2$ for the power of a point.

> The power of a point $A(x_0, y_0)$ with respect to a circle centre $O(h, k)$ and radius r is given by
>
> $$d^2 - r^2 \quad \text{or} \quad (x_0 - h)^2 + (y_0 - k)^2 - r^2$$
>
> where d is the distance OA.

Exercise 10B

1 A common tangent to two circles c_1 and c_2 touches c_1 at S and c_2 at T. Explain why the power of S with respect to c_2 is equal to the power of T with respect to c_1.

2 If O is a point circle, what does the power of A with respect to the circle represent?

3 Two circles intersect at A and B. Prove that, if P is any point on (AB), the power of P with respect to both circles is the same.

Is the converse true? If so, prove it.

4 Find the power of the given point with respect to the circle with the given equation. State whether the point is outside, inside or on the circle. If outside, state also the length of the tangent from the point to the circle.

(a) $(2, 5)$, $x^2 + y^2 + 3x - 4y + 1 = 0$ (b) $(3, -1)$, $x^2 + y^2 - 5x + y + 6 = 0$

(c) $(-2, 0)$, $x^2 + y^2 - 3x + y - 1 = 0$ (d) $(1, -4)$, $x^2 + y^2 + 2x + 5y = 0$

5 Find the points of intersection of the circles c_1 and c_2, with equations $(x + 1)^2 + y^2 - 10 = 0$ and $(x - 4)^2 + y^2 - 25 = 0$. Show that the locus of points whose powers with respect to c_1 and c_2 are in the ratio $k : 1$ is another circle which passes through the same points. What distinguishes those circles for which $k > 0$ from those for which $k < 0$?

6 Points A and B have coordinates $(-6, 0)$ and $(6, 0)$. An Apollonius circle is the locus of points P such that $\dfrac{\text{PA}}{\text{PB}} = k$. Prove that its equation is $x^2 + y^2 - 12 \dfrac{k^2 + 1}{k^2 - 1} x + 36 = 0$.

Two Apollonius circles c_1 and c_2 correspond to the values $k = 2$ and $k = \frac{1}{3}$.

(a) Find the locus of points P such that the powers of P with respect to c_1 and c_2 are equal.

(b) Find the locus of points such that the power of P with respect to c_1 is $\frac{4}{9}$ of the power of P with respect to c_2. Show that your locus is another Apollonius circle, and find the corresponding value of k.

Draw an accurate diagram to illustrate these results, and check by measurement that the lengths of the tangents from P to c_1 and c_2 are in the expected proportion.

11 Vector methods

Another method of proof in geometry is to use vectors. When you have completed this chapter, you should

- be able to use the basic rules of vector algebra to prove results in affine geometry
- be able to use these rules together with the scalar product to prove results in Euclidean geometry.

Throughout this chapter the alphabet convention for position vectors is used; that is, a denotes the position vector of point A, etc. All lengths should be interpreted as sensed lengths (see Section 7.4).

11.1 Parallels and proportions

In Higher Level Book 2 Sections 16.6 and 17.5 it was shown how vectors can be used to prove geometrical theorems. Examples included the concurrence of the medians and of the altitudes of a triangle. In this chapter vector methods will be used more systematically, and vectors will be used to provide alternative proofs for some of the theorems in earlier chapters.

Here is a simple example about well known properties of parallelograms.

Example 11.1.1
A quadrilateral ABCD has [AB] parallel and equal in length to [DC].

(a) Show that [AD] is parallel and equal to [BC].

(b) Show that the mid-points of the diagonals [AC] and [BD] coincide.

(a) Using the alphabet convention, you can write

$$\overrightarrow{AB} = b - a \quad \text{and} \quad \overrightarrow{DC} = c - d.$$

Be careful to label the vectors so that $\overrightarrow{AB}$ and $\overrightarrow{DC}$ are in the same direction, not opposite directions.

The fact that [AB] is parallel and equal to [DC] is expressed by the vector equation $\overrightarrow{AB} = \overrightarrow{DC}$, so

$$b - a = c - d.$$

Therefore

$$d - a = c - b.$$

That is, $\overrightarrow{AD} = \overrightarrow{BC}$. So [AD] is parallel and equal to [BC].

(b) Also, from the same equation, $b - a = c - d$, it follows that $b + d = a + c$, so

$$\tfrac{1}{2}(b + d) = \tfrac{1}{2}(a + c).$$

The left and right sides of this last equation are the position vectors of the mid-points of [BD] and [AC] respectively. Therefore the mid-points of the diagonals coincide.

Part (b) of Example 11.1.1 uses the expression for the position vector of the mid-point. This is a special case of a more general formula.

Suppose that X is a point on the line (AB) such that $AX = qAB$ (where AX and AB are sensed lengths on the line). Thus

$$x - a = q(b - a),$$

so

$$x = a + q(b - a) = (1 - q)a + qb.$$

It is convenient to write $1 - q$ as p, so that

$$x = pa + qb.$$

Notice that, since $AX + XB = AB$ and $AX = qAB$,

$$XB = AB - qAB = (1 - q)AB = pAB,$$

so that $\dfrac{AX}{XB} = \dfrac{q}{p}$.

> If $p + q = 1$, $x = pa + qb$ is the point X on the line (AB) such that $\dfrac{AX}{XB} = \dfrac{q}{p}$.

When you use this formula it is very important to get the coefficients of a and b the right way round. For example, if $p = 0.1$ and $q = 0.9$, so that $\dfrac{AX}{XB} = \dfrac{9}{1}$, then $x = 0.1a + 0.9b$. Since X is much closer to B than to A, it is natural to expect the coefficient of b to outweigh the coefficient of a.

Example 11.1.2
A trapezium BCMN has [BC] parallel to [NM] and twice its length. Find and identify

(a) the intersection of (BN) and (CM),   (b) the intersection of [BM] and [CN].

The fact that [BC] is parallel to [NM] and that $BC = 2NM$ can be expressed in terms of position vectors by the single equation

$$c - b = 2(m - n).$$

Therefore $2n - b = 2m - c$.

(a)   The two sides of this equation each have the form in the shaded box with $p = 2$ and $q = -1$, so that $p + q = 1$. So if you denote $2n - b = 2m - c$ by a, the left side shows that A is the point on (NB) such that $\dfrac{NA}{AB} = \dfrac{-1}{2}$, and the right side shows that A is the point on (MC) such that $\dfrac{MA}{AC} = \dfrac{-1}{2}$. That is, the point A common to (BN) and (CM) is a point on [BN] produced so that $BN = NA$ and on [CM] produced so that $CM = MA$.

(b)　Also, from the equation $2n - b = 2m - c$ above,

$$c + 2n = b + 2m.$$

The two sides of this equation don't represent points on $[CN]$ and $[BM]$, because the sum of the coefficients 1 and 2 is 3, not 1. But if you divide both sides by 3 you get

$$\tfrac{1}{3}c + \tfrac{2}{3}n = \tfrac{1}{3}b + \tfrac{2}{3}m.$$

You can identify this as the position vector of a point G such that $\dfrac{CG}{GN} = \dfrac{BG}{GM} = \dfrac{2}{1}$.

Fig. 11.1 shows the results of both parts of Example 11.1.2. You have seen it before, in Chapter 2, where it is Fig. 2.12. The point G is the centroid of $\triangle ABC$.

You can also use the formula in the shaded box to prove Menelaus's theorem (see Section 7.6). A general proof is given after the following numerical example.

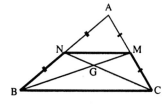

Fig. 11.1

Example 11.1.3

In a triangle ABC, F divides $[AB]$ in the ratio $2:3$, and E divides $[AC]$ in the ratio $2:1$. The transversal (FE) intersects (BC) at D. Find $\dfrac{BD}{DC}$.

In vector notation you are given that

$$f = \tfrac{3}{5}a + \tfrac{2}{5}b \quad \text{and} \quad e = \tfrac{1}{3}a + \tfrac{2}{3}c.$$

A point on (FE) has position vector

$$pf + qe = p\left(\tfrac{3}{5}a + \tfrac{2}{5}b\right) + q\left(\tfrac{1}{3}a + \tfrac{2}{3}c\right),$$

where $p + q = 1$.

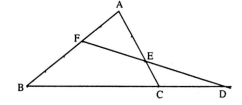

But the position vector of the point D, which is also on (BC), must be expressed in terms of b and c alone, so the coefficient of a in this expression must be 0. That is,

$$\tfrac{3}{5}p + \tfrac{1}{3}q = 0, \quad \text{or} \quad p = -\tfrac{5}{9}q.$$

So you have to find numbers p and q such that

$$p + q = 1 \quad \text{and} \quad p = -\tfrac{5}{9}q.$$

These equations give $p = -\tfrac{5}{4}$, $q = \tfrac{9}{4}$. So

$$d = -\tfrac{5}{4}\left(\tfrac{3}{5}a + \tfrac{2}{5}b\right) + \tfrac{9}{4}\left(\tfrac{1}{3}a + \tfrac{2}{3}c\right)$$
$$= -\tfrac{1}{2}b + \tfrac{3}{2}c.$$

That is, D is the point on (BC) such that $\dfrac{BD}{DC} = \dfrac{\frac{3}{2}}{-\frac{1}{2}} = -3$.

To prove Menelaus's theorem in general, suppose that in the notation of Example 11.1.3 $\dfrac{AF}{FB} = \dfrac{r}{s}$ and that $\dfrac{CE}{EA} = \dfrac{t}{u}$, with $r+s=1$ and $t+u=1$. Using the result in the shaded box for the points F and E,

$$f = sa + rb \quad \text{and} \quad e = ta + uc.$$

Then a point on (FE) has position vector

$$pf + qe = p(sa + rb) + q(ta + uc), \quad \text{where} \quad p+q=1.$$

To find the position vector of D, which must be on (BC), the coefficient of a must be 0, so that p and q satisfy the equations

$$p+q=1 \quad \text{and} \quad ps+qt=0.$$

You can check for yourself that

$$p = \dfrac{t}{t-s} \quad \text{and} \quad q = \dfrac{-s}{t-s}.$$

This gives

$$d = \dfrac{t}{t-s}(sa + rb) - \dfrac{s}{t-s}(ta + uc)$$
$$= \dfrac{tr}{t-s}b - \dfrac{us}{t-s}c.$$

This looks like the position vector of a point on (BC), but to show this you need to check that the sum of the coefficients of b and c is 1. This is where you use the fact that $r+s=1$ and $t+u=1$. The sum of the coefficients is then

$$\dfrac{tr}{t-s} - \dfrac{us}{t-s} = \dfrac{t(1-s)-(1-t)s}{t-s}$$
$$= \dfrac{t-s}{t-s} = 1.$$

So D is the point on (BC) such that

$$\dfrac{BD}{DC} = -\dfrac{us}{t-s} \div \dfrac{tr}{t-s} = -\dfrac{us}{tr}.$$

Therefore

$$\dfrac{BD}{DC} \times \dfrac{CE}{EA} \times \dfrac{AF}{FB} = \left(-\dfrac{us}{tr}\right) \times \dfrac{t}{u} \times \dfrac{r}{s} = -1,$$

which is Menelaus's theorem.

11.2 Ceva's theorem

You can extend the property in the shaded box in Section 11.1 by introducing a third point C, not on (AB), and finding the position vector of a point X in the plane of $\triangle ABC$. For example, suppose that (AX) meets (BC) at D, as in Fig. 11.2. Then

$$x = pa + sd, \quad \text{where } p + s = 1 \text{ and } \frac{AX}{XD} = \frac{s}{p},$$

and

$$d = tb + uc, \quad \text{where } t + u = 1 \text{ and } \frac{BD}{DC} = \frac{u}{t}.$$

So $x = pa + stb + suc$, where

$$p + st + su = p + s(t + u)$$
$$= p + s \times 1 = p + s = 1.$$

Writing $st = q$ and $su = r$, you get

$$s = s(t + u) = st + su = q + r,$$

so that

$$p + q + r = p + s = 1 \quad \text{and} \quad \frac{u}{t} = \frac{su}{st} = \frac{r}{q}.$$

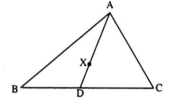

Fig. 11.2

> If $p + q + r = 1$, $x = pa + qb + rc$ is a point in the plane of $\triangle ABC$ such that
> $\dfrac{AX}{XD} = \dfrac{q + r}{p}$, where $\dfrac{BD}{DC} = \dfrac{r}{q}$.

Example 11.2.1
Locate the point X with position vector $x = \frac{1}{6}a + \frac{1}{3}b + \frac{1}{2}c$ in relation to the triangle ABC.

You can write x as

$$x = \tfrac{1}{6}a + \tfrac{5}{6}d,$$

where $d = \frac{6}{5}\left(\frac{1}{3}b + \frac{1}{2}c\right) = \frac{2}{5}b + \frac{3}{5}c$.

So if D is the point on [BC] such that $\dfrac{BD}{DC} = \dfrac{3}{2}$, then X is the point on [AD] such that $\dfrac{AX}{XD} = \dfrac{5}{1}$.

There are other possible answers. For example, you could write

$$x = \tfrac{1}{3}b + \tfrac{2}{3}e, \quad \text{where} \quad e = \tfrac{3}{2}\left(\tfrac{1}{2}c + \tfrac{1}{6}a\right) = \tfrac{3}{4}c + \tfrac{1}{4}a,$$

or $\quad x = \tfrac{1}{2}c + \tfrac{1}{2}f, \quad \text{where} \quad f = \tfrac{2}{1}\left(\tfrac{1}{6}a + \tfrac{1}{3}b\right) = \tfrac{1}{3}a + \tfrac{2}{3}b.$

So if E is the point on [CA] such that $\dfrac{CE}{EA} = \dfrac{1}{3}$, then X is the point on [BE] such that $\dfrac{BX}{XE} = \dfrac{2}{1}$.
And if F is the point on [AB] such that $\dfrac{AF}{FB} = \dfrac{2}{1}$, then X is the mid-point of [CF].

These are the most obvious ways of identifying the position of X. But there are many others. For example, you could split the term $\frac{1}{2}c$ as $\frac{1}{6}c + \frac{1}{3}c$ and write

$$x = \tfrac{1}{6}(a+c) + \tfrac{1}{3}(b+c) = \tfrac{1}{3}u + \tfrac{2}{3}v,$$

where $u = \tfrac{1}{2}(a+c)$ and $v = \tfrac{1}{2}(b+c)$.

What would this tell you about the position of X?

It would be worth drawing an accurate figure for yourself illustrating these various ways of locating the point X.

One by-product of the solution in Example 11.2.1 is a numerical verification of Ceva's theorem, since

$$\frac{BD}{DC} \times \frac{CE}{EA} \times \frac{AF}{FB} = \frac{3}{2} \times \frac{1}{3} \times \frac{2}{1} = 1.$$

In just the same way the general result in the shaded box opposite can be used to give a proof of Ceva's theorem. Suppose that the lines (AD), (BE), (CF) meet at a point X, where D, E, F are points on the sides (possibly produced) opposite A, B, C. If the position vector of X is $pa + qb + rc$, where $p + q + r = 1$, then X is a point on (AD) where $\dfrac{BD}{DC} = \dfrac{r}{q}$. By exactly the same argument, X is a point on (BE) where $\dfrac{CE}{EA} = \dfrac{p}{r}$, and X is a point on (CF) where $\dfrac{AF}{FB} = \dfrac{q}{p}$. So

$$\frac{BD}{DC} \times \frac{CE}{EA} \times \frac{AF}{FB} = \frac{r}{q} \times \frac{p}{r} \times \frac{q}{p} = 1,$$

which is Ceva's theorem.

Exercise 11A

1 Use vectors to prove that the mid-points of the sides of any quadrilateral form a parallelogram. Is this still true if the vertices of the quadrilateral are not all in the same plane?

2 Draw a diagram showing the points with the given position vectors in relation to the triangle ABC.

   (a) $x = \tfrac{1}{5}a + \tfrac{2}{5}b + \tfrac{2}{5}c$ (b) $y = \tfrac{3}{2}a - \tfrac{1}{3}b - \tfrac{1}{6}c$ (c) $z = \tfrac{1}{2}a + \tfrac{3}{4}b - \tfrac{1}{4}c$

3 ABC is a given triangle. D is a point on (BC) such that $CD = \frac{1}{2}BC$, and E is a point on (AC) such that $AC = CE$. State the position vectors of D and E, and deduce the position vector of the point F where (DE) intersects (AB). Hence express AF as a multiple of BA.

4 The position vectors of the vertices of a quadrilateral ABCD are a, b, $a + 2b$ and $\frac{5}{2}a - \frac{1}{2}b$. Find the position vector of the point where the diagonals [AC] and [BD] intersect. How does your answer prove that the quadrilateral is convex?

5   ABCD is a quadrilateral. The centroids of the triangles BCD, CDA, DAB, ABC are P, Q, R, S respectively. Prove that the lines AP, BQ, CR, DS are concurrent. Can you find any other lines which also pass through the point of concurrence?

6   With the notation of Question 5, what can you say about the quadrilateral PQRS?

7   In Section 7.3 (Fig. 7.6) it was shown that the sides of a triangle when produced divide the plane into regions of three types. If a point X has position vector $pa + qb + rc$, where $p + q + r = 1$, what can you say about the signs of p, q, r if X is in

(a)   the J-region whose boundary includes the side [BC],

(b)   the K-region whose boundary includes the vertex A?

8*   In a triangle ABC, D is the point on [BC] such that [AD] bisects $\hat{\text{BAC}}$. Let u, v be unit vectors in the directions of $\overrightarrow{\text{AB}}$ and $\overrightarrow{\text{AC}}$.

(a)   Explain why $u + v$ is a vector in the direction of $\overrightarrow{\text{AD}}$.

(b)   Explain why $\overrightarrow{\text{AB}} = cu$ and $\overrightarrow{\text{AC}} = bv$, where b and c are the lengths of the sides of the triangle opposite B and C.

(c)   Find r and s, with $r + s = 1$, such that $\overrightarrow{\text{AD}} = r\,\overrightarrow{\text{AB}} + s\,\overrightarrow{\text{AC}}$. Use your answer to deduce the angle bisector theorem (see Section 6.1).

(d)   Identify the point in the plane of the triangle with position vector $\dfrac{a}{p}a + \dfrac{b}{p}b + \dfrac{c}{p}c$, where $p = a + b + c$.

11.3   Affine and Euclidean properties

All the vector proofs so far have used only basic vector algebra – addition, subtraction, multiplication by a number. This is because the corresponding geometry has involved only parallel lines and proportions of lengths on a single line or on a pair of parallel lines. These are called 'affine properties', and theorems about them belong to 'affine geometry'.

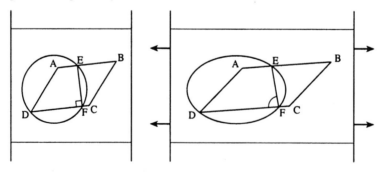

Fig. 11.3

To see what this means, imagine a geometrical figure drawn on an elastic surface which can be stretched uniformly in some direction. For example, Fig. 11.3 shows on the left a parallelogram ABCD, a point of trisection E of the side [AB], a line segment [EF] drawn perpendicular to [DC], and the circle with diameter [DE]. On the right the sheet has been stretched sideways. The basic structure of the figure is still recognisable, and some aspects remain unchanged. For example, ABCD is still a parallelogram, and E is still a point of trisection of [AB]. But many things have changed, such as the lengths AB and BC, the angles $\hat{ADC}$ and $\hat{DFE}$, and the circle has become an ellipse. Affine geometry (as in Sections 11.1 and 11.2) is about the properties of figures that don't change when the sheet is stretched.

To use vectors to describe all the geometrical properties of the figure on the left of Fig. 11.3 you need to introduce the scalar product (see Higher Level Book 2 Chapter 17). For example, the length AB is calculated as the square root of the scalar product $\overrightarrow{AB} \cdot \overrightarrow{AB}$, and the fact that [EF] is perpendicular to [DC] is expressed algebraically by the equation $\overrightarrow{EF} \cdot \overrightarrow{DC} = 0$. These are 'Euclidean properties', and theorems involving the scalar product belong to 'Euclidean geometry'.

The next three sections use vector methods, including the scalar product, to provide alternative proofs of some of the Euclidean results established in earlier chapters by purely geometrical arguments.

11.4 Centres of a triangle

In Chapter 5 it was shown that there was a close connection between several of the centres associated with a triangle. Another way of establishing these properties is to use vectors.

The theory is much simpler if you choose a particular point of the figure, the circumcentre of $\triangle ABC$, to be the origin O. Then $OA = OB = OC = R$, the radius of the circumcircle. So

$$a^2 = \overrightarrow{OA} \cdot \overrightarrow{OA} = OA^2 = R^2, \quad \text{and similarly} \quad b^2 = c^2 = R^2.$$

Beware! The symbol a^2 stands for the square of the distance of A from the origin. It shouldn't be confused with a^2, which would conventionally stand for the square of the length of the side [BC]. In this section the distance OA is denoted by $|a|$, and the use of a, b, c for lengths BC, CA, AB is avoided.

The next simplest centre to describe in vector form is the centroid G, whose position vector is

$$g = \tfrac{1}{3}a + \tfrac{1}{3}b + \tfrac{1}{3}c \qquad \text{(see Higher Level Book 2 Section 16.6).}$$

The orthocentre

Now define a point H on [OG] produced so that $OH = 3 \times OG$, as in Fig. 11.4. Then

$$h = 3g = a + b + c.$$

You know from Chapter 5 that H should be the orthocentre of $\triangle ABC$. To prove this, you have to show that [AH], [BH], [CH] are perpendicular to [BC], [CA], [AB] respectively. That is, in vector notation, that $\overrightarrow{AH} \cdot \overrightarrow{BC} = \overrightarrow{BH} \cdot \overrightarrow{CA} = \overrightarrow{CH} \cdot \overrightarrow{AB} = 0$. So write

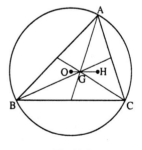

Fig. 11.4

$$\overrightarrow{AH} \cdot \overrightarrow{BC} = (h - a) \cdot (c - b)$$

and use the fact that $h = a + b + c$ to give

$$\overrightarrow{AH} \cdot \overrightarrow{BC} = (c + b) \cdot (c - b)$$
$$= c^2 - b^2 = R^2 - R^2 = 0.$$

The distributive rule in Higher Level Book 2 Section 17.3 ensures that you can multiply out brackets with scalar products just as in ordinary algebra.

This proves that [AH] is perpendicular to [BC]. The argument for the other two scalar products is precisely similar, and it then follows that H is the orthocentre.

Euler's circle

In Fig. 11.5 the mid-points of [OH], [AH] and [BC] have been included, labelled E, U and L, with position vectors

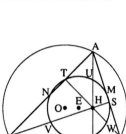

$$e = \tfrac{1}{2}h = \tfrac{1}{2}a + \tfrac{1}{2}b + \tfrac{1}{2}c,$$

$$u = \tfrac{1}{2}a + \tfrac{1}{2}h = \tfrac{1}{2}a + \tfrac{1}{2}(a + b + c) = a + \tfrac{1}{2}b + \tfrac{1}{2}c$$

and $l = \tfrac{1}{2}b + \tfrac{1}{2}c$.

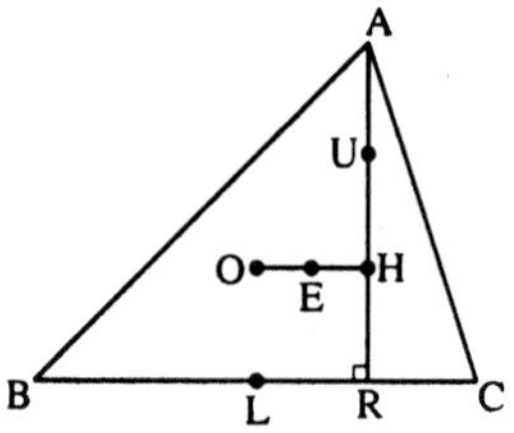

Fig. 11.5

So $\overrightarrow{EU} = u - e = \left(a + \tfrac{1}{2}b + \tfrac{1}{2}c\right) - \left(\tfrac{1}{2}a + \tfrac{1}{2}b + \tfrac{1}{2}c\right) = \tfrac{1}{2}a$

and $\overrightarrow{EL} = l - e = \left(\tfrac{1}{2}b + \tfrac{1}{2}c\right) - \left(\tfrac{1}{2}a + \tfrac{1}{2}b + \tfrac{1}{2}c\right) = -\tfrac{1}{2}a$.

This shows that E is the centre of a circle with diameter [LU] and that the radius of the circle is

$$\left|\tfrac{1}{2}a\right| = \tfrac{1}{2}|a| = \tfrac{1}{2}R.$$

The fact that R, the foot of the perpendicular from A to [BC], lies on the circle follows at once from the converse of the angle in a semicircle theorem.

An exactly similar argument shows that the corresponding points associated with the vertices B and C lie on the same circle. So the nine points L, M, N; U, V, W; R, S, T lie on Euler's circle, with centre E and radius $\tfrac{1}{2}R$. This is shown in Fig. 11.6.

Fig. 11.6

The triangle HBC

You know that [HA], [BA], [CA] are perpendicular to [BC], [CH], [HB] respectively (though some of these line segments were labelled differently before), and this means that A is the orthocentre of $\triangle HBC$. The nine points on Euler's circle for this triangle are

> L, W, V, the mid-points of the sides;
> U, N, M, the mid-points of the line segments joining the vertices to the orthocentre A;
> R, S, T, the feet of the perpendiculars from the vertices to the sides.

These are just the nine points on Euler's circle for $\triangle ABC$, but differently grouped. So $\triangle HBC$ and $\triangle ABC$ share the same Euler circle, with centre E.

Let X be the circumcentre of $\triangle HBC$ (see Fig. 11.7). Then, since A is its orthocentre, E is the mid-point of [XA]. The position vector of X therefore satisfies the equation

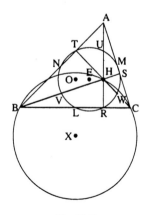

Fig. 11.7

$$e = \tfrac{1}{2}a + \tfrac{1}{2}b + \tfrac{1}{2}c = \tfrac{1}{2}(a+x),$$

so $x = b + c$.

You can check this directly by finding the distances from X to H, B and C.

$$XH = |h - x| = |(a+b+c) - (b+c)| = |a| = R,$$

$$XB = |b - x| = |b - (b+c)| = |-c| = |c| = R,$$

$$XC = |c - x| = |c - (b+c)| = |-b| = |b| = R.$$

So X is the circumcentre of $\triangle HBC$, and its circumradius is R.

There are of course corresponding results for $\triangle HCA$ and $\triangle HAB$. Their circumcentres Y and Z have position vectors $y = c + a$ and $z = a + b$, and these triangles also have circumradius R.

Finally, remember that the addition of position vectors is represented by a parallelogram rule (see Higher Level Book 2 Section 16.6). So, since $x = b + c$ and O is the origin, X is the point such that OBXC is a parallelogram; and since all the sides of this parallelogram have length R, it is in fact a rhombus. So X is the reflection of O in $[BC]$.

11.5 Locus problems

Some locus problems are easily solved using vectors. The method is similar to the analytical method in Chapter 9, but the notation is often more concise.

The process is in two stages. The first is to find the locus in the form of a vector equation. After that you need to be able to interpret that equation geometrically. To start with, consider the second stage.

In Higher Level Book 2 Section 24.2 it was shown how to find the equation of a line in terms of a vector perpendicular to the line and the position vector of a point on it. In Fig. 11.8 v is the position vector of a variable point V on the line, A is a known point on the line, and n is a vector perpendicular to the line.
Then $\overrightarrow{AV}$ is perpendicular to n, so that $(v - a) \cdot n = 0$.

Fig. 11.8

So if the equation of a locus can be put into this form, you know that the locus is a straight line.

If V lies on a circle with centre C and radius r, as in Fig. 11.9, then the length of $\overrightarrow{CV}$ is equal to r, so that

$$(v - c)^2 = r^2,$$

or $v^2 - 2v \cdot c + (c^2 - r^2) = 0.$

Fig. 11.9

So if v satisfies an equation of the form $v^2 - 2v \cdot c + \text{constant} = 0$ (where the constant is less than c^2), you know that the locus of V is a circle.

Example 11.5.1

A and B are given points. Find the locus of points V such that $AV = 2BV$.

This is a particular case of Apollonius's locus (see Section 6.3). To express the equation $AV = 2BV$ in vector form you need to use $AV^2 = (v - a)^2$ and $BV^2 = (v - b)^2$. Since $AV^2 = 4BV^2$,

$$(v - a)^2 = 4(v - b)^2$$

$$v^2 - 2v \cdot a + a^2 = 4v^2 - 8v \cdot b + 4b^2$$

$$3v^2 - 2v \cdot (4b - a) + (4b^2 - a^2) = 0$$

$$v^2 - 2v \cdot (\tfrac{4}{3}b - \tfrac{1}{3}a) + (\tfrac{4}{3}b^2 - \tfrac{1}{3}a^2) = 0.$$

You can now recognise that this has the form $v^2 - 2v \cdot c + (c^2 - r^2) = 0$, which is a circle, with

$$c = \tfrac{4}{3}b - \tfrac{1}{3}a$$

and $(\tfrac{4}{3}b - \tfrac{1}{3}a)^2 - r^2 = \tfrac{4}{3}b^2 - \tfrac{1}{3}a^2$, so that

$$r^2 = \tfrac{16}{9}b^2 - \tfrac{8}{9}b \cdot a + \tfrac{1}{9}a^2 - \tfrac{4}{3}b^2 + \tfrac{1}{3}a^2$$

$$= \tfrac{4}{9}b^2 - \tfrac{8}{9}b \cdot a + \tfrac{4}{9}a^2$$

$$= \tfrac{4}{9}(b - a)^2 = \left(\tfrac{2}{3}\overrightarrow{AB}\right)^2.$$

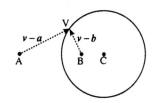

Fig. 11.10

Notice that c is of the form $pa + qb$ with $p + q = -\tfrac{1}{3} + \tfrac{4}{3} = 1$ (see Section 11.1). So C is the point on (AB) such that $\dfrac{AC}{CB} = \dfrac{4}{-1}$. That is, C is on [AB] produced so that $BC = \tfrac{1}{3}AB$. The locus is a circle with centre C and radius $\tfrac{2}{3}AB$ (see Fig. 11.10).

111.6   The power of a point with respect to a circle

The theorems in Chapter 10 are also easily proved using vector methods.

Fig. 11.11 shows a fixed point A and a circle with centre C and radius r. (It is drawn with A outside the circle, but the argument is just the same if it is inside.) A line through A is drawn in any direction such that it meets the circle at P and Q. You want to prove that the product of the sensed lengths AP and AQ is constant, and doesn't depend on the direction of the line.

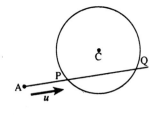

Fig. 11.11

How can you deal with a vector in a variable direction? One method is to introduce a unit vector u and to consider points on the line through A in the direction of u. A point on the line a distance x from A in this direction will have position vector $a + xu$. If this point is on the circle, then its distance from C is equal to r. This is expressed by the equation

$$(a + xu - c)^2 = r^2, \quad \text{or} \quad (xu - (c - a))^2 = r^2.$$

This gives a quadratic equation for x,

$$x^2 u^2 - 2xu \cdot (c-a) + \left((c-a)^2 - r^2\right) = 0.$$

And since u is a unit vector, $u^2 = 1$, so

$$x^2 - 2xu \cdot (c-a) + \left((c-a)^2 - r^2\right) = 0.$$

The argument now continues as in Section 10.5. Comparing the constant term in this equation with that in

$$(x - x_1)(x - x_2) = 0,$$

you can deduce that

$$x_1 x_2 = (c-a)^2 - r^2$$
$$= AC^2 - r^2.$$

Therefore

$$AP \times AQ = AC^2 - r^2,$$

a constant which is independent of the direction of the line.

11.7* A vector expression for sensed area

In Higher Level Book 2 Section 25.3 the vector product was used to calculate the area of a triangle. This can be linked to the idea of sensed area which was used in Section 7.4.

Suppose that a triangle XYZ is labelled anticlockwise as in Fig. 11.12, and that $Y\hat{X}Z = \theta$. Then the vector product $\overrightarrow{XY} \times \overrightarrow{XZ}$ has magnitude $XY \times XZ \times \sin\theta$, which is twice the area of the triangle. Its direction will point out of the plane towards your eye, which would be the direction of the positive normal with the usual right-handed convention. So you could write the sensed area of the triangle as

$$\tfrac{1}{2}(y-x) \times (z-x).$$

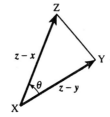

Fig. 11.12

The area is then positive if the product vector points out of the plane, and negative if it points into the plane.

This expression is more symmetrical than it looks. Using the distributive law for vector products,

$$(y-x) \times (z-x) = y \times z - x \times z - y \times x + x \times x$$
$$= y \times z + z \times x + x \times y,$$

since $x \times z = -z \times x$, $y \times x = -x \times y$ and $x \times x = 0$. So the sensed area of $\triangle XYZ$ can be written in a symmetrical form as

$$\tfrac{1}{2}(y \times z + z \times x + x \times y).$$

Exercise 11B

1   With the notation of Section 11.4, B′ is the point on the circumcircle of △ABC diametrically opposite to B. State the position vector of B′, and prove that $\vec{B'C} = \vec{AH}$. Interpret this equation geometrically.

2   With the notation of Section 11.4, X, Y and Z are the circumcentres of △HBC, △HCA and △HAB.

   (a)   Express y, z and $z - y$ in terms of a, b and c. What can you deduce about the triangle XYZ?

   (b)   For △XYZ identify

      (i)   the orthocentre,   (ii)   the circumcentre,   (iii)   the centre of Euler's circle.

   (c)   Of the two sets of nine points identified on Euler's circles for △ABC and △XYZ, which points are common to both?

3   If A and B are fixed points, find the equation of the locus of points V such that AV = BV. Prove that this represents a line through the mid-point M of [AB] perpendicular to [AB].

4   Find the centre and radius of the Apollonius circles which are the locus of points V such that

   (a)   BV = 3AV,   (b)   AV = kBV, where $k > 1$.

5   Use vectors to find the equation of the locus of points V in the plane of △ABC such that $VA^2 + VB^2 + VC^2 = \text{constant}$. Show that this is a circle whose centre is the centroid of the triangle. What is the least value of the constant for which the locus exists?

6   A line through A cuts a circle at P and Q. Show that, whether A is inside, on, or outside the circle, the power of A with respect to the circle can be written as $\vec{AP} \cdot \vec{AQ}$.

7   With the notation of Section 11.6, [MN] is a diameter of the circle with centre C. Prove that $\vec{AM} \cdot \vec{AN}$ is equal to the power of A with respect to the circle.

8*   Use vectors to prove part (b) of the mini-theorem in Section 7.4.

9*   S is a point in the plane of a triangle PQR. Prove that, using sensed areas,
$$\text{area}(\triangle SQR) + \text{area}(\triangle SRP) + \text{area}(\triangle SPQ) = \text{area}(\triangle PQR).$$

Review exercise

1 A and B are fixed points, and $[AT]$ is a tangent to the Apollonius circle of points such that $\dfrac{AP}{BP} = k$, where $k > 1$. Prove that $A\hat{B}T = 90°$.

2 $\triangle ABC$ is an acute-angled triangle, and α is an acute angle greater than $\hat{A}$, $\hat{B}$ and $\hat{C}$. P, Q, R are points on the sides $[BC]$, $[CA]$, $[AB]$ such that $A\hat{P}B = B\hat{Q}C = C\hat{R}A = \alpha$, as shown in the figure.

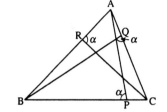

  (a) Prove that the circumcircles of $\triangle AQR$, $\triangle BRP$, $\triangle CPQ$ have a point in common.

  (b) Prove that the point of intersection of $[BQ]$ and $[CR]$ lies on the circumcircle of $\triangle AQR$.

3 The bisectors of the angle at A of a triangle ABC cut (BC) at D and E. If P is any point on the circle with $[DE]$ as diameter, prove that $\dfrac{BP}{CP} = \dfrac{c}{b}$.

  The bisectors of the angle at B cut (CA) at F and G, and the bisectors of the angle at C cut (AB) at H and I. If the circles with diameters $[DE]$ and $[FG]$ meet at X and Y, prove that the circle with diameter $[HI]$ also passes through X and Y.

4 In the figure the circumcircles of $\triangle EAD$ and $\triangle FCD$ intersect at G. Prove that ABCD is a cyclic quadrilateral if, and only if, E, F and G are collinear.

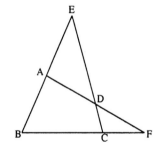

  Prove that, in that case,

  $$EA \times EB + FC \times FB = EF^2.$$

5 (a) X is a point on the side $[BC]$ of $\triangle ABC$ such that $B\hat{A}X = \alpha$. Prove that

  $$\frac{BX}{XC} = \frac{\sin\alpha \sin\hat{C}}{\sin(\hat{A} - \alpha)\sin\hat{B}}.$$

  (b) P is a point inside $\triangle ABC$, and the line segments $[AP]$, $[BP]$, $[CP]$ are produced to meet the sides $[BC]$, $[CA]$, $[AB]$ at X, Y, Z respectively. U, V, W are points on these sides such that $U\hat{A}C = B\hat{A}X$, $V\hat{B}A = C\hat{B}Y$, $W\hat{C}B = A\hat{C}Z$. Prove that $[AU]$, $[BV]$, $[CW]$ are concurrent.

  If the point of concurrence in part (b) is denoted by Q, the points P and Q are called *isogonal conjugates*.

  (c) Which point is its own isogonal conjugate?

  (d) If $\triangle ABC$ is acute-angled, where is the isogonal conjugate of the circumcentre?

  (e) Investigate whether the result of part (b) can be extended to cases in which P is outside the triangle, and whether the result of part (d) remains true if $\triangle ABC$ is obtuse-angled.

6   B and C are fixed points on a circle with centre O and radius r such that the arc BC subtends an angle of $120°$ at O. P is a variable point on the circle. For the triangle PBC, find the locus of

    (a)   the orthocentre,   (b)   the centre of Euler's circle,

    (c)   the centroid,   (d)   the incentre,

    (e)   the e-centre opposite to P.

7   H is the orthocentre of $\triangle ABC$. Prove that the power of H with respect to the Euler circle is

    (a)   one-half of the power of H with respect to the circle with [AB] as diameter,

    (b)   one-quarter of the power of H with respect to the circumcircle.

8   A triangle ABC has sides of length $a = 21$ cm, $b = 10$ cm, $c = 17$ cm. The point X divides [BC] internally in the ratio $3:4$. The line (AX) cuts the circumcircle of $\triangle ABC$ again at D.

    (a)   Use Stewart's theorem to calculate the length AX.

    (b)   Find the length BD.

    (c)   Use the intersecting chords theorem to calculate the length XD.

    (d)   Explain why the triangles XAB, XCD are similar. Hence calculate the length CD.

    (e)   Use Ptolemy's theorem to check your answers to parts (a) to (d).

9   The sides of a cyclic quadrilateral ABCD have lengths $AB = 6$ cm, $BC = 5$ cm, $CD = 3$ cm, $DA = 8$ cm. The sides [AD] and [BC] are produced to meet at X.

    (a)   If $XD = p$ cm, $XC = q$ cm, calculate the values of p and q.

    (b)   Find the length of the tangents from X to the circumcircle of ABCD.

10   Two circles have equations $x^2 + y^2 = 50$ and $x^2 + y^2 - 5x - 15y - 250 = 0$.

    (a)   Show that one circle lies entirely inside the other.

    (b)   Verify that the point $A(-10, 20)$ lies on the larger circle. Find the gradients of the two lines through A which touch the smaller circle.

    (c)   Find the coordinates of the points B and C where the two lines in part (b) meet the larger circle again.

    (d)   Show that the line (BC) touches the smaller circle.

    (e)   Show that the conclusion in part (d) would still follow if the coordinates of A were taken to be $(0, -10)$ instead of $(-10, 20)$.

Examination questions

1   In a $\triangle ABC$, D and E are points on the sides [BC] and [CA] such that $DC = 2BD$ and $EA = 2CE$. If the lines (DE) and (AB) intersect at the point F, then prove that $AB = 3BF$.

(© IBO 2003)

2   (a)   In a $\triangle ABC$, let D be the midpoint of the line segment [BC] and [AD] be a median. Prove Apollonius' theorem, that $AB^2 + AC^2 = 2(AD^2 + BD^2)$.

    (b)   In a quadrilateral ABCD, X and Y are the midpoints of [AC] and [BD], respectively. Prove that $AB^2 + BC^2 + CD^2 + DA^2 = AC^2 + BD^2 + 4XY^2$.   (© IBO 2003)

3 Let Q be a point inside a triangle LMN. Let X, Y, Z be the feet of the perpendiculars from Q to [MN], [NL] and [LM] respectively. The line (MQ) is extended to meet [LN] at the point P.

Prove that $L\hat{Q}N = L\hat{M}N + X\hat{Y}Z$.

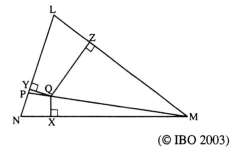

(© IBO 2003)

4 Let M and N be any two points on a circle of centre O and let R be another point on the circle, equidistant from M and N.

Show that (NR) bisects the angle between (MN) and the tangent to the circle at N.

(© IBO 2004)

5 The line $3x + y = 12$ meets the y-axis at P, the x-axis at Q, the line $y - x = 0$ at R and the line $y + x = 0$ at S. Show that P, Q, R, S divide the line segment [PS] in a harmonic ratio.

(© IBO 2005)

6 The diagram shows a triangle ABD and a circle centre O. (BD) is a tangent to the circle at D, so that triangle ABD is isosceles. Also $A\hat{D}B = D\hat{B}A = 2D\hat{A}B$. Let C be the point of intersection of the circle and the line (AB). Prove that AC = DC = DB.

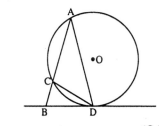

(© IBO 2003)

7 The figure shows a triangle ABC inscribed in a circle. The tangent to the circle at A meets (BC) at D, the tangent at B meets (CA) at E and the tangent at C meets (AB) at F.

(a) Show that $\dfrac{BD}{DC} \times \dfrac{CE}{EA} \times \dfrac{AF}{FB} = -1$.

(b) State briefly, with a reason, what conclusion can be drawn from this result.

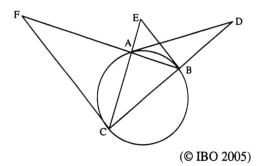

(© IBO 2005)

8 The diagram shows a square ABCD of side a. A circle, centre O, radius r, passes through the vertices A and B. The length of the tangent to the circle from D is $2a$. Find an expression for r in terms of a.

(© IBO 2004)

Answers

1 Preliminaries

Exercise 1 (page 13)

1 L, M, N are collinear. In the three-dimensional model, the line LMN is the intersection of the plane containing X, Y, Z with the floor.

2 (a) If [AC] is perpendicular to [BD], ABCD is a rhombus. False.
 If a parallelogram ABCD has [AC] perpendicular to [BD], then ABCD is a rhombus.
 (b) If the diagonals of a quadrilateral ABCD meet at M, and AM = MC, then ABCD is a parallelogram. False.
 If AM = MC and BM = MD, then ABCD is a parallelogram.
 (c) If triangle ABC and triangle ABD have equal areas, then [AB] is parallel to [CD]. False.
 If triangle ABC and triangle ABD have equal areas and if C and D are on the same side of (AB), then [AB] is parallel to [CD].

3 The bisector of the angle between the part lines.

4 The bisectors of the angles between the lines.

5 The length YZ must be at least as large as the perpendicular distance from X to (YZ).

6 (a) The circle with diameter AB, excluding A and B.
 (b) If ACBD is a square, the major arcs AB of circles with centres C and D, excluding A and B.

7 20 cm, 30 cm. The results are true for any proportion $m:n$ with $m < n$.

8 $\hat{TPO} = 90°$. The points of intersection of the circle having diameter TO with the given circle.

9 If $\dfrac{AP}{PB} = \dfrac{AQ}{QD}$, then [PQ] is parallel to [BD].

2 Some properties of triangles

Exercise 2A (page 19)

1 (a) 15, 4.8 (b) 7.5, 2 (c) 12.5, 4
 (d) 8.4, 4
2 (a) 18, 3 (b) 15.75, 2.5 (c) 6.25, 4.5
5 $BZ = \frac{3}{4} BX$
6 $\hat{ACB} = \hat{AEC} = 90°$

9 (b) For example ABCD could be a square and WXYZ a rectangle.

Exercise 2B (page 22)

1 (a) $q = 5$, $h = 2\sqrt{5}$, $b = 3\sqrt{5}$
 (b) $h = 10$, $a = 10\sqrt{5}$, $b = 5\sqrt{5}$
 (c) $p = \frac{25}{13}$, $q = \frac{144}{13}$, $h = \frac{60}{13}$
 (d) $p = 18$, $q = 8$, $a = 6\sqrt{13}$, $b = 4\sqrt{13}$

Exercise 2C (page 25)

1 $\sqrt{145}$ cm, $\sqrt{112}$ cm, $\sqrt{73}$ cm
5 $c^2 + q^2 = 2p^2 + \frac{2}{9}a^2$, $b^2 + p^2 = 2q^2 + \frac{2}{9}a^2$;
 $b^2 + 2c^2 = 3p^2 + \frac{2}{3}a^2$
6 27.9 km
7 $\frac{1}{3}\left(a^2 + b^2 + c^2\right)$
8 27, 63
9 (a) Circle, centre the mid-point of BC, radius 10 units
 (b) Circle, centre D where BD = 6 and CD = 4, radius 14 units

3 Triangles and circles

Exercise 3A (page 31)

1 3.54 cm
2 3.31 cm
3 3.26 cm
4 4.15 cm, 6.77 cm
7 (b) A parallelogram

Exercise 3B (page 37)

4 Yes; for any polygon circumscribed to a circle, the area is the product of the radius and the semi-perimeter.

6 (b) No; for example, draw a regular hexagon, then double the lengths of AB and DE.

8 (b) Not necessarily; you get a comparable figure if you change the radius of circles centres A and C by x, and the radius of circles centres B and D by $-x$. Only for one value of x will the common tangents be concurrent. Then the points of contact of the circles will coincide with the points of contact of the

sides AB, BC, CD, DA with the inscribed circle.

4 Concyclic points

Exercise 4A (page 43)

1 $60°$

2 $55°$

3 $40°$

5 It must be a rectangle.

10 40 cm

13 $\sin(x - y) = \sin x \cos y - \cos x \sin y$

14 $\hat{A} + \hat{C} + \hat{E} + \hat{G} = 3\pi$ radians

Exercise 4B (page 48)

4 (a) The line through A perpendiclar to [BC].
   (b) The side [BC].

6 (a) $\{C,D,E,P\}$, $\{A,C,P,X\}$
   (c) [PQ] is a diameter of the circumcircle.

5 The orthocentre of a triangle

Exercise 5A (page 51)

2 If $\hat{A}$ is obtuse, $AH = -2R \cos\hat{A}$ and $O\hat{A}H = 180° - \left| \hat{C} - \hat{B} \right|$; no change if $\hat{C}$ is obtuse.

3 (a) AR
   (b) HR if $\hat{C}$ is acute, $-$HR if $\hat{C}$ is obtuse.

Exercise 5B (page 53)

1 The orthocentre of $\triangle$ABC.

4 O is the orthocentre of $\triangle$LMN. The circumcentre of $\triangle$LMN is the mid-point of [OH].

5 If $\hat{B}$ or $\hat{C}$ is obtuse, the angles subtended by [BC] at A and H are equal. H is the circumcentre of $\triangle$XYZ.

Exercise 5C (page 57)

2 $5; \frac{1}{4}a$

3 The two figures have the same Euler circle

4 (a) The reflection of the given circle in (BC).
   (b) The circle with centre at the mid-point of [BC], radius $\frac{1}{2}R$.

6 Internal and external bisectors

Exercise 6A (page 64)

1 (a) $90° - \frac{1}{2}\hat{A}$
   (c) I is the orthocentre of $\triangle$JKL.
   (d) The circumcircle of $\triangle$ABC.

2 (d) $Y_1 Z_1 = (a + b + c) \sin\frac{1}{2}\hat{A}$
   $Z_1 X_1 = (a + b - c) \cos\frac{1}{2}\hat{B}$
   $X_1 Y_1 = (a - b + c) \cos\frac{1}{2}\hat{C}$
   $\hat{X}_1 = 90° + \frac{1}{2}\hat{A}$, $\hat{Y}_1 = \frac{1}{2}\hat{B}$, $\hat{Z}_1 = \frac{1}{2}\hat{C}$

3 (a) 2.5 cm   (b) 15 cm
   (c) $\frac{1}{2}\sqrt{105}$ cm (d) $2\sqrt{70}$ cm

4 (a) $\dfrac{ab}{b + c}$ (b) $\dfrac{ab}{c - b}$
   (c) $\sqrt{bc\left(1 - \dfrac{a^2}{(b + c)^2}\right)}$ (d) $\sqrt{bc\left(\dfrac{a^2}{(c - b)^2} - 1\right)}$

Exercise 6B (page 68)

3 2.26 cm, 3.96 cm

4 The Apollonius circle with fixed points A, C and $k = \dfrac{AB}{BC}$.

7 The theorems of Ceva and Menelaus

Exercise 7A (page 72)

1 3 cm

2 $4{:}1$

3 (c) $3\frac{1}{2}$ cm

Exercise 7B (page 79)

1 (a) WZ   (b) XW   (c) YZ
   (d) YX   (e) XY

4 (a) 2 cm   (b) $5\frac{4}{7}$ cm

Exercise 7C (page 85)

1 (a) $2\frac{2}{5}$ cm (b) $1\frac{1}{3}$ cm   (c) $\frac{6}{7}$ cm

2 3 cm

3 0.9 cm

4 (a) 6 (b) 10

5 $-\frac{9}{4}$

7 The conclusion that J, C, H are collinear corresponds to the conclusion that L, M, N are collinear.

8 Analytical methods

Exercise 8A (page 90)

1 (a) $\left(\dfrac{3x_2-x_1}{2},\dfrac{3y_2-y_1}{2}\right)$

(b) $\left(\dfrac{x_1+2x_3}{3},\dfrac{y_1+2y_3}{3}\right)$, $\left(\dfrac{x_3+2x_1}{3},\dfrac{y_3+2y_1}{3}\right)$

2 (a) $x=3$, $5y=3x+36$, $x+y=12$; $(3,9)$

(b) $y=5x$, $13y=5x+60$, $5x+11y=60$; $(1,5)$

(c) $(0,3)$

(d) All $3\sqrt{17}$; S is the circumcentre of $\triangle ABC$.

(e) $(0,-3)$, $(15,12)$

3 (a) $\left(j,\dfrac{i^2-j^2}{k}\right)$ (b) $\left(\frac{1}{3}j,\frac{1}{3}k\right)$

(c) $\left(0,\dfrac{k^2+j^2-i^2}{2k}\right)$

4 (b) $(5.4,0.2)$, $(3,2)$, $(-0.2,4.4)$; $3x+4y=17$

(c) $(1.8,-1.6)$, $(6,-1)$, $(-2.4,-2.2)$; $y=12$

(d) $45°$

5 $y=12$

Exercise 8B (page 94)

1 (a) $x^2+y^2-4x+10y-20=0$

(b) $x^2+y^2+6y+5=0$

(c) $x^2+y^2-8x-6y=0$

2 (a) Circle centre $(-3,-2)$ radius 4

(b) Circle centre $\left(\frac{3}{2},-\frac{1}{2}\right)$ radius $\frac{1}{2}\sqrt{10}$

(c) Point circle $(1,-3)$

(d) No points satisfy this equation.

3 (a) 4   (b) $\sqrt{p^2+q^2+ap+bq+c}$

4 $2x+3y=12$, $6x-4y=5$

5 (a) Intersect at $(0,0)$, $(-2,4)$

(b) Don't intersect, shortest distance 4

(c) Touch at $\left(\frac{7}{5},\frac{6}{5}\right)$, tangent $4x-3y-2=0$

(d) Intersect at $(2,-1)$, $(4,1)$

(e) Don't intersect, shortest distance 1

6 (a) $y=6x-11$ (b) $y=6x+63$

(c) $x+6y=-29$, $x+6y=45$

7 (a) $3x-4y-6=0$, $3x+4y-6=0$

(b) $9x-40y+18=0$, $x=-2$

8 (a) $(3,8)$ (b) $x^2+y^2-8y-9=0$

(c) $x^2+y^2-3x-4y=0$

9 (a) $(10,10)$, $(24,8)$, $(12,-4)$

(b) All $8\sqrt{2}$; the e-circle opposite B

(c) $\left(\frac{119}{8},\frac{41}{8}\right)$, $\frac{25}{8}\sqrt{2}$

9 Finding loci by analytical methods

Exercise 9 (page 106)

1 $(3,2)$

2 $(2,-1)$, $(12,4)$

3 $(-3,-2)$, $\left(\frac{7}{5},\frac{1}{5}\right)$

4 (a) Circle, centre the mid-point of BC, radius 10 units

(b) Circle, centre D where BD = 6 and CD = 4, radius 14 units

5 Circle, centre $(6,4)$, radius $\sqrt{\dfrac{k-152}{3}}$. Smallest value when P is at $(6,4)$, the centroid of the triangle.

6 Straight line perpendicular to the line through the centres of the two circles. If the circles intersect, only the part of the line outside the circles.

7 (a) The two lines through the centre parallel to the sides of the square.

(b) The line through the centre parallel to [AB] and [CD].

8 Taking A to be $(0,a)$ and the fixed line $y=-a$, the locus is $y=\frac{1}{4}\dfrac{x^2}{a}$, a parabola with vertex half-way between A and l, with axis of symmetry through A perpendicular to l.

10 More properties of circles

Exercise 10A (page 111)

1 (a) 3 cm   (b) 6 cm   (c) 6 cm

2 (a) 5 cm   (b) 18 cm or 5 cm

3 (a) 6 cm   (b) 9 cm, 6 cm

7 (a) $\frac{1}{2}\left(\hat{B}+\hat{C}\right)$ (b) $\frac{1}{2}\left(\hat{A}+\hat{C}\right)$

Exercise 10B (page 115)

2 The square of the distance, OA^2.

3 The converse is true.

4 (a) 16, outside; 4   (b) 0, on

(c) 9, outside; 3(d) -1, inside

5 $(0,\pm3)$. If $k>0$, the circle lies in the region common to the interiors of c_1 and c_2, and in the region external to both c_1 and c_2. If $k<0$, the circle lies in the regions external to one of c_1, c_2 and internal to the other.

6 (a) The y-axis.

  (b) The circle $x^2 + y^2 - 48x + 36 = 0$; $\sqrt{\frac{5}{3}}$

11 Vector methods

Exercise 11A (page 121)

1 Yes, it remains true in 3 dimensions.

2

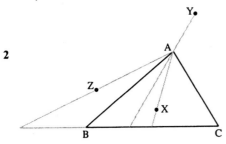

3 $d = \frac{3}{2}c - \frac{1}{2}b$, $e = 2c - a$, $f = 3a - 2b$

  AF = 2BA

4 $a + \frac{2}{5}b$; it is an internal point of both [AC] and [BD].

5 For example, the lines joining the mid-points of opposite sides.

6 It is similar to ABCD, with sides one-third of the lengths.

7 (a) $-,+,+$ (b) $+,-,-$

8 (c) $\frac{b}{b+c}$, $\frac{c}{b+c}$

  (d) It is the incentre of $\triangle$ABC.

Exercise 11B (page 128)

1 $b' = -b$; [B'C] is equal and parallel to [AH], so B'CHA is a parallelogram.

2 (a) $c+a$, $a+b$, $b-c$; $\triangle$XYZ is congruent to $\triangle$ABC; you can get from one to the other by half-turn rotation about E.

  (b) (i) O   (ii) H   (iii) E

  (c) U, V, W are the mid-points of the sides of $\triangle$XYZ; L, M, N are the mid-points of the lines joining the vertices of $\triangle$XYZ to the orthocentre O.

3 $2v \cdot (b-a) = b^2 - a^2$

4 (a) $c = \frac{9}{8}a - \frac{1}{8}b$, so $\frac{AC}{CB} = \frac{-1}{9}$, radius $\frac{3}{8}$AB

  (b) $c = \frac{k^2}{k^2-1}b - \frac{1}{k^2-1}a$, so $\frac{AC}{CB} = \frac{k^2}{-1}$,

  radius $\frac{k}{k^2-1}$AB

5 $\frac{2}{3}(a^2 + b^2 + c^2 - b\cdot c - c\cdot a - a\cdot b)$

11 Review exercise

(page 129)

5 (c) The incentre   (d) The orthocentre

  (e) Yes; the equal angles may both be measured outwards from the sides where appropriate, and the line segments produced if necessary.

6 (a) The reflection of the given circle in (BC) (that is, the circumcircle of $\triangle$OBC).

  (b) The circle with centre M, the mid-point of [BC], and radius $\frac{1}{2}r$, passing through O and touching the given circle.

  (c) The circle with centre N on [OM], where ON $= \frac{2}{3}$OM, and radius $\frac{1}{3}r$, passing through O.

  (d) The minor arc of the circle in part (a), together with the minor arc of a circle at which [BC] subtends 150°, on the opposite side of [BC] from O.

  (e) The major arcs of the two circles in part (d).

8 (a) 10 cm   (b) 9 cm
  (c) 10.8 cm   (d) 20.4 cm

9 (a) 6, 7   (b) $2\sqrt{21}$ cm

10 (b) $-1, -7$ (c) $(15, -5)$, $(-6, -8)$

Examination questions (page 130)

7 (b) D, E, F are collinear.

8 $\frac{1}{2}a\sqrt{10}$

Index

The page numbers refer to the first mention of each term, or the shaded box if there is one.

affine geometry, properties, 122
alternate segment theorem, 109
altitude, 49
    concurrence theorem, 50
analytical proof, 4
angle at the centre theorem, 11
angle bisector as a locus, 32
angle bisector theorems, 58, 62
    converse of, 59
angle in a semicircle, 11
    converse of, 11
angles in the same segment, 39
angles on the same arc theorem, 40
    converse of, 44
Apollonius's (triangle) theorem, 23
Apollonius's circle theorem, 67, 101
arc, 10

centroid, 19
Ceva's theorem, 70, 121
    converse of, 71
    converse of extended, 78
    extended, 76
chord, 10
circle
    as a locus, 10, 96
    equation of, 90, 92, 99
    properties of, 10
    vector equation of, 125
circumcentre, 29
circumcircle, 29
circumradius, 29
circumscribed polygon, 34
collinear points, 1
complete line, 2
concurrent lines, 19
concyclic points, 44
converse, 3
convex quadrilateral, 36

coordinate formulae, 87
cyclic quadrilateral, 40
Désargues property, 13
diagonal points of quadrangle, 57
directed length, 73
directly similar triangles, 16

e-circle, 60
e-centre, 60
equation of circle, 90, 92
    with given diameter, 97
escribed circle, 60
Euclidean geometry, properties, 123
Euclidean proof, 4
Euclid's theorem for proportional segments, 22
Euler's circle, 55, 124
    centre of, 56
Euler's line, 53
exterior angle of cyclic quadrilateral, 40
    converse of, 45
external angle bisector theorem, 62
external bisector, 60
external division of a line segment, 8

Feuerbach's theorem, 56

golden section, 43

harmonic
    conjugates, 82
    construction, 83
    mean, 84
    range, 82
    ratio, 82
hyperbola, 103

incentre, 32
incidence properties, 2
incircle, 32

indirectly similar triangles, 16
inradius, 32
inscribed circle, 34
intercept theorem, 9
internal bisector, 60
internal division of a line segment, 8
intersecting chords theorem, 108
isogonal conjugates, 129

joins, in a quadrangle, 56

line segment, 2
locus, 5, 96

major arc, 10
major segment, 12
mathematical model, 1
median, 18
Menelaus's theorem, 80, 119
    converse of 81
minor arc, 10
minor segment, 12

nine-point circle, 55

opposite angles of cyclic quadrilateral, 40
    converse of, 44
orthocentre, 51, 123
orthocentric quadrangle, 57

Pappus's theorem, 2
parabola, 7
perpendicular bisector
    as a locus, 6
    of sides of triangle, 29
    using co-ordinates, 96
plane geometry, 1
point, 1
    of contact, 12
    of trisection, 8
point circle, 91
power of point with respect to circle, 112
projection, 21
proof, 2

proportional division of line segments, 7
    using vectors, 117
proportional segments
    in a right-angled triangle, 22
Ptolemy's theorem, 42
Pythagoras's theorem, 3
    converse of, 4

quadrangle, 56
    orthocentric, 57

re-entrant quadrilateral, 36
reflex angle, 11
reflex sector, 12

secant, 10
secant-secant theorem, 108
sector, 12
segment, 12
sensed area, 75
    in vector form, 127
sensed length, 73
similar figures, 15
    triangles, 16
Simson's line, 46
Stewart's theorem, 24
straight line, 1
    equation of, 88
    parallel and perpendicular, 87
    vector equation of, 125
subtended angle, 35
supplementary angles, 35

tangent, 12
tangent and chord theorem, 109
tangent-secant theorem, 110
theorem, 2
transversal, 80

vector expression for a point
    on a line, 117
    on a plane, 120

Wallace's line, 47

Topic 2
Statistics and Probability

Hugh Neill and Douglas Quadling

Series Editor Hugh Neill

Contents

	Introduction	v
1	Cumulative distribution functions	1
2	Geometric and exponential probability	10
3	Linear combinations of random variables	25
4	Some properties of normal probability	36
5	Hypothesis testing	45
6	Large sample distributions	58
7	The central limit theorem	72
8	Hypothesis testing with discrete variables	77
9	Errors in hypothesis testing	82
10	The t-distribution	94
11	Confidence intervals	111
12	A survey of probability distributions	126
13	Chi-squared tests	137
	Review exercise	164
	Appendix: some supporting mathematics	169
	Answers	173
	Index	181

Introduction

Statistics and Probability has been written especially for the International Baccalaureate Further Mathematics SL examination. This section covers the syllabus for Topic 2.

It is assumed that students will already have completed the statistics chapters in the Higher Level Books 1 and 2. There is a small amount of material which extends a topic beyond the syllabus as printed, with the aim of enhancing students' appreciation of the subject. This is indicated by an asterisk (*) at the appropriate place in the text.

Occasionally within the text paragraphs appear in *this type style*. These paragraphs are usually outside the main stream of the mathematical argument, but may help to give insight, or suggest extra work or different approaches.

Students are expected to have access to graphic display calculators and the text places considerable emphasis on their potential for supporting the learning of statistics.

Numerical work is presented in a form intended to discourage premature approximation. In ongoing calculations inexact numbers appear in decimal form like 3.456... , signifying that the number is held in a calculator to more places than are given. Numbers are not rounded at this stage; the full display could be, for example, 3.456 123 or 3.456 789. Final answers are then stated with some indication that they are approximate, for example '1.23 correct to 3 significant figures'.

There are plenty of exercises. At the end of the book there is a Review exercise which includes some questions from past International Baccalaureate examinations, but on a different syllabus. At the time of writing, there are few current versions of the Higher Level examinations, so there is no backlog of examination questions on the newer parts of the syllabus.

The author thanks OCR and IBO for permission to use some examination questions and Cambridge University Press for their help in producing this book. Particular thanks are due to Jane Miller for permission to use her material from the Cambridge Advanced Level Mathematics series and to Sharon Dunkley and Linda Moore for their help and advice. However, the responsibility for the text, and for any errors, remains with the author.

1 Cumulative distribution functions

A cumulative distribution function is an alternative way of describing the probability distribution of a random variable. When you have completed this chapter, you should

- know the meaning of a cumulative distribution function and how to find it for both continuous and discrete random variables
- be able to find the probability density from a cumulative distribution function.

1.1 Finding the cumulative distribution from the probability density

When you have statistical data about a continuous random variable, you can represent it either with a histogram or with a cumulative frequency diagram. A similar choice can be made for graphs representing theoretical probability models.

One possibility is to use a probability density function $f(x)$. This is conventionally defined over the complete set $\mathbb{R}$ of real numbers, although often there are intervals $]-\infty,a]$ or $[b,\infty[$ for which $f(x)=0$.

Probability density functions have the following properties (see Higher Level Book 2 Section 10.2).

- $f(x) \geq 0$ for all $x \in \mathbb{R}$.

- The area under the probability density graph is equal to 1. That is,

$$\int_{-\infty}^{\infty} f(x)\,dx = 1.$$

- The probability that the random variable X lies in the interval $[c,d]$ is equal to the area under the probability density graph over this interval. That is,

$$P(c \leq X \leq d) = \int_{c}^{d} f(x)\,dx.$$

Another possibility is to use a **cumulative distribution function** $F(x)$, which is defined as the probability that the random variable X is less than or equal to x. That is,

$$F(x) = P(X \leq x).$$

For a continuous random variable it is not important whether you define the function as $P(X \leq x)$ or $P(X < x)$, since the probability that X is equal to any particular single value x is 0. But the distinction is important if you extend the definition to include discrete random variables.

Example 1.1.1

Fig. 1.1 shows the graph of a probability density function

$$f(x) = \begin{cases} 1 - \frac{1}{2}x & \text{for } 0 \le x \le 2, \\ 0 & \text{otherwise.} \end{cases}$$

Find the cumulative distribution function $F(x)$, and draw its graph.

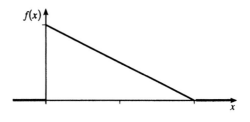

Fig. 1.1

When x is negative the probability density is 0, so $F(x) = 0$ for $x \le 0$. For $0 \le x \le 2$, the cumulative probability is equal to the area under the line in the interval $[0, x]$, which is shown by the shaded region in Fig. 1.2. This is a trapezium with parallel sides of lengths 1 and $1 - \frac{1}{2}x$, at a distance x apart. Therefore

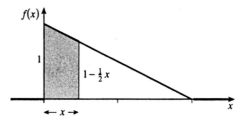

Fig. 1.2

$$F(x) = \frac{1}{2}\left(1 + \left(1 - \frac{1}{2}x\right)\right) \times x = x - \frac{1}{4}x^2.$$

This gives $F(2) = 2 - \frac{1}{4} \times 2^2 = 2 - 1 = 1$; you can check that this is the area of the triangle. Beyond $x = 2$ the probability density is again 0, so that there is no further increase in the cumulative probability. Therefore $F(x) = 1$ for $x > 2$.

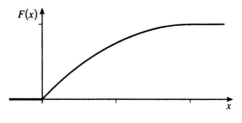

Fig. 1.3

The graph of $F(x)$ is shown in Fig. 1.3.

In most cases finding $F(x)$ for a given $f(x)$ involves integration, but this presents a small problem of notation. If you write the probability $P(X \le x)$ as $\int f(x)\,dx$ evaluated over the interval $]-\infty, x]$, then the letter x appears twice, once inside the integral and the other as one of the limits of integration. Fortunately, in finding a *definite* integral it doesn't matter what letter you use inside the integral: the value of $\int_c^d f(x)\,dx$ is exactly the same as $\int_c^d f(t)\,dt$ or $\int_c^d f(u)\,du$. So it is better to avoid the problem by using a different letter inside the integral, writing the cumulative probability for example as

$$P(X \le x) = \int_{-\infty}^x f(t)\,dt.$$

If a continuous random variable has probability density $f(x)$, the cumulative distribution function $F(x) = P(X \le x)$ is given by

$$\int_{-\infty}^x f(t)\,dt.$$

Example 1.1.2

A probability density function is defined by the equation

$$f(x) = \begin{cases} 0 & \text{for } x < 1, \\ \dfrac{1}{x^2} & \text{for } x \ge 1. \end{cases}$$

(a) Check that this is a valid probability density function.

(b) Find an expression for the cumulative distribution function $F(x)$.

(a)   It is obvious that $f(x) \ge 0$ for all x, so you just have to prove that $\displaystyle\int_{-\infty}^{\infty} f(x)\,dx = 1$.

$$\int_{-\infty}^{\infty} f(x)\,dx = \int_{-\infty}^{1} 0\,dx \; + \int_{1}^{\infty} \frac{1}{x^2}\,dx.$$

The first integral on the right is clearly 0, and the second is the limit as $v \to \infty$ of

$$\int_{1}^{v} \frac{1}{x^2}\,dx = \left[-\frac{1}{x} \right]_{1}^{v} = 1 - \frac{1}{v}.$$

Since $\displaystyle\lim_{v \to \infty}\left(1 - \frac{1}{v}\right) = 1 - 0 = 1$, it follows that

$$\int_{-\infty}^{\infty} f(x)\,dx = 0 + 1 = 1.$$

(b)   If $x < 1$, then clearly $F(x) = 0$.
If $x \ge 1$ then

$$F(x) = P(X \le x)$$

$$= \int_{-\infty}^{1} 0\,dt + \int_{1}^{x} \frac{1}{t^2}\,dt$$

$$= 0 + \left[-\frac{1}{t} \right]_{1}^{x}$$

$$= 1 - \frac{1}{x}.$$

Fig. 1.4

The graph of $f(x)$ is shown in Fig. 1.4,
and that of $F(x)$ in Fig. 1.5.

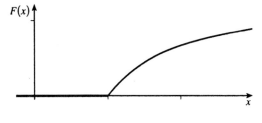

Fig. 1.5

Sometimes to describe $f(x)$ you need different
non-zero expressions over different intervals of the
domain. This is illustrated in the next example.

Example 1.1.3

In a population of a particular breed of dog the age distribution is modelled by the probability density function shown in Fig. 1.6, with equation

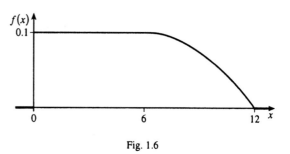

$$f(x) = \begin{cases} \frac{1}{10} & \text{for } 0 < x \le 6, \\ \frac{1}{30}x - \frac{1}{360}x^2 & \text{for } 6 < x \le 12, \\ 0 & \text{otherwise,} \end{cases}$$

Fig. 1.6

where x denotes the age in years. Find expressions for the cumulative distribution function. Hence find the median and quartile ages of the dogs in the population.

Clearly $F(x) = 0$ for $x \le 0$. For $0 < x \le 6$ the region under the probability density graph is a rectangle with width x and height $\frac{1}{10}$, so that $F(x) = \frac{1}{10}x$. For $6 < x \le 12$ the region under the graph is a rectangle of width 6 and height $\frac{1}{10}$ and a region under a curve (see the shaded area in Fig. 1.7) so

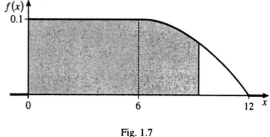

$$F(x) = \frac{6}{10} + \int_6^x \left(\frac{1}{30}t - \frac{1}{360}t^2\right) dt$$

$$= \frac{6}{10} + \left[\frac{1}{60}t^2 - \frac{1}{1080}t^3\right]_6^x$$

$$= \frac{6}{10} + \left(\frac{1}{60}x^2 - \frac{1}{1080}x^3\right) - \left(\frac{36}{60} - \frac{216}{1080}\right)$$

$$= \frac{1}{1080}\left(216 + 18x^2 - x^3\right).$$

Fig. 1.7

For $x > 12$ the probability density is 0, so the value of $F(x)$ remains constant and equal to

$$F(12) = \frac{1}{1080}(216 + 2592 - 1728) = \frac{1}{1080} \times 1080 = 1.$$

Putting all this together,

$$F(x) = \begin{cases} 0 & \text{for } x \le 0, \\ \frac{1}{10}x & \text{for } 0 < x \le 6, \\ \frac{1}{1080}\left(216 + 18x^2 - x^3\right) & \text{for } 6 < x \le 12, \\ 1 & \text{for } x > 12. \end{cases}$$

The graph of $F(x)$ is shown in Fig. 1.8.

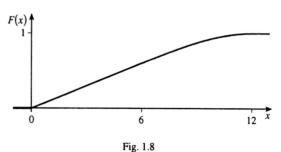

From Higher Level Book 2 Section 10.4 the median M is the value of x such that $P(X \le M) = \frac{1}{2}$, that is $F(M) = \frac{1}{2}$. Since $F(6) = \frac{6}{10} > \frac{1}{2}$, M lies in the interval $]0,6]$, so that $F(M) = \frac{1}{10}M$. Therefore $\frac{1}{10}M = \frac{1}{2}$, so $M = 5$.

Fig. 1.8

Similarly the lower quartile Q_1 lies in the interval $]0,6]$. Therefore $\frac{1}{10}Q_1 = \frac{1}{4}$, so $Q_1 = 2.5$.

However, the upper quartile Q_3 lies in the interval $]6,12]$, so that

$$F(Q_3) = \tfrac{1}{1080}\left(216 + 18Q_3{}^2 - Q_3{}^3\right).$$

Since $F(Q_3)$ has to equal $\frac{3}{4}$, $x = Q_3$ has to satisfy the equation

$$\tfrac{1}{1080}\left(216 + 18x^2 - x^3\right) = \tfrac{3}{4}, \quad \text{which is} \quad x^3 - 18x^2 + 594 = 0.$$

Using a calculator to solve this equation, the root in the interval $]6,12]$ is $7.533\ldots$.

So the upper quartile $Q_3 = 7.53$, correct to 3 significant figures.

1.2 Finding the probability density from the cumulative distribution

Since the cumulative distribution is found from the probability density by integrating, you can find the probability density from the cumulative distribution by differentiating. For example, in Example 1.1.1 the cumulative distribution function over the interval $[0,2]$ is $F(x) = x - \frac{1}{4}x^2$. Differentiating this gives $F'(x) = 1 - \frac{1}{2}x$, which is the equation for the line segment joining $(0,1)$ to $(2,0)$ in the probability density graph.

> If a continuous random variable has cumulative distribution function $F(x)$, the probability density function $f(x)$ is given by
>
> $$f(x) = F'(x).$$

There is one small complication in applying this rule. Although the graph of $F(x)$ is always a continuous line, it may contain isolated points where there is a sudden change of direction, such as $(0,0)$ in Fig. 1.3 and $(1,0)$ in Fig. 1.5. You can't differentiate $F(x)$ at these points, so the equation $f(x) = F'(x)$ doesn't apply there. This doesn't matter, since $f(x)$ is only used to calculate probabilities over an interval, not at isolated points. The usual convention is to define $f(x)$ at these points so that the intervals used to describe $f(x)$ are the same as those used to describe $F(x)$.

In some applications it is easier to begin by finding the cumulative distribution and then to find the probability density by differentiation.

Example 1.2.1
A bad darts player is equally likely to hit any point on the board. (He is allowed to ignore any throws which miss the board completely.) The radius of the board is a. Find the cumulative distribution and the probability density for the random variable R, the distance from the centre at which a dart hits the board.

The distance of any hit from the centre must be between 0 and a, so the probability density is zero in the intervals $r < 0$ and $r > a$.

If r is between 0 and a, the hits for which $R \le r$ lie inside (or on the circumference of) a circle of radius r, shown shaded in Fig. 1.9.

Since the hits are uniformly distributed over the surface of the board, the probability that $R \leq r$ is equal to the ratio of the area of this circle to the area of the whole board. That is,

$$F(r) = P(R \leq r) = \frac{\pi r^2}{\pi a^2} = \frac{r^2}{a^2}.$$

So, over the interval $0 \leq r < a$, the probability density is given by

$$f(r) = F'(r) = \frac{2r}{a^2}.$$

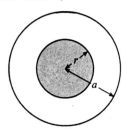

Fig. 1.9

The equations for the cumulative distribution and the probability density are then

$$F(r) = \begin{cases} 0 & \text{for } r < 0, \\ \dfrac{r^2}{a^2} & \text{for } 0 \leq r \leq a, \\ 1 & \text{for } r > a \end{cases} \quad \text{and} \quad f(r) = \begin{cases} 0 & \text{for } r < 0, \\ \dfrac{2r}{a^2} & \text{for } 0 \leq r \leq a, \\ 0 & \text{for } r > a. \end{cases}$$

1.3 Extension to discrete probability distributions

The definition of the cumulative distribution as $P(X \leq x)$ is still valid if the random variable X is discrete, but the value of this probability remains constant in the intervals between successive elements of the sample space. The graph of the cumulative distribution function therefore consists of a set of line segments parallel to the x-axis.

Example 1.3.1

Draw graphs of the probability distribution and of the cumulative distribution function for the Poisson probability $Po(2.5)$.

Your calculator probably has a program to calculate cumulative Poisson probabilities, and you should make sure that you know how to use this. However, you may only be able to use it to find the probability that $X \leq n$ for a particular value of n, and to draw the graph you want a table of values of $P(X \leq n)$ for $n = 0, 1, 2, 3, \ldots$. So it may be more convenient to generate these as a sequence from the Poisson formula

$$P(X = n) = e^{-m} \frac{m^n}{n!}$$

with $m = 2.5$.

This is very simple, because the factor e^{-m} doesn't involve n, and

$$\frac{m^n}{n!} = \frac{m \times m^{n-1}}{n \times (n-1)!} = \frac{m}{n} \times \frac{m^{n-1}}{(n-1)!}.$$

So, if you use u_n to denote the probability $P(X = n)$, values of u_n can be found from the inductive definition

$$u_0 = e^{-m}, \qquad u_n = \frac{m}{n} \times u_{n-1} \text{ for } n = 1, 2, 3, \ldots .$$

Now in this example you want not only values of $P(X = n)$ but also those of $P(X \le n)$, which is the sum sequence of u_n (see Higher Level Book 1 Section 30.4). So if you denote $P(X \le n)$ by v_n, values of v_n can be found from the inductive definition

$$v_0 = u_0 = e^{-m}, \qquad v_n = v_{n-1} + u_n = v_{n-1} + \frac{m}{n} \times u_{n-1} \text{ for } n = 1, 2, 3, \ldots .$$

With $m = 2.5$, these equations give the values (to 3 significant figures) for u_n and v_n in Table 1.10.

n	0	1	2	3	4	5	6	...
$u_n = P(X = n)$	0.082	0.205	0.257	0.214	0.134	0.067	0.028	...
$v_n = P(X \le n)$	0.082	0.287	0.544	0.758	0.891	0.958	0.986	...

Table 1.10

To draw the cumulative distribution graph, you need to define $F(x) = P(X \le x)$ not just when x is a natural number $0, 1, 2, \ldots$ but when x is any real number. Using the values of $P(X \le n)$ given in Table 1.10, it follows that

$$F(x) = \begin{cases} 0 & \text{for } x < 0, \\ 0.082 & \text{for } 0 \le x < 1, \\ 0.287 & \text{for } 1 \le x < 2, \\ 0.544 & \text{for } 2 \le x < 3, \end{cases} \qquad \text{and so on.}$$

The graph of the probability distribution u_n is given in Fig. 1.11, and that of the cumulative distribution is given in Fig. 1.12. In the latter graph, a small dot has been added at the left end of each line segment to make clear that the jump occurs immediately *before* the integer value of x.

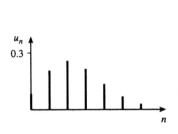

Fig. 1.11

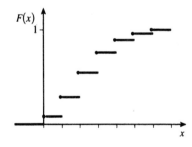

Fig. 1.12

Exercise 1

1   The probability density function of a random variable, X, is

$$f(x) = \begin{cases} \frac{1}{8}x & 0 \le x \le 4, \\ 0 & \text{otherwise.} \end{cases}$$

(a) Find the cumulative distribution function of X.   (b) Find the median.

2 The probability density function of a continuous random variable, X, is

$$f(x) = \begin{cases} \frac{2}{3} & 0 \le x < 1, \\ \frac{4}{3} - \frac{2}{3}x & 1 \le x \le 2, \\ 0 & \text{otherwise.} \end{cases}$$

(a) Find $F(x)$.   (b) Find the lower quartile.   (c) Find the 85th percentile.

3 The probability density function of a continuous random variable, X, is

$$f(x) = \begin{cases} \frac{3}{14}x & 0 \le x < 2, \\ \frac{3}{28}x(4 - x) & 2 \le x \le 4, \\ 0 & \text{otherwise.} \end{cases}$$

(a) Find $F(x)$.   (b) Find the median.   (c) Find $P(2.5 \le X \le 3)$.

4 Daily sales of petrol, X, at a service station (in tens of thousands of litres) are distributed with probability density function

$$f(x) = \begin{cases} \frac{3}{4}x(2 - x)^2 & 0 \le x \le 2, \\ 0 & \text{otherwise.} \end{cases}$$

(a) Find $F(x)$.   (b) Find the median in litres.

5 The cumulative distribution of a random variable, X, is

$$F(x) = \begin{cases} 0 & x < 0, \\ \frac{1}{108}\left(9x^2 - x^3\right) & 0 \le x \le 6, \\ 1 & x > 6. \end{cases}$$

Find the probability density function of X.

6 The cumulative distribution function of a random variable, X, is

$$F(x) = \begin{cases} 0 & x < 0, \\ \frac{1}{18}x^2 & 0 \le x < 3, \\ \frac{2}{3}x - \frac{1}{18}x^2 - 1 & 3 \le x \le 6, \\ 1 & x > 6. \end{cases}$$

Find the probability density function of X.

7 The random variable X metres represents the side of a square. The area of the square is represented by the random variable Y metre^2.

(a) If X has uniform probability density 0.2 over the interval $]0,5[$, find the cumulative distribution function $F(x) = P(X \le x)$.

(b) Deduce the cumulative distribution function for the area, $G(y) = P(Y \le y)$.

(c) Hence find the probability density function $g(y)$ for the area of the square.

8   The random variable X metres represents the base of a rectangle of area 1 metre^2. The height is represented by the random variable Y metres.

(a)   If X has uniform probability density 1 over the interval $]0,1[$, find the cumulative distribution function $F(x) = P(X \le x)$.

(b)   Deduce the cumulative distribution function for the height, $G(y) = P(Y \le y)$.

(c)   Hence find the probability density function $g(y)$ for the height of the rectangle.

9*   In Example 1.1.3, suppose that the probability density function for the age distribution of the dog population remains the same over time, and that the total number of dogs in the population remains constant. It can then be shown that, if the random variable Y represents the age in years to which a dog lives, then the probability density function for Y is

$$g(y) = -yf'(y),$$

where f is the probability density function defined in Example 1.1.3. Use this to find the median age to which a dog of this breed lives.

10   A random variable X has binomial probability $B(3, 0.4)$. Find the values of the cumulative distribution function in the intervals $]-\infty, 0[$, $[0, 1[$, $[1, 2[$, $[2, 3[$ and $[3, \infty[$.

11   Draw the graph of the cumulative distribution function for Poisson probability $Po(1.7)$.

2 Geometric and exponential probability

The two probability models described in this chapter both arise from the same question: how long must you wait until a certain event occurs? When you have completed this chapter, you should

- be able to calculate and apply geometric and exponential probability
- know expressions for the expectation and variance of these probability models
- understand the connection between exponential and Poisson probability.

2.1 The geometric distribution

Consider the following three examples.

1   A dice is rolled until a six is scored. Let X be the number of rolls up to and including the roll on which the first six occurs.

2   A card is selected, with replacement, from a standard pack of cards until an ace is drawn. Let Y be the number of selections up to and including the one on which the first ace occurs.

3   A person has a 1 in 17 chance of winning a prize in a lottery. She keeps playing the lottery once each week. Let W be the number of weeks up to and including the week in which she first wins a prize.

These three random variables have certain similarities.

In the first example,

$$P(X = 1) = P(\text{a six occurs on the first throw}) = \tfrac{1}{6}.$$

Let s represent the event that a six occurs on a trial and let f represent the event that a six does not occur. Then $X = 2$ corresponds to the sequence fs. Similarly the event $X = 3$ corresponds to the sequence ffs. Notice that there is only one possible sequence for each value of X.

You can now calculate the probability distribution for X:

$$P(X = 2) = P(fs) = \left(\tfrac{5}{6}\right) \times \left(\tfrac{1}{6}\right) = \tfrac{5}{36},$$

$$P(X = 3) = P(ffs) = \left(\tfrac{5}{6}\right)^2 \times \tfrac{1}{6} = \tfrac{25}{216},$$

$$P(X = 4) = P(fffs) = \left(\tfrac{5}{6}\right)^3 \times \tfrac{1}{6} = \tfrac{125}{1296},$$

and so on.

You can generalise this as

$$P(X = x) = \left(\tfrac{5}{6}\right)^{x-1} \times \tfrac{1}{6} \quad \text{for } x = 1, 2, 3, \dots .$$

In the second example the probability distribution formula for Y will be $P(Y = y) = \left(\tfrac{12}{13}\right)^{y-1} \times \tfrac{1}{13}$ for values of $y = 1, 2, 3, \dots$ since

$$P(Y = y) = P\left(\overbrace{ff \dots f}^{y-1} s\right) = \overbrace{\tfrac{12}{13} \times \tfrac{12}{13} \times \dots \times \tfrac{12}{13}}^{y-1 \text{ of these}} \times \tfrac{1}{13}.$$

In the third example, by a similar argument,

$$P(W = w) = \left(\tfrac{16}{17}\right)^{w-1} \times \tfrac{1}{17} \quad \text{for } w = 1, 2, 3, \dots \ .$$

You will know from experience that when you roll a dice you may have to wait a long time before a six turns up. In fact, there is no upper limit to the possible values of X, Y and W for these distributions. The sample space is the complete set $\mathbb{Z}^+$ of positive integers.

In general, if you have a sequence of trials for which the probabilities of success and failure are p and q (where $q = 1 - p$), and the random variable X is the number of trials up to and including the first success, then

$$P(X = x) = q^{x-1} \times p.$$

The first few probabilities for this distribution are set down in Table 2.1.

x	1	2	3	4	$\dots$
$P(X = x)$	p	qp	$q^2 p$	$q^3 p$	$\dots$

Table 2.1

You will see that these probabilities form a geometric sequence with first term p and common ratio q (see Higher Level Book 1 Section 30.1). For this reason the probability distribution for X is called a **geometric distribution**. Notice that the values of the probabilities depend on just one parameter p (since q is $1 - p$). A shorthand method of stating that the random variable X has this distribution is to write $X \sim \text{Geo}(p)$.

Fig. 2.2 shows graphs of the distributions $\text{Geo}(0.4)$ and $\text{Geo}(0.6)$. Notice that, because a larger value of p gives a smaller value of q, the graph tails off more rapidly when p is larger. But in both cases the mode of the distribution is 1; before you start to roll the dice, you are more likely to get the first six on the first roll than on any subsequent roll.

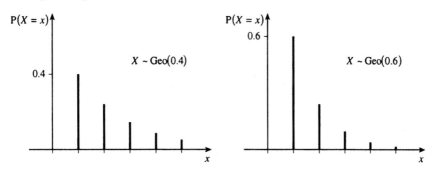

Fig. 2.2

The conditions which have to be satisfied for a set of trials to produce a geometric distribution are the same as those for a binomial distribution (see Higher Level Book 1 Section 34.2). But now, instead of asking how many successes you get in a fixed number of trials, the question is how many trials you must perform until you get a success.

The geometric distribution

- A single trial has exactly two possible outcomes (success and failure) and these are mutually exclusive.
- The outcome of each trial is independent of the outcome of all the other trials.
- The probability of success at each trial is constant.
- The trials are repeated until a success occurs.

The random variable X, which represents the number of trials up to and including the first success, then has a probability distribution given by the formula

$$P(X = x) = pq^{x-1} \quad \text{for } x = 1, 2, 3, \dots ,$$

where p is the probability of success, and $q = 1 - p$ is the probability of failure.

When the random variable X satisfies these conditions $X \sim \text{Geo}(p)$.

Example 2.1.1

A darts player must start a game by getting a dart in a certain region of the dart-board, The probability that any single dart hits this region is $\frac{2}{5}$. The player keeps throwing darts until he hits the required region. Calculate the probability that he needs

(a) exactly 5 throws,

(b) at most 2 throws,

(c) at least 8 throws,

(d) at most 10 throws.

(e) How many throws does the player need to make to be at least 99.999% sure of hitting the required region?

(f) What assumptions have you made in using the geometric distribution to model this situation?

Let X be the number of throws needed to hit the required region of the dartboard. X has a geometric distribution, with parameter $p = \frac{2}{5}$.

(a)   You need to find $P(X = 5)$. From the probability distribution formula

$$P(X = 5) = \frac{2}{5} \times \left(\frac{3}{5}\right)^4 = 0.0518, \text{ correct to 3 significant figures.}$$

(b)   You need to find $P(X \leq 2)$. This can be found by adding probabilities.

$$P(X \leq 2) = P(X = 1) + P(X = 2)$$
$$= \tfrac{2}{5} + \tfrac{3}{5} \times \tfrac{2}{5}$$
$$= 0.64.$$

(c)   Finding $P(X \geq 8)$ is best done by realising that, if the player needs 8 or more throws, the first 7 must have been failures Therefore

$$P(X \geq 8) = \left(\tfrac{3}{5}\right)^7 = 0.0280, \text{ correct to 3 significant figures.}$$

(d)   You can find $P(X \leq 10)$ from the probability of the complementary event, by using $P(X \leq 10) = 1 - P(X \geq 11)$. Then, using a similar argument to that of part (c),

$$P(X \geq 11) = \left(\tfrac{3}{5}\right)^{10}$$

so

$$P(X \leq 10) = 1 - P(X \geq 11)$$
$$= 1 - \left(\tfrac{3}{5}\right)^{10} = 0.994, \text{ correct to 3 significant figures.}$$

(e)   To find m such that $P(X \leq m) \geq 0.999\,99$, use the argument in part (d) to get

$$P(X \leq m) = 1 - P(X \geq m+1) = 1 - \left(\tfrac{3}{5}\right)^m.$$

So, to find m, you must solve the inequality $1 - \left(\tfrac{3}{5}\right)^m \geq 0.999\,99$, which is the same as $\left(\tfrac{3}{5}\right)^m \leq 0.000\,01$, or $\left(\tfrac{5}{3}\right)^m \geq 100\,000$.

Inequalities like this can be solved by taking logarithms of both sides (see Higher Level Book 1 Section 31.5). Using logarithms to base 10,

$$\log\!\left(\tfrac{5}{3}\right)^m \geq \log 100\,000$$
$$m \log\!\left(\tfrac{5}{3}\right) \geq 5$$
$$m \geq \frac{5}{\log \tfrac{5}{3}} = 22.53\ldots\;.$$

The smallest integer satisfying this is 23, so this is the required number of throws.

(f)   The assumptions which have been made are that the probability of success, here $\tfrac{2}{5}$, is constant for every throw. This means that the darts player does not improve with practice, nor does he get worse as he gets tired. The results of individual throws are also assumed to be independent, so that each throw has no effect on any other throw.

You will have noticed that in Example 2.1.1 different methods were used to find $P(X \leq 2)$ and $P(X \leq 10)$. It is interesting to compare the two methods by using them to find $P(X \leq m)$ for a general geometric distribution $\text{Geo}(p)$.

Method 1   This uses the formula for the sum of a geometric series.

$$P(X \leq m) = P(X = 1) + P(X = 2) + P(X = 3) + \ldots + P(X = m)$$
$$= p + pq + pq^2 + \ldots + pq^{m-1}$$
$$= p\left(1 + q + q^2 + \ldots + q^{m-1}\right)$$
$$= p\frac{1 - q^m}{1 - q}$$
$$= p\frac{1 - q^m}{p}$$
$$= 1 - q^m.$$

Method 2   Begin by noting that $P(X \leq m) = 1 - P(X \geq m + 1)$, and that if $m + 1$ or more trials are needed then the first m trials must have resulted in failure. So

$$P(X \geq m + 1) = q^m,$$

and $P(X \leq m) = 1 - q^m.$

For the geometric distribution $X \sim \text{Geo}(p)$

$$P(X \geq x) = (1 - p)^{x-1}.$$

The cumulative geometric distribution function is

$$P(X \leq x) = 1 - (1 - p)^x.$$

2.2   Expectation and variance of a geometric distribution

When you find a new probability distribution it is a good idea to check that the sum of the probabilities for all possible values of the random variable is equal to 1. For geometric probability this sum is an infinite series

$$\sum_{x=1}^{\infty} P(X = x) = p + pq + pq^2 + \ldots$$
$$= p\left(1 + q + q^2 + \ldots\right).$$

The expression in brackets is an infinite geometric series with sum $\dfrac{1}{1 - q}$, so

$$\sum_{x=1}^{\infty} P(X = x) = p \times \frac{1}{1 - q}$$
$$= p \times \frac{1}{p} = 1,$$

as expected.

Your calculator may have programs to find geometric and cumulative geometric probabilities. You could use them to answer questions like those in Example 2.1.1 parts (a) to (d).

The expressions for the expectation and the variance are also found as infinite series. A method of calculating these is given in the Appendix Section A.2.

The results are:

> For the geometric distribution $\text{Geo}(p)$,
>
> $$E(X) = \mu = \frac{1}{p} \quad \text{and} \quad \text{Var}(X) = \sigma^2 = \frac{q}{p^2},$$
>
> where $q = 1 - p$.

As a check, use these expressions to find the expectation and variance in the examples at the beginning of Section 2.1. For example, the distribution for rolling a dice is $\text{Geo}\left(\frac{1}{6}\right)$, for which $E(X) = \frac{1}{\frac{1}{6}} = 6$ and

$\text{Var}(X) = \dfrac{\frac{5}{6}}{\left(\frac{1}{6}\right)^2} = 30$. Is it reasonable that on average the number of rolls needed for a six to come up is 6?

Try carrying out the experiment a lot of times (or simulate it with a computer), and calculate the mean and variance of your results. How well do they agree with the theoretical values?

Example 2.2.1
A brand of cereal has a card in each packet. The cards form a set of 50 different pictures. They are distributed at random in the packets. A child has collected 49 of the picture cards and so needs one more to complete the set. What is the mean number of packets she will need to open to obtain the last picture?

> The probability that the next packet she opens will contain the picture she needs is $\frac{1}{50} = 0.02$. So X, the number of packets opened, up to and including the first one to contain the required picture card, has a geometric distribution with parameter $p = 0.02$.
>
> So $\quad E(X) = \dfrac{1}{p} = \dfrac{1}{0.02} = 50$.
>
> The child can expect to open 50 packets to obtain the last picture.

Example 2.2.2
The random variable Y has a geometric distribution. If $P(Y = 2) = 0.24$ and $P(Y = 3) = 0.144$, find the expected value and the variance of Y.

> If the geometric distribution has parameter p, then
>
> $$P(Y = 2) = qp = 0.24, \quad \text{and} \quad P(Y = 3) = q^2 p = 0.144.$$
>
> Therefore $\dfrac{q^2 p}{qp} = q = \dfrac{0.144}{0.24} = 0.6$.

Thus $p = 0.4$ and $E(Y) = \dfrac{1}{0.4} = 2.5$, $\text{Var}(Y) = \dfrac{0.6}{0.4^2} = 3.75$.

Example 2.2.3

Two children play a game on the beach. They begin by drawing a circle in the sand. Then they each move back 5 metres and pick up a pebble. They throw their pebbles together and try to get them into the circle. Ann's probability of success is 0.25, and Ben's is 0.2. If they throw together again and again, what is the expectation of the number of turns needed until

(a) they both succeed on the same turn,   (b) one or other of them succeeds?

(a) The probability that they will both succeed on the same turn is $0.25 \times 0.2 = 0.05$, and the probability that they won't both succeed is 0.95. So the probability that they first both succeed on the xth turn is $0.95^{x-1} \times 0.05$. The distribution is therefore $\text{Geo}(0.05)$, with expectation

$$\dfrac{1}{0.05} = 20.$$

(b) The probabilities that one of them, Ann or Ben, will fail on any turn are 0.75 and 0.8 respectively. The probability that they will both fail is therefore $0.75 \times 0.8 = 0.6$. If one or other of them (or both) succeeds, then they don't both fail, so the probability is $1 - 0.6 = 0.4$.

The distribution is therefore $\text{Geo}(0.4)$, with expectation $\dfrac{1}{0.4} = 2.5$.

Exercise 2A

In this exercise give probabilities to 4 decimal places.

1   The random variable X represents the number of trials up to and including a success. The probability of a success on any given trial is $p = 0.3$, independently of any other trial. Find the probability that

(a) $X = 5$,   (b) $X = 6$,   (c) $X = 5, 6$ or 7.

2   The random variable Y represents the number of trials up to and including a success. The probability of a success on any given trial is $p = 0.4$, independently of any other trial. Find the probability that

(a) $Y = 3$,   (b) $Y = 4$,   (c) $Y = 2, 3$ or 4.

3   Trials are repeated until a success is obtained. The probability of a success on any given trial is 0.8, independently of any other trial. Find the probability that the total number of trials needed, including the successful one, is

(a) exactly 3,   (b) less than or equal to 3,   (c) more than 5.

4   The random variable G has a geometric distribution, and the probability of a success on the first trial is 0.025. Find the probability that the first success

(a) occurs on the 10th trial,

(b) occurs after the 10th trial,

(c) occurs on or before the 10th trial.

5 It is given that the random variable T, which can take values 1, 2, 3, ... , has a geometric distribution and $P(T = 1) = 0.15$. Calculate

(a) $P(T > 7)$, (b) $P(T > 11)$, (c) $P(T \geq 12)$, (d) $P(T \leq 11)$.

6 A card is chosen at random from an ordinary pack, and replaced after its value has been noted. The process continues until a picture card (K, Q, J) is obtained. Z is the total number of cards drawn, including the picture card. Find

(a) $P(Z = 5)$, (b) $P(Z > 7)$, (c) $P(Z \leq 7)$.

7 In order to start a board game each player must throw at least one six with a pair of dice. Find the probability that for Gaye to start, she needs

(a) one throw, (b) five throws, (c) more than eight throws.

8 Wayne is counting cars going past the front gate of the school. He has been told that, on average, one car in 12 on the roads is green. Assuming that car colours are independent of each other, find the probability that

(a) the first green car he sees is the 8th that passes,

(b) the first green car is not among the first 15 cars,

(c) there is at least one green car among the first 10 cars.

9 A certain irrational number has a decimal expansion in which each digit is randomly chosen from the set {0, 1, 2, 3, 4, 5, 6, 7, 8, 9}. Find the probability that

(a) the first 9 occurs in the 8th place, (b) there is no 9 in the first 10 places.

10 It is known that, on average, one person in three at a shopping centre is wearing trainers. A market researcher observes people entering the shopping centre. Use a geometric distribution, with $p = \frac{1}{3}$, to calculate the probability that

(a) the first person wearing trainers is the fourth person observed,

(b) the first person wearing trainers is not among the first five people observed,

(c) the first person wearing trainers is either the fourth or the fifth person observed.

Give a reason why a geometric distribution might not be suitable in this context.

11 It is known that 9% of the population belongs to blood group B. A hospital consultant visits patients in a hospital and determines their blood groups, stopping when he has found one patient of blood group B.

(a) What is the probability that he needs to examine at least 11 patients?

(b) How many patients must he examine to be 99.8% confident of finding at least one in blood group B?

12 A biologist is collecting data about fruit flies (*Drosophila*). She knows that one fruit fly in 10 has a striped body, and this property occurs at random in the population of fruit flies. She needs to collect one fruit fly with a striped body.

(a) Find the probability that she needs to collect at least 15 fruit flies.

(b) Find the number of fruit flies she must collect to be 99.99% sure of obtaining one with a striped body.

13   An ordinary cubical dice is thrown repeatedly. A six is obtained on the 5th throw. Find the probability that the next six is

    (a) obtained on the 12th throw,   (b) not obtained until at least the 13th throw.

14   The random variable S can take values 1, 2, 3, ... and has a geometric distribution. It is given that $P(S = 2) = 0.2244$. Find the value of $P(S = 1)$, given that it is less than 0.5.

15   The random variable X has a geometric distribution with $P(X > 1) = 0.75$. Find $E(X)$ and $\text{Var}(X)$.

16   A fair coin is tossed until a head is obtained.

    (a) Find the expected value and the variance of the number of tosses required.

    (b) What is the expected value of the number of tails tossed?

17   A box of Chocobix cereal costs $1.50. One box in 25, on average, contains a silver button. If I buy a box of this cereal every week, find the expected total cost of the boxes bought, up to and including the first box with a silver button.

2.3 The exponential distribution

Geometric probability arises when you have a sequence of trials, which you go on performing until a certain event occurs. Exponential probability is similar but, instead of a sequence of separate trials, the event may occur at any instant in a continuous stream of time. Here are some examples.

1 A web site receives on average 15 hits per hour. How long will it be before the next hit?

2 A radioactive substance emits on average 5 particles per second. When you switch on the counter, how long will it be before it registers the first emission?

3 On average a car drives down a village street once every 2 minutes. If a villager opens her front door, how long will it be before the next car passes?

It is not difficult to guess what form the probability density function might take in examples like these. You met a similar situation in the chapter on exponential decay (Higher Level Book 1 Section 32.2) where the equation $f(t) = ab^t$ could be used either with domain $\mathbb{N}$ if values were observed discretely, or with domain $\mathbb{R}^+$ if the decay occurred continuously through time. And it was shown later that, for continuous decay, it is often more convenient to write b as e^k, so that the equation becomes $f(t) = ae^{kt}$ (see Higher Level Book 2 Section 13.3).

You can get from geometric to exponential probability in a similar way. In place of the expression pq^{x-1} for the probability that X takes the value x, you have a probability density function for a continuous random variable X of the form

$$f(x) = ce^{-\lambda x} \quad \text{for } x > 0.$$

The negative sign is inserted so that λ is a positive constant. (Remember that for exponential decay b is between 0 and 1, so that k is negative. Here, similarly, the probability q is between 0 and 1, so the constant in the exponent is negative.)

The next step is to find the constant c. Since f is a probability density, the area under the probability density graph must be 1. So c must be chosen so that

$$\int_0^\infty f(x)\,\mathrm{d}x = 1.$$

Now

$$\int_0^\infty e^{-\lambda x}\,\mathrm{d}x = \lim_{v\to\infty}\int_0^v e^{-\lambda x}\mathrm{d}x$$

$$= \lim_{v\to\infty}\left[-\frac{1}{\lambda}e^{-\lambda x}\right]_0^v$$

$$= \lim_{v\to\infty}\left(-\frac{1}{\lambda}e^{-\lambda v} + \frac{1}{\lambda}\right)$$

$$= 0 + \frac{1}{\lambda} = \frac{1}{\lambda}.$$

So $c \times \dfrac{1}{\lambda}$ must equal 1, that is $c = \lambda$. The equation of exponential probability density for $x > 0$ is therefore

$$f(x) = \lambda e^{-\lambda x}.$$

This is called the **exponential probability distribution.** It is denoted by $\mathrm{Exp}(\lambda)$. Like geometric probability, there is only one parameter λ. This is the average number of occurrences of the event in unit time. For example, in the first example above, x is measured in hours and $\lambda = 15$, so the probability density function is $f(x) = 15e^{-15x}$.

You will already have noticed that exponential probability deals with just the same situations as Poisson probability. But the questions asked about them are different. Poisson probability is concerned with how many events occur in a unit of time; exponential probability is about the time that you have to wait until the next event occurs. But the conditions for the probability model to be valid are the same in both cases.

The exponential distribution

This distribution applies to events which

- occur randomly in space or time
- occur singly, that is they cannot occur simultaneously
- occur independently
- occur at a constant rate.

The random variable X, which represents the distance or time up to the first occurrence of the event, then has a probability density function

$$f(x) = \begin{cases} \lambda e^{-\lambda x} & \text{for } x \geq 0, \\ 0 & \text{otherwise,} \end{cases}$$

where λ is the mean rate at which the event occurs.

When the random variable satisfies these conditions, $X \sim \mathrm{Exp}(\lambda)$.

Often it is more convenient to use the cumulative distribution function than the probability density function. For $x \geq 0$, this is given by

$$F(x) = P(X \leq x) = \int_0^x \lambda e^{-\lambda t} \, dt$$

$$= \left[-e^{-\lambda t} \right]_0^x$$

$$= 1 - e^{-\lambda x}.$$

> If $X \sim \text{Exp}(\lambda)$, the cumulative exponential distribution function for X is
>
> $$F(x) = \begin{cases} 1 - e^{-\lambda x} & \text{for } x \geq 0, \\ 0 & \text{otherwise.} \end{cases}$$

The graph of the probability density function is shown in Fig. 2.3, and that of the cumulative distribution function in Fig. 2.4, both for $\lambda = 1.5$.

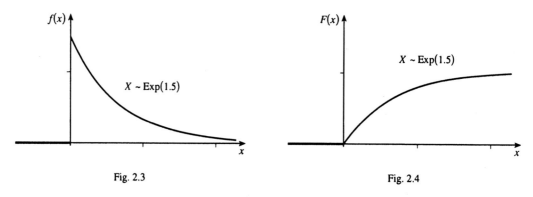

Fig. 2.3   Fig. 2.4

Example 2.3.1

In a packing plant apples are transported along a conveyor belt. On average a checker spots a substandard apple once every 15 seconds. What is the probability that she will miss at least one if her attention is diverted for 6 seconds?

You must begin by choosing what unit of time to use. If you choose a minute, then the mean rate of appearance of substandard apples is 4 per minute, so the appropriate probability distribution is $\text{Exp}(4)$.

The random variable X is the number of minutes until the next substandard apple appears after the checker's attention wanders, and you want to know the probability that this is less than 0.1. From the expression for the cumulative probability,

$$P(X \leq 0.1) = 1 - e^{-4 \times 0.1} = 1 - e^{-0.4} = 0.330, \text{ correct to 3 significant figures.}$$

The probability that the checker will miss at least one substandard apple is 0.330.

(If you had used a second rather than a minute as the unit of time, then λ would equal $\frac{1}{15}$ and you would calculate $P(X \leq 6)$. You can easily check that this gives the same value for the probability.)

2.4 Expectation and variance of an exponential distribution

Calculating the mean and variance for the exponential distribution requires the calculation of infinite integrals (see the Appendix Section A.6.) The results are:

> For the exponential distribution $X \sim \text{Exp}(\lambda)$,
>
> $$E(X) = \mu = \frac{1}{\lambda} \quad \text{and} \quad \text{Var}(X) = \sigma^2 = \frac{1}{\lambda^2}.$$

Example 2.4.1

A traffic census finds that on average a van passes a checkpoint once every 4 minutes. A new person comes on duty. Find the mean and standard deviation of the time he should expect to wait until the next van passes.

Taking a minute as the unit of time, the frequency of vans passing per minute is $\frac{1}{4}$. So the waiting time up to the next van, X minutes, has distribution $\text{Exp}\left(\frac{1}{4}\right)$. This has $\mu = \frac{1}{\frac{1}{4}} = 4$ and

$$\sigma^2 = \frac{1}{\left(\frac{1}{4}\right)^2} = 16, \text{ so that } \sigma = 4.$$

The expectation is 4 minutes and the standard deviation is 4 minutes.

2.5 Combining two exponential distributions

Suppose that a taxi firm has two telephone lines, and that on average the numbers of calls received per hour on these lines are a and b. What is the probability distribution for the time that will elapse before a call comes in on either line?

You will probably guess that it is $\text{Exp}(a + b)$, as it would be if all the calls came in on one line. This is in fact correct, but it is not quite obvious.

Denote by A and B the random variables for the number of hours before the first call comes in on the two lines, and let X be the random variable for all the calls taken together. Then $A \sim \text{Exp}(a)$ and $B \sim \text{Exp}(b)$.

It is easiest to concentrate on the probability that a call has *not* come in. Suppose that after x hours no call has come in to the office. In that case no call has come in on either line. So

$$X > x \quad \Leftrightarrow \quad (A > x) \cap (B > x).$$

Now suppose that the flows of calls on the two lines are independent of each other. (You would have to assume that each call is so short that there is no risk of a customer finding the first line engaged and switching to the second.) Then it follows that

$$P(X > x) = P(A > x) \times P(B > x).$$

And since $A \sim \text{Exp}(a)$ and $B \sim \text{Exp}(b)$, you know that

$$P(A > x) = e^{-ax} \quad \text{and} \quad P(B > x) = e^{-bx},$$

so

$$P(X > x) = e^{-ax} \times e^{-bx} = e^{-(a+b)x},$$

and the cumulative distribution for X is

$$F(x) = P(X \leq x) = 1 - e^{-(a+b)x}.$$

So X has probability distribution $\mathrm{Exp}(a+b)$.

What this means is that, if you have two random sequences of events running in parallel over the same period of time which satisfy the conditions for exponential probability, you can combine them into a single random sequence satisfying the same conditions.

> If two independent sequences of events are taking place in parallel, such that the times to the next occurrence are distributed as $\mathrm{Exp}(a)$ and $\mathrm{Exp}(b)$ respectively, then the time to the next occurrence of one or other event is distributed as $\mathrm{Exp}(a+b)$.

2.6* Proof of the rule for exponential probability

In Section 2.3 the expression for the probability density, $f(x) = \lambda e^{-\lambda x}$, was justified by analogy with exponential decay. This section shows how to get it by a probability argument.

Because the random variable is continuous, the proof uses differentiation. It is simplest to begin by finding the cumulative distribution function, or rather its complement, the probability that the event has *not* occurred up to the time x. If this is denoted by y, then

$$y = P(X > x).$$

The argument is explained in terms of time, because most applications are to events which take place in continuous time. Exponential probability can also be applied to the spacing of points along a line, in which case the wording of the argument would need to be changed, but the essential ideas remain the same.

Now suppose that x is increased to a value $x + \delta x$. Then the value of y will change to $y + \delta y$, and the problem is to find an expression for δy in terms of δx. The basic idea is:

If (1) the event has not occurred up to time $x + \delta x$, then
(2) it has not occurred up to time x, and
(3) it does not occur between times x and $x + \delta x$.

You know the probabilities of (1) and (2): they are $P(X > x + \delta x) = y + \delta y$ and $P(X > x) = y$. To make up an equation, you also need an expression for the probability of (3).

Suppose that δx is a very short interval of time. There is a possibility that an event could occur in this time, but the possibility that more than one event could occur is negligible. (Remember that one of the conditions is that events cannot occur simultaneously.) Also, the probability that an event occurs in this time is proportional to the duration of the interval, δx. So it can be denoted by $\lambda \times \delta x$, where λ is a constant.

The probability of (3), that an event does not occur during this interval is therefore $1 - \lambda \delta x$. Also events occur independently, so (3) is independent of (2). Therefore

$$y + \delta y = y \times (1 - \lambda \delta x),$$

which can be written more simply as

$$\delta y = -y\lambda \delta x, \quad \text{or} \quad \frac{\delta y}{\delta x} = -\lambda y.$$

Although this is written as an exact equation, it is more properly an approximation, because there is still the remote possibility that two events might be fitted into the interval δx. But this becomes more and more improbable as δx gets smaller. So in the limit, as $\delta x \to 0$,

$$\frac{dy}{dx} = -\lambda y.$$

This is a standard differential equation for y in terms of x. It is proved in Higher Level Book 2 Section 23.3 that its solution has the form

$$y = Ce^{-\lambda x}$$

where C is constant. And since $y = P(X > x)$, and you know that $P(X > 0) = 1$, the constant C must be equal to 1. That is,

$$P(X > x) = e^{-\lambda x}.$$

So the cumulative distribution function $F(x) = P(X \le x)$ is

$$F(x) = 1 - e^{-\lambda x}.$$

Finally, the probability density function $f(x) = F'(x)$ is

$$f(x) = \lambda e^{-\lambda x}.$$

Exercise 2B

1   If $X \sim \text{Exp}(0.2)$, find
    (a) $P(X \le 1)$,   (b) $P(X > 10)$,   (c) $P(4 \le X \le 6)$.

2   On average 5 cyclists pass the window each minute. What is the probability that, when you look out of the window, a cyclist will pass in the next 15 seconds?

3   On average a robin visits a garden bird table once every half-hour. Assuming these visits occur randomly, what is the probability that a robin will visit the bird table within the next 5 minutes?

4   An ambulance unit gets an emergency call once every 10 minutes on average. What is the probability that no calls will come in between 10.15 and 10.30?

5 A woman with a cold sneezes randomly 10 times an hour on average. Find the probability that she will not sneeze in the next 5 minutes.

6 Suppose that a major earthquake occurs somewhere in the world once every 4 years on average. What is the probability that a major earthquake will occur next year?

7 On a long street some of the paving stones are damaged. On average there are 25 damaged paving stones per kilometre. Assuming that these are randomly distributed, and that there are no gaps due to side streets, what is the probability that there are no damaged paving stones within 50 metres on either side of the post office entrance?

8 For the distribution $X \sim \text{Exp}(\lambda)$

(a) find (i) the median, (ii) the quartiles, (iii) the mode;

(b) what percentile is represented by the mean?

Show your answers on a sketch of the probability density function for $\text{Exp}(1)$.

9 If X has an exponential distribution, and if $\text{Exp}(X) = 10$, find $P(5 \le x \le 15)$.

10 If $X \sim \text{Exp}(\lambda)$, and $P(X \le 4) = 0.2$, find $E(X)$.

11 If X has an exponential distribution, find the probability that X lies within one standard deviation of the mean.

12 If $X \sim \text{Exp}(\lambda)$ and $P(1 < X < 2) = 0.24$, find two possible values for λ.

13 On average a car alarm goes off accidentally in the neighbourhood once every 2 hours, and a house alarm once every 3 hours. What is the expected time before the next alarm (of either kind) goes off?

14 At a city bus stop buses seem to arrive at random. The average waiting time for a number 10 bus is 10 minutes, and the average waiting time for a number 15 bus is 15 minutes.

(a) How long should a person expect to have to wait before a bus comes along?

(b) What is the probability that the person will have to wait more than 20 minutes?

3 Linear combinations of random variables

This chapter is about the distribution of linear functions and linear combinations of random variables. When you have completed it, you should

- know how to calculate the mean and variance of $aX + b$ when the mean and variance of X are known
- know how to calculate the mean and variance of $aX + bY$ when the mean and variance of X and Y are known.

3.1 Linear functions of a single random variable

Taxi fares are often calculated as the sum of two parts:

- a fixed charge, which appears on the meter as soon as you get in the cab
- an amount proportional to the distance travelled.

So for a journey of x kilometres the total charge $\$y$ is found from an equation of the form $y = ax + b$, where $\$b$ is the fixed charge and a is the distance rate in dollars per kilometre.

Suppose that a taxi firm is reviewing the operation of its fleet of taxis. These will be used for journeys of many different distances, so a variety of fares will be charged. The distances and fares are both random variables, X kilometres and $\$Y$, and the firm could model its business by assigning probabilities to the various values of X. The same probabilities would also apply to the corresponding values of Y; that is, if a journey of x_i kilometres costs $\$y_i$, then $P(Y = y_i)$ is equal to $P(X = x_i)$. From these probabilities the firm could calculate the mean and variance of X and Y.

It is not difficult to guess how these are related. Since each separate value of X is multiplied by a to get the variable part of the charge, the mean will also be multiplied by a. Adding the fixed charge to each fare adds the same amount to the mean. So, if $Y = aX + b$,

$$E(Y) = aE(X) + b.$$

However, adding the fixed charge has no effect on the spread of values of Y, so the variance depends only on the rate per kilometre. And since the variance is calculated from the squares of values of the random variable,

$$\text{Var}(Y) = a^2 \text{Var}(X).$$

Another application of these rules is to situations where the same quantity is measured in two different systems of units, as in Example 3.1.1.

Example 3.1.1
The temperature in degrees Fahrenheit at a seaside resort is a random variable with mean 59 and variance 27. Find the mean and variance of the temperature in degrees Celsius.

Let X be the temperature in $°\text{F}$. Then $E(X) = 59$ and $\text{Var}(X) = 27$.

To convert a temperature from degrees Fahrenheit to degrees Celsius, you subtract 32 then multiply by $\frac{5}{9}$. Thus if $X°F$ is the same as $Y°C$, then $Y = \frac{5}{9}(X - 32) = \frac{5}{9}X - \frac{160}{9}$.

So

$$E(Y) = E\left(\frac{5}{9}X - \frac{160}{9}\right)$$
$$= \frac{5}{9}E(X) - \frac{160}{9}$$
$$= \frac{5}{9} \times 59 - \frac{160}{9} = 15,$$

and

$$\text{Var}(Y) = \left(\frac{5}{9}\right)^2 \text{Var}(X)$$
$$= \frac{25}{81} \times 27 = \frac{25}{3}.$$

The proofs that $E(Y) = aE(X) + b$ and $\text{Var}(Y) = a^2\text{Var}(X)$ are simple if X is a discrete random variable. Suppose that X takes the value x_i with probability p_i. The essential part of the argument is that the values of $y_i = ax_i + b$ are all different, so that each y_i also has probability p_i.

There is a trivial exception to this statement, if $a = 0$. Then all the values of Y are equal to b, so that $E(Y) = b$ and $\text{Var}(Y) = 0$. Obviously the results are true in this case.

The expected value of Y is given by

$$E(Y) = \mu_Y$$
$$= \sum y_i p_i$$
$$= \sum (ax_i + b)p_i$$
$$= a\sum x_i p_i + b\sum p_i$$
$$= aE(X) + b \qquad (\text{since } \sum p_i = 1).$$

Since $Y = aX + b$, $E(Y) = E(aX + b)$; it follows that $E(aX + b) = aE(X) + b$.

Also

$$\text{Var}(Y) = \sum (y_i - \mu_Y)^2 p_i$$
$$= \sum ((ax_i + b) - (a\mu_X + b))^2 p_i \qquad (\text{since } \mu_Y = a\mu_X + b)$$
$$= \sum (a(x_i - \mu_X))^2 p_i$$
$$= \sum a^2 (x_i - \mu_X)^2 p_i$$
$$= a^2 \sum (x_i - \mu_X)^2 p_i$$
$$= a^2 \text{Var}(X).$$

Since $Y = aX + b$, $\text{Var}(Y) = \text{Var}(aX + b)$; it follows that $\text{Var}(aX + b) = a^2\text{Var}(X)$.

These results are still true if X is a continuous random variable. The proof is essentially the same, but it is more difficult to write in terms of integrals and probability density.

For any random variable X,

$$E(aX + b) = aE(X) + b,$$

$$Var(aX + b) = a^2 Var(X),$$

where a and b are constants.

3.2 Linear combinations of more than one random variable

Situations often arise in which you know the expected value and variance of each of several random variables and need to find the expected value and variance of a linear combination of these. For example, you know the expected value and variance of the thickness of the sheets which make up a laminated windscreen and want to find the expected value and variance of the total thickness of the windscreen.

In order to investigate any possible relations between expected values and variances you could start by considering two discrete random variables, X and Y. The question is, if you know the mean and variance of X and Y, how do you find the mean and variance of the random variable $Z = X + Y$?

Example 3.2.1 does this numerically.

Example 3.2.1
Members of a club compete in pairs for a cup. They perform as individuals, and the two scores are then added together. Before the competition one pair reckons the probability distributions for their scores, X and Y, to be as shown in Tables 3.1 and 3.2.

X	50	60	70
Probability	0.2	0.7	0.1

Table 3.1

Y	30	40	50
Probability	0.1	0.3	0.6

Table 3.2

(a) Find the probability distribution for their joint score $X + Y$.

(b) Find the expectation and variance for the individual scores and for the joint score.

(a) The joint score can take the values 80, 90, 100, 110 or 120.

The probabilities of these are calculated as follows.

$$P(X + Y = 80) = P(X = 50 \cap Y = 30)$$
$$= P(X = 50) \times P(Y = 30)$$
$$= 0.2 \times 0.1 = 0.02,$$
$$P(X + Y = 90) = P(X = 50 \cap Y = 40) + P(X = 60 \cap Y = 30)$$
$$= P(X = 50) \times P(Y = 40) + P(X = 60) \times P(Y = 30)$$
$$= 0.2 \times 0.3 + 0.7 \times 0.1 = 0.13, \text{ and so on.}$$

Continuing in this way gives the complete probability distribution shown in Table 3.3.

$X + Y$	80	90	100	110	120
Probability	0.02	0.13	0.34	0.45	0.06

Table 3.3

(b)   You can use a calculator to find the expectations and variances. Check for yourself that

$$E(X) = 59, \qquad E(Y) = 45, \qquad E(X + Y) = 104,$$

$$\text{Var}(X) = 29, \qquad \text{Var}(Y) = 45, \qquad \text{Var}(X + Y) = 74.$$

You will see that in this example

$$E(X + Y) = E(X) + E(Y) \qquad \text{and} \qquad \text{Var}(X + Y) = \text{Var}(X) + \text{Var}(Y).$$

To see if this is true in general you must carry out similar calculations algebraically.

To keep the algebra simple, suppose that X may take just three values x_1, x_2, x_3 and that Y may take just two values y_1, y_2. How many values can Z take?

Since any value of X can be combined with any value of Y, Z can take any of the values

$$x_1 + y_1, \quad x_2 + y_1, \quad x_3 + y_1, \quad x_1 + y_2, \quad x_2 + y_2, \quad x_3 + y_2.$$

A convenient way of showing this is with a two-way table like Table 3.4.

		Values of X			
		x_1	x_2	x_3	Total
Values of Y	y_1	r	s	t	q_1
	y_2	u	v	w	q_2
	Total	p_1	p_2	p_3	1

Table 3.4

The entries r, s, t, u, v, w in the table are the probabilities associated with each of the six values of Z; for example, $r = P(X = x_1 \cap Y = y_1) = P(Z = x_1 + y_1)$. These can be used to write the expectation of Z as

$$E(Z) = (x_1 + y_1)r + (x_2 + y_1)s + (x_3 + y_1)t + (x_1 + y_2)u + (x_2 + y_2)v + (x_3 + y_2)w.$$

It is possible that not all the six values of Z are different; for example, $x_1 + y_2$ might be equal to $x_3 + y_1$. This does not affect the mathematical argument which follows.

If you multiply out the brackets on the right and then rearrange the terms, you can write this as

$$E(Z) = x_1(r + u) + x_2(s + v) + x_3(t + w) + y_1(r + s + t) + y_2(u + v + w).$$

You will see that the first three brackets in this arrangement are the sums of the probabilities in the three columns of Table 3.1, and the last two brackets are the sums of the probabilities in the two rows. If you denote these sums by p_1, p_2, p_3 and q_1, q_2 as shown in Table 3.4, then they are just the probabilities associated with the various values of X and Y. For example,

$$p_1 = r + u = P(X = x_1 \cap Y = y_1) + P(X = x_1 \cap Y = y_2)$$

and

$$q_1 = r + s + t = P(X = x_1 \cap Y = y_1) + P(X = x_2 \cap Y = y_1) + P(X = x_3 \cap Y = y_1),$$

and these are just $P(X = x_1)$ and $P(Y = y_1)$ respectively. Using similar expressions for the other columns and rows in Table 3.4, the equation for $E(Z)$ becomes

$$E(Z) = (x_1 p_1 + x_2 p_2 + x_3 p_3) + (y_1 q_1 + y_2 q_2)$$
$$= E(X) + E(Y).$$

Notice that nothing has been said about the random variables. The result is true whether or not X and Y are independent.

> For any random variables X and Y,
>
> $$E(X + Y) = E(X) + E(Y).$$

This is probably what you would expect. But you may find the corresponding result for variance more surprising.

To start with, it helps to write $E(X)$ as μ_X, and similarly for Y and Z, and to write the variance in the form

$$Var(X) = \sum_{i=1}^{3} x_i^2 p_i - \mu_X^2$$
$$= E(X^2) - \mu_X^2.$$

Similarly

$$Var(Z) = E\left((X + Y)^2\right) - \mu_Z^2.$$

It has just been proved that $\mu_Z = \mu_X + \mu_Y$, so

$$Var(Z) = E(X^2 + 2XY + Y^2) - (\mu_X^2 + 2\mu_X \mu_Y + \mu_Y^2).$$

By extending the result in the shaded box above to the sum of three random variables (remember that they need not be independent), you can write

$$E(X^2 + 2XY + Y^2) = E(X^2) + E(2XY) + E(Y^2),$$

and you have already seen in Section 3.1 that $E(2XY) = 2E(XY)$.

So, rearranging the terms,

$$Var(Z) = \left(E(X^2) - \mu_X^2\right) + \left(E(Y^2) - \mu_Y^2\right) + 2\left(E(XY) - \mu_X \mu_Y\right)$$
$$= Var(X) + Var(Y) + 2\left(E(XY) - \mu_X \mu_Y\right).$$

Now look at the last bracket and go back to Table 3.4. You will see that

$$E(XY) = x_1y_1r + x_2y_1s + x_3y_1t + x_1y_2u + x_2y_2v + x_3y_2w,$$

and

$$\mu_x\mu_y = (x_1p_1 + x_2p_2 + x_3p_3)(y_1q_1 + y_2q_2)$$
$$= x_1y_1p_1q_1 + x_2y_1p_2q_1 + x_3y_1p_3q_1 + x_1y_2p_1q_2 + x_2y_2p_2q_2 + x_3y_2p_3q_2.$$

So $E(XY)$ and $\mu_x\mu_y$ would be the same if

$$r = p_1q_1, \quad s = p_2q_1, \quad t = p_3q_1, \quad u = p_1q_2, \quad v = p_2q_2, \quad w = p_3q_2.$$

What do these equations mean? The first, for example, states that

$$P(X = x_1 \cap Y = y_1) = P(X = x_1) \times P(Y = y_1),$$

and the others are similar. These are just the conditions for the random variables X and Y to be independent. So, if X and Y are independent, then $E(XY) - \mu_x\mu_y = 0$, and

$$Var(Z) = Var(X) + Var(Y).$$

You have probably found this proof rather daunting, but this is largely because of the complicated notation with all the suffixes – hence the decision to restrict X and Y to three and two values respectively. But obviously the proof would be essentially the same however many values there are. Try reading it through again, concentrating on the outline of the argument rather than the details. The result also holds if X and Y are continuous random variables, but it is more difficult to work with integrals rather than sums.

If X and Y are independent random variables, then

$$Var(X + Y) = Var(X) + Var(Y).$$

It is also worth noticing another useful result which has emerged during the proof.

If X and Y are independent random variables, then

$$E(XY) = E(X) \times E(Y).$$

Example 3.2.2
My journey to work is made up of four stages: a walk to the bus-stop, a wait for the bus, a bus journey and a walk at the other end. The times taken for these four stages are independent random variables U, V, W and X with expected values (in minutes) of 4.7, 5.6, 21.6 and 3.7 respectively and standard deviations of 1.1, 1.2, 3.1 and 0.8 respectively. What is the expected time and standard deviation for the total journey?

The expected time for the whole journey is

$$E(U + V + W + X) = E(U) + E(V) + E(W) + E(X)$$
$$= 4.7 + 5.6 + 21.6 + 3.7 = 35.6.$$

Since the variables U, V, W and X are independent,

$$\text{Var}(U + V + W + X) = \text{Var}(U) + \text{Var}(V) + \text{Var}(W) + \text{Var}(X)$$
$$= 1.1^2 + 1.2^2 + 3.1^2 + 0.8^2$$
$$= 12.9,$$

so the standard deviation for the whole journey is $\sqrt{12.9} = 3.59$, correct to 3 significant figures.

The relations between expected values and variances can be generalised to the situation where $Z = aX + bY$ and a and b are constants. By combining the results in this section with those in Section 3.1,

$$E(Z) = E(aX + bY)$$
$$= E(aX) + E(bY)$$
$$= aE(X) + bE(Y);$$

and for independent X and Y

$$\text{Var}(Z) = \text{Var}(aX + bY)$$
$$= \text{Var}(aX) + \text{Var}(bY)$$
$$= a^2\text{Var}(X) + b^2\text{Var}(Y).$$

> For any random variables X and Y, and constants a and b,
>
> $$E(aX + bY) = aE(X) + bE(Y).$$
>
> If X and Y are independent,
>
> $$\text{Var}(aX + bY) = a^2\text{Var}(X) + b^2\text{Var}(Y).$$

Example 3.2.3
The length, L (in cm), of the rectangular panels produced by a machine is a random variable with mean 26 and variance 4 and the width, B (in cm), is a random variable with mean 14 and variance 1. The variables L and B are independent. What are the expected value and variance of

(a) the perimeter of the panels,

(b) the difference between the length and the width?

(c)* What is the expected value of the area of the panels?

    (a)   The perimeter is $2L + 2B$, so

$$E(2L + 2B) = 2E(L) + 2E(B)$$
$$= 2 \times 26 + 2 \times 14 = 80,$$

$$\text{Var}(2L + 2B) = 2^2 \text{Var}(L) + 2^2 \text{Var}(B)$$
$$= 4 \times 4 + 4 \times 1 = 20.$$

(b)   The difference between length and width is $L - B$, so

$$\text{E}(L - B) = \text{E}(L) - \text{E}(B)$$
$$= 26 - 14 = 12,$$

$$\text{Var}(L - B) = 1^2 \text{Var}(L) + (-1)^2 \text{Var}(B)$$
$$= 1 \times 4 + 1 \times 1 = 5.$$

(c)*   The area is LB. Since L and B are independent,

$$\text{E}(LB) = \text{E}(L) \times \text{E}(B)$$
$$= 26 \times 14 = 364.$$

The result in part (b) for the variance is an example of a general rule which applies when variances are combined, namely that they are always added.

Example 3.2.4

If A and B are independent Poisson random variables with distributions $\text{Po}(a)$ and $\text{Po}(b)$, give reasons why the random variables   (a) $Y = 2A$,   (b) $Z = A - B$ are not Poisson random variables.

One property of Poisson random variables is that the mean is equal to the variance. The method is to show that Y and Z do not have this property, so they can't have a Poisson distribution.

(a)   Since $A \sim \text{Po}(a)$, $\text{E}(A) = a$ and $\text{Var}(A) = a$. So, from Section 3.1,

$$\text{E}(Y) = 2\text{E}(A) = 2a \quad \text{and} \quad \text{Var}(Y) = 2^2 \text{E}(A) = 4a.$$

Since $\text{E}(Y) \neq \text{Var}(Y)$, Y does not have a Poisson distribution.

(b)   From the results in this section,

$$\text{E}(Z) = 1\text{E}(A) + (-1)\text{E}(B) = a - b, \quad \text{and} \quad \text{Var}(Z) = 1^2 \text{E}(A) + (-1)^2 \text{E}(B) = a + b.$$

Since b can't be 0, $\text{E}(Z) \neq \text{Var}(Z)$, so Z does not have a Poisson distribution.

3.3   Linear relations involving more than one observation of a random variable

In Section 3.2 the separate random variables may represent different quantities, as in Examples 3.2.1 and 3.2.2, but they may also represent repeated observations of a single random variable. Suppose, for example, you make two observations of a random variable X where $\text{E}(X) = 3$ and $\text{Var}(X) = 4$. Denote these observations by X_1 and X_2. Then the expected values and variances of X_1 and X_2 will be equal to the corresponding values for X. It follows that

$$\text{E}(X_1 + X_2) = \text{E}(X_1) + \text{E}(X_2)$$
$$= \text{E}(X) + \text{E}(X)$$
$$= 3 + 3 = 6,$$

and, providing the observations are independent, that

$$\text{Var}\,(X_1 + X_2) = \text{Var}\,(X_1) + \text{Var}\,(X_2)$$
$$= \text{Var}\,(X) + \text{Var}\,(X)$$
$$= 4 + 4 = 8.$$

It is instructive to compare these results with the values for $E(2X)$ and $\text{Var}\,(2X)$ obtained using the results $E(aX) = aE(X)$ and $\text{Var}\,(aX) = a^2\text{Var}\,(X)$:

$$E(2X) = 2E(X) \qquad \text{and} \qquad \text{Var}\,(2X) = 2^2\text{Var}\,(X)$$
$$= 2 \times 3 = 6, \qquad\qquad\qquad = 2^2 \times 4 = 16.$$

The expected values for $X_1 + X_2$ and $2X$ are the same. This is not surprising since $2X = X + X$ and so $E(2X) = E(X) + E(X) = 6$. Why then do the variances of $X_1 + X_2$ and $2X$ differ? The answer is that $\text{Var}\,(2X)$ is not equal to $\text{Var}\,(X) + \text{Var}\,(X)$, because the variables X and X are not independent: they refer to the *same* observation of the same variable. This means that it is important to distinguish clearly between situations in which a single observation is multiplied by a constant and those in which several different observations of the same random variable are added.

Exercise 3

1   Random points with coordinates (x_i, y_i) lie on the line with equation $y = 4x - 3$. If $E(X) = 2$ and $\text{Var}\,(X) = 0.2$, find $E(Y)$ and $\text{Var}\,(Y)$.

2   A company pension scheme pays former employees a pension of $10\,000 a year plus $500 for each year of service with the company. The directors want to predict the implications of the scheme for the year 2025, and use as a model for its surviving pensioners a distribution with a mean length of service of 17 years with standard deviation of 6 years. What does this predict for the mean and standard deviation of the pensions paid to former employees?

3   Intelligence test scores are scaled to produce a national mean of 100 with standard deviation 15. A new test is devised, and calibrated with a large-scale trial. This suggests that the new test produces national scores with mean 96 and standard deviation 12. What linear scaling formula should be used to convert raw marks R on the new test to scaled marks S? If a girl gets a raw mark of 120 on the new test, what should be her correct intelligence score?

4   The random variable X is the number of even numbers obtained when two ordinary fair dice are thrown. The random variable Y is the number of even numbers obtained when two fair pentagonal spinners, each numbered 1, 2, 3, 4, 5, are spun simultaneously.

Copy and complete the following probability distributions.

x	0	1	2
p	0.25		

y	0	1	2
p	0.36		

$x+y$	0	1	2	3	4
p	0.09				

Find $E(X)$, $\text{Var}\,(X)$, $E(Y)$, $\text{Var}\,(Y)$, $E(X+Y)$, $\text{Var}\,(X+Y)$ by using the probability distributions. Verify that $E(X+Y) = E(X) + E(Y)$ and $\text{Var}\,(X+Y) = \text{Var}\,(X) + \text{Var}\,(Y)$.

5 X and Y are independent random variables with probability distributions as shown.

x	1	2	3
p	0.4	0.2	0.4

y	0	1	2
p	0.3	0.5	0.2

You are given that $E(X) = 2$, $Var(X) = 0.8$, $E(Y) = 0.9$ and $Var(Y) = 0.49$.

The random variable T is defined as $2X - Y$. Find $E(T)$ and $Var(T)$ using the equations in Section 3.2.

Check your answers by completing the following probability distribution and calculating $E(T)$ and $Var(T)$ directly.

t	0	1	2	3	4	5	6
p	0.08						0.12

6   The independent random variables W, X and Y have means 10, 8 and 6 respectively and variances 4, 5 and 3 respectively.

Find $E(W + X + Y)$, $Var(W + X + Y)$, $E(2W - X - Y)$ and $Var(2W - X - Y)$.

7   A piece of laminated plywood consists of three pieces of wood of type A and two pieces of type B. The thickness of A has mean 2 mm and variance 0.04 mm^2. The thickness of B has mean 1 mm and variance 0.01 mm^2. Find the mean and variance of the thickness of the laminated plywood.

8   The random variable S is the score when an ordinary fair dice is thrown. The random variable T is the number of tails obtained when a fair coin is tossed once.

Find $E(S)$, $Var(S)$, $E(6T)$, $Var(6T)$, $E(S + 6T)$ and $Var(S + 6T)$.

9   The random variable X has the probability distribution shown in the table.

x	1	2	3	4
$P(X = x)$	$\frac{3}{8}$	$\frac{1}{4}$	$\frac{1}{4}$	$\frac{1}{8}$

Find the mean and variance of X.

Hence find the mean and variance of the distribution of the sum of three independent observations of X.

10   In American football, the quarterback's rating, Q, is calculated using the formula
$Q = \frac{5}{6}(C + 5Y + 2.5 + 4T - 5I)$, where C, Y, T and I are variables which can be considered independent with means and variances as shown in the table.

Variable	C	Y	T	I
Mean	60.0	6.8	4.5	3.1
Variance	68.5	2.3	9.0	7.1

C, T and I are the percentage completions, touchdown passes and interceptions per pass attempt. Y is the number of yards gained divided by the passes attempted.

Find $E(Q)$ and $Var(Q)$.

11   The random variable Y which can only take the values 0 and 1 is called the Bernoulli distribution. Given that $P(1) = p$, show that $E(Y) = p$ and $Var(Y) = p(1 - p)$.

The binomial distribution can be considered to be a series of Bernoulli trials. That is,

$$X = Y_1 + Y_2 + \ldots + Y_n.$$

Show that $E(X) = np$ and $Var(X) = np(1 - p)$.

12   Let X_1, X_2, $\ldots$, X_n be n values randomly selected from a population, with mean μ and variance σ^2.

By considering $\overline{X} = \dfrac{X_1 + X_2 + \ldots + X_n}{n}$, show that $E(\overline{X}) = \mu$ and $Var(\overline{X}) = \dfrac{\sigma^2}{n}$.

4 Some properties of normal probability

Normal probability has some important properties which no other distributions have. When you have completed this chapter, you should

- know that any linear combination of normal random variables is also normal
- understand what is meant by the sampling distribution of the mean
- be able to apply this to problems involving the location of the mean of a normal population.

4.1 Linear combinations of random variables

When you have a random variable X with a particular kind of distribution, then aX and $X + b$ may or may not have the same kind of distribution.

For example, suppose that X is the uniform distribution of scores which you get when you roll a fair dice, with $P(X = x) = \frac{1}{6}$ for $X = 1,2,3,4,5,6$. Then if you doubled the number of spots on each face of the dice, you would get a random variable $2X$ which also has a uniform distribution, with $P(X = x) = \frac{1}{6}$ for $X = 2,4,6,8,10,12$. And if you put three extra dots on each face, you would get a random variable $X + 3$ with the uniform distribution $P(X = x) = \frac{1}{6}$ for $X = 4,5,6,7,8,9$.

But if X has a Poisson distribution, then $2X$ and $X + 3$ do not have a Poisson distribution (see Example 3.2.4).

Similarly, when you have two independent random variables X and Y with a particular kind of distribution, then $X + Y$ may or may not have the same kind of distribution.

For example, it can be proved that, if X and Y are independent Poisson random variables, then $X + Y$ also has a Poisson distribution. But if X and Y have the uniform distribution of scores on a dice, then $X + Y$ has a triangular, not a uniform, distribution (see Higher Level Book 1 Section 33.1).

So it is a remarkable fact that, if X has a normal distribution, then so does $aX + b$; and if independent random variables X and Y are normally distributed, so is $X + Y$.

You can combine this with the rules given in Chapter 3,

$$E(aX + b) = aE(X) + b, \qquad \text{Var}(aX + b) = a^2\text{Var}(X),$$

$$E(X + Y) = E(X) + E(Y), \quad \text{Var}(X + Y) = \text{Var}(X) + \text{Var}(Y) \qquad \text{(for independent } X, Y)$$

to make precise statements about the distribution of $aX + b$ and $X + Y$.

> If $X \sim N(\mu, \sigma^2)$, then $aX + b$ is a normal random variable $N(a\mu + b, a^2\sigma^2)$.
>
> If X and Y are independent random variables $N(\mu_1, \sigma_1^2)$ and $N(\mu_2, \sigma_2^2)$, then $X + Y$ is a normal random variable $N(\mu_1 + \mu_2, \sigma_1^2 + \sigma_2^2)$.

If you like, you can combine these statements in one more general rule.

> If $X_1, X_2, \dots, X_n$ are independent random variables, and if $X_i \sim N(\mu_i, \sigma_i^2)$, then $a_1 X_1 + a_2 X_2 + \dots + a_n X_n + b$ has normal probability with distribution $N(a_1\mu_1 + a_2\mu_2 + \dots + a_n\mu_n + b, a_1^2\sigma_1^2 + a_2^2\sigma_2^2 + \dots + a_n^2\sigma_n^2)$.

Unfortunately the proofs are too difficult to give here.

Example 4.1.1

The random variable X is distributed $N(10, 5^2)$.

(a) What is the distribution of Y where $Y = 3X - 7$?

(b) Find the probability that a single observation of Y is less than 20.

(a) $E(Y) = E(3X - 7)$
$$= 3E(X) - 7$$
$$= 3 \times 10 - 7 = 23.$$

$\text{Var}(Y) = \text{Var}(3X - 7)$
$$= 3^2 \text{Var}(X)$$
$$= 9 \times 5^2 = 225.$$

Since Y is a linear function of X and X is normally distributed, Y is also normally distributed. Therefore $Y \sim N(23, 225)$.

(b) You have various options for finding $P(Y < 20)$. With some calculators you can simply enter the boundaries of the interval, $-\infty$ and 20, and the values $\mu = 23$ and $\sigma = 15$, and find directly that $P(Y < 20) = 0.421$, correct to 3 significant figures.

You probably can't actually enter '$-\infty$' in your calculator, but any large negative number will do instead, since the areas under the tails of the normal probability density curve are negligible. To be completely safe, you can key in $-1E99$, which stands for -1×10^{99}.

Alternatively you can begin by standardising, writing

$$P(Y < 20) = P\left(Z < \frac{20 - 23}{\sqrt{225}}\right)$$
$$= P(Z < -0.2).$$

You can then either find this directly from the calculator program for the cumulative distribution function for $N(0,1)$, using boundaries $-\infty$ and -0.2, or you can use a table of areas under the standard normal curve. Since the table only gives values of $P(Z \le z)$ for positive values of z, you have to use the symmetry properties of the $N(0,1)$ graph:

$$P(Z < -0.2) = P(Z > 0.2)$$
$$= 1 - P(Z \le 0.2)$$
$$= 1 - 0.5793 \approx 0.421.$$

It is expected that most students will use a calculator to find normal probabilities, so the intermediate algebraic steps in calculations like this will usually be left out.

Example 4.1.2

The mass of an empty lift cage is 210 kg. If the masses (in kg) of adults are distributed as $N(70, 950)$, find the probability that the mass of the lift cage containing 10 adults chosen at random exceeds 1000 kg.

Let the mass in kg of an adult chosen at random be X. Then $X \sim N(70, 950)$.

Let the mass of the cage containing 10 adults be M. Then $M = 210 + X_1 + X_2 + \ldots + X_{10}$.

Assuming that the masses of the adults are independent, M will be normally distributed with mean and variance given by

$$
\begin{aligned}
E(M) &= E(210 + X_1 + X_2 + \ldots + X_{10}) \\
&= 210 + E(X_1) + E(X_2) + \ldots + E(X_{10}) \\
&= 210 + 10 \times E(X) \\
&= 210 + 10 \times 70 = 910,
\end{aligned}
$$

and

$$
\begin{aligned}
\text{Var}(M) &= \text{Var}(210 + X_1 + X_2 + \ldots + X_{10}) \\
&= \text{Var}(X_1) + \text{Var}(X_2) + \ldots + \text{Var}(X_{10}) \\
&= 10 \times \text{Var}(X) \\
&= 10 \times 950 = 9500.
\end{aligned}
$$

So $M \sim N(910, 9500)$.

To find $P(M > 1000)$, either use your calculator as to find the answer directly as described in Example 4.1.1, or standardise first to give

$$
\begin{aligned}
P(M > 1000) &= P\left(Z > \frac{1000 - 910}{\sqrt{9500}}\right) \\
&= P(Z > 0.9233\ldots) = 0.1779.
\end{aligned}
$$

The probability that the mass of the lift cage with 10 adults exceeds 1000 kg is 0.178, correct to 3 significant figures.

Example 4.1.3

An engineering company buys steel rods and steel tubes. Without heating the tubes so that they expand, an insufficient proportion of the rods will fit inside the tubes. Measured in centimetres, the internal diameter at room temperature of a randomly chosen tube is denoted by T, and the diameter at room temperature of a randomly chosen rod is denoted by R. It is given that $T \sim N(4.00, 0.10^2)$, that $R \sim N(4.02, 0.10^2)$, and that T and R are independent.

(a)   Find the probability that a randomly chosen rod would fit inside a randomly chosen tube, without heating the tube.

(b)   The tubes are heated so that the internal diameter of each tube increases by 5%. Find the probability that a randomly chosen rod fits inside a randomly chosen tube, after the tube has been heated.

(OCR)

(a)   In order for a randomly chosen rod to fit inside a randomly chosen tube it is necessary that $T > R$. This inequality can also be expressed as $T - R > 0$, so the problem can be solved by considering the distribution of $T - R$. Since T and R are independent, $T - R$ is normally distributed with

$$E(T - R) = E(T) - E(R)$$
$$= 4.00 - 4.02 = -0.02,$$

and $\text{Var}(T - R) = 1^2 \times \text{Var}(T) + (-1)^2 \times \text{Var}(R)$
$$= (0.10)^2 + (0.10)^2 = 0.02.$$

So $T - R \sim N(-0.02, 0.02)$.

A randomly chosen rod will fit inside a randomly chosen tube if $T - R > 0$.

$$P(T - R > 0) = P\left(Z > \frac{0 - (-0.02)}{\sqrt{0.02}} \right)$$
$$= P(Z > 0.1414\ldots)$$
$$= 0.4437\ldots .$$

The probability that a randomly chosen rod fits inside a randomly chosen tube at room temperature is 0.444, correct to 3 significant figures.

(b)   When the tubes have been heated, their diameter is given by $1.05T$. A rod will now fit inside a tube provided that $1.05T - R > 0$.

$$E(1.05T - R) = 1.05E(T) - E(R)$$
$$= 1.05 \times 4.00 - 4.02$$
$$= 0.18.$$

$$\text{Var}(1.05T - R) = (1.05)^2 \text{Var}(T) + (-1)^2 \text{Var}(R)$$
$$= (1.05)^2 \times (0.1)^2 + (0.1)^2$$
$$= 0.021\,025.$$

Thus $1.05T - R \sim N(0.18, 0.021\,025)$.

$$P(1.05T - R > 0) = P\left(Z > \frac{0 - 0.18}{\sqrt{0.021\,025}} \right)$$
$$= P(Z > -1.241\ldots)$$
$$= 0.8927\ldots .$$

The probability that a randomly chosen rod fits inside a randomly chosen tube after the tube has been heated is 0.893, correct to 3 significant figures.

█ ████████████████████████████████ Exercise 4A ████████████████████████

1 The heights of a population of male students are distributed normally with mean 178 cm and standard deviation 5 cm. The heights of a population of female students are distributed normally with mean 168 cm and standard deviation 4 cm. Find the probability that a randomly chosen female is taller than a randomly chosen male.

2 W is the mass of wine in a fully filled bottle, B is the mass of the bottle and C is the mass of the crate into which 12 filled bottles are placed for transportation, all in grams. It is given that $W \sim N(825, 15^2)$, $B \sim N(400, 10^2)$ and $C \sim N(1500, 20^2)$. Find the probability that a fully filled crate weighs less than 16.1 kg.

3 The times of four athletes for the 400 m are each distributed normally with mean 47 seconds and standard deviation 2 seconds. The four athletes are to compete in a 4×400 m relay race. Find the probability that their total time is less than 3 minutes.

4 The capacities of small bottles of perfume are distributed normally with mean 50 ml and standard deviation 3 ml. The capacities of large bottles of the same perfume are distributed normally with mean 80 ml and standard deviation 5 ml. Find the probability that the total capacity of three small bottles is greater than the total capacity of two large bottles.

5 The diameters of a consignment of bolts are distributed normally with mean 1.05 cm and standard deviation 0.1 cm. The diameters of a consignment of nuts are distributed normally with mean 1.1 cm and standard deviation 0.1 cm. Find the probability that a randomly chosen bolt will not fit inside a randomly chosen nut.

6 The amount of black coffee dispensed by a drinks machine is normally distributed with mean 200 ml and standard deviation 5 ml. If a customer requires white coffee, milk is also dispensed. The amount of milk is distributed normally with mean 20 ml and standard deviation 2 ml. Find the probability that the total amount of liquid dispensed when a customer chooses white coffee is less than 210 ml.

7 Given that $X \sim N(\mu, 10)$, $Y \sim N(12, \sigma^2)$ and $3X - 4Y \sim N(0, 234)$, find μ and σ^2.

4.2 Sampling from a normal population

A researcher for a Ruritanian sock manufacturer states that the average man's foot has a length of 28 cm.

How does she know?

She certainly didn't measure the foot of every Ruritanian man and work out the mean. On the other hand, she didn't just measure the foot of the first Ruritanian man she met in the street, and assume that it was typical of every man in the country.

A practical procedure which comes between these extremes is to select, say, 100 men and take the mean of their foot lengths. They must, of course, be selected randomly; you wouldn't choose too many basketball players or policemen because their feet are likely to be larger than average. There are special techniques to make sure that the selection is free of bias.

But why is it better to take the mean of 100 foot lengths than just one? How many should she select? Would 10 be enough, or should she take 1000? These are questions which can be answered by the results in Section 4.1.

At this stage it is useful to introduce some technical language. The aim of the researcher is to throw light on the complete set of foot lengths of all the men in Ruritania. This set of lengths is called the **population**. (Notice that, in statistics, the population is the set of measurements, *not* the men themselves.) From this population she randomly selects a **sample**. The mean of the sample is then used to give information about the mean of the population.

It is a reasonable assumption that, for the whole population, the lengths can be modelled by a random variable X with a normal distribution $N(\mu, \sigma^2)$. The values of μ and σ^2 are unknown; in fact the researcher is using the sample to help her decide the value of μ.

When the researcher selects her sample, she obtains 100 different lengths $X_1, X_2, \ldots, X_{100}$ from the population. Each of these is an individual random variable whose distribution is the same as that of X; and the random method of selection should ensure that these are independent. (For example, she would not deliberately select two brothers. But there is always the remote possibility that two brothers could be selected by chance, so brothers would not be deliberately excluded either.) She will then take the mean of the 100 lengths, which produces another random variable $\overline{X}$, defined as

$$\overline{X} = \frac{X_1 + X_2 + \ldots + X_{100}}{100}$$
$$= \tfrac{1}{100} X_1 + \tfrac{1}{100} X_2 + \ldots + \tfrac{1}{100} X_{100}.$$

So, from the result in the shaded box in Section 4.1, $\overline{X}$ has normal probability

$$N\left(\tfrac{1}{100}\mu + \tfrac{1}{100}\mu + \ldots + \tfrac{1}{100}\mu, \tfrac{1}{10\,000}\sigma^2 + \tfrac{1}{10\,000}\sigma^2 + \ldots + \tfrac{1}{10\,000}\sigma^2\right),$$

which is $N\left(\mu, \tfrac{1}{100}\sigma^2\right)$. Therefore $\overline{X}$, the mean of the sample, has the same mean as that of the population. But its standard deviation is $\tfrac{1}{10}\sigma$, which is $\tfrac{1}{10}$ of the standard deviation of the population.

This is called the **sampling distribution of the mean**. It is illustrated in Fig. 4.1. The probability density graph on the left is that of $N(\mu, \sigma^2)$, the distribution of the population. The graph on the right is that of $N\left(\mu, \tfrac{1}{100}\sigma^2\right)$, the distribution of the sample mean.

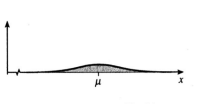
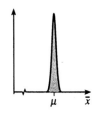

Fig. 4.1

For the theory to be completely valid, the sampling should be carried out 'with replacement'. That is, the method of selection should allow the possibility that the same man's measurement is used more than once. But amongst several million Ruritanian men, the probability of this happening is very small.

The graphs show the advantage of using a sample rather than an individual measurement to make an estimate of μ. Consider the 'two standard deviations' regions which contain more than 95% of the probability of the random variables X and $\overline{X}$. By taking a sample the width of this region has been reduced to one-tenth of its original value.

In general, if a random sample of size n is drawn from a population $N(\mu, \sigma^2)$, then by a similar argument the sampling distribution of the mean is

$$N\left(\frac{1}{n}\mu + \frac{1}{n}\mu + \ldots + \frac{1}{n}\mu, \frac{1}{n^2}\sigma^2 + \frac{1}{n^2}\sigma^2 + \ldots + \frac{1}{n^2}\sigma^2\right), \quad \text{which is} \quad N\left(\mu, \frac{\sigma^2}{n}\right).$$

So if the researcher were to take a sample of 400 foot lengths rather than 100, she would only halve the width of the sampling distribution. Her estimate of μ would certainly be more reliable, but perhaps not enough more to justify the extra expense.

> If the distributions of $X_1, X_2, \ldots, X_n$ are independent $N(\mu, \sigma^2)$ variables, then
>
> the distribution of $\overline{X}$ is $N\left(\mu, \frac{\sigma^2}{n}\right)$.

Example 4.2.1

The mass of a randomly chosen male student in Year 10 at a large secondary school may be modelled by a normal distribution with mean 55 kg and standard deviation 2.2 kg. Four students are chosen at random from this year group. Calculate the probability that the mean mass of the four students is
(a) less than 58 kg,   (b) between 52 kg and 57.5 kg.

Let M_1, M_2, M_3 and M_4 be the masses of four randomly chosen male Year 10 students. Then

$$M_i \sim N(55, 2.2^2) \text{ for } i = 1, 2, 3, 4.$$

Therefore $\overline{M} \sim N\left(55, \frac{2.2^2}{4}\right) = N(55, 1.21)$.

Note that, as the distribution for each M_i is normal, the distribution of $\overline{M}$ is normal.

If you are using normal probability tables, standardise by letting $Z = \dfrac{\overline{M} - 55}{1.1}$, then $Z \sim N(0,1)$.

(a) $P(\overline{M} < 58) = P\left(Z < \dfrac{58 - 55}{1.1}\right)$

$= P(Z < 2.727\ldots)$

$= 0.997$, correct to 3 significant figures.

(b) $P(52 < \overline{M} < 57.5) = P\left(\dfrac{52 - 55}{1.1} < Z < \dfrac{57.5 - 55}{1.1}\right)$

$= P(-2.727\ldots < Z < 2.272\ldots)$

$= 0.985$, correct to 3 significant figures.

If you are using a calculator that gives the answer directly, simply key in $\mu = 55$ and $\sigma = \sqrt{1.21}$, with boundaries $-\infty$ and 58 for part (a), and 52 and 57.5 for part (b).

Example 4.2.2
A second sample of size n is chosen from the male Year 10 students. How large does n have to be for there to be at most a 2% chance that the mean mass of the sample differs from the mean mass of the population by more than 0.6 kg?

Let $M_1, M_2, \ldots, M_n$ be the masses of n randomly chosen Year 10 male students. Then

$$\overline{M} \sim N\left(55, \frac{2.2^2}{n}\right).$$

Then the minimum value of n is required for which

$$P\left(54.4 \le \overline{M} \le 55.6\right) \ge 0.98.$$

Standardising this gives

$$P\left(\frac{-0.6}{2.2/\sqrt{n}} \le Z \le \frac{0.6}{2.2/\sqrt{n}}\right) \ge 0.98.$$

This is illustrated in Fig. 4.2. The shaded area has to be greater than 0.98, so each of the unshaded areas under the graph is less than 0.01. You therefore want to find n such that

$$P\left(Z \le \frac{0.6\sqrt{n}}{2.2}\right) \ge 0.99.$$

Using a calculator or a table of inverse normal probabilities, the number z such that $P(Z \le z) = 0.99$ is $2.326\ldots$. So n must satisfy the inequality

$$\frac{0.6\sqrt{n}}{2.2} \ge 2.326\ldots,$$

$$n \ge \left(\frac{2.326\ldots \times 2.2}{0.6}\right)^2 = 72.7\ldots.$$

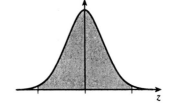

Fig. 4.2

Since n must be an integer, it has to be greater than or equal to 73. So the sample needs to contain at least 73 students for its mean mass to approximate the population's mean mass with the accuracy and certainty desired.

Exercise 4B

1   The body length of a species of ant is normally distributed with mean 3.1 mm and standard deviation 0.2 mm.
   (a) What is the probability that an ant of this species chosen at random has a body length greater than 3.12 mm?
   (b) What is the probability that the mean body length of a sample of
      (i) 9 ants is greater than 3.12 mm,   (ii) 100 ants is greater than 3.12 mm?

2 Random samples of three are drawn from a population of beetles whose lengths have a normal distribution with mean 2.4 cm and standard deviation 0.36 cm. The mean length $\overline{X}$ is calculated for each sample.

(a) State the distribution of $\overline{X}$, giving the values of its parameters.

(b) Find $P(\overline{X} > 2.5)$.

3 The masses of kilogram bags of flour produced in a factory have a normal distribution with mean 1.005 kg and standard deviation 0.0082 kg. A shelf in a store is loaded with 22 of these bags, assumed to be a random sample.

(a) Find the probability that a randomly chosen bag has mass less than 1 kg.

(b) Find the probability that the mean mass of the 22 bags is less than 1 kg.

4 An insurance company offers a pension scheme for retiring executives of large firms. Each firm pays the insurance company $1 200 000 on the day that its executive retires. The insurance company will pay the executives a pension of $10 000 a month for as long as they live. Past experience suggests that the length of retirement enjoyed by executives is normally distributed with a mean of 9 years and a standard deviation of 3 years. If in one year the insurance company sets up 400 such contracts, what is the probability that it will make a loss? (Neglect interest on capital, staff costs, etc.)

One firm decides not to join the scheme, but to pay its retiring executive a pension directly from its own resources. What is the probability that the firm will be better off than if it had joined the scheme?

5 A drink is sold in bottles of nominal capacity 250 ml. A shop takes delivery of 100 bottles. The bottles are filled by a machine which dispenses the drink in quantities which are normally distributed with mean 251.5 ml and standard deviation 5 ml. Find the probabilities that

(a) the delivery does not contain any bottles which are underfilled,

(b) the mean content of all the bottles in the batch is not below the stated capacity.

6 The mean of a random sample of 500 observations of the random variable X, where $X \sim N(25,18)$ is denoted by $\overline{X}$. Find the value of a for which $P(\overline{X} < a) = 0.25$.

7 The life of Powerlong batteries, sold in packs of 6, may be assumed to have a normal distribution with mean 32 hours and standard deviation σ hours. Find the value of σ so that for one box in 100 (on average) the mean life of the batteries is less than 30 hours.

5 Hypothesis testing

An important aim of statistics is to make informed decisions based on data. This chapter uses probability to test hypotheses. When you have completed it, you should

- understand the nature of a hypothesis test
- be able to formulate a null hypothesis and an alternative hypothesis
- understand the difference between a one-tail and a two-tail test
- understand the terms 'critical values', 'significance level', 'rejection region', 'acceptance region' and 'test statistic'
- be able to carry out a hypothesis test of a population mean for a sample drawn from a normal distribution of known variance.

5.1 An introductory example

Over a number of years a primary school has recorded the reading ages of children at the beginning and end of each academic year. The teachers have found that during the third year the increase in reading age is normally distributed with mean 1.14 years and standard deviation 0.16 years. This year they are going to trial a new reading scheme: other schools have tried this scheme and found that it led to a greater increase in reading age. At the end of the year the teachers will use the mean increase in reading age, $\bar{x}$, of the 40 third-year children to help them answer the question: 'Does the new reading scheme give better results than the old one in our school?'

The difficulty in answering this question lies in the fact that each child progresses at a different rate so that different values of $\bar{x}$ will be obtained for different groups of children. It is easy to check whether $\bar{x}$ is greater than 1.14 years. It is not easy to know whether a value of $\bar{x}$ greater than 1.14 years reflects the effectiveness of the new scheme or is just due to random variation between children.

This chapter explores how statistics can be used to arrive at such a decision. The following sections break down the process into several stages.

5.2 Null and alternative hypotheses

There are two theories about how the new reading scheme performs in this particular school. The first is that using the new scheme makes no difference. This theory is called a **null hypothesis**. It is denoted by the symbol H_0. In this example, where the mean of the past increases in reading age is 1.14 years, the null hypothesis can be expressed by $H_0: \mu = 1.14$. Note that H_0 proposes a single value for the population mean, μ, which is based on past experience.

A 'hypothesis' is a theory which is assumed to be true unless evidence is obtained which indicates otherwise. 'Null' means 'nothing' and the term 'null hypothesis' means a 'theory of no change', that is 'no change' from what would be expected from past experience.

The other theory is that the new reading scheme is more effective than the old one, that is that the population mean will increase. This is called the **alternative hypothesis** and is given the symbol H_1. So the alternative hypothesis in this case is $H_1: \mu > 1.14$. The alternative hypothesis proposes the way in which μ will have changed if the new reading scheme is more effective than the old one.

The procedure which is used to decide between these two opposing theories is called a **hypothesis test** or sometimes a **significance test**. In this example the test will be **one-tail** because the alternative hypothesis proposes a change in the mean in only one direction, in this case an increase. It is also possible to have a one-tail test in which the alternative hypothesis proposes a decrease in the mean. Tests in which the alternative hypothesis suggests a difference in the mean in either direction are called **two-tail** tests.

Example 5.2.1

For the following situations give null and alternative hypotheses and say whether a hypothesis test would be one-tail or two-tail.

(a) In the past an athlete has run 100 metres in 10.3 seconds on average. He has been following a new training programme which he hopes will decrease the time he takes to run 100 metres. He is going to time himself on his next six runs.

(b) The bags of sugar coming off a production line have masses which vary slightly but which should have a mean value of 1.01 kg. A sample is to be taken to test whether there has been any change in the mean.

(c) The mean volume of liquid in bottles of lemonade should be at least 2 litres. A sample of bottles is taken in order to test whether the mean volume has fallen below 2 litres.

(a) The null hypothesis proposes a single value for μ, $H_0: \mu = 10.3$, based on the athlete's past performance. The alternative hypothesis proposes how μ might have decreased, $H_1: \mu < 10.3$. This is a one-tail test.

(b) The null hypothesis proposes a single value for μ, $H_0: \mu = 1.01$, based on the mass which the bags should have. The alternative hypothesis proposes how μ might have changed, $H_1: \mu \neq 1.01$. This is a two-tail test.

(c) The null hypothesis proposes that μ should be at least 2, that is $\mu \geq 2$. However, you will see later in the chapter that a single value of μ is needed in order to carry out the calculation in a hypothesis test. So, in this example, the null hypothesis $H_0: \mu = 2$ is taken. This null hypothesis satisfies the criterion that μ is at least 2. A sample is taken in order to test whether the mean has fallen below 2 so the alternative hypothesis is $H_1: \mu < 2$. This is a one-tail test.

For a hypothesis test on the population mean, μ, the null hypothesis, H_0, proposes a value, μ_0, for μ,

$$H_0: \mu = \mu_0.$$

The alternative hypothesis, H_1, suggests the way in which μ might differ from μ_0. H_1 can take three forms:

$H_1: \mu < \mu_0$, a one-tail test for a decrease

$H_1: \mu > \mu_0$, a one-tail test for an increase

$H_1: \mu \neq \mu_0$, a two-tail test for a difference.

In the following situations, state suitable null and alternative hypotheses involving a population with mean μ. You will need some of your answers in Exercise 5B.

1 Bars of Choco are claimed by the manufacturer to have a mean mass of 102.5 grams. A test is carried out to see whether the mean mass of Choco bars is less than 102.5 grams.

2 The mean factory assembly time for a particular electronic component is 84 seconds. It is required to test whether the introduction of a new procedure results in a different assembly time.

3 In a report it was stated that the average age of all hospital patients was 53 years. A newspaper believes that this figure is an underestimate.

4 The manufacturer of a certain battery claims that it has a mean life of 30 hours. A suspicious customer wishes to test the claim.

5 A large batch of capacitors is judged to be satisfactory by an electronics factory if the mean capacitance is at least 5 microfarads. A test is carried out on a batch to determine whether it is satisfactory.

5.3 Critical values

Once you have decided on your null and alternative hypotheses the next step is to devise a rule for choosing between them. Look again at the reading scheme example. The rule will be based on the sample mean, $\bar{x}$. The teachers are only interested in the new scheme if it improves the average increase in reading age and so only values of $\bar{x}$ greater than 1.14 might lead them to drop the old scheme in favour of the new one. Initially, you might think that *any* value of $\bar{x}$ which is greater than 1.14 years would show that the new scheme is more effective. A little more thought shows that is too simple a rule.

It is possible to obtain a sample mean $\bar{x}$ that is greater than 1.14 even if the new reading scheme is not effective at all. To see this suppose that there is no difference between the new reading scheme and the old one. Then both μ and σ will be the same under the two schemes and X will be distributed as $N(1.14, 0.16^2)$.

You have already seen in Section 4.2 that if

$X \sim N(\mu, \sigma^2)$, then $\bar{X} \sim N\left(\mu, \dfrac{\sigma^2}{n}\right)$; so for samples

consisting of 40 children, the mean, $\bar{X}$, will be

distributed as $N\left(1.14, \dfrac{0.16^2}{40}\right)$.

Fig. 5.1 shows the distribution of $\bar{X}$.

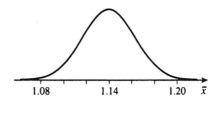

Fig. 5.1

You can see from this diagram that there is a probability of $\frac{1}{2}$ that the sample mean will be greater than 1.14 even though you assumed that there is no change in the population mean.

How big does the sample mean have to be before you can conclude that the population mean is likely to have increased from 1.14? Most people would agree that if a sample mean of 2.00 is obtained then it is unlikely that the population mean is still 1.14; but what about a sample mean of 1.19? One way of tackling this problem is to divide the possible outcomes into two regions: the **rejection** (or **critical**) **region** and the **acceptance region.**

The rejection region will contain values at the top end of the distribution in Fig. 5.1.

If the sample mean is in the rejection region, you reject H_0 in favour of H_1: you conclude that the population mean has increased. If the sample mean is in the acceptance region, you do not reject H_0: there is insufficient evidence to say that the new reading scheme is more effective.

The rejection region is chosen so that it is 'unlikely' for the sample mean to fall in the rejection region when H_0 is true. It is a matter of opinion what you mean by 'unlikely' but a common convention among statisticians is that an event which has a probability of 0.05, that is 1 in 20, or less is 'unlikely'.

Fig. 5.2 shows the rejection region and the acceptance region for the children's reading scheme example. The value, c, which separates the rejection and acceptance regions is called a **critical value**. It can be calculated as follows.

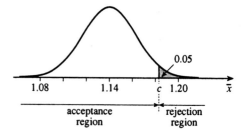

Fig. 5.2

Begin by finding the value of the standardised normal variable, z, such that $P(Z \le z) = 0.95$. Using a calculator or tables, this is $z = 1.645$, correct to 3 decimal places.

The values of the standardised and original variables are related by $z = \dfrac{\bar{x} - \mu}{\sqrt{\dfrac{\sigma^2}{n}}}$ or $z = \dfrac{\bar{x} - \mu}{\dfrac{\sigma}{\sqrt{n}}}$, where $Z \sim N(0,1)$.

Substituting in this equation gives $1.645 = \dfrac{c - 1.14}{\dfrac{0.16}{\sqrt{40}}}$.

Rearranging gives $c = 1.645 \times \dfrac{0.16}{\sqrt{40}} + 1.14 = 1.18$, correct to 3 significant figures.

The rejection region is given by $\bar{X} \ge 1.18$ years.

At the end of the year the observed value for the sample mean was $\bar{x} = 1.19$ years. Since this value is in the rejection region, you can conclude that the observed result is unlikely to be explained by random variation; it is more likely to be due to an increase in the population mean. This suggests that the new reading scheme does give better results than the old one.

In this example a decision is made by considering the value of the sample mean. The sample mean, $\bar{X}$, is called the **test statistic** for this hypothesis test. The rejection region was defined so that the probability of the test statistic falling in it, *if* H_0 *is true*, is at most 0.05, or 5%. This probability is called the **significance level** of the test. It gives the probability of rejecting H_0 when it is in fact true. In this example it gives the probability of concluding that the new reading scheme is better even when it is not. You might feel that this is too high a risk of being wrong and choose instead to use a significance level of, say, 0.01, or 1%.

Example 5.3.1

Find the rejection region for a test at the 1% significance level for the children's reading scheme example.

Now $P(Z \leq z) = 0.99$ gives $z = 2.326$. Substituting into $z = \dfrac{\bar{x} - \mu}{\dfrac{\sigma}{\sqrt{n}}}$ gives

$$2.326 = \dfrac{c - 1.14}{\dfrac{0.16}{\sqrt{40}}}.$$

Rearranging gives $c = 1.20$, correct to 3 significant figures.

The rejection region is $\bar{X} \geq 1.20$.

The observed value of 1.19 years is no longer in the rejection region and so H_0 is not rejected at the 1% significance level.

You may feel that it is unsatisfactory that the result of a hypothesis test should depend on the significance level chosen. This point is discussed in more detail in Section 9.2.

In a two-tail test the rejection region has two parts, because both high and low values of $\bar{X}$ are unlikely if the null hypothesis is true. Example 5.3.2 illustrates this situation.

Example 5.3.2

In the past a machine has produced rope which has a breaking load which is normally distributed with mean 1000 newtons and standard deviation 21 newtons. A new process has been introduced. To test whether the mean breaking load has changed a sample of 50 pieces of rope is taken, the breaking strain of each piece measured and the mean calculated.

(a) Define suitable null and alternative hypotheses for testing whether the breaking load has changed.

(b) Taking the sample mean as the test statistic, find the rejection region for $\bar{X}$ for a hypothesis test at the 5% significance level.

(c) The sample mean for the 50 pieces of rope was 1003 newtons. What can you deduce?

(a) The null hypothesis states the value which the mean breaking load should take, $H_0 : \mu = 1000$.

The alternative hypothesis states how μ might have changed, $H_1 : \mu \neq 1000$.

(b) If H_0 is true, then the sample mean

$\bar{X} \sim N\left(1000, \dfrac{21^2}{50}\right)$. Fig. 5.3 shows the

distribution of $\bar{X}$ with the rejection and acceptance regions. This is a two-tail test so there are two critical values labelled c_1 and c_2.

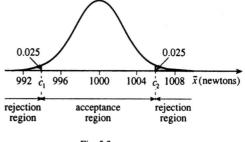

Fig. 5.3

To find the upper critical value, use $P(Z \leq z) = 0.975$, since the 0.05 probability is split equally between the two 'tails' of the distribution. The required value of z is 1.960, correct to 3 decimal places.

Substituting into $z = \dfrac{\bar{x} - \mu}{\dfrac{\sigma}{\sqrt{n}}}$ gives $1.960 = \dfrac{c_2 - 1000}{\dfrac{21}{\sqrt{50}}}$.

Rearranging gives $c_2 = 1006$, to the nearest integer. By symmetry, $c_1 = 994$.

So the rejection region is $\overline{X} \leq 994$ and $\overline{X} \geq 1006$.

(c)   The observed sample mean of $\bar{x} = 1003$ is not in the rejection region. There is not enough evidence to say that the mean has changed and it can be concluded that the new process is satisfactory.

Note that the conclusion to a hypothesis test should always be given in context.

Here is a summary of the terms introduced in this section, followed by a list of the steps involved in carrying out a hypothesis test.

> The **test statistic** is calculated from the sample. Its value is used to decide whether the null hypothesis, H_0, should be rejected.
>
> The **rejection** (or **critical**) **region** gives the values of the test statistic for which the null hypothesis, H_0, is rejected.
>
> The **acceptance region** gives the values of the test statistic for which the null hypothesis, H_0, is not rejected.
>
> The boundary value(s) of the rejection region is (are) called the **critical value(s)**.
>
> The **significance level** of a test gives the probability of the test statistic falling in the rejection region when H_0 is true.

If H_0 is rejected, then H_1 is automatically accepted.

> To carry out a hypothesis test:
>
> **Step 1**   Define the null and alternative hypotheses.
>
> **Step 2**   Decide on a significance level.
>
> **Step 3**   Determine the critical value(s).
>
> **Step 4**   Calculate the test statistic.
>
> **Step 5**   Decide on the outcome of the test depending on whether the value of the test statistic is in the rejection or the acceptance region.
>
> **Step 6**   State the conclusion in words.

Exercise 5B

In the following questions, the rejection (critical) regions should be found in terms of the sample mean, $\overline{X}$.

1   The random variable X has a normal distribution, $N(\mu, 4)$. A test of the null hypothesis $\mu = 10$ against the alternative hypothesis $\mu > 10$ is carried out, at the 5% significance level, using a random sample of 9 observations of X. The rejection region is found to be $\overline{X} \geq 11.10$.

State the conclusion of the test in the following cases.

(a) $\overline{X} = 12.3$ (b) $\overline{X} = 8.6$

2   The random variable Y has a normal distribution, $N(\mu, 9)$. A test of the null hypothesis $\mu = 15$ against the alternative hypothesis $\mu < 15$ is carried out at the 10% significance level, using a random sample of 16 observations. Show that the rejection region is $\overline{Y} < 14.04$.

State the conclusion of the test in the following cases.

(a) $\overline{Y} = 15.5$ (b) $\overline{Y} = 12.7$

3   The random variable X has a normal distribution, $N(\mu, 25)$. A test of the null hypothesis $\mu = 20$ against the alternative hypothesis $\mu \neq 20$ is carried out at the 5% significance level, using a random sample of 4 observations. Show that the rejection region is $\overline{X} < 15.1$ and $\overline{X} > 24.9$.

State the conclusion of the test in the following cases.

(a) $\overline{X} = 17$ (b) $\overline{X} = 13$ (c) $\overline{X} = 30$

4   For the situation in Exercise 5A Question 1, a random sample of 12 bars had a mean mass of 101.4 g. Test, at the 5% significance level, whether the mean mass of all Choco bars is less than 102.5 g, assuming that the mass of a Choco bar is normally distributed with standard deviation 1.7 g.

5   For the situation in Exercise 5A Question 2, a random sample of 40 components had mean assembly time 81.2 s. Assuming that the assembly time of a component has a normal distribution with standard deviation 6.1 s, carry out a test at the 5% significance level of whether the mean for all components differs from 84.0 s.

6   Referring to Exercise 5A Question 5, a random sample of 6 capacitors was selected from the batch. Their capacitances were measured in microfarads with the following results.

       5.12   4.81   4.79   4.85   5.04   4.61

Assuming that the capacitances have a normal distribution with standard deviation 0.35 microfarads, test, at the 2% significance level, whether the batch is satisfactory.

7   The blood pressure of a group of hospital patients with a certain type of heart disease has mean 85.6. A random sample of 25 of these patients volunteered to be treated with a new drug and a week later their mean blood pressure was found to be 70.4. Assuming a normal distribution with standard deviation 15.5 for blood pressures, and using a 1% significance level, test whether the mean blood pressure for all patients treated with the new drug is less than 85.6.

8   Two-litre bottles of a brand of spring water are advertised as containing 6.8 mg of magnesium. In a random sample of 10 of these bottles the mean amount of magnesium was found to be 6.92 mg. Assuming that the amounts of magnesium are normally distributed with standard deviation 0.18 mg, test whether the mean amount of magnesium in all similar bottles differs significantly from 6.8 mg. Use a 5% significance level.

9   The lives of a certain make of battery have a normal distribution with mean 30 h and variance $2.54 \, \text{h}^2$. When a large consignment of these batteries is delivered to a store the quality control manager tests the lives of 8 randomly chosen batteries. The mean life was 28.8 h. Test whether there is cause for complaint. Use a 3% significance level.

10   The birth weights of babies born in a certain large hospital maternity unit during the year 2006 had a normal distribution with mean 3.21 kg and standard deviation 0.73 kg. During the first week of August, there were 24 babies born with a mean weight of 3.17 kg. Using a 5% significance level, test whether the sample is likely to differ from a sample chosen at random from the year's births at the hospital.

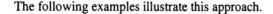

5.4   Standardising the test statistic

In Exercise 5B the rejection region for each question was different and you had to find it before you could obtain the result of the hypothesis test. You may have spotted that the calculation could be shortened by standardising the value of $\overline{X}$ using

$$Z = \frac{\overline{X} - \mu}{\sqrt{\dfrac{\sigma^2}{n}}} = \frac{\overline{X} - \mu}{\dfrac{\sigma}{\sqrt{n}}}$$

and taking Z as the test statistic. For a given type of test, one-tail or two-tail, at a given significance level the rejection region for Z will always be the same.

For example, Fig. 5.4 illustrates the rejection region of Z for a two-tail test at the 5% significance level. The upper critical value is obtained from $P(Z \le z_1) = 0.975$, giving $z_1 = 1.960$, correct to 3 decimal places and, by symmetry, the lower critical value, $z_2 = -1.960$. Thus the rejection region is $Z \ge 1.960$ and $Z \le -1.960$, which you can write more compactly as $|Z| \ge 1.960$.

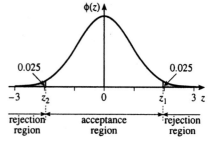

Fig. 5.4

The following examples illustrate this approach.

Example 5.4.1
A test of mental ability has been constructed so that, for adults in the UK, the test score is normally distributed with mean 100 and standard deviation 15. A doctor wishes to test whether sufferers from a particular disease differ in mean from the general population in their performance on this test. She chooses a random sample of 10 sufferers. Their scores on the test are

119   131   95   107   125   90   123   89   103   103.

Carry out a test at the 5% significance level to test whether sufferers from the disease differ from the general population in the way in which they perform at this test.   (OCR, adapted)

The null and alternative hypotheses are $H_0: \mu = 100$ and $H_1: \mu \ne 100$ respectively, where μ is the mean score in a test of mental ability.

This is a two-tail test at the 5% significance level. As explained above, the rejection region for the test statistic, Z, is $|Z| \geq 1.960$.

Under H_0, $\overline{X} \sim N\left(100, \dfrac{15^2}{10}\right)$.

'Under H_0' is another way of saying 'If H_0 is true'.

For this sample,

$$\bar{x} = \tfrac{1}{10}(119 + 131 + 95 + 107 + 125 + 90 + 123 + 89 + 103 + 103) = 108.5.$$

When $\bar{x} = 108.5$, $z = \dfrac{\bar{x} - \mu}{\dfrac{\sigma}{\sqrt{n}}} = \dfrac{(108.5 - 100)}{\dfrac{15}{\sqrt{10}}} = 1.792$, correct to 3 decimal places.

The observed value of Z, 1.792, is not in the rejection region, $|Z| \geq 1.960$, so H_0 is not rejected. There is insufficient evidence, at the 5% significance level, to suggest that sufferers from this disease differ from the general population in their performance on the test.

Example 5.4.2

A manufacturer claims that its light bulbs have a lifetime which is normally distributed with mean 1500 hours and standard deviation 30 hours. A shopkeeper suspects that the bulbs do not last as long as is claimed because he has had a number of complaints from customers. He tests a random sample of six bulbs and finds that their lifetimes are 1472, 1486, 1401, 1350, 1511, 1591 hours. Is there evidence, at the 1% significance level, that the bulbs last a shorter time than the manufacturer claims?

The null and alternative hypotheses are $H_0: \mu = 1500$ and $H_1: \mu < 1500$ respectively, where μ is the mean lifetime of a light bulb in hours.

This is a one-tail test for a decrease at the 1% level. Fig. 5.5 shows the rejection region for Z. The critical value is obtained from $P(Z \leq z) = 0.01$, giving $z = -2.326$ and the rejection region is $Z \leq -2.326$.

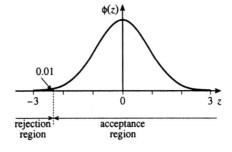

Fig. 5.5

Under H_0, $\overline{X} \sim N\left(1500, \dfrac{30^2}{6}\right)$.

For this sample,

$$\bar{x} = \tfrac{1}{6}(1472 + 1486 + 1401 + 1350 + 1511 + 1591) = 1468.5.$$

When $\bar{x} = 1468.5$, $z = \dfrac{\bar{x} - \mu}{\dfrac{\sigma}{\sqrt{n}}} = \dfrac{1468.5 - 1500}{\dfrac{30}{\sqrt{6}}} = -2.572$, correct to 3 decimal places.

The observed value of Z, -2.572, is in the rejection region, $Z \leq -2.326$. There is evidence, at the 1% significance level, that the manufacturer's bulbs do not last as long as claimed.

You can generalise this method as follows:

The test statistic Z can be used to test a hypothesis about a population mean, $H_0: \mu = \mu_0$, for samples drawn from a normal distribution of known variance σ^2. For a sample of size n, the value of Z is given by

$$z = \frac{\bar{x} - \mu}{\sqrt{\frac{\sigma^2}{n}}} = \frac{\bar{x} - \mu}{\frac{\sigma}{\sqrt{n}}}.$$

The rejection region for Z depends on H_1 and the significance level used. The critical values, correct to 3 decimal places, for some commonly used rejection regions are given below.

Significance level	Two-tail $H_1: \mu \neq \mu_0$	One-tail $H_1: \mu > \mu_0$	One-tail $H_1: \mu < \mu_0$
10%	± 1.645	1.282	-1.282
5%	± 1.960	1.645	-1.645
2%	± 2.326	2.054	-2.054
1%	± 2.576	2.326	-2.326

Exercise 5C

1   Cans of lemonade are filled by a machine which is set to dispense an amount which is normally distributed with mean 330 ml and standard deviation 2.4 ml. A quality control manager suspects that the machine is over-dispensing and tests a random sample of 8 cans. The volumes of the contents, in ml, are as follows:

   329 327 331 326 334 343 328 339.

   Test, at the $2\frac{1}{2}$% significance level, whether the manager's suspicion is justified.

2   The masses of loaves from a certain bakery have a normal distribution with mean μ grams and standard deviation σ grams. When the baking procedure is under control, $\mu = 508$ and $\sigma = 18$. A random sample of 25 loaves from a day's output had a total mass of 12 554 grams. Does this provide evidence at the 10% significance level that the process is not under control?

3   A machine produces elastic bands with breaking tension T newtons, where $T \sim N(45.1, 19.0)$. On a certain day, a random sample of 50 bands was tested and found to have a mean breaking tension of 43.4 newtons. Test, at the 4% significance level, whether this indicates a change in the mean breaking tension.

4   The cholesterol level of healthy males under the age of 21 is normally distributed with mean 160 and standard deviation 10. A random sample of 200 university students, all under age 21, had a mean cholesterol level of 161.8. Test, at the 1% significance level, whether all male university students under age 21 have a mean cholesterol level greater than 160.

5   The mean and standard deviation of the number of copies of *The Daily Courier* sold by a newsagent were 276.4 and 12.2 respectively. During 24 days following an advertising campaign, the total number of copies of *The Daily Courier* sold by the newsagent was 6713. Stating your assumptions, test at the 5% significance level whether the data indicate that the campaign was successful.

5.5   An alternative method of carrying out a hypothesis test

Another way of carrying out a hypothesis test is to calculate the probability that the test statistic takes the observed value (or a more extreme value) and to compare this probability with the significance level. If the probability is less than the significance level then the null hypothesis is rejected. The result is said to be 'significant' at the given significance level. Fig. 5.6 shows that this method will always give the same result as the previous method.

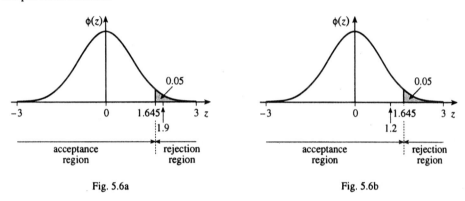

Fig. 5.6a   Fig. 5.6b

Fig. 5.6a shows the rejection region for Z for a one-tail test for an increase at the 5% significance level. If Z takes a value in the rejection region, for example 1.9, then you can see from this figure that $P(Z \geq 1.9)$ is less than 0.05, which would also lead to the rejection of H_0. If Z takes a value in the acceptance region, for example 1.2, as shown in Fig. 5.6b, then $P(Z \geq 1.2)$ is greater than 0.05 and H_0 would not be rejected. To illustrate this idea, look again at Example 5.4.2. In this example, the test statistic took the value -2.572 (correct to 3 decimal places). Low values of Z were of interest so a 'more extreme value' here means a value less than -2.572. The probability that Z took this value or a more extreme value is

$$P(Z \leq -2.572) = 0.005\ 06 = 0.506\%, \text{ correct to 3 significant figures.}$$

Since this probability is less than 1%, the result is significant at the 1% level and so the null hypothesis is rejected. As you would expect this is the same as the conclusion which was reached before. However, this way of quoting the result conveys more information: it shows that the result was significant at the 1% level but not at the 0.5% significance level.

Giving a probability (sometimes called a p -value) rather than using critical values requires a little more work. However, with a calculator it is easy to give a probability and it is becoming more common to give the result of a hypothesis test in this form.

The next example illustrates this approach in a two-tail test.

Example 5.5.1

A machine is designed to produce rods 2 cm long with a standard deviation of 0.02 cm. The lengths may be taken as normally distributed. The machine is moved to a new position in the factory, and in order to check whether the setting for the mean length has altered, the lengths of the first ten rods are measured. The standard deviation may be considered to be unchanged. If these lengths, in cm, are as given below, test at the 5% significance level whether the setting has altered or not.

    2.04 1.97 1.99 2.03 2.04 2.10 2.01 1.98 1.97 2.02   (OCR, adapted)

This is a two-tail test with the null hypothesis assuming that the mean is unaltered.

The null and alternative hypotheses are $H_0: \mu = 2$ and $H_1: \mu \neq 2$ respectively, where μ is the mean length in centimetres of a rod.

Sample mean $= \frac{1}{10}(2.04 + 1.97 + 1.99 + 2.03 + 2.04 + 2.10 + 2.01 + 1.98 + 1.97 + 2.02)$

                 $= 2.015$.

Since the population is normally distributed, $\overline{X}$ is also normally distributed.

Under H_0, $\overline{X} \sim N\left(2, \frac{0.02^2}{10}\right)$.

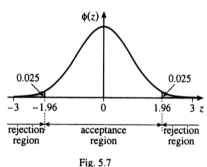

Thus $P(\overline{X} \geq 2.015) = P\left(Z \geq \dfrac{2.015 - 2}{\frac{0.02}{\sqrt{10}}}\right)$

            $= P(Z \geq 2.371\ldots)$

            $= 0.008\,85\ldots$

            $= 0.89\%$, to 2 decimal places.

Fig. 5.7

Since this is a two-tail test, this probability should be compared with half of the value specified in the significance level, that is $2\frac{1}{2}\%$, as shown in Fig. 5.7.

Since 0.89% is less than $2\frac{1}{2}\%$, the result is significant at the 5% level. It can be assumed that the mean length of the rods produced by the machine has been affected by the move.

Some calculators give you the choice of either one-tail or two-tail operation. In that case you would end the calculation in this example by finding the two-tailed probability $P(|Z| \geq 2.371\ldots) = 0.0177\ldots = 1.77\%$ and comparing this with the specified significance level of 5%.

Either method of carrying out a hypothesis test, using critical values or using probabilities, is satisfactory and usually you should use the method which you find easier. However, in later chapters you will meet situations where the probability approach is simpler. For this reason, it is suggested that you carry out Exercise 5D using the probability method.

Exercise 5D

Carry out the hypothesis tests in this exercise by calculating probabilities.

1   The random variable X has a normal distribution with mean μ and variance 25. A random sample of 20 observations of X is taken and the sample mean is denoted by $\overline{X}$. This is used to test the null hypothesis $\mu = 30$ against the alternative hypothesis $\mu < 30$.
(a) Calculate $P(\overline{X} \le 28.4)$.
(b) If the sample mean is, in fact, 28.4, state whether the null hypothesis is rejected at the
    (i) 5% significance level,   (ii) 10% significance level.

2   The alkalinity of soil is measured by its pH value. It has been found from many previous measurements that the pH values in a particular area are normally distributed with mean 8.42 and standard deviation 0.74. After an unusually hot summer the pH values were measured at 36 randomly chosen locations in the area and the sample mean value was found to be 8.63. Calculate $P(\overline{X} > 8.63)$ when $\mu = 8.42$.
What can be concluded
(a) at the 5% significance level,   (b) at the 1% significance level?

3   The average time that I have to wait for the 8.15 bus is 4.3 minutes. A new operator takes over the service, with the same timetable, and my average waiting time for 10 randomly chosen days under the new operator is 3.4 minutes. Assuming that the waiting time has a normal distribution with standard deviation 1.8 minutes, test whether the average waiting time under the new operator has decreased. Use a 10% significance level.

4   The marks of all candidates in an A-Level Statistics examination are normally distributed with mean 42.3 and standard deviation 11.2. The 15 candidates entered from Erehwon High School have a mean mark of 49.8. Test, at the 1% significance level, whether Erehwon High School has unusually good results for this examination.

6 Large sample distributions

Chapter 4 described the effect of drawing samples from a population which is known to be normal. This chapter and the next investigate what happens when samples are drawn from populations which are not normal. When you have completed this chapter, you should

- know that, for large samples, the sum of values of the random variable has a distribution which is approximately normal
- know how to interpret a discrete probability in terms of a continuous random variable
- be able to apply this to find normal approximations to binomial probability distributions.

6.1 The probability distribution for a sample total

Example 6.1.1
A dice has the form of a regular icosahedron, with 20 faces. There are faces with 1, 2, 3, 4 and 5 spots, four faces for each number. Find the probability distribution of the total score when the dice is rolled
(a) once,   (b) twice,   (c) four times.

(a) The probability of getting any one of the scores 1, 2, 3, 4 or 5 is $\frac{4}{20} = 0.2$, so the scores have the probability distribution in Table 6.1.

Score	1	2	3	4	5
Probability	0.2	0.2	0.2	0.2	0.2

Table 6.1

(b) With two rolls the smallest score you can get is $1+1 = 2$ and the largest is $5+5 = 10$.

The probabilities of getting the various scores between 2 and 10 can be found from the two-way table in Fig. 6.2. Above the heavy lines to the left and right are the possible scores on the first and second roll respectively, with their probabilities. Below the heavy lines are nine rows of probabilities, expressed as sums, giving the probabilities of getting a total of 2, 3, ... , 10 when the dice is rolled twice.

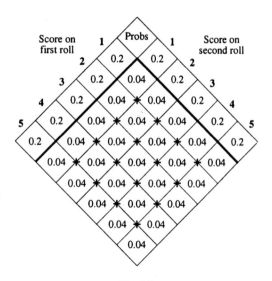

For example, the third row shows the probability of getting a total of 4. This can happen in three ways: 3 on the first roll and 1 on the second, 2 on the first and 2 on the second, 1 on the first and

Fig. 6.2

3 on the second. Each of these outcomes has a probability of $0.2 \times 0.2 = 0.04$, so the probability of getting a total of 4 is

$$0.04 + 0.04 + 0.04 = 0.12.$$

Similar calculations for each of the totals produce the probability distribution in Table 6.3.

Total score	2	3	4	5	6	7	8	9	10
Probability	0.04	0.08	0.12	0.16	0.20	0.16	0.12	0.08	0.04

Table 6.3

(c)   With four rolls the smallest score you can get is 4 and the largest is 20. To find the probabilities you can again use a two-way table, Fig. 6.4. Above the heavy line to the left you have the total scores for the first two rolls, with the probabilities assigned to them in Table 6.3. Above the heavy line to the right you have the total scores for the third and fourth rolls, with the same probability distribution. The rows below the heavy lines are sums giving the probabilities of getting a total of 4, 5, ... when the dice is rolled four times. (In Fig. 6.4 only the first seven rows are shown. It is left to you to complete the table and calculate the remaining probabilities.)

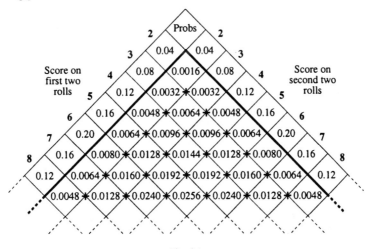

Fig. 6.4

For example, the third row shows the probability of getting a total of 6 with four rolls. This can happen in three ways: 4 on the first two rolls and 2 on the second two, 3 on the first two and 3 on the second two, 2 on the first two and 4 on the second two. From Table 6.3 these outcomes have probabilities of $0.12 \times 0.04 = 0.0048$, $0.08 \times 0.08 = 0.0064$ and $0.04 \times 0.12 = 0.0048$ respectively. So the probability of getting a total of 6 with four rolls is

$$0.0048 + 0.0064 + 0.0048 = 0.0160.$$

Similar calculations for the other rows produce the probability distribution in Table 6.5.

Total score	4	5	6	7	8	9
Probability	0.0016	0.0064	0.0160	0.0320	0.0560	0.0832

Total score	10	11	12	13	14	15
Probability	0.1088	0.1280	0.1360	0.1280	0.1088	0.0832

Total score	16	17	18	19	20
Probability	0.0560	0.0320	0.0160	0.0064	0.0016

Table 6.5

Example 6.1.2

Repeat Example 6.1.1 for an icosahedral dice having eight faces with 2 spots, six with 3 spots, four with 4 spots and two with 5 spots.

(a)   The probabilities of scores of 2, 3, 4, 5 are $\frac{8}{20}$, $\frac{6}{20}$, $\frac{4}{20}$, $\frac{2}{20}$, giving the probability distribution in Table 6.6.

Score	2	3	4	5
Probability	0.4	0.3	0.2	0.1

Table 6.6

(b)   With two rolls the smallest total score is $2+2=4$ and the largest is $5+5=10$. The probabilities can be calculated from Fig. 6.7, in the same way as before, except that the probabilities of different scores for each roll are no longer equal. This gives the probability distribution in Table 6.8.

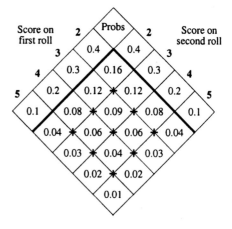

Fig. 6.7

Total score	4	5	6	7	8	9	10
Probability	0.16	0.24	0.25	0.20	0.10	0.04	0.01

Table 6.8

(c)   Proceeding as before, using Fig. 6.9 (which, like Fig. 6.4, is left for you to complete), produces the probability distribution in Table 6.10.

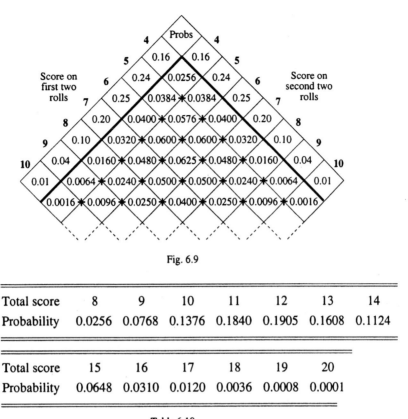

Fig. 6.9

Total score	8	9	10	11	12	13	14
Probability	0.0256	0.0768	0.1376	0.1840	0.1905	0.1608	0.1124

Total score	15	16	17	18	19	20
Probability	0.0648	0.0310	0.0120	0.0036	0.0008	0.0001

Table 6.10

The point of these examples becomes clear when you show these distributions graphically. Figs. 6.11 and Fig. 6.12 show the probability distributions for the dice in Examples 6.1.1 and 6.1.2 respectively.

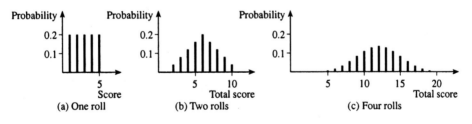

Fig. 6.11

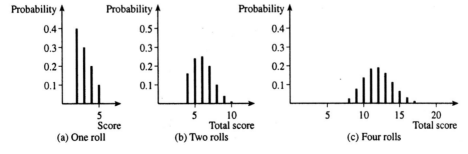

Fig. 6.12

In Fig. 6.11 all the graphs are symmetrical. With one roll the graph is uniform, with two rolls it is triangular, and with four rolls the graph takes a form which will remind you of that of normal probability density.

The graphs in Fig. 6.12 are more surprising, because the graph for one roll is unsymmetrical, with positive skew. However, even with two rolls the mode of the graph has begun to move towards the centre, and with four rolls the graph looks quite symmetrical, and has again begun to resemble the shape of the normal probability graph.

What this illustrates is that the sum of n independent values of a random variable approximates to a normal random variable as the value of n increases. In the examples above, even with four rolls the graphs have begun to take the characteristic bell shape, although the approximation to the actual normal equation is not very close. But if you rolled the dice 100 times, the total scores would approximate very closely to a normal distribution.

From Tables 6.1, 6.3 and 6.5 for Example 6.1.1, and Tables 6.6, 6.8 and 6.10 for Example 6.1.2, you can find the means and variances for the various distributions.

This is a good opportunity to check that you know how to do this using your calculator.

The results are summarised in Tables 6.13 and 6.14 for Examples 6.1.1 and 6.1.2 respectively.

Number of rolls	Mean	Variance
1	3	2
2	6	4
4	12	8

Table 6.13

Number of rolls	Mean	Variance
1	3	1
2	6	2
4	12	4

Table 6.14

There is an obvious pattern here: in both examples the mean and variance are both proportional to the number of rolls. This is what you should expect, since it follows directly by applying the rules of expectation algebra in Section 3.2. If you roll the dice n times, the total score is the sum of the scores in n independent single rolls, each with the probability distribution in Table 6.1 or 6.6. If the distribution of the score X for a single roll has mean μ and variance σ^2, then for the sum of n scores the mean and variance are

$$E(X_1 + X_2 + ... + X_n) = E(X_1) + E(X_2) + ... + E(X_n)$$
$$= \mu + \mu + ... + \mu = n\mu$$

and

$$Var(X_1 + X_2 + ... + X_n) = Var(X_1) + Var(X_2) + ... + Var(X_n)$$
$$= \sigma^2 + \sigma^2 + ... + \sigma^2 = n\sigma^2.$$

You can put this together with the evidence from Fig. 6.11 and Fig. 6.12 that the graphs approach the form of the normal probability density function to obtain the following result.

The sum of n independent values of a random variable with mean μ and variance σ^2 has a distribution which, for large values of n, approximates to the normal distribution $N(n\mu, n\sigma^2)$.

This is true whether the random variable is discrete (as in the examples above) or continuous. There is a small complication when you apply it with a discrete random variable, which is discussed in the next section. Here is an example where it is applied to a continuous random variable.

Example 6.1.3

A map of a motorway shows the distances between successive junctions, each correct to the nearest kilometre. A motorist planning a journey calculates the distance between Junction 1 and Junction 13 by adding twelve of these distances. What is the probability that she gets an answer which is correct to the nearest kilometre?

The error in each recorded distance is between $-\frac{1}{2}$ km and $\frac{1}{2}$ km, with uniform probability distribution. The probability density is therefore

$$f(x) = \begin{cases} 1 & \text{for } -\frac{1}{2} < x < \frac{1}{2}, \\ 0 & \text{otherwise.} \end{cases}$$

The mean of this distribution is obviously 0, and the variance is

$$\int_{-\frac{1}{2}}^{\frac{1}{2}} x^2 \times 1\, dx - 0^2 = \left[\tfrac{1}{3}x^3\right]_{-\frac{1}{2}}^{\frac{1}{2}}$$

$$= \tfrac{1}{24} - \left(-\tfrac{1}{24}\right) = \tfrac{1}{12}.$$

So the sum of twelve of these errors has a distribution which is approximately normal, with mean $12 \times 0 = 0$ and variance $12 \times \frac{1}{12} = 1$.

For the motorist to get an answer correct to the nearest kilometre, the total error must lie between $-\frac{1}{2}$ km and $\frac{1}{2}$ km. You therefore need to find the probability that a $N(0,1)$ random variable is between $-\frac{1}{2}$ and $\frac{1}{2}$. That is,

$$P\left(-\tfrac{1}{2} < x < \tfrac{1}{2}\right) = 0.3829\ldots .$$

The probability that the answer will be correct to the nearest kilometre is approximately 0.383.

The use of the word 'approximately' in the last sentence of the solution is a reminder of a difficulty in applying the result in the shaded box above. There is no general rule for telling whether 12 is a large enough value of n for the normal approximation to give an answer which is accurate to 3 decimal places. This will depend not just on the value of n but also on the nature of the probability distribution for the original random variable X. The more this original distribution resembles normal probability, the smaller n needs to be to give a reasonable approximation. In this example the original distribution is symmetrical about 0, and Fig. 6.11(c) (for a similar discrete distribution) suggests that the sum of 12 errors is likely to produce a distribution which is quite close to the normal form. So the answer of 0.383 obtained from the normal approximation is probably quite close to the actual probability.

Exercise 6A

1   A random variable X has a probability density function

$$f(x) = \begin{cases} \frac{3}{4}(1-x^2) & \text{for } -1 < x < 1, \\ 0 & \text{otherwise.} \end{cases}$$

Find the probability that the sum of 50 independent values of the random variable is greater than 2.

2   A continuous random variable X has a probability density function

$$f(x) = \begin{cases} \frac{1}{2}x & \text{for } 0 < x < 2, \\ 0 & \text{otherwise.} \end{cases}$$

Find the probability that the sum of 90 independent values of the random variable is between 110 and 130.

3   A firm of caterers wishes to buy wine for a wedding reception of 200 guests. They estimate that, on average, each guest will drink 45 cl of wine. The volume of wine in the bottles they buy may be assumed to have a distribution with mean 70.5 cl and standard deviation 1.2 cl. Show that if they buy 128 bottles then the caterers can be more than 95% certain that their requirements will be met.

4   A shoe repairer knows from experience that the mean time that it takes him to complete a job is 25 minutes, with standard deviation 8 minutes. Find the probability that he can get 100 jobs done inside a 40-hour week.

5   An electronic device emits bleeps independently at random at an average rate of one every 10 seconds. State an approximate normal probability model for the time that will elapse before the hundredth bleep occurs. Calculate the probability that there will be at least 100 bleeps in 15 minutes.

6.2 Interpreting discrete probability in continuous terms

You may have thought it rather odd to describe the graphs in Fig. 6.11(c) and Fig. 6.12(c) as 'approximately normal'. These are graphs of discrete distributions, represented by vertical line segments at each integer value of the random variable. How can they resemble the continuous curve which represents normal probability density?

The answer is to represent the discrete distribution in a slightly different way, by a bar chart that looks similar to a histogram. You widen each of the vertical line segments by a $\frac{1}{2}$ unit on either side, so that it becomes a rectangular bar of width 1 unit centred on an integer value. Fig. 6.15 shows this applied to the discrete probability graph in Fig. 6.12(c).

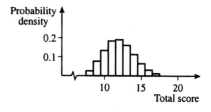

Fig. 6.15

What this does is in effect to replace a discrete random variable X defined by

$$P(X = i) = p_i \quad \text{for } i \in \mathbb{Z}$$

by a continuous random variable X' with probability density defined by

$$f(x') = p_i \quad \text{for } i - \tfrac{1}{2} \le x' < i + \tfrac{1}{2}.$$

It is this random variable X' which is approximated by a normal random variable.

In Fig. 6.16 the graphs of the random variable X' corresponding to Fig. 6.12(c) and the normal probability distribution $N(12,4)$ are shown with the same axes. You can see that, even with just four rolls of the dice, the two graphs are close to each other.

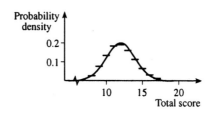

Fig. 6.16

You could object that the graph of X' is made up of horizontal line segments, so it could never really be said to approximate to the smooth normal curve. But in practice what is important about probability density is not the graph itself but the area under the graph, which represents the probability that the random variable lies within a given interval. You would probably agree that if, in Fig. 6.16, you take an interval of values of the random variable, then the areas under the two graphs over this interval would be close to each other.

6.3 A continuity correction

When you use the normal approximation to calculate probabilities in a discrete distribution, you need to take care in choosing the bounds of the interval for which the area under the normal curve is calculated.

Suppose, for example, that for the dice in Example 6.1.2 you want to find the probability of getting a total of 10, 11 or 12 with four rolls. You can, of course, find the exact answer from Table 6.10, as

$$0.1376 + 0.1840 + 0.1905 = 0.5121.$$

What would you get if you used the normal approximation?

In Fig. 6.15, the exact probability is represented by the sum of the areas of the bars extending from 9.5 to 10.5, from 10.5 to 11.5, and from 11.5 to 12.5. So the corresponding area under the normal curve for $N(12,4)$ must be taken over the interval $9.5 \le x \le 12.5$. The calculator gives this as 0.4931.

You might think that 0.4931 is not a very close approximation to the exact value of 0.5121. But considering how skewed the probability distribution is for a single dice, and that four is hardly a 'large number', the agreement between the normal approximation and the exact value is in fact remarkably good.

Example 6.3.1

A boy simulates the results of football matches by rolling a dice. If he throws a 1, 2 or 3, his team wins (3 points). If he throws a 4, the result is a draw (1 point). If he throws a 5 or 6, his team loses (0 points). What is the probability that in this simulation his team will get at least 60 points in a season of 30 matches?

The probability distribution of X, the number of points the boy's team scores in a single match, is shown in Table 6.17.

Points	0	1	3
Probability	$\frac{1}{3}$	$\frac{1}{6}$	$\frac{1}{2}$

Table 6.17

So $E(X) = 0 \times \frac{1}{3} + 1 \times \frac{1}{6} + 3 \times \frac{1}{2} = \frac{5}{3}$

and $\text{Var}(X) = \left(0^2 \times \frac{1}{3} + 1^2 \times \frac{1}{6} + 3^2 \times \frac{1}{2}\right) - \left(\frac{5}{3}\right)^2 = \frac{17}{9}$.

The sum, S, of 30 independent values of X has a distribution which is approximately $N\left(30 \times \frac{5}{3}, 30 \times \frac{17}{9}\right)$, which is $N\left(50, \frac{170}{3}\right)$.

If you represented the exact probabilities of the various values of S by a bar chart, then the bar for 60 points would extend from 59.5 to 60.5, the bar for 61 points from 60.5 to 61.5, and so on. So all the bars for 'at least 60 points' would extend from 59.5 upwards.

Using the normal approximation, the probability of getting at least 60 points is therefore given by $P(S \geq 59.5)$. Using a calculator, with $\mu = 50$ and $\sigma = \sqrt{\frac{170}{3}}$, this probability is $0.1034\ldots$.

The probability that the team will get at least 60 points in the season is approximately 0.103.

The interpretation of 'the probability of at least 60 points' as $P(S \geq 59.5)$ is a natural consequence of replacing the discrete random variable taking only integer values by a continuous random variable. It is called a **continuity correction**. Although the probability 0.103 found in the example is still an approximation to the actual probability, it is considerably closer to the actual value than you would get by calculating $P(S \geq 60)$ with $\mu = 50$ and $\sigma = \sqrt{\frac{170}{3}}$, which gives the value 0.092.

Exercise 6B

1   A dice has the form of a regular icosahedron, with 20 faces. There are faces with 1, 2, 3, 4 and 5 spots, four faces for each number. This dice is rolled four times. Find the probability of getting a total score between 10 and 15 (inclusive)

   (a) exactly,   (b) using the normal approximation.

2   A certain brand of matches has the statement 'average contents 45 matches' printed on the box. In fact, boxes contain 43, 44, 45, 46, 47 matches with probabilities 0.1, 0.2, 0.4, 0.2, 0.1. A customer buys a packet of 30 boxes of these matches. Calculate the probabilities that he gets

   (a) exactly 1350 matches,   (b) between 1345 and 1355 matches (inclusive).

3   A shopkeeper decides to get rid of small change by rounding all payments at the check-out to the nearest 10 cents. If the amount ends in 5 cents, he gives the customer the benefit. On one day he serves 800 customers. Assuming that the numbers of 'odd cents' are randomly distributed, find the probability that on that day he will lose more than 5 dollars as a result of this policy.

4   Two children play games of scissors/paper/stone. (Scissors cut paper, paper wraps stone, stone blunts scissors.) In each game they make their choice randomly, and the outcome is given in the following table.

		B chooses		
		scissors	paper	stone
	scissors	draw	A wins	B wins
A chooses	paper	B wins	draw	A wins
	stone	A wins	B wins	draw

Find the probability that, after 60 games, one player leads the other by more than 10 wins.

5   A table of random digits (between 0 and 9) is arranged in 50 rows and 80 columns. Find the expectation of the number of columns in which the sum of the 50 random digits is less than 200.

6.4   A normal approximation to binomial probability

Example 6.4.1
In a city election there is 35% support for the Happy Party candidate, but only 3% support for the Angry Party candidate. A researcher selects 80 citizens at random and asks them how they propose to vote. Draw graphs (in the form of bar charts) showing the probability distributions of the number of people interviewed who support each candidate.

At each interview the researcher will register 1 Happy supporter with probability 0.35, and 0 with probability 0.65. The total number of pro-Happy responses is equal to the number of 1s she registers in all 80 interviews. This therefore has binomial probability with $n = 80$ and $p = 0.35$, denoted by $B(80, 0.35)$. Its graph is shown in Fig. 6.18.

The probability distribution for the total number of pro-Angry supporters is $B(80, 0.03)$. Its graph is shown in Fig. 6.19.

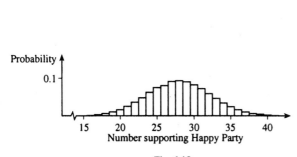

Fig. 6.18

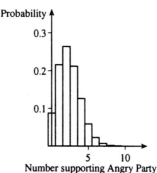

Fig. 6.19

The graphs in Example 6.4.1 look very different. You would probably agree that Fig. 6.18 looks very close to a normal probability graph, but Fig. 6.19 less so. The reason for this is that, for each interview, the probabilities of a 'no' and a 'yes' for the Happy Party are not too unbalanced (0.65 as against 0.35), whereas for the Angry Party the balance is heavily weighted on the 'no' side (0.97 as against 0.03).

In general, binomial probability results from a sequence of separate independent trials, for each of which there are just two possible outcomes – success and failure. A single trial of this kind is called a **Bernoulli trial**. If the random variable X denotes the number of successes in a single trial, then X can take values 0 or 1; and if the probability of success is p and the probability of failure is q (where $q = 1 - p$), the probability distribution for X is given in Table 6.20.

X	0	1
Probability	q	p

Table 6.20

This is the **Bernoulli probability distribution**. It is denoted by $B(1, p)$, because it is simply a binomial distribution $B(n, p)$ with $n = 1$.

Jacob Bernoulli, after whom the distribution is named, was the oldest of a remarkable family of mathematicians which extended over three generations through the late 17th and the 18th century.

From Table 6.20 you can calculate

$$\mu = 0 \times q + 1 \times p = p,$$

and

$$\sigma^2 = \left(0^2 \times q + 1^2 \times p\right) - p^2$$
$$= p - p^2$$
$$= p(1 - p) = pq.$$

> The mean and variance of the Bernoulli probability distribution $B(1, p)$ are
>
> $$\mu = p, \quad \sigma^2 = pq.$$

The general binomial probability distribution gives the probability of the number of successes in a sequence of n independent Bernoulli trials with the same value of p. You can then apply the result in the shaded box in Section 6.1, and deduce a normal distribution to which the binomial approximation approximates when n is large. This normal distribution has mean and variance $n\mu$ and $n\sigma^2$, that is np and npq.

> For large values of n the binomial probability distribution $B(n, p)$ approximates to normal probability density $N(np, npq)$.

For example, the distribution in Fig. 6.18 approximates to $N(80 \times 0.35, 80 \times 0.35 \times 0.65)$, which is $N(28, 18.2)$.

But Example 6.4.1 shows that the validity of this approximation doesn't only depend on the value of n. Both Fig. 6.18 and Fig. 6.19 were drawn with $n = 80$, but you have seen that Fig. 6.18 approximates closely to a normal distribution, but Fig. 6.19 doesn't. A useful working rule is that, for a good approximation, the values of np and nq should both exceed 10.

> The approximation $B(n, p) \approx N(np, npq)$ can be used with confidence if $np > 10$ and $nq > 10$.

That is, binomial probability can be reliably approximated by normal probability if the expected numbers of successes and failures are greater than 10.

Some statisticians have a less demanding criterion, and use the normal approximation if the expected numbers of successes and failures are greater than 5.

Thus for Fig. 6.18, $np = 80 \times 0.35 = 28$ and $nq = 80 \times 0.65 = 52$, both of which are greater than 10, so the normal approximation is valid. But for Fig. 6.19, $np = 80 \times 0.03 = 2.4$ which is less than 10, so the graph is not approximately normal.

Example 6.4.2
It is estimated that 20% of men take size 8 shoes, and 2% take size 12. A shoe store expects 120 male customers in the next week, and buys in

(a) 30 pairs of size 8,   (b) 3 pairs of size 12.

Without using a cumulative binomial program, calculate the probabilities that these will be enough.

(a)   If X denotes the number of size 8 customers, this has probability distribution $B(120, 0.2)$, and you want to find the probability that X is less than or equal to 30.

Since $np = 120 \times 0.2 = 24$ and $nq = 120 \times 0.8 = 96$, and both of these are greater than 10, you can approximate to $B(120, 0.2)$ with the normal probability distribution $N(120 \times 0.2, 120 \times 0.2 \times 0.8)$, which is $N(24, 19.2)$.

The requirement that the discrete random variable X should be less than or equal to 30 is replaced by the requirement that the continuous random variable X' should be less than 30.5. Using the normal approximation, the calculator gives this probability as 0.931, correct to 3 significant figures. Alternatively, using tables of standardised normal probability,

$$P(X' < 30.5) = P\left(Z < \frac{30.5 - 24}{\sqrt{19.2}}\right)$$
$$= P(Z < 1.483...) = 0.931.$$

The probability that the store will have enough size 8 shoes is approximately 0.931.

Compare this with the more accurate answer 0.928 given by the cumulative binomial program.

(b)   The probability distribution for the number Y of size 12 customers is $B(120, 0.02)$, for which $np = 120 \times 0.02 = 2.4$. The normal approximation therefore can't be used, and you must calculate the probability that $Y \leq 3$ directly from the binomial formula. That is,

$$P(Y \leq 3) = P(Y = 0) + P(Y = 1) + P(Y = 2) + P(Y = 3)$$

$$= 0.98^{120} + \binom{120}{1} \times 0.98^{119} \times 0.02 + \binom{120}{2} \times 0.98^{118} \times 0.02^2$$

$$+ \binom{120}{3} \times 0.98^{117} \times 0.02^3$$

$$= 0.0885\ldots + 0.2168\ldots + 0.2632\ldots + 0.2113\ldots$$

$$\approx 0.780.$$

The probability that the store will have enough size 12 shoes is 0.780, correct to 3 significant figures.

Example 6.4.3

(a)   Wine is packed in cases, each holding 12 bottles. Because of a fault at the bottling plant, 10% of the bottles contain less wine than is stated on the label. Find the probability that a case contains two or more underfilled bottles.

(b)   The vineyard sends 500 cases to a wine merchant. What is the probability that more than 150 of these will contain two or more underfilled bottles?

(a)   This is a straight binomial calculation. The distribution of underfilled bottles in a case is $B(12, 0.1)$. The calculator program for cumulative binomial probability gives the probability of one or fewer underfilled bottles as 0.6590, correct to 4 decimal places. So the probability of two or more underfilled bottles in a case is $1 - 0.6590 = 0.3410$.

(b)   The distribution of these cases in a consignment of 500 is $B(500, 0.3410)$, which is approximately $N(500 \times 0.3410, 500 \times 0.3410 \times 0.6590)$, which is $N(170.5, 112.36)$. In terms of a continuous random variable, 'more than 150 cases' is interpreted as 'greater than 150.5'. The calculator program for normal probability gives the probability as 0.970.

There is a 97% probability that more than 150 of the cases will contain at least two underfilled bottles.

Exercise 6C

1   A random variable, X, has a binomial distribution with parameters $n = 40$ and $p = 0.3$. Use a suitable approximation, which you should show is valid, to calculate the following probabilities.

(a) $P(X \geq 18)$ (b) $P(X < 9)$ (c) $P(X = 15)$ (d) $P(11 < X < 15)$

2   The mass production of a cheap pen results in there being 1 defective pen in 20 on average. Use an approximation, which you should show is valid, to find, in a batch of 300 of these pens, the probability of there being

(a)   24 or more defective pens,   (b)   10 or fewer defective pens.

3 A manufacturer states that '3 out of 4 people prefer our product (Acme) to a competitor's product'. To test this claim a researcher asks 80 people about their liking for Acme. Assuming that the manufacturer is correct, find the probability that fewer than 53 prefer Acme. If 1000 researchers each questioned 80 people, how many of these researchers would be expected to record 'fewer than 53 prefer Acme' results?

4 An ordinary unbiased dice is thrown 900 times. Using a suitable approximation, find the probability of obtaining at least 160 sixes.   (OCR)

5 It is given that 40% of the population support the Gamboge Party. One hundred and fifty members of the population are selected at random. Use a suitable approximation to find the probability that more than 55 out of the 150 support the Gamboge Party.   (OCR)

7 The central limit theorem

It is shown in this chapter that the means of large samples from any population have an approximately normal distribution. When you have completed it, you should

- know and be able to apply the central limit theorem
- know how to apply a continuity correction for the means of samples of a discrete random variable.

7.1 The sampling distribution of the mean

It was shown in Section 4.2 that if you take a sample of n values from a normal population with distribution $N(\mu, \sigma^2)$, then the distribution of the mean of the sample is $N\left(\mu, \dfrac{\sigma^2}{n}\right)$.

But how do you know that the population from which you are taking the sample has a normal distribution?

The practical answer to this question is that, if you take a large enough sample, it doesn't matter.

In Section 6.1 you found that the sum, S, of n values of a random variable taken from *any* population with mean μ and variance σ^2 has a distribution which, for large enough values of n, approximates to the normal distribution $N(n\mu, n\sigma^2)$. If the mean of the sample is $\overline{X}$, then $\overline{X} = \dfrac{1}{n} \times S$. So

$$E(\overline{X}) = \frac{1}{n} E(S) = \frac{1}{n} \times n\mu = \mu \quad \text{and} \quad \operatorname{Var}(\overline{X}) = \frac{1}{n^2} \operatorname{Var}(S) = \frac{1}{n^2} \times n\sigma^2 = \frac{\sigma^2}{n}.$$

It follows that, for large values of n, the sample mean $\overline{X}$ has a distribution which approximates to the normal distribution $N\left(\mu, \dfrac{\sigma^2}{n}\right)$. This is called the **central limit theorem.**

> **The central limit theorem** For any sequence of independent identically distributed random variables X_1, X_2, ... , X_n with mean μ and non-zero variance σ^2, provided that n is sufficiently large, $\overline{X} = \dfrac{X_1 + X_2 + ... + X_n}{n}$ has approximately a normal distribution with mean μ and variance $\dfrac{\sigma^2}{n}$.
>
> In symbols, $\overline{X} \sim N\left(\mu, \dfrac{\sigma^2}{n}\right)$.

This theorem is a fundamental result in the theory of statistics and it explains why the normal distribution is so widely studied. The essential point is that it does not matter what distribution X_1, X_2, ... , X_n have individually: as long as they all have the same distribution and are independent of one another, the distribution of the mean $\overline{X}$ will be approximately normal as long as n is sufficiently large. So the theory in Chapter 4 about the distribution of the sample mean and its application in Chapter 5 to hypothesis testing can be used whether or not the background population is normal, provided that you take a large enough sample.

Example 7.1.1

A continuous random variable, X, has a probability density function, $f(x)$, given by

$$f(x) = \begin{cases} 2x & \text{for } 0 \le x \le 1, \\ 0 & \text{otherwise.} \end{cases}$$

Find   (a) the mean, μ,   (b) the variance, σ^2, of this distribution.

A random sample of 100 observations is taken from this distribution, and the mean $\overline{X}$ is found.

(c) Find the mean and variance of $\overline{X}$.   (d) Calculate $P(\overline{X} < 0.68)$.

(a) Using the definition of the mean of a continuous random variable,

$$\mu = \int_0^1 x \times 2x \, dx$$
$$= \int_0^1 2x^2 \, dx$$
$$= \left[\tfrac{2}{3}x^3\right]_0^1 = \tfrac{2}{3}.$$

(b) $\sigma^2 = \int_0^1 x^2 \times 2x \, dx - \left(\tfrac{2}{3}\right)^2$

$$= \int_0^1 2x^3 \, dx - \left(\tfrac{2}{3}\right)^2$$
$$= \left[\tfrac{2}{4}x^4\right]_0^1 - \left(\tfrac{2}{3}\right)^2 = \tfrac{1}{2} - \tfrac{4}{9} = \tfrac{1}{18}.$$

(c) $E(\overline{X}) = \mu = \tfrac{2}{3}$ and $Var(\overline{X}) = \dfrac{\sigma^2}{n} = \dfrac{\frac{1}{18}}{100} = \tfrac{1}{1800}.$

(d) By the central limit theorem, the distribution of $\overline{X}$ is approximately $N\left(\tfrac{2}{3}, \tfrac{1}{1800}\right)$.

Using a calculator, or by using tables to calculate $P\left(Z < \dfrac{0.68 - \frac{2}{3}}{\sqrt{\frac{1}{1800}}}\right)$, you find that

$P(X < 0.68) = 0.714$, correct to 3 significant figures.

7.2* Applying a continuity correction

When you use the central limit theorem with a discrete population you should apply a continuity correction similar to that used for sums in Section 6.3.

If the discrete random variable takes consecutive integer values, then for sums this involves an adjustment of $\pm\tfrac{1}{2}$ (the $\pm$ sign depending on whether you are dealing with a > or a < condition) to interpret the distribution of sums in terms of a continuous random variable. For means, since these are found by dividing sums by n, the amount of the adjustment is $\pm\dfrac{1}{2n}$.

This is illustrated in Example 7.2.1 for the case when the background population has Bernoulli probability.

Example 7.2.1

About 1 in 7 of the words in the English language begin with the letter S. What is the probability that, in an article of 200 words, fewer than 10% begin with an S?

If there are R occurrences of words beginning with the letter S, then the proportion of these in the article is $\dfrac{R}{200}$. This is the mean number of 'successes' (that is, words beginning with S) in a sequence of 200 Bernoulli trials. The condition 'fewer than 10%' means 'fewer than 20 words', which you would interpret in continuous terms as $R < 19.5$. So 'fewer than 10%' would be interpreted as a proportion of less than $\dfrac{19.5}{200}$, which in continuous terms is 'less than 9.75%'.

For a single Bernoulli trial, with $p = \frac{1}{7}$, the mean is $p = \frac{1}{7}$ and the variance is $pq = \frac{1}{7} \times \frac{6}{7} = \frac{6}{49}$. So, by the central limit theorem, the mean for 200 words has approximately normal distribution

$$N\left(\frac{1}{7}, \frac{\frac{6}{49}}{200}\right), \text{ which is } N\left(\frac{1}{7}, \frac{3}{4900}\right).$$

Using the cumulative normal distribution, the probability that the mean is less than 0.0975 is

$$P\left(Z < \frac{0.0975 - \frac{1}{7}}{\sqrt{\frac{3}{4900}}}\right),$$

which is 0.0334, correct to 3 significant figures.

In this example, notice that the continuity correction involves replacing a proportion of 0.1 by 0.0975, a difference of $0.0025 = \frac{1}{400}$. With $n = 200$, this difference is $\dfrac{1}{2n}$.

Example 7.2.2

(a) If X denotes the number of sixes obtained when a fair cubical dice is thrown 12 times, determine $E(X)$ and $Var(X)$.

(b) Forty students each threw a fair cubical dice 12 times. Each student then recorded the number of times that a six occurred in their own 12 throws. The students' lecturer then calculated the mean number of sixes obtained per student. Give an approximate distribution for this mean and find the probability that it exceeds 2.2.

(a) X satisfies the conditions for a binomial distribution to apply. The parameters of the binomial distribution in this case are $n = 12$ and $p = \frac{1}{6}$.

Recall that for a random variable X which has a binomial distribution, $\mu = np$ and $\sigma^2 = npq$.

So, in this case,

$$E(X) = 12 \times \tfrac{1}{6} = 2 \quad \text{and} \quad \text{Var}(X) = 12 \times \tfrac{1}{6} \times \tfrac{5}{6} = \tfrac{5}{3}.$$

(b)   The sample of students' results is drawn from a background population which is binomial, and which has a graph similar to the normal probability graph. So a sample of size 40 is certainly large enough for the normal approximation to give accurate answers. Using the central limit theorem, $\overline{X} \sim N\left(2, \dfrac{\frac{5}{3}}{40}\right) = N\left(2, \tfrac{1}{24}\right)$, approximately.

To find the probability that $\overline{X} > 2.2$ you need to apply a continuity correction. Recall that the lecturer calculates $\overline{X}$ by dividing T by 40, where T is the total number of sixes of all the students. So the condition $\overline{X} > 2.2$ is equivalent to $T > 40 \times 2.2 = 88$.

To apply the normal approximation T is replaced by a continuous variable T', and the condition $T > 88$ is replaced by $T' > 88\tfrac{1}{2}$. In the same way, $\overline{X}$ is replaced by a continuous random variable $\overline{X}'$, and you require the probability that $\overline{X}' > 2.2 + \tfrac{1}{80} = 2.2125$.

Notice that, as in Example 7.2.1, the continuity correction is $\dfrac{1}{2n}$, this time with $n = 40$.

With the usual standardisation,

$$P\left(\overline{X}' > 2.2 + \tfrac{1}{80}\right) = P\left(Z > \frac{2.2125 - 2}{\sqrt{\tfrac{1}{24}}}\right)$$
$$= 0.149, \text{ correct to 3 significant figures.}$$

> When a discrete distribution is approximated by a continuous distribution, the continuity correction for the sample mean, $\overline{X}$, is $\dfrac{1}{2n}$ for a sample of size n.

Exercise 7

1   A random variable X has mean 50 and variance 1000. A random sample of 40 observations of X is taken and the mean, $\overline{X}$, of these observations is calculated. How, approximately, is $\overline{X}$ distributed?
Find
(a) $P(\overline{X} < 55)$,   (b) $P(\overline{X} > 40)$,   (c) $P(40 < \overline{X} < 55)$.

2   A discrete random variable, Y, has the probability distribution shown below.

y	1	2	3	4
$P(Y = y)$	0.1	0.2	0.5	0.2

For this distribution, find

(a) the mean, μ,   (b) the variance, σ^2.

A random sample of 50 observations of Y is taken. Find

(c) $P(\overline{Y} < 2.6)$ (d) $P(|\overline{Y} - \mu| < 0.2)$.

3   An unbiased dice is thrown once. Write down the probability distribution of the score X and show that $\text{Var}(X) = \frac{35}{12}$.

The same dice is thrown 70 times.

(a) Find the probability that the mean score is less than 3.3.

(b) Find the probability that the mean exceeds 3.8.

4   A rectangular field is gridded into squares of side $1\,\text{m}$. At one time of the year the number of snails in the field can be modelled by a Poisson distribution with mean 2.25 per m^2.

(a) A random sample of 120 squares is observed and the number of snails in each square counted. Find the probability that the sample mean number of snails is at most 2.5.

(b) A random sample of 100 squares is observed and the number of snails in each square is counted. Find the probability that the sample mean number of snails is at least 2.

5   The random variable X has a $B(40, 0.3)$ distribution. The mean of a random sample of n observations of X is denoted by $\overline{X}$. Find

(a) $P(\overline{X} \geq 13)$, assuming a sample size of 49,

(b) the smallest value of n for which $P(\overline{X} \geq 13) < 0.001$.

6   The number of tickets sold each day at a city railway station during the winter has mean 512 and variance 1600. For a randomly chosen period of 60 winter days, find the probability that the mean number of tickets sold per day over this period is less than 500.

8 Hypothesis testing with discrete variables

This chapter takes further the idea of hypothesis testing introduced in Chapter 5. When you have completed it, you should

- be able to formulate hypotheses and carry out a hypothesis test of a population proportion by either evaluation of binomial probabilities or by the use of the normal approximation
- understand the difference between a nominal and an actual significance level.

8.1 Testing a population proportion

Advertisements for dairy spreads have claimed that the spread cannot be distinguished from butter. How could you set about testing this claim? One way would be to take pairs of biscuits and put butter on one biscuit in each pair and the dairy spread on the other. The pairs of biscuits would be given to a number of tasters who would be asked to identify the biscuit with butter on it. Half the tasters would be given the 'butter' biscuit first, and the other half the 'butter' biscuit second.

Suppose you decided to use 10 tasters. How would you set about drawing a conclusion from your results? The method of hypothesis testing described in Chapter 5 can be adapted to this situation. First it is necessary to formulate a null hypothesis and an alternative hypothesis. It is usual to start from a position of doubt: you assume that the tasters cannot identify the butter and that they are guessing. In this situation the probability that a taster chosen at random will get the correct result is $\frac{1}{2}$. This can be expressed by the null hypothesis $H_0: p = \frac{1}{2}$. If some of the tasters can actually identify the butter then $p > \frac{1}{2}$. This can be expressed as an alternative hypothesis, $H_1: p > \frac{1}{2}$.

Can you see why it is difficult to take any other null hypothesis?

If H_0 is true, the number, X, of tasters who identify the buttered biscuit correctly is a random variable with distribution $B\left(10, \frac{1}{2}\right)$. Fig. 8.1 shows this distribution.

High values of X would suggest that H_0 should be rejected in favour of H_1. The most straightforward method of carrying out a hypothesis test for a discrete variable is to use the approach of Section 5.5 and calculate the probability that X takes the observed or a more extreme value assuming that H_0 is true and

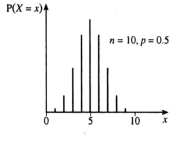

Fig. 8.1

compare this probability with the specified significance level. Suppose that 9 out of the 10 people had identified the butter and you chose a significance level of 5%. Using the cumulative binomial probability program on your calculator gives

$$= 1 - 0.989\,25\ldots = 0.010\,74\ldots = 1.07\%, \text{ correct to 3 significant figures.}$$

This probability is less than 5% so the result is significant at the 5% level. H_0 is rejected and there is evidence, at the 5% significance level, that the proportion of people who can distinguish the butter is greater than $\frac{1}{2}$.

As in Section 5.3 the possible values of X can be divided into an acceptance region and a rejection region. However the situation here is complicated by the fact that X is a discrete variable. Table 8.2 shows the probability distribution of X.

x	0	1	2	3	4	5	6	7	8	9	10
$P(X=x)$	0.0010	0.0098	0.0439	0.1172	0.2051	0.2461	0.2051	0.1172	0.0439	0.0098	0.0010

Table 8.2

For a nominal significance level of, say, 5%, you will find that there is no rejection region which exactly corresponds to this probability. For example, for a rejection region of $X \geq 8$, the probability of a result in the rejection region is $0.0439 + 0.0098 + 0.0010 = 0.0547$ and so the actual significance level of the test is 5.47%; for $X \geq 9$, the actual significance level is 1.07%. This point will be considered in more detail in Section 9.3.

Example 8.1.1
A national opinion poll claims that 40% of the electorate would vote for party R if there were an election tomorrow. A student at a large college suspects that the proportion of young people who would vote for them is lower. She asks 16 fellow students, chosen at random from the college roll, which party they would vote for. Three choose party R. Show, at the 10% significance level, that this indicates that the reported figure is too high for the young people at the student's college.

The null and alternative hypotheses are $H_0: p = 0.4$ and $H_1: p < 0.4$ respectively.

Let X be the number of students who choose party R. Under H_0, $X \sim B(16, 0.4)$.

Using the cumulative binomial probability program on your calculator,

$P(X \leq 3) = 0.0651... = 6.51\%$, correct to 3 significant figures.

This probability is less than 10% so the result is significant at the 10% level. H_0 is rejected, indicating that the reported figure is too high for young people at the student's college.

Example 8.1.2
In order to test a coin for bias it is tossed 20 times. The result is 14 heads and 6 tails. Test, at the 10% significance level, whether the coin is biased.

This is a two-tail test since, before the coin is tossed, there is no indication in which direction, if any, it might be biased. If the coin is unbiased, the probability of a head (or a tail) is $p = 0.5$.

The null and alternative hypotheses are $H_0: p = 0.5$ and $H_1: p \neq 0.5$ respectively.

Let X be the number of heads resulting from 20 tosses. Under H_0, $X \sim B(20, 0.5)$. On average you would expect 10 heads, so the observed value of 14 is on the high side. Using your calculator,

$P(X \geq 14) = 1 - P(X \leq 13)$

$= 1 - 0.942\,34... = 0.057\,65... = 5.77\%$, correct to 3 significant figures.

Since this is a two-tail test at the 10% significance level, this probability must be compared with 5%. Since 5.77% > 5% the result is not significant and the null hypothesis is not rejected: there is insufficient evidence, at the 10% level, to say that the coin is biased.

To carry out a hypothesis test on a discrete variable, calculate the probability of the observed or a more extreme value and compare this probability with the significance level. For a one-tail test, reject the null hypothesis if this probability is less than the significance level; for a two-tail test use the side that produces a probability of less than 50% and reject the null hypothesis if this probability is less than half of the significance level.

Exercise 8A

1   A large housing estate contains a children's playground, and on one particular evening 12 boys and 6 girls were playing there. Assuming these children are a random sample of all children living on the estate, test, at the 10% significance level, whether there are equal numbers of boys and girls on the estate.

2   An advertisement in a newspaper inserted by a car dealer claimed, 'At least 95% of our customers are satisfied with our services.'

In order to check this statement a random sample of 25 of the dealer's customers were contacted and 22 agreed that they were satisfied with the dealer's services. Carry out a test, at the 5% significance level, of whether the data support the claim.

3   The lengths of nails produced by a machine have a normal distribution with mean 2.5 cm. A random sample of 16 nails is selected from a drum containing a large number of these nails. The nails are measured and 13 are found to have length greater than 2.5 cm. Test, at the $2\frac{1}{2}$% significance level, whether the mean length of the nails in the drum is greater than 2.5 cm. State where in the test the information that the nails have a normal distribution is used.

4   A test of 'telepathy' is devised using cards with faces coloured either red, green, blue or yellow, in equal numbers. When a card is placed face down on a table, at random, Ilesh believes he can forecast the colour of the face correctly. The cards are thoroughly mixed, one is selected and placed face down on the table and Ilesh forecasts the colour of the face. This procedure was repeated 20 times.

(a) It is given that Ilesh was correct on 8 occasions. Test, at the 5% significance level, whether Ilesh's results were better than could have been achieved by chance.

(b) How many forecasts would Ilesh have had to make to be significant at the 1% level?

5   A dice is suspected of being loaded to give more sixes when thrown than would be expected from a fair dice. In order to test this suspicion, the dice is thrown 30 times. Ten sixes are obtained. Carry out a test at the 5% significance level to test this suspicion.

6   A magazine article reported that 80% of computer owners use the internet facility regularly. Lisa believed that the true figure was different and she consulted 12 of her friends who owned computers. Six said that they were regular users of the internet facility.

(a) Test Lisa's belief at the 10% significance level.

(b) Comment on the reliability of the test in the light of Lisa's sample.

8.2 Testing a population proportion for large samples

When the sample is large an alternative method of calculating probabilities is to use the fact that the binomial distribution can be approximated by the normal distribution with a continuity correction. This is especially useful in problems for which you need to use the inverse function, because your calculator has an inverse program for normal probability but no corresponding program for binomial probability.

Example 8.2.1

In a multiple choice paper with 100 questions a candidate has to select one of four possible answers to each question. How many questions would a candidate need to answer for the examiner to be persuaded, at the 5% significance level, that he is not guessing the answers?

If the student is guessing the answers, then the probability p that any one answer is correct is $\frac{1}{4}$. If the student is not guessing then the proportion of correct answers should be greater than this.

The null and alternative hypotheses are $H_0: p = \frac{1}{4}$ and $H_1: p > \frac{1}{4}$.

Let X be the number of correct answers. Under H_0, $X \sim B\left(100, \frac{1}{4}\right)$. This can be approximated by a normal distribution with

$$\mu = np = 100 \times \tfrac{1}{4} = 25 \quad \text{and} \quad \sigma^2 = npq = 100 \times \tfrac{1}{4} \times \tfrac{3}{4} = 18.75.$$

So $X \sim B\left(100, \frac{1}{4}\right)$ is approximated by $V \sim N(25, 18.75)$.

Suppose that the student needs to get k answers correct to persuade the examiner that he is not guessing. Then using a significance level of 5% you need to find k such that

$$P(X \geq k) < 0.05.$$

With a continuity correction the condition $X \geq k$ is equivalent to $V > k - 0.5$. So in terms of the normal approximation you want to find an integer k such that

$$P(V > k - 0.5) < 0.05.$$

For a one-tail test at the 5% significance level the rejection region for the test statistic $Z \sim N(0,1)$ is $Z \geq 1.645$ (Section 5.4). So k has to satisfy the inequality

$$\frac{(k - 0.5) - 25}{\sqrt{18.75}} \geq 1.645,$$

that is $k \geq 32.6$. Since k has to be an integer, this means that the smallest number of correct answers the student must get is 33.

You can use the cumulative binomial program for $B\left(100, \frac{1}{4}\right)$ to check this.

$$P(X \geq 32) = 1 - P(X \leq 31)$$
$$= 1 - 0.9306\ldots = 0.069$$

and

$$P(X \geq 33) = 1 - P(X \leq 32)$$
$$= 1 - 0.9554\ldots = 0.045,$$

correct to 3 decimal places. This confirms that the smallest value of k such that $P(X \geq k) < 0.05$ is 33.

Example 8.2.2

If births are equally likely on any day of the week, the proportion of babies born at the weekend should be $\frac{2}{7}$. A researcher suspects that this is not the case, and decides to test it from the records of the 490 births in the city during a recent month. If she uses a two-tail test at the 5% significance level, what numbers of weekend births would confirm her suspicions?

If p is the probability of a birth occurring at a weekend, the null and alternative hypotheses would be $H_0: p = \frac{2}{7}$ and $H_1: p \neq \frac{2}{7}$.

Let X denote the number of babies born at the weekend. Under H_0, $X \sim B\left(490, \frac{2}{7}\right)$. This can be approximated by $V \sim N\left(490 \times \frac{2}{7}, 490 \times \frac{2}{7} \times \frac{5}{7}\right) = N(140, 100)$.

For a two-tail test at the 5% significance level the rejection region is $|Z| > 1.960$, so you would reject values of V such that $\left|\dfrac{V - 140}{\sqrt{100}}\right| > 1.960$; that is, $V < 120.4$ or $V > 159.6$. With a continuity correction, these values correspond to

$$X < 120.4 - 0.5 = 119.9 \quad \text{or} \quad X > 159.6 + 0.5 = 160.1.$$

But X must be an integer, so this gives a rejection region of $X \leq 119$ or $X \geq 161$.

However, since the method involved an approximation, these answers should be checked using the cumulative binomial probabilities. These give

$$P(X \leq 119) = 0.0189\ldots, \quad P(X \leq 120) = 0.0243\ldots, \quad P(X \leq 121) = 0.0308\ldots,$$
$$P(X \geq 160) = 0.0267\ldots, \quad P(X \geq 161) = 0.0212\ldots.$$

This shows that, since $P(X \leq 120) < 0.025$, $X = 120$ should also be included in the rejection region.

So the researcher's suspicions would be confirmed if the number of weekend births was 120 or less, or 161 or more.

Exercise 8B

1   A jar contains a large number of coloured beads. It is claimed that 30% of them are red. A random sample of 80 beads is selected. What numbers of red beads in the sample would be required to support the claim at the 10% significance level?

2   The manufacturers of a new cold relief drug believe that more than 75% of people suffering from a cold will find it effective. They test it with 150 volunteers. How many effective responses would be needed to confirm the manufacturers' belief at the $2\frac{1}{2}\%$ significance level?

3   A parcel delivery service claims that at least 80% of their parcels are delivered within 48 hours of posting. A check was carried out on 200 parcels. What is the smallest number that should be delivered within 48 hours for the claim to be accepted, using a 5% significance level?

4   The drop-out rate of students enrolled at a certain university is reported to be 13.2%. The Dean of Students suspects that the drop-out rate for science students is greater than 13.2%, and she examines the record of a random sample of 95 of these students. How many drop-outs would the Dean need to find in the sample if her suspicions were to be confirmed at the 2% significance level?

9 Errors in hypothesis testing

This chapter investigates the situation where the wrong conclusion is drawn from a hypothesis test. When you have completed it, you should

- know what Type I and Type II errors are
- be able to calculate Type I and Type II errors in the context of the normal and binomial distributions.

9.1 Type I and Type II errors

When you carry out a hypothesis test your final step is to reject or to accept the null hypothesis. For example, the teachers described in Section 5.1, who were trying out a new reading scheme, had to choose between

(a) the new reading scheme is better than the old one, or
(b) the new reading scheme is not better than the old one.

If they came to conclusion (a) they would probably introduce the new scheme; if they came to conclusion (b) they would probably stick to their current reading scheme.

When such a decision is made after carrying out a hypothesis test, it may be either correct or incorrect. You can never be absolutely certain that you have made the right decision because you have to rely on a limited amount of evidence. For example, the reading scheme can only be tested on a sample of children. The situation is similar to that in a trial where the defendant is found either guilty or not guilty on the basis of the evidence brought forward. In this case there are four possible situations (which are mutually exclusive).

The defendant is innocent and is found not guilty: in this case the decision is correct.
The defendant is innocent but is found guilty: in this case the decision is incorrect.
The defendant is guilty but is found not guilty: in this case the decision is incorrect.
The defendant is guilty and is found guilty: in this case the decision is correct.

Suppose that in a criminal court of law a defendant is assumed innocent unless found guilty 'beyond reasonable doubt'. The initial assumption of innocence is equivalent to the null hypothesis, and the theory that the defendant is guilty is equivalent to the alternative hypothesis. Deciding what constitutes 'beyond reasonable doubt' is equivalent to setting a significance level. Similarly in a hypothesis test there are four possible situations, again mutually exclusive.

H_0 is true and H_0 is accepted: in this case the decision is correct.
H_0 is true but H_0 is rejected: in this case the decision is incorrect.
H_0 is not true but H_0 is accepted: in this case the decision is incorrect.
H_0 is not true and H_0 is rejected: in this case the decision is correct.

You can see that there are two different ways in which an incorrect decision could be made. In order to distinguish between them they are called Type I and Type II errors.

> A **Type I error** is made when a true null hypothesis is rejected.
>
> A **Type II error** is made when a false null hypothesis is accepted.

Making an incorrect decision can be costly in various ways. For example, suppose that a fire alarm was tested to see whether it was still functioning correctly after a power cut. You might take as the null and alternative hypotheses

H_0: the alarm is functioning correctly,
H_1: the alarm is not functioning correctly.

A Type II error in this situation would mean that you assumed that the alarm was functioning correctly when in fact it was not. This could result in injury, loss of life or damage to property. A Type I error would mean that you thought the alarm was not working correctly when in fact it was. This could mean expenditure on unnecessary repairs or replacement.

Try to analyse in a similar way the 'costs' of making Type I and Type II errors for the reading scheme example.

The examples given in this chapter should make you appreciate that it is important to assess the risk of making errors when carrying out a hypothesis test. In order to do this you have to calculate

$$P(\text{Type I error}) = P(\text{rejecting } H_0 \,|\, H_0 \text{ true})$$
and $\quad P(\text{Type II error}) = P(\text{accepting } H_0 \,|\, H_0 \text{ false}).$

The following sections show you how these probabilities are calculated for the different types of test which you have met in earlier chapters.

9.2 Type I and Type II errors for tests involving the normal distribution

If you look back to Section 5.3, which considered continuous variables, you will see that the probability of the test statistic falling in the rejection region, when H_0 is true, is equal to the significance level of the test. If the test statistic falls in the rejection region then H_0 will be rejected when it is in fact true; that is, a Type I error will be made.

> When the distribution of the test statistic is continuous, $P(\text{Type I error})$ is equal to the significance level of the test.

The choice of significance level for a hypothesis test is thus related to the value of P(Type I error) which you are prepared to accept. The choice of a significance level should depend in the first instance on how serious the consequences of a Type I error are. The more serious the consequences, the lower the value of the significance level which should be used. For example, if the consequences of a Type I error were not serious, you might use a significance level of 10%; if the consequences were very serious you might use a significance level of 0.1%.

Consider the reading scheme example. A Type I error in this case would mean that the new scheme was adopted even though it did not produce better results. As a result money would be wasted on a new scheme which was no better than the old. If the new scheme is not any better and the teachers use a 5% significance level then there is a 1 in 20 chance that the money will be wasted. If the new material is very costly then the teachers might feel that such a risk is unacceptable and choose a significance level of 1% or even less depending on the resources of their school. If on the other hand the new scheme is not very expensive, or they need to replace their reading material anyway, then they might take a significance level of 10% or even 20%.

A Type II error involves accepting a false null hypothesis, which means that you fail to detect a difference in μ. You would expect the probability of this happening to depend on how much μ has changed: if there is a small difference in μ it could easily go undetected but if there is a big difference in μ then you would expect to detect it. This is why the alternative hypothesis has to be defined more exactly before $P(\text{Type II error})$ can be calculated.

The following example illustrates the method.

Example 9.2.1

A machine fills 'one litre' cola bottles. When the machine is working correctly the contents of the bottles are normally distributed with mean 1.002 litres and standard deviation 0.002 litre. The performance of the machine is tested at regular intervals by taking a sample of 9 bottles and calculating their mean content. If this mean content falls below a certain value, it is assumed that the machine is not performing correctly and it is stopped.

(a) Set up null and alternative hypotheses for a test of whether the machine is working correctly.

(b) For a test at the 5% significance level, find the rejection region taking the sample mean as the test statistic.

(c) Give the value for the probability of making a Type I error.

(d) Find $P(\text{Type II error})$ if the mean content of the bottles has fallen to the nominal value of 1.000 litre.

(e) Find the range of values of μ for which the probability of making a Type II error is less than 0.001.

(a) $H_0 : \mu = 1.002$ (the machine is working correctly);

$H_1 : \mu < 1.002$ (the mean contents has fallen).

(b) Under H_0, $\overline{X} \sim N\left(1.002, \dfrac{0.002^2}{9}\right)$.

For a one-tail test for a decrease at the 5% level, the rejection region for the test statistic Z is $Z \leq -1.645$. Since $Z = \dfrac{\overline{X} - \mu}{\dfrac{\sigma}{\sqrt{n}}}$ this means that $\dfrac{\overline{X} - 1.002}{\dfrac{0.002}{\sqrt{9}}} \leq -1.645$.

Rearranging gives the rejection region for the sample mean as $\overline{X} \leq 1.000\ 90$.

In Fig. 9.1, the broken curve shows the distribution of $\overline{X}$ if H_0 is true and the hatched area shows the $P(\text{Type I error})$.

(c) For a continuous test statistic, $P(\text{Type I error}) = \text{significance level} = 0.05$.

(d) $P(\text{Type II error}) = P(\text{accepting } H_0 \mid H_0 \text{ false})$
$$= P(\overline{X} > 1.000\ 90 \mid \mu = 1.000),$$

that is $P(\overline{X}$ is in acceptance region $\mid \mu$ is no longer 1.002 but 1.000).

This probability is shown by the solid shaded area in Fig. 9.1, where the solid curve shows the distribution of $\overline{X}$ if H_1 is true.

$$P(\overline{X} > 1.0009 \mid \mu = 1.000) = P\left(Z > \frac{1.000\ 90 - 1.000}{\frac{0.002}{\sqrt{9}}}\right)$$
$$= P(Z > 1.35)$$
$$= 0.088, \text{ correct to 3 decimal places.}$$

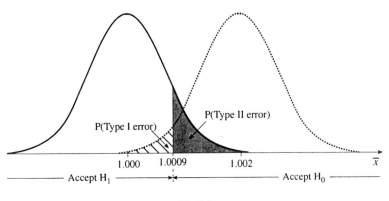

Fig. 9.1

(e) First find the value of z for which the probability of making a Type II error is 0.001. Looking back to part (d) this would require $P(Z > z) = 0.001$. Using the inverse normal distribution in tables or on your calculator, $z = 3.090$.

A Type II error will be made if the test statistic Z is greater than 3.0902, that is if

$$\frac{1.000\ 90 - \mu}{\frac{0.002}{\sqrt{9}}} > 3.0902.$$

Solving gives $\mu < 0.9988$, correct to 4 decimal places.

So for $\mu < 0.9988$ the probability of making a Type II error is less than 0.001.

In Example 9.2.1 the consequence of setting the significance level at 5% is that there is a probability of 5% of stopping the machine unnecessarily when it is working correctly. With this significance level the probability of failing to detect that the mean contents of the bottles has fallen to the nominal value of 1.000 litre is 8.77%. It is interesting to see what happens to P(Type II error) when a lower significance level is used. This is done in the next example.

Example 9.2.2

Repeat Example 9.2.1 parts (b) to (d) with a significance level of 1%.

    (b)   For a one-tail test for a decrease at the 1% level, the rejection region for the test statistic Z is $Z \le -2.326$ so

$$\frac{\overline{X} - 1.002}{\frac{0.002}{\sqrt{9}}} \le -2.326.$$

        Rearranging gives the rejection region for the sample mean as $\overline{X} \le 1.000\ 45$.

    (c) $P(\text{Type I error}) = \text{significance level} = 0.01$.

    (d) $P(\text{Type II error}) = P(\text{accepting } H_0 \mid H_0 \text{ false})$

$$= P(\overline{X} > 1.000\ 45 \mid \mu = 1.000),$$

        that is $P(\overline{X} \text{ is in acceptance region} \mid \mu \text{ is no longer } 1.002 \text{ but } 1.000)$.

$$P(\overline{X} > 1.000\ 4 \ldots \mid \mu = 1.000) = P\left(Z > \frac{1.000\ 45 - 1.000}{\frac{0.002}{\sqrt{9}}} \right)$$

$$= P(Z > 0.675)$$

$$= 0.250, \text{ correct to 3 decimal places.}$$

For this second calculation, at the 1% significance level, the value of $P(\text{Type I error})$ has been reduced but the value of $P(\text{Type II error})$ has increased. You would expect this result from looking at Fig. 9.1. If the critical value is altered so that one type of error increases, the other will decrease. This means that in setting a significance level it may be necessary to assess the risks involved in committing both types of error and balance one against the other. The only way in which both types of error can be reduced at the same time is by taking a larger sample, so that the overlap of the distributions in Fig. 9.1 is reduced.

The following example shows how to calculate $P(\text{Type II error})$ for a two-tail test.

Example 9.2.3

Boxes of a certain breakfast cereal have contents whose masses are normally distributed with mean μ and standard deviation 15 grams. A test of the null hypothesis $\mu = 375$ against the alternative hypothesis $\mu \ne 375$ is carried out at the 5% significance level using a random sample of 16 boxes.

(a) For what values of the sample mean is the alternative hypothesis accepted?

(b) Given that the actual value of μ is 380, find the probability of making a Type II error.

                                                (OCR, adapted)

    (a)   Under H_0, $\overline{X} \sim N\left(375, \frac{15^2}{16} \right)$.

        For a two-tail test at the 5% significance level, the rejection region is $|Z| \ge 1.960$.

Now $Z = \dfrac{\overline{X} - 375}{\dfrac{15}{\sqrt{16}}}$.

You can check that when $Z = 1.96$, $\overline{X} = 382.35$, and when $Z = -1.96$, $\overline{X} = 367.65$. Thus the alternative hypothesis is accepted when $\overline{X} \geq 382.35$ or $\overline{X} \leq 367.65$.

(b) $P(\text{Type II error}) = P(367.65 < \overline{X} < 382.35 \mid \mu = 380)$

$$= P\left(\dfrac{367.65 - 380}{\dfrac{15}{\sqrt{16}}} < Z < \dfrac{382.35 - 380}{\dfrac{15}{\sqrt{16}}} \right)$$

$$= P(-3.293\ldots < Z < 0.626\ldots)$$

$$= 0.734, \text{ correct to 3 significant figures.}$$

Exercise 9A

1   The random variable X has a normal distribution with mean μ and variance 12.8. A test, at the 5% significance level, of the null hypothesis $\mu = 5$ against the alternative hypothesis $\mu > 5$ is carried out using a random sample of 20 observations of X.

(a) Give the rejection region of the test, in terms of the sample mean, $\overline{X}$.

(b) Find the probability of a Type II error in the test when the true value of μ is 7.

2   In a test of the quality of Luxiglow paint, which is intended to cover an area of at least 10 m^2 per litre can, a random sample of 15 cans is tested. The mean area per can covered by the 15 cans is denoted by $\overline{X}$ m^2. It may be assumed that the area covered by a can has a normal distribution with standard deviation 0.51 m^2.

(a) Find, in terms of $\overline{X}$, the rejection region of a test, at the $2\tfrac{1}{2}$% significance level, that the mean area covered by all litre cans of the paint is at least 10 m^2.

(b) For a particular sample, $\overline{X} = 10.3$. State the type of error that could not occur.

(c) Given that the mean cover per can of paint is actually 9.6 m^2, calculate the probability of making a Type II error in the test.

3   In a quality control check 5 randomly selected packs of butter are weighed. The masses of all packs of butter may be assumed to have a normal distribution with mean μ grams and standard deviation 2.7 grams. A test of the null hypothesis $\mu = 247$ against the alternative hypothesis $\mu \neq 247$ is carried out at the α% significance level. It is decided to accept the null hypothesis if the sample mean lies between 245 grams and 249 grams.

(a) Find the value of α.

(b) Given that the actual value of μ is 250, find the probability of making a Type II error in the test.

(c) What can be said about the probability of making a Type II error when the value of μ is greater than 250?

4   The number of daily absences by employees of a large company has mean 1.94 and standard deviation 0.22. A new system of working is introduced in the hope that this will reduce the number of absences, and it is found that there were 68 absences during the first 40 days of the new system. Treating the 40 days as a random sample

(a) test, at the 5% significance level, whether the new system had the desired effect,

(b) calculate the probability of making a Type II error in the test in part (a) when the mean number of absences is actually 1.8,

(c) state, in the context of the question, what is meant by a Type II error.

5   Studies have shown that the time taken for adults to memorise a list of 12 words has mean 3.8 minutes and standard deviation 1.8 minutes. Taking a course in mnemonics is believed to reduce the mean. To investigate this belief a test, at the 5% significance level, is proposed based on a random sample of 36 people who took the course. Each was given the same list of 12 words to memorise.

(a) Find the rejection region of the test in terms of the sample mean time. Assume that the standard deviation remains at 1.8 minutes.

(b) Given that the actual mean time for the 12 words is 2.9 minutes after taking the course, find the probability of making a Type II error in the test.

Suppose now that the test is based on a random sample of 40 people.

(c) Show that the probability of making a Type II error (when the actual mean time is 2.9 minutes) is smaller than that found in part (b).

6*   The breaking strength of lengths of wire required in the manufacture of a certain piece of machinery has a normal distribution with mean $30\,\mathrm{N}$ and standard deviation $0.38\,\mathrm{N}$. A random sample of 9 lengths of the wire is tested to determine whether the population mean breaking strength is less than $30\,\mathrm{N}$. A Type I error for the test has probability 0.04.

(a) Find the set of values of the sample mean breaking strength for which it would be accepted that the mean breaking strength is not less than $30\,\mathrm{N}$.

(b) Given that the probability of making a Type II error in the test is to be less than 0.025, find the set of possible values of the actual mean breaking strength.

9.3   Type I and Type II errors for tests involving the binomial distribution

In Section 8.1 you met the idea that, for a discrete distribution, it is not usually possible to find a rejection region which corresponds exactly to the specified significance level. You may find it helpful to look back at Section 8.1 before going on to the following example.

In this section all binomial probabilities are given correct to 4 decimal places.

Example 9.3.1

An experiment on telepathy is carried out by two people. One person, A, chooses a card at random from a standard pack and concentrates on it. The other person, B, who cannot see the card, has to write down the suit of the card. This is done for 18 cards in all and X, the number of cards whose suit is correctly identified, is counted.

(a)   State suitable hypotheses, involving a probability, for a hypothesis test which could indicate whether person B is able to name the correct suit more often than would be expected by chance.

(b)   What would be the rejection region for the test statistic X for a test at the 10% significance level?

(c)   The nominal significance level of this test is 10%. What is the actual significance level?

    (a)   There are four suits, so if person B is guessing, the probability of being correct is $\frac{1}{4}$; if person B has telepathic powers the probability of being correct will be greater than this, so take $H_0: p = \frac{1}{4}$ and $H_1: p > \frac{1}{4}$.

    (b)   Under H_0, $X \sim B(18, 0.25)$. Let the rejection region for X be denoted by $X \geq c$. You need to find the smallest value of c for which $P(X \geq c)$ is less than the given significance level. From the cumulative binomial probability program on your calculator you will see that, if H_0 is true,

$$P(X \geq 7 \mid p = 0.25) = 1 - P(X \leq 6 \mid p = 0.25)$$
$$= 1 - 0.8610 = 0.1390 = 13.9\% > 10\%,$$

so H_0 is accepted.

$$P(X \geq 8 \mid p = 0.25) = 1 - P(X \leq 7 \mid p = 0.25)$$
$$= 1 - 0.9431 = 0.0569 = 5.69\% < 10\%,$$

so H_0 is rejected.

Thus, the rejection region is $X \geq 8$.

    (c)   The actual significance level of the test is $P(X \geq 8 \mid p = 0.25) = 5.69\%$. This is equal to $P(\text{Type I error})$.

This is not very close to the desired significance level (10% in this example) and this will often be the case in tests involving discrete variables.

> For a hypothesis test involving a discrete variable, for example a variable which has a binomial or Poisson distribution, the rejection region is defined so that
>
> $$P(\text{test statistic falls in rejection region} \mid H_0 \text{ true})$$
> $$\leq \text{nominal significance of the test.}$$
>
> Actual significance level of the test =
> $$P(\text{test statistic falls in rejection region} \mid H_0 \text{ true})$$
>
> and this is also the probability of a Type I error.

The following example shows how to calculate $P(\text{Type II error})$.

Example 9.3.2

A supplier of primrose seeds claims that their germination rate is 0.95. A purchaser of the seeds suspects that the germination rate is lower. To test this claim the purchaser plants 20 seeds in similar conditions, counts the number, X, which germinate and carries out a hypothesis test at the 5% significance level.

(a) Formulate suitable null and alternative hypotheses to test the seed supplier's claim.

(b) For what values of X would the null hypothesis be rejected?

(c) The nominal significance level of this test is 5%. What is the actual significance level?

(d) What is the probability of a Type I error using this test?

(e) Calculate P(Type II error) if the probability that a seed germinates is in fact 0.80.

(a) $H_0: p = 0.95$, $H_1: p < 0.95$.

(b)   Low values of X will lead to the null hypothesis being rejected and so the rejection region takes the form $X \le c$. Under H_0, $X \sim B(20, 0.95)$. The cumulative binomial probability program shows that

$$P(X \le 16 \mid p = 0.95) = 0.0159 = 1.59\% < 5\%, \text{ so } H_0 \text{ is rejected;}$$

$$P(X \le 17 \mid p = 0.95) = 0.0755 = 7.55\% > 5\%, \text{ so } H_0 \text{ is accepted.}$$

So H_0 is rejected if $X \le 16$, and the rejection region for the test is $X \le 16$.

(c) $P(\text{Type I error}) = P(X \le 16 \mid p = 0.95) = 0.0159$.

(d)   The actual significance level $= P(\text{test statistic falls in rejection region} \mid H_0 \text{ is true})$
$$= 0.0159 = 1.59\%.$$

(e) $P(\text{Type II error}) = P(X > 16 \mid p = 0.8)$
$$= 1 - P(X \le 16 \mid p = 0.8)$$
$$= 1 - 0.5886 = 0.4114.$$

The value of P(Type II error) in Example 9.3.2 indicates that there is a fairly high probability that the hypothesis test will fail to detect a fall in the germination rate from 0.95 to 0.80.

The following example illustrates a two-tail test.

Example 9.3.3

The dice used in a board game is rolled 30 times and the number, X, of sixes is counted.

(a) Set up suitable null and alternative hypotheses for testing whether the dice is biased either towards or away from six.

(b) What would be the result of a test at the 10% significance level if $X = 9$?

(c) What is the rejection region for X for a test at the 10% significance level?

(d) What is P(Type I error) for this test?

(e) Find P(Type II error) if the dice is in fact biased so that the probability of getting a six is 0.5.

(a) $H_0: p = \frac{1}{6}$, $H_1: p \ne \frac{1}{6}$.

(b)   Under H_0, $X \sim B(30, \frac{1}{6})$. The value $X = 9$ is on the high side since, on average, you would expect 5 sixes in 30 throws. From the cumulative binomial probability program

$$P(X \geq 9 \mid p = \tfrac{1}{6}) = 1 - P(X \leq 8 \mid p = \tfrac{1}{6})$$
$$= 1 - 0.9494 = 0.0506 = 5.06\% > 5\%,$$

so H_0 is not rejected.

The probability is compared with $\frac{1}{2} \times 10\% = 5\%$ since a two-tail test is being carried out.

There is not enough evidence, at the 10% significance level, that the dice is biased.

(c)   The null hypothesis could be rejected for either high or low values of X (since a two-tail test is being carried out) and so there are two parts to the rejection region. Firstly you need to find a value c such that $P(X \leq c \mid p = \tfrac{1}{6}) \leq 0.05$. The cumulative binomial probability program shows that

$$P(X \leq 2 \mid p = \tfrac{1}{6}) = 0.1028 \geq 0.05, \text{ so accept } H_0,$$

and $P(X \leq 1 \mid p = \tfrac{1}{6}) = 0.0295 \leq 0.05$, so reject H_0.

So the lower part of the rejection region is $X \leq 1$.

Secondly you need a value d such that $P(X \geq d \mid p = \tfrac{1}{6}) \leq 0.05$. You found in part (b) that $X = 9$ is not rejected, so try $X = 10$.

$$P(X \geq 10 \mid p = \tfrac{1}{6}) = 1 - P(X \leq 9 \mid p = \tfrac{1}{6})$$
$$= 1 - 0.9803 = 0.0197 \leq 0.05.$$

So the upper part of the rejection region is $X \geq 10$.

The null hypothesis is rejected when $X \leq 1$ or $X \geq 10$.

(d) $P(\text{Type I error}) = P(X \leq 1 \text{ or } X \geq 10 \mid p = \tfrac{1}{6})$
$$= 0.0295 + 0.0197 = 0.0492 = 4.92\%.$$

This is well below the desired significance level of 10%. It would be possible to get a significance level closer to this value by taking the rejection region as $X \leq 1$ and $X \geq 9$, which gives a significance level of 8.01%. However, it is usual practice if a two-tail test is required to calculate the rejection region as in part (c) unless you are asked to find a rejection region such that $P(\text{Type I error})$ is as close as possible to the nominal significance level.

(e)   Taking the rejection region found in part (c) gives

$$P(\text{Type II error}) = P(1 < X < 10 \mid p = 0.5)$$
$$= P(X \leq 9 \mid p = 0.5) - P(X \leq 1 \mid p = 0.5)$$
$$= 0.0214 - 0.0000 = 0.0214.$$

In Example 9.3.3 the low value of $P(\text{Type II error})$ indicates that the hypothesis test would be effective in detecting a dice biased so that the probability of getting a six is 0.5.

For large samples it becomes easier to find a rejection region which gives $P(\text{Type I error})$ close to the required significance level because you can use the normal approximation to the binomial distribution (see Section 8.2). The following example shows how to calculate P(Type I error) and P(Type II error) in this situation.

Example 9.3.4

It is suspected that a gaming club is running an unfair roulette wheel. The wheel is given 3700 trial spins and X, the number of times that zero (on which the club wins) turns up is counted. There are 37 possible scores on a trial spin, labelled 0 to 36, and these should have equal probability.

(a) For what values of X would you conclude that the wheel was biased in favour of zero if a hypothesis test was carried out at the 5% significance level?

(b) For this test calculate P(Type II error) if the probability of getting zero is in fact $\frac{3}{37}$.

(OCR, adapted)

(a) If the wheel is fair then the probability of getting zero is $\frac{1}{37}$. If the wheel is unfair it will favour the club so the probability of getting zero is greater than this.

The null and alternative hypotheses are $H_0: p = \frac{1}{37}$ and $H_1: p > \frac{1}{37}$ respectively.

Under H_0, $X \sim B\left(3700, \frac{1}{37}\right)$.

Using the normal approximation,

$$\mu = np = 3700 \times \frac{1}{37} = 100, \quad \text{and} \quad \sigma^2 = npq = 3700 \times \frac{1}{37} \times \frac{36}{37} = \frac{3600}{37},$$

so $X \sim B\left(3700, \frac{1}{37}\right)$ is approximated by $V \sim N\left(100, \frac{3600}{37}\right)$.

For a one-tail test for an increase at the 5% significance level, H_0 is rejected if $Z \geq 1.645$. The corresponding rejection region for V is given by

$$\frac{V - 100}{\sqrt{\frac{3600}{37}}} \geq 1.645 \quad \text{giving} \quad V \geq 116.2, \text{ correct to 1 decimal place.}$$

Allowing for the continuity correction, this corresponds to $X \geq 116.2 + 0.5 = 116.7$.

Rounding up to the nearest integer, this suggests that the rejection region is $X \geq 117$. You can check this by using the cumulative binomial program on your calculator, which gives

$$P(X \geq 116) = 0.0605 > 5\% \quad \text{and} \quad P(X \geq 117) = 0.0498 < 5\%.$$

(b) If $p = \frac{3}{37}$, then the distribution of X can be approximated by

$$V \sim N\left(3700 \times \frac{3}{37}, 3700 \times \frac{3}{37} \times \frac{34}{37}\right) = N\left(300, \frac{10\,200}{37}\right).$$

$$P(\text{Type II error}) = P(X \leq 116)$$
$$\approx P(V \leq 116.5) \quad \text{(including the continuity correction)}$$
$$= P\left(Z < \frac{116.5 - 300}{\sqrt{\frac{10\,200}{37}}}\right) = P(Z < -11.05...) \approx 0.$$

The hypothesis test described in Example 9.3.4 would be extremely effective at detecting a degree of bias such that the probability of getting zero is $\frac{3}{37}$.

Exercise 9B

1   A newspaper reported that 55% of households own more than two television sets. Each of a random sample of 30 households in Melchester is contacted and the number of households owning more than two television sets is denoted by N. A test of whether the proportion p of households in Melchester owning more than two television sets is different from 55% is carried out at a nominal 5% significance level.

    (a) Obtain the rejection region of the test in terms of N.

    (b) Calculate P(Type I error).   (c) State the conclusion of the test when $N = 20$.

    (d) Calculate P(Type II error) when the actual value of p is 60%.

2   An election to the presidency of a society of 8000 members is shortly to take place. After a pre-election speech by Mrs Robinson (a candidate), a random sample of 25 people who listened to the speech were asked about their voting intentions. The number who say that they will vote for Mrs Robinson is denoted by R. A test is carried out at a nominal 5% significance level of whether Mrs Robinson will be elected, which will happen if she gets more than 50% of the votes cast.

    (a) Find the rejection region of the test in terms of R and state the conclusion of the test when $R = 19$.

    (b) What is the actual significance level of the test?

    (c) Given that 65% of all members will vote for Mrs Robinson, find the probability of making a Type II error in the test.

3   A drug for treating phlebitis has proved effective in 75% of cases when it has been used. A new drug has been developed which, it is believed, will be more successful and it is used on a sample of 16 patients with phlebitis. A test is carried out to determine whether the new drug has a greater success rate than 75% and the test statistic is X, the number of patients cured by the new drug. It is decided to accept that the new drug is more effective if $X > 14$.

    (a) Find α, the probability of making a Type I error.

    (b) Find β, the probability of making a Type II error when the actual success rate is 80%.

    What can be said about the values of α and β if, with the same decision procedure $(X > 14)$, the sample size were larger than 16?

4   Of a certain make of electric toaster, 10% have to be returned for service within three months of purchase. A modification to the toaster is made in the hope that it will be more reliable. Out of 24 modified toasters sold in a store none was returned for service within three months of purchase. The proportion of all the modified toasters that are returned for service within three months of purchase is denoted by p.

    (a) State, in terms of p, suitable hypotheses for a test.

    (b) Test whether there is evidence, at a nominal 10% significance level, that the modified toaster is more reliable than the previous model in that it requires less service.

    (c) What is the probability of making a Type I error in the test?

    (d) Assuming that, when n is large, $\mathrm{B}(n, p)$ is nearly symmetrical, estimate the set of values of p for which P(Type II error) < 0.25.

10 The *t*-distribution

This chapter explains how you can carry out a hypothesis test when the background population has a normal distribution whose variance is unknown. When you have completed it, you should

- understand the use of $S_{n-1}{}^2$ as an unbiased estimator of the population variance
- know how to use the random variable T to describe the distribution of the sample mean
- understand the idea of degrees of freedom
- be able to apply the *t*-distribution to test hypotheses about the value of the population mean.

10.1 Estimating the population variance

In the last few chapters you have worked many problems like this (Exercise 9A Question 2):

> In a test of the quality of Luxiglow paint,… a random sample of 15 cans is tested…. . It may be assumed that the area covered by a can has a normal distribution with standard deviation 0.51 m^2. Find … the rejection region of a test… that the mean area covered by all litre cans of the paint is at least 10 m^2.

It may have struck you as odd that there should be doubt about the value of the mean, but that the standard deviation (or the variance) should be precisely known. In most situations it is more likely that, when you take a sample to test a hypothesis about the mean of a population, you won't know the variance either. How then could you estimate its value?

The obvious answer is to use the variance of the sample as a guide to the variance of the population. You will remember from Higher Level Book 1 Section 7.8 that a so-called 'unbiased estimate' of the variance of a population can be calculated as $\dfrac{n}{n-1} s_n{}^2$, where $s_n{}^2$ is the variance of a sample of n measurements. This quantity is often denoted by $s_{n-1}{}^2$.

When you use a calculator to find the variance of a sample, it is very important to know whether the quantity calculated is $s_n{}^2$ or $s_{n-1}{}^2$.

This section explores this distinction in more detail. The first example looks at the problem the other way round. It begins with a very simple population with known variance, and finds the variance of all the samples of a given size that can be taken from it. The purpose is to compare the variance of the samples with the variance of the population.

Example 10.1.1

A population consists of just two numbers -1 and $+1$. Write down all the samples (with replacement)
(a) of size 2,   (b) of size 3,
that can be drawn from this population. Compare the variance of the samples with the variance of the population.

Begin by noting that the mean of the population is 0, so the variance is $\dfrac{(-1-0)^2 + (1-0)^2}{2} = 1$.

(a)   There are four samples of size 2 which can be drawn from the population:

$$(-1,-1),(-1,+1),(+1,-1),(+1,+1).$$

The variances of these are 0, 1, 1, 0 respectively.

Notice that two of the samples have the same variance as the population, and two have a smaller variance. The mean of the four variances is $\dfrac{0+1+1+0}{4} = \dfrac{1}{2}$.

(b)   There are eight samples of size 3:

$$(-1,-1,-1),(-1,-1,+1),(-1,+1,-1),(-1,+1,+1),$$
$$(+1,-1,-1),(+1,-1,-1),(+1,+1,-1),(+1,+1,+1).$$

The variances are $0,\dfrac{8}{9},\dfrac{8}{9},\dfrac{8}{9},\dfrac{8}{9},\dfrac{8}{9},\dfrac{8}{9},0$.

None of the samples has a variance as large as the variance of the population. The mean of the variances is $\dfrac{2\times 0+6\times\frac{8}{9}}{8} = \dfrac{2}{3}$.

You may be interested to continue this example by finding the variance of the 16 samples of size 4. What would you guess for the mean of the 16 variances?

The most obvious feature of this example is that, for both $n = 2$ and $n = 3$, the variance of any random sample is not a reliable guide to the variance of the population. But the mean of the variance of all the random samples is, in both cases, $\dfrac{n-1}{n}$ times the variance of the population: $\frac{1}{2}$ for $n = 2$, $\frac{2}{3}$ for $n = 3$. This is in fact true for samples of any size taken from any population.

> The mean of the variance of all independent random samples of size n taken from a population with variance σ^2 is equal to $\dfrac{n-1}{n}\sigma^2$.

A proof of this is given in the next section.

With a larger sample from a more extensive population it is impractical to list all the possible samples, but you can test out the result in the shaded box by finding the variance of a number of samples and taking the mean. You won't expect to get exactly $\dfrac{n-1}{n}\sigma^2$, but you should usually get an answer reasonably close to this.

Example 10.1.2
The population of the 10 single digit numbers from 0 to 9 has $\sigma^2 = 8.25$. Take 10 samples, each of 5 digits, from this population by using random numbers from your calculator or from tables, and calculate their variance. Compare the mean of these variances with the value of $\dfrac{n-1}{n}\sigma^2$ with $n = 5$.

You may find it interesting to work through this example with your own random digits instead of the ones used here.

By reading across a row of a table of random digits the following samples were generated.

(1,8,4,3,9)	(7,3,7,6,8)	(9,7,5,6,5)	(6,5,7,9,5)	(0,1,8,8,1)
(1,8,9,4,8)	(0,7,4,2,6)	(0,1,1,9,2)	(6,7,0,5,1)	(9,5,4,3,2)

For each sample, calculate the variance.

9.20	2.96	2.24	2.24	13.04
9.20	6.56	10.64	7.76	5.84

The mean of these variances is 6.968. This can be compared with the mean over all possible samples, which is $\frac{n}{n-1}\sigma^2 = \frac{4}{5} \times 8.25 = 6.6$.

Reference has already been made in this section to an 'unbiased estimate' of the variance of a population. In statistics the word 'unbiased' has a precise meaning.

> A random variable R is said to be an **unbiased estimator** of a parameter p of a probability distribution if $E(R) = p$.

So the box on the previous page states that $S_n{}^2$, the variance of a random sample of size n, is not an unbiased estimator of the population variance σ^2, because $E(S_n{}^2) = \frac{n-1}{n}\sigma^2 \neq \sigma^2$.

A capital letter S is used in $S_n{}^2$ because the variance of a random sample is itself a random variable.

However, if you multiply both sides of this equation by $\frac{n}{n-1}$, you get

$$E\left(\frac{n}{n-1}S_n{}^2\right) = \frac{n}{n-1}E(S_n{}^2) = \sigma^2.$$

This means that $\frac{n}{n-1}S_n{}^2$ is an unbiased estimator of σ^2

> If $S_n{}^2$ is the variance of a random sample of size n drawn from a population with variance σ^2, then $\frac{n}{n-1}S_n{}^2$ is a unbiased estimator of σ^2.

Don't imagine that this means that, if you take a particular random sample with variance $s_n{}^2$, then $\frac{n}{n-1}s_n{}^2$ will be a good estimate of the population variance. Example 10.1.2 shows this very clearly. If you had picked on the third sample $(9,7,5,6,5)$, this would estimate the population variance as $\frac{5}{4} \times 2.24 = 2.8$; but if you had picked the fifth sample $(0,1,8,8,1)$, you would get an estimate for the population variance of $\frac{5}{4} \times 13.04 = 16.3$. Neither is very close to the actual population variance of 8.25.

For a sample $(x_1, x_2, \ldots, x_n)$ with mean $\bar{x}$, $s_n{}^2$ is calculated as

$$s_n{}^2 = \frac{(x_1 - \bar{x})^2 + (x_2 - \bar{x})^2 + \ldots + (x_n - \bar{x})^2}{n},$$

so

$$\frac{n}{n-1} s_n{}^2 = \frac{(x_1 - \bar{x})^2 + (x_2 - \bar{x})^2 + \ldots + (x_n - \bar{x})^2}{n-1}.$$

Because this is like $s_n{}^2$ but with $n-1$ in the denominator instead of n, the quantity $\frac{n}{n-1} s_n{}^2$ is often denoted by the symbol $s_{n-1}{}^2$. This is the notation used in this book. But in other books and on some calculators you may also meet other notations such as $\hat{\sigma}^2$ (the circumflex is used to stand for 'unbiased estimator'), $\sigma_{n-1}{}^2$, $\sigma_x{}^2$ or $s_x{}^2$.

Before ending this section, it is worth noting that the mean of a sample is an unbiased estimator of the mean of the population. To prove this, begin with a population in which a random variable X has mean μ, and take from it a random sample $(X_1, X_2, \ldots, X_n)$. The mean of this sample is

$$\bar{X} = \frac{X_1 + X_2 + \ldots + X_n}{n}.$$

You want to find the expected value of $\bar{X}$ as $X_1, X_2, \ldots, X_n$ independently range over the whole population. So find

$$\mathrm{E}(\bar{X}) = \frac{1}{n}\left(\mathrm{E}(X_1) + \mathrm{E}(X_2) + \ldots + \mathrm{E}(X_n)\right)$$

$$= \frac{1}{n}\left(\mathrm{E}(X) + \mathrm{E}(X) + \ldots + \mathrm{E}(X)\right)$$

$$= \frac{1}{n} \times n\mathrm{E}(X) = \mathrm{E}(X).$$

And since $\mathrm{E}(X) = \mu$, it follows that

$$\mathrm{E}(\bar{X}) = \mu.$$

> $\bar{X}$ is an unbiased estimator of the population mean μ.

10.2* Proof of the 'mean of variances' formula

This section gives a proof of the result in the first shaded box in Section 10.1. You may omit it if you wish.

With the notation at the end of the last section, suppose that the random variable X has variance σ^2. The problem now is to find the expected value of the variance of the random sample $(X_1, X_2, \ldots, X_n)$ as $X_1, X_2, \ldots, X_n$ independently range over the whole population.

It turns out that the proof is much easier if $\mu = 0$. So it pays to begin by introducing a new random variable Y defined by $Y = X - \mu$. Then

$$
\begin{aligned}
E(Y) &= E(X - \mu) \\
&= E(X) - \mu \\
&= \mu - \mu = 0,
\end{aligned}
$$

and

$$
\begin{aligned}
\text{Var}(Y) &= \text{Var}(X - \mu) \\
&= \text{Var}(X) = \sigma^2.
\end{aligned}
$$

Also, since

$$
\begin{aligned}
\text{Var}(Y) &= E\left((Y - 0)^2\right) \\
&= E\left(Y^2\right),
\end{aligned}
$$

it follows that

$$
E\left(Y^2\right) = \sigma^2.
$$

So now take a random sample $(Y_1, Y_2 \ldots, Y_n)$ of independent values of Y. If the mean of this sample is $\overline{Y}$, the variance V of the sample can be calculated as

$$
V = E\left(Y^2\right) - \overline{Y}^2 = \frac{Y_1^2 + Y_2^2 + \ldots + Y_n^2}{n} - \left(\frac{Y_1 + Y_2 + \ldots + Y_n}{n}\right)^2.
$$

You want the expectation of this as the random variables $Y_1, Y_2, \ldots, Y_n$ range over the population.

Look first at the second term in this expression, whose numerator is $(Y_1 + Y_2 + \ldots + Y_n)^2$. When you multiply this out, you get square terms $Y_1^2, Y_2^2, \ldots, Y_n^2$, and product terms like $2Y_1 Y_2$. Now it was proved in Section 3.2 that the expectation of the product of two independent random variables is equal to the product of the expectations of the two variables separately. So

$$
E(2Y_1 Y_2) = 2E(Y_1) \times E(Y_2).
$$

And since Y_1 and Y_2 both have the distribution of Y, it follows that $E(Y_1) = E(Y) = 0$, and similarly for $E(Y_2)$. Therefore the expectations of all the product terms are 0. It follows that

$$
E\left((Y_1 + Y_2 + \ldots + Y_n)^2\right) = E\left(Y_1^2 + Y_2^2 + \ldots + Y_n^2\right),
$$

so that

$$
\begin{aligned}
E(V) &= \frac{1}{n} E\left(Y_1^2 + Y_2^2 + \ldots + Y_n^2\right) - \frac{1}{n^2} E\left(Y_1^2 + Y_2^2 + \ldots + Y_n^2\right) \\
&= \frac{n-1}{n^2}\left(E\left(Y_1^2\right) + E\left(Y_2^2\right) + \ldots + E\left(Y_n^2\right)\right).
\end{aligned}
$$

Also, for each of the random variables Y_i, $E\left(Y_i^2\right) = E\left(Y^2\right)$. So

$$E(V) = \frac{n-1}{n^2} \times nE(Y^2)$$

$$= \frac{n-1}{n}E(Y^2)$$

$$= \frac{n-1}{n}\sigma^2,$$

using the result $E(Y^2) = \sigma^2$ proved earlier.

10.3 Finding numerical estimates of population parameters

If you have a sample of n numerical values of a random variable, you can now use the results in Section 10.1 to make numerical estimates of the mean and variance of the population from which the sample has been taken. It is important to understand the distinction between the mean and variance of the sample, and the estimated values of the mean and variance of the population.

> If the values $x_1, x_2, \ldots, x_n$ represent a whole population, that is all the values of interest, and you wish to calculate the variance of these values, then use
>
> $$s_n^2 = \sum \frac{x^2}{n} - \bar{x}^2, \text{ or its equivalent } \frac{1}{n}\sum(x - \bar{x})^2.$$
>
> If, on the other hand, you are trying to estimate the variance of a larger population from which the values $x_1, x_2, \ldots, x_n$ are a sample, then use
>
> $$s_{n-1}^2 = \frac{n}{n-1}\left(\sum \frac{x^2}{n} - \bar{x}^2\right), \text{ or its equivalent } \frac{1}{n-1}\sum(x - \bar{x})^2.$$

Example 10.3.1

(a) Nine CDs were played and the playing time of each CD was recorded. The times, in minutes, are given below.

49, 56, 55, 68, 61, 57, 61, 52, 63

Find the mean playing time of the nine CDs and the variance of the playing times.

(b) A student was doing a project on the playing times of CDs. She wished to estimate the mean playing time for CDs sold in the UK and she wished also to estimate the variance of playing times of CDs sold in the UK. She took a sample of nine CDs and recorded their playing times. The results are given below.

49, 56, 55, 68, 61, 57, 61, 52, 63

(i) Use the student's data to estimate the mean playing time for CDs sold in the UK.

(ii) Use the student's data to estimate the variance of the playing times of CDs sold in the UK.

The two parts, (a) and (b) look very similar. However in part (a) you are only interested in the playing times of the nine CDs which have been selected. In part (b) you wish to make estimates of population parameters from the sample data that you have been given.

(a) $\bar{x} = \frac{1}{9}(49 + 56 + ... + 63) = 58$, so the mean is 58 minutes.

$$\text{Variance} = \sum \frac{x^2}{n} - \bar{x}^2 = \frac{1}{9}\left(49^2 + 56^2 + ... + 63^2\right) - 58^2$$
$$= 30.4...,$$

so the variance is 30.4 min^2, correct to 3 significant figures.

(b)   In this part you are estimating the mean and variance of the population.

(i)   The unbiased estimator of the population mean, μ, is the mean of the sample $\bar{x}$, so the estimate of μ will be 58 minutes.

(ii)   To obtain an unbiased estimate of σ^2, you need to use $s_{n-1}^{\;2} = \frac{n}{n-1}\left(\sum \frac{x^2}{n} - \bar{x}^2\right)$.

As $\sum \frac{x^2}{n} - \bar{x}^2$ has already been calculated, to find $s_{n-1}^{\;2}$ all that needs to be done is to

multiply $\sum \frac{x^2}{n} - \bar{x}^2$ by $\frac{n}{n-1}$, which in this case is $\frac{9}{8}$.

Therefore $s_{n-1}^{\;2}$, the unbiased estimate of σ^2, is $\frac{9}{8} \times 30.4... = 34.25$.

Example 10.3.2

A fishing crew recorded the masses in kilograms (kg) of 200 fish of a particular species that were caught on their trawler. The results are summarised in Table 10.1. The weights given are mid-class values.

Weight of fish (kg)	0.5	1.25	1.75	2.25	2.75	3.5	4.5	5.5	7.0	10.5
Number of fish in class	21	32	33	24	18	21	16	12	11	12

Table 10.1

Assuming that these fish are a random sample from the population of this species, estimate

(a) the mean mass, in kilograms, of a fish of this species,

(b) the variance of masses of fish of this species.

(a)   To find the mean of the sample use your calculator or the formula

$$\bar{x} = \frac{\sum xf}{\sum f} = \frac{626.25}{200} = 3.13125, \text{ so the sample mean is } 3.131\,25 \text{ kg.}$$

Since the sample mean is an unbiased estimator of the population mean, you can take this value as the estimate of the mean mass of all fish of this species.

Therefore the estimate of the mean mass of fish of this species is 3.13 kg, correct to 3 significant figures.

(b)   The variance of the sample is given by

$$\text{variance} = \frac{\sum x^2 f}{\sum f} - \bar{x}^2$$

$$= \frac{3220.1875}{200} - 3.131\,25^2 = 6.296\ldots.$$

To obtain the unbiased estimate of the population variance, multiply the variance of the sample by $\dfrac{n}{n-1}$, which in this case is $\frac{200}{199}$.

$$s_{n-1}{}^2 = \frac{200}{199} \left(\frac{\sum x^2 f}{\sum f} - \bar{x}^2 \right)$$

$$= \frac{200}{199} \times 6.296\ldots = 6.33, \text{ correct to 3 significant figures.}$$

Exercise 10A

1   A random sample of 10 people working for a certain company with 4000 employees are asked, at the end of a day, how much they had spent on snacks that day. The results in £ are as follows.

    1.98   1.84   1.75   1.94   1.56   1.88   1.05   2.10   1.85   2.35

Calculate unbiased estimates of the mean and variance of the amounts spent on snacks that day by all workers employed by the company.

2   Fifty boxes of matches were selected at random from a large carton of such boxes. The number of matches in each box was counted. The results are summarised by $\sum x = 2400$, $\sum x^2 = 115\,212$. Calculate

    (a)   the mean and variance of the number of matches in a box for the sample of 50 boxes,

    (b)   unbiased estimates of the mean and variance of the number of matches in a box for all the boxes in the carton.

3   The diameters of 20 randomly chosen plastic doorknobs of a certain make were measured. The results, x cm, are summarised by $\sum (x - 5) = 2.3$ and $\sum (x - 5)^2 = 0.54$. Find

    (a)   the variance of the diameters in the sample,

    (b)   an unbiased estimate of the variance of the diameters of all knobs produced.

4   The number of vehicle accidents occurring along a long stretch of a particular motorway each day was monitored for a period of 100 randomly chosen days. The results are summarised in the following table.

Number of accidents	0	1	2	3	4	5	6
Number of days	8	12	27	35	13	4	1

Find unbiased estimates of the mean and variance of the daily number of accidents.

5   Unbiased estimates of the mean and variance of a population, based on a random sample of 24 observations, are 5.5 and 2.42 respectively. Another random observation of 8.0 is obtained. Find new unbiased estimates of the mean and variance with this new information.

6   A random sample of 150 pebbles was collected from a part of Brighton beach. The masses of the pebbles, correct to the nearest gram, are summarised in the following grouped frequency table.

Mass (g)	10–19	20–29	30–39	40–49	50–59	60–69	70–79	80–89
Frequency	1	4	22	40	49	28	4	2

Find, to 3 decimal places, unbiased estimates of the mean and variance of the masses of all the pebbles on this part of the beach.

10.4 The sampling distribution of the mean

In Chapter 5 you made use of the property that, when you take samples from a normal population with mean μ and known variance σ^2, the test statistic

$$Z = \frac{\overline{X} - \mu}{\dfrac{\sigma}{\sqrt{n}}}$$

has the standardised normal distribution $N(0,1)$. But what happens when you don't know the variance?

The obvious step is to replace σ^2 by the estimated variance $S_{n-1}{}^2$, and to use

$$T = \frac{\overline{X} - \mu}{\dfrac{S_{n-1}}{\sqrt{n}}}$$

as the test statistic.

But when you do this, the test statistic T no longer has a normal distribution. Because the estimate of the standard deviation varies from sample to sample, a second variable S_{n-1} has been introduced into the test statistic. This has the effect of slightly distorting the distribution. Instead of being normal, the test statistic has a distribution called **Student's t-distribution**, of just the **t-distribution**.

The reason for this name is that the distribution of T was studied by the British statistician W.S.Gosset (1876–1937) who wrote under the pen-name 'Student'. Much of Gosset's statistical work was done while he was employed at the Guinness brewery in Dublin.

You use the t-distribution in the same way as you use $N(0,1)$ when the variance is known. Calculators have programs for values of the probability density function and the cumulative distribution for the t-distribution, just as they do for the standardised normal distribution. Some also have programs for the inverse t-distribution. All you need to remember is:

> If the population variance is known, use the test statistic Z with the normal probability distribution.
>
> If the population variance is estimated from the variance of the sample, use the test statistic T with the t-probability distribution.

There is one complication. There is only one normal distribution with mean 0 and variance 1. But there are many different *t*-distributions, and which one you use depends on the size of the sample.

These *t*-distributions involve a positive integer parameter denoted by v, which stands for the number of **degrees of freedom**. (The letter v, pronounced 'nu', is the Greek letter 'n'.) When you use a calculator to find a probability with the *t*-distribution, you have to key in the value of v as well as the number t. The value of t with v degrees of freedom is sometimes denoted by t_v.

The number of degrees of freedom depends on the particular way in which *t*-probability is being applied. When a *t*-test is used to test a hypothesis about the mean of a population, then $v = n - 1$, where n is the size of the sample.

For a random variable from a normal population with mean μ the variable

$$T = \frac{\overline{X} - \mu}{\frac{S_{n-1}}{\sqrt{n}}}$$ has a *t*-distribution with v degrees of freedom, where $v = n - 1$.

That is, $\dfrac{\overline{X} - \mu}{\frac{S_{n-1}}{\sqrt{n}}} \sim t_{n-1}$.

Fig. 10.2 shows the probability density graphs for the distributions t_3, t_5 and $N(0,1)$. For large values of v the graph for t_v is close to that of $N(0,1)$, but the graphs spread out more as v decreases. This means that, in the 'tails', the probabilities are higher for t than for the normal distribution. This is what you should expect; the conclusion is more certain if it is based on a known value of the population variance than on an estimated one.

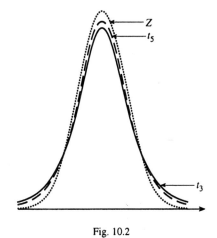

Fig. 10.2

When you use a calculator the only difference between *t*-probability and standard normal probability is that you must also key in the value of v. But to produce tables for *t*-probability like those of normal probability would require a substantial book, because you would need different tables for each v.

To get round this, most *t*-probability tables are much less comprehensive, giving the values of *t* only at the most commonly used significance levels, with one row for each value of v. You can carry out basic hypothesis testing with such tables, but you cannot use them to find *p*-values.

10.5 Hypothesis test of the population mean for a normal population

With a knowledge of the t-distribution it is now possible to extend hypothesis tests on the population mean to the situation in which a sample is taken from a normal population of unknown variance. In this situation the test statistic $\dfrac{\bar{X}-\mu}{\dfrac{S_{n-1}}{\sqrt{n}}}$ is distributed as t_{n-1} and the rejection region is found by using this distribution. The following examples illustrate how rejection regions are found for one- and two-tail tests.

Example 10.5.1

In the past the mean lifetime, X (in hours), of a certain electrical component has been 10.4. A new manufacturing process is introduced which is designed to increase the lifetime. Experimental data collected from a random sample of components manufactured by the new process are summarised by $\sum x = 139.7$, $\sum x^2 = 1858.1$, $n = 11$. Making a suitable assumption, which you should state, test whether there is evidence at the 10% significance level that the new process has increased the lifetime.

This is a one-tail test looking for an increase. The null and alternative hypotheses are $H_0 : \mu = 10.4$, $H_1 : \mu > 10.4$.

The sample mean is $\bar{x} = \dfrac{\sum x}{n} = \dfrac{139.7}{11} = 12.7$,

and an unbiased estimate of the population variance is

$$S_{n-1}^{2} = \frac{n}{n-1}\left(\frac{\sum x^2}{n} - \bar{x}^2\right)$$

$$= \frac{11}{10}\left(\frac{1858.1}{11} - 12.7^2\right) = 8.391\ldots\ .$$

The value of the test statistic is

$$t = \frac{\bar{x}-\mu}{\dfrac{S_{n-1}}{\sqrt{n}}} = \frac{12.7 - 10.4}{\dfrac{\sqrt{8.391\ldots}}{\sqrt{11}}} = 2.633\ldots\ .$$

There are now two ways to complete the test. Method 1 uses the inverse t-program, so if your calculator doesn't have this, use Method 2.

Method 1   For a one-tail test at the 10% significance level you want to find the value of t such that $P(T > t) = 0.10$. So $P(T \le t) = 0.90$, with $\nu = 11 - 1 = 10$, and the 'inverse t' program (or the t-distribution tables) gives the value $t = 1.372$. So the rejection region for this test is $T > 1.372$. This is illustrated in Fig. 10.3.

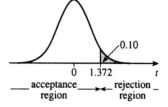

Fig. 10.3

The observed value 2.633 lies in this region, so the null hypothesis is rejected.

Method 2   Using the 't cumulative distribution' program, with $\nu = 10$,

$$P(T \le 2.633\ldots) = 0.9874\ldots\ ,$$

so $P(T > 2.633...) = 1 - 0.9874... = 0.0125...$, or about 1.3%.

Since this is less than 10%, the null hypothesis is rejected.

There is evidence at the 10% significance level that introducing the new process has increased the lifetime of the component.

Example 10.5.2
A student titrates 10 ml of 0.1 M acid against 0.1 M alkali five times and obtains the following results for the volume in ml of alkali.

    9.88   10.18   10.23   10.39   10.25

Assuming that the volume of alkali used has a normal distribution, test at the 5% significance level whether these results show bias from the expected value of 10 ml.

Since the bias can be in either direction a two-tail test is appropriate. The null and alternative hypotheses are $H_0: \mu = 10$, $H_1: \mu \neq 10$.

The sample mean is $\bar{x} = \dfrac{\sum x}{n} = \dfrac{50.93}{5} = 10.186,$

and an unbiased estimate of the population variance is

$$s_{n-1}^2 = \frac{n}{n-1}\left(\frac{\sum x^2}{n} - \bar{x}^2\right)$$

$$= \frac{5}{4}\left(\frac{518.9143}{5} - 10.186^2\right) = 0.035\ 33.$$

The value of the test statistic is $t = \dfrac{\bar{x} - \mu}{\frac{s_{n-1}}{\sqrt{n}}} = \dfrac{10.186 - 10}{\frac{\sqrt{0.035\ 33}}{\sqrt{5}}} = 2.2127...$.

A two-tail test at the 5% significance level has a rejection region divided into two parts, each corresponding to a probability of $2\tfrac{1}{2}\%$. The rejection and acceptance regions are shown in Fig. 10.4.

Method 1   The upper critical value is given by $P(T \leq t) = 0.975$ for 4 degrees of freedom. From the inverse *t* program, $t = 2.776$ and so the rejection region for this test is $|T| \geq 2.776$. The observed value of T does not lie in the rejection region and so the null hypothesis is not rejected.

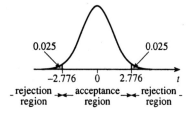

Fig. 10.4

Method 2   Using the *t* cumulative distribution with 4 degrees of freedom

    $P(T \leq 2.2127...) = 0.954...$.

This value is less than 0.975, so T lies in the acceptance region.

The null hypothesis that the student's results do not show bias is accepted.

Example 10.5.3

The weights of packets of a certain brand of breakfast cereal are known to be distributed normally. It is claimed that the net weight of the contents is 450 g. The weights of the contents of seven packets are

445, 453, 447, 451, 440, 460, 449.

Is there any evidence at the 5% level that the population mean is less than 450 g?
What assumption must be made to carry out this test?

The sample mean is $\bar{x} = \dfrac{\sum x}{n} = \dfrac{3145}{7} = 449.28...$, and an unbiased estimate of the population variance is

$$s_{n-1}^2 = \frac{n}{n-1}\left(\frac{\sum x^2}{n} - \bar{x}^2\right)$$

$$= \frac{7}{6}\left(\frac{1\,413\,245}{7} - 449.28...^2\right) = 40.2381.$$

The null and alternative hypotheses are $H_0: \mu = 450$, $H_1: \mu < 450$.

The value of the test statistic is $t = \dfrac{\bar{x} - \mu}{\dfrac{s_{n-1}}{\sqrt{n}}} = \dfrac{449.28... - 450}{\dfrac{\sqrt{40.2381}}{\sqrt{7}}} = -0.2979...$, and the number of

degrees of freedom is $v = 7 - 1 = 6$.

Since the test statistic is negative, the p-value is $P(T \le -0.2979...) = 0.3879...$, or about 38.8%. This is much greater than 5%, so there is no evidence that the population mean is less than 450 g. The assumption made in carrying out this test is that the packets of cereal are randomly chosen.

Here is a summary of the method for carrying out a test of the population mean.

If a random sample of size n is drawn from a normal population of unknown variance, then the null hypothesis $H_0: \mu = \mu_0$ can be tested using the test statistic T. The value of T is given by

$$t = \frac{\bar{x} - \mu}{\dfrac{s_{n-1}}{\sqrt{n}}}, \text{ where } s_{n-1}^2 = \frac{n}{n-1}\left(\frac{\sum x^2}{n} - \bar{x}^2\right).$$

The rejection region for T depends on the form of the alternative hypothesis, H_1, the significance level and the number of degrees of freedom, $v = n - 1$.

- For a two-tail test at the $100\alpha\%$ significance level, the rejection region is given by $|T| \ge t$ where $P(T \le t) = 1 - \frac{1}{2}\alpha$.

- For a one-tail test for an increase at the $100\alpha\%$ significance level, the rejection region is given by $T \ge t$ where $P(T \le t) = 1 - \alpha$.

- For a one-tail test for a decrease at the $100\alpha\%$ significance level, the rejection region is given by $T \le -t$ where $P(T \le t) = 1 - \alpha$.

Exercise 10B

1   A new method for determining the pH value of soil has been developed and is used on a random sample of 15 specimens taken from an area whose pH value has a mean of 6.32. The 15 values give a sample mean of $\bar{x} = 6.14$ and an estimated population variance of $s_{n-1}^2 = 10$. Assuming that the pH values in the area have a normal distribution, test, at the 5% significance level, whether the mean pH value as determined by the new method differs from 6.32.

2   The time taken for a machine to produce a certain plastic bowl has a normal distribution with mean 4.8 seconds. An adjustment is made to the machine which is intended to reduce the mean, and in order to test that it is successful, the times taken to produce 8 bowls are measured. The results, t seconds, are as follows:

    4.2 4.5 4.9 4.3 4.5 4.7 4.6 4.4.

Test, at the $2\frac{1}{2}$% significance level, whether or not the adjustment had the desired effect.

3   The plate glass used in a construction project is required to have a mean thickness greater than 5 mm in order to be acceptable. The thickness of each of 25 samples of a certain kind of plate glass is measured, giving a sample mean of 5.14 mm and estimated population variance of 0.29^2 mm^2. Assuming that the thickness of the glass is distributed normally, carry out a test, at the 5% significance level, to decide whether or not the sampled kind of plate glass is acceptable.

4   The number of minutes late that a Number 38 bus arrives at a city centre stop has a mean of 5.7 during the 'rush hour'. After a reorganisation of the traffic lights in the city, the times of arrival of six Number 38 buses at the city centre bus stop were noted. The number of minutes late were as follows, a negative value indicating that the bus was early.

    2.3 5.6 −1.8 4.3 −1.1 3.2

Assuming that these times comprise a random sample selected from a normal distribution, test, at the 1% significance level, whether or not the new mean is less than 5.7.

5   Haemoglobin levels in females may be modelled by a normal distribution with mean 14.2 (grams per decilitre). As part of a health study, 10 randomly chosen female students from a college had their haemoglobin levels, h, measured. Results summaries are $\sum h = 147.9$ and $\sum h^2 = 2203.19$. Test, at the 5% significance level, whether the mean haemoglobin level of female students in the college differs from the mean level of all females.

6   The mean birth weights of 20 babies born during April 2001 in a London hospital maternity unit was 3.207 kg and gave an unbiased estimate of the population variance of $s_{n-1}^2 = 0.461^2$ kg^2. It may be assumed that these babies form a random sample of all those born in London hospitals during 2001, whose birth weights are distributed normally with mean μ kg. A test of the null hypothesis $\mu = \mu_0$ against the alternative hypothesis $\mu \neq \mu_0$ is carried out at the 10% significance level. Find the set of values of μ_0 for which the null hypothesis is accepted.

10.6   Application to matched pairs

Suppose you want to see whether the time taken to complete a simple task decreases with practice. One way of investigating this would be to take a random sample of people and measure the times which each person takes to perform the task on their first and second attempts. An example of such data is shown in Table 10.5.

Person	A	B	C	D	E	F	G	H
First attempt	6.3	3.5	7.1	3.7	8.4	3.9	4.7	5.2
Second attempt	5.1	3.4	6.2	4.5	7.3	4.0	3.6	5.1
Difference, d	1.2	0.1	0.9	−0.8	1.1	−0.1	1.1	0.1

Table 10.5

The null hypothesis is $H_0 : \mu_x = \mu_y$, where μ_x is the mean time taken by all people on their first attempt and μ_y is the mean time taken by all people on their second attempt. This can be written as $H_0 : \mu_x - \mu_y = 0$. The data collected takes the form of pairs of values, one pair for each person. You can see that there is quite a lot of variation between different people. For example, B is fast on both attempts whereas E is slow. However, it is not the variation between individuals which is of interest but their improvement with practice. If practice does decrease the time taken, then you would expect the first value to be greater than the second. This means that the improvement can be measured by the difference, d, between the first and the second values. The values of these differences are given in the last line of the table. You can check that the average difference, $\bar{d}$, is 0.45 minutes.

The question which now needs to be answered is whether this value indicates that the second time is significantly lower than the first. To do this you need to consider the distribution of $D = X - Y$, where X is the time on the first attempt and Y is the time on the second attempt.

The mean, μ_d, of the sampling distribution of D is given by

$$\begin{aligned}\mu_d &= E(D) = E(X - Y) \\ &= E(X) - E(Y) \\ &= \mu_x - \mu_y.\end{aligned}$$

The null hypothesis $H_0 : \mu_x - \mu_y = 0$ is thus equivalent to $H_0 : \mu_d = 0$. This is just the form of the null hypothesis for a single sample which you met in Section 10.5. So, provided that D has a normal distribution, this null hypothesis can be tested using the statistic T with $n - 1$ degrees of freedom. The variance of the sampling distribution of D is not known, but it can be estimated by S_d^2, where S_d^2 is the unbiased estimator. For the data in Table 10.4 the unbiased estimate of the variance of the differences is $s_d^2 = 0.531...$. You can then calculate

$$t = \frac{\bar{d} - 0}{\frac{s_d}{\sqrt{n}}} = \frac{0.45 - 0}{\frac{\sqrt{0.531...}}{\sqrt{8}}} = 1.7459... \ .$$

The alternative hypothesis is $H_1 : \mu_x > \mu_y$, or $\mu_x - \mu_y > 0$. You therefore have to do a one-tail test with $\nu = 7$. You might choose to use a 10% significance level.

To complete the test you can find, using a calculator or tables, that the rejection region is $T > 1.415$ and that the observed value $t = 1.7459...$ lies in this region; or you can calculate $P(T > 1.7459...) = 0.062\,16...$, and note that 6.22% is less than 10%. The null hypothesis is therefore rejected, and the alternative hypothesis that people take less time with practice is accepted.

*A test like this is called a **matched pairs test**. The word 'matched' is used to indicate that the same people participate in the second trial as in the first.*

Example 10.6.1
To investigate the difference in wear on front and rear tyres of motorcycles, 50 motorcycles of the same model were fitted with new tyres of the same brand. After the motorcycles had been driven for 2000 miles the depths of tread on the front and rear tyres were measured in mm. For each motorcycle the value of d = (depth of front tread – depth of rear tread) was calculated. The results can be summarised by $\sum d = 4.7$ and $\sum d^2 = 3.98$. Test, at the 5% significance level, whether there is a difference in wear on the front and rear tyres.

This is an example of an experiment where the data are collected in pairs. The null hypothesis is $H_0: \mu_x = \mu_y$ where μ_x is the population mean for front tyres and μ_y the population mean for rear tyres. The alternative hypothesis is $H_1: \mu_x \neq \mu_y$.

$$\bar{d} = \frac{4.7}{50} = 0.094 \quad \text{and} \quad s_{n-1}^2 = \frac{50}{49}\left(\frac{3.98}{50} - 0.094^2\right) = 0.0722\ldots .$$

This gives the value of the test statistic $t = \dfrac{0.094 - 0}{\dfrac{\sqrt{0.0722\ldots}}{\sqrt{50}}} = 2.47\ldots .$

Method 1   To find the two-tail rejection region you want the number c such that $P(|T| > c) = 0.05$, so that $P(T > c) = 0.025$. With $\nu = 49$ the inverse *t*-program gives $c = 2.010$. (If you are using tables you may have to get this value by interpolation between 2.021 for $\nu = 40$ and 2.000 for $\nu = 60$.) So the rejection region is $|T| > 2.010$. The calculated value $t = 2.47\ldots$ lies in this region.

Method 2   The cumulative *t*-program gives $P(T > 2.47\ldots) = 0.008\,44\ldots$, so that $P(|T| > 2.47\ldots) = 2 \times 0.008\,44\ldots = 0.016\,89\ldots$, or 1.7%. This is less than the 5% significance level.

Thus H_0 is rejected and H_1, that there is different wear on the front and rear tyres, is accepted.

A matched pairs test can also be used to test whether the mean of paired differences is some constant value, expressed by the null hypothesis $H_0: \mu_x - \mu_y = c$. In this case the test statistic is $T = \dfrac{\bar{D} - c}{\dfrac{S_d}{\sqrt{n}}}$.

Exercise 10C

1   Some psychologists believe that the IQ of the first-born child in a family is significantly greater than the IQ of the last born. In order to investigate this belief, a random sample of 8 families with more than one child agreed to allow their children's IQs to be measured, with the following results.

Family	A	B	C	D	E	F	G	H
IQ of first born	97	121	89	112	138	125	104	114
IQ of last born	101	116	97	108	130	121	101	105

Assuming that the differences have a normal distribution test the psychologists' belief using a 5% significance level.

2   A person's systolic blood pressure is a measure of the pressure exerted by the heart when it contracts and pushes blood around the body. When the heart has just ceased to contract and is dilating ready for the next contraction, the blood pressure drops and is called the diastolic pressure.

The following table gives the systolic and diastolic blood pressures (measured in mm of mercury) of 6 randomly chosen people with diabetes.

Patient	A	B	C	D	E	F
Systolic pressure	141	129	117	115	93	101
Diastolic pressure	83	76	71	59	51	64

Let D denote the amount by which the systolic pressure exceeds the diastolic pressure of a randomly chosen person with diabetes, and let μ_D denote the mean of D. Assuming that D has a normal distribution, test the hypothesis $\mu_D > 40$ at the 5% significance level.

3   The reaction times taken by 10 motorists to apply the brakes of their cars were measured when the motorists had not drunk any alcohol, and after they had drunk a measured amount of alcohol. The reaction times, in hundredths of a second, are given in the following table.

Motorist	A	B	C	D	E	F	G	H	I	J
Without alcohol	40	25	19	23	38	37	28	37	41	27
With alcohol	50	37	35	34	52	50	40	46	53	38

Assuming that the population of differences has a normal distribution, test, at the 1% significance level, whether the drinking of alcohol increases the mean reaction time by more than 0.1 s.

4   An experiment was carried out to compare the difference in the effects of organic and chemical fertilisers on potato yields. Eleven plots of land were selected and two seed potatoes were grown on each plot at a distance of 10 m apart. On one potato an organic fertiliser was used, and on the other, a chemical fertiliser. The choice of which to use was decided by tossing a coin. The differences in yields, d grams, where d = (mass of organic crop − mass of chemical crop), are summarised by

$$\sum d = -310 \quad \text{and} \quad \sum d^2 = 208\ 702.$$

Assuming that the differences have a normal distribution, test, at the 5% significance level, whether there is a difference between the population mean yields.

5   A study of the effect of vitamins on attention span was carried out on 40 sets of identical twins of the same age. One twin was randomly chosen to have the vitamin pill and the other was given a placebo (a pill with no vitamin). Each twin was given a puzzle to solve and the time, in minutes, that each twin remained with the puzzle was measured. The difference in time, d minutes, where d = (vitamin time − placebo time), has mean $\bar{d} = 2.92$ and the unbiased estimate of the variance is 141.23.

If it could be assumed that the differences are distributed normally, what would be the conclusion of the test?

11 Confidence intervals

This chapter introduces the idea of a confidence interval. When you have completed it, you should be able to

- determine a confidence interval for the population mean in the context of a sample drawn from a normal population of known variance
- determine a confidence interval for the population mean in the context of a large sample drawn from any population of known variance
- use a t-distribution, in the context of a sample drawn from a normal population, to determine a confidence interval of the population mean when the variance is unknown
- determine, from a large sample, an approximate confidence interval for a population proportion.

11.1 The concept of a confidence interval

It was shown in Section 10.1 that the mean, $\overline{X}$, of a random sample is an unbiased estimator of the population mean, μ. For example, to estimate the mean amount of pocket money received by all the children in a primary school you could take a random sample of the children and ask each child how much pocket money he or she receives each week. Suppose you find that $\sum x = 111.50$ for a random sample of 50 children, where x is measured in £. Then an unbiased estimate of the population mean, μ, is given by

$$\overline{x} = \frac{\sum x}{n} = \frac{111.50}{50} = 2.23.$$

Such a value is called a **point estimate** because it gives an estimate of the population mean in the form of a single value or 'point' on a number line. Such values are useful, for example, in comparing populations. However, since $\overline{X}$ is a random variable, the value which it takes will vary from sample to sample. As a result you have no idea how close to the actual population mean a point estimate is likely to be. The purpose of a 'confidence interval' is to give an estimate in a form which also indicates the estimate's likely accuracy. A **confidence interval of the mean** is a range of values which has a given probability of 'trapping' the population mean. It is usually taken to be symmetrical about the sample mean. So, if the sample mean takes the value $\overline{x}$, the associated confidence interval would be $[\overline{x} - c, \overline{x} + c]$ where c is a number whose value has yet to be found.

Notice the notation for an interval used here. The interval $[\overline{x} - c, \overline{x} + c]$ means the real numbers from $\overline{x} - c$ to $\overline{x} + c$, including the end-points. For example, $[-2.1, 6.8]$ means real numbers y such that $-2.1 \le y \le 6.8$. See Higher Level Book 1 Section 22.4.

In Fig. 11.1 the sample mean $\overline{X}$ takes a value $\overline{x}_1$ and the confidence interval covers the range of values $[\overline{x}_1 - c, \overline{x}_1 + c]$.

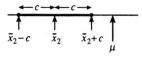

Fig. 11.1   Fig. 11.2

In this case the confidence interval traps the population mean, μ. For a different sample, with a different sample mean, $\overline{x}_2$, the confidence interval might not trap μ. This situation is illustrated in Fig. 11.2.

The end-points of the confidence interval are themselves random variables since they vary from sample to sample. They can be written as $\overline{X} - c$ and $\overline{X} + c$. You can see from Fig. 11.1 and Fig. 11.2 that the confidence interval will trap μ if the difference between the sample mean and the population mean is less than or equal to c. Expressed algebraically this condition is $|\overline{X} - \mu| \leq c$.

The next section explains how the value of c is chosen so as to give a specified probability that the confidence interval traps μ.

11.2 Calculating a confidence interval

Consider the following situation. The masses of tablets produced by a machine are known to be distributed normally with a standard deviation of 0.012 g. The mean mass of the tablets produced is monitored at regular intervals by taking a sample of 25 tablets and calculating the sample mean, $\overline{X}$.

Suppose you wish to find an interval which has a 95% probability of trapping the population mean, μ. The mass, X (in grams), of a single tablet is distributed normally with unknown mean μ and standard deviation 0.012; that is, $X \sim N(\mu, 0.012^2)$. So, for a sample of size 25, $\overline{X} \sim N\left(\mu, \dfrac{0.012^2}{25}\right)$.

Using the notation of the previous section, the population mean is trapped in the interval $\left[\overline{X} - c, \overline{X} + c\right]$, where c is a constant, if $|\overline{X} - \mu| \leq c$. The interval has a probability of 95% of trapping the population mean if, and only if, $P(|\overline{X} - \mu| \leq c) = 0.95$.

Fig. 11.3 shows the sampling distribution of $\overline{X}$ with this probability indicated. The value of c is found by standardising $|\overline{X} - \mu|$ to give $Z = \dfrac{\overline{X} - \mu}{\dfrac{0.012}{\sqrt{25}}}$ where $Z \sim N(0,1)$.

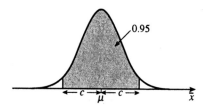

Fig. 11.3

Fig. 11.4 shows the distribution of Z with the probability of 0.95 indicated. If your calculator can operate in two-tail mode, use this to find z such that $P(|Z| \leq z) = 0.95$; if not, convert this to a cumulative normal distribution condition, and find z such that $P(Z < z) = 0.975$. Either way, $z = 1.960$.

Thus $1.960 = \dfrac{\overline{X} - \mu}{\dfrac{0.012}{\sqrt{25}}}$.

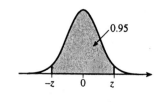

Fig. 11.4

But $\overline{X} - \mu = c$, so

$$1.960 = \dfrac{c}{\dfrac{0.012}{\sqrt{25}}}$$

giving

$$c = 1.960 \times \dfrac{0.012}{\sqrt{25}} = 0.004\ 70, \text{ correct to 3 significant figures.}$$

So the interval which has a 95% probability of trapping μ is $\left[\overline{X} - 0.0047, \overline{X} + 0.0047\right]$.

Suppose that you took a sample of 25 tablets and found that the mean mass was, for example, 0.5642 g. This sample mean would give a value for the interval of $[0.5642 - 0.0047, 0.5642 + 0.0047]$, which is $[0.5595, 0.5689]$. Such an interval is called a **95% confidence interval of the population mean**.

It is important to realise that such a confidence interval may or may not trap μ, depending on the value of $\overline{X}$. Suppose, for a moment, that you know the value of μ and you take a number of different samples of 25 tablets. Fig. 11.5 shows confidence intervals calculated in the way described above for 30 different samples of 25 tablets.

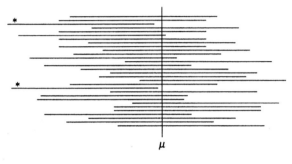

Fig. 11.5

Most of the confidence intervals trap μ but a few (marked *) do not. On average, the proportion of 95% confidence intervals which trap μ is 95%. In practice, of course, you do not know μ and would usually take only one sample and from it calculate one confidence interval. In this situation, you cannot *know* whether your particular confidence interval does include μ: all you can say is that, on average, 95 times out of 100 it will contain μ.

The method which has been described for finding a 95% confidence interval of the mean can be generalised to a sample of size n from a normal population with standard deviation σ. Replacing 25 by n and 0.012 by σ gives

$$1.960 = \frac{c}{\frac{\sigma}{\sqrt{n}}},$$

which, on rearranging, gives $c = 1.960 \frac{\sigma}{\sqrt{n}}$.

> Given a sample of size n from a normal population with variance σ^2, a 95% confidence interval for the population mean is given by
>
> $$\left[\overline{x} - 1.960 \frac{\sigma}{\sqrt{n}}, \overline{x} + 1.960 \frac{\sigma}{\sqrt{n}}\right],$$
>
> where $\overline{x}$ is the sample mean.

Example 11.2.1

The lengths of nails produced by a machine are known to be distributed normally with mean μ mm and standard deviation 0.7 mm. The lengths, in mm, of a random sample of 5 nails are 107.29, 106.56, 105.94, 106.99, 106.47.

(a) Calculate a symmetric 95% confidence interval for μ, giving the end-points to 1 decimal place.

(b) Two hundred random samples of 5 nails are taken and a symmetric 95% confidence interval for μ is calculated for each sample. Find the expected number of intervals which do not contain μ.

(a) The mean of the sample is given by

$$\bar{x} = \frac{107.29 + 106.56 + 105.94 + 106.99 + 106.47}{5} = 106.65.$$

Substituting this value of $\bar{x}$ together with $\sigma = 0.7$ and $n = 5$ into the expression in the shaded box gives a symmetric 95% confidence interval for μ of

$$\left[106.65 - 1.960 \times \frac{0.7}{\sqrt{5}}, \, 106.65 + 1.960 \times \frac{0.7}{\sqrt{5}}\right] = [106.65 - 0.61, 106.65 + 0.61].$$

The symmetric 95% confidence interval for μ, measured in mm, is $[106.0, 107.3]$.

(b) On average, 95% of the confidence intervals should include μ. This means that 5% will not include μ. So out of 200 confidence intervals you would expect $200 \times 5\% = 10$ not to include μ.

It is not easy to suggest a general rule about the accuracy to which confidence intervals are given, so you have to exercise common sense. In Example 11.2.1, since the standard deviation is given to only 1 significant figure, you could not justify giving the bounds of the confidence interval to more than 1 decimal place. But if the standard deviation were known more precisely, an answer correct to 2 decimal places would be appropriate.

Example 11.2.2

For a method of measuring the velocity of sound in air, the results of repeated experiments are known to be distributed normally with standard deviation 6 m s^{-1}. A number of measurements are made using this method, and from these measurements a symmetric 95% confidence interval for the velocity of sound in air is calculated. Find the width of this confidence interval for   (a) 4,   (b) 36 measurements.

A symmetric 95% confidence interval extends from $\bar{x} - 1.960 \frac{\sigma}{\sqrt{n}}$ to $\bar{x} + 1.960 \frac{\sigma}{\sqrt{n}}$, so its width is

$$\bar{x} + 1.960 \frac{\sigma}{\sqrt{n}} - \left(\bar{x} - 1.960 \frac{\sigma}{\sqrt{n}}\right) = 2 \times 1.960 \frac{\sigma}{\sqrt{n}}.$$

In this example $\sigma = 6$, so the width of the confidence interval is $2 \times 1.960 \frac{6}{\sqrt{n}} = \frac{23.52}{\sqrt{n}}$.

(a) For $n = 4$, the width of the confidence interval is $\frac{23.52}{\sqrt{4}} = 11.76$.

(b) For $n = 36$, the width of the confidence interval is $\frac{23.52}{\sqrt{36}} = 3.92$.

Nine times as many measurements are needed to reduce the confidence interval width by a factor of three.

11.3 Different levels of confidence

As Example 11.2.1 makes clear, there is a probability of 5 in 100 that a 95% confidence interval does not include μ. There are circumstances in which you may wish to be more certain that the confidence interval which you have calculated does include μ. For example, you may wish to be 99% certain. Fig. 11.6 is the diagram corresponding to Fig. 11.3 for this situation. The only difference in the calculation of the confidence interval is that a different value of z is needed. In this case $P(|Z| \leq z) = 0.99$ or $P(Z \leq z) = 0.995$, giving $z = 2.576$, so that the 99% confidence interval of the mean is given by

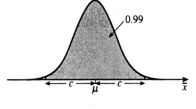

Fig. 11.6

$$\left[\bar{x} - 2.576 \frac{\sigma}{\sqrt{n}}, \bar{x} + 2.576 \frac{\sigma}{\sqrt{n}} \right].$$

Note that this 99% confidence interval is wider than the 95% confidence interval: this is to be expected since the former is more likely to trap μ than the latter. You can see that there is a balance between precision and certainty: if you increase one you decrease the other. This is similar to the balance between Type I and Type II errors in hypothesis testing (see Section 9.2). The only way of decreasing the probabilities of both types of error simultaneously is to increase the sample size. In the same way, to increase both the precision and the certainty of a confidence interval you have to increase the sample size.

For a 90% confidence interval, the appropriate value of z is that value for which $P(|Z| \leq z) = 0.90$ or $P(Z \leq z) = 0.95$, giving $z = 1.645$. You may have spotted that the values of z used in confidence intervals correspond to those used in hypothesis testing. To generalise, the critical value of z for a two-tail test at the $100\alpha\%$ significance level is the same as the value of z used to calculate a symmetric $100(1 - \alpha)\%$ confidence interval (see Fig. 11.7). The critical value of z for a two-tail test at the $100\alpha\%$ level is also the same as the critical value of z for a one-tail test at the $\frac{1}{2} \times 100\alpha\%$ level. These values are given in the shaded box at the end of this section where the probabilities refer to the acceptance region.

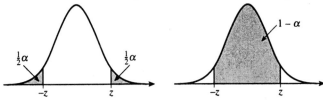

Fig. 11.7

A $100(1 - \alpha)\%$ confidence interval of the population mean for a sample of size n taken from a normal population with variance σ^2 is given by

$$\left[\bar{x} - z \frac{\sigma}{\sqrt{n}}, \bar{x} + z \frac{\sigma}{\sqrt{n}} \right],$$

where $\bar{x}$ is the sample mean and the value of z is such that $P(|Z| \leq z) = 1 - \alpha$ or $P(Z \leq z) = 1 - \frac{1}{2}\alpha$.

Example 11.3.1

The masses of sweets produced by a machine are normally distributed with a standard deviation of 0.5 grams. A sample of 50 sweets had a mean mass of 15.21 grams.

(a) Find a 99% confidence interval for μ, the mean mass of all sweets produced by the machine.

The manufacturer of the machine claims that it produces sweets with a mean mass of 15 grams.

(b) State, giving a reason, whether the confidence interval calculated in part (a) supports this claim.

(a)   From the results given in the shaded box above, a $100(1-\alpha)\%$ confidence interval for μ is

given by $\left[\bar{x} - z\dfrac{\sigma}{\sqrt{n}}, \bar{x} + z\dfrac{\sigma}{\sqrt{n}}\right]$ where the value of z is such that $P(Z \le z) = 1 - \tfrac{1}{2}\alpha$.

For a 99% confidence interval, $100(1-\alpha) = 99$, giving $\alpha = 0.01$. Thus the value of z required is that for which

$$P(Z \le z) = 1 - \tfrac{1}{2}\alpha$$
$$= 1 - \tfrac{1}{2} \times 0.01 = 0.995.$$

From the inverse normal cumulative distribution program, $z = 2.576$.

Substituting $z = 2.576$, $\bar{x} = 15.21$, $\sigma = 0.5$ and $n = 50$ into the expression for the confidence interval gives a 99% confidence interval of

$$\left[15.21 - 2.576 \times \dfrac{0.5}{\sqrt{50}}, 15.21 + 2.576 \times \dfrac{0.5}{\sqrt{50}}\right] = [15.027\ldots, 15.392\ldots]$$
$$= [15.03, 15.39], \text{ correct to 2 decimal places.}$$

(b)   The confidence interval does not include the value 15, which suggests that the manufacturer's claim is untrue.

You can check that the same conclusion is reached if a hypothesis test is carried out at the 1% significance level with $H_0: \mu = 15$ and $H_1: \mu \ne 15$.

Example 11.3.2

The measurement error made in measuring the concentration in parts per million (ppm) of nitrate ions in water by a particular method is known to be distributed normally with mean 0 and standard deviation 0.05.

(a) If 10 measurements on a specimen gave $\sum x = 11.37$ ppm, determine a symmetric 99.5% confidence interval for the true concentration, μ, of nitrate ions in the specimen.

(b) How many measurements would be required in order to reduce the width of this interval to 0.03 ppm at most?

(a)   The measured value, X, of the nitrate ion concentration is equal to $\mu + Y$ where Y is the measurement error. Thus

$$E(X) = E(\mu + Y)$$
$$= \mu + E(Y)$$
$$= \mu + 0 = \mu,$$

and

$$\begin{aligned}
\text{Var}\,(X) &= \text{Var}\,(\mu + Y) \\
&= \text{Var}\,(\mu) + \text{Var}\,(Y) \\
&= 0 + 0.05^2 = 0.05^2.
\end{aligned}$$

This means that $X \sim N(\mu, 0.05^2)$.

For a 99.5% confidence interval, $1 - \alpha = 0.995$, so $\alpha = 0.005$ and $\frac{1}{2}\alpha = 0.0025$.

Thus $P(|Z| \leq z) = 1 - \alpha = 0.995$, or

$$\begin{aligned}
P(Z \leq z) &= 1 - \tfrac{1}{2}\alpha \\
&= 1 - 0.0025 = 0.9975
\end{aligned}$$

which gives

$$z = 2.807.$$

So a 99.5% confidence interval for μ is

$$\begin{aligned}
\left[\bar{x} - 2.807\,\frac{\sigma}{\sqrt{n}}, \bar{x} + 2.807\,\frac{\sigma}{\sqrt{n}}\right] &= \left[\frac{11.37}{10} - 2.807 \times \frac{0.05}{\sqrt{10}}, \frac{11.37}{10} + 2.807 \times \frac{0.05}{\sqrt{10}}\right] \\
&= [1.137 - 0.044,\ 1.137 + 0.044] \\
&= [1.093, 1.181].
\end{aligned}$$

(b) The width of the 99.5% confidence interval for a sample of size n is

$$2 \times 2.807 \times \frac{0.05}{\sqrt{n}}.$$

For this width to be at most 0.03, $2 \times 2.807 \times \dfrac{0.05}{\sqrt{n}} \leq 0.03$.

Rearranging gives

$$\sqrt{n} \geq \frac{2 \times 2.807 \times 0.05}{0.03}, \qquad \text{so} \qquad n \geq 87.5\ldots\ .$$

Since n must be an integer, 88 or more measurements are required to give a confidence interval of width 0.03 ppm at most.

Some values of z for commonly used confidence intervals are given below:

Confidence interval	z
90%	1.645
95%	1.960
98%	2.326
99%	2.576

11.4 Confidence intervals for non-normal populations

So far all the examples of confidence intervals have been obtained from samples drawn from populations with a normal distribution. But if the sample is large enough, that condition can be relaxed.

The reasoning used to establish confidence intervals in Section 11.2 was based on the fact that in a normal population the sample mean $\overline{X}$ is distributed normally. But you know from the central limit theorem (Section 7.1) that, if the sample is large enough, the sample mean has a distribution that is approximately normal whatever the distribution of the underlying population. This means that you can use the same method to find a confidence interval for the mean of any population, provided that the sample is large enough for the normal approximation to be valid.

Example 11.4.1

A supermarket chain has a flexible hours policy for its regular check-out staff. The management is not willing to publish the mean hours worked, but has made it known that the effect of the policy is that the standard deviation of the hours worked per week is 2.9 hours. A trade union researcher asks a random sample of 80 of these employees to record how many hours they work in a typical week. She finds that the total of the working times recorded is 3064 hours. Use these data to find a 90% confidence interval for the mean number of hours per week worked by members of the check-out staff.

The distribution of hours worked by different members of staff is not known, but the sample size of 80 is large enough for the researcher to assume that the distribution of the sample mean is approximately normal.

The mean number of hours worked by a single member of staff is $3064 \div 80$, which is 38.30. The shaded box at the end of Section 11.3 gives the value of z for a 90% confidence interval to be 1.645. The confidence interval is therefore given by

$$\left[38.30 - 1.645 \times \frac{2.9}{\sqrt{80}}, 38.30 + 1.645 \times \frac{2.9}{\sqrt{80}} \right],$$

which is $[37.77, 38.83]$, correct to 2 decimal places.

Exercise 11A

1   Bags of sugar have masses which are distributed normally with mean μ grams and standard deviation 4.6 grams. The sugar in each of a random sample of 5 bags taken from a production line is weighed, with the following results, in grams.

    498.2   501.3   503.7   496.8   502.5

Calculate a symmetric 95% confidence interval for μ.

If a 95% symmetric confidence interval for μ was calculated for each of the 200 samples of 5 bags, how many of the confidence intervals would be expected to contain μ?

2   The volume of milk in litre cartons filled by a machine has a normal distribution with mean μ litres and standard deviation 0.05 litres. A random sample of 25 cartons was selected and the contents, x litres, measured. The results are summarised by $\sum x = 25.11$. Calculate

(a) a symmetric 98% confidence interval for μ,

(b) the width of a symmetric 90% confidence interval for μ based on the volume of milk in a random sample of 50 cartons.

3 The random variable X has a normal distribution with mean μ and variance σ^2. A symmetric 90% confidence interval for μ based on a random sample of 16 observations of X has width 4.24. Find

(a) the value of σ,

(b) the width of a symmetric 90% confidence interval for μ based on a random sample of 4 observations of X,

(c) the width of a symmetric 95% confidence interval for μ based on a random sample of 4 observations of X.

4 The heights of fully-grown British males may be modelled by a normal distribution with mean 178 cm and standard deviation 7.5 cm. The 11 male (fully-grown) biology students present at a university seminar had a mean height of 175.2 cm. Assuming a standard deviation of 7.5 cm, and stating any further assumption, calculate a symmetric 99% confidence interval for the mean height of all fully-grown male biology students.

Does the confidence interval suggest that fully-grown male biology students have a different mean height from 178 cm?

5 A machine is designed to produce metal rods of length 5 cm. In fact, the lengths are distributed normally with mean 5.00 cm and standard deviation 0.032 cm. The machine is moved to a new site and, in order to check whether or not the mean length has altered, the lengths of a random sample of 8 rods are measured. The results, in cm, are as follows.

    5.07 4.95 4.98 5.06 5.13 5.05 4.98 5.06

(a) Assuming that the standard deviation is unchanged, calculate a symmetric 95% confidence interval for the mean length of the rods produced by the machine in its new position.

(b) State, giving a reason, whether you consider that the mean length has changed.

6 A method used to determine the percentage of nitrogen in a fertiliser has an error which is distributed normally with zero mean and standard deviation 0.34%. Ten independent determinations of the percentage of nitrogen gave a mean value of 15.92%.

(a) Calculate a symmetric 98% confidence interval for the percentage of nitrogen in the fertiliser.

(b) Find the smallest number of extra independent determinations that would reduce the width of the symmetric 98% confidence interval to at most 0.4%.

7 Each year a city sets a general knowledge test to all its 10-year-old children. The standard deviation of the marks is always about 23, and the aim is to have a mean mark of 70. This year's test is tried out on 200 randomly chosen children in a neighbouring city, and the mean mark achieved in the trial is 67.8. Find a 90% confidence interval for the true mean for this test. What action should be taken as a result of the trial?

11.5 Populations with unknown variance

So far it has been assumed that the variance of the underlying population is known. In practice you will often not know this variance, and you will have to estimate it from the variance of the sample.

This is just the situation you met in Section 10.5 when testing hypotheses about the population mean, and you deal with it in the same way. That is, the population variance σ^2 is replaced by the estimated population variance s_{n-1}^2, and the multiplier is found from the t-distribution rather than the normal distribution. The rule is then:

> Given a sample of size n from a normal population of unknown variance, a $100(1-\alpha)\%$ confidence interval for the population mean is given by
>
> $$\left[\bar{x} - t \frac{s_{n-1}}{\sqrt{n}}, \bar{x} + t \frac{s_{n-1}}{\sqrt{n}} \right],$$
>
> where $\bar{x}$ is the sample mean and the value of t is such that $P(|T| \le t) = 1 - \alpha$, or $P(T \le t) = 1 - \frac{1}{2}\alpha$, for $\nu = n - 1$ degrees of freedom.

Example 11.5.1

Ten measurements of the zero error on an ammeter yielded the results $+0.13$, -0.09, $+0.06$, $+0.15$, -0.02, $+0.03$, $+0.01$, -0.02, -0.07, $+0.05$. (The zero error is the reading when no electric current is passing through the ammeter.) Assuming that these measurements come from a normal population, calculate a 95% confidence interval for the mean zero error.

First it is necessary to calculate the sample mean and an unbiased estimate of the population variance from the given measurements.

$$\bar{x} = \frac{\sum x}{n} = \frac{0.23}{10} = 0.023,$$

and

$$s_{n-1}^2 = \frac{n}{n-1}\left(\frac{\sum x^2}{n} - \bar{x}^2 \right) \text{ so } s_{n-1} = 0.078\,18\dots\,.$$

For a 95% confidence interval, $\alpha = 0.05$, so $P(T \le t) = 1 - \frac{1}{2} \times 0.05 = 0.975$ for $\nu = n - 1 = 9$ degrees of freedom. Using the inverse cumulative t-distribution program, the value of t is 2.262; so a 95% confidence interval for the population mean is

$$\left[0.023 - 2.262 \times \frac{0.078\,18\dots}{\sqrt{10}}, 0.023 + 2.262 \times \frac{0.078\,18\dots}{\sqrt{10}} \right] = [-0.0329, 0.0789],$$

where the answers have been given to 3 significant figures.

You can also find the value of t for a given confidence level from a table of critical values. In this example you will find the value $t = 2.262$ tabulated for $P(X \le t) = 0.975$ with $\nu = 9$.

========================== **Exercise 11B** ==========================

1   A symmetric $c\%$ confidence interval for a population mean is to be calculated using a random
    sample of n observations of the normal random variable X, which has unknown mean and
    unknown variance. State the values of t used in the following cases.

    (a) $c = 90$, $n = 12$ (b) $c = 95$, $n = 10$ (c) $c = 98$, $n = 25$ (d) $c = 99.5$, $n = 100$

2   Bottles of El Bombero 1999, a Spanish red wine, were advertised as having 'an incredible 15%'
    alcohol content. Wine from a random sample of six bottles was analysed and gave percentage
    alcohol contents of   14.6, 15.1, 14.7, 15.3, 14.9, 15.0.

    Stating any required assumption, calculate a symmetric 95% confidence interval for the mean
    percentage alcohol content in all bottles of El Bombero 1999.

3   The number of calls made in May 2000 to each of 20 randomly chosen ambulance stations in the
    UK was monitored. The resulting sample mean was 2846.6 and an unbiased estimate of the
    population variance was 312.4^2. Calculate a symmetric 90% confidence interval for the mean
    number of calls made to all ambulance stations in the UK in May 2000.

    At the end of the year, the monthly figures for all the ambulance stations were obtained and the
    mean for May was found to lie outside the interval. How might this be explained?

4   The times, t minutes, taken by 18 children in an infant reception class to complete a jigsaw puzzle
    were measured. The results are summarised by $\sum t = 75.6$ and $\sum t^2 = 338.1$.

    (a) Stating your assumptions, calculate a symmetric 95% confidence interval for the population
         mean time for children to complete the puzzle.

    (b) The manufacturers of the puzzle indicate a mean completion time of 5 minutes. What
         conclusion might be made about the children in the class?

5   The acceleration due to gravity, g, is determined experimentally. In 5 independent determinations
    the values, in m s^{-2}, are 9.79, 9.82, 9.80, 9.78, 9.84. It may be assumed that these values are
    observations from a normal distribution whose mean is g.

    (a) Obtain a point estimate for g based on the 5 values.

    (b) Calculate a symmetric 99% confidence interval for g, giving end-points to 3 decimal places.

    (c) State whether or not, apart from rounding errors, the confidence interval found is exact.

6   A random sample of 12 fully-grown swallows (*Hirundo rustica*) were captured and released after
    their lengths, from tip of tail to tip of beak, were measured. The results, x cm, are summarised by
    $\sum x = 229.2$ and $\sum x^2 = 4389.16$.

    (a) Assuming that the lengths are distributed normally, calculate a symmetric 98% confidence
         interval for the mean length of all fully-grown swallows.

    (b) A thirteenth swallow was caught and found to have a length of 15.9 cm. Assuming that the
         mean and variance of the lengths of fully-grown swallows are approximated well by the
         sample estimates, is it likely that this swallow is fully grown?

7   The contents of 140 bags of flour selected randomly from a large batch delivered to a store are weighed and the results, w grams, summarised by $\sum (w - 500) = -266$ and $\sum (w - 500)^2 = 1178$.

(a) Calculate unbiased estimates of the batch mean and variance of the mass of flour in a bag.

(b) Calculate a symmetric 95% confidence interval for the batch mean mass.

The manager of the store believes that the confidence interval indicates a mean less than 500 g and considers the batch to be sub-standard. She has all of the bags in the batch weighed and finds that the batch mean mass is 501.1 g. How can this be reconciled with the confidence interval calculated in part (b)?

8   An environmental science student carried out a study of the incidence of lichens on a stone wall in Derbyshire. She selected, at random, 100 one-metre lengths of wall, all of the same height. The number of lichens in each section was counted and the results are summarised in the following frequency table.

Number of lichens	0	1	2	3	4	5	6
Number of sections	8	22	27	19	13	8	3

(a) Calculate the sample mean and an unbiased estimate of the population variance of the number of lichens per metre length of the wall.

(b) Calculate a symmetric 90% confidence interval for the mean number of lichens per metre length of the wall.

11.6 Confidence interval for a proportion

Many statistical investigations are concerned with finding the proportion of a population which has a specified attribute. Suppose you were a manufacturer of a version of an appliance designed for left-handed people. In order to assess the potential market you would be interested in the proportion of left-handed people in the population. It would be impossible to ask everybody and so you would have to rely on a sample. Suppose that you were able to obtain information from a random sample of 500 people and you found that 60 of them were left-handed. It would seem reasonable to estimate that the proportion, p, of the population who are left-handed is $\frac{60}{500} = 0.12$, or 12%. However, you need to be certain that this method gives you an unbiased estimate of p.

Consider the more general situation where a random sample of n people are questioned. Provided that n is much smaller than the population size the distribution of X, the number of people in a sample of size n who are left-handed, will be B(n, p) since

- there are a fixed number of trials (n people asked)
- each trial has two possible outcomes (left-handed or right-handed)
- the outcomes are mutually exclusive (assuming that no one is ambidextrous)
- the probability of a person being left-handed is constant
- the trials are independent.

Let P be the random variable 'the proportion of people in a sample of size n who are left-handed'. Then $P = \frac{X}{n}$. The expected value of P is

$$E(P) = E\left(\frac{X}{n}\right) = \frac{1}{n}E(X)$$

$$= \frac{1}{n} \times np \qquad \text{(since the mean of a binomial distribution is } np\text{)}$$

$$= p.$$

Thus the proportion in the sample does provide an unbiased point estimate of the population proportion.

It would be more useful, however, to find a confidence interval for p since this gives an idea of the precision of the estimate. In order to do this you need to consider the distribution of P. For a large sample, X will be distributed approximately normally (Section 6.4) and so P will also be distributed approximately normally (see Section 4.1). In order to calculate a confidence interval you also need the variance of P. This can be found as follows.

$$\text{Var}(P) = \text{Var}\left(\frac{X}{n}\right)$$

$$= \frac{1}{n^2} \times \text{Var}(X)$$

$$= \frac{1}{n^2} \times npq \qquad \text{(since the variance of a binomial distribution is } npq\text{)}$$

$$= \frac{pq}{n}.$$

> If $X \sim B(n, p)$, then the sample proportion P, where $P = \frac{X}{n}$, is distributed
>
> approximately as $N\left(p, \frac{pq}{n}\right)$.
>
> This approximation may be used when n is large enough that $np > 10$ and $nq > 10$. In practice, this will be achieved if there are more than 10 successes and 10 failures in n trials.

In Section 11.3 you saw that for the sampling distribution $\overline{X} \sim N\left(\mu, \frac{\sigma^2}{n}\right)$ a confidence interval for the

mean is given by $\left[\overline{x} - z\frac{\sigma}{\sqrt{n}}, \overline{x} + z\frac{\sigma}{\sqrt{n}}\right]$. By analogy a confidence interval for the proportion is found by

replacing $\overline{x}$ by p and $\frac{\sigma}{\sqrt{n}}$ by $\sqrt{\frac{pq}{n}}$ to give an approximate confidence interval $\left[p - z\sqrt{\frac{pq}{n}}, p + z\sqrt{\frac{pq}{n}}\right]$,

where values of z are obtained as before.

This confidence interval is expressed in terms of p and q, which are not known (otherwise a confidence interval would not be required!). However, again similar to finding a confidence interval for the mean, these unknown quantities can be replaced by their estimates from the sample provided that the sample is large. The result is the interval

$$\left[\hat{p} - z\sqrt{\frac{\hat{p}\hat{q}}{n}}, \hat{p} + z\sqrt{\frac{\hat{p}\hat{q}}{n}}\right], \text{ where } \hat{p} = \frac{x}{n} \text{ and } \hat{q} = 1 - \hat{p} = 1 - \frac{x}{n}.$$

Given a large random sample, size n, from a population in which a proportion of members, p, has a particular attribute, an approximate $100(1-\alpha)\%$ confidence interval for p is

$$\left[\hat{p}-z\sqrt{\frac{\hat{p}\hat{q}}{n}}, \hat{p}+z\sqrt{\frac{\hat{p}\hat{q}}{n}}\right],$$

where $\hat{p}$ is the sample proportion with this attribute, $\hat{q}=1-\hat{p}$ and the value of z is such that $P(|Z|\leq z)=1-\alpha$, or $P(Z\leq z)=1-\frac{1}{2}\alpha$.

This rule can now be used to calculate a confidence interval for the proportion of left-handers in the population. For the sample taken, $n=500$, $\hat{p}=0.12$ and $\hat{q}=0.88$, and for a 95% confidence interval, $z=1.96$. This gives a 95% confidence interval

$$\left[0.12-1.960\times\sqrt{\frac{0.12\times0.88}{500}}, 0.12+1.960\times\sqrt{\frac{0.12\times0.88}{500}}\right]=[0.092, 0.148].$$

It is interesting to note that the answer does not depend on the size of the population, only the size of the sample. This will always be true if the sample size is much less than the population size so that the value of p is effectively constant. This fact can be used to calculate the sample size required to give a confidence interval of specified width, as illustrated in the following example.

Example 11.6.1
An opinion poll is to be carried out to estimate the proportion of the electorate of a country who will vote 'yes' in a forthcoming referendum. In a trial run a random sample of 100 people were questioned; 42 said they would vote 'yes'. Estimate the random sample size required to give a 99% confidence interval of the proportion with a width of 0.02.

For a 99% confidence interval, z takes the value 2.576, so the width of this interval is

$2\times2.576\sqrt{\frac{\hat{p}\hat{q}}{n}}$, where $\hat{p}$ and $\hat{q}$ are used to estimate p and q.

The trial run gives $\hat{p}=0.42$ and hence $\hat{q}=0.58$. Thus the required value of n is given by

$$2\times2.576\times\sqrt{\frac{0.42\times0.58}{n}}=0.02.$$

Rearranging and solving for n gives 16 165 to the nearest integer.

It is interesting to think that if this example referred to the UK, where the size of the electorate is about 44 million, then the sample required is only about 0.04% of the electorate. The problem lies in obtaining a random sample. In practice opinion polls do not rely on random samples but use sophisticated techniques which are meant to ensure representative samples.

Exercise 11C

1   In a study of computer usage a random sample of 200 private households in a particular town was selected and the number that own at least one computer was found to be 68. Calculate a symmetric 90% confidence interval of the percentage of households in the town that own at least one computer.

2   Of 500 cars passing under a road bridge on the M1 motorway 92 were found to be red.

(a) Find a symmetric 98% confidence interval of the population proportion of red cars.

(b) State any assumption required for the validity of the interval.

(c) Describe a suitable population to which the interval applies.

(d) If 50 students carried out this experiment at different places and times, what is the expected number of confidence intervals which would contain the population proportion of red cars?

3   A biased dice was thrown 600 times and resulted in 224 sixes. Calculate a symmetric 99% confidence interval of p, the probability of obtaining a six in a single throw of the dice.

Estimate the smallest number of times the dice should be thrown for the width of the symmetric 99% confidence interval of p to be at most 0.08.

4   The board of trustees of a charitable trust wishes to make a change to the trust's constitution. In order for this to happen at least two-thirds of the members must vote for the change. Before the vote is taken, the secretary consults a random sample of 60 members and finds that 75% of them will vote for the change. Calculate a symmetric 95% confidence interval for the proportion of all members who will vote for the change.

Nearer the time at which the vote is to be taken, the secretary consults a random sample of n members and finds, again, that 75% of them will vote for the change. Using this figure, he calculates a symmetric 99% confidence interval for the proportion of members who will vote for the change. This interval does not include the value two-thirds. Find the smallest possible value of n.   (OCR)

5   The compiler of crossword puzzles classifies a puzzle as 'easy' if 60% or more people attempting the puzzle can complete it correctly within 20 minutes. It is classified as 'hard' if fewer than 30% of people can complete it correctly within 20 minutes. All other puzzles are classified as 'average'. A particular puzzle was given to 150 competitors in a contest and 74 completed it correctly within 20 minutes. The compiler wishes to be 90% confident of correctly classifying the puzzle.

(a) How should she classify the puzzle?

(b) Can she be 95% confident that her classification is correct?

12 A survey of probability distributions

This chapter presents a summary of probability distributions and their properties, some of which you have met already. When you have completed it, you should

- know the main properties of a number of probability distributions, and when it is appropriate to use them.

12.1 Uniform distributions

If there is no reason to think that any outcome is more probable than any other, the distribution is said to be uniform. This may occur with either a discrete or a continuous random variable.

(i) The discrete uniform distribution $DU(n)$

In most examples of a discrete uniform distribution the sample space is a set of positive integers $\{1,2,3,\dots,n\}$ for some value of n. When you roll a fair dice the score has a uniform distribution with $n = 6$. When you draw a number out of a hat to find the winner of a raffle, it has a uniform distribution with n equal to the total number of tickets sold.

Since $P(X = x)$ is the same for each number x in the sample space, and the sum of all the probabilities is equal to 1, it follows that

$$P(X = x) = \frac{1}{n} \quad \text{for each } x \in \{1,2,3,\dots,n\}.$$

You can find the mean and variance of this distribution by using the sums

$$\sum_{x=1}^{n} x = \tfrac{1}{2} n(n+1) \quad \text{and} \quad \sum_{x=1}^{n} x^2 = \tfrac{1}{6} n(n+1)(2n+1),$$

which were derived in Higher Level Book 1 Section 2.3 and Higher Level Book 2 Section 1.6.

Then

$$\mu = E(X) = \sum_{x=1}^{n} x \times \frac{1}{n} = \frac{1}{n} \sum_{x=1}^{n} x$$

$$= \frac{1}{n} \times \tfrac{1}{2} n(n+1) = \tfrac{1}{2}(n+1),$$

and

$$\sigma^2 = \text{Var}(X) = \sum_{x=1}^{n} x^2 \times \frac{1}{n} - \mu^2$$

$$= \frac{1}{n} \sum_{x=1}^{n} x^2 - \mu^2$$

$$= \frac{1}{n} \times \tfrac{1}{6} n(n+1)(2n+1) - \left(\tfrac{1}{2}(n+1)\right)^2$$

$$= \tfrac{1}{6}(n+1)(2n+1) - \tfrac{1}{4}(n+1)^2$$

$$= \tfrac{1}{12}(n+1)(2(2n+1) - 3(n+1)) = \tfrac{1}{12}(n+1)(n-1) = \tfrac{1}{12}\left(n^2 - 1\right).$$

For other sample spaces you can find the mean and variance by using the algebra of expectations. For example, if the sample space consists of the 11 even numbers from 60 to 80, the uniform random variable Y can be expressed in terms of $X \sim D(11)$ by $Y = 58 + 2X$, so

$$\begin{aligned} E(Y) &= E(58 + 2X) \\ &= 58 + 2E(X) \\ &= 58 + 2 \times \tfrac{1}{2}(11 + 1) = 70 \end{aligned} \qquad \text{and} \qquad \begin{aligned} \text{Var}(Y) &= \text{Var}(58 + 2X) \\ &= 2^2 \times \text{Var}(X) \\ &= 4 \times \tfrac{1}{12}\left(11^2 - 1\right) = 40. \end{aligned}$$

(ii) The continuous uniform distribution $U(a,b)$

A familiar example of this is the error when people give their age in completed years. This may be anything between 0 and 1 years, and for a randomly selected individual there is no reason to prefer any value to any other. Denoting the error by r, the random variable R has probability density

$$f(r) = \begin{cases} 1 & \text{for } 0 \le r < 1, \\ 0 & \text{otherwise.} \end{cases}$$

From this it is easy to calculate the mean and variance

$$E(R) = \int_0^1 r \times 1 \, dr = \left[\tfrac{1}{2} r^2\right]_0^1 = \tfrac{1}{2},$$

$$\begin{aligned} \text{Var}(R) &= \int_0^1 r^2 \times 1 \, dr - (E(R))^2 \\ &= \left[\tfrac{1}{3} r^3\right]_0^1 - \left(\tfrac{1}{2}\right)^2 = \tfrac{1}{3} - \tfrac{1}{4} = \tfrac{1}{12}. \end{aligned}$$

More generally, a random variable X may take any value in the interval $[a,b]$. If the distribution is uniform, the probability density graph is a horizontal line segment. For the area under this graph to equal 1, the probability density must be given by the equation

$$f(x) = \begin{cases} \dfrac{1}{b-a} & \text{for } a \le x < b, \\ 0 & \text{otherwise.} \end{cases}$$

You can find the mean and variance for the random variable X from that for R. Since $X = a$ corresponds to $R = 0$, and $X = b$ to $R = 1$, these are connected by the equation

$$X = a + (b - a)R.$$

So

$$\begin{aligned} \mu &= E(X) \\ &= a + (b - a)E(R) \\ &= a + (b - a) \times \tfrac{1}{2} = \tfrac{1}{2}(a + b) \end{aligned} \qquad \text{and} \qquad \begin{aligned} \sigma^2 &= \text{Var}(X) \\ &= (b - a)^2 \text{Var}(R) \\ &= \tfrac{1}{12}(b - a)^2. \end{aligned}$$

12.2 Sequences of independent Bernoulli trials

The basis of this set of probability models is the Bernoulli trial, a single trial with two possible outcomes, 'success' or 'failure', with probabilities p and q, where $p + q = 1$. If you carry out a sequence of independent Bernoulli trials, various questions can be asked:

How many successes will there be in a sequence of n trials?
How many trials must you carry out until you get a success?
How many trials must you carry out until you get r successes?

The answers to these questions are given by the binomial, geometric and negative binomial probability distributions. You have already met the first two of these in Higher Level Book 1 Chapter 34 and in Chapter 2 of this book.

(i)   The Bernoulli probability distribution $B(1, p)$

The random variable X used to describe this distribution is the number of successes in the trial. This can take either of two values: 0 if the outcome is failure, 1 if success. So the sample space is the set $\{0,1\}$, with the probability distribution shown in Table 12.1. It is proved in Section 6.4 that $\mu = p$ and $\sigma^2 = pq$.

x	0	1
$P(X = x)$	q	p

Table 12.1

(ii)   The binomial probability distribution $B(n, p)$

The random variable X is now the total number of successes in a sequence of n trials. This can be any number between 0 and n, so the sample space is the set $\{0,1,2,\dots,n\}$ (that is, $x \in \mathbb{N}, x \le n$).

You need to find the probability that the sequence of n trials results in x successes and $n - x$ failures. To do this, consider the whole set of trials $\{T_1, T_2, \dots, T_n\}$ and split it into two subsets, one of x trials and the other of $n - x$ trials. The number of ways of doing this is ^nC_x (see Higher Level Book 1 Section 3.6). For each of these, the probability that all the trials in the first subset have successful outcomes is p^x, and the probability that all the trials in the second subset result in failure is q^{n-x}. So, in the complete sequence of trials, the probability of x successes and $n - x$ failures is $^nC_x q^{n-x} p^x$. And since ^nC_x is equal to the binomial coefficient $\binom{n}{x}$ (Higher Level Book 1 Section 4.3),

$$P(X = x) = \binom{n}{x} q^{n-x} p^x \qquad \text{for } 0 \le x \le n.$$

The reason for the name 'binomial' is that this probability is the term involving p^x when $(q + p)^n$ is expanded by the binomial theorem. Notice that, since $q + p = 1$, the sum of all these probabilities,

$$\sum_{x=0}^{n} P(X = x),$$ is equal to $1^n = 1$, as you would expect.

A simple way of finding the mean and variance for this distribution is to let $X_1, X_2, \dots, X_n$ be the number of successes (0 or 1) in the n independent Bernoulli trials $T_1, T_2, \dots, T_n$. For each of these trials

T_i you know that $E(X_i) = p$ and $\text{Var}(X_i) = pq$, and clearly the total number of successes is $X = X_1 + X_2 + ... + X_n$. So

$$\mu = E(X) \qquad\qquad\qquad \text{and} \qquad \sigma^2 = \text{Var}(X)$$
$$= E(X_1) + E(X_2) + ... + E(X_n) \qquad\qquad = \text{Var}(X_1) + \text{Var}(X_2) + ... + \text{Var}(X_n)$$
$$= p + p + ... + p \qquad\qquad\qquad\qquad = pq + pq + ... + pq$$
$$= np \qquad\qquad\qquad\qquad\qquad\qquad = npq.$$

(iii)   The geometric probability distribution $\text{Geo}(p)$

When you roll a dice you hope that you won't have to wait too long to get the first six, but you know from experience that you may be unlucky. Theoretically the random variable X, the number of the trials needed to achieve the first success, may take any of the values 1, 2, 3,... without limit, so the sample space is the complete set of positive integers $\mathbb{Z}^+$.

If X is equal to x, this means that the outcome of the nth trial is success, but the outcomes of the previous $x - 1$ trials are all failure. The probability that this occurs is therefore pq^{x-1}. That is,

$$P(X = x) = pq^{x-1} \quad \text{for } x \in \mathbb{Z}^+.$$

This is the geometric probability distribution. It is shown in the Appendix Section A.2 that

$$\mu = \frac{1}{p} \qquad \text{and} \qquad \sigma^2 = \frac{q}{p^2}.$$

Another useful result is that the cumulative distribution function for $\text{Geo}(p)$ is

$$P(X \le x) = 1 - q^x = 1 - (1 - p)^x \qquad\qquad \text{(see Section 2.1)}.$$

(iv)   The negative binomial probability distribution $\text{NB}(r, p)$

Just as you can generalise from Bernoulli probability (1 trial) to binomial probability (n trials), you can generalise from geometric probability (the number of trials for the first success) to 'negative binomial' probability (the number of trials for r successes).

The random variable X now denotes the number of trials that you have to carry out so as to achieve r successes. This number must of course be at least r, so the sample space is the set $\{r, r + 1, r + 2, ...\}$ (that is, $x \in \mathbb{Z}^+, x \ge r$).

To find $P(X = x)$, note first that the outcome of the final, xth, trial has to be a success, and that the outcomes of the previous $x - 1$ trials have to include $r - 1$ successes. The number of failures in these $r - 1$ trials must therefore be

$$(x - 1) - (r - 1) = x - r.$$

By an argument similar to that used in subsection (ii) above for finding binomial probabilities, but with $x - 1$ in place of n and $r - 1$ in place of x,

$$P(X = x) = p \times \binom{x-1}{r-1} q^{x-r} p^{r-1}$$
$$= \binom{x-1}{r-1} q^{x-r} p^r \qquad \text{for } x \ge r.$$

The reason for the name 'negative binomial' is given in the Appendix Q2.7, where it is shown that $\binom{x-1}{r-1}q^{x-r}$ is the expression for successive terms of the negative binomial expansion of $(1-q)^{-r}$. It follows that the sum of the probabilities $P(X=x)$ over the sample space is

$$\sum_{x=r}^{\infty}\binom{x-1}{r-1}q^{x-r}p^r = (1-q)^{-r}p^r$$

$$= p^{-r} \times p^r = 1,$$

as you would expect. Geometric probability is the special case of negative binomial probability with $r=1$, so $\text{Geo}(p)$ could also be written as $\text{NB}(1,p)$.

To find the mean and variance you can use an argument like that used for binomial probability in subsection (ii) above, but with the geometric distribution in place of the Bernoulli distribution. You can think of the process of continuing trials up to the rth success as made up of r successive independent sequences of trials up to the first success. If the random variables for these r identical geometric distributions are denoted by $X_1, X_2, \ldots, X_r$, then the total number of trials is

$$X = X_1 + X_2 + \ldots + X_r.$$

And since, for each of these geometric trials $E(X_i) = \dfrac{1}{p}$ and $\text{Var}(X_i) = \dfrac{q}{p^2}$ (see subsection (iii)), the mean and variance for the negative binomial distribution are

$$\mu = E(X) = E(X_1) + \ldots + E(X_r) \quad \text{and} \quad \sigma^2 = \text{Var}(X) = \text{Var}(X_1) + \ldots + \text{Var}(X_r)$$

$$= \frac{1}{p} + \frac{1}{p} + \ldots + \frac{1}{p} \qquad\qquad = \frac{q}{p^2} + \frac{q}{p^2} + \ldots + \frac{q}{p^2}$$

$$= \frac{r}{p} \qquad\qquad\qquad\qquad = \frac{rq}{p^2}.$$

12.3 Sampling without replacement

Suppose you have a bag containing N discs, M of which are green and $N-M$ red. If you draw one disc out of the bag, the probability that it will be green is equal to the proportion of green discs in the bag. So this is a single Bernoulli trial, with $p = \dfrac{M}{N}$.

Now suppose that you repeat this trial n times. What is the probability that x of them will be green and $n-x$ red?

The answer is that it depends on how you carry out the trials. If after each trial you put the disc you have drawn back in the bag, then each trial will be conducted on exactly the same terms, with N discs of which M are green. So the distribution will be binomial, $\text{B}\left(n, \dfrac{M}{N}\right)$. This is called sampling with replacement.

But if you don't put the discs you have drawn back in the bag, the probability distribution for the first draw will be $\text{B}\left(1, \dfrac{M}{N}\right)$, but the probabilities for successive draws will depend on what has happened so far. For example, if the first disc drawn is green, then before the second draw there will be $N-1$ discs in the bag of which $M-1$ are green; but if the first disc is red, then there will be $N-1$ discs in the bag of which M are green. So the probability distribution for the second trial will be $\mathrm{B}\left(1,\dfrac{M-1}{N-1}\right)$ or $\mathrm{B}\left(1,\dfrac{M}{N-1}\right)$ depending on whether the first disc drawn is green or red. This is **sampling without replacement**. The conditions for binomial probability are not satisfied, and a different probability model is needed. This is called the hypergeometric probability model – a rather misleading name, since it is more closely related to binomial probability than to geometric probability.

The hypergeometric probability distribution $\mathrm{Hyp}(n,M,N)$

As with the binomial distribution, the random variable X is the number of successes (that is, green discs) in a sequence of n trials. So the sample space is again $\{0,1,2,\dots,n\}$.

To find the probability of a sample with x successes and $n-x$ failures you can use a counting argument. Fig. 12.2 illustrates the situation when such a sample has been drawn. Out of the M original green discs x have been selected, and out of the $N-M$ red discs $n-x$ have been selected. The numbers of ways of doing this are respectively $^{M}C_{x}$ and $^{N-M}C_{n-x}$, so the total number of possible samples of this kind is $^{M}C_{x}\times{}^{N-M}C_{n-x}$. But the total number of different samples of size n that can be drawn out of the bag is $^{N}C_{n}$.

So $$P(X=x)=\frac{{}^{M}C_{x}\times{}^{N-M}C_{n-x}}{{}^{N}C_{n}}$$

$$=\frac{\dbinom{M}{x}\times\dbinom{N-M}{n-x}}{\dbinom{N}{n}}\qquad\text{for }0\le x\le n.$$

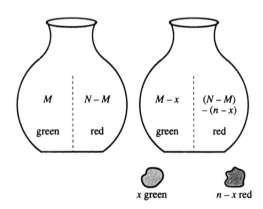

Fig. 12.2

Surprisingly the mean of this distribution is the same as that of the corresponding binomial distribution for sampling with replacement, but the variance is slightly smaller. The formulae are

$$\mu=np\qquad\text{and}\qquad\sigma^{2}=npq\times\frac{N-n}{N-1},$$

where $p=\dfrac{M}{N}$ and $q=1-p$. A method of proving these results is described in the Appendix Section A.5.

12.4   Random events in time

The probability models in this section apply to sequences of events which occur randomly in time, such as the emission of particles from a radioactive source or emergency telephone calls to a fire station. Although the times when these occur are irregular and unpredictable, it will be possible to identify an average rate of occurrence. If the events occur

> singly and independently of each other
> at a constant average rate

then you can ask questions such as:

How many of the events will occur in one unit of time?
How long will it be before the first event occurs?

Answers to these questions are provided by the Poisson and exponential probability distributions. You have already met these in Higher Level Book 1 Chapter 35 and in Chapter 2 of this book.

Both these probability distributions depend on a single parameter m, the average rate of occurrence of the event per unit time.

(i)   The Poisson probability distribution $\mathrm{Po}(m)$

The random variable X denotes the number of times that the event occurs in a unit of time. This is a discrete random variable with sample space $\mathbb{N}$, with probability function

$$P(X = x) = e^{-m} \frac{m^x}{x!}.$$

To show that the sum of these probabilities is equal to 1, and to find the mean and variance, you need to use the exponential series (see the Appendix Section A.3). You can then prove that

$$\mu = m \quad \text{and} \quad \sigma^2 = m.$$

The fact that the mean and variance are equal is a useful pointer to whether or not a Poisson probability model applies in a particular situation. For example, suppose that you count the number of cars passing a checkpoint in successive minutes over a period of three hours. You could then make an estimate of the mean and variance from the data. If these were close to each other, then it would be worth investigating whether the distribution of the data resembled a Poisson distribution. (How to do this is explained in Chapter 13.) But if the estimated mean and variance were very different, you could conclude at once that the conditions for Poisson probability did not apply to this experiment.

An important property of Poisson probability is that, if two random sequences of events are taking place in parallel, with occurrences modelled by Poisson probabilities $P(a)$ and $P(b)$, then the occurrence of one or other event is modelled by Poisson probability $P(a + b)$.

(ii)   The exponential probability distribution $\mathrm{Exp}(m)$

Let X denote the time that you have to wait until the first event occurs. This time must be positive, but it need not of course be an integer. The time can be any positive real number, so X is a continuous random variable and the sample space is $\mathbb{R}^+$. The probability density function for X is

$$f(x) = \begin{cases} me^{-mx} & \text{for } x \geq 0, \\ 0 & \text{otherwise,} \end{cases}$$

and the cumulative distribution function is

$$F(x) = \begin{cases} 1 - e^{-mx} & \text{for } x \geq 0, \\ 0 & \text{otherwise.} \end{cases}$$

The mean and variance are

$$\mu = \frac{1}{m} \quad \text{and} \quad \sigma^2 = \frac{1}{m^2}. \quad \text{(See the Appendix Section A.6.)}$$

(iii) A combined equation for Poisson and exponential probability

If the average rate of occurrence in unit time is m, the average rate of occurrence in x units of time is mx. The probability that the event occurs n times in x units of time is then

$$e^{-mx} \frac{(mx)^n}{n!}.$$

From this expression you can obtain the equations for both Poisson and exponential probability. If you put x equal to 1, you get $e^{-m} \dfrac{m^n}{n!}$, the Poisson probability of n occurrences in unit time. And if you put $n = 0$, you get e^{-mx}, the probability of no occurrences in time x, from which you can deduce the cumulative probability that the event first occurs within the first x units of time,

$$P(X \le x) = 1 - e^{-mx}.$$

12.5 Normal probability

Normal probability was introduced in Higher Level Book 2 Chapter 11. It is important both for its special theoretical properties and also because it provides a good approximate model in many practical situations where measured quantities are subject to random errors. You might think that this is rather surprising, since the sample space for normal probability density is the complete set $\mathbb{R}$ of real numbers, but it is used to model measurements which are restricted to a finite interval. For example, the heights of adult Danish women might be modelled by normal probability with mean 1.64 metres and variance 0.01 metres^2; but you will never meet one with height less than 0 metres or greater than 3 metres. The justification for using a normal model is that, for all practical purposes, the probability of getting values of the random variable more than a few standard deviations away from the mean is negligibly small.

(i) The standardised normal probability distribution $N(0,1)$

It is simplest to begin with $N(0,1)$. You know that it is usual to denote the probability density function by the letter ϕ, so that its equation is

$$\phi(x) = \frac{1}{\sqrt{2\pi}} e^{-\frac{1}{2}x^2}.$$

The reason for the factor $\dfrac{1}{\sqrt{2\pi}}$ is so that the area under the complete graph, given by $\displaystyle\int_{-\infty}^{\infty} \phi(x)\,dx$, is equal to 1. This is quite difficult to prove, but you can verify it numerically with a calculator. The calculator cannot cope with infinite limits of integration, but you should find that if you calculate

$$\int_{-10}^{10} \frac{1}{\sqrt{2\pi}} e^{-\frac{1}{2}x^2} \, dx$$

you get an answer which is as close to 1 as the accuracy of the calculator allows.

Since x appears in the expression for $\phi(x)$ only in the exponent $-\frac{1}{2}x^2$, $\phi(x)$ is an even function. The mean of the distribution is therefore 0. You will find a method of proving that the variance is 1 in the Appendix Section A.4.

(ii)   The general normal probability distribution $N(\mu,\sigma^2)$
To get the most general form for the normal probability function, the first step is to stretch the probability density graph in the x-direction by a factor σ. To keep the total area under the graph equal to 1, there must be a corresponding stretch in the y-direction of factor $\dfrac{1}{\sigma}$. This gives the probability density for $N(0,\sigma^2)$ in the form

$$\frac{1}{\sigma}\phi\left(\frac{x}{\sigma}\right) = \frac{1}{\sigma\sqrt{2\pi}}e^{-\frac{1}{2}x^2/\sigma^2}.$$

A translation of μ in the x-direction then converts this to $N(\mu,\sigma^2)$, with probability density

$$\frac{1}{\sigma}\phi\left(\frac{x-\mu}{\sigma}\right) = \frac{1}{\sigma\sqrt{2\pi}}e^{-\frac{1}{2}(x-\mu)^2/\sigma^2}.$$

The random variable for $N(\mu,\sigma^2)$ is then $\sigma X + \mu$, where $X \sim N(0,1)$, so that

$$E(\sigma X + \mu) = \sigma E(X) + \mu$$
$$= \sigma \times 0 + \mu = \mu$$

and

$$\mathrm{Var}(\sigma X + \mu) = \mathrm{Var}(\sigma X)$$
$$= \sigma^2 \mathrm{Var}(X) = \sigma^2.$$

Important properties of normal probability are that, if X is a normal random variable and a, b are constants, then $aX + b$ is also a normal random variable; and, if X and Y are normal random variables, then so is $X + Y$.

Exercise 12

1   Draw graphs of the probability functions, and the corresponding cumulative distribution functions. (Use a calculator where it would help.)

(a) $DU(5)$ (b) $B(1,0.4)$ (c) $B(10,0.4)$ (d) $Geo(0.4)$

(e) $NB(3,0.4)$ (f) $Hyp(3,4,10)$ (g) $Po(2.4)$

2   Find the mean and variance of the probability functions in Question 1.

3   Use a calculator to display probability density graphs for the following distributions.

(a) $Exp(2.4)$ (b) $N(1,4)$ (c) $N(4,1)$

4   Use (a) graphs (b) algebra to explain why the variance of $U(1,n)$ must be less than that of $DU(n)$ for any integer $n > 1$.

5   The school winter term lasts for ten 5-day weeks. The cook serves chips on average once a week. To decide when to do so, he uses a random number program; chips are served on days when it produces either a 0 or a 9.

(a) Find the probability that during the term there will be three weeks in which chips are served more than once.

(b) In how many weeks of the term would you expect chips to be served at least once?

(c) Find the probability that chips will first be served on the second Wednesday of term.

(d) Find the probability that chips will be served for the tenth time on the last day of term.

6   When Alice and Zebedee play each other at chess, Alice wins three times as often as Zebedee. One year they decide to play one game every Saturday, 52 games in all.

(a) What is the probability that Alice will win exactly 39 times?

(b) Find the probability that Alice will win more than 40 times.

(c) Find the probability that Zebedee will first win on the sixth Saturday.

(d) How many games will they expect to play until Zebedee wins for the first time?

(e) What is the probability that Zebedee will win for the third time on the twelfth Saturday?

(f) Find the expectation and the standard deviation of the number of games they will play until Alice has her 30th win.

7   A box of chocolates contains 20 truffles and 30 caramels, but they all look the same. At a party of 12 people everyone takes a chocolate out of the box.

(a) Find the probability that four people get a truffle.

(b) What are the expectation and the standard deviation of the number of people who get a truffle?

8   In a card game a pile of 20 playing cards is placed face downwards on the table. Of these, six are picture cards. After shuffling one player takes the top four cards.

(a) Find the exact probability distribution of the number of picture cards she takes.

(b) Calculate the mean and variance of this distribution.

(c) Use the formulae for μ and σ^2 in Section 12.3 to check your answers to part (b).

9   A street is home to 100 voters, 30 of whom propose to vote for the Grey Party. Two statistics students each plan to investigate voting intentions by selecting 20 names at random from the list of voters, and asking each how they propose to vote. Their plans differ in one respect: if the same name comes up twice (or more), Abe proposes to count it twice, but Bea proposes only to count it once and to select another name in its place. What difference will this make to the mean and variance of the number of Grey voters they expect to get in their samples?

10 Cars travel at random intervals along a road. On average there are 3 cars going east and 2 going west each minute.

(a) It is safe to cross the road if no cars will come in either direction in the next 15 seconds. What is the probability of being able to cross the road when you want to?

(b) Find the probability that just one car will pass each way in the next half-minute.

(c) Find the probability that not more than 3 cars will pass in the next minute.

11   Random events occur independently in continuous time at an average rate of 6 per minute. Find, in seconds, the mean and standard deviation of the time up to the tenth occurrence.

12   A hall is lit by two kinds of light bulb. On average one Supabulb fails once every 100 days, and one Megalite fails once every 50 days. Find the probability that

(a) a bulb will fail within the next 30 days,

(b) exactly 3 bulbs will fail in the next 100 days.

13*   With the notation of Section 2.6, let y_n be the probability that exactly n events have occurred up to the time x.

(a) Explain why, if $n \geq 1$, $y_n + \delta y_n = y_n \times (1 - m\delta x) + y_{n-1} \times m\delta x$.

(b) Use part (a) to obtain the differential equation $\dfrac{dy_n}{dx} = m(y_{n-1} - y_n)$.

(c) Explain why, when $x = 0$, $y_n = 0$ for $n \geq 1$.

(d) Show that the equations in parts (b) and (c) are satisfied by

$$y_n = e^{-mx} \frac{(mx)^n}{n!} \quad \text{and} \quad y_{n-1} = e^{-mx} \frac{(mx)^{n-1}}{(n-1)!}.$$

(e) Show that, when $x = 1$, y_n is the Poisson probability that n events occur in unit time.

13 Chi-squared tests

This chapter introduces a method of testing whether theory is supported by practice. When you have completed it, you should be able to

- fit a theoretical distribution to given data
- use a χ^2 test with the appropriate number of degrees of freedom to carry out the corresponding goodness of fit test
- use a χ^2 test with the appropriate number of degrees of freedom to test for independence in a contingency table.

13.1 Comparing observed and expected frequencies

Table 13.1 shows the results obtained when a dice was thrown 120 times.

Score	1	2	3	4	5	6
Frequency	26	13	21	25	18	17

Table 13.1

How would you set about deciding whether these results indicate that the dice is a fair one? A start would be to compare these observed frequencies with the theoretical frequencies which you would expect if the dice is fair. The theoretical frequency for each score is found by multiplying the total frequency by the corresponding probability. In this case, the probability of each possible score is $\frac{1}{6}$ and so all the theoretical frequencies are equal to $120 \times \frac{1}{6} = 20$. These theoretical frequencies are usually known as **expected frequencies** and the process of calculating them is called 'fitting a theoretical distribution'. The equation defining expected frequency is

> Expected frequency of a value = total frequency $\times$ probability of that value.

In Table 13.2 the second and third columns give the observed frequencies and the expected frequencies for the results of the dice experiment, where the observed and expected frequencies are denoted by f_o and f_e respectively.

You can see that the agreement between the observed and expected frequencies is not exact. This is what you would expect since the frequencies for each score are random variables: they vary each time the experiment is carried out. What the expected frequency tells you is the mean (or expected value) of each of these random variables.

The fourth column of Table 13.2 gives the difference $f_o - f_e$ for each class. If the agreement between experiment and theory is a good one, then you would expect these differences to be small. You might think that you could measure the total discrepancy between the observed and expected frequencies by finding the total of this column, $\sum (f_o - f_e)$.

Score	f_o	f_e	$f_o - f_e$	$(f_o - f_e)^2 / f_e$
1	26	20	6	1.8
2	13	20	−7	2.45
3	21	20	1	0.05
4	25	20	5	1.25
5	18	20	−2	0.20
6	17	20	−3	0.45
Total	120	120	0	$X^2 = 6.2$

Table 13.2

However, you can see from the table that this total is zero, even though the observed and expected frequencies do not all agree. In fact, this quantity will always equal zero (because the sums of the observed and expected frequencies are both equal to the total frequency) and so it is no use as a measure of discrepancy. This problem could be overcome by squaring the differences and calculating $\sum (f_o - f_e)^2$.

However, this measure of the discrepancy is still not satisfactory because it makes no allowance for the size of the difference relative to the size of the expected frequencies. For example, the difference between an observed frequency of 11 and expected frequency of 10 would give the same contribution to this sum as the difference between an observed frequency of 101 and expected frequency of 100, even though the percentage difference between the two values is 10% in the first instance and 1% in the second. The measure of discrepancy which is actually used is $\sum \dfrac{(f_o - f_e)^2}{f_e}$. It is given the symbol X^2. The square emphasises that this is always a positive quantity.

$$X^2 = \sum \frac{(f_o - f_e)^2}{f_e}$$

The statistic X^2 gives a measure of the **goodness of fit** of the model; that is, how well the observed and theoretical frequencies agree. For perfect agreement it takes the value zero, and it increases as the differences between the observed and expected frequencies increase. The value of X^2 for the dice data is calculated in the last column of Table 13.2 and is equal to 6.2.

If you repeated the experiment with the same dice, you would get different values of f_o and hence a different value of X^2. In other words, X^2 is also a random variable. To decide whether the value 6.2 indicates a significant difference between the observed and expected frequencies it is necessary to study the probability distribution of X^2. This distribution is different from any of the distributions which you have already met. It is approximately related to a new family of continuous distributions which is introduced in the next section.

13.2 The chi-squared (χ^2) family of distributions

Fig. 13.3 shows probability density graphs for some of the members of the χ^2 family of distributions.

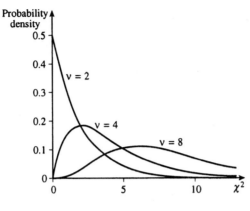

Fig. 13.3

The symbol χ is a Greek letter whose name 'chi' is pronounced as the 'ki' in 'kite'. Thus χ^2 is read as 'chi-squared'. The shape of each member of the family is determined by a single parameter, v, which is known as the **number of degrees of freedom**. You write χ_v^2 to indicate the member of the family with v degrees of freedom. The mean and variance of a χ_v^2 distribution are v and $2v$ respectively (see the Appendix Section A.4). This means that as v increases the location of the distribution shifts to the right and the spread of the distribution increases. You can see this effect in Fig. 13.3, which shows χ_2^2, χ_4^2 and χ_8^2.

As with other distributions used for hypothesis testing, like the t-distribution, you are almost always interested in finding probabilities represented by the area under a χ^2 graph. You can find these directly by using the χ^2 cumulative distribution program on a calculator. You will usually want to find the probability that χ^2 is less or greater than a particular number. For example, $P(\chi_8^2 \leq 10) = 0.735$, or $P(\chi_4^2 \geq 5) = 0.287$.

To decide which member of the χ^2 family gives an approximation to the distribution of X^2 you need to know the value of v. As for the t-distribution, this is given by the number of independent values, in this case expected frequencies (or equivalently, classes), which are used in the calculation of X^2. There are 6 expected frequencies in Table 13.2, but they are not independent. Since the total of the expected frequencies must equal 120, there is 1 constraint. Thus

number of degrees of freedom = number of classes − number of constraints

$$= 6 - 1 = 5,$$

and the distribution of X^2 for this experiment can be approximated by the χ_5^2 distribution.

A useful way of thinking of a constraint in the context of χ^2 tests is as a piece of information which is obtained from the observed frequencies and then used in the calculation of the expected frequencies. In this example the total observed frequency of 120 was multiplied by the probabilities to find the expected frequencies. This gave one constraint. Later in this chapter you will see examples where there is more than one constraint.

To sum up the process so far:

Separate the sample space into a number of mutually exclusive classes.

Obtain n independent values of the random variable experimentally and assign each to its class.

Record the observed frequencies, f_o, in each class.

Calculate the expected frequencies, f_e, in each class from an appropriate probability model.

Then the measure of discrepancy $X^2 = \sum \dfrac{(f_o - f_e)^2}{f_e}$, where the sum is taken over all the classes, has an approximately χ_v^2 distribution, where v is the number of degrees of freedom, calculated as

$v =$ number of classes $-$ number of constraints.

Notice the word 'approximately'. The nature of the approximation is rather like using a normal distribution to approximate to binomial probability (see Section 6.4). You will remember that this approximation was very close provided that the expected numbers of successes and failures were not too small. Similarly the χ^2 approximation is very close provided that the frequencies in every class are not too small.

Most people who use statistics work to the rule that the classes should be chosen so that the expected frequency in any class is not smaller than 5. If it is, then that class should be combined with another to make a class for which the expected frequency is larger.

Classes should be chosen so that the expected frequency in each class is at least 5.

Before you go on to apply the procedure, it is worth noting a different way of calculating the measure of discrepancy, by writing

$$\frac{(f_o - f_e)^2}{f_e} = \frac{f_o^2 - 2f_o f_e + f_e^2}{f_e}$$

$$= \frac{f_o^2}{f_e} - 2f_o + f_e.$$

Now both $\sum f_o$ and $\sum f_e$ are equal to n. It follows that

$$\sum \frac{(f_o - f_e)^2}{f_e} = \sum \frac{f_o^2}{f_e} - 2n + n = \sum \frac{f_o^2}{f_e} - n.$$

It is often quicker to use this form to calculate the discrepancy.

13.3   Carrying out a χ^2 goodness of fit test

For the dice data it was found that $X^2 = 6.2$. This value is based on expected frequencies which assume that the dice is fair and so this assumption forms the null hypothesis. The alternative is that the dice is not fair:

H_0: the dice is fair; H_1: the dice is not fair.

As explained above the distribution of X^2 can be approximated by χ_5^2. If H_0 is true, then the expected and observed frequencies should be similar and so the value of X^2 will be low. A high value of X^2 is unlikely and would lead you to reject H_0. The rejection region thus takes the form $X^2 \geq c$ where the critical value, c, depends on the significance level.

Fig. 13.4 shows the χ_5^2 distribution with acceptance and rejection regions for a 5% significance level.

From the calculator $P\left(\chi_5^2 \geq 6.2\right) = 0.287$. There is a 28.7% probability of getting a discrepancy X^2 as large as 6.2 with a fair dice. Since this is much greater than 5%, $X^2 = 6.2$ is well within the acceptance region with a 5% significance level. There is no reason to think that the dice is unfair.

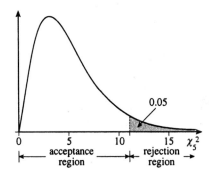

Fig. 13.4

The following example illustrates a χ^2 goodness of fit test in a situation in which the expected frequencies are not all the same.

Example 13.3.1

In genetic work it is predicted that the children with both parents of blood group AB will fall into blood groups AB, A and B in the ratio 2:1:1. Of a random sample of 100 such children 55 were blood group AB, 27 blood group A and 18 blood group B. Test at the 10% significance level whether the observed results agree with the theoretical prediction.

Take
$\qquad$ H_0: the offspring fall into groups AB, A and B in the ratio 2:1:1;
$\qquad$ H_1: the offspring do not fall into groups in the ratio 2:1:1.

The probabilities of falling into the groups AB, A and B are $\frac{1}{2}$, $\frac{1}{4}$ and $\frac{1}{4}$ respectively. The expected frequencies are found by multiplying these probabilities by the total frequency of 100, giving 50, 25 and 25. None of these is less than 5, so the distribution of X^2 can be approximated by a χ^2 distribution.

Table 13.5 sets out the information you need for the calculation of X^2.

Blood group	AB	A	B	Total
f_o	55	27	18	100
f_e	50	25	25	100
$f_o - f_e$	+5	+2	−7	0

Table 13.5

In this example there are 3 classes. There is 1 constraint because the total observed frequency of 100 was used in the calculation of the expected frequencies. Thus

v = number of classes – number of constraints = $3 - 1 = 2$.

To find the discrepancy between the observed and the expected frequencies, calculate

$$\sum \frac{(f_o - f_e)^2}{f_e} = \frac{5^2}{50} + \frac{2^2}{25} + \frac{(-7)^2}{25} = 2.62.$$

Your calculator gives $P(\chi_2^2 \geq 2.62) = 0.270$, or 27.0%. This is greater than the 10% significance level, so 2.62 lies in the acceptance region. The null hypothesis is therefore accepted. The offspring fall into the groups AB, A and B in the ratio 2:1:1 as predicted by genetic theory.

13.4   Goodness of fit tests for discrete probability models

In the dice example in Section 13.1, the observed frequencies were compared with the expected frequencies obtained from the uniform probability distribution $DU(6)$. The question was, whether the experimental evidence is consistent with the hypothesis that the behaviour of the dice is described by this probability model.

The examples show how you can answer similar questions about other discrete probability models.

(i) Testing for a binomial model

Example 13.4.1

A sociologist doing research on family planning decides to investigate the gender make-up of large families. She selects 100 families at random from census data, each with 4 children under 16. Table 13.6 is her record of the girl/boy split in these families.

4g/0b	3g/1b	2g/2b	1g/3b	0g/4b	Total
11	27	23	31	8	100

Table 13.6

(a) Give reasons why a binomial distribution $B(4, \frac{1}{2})$ might be an appropriate model.

(b) Test this hypothesis at significance levels of   (i) 5%,   (ii) 1%.

  (a)   In the population at large boys and girls occur more or less equally. Evidence suggests that, if one child is a boy (say), then the next child is no more likely to be a boy than a girl, or vice versa. So if the parents have decided in advance that they are going to have 4 children, and are happy to 'take what comes', then the basic requirements for a binomial probability model are satisfied.

  • There is a fixed number of trials (in this case 4).
  • The outcome of each trial is independent of the outcomes of other trials.
  • The probability of 'success' on each trial is constant (in this case $\frac{1}{2}$).

  With these assumptions, a $B(4, \frac{1}{2})$ distribution is appropriate.

(b)   The null and alternative hypotheses are

H_0: the gender split has a $B\left(4,\frac{1}{2}\right)$ distribution;

H_1: the gender split does not have a $B\left(4,\frac{1}{2}\right)$ distribution.

Under H_0, the probability of r boys and $4 - r$ girls is

$$\binom{4}{r}\left(\tfrac{1}{2}\right)^{4-r}\left(\tfrac{1}{2}\right)^{r} = \binom{4}{r}\times\left(\tfrac{1}{2}\right)^{4} = \tfrac{1}{16}\times\binom{4}{r}.$$

The probabilities for $r = 0, 1, 2, 3, 4$ are therefore $\frac{1}{16}, \frac{4}{16} = \frac{1}{4}, \frac{6}{16} = \frac{3}{8}, \frac{4}{16} = \frac{1}{4}, \frac{1}{16}$. To get the expected frequencies these probabilities are multiplied by 100, which gives the values of f_e in Table 13.7.

g/b split	4g/0b	3g/1b	2g/2b	1g/3b	0g/4b	Total
f_o	11	27	23	31	8	100
f_e	6.25	25	37.5	25	6.25	100
$f_o - f_e$	4.75	2	−14.5	6	1.75	0

Table 13.7

Notice that the expected frequencies needn't be whole numbers, although the observed frequencies obviously are.

You can work out the discrepancy X^2 either as

$$\sum\frac{(f_o - f_e)^2}{f_e} = \frac{4.75^2}{6.25} + \frac{2^2}{25} + \frac{(-14.5)^2}{37.5} + \frac{6^2}{25} + \frac{1.75^2}{6.25}$$

$$= 3.61 + 0.16 + 5.6066\ldots + 1.44 + 0.49$$

$$= 11.3066\ldots$$

or as

$$\sum\frac{f_o^{\,2}}{f_e} - n = \left(\frac{11^2}{6.25} + \frac{27^2}{25} + \frac{23^2}{37.5} + \frac{31^2}{25} + \frac{8^2}{6.25}\right) - 100$$

$$= (19.36 + 29.16 + 14.1066\ldots + 38.44 + 10.24) - 100$$

$$= 111.3066\ldots - 100 = 11.3066\ldots \ .$$

Both methods have their advantages. The first draws attention to the entries which make the largest contribution to the discrepancy, which are those for 4 girls/0 boys and 2 girls/2 boys. This may suggest where to begin to look for flaws in the model. The second is easier to work out, since you don't need the last line in the table; you can go straight to the answer from the tabulated values of f_o and f_e.

Since there are 5 classes, with the single constraint that $\sum f_e = 100$, the number of degrees of freedom is $5 - 1 = 4$. The calculator then gives

$$P\left(X^2 \geq 11.3066\ldots\right) \approx P\left(\chi_4^{\,2} \geq 11.3066\ldots\right)$$

$$= 0.0233\ldots \ ,$$

or 2.33%.

(i)   Since $2.33 < 5$, the value $X^2 = 11.31$ falls into the rejection region at the 5% significance level. You therefore reject H_0, and conclude that the data do not fit a $B\left(4, \frac{1}{2}\right)$ distribution.

(ii)   Since $2.33 > 1$, the value $X^2 = 11.31$ falls into the acceptance region at the 1% significance level. You therefore accept H_0, and conclude that the data are consistent with the hypothesis of a $B\left(4, \frac{1}{2}\right)$ distribution.

So the sociologist's conclusion depends on the level of significance she chooses. The evidence for rejecting the $B\left(4, \frac{1}{2}\right)$ hypothesis is strong, but not very strong.

In some cases a binomial distribution may appear to be a suitable model, but a value of p is not known at the start. In this case it can be estimated from the data. The mean, μ, of a binomial distribution is given by $\mu = np$. Hence $p = \dfrac{\mu}{n}$. Taking $\bar{x}$ as an estimate of μ gives $p = \dfrac{\bar{x}}{n}$.

> In testing the goodness of fit of a binomial distribution, where p is unknown at the start, an estimate of p is calculated from the data as
>
> $$p = \frac{\bar{x}}{n}.$$

Example 13.4.2

In routine tests of germination rates, parsley seeds are planted in rows of 5 and the number of seeds which have germinated in each row after a fixed time interval is counted. Table 13.8 shows the results for 100 such rows.

Number of seeds germinated (x)	0	1	2	3	4	5
Number of rows f_o	0	0	8	23	43	26

Table 13.8

(a) Use the data to estimate a value for p, the probability that a seed germinates.

(b) Calculate the expected frequencies for the model $B(5, p)$.

(c) Use a χ^2 goodness of fit test at the 5% significance level to test the suitability of the model $B(5, p)$.

(a)   For the data in Table 13.8, $\sum x f_o = 387$, so $\bar{x} = 3.87$. Thus the estimate of p is $\frac{1}{5} \times 3.87 = 0.774$.

(b)   The null and alternative hypotheses are

   H_0: the data can be modelled by $B(5, 0.774)$;
   H_1: the data cannot be modelled by $B(5, 0.774)$.

The expected frequencies are found by multiplying the binomial probabilities by the total observed frequency of 100. You can calculate the binomial probabilities from the binomial formula $\dbinom{5}{r} \times (0.226)^{5-r} \times (0.774)^r$, but with awkward numbers like these you may prefer to use the binomial probability program on your calculator. The values of f_e are given in the bottom row of Table 13.9, correct to 2 decimal places.

Number germinated (x)	0	1	2	3	4	5	Total
f_o	0	0	8	23	43	26	100
f_e	0.06	1.01	6.92	23.68	40.55	27.78	100

Table 13.9

Another step is needed before you go on to calculate v. You will notice that two of the values of f_e are less than 5, so the classes for $x = 0$, $x = 1$ and $x = 2$ should be combined to produce a single class with a large enough expected frequency. This is shown in Table 13.10.

Number germinated (x)	0, 1 or 2	3	4	5	Total
f_o	8	23	43	26	100
f_e	7.99	23.68	40.55	27.78	100

Table 13.10

The number of classes after combination, in this case 4, is used in the calculation of the degrees of freedom. There are 2 constraints because two pieces of information have been obtained from the observed frequencies to calculate the expected frequencies: these are the total frequency (100) and the value of p (0.774). Thus $v = 4 - 2 = 2$.

From Table 13.10 you can calculate that $X^2 = 0.2816...$, and the calculator gives

$$P(X^2 \geq 0.2816...) \approx P(\chi_2^2 \geq 0.2816...) = 0.8686... \text{ , or } 86.9\%.$$

This is far larger than 5%, so the value $X^2 = 0.2816...$ is well within the acceptance region. That is, the binomial distribution $B(5, 0.774)$ is a very good model for the data.

If you combine classes when you do not have to, then you increase the probability of making a Type II error, that is keeping a false null hypothesis.

You may have noticed that the alternative hypothesis for a χ^2 goodness of fit test does not specify the way in which the null hypothesis might be incorrect. If the null hypothesis is rejected, it could be either because the value of the parameter which was used was incorrect or because the conditions for the distribution to be a suitable model are not met. This point is explored further in some of the exercises.

(ii) Testing for a geometric model
Your calculator probably has a program to create a sequence of random numbers. These can be used to pick winners in a lottery, or to provide a strategy in a game of chance, or to simulate values of a random variable in a probability model. People who make use of random numbers professionally take a lot of trouble to make sure that the sequence really is random.

How can you check a sequence for randomness?

One requirement is obviously that, in a long sequence, each number occurs roughly the same number of times. But this doesn't guarantee randomness by itself. For example, in the sequence

123 456 789 123 456 789 123 456 789 123 ...

the frequency of each of the digits from 1 to 9 is the same, but this is hardly a random sequence. So you need to back up the equal frequency test with other more sophisticated tests.

Here are the first 40 of a sequence of 200 digits between 1 and 9 generated by a calculator.

24137 16888 67756 68713 78376 15719 64469 26846 ...

One way of testing this for randomness is to ask, as you read along the sequence, how many digits you have to read until you reach the next multiple of 3. To answer this, rewrite it placing the gaps after each multiple of 3. This has the effect of breaking the sequence into 'runs' so that only the last digit in each run is a multiple of 3.

2413 716 8886 7756 6 8713 783 76 15719 6 446 9 26846 ...

The lengths of the runs are 4, 3, 4, 4, 1, 4, 3, 2, 5, 1, 3, 1, 5, ...

If the digits are random, the length of a run L is a random variable with a geometric distribution (see Section 2.1). If you consider a non-multiple of 3 as a 'failure', and a multiple of 3 as a 'success', then the probability of a success is $p = \frac{3}{9} = \frac{1}{3}$, so $L \sim \text{Geo}\left(\frac{1}{3}\right)$.

Example 13.4.3 investigates this for the complete sequence of 200 digits.

Example 13.4.3
In a sequence of 200 digits the length of runs up to the next multiple of 3 has the frequency distribution in Table 13.11. Test the sequence for randomness, at the 10% level, by finding the goodness of fit to $\text{Geo}\left(\frac{1}{3}\right)$.

Length of run	1	2	3	4	5	6	7	8	9	10	11	Total
f_o	15	14	14	10	5	2	0	1	1	1	1	64

Table 13.11

You may prefer to work this example using your own sequence of 200 digits instead of the one used to produce Table 13.11.

It is encouraging that the sequence of 200 digits split into 64 runs. Since the probability that any digit is a multiple of 3 is $\frac{3}{9} = \frac{1}{3}$, the expected number of multiples of 3 (and therefore of runs) in a sequence of 200 digits is $200 \times \frac{1}{3} = 66\frac{2}{3}$.

The null and alternative hypotheses are

H_0: the data can be modelled by $\text{Geo}\left(\frac{1}{3}\right)$;

H_1: the data cannot be modelled by $\text{Geo}\left(\frac{1}{3}\right)$.

In $\text{Geo}\left(\frac{1}{3}\right)$ the probabilities of runs of length $1,2,3,\dots,x,\dots$ are

$$\frac{1}{3},\frac{1}{3}\times\frac{2}{3}=\frac{2}{9},\frac{1}{3}\times\left(\frac{2}{3}\right)^2=\frac{4}{27},\dots,\frac{1}{3}\times\left(\frac{2}{3}\right)^{x-1},\dots .$$

Multiplying these by 64 gives the expected frequencies in Table 13.12.

Length of run	1	2	3	4	5	6	7	8	9	10	11	Total
f_o	15	14	14	10	5	2	0	1	1	1	1	64
f_e	21.33	14.22	9.48	6.32	4.21	2.81	1.87	1.25	0.83	0.55	0.37	...

Table 13.12

Clearly some classes must be combined to produce expected frequencies greater than 5. There are two possibilities:

- combine all the classes from 5 onwards
- combine the classes for 4 and 5, and all the classes from 6 onwards.

Table 13.13 is based on the second of these. Unlike the binomial distribution, there is no upper limit for the value of X, so the entry for '6 or more' is most simply calculated by subtracting the sum of the entries for 1, 2, 3, 4 and 5 from 64.

Length of run	1	2	3	4 or 5	6 or more	Total
f_o	15	14	14	15	6	64
f_e	21.33	14.22	9.48	10.53	8.44	64

Table 13.13

The calculation then proceeds in the usual way. There are 5 classes and 1 constraint, that $\sum f_e = 64$, so $v = 5 - 1 = 4$. From Table 13.13, $X^2 = 6.639\dots$, and then

$$P\left(X^2 \geq 6.639\dots\right) \approx P\left(\chi_4{}^2 \geq 6.639\dots\right) = 0.156\dots ,$$

or 15.6%.

Since this is greater than the significance level of 10%, the null hypothesis is accepted: the data can be modelled by $\text{Geo}\left(\frac{1}{3}\right)$. So, on this criterion, the method used by the calculator to create sequences of random digits is satisfactory.

(iii) Testing for a Poisson model

The Poisson probability formula was introduced in Higher Level Book 1 Section 35.1 by using data relating to the number of calls arriving at a switchboard in time intervals of 5 minutes. These data are reproduced in Table 13.14.

Number of calls	0	1	2	3	4 or more
Frequency	71	23	4	2	0

Table 13.14

A χ^2 goodness of fit test can now be applied to these data. Use a significance level of 5%. The value of the parameter, m, the population mean, is not known and so it is estimated by the sample mean. You can check that the sample mean is 0.37. So the null and alternative hypotheses for a goodness of fit test are

H_0: the data can be modelled by Po(0.37);
H_1: the data cannot be modelled by Po(0.37).

The expected frequencies are found by multiplying the Poisson probabilities by the total observed frequency, 100. You can find these probabilities either from the formula $P(X = x) = e^{-0.37} \dfrac{0.37^x}{x!}$ or from the calculator program for Poisson probabilities. For example, the expected frequency for 3 calls is $e^{-0.37} \dfrac{0.37^3}{3!} \times 100 = 0.58$. You can check that you agree with the other expected frequencies in Table 13.15. As for the geometric distribution there is no theoretical upper limit on the number of calls and so the expected frequency for 4 or more is found by subtracting the sum of the expected frequencies for $x = 0$, 1, 2 and 3 from the total frequency of 100.

Number of calls	0	1	2	3	4 or more	Total
f_o	71	23	4	2	0	100
f_e	69.07	25.56	4.73	0.58	0.06	100

Table 13.15

In Table 13.16 the last three classes have been combined.

Number of calls	0	1	2 or more	Total
f_o	71	23	6	100
f_e	69.07	25.56	5.37	100

Table 13.16

There are 3 classes after combination, and 2 constraints, since the mean (0.37) and the total frequency (100) are both found from the observed values, so $v = 3 - 2 = 1$. From Table 13.16, $X^2 = 0.384\ldots$, and

$$P(X^2 \geq 0.384\ldots) \approx P(\chi_1^2 \geq 0.384\ldots) = 0.535\ldots,$$

or 53.5%.

This is much larger than the significance level of 5%, so H_0 is accepted: Po(0.37) is a suitable model for the distribution of calls at the switchboard.

If the value of the mean, m, is known or given, this value would be used in the calculation of the expected frequencies and the number of constraints would be 1 rather than 2.

====== **Exercise 13A** ======

1 A dice is rolled 60 times. The results are shown in the table.

Score	1	2	3	4	5	6
Frequency	10	11	9	6	10	14

Use a χ^2 test at the 5% significance level to test the hypotheses

H_0: the dice is fair; H_1: the dice is not fair.

2 In experiments on the breeding of flowers a researcher obtained 95 magenta flowers with a green stigma, 32 magenta flowers with a red stigma, 26 red flowers with a green stigma and 7 red flowers with a red stigma. Genetic theory predicts that flowers of these types should occur in the ratios 9:3:3:1. Carry out a χ^2 test at the 1% significance level to see if the experimental results are in line with the theory.

3 When a tetrahedral dice is thrown the number landing face down counts as the score. Four such dice are thrown 200 times and the numbers of fours obtained are shown.

Number of fours	0	1	2	3	4
Frequency	20	47	83	41	9

(a) Use a χ^2 test at the 5% level to test whether the dice are fair, that is that a $B\left(4, \frac{1}{4}\right)$ model is appropriate.

(b) Use the data to estimate a value for p, the probability that the score is 4. Test at the 5% level whether a $B(4, p)$ model is appropriate.

4 Sixty samples of size 6 are taken after a manufacturing process. The number of defective items in each sample is recorded and the results are shown in the table.

Number of defectives	0	1	2	3	4	5	6
Number of samples	8	24	14	11	1	1	1

Calculate the mean of the frequency distribution and hence find an estimate of p, the probability that an individual item is defective. Using your estimate calculate the expected frequencies corresponding to a binomial distribution and perform a χ^2 goodness of fit test at the 1% level of significance.

5 I wish to investigate the efficiency of the random number generating function on my new calculator. I program it to produce digits from 0 to 9 inclusive, and record the lengths of runs up to the appearance of the next even number. A 10% level is to be used.

The results obtained were the following.

Length of run	1	2	3	4	5	6	7 or more
Frequency	26	13	8	2	0	1	0

Carry out the test and state your conclusion.

6 Despite the result of the test in Question 5, I am not convinced of the randomness of the numbers generated. The digits generated while obtaining the 50 runs yielded the following probability distribution.

Digit	0	1	2	3	4	5	6	7	8	9
Frequency	11	13	5	7	12	6	6	7	6	17

Conduct a χ^2 goodness of fit test at the 10% level using the method of Section 13.1.

7 The number of phone calls I received each day during the first three months of 2006 are recorded in the table.

Number of calls	0	1	2	3	4
Number of days	44	24	14	6	2

It is suspected that they follow a Poisson distribution. Calculate the mean of the frequency distribution and use it to calculate the expected frequencies for $x = 0, 1, 2, 3, 4$ or more. Hence carry out a χ^2 test of goodness of fit at the 5% level.

8 The first 100 draws in the UK National Lottery produced the following results. (Six balls are drawn each time.)

Ball numbers	1–7	8–14	15–21	22–28	29–35	36–42	43–49
Frequency	88	80	80	91	87	78	96

Carry out a χ^2 goodness of fit test at the 5% level to test the null hypothesis
$$P(1\text{–}7) = P(8\text{–}14) = \ldots = P(43\text{–}49) = \tfrac{1}{7}.$$

9 The results of Question 8 could also be grouped according to the colours of the balls used in the draws.

Colour	White	Blue	Pink	Green	Yellow
Ball numbers	1–9	10–19	20–29	30–39	40–49
Frequency	107	125	116	114	138

Carry out a χ^2 goodness of fit test at the 10% level to test the null hypothesis
$$P(W) = \tfrac{9}{49}, \ P(B) = P(P) = P(G) = P(Y) = \tfrac{10}{49}.$$

10 Five drawing pins are thrown onto a table. The number landing point up is recorded. The experiment is conducted 50 times in all, resulting in the following frequency distribution.

Number landing point up	0	1	2	3	4	5
Frequency	3	9	20	15	3	0

Calculate the mean of the frequency distribution, estimate p, the probability of a pin landing point up, and carry out a goodness of fit test at the 5% significance level.

11 The goals scored in each match by a football team during two successive seasons are shown in the table.

Number of goals	0	1	2	3	4	5	6	7
Number of matches	14	32	21	12	3	1	0	1

It is suspected that a Poisson distribution is appropriate.

(a) In the season previous to these two seasons, the mean number of goals scored per match was 1. Carry out a χ^2 goodness of fit test of the model Po(1). Use a 5% significance level.

(b) Calculate the mean of the frequency distribution in the table. Test whether a Poisson distribution with this mean gives a better fit to the data. Use a 5% significance level.

12 A survey is carried out at a supermarket till. When the till opens, the number of customers up to and including the first person to use one of the carrier bags provided by the supermarket is recorded. This is repeated on 100 consecutive days. The data are summarised in the table below.

Number of customers	1	2	3	4	>4
Frequency	79	15	3	3	0

It is thought that this distribution may be modelled by a geometric distribution with parameter p, where p is the probability that a person uses a supermarket carrier bag.

(a) Calculate the mean and hence obtain an estimate of p.

(b) Carry out a test, at the 5% significance level, of the goodness of fit of the model to the data.

13 The number of accidents occurring on a busy road each week is recorded for one year. The results are shown in the table.

Number of accidents (x)	0	1	2	3	4	5
Number of weeks	26	12	10	3	1	0

It is suspected that a Poisson distribution is appropriate. Calculate $\bar{x}$, and use it to find the expected frequencies for $x = 0, 1, 2, 3$ or more. Conduct a χ^2 goodness of fit test at the 2.5% level of significance.

13.5 Testing the goodness of fit of a normal model

So far the goodness of fit tests which have been carried out have been applied to models for discrete variables. It is also possible to apply the method to continuous data which have been grouped into suitable class intervals. Here is an example of testing the goodness of fit of the normal distribution.

Example 13.5.1

The height, in centimetres, gained by a conifer in its first year after planting is denoted by the random variable H. The value of H is measured for a random sample of 86 conifers and the results obtained are summarised in Table 13.17.

H	< 35	35–45	45–55	55–65	> 65
Observed frequency	10	18	28	18	12

Table 13.17

(a) Assuming that the random variable is modelled by a $N(50,15^2)$ distribution, calculate the expected frequencies for each of the five classes.

(b) Carry out a χ^2 goodness of fit analysis to test, at the 5% level, the hypothesis that H can be modelled as in part (a).   (OCR)

(a) If $H \sim N(50,15^2)$ then $Z \sim N(0,1)$ where $Z = \dfrac{H-50}{15}$. The values of Z corresponding to the class boundaries of 35, 45, 55 and 65 are -1, $-\frac{1}{3}$, $\frac{1}{3}$ and 1 respectively.

With a calculator the probabilities that Z lies in the five intervals separated by these class boundaries are 0.1587, 0.2108, 0.2611, 0.2108, 0.1587, correct to 4 decimal places.

To find the expected frequencies, multiply these probabilities by 86, the total number of conifers. This gives expected frequencies of 13.65, 18.13, 22.45, 18.13, 13.65.

(b) The null and alternative hypotheses are

$$H_0: H \sim N(50,15^2); \qquad H_1: H \text{ is not } N(50,15^2).$$

Table 13.18 gives the observed and expected frequencies for the five classes. The expected frequencies don't add up to exactly 86 because the probabilities in part (a) were rounded to 4 decimal places.

H	<35	35–45	45–55	55–65	>65	Total
f_o	10	18	28	18	12	86
f_e	13.65	18.13	22.45	18.13	13.65	86(.01)

Table 13.18

The calculation then proceeds just as in the discrete case. There are 5 classes and 1 constraint, that $\sum f_e = 86$, so $v = 4$. The value of X^2, calculated from Table 13.18, is 2.539... , and $P(\chi_4^2 \geq 2.539...) = 0.637...$, or 63.7%, much greater than the 5% significance level required to reject H_0. The null hypothesis, that H can be modelled by $N(50,15^2)$, is accepted.

To calculate expected frequencies for a normal distribution you need values of μ and σ^2. In the example above these values were given. If either or both of μ and σ^2 are not given, then unbiased estimates are used instead (see Section 10.1). (These estimates should be calculated from the grouped frequency table.) For each estimate used another constraint is added. For example, if both μ and σ^2 are estimated there will be 3 constraints in total.

Example 13.5.2

The lengths (in mm) of 50 leaves that had fallen from an oak were measured. The results are summarised in Table 13.19.

Length (mm)	30–39	40–49	50–59	60–69	70–79	80–89	90–99	100–109
Frequency	3	9	15	9	6	4	3	1

Table 13.19

By carrying out a goodness of fit test at the 5% significance level test whether the length of an oak leaf can be modelled by a normal distribution.

Notice that, in Table 13.19, the lengths are stated to the nearest millimetre. The class boundaries are therefore 29.5–39.5, 39.5–49.5,…, and the mid-class values are 34.5, 44.5, … .

Since the mean, μ, and the variance, σ^2, are not known, they must be estimated from the sample, basing the calculation on the mid-class values. Your calculator probably has a program for calculating $\bar{x}$ and s_{n-1}^2 from a data list, This gives $\bar{x} = 61.5$ and $s_{n-1} = 16.812$. So, if the lengths of leaves can be modelled by a normal distribution, the best guess is that it will be $N(61.5, 16.812^2)$.

So set the null and alternative hypotheses as follows.

H_0: The length, in mm, of oak leaves is distributed as $N(61.5, 16.812^2)$;

H_1: The length, in mm, of oak leaves is not distributed as $N(61.5, 16.812^2)$.

The next step is to calculate the expected frequencies. For this you need to know the probabilities that a random variable X lies in a particular interval, given the known values of μ and σ^2. Some calculators have a program which you can use to find these directly. Otherwise you standardise the class boundaries using the equation

$$Z = \frac{X - 61.5}{16.812}$$

and find the probabilities in the corresponding intervals for $N(0,1)$. To get the expected frequencies you then multiply these probabilities by 50. The results are shown in Table 13.20.

Class boundaries	< 29.5	29.5– 39.5	39.5– 49.5	49.5– 59.5	59.5– 69.5
Probability	0.0285	0.0668	0.1423	0.2150	0.2303
f_e	1.42	3.34	7.12	10.75	11.51

Class boundaries	69.5– 79.5	79.5– 89.5	89.5– 99.5	99.5– 109.5	> 109.5
Probability	0.1749	0.0943	0.0360	0.0098	0.0022
f_e	8.75	4.71	1.80	0.49	0.11

Table 13.20

You can see that it will be necessary to combine some classes, the first three and the last four. Table 13.21 shows the observed and expected frequencies with the classes combined.

Class boundaries	< 49.5	49.5– 59.5	59.5– 69.5	69.5– 79.5	> 79.5	Total
Probability	12	15	9	6	8	50
f_e	11.88	10.75	11.51	8.75	7.11	50

Table 13.21

There are 5 classes and 3 constraints ($\sum f_e = 50$, and μ and σ^2 estimated from the data), so $v = 5 - 3 = 2$. From Table 13.21, $X^2 = 3.204...$, and

$$P\left(X^2 \geq 3.204...\right) \approx P\left(\chi_2^2 \geq 3.204...\right) = 0.2014... \text{ , which is } 20.1\%.$$

This is greater than the significance level of 5%, so the null hypothesis is accepted. The length, in mm, of oak leaves is distributed as $N\left(61.5, 16.812^2\right)$.

Exercise 13B

1   It is thought that the random variable Y is distributed $N(50,100)$. One hundred observations of Y are made and result in the given frequency distribution.

Observations of Y	< 30	30–	40–	50–	60–	> 70
Frequency	3	14	30	35	14	4

It is decided to carry out a goodness of fit test. Some of the expected frequencies are given in the table below.

Value of Y	< 30	30–	40–	50–	60–	> 70
Expected frequency	2.28			34.13		

Complete this table and carry out a goodness of fit test at the 2.5% significance level.

2   Human intelligence is often measured by calculating the Intelligence Quotient (IQ) of an individual, where $IQ \sim N\left(100,15^2\right)$. Three hundred new entrants to a school have IQ scores distributed according to the table.

IQ score	≤ 55	–70	–85	–100	–115	–130	–145	–160	> 160
Frequency	0	10	50	125	82	30	2	1	0

It is decided to test the fit of the model to these data. The expected frequencies (ignoring a continuity correction) are shown below.

IQ score	≤ 55	–70	–85	–100	–115	–130	–145	–160	> 160
Ex. frequency	0.41	6.42	40.77	102.40	102.40	40.77	6.42	0.40	0.01

(a) Show how the expected frequency for the fourth class was calculated.

(b) By carrying out a goodness of fit test at the 5% level, show that the model $IQ \sim N(100, 15^2)$ is not suitable for these data.

(c) It is thought that a better model may be one in which μ is estimated from the data rather than taking $\mu = 100$. Obtain an estimate of μ from the data and test whether a normal distribution with this mean and $\sigma = 15$ gives a better fit to the data.

3   The table below shows the frequency distribution of the lifetimes of a sample of 50 light bulbs.

Lifetime (hours)	< 650	650–659	660–669	670–679	680–689	690–699
Frequency	0	1	3	3	7	15

Lifetime (hours)	700–709	710–719	720–729	730–739	> 739
Frequency	7	7	4	3	0

(a) Show that unbiased estimates of the mean and variance of the population from which this sample was drawn are 698.3 and 354.653 respectively.

It is thought that the lifetime of a light bulb can be modelled by a normal distribution.

(b) Calculate the expected frequencies for the model $N(698.3, 354.653)$ and carry out a goodness of fit test of this model at the 5% level.

4   The amounts of meat eaten per week in a sample of 100 families of four is shown in the table.

Amount of meat (kg)	0–	2–	4–	6–	8–10
Frequency	2	10	20	50	18

It is thought that the amount of meat eaten per week by such families can be modelled by the probability density function $f(w) = 0.0002w^3(10 - w)$, for $0 \le w \le 10$ and zero elsewhere.

(a) Show that the cumulative distribution function for this model is

$$F(w) = \begin{cases} 0 & \text{for } w < 0, \\ 0.000\,04w^4(12.5 - w) & \text{for } 0 \le w \le 10, \\ 1 & \text{for } w > 10. \end{cases}$$

(b) Show that the expected frequency for the class 8–10 is 26.27.

(c) Calculate the expected frequencies for the intervals in the table and conduct a goodness of fit test at the 10% level.

5   The heights of 50 male students aged 18 were recorded correct to the nearest centimetre. The results are summarised in the table.

Heights	156–160	161–165	166–170	171–175	176–180	181–185	186–190
Frequency	2	7	12	14	9	3	3

Find the sample mean and an unbiased estimate of population variance and use them to conduct a goodness of fit test at the 5% level, to see whether height is distributed normally.

6   The durations (in minutes) of 100 phone calls were recorded, resulting in the frequency distribution below.

Duration of calls	0–	1–	2–	3–	4–	5–	10–	20
Frequency	7	18	34	25	13	2	1	0

Are the data normally distributed? Conduct a goodness of fit test at 0.1% level of significance.

13.6   Contingency tables

This section turns to a different kind of significance test which makes use of the χ^2 distribution. The question is whether two attributes of a population tend to be associated, that is to occur together, or whether they occur independently of each other.

Table 13.22 gives some data relating to the income level and the method of getting to work for a random sample of people. The income level is described as 'small' (less than £15 000), 'average' (£15 000 to £25 000), or 'large' (greater than £25 000) and the way of getting to work as 'car' (travelling by car either as driver or passenger), 'public' (using public transport) or 'self' (either cycling or walking). Thus the two attributes are income level and method of transport. A table like this, in which the total frequency has been divided into rows and columns according to the values taken by two attributes, is called a **contingency table**.

		Method of transport			
		Car	Public	Self	Total
	Small	58	21	36	115
Income	Average	199	49	64	312
level	Large	205	32	29	266
	Total	462	102	129	693

Table 13.22

The row and column totals allow you to estimate probabilities of the values for the different attributes. For example, $P(\text{small}) = \frac{115}{693}$ and $P(\text{public}) = \frac{102}{693}$.

Are the variables 'income level' and 'method of transport' independent of each other? This question can be tested by calculating the frequencies which you would expect if the variables *are* independent and then carrying out a χ^2 test. The null and alternative hypotheses are

H_0: the variables 'income level' and 'method of transport' are independent;
H_1: the variables 'income level' and 'method of transport' are not independent.

Suppose you want to find the expected frequency for the group of people with small income who travel by public transport. In order to do this you need an estimate of $P(\text{small and public})$. If H_0 is true and the variables are independent, then

$$P(\text{small and public}) = P(\text{small}) \times P(\text{public}) = \frac{115}{693} \times \frac{102}{693}.$$

Since the total sample size is 693, the corresponding expected frequency is equal to $693 \times \frac{115}{693} \times \frac{102}{693} = 16.93$, correct to 2 decimal places.

The other expected frequencies can be found in a similar fashion. For example,

$$P(\text{large and self}) = P(\text{large}) \times P(\text{self}) = \frac{226}{693} \times \frac{129}{693},$$

so the expected frequency is $693 \times \frac{226}{693} \times \frac{129}{693} = 49.52$, correct to 2 decimal places.

There is a quicker way of calculating the expected frequencies. Look at $693 \times \frac{115}{693} \times \frac{102}{693}$, which is the expression for the expected frequency for people with small income travelling by public transport. Two of the 693s cancel to give $\dfrac{115 \times 102}{693}$. The numerator of this fraction is the product of the row total for small income and the column total for public transport, while the denominator is the total sample size, usually called the 'grand total'. This is an example of a general rule for finding expected frequencies.

> Expected frequencies for a contingency table are given by
>
> $$\text{expected frequency} = \frac{\text{row total} \times \text{column total}}{\text{grand total}}.$$

Table 13.23 shows the calculation of the expected frequencies using this formula.

		Method of transport			
		Car	Public	Self	Total
	Small	$\frac{115 \times 462}{693} = 76.67$	$\frac{115 \times 102}{693} = 16.93$	$\frac{115 \times 129}{693} = 21.41$	115
Income	Average	$\frac{312 \times 462}{693} = 208.00$	$\frac{312 \times 102}{693} = 45.92$	$\frac{312 \times 129}{693} = 58.08$	312
level	Large	$\frac{266 \times 462}{693} = 177.33$	$\frac{266 \times 102}{693} = 39.15$	$\frac{266 \times 129}{693} = 49.52$	266
	Total	462	102	129	693

Table 13.23

A value of X^2 can now be calculated from the observed and expected frequencies as shown in Table 13.24. The total of the expected frequencies is not equal to 693 exactly because of rounding errors.

Income/transport	S/C	S/P	S/S	A/C	A/P	A/S	L/C	L/P	L/S
f_o	58	21	36	199	49	64	205	32	29
f_e	76.67	16.93	21.41	208.00	45.92	58.08	177.33	39.15	49.52

Table 13.24

From this you can work out that $X^2 = 30.78$

You now need to know the number of degrees of freedom of the χ^2 distribution which will approximate the distribution of X^2. As for goodness of fit tests this is calculated from

$\nu = $ number of classes $-$ number of constraints.

There are 9 classes, but how many constraints are there? Look at Table 13.23 again. In this table all three column totals, all three row totals and the grand total were used to calculate the expected frequencies. However, the calculation could have been done with fewer pieces of information as shown in Table 13.25. The missing row and column totals in this table can be found by subtraction and then the expected frequencies calculated as before (check that you agree with this statement). So this table shows that there are 5 constraints, because 5 pieces of information from the observed contingency table are needed in order to calculate the expected frequencies. Thus $v = 9 - 5 = 4$.

| | | Method of transport | | | |
		Car	Public	Self	Total
	Small				115
Income	Average				312
level	Large				
	Total	462	102		693

Table 13.25

So now calculate $P(X^2 \geq 30.78) \approx P(\chi_4^2 \geq 30.78) = 3.4 \times 10^{-6}$. Thus the null hypothesis that the two variables are independent can be rejected at any reasonable significance level: there is very strong evidence that income size and method of transport are related.

Having found that income level and method of transport are not independent it is interesting to see if there is any obvious reason for this. If you look at Table 13.24 and work out X^2 using the formula

$$\sum \frac{(f_o - f_e)^2}{f_e}$$ *, you will see that large contributions to the value of X^2 are made by the first, third, seventh and ninth classes. If you then compare the observed and expected frequencies for these classes you will see that among people with small incomes fewer than expected travel to work by car and more than expected walk or cycle. Among people with large incomes the opposite is true.*

13.7 Degrees of freedom of a contingency table

The method used in the previous section to find the number of degrees of freedom of a contingency table can be generalised. If there are h rows and k columns, then the number of classes is hk. Provided you are given all but one of the column totals, all but one of the row totals and the grand total, you can find all the expected frequencies, using subtraction where appropriate. So the number of constraints is equal to $(h-1) + (k-1) + 1 = h + k - 1$. Thus

v = number of classes − number of constraints

$= hk - (h + k - 1) = hk - h - k + 1$

$= (h-1)(k-1)$.

The number of degrees of freedom of a contingency table is given by

$v = (\text{number of rows} - 1) \times (\text{number of columns} - 1)$.

Applying this rule to the example in Section 13.6, where $h = k = 3$, gives $v = (3-1) \times (3-1) = 4$, as before.

13.8 Combining rows and columns

As for other goodness of fit tests, each expected frequency must be at least 5 in order to carry out a χ^2 test for independence of the two attributes. If necessary, rows or columns in the contingency table can be combined in order to meet this condition.

Note that you should only combine whole rows or columns, not individual entries.

Example 13.8.1

A university sociology department believes that students with a good grade in A level General Studies tend to do well on sociology degree courses. To check this it collected information on a random sample of 100 students who had just graduated and had also taken General Studies at A level. The students' performance in General Studies was divided into two categories, those with grade A or B and 'others'. Their degree classes were recorded as Class I, Class II, Class III and Fail. The data are in Table 13.26.

	Class I	Class II	Class III	Fail	Total
Grade A or B	11	22	6	1	40
Others	4	28	24	4	60
Total	15	50	30	5	100

Table 13.26

Use these data to test, at the 1% significance level, the hypothesis that degree class is independent of General Studies A level performance. State your conclusion clearly.   (OCR, adapted)

Take

H_0: degree class is independent of General Studies A level performance;

H_1: degree class is not independent of General Studies A level performance.

Table 13.27 shows the calculation of the expected frequencies, assuming independence.

	Class I	Class II	Class III	Fail	Total
Grade A or B	$\frac{40\times15}{100}=6$	$\frac{40\times50}{100}=20$	$\frac{40\times30}{100}=12$	$\frac{40\times5}{100}=2$	40
Others	$\frac{60\times15}{100}=9$	$\frac{60\times50}{100}=30$	$\frac{60\times30}{100}=18$	$\frac{60\times5}{100}=3$	60
Total	15	50	30	5	100

Table 13.27

Minimum expected frequencies of 5 can be achieved by combining the columns for Class III and Fail, that is, in each row, adding the frequencies for Class III and Fail.

This combination is logical because it groups 'weak' students together. It would not be sensible, for example, to combine Class I with Fail. Note also that in this example it would be pointless to combine rows since there would then only be one category for General Studies grade. In general, the combination of rows and columns should always be done on the basis of common sense.

Table 13.28 gives the observed and expected frequencies after combination. The values in brackets are the expected frequencies.

	Class I	Class II	Class III and Fail
Grade A or B	11(6)	22(20)	7(14)
Others	4(9)	28(30)	28(21)

Table 13.28

This gives the value $X^2 = 13.111\ldots$.

The number of degrees of freedom is calculated after any combination of rows or columns has been made in the contingency table. So applying the formula in Section 13.7 to Table 13.28,

$$v = (\text{number of rows} - 1) \times (\text{number of columns} - 1)$$
$$= (2-1)(3-1) = 2.$$

So $P(X^2 \geq 13.111\ldots) \approx P(\chi_2^2 \geq 13.111\ldots) = 0.001\,42\ldots$, which is 0.14%. This is less than the significance level of 1%, so 13.111... is in the rejection region.

The null hypothesis that degree class is independent of General Studies A level performance is rejected.

Inspection of Table 13.28 suggests that Class I degree results tend to be associated with grade A or B in General Studies while Class III degrees tend to be associated with lower grades in General Studies.

13.9* Justification for the χ^2 test procedure

All the applications in this chapter have been based on the link between the test statistic $\sum \dfrac{(f_o - f_e)^2}{f_e}$ and χ_v^2 for some value of v. The full theory supporting this can't be given in this book, but here is a proof for the special case $v = 1$. You may omit it if you wish.

The definition of χ^2 is that, if $Z_1, Z_2, \ldots, Z_v$ are v independent variables, each with a N(0,1) distribution, then the sum of their squares, that is $\sum Z_i^2$, has a χ_v^2 distribution. In this chapter you have used the result that the statistic $\sum \dfrac{(f_o - f_e)^2}{f_e}$ has a distribution which is approximately χ_v^2 where there are v degrees of freedom. It is fairly simple to show that this is true for the particular case in which there is one degree of freedom. In this case $\sum \dfrac{(f_o - f_e)^2}{f_e} \sim \chi_1^2$, so $\sum \dfrac{(f_o - f_e)^2}{f_e} = Z^2$.

Consider the situation in which the results fall into one of two classes. Suppose the null hypothesis is that the values are divided between the two classes in the ratio $p:(1-p)$. Denote the observed frequencies by O_1 and O_2, then the total frequency, n, is given by $n = O_1 + O_2$. The corresponding expected frequencies are np and $n(1-p)$. Then

$$\sum \frac{(f_e - f_o)^2}{f_e} = \frac{(O_1 - np)^2}{np} + \frac{(O_2 - n(1-p))^2}{n(1-p)}$$

$$= \frac{(O_1 - np)^2}{np} + \frac{(n - O_1 - n + np)^2}{n(1-p)} \qquad \text{(since } O_2 = n - O_1 \text{)}$$

$$= \frac{(O_1 - np)^2}{np} + \frac{(np - O_1)^2}{n(1-p)}$$

$$= \frac{(O_1 - np)^2}{n}\left(\frac{1}{p} + \frac{1}{1-p}\right)$$

$$= \frac{(O_1 - np)^2}{n}\left(\frac{1-p+p}{p(1-p)}\right)$$

$$= \frac{(O_1 - np)^2}{np(1-p)}.$$

Now O_1 is distributed as $B(n, p)$ since there are n trials and the probability for a result in the first class is p. If n is such that np and $n(1-p)$ are not too small, then this binomial distribution can be approximated by $N(np, np(1-p))$. Thus $O_1 \sim N(np, np(1-p))$ approximately. Standardising this distribution gives

$$Z = \frac{O_1 - np}{\sqrt{np(1-p)}} \sim N(0,1).$$

Squaring gives $Z^2 = \dfrac{(O_1 - np)^2}{np(1-p)}$. It was shown above that $\sum \dfrac{(f_o - f_e)^2}{f_e} = \dfrac{(O_1 - np)^2}{np(1-p)}$ so, in this case,

$\sum \dfrac{(f_o - f_e)^2}{f_e} = Z^2$, approximately.

This result is consistent with the rule for calculating the number of degrees of freedom since there are 2 classes and 1 constraint; that is, that the total observed frequency n is used in the calculation of the expected frequencies.

Exercise 13C

1   The grades achieved at GCSE in maths and English of 500 students are summarised in the table.

		Maths grade		
		A or A*	B	C or worse
English	A or A*	15	30	15
grade	B	33	105	102
	C or worse	27	65	108

Conduct a χ^2 test at the 5% significance level to test the hypothesis that the grades achieved in maths and English are independent.

2 One hundred and thirty people in London were asked to identify their favourite brand of soap from among Brand X, Brand Y and Brand Z. Seventy people in Manchester were asked the same question. The results of the surveys are shown in the table.

	Brand X	Brand Y	Brand Z
London	35	70	25
Manchester	15	35	20

Is there any association between the city and the brand of soap preferred? Use a 5% level of significance.

3 The milk yield from two breeds of cows is classified as 'High', 'Medium' or 'Low'. The yields of 100 cows were classified as in the table.

	Yield		
	High	Medium	Low
Breed A	30	20	18
Breed B	18	10	4

Use these data to test, at the 2.5% level of significance, whether breed of cow and milk yield are independent.

4 Six hundred individuals were classified according to their hair colour and eye colour.

		Eye colour		
		Brown	Green/Grey	Blue
Hair colour	Black	95	56	44
	Brown	78	64	90
	Fair	37	35	61
	Ginger	10	10	20

Conduct a χ^2 test at the 0.1% significance level to test the hypothesis that hair colour and eye colour are independent.

5 The table below gives some data which were obtained from a random sample of men in the course of a study into heart disease. Each man was classified according to his income level and his level of physical activity. The amount of exercise is described as 'Low', 'Medium' or 'High' and the income level as 'Small', 'Average' or 'Large'.

		Level of physical activity		
		Low	Medium	High
Income level	Small	143	56	108
	Average	134	130	188
	Large	53	82	106

Use these data to test, at the 1% significance level, the hypothesis that level of physical activity and income level are independent.

6 The grade achieved at A-level mathematics is recorded for a random sample of 100 students studying at one of three sixth-form colleges in a city. The data are summarised in the table.

		Grade						
		A	B	C	D	E	N	U
	X	12	34	23	7	5	4	1
College	Y	4	45	12	5	3	4	2
	Z	27	23	16	15	5	2	1

It is proposed to test whether there is any association between the college attended and the grade obtained.

(a) Calculate the expected frequencies for a χ^2 test, assuming no association between grade and college.

(b) Explain briefly why some combining of rows or columns should be carried out.

(c) Carry out the test, combining suitable columns and using a 1% significance level.

7 In an investigation into a possible association between hair colour and height, a random sample of 200 adult men was taken, and the data shown in the table were obtained.

		Hair colour			Total
		Dark	Fair	Red	
	Less than 165 cm	16	7	11	34
Height	165 cm to 180 cm	46	39	9	94
	More than 180 cm	33	35	4	72
	Total	95	81	24	200

It is proposed to carry out a χ^2 test for independence between hair colour and height.

(a) Calculate the expected frequencies.

(b) Explain briefly why some combining of rows or columns should be carried out.

(c) Carry out the test, combining suitable rows and using a 5% significance level.   (OCR)

Review exercise

1 X is a random variable with the distribution $X \sim B(12, 0.42)$.

  (a) Anne uses the binomial distribution to calculate the probability that $X < 4$ and gives 4 significant figures in her answer. What answer should she get?

  (b) Ben uses a normal distribution to calculate an approximation for the probability that $X < 4$ and gives 4 significant figures in his answer. What answer should he get?   (OCR, adapted)

2 The time T hours taken to repair a piece of equipment has a probability density function which may be modelled by

$$f(t) = \begin{cases} \dfrac{24}{7t^4} & \text{for } 1 \le t \le 2, \\ 0 & \text{otherwise.} \end{cases}$$

  (a) Find $E(T)$ and $Var(T)$.

  (b) $\overline{T}$ denotes the mean of the times for 30 randomly chosen repairs. Assuming that the central limit theorem holds, estimate $P(\overline{T} < 1.2)$.

  State, giving a reason, whether your answer has little error or considerable error.

3 A machine is set to produce ball-bearings with mean diameter 1.2 cm. Each day a random sample of 50 ball-bearings is selected and the diameters accurately measured. If the sample mean diameter lies outside the range 1.18 cm to 1.22 cm then it will be taken as evidence that the mean diameter of the ball-bearings produced is not 1.2 cm. The machine will then be stopped and adjustments made to it. Assuming that the diameters have standard deviation 0.075 cm, find the probability that

  (a) the machine is stopped unnecessarily,

  (b) the machine is not stopped when the mean diameter of the ball-bearings produced is 1.15 cm.

4 The number of night calls to a fire station serving a small town can be modelled by a Poisson distribution with mean 2.7 calls per night.

  (a) State the expectation and variance of the mean number of night calls over a period of n nights.

  (b) Estimate the probability that during a given year of 365 days the total number of night calls will exceed 1050.

5 Metal struts used in a building are specified to have a mean length of 2.855 m. The lengths have a normal distribution with standard deviation 0.0352 m. A batch of 15 struts is sent to a building site and the lengths are measured. The sample mean length is 2.841 m.

  A test is to be carried out, at the 5% significance level, to decide whether the batch is from the specified population.

  (a) Stating your hypotheses, find the rejection region in terms of Z.

  (b) State the conclusion of the test.

6   A supermarket buys a large batch of plastic bags from a manufacturer to be used in the store. In previous batches 7% of the bags were defective. A quality control manager wishes to test whether the batch has a higher defective rate than 7%, in which case the batch will be returned to the manufacturer. He examines 125 randomly selected bags and finds that 14 are defective. Using a distributional approximation, carry out the manager's test at the 3% significance level and state whether he should return the batch.

7   An employee is accused by his employer of being late for work too often. The employee claims that, on average, he is late on no more than one day in ten. The employer finds that, over a random sample of 20 days, the employee is late on r days. The employer carries out a significance test, at the 5% level, to decide whether, on average, the employee is late on more than one day in ten.

   (a) State suitable null and alternative hypotheses for the test.

   (b) Find the set of values of r for which the null hypothesis would be rejected, and state the conclusion of the test in the case $r = 4$.

   (c) Given that, in fact, the probability that the employee is late for work on a randomly chosen day is 0.2, find the probability of making a Type II error in the test.   (OCR)

8   The time, T, in minutes that a person takes to drive to work is uniformly distributed over the interval 30 to 40. The distance of the journey is 15 km. Let V denote the average speed of the journey in km per hour.

   (a) Write down the relationship between T and V.

   (b) Find the probability density function of V.

   (c) Find (i) the median (ii) the mean of V.

9   Small packets of nails are advertised as having average weight 500 g, and large packets as having average weight 1000 g. Assume that the packet weights are distributed normally with means as advertised, and standard deviations of 10 g for a small packet and 15 g for a large packet. Giving your answers correct to 3 decimal places,

   (a) find the probability that two randomly chosen small packets have a total weight between 990 g and 1020 g,

   (b) find the probability that the weight of one randomly chosen large packet exceeds the total weight of two randomly chosen small packets by at least 25 g,

   (c) find the probability that one half of the weight of one randomly chosen large packet exceeds the weight of one randomly chosen small packet by at least 12.5 g.   (OCR)

10 A slimming regime, consisting of a mixture of diet and exercise, is claimed by the designer to decrease the weight of people using the regime by an average of 4 kg over a three-month period. To support the claim, the designer measures the weight losses of 16 randomly chosen people who used the regime for three months. The results, w kg, are summarised by $\sum w = 46.44$ and $\sum w^2 = 180.5$.

   (a) Test, at the 10% significance level, the null hypothesis that the population mean weight loss is 4 kg against the alternative hypothesis that it is not 4 kg. Weight loss may be assumed to be distributed normally.

   (b) Find the set of values of the population mean weight loss for which the null hypothesis would be rejected in a two-tail test at the 5% significance level using the above data.

11 Ten students were asked to perform a simple task and the times, in seconds, that they took to complete the task were recorded. The next day, the students were asked to perform the same task and the times taken on the second attempt were recorded. A researcher was interested to know whether the practice in the first attempt led to a reduction in time at the second attempt. The times are given in the following table.

Student	1	2	3	4	5	6	7	8	9	10
First attempt	16.3	54.2	63.2	42.0	38.7	48.3	11.2	41.3	52.1	44.9
Second attempt	13.2	57.1	50.1	40.0	36.0	30.2	9.6	44.0	40.3	23.8

(a) Stating your assumptions, use a suitable test, at the 5% significance level, to advise the researcher as to whether there is a reduction in time at the second attempt.

(b) Calculate a 95% confidence interval for the population mean reduction in time for the two attempts.   (OCR, adapted)

12 In a test of car components in which the failure rate is thought to be constant, the numbers of failures in a series of 100-mile intervals are recorded in the following table.

Number of failures	0	1	2	3	4	5	6	7
Frequency	25	30	26	18	9	5	6	1

Calculate the mean number of failures per interval and the expected distribution of failures for the 120 intervals that would be given by a Poisson distribution with this mean.

A good fit between the sets of observed and expected frequencies is taken as evidence of the constancy of the failure rate. Use a χ^2 test to test the goodness of fit.   (OCR)

13 In 1988 the number of new cases of insulin-dependent diabetes in children under the age of 15 years was 1495. The table below breaks down this figure according to age and sex.

	Age (years)			
	0–4	5–9	10–14	Total
Boys	205	248	328	781
Girls	182	251	281	714
Total	387	499	609	1495

Perform a suitable test, at the 5% significance level, to determine whether age and sex are independent factors.   (OCR)

Examination questions

1 The weights of male nurses in a hospital are known to be normally distributed with mean $\mu = 72$ kg and standard deviation $\sigma = 7.5$ kg. The hospital has a lift (elevator) with a maximum recommended load of 450 kg. Six male nurses enter the lift. Calculate the probability p that their combined weight exceeds the maximum recommended load.   (© IBO 2002)

2 The following is a random sample of 16 measurements of the density of aluminium. Assume that the measurements are normally distributed.

2.704	2.709	2.711	2.706
2.708	2.705	2.709	2.701
2.705	2.707	2.710	2.700
2.703	2.699	2.702	2.701

Construct a 95% confidence interval for the density of aluminium, showing all steps clearly.

(© IBO 2002)

3 A sociologist wants to know whether the percentage of sons taking up the profession of their father is the same in every profession. She decides to investigate the situation in each of four professions. She obtained the following data.

63 out of 136 sons of male medical doctors became doctors

42 out of 118 sons of male engineers became engineers

35 out of 96 sons of male lawyers became lawyers

68 out of 150 sons of male businessmen became businessmen

At the 5% level of significance what should her conclusion be?   (© IBO 2002)

4 *Give all numerical answers to this question correct to two decimal places.*

A radar records the speed, v kilometres per hour, of cars on a road. The speed of these cars is normally distributed. The results for 1000 cars are recorded in the following table.

Speed	Number of cars
$40 \le v < 50$	9
$50 \le v < 60$	35
$60 \le v < 70$	93
$70 \le v < 80$	139
$80 \le v < 90$	261
$90 \le v < 100$	295
$100 \le v < 110$	131
$110 \le v < 120$	26
$120 \le v < 130$	11

(a) For the cars on the road, calculate

(i) an unbiased estimate of the mean speed;

(ii) an unbiased estimate of the variance of the speed.

(b) For the cars on the road, calculate

(i) a 95% confidence interval for the mean speed;

(ii) a 90% confidence interval for the mean speed.

(c) Explain why one of the intervals found in part (b) is a subset of the other.   (© IBO 2003)

5 Eggs at a farm are sold in boxes of six. Each egg is either brown or white. The owner believes that the number of brown eggs in a box can be modelled by a binomial distribution. He examines 100 boxes and obtains the following data.

Number of brown eggs in a box	Frequency
0	10
1	29
2	31
3	18
4	8
5	3
6	1

(a) (i) Calculate the mean number of brown eggs in a box.

   (ii) Hence estimate p, the probability that a randomly chosen egg is brown.

(b) By calculating an appropriate statistic, test, at the 2.5% significance level, whether or not the binomial distribution gives a good fit to these data. (© IBO 2003)

6 The random variable Z has probability density function $f(z) = z - \frac{1}{4}z^3$ for $z \in [0,2]$ and 0 elsewhere. A physicist assumes that the lifetime of a certain particle can be modelled by this random variable. The interval $[0, 2]$ is divided into the following equal intervals:

$$I_1 = [0, 0.4[\qquad I_2 = [0.4, 0.8[\qquad I_3 = [0.8, 1.2[\qquad I_4 = [1.2, 1.6[\qquad I_5 = [1.6, 2]$$

The physicist carried out 40 experiments and recorded the number of times the value of Z lay in each of the intervals I_k where $k = 1, 2, 3, 4, 5$ as shown in the following table:

I_1	I_2	I_3	I_4	I_5
2	12	9	8	9

(a) Assuming that the physicist's assumption is correct, for each value of k find $p_k = P(Z \in I_k)$.

(b) At the 5% significance level can his assumption be accepted? (© IBO 2004)

7 Let X and Y be two independent variables with $E(X) = 5$, $Var(X) = 3$, $E(Y) = 4$, $Var(Y) = 2$. Find

(a) $E(2X)$,   (b) $Var(2X)$,   (c) $E(3X - 2Y)$,   (d) $Var(3X - 2Y)$.

(© IBO 2005)

8 A machine shop manufactures steel rods for use in a car production plant. The lengths in metres for a sample of 8 rods are given below.

    0.999, 1.001, 1.005, 1.011, 1.005, 1.001, 0.998, 1.004

Previous observations have shown that the machine settings gave rods with lengths that are normally distributed with standard deviation 0.0028 m.

Stating the type of test used, determine at the 1% significance level if the mean length of the rods produced is 1.005 m. (© IBO 2005)

Appendix: some supporting mathematics

In this book it has been possible to prove some results in probability using mathematics you have already met in the Higher Level books. Other results, such as the central limit theorem or the equation for t-probability, require far more advanced mathematics and must at this stage be taken on trust. This appendix deals with a few mathematical techniques which come between these extremes. They are not an essential part of the course, but they are included so that you can, if you wish, fill in some gaps in the treatment of certain topics.

Most of the material in this appendix takes the form of questions for you to work for yourself. For ease of reference questions are numbered as **Qx.y**, where the number x indicates the section in which it appears, and y tells you the position of the question within the section.

A.1 Mean and variance

This section deals with discrete probability distributions for which the sample space S is $\mathbb{N}$ or a subset of $\mathbb{N}$, such as $\mathbb{Z}^+$ or the finite set $\{0,1,2,\dots,n\}$. If p_x denotes the probability $P(X = x)$, then the standard definitions can be written as

$$\mu = \sum_{x \in S} x p_x \quad \text{and} \quad \sigma^2 = \sum_{x \in S}(x-\mu)^2 p_x, \quad \text{where} \quad \sum_{x \in S} p_x = 1.$$

There are two other ways of finding the variance. You have often used the formula in Q1.1, but Q1.2 may be new to you.

Q1.1 Prove that $\sigma^2 = \sum_{x \in S} x^2 p_x - \mu^2$.

Q1.2 Prove that $\sigma^2 = \sum_{x \in S} x(x-1)p_x + \mu - \mu^2$.

A.2 The negative binomial series

One way of writing the binomial expansion of $(1+x)^n$, where $n \in \mathbb{Z}^+$, is

$$(1+x)^n = 1 + \frac{n}{1!}x + \frac{n(n-1)}{2!}x^2 + \frac{n(n-1)(n-2)}{3!}x^3 + \dots + x^n.$$

If you substitute $x = -q$ and $n = -1$ in this equation, the left side becomes $(1-q)^{-1}$ but the series on the right becomes an infinite series.

Q2.1 Write down the right side with these substitutions, simplifying the coefficients as much as possible. Where have you seen this before?

Q2.2 Show that, if you carry out the the same process with $n = -2$ and $n = -3$, you get

$$(1-q)^{-2} = 1 + 2q + 3q^2 + \dots = \sum_{x=0}^{\infty} xq^{x-1} \quad \text{and} \quad (1-q)^{-3} = 1 + 3q + 6q^2 + \dots = \sum_{x=0}^{\infty} x(x-1)q^{x-2}.$$

Q2.3 Take the expressions on both sides of Q2.1 and differentiate them once and twice with respect to q. (It can be proved that this is valid if $-1 < q < 1$.) Compare your results with those in Q2.2.

Q2.4 Use a calculator to display with the same axes the graphs of $y = (1-x)^{-2}$ and $y = 1 + 2x + 3x^2 + 4x^3 + 5x^4 + 6x^5$. Use a window of $-2 \le x \le 2, -5 \le y \le 10$. For what interval of values of x do the two graphs appear to coincide?

Q2.5 Repeat Q2.4 with the graphs of $y = (1-x)^{-3}$ and $y = 1 + 3x + 6x^2 + 10x^3 + 15x^4 + 21x^5$.

Q2.4 and Q2.5 suggest (as is true) that the equations in Q2.2 are valid if $-1 < q < 1$.

Q2.6 Assuming this, and using the expression for σ^2 in Q1.2, prove that, for the geometric distribution with $P(X = x) = pq^{x-1}$ for $x \in \mathbb{Z}^+$, $\mu = \dfrac{1}{p}$ and $\sigma^2 = \dfrac{q}{p^2}$. (See Section 2.2.)

If you write a series like those in Q2.2 with $n = -r$, you get

$$(1-q)^{-r} = 1 + \frac{r}{1!}q + \frac{r(r+1)}{2!}q^2 + \frac{r(r+1)(r+2)}{3!}q^3 + \dots .$$

Q2.7 Show that the coefficient of q^s can be written as $\dbinom{r+s-1}{r-1}$. Hence the coefficient of q^{x-r} is $\dbinom{x-1}{r-1}$.

This explains the name 'negative binomial' for the probability distribution $\mathrm{NB}(r,p)$ defined by

$$P(X = x) = \binom{x-1}{r-1}q^{x-r}p^r. \text{ (See Section 12.2(iv))}.$$

A.3 The exponential series

Infinite series like those in Q2.2 are called power series, because each term is a multiple of a power of q. Another important power series is

$$E(m) = 1 + \frac{m}{1!} + \frac{m^2}{2!} + \frac{m^3}{3!} + \dots = \sum_{x=0}^{\infty} \frac{m^x}{x!}.$$

This series converges to a limit for all values of m.

Q3.1 Assuming that this series can be differentiated in the same way as in Q2.3, prove that

$$E'(m) = E(m).$$

Q3.2 Use Q3.1 and the fact that $E(0) = 1$ to prove that $E(m) = e^m$. (See Higher Level Book 2 Section 23.3.)

Q3.3 Show that, for Poisson probability $\mathrm{Po}(m)$, with $p_x = e^{-m}\dfrac{m^x}{x!}$, $\displaystyle\sum_{x=0}^{\infty} p_x = 1$.

Q3.4 Using Q1.2, prove that, for Poisson probability $\mathrm{Po}(m)$, $\mu = m$ and $\sigma^2 = m$.

A.4 Normal probability density

The equation for standardised normal probability density $N(0,1)$ is $\phi(x) = \dfrac{1}{\sqrt{2\pi}} e^{-\frac{1}{2}x^2}$.

Q4.1 Use the chain rule to find $\dfrac{d}{dx} e^{-\frac{1}{2}x^2}$.

Q4.2 Find the coordinates of the points of inflexion on the graph of $y = \phi(x)$.

Q4.3 By writing $x^2 e^{-\frac{1}{2}x^2}$ as $(-x) \times \left(-x e^{-\frac{1}{2}x^2}\right)$ and using integration by parts, prove that

$$\int_{-v}^{v} x^2 e^{-\frac{1}{2}x^2}\, dx = -2v e^{-\frac{1}{2}v^2} + \int_{-v}^{v} e^{-\frac{1}{2}x^2}\, dx.$$

Q4.4 Prove that $\displaystyle\int_{-\infty}^{\infty} x^2 \phi(x)\, dx = \int_{-\infty}^{\infty} \phi(x)\, dx$. Hence show that the variance of this probability

distribution is equal to 1, and give a geometrical interpretation of this in terms of the graph of $y = \phi(x)$.

Q4.5 Use a method similar to that in Q4.3 and Q4.4 to show that $\displaystyle\int_{-\infty}^{\infty} x^4 \phi(x)\, dx = 3\int_{-\infty}^{\infty} x^2 \phi(x)\, dx$.

Q4.6 By writing $\mathrm{Var}(Z^2)$ as $\mathrm{E}(Z^4) - \left(\mathrm{E}(Z^2)\right)^2$, prove that $\mathrm{Var}(Z^2) = 2$.

In Section 13.9 it is stated that, if $Z_1, Z_2, \ldots, Z_v$ are v independent variables, each with a $N(0,1)$ distribution, then $\displaystyle\sum_{i=1}^{v} Z_i^2$ has a χ_v^2 distribution.

Q4.7 Use the answer to Q4.6 to show that $\mathrm{E}(\chi_1^2) = 1$ and $\mathrm{Var}(\chi_1^2) = 2$; and, more generally, that $\mathrm{E}(\chi_v^2) = v$ and $\mathrm{Var}(\chi_v^2) = 2v$, as stated in Section 13.2.

A.5 Sampling without replacement

Q5.1 By expanding both sides of the identity $(1+y)^M (1+y)^{N-M} \equiv (1+y)^N$ and equating the coefficients of y^n, prove that $\displaystyle\sum_{x=0}^{n} \binom{M}{x}\binom{N-M}{n-x} = \binom{N}{n}$.

Q5.2 For the hypergeometric probability distribution $\mathrm{Hyp}(n, M, N)$, with

$$p_x = \frac{\dbinom{M}{x}\dbinom{N-M}{n-x}}{\dbinom{N}{n}} \qquad \text{for } x = 0, 1, 2, 3, \ldots, n,$$

show that $\displaystyle\sum_{x=0}^{n} p_x = 1$. (See Section 12.3.)

Q5.3   Write an expression for the mean μ of this probability distribution. By using the identity $x\binom{M}{x} \equiv M\binom{M-1}{x-1}$, show that this mean can be written as $\mu = \dfrac{M}{\binom{N}{n}} \displaystyle\sum_{x=1}^{n} \binom{M-1}{x-1}\binom{N-M}{n-x}$.

Q5.4   Use a method like that in Q5.1 to prove that the sum in Q5.3 is equal to $\binom{N-1}{n-1}$.

Hence show that $\mu = np$, where $p = \dfrac{M}{N}$.

Q5.5   By methods similar to those in Q5.2 to Q5.4, prove that

$$\sum_{x=0}^{n} x(x-1)p_x = \frac{M(M-1)}{\binom{N}{n}} \sum_{x=2}^{n} \binom{M-2}{x-2}\binom{N-M}{n-x} = \frac{M(M-1)}{\binom{N}{n}}\binom{N-2}{n-2} = \frac{M(M-1)}{N(N-1)} \times n(n-1).$$

Q5.6   Hence, using the form for the variance in Q1.2, prove that $\sigma^2 = np(1-p)\left(\dfrac{N-n}{N-1}\right)$.

A.6 Exponential probability

The equation for exponential probability density is

$$f(x) = \begin{cases} me^{-mx} & \text{for } x > 0, \\ 0 & \text{otherwise.} \end{cases}$$

The mean and variance are therefore given by

$$\mu = \int_0^{\infty} mxe^{-mx}\,dx \quad \text{and} \quad \sigma^2 = \int_0^{\infty} mx^2 e^{-mx}\,dx - \mu^2.$$

Q6.1   Use integration by parts to find an expression for $\displaystyle\int_0^{v} mxe^{-mx}\,dx$ in terms of v.

Q6.2   Prove that $\displaystyle\int_0^{v} mx^2 e^{-mx}\,dx = -v^2 e^{-mv} + 2\int_0^{v} xe^{-mx}\,dx$.

In Higher Level Book 2 Review exercise 4 Question 20 you were asked to prove that $\lim_{v \to \infty} ve^{-mv} = 0$ and $\lim_{v \to \infty} v^2 e^{-mv} = 0$.

Q6.3   Use these limits together with Q6.1 and Q6.2 to prove that, for exponential probability $\text{Exp}(m)$, $\mu = \dfrac{1}{m}$ and $\sigma^2 = \dfrac{1}{m^2}$. (See Section 2.4.)

Answers

1 Cumulative distribution functions

Exercise 1 (page 7)

1 (a) $F(x) = 0$ in $]-\infty, 0[$, $\frac{1}{16}x^2$ in $[0,4]$,
    1 in $]4,\infty[$
  (b) 2.83

2 (a) $F(x) = 0$ in $]-\infty, 0[$, $\frac{2}{3}x$ in $[0,1[$,
    $\frac{1}{3}(4x - x^2 - 1)$ in $[1,2]$, 1 in $]2,\infty[$
  (b) $\frac{3}{8}$ (c) 1.33

3 (a) $F(x) = 0$ in $]-\infty, 0[$, $\frac{3}{28}x^2$ in $[0,2[$,
    $\frac{1}{28}(6x^2 - x^3 - 4)$ in $[2,4]$, 1 in $]4,\infty[$
  (b) 2.17   (c) $\frac{41}{224}$

4 (a) $F(x) = 0$ in $]-\infty, 0[$,
    $\frac{1}{16}(24x^2 - 16x^3 + 3x^4)$ in $[0,2]$,
    1 in $]2,\infty[$
  (b) 7710

5 $f(x) = \frac{1}{6}x - \frac{1}{36}x^3$ in $[0,6]$, 0 otherwise

6 $f(x) = \frac{1}{9}x$ in $[0,3[$, $\frac{2}{3} - \frac{1}{9}x$ in $[3,6]$,
    0 otherwise

7 (a) 0 in $]-\infty, 0]$, $0.2x$ in $]0,5[$, 1 in $[5,\infty[$
  (b) 0 in $]-\infty, 0]$, $0.2\sqrt{y}$ in $]0,25[$,
    1 in $[25,\infty[$
  (c) 0 in $]-\infty, 0]$, $\frac{0.1}{\sqrt{y}}$ in $]0,25[$, 1 in $[25,\infty[$

8 (a) 0 in $]-\infty, 0]$, x in $]0,1[$, 1 in $[1,\infty[$
  (b) 0 in $]-\infty, 1]$, $1 - \frac{1}{y}$ in $]1,\infty[$
  (c) 0 in $]-\infty, 1]$, $\frac{1}{y^2}$ in $]1,\infty[$

9 10.5 years

10 0, 0.216, 0.648, 0.936, 1

11 Data for graph:
    $F(x) = 0$ in $]-\infty, 0[$, 0.183 in $[0,1[$,
    0.493 in $[1,2[$, 0.757 in $[2,3[$, 0.907 in $[3,4[$,
    0.970 in $[4,5[$, 0.992 in $[5,6[$, 0.998 in $[6,7[$,
    1.000 in $[7,8[$, ...

2 Geometric and exponential probability

Exercise 2A (page 16)

	(a)	(b)	(c)
1	0.0720	0.0504	0.1577
2	0.144	0.0864	0.4704
3	0.032	0.992	0.0003
4	0.0199	0.7763	0.2237
5	0.3206	0.1673	0.1673
	(d) 0.8327		
6	0.0808	0.1594	0.8406
7	0.3056	0.0711	0.0541
8	0.0453	0.2711	0.5811
9	0.0478	0.3487	
10	0.0988	0.1317	0.1646

   If the people arrive in groups, their choices of footwear may not be independent of each other.

11 (a) 0.3894   (b) 66
12 (a) 0.2288   (b) 88
13 (a) 0.0558   (b) 0.2791
14 0.34
15 4, 12
16 (a) 2, 2   (b) 1
17 $37.50

Exercise 2B (page 23)

1 (a) 0.181   (b) 0.135   (c) 0.148
2 0.713
3 0.154
4 0.223
5 0.435
6 0.221
7 0.082
8 (a) (i) $\frac{1}{\lambda}\ln 2$ (ii) $\frac{1}{\lambda}\ln\frac{4}{3}$, $\frac{1}{\lambda}\ln 4$ (iii) 0
   (b) 63.2%
9 0.383
10 17.9
11 0.865
12 0.916, 0.511
13 1.2 hours

14 (a) 6 minutes   (b) 0.0357

3 Linear combinations of random variables

Exercise 3 (page 33)

1 5, 3.2
2 \$18 500, \$3000
3 $S = \frac{5}{4}R - 20$, 130
4 0.5, 0.25; 0.48, 0.16; 0.3, 0.37, 0.2, 0.04; 1, 0.5, 0.8, 0.48, 1.8, 0.98
5 3.1, 3.69; 0.2, 0.16, 0.1, 0.14, 0.2
6 24, 12, 6, 24
7 8 mm, 0.14 mm^2
8 3.5, $\frac{35}{12}$, 3, 9, 6.5, $\frac{143}{12}$
9 $\frac{17}{8}$, $\frac{71}{64}$; $\frac{51}{8}$, $\frac{213}{64}$
10 82.5, 311

4 Some properties of normal probability

Exercise 4A (page 40)

1 0.0592
2 0.0636
3 0.0228
4 0.127
5 0.362
6 0.0317
7 $\mu = 16$, $\sigma^2 = 9$

Exercise 4B (page 43)

1 (a) 0.460   (b) (i) 0.382   (ii) 0.159
2 (a) N(2.4, 0.0432) (b) 0.3152
3 (a) 0.271   (b) 0.0021
4 1.3×10^{-11}; 0.631
5 (a) 1.2×10^{-21} (b) 0.9987
6 24.872
7 2.11 hours

5 Hypothesis testing

Exercise 5A (page 47)

1 $H_0: \mu = 102.5$, $H_1: \mu < 102.5$
2 $H_0: \mu = 84$, $H_1: \mu \neq 84$
3 $H_0: \mu = 53$, $H_1: \mu > 53$
4 $H_0: \mu = 30$, $H_1: \mu < 30$. A one-tail test is more appropriate for the customer.

5 $H_0: \mu = 5$, $H_1: \mu < 5$. A one-tail test for a decrease is appropriate since the only cause for concern is μ falling below 5.

Exercise 5B (page 51)

The end-points of the critical regions are given correct to 2 decimal places.

1 (a) Reject H_0 and accept that $\mu > 10$.
    (b) Accept $H_0: \mu = 10$.
2 (a) Accept $H_0: \mu = 15$.
    (b) Reject H_0 and accept that $\mu < 15$.
3 (a) Accept $H_0: \mu = 20$.
    (b), (c) Reject H_0 and accept that $\mu \neq 20$.
4 $H_0: \mu = 102.5$, $H_1: \mu < 102.5$; $\overline{X} \leq 101.69$; accept $\mu < 102.5$.
5 $H_0: \mu = 84.0$, $H_1: \mu \neq 84.0$; $\overline{X} \leq 82.11$ or $\overline{X} \geq 85.89$; reject H_0 and accept that mean time differs from 84.0 s.
6 $\overline{x} = 4.87$; $H_0: \mu = 5$, $H_1: \mu < 5$; $\overline{X} \leq 4.71$; accept H_0, mean is at least 5 microfarads.
7 $H_0: \mu = 85.6$, $H_1: \mu < 85.6$; $\overline{X} \leq 78.39$; reject H_0 and accept that the mean is less than 85.6.
8 $H_0: \mu = 6.8$, $H_1: \mu \neq 6.8$; $\overline{X} \leq 6.69$, $\overline{X} \geq 6.91$; reject H_0, and accept that the mean is not equal to 6.8.
9 $H_0: \mu = 30$, $H_1: \mu < 30$; $\overline{X} \leq 28.94$; accept H_1, there is cause for complaint.
10 $H_0: \mu = 3.21$, $H_1: \mu \neq 3.21$; $\overline{X} \leq 2.92$, $\overline{X} \geq 3.50$; accept H_0; the sample does not differ significantly from a random sample drawn from the population of all of the hospital births that year.

Exercise 5C (page 54)

1 $H_0: \mu = 330$, $H_1: \mu > 330$; $z = 2.504 > 1.960$, so accept H_1, manager's suspicion is justified.
2 $H_0: \mu = 508$, $H_1: \mu \neq 508$; $z = -1.622$. This lies between -1.645 and 1.645, so accept H_0, the process is under control.
3 $H_0: \mu = 45.1$, $H_1: \mu \neq 45.1$; $z = -2.758$. This is outside -2.054 to 2.054, so accept H_1, the mean has changed.
4 $H_0: \mu = 160$, $H_1: \mu > 160$; $z = 2.546 > 2.326$, so accept H_1, that the mean is greater than 160.
5 $H_0: \mu = 276.4$, $H_1: \mu > 276.4$; $z = 1.328 < 1.645$, so accept H_0, the campaign was not successful. This assumes that the sample can be treated as random; normal distribution of daily sales; the standard deviation remains unchanged.

Exercise 5D (page 57)

1 (a) 0.076   (b) (i) No   (ii) Yes

2 $H_0 : \mu = 8.42$, $H_1 : \mu > 8.42$; $z = 1.703$,

   $P(\overline{X} > 8.63) = 0.044 = 4.4\%$.

   (a) Accept H_1, mean greater than 8.42.

   (b) Accept H_0, mean not greater than 8.42.

3 $H_0 : \mu = 4.3$; $H_1 : \mu < 4.3$;
   $P(Z < -1.581) = 0.0569 = 5.69\%$, so accept H_1
   that the mean waiting time has decreased.

4 $H_0 : \mu = 42.3$, $H_1 : \mu > 42.3$;
   $P(Z > 2.594) = 0.00475 = 0.475\%$, so accept
   H_1, the results are unusually good.

6 Large sample distributions

Exercise 6A (page 64)

1 0.264

2 0.975

3 $0.961 > 0.95$

4 0.106

5 $N(1000, 10000)$, 0.159

Exercise 6B (page 66)

1 (a) 0.6928   (b) 0.704

2 (a) 0.0664   (b) 0.641

3 0.108

4 0.0969

5 8.37

Exercise 6C (page 70)

1 (a) 0.0289 (b) 0.114   (c) 0.0806 (d) 0.374

2 (a) 0.0122   (b) 0.117

3 0.0264, 26

4 0.198

5 0.773

7 The central limit theorem

Exercise 7 (page 75)

Where appropriate, alternative answers are given; the
second, shown by [*...], includes a continuity
correction.

1 $N(50, 25)$
   (a) 0.841   (b) 0.977   (c) 0.819

2 (a) 2.8   (b) 0.76   (c) 0.0524 [*0.0443]
   (d) 0.895 [*0.911]

3 $P(X = x) = \frac{1}{6}$, $x = 1, 2, 3, 4, 5, 6$
   (a) 0.164 [*0.155]   (b) 0.0708 [*0.0662]

4 (a) 0.966 [*0.968]   (b) 0.952 [*0.955]

5 (a) 0.007 86 [*0.008 41]   (b) 81 [*82]

6 0.0101 [*0.0100]

8 Hypothesis testing with discrete variables

Exercise 8A (page 79)

1 $H_0 : p = \frac{1}{2}$, $H_1 : p \neq \frac{1}{2}$, p is proportion of girls;
   $X \sim B\left(18, \frac{1}{2}\right)$; $P(X \leq 6) = 0.1189 > 0.05$, so
   accept H_0, the numbers of boys and girls are
   equal.

2 $H_0 : p = 0.95$, $H_1 : p < 0.95$; $X \sim B(25, 0.95)$;
   $P(X \leq 22) = 0.1271 > 0.05$, so accept H_0, there
   are at least 95% satisfied customers.

3 $H_0 : p = \frac{1}{2}$, $H_1 : p > \frac{1}{2}$ (or $\mu = 2.5$ and $\mu > 2.5$);
   p is the proportion of nails with length greater
   than 2.5 cm; $X \sim B\left(16, \frac{1}{2}\right)$;
   $P(X \geq 13) = 0.0106 < 0.025$, so accept H_1,
   $p > \frac{1}{2}$ and $\mu > 2.5$.
   The symmetry of the normal distribution about
   its mean is used in the statement $H_0 : p = \frac{1}{2}$.

4 (a) $H_0 : p = \frac{1}{4}$, $H_1 : p > \frac{1}{4}$; $X \sim B\left(20, \frac{1}{4}\right)$;
       $P(X \geq 8) = 0.1018 > 0.05$, so accept H_0,
       the results are no better than those obtained
       by chance.

   (b) 11

5 $H_0 : p = \frac{1}{6}$, $H_1 : p > \frac{1}{6}$; $X \sim B\left(30, \frac{1}{6}\right)$;
   $P(X \geq 10) = 0.0197 < 0.05$, so accept H_1, the
   suspicion is confirmed.

6 (a) $H_0 : p = 0.8$, $H_1 : p \neq 0.8$; $X \sim B(12, 0.8)$;
       $P(X \leq 6) = 0.0194 < 0.05$, so reject H_0
       and accept that the true figure is not 80%.

   (b) Lisa's friends do not comprise a random
       sample, so test is unreliable.

Exercise 8B (page 81)

1 Between 17 and 31.

2 124 or more

3 151

4 21

9 Errors in hypothesis testing

Exercise 9A (page 87)

1 (a) $\bar{X} \geq 6.316$ (b) 0.196

2 (a) $\bar{X} \leq 9.7419$ (b) Type I error
   (c) 0.141

3 (a) 9.78   (b) 0.204   (c) It will be smaller.

4 (a) $H_0: \mu = 1.94$, $H_1: \mu < 1.94$; rejection region:
       $\bar{X} \leq 1.883$; $\bar{x} = 1.7$, reject H_0 and accept
       that new system had the desired effect.
   (b) 0.00866
   (c) Accepting that the mean absence rate is 1.94
       when it is actually less than 1.94.

5 (a) $\bar{T} \leq 3.3065$ (b) 0.0877
   (c) 0.0646, which is less than 0.0877

6 (a) $H_0: \mu = 30$, $H_1: \mu < 30$; $\bar{X} > 29.7782$
   (b) $0 < \mu < 29.53$

Exercise 9B (page 93)

1 (a) $N \leq 10$, $N \geq 23$ (b) 0.0259
   (c) Accept H_0: $p = 0.55$ (d) 0.9536

2 (a) $R \geq 18$, Mrs Robinson should be elected.
   (b) 2.16% (c) 0.694

3 (a) 0.0635 (b) 0.859;
   α is bigger and β is smaller.

4 (a) $H_0: p = 0.1$, $H_1: p < 0.1$
   (b) $P(X = 0) = 0.0798 < 0.10$, so reject H_0 and
       accept that the modified toaster is more reliable.
   (c) 0.0798   (d) $p < 0.0119$

10 The t-distribution

Exercise 10A (page 101)

1 £1.83, 0.119 £^{2}

2 (a) 48, 0.24   (b) 48, 0.245

3 (a) 0.0138 cm^2 (b) 0.0145 cm^2

4 2.49, 1.61

5 5.6, 2.569

6 50.6 g, 147 g^2

Exercise 10B (page 107)

1 $H_0: \mu = 6.32$, $H_1: \mu \neq 6.32$;
   $|t| = |-0.220| < 2.145$, or $p = 82.9\% > 5\%$;
   accept H_0, mean pH does not differ.

2 $H_0: \mu = 4.8$, $H_1: \mu < 4.8$;
   $t = -3.643 < -2.365$, or $p = 0.41\% < 2.5\%$;
   reject H_0 and accept that adjustment has reduced
   time.

3 $H_0: \mu = 5$, $H_1: \mu > 5$;
   $t = 2.414 > 1.711$, or $p = 1.19\% < 5\%$;
   reject H_0, glass is acceptable.

4 $H_0: \mu = 5.7$, $H_1: \mu < 5.7$;
   $t = -2.994 > -3.365$, or $p = 1.52\% > 1\%$;
   accept H_0, reorganisation has not cut delay.

5 $H_0: \mu = 14.2$, $H_1: \mu \neq 14.2$;
   $|t| = |1.410| < 2.262$, or $p = 19.2\% > 5\%$;
   accept H_0, level for students does not differ.

6 $\left| \dfrac{3.207 - \mu}{0.461/\sqrt{20}} \right| < 1.729$; $3.029 < \mu < 3.385$

Exercise 10C (page 109)

1 $H_0: \mu_1 = \mu_2$, $H_1: \mu_1 > \mu_2$;
   $t = 1.279 < 1.895$, or $p = 12.1\% > 5\%$;
   accept H_0, the belief is not suppported.

2 $H_0: \mu_D = 40$, $H_1: \mu_D > 40$;
   $t = 2.547 > 2.015$, or $p = 2.57\% < 5\%$;
   reject H_0 and accept that the difference is more
   than 40.

3 $H_0: \mu_D = 10$, $H_1: \mu_D > 10$;
   $t = 3.162 > 2.821$, or $p = 0.58\% < 1\%$;
   reject H_0 and accept that time goes up by more
   than 0.1 s.

4 $H_0: \mu_o = \mu_c$, $H_1: \mu_o \neq \mu_c$;
   $|t| = |-0.661| < 2.228$, or $p = 52.4\% > 5\%$;
   accept H_0, the mean yields are the same.

5 $H_0: \mu_D = 0$, $H_1: \mu_D > 0$;
   $t = 1.554$, or $p = 6.41\%$;
   accept H_0 at the 5% level, the pill makes no
   difference.

11 Confidence intervals

Exercise 11A (page 118)

1 $[496.5, 504.5]$, 190

2 (a) $[0.981, 1.028]$ (b) 0.0233 litres

3 (a) 5.155   (b) 8.48   (c) 10.10

4 $[169.4, 181.0]$; assumes a random sample;
   no, 178 is within the interval.

5 (a) $[5.013, 5.057]$
   (b) 5.00 cm is outside the interval; this indicates
       that the mean has increased.

6 (a) $[15.67, 16.17]$ (b) Six more

7 [65.1, 70.5]; this includes 70, so the test is
   satisfactory and can be used unchanged.

Exercise 11B (page 121)

1 (a) 1.796   (b) 2.262   (c) 2.492
   (d) 2.871

2 $[14.66, 15.20]$; assumes alcohol content has a normal distribution.

3 $[2725.8, 2967.4]$; 10% chance that interval will not contain population mean.

4 (a) $[3.65, 4.75]$; assumes a normal population and a random sample.
   (b) Class appears better than average, suggesting that they are not a random sample.

5 (a) 9.806   (b) $[9.756, 9.856]$
   (c) Interval is exact; neither the distribution nor parameters are approximated.

6 (a) $[18.3, 19.9]$
   (b) 15.9 is outside 98% interval. The swallow is most unlikely to be fully grown.

7 (a) 498.1 g, 4.839 g^2 (b) $[497.7, 498.5]$
   The confidence interval will not contain the mean 5% of the time.

8 (a) 2.43, 2.288   (b) $[2.18, 2.68]$

Exercise 11C (page 125)

1 $[28.5\%, 39.5\%]$

2 (a) $[0.144, 0.224]$ (b) Sample is random.
   (c) For example, all cars passing under the bridge over a specified period
   (d) 49

3 $[0.322, 0.424]$; $n = 971$

4 $[0.640, 0.860]$, $n = 180$

5 (a) Confidence interval for p is $[0.427, 0.560]$; classify as average.
   (b) 95% confidence interval $[0.413, 0.573]$; yes

12 A survey of probability distributions

Exercise 12 (page 134)

2 (a) 3, 2   (b) 0.4, 0.24
   (c) 4, 2.4   (d) 2.5, 3.75
   (e) 7.5, 11.25 (f) 1.2, 0.56
   (g) 2.4, 2.4

5 (a) 0.258   (b) 6.72   (c) 0.042   (d) 0.0280

6 (a) 0.127   (b) 0.323   (c) 0.0593   (d) 4
   (e) 0.0645   (f) 40, 3.65

7 (a) 0.234   (b) 4.8, 1.49

8 (a) $\frac{1001}{4845}, \frac{2184}{4845}, \frac{1365}{4845}, \frac{280}{4845}, \frac{15}{4845}$
   (b) 1.2, 0.707   (c) $\frac{6}{5}, \frac{336}{475}$

9 Means are both 6; variances are 4.2, 3.39.

10 (a) 0.287   (b) 0.123   (c) 0.265

11 100 s, 31.6 s

12 (a) 0.593   (b) 0.224

13 Chi-squared tests

In all these exercises, the answers are presented in the format: distribution under H_0; expected frequencies (after combination of classes if necessary); value of X^2; $P\left(\chi_v^2 \geq \text{value of } X^2\right)$ as a percentage; accept or reject H_0. Your estimated frequencies and values of χ^2 may differ from those given, depending on how much estimated parameters are rounded. This should not affect your conclusions.

Exercise 13A (page 149)

1 All $\frac{1}{6}$; all 10; 3.4; 63.9%; accept H_0.

2 $p_1 = \frac{9}{16}$, $p_2 = p_3 = \frac{3}{16}$, $p_4 = \frac{1}{16}$; 90, 30, 30, 10; 1.84; 60.6%; accept H_0.

3 (a) $B\left(4, \frac{1}{4}\right)$; 63.28, 84.37, 42.19, 10.16; 241.85; negligible; reject H_0. (3, 4 combined)
   (b) $B(4, 0.465)$; 16.38, 56.96, 74.27, 43.03, 9.35; 3.69; 29.7%; accept H_0.

4 $B\left(6, \frac{5}{18}\right)$; 8.51, 19.65, 18.89, 12.95; 2.34; 31.0%; accept H_0. (3, 4, 5, 6 combined)

5 $Geo\left(\frac{1}{2}\right)$; 25, 12.5, 6.25, 6.25; 2.24; 52.4%; accept H_0. (4, 5, 6, 7 or more combined)

6 All $\frac{1}{10}$; all 9; 16; 6.69%; reject H_0.

7 $Po\left(\frac{13}{15}\right)$; 37.83, 32.79, 14.21, 5.17; 4.91; 8.59%; accept H_0. (3, 4 or more combined)

8 All $\frac{1}{7}$; all 85.71; 3.10; 79.6%; accept H_0.

9 $p_1 = \frac{9}{49}$, remainder $\frac{10}{49}$; 110.2, remainder 122.45; 3.04; 55.1%; accept H_0.

10 $B(5, 0.424)$; 14.84, 17.18, 12.64, 5.34; 2.47; 29.1%; accept H_0. (0, 1 and 4, 5 combined)

11 (a) $Po(1)$; 30.90, 30.90, 15.45, 6.75; 26.84; 0.000 64%,; reject H_0. (3, 4, 5, 6, 7 or more combined)
   (b) $Po\left(\frac{67}{42}\right)$; 17.04, 27.18, 21.68, 11.53, 6.57; 1.81; 61.3%; accept H_0. (4, 5, 6, 7 or more combined)

12 (a) 1.3, 0.769 to 3 sig.fig.
   (b) $Geo(0.769)$; 76.92, 17.75, 5.33; 0.566; 45.2%; accept H_0. (3, 4, >4 combined)

13 $Po\left(\frac{45}{52}\right)$; 21.89, 18.94, $8.20 + 2.97 = 11.17$; 4.03; 4.47%; accept H_0. (2, 3, 4, 5 or more combined)

Exercise 13B (page 154)

1 $N(50, 10^2)$; $2.28 + 13.59 = 15.87$, 34.13, 34.13, $13.59 + 2.28 = 15.87$; 0.89; 82.8%; accept H_0.

2 (b) $N(100, 15^2)$; 6.83, 40.77, 102.40, 102.40, 40.77, 6.83; 17.61; 0.35%; reject H_0.
   (c) $N(96.6, 15^2)$; 11.43, 54.47, 110.99, 90.11, 33.00; 3.04; 38.5%; accept H_0.

3 (b) $N(698.3, 18.83^2)$; 7.95, 8.05, 10.26, 9.93, 7.29, 6.51; 3.36; 33.9%; accept H_0.

4 (c) 8.70, 24.99, 40.03, 26.27; 7.34; 6.2%; reject H_0.

5 $N(172.2, 7.31^2)$; 8.98, 11.42, 13.31, 9.89, 6.40; 0.17; 91.9%; accept H_0.

6 $N(2.915, 1.775^2)$; 14.03, 16.28, 21.60, 21.04, 15.04, 12.01; 18.60; 0.033%; reject H_0.

Exercise 13C (page 161)

1 9, 24, 27, 36, 96, 108, 30, 80, 90; 18.97; 0.08%; reject H_0.

2 32.5, 68.25, 29.25, 17.5, 36.75, 15.75; 2.44; 29.5%; accept H_0.

3 32.64, 20.40, 14.96, 15.36, 9.60, 7.04; 2.62; 27.0%; accept H_0.

4 71.5, 53.6, 69.9, 85.1, 63.8, 83.1, 48.8, 36.6, 47.7, 14.7, 11.0, 14.3; 29.0; 0.0061%; reject H_0.

5 101.31, 82.28, 123.41, 149.16, 121.14, 181.70, 79.53, 64.59, 96.88; 44.28; $5.6 \times 10^{-7}\%$; reject H_0.

6 (a) 14.79, 35.09, 17.54, 9.29, 4.47, 3.44, 1.38, 12.90, 30.60, 15.30, 8.10, 3.90, 3.00, 1.20, 15.31, 36.31, 18.16, 9.61, 4.63, 3.56, 1.42.
   (b) 9 of the expected frequencies are less than 5.
   (c) H_0: 14.79, 35.09, 17.54, 9.29, 9.29, 12.90, 30.60, 15.30, 8.10, 8.10, 15.31, 36.31, 18.16, 9.61, 9.61; 35.148; 0.0025%; reject H_0. (E, N and U combined).

7 (a) 16.15, 13.77, 4.08, 44.65, 38.07, 11.28, 34.20, 29.16, 8.64
   (b) One of the expected frequencies is less than 5.
   (c) H_0: no association; 60.80, 51.84, 15.36, 34.20, 29.16, 8.64; 5.79; 5.5%; accept H_0 (first two rows combined).

Review exercise

(page 164)

1 (a) 0.1853 (b) 0.1839

2 (a) $\frac{9}{7}$, $\frac{3}{49}$
   (b) 0.0289; distribution of T is very skewed so answer has considerable error.

3 (a) 0.0593 (b) 0.0023

4 (a) 2.7, $\dfrac{2.7}{n}$ (b) 0.0192

5 (a) H_0: $\mu = 2.855$, H_1: $\mu \neq 2.855$; $Z \leq -1.96$, $Z \geq 1.96$.
   (b) $z = -1.540$, so accept H_0: $\mu = 2.855$, the batch is from the specified population.

6 H_0: $p = 0.07$, H_1: $p > 0.07$; $X \sim B(125, 0.07)$; $P(X \geq 14) = 0.551 > 0.03$, accept H_0 and retain the batch.

7 (a) H_0: $p = 0.1$, H_1: $p > 0.1$,
   (b) $r > 4$; for $r = 4$ do not reject H_0.
   (c) 0.6296

8 (a) 2
   (b) $f(v) = \begin{cases} \dfrac{90}{v^2} & \text{for } 22.5 \leq v \leq 30, \\ 0 & \text{otherwise.} \end{cases}$
   (c) (i) $25\frac{5}{7}$ km per hour
        (ii) $90 \ln \frac{4}{3}$ km per hour

9 (a) 0.682 (b) 0.113 (c) 0.159

10 (a) $t = -2.515 \notin [-1.753, 1.753]$, or $P(|T| > 2.515) = 2.38\% < 10\%$; reject H_0 and accept that the mean is not 4 kg.
    (b) $\mu < 1.97$, $\mu > 3.83$

11 (a) Assumes students form a random sample and $T_1 - T_2$ has a normal distribution; H_0: $\mu_1 - \mu_2 = 0$, H_1: $\mu_1 - \mu_2 > 0$; $t = 2.504 > 1.833$, or $P(T > 2.504) = 1.68\% < 5\%$, so reject H_0 and accept that there is a reduction in the mean time.
    (b) $[0.66, 12.92]$, to 2 decimal places

12 $Po(2)$; 16.24, 32.48, 32.48, 21.65, 10.83, 6.32; $P(\chi_4^2 \geq 12.24) = 1.57\%$; reject H_0 at 5% significance level (5, 6, 7 combined).

13 H_0: age and sex are independent; 202.2, 260.7, 318.1, 184.8, 238.3, 290.9; $P(\chi_2^2 \geq 2.022) = 36.4\%$; accept H_0.

Examination questions

1 0.164

2 $[2.7030, 2.7070]$

3 $P(\chi_3^2 \geq 4.907) = 17.9\%$; accept that sons follow fathers.

4 (a) (i) $87.13 \ \text{km h}^{-1}$ (ii) $215.58 \left(\text{km h}^{-1}\right)^2$

(b) (i) $[86.22, 88.04]$ (ii) $[86.37, 87.89]$

(c) 95% probability requires a wider interval than 90%.

5 (a) (i) 1.98   (ii) 0.33

(b) $P\left(\chi_3^2 \geq 1.563\right) = 66.8\%$; a good fit.

6 (a) 0.0784, 0.216, 0.296, 0.28, 0.1296

(b) $P\left(\chi_3^2 \geq 4.825\right) = 18.5\%$; accept assumption.

7 (a) 10   (b) 12   (c) 7   (d) 35

8 $P(|Z| \geq 2.020) = 0.0434$; accept H_0, the mean length is 1.005 m.

Appendix

(page 169)

2.1 $1 + q + q^2 + q^3 + \ldots$. This is the infinite geometric series with sum $\dfrac{1}{1-q} = (1-q)^{-1}$, where $-1 < q < 1$.

4.1 $-x e^{-\frac{1}{2}x^2}$

4.2 $\left(\pm 1, \dfrac{1}{\sqrt{2\pi e}} \right)$

4.4 The standard deviation is represented by the distance from a point of inflexion to the y-axis.

5.3 $\mu = \displaystyle\sum_{x=0}^{n} x p_x$, which can also be written as

$\displaystyle\sum_{x=1}^{n} x p_x$.

6.1 $v e^{-mv} - \dfrac{1}{m} e^{-mv} + \dfrac{1}{m}$

Index

The page numbers refer to the first mention of each term, or the box if there is one.

acceptance region, 48
alternative hypothesis, 45

Bernoulli distribution (trial), 68, 128
binomial distribution, 128
    mean and variance, 68, 129
    normal approximation, 68

central limit theorem, 72
chi-squared (χ^2) -distribution, 139
    mean and variance, 139, 171
confidence interval
    for mean, 113, 120
    for proportion, 124
contingency table, 156
continuity correction
    for mean, 75
    for sum, 66
critical region (value), 48
cumulative distribution function, 1

degrees of freedom
    for χ^2 distribution, 139
    for contingency table, 158
    for t-distribution, 103
expectation
    of linear function, 27
    of product of random variables, 30
    of sum of random variables, 29
expected frequency, 137
    for contingency table, 157
exponential distribution, 19, 132
    and Poisson probability, 133
    in combination, 22
    mean and variance, 21, 172

geometric distribution, 12, 129
    mean and variance, 15, 170
goodness of fit, 138

hypergeometric distribution, 131
    mean and variance, 131, 172
hypothesis test, 46
    for a discrete variable, 79

matched pairs test, 108

negative binomial distribution, 129
    mean and variance, 130
normal probability, 134
    approximation to binomial, 68
    in combination, 36, 134
    standardised, 133
null hypothesis, 45

one-tail test, 46

point estimate, 111
Poisson probability, 132
    mean and variance, 170
population, 41
p-value, 55

rejection region, 48

sample, 41
sampling
    with replacement, 130
    without replacement, 131
sampling distribution of mean, 41, 72
significance level, 48
significance test, 46
'Student', 102

t-distribution, 103
test statistic, 48
two-tail test, 46
Type I,II error, 83

unbiased estimator, 96
uniform distribution
    continuous, 127
    discrete, 126

variance
    of linear function, 27
    of sum of random variables, 30

Topic 3
Sets, relations and groups

Hugh Neill and Douglas Quadling

Series Editor Hugh Neill

CAMBRIDGE
UNIVERSITY PRESS

Contents

Introduction   v

1   The language of sets   1

2   Equivalence relations   15

3   Functions   22

4   Binary operations and groups   38

5   Some examples of groups   52

6   Subgroups   63

7   Isomorphisms of groups   78

8   The algebra of sets   89

Review exercise   98

Answers   103

Index   111

Introduction

Sets, Relations and Groups has been written especially for the International Baccalaureate Further Mathematics SL examination. This section covers the syllabus for Topic 3.

Chapters 1 to 7 should be studied in sequence, but Chapter 8, on the algebra of sets, can be studied any time after working through Chapter 1. There is a small amount of material which extends a topic beyond the syllabus as printed, with the aim of enhancing students' appreciation of the subject. This is indicated by an asterisk (*) at the appropriate place in the text.

Occasionally within the text paragraphs appear in *this type style*. These paragraphs are usually outside the main stream of the mathematical argument, but may help to give insight, or suggest extra work or different approaches.

There are plenty of exercises throughout. At the end of the book there is a Review exercise which includes some questions from past International Baccalaureate examinations, but on a different syllabus. At the time of writing, there are few current versions of the Higher Level examinations, so there is no backlog of examination questions on the newer parts of the syllabus.

The author thanks the International Baccalaureate Organization (IBO) and Oxford, Cambridge and RSA Examinations (OCR) for permission to reproduce IBO and OCR intellectual property and Cambridge University Press for their help in producing this book. Particular thanks are due to Sharon Dunkley, for her help and advice. However, the responsibility for the text, and for any errors, remains with the author.

1 The language of sets

This chapter is really a reminder about sets. You probably know most of this material already, and you may wish to use the chapter for reference rather than work through it systematically. When you have completed it, you should

- know that a set needs to be defined so that you can tell clearly whether or not a given element belongs to the set
- be able to list the elements of a finite set
- know the meanings of the symbols $\in$, $\notin$, and the bracket notation for sets
- know the meaning of and notation for the empty set
- know the meaning of and notation for intersection, union, set difference and Cartesian product of two sets
- be able to prove that two sets are equal.

1.1 What is a set?

A **set** is a collection of things; the things are called **elements** or **members** of the set. Sets will be denoted by capital letters such as A, B and S.

A set is determined by its elements. To define a set you can either list its elements or you can describe the elements in words, provided you do so unambiguously. When you define a set, there must never be any uncertainty about what its elements are. If there is no uncertainty, the set is said to be **well-defined**.

If you say for example that the set A consists precisely of the numbers 1, 2 and 3 or alternatively, that 1, 2 and 3 are the elements of A, then it is clear that 4 is not an element of A.

The symbol $\in$ is used to designate 'is an element of' or 'belongs to'; the symbol $\notin$ means 'is not an element of' or 'does not belong to'. So $1 \in A$ means that 1 is an element of A, and $4 \notin A$ means that 4 is not a element of A.

There are some sets, in particular sets of numbers, which will be used so frequently that it is helpful to have some special names for them.

Set of numbers	Symbol	Positive only
Integers	$\mathbb{Z}$	$\mathbb{Z}^+$
Natural numbers, including 0	$\mathbb{N}$	
Rational numbers	$\mathbb{Q}$	$\mathbb{Q}^+$
Real numbers	$\mathbb{R}$	$\mathbb{R}^+$
Complex numbers	$\mathbb{C}$	Not applicable

1.2 Describing sets

When you list the elements of a set, it is usual to put them into curly brackets $\{\ \}$, sometimes called **braces**. For example, the set A consisting of the elements 2, 3 and 4 can be written $A = \{2,3,4\}$. The order in which the elements are written doesn't matter. The set $\{2,4,3\}$ is identical to the set $\{2,3,4\}$, and $A = \{2,3,4\} = \{2,4,3\}$.

If you wrote $A = \{2,2,3,4\}$, it would be the same as saying that $A = \{2,3,4\}$. A set is determined by its *distinct* elements, and any repetition in the list of elements should be avoided.

Two sets A and B are called **equal** if and only if they have the same elements.

Using the brace notation, you can write $\mathbb{Z} = \{\ldots,-2,-1,0,1,2,\ldots\}$.

Another way to describe a set involves specifying properties of its elements. For example,

$$A = \{n \mid n \in \mathbb{Z}, 2 \le n \le 4\}$$

means that A is the set of all elements n such that n is an integer and $2 \le n \le 4$. The symbol | means 'such that'. To the left of the symbol | you are told what a typical element is, while to the right you are given a rule or rules which the typical element must satisfy.

So in A, the elements are the integers which lie between 2 and 4 inclusive. Therefore $A = \{2,3,4\}$.

Sometimes, if there is no room for misunderstanding, you might see in other books the set A of the preceding paragraph defined as

$$A = \{n \in \mathbb{Z}, 2 \le n \le 4\}$$

but that won't be done in this book.

As another example of this notation, the set of rational numbers, $\mathbb{Q}$ (for quotients), can be described as

$$\mathbb{Q} = \left\{ \frac{m}{n} \mid m,n \in \mathbb{Z}, n \ne 0 \right\}.$$

Thus a typical element has the form $\dfrac{m}{n}$, where m and n are integers, and $n \ne 0$.

One more set involving integers will be useful: $\mathbb{Z}_n = \{0,1,2,\ldots,n-1\}$. It may look odd that this set does not contain n, but it does have n members.

Example 1.2.1
List, where possible, the members of each of the following sets.
(a) $A = \{\text{letters in the word 'sets'}\}$
(b) $B = \{x \mid x \in \mathbb{Q}, x^2 = 4\}$
(c) $C = \{n \mid n \in \mathbb{Z}, n = 4m \text{ where } m \in \mathbb{Z}\}$
(d) $D = \{x \mid x \in \mathbb{R}, x > 1\}$
(e) $E = \{\text{molecules} \mid \text{they were part of the dying breath of Julius Caesar}\}$

   (a)   The letters of the word 'sets' are s, e, t and s. But to say that $A = \{\text{s, e, t, s}\}$ would be incorrect, because the letter s is repeated.

   Putting the letters in the set into alphabetical order gives $A = \{\text{e, s, t}\}$.

(b)   If $x^2 = 4$ then $x = 2$ or $x = -2$. Both 2 and -2 are rational ($2 = \dfrac{2}{1}$ and $-2 = \dfrac{-2}{1}$), so

$B = \{-2, 2\}$.

(c) C is a set of integers each of which is $4 \times$ (another integer m).

So $C = \{0, \pm 4, \pm 8, \pm 12, \ldots\}$.

(d)   This is a well-defined set – you know whether or not a given object is an element of the set – but it is not possible to list it because there is no smallest number in the set.

(e)   This is not a well-defined set. There is no method of deciding whether a given molecule was, or was not, part of Julius Caesar's dying breath.

In Example 1.2.1, the numbers of elements in A and B are 3 and 2 respectively. A and B are examples of finite sets, whereas C and D have an infinite number of elements and are examples of infinite sets. The number of elements in a set S is denoted by $n(S)$, so for the sets of Example 1.2.1, $n(A) = 3$, $n(B) = 2$ and $n(\mathbb{Z}_n) = n$; however, in the last case the different use of 'n' is unfortunate, and it will be avoided.

A set with a finite number of elements is called **finite**; sets which are not finite are called **infinite**.

A set with no elements is said to be **empty**. It is usually denoted by $\varnothing$, but it can also be written using the braces notation as $\{\ \}$.

The set which contains all the elements under discussion is called the **universal set** and denoted by U. Every other set will be a subset of U.

Often it is obvious what the universal set is. If you are working with real numbers or complex numbers it is likely to be $\mathbb{R}$ or $\mathbb{C}$ respectively. But if it is not obvious, you will be told the universal set explicitly.

Exercise 1A

1   List the elements of the following sets, stating whether the sets are finite or infinite.

(a) A is the set of positive factors of 32.

(b) B is the set of outcomes when an ordinary dice is thrown.

(c) $C = \left\{x \mid x \in \mathbb{N}, x^2 = 2\right\}$

(d) $D = \left\{x \mid x \in \mathbb{R}^+, x^2 = 2\right\}$

(e) $E = \left\{x \mid x \in \mathbb{R}, x^2 = 2\right\}$

(f) $F = \left\{n \mid n \in \mathbb{Z}, n = 4p + 5q \text{ for some } p, q \in \mathbb{Z}\right\}$

(g) $G = \left\{n \mid n \in \mathbb{Z}, n = 4p + 6q \text{ for some } p, q \in \mathbb{Z}\right\}$

(h) $H = \left\{r \mid r \in \mathbb{Z}_8, r \geq 4\right\}$

2 Some of the following sets are not defined properly in the sense that it is not clear whether a given element belongs to the set or not. Identify these sets.

(a) The set of prime numbers.

(b) People in the world whose birthday is on 1 April.

(c) $A = \{x \mid x \in \mathbb{Z}, x$ is the digit in the 1000th place in the decimal expansion of $\pi\}$

3 The notation $2\mathbb{Z}$ is used to mean the set $\{2n \mid n \in \mathbb{Z}\}$. List the set $2\mathbb{Z}$. List also the members of $\mathbb{Z}$ which are not members of $2\mathbb{Z}$.

1.3 Subsets

In Question 2(a) of Exercise 1A, all the elements in the set of prime numbers $\{2, 3, 5, 7, ...\}$ are also members of $\mathbb{N}$. When this happens, the set $\{2, 3, 5, 7, ...\}$ is called a subset of $\mathbb{N}$. More generally, if all the elements of a set A are also elements of another set B, then A is called a **subset** of B. In this case you write $A \subseteq B$.

You can see from the definition of subset that $A \subseteq A$ for every set A.

Notice that the notation $A \subseteq B$ suggests the notation for inequalities, $a \le b$. This analogy is intentional and helpful. However, you mustn't take the analogy too far: for any two real numbers you have either $a \le b$ or $b \le a$, but the same is not true for sets. For example, for the sets $A = \{1\}$ and $B = \{2\}$ neither $A \subseteq B$ nor $B \subseteq A$ is true.

The notation $A \subset B$ is taken to mean that A is a **proper subset** of B, that is $A \subseteq B$ and $A \ne B$. Thus while A is a subset of A, it is not a proper subset of A. A set is not a proper subset of itself.

Summing up:

> Let A and B be sets. Then
>
> - if $x \in A \ \Rightarrow \ x \in B$, then $A \subseteq B$
>
> - if $x \in A \ \Rightarrow \ x \in B$ and $A \ne B$, then $A \subset B$.
>
> In the first case, A is a **subset** of B.
>
> In the second case, A is a **proper subset** of B.

Example 1.3.1
$U = \{$letters of the alphabet$\}$, $A = \{x \in U \mid x$ is a letter of the word 'table'$\}$,
$B = \{x \in U \mid x$ is a letter of the word 'bleat'$\}$, $C = \{x \in B \mid x$ is a letter of the word 'Beatle'$\}$ and
$D = \{x \in U \mid x$ is a letter of the word 'beetle'$\}$.

Which of the sets, U, A, B, C and D are
(a) equal to each other,   (b) subsets of each other,   (c) proper subsets of each other?

Listing the sets gives $A = \{a,b,e,l,t\}$, $B = \{a,b,e,l,t\}$, $C = \{a,b,e,l,t\}$ and $D = \{b,e,l,t\}$. You can then answer the questions by examining these sets.

(a) $A = B = C$.

(b) $U \subseteq U$, $A \subseteq U$, $B \subseteq U$, $C \subseteq U$, $D \subseteq U$, $A \subseteq A$, $B \subseteq A$, $C \subseteq A$, $D \subseteq A$, $A \subseteq B$, $B \subseteq B$, $C \subseteq B$, $D \subseteq B$, $A \subseteq C$, $B \subseteq C$, $C \subseteq C$, $D \subseteq C$ and $D \subseteq D$.

(c) $A \subset U$, $B \subset U$, $C \subset U$, $D \subset U$, $D \subset A$, $D \subset B$ and $D \subset C$.

1.4   Venn diagrams

Fig. 1.1 and Fig. 1.2 show ways of illustrating sets. They are called **Venn diagrams** after the Englishman John Venn (1834–1923).

The set A is drawn as a circle (or an oval), and x, which is an element of A, is drawn as a point inside A. The outside rectangle indicates the universal set. Fig. 1.1 represents $x \in A$.

In Fig. 1.2, every point inside A is also inside B; this represents the statement that A is a subset of B, or $A \subset B$.

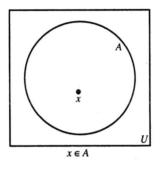

$x \in A$

Fig. 1.1

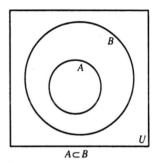

$A \subset B$

Fig. 1.2

These diagrams can be helpful for understanding, seeing and suggesting relationships, but be warned; they can also sometimes be misleading. For example, in Fig. 1.2, the question of whether or not $A = B$ is left open. The fact that in the diagram there are points outside A and inside B does not mean that there are necessarily elements in B which are not in A. Take care when using Venn diagrams!

1.5   Operations on sets: complementation, intersection, union and set difference

In Exercise 1A Question 3 you were asked to list the members of the set $\mathbb{Z}$ which are not members of $2\mathbb{Z}$. As $\mathbb{Z} = \{0, \pm 1, \pm 2, ...\}$ and $2\mathbb{Z} = \{0, \pm 2, \pm 4, ...\}$ the required set was $\{\pm 1, \pm 3, \pm 5, ...\}$. But so far, there is no name for it.

Let A be a set. Then the set of elements in the universal set U which are not in A is called the **complement** of A and denoted by A', pronounced 'A prime, or A dash'.

In Fig. 1.3 the shaded region outside A but within the universal set U illustrates A'.

Formally this is written as:

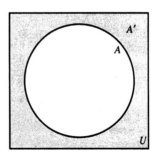

Fig. 1.3

Let A be a set, and let U be the universal set.

Then $A' = \{x \in U \mid x \notin A\}$ is called the **complement** of A.

Example 1.5.1

List the members of A' in the following cases.

(a) $U = \{\text{letters of the alphabet}\}$, $A = \{\text{consonants}\}$

(b) $A = \{n \mid n \in \mathbb{N}, n = 2m + 1 \text{ where } m \in \mathbb{N}\}$

    (a)   Assuming that y is a consonant, $A' = \{a, e, i, o, u\}$.

    (b)   The elements of A are those which are of the form $2m + 1$ where $m \in \mathbb{N}$. So $A = \{1, 3, 5, \ldots\}$. In this case, the universal set is not given explicitly, but you should assume that it is $\mathbb{N}$, as that is the set used in the definition of A.

        So $A' = \{0, 2, 4, \ldots\}$.

Now consider $A = \{x \mid x \in \mathbb{N}, x \text{ is a factor of } 12\}$ and $B = \{x \mid x \in \mathbb{N}, x \text{ is a factor of } 15\}$.

Thus $A = \{1, 2, 3, 4, 6, 12\}$ and $B = \{1, 3, 5, 15\}$.

As you can see, there are elements, 1 and 3, which are members of both sets. These elements, 1 and 3, themselves form a set, called the **intersection** of A and B.

Let A and B be sets.

Then the set $\{x \mid x \in A \text{ and } x \in B\}$ is called the **intersection** of A and B and denoted by $A \cap B$.

It is clear from the definition that $A \cap B = B \cap A$.

$A \cap B$ *is pronounced 'A intersection B'.*

Going back to $A = \{1, 2, 3, 4, 6, 12\}$ and $B = \{1, 3, 5, 15\}$, you can also construct a new set of elements which are in either A or B (or both).

This would be the set $\{1, 2, 3, 4, 5, 6, 12, 15\}$, which is called the **union** of the sets A and B.

Let A and B be sets.

Then the set $\{x \mid x \in A \text{ or } x \in B\}$ is called the **union** of A and B and denoted by $A \cup B$.

It is clear from the definition that $A \cup B = B \cup A$.

Note that in the expression $x \in A$ or $x \in B$, the word 'or' is inclusive, and that $x \in A$ or $x \in B$ means $x \in A$ or $x \in B$ or both.

Figs. 1.4 and 1.5 are Venn diagrams which illustrate the intersection and union of the sets A and B.

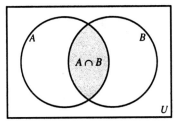

The shaded region is $A \cap B$.

Fig. 1.4

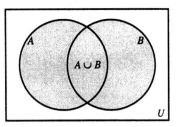

The shaded region is $A \cup B$.

Fig. 1.5

Fig. 1.6 shows a Venn diagram for illustrating three sets. However, don't even think of drawing a Venn diagram for four sets or more as the picture gets much too cluttered.

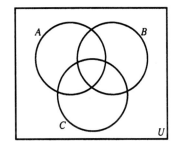

Fig. 1.6

Example 1.5.2

Draw Venn diagrams to illustrate the sets $A \cup B'$, $A' \cap B$ and $A' \cap B \cap C$.

The solutions are shown in Figs. 1.7, 1.8 and 1.9.

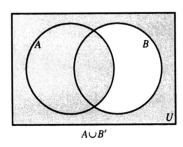

$A \cup B'$

Fig. 1.7

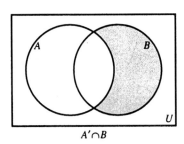

$A' \cap B$

Fig. 1.8

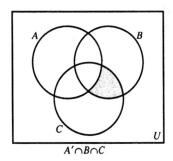

$A' \cap B \cap C$

Fig. 1.9

Example 1.5.3

Let $A = \{2, 3, 4\}$, $B = \{4, 5, 6\}$ and $C = \{6, 7, 8\}$. List the sets $A \cap B$, $A \cup C$ and $A \cap C$.

$A \cap B$ consists of the elements which are in both A and B, so $A \cap B = \{4\}$.

$A \cup C$ consists of the elements in either A or C, so $A \cup C = \{2, 3, 4, 6, 7, 8\}$.

$A \cap C = \{ \ \} = \varnothing$.

In the third case, when there are no elements common to both of the sets, the sets are said to be **disjoint**.

> Let A and B be sets.
>
> Then if $A \cap B = \varnothing$, the sets A and B are said to be **disjoint**.

The question of whether $\varnothing$ is a subset of A or B is somewhat tricky. If you try to use the definition, you have to decide whether 'if $x \in \varnothing$ then $x \in A$' is true. As there is no element x which belongs to $\varnothing$ it is certainly not possible to find an x to show that the statement 'if $x \in \varnothing$ then $x \in A$' is false. So, conventionally, $\varnothing$ is defined to be a subset of every set A.

> Let A be a set. Then $\varnothing \subseteq A$. If $A \neq \varnothing$, then $\varnothing \subset A$.

Example 1.5.4
(a) Let D be the set of plane rhombuses, and R be the set of plane rectangles. Identify $D \cap R$ and $D \cap R'$.
(b) Let Q be the set of plane quadrilaterals and T be the set of triangles. Identify $Q \cap T$.

    (a) $D \cap R$ is the set of those rhombuses which are also rectangles. So $D \cap R$ is the set of squares. $D \cap R'$ are the non-rectangular rhombuses, that is, the rhombuses which are not squares.

Note that if you had been asked to describe $D' \cap R'$ it would have been impossible without knowing the universal set.

    (b)   There are no quadrilaterals which are also triangles, so Q and T are disjoint and $Q \cap T = \varnothing$.

Sometimes you need to be able to consider a set without certain members. For example $\mathbb{N} = \{0, 1, 2, 3, \ldots\}$, but if you want to consider the set $\{1, 2, 3, \ldots\}$, that is $\mathbb{N}$, without the element 0, then $\{1, 2, 3, \ldots\}$ is called the **set difference** of $\mathbb{N}$ and $\{0\}$.

> Let A and B be sets.
>
> Then the set $\{x \mid x \in A \text{ and } x \notin B\}$ is called the **set difference** of A and B and denoted by $A \setminus B$.

It is clear from the definition that $A \setminus B = A \cap B'$.

Example 1.5.5
Let $A = \{1, 2, 3, 4, 6, 12\}$ and $B = \{1, 3, 5, 15\}$. List the sets $A \setminus B$ and $B \setminus A$.

    $A \setminus B = \{2, 4, 6, 12\}$ and $B \setminus A = \{5, 15\}$.

Exercise 1B

1   Let $A = \{2, 4, 6, 8\}$, $B = \{1, 2, 4, 8\}$, $C = \{1, 2, 5\}$ and let the universal set be $\mathbb{Z}_9$. List the members of the following sets.

    (a) $A \cup B$ (b) $A \cap C$ (c) C' (d) $B \setminus C$

    (e) $A \cap C'$ (f) $A' \cup C'$ (g) $B' \cap C'$ (h) $(A \cup B) \setminus C$

2   Let the universal set be the set of triangles, and define the following subsets:
    $S = \{\text{scalene triangles}\}$, $I = \{\text{isosceles triangles}\}$, $E = \{\text{equilateral triangles}\}$ and
    $R = \{\text{right-angled triangles}\}$. Describe in words or symbols each of the following sets.

    (a) $I \cap E$ (b) S' (c) $E \cap R$ (d) $I \setminus E$

    (e) $S' \cap E$ (f) $E' \cap R$ (g) $S \cup I$ (h) $R \setminus I$

3   Let the universal set be the set of plane quadrilaterals, and define the subsets $P = \{\text{parallelograms}\}$,
    $R = \{\text{rectangles}\}$, $D = \{\text{rhombuses}\}$, $S = \{\text{squares}\}$, $K = \{\text{kites}\}$ and $T = \{\text{trapezia}\}$. Describe in
    words or symbols each of the following sets.

    (a) $K \cap D$ (b) $D \cap R$ (c) $K \cap T$ (d) $R \cap P$

1.6 Proving that two sets are equal

To prove that two sets A and B are equal, you have, at this stage, to prove separately that $A \subseteq B$ and
that $B \subseteq A$, that is, that every element of A is also an element of B, and vice versa.

Here are some examples of proofs of this type.

Example 1.6.1
Prove that if A and B are sets, then $A \cap B = B \cap A$.

Proof
The proof that $A \cap B = B \cap A$ has two parts: first, to prove that $A \cap B \subseteq B \cap A$; and secondly, to
prove that $B \cap A \subseteq A \cap B$.

Proof of $A \cap B \subseteq B \cap A$
Suppose that $x \in A \cap B$. Then

$$\begin{aligned} x \in A \cap B \quad &\Rightarrow \quad x \in A \text{ and } x \in B \\ &\Rightarrow \quad x \in B \text{ and } x \in A \\ &\Rightarrow \quad x \in B \cap A. \end{aligned}$$

Thus $A \cap B \subseteq B \cap A$.

Proof of $B \cap A \subseteq A \cap B$
Suppose that $x \in B \cap A$. Then

$$\begin{aligned} x \in B \cap A \quad &\Rightarrow \quad x \in B \text{ and } x \in A \\ &\Rightarrow \quad x \in A \text{ and } x \in B \\ &\Rightarrow \quad x \in A \cap B. \end{aligned}$$

Thus $B \cap A \subseteq A \cap B$.

As $A \cap B \subseteq B \cap A$ and $B \cap A \subseteq A \cap B$, it follows that $A \cap B = B \cap A$.

$A \cap B = B \cap A$ is called the **commutative** rule for intersection of sets. There is a similar commutative
rule for union of sets which you are asked to prove as Question 5 of Exercise 1C.

Example 1.6.2

Prove that if A, B and C are sets, then $(A \cup B) \cup C = A \cup (B \cup C)$.

Proof

The first part is to prove that $(A \cup B) \cup C \subseteq A \cup (B \cup C)$.

Proof of $(A \cup B) \cup C \subseteq A \cup (B \cup C)$

Suppose that $x \in (A \cup B) \cup C$. Then

$$
\begin{aligned}
x \in (A \cup B) \cup C \;\Rightarrow\;& x \in A \cup B \text{ or } x \in C \\
\Rightarrow\;& (x \in A \text{ or } x \in B) \text{ or } x \in C \\
\Rightarrow\;& x \in A \text{ or } x \in B \text{ or } x \in C \\
\Rightarrow\;& x \in A \text{ or } (x \in B \text{ or } x \in C) \\
\Rightarrow\;& x \in A \text{ or } x \in B \cup C \\
\Rightarrow\;& x \in A \cup (B \cup C).
\end{aligned}
$$

Thus $(A \cup B) \cup C \subseteq A \cup (B \cup C)$.

The proof of the second part is similar; it is left for you to prove that

$$A \cup (B \cup C) \subseteq (A \cup B) \cup C.$$

As $(A \cup B) \cup C \subseteq A \cup (B \cup C)$ and $A \cup (B \cup C) \subseteq (A \cup B) \cup C$, it follows that

$$(A \cup B) \cup C = A \cup (B \cup C).$$

This is called the **associative** rule for union of sets. There is a similar associative rule for intersection of sets which you are asked to prove as Question 6 of Exercise 1C.

Example 1.6.3

Prove that, for any sets A and B,
(a) $A \cap A = A$,   (b) $A \cup (A \cap B) = A$.

   (a) **Proof of $A \cap A \subseteq A$**

Suppose that $x \in A \cap A$. Then

$$
\begin{aligned}
x \in A \cap A \;\Rightarrow\;& x \in A \text{ and } x \in A \\
\Rightarrow\;& x \in A.
\end{aligned}
$$

Proof of $A \subseteq A \cap A$

Suppose that $x \in A$.

$$
\begin{aligned}
x \in A \;\Rightarrow\;& x \in A \text{ and } x \in A \\
\Rightarrow\;& x \in A \cap A.
\end{aligned}
$$

As $A \cap A \subseteq A$ and $A \subseteq A \cap A$, it follows that $A \cap A = A$.

(b) **Proof of** $A \cup (A \cap B) \subseteq A$
Suppose that $x \in A \cup (A \cap B)$. Then

$$x \in A \cup (A \cap B) \;\Rightarrow\; x \in A \text{ or } x \in (A \cap B)$$
$$\Rightarrow\; x \in A \text{ or } (x \in A \text{ and } x \in B).$$

Either way, $x \in A$, so $A \cup (A \cap B) \subseteq A$.

Proof of $A \subseteq A \cup (A \cap B)$
Suppose that $x \in A$. Then

$$x \in A \;\Rightarrow\; x \in A \text{ or } (x \in A \text{ and } x \in B)$$
$$\Rightarrow\; x \in A \text{ or } x \in (A \cap B)$$
$$\Rightarrow\; x \in A \cup (A \cap B).$$

Therefore $A \subseteq A \cup (A \cap B)$.

As $A \cup (A \cap B) \subseteq A$ and $A \subseteq A \cup (A \cap B)$, it follows that $A \cup (A \cap B) = A$.

Example 1.6.3(a) shows that $A \cap A = A$, an example of one of the **tautology** rules.

There is another **tautology** rule in Exercise 1C Question 7.

Example 1.6.3(b) shows that $A \cup (A \cap B) = A$, an example of one of the **absorption** rules.

There is another **absorption** rule in Exercise 1C Question 8.

The tautology and absorption rules will be followed up in Section 8.4.

Here is an example suggested by the Venn diagram in Fig. 1.10.

Example 1.6.4
Prove that, for any sets A and B, if $A \subseteq B$ then $A \cap B = A$.

Proof
In this case the hypothesis that $A \subseteq B$ tells you that if $x \in A$ then $x \in B$. This will be used in appropriate places in the proof that $A \cap B = A$.

Proof of $A \cap B \subseteq A$
Suppose that $x \in A \cap B$. Then

$$x \in A \cap B \;\Rightarrow\; x \in A \text{ and } x \in B$$
$$\Rightarrow\; x \in A.$$

Therefore $A \cap B \subseteq A$.

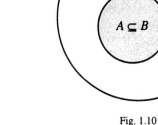

Fig. 1.10

Proof of $A \subseteq A \cap B$

Suppose that $x \in A$. Then

$$x \in A \implies x \in A \text{ and } x \in B \qquad \text{(since } A \subseteq B \text{ is given)}$$
$$\implies x \in A \cap B.$$

Hence $A \subseteq A \cap B$.

As $A \cap B \subseteq A$ and $A \subseteq A \cap B$, it follows that $A \cap B = A$.

It is also true that if $A \cap B = A$, then $A \subseteq B$. This is proved as Example 1.6.5.

Example 1.6.5

Prove that if $A \cap B = A$, then $A \subseteq B$.

Proof

Suppose that $x \in A$. Then

$$x \in A \implies x \in A \text{ and } x \in B \qquad \text{(as } A = A \cap B \text{ is given)}$$
$$\implies x \in B.$$

Thus $A \subseteq B$.

Notice that Examples 1.6.4 and 1.6.5 together show that the two statements $A \subseteq B$ and $A \cap B = A$ are equivalent because each can be deduced from the other.

It follows that

$$A \subseteq B \iff A \cap B = A.$$

Exercise 1C

1   Draw Venn diagrams to illustrate sets P, Q and $P \cap Q'$. What can you say about P, Q if you know that $P \cap Q' = \varnothing$?

2   Draw Venn diagrams to illustrate sets P, Q and $P \cup Q'$. What can you say about P, Q if you know that $P \cup Q' = Q'$?

3   Write down simpler expressions for each of the following.

   (a) $A \cap \varnothing$ 　　　　　(b) $A \cup \varnothing$ 　　　　　(c) $A \cap U$

   (d) $A \cup U$ 　　　　　(e) $\varnothing'$ 　　　　　(f) U'

4   Use a Venn diagram to simplify $A \cap (A \cup B')$.

5   Prove algebraically that $A \cup B = B \cup A$.

6   Prove algebraically that $(A \cap B) \cap C = A \cap (B \cap C)$.

7   Prove that for any set A, $A \cup A = A$. This is the other **tautology** rule.

8   Prove that, for any sets A and B, $A \cap (A \cup B) = A$. This is the other **absorption** rule.

9   Prove that if $A \cup B = A$ then $A \cap B' = \varnothing$, and if $A \cap B' = \varnothing$ then $A \cup B = A$.

10   Use a Venn diagram to simplify $(A \cap B \cap C) \cup A' \cup B' \cup C'$.

1.7 The Cartesian product

You are familiar with the idea of coordinates in the plane consisting of ordered pairs of numbers. You are used to plotting points such as $(3,2)$ and $(\sqrt{2}, -\sqrt{2})$ on coordinate axes on graph paper. Each of the numbers in such a coordinate pair comes from a set: when you plot graphs this set is usually the real numbers $\mathbb{R}$. The set of all pairs of coordinates such as $(3,2)$ and $(\sqrt{2}, -\sqrt{2})$ is called $\mathbb{R} \times \mathbb{R}$, meaning that the first number comes from the set $\mathbb{R}$, as does the second number. The notation $\mathbb{R}^2$ is often used for $\mathbb{R} \times \mathbb{R}$, especially in the context of vectors. The Cartesian product generalises this idea.

> Let A and B be sets.
>
> Then the set $\{(a,b) \mid a \in A, b \in B\}$ is called the **Cartesian product** of A and B and denoted by $A \times B$.

The Cartesian product is named after the Frenchman René Descartes (1596–1650).

Example 1.7.1
Suppose that $A = \{2,3,4\}$ and $B = \{x,y\}$. List the elements of $A \times B$.

$$A \times B = \{(2,x),(2,y),(3,x),(3,y),(4,x),(4,y)\}.$$

Notice that the set $B \times A$ is not the same as $A \times B$, because

$$B \times A = \{(x,2),(y,2),(x,3),(y,3),(x,4),(y,4)\},$$

so the order of the sets in a Cartesian product matters.

Notice also that neither A nor B is a subset of $A \times B$. The set $A \times B$ consists of pairs: the elements of A and B are not pairs, so do not belong to $A \times B$.

If you roll an ordinary fair dice, then the set D of possible outcomes can be written as a set

$$D = \{1,2,3,4,5,6\}.$$

If you roll a pair of dice, and you can distinguish between the dice, then the outcomes can be written as the Cartesian product $D \times D$, with 36 elements, where

$$D \times D = \{(1,1),(1,2),\ldots,(1,6),(2,1),\ldots,(6,5),(6,6)\}.$$

This idea is commonly used in statistics, where the set $D \times D$ is called a sample space.

Example 1.7.2

Suppose that A has m elements and B has n elements. How many elements does $A \times B$ have?

Let $A = \{a_1, a_2, a_3, \dots, a_m\}$ and $B = \{b_1, b_2, b_3, \dots, b_n\}$.

Then the elements of $A \times B$ are

$$\begin{cases} (a_1, b_1) & (a_1, b_2) & \dots & (a_1, b_n) \\ (a_2, b_1) & (a_2, b_2) & \dots & (a_2, b_n) \\ \\ (a_m, b_1) & (a_m, b_2) & \dots & (a_m, b_n) \end{cases}.$$

When you count the elements, you see that there are mn of them.

You can also extend the definition of the Cartesian product in an obvious way to produce a Cartesian product of more than two sets.

Exercise 1D

1 Let C be the set of outcomes when a coin is tossed, and let D be the outcomes when a dice is rolled.

(a) List $C \times D$.   (b) List $D \times C$.

2 Mark each of the following statements about the sets A and B true or false.

(a) The set $A \times B$ always has a finite number of elements.

(b) You cannot form the direct product $A \times B$ if just one of A and B is infinite.

3 Write a definition for the set $A \times B \times C$. If $\mathbb{Z}_2 = \{0, 1\}$, use your definition to write out the elements of $\mathbb{Z}_2 \times \mathbb{Z}_2 \times \mathbb{Z}_2$.

4 Prove that $\mathbb{Z} \times \mathbb{Z} \subseteq \mathbb{Q} \times \mathbb{Q}$.

5 You can interpret the set $\mathbb{R} \times \mathbb{R}$ as all the points on an infinite sheet of paper. How would you interpret $\mathbb{Z} \times \mathbb{Z}$?

2 Equivalence relations

This chapter introduces the idea of a relation between members of a set. When you have completed it, you should

- know and be able to use the definition of an equivalence relation on a set
- know the meaning of 'reflexive', 'symmetric' and 'transitive' in the context of relations
- know the definition of a partition
- know that an equivalence relation on a set partitions the set into equivalence classes and be able to identify them.

2.1 Relations

This section just consists of an example followed by a short exercise to set the scene for later in the chapter. Keep the results for reference.

Example 2.1.1
On paper draw axes from 1 to 6 in each direction, as in Fig. 2.1. The axes are labelled a and b.

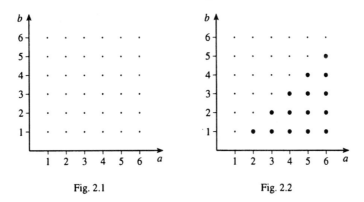

Fig. 2.1   Fig. 2.2

This is the set $D \times D$, where $D = \{1,2,3,4,5,6\}$. (Think of D as standing for dice.)

Take a point (a,b) in $D \times D$. If $a > b$, then a and b will be said to be 'related', and written aRb. In Fig. 2.2, each point (a,b) which has $a > b$ is marked with a blob. Thus the points aRb in $D \times D$ are marked.

What are the values of a which are related to each b? That is, for $b = 1$, what is the set $\{a \mid a \in D, aR1\}$? Call this set $\overline{1}$.

> Then $\overline{1}$ is the set of values of a in Fig. 2.2 with a blob to the right of 1 on the b-axis. There are five of them, so $\overline{1} = \{2,3,4,5,6\}$.

> $\overline{2}$ is the set of values of a with a blob to the right of 2. There are four such values, so $\overline{2} = \{3,4,5,6\}$.

> Similarly, $\overline{3} = \{4,5,6\}$, $\overline{4} = \{5,6\}$, $\overline{5} = \{6\}$, $\overline{6} = \{\ \}$.

Exercise 2A

1   Make a copy of $D \times D$, and repeat Example 2.1.1, including finding $\overline{1}, \overline{2}, \dots, \overline{6}$ when

(a) aRb stands for $a + b$ is an even number,

(b) aRb stands for $2a - b$ is divisible by 3,

(c) aRb stands for $a - b$ is divisible by 3,

(d) aRb stands for ab leaves a remainder of 1 when divided by 7.

2.2   Looking at results

Example 2.1.1 and the four parts of Exercise 2A Question 1 have very different patterns of blobs and lists of sets from one another. In particular in part (a) when $a + b$ is an even number and in part (c) when $a - b$ is divisible by 3 you get symmetrical patterns of blobs in $D \times D$.. You also get symmetrical patterns in parts (b) and (d) but with an important difference: in these cases at least one member of $D \times D$ is not related to itself.

The lists $\overline{1}, \overline{2}, \dots, \overline{6}$ are also very different. In part (a) $\overline{1} = \overline{3} = \overline{5} = \{1,3,5\}$ and $\overline{2} = \overline{4} = \overline{6} = \{2,4,6\}$, and in part (c), $\overline{1} = \overline{4} = \{1,4\}$, $\overline{2} = \overline{5} = \{2,5\}$ and $\overline{3} = \overline{6} = \{3,6\}$. This separation into distinct subsets occurs also in part (b), with the important difference that $1 \notin \overline{1}$, $2 \notin \overline{2}$, $4 \notin \overline{4}$ and $5 \notin \overline{5}$. Similarly, in part (d), $2 \notin \overline{2}$, $3 \notin \overline{3}$, $4 \notin \overline{4}$ and $5 \notin \overline{5}$.

In the remainder of this chapter, the focus will be on the cases like parts (a) and (c), but in rather more general terms.

2.3   Some definitions

In Section 2.1, the word 'related' was not clearly defined. If A is a set, then a **relation** R on A is defined to be a subset of $A \times A$.

This definition turns out to be not especially helpful, except for saying clearly what a relation is: the notation aRb is better, and is connected to the subset idea above by saying that

$$(a,b) \in R \iff aRb.$$

In the remainder of the book, the aRb notation is used for a relation.

In the next section, the idea of an equivalence relation is explored informally.

2.4   Equivalence relations

An equivalence relation is a mathematical way of modelling 'sameness'.

Consider, for example, the set of lower and upper case letters of the alphabet, $\{a, b, c, \dots, A, B, C, \dots\}$. You may wish, for some purposes, to think of e and E as the 'same' as each other; for other purposes, you may wish to think of the lower case letters as the 'same' as each other and for yet other purposes, you may wish to think of vowels as the 'same' as each other. When two things are the 'same' in some way, in that they share some particular property, they are called 'equivalent' with regard to that property. The notion of an equivalence relation provides a means of discussing this abstractly, without referring to any particular property.

In geometry, it is often convenient to think of triangles which are congruent to one another as equivalent, even though they may be located in different places and therefore, strictly, different triangles.

In a school, it is sometimes useful to think of the students in each class as equivalent. Then you have divided the students of the school into subsets matched with the classes.

In Exercise 2A Question 1(a), the values of a divided themselves into subsets which are the even and odd numbers, and in Question 1(c) they were those numbers which leave remainders 1, 2 and 0 on division by 3. If you had found the values of b which were related to given values of a you would have found the same results.

An **equivalence relation** on a set A is a relation R with all three of the following properties.

- xRx for all $x \in A$ Reflexive property

- if xRy, then yRx Symmetric property

- if xRy and yRz, then xRz Transitive property

Here are some examples of relations on a set; some are equivalence relations and some are not.

Example 2.4.1
Let $A = \{$people living in the UK$\}$ and let xRy if $x, y \in A$ and if x and y were born in the same calendar year. Show that R is an equivalence relation. What is the subset of those people related to you?

Clearly x was born in the same year as x, so xRx and R is reflexive.

If x was born in the same year as y, then y was born in the same year as x. So R is symmetric.

And if x was born in the same year as y, and y was born in the same year as z, then x was born in the same year as z. So R is transitive.

Therefore R is an equivalence relation on A.

If you are called a, then $\bar{a}$ is the subset of people related to you, that is the set of people living in the UK who were born in the same year as you.

In fact, A is divided into subsets corresponding to calendar years, each calendar year containing the people who were born in that year.

Example 2.4.2

Show that the relation R on $\mathbb{Z}$ defined by xRy if $x - y$ is divisible by 3 is an equivalence relation. List the sets $\overline{0}$, $\overline{1}$ and $\overline{2}$.

Since $x - x = 0$ which is divisible by 3, xRx. So R is reflexive.

If xRy, then $x - y$ is divisible by 3. Therefore $y - x = -(x - y)$ is divisible by 3, so yRx. So R is symmetric.

Finally if xRy and yRz, then both $x - y$ and $y - z$ are divisible by 3. Therefore $x - y = 3m$ and $y - z = 3n$ for some integers m and n. Adding these two equations gives $x - z = 3(m + n)$, so $x - z$ is divisible by 3. So xRz and R is transitive.

Hence R is an equivalence relation.

In this case, $\overline{0} = \{0, \pm 3, \pm 6, ...\}$, $\overline{1} = \{..., -5, -2, 1, 4, 7, ...\}$ and $\overline{2} = \{..., -4, -1, 2, 5, 8, ...\}$.

Example 2.4.3

Show that the relation on $A = \{\text{people living in the UK}\}$, given by xRy if x is a friend of y, is not an equivalence relation.

In this case, R is not an equivalence relation because you cannot guarantee that the transitive relation holds. x can be friendly with y, and y can be friendly with z without x being friendly with z. So the transitive law doesn't hold and 'is a friend of' is not an equivalence relation.

Example 2.4.4

Define the relation R on $\mathbb{Z}$, by xRy if 5 divides $2x - y$. Show that R is not an equivalence relation on $\mathbb{Z}$.

R is not an equivalence relation because x is not related to x for all $x \in \mathbb{Z}$. If $x = 1$, then $2x - x = x = 1$, and 5 does not divide 1. Hence $1R1$ is false.

In fact, this relation is not symmetric or transitive, as well as not being reflexive, but you only need to show that one of the conditions fails to show R is not an equivalence relation.

In Examples 2.4.1 and 2.4.2, in which the relations were equivalence relations, the underlying sets, A and $\mathbb{Z}$, were divided into subsets containing elements which were related to each other. This idea leads to the following definition and theorem.

The set $\overline{a} = \{x \in A : xRa\}$ is called the **equivalence class** of a.

Theorem 2.1   Let R be an equivalence relation on a set A. Then
(a) for each $a \in A$, $a \in \overline{a}$
(b) for each $a, b \in A$, aRb if, and only if, $\overline{a} = \overline{b}$.

This theorem says first, that a is in its own equivalence class, and secondly, if a is related to b, then the equivalence classes of a and b are identical, and vice versa.

Proof

(a)   Since R is an equivalence relation, aRa, so $a \in \bar{a}$.

(b)   **Proof of 'if'**
Suppose that $\bar{a} = \bar{b}$. Then $\bar{a} \subseteq \bar{b}$. From part (a), $a \in \bar{a}$, so $\bar{a} \subseteq \bar{b}$. Therefore aRb.

Proof of 'only if'
Let aRb. First suppose that $x \in \bar{a}$, so that xRa. Then xRa and aRb, so, by the transitive rule xRb. Therefore $x \in \bar{b}$. So if $x \in \bar{a}$, $x \in \bar{b}$. So $\bar{a} \subseteq \bar{b}$.

Now suppose that $x \in \bar{b}$, so xRb. But, aRb, and, by the symmetric rule, bRa. Hence xRb and bRa, so, by the transitive rule, xRa, giving $x \in \bar{a}$. So if $x \in \bar{b}$, $x \in \bar{a}$, so $\bar{b} \subseteq \bar{a}$.

Therefore, as $\bar{a} \subseteq \bar{b}$ and $\bar{b} \subseteq \bar{a}$, $\bar{a} = \bar{b}$.

In Examples 2.4.1 and 2.4.2, and in Exercise 2A parts (a) and (c) the subsets into which A and $\mathbb{Z}$ were divided were disjoint: they had no elements in common. This is the essence of the idea of a partition.

2.5   Partitions

A **partition** of a set A is a division of A into subsets such that every element of A is in exactly one of the subsets.

The 'exactly' part of the definition ensures that the subsets in a partition are disjoint.

Theorem 2.2   For any equivalence relation R on a set A, the set of equivalence classes forms a partition of A.

Proof
Every element of A is in at least one equivalence class by part (a) of Theorem 2.1. This ensures that no element is 'left out in the cold'.

It remains to prove that each element is in exactly one equivalence class. To do this, the strategy is to suppose that there is an element x which is in two distinct equivalence classes, and then to show that if this is the case, the equivalence classes are identical, and are therefore not distinct. This establishes a contradiction.

Let $a, b \in A$ and suppose that the equivalence classes of a and b are not disjoint, that is, $\bar{a} \cap \bar{b}$ is non-empty. The aim is now to prove that $\bar{a} = \bar{b}$.

As $\bar{a} \cap \bar{b}$ is non-empty, there exists an element $x \in A$, such that $x \in \bar{a}$ and $x \in \bar{b}$.

Therefore xRa and xRb. Therefore, as R is symmetric, aRx.

As aRx and xRb, by the transitive rule, aRb. Therefore, by part (b) of Theorem 2.1, $\bar{a} = \bar{b}$.

Therefore either $\bar{a}$ and $\bar{b}$ are identical or they are disjoint.

Hence the set of equivalence classes is a partition.

This is an important result.

> Let R be an equivalence relation on a set A.
>
> The set $\bar{a} = \{x \in A : xRa\}$ is called the **equivalence class** of a.
>
> The equivalence classes **partition** A.

Example 2.5.1
In Example 2.4.1, $A = \{$people living in the UK$\}$ and it was shown that the relation R defined so that xRy if x and y were born in the same calendar year is an equivalence relation. Find the equivalence classes corresponding to R.

The equivalence classes are those people living in the UK who were born in the same calendar year.

Example 2.5.2
In Example 2.4.2, where the relation R on $\mathbb{Z}$ defined by xRy if $x - y$ is divisible by 3 was shown to be an equivalence relation, find the equivalence classes.

The equivalence classes consist of members of $\mathbb{Z}$ which leave the same remainder on division by 3.

Example 2.5.3
Let $A = $ the set of towns in Great Britain. Let a and b be towns, and let aRb if a and b are in the same county. Identify the equivalence classes.

Each town a is in the same county as itself, so aRa and R is reflexive.

Let a and b be two towns in Great Britain. Then, if aRb, a and b are in the same county. But then b and a are in the same county, so bRa and R is symmetric.

Finally, let a, b and c be three towns in Great Britain. If aRb then a and b are in the same county, and if bRc then b and c are in the same county. It follows that a and c are in the same county, so aRc and R is transitive

The equivalence classes are the counties. Fig. 2.3 shows Great Britain partitioned into counties.

Great Britain partitioned into equivalence classes

Fig. 2.3

Exercise 2B

1   Show that each of the following relations is an equivalence relation. In each case identify the equivalence classes.

(a) On $\mathbb{R}^2 \setminus \{(0,0)\}$, $(a,b)R(c,d)$ if $ad - bc = 0$

(b) On $\mathbb{Q}$, $(p/q)R(r/s)$ if $ps - qr = 0$

(c) On $\mathbb{Z}$, xRy if $x - y$ is divisible by 2

(d) On $\mathbb{Z}$, xRy if $2x + y$ is divisible by 3

(e) On $\mathbb{Z}$, xRy if $|x| = |y|$

2   Decide whether each of the following relations is an equivalence relation, giving the equivalence classes where appropriate.

(a) On $\mathbb{Z}$, xRy if $x - y$ is the square of an integer

(b) On $\mathbb{Z}$, xRy if $xy > 0$

(c) On $\mathbb{Z}^+$, xRy if $xy > 0$

(d) On $\mathbb{Z}$, xRy if $xy \geq 0$

(e) On $\mathbb{R}$, aRb if $|a - b| \leq \frac{1}{2}$

(f) On $\mathbb{R}$, aRb if $z \in \mathbb{Z}$ exists so that $|z - a| \leq \frac{1}{2}$ and $|z - b| \leq \frac{1}{2}$

(g) On the set of lines in a plane, lRm if l is parallel to m

(h) On $\mathbb{R}^2$ $(a,b)R(c,d)$ if $bd = 0$

(i) On the set of triangles, ARB if A is similar to B

(j) On the set of triangles, ARB if A is congruent to B

(k) On the set of lines in a plane, lRm if l is perpendicular to m

3   In $\mathbb{R}^2$, define R by $(a,b)R(c,d)$ if $a - b = c - d$. Show that R is an equivalence relation, and find its equivalence classes.

4   In $\mathbb{R}^2$, define R by $(a,b)R(c,d)$ if $\max(|a|,|b|) = \max(|c|,|d|)$. Show that R is an equivalence relation, find its equivalence classes and describe them geometrically.

5   In $\mathbb{R}^2 \setminus \{(0,0)\}$, define R by $(a,b)R(c,d)$ if $|a| + |b| = |c| + |d|$. Show that R is an equivalence relation, find its equivalence classes and describe them geometrically.

6   In $\mathbb{R}^2$, define R by $(a,b)R(c,d)$ if $a^2 + b^2 = c^2 + d^2$. Show that R is an equivalence relation, find its equivalence classes and describe them geometrically.

3 Functions

This chapter generalises the idea of a function. There is a mass of detail here, some of which you may know already. When you have completed it, you should

- know the meaning of the word 'function' or 'mapping'
- know the language and notation associated with functions
- know the meanings of the terms 'injection', 'surjection' and 'bijection'
- be able to prove whether a given function is an injection, a surjection, a bijection, or none of these
- know what the composition of two functions means, the notation for it, and the conditions under which it exists
- know what an inverse function is, the conditions for the inverse function to exist, and how to find the inverse of a composition of functions
- know that the composition of functions is associative.

Section 3.10 gives an alternative definition of a function which links it to relations. You can omit this if you wish.

3.1 Introduction

You already know a definition of a function, in the context of functions of real numbers and their graphs. So you will see that the definition given in this chapter is a generalisation. If you have already met the generalised idea of a function, then this chapter is likely to be a revision of these ideas, notation and language; in that case, use it mainly for reference.

In some contexts functions are called mappings and the words 'function' and 'mapping' have the same meaning.

3.2 Functions: a discussion

In the context of graphs, people talk about a function of x such as $f(x) = x^2$. But what are the properties that f must have in order to be called a function?

First, what is x? In the case $f(x) = x^2$ there is an understanding that x is a real number, but in the case $g(x) = \sqrt{x}$, the positive square root of x, there is an understanding that x is a positive real number or zero. The point is that in each case x is a member of a starting or object set, although you may not be told explicitly what this starting or object set is. In the generalisation which follows, x will be taken from an object set which will be called the **domain**, and you will be told explicitly what the domain is.

Secondly, what about the result x^2 obtained by operating on x with the function f? It also belongs to a set: this is sometimes called the target set, but more often the **co-domain**. Once again, you should be told explicitly what the co-domain is. In the example $f(x) = x^2$ the co-domain may be $\mathbb{R}$, or it may be $\mathbb{R}^+ \cup \{0\}$. In the context of graphs, you may not be told what the domain is, and often it will not matter precisely what the co-domain is; in this book you will always be told the target set or co-domain.

Thirdly, when you are told that f is a function, you expect that for every value of x you have a rule for calculating the value $f(x)$ of the function corresponding to x. There are two points to emphasise here.

The rule must enable you to calculate the value of $f(x)$ for *every* value of x. And you must be able to calculate *the* value of $f(x)$ for every value of x. Both these aspects are important in the generalised definition of a function. There is a rule which for each value of x in the domain gives you just one value of $f(x)$ in the co-domain. Thus $f(x)$ is called the **image** of x under f.

Fig. 3.1 illustrates these three aspects of the idea of a function. You can see

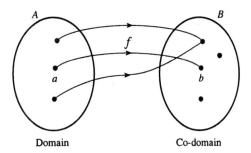

- the starting set, the domain A
- the target set, the co-domain B
- the rule showing the element $b \in B$ corresponding to $a \in A$.

The fact that for each element x in the domain there corresponds just one value of $f(x)$ in the co-domain means that there is exactly one arrow leaving every point in the domain A, with its end in the co-domain B.

A function f with domain A and co-domain B

Fig. 3.1

Notice that it is not necessary for every element in B to be the image of an element of A.

To summarise:

> A **function** f has three components: a starting set A, called the **domain**; a target set B, called the **co-domain**; and a **rule** which assigns to each member a of A a unique member b of B such that
>
> - every element of A has an associated element of B, and
>
> - no element of A has more than one associated element of B.

There is no reason why A and B should not be the same set.

3.3   Notation and language

You write $f : A \rightarrow B$ to show that f is a function for which the domain is A and the co-domain is B.

You say that f maps a to b, and that f maps A into B. The notation to indicate that a maps to b is either $b = f(a)$ or $f : a \mapsto b$.

The set

$$\{b \mid b \in B, b = f(a) \text{ for some } a \in A\}$$

is called the **set of images** or **image set** of A. It is also called the **range** of f.

Two functions $f : A \rightarrow B$ and $g : C \rightarrow D$ are **equal** if and only if $A = C$, $B = D$ and $f(x) = g(x)$ for every element x in A.

In Fig. 3.2 the image set of A is a subset of B containing just two elements.

A natural extension of the idea of image set that you will meet later in the book is that of the **image of a subset** of A. Let $f:A \to B$, and let $X \subseteq A$. Then the image $f(X)$ of the subset X is defined by $f(X) = \{f(x) \mid x \in X\}$.

The function $I_A : A \to A$ given by $I_A(x) = x$ for all $x \in A$ is called the **identity function** on A. If there is no ambiguity, the subscript A can be omitted.

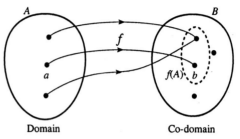

Domain   Co-domain

The image $f(A)$ is shown dotted

Fig. 3.2

Example 3.3.1

For the two examples discussed in Section 3.2, $f(x) = x^2$ and $g(x) = \sqrt{x}$, give complete definitions of f and g.

Possible definitions are

$f : \mathbb{R} \to \mathbb{R}$ such that $f(x) = x^2$

$g : \mathbb{R}^+ \cup \{0\} \to \mathbb{R}$ such that $g(x) = \sqrt{x}$, the positive square root of x.

Notice that for both the functions f and g, the set of images is not the same as the whole domain $\mathbb{R}$. You could have defined the function f differently by saying that

$f : \mathbb{R} \to \mathbb{R}^+ \cup \{0\}$ such that $f(x) = x^2$

but in that case, the two functions called f are different. This illustrates an important fact: that to be equal, two functions must have the same domain, the same co-domain and the same rule.

> Two functions f and g are **equal** if, and only if, they have the same domain, the same co-domain and the same rule.

Example 3.3.2

Explain why $f : \mathbb{Q} \to \mathbb{Z}$ defined by $f(x) =$ the numerator of the fraction x is not a function.

This example fails the uniqueness part of the definition of a function as $f\left(\frac{1}{2}\right) = 1$ and $f\left(\frac{2}{4}\right) = 2$.

Example 3.3.3

Explain why $f : \mathbb{Z} \to \mathbb{Q}$ given by $f(n) = \frac{1}{n}$ is not a function.

The function $f(n)$ is not defined for $n = 0$.

Example 3.3.4

Let $X =$ set of times on a specified day, and $Y =$ set of trains leaving Victoria Station in London on that day. Then let $f : X \to Y$ be given by $f(x) =$ train leaving Victoria Station at time x. Explain why f is not a function.

This example fails on two grounds: given a particular time, there may not be a train leaving Victoria Station at that time; and there may be some times at which more than one train leaves Victoria Station.

3.4   Injections and surjections

A function $f : A \to B$ is called an **injection** if each element of B has at most one element of A mapped into it. The adjective **injective** is used to describe a function which is an injection. An injection is also called a **one-to-one function**.

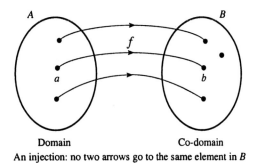

Domain   Co-domain
An injection: no two arrows go to the same element in B

Fig. 3.3

Fig. 3.3 illustrates an injection. Each element of B has at most one arrow coming into it from an element of A. Notice that there may be elements of B which are not images of elements of A.

Proving that a given function f is an injection is equivalent to proving that if $f(a) = f(b)$ then $a = b$. Simply writing down $f(a) = f(b)$ as the first line is often a good way to start the proof. Example 3.4.1 illustrates this.

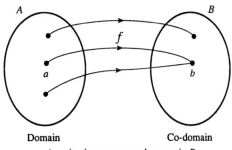

Domain   Co-domain
A surjection: no spare elements in B

Fig. 3.4

A function $f : A \to B$ is called a **surjection** if each element of B has at least one member of A mapped into it, that is, the range of f is the whole of the co-domain. The adjective **surjective** is used to describe a function which is a surjection. A surjection is also called an **onto function**.

Fig. 3.4 illustrates a surjection. Each element of B has at least one arrow coming into it from an element in A. Some elements in B may be the image of more than one element in A.

A function $f : A \to B$ which is both an injection and a surjection is called a **bijection**. The adjective **bijective** is used to describe a function which is a bijection. A bijection is also called a **one-to-one correspondence**.

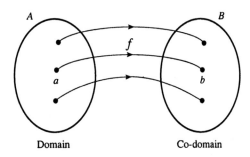

Domain   Co-domain
A bijection: both an injection and a surjection

Fig. 3.5

Fig. 3.5 illustrates a bijection. Each element of B has exactly one arrow coming into it from an element of A.

Example 3.4.1

Prove that the function $f : \mathbb{Z} \to \mathbb{Z}$ such that $f(n) = n + 1$ is both an injection and a surjection.

To prove that f is an injection, suppose that two elements a and b map to the same image under f. Then $f(a) = f(b)$ so $a + 1 = b + 1$, leading to $a = b$.

This method is one you will often use for proving that a function is an injection. Start by supposing that two different elements have identical images, and then show that the elements themselves must be identical.

To prove that f is a surjection, you must find the element in the domain which maps onto any given element in the co-domain. So if you take an element n in the co-domain, consider the element $n - 1$ in the domain. Then $f(n - 1) = (n - 1) + 1 = n$. So every element n in the co-domain has a corresponding element $n - 1$ in the domain.

This method is fairly typical for proving that a function f is a surjection. For any given element of the co-domain, you have to identify an element in the domain which maps onto it.

In Example 3.4.1, as f is both an injection and a surjection, f is a bijection.

Example 3.4.2

Show that the projection function $p : \mathbb{R}^2 \to \mathbb{R}^2$ defined by $p(x, y) = (x, 0)$ is neither an injection nor a surjection.

To prove that p is not an injection, you need to find two elements in the domain which have the same image under p. Since $p(0, 1) = (0, 0)$ and $p(0, 0) = (0, 0)$, p is not an injection.

To prove that p is not a surjection, you need to find an element in the co-domain $\mathbb{R}^2$ which is not the image of any element of the domain $\mathbb{R}^2$. Consider the element $(0, 1)$ and suppose it is the image of (x, y). Then $p(x, y) = (x, 0) = (0, 1)$, which implies that $x = 0$ and $0 = 1$. As the second of these is impossible, no such element exists, and p is not a surjection.

3.5   Injections and surjections of finite sets

Here are two theorems about surjective and injective functions when the domain and co-domain are finite sets.

You may find it useful to draw diagrams like Figs. 3.3 to 3.5 to illustrate the theorems for yourself. The results may then appear to be obvious.

Before the theorems, here is a reminder about notation. If X is a finite set then $n(X)$ means the number of elements in X. Similarly, $n(f(X))$ means the number of elements in $f(X)$.

Theorem 3.1   Let X and Y be finite sets, and let $f : X \to Y$ be a function. Then

(a) $n(f(X)) \le n(X)$

(b) f is injective if, and only if, $n(f(X)) = n(X)$

(c) f is surjective if, and only if, $n(f(X)) = n(Y)$.

(a) **Proof**

By the definition of function, to each $x \in X$ there is assigned one, and only one, element of Y. So to each element of $f(X)$, there corresponds at least one element of X; and no two different elements of $f(X)$ are associated with the same element of X. Therefore $n(f(X)) \leq n(X)$.

(b) **Proof of 'if'**

Suppose that $n(f(X)) = n(X)$. Then X and $f(X)$ have the same number of elements. Suppose that $f(x_1) = f(x_2)$ for $x_1, x_2 \in X$. If $x_1 \neq x_2$, then $n(f(X)) \leq n(X)$, since the images of two different elements in X would be the same. But as $n(f(X)) = n(X)$, $x_1 = x_2$, and f is an injection.

Proof of 'only if'

Suppose that f is injective. Then, if $f(x_1) = f(x_2)$, $x_1 = x_2$. Therefore the elements of $f(X)$ are all different, and $n(f(X)) = n(X)$.

(c) **Proof of 'if'**

Suppose that $n(f(X)) = n(Y)$. Then $f(X)$ and Y have the same number of elements. But $f(X) \subseteq Y$. Therefore $f(X) = Y$. Therefore every element of Y is the image of some member $x \in X$. Therefore f is a surjection.

Proof of 'only if'

Suppose that f is surjective. Then every element of Y is the image of some element of X. So $Y \subseteq f(X)$. But $f(X) \subseteq Y$. Therefore $f(X) = Y$, so $n(f(X)) = n(Y)$.

Since, by definition, $f(X) \subseteq Y$, and so $n(f(X)) \leq n(Y)$, you can deduce that if f is an injection, $n(X) \leq n(Y)$. Or, put an equivalent way, if $n(X) > n(Y)$, then f is not an injection.

This is the **pigeon-hole principle**. It is stated in the following way, with the justification in brackets.

Suppose that you have pigeons which are put into pigeon-holes (that is, a function $f : X \to Y$), and you have more pigeons than pigeon-holes (that is, $n(X) > n(Y)$), then there is at least one pigeon-hole with more than one pigeon (that is, f is not injective).

The pigeon-hole principle has some quite surprising applications. Here is a none-too-serious example.

Example 3.5.1

Let $X =$ the set of non-bald people in England, and let $Y =$ the set of positive integers less than a million. Let $f : X \to Y$ be given by $f(x) =$ the number of hairs on the head of x. Prove that there are at least two people in England with the same number of hairs on their heads.

It is a fact that no-one has more than a million hairs on his or her head, (the number is usually 150 000 to 200 000), so f is well defined.

It is also a fact that $n(X) > n(Y)$, that is, the number of non-bald people in England is greater than a million.

It follows from the pigeon-hole principle that f is not injective, and hence that there are at least two people in England with the same number of hairs on their heads.

Theorem 3.2   Let X and Y be finite sets, let $n(X) = n(Y)$, and let $f : X \rightarrow Y$ be a function. Then f is injective if, and only if, f is surjective.

Proof of 'if'
Suppose that f is surjective. Then, by Theorem 3.1(c), $n(f(X)) = n(Y)$. But, by hypothesis, $n(X) = n(Y)$, so $n(f(X)) = n(X)$. Therefore, by Theorem 3.1(b), f is injective.

Proof of 'only if'
Suppose that f is injective. Then, by Theorem 3.1(b), $n(f(X)) = n(X)$. But, by hypothesis, $n(X) = n(Y)$, so $n(f(X)) = n(Y)$. Then, by Theorem 3.1(c), f is surjective.

Exercise 3A

1   Prove that $f : \mathbb{R} \rightarrow \mathbb{R}$ defined by $f(x) = \sin x$ is neither an injection nor a surjection.

2   Give an example of a function $f : \mathbb{R} \rightarrow \mathbb{R}$ which is an injection, but not a surjection.

3   Give an example of a function $f : \mathbb{R} \rightarrow \mathbb{R}$ which is a surjection, but not an injection.

4   In each of these examples the domain is $\mathbb{R}$ and the co-domain is $\mathbb{R}$. Decide which of them is the definition of a function. If it is a function, decide whether it is injective, and whether it is surjective. Be able to justify your answers. Keep your answers: they will be used in Exercise 3B Question 3.

   (a) $f(x) = x^2$ (b) $f(x) = x^3$ (c) $f(x) = 1/x$ (d) $f(x) = \cos x$

   (e) $f(x) = \tan x$ (f) $f(x) = e^x$ (g) $f(x) = |x|$ (h) $f(x) = \sqrt{x}$

   (i) $f(x) = x + 1$ (j) $f(x) = \text{int } x$ (int x is the largest integer $\leq x$.)

   (k) $f(x) = \sin^{-1} x$ (l) $f(x)$ is the smallest real number greater than x .

5   Prove that the function $f : \mathbb{R}^+ \cup \{0\} \rightarrow \mathbb{R}^+ \cup \{0\}$ defined by $f(x) = \sqrt{x}$ is a bijection.

6   Prove that the function $f : \mathbb{R} \setminus \{0\} \rightarrow \mathbb{R} \setminus \{0\}$ defined by $f(x) = 1/x$ is a bijection.

7   Prove that the function $f : \mathbb{Z} \rightarrow \mathbb{Z}^+$ defined by $f(n) = \begin{cases} 2n, & \text{if } n > 0 \\ 1 - 2n, & \text{if } n \leq 0 \end{cases}$ is a bijection.

8   How can you tell from the graph of a real function $y = f(x)$, whether or not f is

   (a) an injection,   (b) a surjection,   (c) a bijection?

9   Mark each of the following statements true or false.

   (a) The function $f : \mathbb{R} \rightarrow \mathbb{R}$ such that $f(x) = 0$ for all $x \in \mathbb{R}$, is a bijection.

   (b) Every function which is a bijection is also a surjection.

   (c) $f : \mathbb{R} \times \mathbb{R} \rightarrow \mathbb{R} \times \mathbb{R}$ defined by $f(x, y) = (y, x)$, is a bijection.

10   Let $P = \{\text{polynomials in } x \text{ with real coefficients}\}$. Decide whether $f : P \rightarrow P$ defined in the following ways is a function. If it is, decide whether it is injective, and whether it is surjective.

   (a) $f(p) = \dfrac{\text{d}(p(x))}{\text{d}x}$ (b) $f(p) = \displaystyle\int p(t)\, \text{d}t$ (c) $f(p) = \displaystyle\int_0^x p(t)\, \text{d}t$ (d) $f(p) = xp(x)$

3.6   Combining functions

When the co-domain of one function is the domain of another function you can combine the two functions in the way indicated by Fig. 3.6.

In Fig. 3.6, $b = f(a)$ and $c = g(b)$. The composite function is the function which maps a from the set A directly to c in set C.

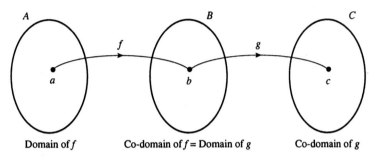

Fig. 3.6

But first you have to establish that the rule which takes a to c is actually a properly defined function.

Theorem 3.3   Let $f : A \to B$ and $g : B \to C$ be functions. Then $h : A \to C$ such that $h(x) = g(f(x))$ is a function.

> **Proof**
>
> To show that h is a function, you need to exhibit its domain and its co-domain, and to show that for every element in the domain there is a unique element in the co-domain.
>
> In this case the domain is A, and the co-domain is C, so it only remains to show the existence and uniqueness properties.
>
> For each element $a \in A$ there exists a unique element $f(a) = b$ in B. Moreover, for that $b \in B$ there is a unique element $g(b) = c$ in C. It follows that for each element $a \in A$ there exists a unique element $c \in C$,, such that $c = g(f(a))$.
>
> This shows that $h : A \to C$ such that $h(x) = g(f(x))$ is a function.

Let $f : A \to B$ and $g : B \to C$ be functions.

Then the function $h : A \to C$ such that $h(x) = g(f(x))$ is called the **composite** of f and g, written sometimes as $g \circ f$ and sometimes as gf.

Then $(g \circ f)(x) = g(f(x))$.

The composite function $g \circ f$ is pronounced 'g blob f'.

Notice that for the composite function to be properly defined it is not necessary that the function $f : A \to B$ is a surjection. For example, let $f : \mathbb{R} \to \mathbb{R}$ be given by $f(x) = \sin x$ and $g : \mathbb{R} \to \mathbb{R}$ be given by $g(x) = 2x$. Then the function $(g \circ f) : \mathbb{R} \to \mathbb{R}$ is defined by $(g \circ f)(x) = g(f(x)) = 2 \sin x$, even though the image set of f is the set $\{x \mid x \in \mathbb{R}, -1 \le x \le 1\}$ and not the whole of $\mathbb{R}$.

Example 3.6.1

Let $f : \mathbb{R} \to \mathbb{R}$ where $f(x) = 2x + 1$ and $g : \mathbb{R} \to \mathbb{R}$ where $g(x) = 2x$. Show that $fg \neq gf$.

To show that two functions are not equal, you do not need a general argument. You only need to find a single value of x for which $fg(x) \neq gf(x)$.

For this case,

$$fg(1) = f(2) = 5 \quad \text{and} \quad gf(1) = g(3) = 6.$$

Hence $fg \neq gf$.

Let $f : A \to A$ and $g : A \to A$ be functions.

Then the functions $fg : A \to A$ and $gf : A \to A$ are not usually equal.

Note that there may be cases when $fg = gf$, but these are exceptions. In general, $fg \neq gf$.

What can you deduce about the composite function $(g \circ f) : A \to C$ when you know some of the properties of the functions $f : A \to B$ and $g : B \to C$? For example, if f and g are both surjections, will $g \circ f$ be a surjection?

The answer is yes. The result itself is not important, but the method of proof is important. As in all proofs about surjections, you have to find an element in A which maps to a given element in the image C.

Example 3.6.2

Prove that if $f : A \to B$ and $g : B \to C$ are surjections, then $(g \circ f) : A \to C$ is also a surjection.

Notice that the conditions for a composite function are satisfied, so the composite function $(g \circ f) : A \to C$ exists.

Now suppose that c is any element in C. Then, since g is surjective, there exists an element $b \in B$ such that $g(b) = c$; and as f is surjective, there exists an element $a \in A$ such that $f(a) = b$. Thus $(g \circ f)(a) = g(f(a)) = g(b) = c$. So $(g \circ f) : A \to C$ is a surjection.

Example 3.6.3

Suppose that $f : A \to B$ is an injection and $g : B \to C$ is a surjection. Can you deduce that
(a) the function $(g \circ f) : A \to C$ is a surjection,   (b) the function $(g \circ f) : A \to C$ is an injection?

(a)   You cannot deduce that $(g \circ f) : A \to C$ is a surjection.

For let $f : \{a, b\} \to \{p, q, r\}$ be given by $f(a) = p$ and $f(b) = q$. Then f is an injection.

And let $g : \{p, q, r\} \to \{s, t\}$ where $g(p) = g(q) = s$ and $g(r) = t$. Then g is a surjection.

Now, $(g \circ f) : \{a, b\} \to \{s, t\}$ is given by $(g \circ f)(a) = s$ and $(g \circ f)(b) = s$. So there is no $x \in A$ such that $(g \circ f)(x) = t$, so $(g \circ f) : A \to C$ is not a surjection.

(b)   Also $(g \circ f) : A \to C$ is not an injection, because a and b are distinct elements of A mapping to the element s in C under $g \circ f$.

This section ends with a proof of an obvious-looking theorem involving the identity function.

Theorem 3.3   For any function $f : A \to A$, $I_A \circ f = f = f \circ I_A$.

Proof
For $a \in A$, $(I_A \circ f)(a) = I_A(f(a)) = f(a)$.

Also $(f \circ I_A)(a) = f(I_A(a)) = f(a)$.

It follows that $I_A \circ f = f = f \circ I_A$.

3.7   Inverse functions

Here is an important question about functions. Suppose that $f : A \to B$ is a function. Under what circumstances is there a reverse function g from B to A which has the opposite effect to f? That is, under what conditions does there exist a function $g : B \to A$ such that $g(b) = a$ whenever $f(a) = b$?

The answer is that there will be a function $g : B \to A$ which reverses the effect of $f : A \to B$, if, and only if, $f : A \to B$ is a bijection.

Proving this apparently straightforward statement is long and detailed. If it would make you feel more comfortable, jump to the end of the section, and come back to study the details later.

Theorem 3.4 $f : A \to B$ is a bijection if, and only if, there exists a function $g : B \to A$ with $g(f(a)) = a$ for all $a \in A$, and $f(g(b)) = b$ for all $b \in B$.

Proof
Consider the following two statements.

(a)   There exists a function $g : B \to A$ such that $g(f(a)) = a$ for all $a \in A$, and $f(g(b)) = b$ for all $b \in B$.

(b) $f : A \to B$ is a bijection.

The proof comes in two stages. The first stage is to show that if statement (a) is true, then statement (b) is true. Thus you need to show that f is injective and surjective.

Suppose that statement (a) is true.

Proof that f is an injection
If $f(x) = f(y)$, then $g(f(x)) = g(f(y))$, so, by the first part of the hypothesis of statement (a), $x = y$. Hence $f : A \to B$ is injective.

Proof that f is a surjection
If $b \in B$, then, from the second part of the hypothesis of statement (a), $b = f(g(b))$ is the image under f of $g(b) \in A$. Hence $f : A \to B$ is surjective.

Hence $f : A \to B$ is both injective and surjective, so it is bijective.

The second stage consists of showing that if statement (b) is true, then statement (a) is true. The first part of this stage consists of showing that the function g is well-defined.

Now suppose that statement (b) is true, that is, $f : A \rightarrow B$ is a bijection.

Proof that g is well-defined

As $f : A \rightarrow B$ is a bijection, for every $b \in B$, there is at least one $a \in A$ such that $f(a) = b$ because f is surjective. But, given b, there cannot be more than one $a \in A$ such that $f(a) = b$ because f is injective. Therefore, specifying $g(b)$ to be that unique $a \in A$ such that $f(a) = b$ gives a well-defined function $g : B \rightarrow A$.

So g is well defined. Now you have to show that the function g has the required properties in (a).

For $b \in B$, $f(g(b)) = f(a) = b$.

Also, for $a \in A$, if you write $b = f(a)$, then $g(b)$ is, by definition, equal to a, so $g(f(a)) = a$.

The theorem tells you that $f : A \rightarrow B$ is a bijection if, and only if, there is a function $g : B \rightarrow A$ such that $g \circ f = I_A$ and $f \circ g = I_B$. And now, from this, you can define an inverse function.

The function $g : B \rightarrow A$ of the previous theorem is called an **inverse** of f.

There are still two more results to prove in this section. These results are the two parts of Theorem 3.5.

Theorem 3.5   Let $f : A \rightarrow B$ be a bijection. Then the function $g : B \rightarrow A$ with $g(f(a)) = a$, for all $a \in A$, and $b = f(g(b))$, for all $b \in B$ is

(a) a bijection,

(b) uniquely determined by f.

Proof

The function f plays the role of an inverse for g, so the previous theorem can be applied to g. This shows that g is a bijection.

Remember in proving part (b), uniqueness, that two functions are equal if they have the same domain, co-domain, and have the same effect on every element of the domain.

To prove the uniqueness, suppose that $g : B \rightarrow A$ and $h : B \rightarrow A$ are both inverses of f. Then $f(g(b)) = b = f(h(b))$ for all $b \in B$. Therefore, since f is injective, $g(b) = h(b)$ for all $b \in B$. Therefore $g = h$.

You can now talk about *the* inverse f^{-1} (rather than *an* inverse) of a bijection $f : A \rightarrow B$. This is the function $f^{-1} : B \rightarrow A$ such that $f \circ f^{-1} = I_B$ and $f^{-1} \circ f = I_A$.

Let $f : A \rightarrow B$ be a bijection.

Then the function $g : B \rightarrow A$ with $g(f(a)) = a$, for all $a \in A$, and $b = f(g(b))$, for all $b \in B$ is a bijection, and is called the **inverse** of f.

The inverse of f is written as f^{-1}.

3.8   Associativity of functions

Suppose that $f: A \to B$, $g: B \to C$ and $h: C \to D$ are three functions. Then you can combine them to form composite functions in two ways: you could combine f and g first to get $g \circ f$ and then combine this with h to get the function $(h \circ (g \circ f)): A \to D$; or you could work the other way round to get $((h \circ g) \circ f): A \to D$. You probably suspect that it doesn't matter which way you write it – the result will be the same. You are right!

To prove it, you need to go back to the definitions in Section 3.6.

Theorem 3.6   Let $f: A \to B$, $g: B \to C$ and $h: C \to D$ be functions. Then $(h \circ g) \circ f = h \circ (g \circ f)$.

Proof
Using the definition of composite function on $((h \circ g) \circ f)(x)$ gives

$$((h \circ g) \circ f)(x) = (h \circ g)(f(x)) = h(g(f(x))).$$

Also $(h \circ (g \circ f))(x)$ gives

$$(h \circ (g \circ f))(x) = h((g \circ f)(x)) = h(g(f(x))).$$

As the domains and co-domains of $(h \circ g) \circ f$ and $h \circ (g \circ f)$ are the same and $((h \circ g) \circ f)(x) = (h \circ (g \circ f))(x)$ for any x in A, it follows that the functions $(h \circ g) \circ f$ and $h \circ (g \circ f)$ are equal.

It is also easy to see, but tedious to write out a proof, that a kind of generalised associative law holds for composite functions. If p, q, r and s are four functions with compatible domains and co-domains so that they can be composed together, you can talk about the function $s \circ r \circ q \circ p$ without brackets.

3.9   Inverse of a composite function

It is useful now to introduce a collapsed form of the usual diagram for sets and functions. Let $f: A \to B$ and $g: B \to C$ be functions. These functions are illustrated in Fig. 3.7, together with $g \circ f: A \to C$.

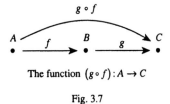

The function $(g \circ f): A \to C$

Fig. 3.7

Now suppose that the functions $f: A \to B$ and $g: B \to C$ are both bijections, so that the inverse functions $f^{-1}: B \to A$ and $g^{-1}: C \to B$ both exist. What can you say about the inverse of the composite function $(g \circ f): A \to C$? Fig. 3.8 helps to make the situation clear.

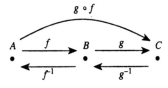

The inverse of $(g \circ f): A \to C$

Fig. 3.8

From Fig. 3.8 you can surmise that the inverse of the function $g \circ f$ is $f^{-1} \circ g^{-1}$. This is proved in the next theorem (Theorem 3.7).

To prove this result you need to go back to Theorem 3.5 and check the details of the theorem are satisfied. You need to check that $(f^{-1} \circ g^{-1}) \circ (g \circ f) = I_A$ and $(g \circ f) \circ (f^{-1} \circ g^{-1}) = I_C$.

Theorem 3.7   Let the two functions $f : A \to B$ and $g : B \to C$ be bijections. Then the inverse of the function $(g \circ f) : A \to C$ exists and is the function $\left(f^{-1} \circ g^{-1}\right) : C \to A$. Furthermore $g \circ f$ and $f^{-1} \circ g^{-1}$ are both bijections.

Proof
You need to show that $\left(f^{-1} \circ g^{-1}\right) \circ (g \circ f) = I_A$. Then you need to show that $(g \circ f) \circ \left(f^{-1} \circ g^{-1}\right) = I_C$.

For the first part,

$$\begin{aligned}
\left(f^{-1} \circ g^{-1}\right) \circ (g \circ f) &= f^{-1} \circ \left(g^{-1} \circ (g \circ f)\right) \\
&= f^{-1} \circ \left(\left(g^{-1} \circ g\right) \circ f\right) \\
&= f^{-1} \circ \left(I_B \circ f\right) \\
&= f^{-1} \circ f \qquad \text{(using Theorem 3.3)} \\
&= I_A .
\end{aligned}$$

Secondly,

$$\begin{aligned}
(g \circ f) \circ \left(f^{-1} \circ g^{-1}\right) &= g \circ \left(f \circ \left(f^{-1} \circ g^{-1}\right)\right) \\
&= g \circ \left(\left(f \circ f^{-1}\right) \circ g^{-1}\right) \\
&= g \circ \left(I_B \circ g^{-1}\right) \\
&= g \circ g^{-1} \qquad \text{(using Theorem 3.3)} \\
&= I_C .
\end{aligned}$$

Therefore $f^{-1} \circ g^{-1}$ is the inverse of $g \circ f$.

Also it follows from Theorem 3.4 that $g \circ f$ and $f^{-1} \circ g^{-1}$ are bijections.

You can think of Theorem 3.7 in terms of doing and un-doing certain actions. For example, if you want to reverse the effect of putting on your socks and then putting on your climbing boots, you would first take off your boots and then take off your socks.

Example 3.9.1
Let $f : \mathbb{R} \to \mathbb{R}$ where $f(x) = 2x + 1$ and $g : \mathbb{R} \to \mathbb{R}$ where $g(x) = 2x$. Assuming that f and g are bijections,
(a) write down the inverses of f and g,
(b) hence find the inverses of $g \circ f$ and $f \circ g$.

(a)   The inverse of f is given by $f^{-1}(x) = \frac{1}{2}(x - 1)$, and the inverse of g is given by $g^{-1}(x) = \frac{1}{2}x$.

(b)   The inverse of $g \circ f$ is $f^{-1} \circ g^{-1}$, so

$$(g \circ f)^{-1}(x) = \left(f^{-1} \circ g^{-1}\right)(x)$$
$$= f^{-1}\left(g^{-1}(x)\right)$$
$$= f^{-1}\left(\tfrac{1}{2}x\right)$$
$$= \tfrac{1}{2}\left(\tfrac{1}{2}x - 1\right)$$
$$= \tfrac{1}{4}x - \tfrac{1}{2}$$

and

$$(f \circ g)^{-1}(x) = \left(g^{-1} \circ f^{-1}\right)(x)$$
$$= g^{-1}\left(f^{-1}(x)\right)$$
$$= g^{-1}\left(\tfrac{1}{2}(x - 1)\right)$$
$$= \tfrac{1}{2}\left(\tfrac{1}{2}(x - 1)\right)$$
$$= \tfrac{1}{4}x - \tfrac{1}{4}.$$

3.10 Functions: an alternative definition

You may omit this section if you wish.

If you look back at the definition of a function in Section 3.2, it mentions a domain, a co-domain and a rule. Some people say that the word 'rule' is not defined. In fact, a rule is hard to define, so here is an alternative way of thinking about functions which gets around this point. You will find this alternative approach in some books.

Let A and B be two sets. A function f which has A as its domain and B as its co-domain is a subset of $A \times B$ with the following properties:

- every $a \in A$ is the first coordinate of some $(a, b) \in f$
- if (a, b_1) and $(a, b_2) \in f$, then $b_1 = b_2$.

You can see, if you think about it, that this definition agrees with the one in Section 3.2, and that it gets round the difficulty of knowing what a rule is. However, you have used functions for some time, so presumably you recognise a rule when you see one, and there is not really a good case for changing the emphasis now.

Exercise 3B

1   Prove that, if $f : A \to B$ and $g : B \to A$ are such that $g \circ f = I_A$, then f is an injection and g is a surjection.

2   Let $f : \mathbb{R} \to \mathbb{R}$ be given by $f(x) = x^2 + 1$. Decide whether or not f is

(a) surjective,   (b) injective,   (c) bijective.

3 In Question 2 of Exercise 3A you decided whether each of the following definitions was the definition of a function and, if so, whether it was injective and whether it was surjective. Use your answer to decide which of the functions have inverses, and give inverses for these functions.

(a) $f(x) = x^2$

(b) $f(x) = x^3$

(c) $f(x) = 1/x$

(d) $f(x) = \cos x$

(e) $f(x) = \tan x$

(f) $f(x) = e^x$

(g) $f(x) = |x|$

(h) $f(x) = \sqrt{x}$

(i) $f(x) = x + 1$

(j) $f(x) = \operatorname{int} x$ ($\operatorname{int} x$ is the largest integer $\le x$.)

(k) $f(x) = \sin^{-1} x$

(l) $f(x)$ is the smallest real number greater than x.

4 Show that the function $g : \mathbb{Z}^+ \to \mathbb{Z}$ defined by

$$g(n) = \begin{cases} n/2, \text{ if } n \text{ is even} \\ (1-n)/2, \text{ if } n \text{ is odd} \end{cases}$$

is inverse to the function $f : \mathbb{Z} \to \mathbb{Z}^+$ of Question 7 in Exercise 3A.

5 Mark each of the following statements true or false. Justify your answers.

(a) The inverse of $f \circ g$ is $f^{-1} \circ g^{-1}$.

(b) If f is a bijection, then f is an injection.

(c) An injection is a bijection if, and only if, it is a surjection.

(d) An injection from a finite set to itself is also a surjection.

(e) An injection from an infinite set to itself is also a surjection.

(f) If $g \circ f$ is a bijection and f is a bijection, then g is a bijection.

(g) If $g \circ f$ is an injection and g is a injection, then f is a injection.

6 Let a function $f(x)$ be defined for all values of $\mathbb{R}$. Prove that the relation xRy defined by xRy if, and only if, $f(x) = f(y)$, is an equivalence relation, and find the equivalence classes.

In particular, find the equivalence classes for the function $f(x) = \sin 2x$ for the case when $\left\{ x \mid x \in \mathbb{R}, f(x) = \dfrac{1}{\sqrt{2}} \right\}$.

7 Let $f : \mathbb{R} \to \mathbb{R}$ be given by $f(x) = \frac{1}{2}x + 1$, and $g : \mathbb{R} \to \mathbb{R}^+$ be given by $g(x) = e^x$.

(a) Show that f and g are both bijections.

(b) Write down the inverses of f and g.

(c) Use the results of part (b) to find the inverse of the real function h where $h(x) = e^{\frac{1}{2}x + 1}$.

8 Show that the function $f : \mathbb{R}^2 \to \mathbb{R}^2$ given by $f(x, y) = (3x + 2y, 5x + 4y)$ is

(a) a surjection,

(b) an injection,

and find an expression for its inverse.

9   Investigate whether the functions $f : \mathbb{R}^2 \to \mathbb{R}^2$ and $g : \mathbb{R}^2 \to \mathbb{R}^2$ defined by

$$f\begin{pmatrix} x \\ y \end{pmatrix} = \begin{pmatrix} 2 & 1 \\ 0 & 1 \end{pmatrix}\begin{pmatrix} x \\ y \end{pmatrix} \quad \text{and} \quad g\begin{pmatrix} x \\ y \end{pmatrix} = \begin{pmatrix} 1 & -2 \\ -2 & 4 \end{pmatrix}\begin{pmatrix} x \\ y \end{pmatrix}$$

are

(a) injective,   (b) surjective,   (c) bijective.

10   For which value of k is the function $f : \mathbb{R}^3 \to \mathbb{R}^3$ defined by

$$f\begin{pmatrix} x \\ y \\ z \end{pmatrix} = \begin{pmatrix} 1 & 2 & -1 \\ 2 & 3 & -2 \\ 1 & 1 & k \end{pmatrix}\begin{pmatrix} x \\ y \\ z \end{pmatrix}$$

(a) injective,   (b) surjective,   (c) bijective?

4 Binary operations and groups

This chapter introduces and develops the ideas of a set with a binary operation and a group. When you have completed it, you should

- know what a binary operation is
- know the axioms for a group
- know how to decide whether a given structure is, or is not, a group.

4.1 Binary operations

Most of the sets you have met so far have had, in addition to the set of elements, an operation: for example, real numbers and the operation of multiplication.

Multiplication of two real numbers is an example of a **binary operation**; another binary operation is the dot product $a \cdot b$ of two vectors a and b.

> A **binary operation** $\circ$ on a set S is a rule which assigns to each ordered pair of elements x, y in S exactly one element denoted by $x \circ y$.

The binary operation $\circ$ is often pronounced 'blob'!

Notice that multiplication, addition and subtraction are binary operations on $\mathbb{Z}$. On the other hand division is not, since $x \div 0$ has no meaning. Multiplication, addition and subtraction are binary operations on $\mathbb{R}$, $\mathbb{C}$ and $\mathbb{Q}$, but division is not, because you cannot divide by zero.

However, if you use the notation $A \setminus B$ to mean the set which consists of elements of A which are not elements of B, that is,

$$A \setminus B = \{x \mid x \in A \text{ and } x \notin B\},$$

you can then say that division is a binary operation on $\mathbb{R} \setminus \{0\}$, $\mathbb{C} \setminus \{0\}$ and $\mathbb{Q} \setminus \{0\}$.

In the definition of binary operation, notice that $x \circ y$ does not have to be an element of the set S. For example, the scalar product of two vectors is not a vector. However, in cases where the binary operation on S always gives a result which is in the set S, the operation is said to be **closed** within the set.

In some books, the term 'binary operation' is used to mean a closed binary operation.

Example 4.1.1
Decide which of the following operations on the given sets are binary operations. For those which are binary operations, say whether or not they are closed.
(a) $\mathbb{N}$, where $a \circ b$ means $a - b$
(b) $\mathbb{N} \setminus \{0\}$, where $a \circ b$ means the lowest common multiple (lcm) of a and b
(c) $\mathbb{R}$, where $a \circ b$ means the greater of a and b
(d) $\mathbb{R}$, where $a \circ b = \dfrac{a + b}{1 - ab}$

(e) $\mathbb{Z}$, where $a \circ b$ means a

(f) $\mathbb{R}^2$, where $(a,b) \circ (c,d) = (ac - bd, ad + bc)$

(a) A binary operation. Since, for example, $1-2$ is not defined in $\mathbb{N}$, the operation is not closed.

(b) A binary operation. The lowest common multiple (lcm) of two positive integers a and b is always defined. As the lcm is a positive integer, the operation is closed.

(c) A binary operation. The greater of a and b is defined, except when $a = b$ when it is understood that $a \circ b$ is equal to either a or b. It is closed since the result is in $\mathbb{R}$.

(d) Not a binary operation, since you cannot calculate $1 \circ 1$.

(e) A binary operation. As a is in $\mathbb{Z}$ the result $a \circ b = a$ is also in $\mathbb{Z}$, so the binary operation is closed.

(f) A binary operation. As $ac - bd$ and $ad + bc$ are both in $\mathbb{R}$, $(ac - bd, ad + bc) \in \mathbb{R}^2$, so the binary operation is closed.

In Example 4.1.1 operations (b) and (c), the order in which a and b are written does not matter since $a \circ b = b \circ a$, but in operations (a) and (e) the order does matter.

> A binary operation $\circ$ on a set S is **commutative** if $a \circ b = b \circ a$ for all $a, b \in S$; otherwise it is **not commutative**.

Important examples of non-commutative binary operations are

- division on $\mathbb{R} \setminus \{0\}$; a counterexample is $2 \div 1 = 2$ and $1 \div 2 = \frac{1}{2}$

- subtraction on $\mathbb{R}$; a counterexample is $3 - 2 = 1$ and $2 - 3 = -1$

- the multiplication of square matrices; a counterexample is $\begin{pmatrix} 1 & 0 \\ 1 & 0 \end{pmatrix}\begin{pmatrix} 0 & 1 \\ 0 & 1 \end{pmatrix} = \begin{pmatrix} 0 & 1 \\ 0 & 1 \end{pmatrix}$ and

$\begin{pmatrix} 0 & 1 \\ 0 & 1 \end{pmatrix}\begin{pmatrix} 1 & 0 \\ 1 & 0 \end{pmatrix} = \begin{pmatrix} 1 & 0 \\ 1 & 0 \end{pmatrix}$.

If you have expressions of the form $(a \circ b) \circ c$ and $a \circ (b \circ c)$ where $\circ$ is a closed binary operation and $a, b, c \in S$, it may or may not be true that $(a \circ b) \circ c = a \circ (b \circ c)$. For example, for the binary operation $+$ on $\mathbb{R}$, you can say that $(a + b) + c = a + (b + c)$, but for the binary operation $-$ on $\mathbb{R}$, the counterexample $(4 - 2) - 1 = 1$ and $4 - (2 - 1) = 3$; shows that in general, $(a - b) - c \neq a - (b - c)$.

> A closed binary operation $\circ$ on a set S is **associative** if $(a \circ b) \circ c = a \circ (b \circ c)$ for all $a, b, c \in S$; otherwise it is **not associative**.

When a binary operation is associative, you may leave out the brackets and write $a \circ b \circ c$, since both ways of evaluating it give the same answer.

Example 4.1.2
Say whether or not the following closed binary operations are commutative and associative.
(a) $\mathbb{N}$: multiplication
(b) Matrices of the form $\begin{pmatrix} x & x \\ 0 & 0 \end{pmatrix}$, where $x \in \mathbb{R}$: matrix multiplication
(c) Vectors in three dimensions: vector product
(d) $\mathbb{Z}$: the operation $a \circ b$ defined as $a + b - ab$

(a) For natural numbers $ab = ba$ and $(ab)c = a(bc)$, so the operation is commutative and associative.

(b) $\begin{pmatrix} x & x \\ 0 & 0 \end{pmatrix}\begin{pmatrix} y & y \\ 0 & 0 \end{pmatrix} = \begin{pmatrix} xy & xy \\ 0 & 0 \end{pmatrix}$ and $\begin{pmatrix} y & y \\ 0 & 0 \end{pmatrix}\begin{pmatrix} x & x \\ 0 & 0 \end{pmatrix} = \begin{pmatrix} yx & yx \\ 0 & 0 \end{pmatrix}$. As $x, y \in \mathbb{R}$, $xy = yx$, and

$\begin{pmatrix} x & x \\ 0 & 0 \end{pmatrix}\begin{pmatrix} y & y \\ 0 & 0 \end{pmatrix} = \begin{pmatrix} y & y \\ 0 & 0 \end{pmatrix}\begin{pmatrix} x & x \\ 0 & 0 \end{pmatrix}$, so the operation is commutative. Since matrix

multiplication is associative, this operation is associative.

(c) Since $i \times j = k$ and $j \times i = -k$, the operation is not commutative. Since $(i \times j) \times j = k \times j = -i$ and $i \times (j \times j) = i \times 0 = 0$, the operation is not associative.

(d) $a \circ b = a + b - ab = b + a - ba = b \circ a$ so the operation is commutative.

$$(a \circ b) \circ c = (a + b - ab) \circ c = (a + b - ab) + c - (a + b - ab)c$$
$$= a + b - ab + c - ac - bc + abc$$

and

$$a \circ (b \circ c) = a \circ (b + c - bc) = a + (b + c - bc) - a(b + c - bc)$$
$$= a + b + c - bc - ab - ac + abc.$$

As these expressions are equal, the operation is associative.

Sometimes, if you have two binary operations on a set, such as addition and multiplication for real numbers, you might need to know whether the distributive rule holds. If one operation is denoted by $*$ and the other is denoted by $\circ$, then $*$ is said to be distributive over $\circ$ if $a * (b \circ c) = (a * b) \circ (a * c)$.

> Let $*$ and $\circ$ be two binary operations on a set S. Then $*$ is said to be **distributive** over $\circ$ if $a * (b \circ c) = (a * b) \circ (a * c)$ for all $a, b, c \in S$.

Example 4.1.3
Let $*$ and $\circ$ be defined on $\mathbb{R}$ by $a * b = ab + a + b$ and $a \circ b = a + b + 1$. Investigate whether $*$ is distributive over $\circ$.

Using the definitions,

$$a * (b \circ c) = a * (b + c + 1)$$
$$= a(b + c + 1) + a + (b + c + 1)$$
$$= ab + ac + a + a + b + c + 1$$
$$= ab + ac + 2a + b + c + 1$$

and

$$(a * b) \circ (a * c) = (ab + a + b) \circ (ac + a + c)$$
$$= (ab + a + b) + (ac + a + c) + 1$$
$$= ab + a + b + ac + a + c + 1$$
$$= ab + ac + 2a + b + c + 1.$$

As these two expressions are equal, $*$ is distributive over $\circ$.

You can also define binary operations for sets which have only a finite number of elements.

You can use an **operation table** to show the details of a closed binary operation on a small set. Table 4.1 shows the result of 'last digit arithmetic' on $\{2,4,6,8\}$. For example, $2 \times 8 = 16$ has last digit 6, so $2 \circ 8 = 6$. This is shown in the shaded cell in Table 4.1. Stated formally, the binary operation $\circ$ on the set $\{2,4,6,8\}$ given by $a \circ b$ is the remainder after the product ab is divided by 10.

			Second number		
	$\circ$	2	4	6	8
	2	4	8	2	6
First	4	8	6	4	2
number	6	2	4	6	8
	8	6	2	8	4

Table 4.1

A binary operation can actually be *defined* by an operation table. For example, Table 4.2 defines a binary operation $\circ$ on the set $\{a,b,c\}$.

$\circ$	a	b	c
a	b	a	c
b	a	c	b
c	b	b	a

Table 4.2

You can see immediately that $\circ$ is a binary operation, and also that it is closed, because Table 4.2 shows the result of every possible combination of two members of the set.

Operation tables are also called **Cayley tables**, after the Englishman Arthur Cayley, 1821–1895. If each element appears exactly once in each row and column, the table is said to be a **Latin square**.

You can also tell quickly from an operation table if a binary operation is commutative by looking for symmetry about the leading diagonal from top left to bottom right. Table 4.2 is not symmetrical since $c \circ a = b$ and $a \circ c = c$ and therefore the operation is not commutative.

Without detailed checking you can't tell from a table whether a binary operation is associative. It is usually easier to exploit some other knowledge you may have about what is described by the table.

1 Decide which of the following operations are binary operations on the given sets. If an operation is not a binary operation, give one reason. For those which are binary operations, check whether they are closed, commutative and associative.

(a) $-$ on $\mathbb{Z}^+$

(b) matrix multiplication on 2×2 matrices

(c) $\circ$ on $\mathbb{Z}^+$, where $a \circ b = a^b$

(d) $\circ$ on $\mathbb{R}$, where $a \circ b = |a - b|$

(e) $\circ$ on $\mathbb{R}$, where $a \circ b = 0$ for all $a, b \in \mathbb{R}$

(f) $\circ$ on 2×2 matrices where $A \circ B = AB^{-1}$ for all A and B

(g) $\circ$ on $\mathbb{R}$, where $a \circ b = b$ for all $a, b \in \mathbb{R}$

(h) $\circ$ on $\mathbb{R}^+$, where $a \circ b = a^b$

(i) $\circ$ on $\{1, 3, 7, 9\}$, where $a \circ b$ is the remainder when $a \times b$ is divided by 10

(j) $\circ$ on $\mathbb{R}$, where $a \circ b$ is the smallest number greater than $a + b$

2 Let A, B and C be any three subsets of a universal set U. Use Venn diagrams to investigate whether it is true that

(a) $A \cup (B \cap C) = (A \cup B) \cap (A \cup C)$,   (b) $A \cap (B \cup C) = (A \cap B) \cup (A \cap C)$.

3 Let $\mathbb{Z}_5$ be the set $\{0, 1, 2, 3, 4\}$, and define the operations $\otimes$ and $\oplus$ on $\mathbb{Z}_5$ as follows.

$x \otimes y$ is the remainder when xy is divided by 5, $x \oplus y$ is the remainder when $x + y$ is divided by 5.

Investigate whether

(a) $\otimes$ is distributive over $\oplus$,   (b) $\oplus$ is distributive over $\otimes$.

4.2 Identity elements

The numbers 0 and 1 in $\mathbb{R}$ are very special. When the operation is addition, the number 0 has the property that

$$a + 0 = 0 + a = a$$

for every number a in $\mathbb{R}$.

Similarly, when the operation is multiplication, the number 1 has the property that

$$a \times 1 = 1 \times a = a$$

for every number a in $\mathbb{R} \setminus \{0\}$.

In each of these examples you have a set S that is closed under a binary operation $\circ$ and an element, often denoted by e, with the property that $a \circ e = e \circ a = a$ for all members of the set S. This element e is called an **identity element** for the set S with the operation $\circ$.

A set with a closed binary operation need not have an identity element.

Example 4.2.1
Show that the set $\mathbb{Z}$ with the operation of subtraction does not have an identity element.

The element 0 is the only element with the property that $a - 0 = a$ for every $a \in \mathbb{Z}$, but as $0 - a = -a$, 0 is not an identity element for $\mathbb{Z}$ under subtraction.

Example 4.2.2
Find the identity element in $\mathbb{R} \setminus \{1\}$ with the binary operation $a \circ b = a + b - ab$.

Let e be an identity element with this binary operation.

$$a \circ e = a \quad \Leftrightarrow \quad a + e - ae = a$$
$$\Leftrightarrow \quad e - ae = 0$$
$$\Leftrightarrow \quad e(1 - a) = 0.$$

For this to be true for all a in $\mathbb{R} \setminus \{1\}$, you need $e = 0$.

As $a \circ b = b \circ a$, there is no need to check separately that $e \circ a = a$.

4.3 Inverse elements

Consider again the two numbers discussed at the beginning of Section 4.2, that is 0 and 1 in $\mathbb{R}$.

For each number $a \in \mathbb{R}$, there exists a number $(-a) \in \mathbb{R}$ such that

$$(-a) + a = a + (-a) = 0.$$

For each number $\mathbb{R} \setminus \{0\}$, there exists a number $a^{-1} \in \mathbb{R} \setminus \{0\}$ such that

$$a^{-1} \times a = a \times a^{-1} = 1.$$

In ordinary algebraic notation these statements look quite different, but $\mathbb{R}$ and $\mathbb{R} \setminus \{0\}$ are both examples of a set S closed under a binary operation $\circ$, with an identity element e. The two statements mean that for each element a in S there exists an element b with the property that $a \circ b = b \circ a = e$. This element b is called an **inverse** of a.

Example 4.3.1
Find an inverse of a in $\mathbb{R} \setminus \{1\}$ with the binary operation $a \circ b = a + b - ab$.

In Example 4.2.2, it was shown that the identity element is 0.

$$b \circ a = e \quad \Leftrightarrow \quad b + a - ba = 0 \quad \Leftrightarrow \quad b = \frac{a}{a - 1}$$

so, as $a \neq 1$, $\dfrac{a}{a - 1}$ is an inverse of a.

As $a \circ b = b \circ a$, there is no need to check separately that $a \circ b = e$.

Example 4.3.2
In Table 4.1, find the identity element and the inverse of 8.

The identity element e is given by $2 \circ e = 2$, $4 \circ e = 4$, $6 \circ e = 6$ and $8 \circ e = 8$. From the table $e = 6$.

The inverse of 8, 8^{-1}, is given by $8^{-1} \circ 8 = e = 6$. From the table, $2 \circ 8 = 6$, so $8^{-1} = 2$.

Summarising the discussion in this and the previous section gives the following:

> Let S be a set with a closed binary operation $\circ$.
>
> If there exists an element $e \in S$ such that, for all $a \in S$, $e \circ a = a \circ e = a$, then e is an **identity element** for S with the operation $\circ$.
>
> If for each element $a \in S$ there exists an element $b \in S$ such that $b \circ a = a \circ b = e$, where e is an identity element for S, then b is called an **inverse** of a in S with the operation $\circ$.

Exercise 4B

1 In each of these operation tables, identify the products $s \circ t$, $t \circ s$, $(p \circ q) \circ s$ and $p \circ (q \circ t)$, find the identity element and the inverse of s. Find also the solution for the equations $x \circ t = s$ and $u \circ y = t$.

	p	q	r	s	t	u
p	q	r	p	t	u	s
q	r	p	q	u	s	t
r	p	q	r	s	t	u
s	u	t	s	r	p	q
t	s	u	t	q	r	p
u	t	s	u	p	q	r

	p	u	s	r	q	t
p	r	t	q	p	u	s
u	q	s	r	u	t	p
s	t	r	u	s	p	q
r	p	u	s	r	q	t
q	s	p	t	q	r	u
t	u	q	p	t	s	r

2 In each part of this question a set with a closed binary operation is given. Find the identity element, if it exists, and if it does exist, find the inverse of a general element a, if it exists.

  (a) Vectors with 3 components: vector product

  (b) 2×2 matrices: matrix multiplication

  (c) $\mathbb{C}$: multiplication

  (d) $\mathbb{R}$: $\circ$ where $a \circ b = |a - b|$

  (e) $\mathbb{R}$: $\circ$ where $a \circ b = b$ for all $a, b \in \mathbb{R}$

3 In each part of this question a set with a closed binary operation is given. Find the identity element, if it exists, and if it does exist, find the inverse of a general element a, if it exists.

  (a) The set of matrices of the form $\begin{pmatrix} x & x \\ 0 & 0 \end{pmatrix}$, where $x \in \mathbb{R} \setminus \{0\}$: matrix multiplication

  (b) $\{2,4,6,8\}$: $\circ$ where $a \circ b$ is the remainder when $a \times b$ is divided by 10

  (c) $\{0,2,4,6,8\}$: $\circ$ where $a \circ b$ is the remainder when $a + b$ is divided by 10

  (d) $\{1,3,7,9\}$: $\circ$ where $a \circ b$ is the remainder when $a \times b$ is divided by 10

4.4   Groups

You have seen that sets with binary operations can be distinguished by various properties: the binary operations may or may not be closed or associative, and the sets may or may not have identity and inverse elements. Sets with binary operations which are associative and have identity and inverse elements are especially important.

> A set G, with a binary operation $\circ$, is called a **group** if it has four properties, called **axioms**.
>
> 1 **Closure**: $a \circ b \in G$ for all $a, b \in G$; that is, the operation is closed.
>
> 2 **Associativity**: $a \circ (b \circ c) = (a \circ b) \circ c$ for all $a, b, c \in G$; that is, the binary operation is associative.
>
> 3 **Identity**: there exists an identity element $e \in G$ such that for all $a \in G$, $e \circ a = a \circ e = a$.
>
> 4 **Inverse**: for each element $a \in G$, there exists an inverse element $b \in G$ such that $b \circ a = a \circ b = e$.
>
> The group G with binary operation $\circ$ is denoted by $(G, \circ)$.

Notice that a group operation need not be commutative.

It is an important fact that there is only one element $e \in G$ with the property that for all $a \in G$, $e \circ a = a \circ e = a$. Once you know that there is only one such element, you can call it *the* identity element for $(G, \circ)$. Similarly, given an element $a \in G$, there is only one inverse element $b \in G$ such that $b \circ a = a \circ b = e$, so you can talk about *the* inverse of a. The notation a^{-1} is used for the inverse of a.

These facts about the uniqueness of the identity and the uniqueness of the inverse for each element are proved at end of the section (see Theorem 4.2). Assume them for now.

Groups may have a finite or an infinite number of elements. Examples of infinite groups are $(\mathbb{Z}, +)$, $(\mathbb{R} \setminus \{0\}, \times)$ and $(\{z \mid z \in \mathbb{C}, |z| = 1\}, \times)$. The set in Example 4.4.1 is an example of a finite group.

> The number of elements in a group is called its **order**.
>
> If a group has an infinite number of elements, it is said to have **infinite order**.

To prove that a set with an infinite number of elements is a group, you cannot use arguments based on operation tables.

Example 4.4.1
Prove that the set $\{1, i, -1, -i\}$ with the operation of multiplication is a group.

For a set as small as this, it is often easiest to show that the binary operation is closed by using a table.

Table 4.3 shows the operation table for the set $\{1, i, -1, -i\}$.

$\times$	1	i	-1	$-i$
1	1	i	-1	$-i$
i	i	-1	$-i$	1
-1	-1	$-i$	1	i
$-i$	$-i$	1	i	-1

Table 4.3

To show that the set is a group, there are four properties to establish, namely the four group axioms.

1   **Closure**: The table shows that the operation of multiplication is closed since every possible product is a member of the set $\{1, i, -1, -i\}$.

2   **Associativity**: Multiplication of complex numbers is associative, so multiplication of these elements is associative.

3   **Identity**: The element 1 is the identity element, since $1 \times z = z \times 1 = z$ for every complex number z.

4   **Inverse**: The inverses of 1, -1, i and $-i$ are 1, -1, $-i$ and i respectively, so every element has an inverse which is in the set $\{1, i, -1, -i\}$.

Therefore $\{1, i, -1, -i\}$ with the operation of multiplication is a group.

The row corresponding to the identity element is the same as the row of 'column labels' at the top of the operation table; the column corresponding to the identity element is the same as the column of 'row labels' at the left of the table.

You may have noticed that each element of the group in Table 4.3 appears just once in every row and once in every column, that is, its operation table is a Latin square. This is necessary for a group, as the following theorem shows. However, for a group to have a group table it must be finite.

Theorem 4.1   In the operation table for a finite group, each element appears just once in every row.

In the following argument, a very brief justification is given for each step by referring to one of the group axioms.

Proof
The elements which appear in a row are those of the form $a \circ x$ where a is fixed and x ranges over the elements of the group. Suppose that two elements in a row are the same. Then $a \circ x = a \circ y$ for some x and y, with $x \neq y$. Therefore

$$a \circ x = a \circ y \;\; \Rightarrow \;\; a^{-1} \circ (a \circ x) = a^{-1} \circ (a \circ y) \quad \text{(inverse } a^{-1} \text{ exists)}$$
$$\Rightarrow \;\; \left(a^{-1} \circ a\right) \circ x = \left(a^{-1} \circ a\right) \circ y \quad \text{(associative property)}$$
$$\Rightarrow \;\; e \circ x = e \circ y \quad\quad\quad\quad\quad \text{(property of inverse)}$$
$$\Rightarrow \;\; x = y. \quad\quad\quad\quad\quad\quad\;\; \text{(property of identity)}$$

This is a contradiction, so no element appears more than once in each row.

So, if there are n elements in the group, then there are n elements in the row of the group table, which must all be different. Therefore each element appears just once in each row.

The proof for columns is left to you in Exercise 4C Question 5.

Theorem 4.1 has no meaning for infinite groups, because you can't draw up a table, but the part of the theorem which involves the cancelling argument that

$$a \circ x = a \circ y \;\; \Rightarrow \;\; x = y$$

is valid for infinite groups.

Suppose that a and b are known and that you want to solve the equation $a \circ x = b$ for x.

$$a \circ x = b \;\; \Leftrightarrow \;\; a^{-1} \circ (a \circ x) = a^{-1} \circ b \quad \text{(inverse } a^{-1} \text{ exists)}$$
$$\Leftrightarrow \;\; \left(a^{-1} \circ a\right) \circ x = a^{-1} \circ b \quad \text{(associative property)}$$
$$\Leftrightarrow \;\; e \circ x = a^{-1} \circ b \quad\quad\quad \text{(property of inverse)}$$
$$\Leftrightarrow \;\; x = a^{-1} \circ b. \quad\quad\quad\;\; \text{(property of identity)}$$

There are corresponding results if the order of a and x is reversed:

$$x \circ a = y \circ a \;\; \Rightarrow \;\; x = y \quad \text{and} \quad x \circ a = b \;\; \Leftrightarrow \;\; x = b \circ a^{-1}.$$

> In a finite group, each element appears exactly once in each row and each column of the group table.
>
> For any group, $a \circ x = a \circ y \;\; \Rightarrow \;\; x = y$ and $x \circ a = y \circ a \;\; \Rightarrow \;\; x = y$. This is called the **cancellation law**.
>
> For any group, $a \circ x = b \;\; \Leftrightarrow \;\; x = a^{-1} \circ b$ and $x \circ a = b \;\; \Leftrightarrow \;\; x = b \circ a^{-1}$.

Although the operation table for a group is always a Latin square, the reverse is not necessarily true. See Exercise 4C Question 2.

Example 4.4.2

Prove that the set of non-singular 2×2 matrices with the operation of matrix multiplication is a group.

The matrices must be non-singular so that inverse matrices exist.

1   **Closure**: The product of two non-singular 2×2 matrices M and N is a 2×2 matrix MN. As M and N are non-singular, $\det M \neq 0$ and $\det N \neq 0$, and since $\det MN = \det M \det N$, $\det MN \neq 0$, so MN is non-singular. So the operation of matrix multiplication is closed.

2   **Associativity**: Since matrix multiplication is associative the group operation is associative.

3   **Identity**: The 2×2 identity matrix I is non-singular and is a member of the set. It has the property that for any matrix M in the set, $IM = MI = M$.

4   **Inverse**: If M is non-singular, then M^{-1} exists and is non-singular, so there exists an element in the set such that $M^{-1}M = MM^{-1} = I$.

Therefore the set of non-singular 2×2 matrices with the operation of matrix multiplication is a group.

There is an important difference between the groups in Examples 4.4.1 and 4.4.2. In Example 4.4.1 the binary operation is commutative, while in Example 4.4.2 it is not.

In a group $(G, \circ)$, if $a \circ b = b \circ a$ for all $a, b \in G$, the group $(G, \circ)$ is said to be **Abelian** or **commutative**.

The word 'Abelian' is in honour of the Norwegian mathematician Niels Abel (1802–1829).

The next example gives you practice in carrying out calculations in a group. Index notation, which is defined in Section 6.2, is used informally, so that $a^2 = a \circ a$, and so on.

Example 4.4.3

Let $(G, \circ)$ be a group in which $a^3 = e$, $b^2 = e$ and $a \circ b = b \circ a^2$. Show that $b \circ (a^2 \circ b) = a$, $b \circ a = a^2 \circ b$, and simplify the product $(a \circ b)^2$.

Note that, as $a^3 = e$, $a^{-1} = a^2$, and as $b^2 = e$, $b^{-1} = b$.

$$
\begin{aligned}
b \circ (a^2 \circ b) &= b \circ a \circ (a \circ b) && \text{(associative property)} \\
&= b \circ a \circ (b \circ a^2) && \text{(since } a \circ b = b \circ a^2) \\
&= b \circ (a \circ b) \circ a^2 && \text{(associative property)} \\
&= b \circ (b \circ a^2) \circ a^2 && \text{(since } a \circ b = b \circ a^2) \\
&= b^2 \circ a^4 && \text{(associative property)} \\
&= a. && \text{(since } a^3 = e \text{ and } b^2 = e)
\end{aligned}
$$

Since $b \circ (a^2 \circ b) = a$,

$$
\begin{aligned}
b \circ a &= b \circ (b \circ (a^2 \circ b)) && (a = b \circ (a^2 \circ b) \text{ from the first part)} \\
&= b^2 \circ a^2 \circ b && \text{(associative property)} \\
&= e \circ a^2 \circ b && \text{(since } b^2 = e) \\
&= a^2 \circ b. && \text{(} e \text{ is the identity)}
\end{aligned}
$$

Notice the strategy: in the first case, the bs were moved steadily across the expression from right to left using the given result $a \circ b = b \circ a^2$ until the results $a^3 = e$, $b^2 = e$ could be used; the second case was simpler, but only because the first part had already been proved.

Now

$$(a \circ b)^2 = (a \circ b) \circ (a \circ b) \qquad \text{(definition of } (a \circ b)^2)$$
$$= a \circ (b \circ a) \circ b \qquad \text{(associative property)}$$
$$= a \circ (a^2 \circ b) \circ b \qquad (b \circ a = a^2 \circ b \text{ from the second part)}$$
$$= a^3 \circ b^2 \qquad \text{(associative property)}$$
$$= e \circ e \qquad \text{(since } a^3 = e \text{ and } b^2 = e)$$
$$= e. \qquad (e \text{ is the identity)}$$

Here are the important algebraic results about groups and inverses promised earlier in this section. These results will be used continually in the chapters which follow.

Theorem 4.2   A group $(G, \circ)$ has the following properties.

(a)   The identity element for a group $(G, \circ)$ is unique.

(b)   For any $a \in G$, the inverse of a is unique.

(c)   For $a, b \in G$, if $a \circ b = e$, then $a = b^{-1}$ and $b = a^{-1}$ and $b \circ a = e$.

(d)   For $a, b \in G$, $(a \circ b)^{-1} = b^{-1} \circ a^{-1}$.

(e)   For $a \in G$, $\left(a^{-1}\right)^{-1} = a$.

One strategy for showing that an element is unique is to suppose that there are two such elements, and then to prove that they must be the same.

Proof

(a)   Suppose that there are two identity elements, e and f.
Since e is an identity, $e \circ a = a$ for any a.
Putting $a = f$ gives $e \circ f = f$.

Since f is an identity, $a \circ f = a$.
Putting $a = e$ gives $e \circ f = e$.

Therefore $f = e$, and the identity element for a group is unique.

(b)   Suppose that a has two inverses, b and c.
Then $a \circ b = b \circ a = e$ and $a \circ c = c \circ a = e$.

So

$$c = c \circ e \qquad (e \text{ is the identity)}$$
$$= c \circ (a \circ b) \qquad \text{(since } a \circ b = e)$$
$$= (c \circ a) \circ b \qquad \text{(associative property)}$$
$$= e \circ b \qquad \text{(since } c \circ a = e)$$
$$= b, \qquad (e \text{ is the identity)}$$

a contradiction, which shows that the inverse of a is unique.

(c)   To prove $a = b^{-1}$, multiply $a \circ b = e$ on the right by b^{-1}. Then

$$a \circ b = e \;\Rightarrow\; (a \circ b) \circ b^{-1} = e \circ b^{-1} \qquad \text{(associative \& identity properties)}$$
$$\Rightarrow\; a \circ \left(b \circ b^{-1} \right) = b^{-1} \qquad \text{(associative property)}$$
$$\Rightarrow\; a \circ e = b^{-1} \qquad \text{(since } b \circ b^{-1} = e)$$
$$\Rightarrow\; a = b^{-1}. \qquad (e \text{ is the identity)}$$

The proof of the second part, $b = a^{-1}$, is similar. Then

$$b \circ a = b \circ b^{-1} = e. \qquad \text{(since } a = b^{-1})$$

(d)   The proof involves showing that $(a \circ b) \circ \left(b^{-1} \circ a^{-1} \right)$ is e, and using part (c).

$$(a \circ b) \circ \left(b^{-1} \circ a^{-1} \right) = a \circ \left(b \circ \left(b^{-1} \circ a^{-1} \right) \right) \qquad \text{(associative property)}$$
$$= a \circ \left(\left(b \circ b^{-1} \right) \circ a^{-1} \right) \qquad \text{(associative property)}$$
$$= a \circ \left(e \circ a^{-1} \right) \qquad \text{(since } b \circ b^{-1} = e)$$
$$= a \circ a^{-1} \qquad (e \text{ is the identity)}$$
$$= e. \qquad \text{(since } a \circ a^{-1} = e)$$

Then, using part (c) with $a \circ b$ in place of a and $b^{-1} \circ a^{-1}$ in place of b, $(a \circ b)^{-1} = b^{-1} \circ a^{-1}$.

(e)   Since $a \circ a^{-1} = e$, using part (c) with $b = a^{-1}$, $\left(a^{-1} \right)^{-1} = a$.

Exercise 4C

1   Which of the following sets with the given operations are not groups? Give what you believe to be the simplest reason why each is not a group.

(a) $\mathbb{N}$, under addition

(b) $\mathbb{Q}^{+}$, under multiplication

(c) $\{1,2,3,4,5\} : \circ$ where $a \circ b$ is the remainder after ab is divided by 6

(d) $\{1,2,3,4,5,6\} : \circ$ where $a \circ b$ is the remainder after ab is divided by 7

(e) $\{1,2,3,4,5,6\} : \circ$ where $a \circ b$ is the remainder after $a + b$ is divided by 6

(f) $\{0,1,2,3,4,5\} : \circ$ where $a \circ b$ is the remainder after $a + b$ is divided by 6

(g) $\{1,3,5,7,9\} : \circ$ where $a \circ b$ is the remainder after ab is divided by 10

(h)   Rational numbers of the form $\dfrac{m}{2^n}$, where $m, n \in \mathbb{Z}$, under addition

(i)   Rational numbers of the form $\dfrac{m}{2^n}$, where $m, n \in \mathbb{Z}$, under multiplication

(j)   Numbers of the form 2^n, $n \in \mathbb{Z}$, under multiplication

(k)   Matrices of the form $\begin{pmatrix} a & -b \\ b & a \end{pmatrix}$, where $a, b \in \mathbb{R}$, $a^2 + b^2 \neq 0$ under matrix multiplication

(l)   Even integers under addition

2 Show that this table is not a group table.

	e	a	b	c
e	e	a	c	b
a	a	c	b	e
b	c	b	e	a
c	b	e	a	c

3 Let the following functions be defined for the domain $x \in \mathbb{R} \setminus \{0,1\}$.

$$i : x \mapsto x \qquad\qquad p : x \mapsto 1 - x \qquad\quad q : x \mapsto \frac{1}{x} \qquad\qquad r : x \mapsto \frac{1}{1-x}$$

Show that these functions, together with two more functions which you should find, form a group under composition of functions.

4 Prove that in a finite group table, each element appears just once in every column.

5 Prove that $(\mathbb{Z} \setminus \{0\}, \times)$ is not a group.

6 A group G has four elements. Three of these are e (the identity), a and b. Give reasons why the element $a \circ b$ cannot be equal to e, to a or to b.

7 Prove that the set of nth roots of unity forms a group under multiplication.

8 Show that functions of the form $f(x) = ax + b$, where $a, b \in \mathbb{R}$ and $a \neq 0$, form a group under the operation of composition of functions. What is the inverse of $x \mapsto ax + b$?

9 Let $(G, \circ)$ be a group in which $a^4 = e$, $b^2 = e$ and $a \circ b = b \circ a^3$.
Show that $b \circ a = a^3 \circ b$, $b \circ (a^2 \circ b) = a^2$, and simplify the product $(a \circ b) \circ (a^2 \circ b)$.

10 Consider the set $(\mathbb{R} \times \mathbb{R}) \setminus \{0,0\}$ with the binary operation $\circ$ defined by

$$(a,b) \circ (c,d) = (ad + bc, bd - ac).$$

Show that this set with this operation is a group.

11 Let $(G, \circ)$ and $(H, *)$ be groups, and consider the set $G \times H$ with the binary operation $\times$ defined by $(g_1, h_1) \times (g_2, h_2) = (g_1 \circ g_2, h_1 * h_2)$. Show that $G \times H$ with this operation is a group.

5 Some examples of groups

This chapter introduces you to a variety of groups. When you have completed it, you should

- know that the integers modulo n under addition form a group
- know the groups of symmetries of an equilateral triangle, rectangle and square
- know that permutations form a group.

5.1 Modular arithmetic and addition

Modular arithmetic is a kind of 'arithmetic with remainders'. When you divide a natural number by n, the remainder is one of the numbers $0, 1, 2, \dots, n-1$. So consider the set $\mathbb{Z}_n = \{0, 1, 2, \dots, n-1\}$ with the following rule for combining the elements:

$a \oplus b$ is the remainder when $a + b$ is divided by n.

To show that $\mathbb{Z}_n$ with this rule is a group, use the axioms in Section 4.4.

1   **Closure:** As the remainder after division by n belongs to $\mathbb{Z}_n$, the operation is closed.

2   **Associativity:** Suppose that $a + b = nr + x$, where $x \in \mathbb{Z}_n$, and $x + c = ns + y$, where $y \in \mathbb{Z}_n$.

Then $x = a \oplus b$, and $y = x \oplus c = (a \oplus b) \oplus c$.

Now
$$
\begin{aligned}
(a + b) + c &= (nr + x) + c \\
&= nr + (x + c) \\
&= nr + (ns + y) \\
&= (nr + ns) + y \\
&= n(r + s) + y,
\end{aligned}
$$

so $y = (a \oplus b) \oplus c$ is the remainder when $(a + b) + c$ is divided by n.

Similarly, $a \oplus (b \oplus c)$ is the remainder when $a + (b + c)$ is divided by n.

But $(a + b) + c = a + (b + c)$, so $(a \oplus b) \oplus c = a \oplus (b \oplus c)$.

3   **Identity:** The number 0 acts as the identity since $a \oplus 0 = 0 \oplus a = a$ for all $a \in \mathbb{Z}_n$.

4   **Inverse:** If $a = 0$, consider 0. Then $0 \oplus 0 = 0$, so 0 is the inverse of 0.

Now consider $a \neq 0$, where $a \in \mathbb{Z}_n$. Consider $n - a$.

As $n > n - a > 0$, $n - a \in \mathbb{Z}_n$; and $(n - a) \oplus a = ((n - a) + a) - n = 0$ and $a \oplus (n - a) = (a + (n - a)) - n = 0$.

Therefore $n - a$ is the inverse of a.

Therefore $\mathbb{Z}_n$ with this rule is a group.

The group is called $(\mathbb{Z}_n, \oplus)$, the group of **integers modulo n (mod n) under addition**, and the operation is sometimes written as $+ (\mathrm{mod}\, n)$.

Notice that, now that the basic properties of modular arithmetic have been established, there is no need to go on using the 'ringed' addition sign. You can use the ordinary addition sign without ambiguity, and write $(\mathbb{Z}_n,+)$.

The word 'modulo' is used in a totally different way from the word 'modulus'.

Example 5.1.1
Find the remainder when the numbers 23 and −23 are written in modulo 4 .

$23 = 5 \times 4 + 3$, so the remainder is 3.

$-23 = (-6) \times 4 + 1$, so the remainder is 1.

Example 5.1.2
(a) Write out the group table for $(\mathbb{Z}_4,+)$.   (b) Solve the equations $x + 1 = 0$ and $2 + y = 1$.

(a)

+	0	1	2	3
0	0	1	2	3
1	1	2	3	0
2	2	3	0	1
3	3	0	1	2

Table 5.1

(b)   From Table 5.1, the inverse of 1 is 3, so

$$(x+1)+3 = 0+3$$
$$x+(1+3) = 0+3$$
$$x+0 = 3$$
$$x = 3.$$

The inverse of 2 is 2, so

$$2+(2+y) = 2+1$$
$$(2+2)+y = 3$$
$$0+y = 3$$
$$y = 3.$$

5.2* Modular arithmetic and multiplication

If you wish you can omit the theory of this section. However in order to do some of the exercises, you will need to know that $(\mathbb{Z}_p \setminus \{0\}, \times)$, where p is prime, is a group.

As well as doing modular arithmetic with addition, you can also do it with multiplication, using the definition

$a \otimes b$ is the remainder when ab is divided by n.

However, there are two important differences between multiplication and addition.

- The number 0 has the property that $0 \times a = a \times 0 = 0$ for all $a \in \mathbb{Z}_n$. It follows that $(\mathbb{Z}_n, \otimes)$ cannot be a group, since 0 does not have an inverse. So it is best to consider $\mathbb{Z}_n \setminus \{0\}$, that is the set $\{1, 2, \ldots, n-1\}$.

- If n is not prime, then $(\mathbb{Z} \setminus \{0\}, \otimes)$ is not closed. For example, in $\mathbb{Z}_6$, $2 \otimes 3 = 0$ which is not in $\mathbb{Z}_6 \setminus \{0\}$. So you can only get a group if n is a prime number.

So consider the set $\mathbb{Z}_p \setminus \{0\} = \{1, 2, \ldots, p-1\}$, where p is a prime number.

1   **Closure**: Since the remainder after division by p belongs to $\mathbb{Z}_n \setminus \{0\}$, the operation is closed.

Note that the remainder cannot be 0 because that would mean that $ab = xp$ and as the right side is divisible by p, the left side is also divisible by p. But $0 < a, b \leq p-1$ so this is impossible.

2   **Associativity**: Let $ab = pr + x$, where $x \in \mathbb{Z}_p \setminus \{0\}$, and $xc = ps + y$ where $y \in \mathbb{Z}_p \setminus \{0\}$.

Then $x = a \otimes b$, and $y = x \otimes c = (a \otimes b) \otimes c$.

Now $(ab)c = (pr + x)c$
$$= (pr)c + (xc)$$
$$= p(rc) + (ps + y)$$
$$= (p(rc) + ps) + y$$
$$= p(rc + s) + y,$$

so $y = (a \otimes b) \otimes c$ is the remainder when $(ab)c$ is divided by p.

Similarly, $a \otimes (b \otimes c)$ is the remainder when $a(bc)$ is divided by p.

But $(ab)c = a(bc)$, so $(a \otimes b) \otimes c = a \otimes (b \otimes c)$.

3   **Identity**: The number 1 acts as the identity since $a \otimes 1 = 1 \otimes a = a$ for all $a \in \mathbb{Z}_p \setminus \{0\}$.

4   **Inverse**: For $a \in \mathbb{Z}_p \setminus \{0\}$, consider the elements $\{1 \otimes a, 2 \otimes a, \ldots, (p-1) \otimes a\}$.

These elements are all different, since if two of them, say $r \otimes a$ and $s \otimes a$, are equal, then $r \otimes a$ and $s \otimes a$ have the same remainder on division by p.

Suppose that $ra = kp + x$ and $sa = lp + x$ where k and l are integers and $x \in \mathbb{Z}_p \setminus \{0\}$. Then

$$ra - kp = sa - lp,$$

so $$ra - sa = kp - lp,$$

that is,

$$(r - s)a = (k - l)p.$$

Now p divides the right side; so p divides the left side, and must divide either a or $r - s$.

But $a \in \mathbb{Z}_p \setminus \{0\}$, so p does not divide a; and $-(p-1) \leq r - s \leq p-1$, so the only possibility is that $r - s = 0$, or $r = s$.

So no two members of the set $\{1 \otimes a, 2 \otimes a, \dots, (p-1) \otimes a\}$ are equal.

As they are all different, and there are $p-1$ of them, one of them must be 1.

Suppose that $b \otimes a = 1$.

Then $a \otimes b = 1$, from the definition of $\otimes$, so b is the inverse of a.

The proof that the inverse exists is interesting because it does not actually produce the inverse of each element. It only shows that each element must have an inverse.

So $\mathbb{Z}_p \setminus \{0\}$ with this rule is a group which is called $(\mathbb{Z}_n \setminus \{0\}, \otimes)$, the group of **non-zero integers modulo p (mod p) under multiplication**. In order to distinguish this operation from ordinary multiplication, it is sometimes written as $\times (\bmod\, n)$.

Notice that, as for addition, the multiplication sign rather than the 'ringed' multiplication sign is used. Table 5.2 shows $(\mathbb{Z}_5 \setminus \{0\}, \times)$.

$\times$	1	2	3	4
1	1	2	3	4
2	2	4	1	3
3	3	1	4	2
4	4	3	2	1

Table 5.2

From Table 5.2, the inverse of 3 is 2, and vice versa. But if you had to find, say, the inverse of 7 in $(\mathbb{Z}_{59} \setminus \{0\}, \times)$, it would not be so easy.

Example 5.2.1
Find the inverse of 5 in $(\mathbb{Z}_{11} \setminus \{0\}, \times)$.

$2 \times 5 = 10$, $3 \times 5 = 4$, $4 \times 5 = 9$, $5 \times 5 = 3$, $6 \times 5 = 8$, $7 \times 5 = 2$, $8 \times 5 = 7$, $9 \times 5 = 1$.

Since $5^{-1} \times 5 = 1$ and $9 \times 5 = 1$, the inverse of 5 is 9.

You can often use 'brute force' in this way to find inverses in a small group.

Note that in Example 5.2.1, if you want inverses of other elements, things get progressively easier. You now know that the inverse of 5 is 9, so the inverse of 9 is 5. To find 3^{-1} use $5 \times 5 = 3$ to give

$$3^{-1} = (5 \times 5)^{-1} = 5^{-1} \times 5^{-1} = 9 \times 9 = 4,$$

so $3^{-1} = 4$. And this also shows that $4^{-1} = 3$.

If you want 2^{-1}, you need now try only 2, 6, 7, 8 and 10. Once you spot $2^{-1} = 6$, you can deduce from $6 \times 5 = 8$ that

$$8^{-1} = (6 \times 5)^{-1} = 5^{-1} \times 6^{-1} = 9 \times 2 = 7.$$

This leaves 10 as its own inverse.

Example 5.2.2

Construct an operation table for the numbers 1, 5, 7, 11, 13, 17 when combined under the operation $\times\,(\text{mod}\,18)$. Show that these numbers with this operation form a group, and write down the inverse of each element. Solve the equation $13x = 11$.

The operation table is shown in Table 5.3.

$\times\,(\text{mod}\,18)$	1	5	7	11	13	17
1	1	5	7	11	13	17
5	5	7	17	1	11	13
7	7	17	13	5	1	11
11	11	1	5	13	17	7
13	13	11	1	17	7	5
17	17	13	11	7	5	1

Table 5.3

The numbers form a group, because

- the table shows that the operation is a closed binary operation
- the operation is associative, because ordinary multiplication is associative
- the identity is 1
- each element has an inverse; the inverses of 1, 5, 7, 11, 13 and 17 are respectively, 1, 11, 13, 5, 7 and 17.

As the inverse of 13 is 7, multiplying $13x = 11$ by 7 gives $x = 7 \times 11 = 5$.

It is true, but won't be proved here, that the positive integers which are less than n and have no factors in common with n form a group under the operation $\times\,(\text{mod}\,n)$.

██████████████ **Exercise 5A** ██████████████

1 Write out the group table for $(\mathbb{Z}_5, +)$, and write down the inverse of 2. Solve the equations $x + 2 = 1$ and $4 + y = 2$.

2 Write out a group table for $(\mathbb{Z}_7 \setminus \{0\}, \times)$. Write down the inverses of 3 and 4.

3 Write out a table of operations for $(\mathbb{Z}_6 \setminus \{0\}, \times)$. Give one reason why $(\mathbb{Z}_6 \setminus \{0\}, \times)$ is not a group. Give a reason why $(\mathbb{Z}_q \setminus \{0\}, \times)$ is not a group if q is not prime.

4 Construct a combination table for the integers $\{1, 2, 4, 7, 8, 11, 13, 14\}$ under the operation $\times\,(\text{mod}\,15)$. Use your table to solve the equation $13x = 8\ (\text{mod}\,15)$.

5 Solve the equation $13x = 17$ using the operation $\times\,(\text{mod}\,20)$.

6 Calculate 7×9 and 4×15 in $(\mathbb{Z}_{59} \setminus \{0\}, \times)$. Use your answers to find the inverses of

    (a) 4,   (b) 7,   (c) 28,   (d) 49.

7 Construct a combination table for the numbers $\{0,1,2,3,4\}$ under the operation $\oplus$ where $a \oplus b = (a+b+2)(\mathrm{mod}\,5)$, and verify that it is a group table. Write down the identity element and the inverse of each element.

5.3 A group of symmetries

Let **E** be the equilateral triangle ABC shown in Fig. 5.4, and let the lines x, y and z and the points 1, 2 and 3 be fixed in the plane. Define the following transformations of the plane containing **E**.

- X is 'reflect in the line x'.
- Y is 'reflect in the line y'.
- Z is 'reflect in the line z'.
- R is 'rotate by $\frac{2}{3}\pi$ anticlockwise about O'.
- S is 'rotate by $\frac{4}{3}\pi$ anticlockwise about O'.
- I is 'do nothing'.

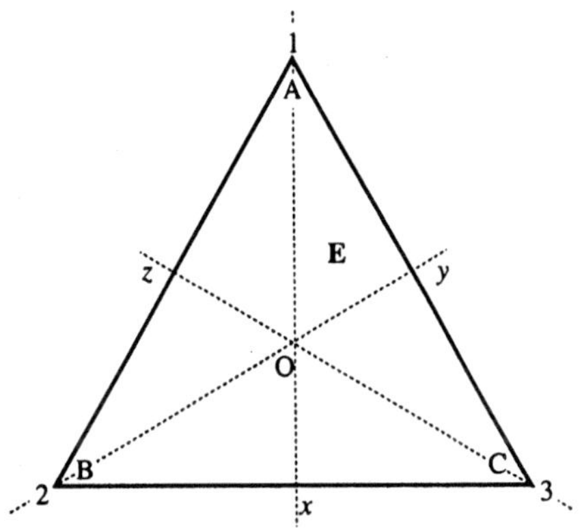

Each of these transformations of the plane leaves the triangle where it is now, although it may change the positions of the vertices which make up the triangle **E**. This kind of transformation is called a **symmetry** of **E**.

Fig. 5.4

You can describe the transformation X by writing

$$\begin{pmatrix} 1 & 2 & 3 \\ A & B & C \end{pmatrix} \xrightarrow{\;X\;} \begin{pmatrix} 1 & 2 & 3 \\ A & C & B \end{pmatrix}$$

where the notation in the first bracket shows that A started in position 1, B in position 2 and C in position 3, and after the transformation by X, A is still in position 1, B is now in position 3 and C is in position 2.

To combine operations use the rule 'followed by', that is the usual rule for combining functions.

The transformation RX (X followed by R) is

$$\begin{pmatrix} 1 & 2 & 3 \\ A & B & C \end{pmatrix} \xrightarrow{\;X\;} \begin{pmatrix} 1 & 2 & 3 \\ A & C & B \end{pmatrix} \xrightarrow{\;R\;} \begin{pmatrix} 1 & 2 & 3 \\ B & A & C \end{pmatrix}$$

which is the same as transformation Z. Thus $RX = Z$. Similarly $SR = I$.

You can make up Table 5.5, which shows how each of the transformations I, R, S, X, Y and Z combines with the others, using the rule 'followed by'. The result is always one of I, R, S, X, Y and Z, so 'followed by' is a closed binary operation on the set $\{I, R, S, X, Y, Z\}$.

In Table 5.5, the result $RX = Z$ is shown by going along the row containing R and down the column containing X.

		First operation performed					
		I	R	S	X	Y	Z
	I	I	R	S	X	Y	Z
Second	R	R	S	I	Z	X	Y
operation	S	S	I	R	Y	Z	X
performed	X	X	Y	Z	I	R	S
	Y	Y	Z	X	S	I	R
	Z	Z	X	Y	R	S	I

Table 5.5

As 'followed by' is the rule of combination of functions, it is associative.

The transformation I is the identity element.

Each element has an inverse. The inverses of I, R, S, X, Y and Z are I, S, R, X, Y and Z respectively.

So the set $\{I, R, S, X, Y, Z\}$ together with the operation 'followed by' is a group. It is called the **dihedral group of the triangle** and is given the symbol D_3. Similar groups are defined for all regular polygons: the symbol for the dihedral group of the n-sided polygon is D_n.

The word 'dihedral' means having or being contained by two plane faces.

━━━━━━━━━━━━━━━━━━━━ **Exercise 5B** ━━━━━━━━━━━━━━━━━━━━

1 Write out the group table for the symmetries of a non-square rectangle. Use X and Y for reflections in the x- and y-axes respectively, and H for half-turn.

2 In the group D_3 in Table 5.5 find the elements R^{-1} and X^{-1}. Calculate the products RAR^{-1} and XAX^{-1} when $A = I, R, S, X, Y$ and Z in turn. Solve for A the equation $RAX = Y$.

3 Write out the group table for D_4, the dihedral group of the square. (Keep this group table for use with Question 4 and future exercises.)
   (Take the origin to be at the centre of the square and let R be an anticlockwise quarter-turn about the origin, and use the notation R^2 and R^3 for the other rotations. Let H and V be reflections in the x- and y-axes, and L and M be reflections in the lines $y = -x$ and $y = x$. Put the operations in the order, I, R, R^2, R^3, H, L, V, M. Your table should then match the one given in the answers.)

4 In D_4 solve for A the equation $RAV = H$. (Use your table from Question 3.)

5.4 Permutations

Suppose that you have a set of four distinct objects. A permutation of these objects is a rearrangement of them among themselves. Thus if the objects are red, white, blue and green counters, then you could permute them by replacing the green counter by the blue one, and vice versa. Or you could replace blue by green, red by blue, and green by red. Both of these are examples of permutations. In practice, it is more convenient to label the four objects 1, 2, 3 and 4. Then the permutation which interchanges blue and green would be 'replace 1, 2, 3, 4 by 1, 2, 4, 3'. This permutation is called

$$\begin{pmatrix} 1 & 2 & 3 & 4 \\ 1 & 2 & 4 & 3 \end{pmatrix}$$

where each number is replaced by the number underneath it, to show that 4 replaces 3 and 3 replaces 4.

Similarly the permutation which replaces 1, 2, 3, 4 by 3, 2, 4, 1 is called

$$\begin{pmatrix} 1 & 2 & 3 & 4 \\ 3 & 2 & 4 & 1 \end{pmatrix}$$

showing that 3 replaces 1, 4 replaces 3 and 1 replaces 4.

Notice that the original order 1, 2, 3, 4 is not important. The permutation $\begin{pmatrix} 4 & 2 & 1 & 3 \\ 3 & 2 & 1 & 4 \end{pmatrix}$ means the same as $\begin{pmatrix} 1 & 2 & 3 & 4 \\ 1 & 2 & 4 & 3 \end{pmatrix}$; both of them show that 4 replaces 3 and 3 replaces 4. Similarly, $\begin{pmatrix} 1 & 2 & 3 & 4 \\ 3 & 2 & 4 & 1 \end{pmatrix}$, $\begin{pmatrix} 4 & 2 & 1 & 3 \\ 1 & 2 & 3 & 4 \end{pmatrix}$, $\begin{pmatrix} 2 & 3 & 4 & 1 \\ 2 & 4 & 1 & 3 \end{pmatrix}$ and $\begin{pmatrix} 2 & 1 & 4 & 3 \\ 2 & 3 & 1 & 4 \end{pmatrix}$ are identical permutations.

If the permutation $\begin{pmatrix} 1 & 2 & 3 & 4 \\ 1 & 2 & 4 & 3 \end{pmatrix}$ is followed by $\begin{pmatrix} 1 & 2 & 3 & 4 \\ 3 & 2 & 4 & 1 \end{pmatrix}$, then the effect is the permutation $\begin{pmatrix} 1 & 2 & 3 & 4 \\ 3 & 2 & 1 & 4 \end{pmatrix}$. It can be useful to consider the two permutations in the product 'above' one another, in the form

$$\begin{pmatrix} 1 & 2 & 3 & 4 \\ 1 & 2 & 4 & 3 \\ 3 & 2 & 1 & 4 \end{pmatrix}.$$

The first two rows show the effect of the first permutation, while the second two rows show the effect of the second permutation. The result of the first permutation followed by the second permutation is the permutation formed by taking the first and last rows, namely $\begin{pmatrix} 1 & 2 & 3 & 4 \\ 3 & 2 & 1 & 4 \end{pmatrix}$, showing that 3 replaces 1, and 1 replaces 3.

5.5 Another look at permutations

You can think of the ideas in Section 5.4 in a different way. Let A be the set $\{1, 2, 3, 4\}$. Then the permutation $\begin{pmatrix} 1 & 2 & 3 & 4 \\ 1 & 2 & 4 & 3 \end{pmatrix}$ is really a bijection of the set A to itself, defined in Fig. 5.6.

In the same way, Fig. 5.7 shows the effect of the permutation $\begin{pmatrix} 1 & 2 & 3 & 4 \\ 3 & 2 & 4 & 1 \end{pmatrix}$.

This leads to the following definition.

A **permutation** of a set A is a bijection from A to A.

1	$\rightarrow$	1
2	$\rightarrow$	2
3	$\rightarrow$	2
4	$\rightarrow$	4

Fig. 5.6

1	$\rightarrow$	3
2	$\rightarrow$	2
3	$\rightarrow$	4
4	$\rightarrow$	1

Fig. 5.7

Looking at it this way, you can see that the composition of permutations described in Section 5.4 is nothing more than the composition of functions from Section 3.6.

For example, returning to the case when $A = \{1, 2, 3, 4\}$, for the permutation $\begin{pmatrix} 1 & 2 & 3 & 4 \\ 1 & 2 & 4 & 3 \end{pmatrix}$ followed by $\begin{pmatrix} 1 & 2 & 3 & 4 \\ 3 & 2 & 4 & 1 \end{pmatrix}$, you could draw the diagram in Fig. 5.8.

$$
\begin{array}{ccccc}
1 & \rightarrow & 1 & \rightarrow & 3 \\
2 & \rightarrow & 2 & \rightarrow & 2 \\
3 & \rightarrow & 4 & \rightarrow & 1 \\
4 & \rightarrow & 3 & \rightarrow & 4
\end{array}
$$

Fig. 5.8

This leads, as before, to the permutation $\begin{pmatrix} 1 & 2 & 3 & 4 \\ 3 & 2 & 1 & 4 \end{pmatrix}$.

You may think that it is easier to think of a permutation as a function, and to use the notation of Fig. 5.8 instead of the bracket notation. You may be right, but the bracket notation is traditional, and a little reflection should convince you that they are equivalent. Moreover, the bracket notation saves space.

It follows immediately the work on functions in Chapter 3 that the set S_A of permutations of a set A under the operation of composition of functions is a group.

In the particular case when A is the finite set $\{1, 2, \dots, n\}$, the group of all permutations of A is called the **symmetric group of degree n**, and is written S_n.

Example 5.5.1

Calculate the result of the permutation $\begin{pmatrix} 1 & 2 & 3 \\ 2 & 3 & 1 \end{pmatrix}$ on three elements followed by the permutation $\begin{pmatrix} 1 & 2 & 3 \\ 3 & 1 & 2 \end{pmatrix}$.

To do this you need to 'chase' each element through both permutations.

In the first permutation $1 \rightarrow 2$, and in the second, $2 \rightarrow 1$, so composing the two permutations gives $1 \rightarrow 1$. Similarly, $2 \rightarrow 3 \rightarrow 2$, and $3 \rightarrow 1 \rightarrow 3$. So the combined permutation is $\begin{pmatrix} 1 & 2 & 3 \\ 1 & 2 & 3 \end{pmatrix}$.

This is the identity permutation, in which each element is mapped to itself. Notice also that the permutations $\begin{pmatrix} 1 & 2 & 3 \\ 2 & 3 & 1 \end{pmatrix}$ and $\begin{pmatrix} 1 & 2 & 3 \\ 3 & 1 & 2 \end{pmatrix}$ are inverse.

The word 'inverse' is used in two senses here, and these two senses coincide. The two permutations, which are bijections, are inverse bijections. And each of them is also the inverse element of the other in the group sense of the word inverse.

Example 5.5.2

Let $x = \begin{pmatrix} 1 & 2 & 3 & 4 & 5 \\ 3 & 1 & 5 & 4 & 2 \end{pmatrix}$ and $y = \begin{pmatrix} 1 & 2 & 3 & 4 & 5 \\ 2 & 3 & 4 & 5 & 1 \end{pmatrix}$. Calculate xy and yx.

Notice how the use of product notation has been slipped into permutations. As usual xy means permutation y followed by permutation x. This notation is consistent with the notation for functions $f(g(a)) = (fg)(a)$.

Chasing through the elements again, for the permutation xy, $1 \to 2 \to 1$, $2 \to 3 \to 5$, $3 \to 4 \to 4$, $4 \to 5 \to 2$, and $5 \to 1 \to 3$. The permutation xy is given by

$$xy = \begin{pmatrix} 1 & 2 & 3 & 4 & 5 \\ 1 & 5 & 4 & 2 & 3 \end{pmatrix}.$$

Similarly, the permutation yx is given by

$$yx = \begin{pmatrix} 1 & 2 & 3 & 4 & 5 \\ 4 & 2 & 1 & 5 & 3 \end{pmatrix}.$$

Notice that for permutations, just as for all functions, xy is not generally equal to yx.

> Composition of permutations of three or more elements is not commutative.

Example 5.5.3

Let $x = \begin{pmatrix} 1 & 2 & 3 & 4 & 5 \\ 3 & 1 & 5 & 4 & 2 \end{pmatrix}$. Find the permutation x^{-1}.

You could do this in one of two ways. You might notice that $x^{-1} = \begin{pmatrix} 3 & 1 & 5 & 4 & 2 \\ 1 & 2 & 3 & 4 & 5 \end{pmatrix}$ and then rearrange the elements in the top row so that they come in the conventional order, at the same time moving the bottom row in a corresponding way.

Thus $x^{-1} = \begin{pmatrix} 1 & 2 & 3 & 4 & 5 \\ 2 & 5 & 1 & 4 & 3 \end{pmatrix}$.

On the other hand, you could chase elements.

Starting with 1, since x takes $1 \to 3$, x^{-1} takes $3 \to 1$. So x^{-1} starts $x^{-1} = \begin{pmatrix} & & 3 & & \\ & & 1 & & \end{pmatrix}$. Then x takes $2 \to 1$, so x^{-1} takes $1 \to 2$. So x^{-1} continues with $x^{-1} = \begin{pmatrix} 1 & & 3 & & \\ 2 & & 1 & & \end{pmatrix}$.

And so on until $x^{-1} = \begin{pmatrix} 1 & 2 & 3 & 4 & 5 \\ 2 & 5 & 1 & 4 & 3 \end{pmatrix}$.

Example 5.5.4

Write out a Cayley table (or group table) for the composition of permutations in S_3.

The possible permutations in S_3 are given by the six possible ways of ordering the numbers a, b and c as 1, 2 and 3 in the second row of the permutation $\begin{pmatrix} 1 & 2 & 3 \\ a & b & c \end{pmatrix}$.

They are therefore the six permutations below.

$$e = \begin{pmatrix} 1 & 2 & 3 \\ 1 & 2 & 3 \end{pmatrix} \quad r = \begin{pmatrix} 1 & 2 & 3 \\ 2 & 3 & 1 \end{pmatrix} \quad s = \begin{pmatrix} 1 & 2 & 3 \\ 3 & 1 & 2 \end{pmatrix}$$

$$x = \begin{pmatrix} 1 & 2 & 3 \\ 1 & 3 & 2 \end{pmatrix} \quad y = \begin{pmatrix} 1 & 2 & 3 \\ 3 & 2 & 1 \end{pmatrix} \quad z = \begin{pmatrix} 1 & 2 & 3 \\ 2 & 1 & 3 \end{pmatrix}$$

The group table for S_3 is shown in Table 5.9.

S_3	e	r	s	x	y	z
e	e	r	s	x	y	z
r	r	s	e	z	x	y
s	s	e	r	y	z	x
x	x	y	z	e	r	s
y	y	z	x	s	e	r
z	z	x	y	r	s	e

Table 5.9

Exercise 5C

1 The permutations a, b and c are taken from S_5.

$$a = \begin{pmatrix} 1 & 2 & 3 & 4 & 5 \\ 5 & 3 & 4 & 1 & 2 \end{pmatrix} \qquad b = \begin{pmatrix} 1 & 2 & 3 & 4 & 5 \\ 2 & 3 & 4 & 5 & 1 \end{pmatrix} \qquad c = \begin{pmatrix} 1 & 2 & 3 & 4 & 5 \\ 5 & 3 & 2 & 4 & 1 \end{pmatrix}$$

Calculate the permutations: ab, ba, a^2b, ac^{-1}, $(ac)^{-1}$, $c^{-1}ac$.

2 Using the permutations from Question 1, solve for x the equations $ax = b$ and $axb = c$.

3 In S_3, let $a = \begin{pmatrix} 1 & 2 & 3 \\ 2 & 3 & 1 \end{pmatrix}$ and $b = \begin{pmatrix} 1 & 2 & 3 \\ 3 & 2 & 1 \end{pmatrix}$.

Calculate the following permutations.

(a) ab
(b) ba
(c) a^{-1}
(d) b^{-1}
(e) aba^{-1}
(f) bab^{-1}
(g) ab^2a^{-1}
(h) ba^2b^{-1}

6 Subgroups

This chapter extends the study of groups by investigating groups within other groups. When you have completed it, you should know

- what is meant by the order of an element
- what is meant by a cyclic group, and how to show that a group is, or is not, cyclic
- what a subgroup is, and how to test for a subgroup
- that the order of a subgroup divides the order of the group
- that the order of an element divides the order of the group
- that all groups of prime order are cyclic.

6.1 Notation

It can be tedious to use the notation $(G, \circ)$ for a group, and it is quite usual to leave out the symbol for the operation and to use multiplicative notation. From now on, provided there is no ambiguity, the symbol G will be used for a group and ab will be used instead of $a \circ b$.

However, in some groups, such as $\mathbb{Z}$, the operation is addition, and then it is usual to retain the $+$ sign. It is a convention that, whenever additive notation is used, the group is commutative. If multiplicative notation is used, the group may be either commutative or not commutative.

Here is an example of a proof in the new notation.

Example 6.1.1
Let G be a group in which every element is its own inverse. Prove that G is commutative.

> Let $a, b \in G$. Then $ab \in G$. As $ab \in G$, it is its own inverse, so $(ab)^{-1} = ab$. But the inverse of ab is $b^{-1}a^{-1}$ so $b^{-1}a^{-1} = ab$, and as $a^{-1} = a$ and $b^{-1} = b$, $ba = ab$. So G is commutative.

6.2 Powers of elements

In Example 4.4.3, you saw that when you multiply an element a of a group G by itself, you obtain aa, which is written as a^2. This leads to the following definition.

> Let a be an element of a group G. If n is a positive integer, then
>
> $$a^n = \overbrace{aa \ldots a}^{n \text{ times}} \quad \text{and} \quad a^{-n} = \overbrace{a^{-1}a^{-1} \ldots a^{-1}}^{n \text{ times}}.$$
>
> The power a^0 is defined to be e.

Many of the usual index rules are satisfied for all integers $m, n \in \mathbb{Z}$, but they require proof. Here are two examples of such proofs. If you wish, you may omit them and assume the results of the next shaded box.

Example 6.2.1*

Show that $a^m a^n = a^{m+n}$ when m is a positive integer and n is a negative integer.

Let $n = -N$, so that N is positive. Then $a^m a^{-N} = \overbrace{aa \ldots aa^{-1}}^{m \text{ times}} \overbrace{a^{-1} \ldots a^{-1}}^{N \text{ times}}$.

Case 1   Suppose that $m > N$. Then

$$a^m a^{-N} = \overbrace{aa \ldots a}^{m \text{ times}} \overbrace{a^{-1} a^{-1} \ldots a^{-1}}^{N \text{ times}} = \overbrace{aa \ldots a}^{(m-N) \text{ times}} = \overbrace{aa \ldots a}^{(m+n) \text{ times}} = a^{m+n}.$$

Case 2   Suppose that $m = N$. Then

$$a^m a^{-N} = \overbrace{aa \ldots a}^{m \text{ times}} \overbrace{a^{-1} a^{-1} \ldots a^{-1}}^{m \text{ times}} = e = a^0 = a^{m-N} = a^{m+n}.$$

Case 3   Suppose that $m < N$. Then

$$a^m a^{-N} = \overbrace{aa \ldots a}^{m \text{ times}} \overbrace{a^{-1} a^{-1} \ldots a^{-1}}^{N \text{ times}} = \overbrace{a^{-1} a^{-1} \ldots a^{-1}}^{(N-m) \text{ times}} = a^{-(N-m)} = a^{m-N} = a^{m+n}.$$

Therefore, in all cases, $a^m a^n = a^{m+n}$ when m is a positive integer and n is a negative integer.

Example 6.2.2*

Show that $a^{-m} = (a^m)^{-1} = (a^{-1})^m$ when m is a positive integer.

From Case 2 above, $a^m a^{-m} = e$, so a^{-m} is the inverse of a^m, that is $a^{-m} = (a^m)^{-1}$.

By definition, $\overbrace{a^{-1} a^{-1} \ldots a^{-1}}^{m \text{ times}} = a^{-m}$; but $\overbrace{a^{-1} a^{-1} \ldots a^{-1}}^{m \text{ times}} = (a^{-1})^m$. So $a^{-m} = (a^{-1})^m$.

Therefore $a^{-m} = (a^m)^{-1} = (a^{-1})^m$ when m is a positive integer.

The results of the above examples, and others like them, are summarised by:

> In a group G, $a^m a^n = a^{m+n}$, $(a^m)^n = a^{mn}$, $a^{-m} = (a^m)^{-1} = (a^{-1})^m$, where m and $n \in \mathbb{Z}$.
>
> In general $(ab)^m \neq a^m b^m$, unless the group G is commutative.

It is clear that in a finite group the powers of an element cannot all be different from each other.

For example, in $(\mathbb{Z}_7 \setminus \{0\}, \times)$,

$$2^2 = 4, \quad 2^3 = 2 \times 4 = 1, \quad 2^4 = 2 \times 1 = 2, \quad 2^5 = 2 \times 2^4 = 2 \times 2 = 4, \quad 2^6 = 2^2 \times 2^4 = 4 \times 2 = 1,$$

and so on.

In D_3 (from Section 5.3) which is reproduced as Table 6.1 in Example 6.2.3,

$$R^2 = S, \quad R^3 = RS = I, \quad R^4 = RI = R, \quad R^5 = RR = S, \quad \text{and so on.}$$

Theorem 6.1   Let a be an element of a finite group G. Then the powers of a cannot all be different, and there is a smallest positive integer k such that $a^k = e$.

Proof

Consider the set of all possible powers of a.

There are infinitely many of them, and all of them are elements of G.

Since G is finite they cannot all be different.

Let r and s be two positive integers, with $r < s$, such that $a^r = a^s$. Then

$$a^{s-r} = a^s a^{-r} = a^r a^{-r} = e.$$

Therefore there is at least one positive power, $s - r$, of a which gives the identity element. Let k be the smallest of these powers, so that $a^k = e$.

There is always a smallest power. See Exercise 6A Question 11.

Let a be an element of a group G. Then a is said to have **finite order** if $a^n = e$ for some positive integer n. The least such n is called the **order** of a.

If no such n exists, the element a has **infinite order**.

'Order' is used quite differently here from its use in the context of 'order of a group'. Some books use the word 'period' instead of 'order' in this context.

Note that, from the definition, in any group the order of the identity e is 1.

Example 6.2.3

Find the orders of the elements of   (a) $(\mathbb{Z}_5, +)$ (b) $(\mathbb{Z}_7 \setminus \{0\}, \times)$,   (c) D_3.

(a)   In $(\mathbb{Z}_5, +)$ use additive notation. The orders of the elements are as follows:

The identity element, 0, has order 1.
As $1 + 1 = 2$, $2 + 1 = 3$, $3 + 1 = 4$, $4 + 1 = 0$, the order of 1 is 4.
As $2 + 2 = 4$, $4 + 2 = 1$, $1 + 2 = 3$, $3 + 2 = 0$, the order of 2 is 4.
As $3 + 3 = 1$, $1 + 3 = 4$, $4 + 3 = 2$, $2 + 3 = 0$, the order of 3 is 4.
As $4 + 4 = 3$, $3 + 4 = 2$, $2 + 4 = 1$, $1 + 4 = 0$, the order of 4 is 4.

(b)   The orders of the elements of $(\mathbb{Z}_7 \setminus \{0\}, \times)$ can be worked out in a similar way:

The identity element, 1, has order 1.
As $2^1 = 2$, $2^2 = 4$, $2^3 = 1$, the order of 2 is 3.
As $3^1 = 3$, $3^2 = 2$, $3^3 = 6$, $3^4 = 4$, $3^5 = 5$, $3^6 = 1$, the order of 3 is 6.
As $4^1 = 4$, $4^2 = 2$, $4^3 = 1$, the order of 4 is 3.
As $5^1 = 5$, $5^2 = 4$, $5^3 = 6$, $5^4 = 2$, $5^5 = 3$, $5^6 = 1$, the order of 5 is 6.
As $6^1 = 6$, $6^2 = 1$, the order of 6 is 2.

(c)   The orders of the elements can be found from the D_3 group table in Table 6.1.

The orders of I, X, Y and Z are respectively $1, 2, 2$ and 2.

Since $R^2 = S$ and $R^3 = RS = I$, the order of R is 3.

Finally $S^2 = R$ and $S^3 = SR = I$, so the order of S is 3.

D_3		First operation performed					
		I	R	S	X	Y	Z
	I	I	R	S	X	Y	Z
Second	R	R	S	I	Z	X	Y
operation	S	S	I	R	Y	Z	X
performed	X	X	Y	Z	I	R	S
	Y	Y	Z	X	S	I	R
	Z	Z	X	Y	R	S	I

Table 6.1

Example 6.2.4
In $(\mathbb{R} \setminus \{0\}, \times)$, give an element of   (a) finite order greater than 1,   (b) infinite order.

(a)   As an element a of finite order has to satisfy the equation $a^n = 1$ and belong to $\mathbb{R} \setminus \{0\}$, the only possibilities are ± 1. Since 1 has order 1 and -1 has order 2, the only example is -1.

(b)   The element 2 has infinite order since $2^n \neq 1$ for any positive integer n.

6.3 Cyclic groups

If G is a group, it is sometimes the case that G consists entirely of the powers of a single element. In this case the group is said to be **generated** by this element.

An example of a finite group of this type is the group of symmetries of an object such as the Manx symbol in Fig. 6.2.

This group consists of the set $\{I, R, R^2\}$, where R is a rotation of $\frac{2}{3}\pi$, together with the operation 'followed by'. Note that R^2, which is a rotation of $-\frac{2}{3}\pi$, is also a generator.

Groups like this are called **cyclic groups**. In the definition of a cyclic group which follows, recall that from the definition of the powers of an element a, $a^0 = e$.

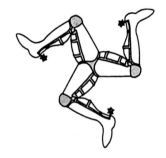

Fig. 6.2

> Let G be a group. If there is an element $a \in G$ such that every element of G has the form a^n for $n \in \mathbb{Z}$, then G is called a **cyclic** group. The element a is called a **generator** for G.

If you can find an element of a group whose order is equal to the order of the group (that is, the number of elements of the group), then it follows that the group is cyclic. One way of showing that a group is not cyclic is to find the order of each element and show that none of them is equal to the order of the group. But there may be simpler ways of showing that a group is not cyclic; for example, if a group is not commutative it can't be cyclic, because all cyclic groups are commutative (why?).

Example 6.3.1
Show that the groups $(\mathbb{Z}_7,+)$ and $(\mathbb{Z}_7 \setminus \{0\},\times)$ are cyclic groups.

To show that $(\mathbb{Z}_7,+)$ is cyclic, you need to interpret the multiplicative notation of the definition of cyclic groups so that you can apply it to a group which uses additive notation.

In $(\mathbb{Z}_7,+)$, 1 is a generator because $1+1=2$, $1+1+1=3$, $1+1+1+1=4$, $1+1+1+1+1=5$, $1+1+1+1+1+1=6$ and $1+1+1+1+1+1+1=0$. As $(\mathbb{Z}_7,+)$ has a generator, it is cyclic.

In $(\mathbb{Z}_7 \setminus \{0\},\times)$, 3 is a generator because its order, 6, is equal to the order of the group (see Example 6.2.3(b)). As $(\mathbb{Z}_7 \setminus \{0\},\times)$ has a generator, it is cyclic.

Note that 5 is also a generator for $(\mathbb{Z}_7 \setminus \{0\},\times)$, but one generator is enough to show it is cyclic.

Example 6.3.2
Show that $(\mathbb{Z},+)$ is a cyclic group.

If an element a is a generator, the group consists of the set of elements $\{...,a^{-3},a^{-2},a^{-1},e,a,a^2,a^3,...\}$. When $a=1$, $a^2=1+1=2$, $a^3=1+1+1=3$ etc., and $a^{-1}=-1$, $a^{-2}=(-1)+(-1)=-2$ etc. Therefore 1 is a generator for $(\mathbb{Z},+)$, and so $(\mathbb{Z},+)$ is a cyclic group.

Note that -1 is also a generator for $(\mathbb{Z},+)$.

Example 6.3.3
Show that the group $(\mathbb{Q}^+,\times)$ is not a cyclic group.

Notice first that 1 is not a generator, since all its powers are 1, and that -1 is not a generator since all its powers are 1 or -1.

Suppose now that x is a generator, where $x \neq 1$ or -1. Then $x^n = -1$ for some value of n, so $|x^n| = |-1| = 1$, giving $|x|^n = 1$. But $x \neq 1$ or -1, so this is a contradiction. So $(\mathbb{Q}^+,\times)$ is not a cyclic group.

Exercise 6A

1 Find the powers of 5 in the group G consisting of the elements 1, 2, 4, 5, 7, 8 where $a \circ b$ is the remainder when ab is divided by 9. How many distinct powers of 5 are there?

2 Find the orders of the elements in the groups
(a) $(\mathbb{Z}_6,+)$, (b) $(\mathbb{Z}_{11} \setminus \{0\},\times)$, (c) D_4 (see Exercise 5B Question 3).
Keep your answer to part (c) for Exercise 6B Question 1.

3 Find all the elements of order 2 in the group of symmetries of a non-square rectangle (see Exercise 5B Question 1.)

4 Find all the elements of order 4 in the group $(\mathbb{C} \setminus \{0\}, \times)$. How many elements of $(\mathbb{C} \setminus \{0\}, \times)$ have order 3?

5 In $(\mathbb{Q} \setminus \{0\}, \times)$, write down all the elements of finite order.

6 Given that the set of non-singular matrices with the operation of matrix multiplication forms a group, show there is an infinite number of elements of order 2.

7 Is the group in Question 1 a cyclic group? Give a reason for your answer.

8 The set $2\mathbb{Z}$ is the set of even integers. Prove that $(2\mathbb{Z}, +)$ is a cyclic group. (You may assume that $(2\mathbb{Z}, +)$ is a group.)

9 The tables below show two groups: one of them is cyclic and one is not. Identify which is which, find all the generators of the cyclic group, and prove that the other group is not cyclic.

	e	a	b	c
e	e	a	b	c
a	a	e	c	b
b	b	c	e	a
c	c	b	a	e

	e	a	b	c
e	e	a	b	c
a	a	b	c	e
b	b	c	e	a
c	c	e	a	b

10 Prove that the groups $(\mathbb{Z}_5, +)$ and $(\mathbb{Z}_6, +)$ are cyclic, and find all their generators.

11* Prove by induction that, in any set of positive integers, there is always a least member.

6.4 Subgroups

Look again at Table 5.5 for the group D_3, reprinted here as Table 6.3 with the title D_3 in the top left corner. Part of the table is shaded; as $S = R^2$, this is the group $\{I, R, R^2\}$ of Fig. 6.2.

D_3	I	R	S	X	Y	Z
I	I	R	S	X	Y	Z
R	R	S	I	Z	X	Y
S	S	I	R	Y	Z	X
X	X	Y	Z	I	R	S
Y	Y	Z	X	S	I	R
Z	Z	X	Y	R	S	I

Table 6.3

The set $\{I, R, S\}$ with the operation 'followed by' is a smaller group inside the whole group; this is called a **subgroup** of D_3.

If you re-drew the table with the elements in the order $\{I, X, R, S, Y, Z\}$ you would find that there is also a small group $\{I, X\}$ in the top left corner. So $\{I, X\}$ is another subgroup of D_3. So too are $\{I, Y\}$ and $\{I, Z\}$.

In addition to these subgroups of D_3, the identity group $\{I\}$, and the whole group $\{I, R, S, X, Y, Z\}$ are also regarded as subgroups of D_3. The subgroups $\{I\}$ and D_3 are called **trivial** subgroups of D_3. The remaining subgroups are called **proper** subgroups of D_3.

> If H is a subset of a group G with operation $\circ$, such that H is a group with operation $\circ$, then H is a **subgroup** of G.
>
> Every group G has two **trivial** subgroups, $\{e\}$ and G itself.
>
> Subgroups of G other than $\{e\}$ and G are called **proper** subgroups.

Example 6.4.1
Explain why $(\mathbb{Q} \setminus \{0\}, \times)$ is not a subgroup of $(\mathbb{Q}, +)$.

Although $\mathbb{Q} \setminus \{0\}$ is a subset of $\mathbb{Q}$, the operations in the two groups are different, so $(\mathbb{Q} \setminus \{0\}, \times)$ is not a subgroup of $(\mathbb{Q}, +)$.

Example 6.4.2
Find all the subgroups of $(\mathbb{Z}_6, +)$, saying which are proper subgroups.

The subgroups are $\{0\}$, $\{0, 3\}$, $\{0, 2, 4, 6\}$ and $\mathbb{Z}_6$ itself. Of these the proper subgroups are $\{0, 3\}$ and $\{0, 2, 4, 6\}$ with the operation of addition modulo 6.

Example 6.4.3
Find a finite proper subgroup and an infinite proper subgroup of $(\mathbb{C} \setminus \{0\}, \times)$.

A finite proper subgroup is $\{1, -1\}$. An infinite proper subgroup is $(\mathbb{R} \setminus \{0\}, \times)$.

Theorem 6.2   Let G be a group, and let H be a non-empty subset of G. Then H is a subgroup of G if

- $a \in H$ and $b \in H \implies ab \in H$
- $e \in H$
- $a \in H \implies a^{-1} \in H$.

Proof

If $a \in H$ and $b \in H \implies ab \in H$, then the operation of G is closed in H.

Suppose that $a, b, c \in H$. Then, since H is a subset of G, $a, b, c \in G$. But the group operation in G is associative, so $(ab)c = a(bc)$. Therefore the operation is associative in H.

Since $ea = ae = a$ for each $a \in G$, $ea = ae = a$ is also true for each $a \in H$.

For $a \in H$, and hence $a^{-1} \in H$, $a^{-1}a = aa^{-1} = e$ because a^{-1} is the inverse of a in G.

Therefore H is a subgroup of G.

Theorem 6.3 shows another way of proving that a non-empty subset H of a group G is a subgroup. It appears easier than the three conditions of Theorem 6.2, but it is less intuitive than Theorem 6.2. Which you decide to use is up to you.

Theorem 6.3   Let G be a group, and let H be a non-empty subset of G. Then H is a subgroup of G if $ab^{-1} \in H$ whenever $a, b \in H$.

Proof
If $a, b \in H \implies ab^{-1} \in H$, then, by writing $b = a$, $aa^{-1} \in H$, so $e \in H$.

If $a, b \in H \implies ab^{-1} \in H$, then, by writing $a = e$ and $b = a^{-1}$,

$$e, a \in H \implies ea^{-1} \in H, \text{ so } a^{-1} \in H. \text{ Similarly, } b^{-1} \in H.$$

So if $a, b^{-1} \in H$, then $a(b^{-1})^{-1} \in H$, so $ab \in H$.

The three conditions of Theorem 6.2 hold, so H is a subgroup of G.

Example 6.4.4
Verify that $(\mathbb{Z}^+ \cup \{0\}, +)$, which satisfies the first two conditions of Theorem 6.2 but not the third, is not a subgroup of $(\mathbb{Z}, +)$.

Since $-1 \notin (\mathbb{Z}^+ \cup \{0\}, +)$, the element 1 in $(\mathbb{Z}^+ \cup \{0\}, +)$ has no inverse, so $(\mathbb{Z}^+ \cup \{0\}, +)$ is not a group and therefore is not a subgroup of $(\mathbb{Z}, +)$.

Example 6.4.5
Prove that $H = \{12x + 21y : x, y \in \mathbb{Z}\}$ is a subgroup of $(\mathbb{Z}, +)$.

As x and y are integers, $12x + 21y$ is an integer, so H is a non-empty subset of $\mathbb{Z}$.

First note that 0 is the identity in $(\mathbb{Z}, +)$ and that $0 = 12 \times 0 + 21 \times 0$ is a member of H.

Method 1   Using Theorem 6.2

If $p, q \in H$, then $p = 12x_1 + 21y_1$ and $q = 12x_2 + 21y_2$ for integers x_1, y_1, x_2 and y_2. So $p + q = (12x_1 + 21y_1) + (12x_2 + 21y_2) = 12(x_1 + x_2) + 21(y_1 + y_2)$ where $x_1 + x_2$ and $y_1 + y_2$ are integers. Therefore $p + q \in H$.

If $p = 12x_1 + 21y_1 \in H$, then $-p = -(12x_1 + 21y_1) = 12(-x_1) + 21(-y_1)$. As $-x_1$ and $-y_1$ are integers, $12(-x_1) + 21(-y_1)$ is also an integer, so $-p \in H$. Also $(-p) + p = p + (-p) = 0$ so $-p$ is the inverse of p. Therefore the inverse of p is a member of H.

Therefore, using Theorem 6.2, H is a subgroup of $(\mathbb{Z}, +)$.

Method 2   Using Theorem 6.3

If $p, q \in H$, then $p = 12x_1 + 21y_1$ and $q = 12x_2 + 21y_2$ for integers x_1, y_1, x_2 and y_2.

Since $0 = 12 \times 0 + 21 \times 0$, and 0 is an integer, $0 \in H$.

If $q = 12x_2 + 21y_2 \in H$, then $-q = -(12x_2 + 21y_2) = 12(-x_2) + 21(-y_2)$. As $-x_2$ and $-y_2$ are integers, $12(-x_2) + 21(-y_2)$ is also an integer, so $-q \in H$. Also $p + (-q) = (-q) + p = 0$ so $-q$ is the inverse of q.

Then $p - q = (12x_1 + 21y_1) + 12(-x_2) + 21(-y_2) = 12(x_1 - x_2) + 21(y_1 - y_2)$ where $x_1 - x_2$ and $y_1 - y_2$ are integers, so $p - q$ is a member of H.

Therefore, using Theorem 6.3, H is a subgroup of $(\mathbb{Z}, +)$.

What is this subgroup? Notice first that any factor of both 12 and 21 divides $12x + 21y$, so the highest common factor of 12 and 21, namely 3, divides every member of H.

If you take $x = 2$ and $y = -1$, you find that $2 \times 12 + (-1) \times 21 = 3$ is a member of H, so H consists of all multiples of 3.

This argument can be generalised to show that for positive integers a and b, $H = \{ax + by : x, y \in \mathbb{Z}\}$ is a subgroup of $(\mathbb{Z}, +)$, and consists of multiples of the highest common factor of a and b.

Subgroups of a finite group

For a finite group G it is usually easy to check from a table whether a subset H is a subgroup. You need only check that the operation on the subset H is closed. For example, in Table 6.3, once you have seen that $\{I, R, S\}$ is closed, you do not need to check the other group properties. This is summarised in the following theorem.

Theorem 6.4   Let G be a group, and let H be a finite subset of G. Then H is a subgroup of G if
$$a \in H \text{ and } b \in H \implies ab \in H.$$

Theorem 6.2 proved that any subset H (not necessarily finite) of G which satisfies

- $a \in H$ and $b \in H \implies ab \in H$
- $e \in H$
- $a \in H \implies a^{-1} \in H$

is a subgroup. So what remains to be proved is that the first condition, which is given, together with the fact that the set H is finite is sufficient to prove the second and third conditions.

Proof

If, in the statement '$a \in H$ and $b \in H \implies ab \in H$', you put $a, a^2, a^3, \ldots$ in turn instead of b, you find that $a^2 \in H$, $a^3 \in H$, $a^4 \in H$ for all positive powers of a. Using Theorem 6.1, let the order of a be k, so $a^k = e$, and $e \in H$.

Now consider a^{k-1}. Since $a^{k-1}a = a^k = e$, a^{k-1} is the inverse of a. But $a^{k-1} \in H$, so $a^{-1} \in H$.

By Theorem 6.2, H is a subgroup of G.

6.5   The subgroup generated by an element

In D_3 the set of powers of R is $\{R, R^2 = S, R^3 = I\}$, that is $\{R, S, I\}$, and you saw in Section 6.4 that this is a subgroup of D_3.

Similarly, in $(\mathbb{Z}_7 \setminus \{0\}, \times)$, the powers of 2 are $\{2, 2^2 = 4, 2^3 = 1\}$ which is a subgroup of $(\mathbb{Z}_7 \setminus \{0\}, \times)$.

Also, in $(\mathbb{Q}, \times)$, the powers of 2, $\{\ldots, 2^{-s}, \ldots, 2^{-1}, 1, 2, \ldots, 2^r, \ldots\}$, form a subgroup.

In fact, the set of powers of an element is always a subgroup.

Theorem 6.5   Let a be an element of a group G. Then the set of all powers of a, $H = \{a^n : n \in \mathbb{Z}\}$ is a subgroup of G.

Proof

If $p, q \in H$, then $p = a^r$ and $q = a^s$ for integers r and s. Then $pq = a^r a^s = a^{r+s}$, and since $r + s$ is an integer, $pq \in H$.

Since 0 is an integer, $a^0 \in H$. And since $a^0 = e$ by definition, $e \in H$.

If $p \in H$, then $p = a^r$ for an integer r. Therefore $-r$ is an integer, and so $a^{-r} \in H$. But $a^{-r}a^r = a^{r-r} = e$, so a^{-r} is the inverse of p, and belongs to H.

Therefore $H = \{a^n : n \in \mathbb{Z}\}$ is a subgroup of G.

This proof applies to both finite and infinite groups.

> The subgroup H of a group G defined by $H = \{a^n : n \in \mathbb{Z}\}$ is said to be the subgroup **generated** by a.

If an element a has infinite order, then the group generated by a is $\{...,a^{-2},a^{-1},e,a,a^2,...\}$ and is infinite.

If an element a has finite order n, then the group generated by a is $\{e,a,a^2,...,a^{n-1}\}$. The order of the subgroup generated by a is then the same as the order of a.

Notice that the subgroup generated by an element is a cyclic subgroup, and that the order of the cyclic subgroup is the same as the order of the generating element.

Exercise 6B

1 (a) Find the orders of the elements of the group D_4 (see Exercise 6A Question 2(c)).

(b) Find the cyclic subgroups of D_4.

(c) Find two proper non-cyclic subgroups of D_4.

2 Find all the subgroups of   (a) $(\mathbb{Z}_4,+)$,   (b) $(\mathbb{Z}_5,+)$.

3 Find all the proper subgroups of S_3 (see Table 5.9).

4 Find a finite subgroup, apart from $\{1\}$, of the group $(\mathbb{R} \setminus \{0\},\times)$.

5 Prove that the set $(\{...,-3n,-2n,-n,0,n,2n,3n,...\},+)$, where $n \in \mathbb{N}$, is a cyclic group.

6 Show that the group of functions $\{x \mapsto ax \mid a \in \mathbb{R}, a \neq 0\}$ is a subgroup of the group $\{x \mapsto ax + b \mid a,b \in \mathbb{R}, a \neq 0\}$ under the operation of composition of functions.

7 Prove that if G is cyclic it is commutative.

8 Let G be a group, and let g be a fixed element of G. Prove that the set of elements which commute with g, that is $H = \{x \in G : gx = xg\}$ is a subgroup of G. Identify H in the following examples.

(a) G is D_3 and g is R.

(b) G is D_3 and g is X.

(c) G is the set of 2×2 matrices under multiplication and g is $\begin{pmatrix} 1 & 1 \\ 0 & 1 \end{pmatrix}$.

(d) G is Q_4 (see Question 9) and g is q.

(e) G is A_4 (see Question 10) and g is x.

9 Find all the subgroups of the quaternion group denoted by Q_4, shown in the table. Keep a note of their orders for the next section.

Q_4	e	a	b	c	p	q	r	s
e	e	a	b	c	p	q	r	s
a	a	b	c	e	s	p	q	r
b	b	c	e	a	r	s	p	q
c	c	e	a	b	q	r	s	p
p	p	q	r	s	b	c	e	a
q	q	r	s	p	a	b	c	e
r	r	s	p	q	e	a	b	c
s	s	p	q	r	c	e	a	b

10 The group A_4 of rotational symmetries of the regular tetrahedron has order 12 and is shown in the table below. Find all the subgroups, and make a note of their orders for the next section. Check that A_4 has no subgroup of order 6.

A_4	e	a	b	c	x	y	z	t	p	q	r	s
e	e	a	b	c	x	y	z	t	p	q	r	s
a	a	e	c	b	z	t	x	y	s	r	q	p
b	b	c	e	a	t	z	y	x	q	p	s	r
c	c	b	a	e	y	x	t	z	r	s	p	q
x	x	t	y	z	p	s	q	r	e	c	a	b
y	y	z	x	t	r	q	s	p	c	e	b	a
z	z	y	t	x	s	p	r	q	a	b	e	c
t	t	x	z	y	q	r	p	s	b	a	c	e
p	p	r	s	q	e	b	c	a	x	z	t	y
q	q	s	r	p	b	e	a	c	t	y	x	z
r	r	p	q	s	c	a	e	b	y	t	z	x
s	s	q	p	r	a	c	b	e	z	x	y	t

6.6 Lagrange's theorem

If you look back at some of the results of Exercise 6B in which you found subgroups of finite groups, and at the examples before Exercise 6B, you find that

- the subgroups of D_3, which has order 6, have orders 1, 2, 3 and 6
- the subgroups of $(\mathbb{Z}_4, +)$, which has order 4, have orders 1, 2 and 4
- the subgroups of $(\mathbb{Z}_5, +)$, which has order 5, have orders 1 and 5
- the subgroups of D_4, which has order 8, have orders 1, 2, 4 and 8
- the subgroups of Q_4, which has order 8, have orders 1, 2, 4 and 8
- the subgroups of A_4, which has order 12, have orders 1, 2, 3, 4 and 12.

You have enough evidence to conjecture that, for finite groups, the order of a subgroup divides the order of the group. This result is called Lagrange's theorem after Joseph-Louis Lagrange (1736–1813).

> **Lagrange's theorem**   Let H be a subgroup of a finite group G. Then the order of H divides the order of G.

Lagrange's theorem is proved in Section 6.7.

Lagrange's theorem has a number of immediate consequences, called **corollaries**.

Corollary 1   The order of an element of a finite group G divides the order of G.

The order of an element a is equal to the order of the subgroup generated by a.

By Lagrange's theorem, the order of a divides the order of the group.

Corollary 2   A group of prime order has no proper subgroups.

If the order of a group G is a prime number, p, by Lagrange's theorem the only possible subgroups will have orders 1 and p.

But these subgroups will be the trivial subgroups consisting of the identity only and the whole group.

Therefore there are no proper subgroups.

Corollary 3   Every group G of prime order p is cyclic.

Consider an element $a \in G$ other than the identity.

As the order of a divides p, and a is not the identity, the order of a must be p itself.

Therefore a is a generator for G, and G is cyclic.

It is tempting to think that the converse of Lagrange's theorem might be true, that if the order of a finite group G has a factor n, then there is a subgroup of G with order n; but this is actually false. A_4, the group with 12 elements in Exercise 6B Question 10, has no subgroup of order 6.

Exercise 6C

1   Use Lagrange's theorem to state the possible orders of subgroups of a group of order 24.

2   Explain why a group of order 15 cannot have a subgroup of order 9.

3   G is a finite cyclic group of order pq, where p and q are prime. What are the possible orders of subgroups of G?

4   Prove that the order of a finite group with at least two elements but no proper subgroups is prime.

5   Let p be a prime number. What are the possible orders of subgroups of $\mathbb{Z}_p \times \mathbb{Z}_p$ and $\mathbb{Z}_p \times \mathbb{Z}_{p^2}$?

6.7* Proof of Lagrange's theorem

You may, if you wish, omit this section.

Let H be a subgroup of a finite group G. The idea of the proof of Lagrange's theorem is to show that the elements of the finite group G can be parcelled up into separate packages, called cosets, one of which is the subgroup H itself. It will turn out that all these packages have the same number of elements as H. Lagrange's theorem then follows easily.

If $a \in G$, then the set $Ha = \{ha : h \in H\}$ is called a **right coset** of H in G.

Example 6.7.1

Find the right cosets of the subgroup $\{I, X\}$ in D_3.

To find the right cosets, write out part of the group table of D_3 with the elements of the subgroup $\{I, X\}$ in the top places in the left column, as shown in Table 6.4.

	I	R	S	X	Y	Z
I	I	R	S	X	Y	Z
X	X	Y	Z	I	R	S

Table 6.4

Each column of the table is a right coset of the subgroup $\{I, X\}$ in D_3.

To see that this is true, notice that the first column consists of the subgroup multiplied on the right by I; the second column consists of the elements $IR = R$ and $XR = Y$, that is the elements I and X of the subgroup $\{I, X\}$ multiplied on the right by R; and so on.

Recall that, as the order in which the elements of a set are written is irrelevant, the set $\{I, X\}$ is the same as the set $\{X, I\}$. Similarly $\{R, Y\} = \{Y, R\}$ and $\{S, Z\} = \{Z, S\}$.

There are three distinct right cosets: $\{I, X\}$, $\{R, Y\}$ and $\{S, Z\}$.

Notice that the elements of the group are divided equally among three cosets.

Example 6.7.2

The group Q_4, called the quaternion group, is shown in Table 6.5. Find the right cosets of the subgroups $H_1 = \{e, b\}$ and $H_2 = \{e, a, b, c\}$.

Q_4	e	a	b	c	p	q	r	s
e	e	a	b	c	p	q	r	s
a	a	b	c	e	s	p	q	r
b	b	c	e	a	r	s	p	q
c	c	e	a	b	q	r	s	p
p	p	q	r	s	b	c	e	a
q	q	r	s	p	a	b	c	e
r	r	s	p	q	e	a	b	c
s	s	p	q	r	c	e	a	b

Table 6.5

Proceed as in Example 6.7.1, and write out just those rows of the group table for Q_4 which contain the elements of the subgroup in the column on the left. This is shown in Table 6.6.

	e	a	b	c	p	q	r	s
e	e	a	b	c	p	q	r	s
b	b	c	e	a	r	s	p	q

Table 6.6

The right cosets of H_1 are $\{e,b\}$, $\{a,c\}$, $\{p,r\}$ and $\{q,s\}$.

Working in the same way with the subgroup $H_2 = \{e,a,b,c\}$ gives Table 6.7.

	e	a	b	c	p	q	r	s
e	e	a	b	c	p	q	r	s
a	a	b	c	e	s	p	q	r
b	b	c	e	a	r	s	p	q
c	c	e	a	b	q	r	s	p

Table 6.7

The right cosets of H_2 are $\{e,a,b,c\}$ and $\{p,q,r,s\}$.

Notice that, for both H_1 and H_2, the order of the subgroup multiplied by the number of cosets gives the order of the group.

Lagrange's theorem follows from the three parts of the following theorem.

Theorem 6.6   Let H be a subgroup of a finite group G. Then

(a) any two right cosets of H in G are either identical or have no elements in common,
(b) all the right cosets of H in G have the same number of elements,
(c) every element of G is in some right coset of H in G.

Proof

(a)   Let a and b be elements of G. Then either b belongs to Ha, or it doesn't.

Case 1 b belongs to Ha. Then $b = ha$ for some $h \in H$. Let x be any element of Hb. Then $x = h_1 b = h_1 ha = h_2 a$, where $h_2 \in H$, since H is a subgroup. But $h_2 a \in Ha$, so $x \in Ha$, and all the elements of Hb are members of Ha.

Case 2 b does not belong to Ha. Then no element of Hb belongs to Ha, since if $h_1 b = h_2 a$, then $b = h_1^{-1} h_2 a = h_3 a$ where $h_3 \in H$, a contradiction.

So either all elements of Hb are in Ha or no elements of Hb are in Ha. Now notice the symmetrical roles of a and b, in the sense that you could also prove that either all elements of Ha are in Hb or no elements of Ha are in Hb. Thus any two right cosets of H in G are either identical or have no elements in common.

(b) G is finite, so H is finite. Let H have n elements, $H = \{h_1, h_2, \ldots, h_n\}$. Then the elements of Ha are $\{h_1 a, h_2 a, \ldots, h_n a\}$. No two of these are the same, since if $h_r a = h_s a$ then $h_r = h_s$ by the cancellation law; so Ha also has n elements. So every right coset of H has n elements.

(c)   Let a be any element of G. Then the coset Ha contains a because $e \in H$ and you can write $a = ea$.

All the bricks are now to hand to prove Lagrange's theorem.

Theorem 6.7 (Lagrange's theorem)   Let H be a subgroup of a finite group G. Then the order of H divides the order of G.

Proof

Let G and H have orders m and n respectively. Then by Theorem 6.6(b), each right coset of H has exactly n elements.

By Theorem 6.6(a), any two of the right cosets either are identical or have no elements in common. Suppose that there are d distinct cosets.

These d cosets therefore account for nd elements of the group G. But part (c) of Theorem 6.6 states that every element of the group is in some coset, so these nd elements account for all the elements of the group. Thus $nd = m$, so n divides m.

Therefore the order of H divides the order of G.

Exercise 6D*

1   Find the right cosets of the subgroups $\{I, R, S\}$, $\{I\}$ and D_3 itself in the group D_3.

2   Find the right cosets of $\{0,3\}$ in $(\mathbb{Z}_6, +)$. (You will have to use additive notation.)

3   The table in Exercise 6B Question 10 shows the group A_4, the symmetry group of the tetrahedron. Find the right cosets of

   (a) $H_1 = \{e, a, b, c\}$,   (b) the subgroup H_2 generated by x.

4   Find the right cosets of the subgroup $\{0, \pm 3, \pm 6, \ldots\}$ of the group $(\mathbb{Z}, +)$.

7 Isomorphisms of groups

This chapter is about groups that are identical to each other as regards their structure. When you have completed it, you should

- know what is meant by isomorphic groups or an isomorphism between groups
- know all the different (non-isomorphic) groups with orders up to 7.

7.1 What are isomorphic groups?

The word 'isomorphic' literally means 'equal in form'. When the word is applied to a pair of groups it means that the groups are structurally the same as each other.

For example, consider the groups $(\mathbb{Z}_4, +)$ and $(\{1, i, -1, -i\}, \times)$ in Tables 7.1 and 7.2.

+	0	1	2	3
0	0	1	2	3
1	1	2	3	0
2	2	3	0	1
3	3	0	1	2

Table 7.1

×	1	i	-1	-i
1	1	i	-1	-i
i	i	-1	-i	1
-1	-1	-i	1	i
-i	-i	1	i	-1

Table 7.2

You can see that these tables, apart from their labelling, are identical. The symbol 1 appears in Table 7.2 in every place that the symbol 0 appears in Table 7.1. Similarly i appears in place of 1, −1 appears in place of 2 and −i in place of 3.

Groups with tables that are related in this way are said to be **isomorphic** to each other. In applying this statement, however, you need to take care. Table 7.3 shows the group $(\{2, 4, 6, 8\}, \times (\mathrm{mod}\,10))$.

×(mod 10)	2	4	6	8
2	4	8	2	6
4	8	6	4	2
6	2	4	6	8
8	6	2	8	4

Table 7.3

×(mod 10)	6	2	4	8
6	6	2	4	8
2	2	4	8	6
4	4	8	6	2
8	8	6	2	4

Table 7.4

You might think that the group defined by this table is not isomorphic to $(\mathbb{Z}_4, +)$, but in fact, it is. The group identity is 6, so try rearranging the elements as in Table 7.4, so that they are in the order 6, 2, 4, 8, with the group identity first. You can now see, by comparing Table 7.4 with Table 7.1, that the group *is* isomorphic to $(\mathbb{Z}_4, +)$.

So tables can be helpful for detecting isomorphisms between small groups, but you must not be misled by the way the elements are arranged in the table. For larger groups, tables are cumbersome to use. For infinite groups, tables cannot be used at all.

However, you can use tables to develop a general definition of isomorphism of groups G and H. The important idea is that to every $a \in G$ in Table 7.5, there corresponds an $A \in H$ in Table 7.6. Moreover, if an element x in G is the product of two elements a and b, that is $x = ab$, an X must appear in the corresponding position in H, as the product of the image of a and the image of b, that is $X = AB$.

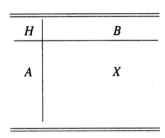

G	b
a	x

Table 7.5

H	B
A	X

Table 7.6

The language of the previous paragraph should remind you of the language of functions in Chapter 3.

Looking again at Tables 7.5 and 7.6, and the paragraph above them, you can define a function $f : G \to H$, such that $f(a) = A$, $f(b) = B$ and $f(x) = X$. You can now write the condition $X = AB$ as $f(x) = f(a)f(b)$, and since $x = ab$, it follows that $f(ab) = f(a)f(b)$.

7.2 A definition of isomorphism

In addition to the condition that $f(ab) = f(a)f(b)$ you would also expect isomorphic finite groups to have the same order. You can make sure that this happens by imposing two conditions: by allowing no spare elements in H which are not the images of elements in G, that is, f is a surjection; and by requiring that different elements of G be sent to different elements of H, that is, f is an injection. Note that since f is both an injection and a surjection, it is a bijection (see Section 3.4). Summarising:

> Two groups $(G, \circ)$ and $(H, *)$ are **isomorphic** if there exists a function $f : G \to H$ such that
>
> - f is a bijection
> - $f(a \circ b) = f(a) * f(b)$ for all $a, b \in G$.
>
> The function $f : G \to H$ is called an **isomorphism**.

The definition looks oddly asymmetrical between the two groups G and H, but it isn't really. If you write $f^{-1} = F$, the definition could be reversed in terms of F by writing $F : H \to G$, with $F(A * B) = F(A)F(B) = a \circ b$.

It is usual to drop the group operation symbols $\circ$ and $*$, and to use multiplicative notation for both groups. Then $f(a \circ b) = f(a) * f(b)$ becomes $f(ab) = f(a)f(b)$.

It is comforting that many of the things that you would expect to be true about isomorphic groups are indeed true.

Here are three important examples.

Theorem 7.1   If $f : G \rightarrow H$ is an isomorphism of G and H, and e is the identity in G, then $f(e)$ is the identity in H. If $a \in G$, then $f\left(a^{-1}\right)$ is the inverse of $f(a)$ in H.

You must expect to use the relation $f(ab) = f(a)f(b)$ somewhere in this proof.

Proof
Let e be the identity in G.

If $a \in G$, then

$$f(e)f(a) = f(ea) \qquad \text{(using } f(ab) = f(a)f(b)\text{)}$$
$$= f(a) \qquad \text{(} e \text{ is the identity in } G\text{)}$$

and

$$f(a)f(e) = f(ae) \qquad \text{(using } f(ab) = f(a)f(b)\text{)}$$
$$= f(a). \qquad \text{(} e \text{ is the identity in } G\text{)}$$

Therefore $f(e)f(a) = f(a)f(e) = f(a)$, so $f(e)$ is the identity in H. Call it e_H.

To prove that $f\left(a^{-1}\right)$ is the inverse of $f(a)$, you must prove that

$$f\left(a^{-1}\right)f(a) = f(a)f\left(a^{-1}\right) = e_H .$$

Starting with $f\left(a^{-1}\right)f(a)$, you find that

$$f\left(a^{-1}\right)f(a) = f\left(a^{-1}a\right) \qquad \text{(using } f(ab) = f(a)f(b)\text{)}$$
$$= f(e) \qquad \text{(as } a^{-1}a = e\text{)}$$
$$= e_H . \qquad \text{(already proved)}$$

Similarly, $f(a)f\left(a^{-1}\right) = e_H$, so $f(a)f\left(a^{-1}\right) = f\left(aa^{-1}\right) = f(e) = e_H$ and the theorem is proved.

Theorem 7.2   If $f : G \rightarrow H$ is an isomorphism of G and H, the order of the element $a \in G$ is the same as the order of $f(a) \in H$.

Proof
Let n be the order of a. Then n is the smallest positive integer such that $a^n = e$. Consider

$$\overbrace{(f(a))^n = f(a)f(a)\ldots f(a)}^{n \text{ of these}} \qquad \text{(by definition of } n\text{th power)}$$
$$= f(aa\ldots a) \qquad \text{(using } f(ab) = f(a)f(b)\text{)}$$
$$= f\left(a^n\right) \qquad \text{(by definition of } n\text{th power)}$$
$$= f(e) \qquad \text{(the order of } a \text{ is } n\text{)}$$
$$= e_H .$$

But is n the *least* positive integer such that $(f(a))^n = e_H$?

Suppose that the order of $f(a)$ is m where $m < n$. Then $(f(a))^m = e_H$.

As $f(a^m) = (f(a))^m = e_H$, there are two elements, a^n and a^m, with image e_H.

But $a^n \neq a^m$, since $a^n = e$ and n is the smallest positive integer such that $a^n = e$ and $m < n$.

This contradicts the fact that the isomorphism $f : G \to H$ is one-to-one.

Therefore the order of $a \in G$ is the same as the order of $f(a) \in H$.

This theorem is particularly useful for proving that two groups are not isomorphic. Just look at the elements of each group and find their orders. If they don't match, the groups are not isomorphic.

The converse of this result is false. You can have two groups G and H of the same order and set up a function $f : G \to H$ such that the range of f is H, f is one-to-one and elements of G and their images in H have the same orders, but G and H are not isomorphic. The order of the lowest example is 16.

Example 7.2.1
Prove that $(\mathbb{Z}_6, +)$ is not isomorphic to D_3.

The elements $0, 1, 2, 3, 4, 5 \in \mathbb{Z}_6$ have orders $1, 6, 3, 2, 3, 6$ respectively.

The elements $I, R, R^2, X, Y, Z \in D_3$ have orders $1, 3, 3, 2, 2, 2$ respectively.

Therefore the groups are not isomorphic.

Example 7.2.2
Prove that $(\mathbb{R}, +)$ is not isomorphic to $(\mathbb{C} \setminus \{0\}, \times)$.

The only element of finite order in $(\mathbb{R}, +)$ is 0, which has order 1. In $(\mathbb{C} \setminus \{0\}, \times)$ the element -1 has order 2. Therefore the groups are not isomorphic.

Theorem 7.3 (a) Every infinite cyclic group is isomorphic to $(\mathbb{Z}, +)$.
(b) Every finite cyclic group of order n is isomorphic to $(\mathbb{Z}_n, +)$.

To prove that two groups are isomorphic, produce a function from the first group to the second, and show that the function is an isomorphism.

Proof
For both parts (a) and (b), the method is to take a generator a of the cyclic group G, and to define a function $f : \mathbb{Z} \to G$ or $f : \mathbb{Z}_n \to G$ such that $f(r) = a^r$. Then every element of G is the image of some element of $\mathbb{Z}$ or $\mathbb{Z}_n$, so that the range of f is G.

(a) **Infinite case**
To prove that f is injective, suppose that $f(r) = f(s)$ with $r > s$.

Then $a^r = a^s$, so $a^{r-s} = e$ for $r - s \neq 0$.

But this contradicts the fact that G is an infinite cyclic group, so f is injective.

To prove that $f(r + s) = f(r)f(s)$, consider first $f(r + s) = a^{r+s}$.

But $a^{r+s} = a^r a^s = f(r)f(s)$, so $f : \mathbb{Z} \to G$ is an isomorphism.

(b)   **Finite case**

Let the order of G be n. Define $f : \mathbb{Z}_n \to G$ by $f(r) = a^r$ for $0 \le r < n$.

To prove that f is injective, suppose that $f(r) = f(s)$ with $r > s$.

Then $a^r = a^s$, so $a^{r-s} = e$.

But as $0 \le s < r < n$, then $0 < r - s < n$, which contradicts the fact that n is the order of G.

Therefore f is injective.

Finally, to prove that $f(r + s) = a^{r+s}$ there are two cases to consider. Notice first that $0 \le r + s < 2n$, so that either $0 \le r + s < n$ or $n \le r + s < 2n$.

If $0 \le r + s < n$, then $f(r + s) = a^{r+s} = a^r a^s = f(r)f(s)$.

However, if $n \le r + s < 2n$, then the sum of r and s in $\mathbb{Z}_n$ is $r + s - n$, so

$$f(r + s) = f(r + s - n) = a^{r+s-n} = a^r a^s e = a^r a^s = f(r)f(s).$$

Therefore $f : \mathbb{Z}_n \to G$ is an isomorphism.

This theorem says that cyclic groups of a given order are isomorphic. This is sometimes stated as, 'there is only one cyclic group of a given order, up to isomorphism'.

Example 7.2.3
Prove that the following groups are isomorphic to each other.
(a) Rotational symmetries of a wheel with 10 equally spaced spokes
(b) $(\mathbb{Z}_{11} \setminus \{0\}, \times)$
(c) $(\mathbb{Z}_{10}, +)$
(d) 10th roots of unity under multiplication

The groups are all cyclic. Possible generators are (a) rotation through $\frac{1}{5}\pi$, (b) 2, (c) 1, (d) $\exp\left(\frac{1}{5}\pi i\right)$.

The groups all have 10 elements, so they are isomorphic.

Example 7.2.4
Prove that the subgroup $\{0, \pm 2, \pm 4, \pm 6, ...\}$ of $(\mathbb{Z}, +)$ is isomorphic to $(\mathbb{Z}, +)$.

Method 1   The subgroup $\{0, \pm 2, \pm 4, \pm 6, ...\}$ is infinite, and 2 is a generator, so by Theorem 7.3(a) it is isomorphic to $(\mathbb{Z}, +)$.

Method 2   Consider the function $f : \mathbb{Z} \to \{0, \pm 2, \pm 4, \pm 6, ...\}$ defined by $f(n) = 2n$.

To prove that f is injective, suppose that $f(i) = f(j)$. Then $2i = 2j$, so $i = j$.

To prove that f is surjective, suppose that there is an element $n \in \{0, \pm 2, \pm 4, \pm 6, ...\}$ which is not the image of an element of $\mathbb{Z}$. Since $n \in \{0, \pm 2, \pm 4, \pm 6, ...\}$ this element is of the form $n = 2m$ for some integer m, so $f(m) = 2m = n$, and f is surjective.

Hence f is an injection and a surjection, and so it is a bijection.

Finally, $f(i + j) = 2(i + j) = 2i + 2j = f(i) + f(j)$, so f is an isomorphism.

Exercise 7A

1 Show that the group $(\{1,-1\},\times)$ is isomorphic to $(\mathbb{Z}_2,+)$.

2 Use the function $f(x)=e^x$ to show that $(\mathbb{R},+)$ is isomorphic to $(\mathbb{R}^+,\times)$.

3 Show that $(\mathbb{Z}_{13}\setminus\{0\},\times(\mathrm{mod}\,13))$ is isomorphic to $(\mathbb{Z}_{12},+)$.

4 Prove that the group of even integers under addition is isomorphic to the group of integers under addition.

5 Prove that $(\mathbb{R}\setminus\{0\},\times)$ is not isomorphic to $(\mathbb{C}\setminus\{0\},\times)$.

6 Let g be a fixed element of the group G. Prove that $f:G\rightarrow G$ defined by $f(a)=g^{-1}ag$ is an isomorphism from G to itself.

7.3   Group generators

You met the idea of a group generator in the context of cyclic groups in Section 6.3. However, you can extend the idea to non-cyclic groups.

Consider the group of symmetries of a rectangle which is not a square. The individual symmetries are the identity e, the reflections a and b in the axes of symmetry, and the rotation of $180°$ about the centre, which you can obtain by carrying out either first a then b or first b then a. In fact, you can describe this group by saying that it is generated by a and b given that $a^2=b^2=e$ and $ab=ba$. You can then simplify any expression in a and b, such as bab^2aba^2 by moving all the b terms to the left using the relation $ab=ba$ to get b^4a^4. Using $a^2=b^2=e$ simplifies this to e.

Similarly, the group D_3 is generated by R and X. A copy of D_3 (from Table 5.5) is shown in Table 7.7 on the next page. Notice first that $S=R^2$, $Y=XR$, $Z=XS=XR^2$ and $R^3=X^2=I$, so that every element can be written in terms of R and X. But notice also that the two equations $XR=Y$ and $R^2X=SX=Y$ give the relation $XR=R^2X$ between R and X.

These relations are sufficient to carry out any calculations within the group.

Now consider XR^2.

$$XR^2=(XR)R=(R^2X)R=R^2(XR)=R^2(R^2X)=R^4X=RX.$$

You can construct a table for D_3 using only R and X. The entries shown in Table 7.8 are easy to supply. These entries come from calculations such as

$$(XR)(XR^2)=X(RX)R^2=X(XR^2)R^2=X^2R^4=R,$$

and

$$(R^2)(XR)=(R^2X)R=(XR)R=XR^2,$$

in which the terms in X are progressively moved to the left using the given relation $XR=R^2X$ and the relation $RX=XR^2$, which was derived from it. Try filling in the rest of Table 7.8 for yourself.

D_3	I	R	S	X	Y	Z
I	I	R	S	X	Y	Z
R	R	S	I	Z	X	Y
S	S	I	R	Y	Z	X
X	X	Y	Z	I	R	S
Y	Y	Z	X	S	I	R
Z	Z	X	Y	R	S	I

Table 7.7

	I	R	R^2	X	XR	XR^2
I	I	R	R^2	X	XR	XR^2
R	R	R^2	I			
R^2	R^2	I	R			
X	X	XR	XR^2	I		
XR	XR	XR^2	X		I	
XR^2	XR^2	X	XR			I

Table 7.8

Thus the group D_3 is generated by R and X where $R^3 = X^2 = I$ and $XR = R^2 X$.

In the next section, the idea of generators will be used extensively.

7.4   Classifying groups of order up to 7

The only group of order 1 is the group consisting of the identity element only.

As every group of prime order is cyclic (Section 6.6) the only groups of orders 2, 3, 5 and 7 are cyclic.

This leaves groups of orders 4 and 6. They need a much more detailed treatment.

Groups of order 4
Let G be a group of order 4. As the orders of the elements must divide the order of the group, all the elements of G, other than the identity, have order 4 or 2.

If there is an element of order 4, the group G is cyclic, and is isomorphic to $(\mathbb{Z}_4, +)$.

If there is no element of order 4, all the elements other than the identity have order 2.

Now an element of order 2 is its own inverse; that is, $a^2 = e \Leftrightarrow a = a^{-1}$. Recall from Example 6.1.1 that a group in which every element is its own inverse is commutative.

Let a and b be two distinct non-identity elements of G, and consider the element ba.

As the group is commutative, $ba = ab$.

At this stage the group table shown in Table 7.9 is incomplete.

	e	a	b
e	e	a	b
a	a	e	
b	b	ba	e

Table 7.9

	e	a	b	ba
e	e	a	b	ba
a	a	e	ba	b
b	b	ba	e	a
ba	ba	b	a	e

Table 7.10

The element ba in Table 7.9, shown shaded, cannot be b or e because b and e are already in the same row. And it cannot be a since a is in the same column. So ba is distinct from the other elements, and $G = \{e, a, b, ba\}$.

Complete the table for yourself using similar arguments. You should end up with Table 7.10.

This group is called the four-group or occasionally the Klein four-group. It is denoted by V after the German word *vier* meaning 'four'. It is isomorphic to the group of symmetries of the rectangle. See Exercise 5B Question 1.

There are thus two, and only two, distinct groups of order 4, the cyclic group $(\mathbb{Z}_4, +)$, and V. Every group of order 4 is isomorphic to one of them.

Groups of order 6

Let G be a group of order 6. As the orders of the elements must divide the order of the group, all the elements of G, other than the identity, have order 6, 3 or 2.

If there is an element of order 6, the group G is cyclic, and is isomorphic to $(\mathbb{Z}_6, +)$.

If there is no element of order 6, suppose that there is an element a of order 3. Then the group includes the elements e, a and a^2, and there must be another element b such that $b \neq e$, a or a^2. Thus the elements of G are $\{e, a, a^2, b, ba, ba^2\}$. It is easy to check that none of these six elements can be equal to one another.

At this stage the incomplete group table appears as in Table 7.11.

	e	a	a^2	b	ba	ba^2
e	e	a	a^2	b	ba	ba^2
a	a	a^2	e			
a^2	a^2	e	a			
b	b	ba	ba^2			
ba	ba	ba^2	b			
ba^2	ba^2	b	ba			

Table 7.11

Now consider b^2. It is in the same row as b, ba and ba^2, so it can't be any of them. This leaves only $b^2 = a$, $b^2 = a^2$ or $b^2 = e$ as possibilities.

Suppose first that $b^2 = a$. Then $b^3 = b(b^2) = ba$, $b^4 = b(b^3) = b(ba) = b^2a = a^2$, $b^5 = b(b^4) = ba^2$ and $b^6 = b(b^5) = b(ba^2) = b^2a^2 = aa^2 = a^3 = e$. As these powers of b are all different, the order of b would be 6, contrary to hypothesis.

A similar argument shows that if $b^2 = a^2$, the order of b would also be 6. Try it!

Therefore $b^2 = e$.

Now consider the product ab. It is in the same row as a, a^2 and e and in the same column as b, so it can't be any of them. That leaves two cases, $ab = ba$ and $ab = ba^2$.

Suppose $ab = ba$ and consider the various powers of ab:

$$(ab)^2 = abab = a(ba)b = aabb = a^2b^2 = a^2e = a^2,$$

$$(ab)^3 = (ab)^2 ab = a^2 ab = a^3 b = b, \qquad (ab)^4 = (ab)^2 (ab)^2 = a^2 a^2 = a,$$

$$(ab)^5 = (ab)^3 (ab)^2 = ba^2, \qquad (ab)^6 = (ab)^2 (ab)^4 = a^2 a = a^3 = e.$$

So the order of ab is 6, contrary to hypothesis. Thus $ab \neq ba$.

If $ab = ba^2$, you can construct a table, using computations such as

$$\left(ba^2\right)(ba) = ba^2 ba = ba(ab)a = baba^2 a = bab = bba^2 = a^2;$$

$$(ba)\left(ba^2\right) = baba^2 = b(ab)a^2 = bba^2 a^2 = b^2 a^4 = a.$$

Complete the table for yourself. You should get the result shown in Table 7.12.

	e	a	a^2	b	ba	ba^2
e	e	a	a^2	b	ba	ba^2
a	a	a^2	e	ba^2	b	ba
a^2	a^2	e	a	ba	ba^2	b
b	b	ba	ba^2	e	a	a^2
ba	ba	ba^2	b	a^2	e	a
ba^2	ba^2	b	ba	a	a^2	e

Table 7.12

Comparing Table 7.12 with the completed version of Table 7.8, you can easily see that this group is isomorphic to the group D_3.

Suppose now that G has no elements of order 6 or of order 3. Then all the elements other than the identity have order 2, and the group is commutative (see Example 6.1.1).

Then, if a and b are two distinct, non-identity elements in G, the argument goes precisely as for the non-cyclic group of order 4: G contains e, a, b and ba, but there are no more products of a and b with results distinct from these. But $\{e, a, b, ab\}$ is V, a group of order 4 and, by Lagrange's theorem, a group of order 6 cannot have a subgroup of order 4. So the supposition that all the elements have order 2 leads to a contradiction.

Therefore the only distinct groups of order 6 are $(\mathbb{Z}_6, +)$ and D_3. Every group of order 6 is isomorphic to one or the other of them.

> The groups of order up to and including 7 are
>
> $(\mathbb{Z}_2, +)$ of order 2, $(\mathbb{Z}_3, +)$ of order 3, $(\mathbb{Z}_4, +)$ and V of order 4,
>
> $(\mathbb{Z}_5, +)$ of order 5, $(\mathbb{Z}_6, +)$ and D_3 of order 6, $(\mathbb{Z}_7, +)$ of order 7.

1 The set $\{2,4,6,8\}$ forms a group G under multiplication modulo 10.

   (a) Write down the operation table for G.

   (b) State the identity element and the inverse of each element in G.

   The set $\{1,i,-1,-i\}$, where $i^2 = -1$, forms a group H under multiplication of complex numbers.

   (c) Determine whether or not G and H are isomorphic, giving a reason for your answer.   (OCR)

2 A group D, of order 8, has the operation table shown below.

	e	a	b	b^2	b^3	ab	ab^2	ab^3
e	e	a	b	b^2	b^3	ab	ab^2	ab^3
a	a	e	ab	ab^2	ab^3	b	b^2	b^3
b	b	ab^3	b^2	b^3	e	a	ab	ab^2
b^2	b^2	ab^2	b^3	e	b	ab^3	a	ab
b^3	b^3	ab	e	b	b^2	ab^2	ab^3	a
ab	ab	b^3	ab^2	ab^3	a	e	b	b^2
ab^2	ab^2	b^2	ab^3	a	ab	b^3	e	b
ab^3	ab^3	b	a	ab	ab^2	b^2	b^3	e

   (a) Find the orders of the eight elements of D.

   (b) Write down the number of subgroups of order 2.

   (c) Find two subgroups of order 4.

   (d) Give a reason why there is no subgroup of order 6.

   (e) Explain how you can tell that the group D is not isomorphic to the group M, in which the elements $\{1,3,7,9,11,13,17,19\}$ are combined by multiplication modulo 20.   (OCR)

3 (a) The set S consists of the eight elements 9^1, 9^2, ... , 9^8 written in arithmetic modulo 64. Determine each of the elements of S as an integer between 0 and 63.

      Under multiplication modulo 64, the set S forms a group G, with identity 1. Write down the orders of each of the remaining elements of G.

      Write down all the possible generators for G, and list all the subgroups of G.

   (b) The group H consists of the set $\{1,9,31,39,41,49,71,79\}$ under multiplication modulo 80. Determine, with justification, whether G and H are isomorphic.   (OCR)

4 The set $S = \{1,2,p,q,7,8\}$ with the operation of multiplication modulo 9 forms a group G.

   (a) By considering the closure of G, find the integers p and q where $0 < p < q < 9$.

   (b) State the inverse of each element of G, and write down all the subgroups of G.

   (c) Given that $\omega = \cos\frac{1}{3}\pi + i\sin\frac{1}{3}\pi$, and H is the group $\{\omega,\omega^2,\omega^3,\omega^4,\omega^5,\omega^6\}$ under multiplication of complex numbers, find with reasons whether G and H are isomorphic.   (OCR)

5 (a) Prove that the set $\{1,3,5,9,11,13\}$ together with the operation of multiplication modulo 14 forms a group G. (You may assume that the operation is associative.)

List all the subgroups of G with fewer than three elements.

(b) The group of symmetry transformations of the equilateral triangle under the operation of composition is H. Describe geometrically the six elements of H.

(c) Determine, with reasons, whether G and H are isomorphic.

Find a subgroup of G with three elements. Is it isomorphic to a subgroup of H?   (OCR)

6 Prove that the set $\{1,2,4,7,8,k,13,14\}$ together with the operation multiplication modulo 15 forms a group G, provided k takes one particular value. State this value of k. (You may assume that the operation is associative, but the other axioms for a group must be clearly verified.)

If H is a subgroup of G of order n, use Lagrange's theorem to find all the possible values of n.

Find three subgroups of order 4, each containing the elements 1 and 4, and prove that exactly two of them are isomorphic.   (OCR)

7 Given that the multiplication of complex numbers is associative, show that the set $\{1,-1,i,-i\}$ forms a group G under multiplication of complex numbers.

Prove also that the set $\{1,7,18,24\}$ under multiplication modulo 25 forms a group H.

Determine, with reasons, whether G and H are isomorphic.   (OCR)

8 (a) The law of composition $*$ is defined by $a*b = a+b-ab$. Given that a, b and c are real numbers, prove that $a*(b*c) = (a*b)*c$.

(b) The law of composition $\circ$ is defined by $a \circ b = a+b-ab$ evaluated modulo 7 so that $2 \circ 4 = 5$ for example.

Copy and complete the combination table for the set $\{0,2,3,4,5,6\}$ with law of composition $\circ$.

$\circ$	0	2	3	4	5	6
0	0	2	3	4	5	6
2	2	0	6	5	4	3

(c) Prove that the set $\{0,2,3,4,5,6\}$ forms a group G under $\circ$.

(d) Determine, with reasons, whether G is isomorphic to the group of rotations of the regular hexagon.   (OCR)

9 The elements of the group G_n are the number 1 and the integers between 1 and n which have no factor in common with n; for example, the elements of G_4 are 1, 3. The operation of the group is multiplication modulo n. Write out the tables of G_5, G_8, G_{10} and G_{12}.

State which groups are isomorphic, giving your reasons.   (OCR)

8 The algebra of sets

In Chapter 1 you learnt to use set language and found how to prove that two sets are equal. This chapter develops an algebra which enables you to simplify expressions involving sets and gives you another method for proving that sets are equal. When you have completed it, you should

- know, be able to prove and use the rules of set algebra
- know and be able to use De Morgan's laws
- know the definition of symmetric difference.

8.1 Strategy

In Example 1.6.1 you saw a proof that for any sets A and B, $A \cap B = B \cap A$. This proof enabled you to use $A \cap B = B \cap A$ to simplify expressions involving sets.

Also in Exercise 1C Question 5, if you tackled it, you proved that $A \cup B = B \cup A$.

$A \cap B = B \cap A$ and $A \cup B = B \cup A$ are the commutative rules for intersection and union.

Similarly, $(A \cap B) \cap C = A \cap (B \cap C)$ and $(A \cup B) \cup C = A \cup (B \cup C)$. These are the associative rules for intersection and union.

In this chapter, a number of similar rules are developed, and you will learn how to use them to simplify expressions involving sets and to prove that sets are equal.

8.2 Complementation

In Section 1.5 you met the idea of the complement of a set A. Fig. 8.1 shows the sets A and A', and the universal set U.

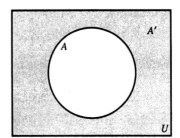

From Fig. 8.1 it looks as though $A \cup A' = U$ and $A \cap A' = \varnothing$. Example 8.2.1 proves the first of these relations.

Fig. 8.1

Example 8.2.1
Prove that $A \cup A' = U$.

Proof
Remember, that to prove two sets are equal, you need to prove that each is a subset of the other, that is $A \cup A' \subseteq U$ and $U \subseteq A \cup A'$.

Proof of $A \cup A' \subseteq U$
All sets are a subset of U (definition of U), so $A \cup A' \subseteq U$.

Proof of $U \subseteq A \cup A'$
Suppose $x \in U$.

$$x \in U \quad \Rightarrow \quad x \in A \text{ or } x \in A' \qquad \text{(definition of } A')$$
$$\Rightarrow \quad x \in A \cup A'.$$

Thus $U \subseteq A \cup A'$.

As $A \cup A' \subseteq U$ and $U \subseteq A \cup A'$, it follows that $A \cup A' = U$.

The proof of the result $A \cap A' = \varnothing$ is left to you in Exercise 8A Question 5.

The rules $A \cup A' = U$ and $A \cap A' = \varnothing$ are called the **complementation rules**.

Finally in this section, what can you say about the complement of a complement? Looking back at Fig. 8.1, the set of elements not in A', are in A. But remember, Venn diagrams do not constitute proof.

Example 8.2.2
Prove that $\left(A'\right)' = A$.

Proof of $\left(A'\right)' \subseteq A$
Suppose that $x \in \left(A'\right)'$.

For the moment let $B = A'$. Then $x \in \left(A'\right)'$ is the same as $x \in B'$, so $x \notin B$.

Using $B = A'$, this is $x \notin A'$, so $x \in A$.

Therefore, $\left(A'\right)' \subseteq A$.

Proof of $A \subseteq \left(A'\right)'$
Suppose that $x \in A$. Then $x \notin A'$.

For the moment let $B = A'$. Then $x \notin A'$ is the same as $x \notin B$, so $x \in B'$.

Using $B = A'$, $x \in B'$ is the same as $x \in \left(A'\right)'$.

So, $A \subseteq \left(A'\right)'$.

As $\left(A'\right)' \subseteq A$ and $A \subseteq \left(A'\right)'$, it follows that $\left(A'\right)' = A$.

The rule $\left(A'\right)' = A$ is called the **complement of a complement rule**.

8.3 The distributive rules

The commutative and associative rules for sets are very like those of addition and multiplication in arithmetic. Is there an equivalent set rule for the arithmetic rule $a \times (b + c) = (a \times b) + (a \times c)$, that is, the distributive rule?

Have a look at the Venn diagrams in Fig. 8.2.

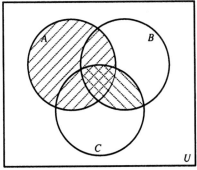
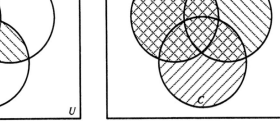

The region with any shading is $A \cup (B \cap C)$ The cross-shaded region is $(A \cup B) \cap (A \cup C)$

Fig. 8.2

From the diagram it certainly looks as though $A \cup (B \cap C) = (A \cup B) \cap (A \cup C)$.

Example 8.3.1 proves that this is true.

Example 8.3.1*
Prove that $A \cup (B \cap C) = (A \cup B) \cap (A \cup C)$.

Proof
There are two parts: the second part is left for you to prove in Exercise 8A Question 4.

Proof of $A \cup (B \cap C) \subseteq (A \cup B) \cap (A \cup C)$
Suppose $x \in A \cup (B \cap C)$.

$$x \in A \cup (B \cap C) \Rightarrow x \in A \text{ or } x \in B \cap C.$$

So there are two possibilities: either $x \in A$, or $x \in B \cap C$.

Taking the first of these,

$$x \in A \Rightarrow x \in A \cup B \text{ and } x \in A \cup C$$
$$\Rightarrow x \in (A \cup B) \cap (A \cup C).$$

The other possibility, $x \in B \cap C$, gives

$$x \in B \cap C \Rightarrow x \in B \text{ and } x \in C$$
$$\Rightarrow x \in A \cup B \text{ and } x \in A \cup C$$
$$\Rightarrow x \in (A \cup B) \cap (A \cup C).$$

So either way, $x \in (A \cup B) \cap (A \cup C)$.

Hence $A \cup (B \cap C) \subseteq (A \cup B) \cap (A \cup C)$.

Proof of $(A \cup B) \cap (A \cup C) \subseteq A \cup (B \cap C)$
See Exercise 8A Question 4.

As $A \cup (B \cap C) \subseteq (A \cup B) \cap (A \cup C)$ and $(A \cup B) \cap (A \cup C) \subseteq A \cup (B \cap C)$, it follows that

$$A \cup (B \cap C) = (A \cup B) \cap (A \cup C).$$

$A \cup (B \cap C) = (A \cup B) \cap (A \cup C)$ is called the **distributive rule for union over intersection**.

However, it is also true that intersection is distributive over union.

So $A \cap (B \cup C) = (A \cap B) \cup (A \cap C)$. This is called the **distributive rule for intersection over union**.

8.4 Using the rules for the algebra of sets

You met the tautology and absorption rules in Example 1.6.3 and Exercise 1C Questions 7 and 8.

The tautology rules are $A \cap A = A$ and $A \cup A = A$,

and the absorption rules are $A \cap (A \cup B) = A$ and $A \cup (A \cap B) = A$.

Here is a summary of the rules proved (or established through an exercise) so far.

Given any sets, A, B, C, and the universal set U then the following are true.

The complementation rules

$A \cap A' = \emptyset$ $A \cup A' = U$

Complement of complement rule

$(A')' = A$

The commutative rules

$A \cap B = B \cap A$ $A \cup B = B \cup A$

The associative rules

$(A \cap B) \cap C = A \cap (B \cap C)$ $(A \cup B) \cup C = A \cup (B \cup C)$

The distributive rules

$A \cup (B \cap C) = (A \cup B) \cap (A \cup C)$ $A \cap (B \cup C) = (A \cap B) \cup (A \cap C)$

The tautology rules

$A \cap A = A$ $A \cup A = A$

The absorption rules

$A \cap (A \cup B) = A$ $A \cup (A \cap B) = A$

Rules involving $\emptyset$ and U

$A \cap \emptyset = \emptyset$ $A \cup \emptyset = A$

$A \cap U = A$ $A \cup U = U$

$\emptyset' = U$ $U' = \emptyset$

The examples in the remainder of this section show how these rules can be used to simplify expressions involving sets.

Example 8.4.1
Simplify $\varnothing \cap A$.

$$\varnothing \cap A = A \cap \varnothing \qquad \text{(commutative rule)}$$
$$= \varnothing. \qquad \text{(rule involving } \varnothing)$$

Example 8.4.2
Prove that $(B \cup A') \cap B = B$.

$$(B \cup A') \cap B = B \cap (B \cup A') \qquad \text{(commutative rule)}$$
$$= (B \cap B) \cup (B \cap A') \qquad \text{(distributive rule)}$$
$$= B. \qquad \text{(absorption rule)}$$

Example 8.4.3
Simplify $A \cup (A' \cap B)$.

$$A \cup (A' \cap B) = (A \cup A') \cap (A \cup B) \qquad \text{(distributive rule)}$$
$$= U \cap (A \cup B) \qquad \text{(complementation rule)}$$
$$= A \cup B. \qquad \text{(rule involving } U)$$

Example 8.4.4
Simplify $(A \cup B) \cap (A' \cup B) \cap (A \cup B') \cap (A' \cup B')$.

$$(A \cup B) \cap (A \cup B') \cap (A' \cup B) \cap (A' \cup B')$$
$$= (A \cap (B \cup B')) \cap (A' \cup B) \cap (A' \cup B') \qquad \text{(distributive rule)}$$
$$= (A \cap U) \cap (A' \cup B) \cap (A' \cup B') \qquad \text{(complementation rule)}$$
$$= A \cap (A' \cup B) \cap (A' \cup B') \qquad \text{(rule involving } U)$$
$$= A \cap (A' \cup (B \cap B')) \qquad \text{(distributive rule)}$$
$$= A \cap (A' \cup \varnothing) \qquad \text{(complementation rule)}$$
$$= A \cap A' \qquad \text{(rule involving } \varnothing)$$
$$= \varnothing. \qquad \text{(complementation rule)}$$

Example 8.4.5
Simplify $(A' \cap (A \cup B')) \cup (B' \cap (B' \cup C)) \cup B'$.

$$(A' \cap (A \cup B')) \cup (B' \cap (B' \cup C)) \cup B'$$
$$= (A' \cap A) \cup (A' \cap B') \cup (B' \cap (B' \cup C)) \cup B' \qquad \text{(distributive rule)}$$
$$= \varnothing \cup (A' \cap B') \cup (B' \cap (B' \cup C)) \cup B' \qquad \text{(complementation rule)}$$
$$= (A' \cap B') \cup (B' \cap (B' \cup C)) \cup B' \qquad \text{(rule involving } \varnothing)$$
$$= (A' \cap B') \cup B' \cup B' \qquad \text{(absorption rule)}$$
$$= (A' \cap B') \cup B' \qquad \text{(tautology rule)}$$
$$= B'. \qquad \text{(absorption rule)}.$$

Exercise 8A

1 Simplify the following.

(a) $\varnothing \cup A$ (b) $U \cap B$ (c) $U \cup B'$ (d) $A \cap (A \cup \varnothing)$

2 Prove that the following equations are correct.

(a) $(A \cup B') \cap B' = B'$

(b) $(A' \cup B') \cap (A \cup B) = (A \cap B') \cup (A' \cap B)$

(c) $A \cap (A' \cup B) \cap (A \cup B') = A \cap B$

3 Simplify each of the following expressions down to a single letter or symbol.

(a) $A' \cap B' \cap A$ (b) $B \cup (A \cup A')$

(c) $A' \cup B' \cup A' \cup B$ (d) $(A' \cup C) \cap (A' \cup B' \cup C') \cap (A' \cup C')$

4* Prove that $(A \cup B) \cap (A \cup C) \subseteq A \cup (B \cap C)$.

5 Prove that $A \cap A' = \varnothing$.

8.5 De Morgan's laws

De Morgan's laws are about simplifying $(A \cap B)'$ and $(A \cup B)'$. For example, how can you write them in terms of A, A', B and B'?

The Englishman Augustus De Morgan lived from 1806 to 1871.

Using Venn diagrams can help. See Fig. 8.3.

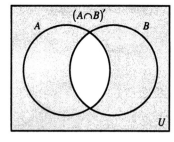 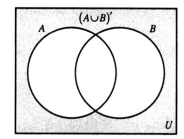

Fig. 8.3

The left diagram represents $(A \cap B)'$ and the right $(A \cup B)'$. The diagrams suggest that

$$(A \cap B)' = A' \cup B' \quad \text{and} \quad (A \cup B)' = A' \cap B'.$$

Theorem 8.1 shows how to prove the first of these. The second is left for you to prove Exercise 8B Question 5.

Theorem 8.1 (De Morgan's law)* $(A \cap B)' = A' \cup B'$

    Proof of $(A \cap B)' \subseteq A' \cup B'$

    Suppose that $x \in (A \cap B)'$. Then

$$x \in (A \cap B)' \implies x \notin (A \cap B)$$
$$\implies x \in A' \text{ or } x \in B'$$
$$\implies x \in (A' \cup B').$$

Thus $(A \cap B)' \subseteq A' \cup B'$.

Proof of $A' \cup B' \subseteq (A \cap B)'$

Suppose that $x \in A' \cup B'$.

$$x \in A' \cup B' \implies x \in A' \text{ or } x \in B'.$$

If $x \in A'$, then $x \notin A$, so $x \notin (A \cap B)$, showing $x \in (A \cap B)'$.

Similarly, if $x \in B'$, then $x \notin B$, so $x \notin A \cap B$, showing $x \in (A \cap B)'$.

Either way, $x \in (A \cap B)'$, so $A' \cup B' \subseteq (A \cap B)'$.

As $(A \cap B)' \subseteq A' \cup B'$ and $A' \cup B' \subseteq (A \cap B)'$, it follows that $(A \cap B)' = A' \cup B'$.

This is one of De Morgan's laws. The other is $(A \cup B)' = A' \cap B'$. They should be added to the list in Section 8.4.

> **De Morgan's laws**   If A and B are two subsets of a universal set,
>
> $$(A \cap B)' = A' \cup B' \quad \text{and} \quad (A \cup B)' = A' \cap B'.$$

De Morgan's laws give you another method for proving that sets are equal without needing to go back to first principles.

Example 8.5.1

Prove that if A and B are two subsets of a universal set, U, then

(a) $(A \cap B')' = A' \cup B$,   (b) $A \cap (A \cup B)' = \varnothing$.

(a)   Using De Morgan's law $(A \cap B)' = A' \cup B'$ with B' in place of B gives

$$(A \cap B')' = A' \cup (B')' \qquad \text{(De Morgan's law)}$$
$$= A' \cup B. \qquad \text{(complement of complement rule)}$$

(b)   Using De Morgan's second law on $(A \cup B)'$ and starting with the left side gives

$$A \cap (A \cup B)' = A \cap (A' \cap B') \qquad \text{(De Morgan's law)}$$
$$= (A \cap A') \cap B' \qquad \text{(associative rule)}$$
$$= \varnothing \cap B' \qquad \text{(complementation rule)}$$
$$= \varnothing. \qquad \text{(rule involving } \varnothing\text{)}$$

8.6   Set difference and symmetric difference

In Section 1.5 you were introduced to set difference, which was defined to be those elements of A which were not in B. That is, set difference $A \setminus B$ is defined by $A \setminus B = A \cap B'$. This is illustrated in Fig. 8.4.

Another operation on two sets, closely related to the set difference, is the **symmetric difference**. This is illustrated in Fig. 8.5.

The shaded region is the symmetric difference of A and B. It is denoted by $A \Delta B$ and defined by

$$A \Delta B = (A \setminus B) \cup (B \setminus A).$$

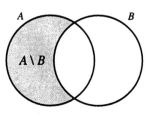

Fig. 8.4

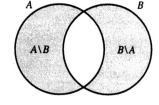

Fig. 8.5

> Let A and B be sets.
>
> Then the set $A \Delta B = (A \setminus B) \cup (B \setminus A)$ is called the **symmetric difference** of A and B and is denoted by $A \Delta B$.

Alternatively, by substituting $A \cap B'$ and $A' \cap B$ for $A \setminus B$ and $B \setminus A$ respectively,

$$A \Delta B = (A \cap B') \cup (A' \cap B).$$

Example 8.6.1
Simplify $A \Delta \varnothing$.

$$
\begin{aligned}
A \Delta \varnothing &= (A \cap \varnothing') \cup (A' \cap \varnothing) && \text{(using the alternative form)} \\
&= (A \cap U) \cup (A' \cap \varnothing) && \text{(rules involving } \varnothing \text{ and } U) \\
&= A \cup (A' \cap \varnothing) && \text{(rule involving } U) \\
&= A \cup \varnothing && \text{(rule involving } \varnothing) \\
&= A. && \text{(rule involving } \varnothing)
\end{aligned}
$$

Example 8.6.2
Prove that $(A \setminus B) \cup (B \setminus A) = (A \cup B) \cap (A \cap B)'$.

$$
\begin{aligned}
&(A \setminus B) \cup (B \setminus A) \\
&= (A \cap B') \cup (A' \cap B) && \text{(alternative form)} \\
&= ((A \cap B') \cup A') \cap ((A \cap B') \cup B) && \text{(distributive rule)} \\
&= (A' \cup (A \cap B')) \cap (B \cup (A \cap B')) && \text{(commutative rule (×2))} \\
&= ((A' \cup A) \cap (A' \cup B')) \cap ((B \cup A) \cap (B \cup B')) && \text{(distributive rule (×2))} \\
&= (U \cap (A' \cup B')) \cap ((B \cup A) \cap U) && \text{(complementation rule (×2))} \\
&= (A' \cup B') \cap (B \cup A) && \text{(rule involving } U \text{ (×2))} \\
&= (A \cup B) \cap (A' \cup B') && \text{(commutative rule (×2))} \\
&= (A \cup B) \cap (A \cap B)'. && \text{(De Morgan's law)}
\end{aligned}
$$

Exercise 8B

1 Simplify the following.

   (a) $(A' \cup B)'$

   (b) $(A' \cap B')'$

2 Simplify the following.

   (a) $A \Delta A$

   (b) $A \Delta \varnothing$

   (c) $A \Delta U$

   (d) $B \cup (A \setminus B)$

   (e) $A \setminus (A \setminus B)$

   (f) $A \Delta (A \setminus B)$

3 Prove that if A, B and C are three sets, and if $A \cap B = A \cap C$ and $A \cup B = A \cup C$, then $B = C$.
   (Hint: start with $B = B \cap (A \cup B)$ and use $A \cup B = A \cup C$.)

4 Prove that $B \cap (A \setminus B) = \varnothing$.

5* Prove that $(A \cup B)' = A' \cap B'$.

6 Let $A = \{1, 2, 3, 4\}$ and $B = \{3, 4, 5, 6\}$. List the elements of

   (a) $A \Delta B$,

   (b) $A \setminus B$,

   (c) $B \setminus A$,

   (d) $(A \Delta B) \setminus B$.

7 Draw a Venn diagram to illustrate $A \Delta (B \Delta C)$. Explain why the result suggests that
   $A \Delta (B \Delta C) = (A \Delta B) \Delta C$.

   Prove the result algebraically.

8 Simplify the following expressions.

   (a) $(A \cap B')' \cup A'$

   (b) $(A' \cap B)' \cup A'$

9 Prove that $((A \cap C) \cup (B \cap C'))' = (A' \cap C) \cup (B' \cap C')$.

10 Prove that $(A \setminus B) \setminus C = (A \setminus C) \setminus (B \setminus C)$.

Review exercise

1 Let G be a commutative group. Prove that the set of elements of order 2 together with the identity element, that is $H = \{a \in G : a^2 = e\}$, is a subgroup of G.

2 G is a commutative group, and $H = \{x \in G : x^3 = e\}$. Prove that H is a subgroup of G.

3 The binary operation $*$ on $\mathbb{R} \times \mathbb{R}$ is defined by $(a,b) * (c,d) = (ac - bd, ac + bd)$.

   (a) Prove that $*$ is closed.

   (b) What would you need to do to prove that $*$ is associative? (You do not need to prove this.)

   (c) Assuming that $*$ is associative, prove that $\mathbb{R} \times \mathbb{R}$ with the operation $*$ is a group, and write down its identity element.

4 (a) Sketch the graph of the function f defined by $f : \mathbb{R} \to \mathbb{R}$ where $f(x) = e^{-x^2}$, and state its range.

   (b) Determine whether f is injective and whether f is surjective, and justify your answers.

   (c) A new function g is to be defined such that $g : A \to B$, where $A \subseteq \mathbb{R}$ and $B \subseteq \mathbb{R}$ such that $g(x) = e^{-x^2}$ has an inverse. Give examples of suitable sets A and B.

5 The relation R is defined on $\mathbb{C}$ by $(a + bi)R(c + di) \iff a^2 + b^2 = c^2 + d^2$, where $a, b, c, d \in \mathbb{R}$. Investigate whether or not R is an equivalence relation: if R is not an equivalence relation, say why; if R is an equivalence relation, find its equivalence classes.

6 In S_4, the permutations a and b are given by $a = \begin{pmatrix} 1 & 2 & 3 & 4 \\ 2 & 4 & 1 & 3 \end{pmatrix}$ and $b = \begin{pmatrix} 1 & 2 & 3 & 4 \\ 1 & 4 & 3 & 2 \end{pmatrix}$.

   (a) Using a similar notation, calculate the permutations a^2, a^{-1}, ab and ab^{-1}.

   (b) Calculate the orders of a and b.

7 You are given that the set $\{1, 2, 3, \ldots, 12\}$ forms a group G under multiplication modulo 13. A subgroup with n elements is said to have order n. Find, or explain why none exists, a subgroup of G with order

   (a) 2,   (b) 3,   (c) 5.   (OCR)

8 The set $\{a, b, c, d\}$ under the binary operation $*$ forms a group G of order 4 with the following operation table.

$*$	a	b	c	d
a	d	a	b	c
b	a	b	c	d
c	b	c	d	a
d	c	d	a	b

   (a) Find the order of each element of G.

   (b) Write down a proper subgroup of G.   (OCR)

9 The functions $i(x)$, $a(x)$, $b(x)$, $c(x)$ are defined for all $x \neq 0$, $x \neq 1$ by

$$i(x) = x, \quad a(x) = \frac{1}{x}, \quad b(x) = 1 - x \quad \text{and} \quad c(x) = \frac{1}{1-x}.$$

The operation $\otimes$ is defined as the composition of functions: that is,

$$(p \otimes q)(x) = pq(x) = p\{q(x)\}.$$

(a) Show that the set of functions $\{i,a,b,c\}$ is not closed under $\otimes$, and find two further functions $d(x)$ and $e(x)$ such that $\{i,a,b,c,d,e\}$ is closed under $\otimes$.

(b) Copy and complete the composition table for the set $G = \{i,a,b,c,d,e\}$, under $\otimes$.

$\otimes$	i	a	b	c	d	e
i	i	a	b	c	d	e
a	a	i		b		
b	b		i			
c	c		a		i	
d	d			i		a
e	e	c			a	i

(c) Hence show that $(G, \otimes)$ forms a group. (You may assume that the composition of functions is associative.)

(d) Find whether G is a commutative group, giving reasons.

(e) Find whether G is a cyclic group, giving reasons.

(f) Write down all the subgroups of G. (OCR)

10 Show that the matrices $\begin{pmatrix} a & b \\ c & d \end{pmatrix}$, where $ad \neq bc$, form a group G under matrix multiplication. Show that the following subsets of G form subgroups of G.

(a) $\begin{pmatrix} a & b \\ 0 & 1 \end{pmatrix}$ (b) $\begin{pmatrix} 1 & b \\ 0 & 1 \end{pmatrix}$ (c) $\begin{pmatrix} a & 0 \\ 0 & 1 \end{pmatrix} (a \neq 0)$

(d) Find a proper subgroup of (a) which contains (b) as a proper subgroup.

(e) Find a subgroup of G of order 4.

11 (a) The elements a, b and c are elements of a non-commutative group G. Prove that $(abc)^{-1} = c^{-1}b^{-1}a^{-1}$.

(b) A group H contains distinct elements x, y and e, where e is the identity element. Given that $xy = y^2 x$, prove that $xy \neq yx$. (OCR)

12 The law of composition $*$ is defined by $a*b = a+b-2$ where a and b are numbers in arithmetic modulo 6.

(a) Show that the set $\{0,1,2,3,4,5\}$ forms a group G under $*$ in arithmetic modulo 6.

(b) Find all the subgroups of G.

13 Let $S = \{1,2,3,4\}$ and f be a function whose domain and range are both S, defined by

$f(x) =$ the remainder when $2x$ is divided by 5.

(a) Prove that f is a bijection.   (b) Show that the composite function $f \circ f$ is the identity.

14 The set S consists of the eight elements 9^1, 9^2, ... , 9^8 where the operation is multiplication modulo 64. Determine each of the elements of S as an integer between 0 and 63.

Under multiplication modulo 64, the set S forms a group G with identity 1. Write down the inverses of each of the remaining elements of G.

A group in which each element x can be written as a power of a particular element g of the group is said to be a cyclic group; and such an element g is called a generator of the group. Write down all the possible generators of G.

15 Construct the composition table for $(S, \circ)$, where the binary operation $\circ$ is defined on the set $S = \{0,1,2,3,4,5,6\}$ by $x \circ y = x + y - xy$ modulo 7.

One of the elements of S is removed to form a set S' of order 6, such that $(S', \circ)$ forms a group. State which element is to be deleted, and prove that $(S', \circ)$ is a group.

16 Let A and B be sets. Show that A and B with the operation of symmetric difference generate a group (G, Δ). (You may assume that sets are associative under the operation Δ.)

Write down the order of each element of G.

17 Let G be a group and H be a subgroup of G. The relation R is defined on the elements of G by $aRb \iff ab^{-1} \in H$. Prove that R is an equivalence relation, and find the equivalence classes.

18 Let H and K be finite subgroups of a finite group G, and let the orders of H and K be relatively prime; that is, they have no common factors apart from 1. Prove that the only element common to H and K is the identity element.

<hr>

Examination questions

1 (a) The difference, $A - B$, of two sets A and B is defined as the set of all elements of A which do not belong to B.

(i)   Show by means of a Venn diagram that $A - B = A \cap B'$.

(ii)   Using set algebra, prove that $A - (B \cup C) = (A - B) \cap (A - C)$.

(b) Let S be the set of all 2×2 non-singular matrices each of whose elements is either 0 or 1.

Two matrices belonging to S are $\begin{pmatrix} 0 & 1 \\ 1 & 0 \end{pmatrix}$ and $\begin{pmatrix} 1 & 1 \\ 0 & 1 \end{pmatrix}$.

Write down the other four members of S.

(c) You are given that S forms a group under matrix multiplication, when the elements of the matrix product are calculated modulo 2.

(i)   Find the order of all the members of S whose determinant is negative.

(ii)   Hence find a subgroup of S of order 3.

(d) The group $(G, *)$ is defined on the set $\{e,a,b,c\}$, where e denotes the identity element. Prove that $a * b = b * a$.

(© IBO 2004)

2 (a) Let A, B and C be subsets of a given universal set.

   (i) Use a Venn diagram to show that $(A \cap B) \cup C = (A \cup C) \cap (B \cup C)$.

   (ii) Hence, and by using De Morgan's laws, show that $(A' \cap B) \cup C' = (A \cap C)' \cap (B' \cap C)'$.

   (b) Let R be a relation on $\mathbb{Z}$ such that for $m \in \mathbb{Z}^+$, xRy if and only if m divides $x - y$, where $x, y \in \mathbb{Z}$.

   (i) Prove that R is an equivalence relation on $\mathbb{Z}$.

   (ii) Prove that this equivalence relation partitions $\mathbb{Z}$ into m distinct classes.

   (iii) Let $\mathbb{Z}_m$ be the set of all the equivalence classes found in part (b). Define a suitable binary operation $+_m$ on $\mathbb{Z}_m$ and prove that $(\mathbb{Z}_m, +_m)$ is an additive Abelian group.

   (iv) Let $(K, \lozenge)$ be a cyclic group of order m. Prove that $(K, \lozenge)$ is isomorphic to $\mathbb{Z}_m$.

   (c) Let $(G, \circ)$ be a group with subgroups $(H, \circ)$ and $(K, \circ)$. Prove that $(H \cup K, \circ)$ is a subgroup of $(G, \circ)$ if and only if one of the sets H and K is contained in the other.   (© IBO 2002)

3 The operation # defined on the set $\{a,b,c,d,e\}$ has the following operation table.

#	a	b	c	d	e
a	d	c	e	a	b
b	e	d	a	b	c
c	b	e	d	c	a
d	a	b	c	d	e
e	c	a	b	e	d

   (a) Show that only three of the four group axioms are satisfied.

   Let R be a relation defined on 2×2 matrices such that, given the matrices A and B, ARB if and only if there exists a matrix H such that $A = HBH^{-1}$.

   (b) Show that R is an equivalence relation.

   (c) Show that all matrices in the same equivalence class have equal determinants.

   (d) Given the matrix $M = \begin{pmatrix} 1 & 2 \\ 1 & 3 \end{pmatrix}$, find a 2×2 matrix that is

   (i) related to M (excluding M itself),

   (ii) not related to M.

   (e) Let $(G, *)$ be a group, and H a subset of G. Given that for all $a, b \in H$, $a^{-1}b \in H$, prove that $(H, *)$ is a subgroup of $(G, *)$.   (© IBO 2005)

4 Let $S = \{2, 4, 6, 8, 10, 12, 14\}$. The relation R is defined on S such that for $a, b \in S$, aRb if and only if $a^2 = b^2 \pmod{\text{modulo } 6}$.

   (a) Show that R is an equivalence relation.

   (b) Find all the equivalence classes.   (© IBO 2006)

5 The function f is defined by $f : \mathbb{R} \to \mathbb{R}$ where $f(x) = e^{\sin x} - 1$.

   (a) Find the exact range, A, of f.

   (b) (i)   Explain why f is not an injection.

         (ii)   Giving a reason, state whether or not f is a surjection.

   (c) The function g is now defined to be $g : [-k,k] \to A$, where $g(x) = e^{\sin x} - 1$ and $k > 0$.

         (i)   Find the maximum value of k for which g is an injection.

         For this value of k,

         (ii)   find an expression for $g^{-1}(x)$,

         (iii) write down the domain of g^{-1}.   (© IBO 2006)

Answers

1 The language of sets

Exercise 1A (page 3)

1. (a) $A = \{1, 2, 4, 8, 16, 32\}$
   (b) $B = \{1, 2, 3, 4, 5, 6\}$
   (c) $C = \varnothing$
   (d) $D = \{\sqrt{2}\}$
   (e) $E = \{-\sqrt{2}, \sqrt{2}\}$
   (f) $F = \{0, \pm 1, \pm 2, \dots\} = \mathbb{Z}$
   (g) $G = \{0, \pm 2, \pm 4, \dots\}$
   (h) $H = \{4, 5, 6, 7\}$

   Sets F and G are infinite; all the others are finite.

2. (a) Well-defined
   (b) This may be well-defined in a particular country, but given different time zones, and the difficulty of determining the exact time of birth, it is probably better avoided.
   (c) Well-defined. Note that it may be very difficult to find out what it is.

3. $2\mathbb{Z} = \{0, \pm 2, \pm 4, \dots\}$, $\{\pm 1, \pm 3, \pm 5, \dots\}$

Exercise 1B (page 8)

1. (a) $\{1, 2, 4, 6, 8\}$ (b) $\{2\}$
   (c) $\{0, 3, 4, 6, 7, 8\}$ (d) $\{4, 8\}$
   (e) $\{4, 6, 8\}$ (f) $\{0, 1, 3, 4, 5, 6, 7, 8\}$
   (g) $\{0, 3, 6, 7\}$ (h) $\{4, 6, 8\}$

2. (a) E (b) I (c) $\varnothing$
   (d) Isosceles triangles, but not equilateral ones
   (e) E (f) R (g) $\varnothing$
   (h) Non-isosceles right-angled triangles

3. (a) S (b) S (c) D (d) R

Exercise 1C (page 12)

1. $P \subsetneq Q$
2. $P \subseteq Q$
3. (a) $\varnothing$ (b) A (c) A
   (d) U (e) U (f) $\varnothing$
4. A
10. U

Exercise 1D (page 14)

1. (a) $\{(H,1),(H,2),(H,3),(H,4),(H,5),(H,6),$
      $(T,1),(T,2),(T,3),(T,4),(T,5),(T,6)\}$

(b) $\{(1,H),(1,T), (2,H),(2,T), (3,H),(3,T),$
    $(4,H),(4,T), (5,H),(5,T), (6,H),(6,T)\}$

2. (a) False   (b) False

3. $A \times B \times C = \{(a, b, c) \mid a \in A, b \in B, c \in C\}$
   $(0,0,0),(0,0,1),(0,1,0),(1,0,0),(0,1,1),(1,0,1),$
   $(1,1,0),(1,1,1)$

5. $\mathbb{Z} \times \mathbb{Z}$ is the set of points in the plane which have integer coordinates for both x and y.

2 Equivalence relations

Exercise 2A (page 16)

1. (a)
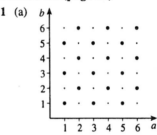
$\overline{1} = \overline{3} = \overline{5} = \{1, 3, 5\}$, $\overline{2} = \overline{4} = \overline{6} = \{2, 4, 6\}$

(b)
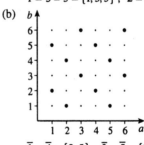
$\overline{1} = \overline{4} = \{2, 5\}$, $\overline{2} = \overline{5} = \{1, 4\}$,
$\overline{3} = \overline{6} = \{3, 6\}$

(c)
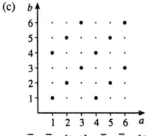
$\overline{1} = \overline{4} = \{1, 4\}$, $\overline{2} = \overline{5} = \{2, 5\}$,
$\overline{3} = \overline{6} = \{3, 6\}$

(d)

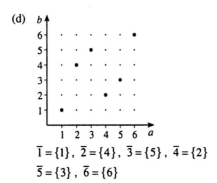

$\overline{1} = \{1\}$, $\overline{2} = \{4\}$, $\overline{3} = \{5\}$, $\overline{4} = \{2\}$

$\overline{5} = \{3\}$, $\overline{6} = \{6\}$

Exercise 2B (page 21)

1 The equivalence classes are
   (a) lines passing through the origin, but not including the origin;
   (b) equivalent fractions, that is, the elements of $\mathbb{Q}$;
   (c) even integers and odd integers;
   (d) integers which leave remainders 0, 1 and 2 when divided by 3;
   (e) $\left\{\pm x \,|\, x \in \mathbb{Z}\right\}$.

2 (a) Not an equivalence relation, since $1R0$ but 0 is not related to 1, since -1 is not a perfect square.
   (b) Not an equivalence relation, since 0 is not related to 0, as $0 \times 0 \not> 0$.
   (c) This is an equivalence relation, as, trivially, all the conditions are satisfied. There is just one equivalence class, that of $\mathbb{Z}^+$ itself.
   (d) Not an equivalence relation, since $1R0$ and $0R-1$, but 1 is not related to -1.
   (e) Not an equivalence relation, since $0R\frac{1}{2}$ and $\frac{1}{2}R1$, but 0 is not related to 1.
   (f) Not an equivalence relation, since $1R2$ and $2R3$, but 1 is not related to 3.
   (g) This is an equivalence relation provided you agree that a line is parallel to itself. The equivalence classes are sets of parallel lines in the plane.
   (h) Not an equivalence relation, since $(1,1)$ is not related to $(1,1)$.
   (i) This is an equivalence relation if you agree that a triangle is similar to itself. The equivalence classes are sets of similar triangles.
   (j) This is an equivalence relation. The solution is identical to that of part (i), with the word 'congruent' replacing 'similar'.
   (k) Not an equivalence relation, since l is not perpendicular to itself.

3 The equivalence classes are lines in the plane $\mathbb{R}^2$ which are parallel to $y = x$.

4 The equivalence classes are squares with centres at the origin. The sides of the squares are parallel to the axes.

5 The equivalence classes are squares with centres at the origin. The vertices of the squares lie on the axes.

6 The equivalence classes are circles with centres at the origin.

3 Functions

Exercise 3A (page 28)

2 For example, $f:\mathbb{R} \to \mathbb{R}$, where $f(x) = e^x$

3 For example, $f:\mathbb{R} \to [-1,1]$, where $f(x) = \sin x$

4 (a) Function; not an injection; not a surjection
   (b) Function; injection; surjection
   (c) Not a function (undefined at 0)
   (d) Function; not an injection; not a surjection
   (e) Not a function (undefined at $\left(n+\frac{1}{2}\right)\pi$, $n \in \mathbb{Z}$)
   (f) Function; injection; not a surjection
   (g) Function; not an injection; not a surjection
   (h) Not a function (undefined for $x \in \mathbb{R} \setminus \left(\mathbb{R}^+ \cup \{0\}\right)$)
   (i) Function; injection; surjection
   (j) Function; not an injection; not a surjection
   (k) Not a function (undefined for $x \in \mathbb{R} \setminus [-1,1]$)
   (l) Not a function (no such number exists)

8 (a) Every y-value of the function has at most one x-value corresponding to it.
   (b) Every y-value of the function has at least one x-value corresponding to it.
   (c) Every y-value of the function has exactly one x-value corresponding to it.

9 (a) False   (b) True   (c) True

10 (a) Function; not an injection; surjection
   (b) Not a function; $f(p)$ is not uniquely specified
   (c) Function; injection; not a surjection
   (d) Function; injection; not a surjection

Exercise 3B (page 35)

2 (a) Not surjective
   (b) Not injective
   (c) Not bijective

3 The only bijections are (b) and (i).

(b) The inverse is $f^{-1}:\mathbb{R} \to \mathbb{R}$ where
$$f^{-1}(x) = x^{\frac{1}{3}}.$$

(i) The inverse is $f^{-1}:\mathbb{R} \to \mathbb{R}$ where
$$f^{-1}(x) = x - 1.$$

5 (a) False   (b) True   (c) True   (d) True
(e) False   (f) True   (g) False

6 The equivalence classes are
$\{x \mid x \in \mathbb{R}, f(x) = k, k \in \text{range} f\}.$
$\{\frac{1}{8}\pi + n\pi, \frac{3}{8}\pi + n\pi \mid n \in \mathbb{Z}\}$

7 (b) $f^{-1}(x) = 2(x-1)$, $g^{-1}(x) = \ln x$
(c) $h^{-1}(x) = 2(\ln x - 1)$

8 $f^{-1}(x,y) = (4x - 2y, -5x + 3y)$

9 f is injective, surjective and bijective;
g is none of these.

10 (a) -1 (b) -1 (c) -1

4 Binary operations and groups

Exercise 4A (page 42)

1 (a) Binary operation: not closed;
not commutative; not associative
(b) Binary operation: closed;
not commutative; associative
(c) Binary operation: closed;
not commutative; not associative
(d) Binary operation: closed;
commutative; not associative
(e) Binary operation: closed;
commutative; associative
(f) Not a binary operation as B^{-1} does not exist
for all 2×2 matrices
(i) Binary operation: closed; commutative;
associative
(g) Binary operation: closed;
not commutative; associative
(h) Binary operation: closed;
not commutative; not associative
(i) Binary operation: closed;
commutative; associative
(j) Not a binary operation as there is no
smallest number greater than $a + b$

2 (a) True   (b) True

3 (a) True   (b) True

Exercise 4B (page 44)

1 $s \circ t = p$, $t \circ s = q$, $(p \circ q) \circ s = s$, $p \circ (q \circ t) = t$,
r, s; q, p

$s \circ t = q$, $t \circ s = p$, $(p \circ q) \circ s = r$, $p \circ (q \circ t) = t$,
r, u; p, q

2 (a) No identity
(b) Identity I; no general inverse
(c) Identity $1 + 0i$; no general inverse, e.g. 0
(d) No identity
(e) No identity

3 (a) Identity $\begin{pmatrix} 1 & 1 \\ 0 & 0 \end{pmatrix}$; inverse $\begin{pmatrix} x^{-1} & x^{-1} \\ 0 & 0 \end{pmatrix}$

(b) Identity 6; inverses of 2, 4, 6 and 8 are 8, 4,
6 and 2.
(c) Identity 0; inverses of 0, 2, 4, 6 and 8 are 0,
8, 6, 4 and 2.
(d) Identity 1; inverses of 1, 3, 7 and 9 are 1, 7,
3 and 9.

Exercise 4C (page 50)

1 (a) Not a group; no identity element.
(c) Not a group; 2 has no inverse.
(e) Not a group; not closed.
(g) Not a group; 5 has no inverse.
(i) Not a group; 0 has no inverse.
All the rest are groups.

2 There is no identity element.

3 $x \mapsto \dfrac{x-1}{x}$, $x \mapsto \dfrac{x}{x-1}$

6 If $a \circ b = e$, a and b would be inverse elements
of G and e, a and b would form a group with
three elements.
If $a \circ b = a$, then b would be the identity, a
contradiction. Similarly, if $a \circ b = b$, then a
would be the identity.

8 $x \mapsto a^{-1}(x - b)$

9 a^3

5 Some examples of groups

Exercise 5A (page 56)

1

	0	1	2	3	4
0	0	1	2	3	4
1	1	2	3	4	0
2	2	3	4	0	1
3	3	4	0	1	2
4	4	0	1	2	3

The inverse of 2 is 3. $x = 4$; $y = 3$

2

	1	2	3	4	5	6
1	1	2	3	4	5	6
2	2	4	6	1	3	5
3	3	6	2	5	1	4
4	4	1	5	2	6	3
5	5	3	1	6	4	2
6	6	5	4	3	2	1

The inverse of 3 is 5, and the inverse of 4 is 2.

3

	1	2	3	4	5
1	1	2	3	4	5
2	2	4		2	4
3	3		3		3
4	4	2		4	2
5	5	4	3	2	1

The operation is not closed as 2×3 is not in the set. If q is not prime, then $q = mn$ for some

$$q = m, n \in \left(\mathbb{Z}_q \setminus \{0\}, \times\right); \; mn = q \notin \left(\mathbb{Z}_q \setminus \{0\}, \times\right),$$

so the operation is not closed.

4

	1	2	4	7	8	11	13	14
1	1	2	4	7	8	11	13	14
2	2	4	8	14	1	7	11	13
4	4	8	1	13	2	14	7	11
7	7	14	13	4	11	2	1	8
8	8	1	2	11	4	13	14	7
11	11	7	14	2	13	1	8	4
13	13	11	7	1	14	8	4	2
14	14	13	11	8	7	4	2	1

11

5 9

6 4, 1;   (a) 15 (b) 17 (c) 19 (d) 53

7

	0	1	2	3	4
0	2	3	4	0	1
1	3	4	0	1	2
2	4	0	1	2	3
3	0	1	2	3	4
4	1	2	3	4	0

The identity is 3, and the inverses of 0, 1, 2, 3 and 4 are 1, 0, 4, 3 and 2 respectively.

Exercise 5B (page 57)

1

	I	X	Y	H
I	I	X	Y	H
X	X	I	H	Y
Y	Y	H	I	X
H	H	Y	X	I

2 S and X; for RAR^{-1} the elements are I, R, S, Y, X and Z and for XAX^{-1} they are I, S, R, X, Z and Y. $A = R$

3

D_4	I	R	R^2	R^3	H	L	V	M
I	I	R	R^2	R^3	H	L	V	M
R	R	R^2	R^3	I	M	H	L	V
R^2	R^2	R^3	I	R	V	M	H	L
R^3	R^3	I	R	R^2	L	V	M	H
H	H	L	V	M	I	R	R^2	R^3
L	L	V	M	H	R^3	I	R	R^2
V	V	M	H	L	R^2	R^3	I	R
M	M	H	L	V	R	R^2	R^3	I

4 R

Exercise 5C (page 62)

1 $ab = \begin{pmatrix} 1 & 2 & 3 & 4 & 5 \\ 3 & 4 & 1 & 2 & 5 \end{pmatrix}$

$ba = \begin{pmatrix} 1 & 2 & 3 & 4 & 5 \\ 1 & 4 & 5 & 2 & 3 \end{pmatrix}$

$a^2b = \begin{pmatrix} 1 & 2 & 3 & 4 & 5 \\ 4 & 1 & 5 & 3 & 2 \end{pmatrix}$

$ac^{-1} = \begin{pmatrix} 1 & 2 & 3 & 4 & 5 \\ 2 & 4 & 3 & 1 & 5 \end{pmatrix}$

$(ac)^{-1} = \begin{pmatrix} 1 & 2 & 3 & 4 & 5 \\ 4 & 1 & 3 & 2 & 5 \end{pmatrix}$

$c^{-1}ac = \begin{pmatrix} 1 & 2 & 3 & 4 & 5 \\ 3 & 4 & 2 & 5 & 1 \end{pmatrix}$

2 $x = a^{-1}b = \begin{pmatrix} 1 & 2 & 3 & 4 & 5 \\ 5 & 2 & 3 & 1 & 4 \end{pmatrix}$

$x = a^{-1}cb^{-1} = \begin{pmatrix} 1 & 2 & 3 & 4 & 5 \\ 4 & 1 & 2 & 5 & 3 \end{pmatrix}$

3 (a) $\begin{pmatrix} 1 & 2 & 3 \\ 1 & 3 & 2 \end{pmatrix}$ (b) $\begin{pmatrix} 1 & 2 & 3 \\ 2 & 1 & 3 \end{pmatrix}$

(c) $\begin{pmatrix} 1 & 2 & 3 \\ 3 & 1 & 2 \end{pmatrix}$ (d) $\begin{pmatrix} 1 & 2 & 3 \\ 3 & 2 & 1 \end{pmatrix}$

(e) $\begin{pmatrix} 1 & 2 & 3 \\ 2 & 1 & 3 \end{pmatrix}$ (f) $\begin{pmatrix} 1 & 2 & 3 \\ 3 & 1 & 2 \end{pmatrix}$

(g) $\begin{pmatrix} 1 & 2 & 3 \\ 1 & 2 & 3 \end{pmatrix}$ (h) $\begin{pmatrix} 1 & 2 & 3 \\ 2 & 3 & 1 \end{pmatrix}$

6 Subgroups

Exercise 6A (page 67)

1 $5^1 = 5,\ 5^2 = 7,\ 5^3 = 8,\ 5^4 = 4,\ 5^5 = 2,\ 5^6 = 1$; there are six distinct powers.

2 (a) 0, 1; 1, 6; 2, 3; 3, 2; 4, 3; 5, 6
   (b) 1, 1; 2, 10; 3, 6; 4, 5; 5, 5; 6, 10; 7, 10; 8, 10; 9, 5; 10, 2
   (c) I, 1; R, 4; R^2, 2; R^3, 4; H, 2; L, 2; V, 2; M, 2

3 X, Y, H

4 $i, -i;$ 2

5 $1, -1$

6 For example, any matrix of the form $\begin{pmatrix} 1 & k \\ 0 & -1 \end{pmatrix}$ where $k \in \mathbb{N}$ has order 2.

7 Yes; 5 is a generator.

8 2 (and -2) are both generators.

9 The first is not cyclic, since $a^2 = b^2 = c^2 = e$; the second is cyclic, with a and c as generators.

10 1, 2, 3 and 4 are generators of $(\mathbb{Z}_5, +)$; 1 and 5 are generators of $(\mathbb{Z}_6, +)$.

Exercise 6B (page 72)

1 (a) I, 1; R, 4; R^2, 2; R^3, 4; H, 2; L, 2; V, 2; M, 2
   (b) $\{I\},\ \{I, R^2\},\ \{I, H\},\ \{I, L\},\ \{I, V\},$ $\{I, M\},\ \{I, R, R^2, R^3\}$
   (c) $\{I, H, R^2, V\},\ \{I, L, R^2, M\}$

2 (a) $(\{0\}, +),\ (\{0, 2\}, +),\ (\mathbb{Z}_4, +)$
   (b) $(\{0\}, +),\ (\mathbb{Z}_5, +)$

3 $\left\{\begin{pmatrix} 1 & 2 & 3 \\ 1 & 2 & 3 \end{pmatrix}, \begin{pmatrix} 1 & 2 & 3 \\ 3 & 1 & 2 \end{pmatrix}, \begin{pmatrix} 1 & 2 & 3 \\ 2 & 3 & 1 \end{pmatrix}\right\},$

$\left\{\begin{pmatrix} 1 & 2 & 3 \\ 1 & 2 & 3 \end{pmatrix}, \begin{pmatrix} 1 & 2 & 3 \\ 1 & 3 & 2 \end{pmatrix}\right\},$

$\left\{\begin{pmatrix} 1 & 2 & 3 \\ 1 & 2 & 3 \end{pmatrix}, \begin{pmatrix} 1 & 2 & 3 \\ 3 & 2 & 1 \end{pmatrix}\right\},$

$\left\{\begin{pmatrix} 1 & 2 & 3 \\ 1 & 2 & 3 \end{pmatrix}, \begin{pmatrix} 1 & 2 & 3 \\ 2 & 1 & 3 \end{pmatrix}\right\}$

4 $\{1, -1\}$

8 (a) $\{I, R, S\}$ (b) $\{I, X\}$

(c) $\left\{\begin{pmatrix} a & b \\ 0 & a \end{pmatrix} : a, b \in \mathbb{R}\right\}$ (d) $\{e, b, q, s\}$

(e) $\{e, x, p\}$

9 $\{e\},\ \{e, b\},\ \{e, a, b, c\},\ \{e, b, p, r\},\ \{e, b, q, s\},$ Q_4

10 $\{e\},\ \{e, a\},\ \{e, b\},\ \{e, c\},\ \{e, x, p\},\ \{e, y, q\},$ $\{e, z, r\},\ \{e, t, s\},\ \{e, a, b, c\},\ A_4$

Exercise 6C (page 74)

1 1, 2, 3, 4, 6, 8, 12, 24

2 As 9 is not a factor of 15, Lagrange's theorem shows that a group of order 15 cannot have a subgroup of order 9.

3 $1, p, q$ and pq

5 $1,\ p$ and p^2; $1,\ p,\ p^2$ and p^3

Exercise 6D (page 77)

1 $\{I, R, S\},\ \{X, Y, Z\}$; $\{I\},\ \{R\},\ \{S\},\ \{X\},\ \{Y\},\ \{Z\}$ D_3

2 $\{0, 3\},\ \{1, 4\},\ \{2, 5\}$

3 (a) $\{e, a, b, c\},\ \{x, y, z, t\},\ \{p, q, r, s\}$
   (b) $\{e, x, p\},\ \{a, t, r\},\ \{b, y, s\},\ \{c, z, q\}$

4 $\{0, \pm 3, \pm 6, \dots\},\ \{\dots, -2, 1, 4, \dots\},\ \{\dots, -1, 2, 5, \dots\}$

7 Isomorphisms of groups

Exercise 7A (page 83)

3 2 is a generator of $(\mathbb{Z}_{13} \setminus \{0\}, \times (\bmod 13))$. Define a function $f : \mathbb{Z}_{13} \to \mathbb{Z}_{12}$ by the rule $f(2^n) = n$ and show that it is an isomorphism.

Exercise 7B (page 87)

1 (a)

	2	4	6	8
2	4	8	2	6
4	8	6	4	2
6	2	4	6	8
8	6	2	8	4

(b) 6; $2^{-1} = 8$, $4^{-1} = 4$, $6^{-1} = 6$, $8^{-1} = 2$

(c) Both groups are cyclic with generators 2 and i respectively, so they are isomorphic.

2 (a) $e, 1$; $a, 2$; $b, 4$; $b^2, 2$; $b^3, 4$; $ab, 2$; $ab^2, 2$; $ab^3, 3$

(b) 5 subgroups; $\{e, a\}$, $\{e, ab\}$, $\{e, ab^2\}$, $\{e, b^2\}$ and $\{e, ab^3\}$ all have order 2.

(c) $\{e, b, b^2, b^3\}$ and $\{e, ab, b^2, ab^3\}$

(d) By Lagrange's theorem the order of a subgroup of a finite group divides the order of the group. As 6 does not divide 8, there is no subgroup of order 6.

(e) M is commutative and D is not, $ab \neq ba$.

3 (a) 9, 17, 25, 33, 41, 49, 57, 1
Orders are 1, 1; 9, 8; 17, 4; 25, 8; 33, 2; 41, 8; 49, 4; 57, 8.
The possible generators are 9, 25, 41, 57.
The subgroups are $\{1\}$, $\{1, 33\}$, $\{1, 17, 33, 49\}$, G.

(b) G contains a generator, so it is cyclic. Every element of H apart from the identity has order 2, so H is not cyclic. Therefore G and H are not isomorphic.

4 (a) $p = 4$, $q = 5$

(b) 1 and 8 are self-inverse; the other inverses occur in pairs, 2, 5 and 4, 7; $\{1\}$, $\{1, 8\}$, $\{1, 4, 7\}$, G.

(c) The order of the element 2 of G is 6, so G is cyclic. $\omega \in H$ has order 6, so H is cyclic. Therefore G and H are isomorphic.

5 (a) $\{1\}$, $\{1, 13\}$

(b) The elements are the rotations of $\frac{2}{3}\pi$, $\frac{4}{3}\pi$ and 0 about the centre of the triangle, plus reflections in the lines of symmetry.

$\{1, 9, 11\}$ is a subgroup of G which is isomorphic to the subgroup of rotations of H.

6 $k = 11$. The possible values of n are 1, 2, 4 and 8. $\{1, 4, 7, 13\}$, $\{1, 2, 4, 8\}$ and $\{1, 4, 11, 14\}$. The orders of the elements in these groups are 1, 2, 4, 4, 1, 4, 2, 4 and 1, 2, 2, 2. The first two groups both have generators, and are therefore cyclic

and isomorphic. The third group does not have a generator, and is not isomorphic to the other two.

7 The orders of the elements $\{1, -1, i, -i\}$ are 1, 2, 4, 4. The orders of the elements $\{1, 7, 18, 24\}$ are 1, 4, 4, 2. Both groups have generators, and are therefore both cyclic and isomorphic.

8 (b)

	0	2	3	4	5	6
0	0	2	3	4	5	6
2	2	0	6	5	4	3
3	3	6	4	2	0	5
4	4	5	2	6	3	0
5	5	4	0	3	6	2
6	6	3	5	0	2	4

(d) 3 is a generator for G, so G is a cyclic group. The group of rotations of the regular hexagon has an element (rotation of angle $\frac{1}{3}\pi$) of order 6 and is cyclic. Therefore the groups are isomorphic.

9

G_5	1	2	3	4
1	1	2	3	4
2	2	4	1	3
3	3	1	4	2
4	4	3	2	1

G_8	1	3	5	7
1	1	3	5	7
3	3	1	7	5
5	5	7	1	3
7	7	5	3	1

G_{10}	1	3	7	9
1	1	3	7	9
3	3	9	1	7
7	7	1	9	3
9	9	7	3	1

G_{12}	1	5	7	11
1	1	5	7	11
5	5	1	11	7
7	7	11	1	5
11	11	7	5	1

There are only two groups of order 4, up to isomorphism, the cyclic group $\mathbb{Z}_4$ and the four-group V. The groups G_5 and G_{10} have generators 2 and 3 respectively, so they are cyclic and isomorphic to $\mathbb{Z}_4$. The elements of G_8 and G_{12}, apart from the identity elements, all have order 2, so these groups are not cyclic, and are isomorphic to the four-group V.

8 The algebra of sets

Exercise 8A (page 94)

1 (a) A (b) B (c) U (d) A
3 (a) $\varnothing$ (b) U (c) U (d) A'

Exercise 8B (page 97)

1 (a) $A \cap B'$ (b) $A \cup B$
2 (a) $\varnothing$ (b) A
   (c) A' (d) $A \cup B$
   (e) $A \cap B$ (f) $A \cap B$
6 (a) $\{1,2,5,6\}$ (b) $\{1,2\}$
   (c) $\{5,6\}$ (d) $\{1,2\}$

7

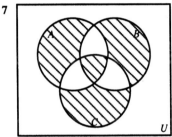

The region representing $A \,\Delta\,(B \,\Delta\, C)$ is symmetrical with regard to the sets A, B and C. This suggests that Δ is associative.

8 (a) $A' \cup B$ (b) U

Review exercise

(page 98)

3 (b) Show that
$$\big((a,b)*(c,d)\big)*(e,f)=(a,b)*\big((c,d)*(e,f)\big).$$
   (c) $(1,0)$
4 (a) $\{y \in \mathbb{R} \mid 0 < y \le 1\}$ or $]0,1]$
   (b) Not injective, as $f(1) = f(-1)$; not surjective as no element maps to 2.
   (c) $A = \mathbb{R}^+ \cup \{0\}$ or $A = [0,\infty[$;
        $B = \{y \in \mathbb{R} \mid 0 < y \le 1\}$ or $B =]0,1]$
5 R is an equivalence relation. The equivalence classes are numbers of equal modulus.
6 (a) $\begin{pmatrix} 1 & 2 & 3 & 4 \\ 4 & 3 & 2 & 1 \end{pmatrix}$, $\begin{pmatrix} 1 & 2 & 3 & 4 \\ 3 & 1 & 4 & 2 \end{pmatrix}$
        $\begin{pmatrix} 1 & 2 & 3 & 4 \\ 2 & 3 & 1 & 4 \end{pmatrix}$, $\begin{pmatrix} 1 & 2 & 3 & 4 \\ 2 & 3 & 1 & 4 \end{pmatrix}$
   (b) 4, 2

7 (a) $\{1,12\}$ (b) $\{1,3,9\}$
   (c) By Lagrange's theorem, the order of a subgroup divides the order of a group. As 5 does not divide 12, there is no subgroup of order 5.

8 (a) a, 4; b, 1; c, 4; d, 2
   (b) $\{b,d\}$

9 (a) $(b \otimes c)(x) = 1 - \dfrac{1}{1-x} = \dfrac{1-x-1}{1-x} = \dfrac{x}{x-1}$
        $d(x) = \dfrac{x-1}{x}$; $e(x) = \dfrac{x}{x-1}$

   (b)

G	i	a	b	c	d	e
i	i	a	b	c	d	e
a	a	i	c	b	e	d
b	b	d	i	e	a	c
c	c	e	a	d	i	b
d	d	b	e	i	c	a
e	e	c	d	a	b	i

   (d) Not commutative as $d \otimes a = b$ and $a \otimes d = e$.
   (e) Not cyclic since it is not commutative.
   (f) $\{i\}$, $\{i,a\}$, $\{i,b\}$, $\{i,e\}$, $\{i,c,d\}$, G

10 (d) $\begin{pmatrix} \pm 1 & b \\ 0 & 1 \end{pmatrix}$
    (e) $\left\{ \begin{pmatrix} 1 & 0 \\ 0 & 1 \end{pmatrix}, \begin{pmatrix} 0 & -1 \\ 1 & 0 \end{pmatrix}, \begin{pmatrix} -1 & 0 \\ 0 & -1 \end{pmatrix}, \begin{pmatrix} 0 & 1 \\ -1 & 0 \end{pmatrix} \right\}$
         This is the subgroup generated by a rotation of $\frac{1}{2}\pi$ anticlockwise about the origin.

12 (b) $\{2\}$, $\{2,5\}$, $\{2,4,0\}$, G
14 In order, 9, 17, 25, 33, 41, 49, 57, 1.
    Inverses are in pairs, 9, 57; 17, 49; 25, 41; and 33 is self-inverse.
    Generators are 9, 25, 41, 57.

15	0	1	2	3	4	5	6
0	0	1	2	3	4	5	6
1	1	1	1	1	1	1	1
2	2	1	0	6	5	4	3
3	3	1	6	4	2	0	5
4	4	1	5	2	6	3	0
5	5	1	4	0	3	6	2
6	6	1	3	5	0	2	4

Remove the element 1.

16 $\varnothing$, 1; A, 2; B, 2; $A\Delta B$, 2
17 The equivalence classes are the sets $aH = \{ah \mid h \in H\}$ for each element $a \in G$.

Examination questions

1 (b) $\begin{pmatrix} 1 & 0 \\ 0 & 1 \end{pmatrix}, \begin{pmatrix} 1 & 0 \\ 1 & 1 \end{pmatrix}, \begin{pmatrix} 0 & 1 \\ 1 & 1 \end{pmatrix}, \begin{pmatrix} 1 & 1 \\ 1 & 0 \end{pmatrix}$

(c) (i) $\begin{pmatrix} 0 & 1 \\ 1 & 0 \end{pmatrix}$ has order 2;

$\begin{pmatrix} 1 & 1 \\ 1 & 0 \end{pmatrix}$ and $\begin{pmatrix} 0 & 1 \\ 1 & 1 \end{pmatrix}$ have order 3.

(ii) $\begin{pmatrix} 1 & 0 \\ 0 & 1 \end{pmatrix}, \begin{pmatrix} 1 & 1 \\ 1 & 0 \end{pmatrix}, \begin{pmatrix} 0 & 1 \\ 1 & 1 \end{pmatrix}$

2 (b) (iii) In $\mathbb{Z}_m$, $p +_m q = p + q \pmod{m}$

3 (a) Closure is satisfied as the result of multiplying any two members of the set is still a member of the set. d is the identity. The inverses of a, b, c, d, e are respectively a, b, c, d, e. However, $a(be) = ac = e$ and $(ab)e = ce = a$, so the associative rule is not satisfied. Hence three but not four of the axioms are satisfied.

(d) (i) $\begin{pmatrix} 2 & 1 \\ 1 & 1 \end{pmatrix}$ (ii) $\begin{pmatrix} 0 & 1 \\ 1 & 0 \end{pmatrix}$

4 (b) $\{2, 4, 8, 10, 14\}$ and $\{6, 12\}$

5 (a) $[e^{-1} - 1, e - 1]$

(b) (i) $f(0) = f(\pi) = 0$

(ii) Not a surjection; no element maps to 2.

(c) (i) $\frac{1}{2}\pi$

(ii) $g^{-1}(x) = \arcsin(\ln(1 + x))$

(iii) $\left[-\frac{1}{2}\pi, \frac{1}{2}\pi\right]$

Index

The page numbers refer to the first mention of each term, or the box if there is one.

Abelian group, 48
absorption rule, 11
associative binary operation, 39
associative rule, 10
    for functions, 33
axioms of a group, 45

bijection, 25
binary operation, 38

cancellation law, 47
Cayley table, 41
closed binary operation, 38
co-domain, 23
commutative, 39
    group, 48
    rule, 9
complement, 6
complement of a complement rule, 90
complementation rules, 90
composite function, 29
    inverse of, 33
cyclic group, 66

De Morgan's laws, 95
dihedral group of the triangle, 57
disjoint sets, 8
distributive rule, 40
    for intersection over union, 92
    for union over intersection, 91
domain, 23

element of a set, 1
empty set, 3
equal functions, 24
equal sets, 2
    proof of, 9

equivalence class, 18
equivalence relation, 17

finite order, 65
finite set, 3
function, 23, 35

generator, 66
group(s), 45
    A_4, 73
    cyclic, 66
    D_n, 57
    isomorphic, 79
    Klein four-, 85
    of order 4, 84
    of order 6, 85
    Q_4, 73
    S_n, 60
group axioms, 45
group notation, 63

identity element, 44
identity function, 24
image of a subset, 24
image set, 23
infinite order
    of an element, 65
    of a group, 45
infinite set, 3
injection, 25
intersection, 6
inverse
    of a composite function, 33
    element, 44
    function, 32
isomorphism, 79

Klein four-group, 85

Lagrange's theorem, 74
Latin square, 41

mapping, 22
member of a set, 1
modular arithmetic, 52

operation table, 41
order,
    of an element, 65
    of a group, 45

partition, 19
permutation, 59
pigeon-hole principle, 27
proper subgroup, 69
proper subset, 4

range, 23
reflexive property, 17
relation, 16
right coset, 75
rules for algebra of sets, 92

sample space, 13
set, 1
set difference, 8
set of images, 23
subgroup, 69
    of a finite group, 71
    generated by an element, 72
subset, 4
surjection, 25
symmetric difference, 96
symmetric group, 60
symmetric property, 17
symmetry, 56

tautology rule, 11
transitive property, 17
trivial subgroup, 69

union, 6
universal set, 3

Venn diagram, 5

well-defined set, 1

Topic 4
Series and differential equations

Hugh Neill and Douglas Quadling

Series Editor Hugh Neill

CAMBRIDGE
UNIVERSITY PRESS

Contents

Introduction   v

1   Summing finite series   1

2   Infinite series   12

3   Tests for convergence   23

4   Series and integrals   32

5   Infinite integrals and infinite series   45

6   Series with positive and negative terms   55

7   The theory of limits   65

8   Power series   79

9   Maclaurin series   85

10   The error term   102

11   Taylor series and l'Hôpital's rule   115

12   Homogeneous differential equations   121

13   Linear differential equations   133

14   Approximate methods   142

Review exercise   150

Answers   154

Index   161

Introduction

Series and differential equations has been written especially for the International Baccalaureate Further Mathematics examination. This book covers the syllabus for Topic 4.

There are 11 chapters on series followed by 3 chapters on differential equations, and these are completely independent of each other. Students could, if they wish, begin work on the differential equations chapters as soon as they have completed the associated chapters 23 and 27 in Higher Level Book 2. There is a small amount of material which extends a topic beyond the syllabus as printed, with the aim of enhancing students' appreciation of the subject. This is indicated by an asterisk (*) at the appropriate place in the text.

Occasionally within the text paragraphs appear in *this type style*. These paragraphs are usually outside the main stream of the mathematical argument, but may help to give insight, or suggest extra work or different approaches.

Students are expected to have access to graphic display calculators and the text places considerable emphasis on their potential for supporting the learning of mathematics.

There are plenty of exercises throughout. At the end of the book there is a Review exercise which includes some questions from past International Baccalaureate examinations, but on a different syllabus. At the time of writing, there are few current versions of the Higher Level examinations, so there is no backlog of examination questions on the newer parts of the syllabus.

The authors thank OCR and IBO for permission to use some examination questions and Cambridge University Press for their help in producing this book. Particular thanks are due to Brian Fugard, for his help and advice. However, the responsibility for the text, and for any errors, remains with the authors.

1 Summing finite series

When the terms of a series are given algebraically, it may be possible to find a formula for the sum of n terms. When you have completed this chapter, you should

- know how to use the method of differences to find the sums of series
- be able to express algebraic fractions as the sum of partial fractions, and use these in conjunction with the method of differences to sum series.

1.1 The method of differences

You already know a number of formulae for the sums of series of different kinds. Here are some examples.

Sums of powers of integers:

$$\sum_{i=1}^{n} i = 1 + 2 + 3 + \ldots + n = \tfrac{1}{2}n(n+1) \qquad \text{(HL Book 1 Section 2.3)}$$

$$\sum_{i=1}^{n} i^2 = 1^2 + 2^2 + 3^2 + \ldots + n^2 = \tfrac{1}{6}n(n+1)(2n+1) \qquad \text{(HL Book 2 Section 1.6)}$$

Geometric series:

$$\sum_{i=1}^{n} r^{i-1} = 1 + r + r^2 + \ldots + r^{n-1} = \frac{1-r^n}{1-r} \quad (r \neq 1) \qquad \text{(HL Book 1 Section 30.3)}$$

Various methods have been used to prove these: from a diagram, by mathematical induction, or by a special algebraic method which depends on a particular property of the sequence of terms.

Finding a formula for the sum of a series is called 'summing' the series.

This section describes a general method which can be used to sum a number of series. It depends on being able to find a function f so that a general term u_i of the series can be expressed in the form

$$u_i = f(i) - f(i-1).$$

Then the sum of the series is

$$\sum_{i=1}^{n} u_i = (f(1) - f(0)) + (f(2) - f(1)) + (f(3) - f(2)) + \ldots + (f(n) - f(n-1)).$$

Now in this sum you have $f(1)$ in the first bracket and $-f(1)$ in the second, $f(2)$ in the second bracket and $-f(2)$ in the third, and so on. All that is left is $-f(0)$ in the first bracket and $f(n)$ in the last. So

$$\sum_{i=1}^{n} u_i = f(n) - f(0).$$

This is called the **method of differences**, and the series is summed by **telescoping**.

> **Method of differences**   If, given a sequence u_i, you can find a function f such that $u_i = f(i) - f(i-1)$, then
>
> $$\sum_{i=1}^{n} u_i = f(n) - f(0).$$

The difficult part, of course, is finding a function f with the required property. This is a 'trial and error' process (or perhaps better, 'trial and modify'). The following examples suggest some methods which often work.

Example 1.1.1

Sum $\displaystyle\sum_{i=1}^{n} i(i+1)$.

The general term u_i is the product of two consecutive integers, so try taking for $g(i)$ the product of three consecutive integers $i(i+1)(i+2)$. (Think 'g stands for guess'!) Then

$$g(i-1) = (i-1)(i-1+1)(i-1+2)$$
$$= (i-1)i(i+1).$$

Notice that both $g(i)$ and $g(i-1)$ have $i(i+1)$ as a factor. So

$$g(i) - g(i-1) = i(i+1)(i+2) - (i-1)i(i+1)$$
$$= i(i+1)((i+2) - (i-1))$$
$$= i(i+1) \times 3.$$

The first guess is just 3 times u_i. So modify the guess by dividing the first guess by 3. If $f(i) = \frac{1}{3}g(i) = \frac{1}{3}i(i+1)(i+2)$, then

$$f(i) - f(i-1) = \tfrac{1}{3}(g(i) - g(i-1))$$
$$= \tfrac{1}{3} \times i(i+1) \times 3$$
$$= i(i+1).$$

You have now found a function with the desired property, so by the result in the shaded box

$$\sum_{i=1}^{n} i(i+1) = f(n) - f(0)$$
$$= \tfrac{1}{3}n(n+1)(n+2) - \tfrac{1}{3} \times 0 \times 1 \times 2$$
$$= \tfrac{1}{3}n(n+1)(n+2).$$

It is a good idea to check your answer numerically with a small value for n. For example, if $n = 2$, the left side is $1 \times 2 + 2 \times 3 = 2 + 6 = 8$, and the right side is $\frac{1}{3} \times 2 \times 3 \times 4 = 8$.

It is worth noticing that the result of Example 1.1.1 gives another method of summing $\sum_{i=1}^{n} i^2$. Since, by the addition rule (Higher Level Book 1 Section 2.6),

$$\sum_{i=1}^{n} i(i+1) = \sum_{i=1}^{n} \left(i^2 + i\right) = \sum_{i=1}^{n} i^2 + \sum_{i=1}^{n} i,$$

it follows that

$$\sum_{i=1}^{n} i^2 = \sum_{i=1}^{n} i(i+1) - \sum_{i=1}^{n} i$$
$$= \tfrac{1}{3} n(n+1)(n+2) - \tfrac{1}{2} n(n+1)$$
$$= \tfrac{1}{6} n(n+1)(2(n+2) - 3)$$
$$= \tfrac{1}{6} n(n+1)(2n+1).$$

Example 1.1.2

Write $\dfrac{1}{1 \times 2} + \dfrac{1}{2 \times 3} + \dfrac{1}{3 \times 4} + \ldots + \dfrac{1}{98 \times 99} + \dfrac{1}{99 \times 100}$ as a single fraction.

This sum could be written as $\sum_{i=1}^{99} \dfrac{1}{i(i+1)}$, so you want to find a function f such that

$$f(i) - f(i-1) = \frac{1}{i(i+1)}.$$

It is obviously no good starting as in Example 1.1.1 by guessing $g(i) = \dfrac{1}{i(i+1)(i+2)}$, since then $g(i-1)$ would be $\dfrac{1}{(i-1)i(i+1)}$ and $g(i) - g(i-1)$ would be a fraction with four factors in the denominator, $(i-1)i(i+1)(i+2)$.

But this gives a hint how you might find $f(i)$. To get a fraction so that $f(i) - f(i-1)$ has just two factors in the denominator, perhaps you should begin with fractions $f(i)$ and $f(i-1)$ each having one factor in the denominator.

The obvious guess is that $g(i)$ is $\dfrac{1}{i+1}$. Then $g(i-1) = \dfrac{1}{i-1+1} = \dfrac{1}{i}$. So

$$g(i) - g(i-1) = \frac{1}{i+1} - \frac{1}{i}$$
$$= \frac{i - (i+1)}{(i+1)i} = \frac{-1}{i(i+1)}.$$

This is almost what you want, except for the minus sign. So take $f(i) = -g(i) = \dfrac{-1}{i+1}$. Then

$$f(i) - f(i-1) = \frac{-1}{i+1} - \frac{-1}{i}$$
$$= \frac{-i + (i+1)}{(i+1)i} = \frac{1}{i(i+1)}.$$

Using $\dfrac{1}{i(i+1)} = \dfrac{-1}{i+1} - \dfrac{-1}{i}$ with $i = 1, 2, 3, \ldots , 99$ in turn,

$$\frac{1}{1\times 2} + \frac{1}{2\times 3} + \frac{1}{3\times 4} + \ldots + \frac{1}{98\times 99} + \frac{1}{99\times 100}$$

$$= \left(\frac{-1}{2} - \frac{-1}{1}\right) + \left(\frac{-1}{3} - \frac{-1}{2}\right) + \left(\frac{-1}{4} - \frac{-1}{3}\right) + \ldots + \left(\frac{-1}{99} - \frac{-1}{98}\right) + \left(\frac{-1}{100} - \frac{-1}{99}\right)$$

$$= \left(1 - \tfrac{1}{2}\right) + \left(\tfrac{1}{2} - \tfrac{1}{3}\right) + \left(\tfrac{1}{3} - \tfrac{1}{4}\right) + \ldots + \left(\tfrac{1}{98} - \tfrac{1}{99}\right) + \left(\tfrac{1}{99} - \tfrac{1}{100}\right)$$

$$= 1 - \tfrac{1}{100} = \tfrac{99}{100}.$$

Example 1.1.3

Simplify $f(i) - f(i-1)$ when $f(i) = i^2(i+1)^2$. Use your answer to sum $\displaystyle\sum_{i=1}^{n} i^3$.

$$f(i) - f(i-1) = i^2(i+1)^2 - (i-1)^2 i^2$$

$$= i^2\big((i+1)^2 - (i-1)^2\big)$$

$$= i^2\big((i+1) - (i-1)\big)\big((i+1) + (i-1)\big) \qquad \text{(difference of two squares)}$$

$$= i^2 \times 2 \times 2i = 4i^3.$$

Then, using the method of differences,

$$f(n) - f(0) = \sum_{i=1}^{n} 4i^3 = 4\sum_{i=1}^{n} i^3,$$

so

$$\sum_{i=1}^{n} i^3 = \tfrac{1}{4}\big(n^2(n+1)^2 - 0^2 \times (0+1)^2\big)$$

$$= \tfrac{1}{4}n^2(n+1)^2.$$

You may have noticed that the process of finding a function f such that $u_i = f(i) - f(i-1)$ is rather like finding an indefinite integral. Compare $\displaystyle\sum_{i=1}^{n} u_i = f(n) - f(0)$ with $\displaystyle\int_a^b f(x)\,dx = I(b) - I(a)$. Can you see any other similarities?

Exercise 1A

1 Use the method of Example 1.1.2 to prove that $\displaystyle\sum_{i=1}^{n} \frac{1}{i(i+1)} = \frac{n}{n+1}$.

2 (a) Find a function f such that $f(i) - f(i-1) = i(i+1)(i+2)$. Hence sum $\displaystyle\sum_{i=1}^{n} i(i+1)(i+2)$.

(b) Find a function f such that $f(i) - f(i-1) = \dfrac{1}{i(i+1)(i+2)}$. Hence sum $\displaystyle\sum_{i=1}^{n} \frac{1}{i(i+1)(i+2)}$.

3 Simplify $i^3(i+1)^3 - (i-1)^3 i^3$. Hence, using the result of Example 1.1.3, sum $\displaystyle\sum_{i=1}^{n} i^5$.

Check your answer with a numerical value for n.

4 Sum the series

(a) $\displaystyle\sum_{i=1}^{n} \ln\left(1+\frac{1}{i}\right)$,   (b) $\displaystyle\sum_{i=1}^{n} \frac{i-1}{i!}$.

5 If $f(i) = (i+1)!$, show that $f(i) - f(i-1) = i \times i!$. Hence sum $\displaystyle\sum_{i=1}^{n} i \times i!$.

6 Find the value of $\displaystyle\sum_{i=1}^{100} \frac{1}{(2i-1)(2i+1)}$.

7 Simplify $(2i+1)^5 - (2i-1)^5$. Hence sum $\displaystyle\sum_{i=1}^{20} i^4$.

Check your answer by using a calculator to sum the series.

8 (a) Show that $ir^i - (i-1)r^{i-1} = r^{i-1} - (1-r)ir^{i-1}$. Use this result to find $\displaystyle\sum_{i=1}^{n} ir^{i-1}$.

(b) Check your answer by differentiating the sum $\displaystyle\sum_{i=0}^{n} r^i$.

9 Prove that $\sin\left(i+\tfrac{1}{2}\right)\theta - \sin\left(i-\tfrac{1}{2}\right)\theta = 2\cos i\theta \sin\tfrac{1}{2}\theta$. Hence sum $\displaystyle\sum_{i=1}^{n} \cos i\theta$.

1.2 Partial fractions

In Example 1.1.2 the expression $\dfrac{1}{i(i+1)}$ was split into two simpler fractions as $\dfrac{-1}{i+1} - \dfrac{-1}{i}$, which is

$\dfrac{1}{i} - \dfrac{1}{i+1}$. This process is called **splitting into partial fractions**. It is a very useful technique, not only for summing series but also for differentiation, integration, curve sketching and many other applications.

When you add two fractions $\dfrac{a}{x-p} + \dfrac{b}{x-q}$ you get a single fraction

$$\frac{a(x-q)+b(x-p)}{(x-p)(x-q)}, \quad \text{which can be written as} \quad \frac{(a+b)x-(aq+bp)}{(x-p)(x-q)}.$$

The denominator is a quadratic polynomial in factor form. The numerator is usually a linear polynomial, but if $a+b=0$ it is simply a constant. In any case, the degree of the numerator is 1 or less.

If you increase the number of fractions to three, $\dfrac{a}{x-p} + \dfrac{b}{x-q} + \dfrac{c}{x-r}$, you get

$$\frac{a(x-q)(x-r)+b(x-p)(x-r)+c(x-p)(x-q)}{(x-p)(x-q)(x-r)}.$$

The denominator is now a cubic polynomial. The numerator is a polynomial of degree 2, or possibly less. The important point is that the degree of the numerator is less than the number of factors in the denominator.

If you have a fraction with two or more linear factors in the denominator and a polynomial of lower degree in the numerator, you can reverse the process and express it as the sum of partial fractions of the form $\dfrac{a}{x-p}$.

Example 1.2.1

Split $\dfrac{4}{(x-1)(3x+1)}$ into partial fractions.

The aim is to find numbers A and B such that

$$\frac{A}{x-1} + \frac{B}{3x+1} \equiv \frac{4}{(x-1)(3x+1)}.$$

Notice the use of $\equiv$ to denote an identity. The two sides have to be equal for all the values of x for which they have a meaning.

Begin by finding A. To do this, multiply both sides of the identity by $x-1$ to get another identity

$$A + \frac{B(x-1)}{3x+1} \equiv \frac{4}{3x+1}.$$

Notice that on the right the effect of multiplying by $x-1$ is simply to remove the factor $(x-1)$ from the denominator.

Now, to find A without involving B, you want to cut out the second term on the left side. You can do this by putting x equal to 1, which makes $x-1=0$. This gives

$$A + \frac{B \times 0}{3 \times 1 + 1} = \frac{4}{3 \times 1 + 1},$$

so $A + 0 = \dfrac{4}{4}$,   giving $A = 1$.

You can use a similar method to find B. This time multiply both sides of the original identity by $3x+1$ to get

$$\frac{A(3x+1)}{x-1} + B \equiv \frac{4}{x-1}.$$

The effect of this is to remove the factor $(3x+1)$ from the denominator on the right.

To find B without involving A, put $x = -\frac{1}{3}$, which makes $3x+1=0$. This gives

$$\frac{A \times 0}{-\frac{1}{3}-1} + B = \frac{4}{-\frac{1}{3}-1},$$

so $0 + B = \dfrac{4}{-\frac{4}{3}}$,   giving $B = -3$.

Putting all this together,

$$\frac{4}{(x-1)(3x+1)} \equiv \frac{1}{x-1} + \frac{-3}{3x+1}$$

$$\equiv \frac{1}{x-1} - \frac{3}{3x+1}.$$

Example 1.2.2

Split $\dfrac{4x+1}{(x-2)(2x-1)}$ into partial fractions.

You want to find A and B such that

$$\frac{A}{x-2} + \frac{B}{2x-1} \equiv \frac{4x+1}{(x-2)(2x-1)}.$$

To find A, multiply by $x-2$:

$$A + \frac{B(x-2)}{2x-1} \equiv \frac{4x+1}{2x-1}.$$

The factor $(x-2)$ has disappeared from the denominator on the right. Now put $x=2$:

$$A + \frac{B \times 0}{2 \times 2 - 1} = \frac{4 \times 2 + 1}{2 \times 2 - 1}.$$

So $\quad A + 0 = \dfrac{9}{3}, \quad$ giving $\quad A = 3$.

To find B, multiply by $2x-1$:

$$\frac{A(2x-1)}{x-2} + B \equiv \frac{4x+1}{x-2}.$$

The factor $(2x-1)$ has disappeared from the denominator on the right. Now put $x = \frac{1}{2}$:

$$\frac{A \times 0}{\frac{1}{2} - 2} + B = \frac{4 \times \frac{1}{2} + 1}{\frac{1}{2} - 2}.$$

So $\quad 0 + B = \dfrac{3}{-\frac{3}{2}}, \quad$ giving $\quad B = -2$.

Therefore, in partial fractions,

$$\frac{4x+1}{(x-2)(2x-1)} \equiv \frac{3}{x-2} - \frac{2}{2x-1}.$$

It is worth checking the answer, by combining the partial fractions to make sure that they give the correct numerator. In Example 1.2.2 the numerator is $3(2x-1) - 2(x-2)$, which can be simplified as $6x - 3 - 2x + 4 \equiv 4x + 1$, as required.

You will soon find that you can write down the partial fractions without setting out the intermediate steps in full. In Example 1.2.2, to find A you remove $(x-2)$ from the denominator and then put $x=2$. To find B you remove $(2x-1)$ from the denominator and put $x=\frac{1}{2}$.

Example 1.2.3

Split $\dfrac{x^2+2}{x(x+1)(x-2)}$ into partial fractions.

You want

$$\frac{A}{x}+\frac{B}{x+1}+\frac{C}{x-2}\equiv\frac{x^2+2}{x(x+1)(x-2)}.$$

To find A, remove x from the denominator on the right and put $x=0$:

$$A=\frac{0^2+2}{(0+1)(0-2)}=\frac{2}{-2}=-1.$$

To find B, remove $(x+1)$ from the denominator on the right and put $x=-1$:

$$B=\frac{(-1)^2+2}{(-1)(-1-2)}=\frac{3}{3}=1.$$

To find C, remove $(x-2)$ from the denominator on the right and put $x=2$:

$$C=\frac{2^2+2}{2(2+1)}=\frac{6}{6}=1.$$

So $\dfrac{x^2+2}{x(x+1)(x-2)}\equiv-\dfrac{1}{x}+\dfrac{1}{x+1}+\dfrac{1}{x-2}.$

Exercise 1B

1   Split the following into partial fractions.

(a) $\dfrac{2x+8}{(x+5)(x+3)}$ (b) $\dfrac{10x+8}{(x-1)(x+5)}$ (c) $\dfrac{x}{(x-4)(x-5)}$ (d) $\dfrac{28}{(2x-1)(x+3)}$

2   Split the following into partial fractions.

(a) $\dfrac{8x+1}{x^2+x-2}$ (b) $\dfrac{25}{x^2-3x-4}$ (c) $\dfrac{10x-6}{x^2-9}$ (d) $\dfrac{3}{2x^2+x}$

3   Split into partial fractions

(a) $\dfrac{35-5x}{(x+2)(x-1)(x-3)}$,   (b) $\dfrac{8x^2}{(x+1)(x-1)(x+3)}$,   (c) $\dfrac{15x^2-28x-72}{x^3-2x^2-24x}$.

1.3   Summation using partial fractions

You can often use partial fractions to express the terms of a series in the form $f(i) - f(i-1)$, and hence to sum the series.

Example 1.3.1

Find the sum of the first n terms of the series $\dfrac{1}{1 \times 4} + \dfrac{1}{4 \times 7} + \dfrac{1}{7 \times 10} + \cdots$.

The numbers $1, 4, 7, \ldots$ form an arithmetic sequence, and the ith number in the sequence is $1 + 3(i-1) = 3i - 2$. So a general term of the series is $\dfrac{1}{(3i-2)(3i+1)}$, which can be expressed in partial fractions as

$$\frac{\frac{1}{3}}{3i-2} - \frac{\frac{1}{3}}{3i+1}.$$

You can write this as

$$\frac{\frac{1}{3}}{3(i-1)+1} - \frac{\frac{1}{3}}{3i+1},$$

which is $f(i) - f(i-1)$ with $f(i) = -\dfrac{\frac{1}{3}}{3i+1}$.

So, using the method of differences, the sum of the series is

$$f(n) - f(0) = -\frac{\frac{1}{3}}{3n+1} + \frac{\frac{1}{3}}{1} = \frac{1}{3} - \frac{1}{3(3n+1)}.$$

Example 1.3.2

Find the value of $\displaystyle\sum_{i=1}^{50} \frac{i}{(i+1)(i+2)(i+3)}$.

You can check for yourself that, in partial fractions,

$$\frac{i}{(i+1)(i+2)(i+3)} \equiv -\frac{\frac{1}{2}}{i+1} + \frac{2}{i+2} - \frac{\frac{3}{2}}{i+3}.$$

There are two possible ways to continue.

Method 1   You may not see how this expression can be put into the form $f(i) - f(i-1)$. But if you write out the first few and the last few terms using the partial fraction form you may spot a way of finding the sum.

$$\sum_{i=1}^{50} \frac{i}{(i+1)(i+2)(i+3)} = \frac{1}{2 \times 3 \times 4} + \frac{2}{3 \times 4 \times 5} + \frac{3}{4 \times 5 \times 6} + \cdots$$

$$+ \frac{48}{49 \times 50 \times 51} + \frac{49}{50 \times 51 \times 52} + \frac{50}{51 \times 52 \times 53}.$$

Writing the terms on the right downwards, and using the identity above, you get

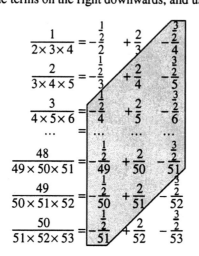

$$\frac{1}{2\times 3\times 4}=-\frac{\frac{1}{2}}{2}+\frac{2}{3}-\frac{\frac{3}{2}}{4}$$

$$\frac{2}{3\times 4\times 5}=-\frac{\frac{1}{2}}{3}+\frac{2}{4}-\frac{\frac{3}{2}}{5}$$

$$\frac{3}{4\times 5\times 6}=-\frac{\frac{1}{2}}{4}+\frac{2}{5}-\frac{\frac{3}{2}}{6}$$

$$\cdots = \cdots \cdots$$

$$\frac{48}{49\times 50\times 51}=-\frac{\frac{1}{2}}{49}+\frac{2}{50}-\frac{\frac{3}{2}}{51}$$

$$\frac{49}{50\times 51\times 52}=-\frac{\frac{1}{2}}{50}+\frac{2}{51}-\frac{\frac{3}{2}}{52}$$

$$\frac{50}{51\times 52\times 53}=-\frac{\frac{1}{2}}{51}+\frac{2}{52}-\frac{\frac{3}{2}}{53}$$

Look at the terms inside the shaded region. If you add these up along lines parallel to the sloping sides you get a lot of sums running from $-\frac{\frac{1}{2}}{4}+\frac{2}{4}-\frac{\frac{3}{2}}{4}$ to $-\frac{\frac{1}{2}}{51}+\frac{2}{51}-\frac{\frac{3}{2}}{51}$, all of which are 0. So the sum of all the numbers inside the shaded region is 0, and all that is left is

$$-\frac{\frac{1}{2}}{2}-\frac{\frac{1}{2}}{3}+\frac{2}{3}+\frac{2}{52}-\frac{\frac{3}{2}}{52}-\frac{\frac{3}{2}}{53}=-\frac{\frac{1}{2}}{2}+\frac{\frac{3}{2}}{3}+\frac{\frac{1}{2}}{52}-\frac{\frac{3}{2}}{53},$$

which is $\frac{1275}{5512}$.

Method 2   You might notice that, if you split 2 as $-\left(-\frac{3}{2}\right)+\frac{1}{2}$, the expression in partial fractions for the general term of the series could be written as $f(i)-f(i-1)$, with $f(i)=\frac{\frac{1}{2}}{i+2}-\frac{\frac{3}{2}}{i+3}$. So, by the method of differences,

$$\sum_{i=1}^{50}\frac{i}{(i+1)(i+2)(i+3)}=f(50)-f(0)$$

$$=\left(\frac{\frac{1}{2}}{52}-\frac{\frac{3}{2}}{53}\right)-\left(\frac{\frac{1}{2}}{2}-\frac{\frac{3}{2}}{3}\right)=\frac{1275}{5512}.$$

Example 1.3.3*

Sum $\displaystyle\sum_{i=1}^{n}\frac{2i+1}{(i+1)(i+2)}3^{i}$.

In partial fractions,

$$\frac{2i+1}{(i+1)(i+2)}\equiv-\frac{1}{i+1}+\frac{3}{i+2}.$$

So $\dfrac{2i+1}{(i+1)(i+2)}3^i = -\dfrac{3^i}{i+1}+\dfrac{3^{i+1}}{i+2}.$

This is $f(i)-f(i-1)$ with $f(i)=\dfrac{3^{i+1}}{i+2}.$

So, by the method of differences,

$$\sum_{i=1}^{n}\dfrac{2i+1}{(i+1)(i+2)}3^i = f(n)-f(0)$$

$$= \dfrac{3^{n+1}}{n+2}-\dfrac{3}{2}.$$

Exercise 1C

1   Find the sum of the first n terms of the following series.

(a) $\dfrac{1}{1\times 3}+\dfrac{1}{3\times 5}+\dfrac{1}{5\times 7}+\ldots$

(b) $\dfrac{1}{2\times 5}+\dfrac{1}{5\times 8}+\dfrac{1}{8\times 11}+\ldots$

(c) $\dfrac{1}{1\times 3\times 5}+\dfrac{1}{3\times 5\times 7}+\dfrac{1}{5\times 7\times 9}+\ldots$

(d) $\dfrac{1}{3\times 5\times 7}+\dfrac{3}{5\times 7\times 9}+\dfrac{5}{7\times 9\times 11}+\ldots$

2*   Sum the following series.

(a) $\displaystyle\sum_{i=1}^{n}\dfrac{i}{(i+1)(i+2)}2^i$

(b) $\displaystyle\sum_{i=1}^{n}\dfrac{i+3}{(i+1)(i+2)}\left(\tfrac{1}{2}\right)^i$

(c) $\displaystyle\sum_{i=1}^{n}\dfrac{i+1}{(2i-1)(2i+1)}\left(\tfrac{1}{3}\right)^i$

2 Infinite series

This chapter introduces methods of determining whether infinite series are convergent or divergent. When you have completed it, you should

- be able to deduce the sums of convergent infinite series when the sum to n terms can be found
- be able to use comparison methods to decide whether a series of positive terms is convergent or divergent
- be able to use inequalities to find an upper bound for the sum to infinity of a series of positive terms.

2.1 From n to infinity

You will remember that the sum of the geometric series

$$1 + r + r^2 + r^3 + \dots$$

converges to a limit as the number of terms tends to infinity, provided that the common ratio r is between -1 and 1 (Higher Level Book 1 Section 30.4). The way you proved this was to begin with the formula for the sum of n terms,

$$S_n = \frac{1 - r^n}{1 - r}.$$

S_n is called a **partial sum** of the infinite geometric series, and its values for $n = 1, 2, 3, \dots$ form the **sum sequence**. You can split S_n into two terms, the first of which doesn't involve n, as

$$S_n = \frac{1}{1-r} - \frac{1}{1-r} \times r^n.$$

Then, if $-1 < r < 1$, the factor r^n in the second term tends to 0 as n tends to infinity, so that

$$\lim_{n \to \infty} S_n = \frac{1}{1-r}.$$

This is the **sum to infinity** of the series, and it is usually denoted by $S_\infty = \sum_{i=1}^{\infty} r^{i-1}$. You say that the infinite series $\sum r^{i-1}$ is **convergent** if $-1 < r < 1$.

You can use a similar argument with other series which you know how to sum.

In the rest of this chapter all the series have positive terms.

Example 2.1.1

Investigate whether the series $\dfrac{1}{1 \times 4} + \dfrac{1}{4 \times 7} + \dfrac{1}{7 \times 10} + \dots$ converges to a limit as $n \to \infty$.

It was shown in Example 1.3.1 that the sum of n terms of this series is $S_n = \frac{1}{3} - \dfrac{1}{3(3n+1)}$.

The second term of this expression can be made as small as you like by making n large enough, so that $\lim\limits_{n \to \infty} \dfrac{1}{3(3n+1)} = 0$. So the series is convergent and the sum to infinity is

$$S_\infty = \lim_{n \to \infty} S_n = \tfrac{1}{3} - 0 = \tfrac{1}{3}.$$

The series converges to a limit of $\tfrac{1}{3}$ as $n \to \infty$.

Example 2.1.2*

Investigate the convergence of $\displaystyle\sum \dfrac{2i+3}{(2i-1)(2i+1)}\left(\tfrac{1}{2}\right)^i$.

The symbol $\sum$ without stating the values of i is used because you don't yet know whether the series is convergent or not. Once it has been proved convergent, you can use $\displaystyle\sum_{i=1}^{\infty}$ to denote its sum to infinity.

It is often worth beginning by calculating a few terms.

$$S_1 = \frac{5}{1 \times 3} \times \tfrac{1}{2} = 0.8333\ldots, \qquad S_2 = S_1 + \frac{7}{3 \times 5} \times \tfrac{1}{4} = 0.95,$$

$$S_3 = S_2 + \frac{9}{5 \times 7} \times \tfrac{1}{8} = 0.9821\ldots, \qquad S_4 = S_3 + \frac{11}{7 \times 9} \times \tfrac{1}{16} = 0.9930\ldots .$$

It looks as if the sum sequence might tend to a limit, possibly 1. To test this, try to sum the series to find a formula for S_n.

In partial fractions, $\dfrac{2i+3}{(2i-1)(2i+1)} \equiv \dfrac{2}{2i-1} - \dfrac{1}{2i+1}$,

so $\quad \dfrac{2i+3}{(2i-1)(2i+1)}\left(\tfrac{1}{2}\right)^i \equiv \dfrac{\left(\tfrac{1}{2}\right)^{i-1}}{2i-1} - \dfrac{\left(\tfrac{1}{2}\right)^i}{2i+1}.$

The expression on the right has the form $f(i) - f(i-1)$ where $f(i) = \dfrac{-\left(\tfrac{1}{2}\right)^i}{2i+1}$. It follows that

$$S_n = \sum_{i=1}^{n} \frac{2i+3}{(2i-1)(2i+1)}\left(\tfrac{1}{2}\right)^i$$

$$= f(n) - f(0)$$

$$= \frac{-\left(\tfrac{1}{2}\right)^n}{2n+1} - \frac{-1}{1}.$$

You can see at once that S_n is less than 1 for all values of n. In the first term, the numerator $-\left(\tfrac{1}{2}\right)^n$ tends to 0 as $n \to \infty$, and the denominator increases without limit, so this term certainly tends to 0. So $S_n \to 0 - (-1) = 1$, and the sum to infinity is

$$\sum_{i=1}^{\infty} \frac{2i+3}{(2i-1)(2i+1)}\left(\tfrac{1}{2}\right)^i = 1.$$

The series converges to a limit of 1.

Exercise 2A

1 Find the sums of the following infinite series.

(a) $\displaystyle\sum_{i=1}^{\infty} \frac{1}{i(i+1)}$

(b) $\displaystyle\sum_{i=1}^{\infty} \frac{1}{i(i+1)(i+2)}$

(c) $\displaystyle\sum_{i=1}^{\infty} \frac{1}{(2i-1)(2i+1)}$

(d) $\displaystyle\sum_{i=1}^{\infty} \frac{1}{(3i-1)(3i+2)}$

(e) $\displaystyle\sum_{i=1}^{\infty} \frac{1}{(4i-3)(4i+1)}$

(f) $\displaystyle\sum_{i=1}^{\infty} \frac{1}{(2i-1)(2i+1)(2i+3)}$

2* Find the sums of the following infinite series.

(a) $\displaystyle\sum_{i=1}^{\infty} \frac{i-1}{(i+1)(i+2)(i+3)}$

(b) $\displaystyle\sum_{i=1}^{\infty} \frac{i+1}{(2i-1)(2i+1)} \left(\frac{1}{3}\right)^i$

(c) $\displaystyle\sum_{i=1}^{\infty} \frac{i+3}{i(i+1)} \left(\frac{2}{3}\right)^i$

3 (a) Prove that $\displaystyle\sum_{i=1}^{\infty} \frac{i-1}{i!} = 1$.   (b) Find $\displaystyle\sum_{i=1}^{\infty} \frac{i^2-i-1}{i!}$.

2.2 Series which cannot be summed

The series in the last section were easy to deal with because it was possible to find a formula for S_n. But there are many series which can't be summed in this way, which may or may not converge to a limit. The examples in this section illustrate both possibilities.

Example 2.2.1

Investigate whether the series $\dfrac{1}{\sqrt{1}} + \dfrac{1}{\sqrt{2}} + \dfrac{1}{\sqrt{3}} + \dots$ converges to a limit.

What do you think? In some respects this series resembles those in the last section; for example, the terms get steadily smaller, and tend to 0 as $n \to \infty$. Is this enough to ensure that the series converges?

It is worth beginning experimentally. Your calculator may have a program for finding the sum of a given number of terms of a series defined by a formula. Table 2.1 gives some values of $S_n = \displaystyle\sum_{i=1}^{n} \frac{1}{\sqrt{i}}$ found in this way.

n	50	100	200	500	999
S_n	12.752...	18.589...	26.859...	43.283...	61.769...

Table 2.1

The reason for stopping at 999 is that the 'sum sequence' program on the calculator used to make this table was limited to values of n less than 1000. If you want to go further you may have to split the sum into several parts, or write a program to do the calculations. If 'sum sequence' is not available you can use the $\sum$ program to find each value of S_n separately.

Another possibility is to use a calculator to produce a graph of the sum sequence, defined by

$$S_1 = 1, \quad S_n = S_{n-1} + \frac{1}{\sqrt{n}}.$$

This is shown, for $1 \le n \le 50$, in Fig. 2.2. Again, the calculator may restrict the values of n for which you can do this.

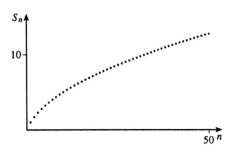

Fig. 2.2

You would probably suspect by now that the series doesn't converge to a limit, but the experimental evidence isn't conclusive. What is needed is an algebraic argument.

For this series it is quite easy to prove that the series doesn't converge. It has already been remarked that the terms get steadily smaller, and this means that all the terms $\frac{1}{\sqrt{1}}, \frac{1}{\sqrt{2}}, \frac{1}{\sqrt{3}}, \dots, \frac{1}{\sqrt{n-1}}$ are greater than $\frac{1}{\sqrt{n}}$. It follows that, if $n > 1$,

$$S_n = \frac{1}{\sqrt{1}} + \frac{1}{\sqrt{2}} + \frac{1}{\sqrt{3}} + \dots + \frac{1}{\sqrt{n-1}} + \frac{1}{\sqrt{n}}$$
$$> \frac{1}{\sqrt{n}} + \frac{1}{\sqrt{n}} + \frac{1}{\sqrt{n}} + \dots + \frac{1}{\sqrt{n}} + \frac{1}{\sqrt{n}}$$
$$= n \times \frac{1}{\sqrt{n}} = \sqrt{n}.$$

You can show this inequality numerically by adding a third row to Table 2.1, to give Table 2.3.

n	50	100	200	500	999
S_n	12.752...	18.589...	26.859...	43.283...	61.769...
$\sqrt{n}$	7.071...	10	14.142...	22.360...	31.606...

Table 2.3

Now $\sqrt{n}$ doesn't tend to a limit as $n \to \infty$. You can make it as large as you like by taking a large enough value for n. Since S_n is larger than $\sqrt{n}$, the same is true of the sum sequence S_n. This means that the series $\sum \frac{1}{\sqrt{i}}$ is not convergent.

A series which does not converge is said to be **divergent**. In Example 2.2.1 the sum sequence 'diverges to infinity'. You write $S_n \to \infty$ as $n \to \infty$.

Example 2.2.2
Investigate whether the series $\sum \frac{1}{i^2}$ is convergent.

As in the previous example, begin with some numerical calculations. Table 2.4 gives the values of $S_n = \sum_{i=1}^{n} \frac{1}{i^2}$ for a selection of values of n, and Fig. 2.5 shows the graph of S_n for $1 \le n \le 50$.

n	50	100	200	500	999
S_n	1.6251...	1.6349...	1.6399...	1.6429...	1.6439...

Table 2.4

This series behaves quite differently from $\sum \dfrac{1}{\sqrt{i}}$.

It is clearly convergent, though the value of the sum to infinity is not at all obvious.

You have in fact seen Fig. 2.5 before. It is Fig. 9.14 in Higher Level Book 1 Section 9.6, and it was stated there that the series converges to the limit $\frac{1}{6}\pi^2$.

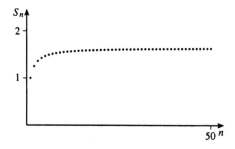

Fig. 2.5

In Example 2.2.1, where you wanted to prove that the series is divergent, you found an inequality which showed that the partial sums are greater than another function which tends to infinity. To prove that a series is convergent, you try to prove that the partial sums are less than another function which tends to a limit as $n \to \infty$. In this example you can do this by finding another series which is convergent and whose terms are greater than those of $\sum \dfrac{1}{i^2}$.

To get a fraction $\dfrac{1}{\cdots}$ greater than $\dfrac{1}{i^2}$, the denominator has to be *less* than i^2. A good choice is to take a denominator of $i^2 - \frac{1}{4}$. The reason for this is that you can then express the fraction in partial fractions as

$$\frac{1}{i^2 - \frac{1}{4}} \equiv \frac{1}{\left(i - \frac{1}{2}\right)\left(i + \frac{1}{2}\right)} \equiv \frac{1}{i - \frac{1}{2}} - \frac{1}{i + \frac{1}{2}};$$

and these partial fractions have the form $f(i) - f(i-1)$, with $f(i) = -\dfrac{1}{i + \frac{1}{2}}$. So

$$\sum_{i=1}^{n} \frac{1}{i^2 - \frac{1}{4}} = f(n) - f(0) = -\frac{1}{n + \frac{1}{2}} + \frac{1}{\frac{1}{2}} = 2 - \frac{1}{n + \frac{1}{2}}.$$

And since $\dfrac{1}{n + \frac{1}{2}} \to 0$ as $n \to \infty$, this series is convergent, and $\displaystyle\sum_{i=1}^{\infty} \frac{1}{i^2 - \frac{1}{4}} = 2$.

This completes the argument. You know that, for each positive integer i,

$$\frac{1}{i^2} < \frac{1}{i^2 - \frac{1}{4}}, \quad \text{so that} \quad S_n = \sum_{i=1}^{n} \frac{1}{i^2} < \sum_{i=1}^{n} \frac{1}{i^2 - \frac{1}{4}}.$$

Also the series on the right converges to the limit 2. So S_n converges to a limit which is less than or equal to 2.

2.3   Some general rules

The examples in the last two sections will have suggested to you some properties which are true of many infinite series. One almost obvious property is that, if a series is convergent, then the size of the individual terms u_i must tend to 0 as $n \to \infty$. This is easy to prove. If S_n and S_{n-1} are the partial sums of n and $n-1$ terms of the series $\sum u_i$, then

$$S_n = S_{n-1} + u_n, \quad \text{so that} \quad u_n = S_n - S_{n-1}.$$

But if the series is convergent, both S_n and S_{n-1} tend to the sum to infinity S_∞. So

$$\lim_{n \to \infty} (S_n - S_{n-1}) = \lim_{n \to \infty} S_n - \lim_{n \to \infty} S_{n-1} = S_\infty - S_\infty = 0.$$

It follows that $\lim_{n \to \infty} u_n = 0$.

What is less obvious is that the converse is not true. You can have series, such as the one in Example 2.2.1, for which $\lim_{n \to \infty} u_n = 0$ but which are not convergent. One way of expressing this in words is:

> For $\sum u_i$ to be convergent it is necessary, but not sufficient, that $\lim_{n \to \infty} u_n = 0$.

All the examples in this chapter are series of positive terms, but this rule is still true for series with some terms positive and some negative. The proof is exactly the same.

It follows from this that:

> If $\lim_{n \to \infty} u_n \neq 0$, or if the limit does not exist, the series is divergent.

Example 2.3.1
Prove that $\sum \cos^2 i$ is divergent.

The method is to show that there are numbers i as large as you like for which $\cos^2 i$ is greater than a positive constant, so that it cannot tend to 0 as $i \to \infty$.

Since $\pi > 3$, $\frac{1}{6}\pi > \frac{1}{2}$. So, for every positive integer m, there is at least one integer i between $m\pi - \frac{1}{6}\pi$ and $m\pi + \frac{1}{6}\pi$. For these values of i,

$$\cos^2 i > \cos^2\left(m\pi \pm \tfrac{1}{6}\pi\right) = \cos^2 \tfrac{1}{6}\pi = \left(\tfrac{1}{2}\sqrt{3}\right)^2 = \tfrac{3}{4}.$$

Therefore $\lim_{i \to \infty} \cos^2 i \neq 0$; in fact the limit doesn't exist. So $\sum \cos^2 i$ is divergent.

The next two rules are illustrated by Example 2.2.2. These are only true for series with all positive terms.

> If $\sum u_i$ is a series of positive terms, and if there is a number A such that all the partial sums S_n are less than A, then the series is convergent, and the sum to infinity is less than or equal to A.

You may be surprised by the words 'less than or equal to' in this rule. In Example 2.2.2 all the partial sums are less than 2, and the sum to infinity is less than 2. But if you take a series like the geometric series

$$1 + \tfrac{1}{2} + \left(\tfrac{1}{2}\right)^2 + \ldots + \left(\tfrac{1}{2}\right)^{n-1},$$

all the partial sums are less than 2, but the sum to infinity is equal to 2. So in stating the general rule, the conclusion must be $S_\infty \le A$ rather than $S_\infty < A$.

The inequality in Example 2.2.2 was obtained by comparing the terms of the series $\sum \dfrac{1}{i^2}$ with those of

$\sum \dfrac{1}{i^2 - \frac{1}{4}}$. This is an example of the **comparison test** for convergence.

> **The comparison test**   If $\sum u_i, \sum v_i$ are two series of positive terms such that, for all i, $u_i \le v_i$, and if $\sum v_i$ converges to a limit S, then $\sum u_i$ converges to a limit less than or equal to S.

There is a corresponding test for divergence:

> If $\sum u_i, \sum v_i$ are two series of positive terms such that, for all i, $u_i \le v_i$, and if $\sum u_i$ is divergent, then $\sum v_i$ is divergent.

For example, you know from Example 2.2.1 that $\sum \dfrac{1}{\sqrt{i}}$ is divergent. And if i is any number greater than

1, $\sqrt[4]{i} < \sqrt{i}$, so that $\dfrac{1}{\sqrt[4]{i}} > \dfrac{1}{\sqrt{i}}$. Taking $u_i = \dfrac{1}{\sqrt{i}}$ and $v_i = \dfrac{1}{\sqrt[4]{i}}$, it follows that $\sum \dfrac{1}{\sqrt[4]{i}}$ is divergent.

Exercise 2B

1   Give reasons why the following infinite series are divergent.

   (a) $\sum \dfrac{i}{2i - 1}$

   (b) $\sum \dfrac{1}{\sqrt[3]{i}}$

2   Give reasons why the following infinite series are convergent.

   (a) $\sum \dfrac{1}{i^{2.5}}$

   (b) $\sum \dfrac{1}{i^2 + 1}$

   (c) $\sum \dfrac{1}{2^i + 1}$

3   (a) Prove that, for $i > 1$, $\dfrac{1 \times 2 \times 3 \times \ldots \times i}{i \times i \times i \times \ldots \times i} \le \dfrac{2}{i^2}$.

   (b) Prove that $\sum \dfrac{i!}{i^i}$ is convergent. Can you find a number M such that $\displaystyle\sum_{i=1}^{\infty} \dfrac{i!}{i^i} \le M$?

   (c) Use a calculator to evaluate $\displaystyle\sum_{i=1}^{n} \dfrac{i!}{i^i}$ for as large a value of n as you can.

4 (a) Give a reason why $\sum \dfrac{1}{i^4}$ is convergent.

   (b) Use a calculator to find $\displaystyle\sum_{i=1}^{n} \dfrac{1}{i^4}$ for a large value of n.

   (c) It can be proved that $\displaystyle\sum_{i=1}^{\infty} \dfrac{1}{i^4} = \dfrac{1}{N}\pi^4$ where N is an integer. Use your answer to part (b) to identify the value of N.

5 (a) Give a reason why $\sum \dfrac{1}{i^3}$ is convergent.

   (b) Use a calculator to find $\displaystyle\sum_{i=1}^{n} \dfrac{1}{i^3}$ for a large value of n.

   (c) Show that, for $i \in \mathbb{Z}^{+}$, $i^3 > (i-1)i(i+1)$.

   (d) A student tries to find an upper bound to the value of $\displaystyle\sum_{i=1}^{\infty} \dfrac{1}{i^3}$ by comparing it with

   $\displaystyle\sum_{i=1}^{\infty} \dfrac{1}{(i-1)i(i+1)}$. What goes wrong?

   (e) Modify the method in part (d) to find an upper bound for $\displaystyle\sum_{i=1}^{\infty} \dfrac{1}{i^3}$. Compare this with your answer to part (b).

6 (a) The terms of the finite series $S_n = \displaystyle\sum_{i=1}^{n} \dfrac{1}{i}$ can be grouped as

   $$1 + \frac{1}{2} + \left(\frac{1}{3} + \frac{1}{4}\right) + \left(\frac{1}{5} + \frac{1}{6} + \frac{1}{7} + \frac{1}{8}\right) + \dots + \left(\frac{1}{2^{j-1}+1} + \frac{1}{2^j}\right) + \frac{1}{2^j+1} + \dots + \frac{1}{n},$$

   where j is the highest power of 2 less than or equal to n. Explain why the sum in each of the brackets is greater than $\frac{1}{2}$. Hence show that $S_n > 1 + \frac{1}{2}j$. What can you deduce about the infinite series $\sum \dfrac{1}{i}$?

   (b) Use part (a) to find a lower bound for the value of S_{1000}. By grouping the terms in a different way, prove that $S_{1000} < 10$.

   (c) Use a calculator to find S_{1000} correct to 6 decimal places.

7 (a) Prove that, for $i \in \mathbb{Z}^{+}$, $i! \geq 2^{i-1}$; for what values of i are the two sides equal? Hence prove that

   $\sum \dfrac{1}{i!}$ is convergent. What can you say about $\displaystyle\sum_{i=1}^{\infty} \dfrac{1}{i!}$?

   (b) Use an inequality similar to that in part (a) to prove that $\sum \dfrac{2^i}{i!}$ is convergent. Can you find a

   number M such that $\displaystyle\sum_{i=1}^{\infty} \dfrac{2^i}{i!} \leq M$?

8 (a) Prove that, for $i > 1$, $\dfrac{(2i)!}{(i!)^2} > 2^i$.

   (b) Prove that, if $u_i = \dfrac{1}{2^i C_i}$, $\displaystyle\sum u_i$ is convergent, and that $\displaystyle\sum_{i=1}^{\infty} u_i \le 1$.

   (c) Use a calculator to evaluate $\displaystyle\sum_{i=1}^{n} u_i$ for as large a value of n as you can.

2.4 Some important limits

In Example 2.1.2 you needed to find the limit as $n \to \infty$ of $\dfrac{-\left(\frac{1}{2}\right)^n}{2n+1}$. This was simple, because the numerator of the fraction tends to 0 and the denominator tends to infinity, so $\dfrac{1}{2n+1}$ also tends to 0.

But what would happen if $(2n+1)$ had been in the numerator? You would then have the product of two factors, one tending to 0 and the other to infinity. Which would prevail?

You would have a similar problem if $\frac{1}{2}$ is replaced by 2. You would then have a fraction with both numerator and denominator tending to infinity. Will this tend to infinity, to 0, or somewhere in between?

The answer is that 'powers prevail over polynomials'. In the product $(2n+1) \times \left(\frac{1}{2}\right)^n$, the fact that $\left(\frac{1}{2}\right)^n$ tends to 0 is more powerful than that $(2n+1)$ tends to infinity. And the fact that 2^n tends to infinity is what determines the behaviour of the function $\dfrac{2^n}{2n+1}$.

You can easily check these statements numerically with a calculator, but they need to be proved algebraically. The basic results are:

> If $a > 1$, then $\dfrac{a^n}{n} \to \infty$ as $n \to \infty$.
>
> If $0 < b < 1$, then $nb^n \to 0$ as $n \to \infty$.

You can prove both of these by using the binomial theorem. For the first, since $a > 1$, you can write $a = 1 + c$, where $c > 0$. Then

$$a^n = 1 + nc + \frac{n(n-1)}{2}c^2 + \ldots + c^n,$$

and all the terms on the right are positive. So a^n is greater than any one of the terms. In particular,

$$a^n > \frac{n(n-1)}{2}c^2, \quad \text{so} \quad \frac{a^n}{n} > \frac{n-1}{2}c^2.$$

This inequality produces the desired result. Since c is constant, $\frac{n-1}{2}c^2$ tends to infinity as $n \to \infty$.

Therefore $\frac{a^n}{n}$, which is greater than $\frac{n-1}{2}c^2$, also tends to infinity.

The second result is proved in a similar way. If $0 < b < 1$, then $\frac{1}{b} > 1$, so write $\frac{1}{b} = 1 + c$.

Then

$$nb^n = \frac{n}{(1+c)^n} < \frac{n}{\frac{n(n-1)}{2}c^2} = \frac{2}{(n-1)c^2},$$

and since c is constant this tends to 0 as $n \to \infty$.

The next example shows how this can be used to find the sum of an infinite series.

Example 2.4.1

Show that $\sum i\left(\frac{1}{2}\right)^i$ is convergent, and find the sum to infinity.

If you can find a function f such that $f(i) - f(i-1) = i\left(\frac{1}{2}\right)^i$, you could sum the first n terms of the series. You would probably expect $f(i)$ to have $\left(\frac{1}{2}\right)^i$ as a factor, and perhaps another factor which is a linear polynomial in i. So try $f(i) = (Ai + B)\left(\frac{1}{2}\right)^i$ for some unknown coefficients A and B. These have to satisfy the identity

$$(Ai + B)\left(\tfrac{1}{2}\right)^i - (A(i-1) + B)\left(\tfrac{1}{2}\right)^{i-1} \equiv i\left(\tfrac{1}{2}\right)^i.$$

Dividing by $\left(\frac{1}{2}\right)^{i-1}$, A and B must satisfy

$$(Ai + B)\left(\tfrac{1}{2}\right) - A(i-1) - B \equiv i\left(\tfrac{1}{2}\right).$$

Equating coefficients of i and the constant term,

$$\tfrac{1}{2}A - A = \tfrac{1}{2} \quad \text{and} \quad \tfrac{1}{2}B + A - B = 0.$$

So $A = -1$ and $B = -2$.

Therefore $f(i) = -(i+2)\left(\frac{1}{2}\right)^i$, and the partial sum is

$$\sum_{i=1}^{n} i\left(\tfrac{1}{2}\right)^i = f(n) - f(0) = -(n+2)\left(\tfrac{1}{2}\right)^n + 2.$$

Now, since $\frac{1}{2}$ is between 0 and 1, $2 \times \left(\frac{1}{2}\right)^n \to 0$ and $n \times \left(\frac{1}{2}\right)^n \to 0$ as $n \to \infty$, so $(n+2)\left(\frac{1}{2}\right)^n \to 0$.

The series is therefore convergent, and $\sum_{i=1}^{\infty} i\left(\frac{1}{2}\right)^i = 2$.

A series like $\sum i\left(\frac{1}{2}\right)^i$ is sometimes described as 'arithmetico-geometric', because its terms are the product of an arithmetic sequence $u_i = i$ and a geometric sequence $v_i = \left(\frac{1}{2}\right)^i$.

The results in the previous shaded box can be generalised, with n raised to any positive power.

> If $a > 1$ and k is any positive number, then $\dfrac{a^n}{n^k} \to \infty$ as $n \to \infty$.
>
> If $0 < b < 1$ and k is any positive number, then $n^k b^n \to 0$ as $n \to \infty$.

To prove this, notice first that $\sqrt[k]{a} > 1$ and that $0 < \sqrt[k]{b} < 1$. So, applying the previous results with $a^{\frac{1}{k}} = \sqrt[k]{a}$ and $b^{\frac{1}{k}} = \sqrt[k]{b}$ in place of a and b, you can deduce that

$$\frac{\left(a^{\frac{1}{k}}\right)^n}{n} \to \infty \quad \text{and} \quad n\left(b^{\frac{1}{k}}\right)^n \to 0.$$

That is,

$$\frac{a^{\frac{n}{k}}}{n} \to \infty \quad \text{and} \quad nb^{\frac{n}{k}} \to 0 \quad \text{as } n \to \infty.$$

Now raise the expressions on the left to the power k. Since k is positive, the limits are still ∞ and 0 respectively, and

$$\left(\frac{a^{\frac{n}{k}}}{n}\right)^k = \frac{a^n}{n^k} \quad \text{and} \quad \left(nb^{\frac{n}{k}}\right)^k = n^k b^n.$$

So $\dfrac{a^n}{n^k} \to \infty \quad \text{and} \quad n^k b^n \to 0 \quad \text{as } n \to \infty.$

Exercise 2C

1 Prove that, if $p(x)$ is a polynomial of any degree, and $0 < b < 1$, then $p(n) \times b^n \to 0$ as $n \to \infty$.

2 (a) Use the method of Example 2.4.1 to evaluate $\displaystyle\sum_{i=1}^{\infty} i\left(\frac{1}{3}\right)^i$.

(b) Use the same method to prove that, if $0 < q < 1$, $\displaystyle\sum_{i=1}^{\infty} iq^i = \frac{q}{(1-q)^2}$.

3 Use a method similar to that in Example 2.4.1 to find $\displaystyle\sum_{i=1}^{\infty} i^2\left(\frac{1}{2}\right)^i$. Check your answer with a calculator.

3 Tests for convergence

There are a number of tests which you can use to investigate whether a series is convergent. Two of these are described in this chapter. When you have completed it, you should

- be able to use the ratio test to prove that an infinite series is convergent
- be able to use the limit comparison test to prove that an infinite series is either convergent or divergent.

3.1 The ratio test

You saw in Example 2.2.1 that, for a series of positive terms to converge, it is not sufficient for the terms to get steadily smaller and tend to 0. For the series $\sum u_i$, where $u_i = \dfrac{1}{\sqrt{i}}$, you know that $u_i < u_{i-1}$ and that $\lim\limits_{i\to\infty} u_i = 0$, but $\sum u_i$ is divergent.

But suppose you have a series such that $u_i \leq \frac{1}{2} u_{i-1}$ for all values of i. Will this be sufficient to guarantee that $\sum u_i$ converges?

Putting $i = 2, 3, 4, \dots$ in turn, you know that

$$u_2 \leq \tfrac{1}{2} u_1, \qquad u_3 \leq \tfrac{1}{2} u_2, \qquad u_4 \leq \tfrac{1}{2} u_3, \text{ and so on.}$$

By putting these inequalities together, you can find inequalities connecting all the terms $u_2, u_3, u_4, \dots$ in terms of u_1. Thus

$$u_3 \leq \tfrac{1}{2} u_2 \leq \tfrac{1}{2}\left(\tfrac{1}{2} u_1\right) = \left(\tfrac{1}{2}\right)^2 u_1,$$

$$u_4 \leq \tfrac{1}{2} u_3 \leq \tfrac{1}{2}\left(\left(\tfrac{1}{2}\right)^2 u_1\right) = \left(\tfrac{1}{2}\right)^3 u_1,$$

and in general

$$u_i \leq \left(\tfrac{1}{2}\right)^{i-1} u_1.$$

Denote $\left(\tfrac{1}{2}\right)^{i-1} u_1$ by v_i, so that $u_i \leq v_i$ for all i. Then you have the situation of the comparison test in Section 2.3, since

$$\sum_{i=1}^{\infty} v_i = u_1 \sum_{i=1}^{\infty} \left(\tfrac{1}{2}\right)^{i-1}$$

is a convergent geometric series, with sum

$$u_1 \times \frac{1}{1 - \tfrac{1}{2}} = \frac{u_1}{\tfrac{1}{2}} = 2u_1.$$

It follows by the comparison test that $\sum u_i$ converges to a limit which is less than or equal to $2u_1$.

There is nothing special about the factor $\frac{1}{2}$. Any factor r less than 1 would do just as well, with $u_i \leq ru_{i-1}$ for all values of i. You would then define v_i as $r^{i-1}u_1$, so that $u_i \leq v_i$ for all i, and

$$\sum_{i=1}^{\infty} v_i = u_1 \sum_{i=1}^{\infty} r^{i-1} = u_1 \times \frac{1}{1-r}.$$

This is called the **ratio test**, because the condition $u_i \leq ru_{i-1}$ can be written in ratio form as $\dfrac{u_i}{u_{i-1}} \leq r$.

> **The ratio test**   If $\sum u_i$ is a series of positive terms such that, for all $i > 1$,
>
> $\dfrac{u_i}{u_{i-1}} \leq r$ where $r < 1$, then the series converges to a limit S_∞ such that
>
> $S_\infty \leq \dfrac{u_1}{1-r}.$

Example 3.1.1

Prove that the series $\sum \dfrac{1}{{}^{2i}C_i}$ is convergent. (See Exercise 2B Question 7.)

Since ${}^nC_r = \dfrac{n!}{r! \times (n-r)!}$ (see Higher Level Book 1 Section 3.6), ${}^{2i}C_i = \dfrac{(2i)!}{i! \times i!}$, and

$$u_i = \frac{1}{{}^{2i}C_i} = \frac{i! \times i!}{(2i)!}.$$

So

$$\frac{u_i}{u_{i-1}} = \frac{i! \times i!}{(2i)!} \div \frac{(i-1)! \times (i-1)!}{(2i-2)!}$$

$$= \frac{i!}{(i-1)!} \times \frac{i!}{(i-1)!} \times \frac{(2i-2)!}{(2i)!}$$

$$= i \times i \times \frac{1}{(2i) \times (2i-1)}$$

$$= \frac{1}{2} \times \frac{i}{2i-1}.$$

Now if $i > 1$, $i < 2i - 1$, so $\dfrac{u_i}{u_{i-1}} \leq \frac{1}{2}$ for $i = 2,3,4,\dots$. Therefore, by the ratio test, $\sum \dfrac{1}{{}^{2i}C_i}$ is convergent, and

$$\sum_{i=1}^{\infty} \frac{1}{{}^{2i}C_i} \leq \frac{1}{{}^2C_1} \times \frac{1}{1-\frac{1}{2}} = \frac{1}{2} \times 2 = 1.$$

Example 3.1.2

Investigate the convergence of the infinite series $\displaystyle\sum \frac{1}{3^i - 2}$.

If $u_i = \dfrac{1}{3^i - 2}$, then $u_{i-1} = \dfrac{1}{3^{i-1} - 2}$, and

$$\frac{u_i}{u_{i-1}} = \frac{3^{i-1} - 2}{3^i - 2}.$$

It is not immediately obvious that this is always less than a number r less than 1. So try working out the first few values of the ratio:

$$\frac{u_2}{u_1} = \frac{3 - 2}{3^2 - 2} = \frac{1}{7} = 0.142\ldots, \qquad \frac{u_3}{u_2} = \frac{3^2 - 2}{3^3 - 2} = \frac{7}{25} = 0.28,$$

$$\frac{u_4}{u_3} = \frac{3^3 - 2}{3^4 - 2} = \frac{25}{79} = 0.316\ldots, \qquad \frac{u_5}{u_4} = \frac{3^4 - 2}{3^5 - 2} = \frac{79}{241} = 0.327\ldots\,.$$

It looks as if the ratio might always be less than $\frac{1}{3}$. So try working out

$$\begin{aligned}
\frac{1}{3} - \frac{u_i}{u_{i-1}} &= \frac{1}{3} - \frac{3^{i-1} - 2}{3^i - 2} \\
&= \frac{3^i - 2 - 3\left(3^{i-1} - 2\right)}{3\left(3^i - 2\right)} \\
&= \frac{3^i - 2 - 3^i + 6}{3\left(3^i - 2\right)} = \frac{4}{3\left(3^i - 2\right)}.
\end{aligned}$$

This is obviously positive, which proves that, for all $i > 1$, $\dfrac{u_i}{u_{i-1}} < \frac{1}{3}$. So the series converges.

Also, since $u_1 = \dfrac{1}{3^1 - 2} = 1$, $\displaystyle\sum_{i=1}^{\infty} \frac{1}{3^i - 2} \leq 1 \times \frac{1}{1 - \frac{1}{3}} = \frac{3}{2}$.

You can check this with a calculator. For example, $S_{50} = 1.2017\ldots$. By the time that i reaches the value 50 the terms are very small indeed, so it is likely that the value of S_∞ is close to this.

3.2 Modifications of the ratio test

You often want to investigate the convergence of series for which the use of the ratio test doesn't exactly fit the wording in Section 3.1. This section discusses some possible modifications.

(i) Ignoring the early terms

If you want to know whether a series is convergent, what is important is the size of the terms u_i when i is large. It doesn't matter if some of the early terms don't fit the pattern.

So it isn't necessary to insist that the inequality $\dfrac{u_i}{u_{i-1}} \leq r$ holds 'for all $i > 1$'. Provided that you can find a number m such that the inequality holds 'for all $i > m$', the series will still converge.

The only difference is that the inequality for S_∞ will have to be modified by detaching the first $m-1$ terms and summing them separately. It then becomes

$$S_\infty \leq \sum_{i=1}^{m-1} u_i + \frac{u_m}{1-r}.$$

Example 3.2.1

Show that $\sum \frac{3^i}{i!}$ is convergent, and that the sum to infinity is not greater than $25\frac{1}{2}$.

If $u_i = \frac{3^i}{i!}$, then $\frac{u_i}{u_{i-1}} = \frac{3^i}{i!} \times \frac{(i-1)!}{3^{i-1}} = \frac{3}{i}$. So $\quad \frac{u_2}{u_1} = \frac{3}{2}, \quad \frac{u_3}{u_2} = \frac{3}{3} = 1, \quad \frac{u_4}{u_3} = \frac{3}{4}, \ldots$.

To prove convergence, the ratio of successive terms must be less than a number less than 1, and this happens from $i = 4$ onwards; that is, for all $i > 3$. The ratio is then less than or equal to $\frac{3}{4}$, so the series is convergent, and

$$S_\infty \leq \sum_{i=1}^{2} \frac{3^i}{i!} + \frac{3^3}{3!} \times \frac{1}{1 - \frac{3}{4}}$$

$$\leq \frac{3}{1!} + \frac{3^2}{2!} + \frac{3^3}{3!} \times 4$$

$$= 3 + \frac{9}{2} + \frac{27}{6} \times 4 = 25\frac{1}{2}.$$

(You will find in Section 9.3 that the exact sum to infinity is $e^3 - 1 = 19.08\ldots$.)

(ii) A limit form of the ratio test

When you use the ratio test, it is sometimes rather tricky to find a suitable value of r and to obtain the inequality $\frac{u_i}{u_{i-1}} \leq r$. But it quite often happens that $\frac{u_i}{u_{i-1}}$ tends to a limit as $i \to \infty$. If this limit is l, and if $l < 1$, then you can be sure that the ratio is as close as you like to l by making i large enough. So if you choose a number r between l and 1, you know that beyond some number m all the values of $\frac{u_i}{u_{i-1}}$ are less than r. This is illustrated in Fig. 3.1.

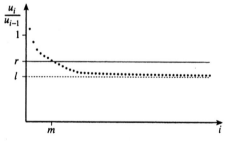

Fig. 3.1

The conditions given in (i) above for $\sum u_i$ to converge are therefore satisfied. The ratio test then takes the form:

The ratio test (limit form)   If $\sum u_i$ is a series of positive terms such that $\lim_{i \to \infty} \frac{u_i}{u_{i-1}} < 1$, then the series is convergent.

This is often a simpler form of the ratio test to use. The only drawback is that it requires the limit to exist. Occasionally you come across series for which $\dfrac{u_i}{u_{i-1}}$ doesn't tend to a limit, even though $\dfrac{u_i}{u_{i-1}} < r < 1$ for all $i > 1$.

Example 3.2.2

Investigate the convergence of the infinite series $\sum \dfrac{1}{3^i - 2}$.

This is a repeat of Example 3.1.2. In that example the most difficult part was to decide on a value for r and to prove the inequality. But it is quite easy to find the limit as $i \to \infty$ of $\dfrac{u_i}{u_{i-1}} = \dfrac{3^{i-1} - 2}{3^i - 2}$.

When you have a fraction where numerator and denominator have a similar form and both tend to infinity, a useful move is often to divide top and bottom by the same quantity so as to get expressions which tend to a finite limit. In this case, if you divide top and bottom by 3^{i-1}, you get

$$\frac{u_i}{u_{i-1}} = \frac{1 - \dfrac{2}{3^{i-1}}}{3 - \dfrac{2}{3^{i-1}}}.$$

Since $3^{i-1} \to \infty$ as $i \to \infty$, $\dfrac{2}{3^{i-1}} \to 0$. So

$$\lim_{i \to \infty} \frac{u_i}{u_{i-1}} = \frac{1 - 0}{3 - 0} = \tfrac{1}{3}.$$

And since $\tfrac{1}{3} < 1$, the limit form of the ratio test proves that $\sum \dfrac{1}{3^i - 2}$ is convergent.

(iii)   A test for divergence?

In Section 3.1 the ratio test was proved by using the comparison test from Section 2.3. There was another part of the comparison test which could be used to prove a series divergent. So you might ask whether a ratio test can be used to prove a series divergent.

The answer is that it can, but there is not much point in doing so. For if $\dfrac{u_i}{u_{i-1}} > 1$ for all i, then $u_i > u_{i-1}$, so the terms are getting steadily larger as i increases. In that case, u_i can't tend to 0 as $i \to \infty$, so the series can't possibly converge. So rather than using a ratio test to prove the series divergent, it is usually simpler just to show that u_i doesn't tend to 0.

Finally, what happens if $\lim\limits_{i \to \infty} \dfrac{u_i}{u_{i-1}} = 1$?

In that case the ratio test is useless. To show this, look at the two examples in Section 2.2, $\sum \dfrac{1}{\sqrt{i}}$ and $\sum \dfrac{1}{i^2}$.

For the first series,

$$\frac{u_i}{u_{i-1}} = \frac{\sqrt{i-1}}{\sqrt{i}} = \sqrt{\frac{i-1}{i}} = \sqrt{1-\frac{1}{i}}, \qquad \text{so} \qquad \lim_{i\to\infty} \frac{u_i}{u_{i-1}} = \sqrt{1-0} = 1.$$

And for the second series,

$$\frac{u_i}{u_{i-1}} = \frac{(i-1)^2}{i^2} = \left(\frac{i-1}{i}\right)^2 = \left(1-\frac{1}{i}\right)^2, \qquad \text{so} \qquad \lim_{i\to\infty} \frac{u_i}{u_{i-1}} = (1-0)^2 = 1.$$

But the first series is divergent and the second is convergent.

If $\lim\limits_{i\to\infty} \dfrac{u_i}{u_{i-1}} = 1$, the ratio test tells you nothing about the convergence of $\sum u_i$.

Example 3.2.3

For what positive values of q is the infinite series $\sum \dfrac{q^i}{i^2}$ convergent?

If $u_i = \dfrac{q^i}{i^2}$,

$$\frac{u_i}{u_{i-1}} = \frac{q^i}{i^2} \times \frac{(i-1)^2}{q^{i-1}} = q \times \left(1-\frac{1}{i}\right)^2,$$

so $\lim\limits_{i\to\infty} \dfrac{u_i}{u_{i-1}} = q(1-0)^2 = q.$

By the ratio test, the series converges if $q < 1$.

If $q > 1$, you know from Section 2.4 that $u_i = \dfrac{q^i}{i^2} \to \infty$ as $i \to \infty$. So the series is divergent if $q > 1$.

If $q = 1$, the series is $\sum \dfrac{1}{i^2}$. It was proved in Example 2.2.2 that this is convergent.

Therefore, if q is positive, $\sum \dfrac{q^i}{i^2}$ is convergent for $q \le 1$.

Notice that in this example a different argument has to be used for each of the three cases.

Exercise 3A

1   Use the ratio test to prove that the following series are convergent. Find an upper bound for the sum to infinity, and compare it with a suitable partial sum found with a calculator.

(a) $\sum \dfrac{1}{5^i - 1}$ (b) $\sum \dfrac{1}{2^{i^2}}$ (c) $\sum \dfrac{i^2}{2^i}$

2   Use the limit form of the ratio test to prove that the following series are convergent.

   (a) $\sum \dfrac{1}{2^i - i}$ (b) $\sum \dfrac{1}{3^i - i^2}$

3   Prove that, if $u_i = \dfrac{1}{i}$, then $\dfrac{u_i}{u_{i-1}} < 1$ for all $i > 1$. Does this prove that $\sum \dfrac{1}{i}$ converges?

4   (a) Prove that $\dfrac{1}{\sqrt{i} + \sqrt{i-1}} = \sqrt{i} - \sqrt{i-1}$.

   (b) Explain why you can't use the ratio test to investigate the convergence of $\sum \dfrac{1}{2^{\sqrt{i}}}$.

5   For what positive values of q are the following series convergent?

   (a) $\sum \dfrac{q^i}{\sqrt{i}}$ (b) $\sum \dfrac{q^i}{i!}$ (c) $\sum i^3 q^i$

3.3   The limit comparison test

If $\sum u_i$ and $\sum v_i$ are infinite series and if, for all i, $v_i = ku_i$, where k is a positive constant, then if $\sum u_i$ is divergent, so is $\sum v_i$; and if $\sum u_i$ is convergent, so is $\sum v_i$.

This may seem trivial, but it is worth mentioning because of two possible modifications.

First, as already noted in Section 3.2(i), what is important is the size of the terms when i is large. It doesn't matter if the early terms don't fit the pattern. So in the statement in the first paragraph, you can replace 'for all i' by 'for all $i > m$' where m is some fixed number.

Secondly, the multiplier k doesn't have to be 'absolutely constant', provided that it is not very different from k. If you choose two numbers, one above k and one below, as close as you like to k, and if the ratio $\dfrac{v_i}{u_i}$ is always between these two numbers when i is large enough, it would still be true that the two series diverge together, or converge together.

Putting these two modifications together, the multiplier has to be very close to k for values of i greater than m. What this means is that the multiplier can be different for each value of i, but it has to tend to k as a limit as $i \to \infty$.

So denote the multiplier by k_i, where $\lim\limits_{i \to \infty} k_i = k$ is a positive constant. Then you can amend the statement in the first paragraph as follows.

> If $\sum u_i$ and $\sum v_i$ are infinite series and if $v_i = k_i u_i$, where $\lim\limits_{k \to \infty} k_i = k > 0$, then if $\sum u_i$ is divergent, so is $\sum v_i$; and if $\sum u_i$ is convergent, so is $\sum v_i$.
>
> This is called the **limit comparison test**.

You can use the limit comparison test when you have a series whose terms v_i are given by a rather complicated expression. The idea is to compare this with a series with simpler terms u_i which have the same order of magnitude as v_i.

Example 3.3.1

Prove that $\sum \dfrac{1}{i^2 - i + 1}$ is convergent.

When i is large, the dominant term in $i^2 - i + 1$ is the quadratic term i^2, since

$$i^2 - i + 1 = i^2 \left(1 - \frac{1}{i} + \frac{1}{i^2} \right),$$

and both $\dfrac{1}{i}$ and $\dfrac{1}{i^2}$ are small when i is large. So you can write

$$\frac{1}{i^2 - i + 1} = \frac{1}{1 - \frac{1}{i} + \frac{1}{i^2}} \times \frac{1}{i^2} \quad \text{as} \quad k_1 \times \frac{1}{i^2}, \quad \text{where} \quad \lim_{i \to \infty} k_1 = 1.$$

You already know from Example 2.2.2 that $\sum \dfrac{1}{i^2}$ is convergent. It follows, by the limit comparison test, that $\sum \dfrac{1}{i^2 - i + 1}$ is convergent.

By now you are familiar with a number of convergent series, for example:

$$\sum \frac{1}{i^2}, \ \sum \frac{1}{i^3}, \ \sum \frac{1}{i^4}, \ \ldots \ ; \ \sum \frac{1}{i(i+1)}, \ \sum \frac{1}{i(i+1)(i+2)}, \ \ldots \ ; \ \sum ar^{i-1} \quad \text{for} \quad 0 < r < 1.$$

You also know some divergent series:

$$\sum \frac{1}{\sqrt{i}}, \ \sum \frac{1}{\sqrt[3]{i}}, \ \sum \frac{1}{\sqrt[4]{i}}, \ \ldots \ ; \ \sum i, \ \sum i(i+1), \ \sum i(i+1)(i+2), \ \ldots \ ; \ \sum ar^{i-1} \quad \text{for} \quad r > 1.$$

And you have met some sequences which tend to a positive limit. A good way of finding such limits is to notice that, as $i \to \infty$, $\dfrac{1}{i} \to 0$. If you can express a sequence k_i in terms of $\dfrac{1}{i}$, then you can usually find the limit of the sequence by replacing $\dfrac{1}{i}$ by 0. Here are some examples.

$$\frac{ai + b}{pi + q} \quad \text{can be written as} \quad \frac{a + \frac{b}{i}}{p + \frac{q}{i}}, \quad \text{so} \quad \lim_{i \to \infty} \frac{ai + b}{pi + q} = \frac{a + 0}{p + 0} = \frac{a}{p}.$$

If a is a positive number, $\displaystyle \lim_{i \to \infty} \sqrt[i]{a} = \lim_{i \to \infty} a^{\frac{1}{i}} = a^0 = 1.$

Since $\lim\limits_{x\to 0} \dfrac{\sin x}{x} = 1$ (see Higher Level Book 2 Section 21.1), $\lim\limits_{i\to\infty} i \sin\left(\dfrac{1}{i}\right) = \lim\limits_{i\to\infty} \dfrac{\sin\left(\dfrac{1}{i}\right)}{\dfrac{1}{i}} = 1$.

So if you take one of the series as $\sum u_i$, and one of the sequences as the multiplier k_i, then you get another series $\sum v_i$ which diverges if $\sum u_i$ diverges, and converges if $\sum u_i$ converges.

Example 3.3.2

Investigate whether the following series are convergent or divergent.

(a) $\sum \dfrac{\sqrt{i}}{2i-1}$ (b) $\sum \dfrac{1}{i}\sin\left(\dfrac{1}{i}\right)$ (c) $\sum 2^{\frac{1}{i}} \times \left(\dfrac{1}{2}\right)^i$

(a) You can write $\dfrac{\sqrt{i}}{2i-1}$ as $\dfrac{i}{2i-1} \times \dfrac{1}{\sqrt{i}}$, and

$$\lim_{i\to\infty} \frac{i}{2i-1} = \lim_{i\to\infty} \frac{1}{2-\dfrac{1}{i}} = \frac{1}{2-0} = \frac{1}{2}.$$

Since $\sum \dfrac{1}{\sqrt{i}}$ is divergent, the limit comparison test shows that $\sum \dfrac{\sqrt{i}}{2i-1}$ is divergent.

(b) You can write $\dfrac{1}{i}\sin\left(\dfrac{1}{i}\right)$ as $i\sin\left(\dfrac{1}{i}\right) \times \dfrac{1}{i^2}$.

Since $\lim\limits_{i\to\infty} i\sin\left(\dfrac{1}{i}\right) = 1$ and $\sum \dfrac{1}{i^2}$ is convergent, it follows by the limit comparison test that $\sum \dfrac{1}{i}\sin\left(\dfrac{1}{i}\right)$ is convergent.

(c) Since $\lim\limits_{i\to\infty} 2^{\frac{1}{i}} = 2^0 = 1$ and $\sum \left(\dfrac{1}{2}\right)^i$ is convergent, $\sum 2^{\frac{1}{i}} \times \left(\dfrac{1}{2}\right)^i$ is convergent.

Exercise 3B

1 Find the limits as $i \to \infty$ of

(a) $\cos\left(\dfrac{1}{i}\right)$, (b) $\dfrac{2i^2+3i+4}{4i^2+3i+2}$.

2 Use the limit comparison test to prove the results in Exercise 3A Question 2.

3 Investigate whether the following infinite series are convergent or divergent.

(a) $\sum \sin^2\left(\dfrac{1}{i}\right)$ (b) $\sum \dfrac{i+2}{i(i+1)^2}$ (c) $\sum \sqrt{\dfrac{(i+1)(i+3)}{i(i+2)(i+4)}}$

(d) $\sum \dfrac{1}{i^2}\cos\left(\dfrac{1}{i}\right)$ (e) $\sum \dfrac{i(i+2)}{i+1}$ (f) $\sum \dfrac{2^i+3}{3^i+4}$

4 Series and integrals

This chapter introduces definite integrals and their links with finite series. When you have completed it, you should

- know how to define a definite integral in terms of lower and upper sums
- be able to use lower and upper sums to find bounds for the sums of finite series.

4.1 Defining a definite integral

If you were asked to say what you mean by $\int_a^b f(x)\,dx$, you would probably begin by describing how to

find it. You might say something like 'find a function $I(x)$ whose derivative is $f(x)$, then $\int_a^b f(x)\,dx$

is $I(b) - I(a)$'.

That may do well enough for a function like $f(x) = x^3$, for which you can take $I(x)$ to be $\frac{1}{4}x^4$. But it

doesn't help for a function like $f(x) = \sqrt{1 + x^3}$, because you don't know any function $I(x)$ such that

$I'(x) = \sqrt{1 + x^3}$, or even that such a function exists.

In fact such a function does exist, and it is $\int_0^x \sqrt{1 + t^3}\,dt$. But that doesn't help with the problem of

defining a definite integral, because it is itself a definite integral! You are just chasing yourself round in circles.

The reason for using the letter t rather than x inside the integral is to avoid using x in two different

senses in the same expression. Inside a definite integral it doesn't matter what letter you use; $\int_a^b t^3\,dt$ is

the same as $\int_a^b x^3\,dx$, that is $\frac{1}{4}(b^4 - a^4)$. So $\int_0^x t^3\,dt = \frac{1}{4}x^4$ is a function of x, whose derivative is x^3.

So what you need is a way of defining a definite integral that doesn't depend on the idea of

differentiation. The way to do this is to go back to the idea of $\int_a^b f(x)\,dx$ as the area under the graph of

$y = f(x)$ over the interval $[a,b]$.

Begin by trying to fill the region under the graph as well as you can with rectangles, as in Fig. 4.1. Each rectangle must be completely inside the region, but as tall as possible. If there are n rectangles in all, what you are doing is in effect to split the interval $[a,b]$ on the x-axis into n small subintervals, and then to make the height of each rectangle equal to the smallest value which $f(x)$ takes in that subinterval.

This is called the 'lower bound' of $f(x)$ in the subinterval.

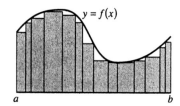

Fig. 4.1

You need a notation to express this. First, since a is at the left end of the first subinterval and b is at the right end of the last, nth, subinterval, it is useful to write $a = x_0$ and $b = x_n$. You can then denote the ith subinterval by $[x_{i-1}, x_i]$, and its width by $w_i = x_i - x_{i-1}$. There is no need for all the rectangles to have the same width, but there is no reason why they shouldn't if you choose. If they do, then this width can be denoted by w, where

$$w = \frac{b-a}{n},$$

and $x_i - x_{i-1} = w$ for each i. Then $b = a + nw$ and

$$x_i = x_0 + iw = a + iw.$$

The height of the ith rectangle is the lower bound of $f(x)$ in the subinterval. Denoting this by m_i,

$$x_{i-1} \le x \le x_i \quad \Rightarrow \quad f(x) \ge m_i.$$

The notation is illustrated in Fig. 4.2.

The total area of all the rectangles is then

$$s = m_1 w_1 + m_2 w_2 + \dots + m_n w_n$$

$$= \sum_{i=1}^{n} m_i (x_i - x_{i-1}).$$

Fig. 4.2

This is called the **lower sum** for this particular subdivision.

It is sometimes called the lower Riemann sum, after Bernhard Riemann (1826–1866), who was a professor at the University of Göttingen in Germany. The basic idea goes back to Archimedes (3rd century BC), but Riemann developed it into a general and mathematically rigorous definition.

This particular lower sum is of course not greater than the actual area of the region under the graph. But if you imagine every possible way of subdividing the interval $[a,b]$ into any number of subintervals, you could get some for which the corresponding lower sum is as close as you like to the area under the graph. That is, the area can be found as the limit of all the possible lower sums as the width of the subintervals tends to 0.

Will this always work? Might there be some functions, perhaps with very spiky graphs, for which the limit doesn't exist, or doesn't give the area you want?

To be quite sure, you can try another way of finding the area. Instead of drawing rectangles which fit inside the region, you could draw rectangles which completely cover the region but are as short as possible. To do this, begin by splitting the interval $[a,b]$ into subintervals as before, but then construct rectangles whose height is the upper bound of $f(x)$ in each subinterval. If this height is denoted by M_i, then

$$x_{i-1} \le x \le x_i \quad \Rightarrow \quad f(x) \le M_i.$$

This is illustrated in Fig. 4.3. The total area of all these rectangles is the **upper sum**,

$$S = M_1 w_1 + M_2 w_2 + \ldots + M_n w_n$$

$$= \sum_{i=1}^{n} M_i (x_i - x_{i-1}).$$

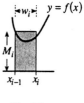

Fig. 4.3

Fig. 4.4 shows the upper sum, which is certainly not less than the actual area of the region under the graph.

Taking the limit of all possible upper sums as the width of the subintervals tends to 0 gives another way of finding the area you want. For any subdivision of $[a,b]$,

$$s \leq \text{area under the graph} \leq S.$$

So if the limit of the lower sums is equal to the limit of the upper sums, there can be no doubt that the area under the graph is equal to this common limit.

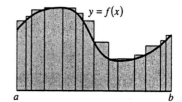

Fig. 4.4

The first example illustrates the idea with a numerical calculation.

Example 4.1.1

Find $\displaystyle\int_0^2 \sqrt{1+x^3}\, dx$ correct to 3 significant figures.

Since $\sqrt{1+x^3}$ is an increasing function (see Fig. 4.5), the lower bound for each subinterval is the value at the left end of the subinterval and the upper bound is the value at the right end.

Try splitting the interval $[0,2]$ into 100 equal subintervals, each of width 0.02. The ith subinterval runs from $0.02(i-1)$ to $0.2i$, so

$$m_i = \sqrt{1 + (0.02(i-1))^3}$$

and

$$M_i = \sqrt{1 + (0.02i)^3}.$$

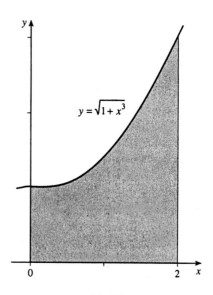

Fig. 4.5

The lower and upper sums are then

$$s = \sum_{i=1}^{100} \sqrt{1 + (0.02(i-1))^3} \times 0.02 \quad \text{and} \quad S = \sum_{i=1}^{100} \sqrt{1 + (0.02i)^3} \times 0.02$$

$$= 3.221\ldots \qquad\qquad\qquad\qquad = 3.261\ldots,$$

using a calculator to find the sums.

These values are not close enough to give the area correct to 3 significant figures, so you will need to split the interval $[0,2]$ into a larger number of narrower intervals. If you take 800 intervals, each of width 0.0025, then the ith subinterval runs from $0.0025(i-1)$ to $0.0025i$. Reasoning as before, the lower and upper sums are then

$$s = \sum_{i=1}^{800} \sqrt{1 + (0.0025(i-1))^3} \times 0.0025 \quad \text{and} \quad S = \sum_{i=1}^{800} \sqrt{1 + (0.0025i)^3} \times 0.0025$$
$$= 3.2388\ldots \qquad\qquad\qquad\qquad\qquad = 3.2438\ldots\ .$$

Correct to 3 significant figures both of these are 3.24, so the area under the graph must also be 3.24, correct to 3 significant figures.

Notice how in Example 4.1.1 the increase in the number of subintervals from 100 to 800 brings the lower sum and upper sum closer together, and therefore closer to the limiting value. In the second calculation there are 8 new subintervals for each of the subintervals in the first calculation. Fig. 4.6 shows how the effect of this is to increase the lower sum and decrease the upper sum.

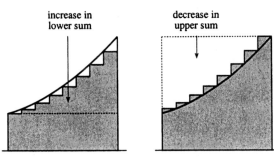

Fig. 4.6

But the numerical calculation doesn't by itself prove that s and S are tending to the same limit. To do this, you can use the fact that $\sqrt{1 + x^3}$ is an increasing function. This means that the height of the ith rectangle contributing to the lower sum is the same as the height of the $(i-1)$th rectangle contributing to the upper sum. So the 2nd, 3rd, ... , nth terms in the sum for s are the same as the 1st, 2nd, ... , $(n-1)$th terms in the sum for S. This is illustrated by Fig. 4.7; because the function is increasing, the rectangles for the upper sum are just the same as the rectangles for the lower sum, but translated to the left by the width of one subinterval.

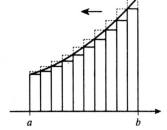

Fig. 4.7

So the only difference between the sums for s and S is that the first term of s is replaced by the last term of S.

That is, with n subintervals each of width $\dfrac{2}{n}$,

$$S - s = \sqrt{1 + 2^3} \times \frac{2}{n} - \sqrt{1 + 0^3} \times \frac{2}{n}$$
$$= (3-1) \times \frac{2}{n} = \frac{4}{n}.$$

And since $\lim\limits_{n\to\infty}\dfrac{4}{n}=0$, it follows that s and S tend to the same limit, which is $\displaystyle\int_0^2 \sqrt{1+x^3}\,dx$.

But you can't find the value of this limit precisely, because you can't find a formula for a sum like

$\displaystyle\sum_{i=1}^{n}\sqrt{1+\left(\dfrac{2}{n}i\right)^3}$. If you could sum the series, you could then find a formula for the definite integral. This is what happens in the next example.

Example 4.1.2

Use the summation method to find $\displaystyle\int_0^a x^3\,dx$, where $a>0$.

The function x^3 is increasing in the interval $[0,a]$, so as in Example 4.1.1 the lower bound in each subinterval is on the left and the upper bound is on the right.

Split the interval $[0,a]$ into n subintervals, each of width $\dfrac{a}{n}$. The ith subinterval runs from $x=(i-1)\dfrac{a}{n}$ to $x=i\dfrac{a}{n}$, so for this subinterval

$$m_i = (i-1)^3\frac{a^3}{n^3} \quad\text{and}\quad M_i = i^3\frac{a^3}{n^3}.$$

The upper and lower sums are then

$$s = \sum_{i=1}^{n}(i-1)^3\frac{a^3}{n^3}\times\frac{a}{n} \qquad\qquad S = \sum_{i=1}^{n}i^3\frac{a^3}{n^3}\times\frac{a}{n}$$

$$\text{and}$$

$$= \frac{a^4}{n^4}\sum_{i=1}^{n}(i-1)^3 \qquad\qquad = \frac{a^4}{n^4}\sum_{i=1}^{n}i^3.$$

Now you know that $\displaystyle\sum_{i=1}^{n}i^3 = \tfrac{1}{4}n^2(n+1)^2$ (see Example 1.1.3). Also

$$\sum_{i=1}^{n}(i-1)^3 = 0^3 + 1^3 + \ldots + (n-1)^3$$

$$= 0 + \sum_{i=1}^{n-1}i^3 = \tfrac{1}{4}(n-1)^2 n^2.$$

So

$$s = \frac{a^4}{n^4}\times\tfrac{1}{4}(n-1)^2 n^2 \qquad\qquad S = \frac{a^4}{n^4}\times\tfrac{1}{4}n^2(n+1)^2$$

$$= \tfrac{1}{4}a^4\times\frac{(n-1)^2}{n^2} \qquad\text{and}\qquad = \tfrac{1}{4}a^4\times\frac{(n+1)^2}{n^2}$$

$$= \tfrac{1}{4}a^4\left(1-\frac{1}{n}\right)^2 \qquad\qquad = \tfrac{1}{4}a^4\times\left(1+\frac{1}{n}\right)^2.$$

Since $\lim\limits_{n \to \infty} \dfrac{1}{n} = 0$, it follows that

$$\lim_{n \to \infty} s = \tfrac{1}{4}a^4(1-0)^2 = \tfrac{1}{4}a^4 \quad \text{and} \quad \lim_{n \to \infty} S = \tfrac{1}{4}a^4(1+0)^2 = \tfrac{1}{4}a^4.$$

And since these limits are the same, both are equal to the definite integral,

$$\int_0^a x^3 \, \mathrm{d}x = \tfrac{1}{4}a^4.$$

Of course, it is much easier to get the result in Example 4.1.2 by the anti-differentiation method than by the summation method. And the latter only works because you know how to sum $\sum\limits_{i=1}^{n} i^3$. You couldn't use the summation method to find $\int_0^a \sqrt{x} \, \mathrm{d}x$, for example, because you don't know how to sum $\sum\limits_{i=1}^{n} \sqrt{i}$; but it is simple by anti-differentiation. In fact, the great breakthrough by Newton and Leibniz was to show that the anti-differentiation method provides a far more powerful way of finding areas than the summation method initiated by Archimedes.

So the purpose of this section is to find a *definition* for $\int_a^b f(x) \, \mathrm{d}x$, not to suggest a new way of calculating it. Once you know that the definition is secure, you can go on to prove, just as in Higher Level Book 1 Section 29.4, that $\dfrac{\mathrm{d}}{\mathrm{d}x} \int_a^x f(t) \, \mathrm{d}t = f(x)$. And once you have done that, this is the property which you use to find definite integrals.

But the summation method does have one other advantage. It provides you with a way of finding a numerical value for definite integrals when you can't find a function $I(x)$ such that $I'(x) = f(x)$. You can then use the method of Example 4.1.1 to find bounds within which the value of $\int_a^b f(x) \, \mathrm{d}x$ must lie.

Exercise 4A

1   Areas under the following graphs over the given intervals are estimated by lower and upper sums with subintervals of equal widths. Calculate these sums for the stated widths, and compare them with the exact values of the areas.

(a) $y = 2x + 3$, $0 \le x \le 1$; widths $0.5, 0.1, 0.01$

(b) $y = 3x^2$, $1 \le x \le 2$; widths $0.5, 0.1, 0.01$

(c) $y = \sqrt{x}$, $1 \le x \le 4$; widths $1, 0.1, 0.01$

(d) $y = 12x - x^3$, $0 \le x \le 3$; widths $1, 0.5$

2 By finding lower and upper sums, with n intervals of equal width, find the following integrals.

(a) $\displaystyle\int_0^{10} x\,dx$ (b) $\displaystyle\int_0^a x^2\,dx$ (c) $\displaystyle\int_0^1 e^x\,dx$

(In part (c), remember that, from the definition of e, $\displaystyle\lim_{h\to0}\frac{e^h-1}{h}=1$. See Higher Level Book 2 Section 13.2.)

3 A value for $\displaystyle\int_0^1 2^x\,dx$ is estimated by finding lower and upper sums with subintervals of equal width. Find the difference between the lower and upper sums if the number of subintervals is

(a) 5,   (b) 100,   (c) n.

4 Repeat Question 3 for the integral $\displaystyle\int_1^4 \frac{1}{\sqrt{x}}\,dx$.

5 A function f is increasing over the interval $[a,b]$. A value for $\displaystyle\int_a^b f(x)\,dx$ is obtained by finding the lower sums s and the upper sum S when the interval $[a,b]$ is split into n subintervals of equal width. Prove that

$$S-s=\frac{(f(b)-f(a))(b-a)}{n}.$$

Deduce that $\displaystyle\lim_{n\to\infty} S = \lim_{n\to\infty} s = \int_a^b f(x)\,dx$.

What would be the corresponding result if f were a decreasing function over $[a,b]$?

4.2 Finding bounds for the sums of series

The idea of lower and upper sums can be adapted to find upper and lower bounds for the sums of finite series which cannot be summed exactly. By representing each term as the area of a rectangle of width 1, the sum can be compared with an integral over the same interval.

Example 4.2.1
Find upper and lower bounds for $\sqrt{1}+\sqrt{2}+\sqrt{3}+\ldots+\sqrt{10}$.

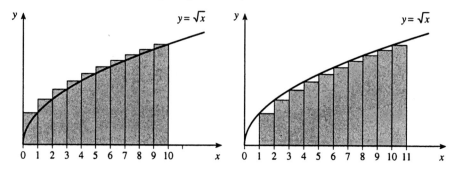

Fig. 4.8

In the left diagram of Fig. 4.8 the sum is represented as the area of a set of 10 rectangles, each having width 1 and with heights $\sqrt{1}$, $\sqrt{2}$, $\sqrt{3}$, ... , $\sqrt{10}$. These cover the interval $0 \le x \le 10$ of the x-axis.

The top right corners of these rectangles have coordinates $\left(1, \sqrt{1}\right)$, $\left(2, \sqrt{2}\right)$, $\left(3, \sqrt{3}\right)$, ... , $\left(10, \sqrt{10}\right)$ all of which lie on the curve $y = \sqrt{x}$.

Clearly the sum of the areas of the rectangles is greater than the area under the curve, so that

$$\sum_{i=1}^{10} \sqrt{i} > \int_0^{10} \sqrt{x}\,dx$$

$$= \left[\tfrac{2}{3} x^{\frac{3}{2}}\right]_0^{10}$$

$$= \tfrac{2}{3} \times 10\sqrt{10} = \tfrac{20}{3}\sqrt{10},$$

giving

$$\tfrac{20}{3}\sqrt{10} < \sum_{i=1}^{10} \sqrt{i}.$$

This gives a lower bound for the sum.

To find an upper bound, push all the rectangles to the right by 1 unit, so that they cover the interval $1 \le x \le 11$. The right diagram of Fig. 4.8 shows that the top left corners of the rectangles now lie on $y = \sqrt{x}$, and it is easy to see that

$$\sum_{i=1}^{n} \sqrt{i} < \int_1^{11} \sqrt{x}\,dx$$

$$= \left[\tfrac{2}{3} x^{\frac{3}{2}}\right]_1^{11}$$

$$= \tfrac{2}{3}\left(11\sqrt{11} - 1\right) = \tfrac{22}{3}\sqrt{11} - \tfrac{2}{3},$$

giving

$$\sum_{i=1}^{n} \sqrt{i} < \tfrac{22}{3}\sqrt{11} - \tfrac{2}{3}.$$

as an upper bound for the sum.

So $\tfrac{20}{3}\sqrt{10} < \sum_{i=1}^{n} \sqrt{i} < \tfrac{22}{3}\sqrt{11} - \tfrac{2}{3}$

You could of course find $\sqrt{1} + \sqrt{2} + \ldots + \sqrt{10}$ with a calculator. But you can use the same method to find a general inequality for the sum of the first n square roots, as in the next example.

Example 4.2.2

Find lower and upper bounds for the sum $\sqrt{1}+\sqrt{2}+\sqrt{3}+\ldots+\sqrt{n}$.

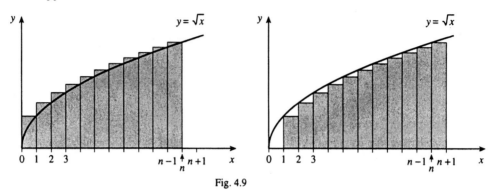

Fig. 4.9

In the left diagram of Fig. 4.9 the sum is represented as the area of a set of n rectangles, each having width 1 and with heights $\sqrt{1}$, $\sqrt{2}$, $\sqrt{3}$, ... , $\sqrt{n}$. These cover the interval $0 \le x \le n$ of the x-axis.

The top right corners of these rectangles have coordinates $\left(1,\sqrt{1}\right)$, $\left(2,\sqrt{2}\right)$, $\left(3,\sqrt{3}\right)$, ... , $\left(n,\sqrt{n}\right)$ all of which lie on the curve $y=\sqrt{x}$.

Clearly the sum of the areas of the rectangles is greater than the area under the curve, so that

$$\sum_{i=1}^{n}\sqrt{i} > \int_{0}^{n}\sqrt{x}\,dx$$
$$=\left[\tfrac{2}{3}x^{\frac{3}{2}}\right]_{0}^{n} = \tfrac{2}{3}n\sqrt{n},$$

giving

$$\tfrac{2}{3}n\sqrt{n} < \sum_{i=1}^{n}\sqrt{i}.$$

This gives a lower bound for the sum.

To find an upper bound, push all the rectangles to the right by 1 unit, so that they cover the interval $1 \le x \le n+1$. The right diagram of Fig. 4.9 shows that the top left corners of the rectangles now lie on $y=\sqrt{x}$, and it is easy to see that

$$\sum_{i=1}^{n}\sqrt{i} < \int_{1}^{n+1}\sqrt{x}\,dx$$
$$=\left[\tfrac{2}{3}x^{\frac{3}{2}}\right]_{1}^{n+1} = \tfrac{2}{3}\left((n+1)\sqrt{n+1}-1\right),$$

giving

$$\sum_{i=1}^{n}\sqrt{i} < \tfrac{2}{3}\left((n+1)\sqrt{n+1}-1\right)$$

as an upper bound.

So $\frac{2}{3}n\sqrt{n} < \sum_{i=1}^{n} \sqrt{i} < \frac{2}{3}\left((n+1)\sqrt{n+1}-1\right)$.

This method gives remarkably good approximations. For example, if you put $n = 100$ in Example 4.2.2, you find that the sum of the square roots of the first 100 natural numbers lies between

$$\frac{2}{3} \times 100\sqrt{100} = 666.66\ldots \qquad \text{and} \qquad \frac{2}{3} \times \left(101\sqrt{101} - 1\right) = 676.02\ldots.$$

The correct value of the sum is $671.46\ldots$. Both bounds are within 1% of this.

Things are slightly different if the graph of the function is decreasing.

Example 4.2.3

Show that $\ln 101 < 1 + \dfrac{1}{2} + \dfrac{1}{3} + \ldots + \dfrac{1}{100} < 1 + \ln 100$.

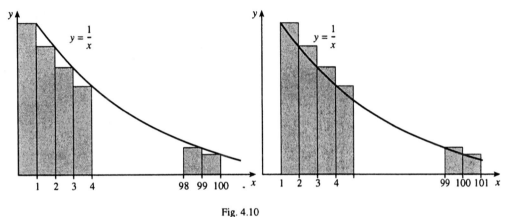

Fig. 4.10

The right diagram of Fig. 4.10 shows the sum $1 + \dfrac{1}{2} + \dfrac{1}{3} + \ldots + \dfrac{1}{100}$ represented as a set of 100

rectangles, each having width 1 and heights $1, \dfrac{1}{2}, \dfrac{1}{3}, \ldots, \dfrac{1}{100}$. These cover the interval $1 \le x \le 101$

of the x-axis. The top left corners of these rectangles have coordinates $(1,1)$, $\left(2, \dfrac{1}{2}\right)$, $\left(3, \dfrac{1}{3}\right)$, $\ldots$,

$\left(100, \dfrac{1}{100}\right)$ all of which lie on the curve $y = \dfrac{1}{x}$. Clearly the sum of the areas of the rectangles is

greater than the area under the curve, so that

$$1 + \frac{1}{2} + \frac{1}{3} + \ldots + \frac{1}{100} > \int_{1}^{101} \frac{1}{x}\,dx$$
$$= [\ln x]_{1}^{101}$$
$$= \ln 101,$$

or $\quad \ln 101 < 1 + \dfrac{1}{2} + \dfrac{1}{3} + \ldots + \dfrac{1}{100}$.

The left diagram shows all the shaded rectangles having moved to the left by 1 unit.

However, there is a problem, because you cannot have 0 as the lower limit of this integral which would then not exist. The solution is to ignore the first rectangle: the area under the curve between 1 and 100 is greater than the sum of the areas of the remaining rectangles, so

$$\frac{1}{2}+\frac{1}{3}+...+\frac{1}{100} < \int_1^{100} \frac{1}{x}dx$$

$$= [\ln x]_1^{100} = \ln 100,$$

giving

$$\frac{1}{2}+\frac{1}{3}+...+\frac{1}{100} < \ln 100.$$

Therefore, adding 1 (the area of the first rectangle) to both sides,

$$1+\frac{1}{2}+\frac{1}{3}+...+\frac{1}{100} < 1+\ln 100.$$

So $$\ln 101 < 1+\frac{1}{2}+\frac{1}{3}+...+\frac{1}{100} < 1+\ln 100.$$

Example 4.2.4

Find lower and upper bounds for $\displaystyle\sum_{i=m}^{n} \frac{1}{i^2}$, where $n > m \geq 2$. Hence find bounds for $\displaystyle\sum_{i=m}^{\infty} \frac{1}{i^2}$.

Sketch for yourself the graph of $y = \dfrac{1}{x^2}$, and mark on it points with coordinates $\left(m, \dfrac{1}{m^2}\right)$, $\left(m+1, \dfrac{1}{(m+1)^2}\right), \left(m+2, \dfrac{1}{(m+2)^2}\right), ..., \left(n, \dfrac{1}{n^2}\right)$.

Since $\dfrac{1}{x^2}$ is a decreasing function, you will get a lower bound by representing the sum by rectangles with these points at the top left corners, so that they cover the interval $m \leq x \leq n+1$.

The curve then lies inside the rectangles, so the sum of the areas of the rectangles is greater than the area under the curve, that is

$$\sum_{i=m}^{n} \frac{1}{i^2} > \int_m^{n+1} \frac{1}{x^2}dx$$

$$= \left[-\frac{1}{x}\right]_m^{n+1}$$

$$= \frac{1}{m} - \frac{1}{n+1},$$

which gives

$$\frac{1}{m} - \frac{1}{n+1} < \sum_{i=m}^{n} \frac{1}{i^2}.$$

To get an upper bound, push all the rectangles to the left by 1 unit. They then cover the interval $m - 1 \le x \le n$, and have their top right corners on the curve, so that the curve lies above the rectangles. (Since $m \ge 2$, the interval does not include the awkward value $x = 0$.)

Therefore

$$\sum_{i=m}^{n} \frac{1}{i^2} < \int_{m-1}^{n} \frac{1}{x^2} \, dx$$

$$= \left[-\frac{1}{x} \right]_{m-1}^{n}$$

$$= \frac{1}{m-1} - \frac{1}{n},$$

giving

$$\sum_{i=m}^{n} \frac{1}{i^2} < \frac{1}{m-1} - \frac{1}{n}.$$

Combining these results,

$$\frac{n-m+1}{m(n+1)} < \sum_{i=m}^{n} \frac{1}{i^2} < \frac{n-m+1}{(m-1)n}.$$

By letting $n \to \infty$ you can find bounds for the sum of the infinite series $\sum_{i=m}^{\infty} \frac{1}{i^2}$. Since

$$\lim_{n \to \infty} \frac{n-m+1}{n+1} = \lim_{n \to \infty} \frac{1 - \frac{m-1}{n}}{1 + \frac{1}{n}} = \frac{1-0}{1+0} = 1 \quad \text{and} \quad \lim_{n \to \infty} \frac{n-m+1}{n} = \lim_{n \to \infty} \left(1 - \frac{m-1}{n} \right) = 1 - 0 = 1,$$

it follows that

$$\frac{1}{m} \le \sum_{i=m}^{\infty} \frac{1}{i^2} \le \frac{1}{m-1}.$$

When you reason by taking limits as $n \to \infty$, $<$ must be replaced by $\le$. See Section 2.3. But you should be able to see from your figure that in this example the strong inequality $<$ is in fact valid.

Exercise 4B

1 Establish the following upper and lower bounds for the given sums.

(a) $4 - \ln 3 < \dfrac{2}{3} + \dfrac{3}{4} + \dfrac{4}{5} + \dfrac{5}{6} < 4 - \ln\left(\dfrac{7}{3}\right)$

(b) $2 - \dfrac{2}{\sqrt{5}} < \dfrac{1}{1\sqrt{1}} + \dfrac{1}{2\sqrt{2}} + \dfrac{1}{3\sqrt{3}} + \dfrac{1}{4\sqrt{4}} < 2$

(c) $20 - 2\sqrt{10} < \dfrac{1}{\sqrt{10}} + \dfrac{1}{\sqrt{11}} + \dfrac{1}{\sqrt{12}} + \dots + \dfrac{1}{\sqrt{99}} < 6\sqrt{11} - 6$

2 Find upper and lower bounds for the following sums. Give your answers in decimal form to 4 significant figures, rounding upper bounds up and lower bounds down.

(a) $\sqrt[4]{100} + \sqrt[4]{101} + \sqrt[4]{102} + \dots + \sqrt[4]{999}$

(b) $\dfrac{1}{101} + \dfrac{2}{102} + \dfrac{3}{103} + \dots + \dfrac{99}{199}$

(c) $\displaystyle\sum_{i=1}^{89} \sin i^\circ$

(d) $\displaystyle\sum_{i=1}^{100} \dfrac{1}{100^2 + i^2}$

3 If $n > m > 1$, find upper and lower bounds for

(a) $\displaystyle\sum_{i=m}^{n} \dfrac{1}{i^3}$

(b) $\displaystyle\sum_{i=m}^{n} \dfrac{i}{1+i^2}$

(c) $\dfrac{n!}{m!}$

4 (a) Use your answer to Question 3(a) to prove that $\displaystyle\sum_{i=1}^{\infty} \dfrac{1}{i^3} \le 1\tfrac{1}{2}$.

(b) Use your answer to Question 3(b) to prove that $\displaystyle\sum_{i=1}^{\infty} \dfrac{i}{1+i^2}$ is divergent.

5 (a) By considering a suitable integral, show that $12 < \sqrt[3]{1} + \sqrt[3]{2} + \sqrt[3]{3} + \dots + \sqrt[3]{8}$.

(b) Find an upper bound for $\displaystyle\sum_{i=1}^{8} \sqrt[3]{i}$.

(c) Use a similar method to find upper and lower bounds for $\displaystyle\sum_{i=101}^{200} \sqrt[3]{i}$.

6 Show that $\displaystyle\int_{n}^{2n} \dfrac{1}{x}\,dx - \dfrac{1}{2n} < \dfrac{1}{n+1} + \dfrac{1}{n+2} + \dots + \dfrac{1}{2n} < \int_{n}^{2n} \dfrac{1}{x}\,dx.$

Hence prove that $\displaystyle\lim_{n\to\infty}\left(\dfrac{1}{n+1} + \dfrac{1}{n+2} + \dots + \dfrac{1}{2n}\right) = \ln 2.$

5 Infinite integrals and infinite series

You already know how to find the sum of an infinite series as the limit of a finite sum. This chapter describes how, in a similar way, you can define an infinite integral as a limit. When you have completed it, you should

- know the definition of an infinite integral, and be able to calculate infinite integrals
- know how to use infinite integrals to determine whether an infinite series is convergent or divergent
- know what is meant by a *p*-series, and for what values of *p* it is convergent
- be able to use infinite integrals to find approximations to the sums of infinite series.

5.1 Infinite integrals

In the definition of a definite integral in Section 4.1 it seemed hardly necessary to mention that the interval $[a,b]$ has to be finite. You can't split an interval $[a,\infty]$ into n subintervals whose width tends to 0 as $n \to \infty$.

But provided that b remains a real number, it can be as large as you like. The definition of integral can be used to find integrals such as $\displaystyle\int_0^{10^6} f(x)\,dx$.

And if you write $\displaystyle\int_a^b f(x)\,dx$ as $I(b) - I(a)$, where $I'(x) = f(x)$, it may happen that $I(b)$ tends to a limit as $b \to \infty$. If so, then

$$\lim_{b \to \infty} \int_a^b f(x)\,dx = \left(\lim_{b \to \infty} I(b) \right) - I(a).$$

This is called an **infinite** (or **improper**) **integral**, and it is denoted by $\displaystyle\int_a^\infty f(x)\,dx$. The integral $\displaystyle\int_a^b f(x)\,dx$ is said to be **convergent** as $b \to \infty$.

The description 'improper' is sometimes reserved for a different kind of definite integral, in which the integrand is unbounded within the interval of integration.

Example 5.1.1

Show that $\displaystyle\int_0^b e^{-2x}\,dx$ is convergent, and find $\displaystyle\int_0^\infty e^{-2x}\,dx$.

The integral is found in the usual way, as

$$\int_0^b e^{-2x}\,dx = \left[-\tfrac{1}{2}e^{-2x} \right]_0^b = -\tfrac{1}{2}e^{-2b} + \tfrac{1}{2}.$$

Since $\lim\limits_{b \to \infty} e^{-2b} = 0$, this integral is convergent, and

$$\int_0^\infty e^{-2x}\,dx = \lim_{b \to \infty} \int_0^b e^{-2x}\,dx = -\tfrac{1}{2} \times 0 + \tfrac{1}{2} = \tfrac{1}{2}.$$

Fig. 5.1 shows the graph of $y = e^{-2x}$.
However large the value of b, the shaded area
is less than $\tfrac{1}{2}$, and it tends to $\tfrac{1}{2}$ as $b \to \infty$.

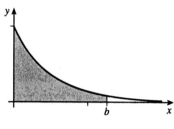

Fig. 5.1

Exercise 5A

1   Find which of the following integrals converge as $b \to \infty$. For those which do, give the
values of the infinite integral.

(a) $\displaystyle\int_1^b \frac{1}{x^2}\,dx$

(b) $\displaystyle\int_0^b \frac{1}{1+x}\,dx$

(c) $\displaystyle\int_0^b e^{-\frac{1}{3}x}\,dx$

(d) $\displaystyle\int_0^b \frac{1}{(2x+1)^{\frac{3}{2}}}\,dx$

(e) $\displaystyle\int_0^b \frac{1}{\sqrt{x+1}}\,dx$

(f) $\displaystyle\int_0^b xe^{-x}\,dx$

2   Find for what values of p the following infinite integrals exist.

(a) $\displaystyle\int_0^\infty e^{px}\,dx$

(b) $\displaystyle\int_1^\infty x^p\,dx$

3   Find the values of the following infinite integrals.

(a) $\displaystyle\int_1^\infty \frac{1}{x^3}\,dx$

(b) $\displaystyle\int_0^\infty xe^{-\frac{1}{2}x^2}\,dx$

(c) $\displaystyle\int_0^\infty \frac{1}{1+x^2}\,dx$

(d) $\displaystyle\int_0^\infty \frac{x}{\left(1+x^2\right)^2}\,dx$

(e) $\displaystyle\int_0^\infty \frac{x}{(x+2)^3}\,dx$

(f) $\displaystyle\int_1^\infty \frac{1}{\sqrt{x}}e^{-\sqrt{x}}\,dx$

4   If $f(x)$ tends to a limit L as $x \to \infty$, prove that $\displaystyle\int_a^\infty f(x)\,dx$ can only exist if $L = 0$.

Is it true that, if $L = 0$, then $\displaystyle\int_a^\infty f(x)\,dx$ exists? Give a reason for your answer.

5   If $0 < f(x) < g(x)$ for all $x > a$, and if $\displaystyle\int_a^\infty g(x)\,dx$ exists, show that $\displaystyle\int_a^\infty f(x)\,dx$ exists.

5.2   The integral test

Infinite integrals and infinite series have a lot in common. For example, Question 4 in Exercise 5A will have reminded you of the property in Section 2.3 that, if $\sum u_i$ is convergent, then $\lim_{n\to\infty} u_n = 0$, but the converse is not true. And Question 5 is a comparison test for infinite integrals similar to the comparison test for infinite series in Section 2.3.

The links are not confined to general properties like this. In Section 4.2 the value of $\sum_{i=1}^{n} f(i)$ was found by sandwiching it between $\int_{0}^{n} f(x)\,dx$ and $\int_{1}^{n+1} f(x)\,dx$. This section extends this idea, and gives a way of comparing $\sum_{i=1}^{\infty} f(i)$ with $\int_{1}^{\infty} f(x)\,dx$, where these exist.

Suppose that f is a function defined for $x > 0$ which has the two properties

- $f(x)$ is a decreasing function
- $f(x)$ tends to 0 as $x \to \infty$.

You know many functions with these properties, such as $\dfrac{1}{x}$, $\dfrac{1}{\sqrt{x}}$, e^{-x}, $\dfrac{1}{x^2+1}$. Obviously such a function must have $f(x) > 0$ for all $x > 0$.

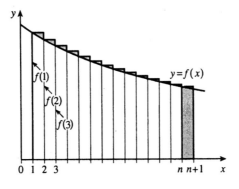

Fig. 5.2

Fig. 5.2 shows the graph of such a function, and a set of n rectangles of width 1 whose area represents the sum $\sum_{i=1}^{n} f(i)$. These rectangles cover the interval $1 \le x \le n+1$ on the x-axis. It is clear from Fig. 5.2 that this sum is greater than the area under the curve from $x = 1$ to $x = n$. The shaded regions have an area which represents the difference

$$d_n = \sum_{i=1}^{n} f(i) - \int_{1}^{n} f(x)\,dx,$$

so $d_n > 0$.

Now d_n is also a sequence. Notice that

$$d_1 = f(1) - 0 = f(1).$$

The term of the sequence after d_n is

$$d_{n+1} = \sum_{i=1}^{n+1} f(i) - \int_1^{n+1} f(x)\,dx,$$

so $$d_{n+1} - d_n = f(n+1) - \int_n^{n+1} f(x)\,dx.$$

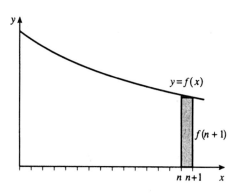

Fig. 5.3

The quantity on the right side of this equation is the difference between the area of the rectangle and the area under the curve in Fig. 5.3, and this shows that $d_{n+1} - d_n < 0$, that is $d_{n+1} < d_n$.

You now know three things about the sequence d_n:

- $d_1 = f(1)$
- $d_n > 0$ for all n
- the terms of the sequence decrease as n increases.

Example 5.2.1

Demonstrate these properties of the sequence d_n when $f(x) = \dfrac{1}{x}$.

Table 5.4 gives the values of $S_n = \sum_{i=1}^{n} \dfrac{1}{i}$ and of $\int_1^n \dfrac{1}{x}\,dx = \ln n$ for values of $n = 10^k$ for $k = 0, 1, 2, 3, 4, 5$ and 6. The last line gives the difference $d_n = S_n - \ln n$. All entries are rounded correct to 5 decimal places.

n	1	10	10^2	10^3	10^4	10^5	10^6
S_n	1	2.928 97	5.187 38	7.485 47	9.787 61	12.090 15	14.392 73
$\ln n$	0	2.302 59	4.605 17	6.907 76	9.210 34	11.512 93	13.815 51
d_n	1	0.626 38	0.582 21	0.577 72	0.577 27	0.577 22	0.577 22

Table 5.4

You can see from the last line of the table that the values of $d_n = S_n - \ln n$ tend to a limit of about 0.577 22 as $n \to \infty$. This limit is called **Euler's constant**, after the 18th-century Swiss mathematician who first discovered it; it is usually denoted by γ, the Greek letter gamma.

The fact that d_n tends to a limit as $n \to \infty$, shown in this example for the function $f(x) = \dfrac{1}{x}$, is an inevitable consequence of the properties of d_n listed above. If a sequence is decreasing and positive, it must tend to a limit.

These results can be summed up as follows:

> If a function $f(x)$ is decreasing for $x > 0$ and $f(x)$ tends to 0 as $x \to \infty$, then
>
> $$\sum_{r=1}^{n} f(r) - \int_{1}^{n} f(x)\,dx \quad \text{tends to a limit between 0 and } f(1) \text{ as } n \to \infty.$$

Now suppose that the infinite integral $\int_{1}^{\infty} f(x)\,dx$ exists. Then, by letting $n \to \infty$ in the equation

$$\sum_{i=1}^{n} f(i) = d_n + \int_{1}^{n} f(x)\,dx,$$

it follows that the sum of the series tends to a limit as $n \to \infty$. On the other hand, if $\int_{1}^{n} f(x)\,dx$ diverges to infinity, then so does the sum of the series. This is called the **integral test**.

> **The integral test**   If a function $f(x)$ is decreasing for $x > 0$ and $f(x)$ tends to 0 as $x \to \infty$, then the infinite series $\sum f(i)$ converges if and only if
>
> $$\int_{1}^{\infty} f(x)\,dx \quad \text{exists, and then}$$
>
> $$\int_{1}^{\infty} f(x)\,dx < \sum_{i=1}^{\infty} f(i) < f(1) + \int_{1}^{\infty} f(x)\,dx.$$

Example 5.2.2

Prove that $\displaystyle\sum_{i=1}^{\infty} \frac{1}{i(3i-1)}$ exists, and find bounds for its value.

You found the sums of some series like this in Chapter 2. A useful first step is to express the terms in partial fractions. So begin by writing

$$\frac{1}{i(3i-1)} \equiv \frac{3}{3i-1} - \frac{1}{i}.$$

Substituting $i = 1, 2, 3, \ldots$ you get

$$\frac{1}{1 \times 2} = \frac{3}{2} - \frac{1}{1}, \quad \frac{1}{2 \times 5} = \frac{3}{5} - \frac{1}{2}, \quad \frac{1}{3 \times 8} = \frac{3}{8} - \frac{1}{3}, \ldots .$$

If you write $\frac{1}{1}$ as $\frac{3}{3}$, $\frac{1}{2}$ as $\frac{3}{6}$, $\frac{1}{3}$ as $\frac{3}{9}$, ... , the sum is

$$\sum_{i=1}^{\infty} \frac{1}{i(3i-1)} = \left(\frac{3}{2} - \frac{3}{3}\right) + \left(\frac{3}{5} - \frac{3}{6}\right) + \left(\frac{3}{8} - \frac{3}{9}\right) + \cdots$$

$$= 3\left(\frac{1}{2} - \frac{1}{3} + \frac{1}{5} - \frac{1}{6} + \frac{1}{8} - \frac{1}{9} + \cdots\right).$$

Unfortunately none of these fractions cancel out as they did in the examples in Chapter 2, so you can't get any further along this route.

But you can find an exact expression for the infinite integral $\int_1^\infty \frac{1}{x(3x-1)}\,dx$. Using the same partial fractions as before,

$$\int_1^n \frac{1}{x(3x-1)}\,dx = \int_1^n \left(\frac{3}{3x-1} - \frac{1}{x}\right)dx$$
$$= \left[\ln(3x-1) - \ln x\right]_1^n$$
$$= (\ln(3n-1) - \ln n) - (\ln 2 - \ln 1)$$
$$= \ln\left(\frac{3n-1}{2n}\right) = \ln\left(\frac{3}{2} - \frac{1}{2n}\right).$$

As $n \to \infty$, $\frac{1}{2n} \to 0$, so $\lim_{n \to \infty} \ln\left(\frac{3}{2} - \frac{1}{2n}\right) = \ln\frac{3}{2}$. Therefore

$$\int_1^\infty \frac{1}{x(3x-1)}\,dx = \ln\frac{3}{2}.$$

Also $f(1) = \frac{1}{1 \times 2} = \frac{1}{2}$. Therefore, by the integral test, $\sum \frac{1}{i(3i-1)}$ converges, and

$$\ln\frac{3}{2} < \sum_{i=1}^\infty \frac{1}{i(3i-1)} < \frac{1}{2} + \ln\frac{3}{2}.$$

As a check, the calculator gives for this series $S_{999} = 0.7406\ldots$, so S_∞ will be a little greater than this. The bounds for the sum to infinity are $\ln\frac{3}{2} = 0.4054\ldots$ and $\frac{1}{2} + \ln\frac{3}{2} = 0.9054\ldots$.

5.3   The p-series

An important application of the integral test is to the series

$$\sum \frac{1}{i^p} = \frac{1}{1^p} + \frac{1}{2^p} + \frac{1}{3^p} + \ldots , \qquad \text{where } p > 0, \text{ which is known as the } \textbf{\textit{p}-series.}$$

It was shown in Section 2.2 that $\sum \frac{1}{i^2}$ is convergent, and that $\sum \frac{1}{\sqrt{i}} = \sum \frac{1}{i^{\frac{1}{2}}}$ is divergent. So whether the series converges or diverges depends on the value of p. There is no easy way to sum the series exactly for a general value of p.

But the infinite integral $\int_1^\infty \frac{1}{x^p}\,dx$, where it exists, can be found exactly. It helps to consider three cases separately.

If $p < 1$,

$$\int_1^n x^{-p}\,dx = \left[\frac{1}{1-p}x^{1-p}\right]_1^n = \frac{1}{1-p}\left(n^{1-p} - 1\right).$$

Since $1 - p > 0$, n^{1-p} increases without limit as $n \to \infty$, so the infinite integral doesn't exist.

If $p = 1$,

$$\int_1^n x^{-1}\, dx = [\ln x]_1^n = \ln n.$$

This also increases without limit as $n \to \infty$, so the infinite integral doesn't exist.

If $p > 1$,

$$\int_1^n x^{-p}\, dx = \left[-\frac{1}{p-1} x^{-(p-1)} \right]_1^n = \frac{1}{p-1}\left(-n^{-(p-1)} + 1 \right).$$

Since $p - 1 > 0$, $n^{-(p-1)} \to 0$ as $n \to \infty$, so the integral converges to $\frac{1}{p-1}(-0 + 1)$, and

$$\int_1^\infty \frac{1}{x^p}\, dx = \frac{1}{p-1}.$$

The infinite integral $\int_1^n \frac{1}{x^p}\, dx$ converges as $n \to \infty$ if $p > 1$, and

$$\int_1^\infty \frac{1}{x^p}\, dx = \frac{1}{p-1}.$$

You can now apply the integral test to $\sum \frac{1}{i^p}$. Note that the function $\frac{1}{x^p}$ with $p > 0$ is decreasing for $x > 0$, and tends to 0 as $x \to \infty$, so the conditions for the test are satisfied.

The infinite series $\sum \frac{1}{i^p}$ is convergent if $p > 1$, and

$$\frac{1}{p-1} < \sum_{i=1}^\infty \frac{1}{i^p} < 1 + \frac{1}{p-1}.$$

The series is divergent if $p \le 1$.

This shows that $\sum_{i=1}^\infty \frac{1}{i^p}$ is a function of p with domain $p > 1$. It is usually denoted by $\zeta(p)$, and is called *Riemann's zeta-function*. (ζ (zeta) is the Greek letter z.)

When $p = 1$ the series becomes $1 + \frac{1}{2} + \frac{1}{3} + \frac{1}{4} + \ldots$, which is known as the *harmonic series*.

<hr />

Exercise 5B

1   Use the integral test to prove that the following series are divergent.

(a) $\sum \dfrac{i}{i^2+3}$

(b) $\sum \dfrac{i^2}{(i+1)^3}$

(c) $\sum \dfrac{i}{(i+1)(2i-1)}$

Keep your solutions to Question 2 for use in Exercise 5C Question 2.

2   Use the integral test to prove that the following series $\sum f(i)$ are convergent, and find lower and upper bounds for the value of $\displaystyle\sum_{i=1}^{\infty} f(i)$. Check these by finding approximations to the sum to infinity with a calculator.

(a) $\sum \dfrac{1}{i(2i-1)}$

(b) $\sum \dfrac{1}{i^2+9}$

(c) $\sum \dfrac{1}{(2i-1)(3i-2)}$

(d) $\sum \dfrac{1}{i^2}\cos\left(\dfrac{1}{i}\right)$

(e) $\sum \dfrac{i}{\left(i^2+24\right)^{\frac{3}{2}}}$

3   Prove that the infinite series

$$\dfrac{1}{2(\ln 2)^p}+\dfrac{1}{3(\ln 3)^p}+\dfrac{1}{4(\ln 4)^p}+\dots$$

is convergent for $p>1$ and divergent for $p\le1$.

4   Find $\dfrac{d}{dx}\ln\left(x+\sqrt{1+x^2}\right)$ and $\dfrac{d}{dx}\dfrac{x}{\sqrt{1+x^2}}$. Hence show that $\displaystyle\sum \dfrac{1}{\left(1+i^2\right)^{\frac{1}{2}}}$ is divergent and that

$\displaystyle\sum \dfrac{1}{\left(1+i^2\right)^{\frac{3}{2}}}$ is convergent. Find lower and upper bounds for the value of $\displaystyle\sum_{i=1}^{\infty} \dfrac{1}{\left(1+i^2\right)^{\frac{3}{2}}}$.

5   Use the integral test to prove that the infinite integral $\displaystyle\int_1^{\infty} r^x \, dx$ exists if $0<r<1$.

<hr />

5.4 Calculating sums to infinity

The integral test is a useful way of proving that an infinite series is convergent, but the lower and upper bounds are too far apart to give an accurate value of the sum to infinity. This is because they differ by $f(1)$, and since the terms of the series are decreasing the first term will usually be comparatively large.

You will probably have experienced occasional difficulties in using a calculator to estimate the sum to infinity of a series. These are of two kinds.

- The program for finding sums may impose a restriction on the number of terms that can be added. For the calculator used in writing this book the largest permitted number of terms is 999.
- There is a ceiling over the size of numbers that the calculator can handle. On many calculators this is 10^{100}. If the expression for the terms involves a function such as $i!$ or i^i this ceiling will soon be reached. For example, $70!$ and 57^{57} both exceed it.

However, by combining the use of a calculator with the integral test inequalities you can often find the sum to infinity of a series to a high degree of accuracy.

In Section 5.2 the series and the integral started at $i = 1$ and $x = 1$, but they could have started at any integer m. The argument would be exactly the same, but the inequalities in the shaded box at the end of the section would then become

$$\int_m^\infty f(x)\,dx < \sum_{i=m}^\infty f(i) < f(m) + \int_m^\infty f(x)\,dx.$$

The important change is that the difference between the upper and lower bounds is now $f(m)$ instead of $f(1)$. Since $f(x)$ is a decreasing function, the difference between the upper and lower bounds gets smaller as m gets larger.

Now the sum to infinity of the series can be split into two parts, as

$$\sum_{i=1}^\infty f(i) = \sum_{i=1}^{m-1} f(i) + \sum_{i=m}^\infty f(i).$$

So, adding $\sum_{i=1}^{m-1} f(i)$ to the expressions in the inequality, you get

$$\sum_{i=1}^{m-1} f(i) + \int_m^\infty f(x)\,dx < \sum_{i=1}^\infty f(i) < f(m) + \sum_{i=1}^{m-1} f(i) + \int_m^\infty f(x)\,dx.$$

The method is to use a calculator to find $\sum_{i=1}^{m-1} f(i)$, taking as large a value for m as you can, and to add to this the infinite integral $\int_m^\infty f(x)\,dx$. You can then be sure that you have a value for $\sum_{i=1}^\infty f(i)$, with a maximum possible error of $f(m)$.

Example 5.4.1

Find $\sum_{i=1}^\infty \dfrac{1}{i(3i-1)}$ correct to as many decimal places as you can. (See Example 5.2.2.)

If the calculator program for summing series is restricted to 999 terms, take $m = 1000$. Then, from the calculator,

$$\sum_{i=1}^{999} \frac{1}{i(3i-1)} = 0.740\,685\,195, \quad \text{correct to 9 decimal places.}$$

You have to add to this the infinite integral $\int_{1000}^\infty \dfrac{1}{x(3x-1)}\,dx$, using partial fractions to do the integration as in Example 5.2.2. Begin by finding the integral from 1000 to n, as

$$\int_{1000}^n \frac{1}{x(3x-1)}\,dx = \left[\ln(3x-1) - \ln x\right]_{1000}^n$$

$$= \ln\!\left(\frac{3n-1}{n}\right) - \ln\frac{2999}{1000} = \ln\!\left(3 - \frac{1}{n}\right) - \ln\frac{2999}{1000}.$$

The limit as $n \to \infty$ is

$$\int_{1000}^{\infty} \frac{1}{x(3x-1)} \, dx = \ln 3 - \ln \frac{2999}{1000} = \ln \frac{3000}{2999}$$

$$= 0.000\,333\,389.$$

So the lower bound is

$$\sum_{i=1}^{999} \frac{1}{i(3i-1)} + \int_{1000}^{\infty} \frac{1}{x(3x-1)} \, dx = 0.740\,685\,195\ldots + 0.000\,333\,389\ldots$$

$$= 0.741\,018\,583\ldots \ .$$

For the upper bound you have to add on the value of the 1000th term, which is

$$\frac{1}{1000(3 \times 1000 - 1)} = \frac{1}{1000 \times 2999} = 0.000\,000\,333.$$

So the upper bound is $0.741\,018\,916$.

It follows that

$$0.741\,018\,583 < \sum_{i=1}^{\infty} \frac{1}{i(3i-1)} < 0.741\,018\,916.$$

The sum to infinity is $0.741\,019$, correct to 6 decimal places.

Exercise 5C

1   Find lower and upper bounds for

(a) $\displaystyle\sum_{i=1}^{\infty} \frac{1}{i^2}$,   (b) $\displaystyle\sum_{i=1}^{\infty} \frac{1}{(4i-3)(4i-1)}$,

keeping as many decimal places in your answers as the calculator allows.

The exact values of these sums are   (a) $\frac{1}{6}\pi^2$ and   (b) $\frac{1}{8}\pi$. Check that these lie within the bounds you have calculated.

2   For the series in Exercise 5B Question 2 find the sum to infinity correct to as many decimal places as you can.

6 Series with positive and negative terms

This chapter extends the study of infinite series to series with some positive and some negative terms. When you have completed it, you should

- know what is meant by an alternating series, and that alternating series with terms decreasing in absolute value with limit 0 are convergent
- be familiar with the various ways in which a series may diverge
- be able to distinguish between absolutely convergent and conditionally convergent series.

6.1 Alternating series

So far in this book all the infinite series have had only positive terms. The only exceptions you have seen have been geometric series with a negative common ratio. Fig. 6.1 is a copy of the graph in Higher Level Book 1 Section 30.4, and shows the sum sequence for the series $\sum 10 \times (-0.9)^{i-1}$, that is, $\sum u_i$ defined by

$$u_1 = 10, \quad u_i = -0.9u_{i-1} \text{ for } i > 1.$$

The partial sum of n terms for this series is

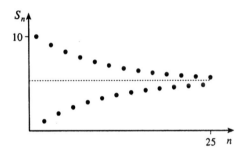

$$S_n = 10 \times \frac{1 - (-0.9)^n}{1 - (-0.9)}$$
$$= \tfrac{100}{19} - \tfrac{100}{19} \times (-0.9)^n.$$

Fig. 6.1

The sum to infinity is $\tfrac{100}{19}$; S_n is greater than $\tfrac{100}{19}$ when n is odd and less than $\tfrac{100}{19}$ when n is even.

Series like this, whose terms are alternately positive and negative, are called **alternating series**. They are an important special case of infinite series with both positive and negative terms.

There are a lot of series whose sum series have graphs similar to Fig. 6.1. For example, Fig. 6.2 shows the graph of S_n for the series $1 - \tfrac{1}{2} + \tfrac{1}{3} - \tfrac{1}{4} + \dots$, with $u_i = \frac{(-1)^{i-1}}{i}$.

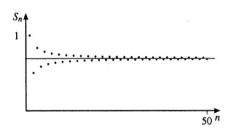

As in Fig. 6.1, the sequence $S_1, S_3, S_5, \dots$ of partial sums for odd n is decreasing. This is because in absolute value the terms are getting steadily smaller: for all i, $|u_i| < |u_{i-1}|$. So to get from S_1 to S_3 you go down by $|u_2| = \tfrac{1}{2}$ and then up by $|u_3| = \tfrac{1}{3}$, so $S_3 < S_1$. Similarly $S_5 < S_3$, $S_7 < S_5$ and so on.

Fig. 6.2

A similar argument shows that the sequence of partial sums for even n is increasing.

But also the odd-suffix partial sums are all greater than the even-suffix ones. For example, to show that $S_{11} > S_6$, you have only to remark that $S_6 < S_8 < S_{10}$ because the even-suffix sequence is increasing, and $S_{11} > S_{10}$ because $S_{11} = S_{10} + u_{11}$ and u_{11} is positive.

It follows that the sequence of odd-suffix partial sums tends to a limit, and so does the even-suffix sequence. And because $\lim_{i \to \infty} u_i = 0$, these limits must be the same. So S_n tends to a limit as $n \to \infty$; that is, $\sum u_i$ is convergent.

You can also say something about the value of the sum to infinity S_∞.

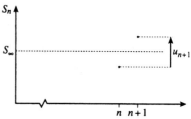

Fig. 6.3 illustrates the case in which n is even, so that $S_n < S_\infty$. Also $n + 1$ is odd, so $S_{n+1} > S_\infty$. And $S_{n+1} = S_n + u_{n+1}$, so

$$S_\infty - S_n < S_{n+1} - S_n = u_{n+1}.$$

Fig. 6.3

If n is odd (Fig. 6.4) then the corresponding inequalities are $S_n > S_\infty$ and $S_{n+1} < S_\infty$, so

$$S_n - S_\infty < S_n - S_{n+1} = -u_{n+1},$$

and $-u_{n+1} = |u_{n+1}|$ because $u_{n+1} < 0$.

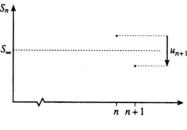

These inequalities show that, in either case, the error in using S_n as an approximation to S_∞ is less than the absolute value of the next term. This is called the **truncation error**.

Fig. 6.4

For example, you can calculate for the series $\sum \dfrac{(-1)^{i-1}}{i}$ in Fig. 6.2 that $S_{999} = 0.6936\ldots$ and $S_{1000} = 0.6926\ldots$. In Section 6.3 you will find that the sum to infinity of this series is $\ln 2 = 0.6931\ldots$. The error in using S_{999} as an approximation to $\ln 2$ is about 0.0005, which is less than the absolute value of the 1000th term, which is $\left| -\dfrac{1}{1000} \right| = 0.001$.

The argument above depends on just three properties: that the terms are alternately positive and negative, that they get steadily smaller in absolute value, and that they tend to 0. So you can sum it up in a general statement.

If an infinite series $\sum u_i$ has

- terms which are alternately positive and negative

- for all $i > 1$, $|u_i| < |u_{i-1}|$

- $\lim_{i \to \infty} u_i = 0$,

then the series is convergent.

The error in taking the sum of n terms as an approximation to the sum to infinity (the truncation error) is less than the absolute value of the $(n + 1)$th term.

Example 6.1.1

How many terms of the series $\frac{1}{1^2} - \frac{1}{2^2} + \frac{1}{3^2} - \ldots$ should you take to be sure of finding the sum to infinity with truncation error whose absolute value is less than 0.001?

This series satisfies the three conditions listed in the shaded box. The absolute value of the $(n+1)$th term is $\frac{1}{(n+1)^2}$, so the magnitude of the truncation error is less than this. To be sure that the absolute error is less than 0.001, you should choose n to satisfy the inequality

$$\frac{1}{(n+1)^2} < 0.001,$$

so that $(n+1)^2 > 1000$, that is $n > \sqrt{1000} - 1 = 30.6\ldots$. Since n must be an integer, you should take 31 terms.

If you work out the sum of 31 terms in this example you get $S_{31} = 0.822\,97\ldots$. The exact sum to infinity is in fact $\frac{1}{12}\pi^2 = 0.822\,46\ldots$, so the absolute value of the truncation error is $0.000\,51\ldots$, considerably less than the 0.001 required. To get an error less than 0.001 you need only 22 terms, since $S_{22} = 0.821\,48\ldots$ and $S_{23} = 0.823\,37\ldots$, with truncation errors of absolute value $0.000\,98\ldots$ and $0.000\,90\ldots$ respectively. Any subsequent partial sums are closer than this to the sum to infinity. But the critical words in the question asked are 'to be *sure*'; and for this, using the methods of this section, you must take 31 terms.

6.2 Different forms of divergence

If all the terms of an infinite series are positive, there are only two possibilities: either the series converges, or it diverges to infinity.

But if some terms are positive and some are negative, there are other possibilities. Some of these are illustrated by the examples in this section.

Example 6.2.1

Display the graph of the partial sums S_n for the infinite geometric series $\sum 10 \times (-1.1)^{i-1}$.

This series cannot converge, because the terms do not tend to 0 as $i \to \infty$.

If you compare the graph in Fig. 6.5 with Fig. 6.1, you will see that the odd-suffix partial sums form an increasing sequence which tends to ∞, and the even-suffix partial sums form a decreasing sequence which tends to $-\infty$. This is because the absolute value of the terms increases as i increases, so each jump (up or down) from S_{n-1} to S_n is larger than the one before.

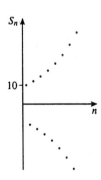

Fig. 6.5

A sequence like the one in Example 6.2.1 is said to **oscillate**. Because there are no bounds for the values of S_n, it is described as 'oscillating infinitely'.

Example 6.2.2

Describe the behaviour of the sequence of partial sums for the infinite series $\sum\left(1+2\times(-1)^{i-1}\right)\times i$.

The expression in brackets, $1+2\times(-1)^{i-1}$, takes alternately the values 3 when i is odd and -1 when i is even. So successive terms of the series are

$$3\times1, \quad -1\times2, \quad 3\times3, \quad -1\times4, \quad 3\times5, \quad -1\times6, \quad \dots$$

and the partial sums are

$$3, \quad 1, \quad 10, \quad 6, \quad 21, \quad 15, \quad \dots .$$

You can write separate formulae for the partial sum S_n according as n is an even or an odd number.

If $n = 2m$, then

$$S_n = 3\times(1+3+5+\dots+(2m-1))-(2+4+6+\dots+2m).$$

Both brackets contain arithmetic series, with sums $\frac{1}{2}m(1+(2m-1)) = m^2$ and $2\left(\frac{1}{2}m(m+1)\right) = m(m+1)$ respectively. So

$$S_n = 3m^2 - m(m+1) = 2m^2 - m$$
$$= 2\left(\frac{1}{2}n\right)^2 - \frac{1}{2}n = \frac{1}{2}n(n-1).$$

If $n = 2m-1$, then

$$S_n = 3\times(1+3+5+\dots+(2m-1))-(2+4+6+\dots+2(m-1))$$
$$= 3m^2 - (m-1)m = 2m^2 + m$$
$$= 2\left(\frac{1}{2}(n+1)\right)^2 + \frac{1}{2}(n+1) = \frac{1}{2}(n+1)(n+2).$$

So

$$S_n = \begin{cases} \frac{1}{2}(n+1)(n+2) & \text{if } n \text{ is odd,} \\ \frac{1}{2}n(n-1) & \text{if } n \text{ is even.} \end{cases}$$

Although the terms alternate in sign, so that the values of S_n successively increase and decrease, this series does *not* oscillate. The expressions for S_n both tend to infinity as $n \to \infty$, so this series diverges to infinity. This is shown graphically in Fig. 6.6.

All the series so far in this chapter have been alternating series, but the third example in this section is more erratic. Positive and negative terms occur in blocks, mostly of 3 terms but occasionally of 4.

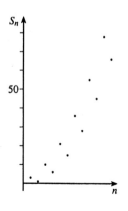

Fig. 6.6

Example 6.2.3

For the infinite series $\sum \cos i$, display graphs of $u_i = \cos i$ and $S_n = \sum_{i=1}^{n} \cos i$.

This series cannot converge because $\cos i$ doesn't tend to 0 as $i \to \infty$.

In Exercise 1A Question 9 you found that

$$\sum_{i=1}^{n} \cos i\theta = \frac{\sin\left(n + \frac{1}{2}\right)\theta}{2\sin\frac{1}{2}\theta} - \frac{1}{2}.$$

So, putting $\theta = 1$,

$$S_n = \sum_{i=1}^{n} \cos i = \frac{1}{2}\left(\frac{\sin\left(n + \frac{1}{2}\right)}{\sin\frac{1}{2}} - 1\right).$$

Figs. 6.7 and 6.8 are the graphs of u_i and S_n respectively. They consist of the points for which $x \in \mathbb{Z}^+$ on the graphs of $y = \cos x$ and $y = \frac{1}{2}\left(\frac{\sin\left(x + \frac{1}{2}\right)}{\sin\frac{1}{2}} - 1\right)$, which are shown grey in the figures.

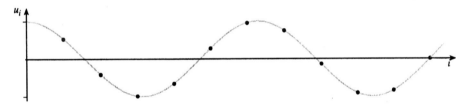

Fig. 6.7

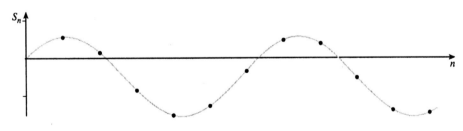

Fig. 6.8

The values of u_i are all between -1 and $+1$. They never equal these bounding values (because π is an irrational number) but they sometimes get very close; for example, $u_{22} = -0.999\,96...$. Since $\sin\left(n + \frac{1}{2}\right)$ is always between -1 and $+1$, the values of S_n lie between $\frac{1}{2}\left(-\frac{1}{\sin\frac{1}{2}} - 1\right) = -1.5429...$

and $\frac{1}{2}\left(\frac{1}{\sin\frac{1}{2}} - 1\right) = 0.5429...$.

In Example 6.2.3 the series oscillates as $n \to \infty$, but it differs from Example 6.2.1 in that the values of S_n always lie within fixed bounds. The series is said to 'oscillate finitely'.

> If an infinite series has some positive and some negative terms, then it may converge, diverge to $+\infty$ or to $-\infty$, or oscillate (finitely or infinitely).

6.3 Absolute and conditional convergence

The two series $\sum 10 \times (-0.9)^{i-1}$ and $\sum \frac{(-1)^{i-1}}{i}$, whose graphs are drawn in Fig. 6.1 and Fig. 6.2, could both be proved convergent by using the alternating series property in the shaded box in Section 6.1. But although they are similar in this respect, in other ways they are very different.

The essential distinction between the two is that if you make new series by taking the absolute value of each term, the first series becomes $\sum 10 \times 0.9^{i-1}$, which is just another convergent geometric series with common ratio 0.9 rather than –0.9; but the second becomes $\sum \frac{1}{i}$, which was shown in Section 5.3 to be divergent.

> If $\sum u_i$ is a series with a mixture of positive and negative terms, and if $\sum |u_i|$ is convergent, then $\sum u_i$ is said to be **absolutely convergent**; however, if $\sum |u_i|$ is divergent but $\sum u_i$ is convergent, then $\sum u_i$ is **conditionally convergent**.

So with these definitions $\sum 10 \times (-0.9)^{i-1}$ is absolutely convergent, but $\sum \frac{(-1)^{i-1}}{i}$ is conditionally convergent.

With conditionally convergent series it is possible to reach absurd conclusions when you carry out what seem to be quite normal algebraic procedures. Here are two examples.

Example 6.3.1
A 'proof' that $0 > \frac{1}{2}$.

It is clear from Fig. 6.2 that $\sum \frac{(-1)^{i-1}}{i}$ converges to a limit which is certainly greater than $\frac{1}{2}$. But

$$1 - \tfrac{1}{2} + \tfrac{1}{3} - \tfrac{1}{4} + \tfrac{1}{5} - \tfrac{1}{6} + \tfrac{1}{7} - \tfrac{1}{8} + \ldots = \left(1 + \tfrac{1}{2} + \tfrac{1}{3} + \tfrac{1}{4} + \tfrac{1}{5} + \tfrac{1}{6} + \tfrac{1}{7} + \tfrac{1}{8} + \ldots\right) - 2 \times \left(\tfrac{1}{2} + \tfrac{1}{4} + \tfrac{1}{6} + \tfrac{1}{8} + \ldots\right)$$

$$= \left(1 + \tfrac{1}{2} + \tfrac{1}{3} + \tfrac{1}{4} + \ldots\right) - \left(1 + \tfrac{1}{2} + \tfrac{1}{3} + \tfrac{1}{4} + \ldots\right)$$

$$= 0.$$

'Therefore' $0 > \frac{1}{2}$.

It is not very hard to find the flaw in this argument. Notice that in line 2 both brackets contain the divergent (and therefore meaningless) series $\sum \frac{1}{i}$. If you write out the argument in terms of partial sums, it takes the form

$$1 - \tfrac{1}{2} + \tfrac{1}{3} - \tfrac{1}{4} + \tfrac{1}{5} - \tfrac{1}{6} + \tfrac{1}{7} - \tfrac{1}{8} + \dots + \frac{1}{2n-1} - \frac{1}{2n}$$

$$= \left(1 + \tfrac{1}{2} + \tfrac{1}{3} + \tfrac{1}{4} + \tfrac{1}{5} + \tfrac{1}{6} + \tfrac{1}{7} + \tfrac{1}{8} + \dots + \frac{1}{2n} \right) - 2 \times \left(\tfrac{1}{2} + \tfrac{1}{4} + \tfrac{1}{6} + \tfrac{1}{8} + \dots + \frac{1}{2n} \right)$$

$$= \left(1 + \tfrac{1}{2} + \tfrac{1}{3} + \tfrac{1}{4} + \dots + \frac{1}{2n} \right) - \left(1 + \tfrac{1}{2} + \tfrac{1}{3} + \tfrac{1}{4} + \dots + \frac{1}{n} \right)$$

$$= \frac{1}{n+1} + \frac{1}{n+2} + \dots + \frac{1}{2n}.$$

This is quite an interesting result in itself. It was stated in Section 6.1 that the sum to infinity of $\sum \dfrac{(-1)^{i-1}}{i}$ is $\ln 2$; this can now be proved, since you showed in Exercise 4B Question 6 that

$$\lim_{n \to \infty} \left(\frac{1}{n+1} + \frac{1}{n+2} + \dots + \frac{1}{2n} \right) = \ln 2.$$

But what is more surprising is that if you carry out the 'illegal' algebra in Example 6.3.1 with the series $\sum 10 \times (-0.9)^{i-1}$ (which is absolutely convergent), you *don't* arrive at an absurd conclusion. (See Exercise 6 Question 5.) You can carry out algebraic operations much more freely when the series are absolutely convergent than when they are conditionally convergent.

Example 6.3.2
The multiplication paradox: the product of two convergent series may not be convergent.

If you square the conditionally convergent series $\sum \dfrac{(-1)^{i-1}}{\sqrt{i}}$, multiplying out the brackets in the same way as you do with polynomials, you get

$$\left(\frac{1}{\sqrt{1}} - \frac{1}{\sqrt{2}} + \frac{1}{\sqrt{3}} - \dots \right) \left(\frac{1}{\sqrt{1}} - \frac{1}{\sqrt{2}} + \frac{1}{\sqrt{3}} - \dots \right)$$

$$= \left(\frac{1}{\sqrt{1}} \times \frac{1}{\sqrt{1}} \right) - \left(\frac{1}{\sqrt{1}} \times \frac{1}{\sqrt{2}} + \frac{1}{\sqrt{2}} \times \frac{1}{\sqrt{1}} \right) + \left(\frac{1}{\sqrt{1}} \times \frac{1}{\sqrt{3}} + \frac{1}{\sqrt{2}} \times \frac{1}{\sqrt{2}} + \frac{1}{\sqrt{3}} \times \frac{1}{\sqrt{1}} \right) - \dots \ .$$

You could write this as $\sum (-1)^{i-1} v_i$, where

$$v_i = \frac{1}{\sqrt{1}} \times \frac{1}{\sqrt{i}} + \frac{1}{\sqrt{2}} \times \frac{1}{\sqrt{i-1}} + \dots + \frac{1}{\sqrt{i}} \times \frac{1}{\sqrt{1}}$$

$$= \frac{1}{\sqrt{1 \times i}} + \frac{1}{\sqrt{2 \times (i-1)}} + \dots + \frac{1}{\sqrt{i \times 1}}.$$

There are i terms in this sum, and it can be written as $\displaystyle\sum_{k=1}^{i} \frac{1}{\sqrt{k(i+1-k)}}$.

Now if you write the expression under the $\sqrt{}$ sign in completed square form, you get

$$k(i+1-k) = \left(\frac{i+1}{2} \right)^2 - \left(k - \frac{i+1}{2} \right)^2.$$

It follows that, for each value of k,

$$k(i+1-k) \le \left(\frac{i+1}{2}\right)^2, \quad \text{so} \quad \frac{1}{\sqrt{k(i+1-k)}} \ge \frac{2}{i+1}.$$

Therefore

$$v_i \ge i \times \frac{2}{i+1} = \frac{2}{1+\frac{1}{i}},$$

and $\lim_{i \to \infty} v_i = 2$.

But it was shown in Section 2.3 that for the series $\sum (-1)^{i-1} v_i$ to converge it is necessary that $\lim_{i \to \infty} v_i = 0$. So the product series $\sum (-1)^{i-1} v_i$ is not convergent.

Again, this could not happen when you square an absolutely convergent series. If you square an absolutely convergent series using the method in Example 6.3.2, the result is another absolutely convergent series. (See Exercise 6 Question 6.)

You can use the comparison test in Section 2.3 to find some properties of absolutely and conditionally convergent series which help to explain the differences in their behaviour.

Suppose that u_i is a series with some positive and some negative terms, with a sum sequence $S_n = \sum_{i=1}^{n} u_i$.

From this you can obtain three other series:

- the absolute term series, with terms $v_i = |u_i|$ and sum sequence $A_n = \sum_{i=1}^{n} v_i$

- the positive term series, with terms $y_i = u_i$ when u_i is positive or zero and 0 when u_i is negative, and sum sequence $P_n = \sum_{i=1}^{n} y_i$

- the negative term series, with terms $z_i = u_i$ when u_i is negative or zero and 0 when u_i is positive, and sum sequence $Q_n = \sum_{i=1}^{n} z_i$.

For example, if u_i is the sequence $1, \; -\frac{1}{2}, \; \frac{1}{3}, \; \frac{1}{4}, \; -\frac{1}{5}, \; \frac{1}{6}, \; \dots$, then

$$S_6 = 1 - \tfrac{1}{2} + \tfrac{1}{3} + \tfrac{1}{4} - \tfrac{1}{5} + \tfrac{1}{6}, \qquad A_6 = 1 + \tfrac{1}{2} + \tfrac{1}{3} + \tfrac{1}{4} + \tfrac{1}{5} + \tfrac{1}{6},$$

$$P_6 = 1 + 0 + \tfrac{1}{3} + \tfrac{1}{4} + 0 + \tfrac{1}{6}, \qquad Q_6 = 0 - \tfrac{1}{2} + 0 + 0 - \tfrac{1}{5} + 0.$$

These are of course not independent. You can easily check that

$$u_i = y_i + z_i \qquad \text{and} \qquad v_i = y_i - z_i,$$

so $\quad S_n = P_n + Q_n \qquad \text{and} \qquad A_n = P_n - Q_n.$

Begin by supposing that $\sum v_i = \sum |u_i|$ is convergent. What can you deduce about $\sum y_i$ and $\sum z_i$?

Clearly $y_i \geq 0$, and $y_i \leq v_i$ for all i. So by the comparison test, since $\sum v_i$ is convergent, $\sum y_i$ is convergent. Call its sum P_∞.

Also $-z_i \geq 0$, and $-z_i \leq v_i$ for all i. So by the comparison test, since $\sum v_i$ is convergent, $\sum -z_i$ is convergent, and therefore $\sum z_i$ is convergent. Call its sum Q_∞.

Then $\lim_{n \to \infty} (P_n + Q_n) = P_\infty + Q_\infty$, so that $S_n = P_n + Q_n$ tends to a limit. That is, $\sum u_i$ is convergent.

Here is a summary of what has been proved so far.

> If $\sum |u_i|$ is a convergent series, then
>
> - the positive sum series $\sum y_i$ is convergent,
> - the negative sum series $\sum z_i$ is convergent,
> - the series $\sum u_i$ is convergent.
>
> That is, an absolutely convergent series is convergent.

You may think that the last statement is obvious. Perhaps it is, but it still needs proving!

Now suppose that $\sum u_i$ is convergent but not absolutely convergent. Then, because $A_n = P_n - Q_n$ is divergent, $\sum y_i$ and $\sum z_i$ can't both be convergent. But it is impossible for one of them to be convergent but not the other. For example, if $\sum y_i$ is convergent with sum to infinity P_∞, then $Q_n = S_n - P_n$ tends to $S_\infty - P_\infty$ as $n \to \infty$; that is, $\sum z_i$ is convergent. So, since $\sum u_i$ is not absolutely convergent, both $\sum y_i$ and $\sum z_i$ are divergent.

> If $\sum u_i$ is a conditionally convergent series, then the series of positive terms diverges to $+\infty$ and the series of negative terms diverges to $-\infty$.

A remarkable consequence of this is that, by rearranging the order of the terms, you can convert a conditionally convergent series $\sum u_i$ into another series $\sum w_i$ which converges to any sum L that you like. The process is described by the following algorithm.

Let $T_n = \sum_{i=1}^{n} w_i$, and define $T_0 = 0$. Start with $n = 0$.

Step 1 If $T_n \geq L$, define w_{n+1} as the next negative (or zero) term of $\sum u_i$.

If $T_n < L$, define w_{n+1} as the next positive (or zero) term of $\sum u_i$.

Step 2 Increase n by 1, and go back to Step 1.

So you need to be very careful when you work with conditionally convergent series!

Exercise 6

1   For the following alternating series, find a value of n for which you can be sure that the partial sum S_n approximates to the sum to infinity with an error less than 0.0001. Hence find bounds between which you can be sure that the sum to infinity lies. Give these bounds to 6 decimal places, rounding the lower bound down and the upper bound up.

(a) $\sum \dfrac{(-1)^{i-1}}{i^3}$ 　　(b) $\sum \dfrac{(-1)^{i-1}}{i^i}$ 　　(c) $\sum \dfrac{(-1)^{i-1}}{i!}$ 　(d) $\sum \dfrac{(-1)^{i-1}2^i}{i!}$

2   For the following infinite series, state if they are absolutely convergent or conditionally convergent. If they are neither, describe their limiting behaviour as the number of terms tends to infinity.

(a) $\sum \dfrac{(-1)^{i-1}}{i^2}$ 　　(b) $\sum \dfrac{(-1)^{i-1}}{i+10}$ 　　(c) $\sum \sin\left(\tfrac{1}{2}\pi i\right)$ 　(d) $\sum \dfrac{\sin\left(\tfrac{1}{2}\pi i\right)}{i}$

(e) $\sum (-1)^{i-1} i$ 　　(f) $\sum (-1)^{i-1} i^2$ 　　(g) $\sum (-2)^{i-1}$ 　(h) $\sum \dfrac{(-1)^{i-1} i}{(i+1)(i+2)}$

(i) $\sum \dfrac{(-1)^{i-1} i}{(i+1)(i+2)(i+3)}$ 　(j) $\sum \dfrac{1+3\times(-1)^{i-1}}{i}$ 　(k) $\sum (-1)^{\frac{1}{2}i(i+1)}$ 　(l) $\sum (-1)^{\frac{1}{2}i(i+1)} i$

3   You are given that $\sum\limits_{i=1}^{\infty} \dfrac{1}{i^4} = \dfrac{1}{90}\pi^4$. For the infinite series $\sum \dfrac{(-1)^{i-1}}{i^4}$, find (with the notation of Section 6.3)

(a) Q_∞, 　　　　(b) P_∞, 　　　　(c) S_∞.

4   Use the algorithm at the end of Section 6.3 to find the first 10 terms of a rearrangement of the series $1-\tfrac{1}{2}+\tfrac{1}{3}-\tfrac{1}{4}+\tfrac{1}{5}-\tfrac{1}{6}+\dots$ which converges to

(a) 0.4, 　　　　(b) 1.1, 　　　　(c) –0.2.

What property of conditionally convergent series makes such rearrangements possible?

5   Show that if you carry out steps on the absolutely convergent series $\sum\left(-\tfrac{1}{2}\right)^{i-1}$ similar to those carried out on $\sum \dfrac{(-1)^{i-1}}{i}$ in Example 6.3.1, you can arrive at the conclusion

$$1-\tfrac{1}{2}+\tfrac{1}{4}-\tfrac{1}{8}+\tfrac{1}{16}-\dots = \tfrac{1}{2}+\tfrac{1}{8}+\tfrac{1}{32}+\tfrac{1}{128}+\dots .$$

Use the formula for the sum to infinity of a geometric series to show that this equation is in fact true.

6* (a) Find the series $\sum u_i$ which results when the series $\sum\left(-\tfrac{1}{2}\right)^{i-1}$ is squared using the method of Example 6.3.2.

(b) Use the result in Example 2.4.1 to show that $\sum u_i$ is absolutely convergent, and state the value of $\sum |u_i|$.

(c) Use the result of Exercise 2C Question 2(b) to calculate the sum of the series of negative terms in the series $\sum u_i$.

(d) Hence calculate $\sum\limits_{i=1}^{\infty} u_i$, and show that it is equal to the square of $\sum\limits_{i=1}^{\infty}\left(-\tfrac{1}{2}\right)^{i-1}$.

7 The theory of limits

This chapter develops and shows how to apply a definition of the limit of a sequence. When you have completed it, you should

- know how to define the limit of a sequence as $n \to \infty$
- be able to use the definition to give proofs of the limits of particular sequences
- understand how the definition can be used to prove general theorems about limits of sequences.

7.1 The definition of a limit

You have been using limits for a long time: as $\delta x \to 0$ for differentiation, as $x \to a$ for asymptotes, as $n \to \infty$ for convergence of sequences. Sometimes various properties of limits have been assumed, for example that the limit of the product of two functions is equal to the product of the limits. But to justify these properties you need to have a definition of what is meant by a limit.

This chapter gives a definition for the limit of a sequence u_n as $n \to \infty$. Definitions of other limits, such as $\lim_{x \to a} f(x)$, are very similar, and proofs of the various properties are almost identical to those for $\lim_{n \to \infty} u_n$.

The basic idea of what is meant by $\lim_{n \to \infty} u_n = L$ is illustrated by the graph in Fig. 7.1. This shows a set of points with coordinates (n, u_n) approaching the line $y = L$ as n increases, and two lines $y = p$ and $y = q$ with $p < L < q$, so that $y = L$ lies inside the shaded strip between them. The numbers p and q are not fixed: p can be any number less than L, and q can be any number greater than L. But whatever numbers you take for p and q, there is a number m such that, beyond $n = m$, all the points (n, u_n) are inside the shaded strip.

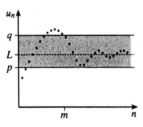

Fig. 7.1

Example 7.1.1

Show that, if $u_n = \dfrac{3n+1}{n}$, then $\lim_{n \to \infty} u_n = 3$.

Suppose that you take $p = 2.9$ and $q = 3.2$. Since $\dfrac{3n+1}{n} = 3 + \dfrac{1}{n}$, clearly u_n is less than 3.2 when n is greater than 5. Also u_n is always greater than 3, so it is certainly greater than 2.9. That is, $2.9 < u_n < 3.2$ if $n > 5$. To the right of $n = 5$, all the points (n, u_n) are inside the strip between the lines $y = 2.9$ and $y = 3.2$.

This doesn't of course prove that $u_n \to 3$. If you were to take a larger value of p and a smaller value of q, you would need a larger value of m so that $p < u_n < q$ for $n > m$. For example, if $p = 2.99$ and $q = 3.02$, you need to take n greater than 50 to get $p < u_n < q$.

For a proof you have to show that you can find such an inequality whatever numbers p and q you take such that $p < 3 < q$. In this example, the value of p doesn't affect the choice of m; since $\frac{1}{n} > 0$, $u_n > 3 > p$ for all n. So you merely have to find the values of n for which $u_n < q$, that is $3 + \frac{1}{n} < q$.

$$3 + \frac{1}{n} < q \iff q - 3 > \frac{1}{n} \iff n > \frac{1}{q-3} \qquad \text{(since } q - 3 \text{ is positive).}$$

Therefore, if $n > \frac{1}{q-3}$, $p < u_n < q$. Since this works for any numbers p and q with $p < 3$ and $q > 3$, this proves that $\lim_{n \to \infty} u_n = 3$.

Example 7.1.2

Show that, if $u_n = \frac{3n + (-1)^n}{n}$, then $\lim_{n \to \infty} u_n = 3$.

Since $\frac{3n + (-1)^n}{n} = 3 + \frac{(-1)^n}{n}$, u_n is greater than 3 when n is even and less than 3 when n is odd. So you must consider even and odd values of n separately.

If n is even, then $u_n = 3 + \frac{1}{n}$, and you have the same situation as in Example 7.1.1. That is, if n is even and greater than $\frac{1}{q-3}$, then $p < u_n < q$.

If n is odd, then $u_n = 3 - \frac{1}{n}$. This is certainly less than q, since $q > 3$. Also

$$3 - \frac{1}{n} > p \iff 3 - p > \frac{1}{n} \iff n > \frac{1}{3-p} \qquad \text{(since } 3 - p \text{ is positive).}$$

Therefore, if n is odd and greater than $\frac{1}{3-p}$, then $p < u_n < q$.

So to be certain of getting $p < u_n < q$, you need to have $n > \frac{1}{q-3}$ if n is even, and $n > \frac{1}{3-p}$ if n is odd. The safe way of ensuring that both inequalities are satisfied is to define m as the greater of $\frac{1}{q-3}$ and $\frac{1}{3-p}$. This is sometimes written as $\max\left(\frac{1}{q-3}, \frac{1}{3-p}\right)$. Then, when $n > m$, $p < u_n < q$, whether n is odd or even.

What these examples illustrate is how the proof depends on the definition. This can now be stated formally.

> **Limit of a sequence**   If, for any numbers p and q such that $p < L < q$, there is a positive number m such that, for all $n > m$, $p < u_n < q$, then $\lim\limits_{n \to \infty} u_n = L$.

There are several points to notice about this definition.

- Once the value of m has been settled, the inequality $p < u_n < q$ has to hold for *all* n greater than m, without exception.
- The value of m usually depends on p and q. Generally, the closer that p and q are to L, the larger the value of m.
- Although $n \in \mathbb{Z}^+$, there is no requirement for m to be an integer.
- There may also be some values of n less than m for which $p < u_n < q$, but they are not relevant. This is shown in Fig. 7.1, where you can see that there are some points to the left of m inside the shaded strip. In Example 7.1.2, if you take $p = 2.99$ and $q = 3.02$, then u_n is between p and q for $n = 52, 54, 56, \ldots$, but not for $n = 53, 55, 57, \ldots, 99$. The conditions are not satisfied for all $n > m$ until $n = 100$.
- You aren't allowed to place restrictions on the values chosen for p and q such as that 'they may not be too close to L'. But you will find in later examples that it is sometimes convenient to specify that 'they may not be too far from L'. There is no objection to that.
- There is no special merit in trying to find the smallest possible value of m which satisfies the conditions. All that is required is to be able to find *some* number m. It can be as large as you like. This is illustrated in Example 7.1.3.

In Examples 7.1.1 and 7.1.2 you may have wondered why p and q were not taken at equal distances from L above and below. The answer is that they could have been, and indeed the definition is often given by writing p as $L - \varepsilon$ and q as $L + \varepsilon$. (The Greek letter ε, 'epsilon', is like the English short 'e'.) The condition $p < u_n < q$ then becomes $L - \varepsilon < u_n < L + \varepsilon$, which can be written more neatly as $|u_n - L| < \varepsilon$. You can then write the definition of a limit in a different way:

> **Limit of a sequence (alternative definition)**   If, for any positive number ε there is a positive number m such that, for all $n > m$, $|u_n - L| < \varepsilon$, then $\lim\limits_{n \to \infty} u_n = L$.

You might think that this is a less demanding requirement than the previous definition, since it restricts the number of shaded strips you can use. But this isn't so. The two definitions are in fact logically equivalent to each other. If a sequence u_n tends to L according to one definition, then it does so according to the other definition, so you can use whichever definition you prefer. In practice, proofs are sometimes a little shorter if you use one definition rather than the other. Some of the proofs in this chapter use the p, q definition, while others use ε.

Example 7.1.3

Prove that $\lim\limits_{n \to \infty} \dfrac{\cos n}{n} = 0$.

Before reading on, display the graph of $u_n = \dfrac{\cos n}{n}$ on your calculator. Remember to put it into radian mode first.

The proof is given using the ε definition.

One difference between this and the examples earlier in this chapter is that you can't solve the inequalities $\dfrac{\cos n}{n} < \varepsilon$ and $\dfrac{\cos n}{n} > -\varepsilon$. But you know that, for all $n \in \mathbb{Z}^+$, $\left| \cos n \right| < 1$, so that

$$\left| \frac{\cos n}{n} \right| < \frac{1}{n}.$$

You can also solve the inequality $\dfrac{1}{n} < \varepsilon$, as

$$\frac{1}{n} < \varepsilon \iff n > \frac{1}{\varepsilon}.$$

(Recall that, in the definition, ε has to be a positive number.) So it is certainly true that, if $n > \dfrac{1}{\varepsilon}$,

$$\left| \frac{\cos n}{n} \right| < \frac{1}{n} < \varepsilon.$$

This is all you need. You have found a number $m = \dfrac{1}{\varepsilon}$ such that, for all $n > m$, $\left| \dfrac{\cos n}{n} - 0 \right| < \varepsilon$.

Therefore, from the definition, $\lim\limits_{n \to \infty} \dfrac{\cos n}{n} = 0$.

This is an example of a sequence for which it is very likely that there will also be values of n less than m for which the inequality is satisfied. And for some values of ε, m will not be the smallest number such that the inequality is satisfied 'for all $n > m$'. For example, if you take $\varepsilon = 0.01$, you will find that $\left| \dfrac{\cos n}{n} \right| < 0.01$ when n is equal to 95, 96, 97, 98, 99 and 100 as well as for all $n > 100$; that is, the inequality holds for all $n > 94$. But, as stated above, this is of no importance. Once you have found that $m = 100$ satisfies the conditions, it is a waste of time to look any further.

Exercise 7A

1 Prove that

(a) $\lim\limits_{n \to \infty} \dfrac{2n+3}{n+2} = 2,$

(b) $\lim\limits_{n \to \infty} \dfrac{n}{2n-1} = \frac{1}{2}.$

2 If $u_n = \dfrac{2+(-1)^n}{n}$, find a number m such that

(a) $u_n < 0.01$ for all $n > m$,

(b) $u_n < 0.001$ for all $n > m$,

(c) $u_n < q$ for all $n > m$, where $q > 0$.

3 If $u_n = \dfrac{1+2\times(-1)^n}{n}$, find a number m such that

(a) $-0.05 < u_n < 0.1$ for all $n > m$,

(b) $p < u_n < q$ for all $n > m$, where $p < 0$ and $q > 0$.

4 Find

(a) $\lim\limits_{n \to \infty} \dfrac{3n-4}{2n+1},$

(b) $\lim\limits_{n \to \infty} \dfrac{n+2\times(-1)^n}{n+1}.$

Use the definition to prove your answers.

5   (a)   Prove that $\lim\limits_{n\to\infty} \dfrac{1}{\sqrt{n}} = 0$.

    (b)   Use the identity $\left(\sqrt{n+1} - \sqrt{n}\right)\left(\sqrt{n+1} + \sqrt{n}\right) \equiv 1$ to prove that $\lim\limits_{n\to\infty}\left(\sqrt{n+1} - \sqrt{n}\right) = 0$.

6   By comparing the area under $y = \dfrac{1}{x}$ with the area of two rectangles, prove that (for $n > 0$)

$$\frac{1}{n+1} < \ln\left(1 + \frac{1}{n}\right) < \frac{1}{n}.$$

Hence find $\lim\limits_{n\to\infty} n \ln\left(1 + \dfrac{1}{n}\right)$, and prove that your answer is correct.

7   Prove that, if $x > 0$, $(1+x)^n > nx$. Hence show that, if $\sqrt[n]{2} = 1 + x$, then $nx < 2$.
    Use this inequality to prove that $\lim\limits_{n\to\infty}\sqrt[n]{2} = 1$.

8   Prove that, if $\sqrt[n]{n} = 1 + y$, then $(n-1)y^2 < 2$. Use this inequality to find $\lim\limits_{n\to\infty}\sqrt[n]{n}$.

7.2   Theorems about limits

You would probably think it obvious that, if $\lim\limits_{n\to\infty} u_n = L$, then $\lim\limits_{n\to\infty}(-u_n) = -L$, $\lim\limits_{n\to\infty}(5u_n) = 5L$ and $\lim\limits_{n\to\infty} u_n{}^2 = L^2$, These conclusions are in fact correct, and now that you have a definition of $\lim\limits_{n\to\infty} u_n$ you can prove them.

To show the logical structure these proofs are set out as a sequence of theorems. The paragraphs in italic are not part of the proofs, but remarks to help you understand how such proofs are constructed.

The first theorem is very simple, since the results follow directly from the definition.

Theorem 1   If $\lim\limits_{n\to\infty} u_n = L$ and b is constant, then

(a) $\lim\limits_{n\to\infty}(u_n + b) = L + b$,   (b) $\lim\limits_{n\to\infty}(-u_n) = -L$.

Proof
You are given that $\lim\limits_{n\to\infty} u_n = L$. So, if you are given any positive number ε, there is a number m such that, for all $n > m$, $|u_n - L| < \varepsilon$.

Now (a) $\left|(u_n + b) - (L + b)\right| = |u_n - L|$ and   (b) $\left|(-u_n) - (-L)\right| = \left|-(u_n - L)\right| = |u_n - L|$.

It follows that, for the given number ε, there is a number m such that, for all $n > m$,

(a) $\left|(u_n + b) - (L + b)\right| < \varepsilon$ and   (b) $\left|(-u_n) - (-L)\right| < \varepsilon$.

And these are just the properties you need to prove that

(a) $\lim\limits_{n\to\infty}(u_n + b) = L + b$ and   (b) $\lim\limits_{n\to\infty}(-u_n) = -L$.

Before proving the next theorem it may be useful to illustrate it with a trivial example.

Example 7.2.1

Find numbers m such that, for all $n > m$,   (a) $\dfrac{1}{n^2} < 0.01$,   (b) $\dfrac{4}{n^2} < 0.01$.

(a) $\dfrac{1}{n^2} < 0.01 \iff n^2 > 100 \iff n > 10$ (since $n \in \mathbb{Z}^+$).

So $m = 10$ satisfies the condition.

(b) $\dfrac{4}{n^2} < 0.01 \iff \dfrac{1}{n^2} < 0.0025 \iff n > 20$.

So $m = 20$ satisfies the condition.

The point of this example is that, since $\dfrac{4}{n^2}$ is $4 \times \dfrac{1}{n^2}$, you have to solve the inequality $\dfrac{1}{n^2} < \dfrac{1}{4} \times 0.01$.

Because $\lim\limits_{n \to \infty} \dfrac{1}{n^2} = 0$, this is certainly possible, but you are using a different value for 'ε', so you need a different value of m.

Theorem 2   If $\lim\limits_{n \to \infty} u_n = L$ and a is a positive constant, then $\lim\limits_{n \to \infty} (au_n) = aL$.

This is slightly more complicated, since if you know that $|u_n - L| < \varepsilon$ you can only deduce that $|au_n - aL| < a\varepsilon$. But to prove that $\lim\limits_{n \to \infty} (au_n) = aL$ you have to show that, if you are given any positive number ε, $|au_n - aL| < \varepsilon$ for all $n > m$. To do this you need to begin with the inequality $|u_n - L| < \dfrac{\varepsilon}{a}$.

What you are given is that $\lim\limits_{n \to \infty} u_n = L$. This means that, for any positive number whatever, you can make $|u_n - L|$ less than this number. So begin the proof by applying this, not with the number ε, but with $\dfrac{\varepsilon}{a}$.

Proof
Let ε be any positive number. Since $\lim\limits_{n \to \infty} u_n = L$, there is a number m such that, for all $n > m$, $|u_n - L| < \dfrac{\varepsilon}{a}$. Therefore, for all $n > m$,

$$|au_n - aL| = |a(u_n - L)| = a \times |u_n - L| < a \times \dfrac{\varepsilon}{a} = \varepsilon.$$

That is, $\lim\limits_{n \to \infty} (au_n) = aL$.

By putting Theorems 1 and 2 together you can establish the limit of any linear function of u_n. For example, if $\lim\limits_{n \to \infty} u_n = L$, then

$$\begin{aligned}
\lim_{n \to \infty} (-5u_n + 2) &= \lim_{n \to \infty} (-5u_n) + 2 & \text{(by Theorem 1(a))} \\
&= -\lim_{n \to \infty} (5u_n) + 2 & \text{(by Theorem 1(b))} \\
&= -5 \lim_{n \to \infty} u_n + 2 & \text{(by Theorem 2)} \\
&= -5L + 2.
\end{aligned}$$

What about other functions of u_n? Is it generally true that, if $\lim_{n\to\infty} u_n = L$, then $\lim_{n\to\infty} f(u_n) = f(L)$?

The answer is yes, provided that the function f is continuous. To prove this, you need to define what you mean by a continuous function, and that would go beyond the scope of this book. However, it is possible to give proofs for particular functions. The next theorem does this for the reciprocal function. In this case it is simpler to use the p, q definition.

Theorem 3   If $\lim_{n\to\infty} u_n = L$, then $\lim_{n\to\infty} \dfrac{1}{u_n} = \dfrac{1}{L}$ (a) if $L > 0$,   (b) if $L < 0$.

The logic is similar to that in Theorem 2. You start with given numbers p and q such that $p < \dfrac{1}{L}$ and

$q > \dfrac{1}{L}$, and have to prove that, beyond a certain number m, $\dfrac{1}{u_n}$ lies between p and q. The proof has to be constructed by using the given fact that $\lim_{n\to\infty} u_n = L$.

In part (a) it is helpful to restrict p to be a positive number. Since $\dfrac{1}{L} > 0$, there is no problem with this. As

mentioned in Section 7.1, it is quite acceptable to specify that p should be 'not too far from $\dfrac{1}{L}$'.

Proof

(a)   Let p, q be any numbers such that $0 < p < \dfrac{1}{L} < q$. Then $L > \dfrac{1}{q}$ and $L < \dfrac{1}{p}$. This is illustrated in Fig. 7.2, where the graph on the left shows values of u_n and the graph on the right shows values of $\dfrac{1}{u_n}$.

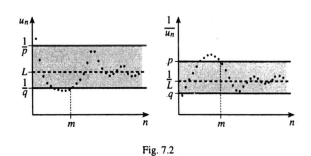

Fig. 7.2

You are given that $\lim_{n\to\infty} u_n = L$. This means that, from the definition, there is a number m such that, for all $n > m$,

$$\frac{1}{q} < u_n < \frac{1}{p}.$$

It follows that $\dfrac{1}{u_n} < q$ and $\dfrac{1}{u_n} > p$, that is

$$p < \frac{1}{u_n} < q \qquad \text{for all } n > m.$$

And since p and q are any numbers such that $p < \dfrac{1}{L} < q$, it follows from the definition that

$$\lim_{n\to\infty} \frac{1}{u_n} = \frac{1}{L}.$$

(b)   If L is negative, you can combine Theorem 1(b) with the result of part (a). Since $\lim\limits_{n \to \infty} u_n = L < 0$, $\lim\limits_{n \to \infty} (-u_n) = -L > 0$ by Theorem 1(b). So you can apply part (a) to the sequence $-u_n$, and deduce that

$$\lim_{n \to \infty} \frac{1}{-u_n} = \frac{1}{-L} = -\frac{1}{L}.$$

But $\lim\limits_{n \to \infty} \dfrac{1}{-u_n} = \lim\limits_{n \to \infty} \left(-\dfrac{1}{u_n} \right)$

$$= -\lim_{n \to \infty} \frac{1}{u_n},$$

using Theorem 1(b) a second time. Therefore

$$-\lim_{n \to \infty} \frac{1}{u_n} = -\frac{1}{L}, \quad \text{that is} \quad \lim_{n \to \infty} \frac{1}{u_n} = \frac{1}{L}.$$

Theorem 3 is clearly meaningless if $L = 0$. In fact, if $\lim\limits_{n \to \infty} u_n = 0$, the sequence $\dfrac{1}{u_n}$ may diverge either to $-\infty$ or to ∞, or it may oscillate infinitely. But it cannot tend to a finite limit.

Exercise 7B

1   If $\lim\limits_{n \to \infty} u_n = 3$, find

(a) $\lim\limits_{n \to \infty} (2u_n - 5)$,   (b) $\lim\limits_{n \to \infty} \dfrac{1}{1 - 2u_n}$,   (c) $\lim\limits_{n \to \infty} \left(1 - \dfrac{2}{u_n} \right)$.

State at each step which of Theorems 1–3 you are using.

2   Use the result of Exercise 7A Question 7 to find

(a) $\lim\limits_{n \to \infty} \left(\sqrt[n]{2} - 1 \right)$,   (b) $\lim\limits_{n \to \infty} \dfrac{1}{1 + \sqrt[n]{2}}$,   (c) $\lim\limits_{n \to \infty} \dfrac{\sqrt[n]{2}}{1 + \sqrt[n]{2}}$,   (d) $\lim\limits_{n \to \infty} \sqrt[n]{0.5}$.

State at each step which of Theorems 1–3 you are using.

3   Give examples of sequences u_n such that $\lim\limits_{n \to \infty} u_n = 0$ for which $\lim\limits_{n \to \infty} \dfrac{1}{u_n}$

(a) diverges to $+\infty$,   (b) diverges to $-\infty$,   (c) oscillates infinitely.

7.3 Combinations of two sequences

The theorems in Section 7.2 were concerned with functions of one sequence u_n whose limit L was known. This section considers a pair of sequences u_n and v_n whose limits L_1 and L_2 are known and investigates the limits of combinations of these sequences such as $u_n + v_n$, $u_n \times v_n$ and $\dfrac{u_n}{v_n}$.

The next example illustrates what is involved.

Example 7.3.1

(a) Find a number m such that $\sqrt[n]{2} + \sqrt[n]{3} < 2.01$ for all $n > m$.   (b) Prove that $\lim\limits_{n \to \infty} \left(\sqrt[n]{2} + \sqrt[n]{3} \right) = 2$.

(a)   Both $\sqrt[n]{2}$ and $\sqrt[n]{3}$ are greater than 1 for all $n \in \mathbb{Z}^+$, so for their sum to be less than 2.01 each must certainly be less than 1.01. It would be simplest to find n such that each is less than 1.005, though there are of course other possibilities; for example, you could if you prefer make $\sqrt[n]{2}$ less than 1.004 and $\sqrt[n]{3}$ less than 1.006. This might produce a smaller value for m, but that is not required.

In Exercise 7A Question 7 you proved that, if $\sqrt[n]{2} = 1 + x$, then $nx < 2$. So if n is a number greater than $\dfrac{2}{0.005} = 400$,

$$\sqrt[n]{2} = 1 + x < 1 + \frac{2}{n} < 1 + \frac{2}{400} = 1.005.$$

In just the same way, if $\sqrt[n]{3} = 1 + y$, then $ny < 3$. So if n is a number greater than $\dfrac{3}{0.005} = 600$,

$$\sqrt[n]{3} = 1 + y < 1 + \frac{3}{n} < 1 + \frac{3}{600} = 1.005.$$

You want both of these inequalities to hold simultaneously, and this will happen if n is greater than both 400 and 600; that is, if $n > \max(400, 600) = 600$. So,

$$\text{if } n > 600, \qquad \sqrt[n]{2} + \sqrt[n]{3} < 1.005 + 1.005 = 2.01.$$

That is, $m = 600$ satisfies the requirement.

In fact, you can check with a calculator that the inequality is satisfied by $n = 180$ but not by $n = 179$, so $m = 179$ would do. But there is no way of finding this by an algebraic method.

(b)   If you are given a positive number ε, you have to find a number m such that, for all $n > m$, $\left| \sqrt[n]{2} + \sqrt[n]{3} - 2 \right| < \varepsilon$. Since $\sqrt[n]{2} + \sqrt[n]{3}$ is always greater than 2, it is certainly greater than the lower bound $2 - \varepsilon$. So all that is needed is to find values of n such that $\sqrt[n]{2} + \sqrt[n]{3} < 2 + \varepsilon$.

This is the problem in part (a) with ε in place of 0.01. So it can be solved by finding values of n such that both $\sqrt[n]{2} < 1 + \frac{1}{2}\varepsilon$ and $\sqrt[n]{3} < 1 + \frac{1}{2}\varepsilon$. This will certainly be true if n is greater than both $\dfrac{2}{\frac{1}{2}\varepsilon} = \dfrac{4}{\varepsilon}$ and $\dfrac{3}{\frac{1}{2}\varepsilon} = \dfrac{6}{\varepsilon}$.

So take $m = \max\left(\dfrac{4}{\varepsilon}, \dfrac{6}{\varepsilon} \right) = \dfrac{6}{\varepsilon}$. Then, for all $n > m$,

$$\sqrt[n]{2} + \sqrt[n]{3} < \left(1 + \frac{2}{n} \right) + \left(1 + \frac{3}{n} \right) < 2 + \frac{2}{\left(\frac{6}{\varepsilon} \right)} + \frac{3}{\left(\frac{6}{\varepsilon} \right)} = 2 + \frac{5}{6}\varepsilon < 2 + \varepsilon.$$

Since also $\sqrt[n]{2} + \sqrt[n]{3} > 2 > 2 - \varepsilon$, it follows that $\lim\limits_{n \to \infty} \left(\sqrt[n]{2} + \sqrt[n]{3} \right) = 2$.

To prove that the limit of the sum of two sequences is equal to the sum of the limits, you can use the method in Example 7.3.1 in a general form. The essential idea is to split the number ε into two parts of $\frac{1}{2}\varepsilon$, and to use one of these parts with each of the separate sequences.

Theorem 4   If $\lim_{n\to\infty} u_n = L_1$ and $\lim_{n\to\infty} v_n = L_2$, then $\lim_{n\to\infty}(u_n + v_n) = L_1 + L_2$.

Proof

Let ε be any positive number. Then, since $\lim_{n\to\infty} u_n = L_1$, there is a number m_1 such that, for all $n > m_1$,

$$L_1 - \tfrac{1}{2}\varepsilon < u_n < L_1 + \tfrac{1}{2}\varepsilon.$$

Similarly, since $\lim_{n\to\infty} v_n = L_2$, there is a number m_2 such that, for all $n > m_2$,

$$L_2 - \tfrac{1}{2}\varepsilon < v_n < L_2 + \tfrac{1}{2}\varepsilon.$$

Let $m = \max(m_1, m_2)$. Then, for all $n > m$, both sets of inequalities hold. So

$$\left(L_1 - \tfrac{1}{2}\varepsilon\right) + \left(L_2 - \tfrac{1}{2}\varepsilon\right) < u_n + v_n < \left(L_1 + \tfrac{1}{2}\varepsilon\right) + \left(L_2 + \tfrac{1}{2}\varepsilon\right).$$

That is, $(L_1 + L_2) - \varepsilon < u_n + v_n < (L_1 + L_2) + \varepsilon$.

Since this is true for any positive number ε, it follows that $\lim_{n\to\infty}(u_n + v_n) = L_1 + L_2$.

There is an exactly similar theorem for the product of two sequences. It is simplest to begin with the special case in which L_1 and L_2 are both 0. Then what you have to do is to write ε as the product of two numbers, rather than (as in Theorem 4) as the sum of two numbers. The most obvious choice is to split it as $\varepsilon = \sqrt{\varepsilon} \times \sqrt{\varepsilon}$. The proof is then very similar to that of Theorem 4, with multiplication in place of addition.

Theorem 5   If $\lim_{n\to\infty} u_n = 0$ and $\lim_{n\to\infty} v_n = 0$, then $\lim_{n\to\infty}(u_n v_n) = 0$.

Proof

Let ε be any positive number. Then, since $\lim_{n\to\infty} u_n = 0$, there is a number m_1 such that, for all $n > m_1$,

$$|u_n - 0| < \sqrt{\varepsilon}, \quad \text{that is} \quad |u_n| < \sqrt{\varepsilon}.$$

Similarly, since $\lim_{n\to\infty} v_n = 0$, there is a number m_2 such that, for all $n > m_2$,

$$|v_n| < \sqrt{\varepsilon}.$$

Let $m = \max(m_1, m_2)$. Then, for all $n > m$, both inequalities hold. So

$$|u_n v_n| = |u_n| \times |v_n| < \sqrt{\varepsilon} \times \sqrt{\varepsilon} = \varepsilon.$$

Since this is true for any positive number ε, it follows that $\lim_{n\to\infty}(u_n v_n) = 0$.

You need just two more theorems, about multiplication in general and division, but these can be easily deduced from what has already been proved. No more 'ε' or 'p, q' type proofs are needed.

Theorem 6   If $\lim\limits_{n \to \infty} u_n = L_1$ and $\lim\limits_{n \to \infty} v_n = L_2$, then $\lim\limits_{n \to \infty} (u_n v_n) = L_1 L_2$.

Proof
Define two new sequences, a_n and b_n, by

$$a_n = u_n - L_1 \qquad \text{and} \qquad b_n = v_n - L_2.$$

Then, by Theorem 1(a),

$$\lim_{n \to \infty} a_n = \lim_{n \to \infty} u_n - L_1 = L_1 - L_1 = 0 \qquad \text{and} \qquad \lim_{n \to \infty} b_n = \lim_{n \to \infty} v_n - L_2 = L_2 - L_2 = 0.$$

So

$$
\begin{aligned}
\lim_{n \to \infty} u_n v_n &= \lim_{n \to \infty} (a_n + L_1)(b_n + L_2) \\
&= \lim_{n \to \infty} (a_n b_n) + \lim_{n \to \infty} (L_1 b_n) + \lim_{n \to \infty} (a_n L_2) + L_1 L_2 \quad \text{(by Theorems 1(a) and 4)} \\
&= 0 + L_1 \times \lim_{n \to \infty} b_n + L_2 \times \lim_{n \to \infty} a_n + L_1 L_2 \qquad \text{(by Theorems 2 and 5)} \\
&= 0 + L_1 \times 0 + L_2 \times 0 + L_1 L_2 \\
&= L_1 L_2.
\end{aligned}
$$

Theorem 7   If $\lim\limits_{n \to \infty} u_n = L_1$ and $\lim\limits_{n \to \infty} v_n = L_2$, where $L_2 \neq 0$, then $\lim\limits_{n \to \infty} \dfrac{u_n}{v_n} = \dfrac{L_1}{L_2}$.

Proof
By Theorem 3, since $L_2 \neq 0$, $\lim\limits_{n \to \infty} \dfrac{1}{v_n} = \dfrac{1}{L_2}$.

Therefore, by Theorem 6,

$$
\begin{aligned}
\lim_{n \to \infty} \frac{u_n}{v_n} &= \lim_{n \to \infty} \left(u_n \times \frac{1}{v_n} \right) \\
&= \lim_{n \to \infty} u_n \times \lim_{n \to \infty} \frac{1}{v_n} \\
&= L_1 \times \frac{1}{L_2} = \frac{L_1}{L_2}.
\end{aligned}
$$

7.4 The squeeze theorem

A method of finding limits that is sometimes useful is to show that a sequence can be squeezed between two other sequences, each of which tends to the same limit.

You have already met special cases of this process. In Higher Level Book 2 Section 21.1 the inequality $\cos \theta < \dfrac{\sin \theta}{\theta} < 1$ was used to prove that $\lim\limits_{\theta \to 0} \dfrac{\sin \theta}{\theta} = 1$. The graph of $y = \dfrac{\sin \theta}{\theta}$ was squeezed between the graph of $y = \cos \theta$ and the line $y = 1$, its tangent where $\theta = 0$. There is another example in Section 4.1 of this book, where the area under a curve was shown to be squeezed between lower and upper sums, both having the same limits.

In these examples one of the three elements is constant: the line $y = 1$ in the first case, and the actual value of the area under the curve in the second. But in general applications all three may vary.

Theorem 8   (the squeeze theorem)   If two sequences u_n and v_n have the same limit L as $n \to \infty$, and if w_n is between u_n and v_n for all n, then $\lim\limits_{n \to \infty} w_n = L$.

This theorem is perhaps the most 'obvious' of all. The proof follows directly from the definition of a limit.

Let p and q be any two numbers such that $p < L < q$.

Since $\lim\limits_{n \to \infty} u_n = L$, there is a number m_1 such that $p < u_n < q$ for all $n > m_1$.

Since $\lim\limits_{n \to \infty} v_n = L$, there is a number m_2 such that $p < v_n < q$ for all $n > m_2$.

Therefore, if $m = \max\left(m_1, m_2\right)$, both $p < u_n < q$ and $p < v_n < q$ for all $n > m$.

Suppose that $u_n \le v_n$, so that $u_n \le w_n \le v_n$, Then, if $n > m$,

$$w_n \le v_n < q \qquad \text{and} \qquad w_n \ge u_n > p,$$

so $p < w_n < q$. This conclusion follows similarly if $u_n > v_n$.

Therefore, for all $n > m$, $p < w_n < q$. And since p and q are any numbers such that $p < L < q$, it follows from the definition that $\lim\limits_{n \to \infty} w_n = L$.

Example 7.4.1

Prove that $\lim\limits_{n \to \infty} \dfrac{\cos n}{n} = 0.$ (See Example 7.1.3.)

Let $w_n = \dfrac{\cos n}{n}$. Since, for all $n \in \mathbb{Z}^+$, $-1 < \cos n < 1$,

$$-\frac{1}{n} < \frac{\cos n}{n} < \frac{1}{n}.$$

But $\lim\limits_{n \to \infty} \dfrac{1}{n} = 0$ and $\lim\limits_{n \to \infty}\left(-\dfrac{1}{n}\right) = -\lim\limits_{n \to \infty} \dfrac{1}{n} = 0$ (Theorem 1(b)).

Therefore, by the squeeze theorem, $\lim\limits_{n \to \infty} w_n = 0$.

Example 7.4.2

If $s_n = \dfrac{1}{n^2} + \dfrac{1}{(n+1)^2} + \dfrac{1}{(n+2)^2} + \ldots + \dfrac{1}{(2n)^2}$, find $\lim\limits_{n \to \infty}\left(n s_n\right)$.

In Fig. 7.3 s_n is represented as the sum of the areas of rectangles of width 1 and heights

$\dfrac{1}{n^2}, \dfrac{1}{(n+1)^2}, \dfrac{1}{(n+2)^2}, \ldots, \dfrac{1}{(2n)^2}$. The graph on the left shows this sum as a lower sum for the area under $y = \dfrac{1}{x^2}$ from $x = n-1$ to $x = 2n$. The graph on the right shows it as an upper sum for the area under the same curve from $x = n$ to $x = 2n+1$.

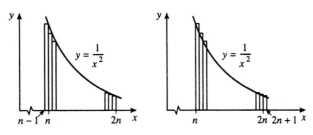

Fig. 7.3

Therefore

$$\int_n^{2n+1} \frac{1}{x^2}\,dx < s_n < \int_{n-1}^{2n} \frac{1}{x^2}\,dx,$$

and

$$\int_n^{2n+1} \frac{1}{x^2}\,dx = \left[-\frac{1}{x}\right]_n^{2n+1}$$

$$= -\frac{1}{2n+1} + \frac{1}{n}$$

$$= \frac{-n+(2n+1)}{n(2n+1)}$$

$$= \frac{n+1}{n(2n+1)},$$

and

$$\int_{n-1}^{2n} \frac{1}{x^2}\,dx = \left[-\frac{1}{x}\right]_{n-1}^{2n}$$

$$= -\frac{1}{2n} + \frac{1}{n-1}$$

$$= \frac{-(n-1)+2n}{2n(n-1)}$$

$$= \frac{n+1}{2n(n-1)}.$$

So

$$\frac{n+1}{n(2n+1)} < s_n < \frac{n+1}{2n(n-1)}.$$

Multiplying by n,

$$\frac{n+1}{2n+1} < ns_n < \frac{n+1}{2n-2}.$$

Now, using Theorem 7,

$$\lim_{n\to\infty} \frac{n+1}{2n+1} = \lim_{n\to\infty} \frac{1+\dfrac{1}{n}}{2+\dfrac{1}{n}}$$

$$= \frac{\displaystyle\lim_{n\to\infty}\left(1+\frac{1}{n}\right)}{\displaystyle\lim_{n\to\infty}\left(2+\frac{1}{n}\right)} = \frac{1}{2}$$

and

$$\lim_{n\to\infty} \frac{n+1}{2n-2} = \lim_{n\to\infty} \frac{1+\dfrac{1}{n}}{2-\dfrac{2}{n}}$$

$$= \frac{\displaystyle\lim_{n\to\infty}\left(1+\frac{1}{n}\right)}{\displaystyle\lim_{n\to\infty}\left(2-\frac{2}{n}\right)} = \frac{1}{2}.$$

Therefore, by the squeeze theorem,

$$\lim_{n\to\infty}(ns_n) = \tfrac{1}{2}.$$

Exercise 7C

1 If $\lim\limits_{n\to\infty} u_n = 4$ and $\lim\limits_{n\to\infty} v_n = -1$, find

(a) $\lim\limits_{n\to\infty} \dfrac{u_n + v_n}{u_n - v_n}$,   (b) $\lim\limits_{n\to\infty} (u_n + 2v_n)^2$.

State at each step which theorem you are using.

2 Find

(a) $\lim\limits_{n\to\infty} \dfrac{n^2 + 2n}{3n^2 - 4}$,   (b) $\lim\limits_{n\to\infty} \sqrt[n]{n^2}$,   (c) $\lim\limits_{n\to\infty} \left(\sqrt[n]{10} - \sqrt[n]{0.1} \right)$,   (d) $\lim\limits_{n\to\infty} \dfrac{e^n - n^2}{e^n + n^2}$.

3 By comparing the area under the graph of $y = \dfrac{1}{x}$ with the area of two rectangles, prove that, if $a > 0$ and $n > 0$,

$$\frac{a}{n + a} < \ln\!\left(1 + \frac{a}{n} \right) < \frac{a}{n}.$$

Hence find $\lim\limits_{n\to\infty} \ln\!\left(1 + \dfrac{a}{n} \right)^{\!n}$, and deduce $\lim\limits_{n\to\infty} \left(1 + \dfrac{a}{n} \right)^{\!n}$.

In the last step, what assumption are you making that you have not proved?

4 Find the limits, as $n \to \infty$, of

(a) $n \times \sum\limits_{i=n}^{3n} \dfrac{1}{i^2}$,   (b) $n^2 \times \sum\limits_{i=n}^{3n} \dfrac{1}{i^3}$,   (c) $\sum\limits_{i=n}^{3n} \dfrac{1}{i}$.

Check your answers with a calculator.

5* (a) Use the fact that $\lim\limits_{n\to\infty} \sqrt[n]{n} = 1$ (see Exercise 7A Question 8) to find $\lim\limits_{n\to\infty} \dfrac{\ln n}{n}$.

(b) By writing $\dfrac{\ln(n+1)}{n}$ as $\dfrac{n+1}{n} \times \dfrac{\ln(n+1)}{n+1}$, find $\lim\limits_{n\to\infty} \dfrac{\ln(n+1)}{n}$.

(c) Draw a diagram to show that $\displaystyle\int_1^n \ln x \, dx < \ln n! < \int_1^{n+1} \ln x \, dx$.

(d) Deduce from part (c) that $-1 + \dfrac{1}{n} < \ln\dfrac{\sqrt[n]{n!}}{n} < \ln\!\left(1 + \dfrac{1}{n} \right) + \dfrac{\ln(n+1)}{n} - 1$.

(e) Hence show that $\lim\limits_{n\to\infty} \dfrac{\sqrt[n]{n!}}{n} = \dfrac{1}{e}$.

(f) Use a calculator to check that, when n is large, $\dfrac{\sqrt[n]{n!}}{n} \approx \dfrac{1}{e}$.

8 Power series

In this chapter the terms of the series include powers of a variable x. When you have completed it, you should

- know what is meant by a power series
- understand that a power series defines a function whose natural domain is the interval of convergence
- be able to use the ratio test and understand other methods to find the interval of convergence.

8.1 Definitions

So far the terms of almost all series have been functions simply of a positive integer variable i, and for convergent series the sum has been a number.

The series in this chapter are different, since each term also includes a power of a real (or possibly complex) variable x, so that

$$u_i = a_i x^i,$$

where a_i is a sequence of numbers.

One example which you will recognise is the infinite geometric series

$$1 + x + x^2 + x^3 + \ldots,$$

for which $a_i = 1$ for all i. This is convergent if $|x| < 1$. If you replace x by $-2x$ or $\frac{1}{3}x$ you get other infinite geometric series,

$$1 - 2x + 4x^2 - 8x^3 + \ldots \quad \text{or} \quad 1 + \tfrac{1}{3}x + \tfrac{1}{9}x^2 + \tfrac{1}{27}x^3 + \ldots,$$

with $a_i = (-2)^i$ and $a_i = \left(\tfrac{1}{3}\right)^i$ respectively. These are convergent if $|-2x| < 1$ and $\left|\tfrac{1}{3}x\right| < 1$, that is if $-\tfrac{1}{2} < x < \tfrac{1}{2}$ and $-3 < x < 3$.

You will notice one difference between these examples and the series in earlier chapters. As well as terms with powers of x, there is also a 'constant term', $u_0 = a_0 x^0$. When you use sigma notation to describe the series, the values of i will start at 0 rather than 1. You could think of the series as 'infinite polynomials', and the partial sum

$$S_n = \sum_{i=0}^{n} a_i x^i$$

is a polynomial of degree n, written with ascending powers of x.

> A **power series** is an infinite series $\sum u_i$ where $u_i = a_i x^i$ for $i = 0, 1, 2, \ldots$.

Obviously all power series are convergent when $x = 0$, since there is then only one non-zero term a_0. There are some power series which are convergent for all $x \in \mathbb{R}$. But many power series are convergent for some values of x but not for others. In that case there is an **interval of convergence**, denoted by I.

For the geometric series above you can use the formula for S_n to write down algebraic expressions for the sum over the interval of convergence. Thus

$$\sum_{i=0}^{\infty} x^i = \frac{1}{1-x} \text{ for } -1 < x < 1, \qquad \sum_{i=0}^{\infty} (-2)^i x^i = \frac{1}{1+2x} \text{ for } -\tfrac{1}{2} < x < \tfrac{1}{2}$$

and $\displaystyle\sum_{i=0}^{\infty} \left(\tfrac{1}{3}\right)^i x^i = \frac{1}{1 - \tfrac{1}{3}x} \text{ for } -3 < x < 3.$

Notice that the expressions for the sum also have a meaning when x is outside the interval of convergence (except at $x = 1$, $-\tfrac{1}{2}$ and 3 respectively), but the function is not then represented by the series.

In the same way, any power series defines a function of x. But unlike the geometric series, it is unusual to be able to give an algebraic expression for the sum. In that case the power series itself serves as the definition of the function.

> A power series $\sum a_i x^i$ is convergent within an interval of convergence I. It then defines a function
>
> $$S(x) = \sum_{i=0}^{\infty} a_i x^i$$
>
> whose natural domain is I.

8.2   The interval of convergence

For the geometric series in Section 8.1 it was possible to write down the intervals of convergence because you know formulae for the partial sums S_n. Usually you don't, and then you have to use another method. One way of finding the interval of convergence which often works is to use the ratio test in Section 3.2:

If $\sum u_i$ is a series of positive terms such that $\lim\limits_{i \to \infty} \dfrac{u_i}{u_{i-1}} < 1$, then the series is convergent.

You might object that in a power series the coefficients a_i may not all be positive, and also x might be negative. To get round this, begin by asking for what values of x the series is *absolutely* convergent. The ratio test then becomes:

If $\lim\limits_{i \to \infty} \left| \dfrac{u_i}{u_{i-1}} \right| < 1$, then the series $\sum u_i$ is absolutely convergent.

To apply this to a power series, write $u_i = a_i x^i$ and remember the rules for the modulus, that

$$\left| s \times t \right| = \left| s \right| \times \left| t \right| \text{ and } \left| \frac{s}{t} \right| = \frac{\left| s \right|}{\left| t \right|}.$$

Then

$$\frac{|u_i|}{|u_{i-1}|} = \frac{|a_i x^i|}{|a_{i-1} x^{i-1}|} = \left|\frac{a_i}{a_{i-1}}\right| \times |x|.$$

The condition $\displaystyle\lim_{i\to\infty}\frac{|u_i|}{|u_{i-1}|} < 1$ then becomes $\displaystyle\lim_{i\to\infty}\left(\left|\frac{a_i}{a_{i-1}}\right| \times |x|\right) < 1$. You can use the results of Theorems 2 and 3 in Section 7.2 to write this as

$$|x| < \lim_{i\to\infty}\left|\frac{a_{i-1}}{a_i}\right|.$$

You can also reverse the argument to find what happens if $|x| > \displaystyle\lim_{i\to\infty}\left|\frac{a_{i-1}}{a_i}\right|$. Working backwards, you

reach the conclusion that $\displaystyle\lim_{i\to\infty}\frac{|u_i|}{|u_{i-1}|} > 1$. This means that, for values of i beyond a certain point,

$|u_i| > |u_{i-1}|$. That is, the terms of the series increase in absolute value, and therefore can't tend to 0, so the series is not convergent.

These results can be summarised as follows.

> If $\displaystyle\lim_{i\to\infty}\left|\frac{a_{i-1}}{a_i}\right| = R$, then the power series $\sum a_i x^i$ is convergent for $|x| < R$ and
>
> divergent for $|x| > R$.

This is illustrated in Fig. 8.1. The interval of convergence certainly includes the whole of the open interval $]-R,R[$ and doesn't extend outside the closed interval $[-R,R]$. But there are question marks over what happens when $x = -R$ and $x = R$. The ratio test doesn't help here, and you need to consider each case individually.

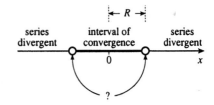

Fig. 8.1

Example 8.2.1

Find the intervals of convergence for the power series   (a) $\displaystyle\sum\frac{x^i}{(i+1)^2}$,   (b) $\displaystyle\sum\frac{x^i}{i+1}$,   (c) $\displaystyle\sum i x^i$.

(a)   Since $a_i = \dfrac{1}{(i+1)^2}$, $R = \displaystyle\lim_{i\to\infty}\left|\dfrac{\dfrac{1}{(i)^2}}{\dfrac{1}{(i+1)^2}}\right| = \lim_{i\to\infty}\dfrac{(i+1)^2}{i^2} = \lim_{i\to\infty}\left(1+\dfrac{1}{i}\right)^2 = 1.$

The series is therefore convergent for $|x| < 1$ and divergent for $|x| > 1$. When $x = 1$ and $x = -1$ the series becomes

$$\frac{1}{1^2}+\frac{1}{2^2}+\frac{1}{3^2}+\dots \quad\text{and}\quad \frac{1}{1^2}-\frac{1}{2^2}+\frac{1}{3^2}-\dots ,$$

and you know from Sections 2.2 and 6.1 that these are convergent. The interval of convergence is therefore the closed interval $[-1,1]$.

(b)   Since $a_i = \frac{1}{i+1}$, $R = \lim\limits_{i\to\infty}\left|\dfrac{\frac{1}{i}}{\frac{1}{i+1}}\right| = \lim\limits_{i\to\infty}\left|\dfrac{i+1}{i}\right| = \lim\limits_{i\to\infty}\left|1+\dfrac{1}{i}\right| = 1$.

When $x = 1$ the series becomes

$$\frac{1}{1} + \frac{1}{2} + \frac{1}{3} + \dots,$$

which is not convergent. But when $x = -1$ the series is

$$\frac{1}{1} - \frac{1}{2} + \frac{1}{3} - \dots,$$

which was shown to be convergent in Section 6.1. So the interval of convergence is $[-1,1[$.

(c)   Since $a_i = i$, $R = \lim\limits_{i\to\infty}\left|\dfrac{i-1}{i}\right| = \lim\limits_{i\to\infty}\left|1-\dfrac{1}{i}\right| = 1$.

But this series cannot converge when $x = 1$ or $x = -1$, because then $|u_i| = |a_i x^i| = i$, which does not tend to 0 as $i \to \infty$. So the interval of convergence is the open interval $]-1,1[$.

You will see from Example 8.2.1 that the ratio test can be very effective when $\lim\limits_{i\to\infty}\left|\dfrac{a_{i-1}}{a_i}\right|$ exists. But sometimes it doesn't, as in the next two examples. You then need to find the interval of convergence by another method.

Example 8.2.2
Find the interval of convergence of the power series $\sum\left(2-(-1)^i\right)x^i$.

The series begins

$$1 + 3x + x^2 + 3x^3 + x^4 + 3x^5 + \dots,$$

with $a_i = 1$ when i is even and $a_i = 3$ when i is odd. So the ratio $\dfrac{a_{i-1}}{a_i}$ takes alternately the values $\frac{1}{3}, 3, \frac{1}{3}, 3, \frac{1}{3}, \dots$. This clearly does not tend to a limit.

The series consists of two interleaved geometric series,

$$1 + x^2 + x^4 + \dots \quad \text{and} \quad 3x + 3x^3 + 3x^5 + \dots,$$

each with common ratio x^2. These are convergent when $x^2 < 1$, that is when $-1 < x < 1$. The interval of convergence is therefore $]-1,1[$.

Example 8.2.3

Find the interval of convergence of the power series $\sum(\cos i)x^i$.

A glance at the graph of the sequence $a_i = \cos i$ (see Section 6.2, Fig. 6.7) will convince you that $\left|\dfrac{\cos(i-1)}{\cos i}\right|$ doesn't tend to a limit as $i \to \infty$. So you can't use the ratio test.

But since $|\cos i| \le 1$ for all $i \in \mathbb{N}$, you know that, for any value of x, $\left|(\cos i)x^i\right| \le |x|^i$. And since the geometric series $\sum|x|^i$ is convergent for $|x| < 1$, you can use the comparison test in Section 2.3 to deduce that $\sum\left|(\cos i)x^i\right|$ is convergent for $|x| < 1$.

When $x = 1$ and $x = -1$ the series becomes $\sum \cos i$ and $\sum(-1)^i \cos i$ respectively. Neither of these can converge, since $\cos i$ doesn't tend to a limit as $i \to \infty$ (see Example 6.2.3). So the interval of convergence is $\,]-1,1[\,$.

What these examples illustrate is that, even when $\lim\limits_{i\to\infty}\left|\dfrac{a_{i-1}}{a_i}\right|$ does not exist, there is still a number R which separates the values of $|x|$ for which the series is absolutely convergent from those for which it is divergent. This is in fact true for almost any power series, but it is not so easy to prove.

There are just two exceptions. If $\lim\limits_{i\to\infty}\left|\dfrac{a_{i-1}}{a_i}\right| = 0$, then the ratio

$$\frac{|u_i|}{|u_{i-1}|} = \left|\frac{a_i}{a_{i-1}}\right| \times |x|$$

tends to infinity for every value of x except 0. In that case the power series converges only when $x = 0$. And if $\left|\dfrac{a_{i-1}}{a_i}\right|$ tends to infinity as $i \to \infty$, then the ratio $\dfrac{|u_i|}{|u_{i-1}|}$ tends to 0 whatever the value of x, so the power series converges for all values of x.

Example 8.2.4

For what values of x are the following infinite series convergent?

(a) $\sum\dfrac{x^i}{(i+1)^i}$ (b) $\sum(i+1)^i x^i$

(a) If $a_i = \dfrac{1}{(i+1)^i}$, then $\left|\dfrac{a_{i-1}}{a_i}\right| = \dfrac{(i+1)^i}{i^{i-1}} = \left(\dfrac{i+1}{i}\right)^i \times i$. The first factor of this expression is greater than 1 and the second tends to infinity, so $\left|\dfrac{a_{i-1}}{a_i}\right|$ tends to infinity as $i \to \infty$. The series therefore converges for all values of x.

(b)   If $a_i = (i+1)^i$, then $\left|\dfrac{a_{i-1}}{a_i}\right| = \dfrac{i^{i-1}}{(i+1)^i} = \left(\dfrac{i}{i+1}\right)^i \times \dfrac{1}{i}$. The first factor of this expression is less

than 1 and the second tends to 0, so $\displaystyle\lim_{i\to\infty}\left|\dfrac{a_{i-1}}{a_i}\right| = 0$. The series converges only if $x = 0$, and

its value is then the constant term $(0+1)^0 = 1^0 = 1$.

To summarise:

> For any power series $\sum a_i x^i$,
>
> *either*   the series converges only when $x = 0$,
>
> *or*   the series converges for all values of x,
>
> *or*   there is a number R such that the series is convergent for $|x| < R$ and
>   divergent for $|x| > R$.
>
> The number R is called the **radius of convergence** of the series.

You may be surprised at the use of the word 'radius'. The reason is that the theory of power series can be extended to allow x to be a complex number (see Higher Level Book 2 Section 36.5), and sometimes also to series where the coefficients a_i may be complex. The number R is then the radius of a circle in the complex plane which separates the points for which the series converges from those for which it diverges. The corresponding property when x is real is that the points on the number line which separate the interval of convergence from the intervals of divergence are at a distance R from the origin.

Exercise 8

1   Find the interval of convergence for the following power series.

(a) $\displaystyle\sum\frac{x^i}{(i+1)(i+2)}$ (b) $\displaystyle\sum\frac{x^i}{\sqrt{i+1}}$ (c) $\displaystyle\sum\frac{x^i}{i!}$

(d) $\displaystyle\sum\frac{2^i}{i+1}x^i$ (e) $\displaystyle\sum i!\,x^i$ (f) $\displaystyle\sum\frac{i+1}{2i+1}x^i$

(g) $\displaystyle\sum\frac{x^i}{1+2\times(-1)^i}$ (h) $\displaystyle\sum\binom{n+i}{i}x^i$ for $n \in \mathbb{Z}^+$ (i) $\displaystyle\sum\binom{2i}{i}x^i$

[To decide about the end points in part (i), you may find it helpful to use *Stirling's approximation*, that $n! \approx \sqrt{2\pi}\,n^{n+\frac{1}{2}}e^{-n}$ when n is large.]

2   Find the radius of convergence for the following power series.

(a) $\displaystyle\sum\frac{x^i}{3i+1}$ (b) $\displaystyle\sum\frac{x^i}{2+(-1)^i}$ (c) $\displaystyle\sum\frac{x^i}{1+(-2)^i}$ (d) $\displaystyle\sum\frac{x^{2i}}{2^i}$

9 Maclaurin series

In this chapter functions are associated with power series. When you have completed it, you should

- be able to find Maclaurin polynomials, and understand why they give good approximations to functions
- know the Maclaurin series for a number of functions, and be able to extend these by using substitutions
- understand what is meant by the interval of validity of a series
- know how to find series using integration
- be able to use series to find limits.

9.1 Agreement between functions

Suppose that $n \in \mathbb{Z}^+$, and that you want to expand $(1+x)^n$ in ascending powers of x as

$$1 + a_1 x + a_2 x^2 + \ldots + a_i x^i + \ldots + a_n x^n.$$

It was shown in Higher Level Book 1 Section 4.4 that the terms can be generated inductively, each coefficient being found from the one before:

$$1 \xrightarrow{\times \frac{n}{1}} a_1 \xrightarrow{\times \frac{n-1}{2}} a_2 \xrightarrow{\times \frac{n-2}{3}} a_3 \rightarrow \ldots \rightarrow a_{i-1} \xrightarrow{\times \frac{n-i+1}{i}} a_i \rightarrow \ldots \xrightarrow{\times \frac{1}{n}} a_n.$$

In the sequence of multipliers $\dfrac{n}{1}, \dfrac{n-1}{2}, \dfrac{n-2}{3}, \ldots, \dfrac{1}{n}$ the denominators go up by 1 at each step, and the numerators go down by 1. The sequence of coefficients stops at a_n, because the next multiplier would be $\dfrac{1-1}{n+1}$, which is 0.

But if you generate a series by the same rule with a value of n which is not a positive integer, the sequence of coefficients will never end, and the expression would be an infinite power series. For example, if $n = \frac{1}{2}$, the multipliers would be

$$\frac{\frac{1}{2}}{1}, \frac{-\frac{1}{2}}{2}, \frac{-\frac{3}{2}}{3}, \frac{-\frac{5}{2}}{4}, \ldots$$

which would produce coefficients

$$1 \xrightarrow{\times \frac{1}{2}} \frac{1}{2} \xrightarrow{\times (-\frac{1}{4})} -\frac{1}{8} \xrightarrow{\times (-\frac{1}{2})} \frac{1}{16} \xrightarrow{\times (-\frac{5}{8})} -\frac{5}{128} \rightarrow \ldots$$

and an infinite series $S(x)$ whose first few terms are

$$S(x) = 1 + \frac{1}{2}x - \frac{1}{8}x^2 + \frac{1}{16}x^3 - \frac{5}{128}x^4 + \ldots .$$

This is called a **binomial series**. But does it have any connection with $(1+x)^{\frac{1}{2}}$?

To investigate this, Fig. 9.1, Fig. 9.2 and Fig. 9.3 compare the graph of $f(x) = (1+x)^{\frac{1}{2}}$, or $\sqrt{1+x}$, with the graphs of the partial sums of degrees 1, 2 and 3 of $S(x)$. These are

$$S_1(x) = 1 + \tfrac{1}{2}x,$$
$$S_2(x) = 1 + \tfrac{1}{2}x - \tfrac{1}{8}x^2,$$
$$S_3(x) = 1 + \tfrac{1}{2}x - \tfrac{1}{8}x^2 + \tfrac{1}{16}x^3.$$

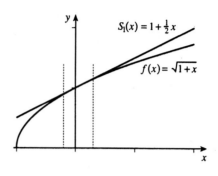

Fig. 9.1

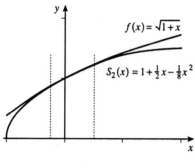

Fig. 9.2

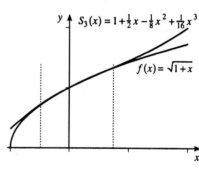

Fig. 9.3

The dotted lines indicate the intervals of values of x for which you can't distinguish the pairs of graphs by eye. You can see that the more terms you take, the wider the interval over which the polynomial gives a good approximation to $\sqrt{1+x}$.

The polynomial $S_1(x)$ has the same value as $f(x)$ when $x = 0$, and also the same gradient. Thus $f(0) = \sqrt{1+0} = 1$ and $S_1(0) = 1$. Also, since

$$f'(x) = \tfrac{1}{2}(1+x)^{-\frac{1}{2}} \quad \text{and} \quad S_1'(x) = \tfrac{1}{2},$$

you find that $f'(0) = S_1'(0) = \tfrac{1}{2}$.

The reason why $S_2(x)$ fits $f(x)$ better than $S_1(x)$ is that, by adding a term in x^2, the graph can be made to bend into a curve. The coefficient of x^2 ensures that the two graphs bend at the same rate when $x = 0$; that is, their second derivatives are the same. Thus

$$f''(x) = -\tfrac{1}{4}(1+x)^{-\frac{3}{2}} \quad \text{and} \quad S_2''(x) = -\tfrac{1}{4},$$

so that $f''(0) = S_2''(0) = -\tfrac{1}{4}$.

The functions $S_3(x)$ and $f(x)$ agree even better, since they not only bend at the same rate at $x = 0$, but also their rates of bending are changing at the same rate. You can check for yourself that $f'''(0) = S_3'''(0) = \tfrac{3}{8}$.

The ideas above can be summarised with the help of a definition:

Definition   The functions f and g **agree to the nth degree** at $x = 0$ if

$$f(0) = g(0), \quad f'(0) = g'(0), \quad f''(0) = g''(0), \quad \ldots, \quad f^{(n)}(0) = g^{(n)}(0);$$

that is, if $f^{(i)}(0) = g^{(i)}(0)$ where i is an integer and $0 \le i \le n$.

Thus $f(x)$ and $S_1(x)$ agree to the first degree, $f(x)$ and $S_2(x)$ agree to the second degree, and $f(x)$ and $S_3(x)$ agree to the third degree.

You can extend this idea to other functions.

Example 9.1.1
Find a cubic polynomial which agrees with $\tan x$ to the third degree.

Writing $\tan x$ as $f(x)$, use the chain rule and the product rule to find

$$f'(x) = \sec^2 x,$$
$$f''(x) = \sec x \tan x \times 2 \sec x$$
$$= 2 \sec^2 x \tan x,$$
$$f'''(x) = \sec x \tan x \times 4 \sec x \times \tan x + 2 \sec^2 x \times \sec^2 x$$
$$= 2 \sec^2 x \left(2 \tan^2 x + \sec^2 x \right).$$

Since $\tan 0 = 0$ and $\sec 0 = 1$,

$$f(0) = 0, \quad f'(0) = 1, \quad f''(0) = 0, \quad f'''(0) = 2.$$

If the required cubic polynomial is $p(x) = a + bx + cx^2 + dx^3$, then

$$p'(x) = b + 2cx + 3dx^2, \quad p''(x) = 2c + 6dx, \quad p'''(x) = 6d.$$

So

$$p(0) = a, \quad p'(0) = b, \quad p''(0) = 2c, \quad p'''(0) = 6d.$$

For $p(x)$ and $f(x)$ to agree at $x = 0$, you need

$$a = 0, \quad b = 1, \quad 2c = 0, \quad 6d = 2.$$

Therefore $p(x) = x + \frac{1}{3}x^3$.

It is interesting to plot the graphs of $\tan x$ and $p(x) = x + \frac{1}{3}x^3$ on a calculator, and to suggest an interval over which you would consider that $p(x)$ is a good approximation to $\tan x$.

9.2 Maclaurin polynomials

You can generalise the argument in the last section to give polynomial approximations to any function $f(x)$ around $x = 0$, provided that all the derivatives of the function are defined.

The polynomial of degree n which agrees with $f(x)$ to the nth degree at $x = 0$ is

$$p_n(x) = f(0) + \frac{f'(0)}{1!}x + \frac{f''(0)}{2!}x^2 + \ldots + \frac{f^{(i)}(0)}{i!}x^i + \ldots + \frac{f^{(n)}(0)}{n!}x^n.$$

This is called the **Maclaurin polynomial for $f(x)$ of degree n**.

In sigma notation it can be written as $p_n(x) = \sum_{i=0}^{n} \frac{f^{(i)}(0)}{i!}x^i$.

It is named after Colin Maclaurin, a Scottish mathematician who lived in the first half of the 18th century.

A proof of this result is given below. First, here is an example to show how it can be used.

Example 9.2.1
Find the Maclaurin polynomial of degree 4 for the function $f(x) = (1 + x)^{-3}$.

The first four derivatives are

$$f'(x) = -3(1 + x)^{-4}, \quad f''(x) = 12(1 + x)^{-5},$$

$$f'''(x) = -60(1 + x)^{-6}, \quad f^{(4)}(x) = 360(1 + x)^{-7}.$$

Therefore

$$f(0) = 1, \quad f'(0) = -3, \quad f''(0) = 12, \quad f'''(0) = -60, \quad f^{(4)}(0) = 360.$$

This gives

$$p_4(x) = 1 + \frac{(-3)}{1!}x + \frac{12}{2!}x^2 + \frac{(-60)}{3!}x^3 + \frac{360}{4!}x^4$$

$$= 1 - 3x + 6x^2 - 10x^3 + 15x^4.$$

You can check that this is the same as the partial sum of degree 4 of the binomial series for $(1 + x)^{-3}$ up to and including the term in x^4.

To prove the result in the shaded box, what you have to show is that if the polynomial

$$p_n(x) \equiv a_0 + a_1 x + a_2 x^2 + \ldots + a_i x^i + \ldots + a_n x^n$$

agrees with $f(x)$ to the nth degree at $x = 0$, then the coefficient a_i is equal to $\frac{f^{(i)}(0)}{i!}$ for $i = 0, 1, 2, \ldots, n$. To do this, bracket off the terms as

$$p_n(x) \equiv \left(a_0 + a_1 x + a_2 x^2 + \ldots + a_{i-1}x^{i-1}\right) + \left(a_i x^i\right) + \left(a_{i+1}x^{i+1} + \ldots + a_n x^n\right)$$

and consider what happens to each bracket when you differentiate the identity i times.

Each time that you differentiate a term $a_r x^r$ the index goes down by 1. After r differentiations the index is 0 so that the term is reduced to a constant, and after $r + 1$ differentiations the term vanishes.

- In the first bracket all the terms have $r \leq i-1$, so $r+1 \leq i$. Therefore after i differentiations all the terms in this bracket have vanished.
- In the last bracket all the terms have $r \geq i+1$, so after i differentiations the index is $r-i \geq 1$. So x is a factor of all the terms in this bracket.
- After i differentiations the index in the term $a_i x^i$ becomes $i-i=0$, so that this term becomes a constant. Successive derivatives of x^i are

$$ix^{i-1}, \quad i(i-1)x^{i-2}, \quad i(i-1)(i-2)x^{i-3}, \dots , \quad i(i-1)(i-2)\dots 1x^0,$$

so $\dfrac{\mathrm{d}^i}{\mathrm{d}x^i}\left(a_i x^i\right) = a_i \times i!.$

Combining these, you find that

$$p_n^{(i)}(x) \equiv (0) + \left(a_i \times i!\right) + (\text{terms having a factor } x).$$

So, putting x equal to 0,

$$p_n^{(i)}(0) = 0 + a_i \times i! + 0 = a_i \times i!.$$

Now the aim is to make $p_n(x)$ agree with $f(x)$ to the nth degree at $x=0$, that is

$$p_n^{(i)}(0) = f^{(i)}(0) \quad \text{for } i = 0,1,2,\dots,n.$$

So you must choose a_i so that

$$a_i \times i! = f^{(i)}(0).$$

That is, $a_i = \dfrac{f^{(i)}(0)}{i!}$, which is what you set out to prove.

Example 9.2.2
Find the Maclaurin polynomial of degree 4 for $f(x) = \cos x$.

Differentiating four times in succession,

$$f'(x) = -\sin x, \quad f''(x) = -\cos x, \quad f'''(x) = \sin x, \quad f^{(4)}(x) = \cos x.$$

So

$$f(0) = 1, \quad f'(0) = 0, \quad f''(0) = -1, \quad f'''(0) = 0, \quad f^{(4)}(0) = 1.$$

Using the equation in the shaded box with $n = 4$, the Maclaurin polynomial is

$$p_4(x) = 1 + \frac{0}{1!}x + \frac{-1}{2!}x^2 + \frac{0}{3!}x^3 + \frac{1}{4!}x^4$$
$$= 1 - \tfrac{1}{2}x^2 + \tfrac{1}{24}x^4.$$

Use a calculator to display the graphs of $y = \cos x$ and $y = p_4(x)$ with the same axes. Over what interval would you say that $p_4(x)$ is a good approximation to $\cos x$?

1   For the following expressions $f(x)$ write down the partial sums $S_3(x)$ of the binomial series. Verify that $f(x)$ and $S_3(x)$ agree to the third degree at $x = 0$. Display graphs of $f(x)$ and $S_3(x)$ on a calculator, and estimate the interval over which you cannot distinguish between the graphs.

   (a) $(1+x)^{\frac{3}{2}}$ (b) $(1-x)^{-\frac{3}{2}}$

2   For the following expressions $f(x)$ find the Maclaurin polynomial $p_n(x)$ of the given degree n. Illustrate your answers by comparing the graphs of $f(x)$ and $p_n(x)$.

   (a) $\sin x$, $n = 5$ (b) $\sin 2x$, $n = 5$ (c) e^x, $n = 4$

   (d) e^{-3x}, $n = 4$ (e) $\sin^2 x$, $n = 3$ (f) $\cos^2 x$, $n = 3$

   (g) $\ln(1-x)$, $n = 4$ (h) $\dfrac{1}{\sqrt{1-2x}}$, $n = 3$ (i) $e^{-\frac{1}{2}x^2}$, $n = 4$

   (j) $\ln\left(1+x^2\right)$, $n = 4$

3   For the binomial series with $n = \frac{1}{2}$ in Section 9.1, use the multiplier from a_{i-1} to a_i to show that the radius of convergence is 1.

4   Show that it is possible to find numbers a and b such that $a + bx^2$ and $\sec x$ agree to degree 3 at $x = 0$.

5   Find the Maclaurin polynomial of degree 4 for $(1+x)^p$, where p is not a positive integer. Verify that this agrees with the first five terms of the binomial series for $(1+x)^p$.

9.3   Maclaurin series and intervals of validity

The power series

$$f(0) + \frac{f'(0)}{1!}x + \frac{f''(0)}{2!}x^2 + \dots + \frac{f^{(i)}(0)}{i!}x^i + \dots,$$

continued indefinitely, is called the **Maclaurin series** of $f(x)$. The partial sums obtained by cutting off the series after the second, third, fourth, ... terms produce a sequence of Maclaurin polynomials $p_1(x)$, $p_2(x)$, $p_3(x)$, ...

Fig. 9.1, Fig. 9.2 and Fig. 9.3 showed how such a sequence of polynomials can give better and better approximations to $f(x)$ for certain values of x. In such cases you can say that $f(x)$ is the limit of the sequence of polynomial values as n tends to infinity. Thus

$$f(x) = \lim_{n \to \infty} p_n(x) = \lim_{n \to \infty} \sum_{i=0}^{n} \frac{f^{(i)}(0)}{i!}x^i, \quad \text{or} \quad \sum_{i=0}^{\infty} \frac{f^{(i)}(0)}{i!}x^i.$$

This means that, by taking n large enough, you can (for a particular value of x) make $p_n(x)$ as close as you like to $f(x)$.

For many functions this is true for some but not all values of x. For example, if $f(x) = \ln(1 + x)$, then

$$f'(x) = (1+x)^{-1}, \quad f''(x) = -(1+x)^{-2}, \quad f'''(x) = 2(1+x)^{-3}, \quad \dots ,$$

so that

$$f'(0) = 1, \quad f''(0) = -1, \quad f'''(0) = 2, \quad \dots .$$

The general term is positive when i is odd and negative when i is even. It is not difficult to check that

$$f^{(i)}(x) = (-1)^{i-1}(i-1)!(1+x)^{-i},$$

so that

$$\frac{f^{(i)}(0)}{i!} = \frac{(-1)^{i-1}(i-1)!}{i!} = (-1)^{i-1}\frac{1}{i}.$$

The Maclaurin series is therefore

$$\ln(1 + x) = x - \tfrac{1}{2}x^2 + \tfrac{1}{3}x^3 - \tfrac{1}{4}x^4 + \dots .$$

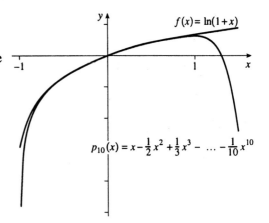

Fig. 9.4

Fig. 9.4 shows a comparison of the graphs of $\ln(1 + x)$ and the 10th Maclaurin polynomial, ending with the term $-\tfrac{1}{10}x^{10}$. It is striking how closely the Maclaurin polynomial follows the function from just above -1 to just below 1, but that beyond 1 the two functions separate very sharply. However many terms you take, you can never get $p_n(x)$ to come close to $\ln(1 + x)$ for $x > 1$.

Contrast this with the function $f(x) = \sin x$. Since the derivatives are successively

$$\cos x, \ -\sin x, \ -\cos x, \ \sin x, \dots$$

and then repeat through the same cycle, the values of $f^{(i)}(0)$ are successively

$$1, \ 0, \ -1, \ 0, \ 1, \ 0, \ \dots .$$

Also $f(0) = 0$. The Maclaurin series is therefore

$$\sin x = \frac{x}{1!} - \frac{x^3}{3!} + \frac{x^5}{5!} - \frac{x^7}{7!} + \dots .$$

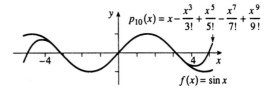

Fig. 9.5

Fig. 9.5 shows a comparison of the graphs of $\sin x$ and the 10th Maclaurin polynomial. (The last non-zero term of $p_{10}(x)$ is $\frac{x^9}{9!}$, because $f^{(10)}(0) = 0$.) You can see that already the graphs cannot be distinguished from each other by eye between about -4 and $+4$. And in fact, by taking enough terms, you can get a Maclaurin polynomial which fits the $\sin x$ graph over as wide an interval as you like.

The set of values of x for which the Maclaurin series can be made to fit a function, provided that enough terms are taken, is called the **interval of validity** of the series. For the function $\ln(1 + x)$ the interval of validity is $-1 < x \le 1$; the series for $\sin x$ is valid for all real values of x, so its interval of validity is $\mathbb{R}$.

Obviously the interval of validity for a Maclaurin series can't be larger than the interval of convergence of the power series. In fact, the two intervals are generally the same, though this is not easy to prove. For example, the Maclaurin series for $\ln(1+x)$ has $|a_{i-1}| = \frac{1}{i-1}$ and $|a_i| = \frac{1}{i}$, so the radius of convergence is $\lim_{i \to \infty} \left| \frac{a_{i-1}}{a_i} \right| = \lim_{i \to \infty} \frac{i}{i-1} = 1$. You know that the series is convergent when $x = 1$ but not when $x = -1$, so the interval of convergence is $-1 < x \leq 1$. This is the same as the interval of validity.

The only condition for a function to have a Maclaurin series is that $f(0)$ and all the derivatives $f^{(i)}(0)$ must be defined. So $\csc x$ and $\ln x$ do not have Maclaurin series, because they are not defined when $x = 0$; and $|x|$ does not have one, since $\dfrac{d}{dx}(|x|)$ is not defined when $x = 0$.

But many of the standard functions do have Maclaurin series, and the most important ones are listed below. Before reading on, you should check these for yourself; it is worth remembering the first few terms of each series, but not the expression for the general term.

> **Maclaurin series for some standard functions**
>
> $$e^x = 1 + \frac{x}{1!} + \frac{x^2}{2!} + \frac{x^3}{3!} + \ldots + \frac{x^i}{i!} + \ldots, \quad \text{for } x \in \mathbb{R}.$$
>
> $$\sin x = \frac{x}{1!} - \frac{x^3}{3!} + \frac{x^5}{5!} - \frac{x^7}{7!} + \ldots + (-1)^i \frac{x^{2i+1}}{(2i+1)!} + \ldots, \quad \text{for } x \in \mathbb{R}.$$
>
> $$\cos x = 1 - \frac{x^2}{2!} + \frac{x^4}{4!} - \frac{x^6}{6!} + \ldots + (-1)^i \frac{x^{2i}}{(2i)!} + \ldots, \quad \text{for } x \in \mathbb{R}.$$
>
> $$\ln(1+x) = x - \tfrac{1}{2}x^2 + \tfrac{1}{3}x^3 - \tfrac{1}{4}x^4 + \ldots + (-1)^{i-1}\tfrac{1}{i}x^i + \ldots, \quad \text{for } -1 < x \leq 1.$$
>
> $$(1+x)^p = 1 + px + \frac{p(p-1)}{2!}x^2 + \frac{p(p-1)(p-2)}{3!}x^3 + \ldots$$
>
> $$+ \frac{p(p-1)(p-2)\ldots(p-(i-1))}{i!}x^i + \ldots, \quad \text{for } x \in \mathbb{R} \text{ if } p \in \mathbb{N},$$
>
> otherwise for $-1 < x < 1$ (and, in some cases, also for $x = -1$ or $x = 1$).

Example 9.3.1

Use Maclaurin series to find e and $\dfrac{1}{e}$, correct to 4 decimal places.

You can evaluate these by substituting $x = 1$ and $x = -1$ in the series for e^x:

$$e = 1 + \frac{1}{1!} + \frac{1}{2!} + \frac{1}{3!} + \frac{1}{4!} + \ldots,$$

$$\frac{1}{e} = 1 - \frac{1}{1!} + \frac{1}{2!} - \frac{1}{3!} + \frac{1}{4!} - \ldots.$$

The calculation is very simple, since $(i+1)! = (i+1) \times i!$, so that you can find $\dfrac{1}{(i+1)!}$ by dividing $\dfrac{1}{i!}$ by $i+1$.

Table 9.6 lists values of $\dfrac{1}{i!}$ up to $r = 9$.

$1 = 1$	$\frac{1}{1!} = 1$
$\frac{1}{2!} = 0.5$	$\frac{1}{3!} = 0.166667$
$\frac{1}{4!} = 0.041667$	$\frac{1}{5!} = 0.008333$
$\frac{1}{6!} = 0.001389$	$\frac{1}{7!} = 0.000198$
$\frac{1}{8!} = 0.000025$	$\frac{1}{9!} = 0.000003$
1.543081	1.175201

Table 9.6

So $e \approx 1.543\,081 + 1.175\,201 \approx 2.7183$,

$\dfrac{1}{e} \approx 1.543\,081 - 1.175\,201 \approx 0.3679$, both correct to 4 decimal places.

Exercise 9B

1   Use Maclaurin series to find, correct to 4 decimal places, the values of

(a) $\sqrt{e}$,   (b) $\sin 1$,   (c) $\sqrt[3]{0.9}$,   (d) $\cos 20°$,

(e) $\ln 0.95$,   (f) $\ln 2.25$,   (g) $\cos 3$.

2   Find the Maclaurin series for $\ln\dfrac{1+x}{1-x}$, and state its interval of validity. By choosing a suitable value

for x, calculate the value of $\ln 3$, correct to 3 decimal places.

Why can't you find $\ln 3$ directly from the Maclaurin series for $\ln(1+x)$?

3   Find, as far as the term in x^4, Maclaurin series for

(a) $\sec x$ (b) $\arctan x$.

For each function, find the percentage error in using the Maclaurin series as an approximation when $x = 0.1$, correct to 2 significant figures.

4   An approximate value for π can be found by putting $x = \frac{1}{2}\pi$ in the Maclaurin series of $\cos x$ and

neglecting all the terms of degree greater than 4, and then solving a quartic polynomial equation for π. How accurate is the approximation?

An alternative method is to use the substitution $x = \frac{1}{3}\pi$. How accurate is the resulting approximation?

Which method gives the better approximation? Suggest a reason why.

9.4 Modifying Maclaurin series

If you want to find the Maclaurin series for a function such as $\sin 5x$ or $\ln(1 + x^2)$, you could use the general expression at the beginning of Section 9.3 with $f(x) = \sin 5x$ or $f(x) = \ln(1 + x^2)$. This is quite easy for $\sin 5x$, since the derivatives are successively $5\cos 5x$, $-5^2 \sin 5x$, $-5^3 \cos 5x$, ... , whose values for $x = 0$ are 5, 0, -5^3, ... It is easy to see how this continues. The Maclaurin series then begins

$$\frac{5}{1!}x - \frac{5^3}{3!}x^3 + \frac{5^5}{5!}x^5 - \dots \ .$$

You can write this as

$$\frac{(5x)}{1!} - \frac{(5x)^3}{3!} + \frac{(5x)^5}{5!} - \dots \ ,$$

which is (as you would probably expect) what you would get by simply replacing x by $5x$ in the Maclaurin expansion for $\sin x$.

Differentiating $\ln(1 + x^2)$ several times is a lot more difficult, and you might not recognise the general pattern. But, just as with $\sin 5x$, you can find the Maclaurin series by substitution, in this case by simply replacing x by x^2 in the Maclaurin series of $\ln(1 + x)$. This gives

$$\ln(1 + x^2) = (x^2) - \tfrac{1}{2}(x^2)^2 + \tfrac{1}{3}(x^2)^3 - \tfrac{1}{4}(x^2)^4 + \ldots$$
$$= x^2 - \tfrac{1}{2}x^4 + \tfrac{1}{3}x^6 - \tfrac{1}{4}x^8 + \ldots \; .$$

Since the series for $\ln(1 + x)$ is valid when $-1 < x \le 1$, this series is valid when $-1 < x^2 \le 1$, that is when $-1 \le x \le 1$.

Sometimes it is worth using some special property of the function before finding the Maclaurin series, as in the following example.

Example 9.4.1
Find Maclaurin series for   (a) $\sin\left(x + \tfrac{1}{4}\pi\right)$,   (b) $\ln(2 - 4x)$.

(a)   By the addition formula, $\sin\left(x + \tfrac{1}{4}\pi\right) = \sin x \cos \tfrac{1}{4}\pi + \cos x \sin \tfrac{1}{4}\pi$.

Since $\sin \tfrac{1}{4}\pi = \cos \tfrac{1}{4}\pi = \dfrac{1}{\sqrt{2}}$,

$$\sin\left(x + \tfrac{1}{4}\pi\right) = \frac{1}{\sqrt{2}}(\sin x + \cos x)$$
$$= \frac{1}{\sqrt{2}}\left(\left(\frac{x}{1!} - \frac{x^3}{3!} + \frac{x^5}{5!} - \ldots\right) + \left(1 - \frac{x^2}{2!} + \frac{x^4}{4!} - \ldots\right)\right)$$
$$= \frac{1}{\sqrt{2}}\left(1 + \frac{x}{1!} - \frac{x^2}{2!} - \frac{x^3}{3!} + \frac{x^4}{4!} + \frac{x^5}{5!} - \ldots\right).$$

(b)   Use the multiplication rule of logarithms to write

$$\ln(2 - 4x) = \ln 2 + \ln(1 - 2x).$$

Then use the Maclaurin series for $\ln(1 + x)$, replacing x by $-2x$, to get

$$\ln(2 - 4x) = \ln 2 + (-2x) - \tfrac{1}{2}(-2x)^2 + \tfrac{1}{3}(-2x)^3 - \tfrac{1}{4}(-2x)^4 - \ldots$$
$$= \ln 2 - 2x - 2x^2 - \tfrac{8}{3}x^3 - 4x^4 - \ldots \; .$$

This is valid if $-1 < -2x \le 1$, that is if $\dfrac{(-1)}{(-2)} > x \ge \dfrac{1}{(-2)}$, or $-\tfrac{1}{2} \le x < \tfrac{1}{2}$.

Sometimes you want to find a Maclaurin series for a function which is the product of two simpler functions. Although you could do this by the usual Maclaurin method, finding the derivatives by the rule for differentiating a product, it is often simpler to expand the two functions separately as far as is needed and then to multiply the two polynomials together.

The next example compares the two methods.

Example 9.4.2
Find the Maclaurin series, as far as the term in x^4, for $f(x) = e^{2x} \cos 3x$
(a) by direct application of the Maclaurin series formula,
(b) by multiplying together the series for the separate factors.

(a)   Differentiating four times in succession, using the product rule,

$$f'(x) = 2e^{2x} \cos 3x + e^{2x}(-3\sin 3x)$$
$$= e^{2x}(2\cos 3x - 3\sin 3x);$$

$$f''(x) = 2e^{2x}(2\cos 3x - 3\sin 3x) + e^{2x}(-6\sin 3x - 9\cos 3x)$$
$$= e^{2x}(-5\cos 3x - 12\sin 3x);$$

$$f'''(x) = 2e^{2x}(-5\cos 3x - 12\sin 3x) + e^{2x}(15\sin 3x - 36\cos 3x)$$
$$= e^{2x}(-46\cos 3x - 9\sin 3x);$$

$$f^{(4)}(x) = 2e^{2x}(-46\cos 3x - 9\sin 3x) + e^{2x}(138\sin 3x - 27\cos 3x)$$
$$= e^{2x}(-119\cos 3x + 120\sin 3x).$$

So $f(0) = 1$, $f'(0) = 2$, $f''(0) = -5$, $f'''(0) = -46$, $f^{(4)}(0) = -119$.

Using the formula in Section 9.3, the Maclaurin series as far as the term in x^4 is

$$e^{2x} \cos 3x = 1 + \frac{2}{1!}x + \frac{-5}{2!}x^2 + \frac{-46}{3!}x^3 + \frac{-119}{4!}x^4$$
$$= 1 + 2x - \tfrac{5}{2}x^2 - \tfrac{23}{3}x^3 - \tfrac{119}{24}x^4.$$

(b)   Using the standard series for e^x and $\cos x$, with x replaced by $2x$ and $3x$ respectively, gives

$$e^{2x} = 1 + \frac{(2x)}{1!} + \frac{(2x)^2}{2!} + \frac{(2x)^3}{3!} + \frac{(2x)^4}{4!} + \dots$$
$$= 1 + 2x + 2x^2 + \tfrac{4}{3}x^3 + \tfrac{2}{3}x^4 + \dots ,$$

and

$$\cos 3x = 1 - \frac{(3x)^2}{2!} + \frac{(3x)^4}{4!} - \dots$$
$$= 1 - \tfrac{9}{2}x^2 + \tfrac{27}{8}x^4 - \dots .$$

So

$$e^{2x} \cos 3x = \left(1 + 2x + 2x^2 + \tfrac{4}{3}x^3 + \tfrac{2}{3}x^4 + \dots\right)\left(1 - \tfrac{9}{2}x^2 + \tfrac{27}{8}x^4 - \dots\right)$$
$$= 1 + 2x + \left(2 - \tfrac{9}{2}\right)x^2 + \left(\tfrac{4}{3} - 2\times\tfrac{9}{2}\right)x^3 + \left(\tfrac{27}{8} - 2\times\tfrac{9}{2} + \tfrac{2}{3}\right)x^4 + \dots$$
$$= 1 + 2x - \tfrac{5}{2}x^2 - \tfrac{23}{3}x^3 - \tfrac{119}{24}x^4,$$

as far as the term in x^4.

Example 9.4.3
Find the Maclaurin polynomial of degree 4 for $\ln \cos x$.

The function in this example involves two expansions. The work can be eased by discarding powers of x higher than x^4 as you go along.

$$\ln \cos x = \ln\left(1 - \frac{x^2}{2!} + \frac{x^4}{4!} - \ldots\right)$$

$$= \ln\left(1 + \left(-\tfrac{1}{2}x^2 + \tfrac{1}{24}x^4 - \ldots\right)\right)$$

$$= \left(-\tfrac{1}{2}x^2 + \tfrac{1}{24}x^4 - \ldots\right) - \tfrac{1}{2}\left(-\tfrac{1}{2}x^2 + \tfrac{1}{24}x^4 - \ldots\right)^2 + \ldots$$

$$= \left(-\tfrac{1}{2}x^2 + \tfrac{1}{24}x^4\right) - \tfrac{1}{2}\left(\tfrac{1}{4}x^4\right) \text{ to degree 4}$$

$$= -\tfrac{1}{2}x^2 + \left(\tfrac{1}{24} - \tfrac{1}{8}\right)x^4 = -\tfrac{1}{2}x^2 - \tfrac{1}{12}x^4.$$

9.5 Differentiating and integrating series

Another way of obtaining series is to use differentiation and integration. Suppose for example that you want to find the function represented by the infinite series

$$S(x) = \frac{x}{1^2} + \frac{x^2}{2^2} + \frac{x^3}{3^2} + \ldots + \frac{x^i}{i^2} + \ldots \; .$$

If the series were a finite series, you could find the derivative by differentiating each term separately. Assuming that you can still do this with an infinite series, you would get

$$S'(x) = \frac{1}{1^2} + \frac{2x}{2^2} + \frac{3x^2}{3^2} + \ldots + \frac{ix^{i-1}}{i^2} + \ldots$$

$$= 1 + \frac{x}{2} + \frac{x^2}{3} + \ldots + \frac{x^{i-1}}{i} + \ldots \; .$$

You know the sum of this last series. If you substitute $-x$ for x in the series for $\ln(1 + x)$, you get

$$\ln(1 - x) = -x - \frac{x^2}{2} - \frac{x^3}{3} - \ldots - \frac{x^i}{i} - \ldots$$

$$= -x\left(1 + \frac{x}{2} + \frac{x^2}{3} + \ldots + \frac{x^{i-1}}{i} + \ldots\right),$$

which is $-xS'(x)$. So

$$S'(x) = -\frac{1}{x}\ln(1 - x).$$

There are two ways you might continue from here. You could write $S(x)$ as an indefinite integral,

$$S(x) = \int -\frac{1}{x}\ln(1 - x)\,dx,$$

remembering that you need an arbitrary constant to ensure that $S(0) = 0$. This would be fine if you knew an expression for the indefinite integral, but unfortunately you don't in this case.

So a better method is to write $S(x)$ as a definite integral,

$$S(x) = \int_0^x -\frac{1}{t}\ln(1-t)\,dt.$$

Taking the lower limit of integration to be 0 ensures that $S(0) = 0$. Although you can't get any further by expressing the integral in terms of known functions, you do at least have a definite expression for $S(x)$. You could, for example, now use the integration program on your calculator to find the value of the sum for a particular numerical value of x.

See the note in Section 4.1 about the use of the letter t *rather than* x *inside the integral.*

But is the process valid? The answer is 'yes, but with reservations'. One point to notice is that the interval of convergence for the original series $S(x)$ is $-1 \le x \le 1$, but the interval of convergence for the $\ln(1-x)$ series is only $-1 \le x < 1$. So although the radius of convergence of both series is 1, there is a value of x on the boundary for which the original series converges but the differentiated series does not converge.

These features are true in general for power series.

> If a power series $\sum a_i x^i$ converges to $S(x)$ with radius of convergence R, then its differentiated series $\sum i a_i x^{i-1}$ converges to $S'(x)$ with the same radius of convergence. There may, however, be values of x such that $|x| = R$ for which the original series converges but the differentiated series does not converge.

This process is known as **term-by-term differentiation**.

Example 9.5.1

Write Maclaurin series, $M_2(x)$ and $M_3(x)$, for $(1+x)^{-2}$ and $(1+x)^{-3}$. Show that $M_3(x)$ could be obtained from $M_2(x)$ using term-by-term differentiation.

Using the series for $(1+x)^p$ in Section 9.3 with $p = -2$ and -3,

$$M_2(x) = 1 + \frac{(-2)}{1!}x + \frac{(-2)\times(-3)}{2!}x^2 + \dots + \frac{(-2)\times(-3)\times\dots\times(-i-1)}{i!}x^i + \dots$$
$$= 1 - 2x + 3x^2 - 4x^3 + \dots + (-1)^i(i+1)x^i + \dots ,$$

$$M_3(x) = 1 + \frac{(-3)}{1!}x + \frac{(-3)\times(-4)}{2!}x^2 + \dots + \frac{(-3)\times(-4)\times\dots\times(-i-2)}{i!}x^i + \dots$$
$$= 1 - 3x + 6x^2 - 10x^3 + \dots + (-1)^i\frac{(i+1)(i+2)}{2}x^i + \dots .$$

Term-by-term differentiation of $M_2(x)$ gives

$$\frac{d}{dx}M_2(x) = -2 + 6x - 12x^2 + \ldots + (-1)^i i(i+1)x^{i-1} + \ldots$$

$$= -2\left(1 - 3x + 6x^2 - \ldots + (-1)^{i-1}\frac{i(i+1)}{2}x^{i-1} + \ldots\right).$$

To compare the general terms, replace $i-1$ by i. Then this becomes

$$\frac{d}{dx}M_2(x) = -2\left(1 - 3x + 6x^2 - \ldots + (-1)^i\frac{(i+1)(i+2)}{2}x^i + \ldots\right)$$

$$= -2M_3(x).$$

This is what you would expect, since $\frac{d}{dx}(1+x)^{-2} = -2(1+x)^{-3}$.

But term-by-term differentiation does not work for all series. For example, it can be proved that the series

$$\sin x - \tfrac{1}{2}\sin 2x + \tfrac{1}{3}\sin 3x - \ldots$$

is convergent with sum $\tfrac{1}{2}x$ in the interval $-\pi < x < \pi$. But the series of differentiated terms,

$$\cos x - \cos 2x + \cos 3x - \ldots$$

is not convergent because $\lim_{i\to\infty}\cos ix$ is not equal to 0. So you should not think that the statement in the shaded box is obvious; it has to be proved, though the proof is too difficult to give here.

Example 9.5.2
Find the Maclaurin series for $\arctan x$.

Since $\int_0^x \frac{1}{1+t^2}\,dt = [\arctan t]_0^x = \arctan x - \arctan 0 = \arctan x$, you can find the series for $\arctan x$ by integrating the terms of the binomial series for $(1+t^2)^{-1} = 1 - t^2 + t^4 - t^6 + \ldots$ from 0 to x.

That is,

$$\arctan x = x - \tfrac{1}{3}x^3 + \tfrac{1}{5}x^5 - \tfrac{1}{7}x^7 + \ldots$$

$$= \sum_{i=0}^{\infty}(-1)^i\frac{1}{2i+1}x^{2i+1}.$$

When you integrate a power series term-by-term, the interval of validity of the result may include more values than the original series. In Example 9.5.2, the binomial series for $(1+x^2)^{-1}$ is valid for $-1 < x < 1$, but the $\arctan x$ series is also valid when $x = \pm 1$. The value $x = 1$ produces the delightful (but not very useful) result

$$\tfrac{1}{4}\pi = 1 - \tfrac{1}{3} + \tfrac{1}{5} - \tfrac{1}{7} + \ldots \ .$$

Example 9.5.3
Use term-by-term integration of a Maclaurin series to find the value of $\frac{1}{\sqrt{2\pi}}\int_{-1}^{1}e^{-\frac{1}{2}t^2}\,dt.$

This integral is important in probability. It gives the probability that a normal random variable takes a value within one standard deviation of the mean.

Using the Maclaurin series for e^x with $x = -\frac{1}{2}t^2$,

$$e^{-\frac{1}{2}t^2} = 1 - \frac{1}{1!}\frac{t^2}{2} + \frac{1}{2!}\left(\frac{t^2}{2}\right)^2 - \cdots .$$

So

$$\int_0^1 e^{-\frac{1}{2}t^2}\,dt = \left[t - \frac{1}{2}\frac{t^3}{3} + \frac{1}{8}\frac{t^5}{5} - \frac{1}{48}\frac{t^7}{7} + \frac{1}{384}\frac{t^9}{9} - \frac{1}{3840}\frac{t^{11}}{11} + \cdots\right]_0^1$$

$$= 1 - \frac{1}{6} + \frac{1}{40} - \frac{1}{336} + \frac{1}{3456} - \frac{1}{42240} + \cdots = 0.85562\ldots .$$

Since $e^{-\frac{1}{2}t^2}$ is an even function, the integral from -1 to 1 is double the integral from 0 to 1. The probability required is therefore

$$\frac{1}{\sqrt{2\pi}} \times 2 \times 0.85562\ldots \approx 0.683, \text{ correct to 3 decimal places.}$$

9.6 Using series to find limits

A useful application of Maclaurin series is to find limits as $x \to 0$ of expressions of the form $\dfrac{f(x)}{g(x)}$ where both $f(0)$ and $g(0)$ are equal to 0. Then both $f(x)$ and $g(x)$ have x (or a power of x) as a factor. This can be cancelled so as to replace the expression by a function whose value can be calculated at $x = 0$.

Example 9.6.1

Find   (a) $\displaystyle\lim_{x \to 0} \frac{\sqrt{1 + 2x} - \sqrt{1 + x}}{x}$,   (b) $\displaystyle\lim_{x \to 0} \frac{x(1 - \cos x)}{x - \sin x}$.

(a)   Using the Maclaurin series for $(1 + x)^p$ with $p = \frac{1}{2}$,

$$\sqrt{1 + x} = 1 + \tfrac{1}{2}x - \tfrac{1}{8}x^2 + \cdots .$$

Also, substituting $2x$ for x,

$$\sqrt{1 + 2x} = 1 + \tfrac{1}{2}(2x) - \tfrac{1}{8}(2x)^2 + \cdots$$

$$= 1 + x - \tfrac{1}{2}x^2 + \cdots .$$

So $\sqrt{1 + 2x} - \sqrt{1 + x} = \tfrac{1}{2}x - \tfrac{3}{8}x^2 + \cdots ,$

and $\dfrac{\sqrt{1 + 2x} - \sqrt{1 + x}}{x} = \tfrac{1}{2} - \tfrac{3}{8}x + \cdots .$

Therefore $\displaystyle\lim_{x \to 0} \frac{\sqrt{1 + 2x} - \sqrt{1 + x}}{x} = \lim_{x \to 0}\left(\tfrac{1}{2} - \tfrac{3}{8}x + \cdots\right) = \tfrac{1}{2}.$

(b)   Using the Maclaurin series for $\cos x$ and $\sin x$,

$$\lim_{x \to 0} \frac{x(1 - \cos x)}{x - \sin x} = \lim_{x \to 0} \frac{x\left(1 - \left(1 - \frac{1}{2}x^2 + \frac{1}{24}x^4 - \ldots\right)\right)}{x - \left(x - \frac{1}{6}x^3 + \frac{1}{120}x^5 - \ldots\right)}$$

$$= \lim_{x \to 0} \frac{\frac{1}{2}x^3 - \frac{1}{24}x^5 + \ldots}{\frac{1}{6}x^3 - \frac{1}{120}x^5 + \ldots}$$

$$= \lim_{x \to 0} \frac{\frac{1}{2} - \frac{1}{24}x^2 + \ldots}{\frac{1}{6} - \frac{1}{120}x^2 + \ldots}$$

$$= \frac{\frac{1}{2}}{\frac{1}{6}} = 3.$$

Exercise 9C

1   Each of the following expressions $f(x)$ can be written as $g(h(x))$, where g is one of the functions whose Maclaurin series is listed in Section 9.3. Expand $f(x)$ as far as the term in x^4 by two methods: (i) by finding $f^{(r)}(x)$ for $r = 1, 2, 3, 4$ and using the general formula for a Maclaurin series, and (ii) by substituting $h(x)$ in place of x in the series for $g(x)$. Verify that both methods give the same answer.

(a) $f(x) = (1 + 2x)^{\frac{3}{2}}$ (b) $f(x) = e^{-2x}$

(c) $f(x) = \ln\left(1 + x^3\right)$ (d) $f(x) = \sin x^3$

2   Write the Maclaurin series for the following, in each case giving the first three non-zero terms, an expression for the general term and the interval of validity.

(a) e^{3x} (b) $\cos \frac{1}{2}x$ (c) $\sqrt{x} \sin \sqrt{x}$ (d) $\ln(1 - x)$

(e) $\ln(1 + 2x)$ (f) e^{1+x} (g) $\cos^2 x$ (h) $\ln(e + x)$

(i) $\cos(1 + x)$

3   Find the Maclaurin series for the following functions as far as the term in x^4.

(a) $e^{-x} \sin x$ (b) $\sqrt{1 - x} \cos x$ (c) $\dfrac{e^x}{1 + x}$

(d) $(1 + x)^2 \ln(1 + x)$ (e) $e^{-2x} \ln(1 + 3x)$ (f) $\ln(1 - 2x) \sin 3x$

4   Find the Maclaurin polynomials of degree 4 for the following.

(a) $\cos(\sin x)$ (b) $\ln\left(1 + e^x\right)$

5   Use the property $\arcsin x = \displaystyle\int_0^x \frac{1}{\sqrt{1 - t^2}}\, dt$ to find the Maclaurin series for $\arcsin x$. Hence find the series for $\arccos x$. By taking $x = \frac{1}{2}$, use your Maclaurin series to find the value of π, correct to 4 decimal places.

6 A function called the *sine integral* is defined by $\mathrm{Si}\,(x) = \int_0^x \frac{\sin u}{u}\,du$. Find the Maclaurin series for $\mathrm{Si}\,(x)$, and use this to obtain the graph of $y = \mathrm{Si}\,(x)$ for $x > 0$.

7 Find the Maclaurin series for $\int_0^x \frac{e^t - 1}{t}\,dt$. Hence evaluate $\int_0^{\frac{1}{2}} \frac{e^t - 1}{t}\,dt$, correct to 3 decimal places.

8 Show that, if you assume that a function can be differentiated by differentiating each term of its Maclaurin series, you get correct results for

    (a) $\dfrac{d}{dx}e^x$,   (b) $\dfrac{d}{dx}\sin x$,   (c) $\dfrac{d}{dx}\ln(1 + x)$,   (d) $\dfrac{d}{dx}\sqrt{1 + x}$.

9 Use the standard Maclaurin series to find the first two non-zero terms in the series for $x\cos x - \sin x$. Hence find the limit, as $x \to 0$, of $\dfrac{x\cos x - \sin x}{x^3}$.

10 Find the limit, as $x \to 0$, of

    (a) $\dfrac{e^x - e^{-x}}{x}$,   (b) $\dfrac{1 - \cos x}{x^2}$,   (c) $\dfrac{\ln(1 + x)}{x}$,   (d) $\dfrac{\ln(1 + x) - x}{x^2}$.

11* The following construction is suggested to trisect a given angle θ. Make a triangle ABC with angle BAC equal to θ and angle ABC a right angle. Divide the side [BC] into three equal parts at X and Y, so that $\mathrm{BX} = \mathrm{XY} = \mathrm{YC}$. Then angle XAY is approximately $\frac{1}{3}\theta$.

Prove that angle XAY is exactly $\arctan\!\left(\frac{2}{3}\tan\theta\right) - \arctan\!\left(\frac{1}{3}\tan\theta\right)$. Find the Maclaurin polynomial of degree 3 for this function, and use this to estimate the greatest value of θ for which the construction is accurate to within 5%.

12 A power series $S(x) = \displaystyle\sum_{i=0}^{\infty} a_i x^i$ has radius of convergence $R = \lim_{i \to \infty}\left|\dfrac{a_{i-1}}{a_i}\right|$. Prove that the derivative series $S'(x) = \displaystyle\sum_{i=1}^{\infty} i a_i x^{i-1}$ also has radius of convergence R.

10 The error term

This chapter gives two formulae for the truncation error when a Maclaurin polynomial is used to find an approximation to the value of a function. When you have completed it, you should

- be familiar with the integral and the Lagrange expressions for the error term
- understand how the error term can be used to determine the interval of validity of a Maclaurin series.

10.1 Approximation by a Maclaurin polynomial

In Chapter 9 you used Maclaurin polynomials to find approximations to the values of functions such as e^x and $\sin x$. But an approximation is not much use unless you have some idea of the size of the error, which is defined by the equation

error = exact value – approximate value.

You can't of course find the error exactly, because if you did you would know the exact value of the function, and there would be no point in calculating the approximation. So what is wanted is a statement like 'if you use the nth Maclaurin polynomial as an approximation to $f(x)$ for a particular value of x, the error is not greater than such-and-such'.

So you have a function $f(x)$ represented by a Maclaurin series

$$f(x) = \sum_{i=0}^{\infty} \frac{f^{(i)}(0)}{i!} x^i,$$

and you approximate to it by the nth Maclaurin polynomial, or partial sum,

$$p_n(x) = \sum_{i=0}^{n} \frac{f^{(i)}(0)}{i!} x^i.$$

These differ by an amount called the **error term**, or the **remainder**, denoted by $R_n(x)$, so that

$$f(x) = p_n(x) + R_n(x).$$

The problem is to find an expression for $R_n(x)$ in terms of the function f and the numbers x and n.

Up to now, when working with power series, you have treated x as a variable, but in this chapter it is helpful to think of x as a fixed number, and to introduce a new variable t. The function $y = f(t)$ will then be considered in the interval $0 \le t \le x$. Fig. 10.1 shows its graph passing through the points with coordinates $(0, f(0))$ and $(x, f(x))$.

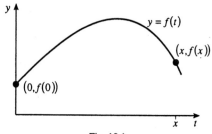

Fig. 10.1

It will be assumed that the function $f(t)$ is a 'well-behaved' function with no discontinuities in the interval $[0, x]$, for which it is possible to find as many higher derivatives $f^{(i)}(t)$ as you need.

The figure is drawn with $x > 0$, but the theory in this chapter also applies when $x < 0$.

10.2 The integral form

Begin with the very simplest case, with $n = 0$, so that $p_0(x)$ is just the constant term $f(0)$, and

$$f(x) = p_0(x) + R_0(x) = f(0) + R_0(x).$$

So $R_0(x) = f(x) - f(0).$

One way of writing the right side is as $[f(t)]_0^x$, which is the value of the definite integral $\displaystyle\int_0^x f'(t)\,dt$. You are going to find successive values of the error term $R_n(x)$ using integration by parts.

This may seem an odd suggestion, since the integrand $f'(t)$ is not the product of two functions. But you met a similar situation in Higher Level Book 2 Section 22.1, where $\displaystyle\int \ln x\,dx$ was found by writing the integrand $\ln x$ as $\ln x \times 1$. In just the same way you could write

$$R_0(x) = \int_0^x f'(t) \times 1\,dt,$$

and use integration by parts with $u = f'(t)$ and taking for v a function such that $\dfrac{dv}{dt} = 1$.

You now come to the ingenious part of the argument, which is to choose for v not the obvious function $v = t$, but to take $v = -(x - t)$. (Remember that x is being treated as a constant.) Then

$$R_0(x) = [f'(t) \times (-(x - t))]_0^x - \int_0^x f''(t) \times (-(x - t))\,dt$$

$$= f'(x) \times (-0) - f'(0) \times (-x) - \int_0^x -f''(t) \times (x - t)\,dt$$

$$= f'(0)x + \int_0^x f''(t) \times (x - t)\,dt.$$

Now recall that $R_0(x)$ is equal to $f(x) - f(0)$, so this equation can be written as

$$f(x) = \{f(0) + f'(0)x\} + \int_0^x f''(t) \times (x - t)\,dt.$$

You will recognise the expression in the curly brackets – it is just the Maclaurin polynomial $p_1(x)$. And since by definition $f(x) = p_1(x) + R_1(x)$, the integral on the right side must be the error term $R_1(x)$.

This looks promising, so try repeating the process with $R_1(x)$ rather than $R_0(x)$. If you integrate by parts again, with $u = f''(t)$ and $v = -\frac{1}{2}(x - t)^2$, so that $\dfrac{dv}{dt} = x - t$, you get

$$R_1(x) = \left[f''(t) \times \left(-\tfrac{1}{2}(x - t)^2\right)\right]_0^x - \int_0^x f'''(t) \times \left(-\tfrac{1}{2}(x - t)^2\right)dt$$

$$= \frac{f''(0)}{2}x^2 + \int_0^x \frac{f'''(t)}{2} \times (x - t)^2\,dt.$$

That is,

$$f(x) = \left\{ f(0) + f'(0)x + \frac{f''(0)}{2}x^2 \right\} + \int_0^x \frac{f'''(t)}{2} \times (x-t)^2 \, dt.$$

The expression in curly brackets is now the Maclaurin polynomial $p_2(x)$, so the integral is the error term $R_2(x)$.

If you go on like this you can reach a similar equation for any value of n.

> The function $f(x)$ can be expressed as the sum of the nth Maclaurin polynomial
>
> $$p_n(x) = f(0) + f'(0)x + \frac{f''(0)}{2!}x^2 + \ldots + \frac{f^{(n)}(0)}{n!}x^n$$
>
> and an error term
>
> $$R_n(x) = \int_0^x \frac{f^{(n+1)}(t)}{n!} \times (x-t)^n \, dt.$$

The way in which this was obtained by going from $n = 0$ to $n = 1$, and then from $n = 1$ to $n = 2$, suggests that the general result could be proved by mathematical induction. You would begin by assuming the expression for $p_n(x)$ and R_n with $n = k$, and then use integration by parts to show that

$$\int_0^x \frac{f^{(k+1)}(t)}{k!} \times (x-t)^k \, dt = \frac{f^{(k+1)}(0)}{(k+1)!}x^{k+1} + \int_0^x \frac{f^{(k+2)}(t)}{(k+1)!} \times (x-t)^{k+1} \, dt.$$

On the right the first term is the final term of $p_n(x)$ with $n = k+1$ and the integral is R_{k+1}. The details are left for you to verify.

10.3 The Lagrange form

There are drawbacks in using the integral form of the error term. For one thing, although the expression is exact its use is limited, since the integral can't be evaluated. It is not even obvious that its value is small, or that $p_n(x)$ is an increasingly good approximation to $f(x)$.

The form for the error term described in this section, known as Lagrange's form, is based directly on the idea of polynomial approximation. The idea is to try to find the polynomial of a given degree which agrees with $y = f(t)$ to the highest possible degree at $t = 0$ but whose graph also passes through the point $(x, f(x))$.

The proof depends on an idea which is very easy to understand (though not to prove!), illustrated in Fig. 10.2. This is that, if you have a function $\phi(t)$ for which $\phi(a)$ and $\phi(b)$ are both 0, then somewhere in the interval $a < x < b$ there is a number c for which $\phi'(c) = 0$. (There may of course be more than one such number.) This is known as Rolle's theorem.

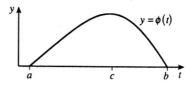

Fig. 10.2

Michel Rolle was a French mathematician at the end of the 17th century. His theorem appeared in a book on solving polynomial equations. Joseph-Louis Lagrange was probably the greatest French mathematician of the 18th century.

Turn back to Fig. 10.1 in Section 10.1. The simplest polynomial which approximates to $y = f(t)$ at $t = 0$ and also passes through $(x, f(x))$ is a linear polynomial $q_0(t) = a_0 + a_1 t$. There are two coefficients available, which can be chosen from two equations; you can make $q_0(0) = f(0)$ and $q_0(x) = f(x)$. So

$$f(0) = a_0 \quad \text{and} \quad f(x) = a_0 + a_1 x.$$

Fig. 10.3 shows the graphs of $y = f(t)$ and $y = q_0(t)$. The amount by which the first graph exceeds the second is denoted by $g_0(t)$. That is, $g_0(t) = f(t) - q_0(t)$.

The graph of $y = g_0(t)$ is shown in Fig. 10.4. You will see that it is similar to Fig. 10.2, with $g_0(t)$ in place of $\phi(t)$. Since $g_0(0) = 0$ and $g_0(x) = 0$, there is a number c_1 between 0 and x at which $g_0'(c_1) = 0$. That is,

$$f'(c_1) = q_0'(c_1) = a_1.$$

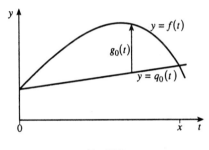

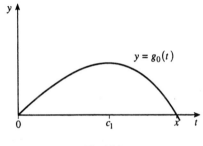

Fig. 10.3   Fig. 10.4

Now combine this with the two equations for a_0 and a_1 above. Substituting $a_0 = f(0)$ and $a_1 = f'(c_1)$ in the equation $f(x) = a_0 + a_1 x$,

$$f(x) = f(0) + f'(c_1)x.$$

You may just recognise a slight resemblance to the Maclaurin series. You can get closer to it by taking a quadratic polynomial $q_1(t) = a_0 + a_1 t + a_2 t^2$ in place of $q_0(t)$.

You now have another coefficient at your disposal, so you can make the polynomial $q_1(t)$ satisfy another condition. To make it agree better with $y = f(t)$ at $t = 0$, you can choose the coefficients so that, as well as $q_1(0) = f(0)$ and $q_1(x) = f(x)$, the derivatives at 0 are equal, that is $q_1'(0) = f'(0)$. This is illustrated in Fig. 10.5.

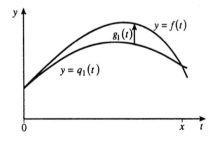

Fig. 10.5

You now have three equations for the coefficients of $q_1(t)$:

$$f(0) = a_0, \quad f'(0) = a_1 \quad \text{and} \quad f(x) = a_0 + a_1 x + a_2 x^2.$$

As before, define a function to represent the amount by which $f(t)$ exceeds $q_1(t)$, writing $g_1(t) = f(t) - q_1(t)$. Its graph is shown in Fig. 10.6. You will notice that it has the same two properties as $g_0(t)$, that $g_0(0) = 0$ and $g_0(x) = 0$. But, because $q_1'(0) = f'(0)$, it also has the additional property that $g_1'(0) = 0$.

This makes it possible to use Rolle's theorem twice. First, as before taking $\phi(t)$ to be $g_1(t)$, there is a number c_1 between 0 and x at which $g_1'(c_1) = 0$. (This isn't of course the same c_1 as before; compare Fig. 10.6 with Fig. 10.4.)

Then, since both $g_1'(0)$ and $g_1'(c_1) = 0$, you can use Rolle's theorem a second time taking $\phi(t)$ to be $g_1'(t)$. The conclusion is that there is a number c_2 between 0 and c_1 (and therefore between 0 and x) at which $g_1''(c_2) = 0$. That is,

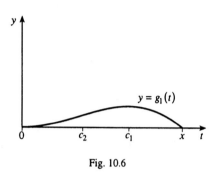

Fig. 10.6

$$f''(c_2) = q_1''(c_2) = 2a_2.$$

Now combine this with the three equations for a_0, a_1 and a_2 above. Substituting $a_0 = f(0)$, $a_1 = f'(0)$ and $a_2 = \frac{1}{2} f''(c_2)$ in the equation for $f(x)$, you get

$$f(x) = f(0) + f'(0)x + \tfrac{1}{2} f''(c_2)x^2.$$

Now it is easy to see Maclaurin's series emerging. The first two terms on the right make up the Maclaurin polynomial $p_1(x)$, and the last term is the error term $R_1(x)$.

This is a special case with $n = 1$ of a general result.

> The function $f(x)$ can be expressed as the sum of the nth Maclaurin polynomial
>
> $$p_n(x) = f(0) + f'(0)x + \frac{f''(0)}{2!} x^2 + \ldots + \frac{f^{(n)}(0)}{n!} x^n$$
>
> and an error term
>
> $$R_n(x) = \frac{f^{(n+1)}(c)}{(n+1)!} x^{n+1}, \quad \text{where } c \text{ is a number between 0 and } x.$$
>
> This form of the error term is known as Lagrange's form.

To prove this, you would define a polynomial function $q_n(t) = a_0 + a_1t + \ldots + a_{n+1}t^{n+1}$ which agrees with $f(t)$ to the nth degree at 0 and such that $q_n(x) = f(x)$. Then $g_n(t) = f(t) - q_n(t)$ would have $g_n(0) = g_n'(0) = g_n''(0) = \ldots = g_n^{(n)}(0) = 0$ and also $g_n(x) = 0$. Then apply Rolle's theorem $n + 1$ times and find a sequence of numbers $c_1, c_2, \ldots, c_{n+1}$ at which $g_n'(c_1) = 0, g_n''(c_2) = 0, g_n^{(n+1)}(c_{n+1}) = 0$, and this last equation would be shown to be $f^{(n+1)}(c_{n+1}) = (n+1)!a_{n+1}$. All of this is a direct extension of the proof given above with $n = 1$; the algebra looks more complicated, but the ideas are just the same. (In the shaded box the suffix has been dropped from c_{n+1}; it is useful in the proof to make the notation consistent, but there is no point in keeping it when you apply the result.)

Example 10.3.1

Give the error term if the nth Maclaurin polynomial is used as an approximation for $f(x) = e^x$ for $x > 0$,
(a) in the integral form,   (b) in the Lagrange form.
Use this to find an upper bound for the relative error in using the 4th Maclaurin polynomial to estimate
the value of $e^{0.2}$.

Since $f'(x) = e^x$, it follows that $f^{(i)}(x) = e^x$ for all $i \in \mathbb{Z}^+$. So the error term $R_n(x)$ can be written
as

(a) $\displaystyle \int_0^x \frac{e^t}{n!}(x-t)^n \, dt$,   or as   (b) $\displaystyle \frac{e^c}{(n+1)!} x^{n+1}$, where $0 < c < x$.

You might think that you could find the integral in part (a) by integrating by parts, but if you try
you will just get back to the equation $e^x = e^x$!

To use the formula to estimate an error you need to find an inequality for $R_n(x)$. For $0 < t < x$,
$(x - t)^n$ is positive and $e^t < e^x$, so

$$0 < e^t (x-t)^n < e^x (x-t)^n .$$

Therefore

$$0 < R_n(x) < \int_0^x \frac{e^x}{n!}(x-t)^n \, dt$$

$$= \frac{e^x}{n!} \times \int_0^x (x-t)^n \, dt$$

$$= \frac{e^x}{n!} \times \left[-\frac{1}{n+1}(x-t)^{n+1} \right]_0^x$$

$$= \frac{e^x}{(n+1)!} x^{n+1} .$$

You get just the same inequality if you use the Lagrange formula. The only thing you know about
the number c is that it is between 0 and x, so that $e^c < e^x$ since $x > 0$. This again gives the
inequality

$$0 < R_n(x) < \frac{e^x}{(n+1)!} x^{n+1} .$$

With $x = 0.2$ and $n = 4$,

$$0 < R_4(0.2) < \frac{e^{0.2}}{5!} \times 0.2^5$$

$$= e^{0.2} \times 2.67 \times 10^{-6} .$$

You might think that this is not much use, since the purpose of using the Maclaurin polynomial in
the first place is to calculate the value of $e^{0.2}$. But what it does do is to give an upper bound for the
relative error, that is the error as a proportion of the exact value. The equation shows that the
relative error is less than 2.67×10^{-6}. (This is often given as a percentage, as $2.67 \times 10^{-4}\%$, or
about 0.0003%.)

10.4   The interval of validity of Maclaurin series

The sum of an infinite series is defined as the limit of the sum of the first n terms (or the first $n+1$, if $i = 0$ is included). That is, the difference between the sum of the infinite series and the finite sum is always smaller than any positive number ε when n is greater than some number m.

So when you say that $f(x)$ is the sum of an infinite Maclaurin series for a certain value of x, and write

$$f(x) = p_n(x) + R_n(x),$$

you are in effect stating that the limit as $n \to \infty$ of the error term $R_n(x)$ is 0.

Now that you have expressions for $R_n(x)$ you can use these to find the values of x for which the Maclaurin series is valid (the interval of validity). The examples in this section demonstrate the method for the two functions in Section 9.3 illustrated by the graphs in Fig. 9.5 and Fig. 9.4 respectively.

Example 10.4.1
Prove that the Maclaurin series for $\sin x$ is valid for all values of x.

If $f(x) = \sin x$, the derivatives are successively $\cos x, -\sin x, -\cos x, \sin x,\dots$. So for any value of r and any value of x you can be certain that $\left| f^{(r)}(x) \right| \le 1$.

The Lagrange formula for the error term is $R_n(x) = \dfrac{f^{(n+1)}(c)}{(n+1)!} x^{n+1}$. For any particular values of x and n you don't know the value of c, but you do know that $\left| f^{(n+1)}(c) \right| \le 1$, and therefore that

$$\left| R_n(x) \right| \le \frac{\left| x^{n+1} \right|}{(n+1)!} = \frac{\left| x \right|^{n+1}}{(n+1)!}.$$

If you can prove that this tends to 0 for all x, then it will follow that the Maclaurin series is valid for all x.

Before giving a general proof of this, it may help to consider a numerical example, such as $x = \pi$. Then you could write

$$\frac{\pi^{n+1}}{(n+1)!} \quad \text{as} \quad \frac{\pi \times \pi \times \pi \times \dots \times \pi}{1 \times 2 \times 3 \times \dots \times (n+1)} = \left(\frac{\pi \times \pi \times \pi}{1 \times 2 \times 3} \right) \times \left(\frac{\pi}{4} \times \frac{\pi}{5} \times \dots \times \frac{\pi}{n+1} \right).$$

The first bracket is the same whatever value you take for n, and all the $(n-2)$ factors in the second bracket except the first are less than $\dfrac{\pi}{4}$. So

$$\frac{\pi^{n+1}}{(n+1)!} < \frac{\pi^3}{3!} \times \left(\frac{\pi}{4} \right)^{n-2} = \frac{\pi^3}{3!} \div \left(\frac{\pi}{4} \right)^2 \times \left(\frac{\pi}{4} \right)^n,$$

which has the form, constant $\times a^n$, where $0 < a < 1$.

Then, for the general proof, you can do the same with any value of $|x|$. If K is the positive integer such that $K - 1 \le |x| < K$, you can write

$$\frac{|x|^{n+1}}{(n+1)!} \quad \text{as} \quad \left(\frac{|x|\times|x|\times|x|\times\ldots\times|x|}{1\times 2\times\ldots\times(K-1)}\right)\times\left(\frac{|x|}{K}\times\frac{|x|}{K+1}\times\ldots\times\frac{|x|}{n+1}\right),$$

so

$$\frac{|x|^{n+1}}{(n+1)!} < \frac{|x|^{K-1}}{(K-1)!}\times\left(\frac{|x|}{K}\right)^{n-K+2} = \frac{|x|^{K-1}}{(K-1)!}\div\left(\frac{|x|}{K}\right)^{K-2}\times\left(\frac{|x|}{K}\right)^{n},$$

which again has the form, constant $\times a^n$, where $0 < a < 1$. And since $\lim\limits_{n\to\infty} a^n = 0$ when $0 < a < 1$,

it follows that $\lim\limits_{n\to\infty}\dfrac{|x|^{n+1}}{(n+1)!} = 0$, so that $\lim\limits_{n\to\infty} R_n(x) = 0$.

That is, the Maclaurin series for $\sin x$ is valid for all values of x.

Example 10.4.2
Prove that the Maclaurin series for $\ln(1+x)$ is valid   (a) for $0 < x \le 1$,   (b) for $-1 < x < 0$.

(a)   If $f(x) = \ln(1+x)$, then

$$f'(x) = \frac{1}{1+x}, \quad f''(x) = \frac{-1}{(1+x)^2}, \quad f'''(x) = \frac{2}{(1+x)^3}, \quad \ldots \quad, f^{(n+1)}(x) = \frac{(-1)^n \times n!}{(1+x)^{n+1}}.$$

So, in Lagrange's form,

$$R_n(x) = \frac{(-1)^n \times n!}{(1+c)^{n+1}\times(n+1)!}\times x^{n+1} = (-1)^n\times\frac{x^{n+1}}{(1+c)^{n+1}\times(n+1)}.$$

You want to prove that $\lim\limits_{n\to\infty}\big|R_n(x)\big| = 0$ when $0 < x \le 1$.

Look first at the factor $(1+c)^{n+1}$. All that you know about the number c is that it is between 0 and x. Since $x > 0$, this means that $c > 0$, so that $1 + c > 1$.

Therefore $(1+c)^{n+1} > 1$ and, since $x \le 1$, $\big|x^{n+1}\big| \le 1$, so

$$|R_n(x)| < \frac{1}{n+1}.$$

And since $\lim\limits_{n\to\infty}\dfrac{1}{n+1} = 0$, it follows that $\lim\limits_{n\to\infty} R_n(x) = 0$. That is, the Maclaurin series for $\ln(1+x)$ is valid for $0 < x \le 1$.

(b)   The proof in part (a) cannot be used if x is negative, since then c is negative, so that $1 + c$ is not greater than 1.

It is easier to work with positive rather than negative numbers, so substitute $-x$ for x and consider the Maclaurin series for $f(x) = -\ln(1-x)$, which is

$$f(x) = x + \tfrac{1}{2}x^2 + \tfrac{1}{3}x^3 + \ldots, \quad \text{where } 0 < x < 1.$$

For this function,

$$f'(x) = \frac{1}{1-x}, \quad f''(x) = \frac{1}{(1-x)^2}, \quad f'''(x) = \frac{2}{(1-x)^3}, \quad \ldots, \quad f^{(n+1)}(x) = \frac{n!}{(1-x)^{n+1}}.$$

It is simpler to use the integral form for $R_n(x)$, which is

$$R_n(x) = \int_0^x \frac{n!}{(1-t)^{n+1} \times n!}(x-t)^n \, dt$$

$$= \int_0^x \frac{(x-t)^n}{(1-t)^{n+1}} \, dt$$

$$= \int_0^x \left(\frac{x-t}{1-t}\right)^n \times \frac{1}{1-t} \, dt.$$

Notice that, in the interval $0 < t < x$, $x - t > 0$ and $1 - t > 1 - x > 0$, so the integrand is positive. Therefore $R_n(x) > 0$.

To find an upper bound for $R_n(x)$, consider the function $g(t) = \frac{x-t}{1-t}$ whose graph is shown in Fig. 10.7. The important things to notice are that $g(0) = x$, $g(x) = 0$ and that the function is decreasing in the interval $0 < t < x$. Therefore, in this interval,

$$0 < \frac{x-t}{1-t} < x,$$

so the integrand is less than $x^n \times \frac{1}{1-t}$.

Therefore

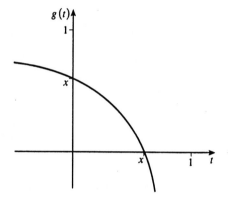

Fig. 10.7

$$0 < R_n(x) < \int_0^x x^n \times \frac{1}{1-t} \, dt$$

$$= x^n \times [-\ln(1-t)]_0^x$$

$$= -x^n \ln(1-x).$$

This is all you need. Since $0 < x < 1$, $\lim_{n \to \infty} x^n = 0$, and $-\ln(1-x)$ is a positive constant. So $\lim_{n \to \infty} R_n(x) = 0$, which means that the Maclaurin series is valid.

10.5   Other ways of finding errors

The advantage of the formulae for the error terms in Sections 10.2 and 10.3 is that they can be used with any function $f(x)$. But they are not the only way to find truncation errors. For some functions simpler methods are available.

Suppose, for example, that a power series has alternately positive and negative signs for some values of x, and that the terms are decreasing in absolute value. Then you can use the property of alternating series in Section 6.1, that the size of the error in taking the sum to n terms as an approximation to the sum to infinity is less than the absolute value of the next term.

Example 10.5.1

How many terms of the Maclaurin series for $\cos x$ would you need to take to find the value of $\cos 6$ with an error less than 10^{-4} in absolute value, using   (a) $x = 6$,   (b) $x = 2\pi - 6$?

(a)   With $x = 6$ the first few terms of the series increase in absolute value:

$$1 - \frac{6^2}{2!} + \frac{6^4}{4!} - \frac{6^6}{6!} + \ldots = 1 - 18 + 54 - 64.8 + \ldots \ .$$

But beyond the term $-\dfrac{6^6}{6!}$ they begin to decrease. And since $\dfrac{|x|^n}{n!}$ tends to 0 for any x (which was proved in Example 10.4.1) the alternating series property can then be used to find an upper bound for the error.

The nth term of the Maclaurin series for $\cos x$ is $(-1)^{n-1} \dfrac{x^{2n-2}}{(2n-2)!}$. So the error in using the first n terms as an approximation to $\cos x$ is less in magnitude than the $(n+1)$th term, which has absolute value $\dfrac{x^{2n}}{(2n)!}$. With $x = 6$, you want the smallest value of n for which $\dfrac{6^{2n}}{(2n)!} < 10^{-4}$, that is

$$(2n)! > 10\,000 \times 6^{2n}.$$

You can't solve this inequality algebraically, so n must be found by numerical experiment:

n	10	11	12
$(2n)!$	$2.43\ldots \times 10^{18}$	$1.12\ldots \times 10^{21}$	$6.20\ldots \times 10^{23}$
$10\,000 \times 6^{2n}$	$3.65\ldots \times 10^{19}$	$1.31\ldots \times 10^{21}$	$4.73\ldots \times 10^{22}$

You must take 12 terms of the series to be sure of finding $\cos 6$ with an error less than 10^{-4}.

(b)   With $x = 2\pi - 6 = 0.283\ldots$ the terms decrease in absolute value from the start. So you want the smallest value of n for which

$$(2n)! > 10\,000 \times (2\pi - 6)^{2n}.$$

By numerical experiment the smallest value of n is 3. You must take 3 terms of the series to be sure of finding $\cos 6$ with an error less than 10^{-4}.

Notice how much work can be saved by calculating $\cos 6$ *with* $x = 2\pi - 6$ *rather than* $x = 6$.

Another method that can sometimes be used is to integrate or differentiate a series for which an exact form for the error is known. For example, from the formula for the sum of a finite geometric series,

$$1 + x + x^2 + \ldots + x^{n-1} = \frac{1 - x^n}{1 - x},$$

you can deduce

$$\frac{1}{1 - x} = 1 + x + x^2 + \ldots + x^{n-1} + \frac{x^n}{1 - x}.$$

So if $f(x) = (1 - x)^{-1}$, the $(n-1)$th Maclaurin polynomial is $p_{n-1}(x) = 1 + x + x^2 + \ldots + x^{n-1}$, and the error term is $R_{n-1}(x) = f(x) - p_{n-1}(x) = \frac{x^n}{1 - x}.$

Example 10.5.2
Find bounds for the error term in the Maclaurin series for $-\ln(1 - x)$, where $0 < x < 1$.

Since $\int_0^x \frac{1}{1 - u} \, du = [-\ln(1 - u)]_0^x = -\ln(1 - x),$

$$-\ln(1 - x) = \int_0^x \left(1 + u + u^2 + \ldots + u^{n-1} + \frac{u^n}{1 - u} \right) du$$

$$= \left(x + \frac{1}{2} x^2 + \frac{1}{3} x^3 + \ldots + \frac{1}{n} x^n \right) + \int_0^x \frac{u^n}{1 - u} \, du.$$

The series in brackets is the Maclaurin polynomial $p_n(x)$ for $-\ln(1 - x)$, so the integral is the error term $R_n(x)$. You will notice that it is much simpler than the error term $\int_0^x \left(\frac{x - t}{1 - t} \right)^n \times \frac{1}{1 - t} \, dt$ found in Example 10.4.2(b).

To find bounds for the error term, note that if $0 < u < x$, then $1 > 1 - u > 1 - x$, so that $1 < \frac{1}{1 - u} < \frac{1}{1 - x}$ (since $x < 1$). Therefore

$$\int_0^x u^n \, du < \int_0^x \frac{u^n}{1 - u} \, du < \int_0^x \frac{u^n}{1 - x} \, du.$$

This gives both a lower and an upper bound for the error. A lower bound is

$$\int_0^x u^n \, du = \frac{1}{n + 1} x^{n+1}$$

and an upper bound is

$$\frac{1}{1 - x} \int_0^x u^n \, du.$$

Therefore the bounds for the error term are given by

$$\frac{1}{n+1}x^{n+1} < R_n(x) < \frac{1}{n+1} \times \frac{x^{n+1}}{1-x}.$$

Exercise 10

1   The Maclaurin polynomial of degree 4 is used to estimate the value of e^x for $x = -0.2$.

   (a) Find the value of $p_4(-0.2)$.

   (b) Use a calculator to find the error $R_4(-0.2)$.

   (c) Use the Lagrange form for $R_n(x)$ to write an expression for the error, and give an upper bound for its magnitude.

   (d) Use the alternating series property to find an upper bound for the magnitude of the error.

2   The Maclaurin polynomial of degree 5 is used to estimate the value of $\sin x$ for $x = 0.5$.

   (a) Find the value of $p_5(0.5)$.

   (b) Use a calculator to find the error $R_5(0.5)$.

   (c) Use the Lagrange form for $R_n(x)$ to write an expression for the error, and give an upper bound for its magnitude.

   (d) Use the alternating series property to find an upper bound for the magnitude of the error.

   (e) Compare your answers to parts (c) and (d) and comment on the difference.

3   Use the analysis in Examples 10.4.2 and 10.5.2 to find

   (a) an upper bound for the magnitude of the error when the Maclaurin polynomial of degree 5 is used to calculate $\ln 1.2$;

   (b) an upper bound for the value of the relative error when the Maclaurin polynomial of degree 5 is used to calculate $\ln 0.8$;

   (c) lower and upper bounds for the magnitude of the error when the Maclaurin polynomial of degree 5 is used to calculate $\ln 0.8$.

4   In Chapter 9, Fig. 9.5 and Fig. 9.4 respectively compare graphs of

   (a) $y = \sin x$,

   (b) $y = \ln(1 + x)$

   with the corresponding Maclaurin polynomial approximations of degree 10. Use upper bounds for the remainders in Example 10.4.1 and Example 10.4.2 to find intervals of values of x within which you can be sure that the error in the approximation is less than 0.001 in absolute value.

5   How many terms of the Maclaurin series should you take to be sure of finding the value of e^x with an error of less than 0.0001 in absolute value

   (a) when $x = 2.5$,

   (b) when $x = -2.5$?

6 (a) Find an expression for the coefficient of x^i (where $i \geq 2$) in the Maclaurin series for $\sqrt{1-x}$.

   (b) Find the Lagrange form for the error $R_n(x)$ if the Maclaurin polynomial $p_n(x)$ of degree n is used as an approximation for $\sqrt{1-x}$.

   (c) Prove that, if $0 < x < 1$, then $|R_n(x)| < A_n(x)$, where $A_1(x) = \frac{1}{8}\dfrac{x^2}{(1-x)^{\frac{3}{2}}}$ and

$$A_n(x) = \frac{2n-1}{2n+2} \times \frac{x}{1-x} A_{n-1}(x).$$

   (d) Find the smallest value of n for which you can be sure that the difference between $\sqrt{0.8}$ and $p_n(0.2)$ is less than 10^{-5}.

   (e) For the value of n you found in part (d) calculate the actual difference between $\sqrt{0.8}$ and $p_n(0.2)$.

7 (a) For the binomial series $(1+x)^{-3}$ use the Lagrange form of the remainder to find an upper bound for the magnitude of the error term. Hence prove that the series is valid for $0 < x < 1$.

   (b) For the binomial series $(1-x)^{-3}$ use the integral form of the remainder to find an upper bound for the error term. Hence prove that the series is valid for $0 < x < 1$.

8 By finding the second derivative of the expression for $(1-x)^{-1}$ as the sum of a polynomial of degree $n+2$ and a remainder term, obtain an expression for $(1-x)^{-3}$ in the form $p_n(x) + R_n(x)$. By using the result in Exercise 2C Question 1, deduce that the infinite binomial series for $(1-x)^{-3}$ is valid for $-1 < x < 1$.

9 For the function $-\ln(1-x)$, show that the form of the error term given in Example 10.4.2(b) can be found from the form given in Example 10.5.2 by substituting $u = \dfrac{x-t}{1-t}$.

10 What difficulty arises if you try to use the Maclaurin formula to find a series for $\arctan x$?

In Example 9.5.2 a series for $\arctan x$ was found by integrating the series for $\dfrac{1}{1+x^2}$. Prove that the difference between $\arctan x$ and the first n non-zero terms of its Maclaurin series has absolute value $\displaystyle\int_0^{|x|} \frac{t^{2n}}{1+t^2}\,dt$, and show that this is less than $\dfrac{|x|^{2n+1}}{2n+1}$.

Use this to estimate the smallest number of terms of the $\arctan x$ series that you might need to use to compute $\arctan 0.2$ with an error less than 10^{-10} in absolute magnitude.

11 Taylor series and l'Hôpital's rule

Maclaurin series can be modified to give approximations to a function around a general value of x. When you have completed this chapter, you should

- be able to find infinite series, polynomial approximations and error terms centred on a value of x other than 0
- understand how these approximations can be adapted to obtain a rule for finding limits.

11.1 Taylor series

An important use of Maclaurin series is to find approximations to values of a function in the neighbourhood of $x = 0$, when $|x|$ is small. Sometimes you want a similar approximation in the neighbourhood of some other value $x = a$, when $|x - a|$ is small.

Fig. 11.1 shows a graph $y = f(x)$ passing through a point $(a, f(a))$. The aim is to find a polynomial of degree n whose graph fits that of $y = f(x)$ as closely as possible around $x = a$. The figure shows another point on the curve close to $(a, f(a))$ with x-coordinate j and y-coordinate k, so that $k = f(j)$.

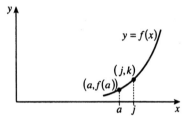

Fig. 11.1

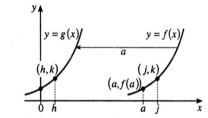

Fig. 11.2

In Fig. 11.2 the graph $y = f(x)$ has been translated by an amount a in the negative x-direction to produce another graph $y = g(x)$. The point (j, k) is then translated to (h, k), where $h = j - a$.

The two curves are identical in shape, so all the derivatives of $g(x)$ at $x = 0$ are equal to the corresponding derivatives of $f(x)$ at $x = a$.

Now you can find k in terms of h by a Maclaurin series, as

$$k = g(0) + \frac{g'(0)}{1!}h + \frac{g''(0)}{2!}h^2 + \dots .$$

Substituting $g(0) = f(a)$, $g'(0) = f'(a)$, $g''(0) = f''(a)$, ... and $h = j - a$, this becomes

$$k = f(a) + \frac{f'(a)}{1!}(j - a) + \frac{f''(a)}{2!}(j - a)^2 + \dots .$$

This last equation contains only quantities which appear in Fig. 11.1. And as j is the x-coordinate of any point on the curve around $(a, f(a))$, and $k = f(j)$, you can now change j to x and k to $f(x)$ and write

$$f(x) = f(a) + \frac{f'(a)}{1!}(x-a) + \frac{f''(a)}{2!}(x-a)^2 + \ldots = \sum_{i=0}^{\infty} \frac{f^{(i)}(a)}{i!}(x-a)^i.$$

This is known as a **Taylor series**.

Like Maclaurin, Brook Taylor belonged to the generation of mathematicians following Isaac Newton; but in fact the series attributed to them were known by an earlier Scottish mathematician, James Gregory.

Everything in the last three chapters about power series, Maclaurin series, Maclaurin polynomials and the error term can be generalised in this way. For example, if a power series $\sum c_i x^i$ is convergent for $|x| < R$, the power series $\sum c_i (x-a)^i$ is convergent for $|x-a| < R$, that is for $a - R < x < a + R$. The integral form for the error term has $\int_a^x$ in place of $\int_0^x$, and in the Lagrange form x^{n+1} is replaced by $(x-a)^{n+1}$ and c lies between a and x rather than between 0 and x. This is summarised below.

A function $f(x)$ can be expressed as a **Taylor series**

$$f(x) = \sum_{i=0}^{\infty} \frac{f^{(i)}(a)}{i!}(x-a)^i$$

within an interval of validity, or as the sum of a Taylor polynomial

$$f(x) = \sum_{i=0}^{n} \frac{f^{(i)}(a)}{i!}(x-a)^i$$

and an error term

$$R_n(x) = \int_a^x \frac{f^{(n+1)}(t)}{n!} \times (x-t)^n \, dt$$

or $R_n(x) = \frac{f^{(n+1)}(c)}{(n+1)!}(x-a)^{n+1}$ where c is a number between a and x.

Example 11.1.1
Find a Taylor series for $\ln x$ at $x = a$, where $a > 0$, and determine its interval of validity.

If $f(x) = \ln x$, then $f'(x) = \frac{1}{x}$, $f''(x) = -\frac{1}{x^2}$, $f'''(x) = \frac{2}{x^3}$, $\ldots$, $f^{(i)}(x) = (-1)^{i-1}\frac{(i-1)!}{x^i}$.

So $\ln x = \ln a + \frac{1}{a}(x-a) - \frac{1}{2a^2}(x-a)^2 + \frac{1}{3a^3}(x-a)^3 - \ldots + (-1)^{i-1} \times \frac{1}{ia^i}(x-a)^i + \ldots .$

The radius of convergence is given by

$$R = \lim_{i\to\infty} \left| \frac{(-1)^{i-2} \times \frac{1}{(i-1)a^{i-1}}}{(-1)^{i-1} \times \frac{1}{ia^i}} \right| = \lim_{i\to\infty} \frac{i}{i-1} \times a = 1 \times a = a \qquad \text{(see Section 8.2).}$$

So the series is convergent when $|x - a| < a$, that is if $0 < x < 2a$. It is also convergent when $x - a = a$, by the alternating series property (see Section 6.1). The complete interval of convergence, which is the same as the interval of validity, is $0 < x \le 2a$.

Although the series in this example looks unfamiliar, it is not really new. Suppose for example that you put $x = 11$ and $a = 10$. Then you get

$$\ln 11 = \ln 10 + \tfrac{1}{10} \times 1 - \tfrac{1}{200} \times 1^2 + \tfrac{1}{3000} \times 1^3 - \dots ,$$

or

$$\ln\left(\tfrac{11}{10}\right) = \tfrac{1}{10} - \tfrac{1}{2} \times \left(\tfrac{1}{10}\right)^2 + \tfrac{1}{3} \times \left(\tfrac{1}{10}\right)^3 - \dots .$$

This is just the Maclaurin series for $\ln\left(1 + \tfrac{1}{10}\right)$.

In general, you can write $\ln\left(\dfrac{x}{a}\right)$ as $\ln\left(1 + \dfrac{x - a}{a}\right)$, so the Maclaurin series is

$$\ln\left(\frac{x}{a}\right) = \frac{x - a}{a} - \frac{1}{2}\left(\frac{x - a}{a}\right)^2 + \frac{1}{3}\left(\frac{x - a}{a}\right)^3 - \dots .$$

And if you write $\ln\left(\dfrac{x}{a}\right)$ as $\ln x - \ln a$, this is the same as the series in Example 11.1.1. The Taylor series is a disguised version of the Maclaurin series.

11.2 Another form for Taylor series

Look back to the equations in Section 11.1 which begin ' $k = \dots$ '. Since $j - a = h$, and $k = f(j)$, you can write k as $f(a + h)$, and the equation for k then becomes

$$f(a + h) = f(a) + \frac{f'(a)}{1!} h + \frac{f''(a)}{2!} h^2 + \dots = \sum_{i=0}^{\infty} \frac{f^{(i)}(a)}{i!} h^i .$$

Sometimes this is a more convenient way of writing a Taylor series, and it is worth learning to recognize it in this form as well as the form given in Section 11.1.

The Lagrange form for the error term will then be

$$\frac{f^{(n+1)}(c)}{(n+1)!} h^{n+1},$$

where c is a number between a and $a + h$. It is quite common to write c as $a + \theta h$, where θ is a number between 0 and 1. This has the advantage that it always stands for a number between a and $a + h$, whether h is positive or negative. You can therefore write the error term as

$$\frac{f^{(n)}(a + \theta h)}{(n+1)!} h^{n+1}, \text{ where } 0 < \theta < 1.$$

11.3   l'Hôpital's rule

In Section 9.6 Maclaurin series were used to find limits as $x \to 0$ of expressions of the form $\dfrac{f(x)}{g(x)}$ when $f(0)$ and $g(0)$ are both 0. If you want limits as $x \to a$ when $f(a)$ and $g(a)$ are both 0 you would use Taylor series. Since $f(a) = 0$ and $g(a) = 0$ the first terms of the series are 0, so

$$\frac{f(x)}{g(x)} = \frac{f'(a)(x-a) + \frac{1}{2!}f''(a)(x-a)^2 + \frac{1}{3!}f'''(a)(x-a)^3 + \dots}{g'(a)(x-a) + \frac{1}{2!}g''(a)(x-a)^2 + \frac{1}{3!}g'''(a)(x-a)^3 + \dots}.$$

You can then cancel a factor $(x-a)$, so

$$\frac{f(x)}{g(x)} = \frac{f'(a) + \frac{1}{2!}f''(a)(x-a) + \frac{1}{3!}f'''(a)(x-a)^2 + \dots}{g'(a) + \frac{1}{2!}g''(a)(x-a) + \frac{1}{3!}g'''(a)(x-a)^2 + \dots}.$$

As $x \to a$ all the terms after the first in each series tend to 0, so provided that $g'(a)$ is not zero,

$$\lim_{x \to a} \frac{f(x)}{g(x)} = \frac{f'(a)}{g'(a)}.$$

> **l'Hôpital's rule**   If $f(a) = 0$ and $g(a) = 0$, and $g'(a) \neq 0$, then
> $$\lim_{x \to a} \frac{f(x)}{g(x)} = \frac{f'(a)}{g'(a)}.$$

The French mathematician Guillaume l'Hôpital published this rule in a textbook which appeared in 1696.

Example 11.3.1

Find $\lim\limits_{x \to 1} \dfrac{\sqrt[3]{x} - 1}{\sqrt{x} - 1}$.

If $f(x) = \sqrt[3]{x} - 1$ and $g(x) = \sqrt{x} - 1$, then both $f(1) = 0$ and $g(1) = 0$, and

$$f'(x) = \frac{1}{3\sqrt[3]{x^2}}, \quad g'(x) = \frac{1}{2\sqrt{x}}.$$

So $f'(1) = \frac{1}{3}$ and $g'(1) = \frac{1}{2}$. Therefore, by l'Hôpital's rule,

$$\lim_{x \to 1} \frac{\sqrt[3]{x} - 1}{\sqrt{x} - 1} = \frac{\frac{1}{3}}{\frac{1}{2}} = \frac{2}{3}.$$

What happens if in addition $f'(a)$ and $g'(a)$ are both 0?

In that case

$$\frac{f(x)}{g(x)} = \frac{\frac{1}{2!}f''(a)(x-a) + \frac{1}{3!}f'''(a)(x-a)^2 + \ldots}{\frac{1}{2!}g''(a)(x-a) + \frac{1}{3!}g'''(a)(x-a)^2 + \ldots}.$$

You can now cancel $\frac{1}{2}(x-a)$, which gives

$$\frac{f(x)}{g(x)} = \frac{f''(a) + \frac{1}{3}f'''(a)(x-a) + \ldots}{g''(a) + \frac{1}{3}g'''(a)(x-a) + \ldots}.$$

Then, if $g''(a) \neq 0$,

$$\lim_{x \to a} \frac{f(x)}{g(x)} = \frac{f''(a)}{g''(a)}.$$

But also, by using $f'(x)$ and $g'(x)$ in place of $f(x)$ and $g(x)$ in the previous shaded box,

$$\lim_{x \to a} \frac{f'(x)}{g'(x)} = \frac{f''(a)}{g''(a)}.$$

From this you can obtain a more general form of l'Hôpital's rule which includes the form given earlier as a special case.

> **l'Hôpital's rule (general form)**
>
> If $f(a) = 0$ and $g(a) = 0$, and if $\lim_{x \to a} \dfrac{f'(x)}{g'(x)} = L$, then $\lim_{x \to a} \dfrac{f(x)}{g(x)} = L$.

Example 11.3.2

Find (a) $\displaystyle\lim_{x \to \pi} \frac{(x-\pi)^2}{1 + \cos x}$,   (b) $\displaystyle\lim_{x \to 1} \frac{(\ln x)^2}{x^3 - x^2 - x + 1}$.

(a)   If $f(x) = (x-\pi)^2$ and $g(x) = 1 + \cos x$, then $f'(x) = 2(x-\pi)$ and $g'(x) = -\sin x$, and $f''(x) = 2$ and $g''(x) = -\cos x$. So $f(\pi) = g(\pi) = 0$, $f'(\pi) = g'(\pi) = 0$ and $f''(\pi) = 2$, $g''(\pi) = -(-1) = 1$. Therefore, by l'Hôpital's rule,

$$\lim_{x \to \pi} \frac{f'(x)}{g'(x)} = \frac{f''(\pi)}{g''(\pi)} = 2, \quad \text{so} \quad \lim_{x \to \pi} \frac{f(x)}{g(x)} = 2.$$

(b)   If $f(x) = (\ln x)^2$ and $g(x) = x^3 - x^2 - x + 1$, then $f'(x) = \dfrac{2\ln x}{x}$ and $g'(x) = 3x^2 - 2x - 1$. So $f(1) = g(1) = 0$, and $f'(1) = g'(1) = 0$.

You could go on to find $f''(x)$ and $g''(x)$ as in part (a), but it is slightly simpler to note that

$$\frac{f'(x)}{g'(x)} = \frac{2\ln x}{3x^3 - 2x^2 - x},$$

and to write $F(x) = 2\ln x$ and $G(x) = 3x^3 - 2x^2 - x$, where $F(1) = G(1) = 0$. Then $F'(x) = \dfrac{2}{x}$ and $G'(x) = 9x^2 - 4x - 1$. So $F'(1) = 2$ and $G'(1) = 4$. Therefore, by l'Hôpital's rule,

$$\lim_{x \to 1} \frac{F(x)}{G(x)} = \frac{F'(1)}{G'(1)} = \tfrac{1}{2}.$$

And since $\dfrac{F(x)}{G(x)} = \dfrac{f'(x)}{g'(x)}$,

$$\lim_{x \to 1} \frac{f'(x)}{g'(x)} = \tfrac{1}{2}, \quad \text{so} \quad \lim_{x \to 1} \frac{f(x)}{g(x)} = \tfrac{1}{2}.$$

Exercise 11

1   Find a Taylor series for e^x around $x = a$. Show how your series is related to the Maclaurin series for e^x.

   If e^x is approximated by a Taylor approximation around $x = a$ of degree n, write expressions for the error term in both integral and Lagrange forms.

2   Write a Taylor polynomial of degree 6 for $\sin x$ around $x = \tfrac{1}{4}\pi$. Write an expression for the error term in the form of an integral. Use integration by parts to obtain the Taylor polynomial of degree 7 and the corresponding error term.

3   Expand $\sqrt[3]{1+h}$ as a series of powers of h as far as the term in h^3, and give an expression for the remainder. Use the series to find an approximation for $\sqrt[3]{1.15}$. State whether your answer is too large or too small, and find an upper bound for the error.

4   If $f(x) = x^3 - 5x + 2$ and $g(x) = x^3 - x^2 - 4$, show that $f(2) = g(2) = 0$. Hence factorise $f(x)$ and $g(x)$. Find $\displaystyle\lim_{x \to 2} \frac{f(x)}{g(x)}$

   (a) by cancelling a common factor,   (b) by using l'Hôpital's rule.

5   Repeat Question 4 with $f(x) = x^3 - 3x^2 + 4$ and $g(x) = x^3 - 12x + 16$.

6   Find

   (a) $\displaystyle\lim_{x \to 2} \frac{x^2 - 4}{\sin(x - 2)}$,

   (b) $\displaystyle\lim_{x \to \pi} \frac{\tan x}{\cos \tfrac{1}{2} x}$,

   (c) $\displaystyle\lim_{x \to e} \frac{1 - \ln x}{\sqrt{x} - \sqrt{e}}$,

   (d) $\displaystyle\lim_{x \to 0} \frac{e^x - e^{-x}}{\sin x}$.

7   Find

   (a) $\displaystyle\lim_{x \to 1} \frac{(x - 1)^2}{1 + \sin \tfrac{3}{2} \pi x}$,

   (b) $\displaystyle\lim_{x \to \frac{1}{2}\pi} \frac{1 - \sin 5x}{1 + \cos 2x}$,

   (c) $\displaystyle\lim_{x \to 1} \frac{\ln x + \ln(2 - x)}{1 - \cos(1 - x)}$,

   (d) $\displaystyle\lim_{x \to 1} \frac{\sqrt{x} + \sqrt{2 - x} - 2}{(x - 1)\ln x}$.

12 Homogeneous differential equations

Higher Level Book 2, Chapters 23 and 27, showed how to solve certain types of differential equation. This chapter introduces another type. When you have completed it, you should

- know what is meant by a homogeneous differential equation, and that it can (if necessary) be solved by a substitution
- understand the geometrical significance of the differential equation, and that solution curves can be obtained from others by enlargement from the origin.

12.1 Some examples of homogeneous equations

You already know how to solve differential equations which have the forms $\dfrac{dy}{dx} = f(x)$ and $\dfrac{dy}{dx} = f(y)$ (Higher Level Book 2 Chapter 23), and $\dfrac{dy}{dx} = \dfrac{f(x)}{g(y)}$ (Higher Level Book 2 Section 27.3). Another type of differential equation for which there is a standard method of solution has the form $\dfrac{dy}{dx} = f\!\left(\dfrac{y}{x}\right)$. This is called a **homogeneous differential equation**.

The basic meaning of the word homogeneous is 'having the same degree'. In algebra, an equation such as $y^3 + 4x^2y - 3x^3 = 0$ is homogeneous, as each term has degree 3 in x and/or y. But $y^3 + 4x^2 - 3 = 0$ is not homogeneous, because the first term has degree 3, the second has degree 2 and the third has degree 0.

Notice that the homogeneous equation $y^3 + 4x^2y - 3x^3 = 0$ can be rewritten as $\left(\dfrac{y}{x}\right)^3 + 4\left(\dfrac{y}{x}\right) - 3 = 0$, that is as $f\!\left(\dfrac{y}{x}\right) = 0$. This is why the name 'homogeneous' is used to describe these differential equations.

Differential equations of this type are more common than you might at first think. Besides obvious examples such as $\dfrac{dy}{dx} = \left(\dfrac{y}{x}\right)^2$ (solved in Higher Level Book 2 Example 27.3.1) and $\dfrac{dy}{dx} = \sin\!\left(\dfrac{y}{x}\right)$ (for which no exact solution exists in terms of functions that you know), the description homogeneous includes differential equations such as

$$\frac{dy}{dx} = \ln x - \ln y, \qquad \frac{dy}{dx} = \frac{2x+y}{y} \qquad \text{and} \qquad \frac{dy}{dx} = \frac{xy}{x^2 - 3y^2},$$

because

$$\ln x - \ln y = -\ln\!\left(\frac{y}{x}\right), \qquad \frac{2x+y}{y} = \frac{2 + \dfrac{y}{x}}{\dfrac{y}{x}} \qquad \text{and} \qquad \frac{xy}{x^2 - 3y^2} = \frac{\dfrac{y}{x}}{1 - 3\left(\dfrac{y}{x}\right)^2}.$$

These all have the form $f\!\left(\dfrac{y}{x}\right)$ with $f(u) = -\ln u$, $\dfrac{2+u}{u}$ and $\dfrac{u}{1-3u^2}$ respectively.

You already know how to solve homogeneous equations of the special form $\dfrac{dy}{dx} = a\left(\dfrac{y}{x}\right)^m$, because this differential equation can be written with separable variables as $\dfrac{1}{y^m}\dfrac{dy}{dx} = \dfrac{a}{x^m}$.

Example 12.1.1

Find the solution curves of the differential equation $\dfrac{dy}{dx} = -\dfrac{y}{x}$ which pass through the points

(a) $(1,2)$, (b) $(1,1)$, (c) $(1,-1)$, (d) $(1,0)$.

Note that the expression for $\dfrac{dy}{dx}$ is undefined when $x = 0$, so that the solution curves cannot cross from positive to negative values of x. So in solving the differential equation you need only consider $x > 0$.

The differential equation can be written as

$$\frac{1}{y}\frac{dy}{dx} = -\frac{1}{x}.$$

The left side is the derivative with respect to x of $\ln|y|$, so the equation can be integrated as

$$\ln|y| = -\ln x + k.$$

(Notice that, since $x > 0$, it is not necessary to write $\ln|x|$ on the right side.)

(a) To pass through $(1,2)$ the constant k must satisfy

$$\ln|2| = -\ln 1 + k, \quad \text{so} \quad k = \ln 2.$$

Therefore

$$\ln|y| = -\ln x + \ln 2,$$

which gives

$$|y| = \frac{2}{x}, \quad \text{or} \quad y = \pm\frac{2}{x}.$$

Since the curve has to pass through $(1,2)$, the positive sign must be taken. The solution curve therefore has equation

$$y = \frac{2}{x}, \; x > 0.$$

(b) Using a similar method, to pass through $(1,1)$ the constant k must satisfy

$$\ln|1| = -\ln 1 + k,$$

so $k = 0$.

Therefore

$$\ln|y| = -\ln x,$$

which gives

$$y = \pm\frac{1}{x}.$$

As in part (a) the positive sign must be taken, so the equation of the solution curve is

$$y = \frac{1}{x}, \ x > 0.$$

(c)   To pass through $(1,-1)$, k must satisfy

$$\ln|-1| = \ln 1 + k,$$

which again gives $k = 0$, so $y = \pm\frac{1}{x}$. But to pass through $(1,-1)$ the negative sign must be taken, so the solution curve has equation

$$y = -\frac{1}{x}, \ x > 0.$$

(d)   The method used in parts (a) to (c) breaks down, because $\ln|0|$ has no meaning. The problem lies at the very first step of the solution, where the equation $\frac{dy}{dx} = -\frac{y}{x}$ is replaced by

$\frac{1}{y}\frac{dy}{dx} = -\frac{1}{x}$, dividing both sides by y. This is not valid if $y = 0$, which occurs at the given point $(1,0)$. So you need a different approach.

Notice that in parts (a) to (c) the solution has the form $y = \frac{A}{x}$ for some constant A. So try an equation of this form satisfied by $x = 1$ and $y = 0$. This would require $A = 0$, giving the solution of the equation as

$$y = 0, \ x > 0.$$

The corresponding graph is the positive x-axis.

You can easily check that this satisfies the differential equation, since the axis has gradient 0, which is equal to $-\frac{y}{x}$ when $y = 0, \ x > 0$.

The four solution curves are shown in Fig. 12.1.

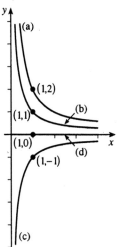

Fig. 12.1

12.2 Solution by substitution

The homogeneous differential equation in Example 12.1.1 is a very special case, because the variables are separable. If you try to use a similar method with an equation such as $\dfrac{dy}{dx} = 1 - \dfrac{y}{x}$, you will find that there is no way of expressing this in the form $g(y)\dfrac{dy}{dx} = f(x)$, so you need a different method.

A way of simplifying the equation would be to replace the $\dfrac{y}{x}$ in the expression $f\!\left(\dfrac{y}{x}\right)$ by a single letter. It could not of course be a constant, but you could write $\dfrac{y}{x}$ as a single variable z.

The question is then what happens to the other quantity in the equation, $\dfrac{dy}{dx}$. Since $y = xz$, you can use the product rule of differentiation to write this as

$$\frac{dy}{dx} = 1 \times z + x \times \frac{dz}{dx}$$
$$= z + x\frac{dz}{dx}.$$

The differential equation $\dfrac{dy}{dx} = f\!\left(\dfrac{y}{x}\right)$ then becomes

$$z + x\frac{dz}{dx} = f(z),$$

which can be rearranged as

$$x\frac{dz}{dx} = f(z) - z.$$

And now you have a differential equation in separable variables form, as

$$\frac{1}{f(z) - z}\frac{dz}{dx} = \frac{1}{x}.$$

So if you can find $\displaystyle\int \frac{1}{f(z) - z}\,dz$, you could integrate this differential equation as an equation connecting z and x. Finally, since $y = xz$, this can be written as an equation connecting $\dfrac{y}{x}$ and x; that is, as an equation connecting y and x.

Example 12.2.1

Find the solution curves of the differential equation $\dfrac{dy}{dx} = 1 - \dfrac{y}{x}$ which pass through the points
(a) $(1,2)$,   (b) $(1,1)$,   (c) $(1,-1)$,   (d) $(1,0)$.

If you write $\dfrac{y}{x} = z$, that is $y = xz$, you can differentiate with respect to x to get

$$\frac{dy}{dx} = z + x\frac{dz}{dx}.$$

The differential equation then becomes

$$z + x\frac{dz}{dx} = 1 - z,$$

which can be rearranged as

$$\frac{1}{2z-1}\frac{dz}{dx} = -\frac{1}{x}.$$

Notice that, as in Example 12.1.1, $\frac{dz}{dx}$ is undefined when $x = 0$, so the solution curves cannot pass from positive to negative values of x. You can therefore restrict the solution to $x > 0$, and the integral of $\frac{1}{x}$ can be taken as $\ln x$ rather than $\ln|x|$.

Integrating the differential equation for z,

$$\tfrac{1}{2}\ln|2z-1| = -\ln x + k,$$

which you can write as

$$\ln|2z-1| + 2\ln x = 2k.$$

This can be simplified by noting that

$$\ln|2z-1| + 2\ln x = \ln\left(\left|2\frac{y}{x}-1\right| \times x^2\right)$$
$$= \ln|2xy - x^2|.$$

So

$$\left|2xy - x^2\right| = e^{2k},$$

$$2xy - x^2 = \pm\, e^{2k}.$$

Write the constant on the right more simply as A. This can be found for the four solution curves by substituting the given values of x and y, as

(a) $A = 2\times 1\times 2 - 1^2 = 3,$ (b) $A = 2\times 1\times 1 - 1^2 = 1,$

(c) $A = 2\times 1\times (-1) - 1^2 = -3,$ (d) $A = 2\times 1\times 0 - 1^2 = -1.$

Then rearranging $2xy - x^2 = A$ as $y = \tfrac{1}{2}\left(x + \frac{A}{x}\right)$, the four solution curves have equations

(a) $y = \tfrac{1}{2}\left(x + \frac{3}{x}\right),$ (b) $y = \tfrac{1}{2}\left(x + \frac{1}{x}\right),$

(c) $y = \tfrac{1}{2}\left(x - \frac{3}{x}\right),$ (d) $y = \tfrac{1}{2}\left(x - \frac{1}{x}\right).$

It is a good idea to check these solutions, as it is easy to make a slip along the way.

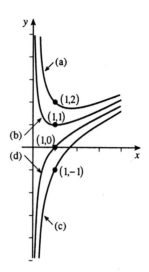

If $y = \frac{1}{2}\left(x + \frac{A}{x}\right),$

then $\frac{dy}{dx} = \frac{1}{2}\left(1 - \frac{A}{x^2}\right),$

and $1 - \frac{y}{x} = 1 - \frac{1}{2}\left(1 + \frac{A}{x^2}\right) = \frac{1}{2}\left(1 - \frac{A}{x^2}\right),$

so $\frac{dy}{dx} = 1 - \frac{y}{x}$, as required.

The four solution curves are shown in Fig. 12.2.

Fig. 12.2

Example 12.2.2

For the differential equation $\frac{dy}{dx} = \frac{y}{x+y}$, find the solution curve through $(1,1)$.

It is useful to note, for later reference, that $\frac{dy}{dx}$ is not defined when $x + y = 0$, so the solution curve cannot cross from positive to negative values of $x + y$. The whole solution curve must lie above the line with equation $x + y = 0$.

Writing $\frac{y}{x} = z,$

$$\frac{y}{x+y} = \frac{xz}{x+xz} = \frac{z}{1+z}.$$

So, using $\frac{dy}{dx} = z + x\frac{dz}{dx}$, the differential equation becomes

$$z + x\frac{dz}{dx} = \frac{z}{1+z},$$

$$x\frac{dz}{dx} = \frac{z}{1+z} - z = \frac{z - z(1+z)}{1+z} = \frac{-z^2}{1+z}.$$

This can be rearranged as

$$-\frac{1+z}{z^2}\frac{dz}{dx} = \frac{1}{x},$$

or $\left(-\frac{1}{z^2} - \frac{1}{z}\right)\frac{dz}{dx} = \frac{1}{x}.$

This is now in a form which you can integrate, as

$$\frac{1}{z} - \ln|z| = \ln|x| + k.$$

You can find the constant k by noting that, when $x = 1$ and $y = 1$, then $z = \frac{1}{1} = 1$, so

$$1 - \ln|1| = \ln|1| + k, \quad \text{which gives} \quad k = 1.$$

The solution is therefore

$$\frac{1}{z} - \ln|z| = \ln|x| + 1,$$

$$\frac{1}{z} = \ln|xz| + 1.$$

Writing $z = \dfrac{y}{x}$, the equation of the solution curve is

$$\frac{x}{y} = \ln|y| + 1, \quad \text{which is} \quad x = y(\ln|y| + 1).$$

When you solve differential equations it often happens that you can't write the solution in function form as $y = F(x)$, and this sometimes makes it difficult to draw the graph of the solution curve. But in this case the equation comes out in the form $x = F(y)$. So you could find its shape by drawing the graph of

$$y = x(\ln|x| + 1)$$

and then swopping the x- and y-axes by reflecting the graph in the line $y = x$. (Your calculator may have a program which does this for you.)

Fig. 12.3 shows the resulting graph. The part with $y > 0$ has equation $x = y(\ln y + 1)$, and the part with $y < 0$ has equation $x = y(\ln(-y) + 1)$. And since the graph of $y = x(\ln x + 1)$ has a minimum point at $\left(e^{-2}, -e^{-2}\right)$, the graph of $x = y(\ln y + 1)$ has a tangent parallel to the y-axis at $\left(-e^{-2}, e^{-2}\right)$.

This is where the remark at the beginning of the solution becomes relevant. You will notice that $\left(-e^{-2}, e^{-2}\right)$ lies on the line $x + y = 0$, and it is only the part of the curve through $(1,1)$ for which $x + y > 0$ that forms the solution curve. This is the curve shown with the solid line in Fig. 12.3. The required solution is therefore given by

$$x = y(\ln y + 1), \quad y > e^{-2}.$$

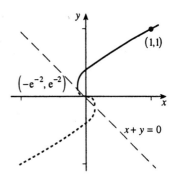

Fig. 12.3

Exercise 12A

Keep your answers to Questions 2(a), 4 and 6 for use in Exercise 12B Questions 2, 3 and 4.

1 Solve the differential equation $\dfrac{dy}{dx} = \dfrac{x}{y}$ for $y > 0$. Use a calculator to display the solution curves through $(0,1)$, $(0,2)$, $(1,1)$, $(-1,1)$, $(1,2)$, $(-1,2)$, $(2,1)$ and $(3,1)$.

2 Find equations of the solution curves in the first quadrant of the differential equations

(a) $\dfrac{dy}{dx} = \sqrt{\dfrac{y}{x}}$,

(b) $\dfrac{dy}{dx} = \sqrt{\dfrac{x}{y}}$

through the points $(1,9)$, $(1,4)$, $(1,1)$, $(4,1)$, $(9,1)$. State any restrictions on the values of x for which your solution is valid, and sketch the solution curves.

3 Find an equation for the general solution of the differential equation $\dfrac{dy}{dx} = \dfrac{x^2 + y^2}{xy}$ for $x > 0$, $y > 0$. Check your answer by substitution in the two sides of the differential equation.

4 Find the equations of the solution curves through $(1,2)$, $(2,4)$ and $(4,6)$ of the differential equations

(a) $\dfrac{dy}{dx} = \dfrac{x^2 + y^2}{2xy}$,

(b) $\dfrac{dy}{dx} = \dfrac{y^2 - x^2}{2xy}$.

5 Find the equation of the solution curve through $(1,1)$ of the differential equation $\dfrac{dy}{dx} = \dfrac{xy}{x^2 + y^2}$.

6 Solve the differential equation $\dfrac{dy}{dx} = \dfrac{xy - y^2}{x^2}$ for $x > 0$.

7 Find in the form of an implicit equation the solution of the differential equation $\dfrac{dy}{dx} = \dfrac{y - x}{y + x}$.

Check the answer by differentiating your equation with respect to x.

12.3* Geometrical properties of the solution curves

Fig. 12.4 shows the solution curves of the differential equation $\dfrac{dy}{dx} = 1 - \dfrac{y}{x}$ which were found in Example 12.2.1.

A number of lines through the origin have been added to the figure, together with the tangents to the solution curves at the points of intersection. What this demonstrates is that, for each of these lines, the tangents to the solution curves which they intersect are parallel.

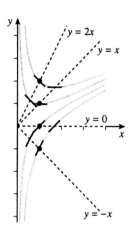

Fig. 12.4

It is easy to see why. Consider for example the line $y = 2x$, which intersects the solution curves $y = \frac{1}{2}\left(x + \frac{1}{x}\right)$ and $y = \frac{1}{2}\left(x + \frac{3}{x}\right)$. At each point of intersection $\frac{y}{x} = 2$, and from the differential equation $\frac{dy}{dx} = 1 - \frac{y}{x} = 1 - 2 = -1$. So the tangent to any solution curve at its intersection with $y = 2x$ has gradient -1.

Similarly for the other lines. At the intersection of a solution curve with $y = x$, $\frac{y}{x} = 1$ so that $\frac{dy}{dx} = 1 - 1 = 0$. You can see from Fig. 12.4 that the minimum points of each solution curve which intersects $y = x$ lie on this line.

The lines $y = 2x$ and $y = x$ don't intersect all the solution curves. But other solution curves have intersections with other lines through the origin. Fig. 12.4 shows the solution curves $y = \frac{1}{2}\left(x - \frac{1}{x}\right)$ and $y = \frac{1}{2}\left(x - \frac{3}{x}\right)$ intersected by $y = -x$ and $y = 0$. At these intersections the gradients of the tangents are respectively $1 - (-1) = 2$ and $1 - 0 = 1$.

You can use the same argument for any homogeneous differential equation and any line through the origin. If a solution curve of the differential equation $\frac{dy}{dx} = f\left(\frac{y}{x}\right)$ is intersected by a line $y = mx$ through the origin, then at the point of intersection $\frac{y}{x} = m$, so the gradient of the solution curve is $f(m)$. It follows that the tangents to all the solution curves which intersect $y = mx$ have the same gradient at the points of intersection, and are therefore parallel.

You can use this idea to draw sketches of solution curves for homogeneous differential equations when you can't find an exact equation for the solution. The method is described in the following example.

Example 12.3.1

For the differential equation $\frac{dy}{dx} = e^{\frac{y}{x}}$, sketch the solution curve through the point $(2, 0)$.

Begin by drawing at the point $(2, 0)$ a short line segment indicating the tangent to the solution curve, with gradient $e^{\frac{0}{2}} = e^0 = 1$.

Now draw a number of lines through the origin. In Fig. 12.5 these are $y = x$, $y = \frac{1}{2}x$, $y = \frac{1}{4}x$, $y = -\frac{1}{4}x$, $y = -\frac{1}{2}x$, $y = -x$ and $y = -2x$. On each of these lines draw several short line segments whose direction is that of the tangents to the solution curves which intersect the line; that is, with gradients e^1, $e^{\frac{1}{2}}$, $e^{\frac{1}{4}}$, $e^{-\frac{1}{4}}$, $e^{-\frac{1}{2}}$, e^{-1} and e^{-2}.

Finally, draw a curve so that the tangent at the intersection with each of the lines is parallel to the corresponding line segments. Although this can only be done approximately, the sketch gives a good idea of the shape of the solution curve.

Now suppose that in Example 12.3.1 you want to add a sketch of the solution curve through $(3,0)$. Using the same method, the tangent as the curve crosses each of the dotted lines in Fig. 12.5 would be parallel to that for the curve already drawn. You might guess that the new solution curve would have the same shape as the one already sketched, but enlarged in the ratio 3 to 2.

This is in fact correct. The property is illustrated by the exact solution curves in the next example.

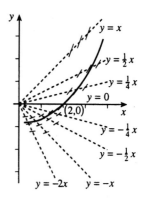

Fig. 12.5

Example 12.3.2

Find the general solution of the homogeneous differential equation $\dfrac{dy}{dx} = \dfrac{y}{x} - 2$ for $x > 0$.

Using the substitution $y = xz$, the equation becomes

$$z + x\frac{dz}{dx} = z - 2,$$

which reduces to

$$\frac{dz}{dx} = -\frac{2}{x}.$$

Integrating,

$$z = k - 2\ln x,$$

where k is an arbitrary constant. (No modulus sign is needed, since $x > 0$.) Finally, writing $z = \dfrac{y}{x}$ gives the general solution

$$y = x(k - 2\ln x).$$

Fig. 12.6 shows the solution curves for the equation in Example 12.3.2 with $k = 0, 1, 2$ and 3. The last three of these are enlargements of the first.

To show this, recall that replacing x by $\dfrac{x}{c}$ in an equation $y = f(x)$ stretches the graph by a factor c in the x-direction; and replacing y by $\dfrac{y}{c}$ stretches the graph by a factor c in the y-direction. So replacing both x and y by $\dfrac{x}{c}$ and $\dfrac{y}{c}$ produces stretches of factor c in both directions, that is an enlargement of factor c from the origin.

So the enlargement of the graph $y = -2x \ln x$ by a factor c produces the graph of $\dfrac{y}{c} = -2\dfrac{x}{c}\ln\left(\dfrac{x}{c}\right)$, which is $y = x(k - 2\ln x)$ with $k = 2\ln c$, that is $c = e^{\frac{1}{2}k}$.

So the graphs in Fig. 12.6 of

$$y = x(1 - 2\ln x),$$

$$y = x(2 - 2\ln x)$$

and $y = x(3 - 2\ln x)$

are enlargements of $y = -2x \ln x$ with factors $e^{\frac{1}{2}}$, e and $e^{\frac{3}{2}}$ respectively.

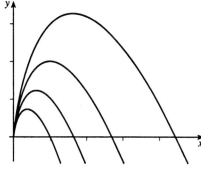

Fig. 12.6

What this illustrates is:

> If S is a solution curve of a homogeneous differential equation, then any curve obtained from S by enlargement from the origin is also a solution curve.

You can prove this by using the chain rule. Suppose that (x, y) are the coordinates of a point on S, and that $X = cx$, $Y = cy$. Then you can find $\dfrac{\mathrm{d}Y}{\mathrm{d}x}$ either as $\dfrac{\mathrm{d}X}{\mathrm{d}x} \times \dfrac{\mathrm{d}Y}{\mathrm{d}X} = c \times \dfrac{\mathrm{d}Y}{\mathrm{d}X}$ or as $\dfrac{\mathrm{d}y}{\mathrm{d}x} \times \dfrac{\mathrm{d}Y}{\mathrm{d}y} = \dfrac{\mathrm{d}y}{\mathrm{d}x} \times c$. It follows that $\dfrac{\mathrm{d}Y}{\mathrm{d}X} = \dfrac{\mathrm{d}y}{\mathrm{d}x}$. Also $\dfrac{Y}{X} = \dfrac{y}{x}$. So if (x, y) satisfies the homogeneous differential equation $\dfrac{\mathrm{d}y}{\mathrm{d}x} = f\left(\dfrac{y}{x}\right)$, (X, Y) satisfies $\dfrac{\mathrm{d}Y}{\mathrm{d}X} = f\left(\dfrac{Y}{X}\right)$. That is, the curve obtained from S by enlargement of factor c from the origin is also a solution curve of the differential equation.

Exercise 12B *

1   In Example 12.2.1, find the enlargement factor which transforms the solution curve $y = \tfrac{1}{2}\left(x + \dfrac{1}{x}\right)$ to $y = \tfrac{1}{2}\left(x + \dfrac{3}{x}\right)$.

2   In Exercise 12A Question 2(a), show that there are two pairs of solution curves which are enlargements of each other.

3   In Exercise 12A Question 4 parts (a) and (b), show that the last two solution curves can be obtained from the first by enlargement from the origin, and find the enlargement factors.

4   In Exercise 12A Question 6, investigate whether all the solution curves can be obtained from the others by enlargement from the origin.

5   Use the method of Example 12.3.1 to sketch the solution curve of the differential equation $\dfrac{dy}{dx} = \dfrac{\sqrt{x^2 + y^2}}{x}$ through the point $(5,0)$.

6   Show that, if a solution curve of $\dfrac{dy}{dx} = \dfrac{y}{x} + \dfrac{y^2}{x^2}$ has any stationary points, then they lie on one of two lines, and state their equations.

Verify your answer by solving the equation and finding the coordinates of the stationary points on the solution curves.

13 Linear differential equations

This chapter describes another method which can be used to solve some differential equations. When you have completed it, you should

- be able to solve first order linear differential equations by using an integrating factor.

13.1 Solution using the product rule

Example 13.1.1

Find the general solution of the differential equation $3x^2y + x^3\dfrac{dy}{dx} = x^4$.

When you have a differential equation to solve, you should begin by asking whether it is one of a type for which you already know a special method. For example, is $\dfrac{dy}{dx}$ a function of just x, or just y? Are the variables separable? Is the equation homogeneous?

With the given differential equation, the answer to all these questions is 'no'. So where do you go next?

Look at the left side of the equation. Does it remind you of anything? The factors involving x, that is $3x^2$ and x^3, should give you a clue, since $3x^2 = \dfrac{d}{dx}x^3$. So the left side could be written as

$$\frac{d}{dx}x^3 \times y + x^3 \times \frac{dy}{dx}.$$

This is just what you get when you differentiate x^3y using the product rule. So the differential equation is

$$\frac{d}{dx}\left(x^3y\right) = x^4.$$

It is now easy to complete the solution. Integrating with respect to x,

$$x^3y = \tfrac{1}{5}x^5 + k.$$

That is,

$$y = \tfrac{1}{5}x^2 + \frac{k}{x^3}.$$

Check this answer for yourself by substitution into the original differential equation.

The trouble with this example is that it is most unlikely that you will be asked to solve

$$3x^2y + x^3\frac{dy}{dx} = x^4,$$

because all the terms of this equation have a common factor x^2. It is more likely that the equation will be presented as

$$3y + x\frac{dy}{dx} = x^2,$$

and then the left side is not the derivative of a product. How could you tell that the key to solving this equation is to multiply each term by x^2? Read on!

13.2 Integrating factors

This chapter is concerned with the general problem of solving differential equations of the form

$$f(x)\frac{dy}{dx} + g(x)y = h(x),$$

where f, g and h are given functions. Example 13.1.1 is such an equation with $f(x) = x^3$, $g(x) = 3x^2$ and $h(x) = x^4$. A differential equation like this is said to be **linear**, because $\frac{dy}{dx}$ and y appear only to the first degree; the equation has no terms involving $\left(\frac{dy}{dx}\right)^m$ or y^m with $m \neq 1$, nor are there any products like $y\frac{dy}{dx}$.

It isn't necessary to write this equation with three given functions, because you can divide through by $f(x)$ to get

$$\frac{dy}{dx} + \frac{g(x)}{f(x)}y = \frac{h(x)}{f(x)}$$

and then express $\frac{g(x)}{f(x)}$ as a single function $p(x)$, and $\frac{h(x)}{f(x)}$ as $q(x)$.

> The **standard form** of a first order linear differential equation is
>
> $$\frac{dy}{dx} + p(x)y = q(x),$$
>
> where $p(x)$ and $q(x)$ are given functions of x.

For example, the standard form of the equation discussed in Example 13.1.1 would be

$$\frac{dy}{dx} + \frac{3}{x} \times y = x.$$

You already know that this can be integrated by multiplying by x^3, which makes the left side $3x^2y + x^3\frac{dy}{dx}$. The question is, how can you find this multiplying factor x^3 from the knowledge that $p(x) = \frac{3}{x}$?

The answer comes in two steps. First, notice that

$$\int \frac{3}{x}\,dx = 3\ln x + k = \ln x^3 + k.$$

So you could say that the 'simplest' integral of $\frac{3}{x}$ is $\ln x^3$.

The second step is to get from $\ln x^3$ to the multiplying factor x^3, and to do this you simply have to take the exponential, since $e^{\ln x^3} = x^3$.

This works as a general rule. The multiplier x^3 is an example of an **integrating factor**. It is a function that you can use to convert a first order differential equation in standard form into a form which can be integrated.

> To find an integrating factor for the differential equation
>
> $$\frac{dy}{dx} + p(x)y = q(x)$$
>
> first find the simplest integral of $p(x)$, and call it $I(x)$; then $e^{I(x)}$ is an integrating factor.

Example 13.2.1

Find the general solution of the differential equation $\dfrac{dy}{dx} - \dfrac{y}{x} = x$.

This is already in standard form, with $p(x) = -\dfrac{1}{x}$. So find the simplest integral of $-\dfrac{1}{x}$, which is $-\ln x$, or $\ln\dfrac{1}{x}$. An integrating factor is therefore $e^{\ln\frac{1}{x}}$, which is simply $\dfrac{1}{x}$.

Multiplying the differential equation by $\dfrac{1}{x}$ gives

$$\frac{dy}{dx} \times \frac{1}{x} + y \times \left(-\frac{1}{x^2}\right) = 1.$$

The left side of this is $\dfrac{d}{dx}\left(y \times \dfrac{1}{x}\right)$, so the equation can be written as

$$\frac{d}{dx}\left(y \times \frac{1}{x}\right) = 1.$$

This can be integrated as

$$y \times \frac{1}{x} = x + k,$$

or more conveniently

$$y = x^2 + kx.$$

In an example like this, since the process is quite complicated, it is a good idea to check the answer by direct substitution. If $y = x^2 + kx$, then $\dfrac{dy}{dx} = 2x + k$ and $\dfrac{y}{x} = x + k$, so $\dfrac{dy}{dx} - \dfrac{y}{x} = (2x + k) - (x + k) = x$, as required.

In Example 13.2.1 all the solution curves are parabolas through the origin, including $y = x^2$ when $k = 0$. Fig. 13.1 shows a selection of these curves for various values of k.

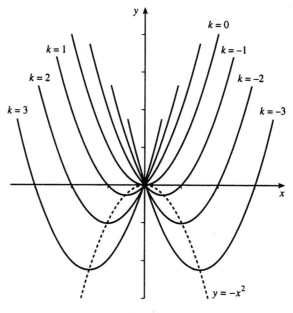

Fig. 13.1

It is interesting to notice that the minimum points on all the solution curves lie on the curve $y = -x^2$, shown dotted in Fig. 13.1. You can see the reason for this by going back to the differential equation and putting $\dfrac{dy}{dx} = 0$. This gives $-\dfrac{y}{x} = x$, which is $y = -x^2$.

The next example requires you to find the particular solution curve which passes through a given point.

Example 13.2.2

Find the curve through $(0,1)$ whose equation satisfies the differential equation $\dfrac{dy}{dx} + y = e^x$.

For this differential equation $p(x)$ is simply 1, and the simplest integral of this is x. So an integrating factor is e^x.

Multiplying the equation by e^x gives

$$\frac{dy}{dx} \times e^x + y \times e^x = e^{2x}.$$

The left side is $\dfrac{\mathrm{d}}{\mathrm{d}x}\left(ye^x\right)$, so the equation can be written as $\dfrac{\mathrm{d}}{\mathrm{d}x}\left(ye^x\right)=e^{2x}$, and then integrated to give the general solution

$$ye^x = \tfrac{1}{2}e^{2x}+k.$$

The question asks for the solution for which $y=1$ when $x=0$, so substitute these values to obtain $1=\tfrac{1}{2}+k$, giving $k=\tfrac{1}{2}$.

The required solution is therefore

$$ye^x = \tfrac{1}{2}e^{2x}+\tfrac{1}{2},$$

which is best written as

$$y = \tfrac{1}{2}e^x+\tfrac{1}{2}e^{-x}.$$

Fig. 13.2 shows a number of solution curves for the differential equation in Example 13.2.2, with the curve through $(0,1)$ emphasised as a heavier line. In this case not all the curves have stationary points; for those which do, these points lie on $y=e^x$ (shown dotted in Fig. 13.2), which you get by putting $\dfrac{\mathrm{d}y}{\mathrm{d}x}=0$ in the differential equation.

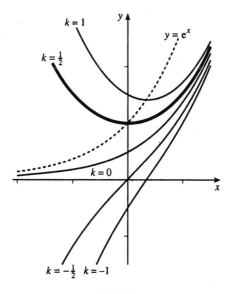

Fig. 13.2

It is important to remember that, to use the integrating factor rule, you have to begin with the differential equation in standard form. But it is always worth checking first that the equation isn't already in a form which can be integrated directly, as was the case with the example in Section 13.1. This is the point of the first step in the following algorithm, which summarises the method of using an integrating factor to solve first order linear differential equations..

To find the general solution of the differential equation $\dfrac{dy}{dx} f(x) + y g(x) = h(x)$ using an integrating factor:

Step 1 If $g(x) = f'(x)$, write the equation as $\dfrac{d}{dx}(y f(x)) = h(x)$ and go to Step 6.

Step 2 Divide the equation by $f(x)$ to obtain the standard form
$$\frac{dy}{dx} + y\, p(x) = q(x).$$

Step 3 Find the simplest integral of $p(x)$; denote it by $I(x)$.

Step 4 Write $u(x) = e^{I(x)}$, and simplify this if possible. This is the integrating factor.

Step 5 Multiply the equation (in its form after Step 2) by $u(x)$, and write the equation as $\dfrac{dy}{dx}(y u(x)) = q(x) u(x)$.

Step 6 Integrate the equation with respect to x, including an arbitrary constant.

Step 7 Put the solution into the form $y = \ldots$ by dividing by the function which multiplies y (that is $u(x)$ or $f(x)$).

Example 13.2.3

Find the general solution of $\dfrac{dy}{dx} \cos x + y \sin x = \tan x$.

Step 1 $f'(x)$ is $\dfrac{d}{dx}\cos x = -\sin x$, which does not equal $g(x) = \sin x$.

Step 2 Divide by $\cos x$ to obtain $\dfrac{dy}{dx} + y \tan x = \tan x \sec x$.

Step 3 $p(x) = \tan x$; $\displaystyle\int \tan x\, dx = \ln \sec x + k$, so take $I(x) = \ln \sec x$.

Step 4 The integrating factor is $u(x) = e^{\ln \sec x} = \sec x$.

Step 5 Multiply by $\sec x$: $\dfrac{dy}{dx}\sec x + y \sec x \tan x = \tan x \sec^2 x$, which is

$$\frac{d}{dx}(y \sec x) = \tan x \sec^2 x.$$

Step 6 Integrating, $y \sec x = \frac{1}{2}\tan^2 x + k$.

Step 7 Dividing by $\sec x$, $y = \dfrac{\sin^2 x}{2 \cos x} + k \cos x$.

This is a perfectly acceptable answer to the question. However, it is worth noticing that it can be written as

$$y = \frac{1 - \cos^2 x}{2 \cos x} + k \cos x,$$

which is

$$y = \tfrac{1}{2}(\sec x - \cos x) + k \cos x = \tfrac{1}{2}\sec x + \left(k - \tfrac{1}{2}\right)\cos x.$$

Since k is an arbitrary constant, $k - \tfrac{1}{2}$ can be replaced by a single arbitrary constant c, giving the simplest form of the solution as

$$y = \tfrac{1}{2}\sec x + c \cos x.$$

After such a complicated calculation it is worth checking the answer to make sure you have not made a mistake. If $y = \tfrac{1}{2}\sec x + c \cos x$, then $\dfrac{dy}{dx} = \tfrac{1}{2}\sec x \tan x - c \sin x$, so that the left side of the original equation is

$$\left(\tfrac{1}{2}\sec x \tan x - c \sin x\right)\cos x + \left(\tfrac{1}{2}\sec x + c \cos x\right)\sin x$$

$$= \tfrac{1}{2}\tan x - c \sin x \cos x + \tfrac{1}{2}\tan x + c \cos x \sin x$$

$$= \tan x, \quad \text{as required.}$$

One small point to notice at Step 3 is that strictly the integral of $\tan x$ is $\ln|\sec x|$; that is, it is $\ln \sec x$ or $\ln(-\sec x)$ depending on whether $\sec x$ is positive or negative. If you use the minus sign, then at Step 4 you get $u(x) = -\sec x$ rather than $\sec x$. But this is not important, since it clearly makes no difference at Step 5 whether you multiply the equation by $\sec x$ or $-\sec x$.

13.3 Why the method works

It is quite easy to see why the rule for finding the integrating factor works. Since $I(x)$ is an integral of $p(x)$, it follows that $p(x) = I'(x)$. The left side of the differential equation, in standard form, is therefore

$$\frac{dy}{dx} + yI'(x).$$

After multiplying by $e^{I(x)}$, this becomes

$$\frac{dy}{dx}e^{I(x)} + ye^{I(x)}I'(x).$$

Now if $u(x) = e^{I(x)}$, then differentiation by the chain rule gives $u'(x) = I'(x) \times e^{I(x)}$.

So

$$\frac{dy}{dx}e^{I(x)} + yI'(x) \times e^{I(x)} = \frac{dy}{dx}u(x) + yu'(x), \text{ which is } \frac{d}{dx}\big(y\,u(x)\big).$$

You may also question why the algorithm in Section 13.2 specifies that you should choose $I(x)$ to be the *simplest* integral of $p(x)$. The answer is that you needn't. But if you chose some other integral of $p(x)$, this would have the form $I(x) + c$, for some constant c. The integrating factor would then be $e^{I(x)+c}$, which is $e^{I(x)} \times e^c$. So the only effect of taking one of the other integrals of $p(x)$ for $I(x)$ is to multiply the equation through by an additional numerical constant e^c, which is pointless.

Exercise 13

1   For each of the following differential equations, show that the left side is the derivative of a product. Hence find the general solution of the differential equation.

(a) $y + x\dfrac{dy}{dx} = x^2$

(b) $x\cos t + \dfrac{dx}{dt}\sin t = 1$

(c) $\dfrac{1}{x}\dfrac{dy}{dx} - \dfrac{1}{x^2}y = \dfrac{1}{x^3}$

(d) $e^{x^2}\dfrac{du}{dx} + 2xe^{x^2}u = 2$

2   Find the equation of the solution curve through the given point for each of the following differential equations.

(a) $2xy + x^2\dfrac{dy}{dx} = 1$ through $(1,0)$

(b) $2y\sin x\cos x + \dfrac{dy}{dx}\sin^2 x = \cos x$ through $\left(\frac{1}{2}\pi, 1\right)$

(c) $\dfrac{y}{\sqrt{x}} + 2\sqrt{x}\dfrac{dy}{dx} = x$ through $(1,1)$

3   Use integrating factors to find the general solutions of the following differential equations. Check your answers by substituting back into the original equations.

(a) $\dfrac{du}{dx} + \dfrac{2u}{x} = 1$

(b) $\dfrac{dy}{dx} - y\tan x = 2\sin x$

(c) $\dfrac{dx}{dt} - 4x = e^{2t}$

(d) $\dfrac{dy}{dx} - \dfrac{3y}{x} = x$

(e) $\dfrac{dy}{dt} + y\tan t = \cos t$

(f)* $\dfrac{dy}{dx}\sin x + y\sec x = \cos^2 x$

4   For the following differential equations, find the equations of the solution curves which pass through the given points. Use a calculator to display them on a single diagram.

(a) $\dfrac{dy}{dx} + 3y = 9x$ through $(0,-2), (0,-1), (0,0), (0,1), (0,2)$

(b) $x\dfrac{dy}{dx} + 2y = x^2$, for $x > 0$, through $(1,0), (1,1), (1,2), (2,0), (2,1), (2,2)$

(c) $y\sin x + \dfrac{dy}{dx}\cos x = 2\tan x$, for $-\frac{1}{2}\pi < x < \frac{1}{2}\pi$, through $(0,-2),(0,-1),(0,0),(0,1),(0,2)$

(d) $x\dfrac{dy}{dx} = 3y + 2x$, for $x \neq 0$, through $(-1,-1), (-1,0), (-1,1), (1,-1), (1,0), (1,1)$

5   A curve passing through the point $(1,1)$ has the property that, at each point P of the curve, the gradient of the curve is 1 less than the gradient of (OP), where O is the origin. Find the equation of the curve, and illustrate your answer with a graph.

6 A sack containing a liquid chemical is placed in an empty tank. The chemical seeps out of the sack at a rate of $0.1x$ litres per hour, where x is the number of litres of the chemical remaining in the sack after t hours. The chemical in the tank evaporates at a rate $0.2y$ litres per hour, where y is the number of litres of the chemical in the tank after t hours. If the sack originally contained 50 litres of the chemical, find differential equations for x and for y, and solve them. Find the greatest amount of chemical in the tank, and when this occurs.

7 A will-o'-the-wisp is oscillating in a straight line so that its displacement from the origin at time t is $a + b\sin ct$, where a, b and c are positive constants. It is chased by a kitten which moves so that its velocity at any time is equal to cy, where y is the displacement of the will-o'-the-wisp from the kitten. If x denotes the displacement of the kitten from the origin at time t, find a differential equation connecting x and t. Show that, after some time, x is approximately equal to $a + \dfrac{1}{\sqrt{2}} b\sin\left(ct - \tfrac{1}{4}\pi\right)$. Draw graphs to illustrate the positions of the kitten and the will-o'-the-wisp during the chase.

8 A rope hangs over a rough circular peg of radius r. It is just about to slip with a vertical length p on one side and a vertical length q on the other, where $q > p$. It can be shown that, if the coefficient of friction is 1, the quantity $u = \dfrac{T}{\gamma g}$ satisfies the differential equation

$\dfrac{du}{d\theta} - u = r(\cos\theta - \sin\theta)$. ($\gamma$ is the mass of the rope per unit length, g is the acceleration due to gravity, θ is the angle that the radius to a point on the peg makes with the vertical and T is the tension in the rope at that point.) Given that $u = p$ when $\theta = -\tfrac{1}{2}\pi$, and $u = q$ when $\theta = \tfrac{1}{2}\pi$, prove that $q = pe^{\pi} + r\left(1 + e^{\pi}\right)$.

9 Find the general solution of the differential equation $x\dfrac{dy}{dx} = 2(y - x)$ for $x \neq 0$. Investigate the regions in which the gradient of the solution curve is positive, and those in which it is negative,

(a) from the equation of the solution,

(b) from the differential equation.

Illustrate your answers with sketches of some solution curves.

10 Find the general solution of the differential equation $x\dfrac{dy}{dx} + y = \dfrac{1}{x^2}$ for $x > 0$. Use the differential equation to show that the stationary points on the solution curves all lie on $y = \dfrac{1}{x^2}$, and verify this from your equation for the general solution. Draw graphs to illustrate this property.

By differentiating the differential equation, show that $\dfrac{d^2y}{dx^2} = \dfrac{2}{x^2}\left(y - \dfrac{2}{x^2}\right)$. Hence identify the regions in which the solution curves are concave up, and those in which they are concave down. Check your answer from your graphs.

14 Approximate methods

This chapter develops techniques for numerical and graphical solutions of differential equations. When you have completed it, you should

- be able to use Euler's method to find numerical approximations to the solutions of differential equations
- understand that the errors can be reduced by shortening the step length, the amount of reduction that can be expected, and why
- understand what is meant by a slope field, and how it can be used to sketch approximate solution curves.

14.1 Euler's method

You now know how to solve many differential equations, but there are some whose solutions can't be written as exact algebraic equations. However, you can still solve particular equations as accurately as you want by numerical methods. The first example illustrates the idea with an application in kinematics.

Example 14.1.1

A rocket is launched vertically into space. Table 14.1 gives the speed at 10-second intervals after lift-off for 50 seconds. Estimate the height of the rocket at these times.

Time, t (seconds)	0	10	20	30	40	50
Speed, v (km s^{-1})	0	0.63	1.42	2.47	3.99	6.67

Table 14.1

The speed is the rate at which the height of the rocket is increasing. So if the rocket is at height z km after t seconds, its speed is given by $v = \dfrac{dz}{dt}$. But as only numerical values of $\dfrac{dz}{dt}$ are available, you can't solve this algebraically to find z in terms of t. As a first approximation you can split the period into 5 time-steps of 10 seconds each, and suppose that over each step the rocket travels with the speed given in the table for the beginning of the step. The calculation can then be set out as in Table 14.2.

Time, t	0	10	20	30	40	50
Height, z	0	0	6.3	20.5		85.1
Speed, $v = \dfrac{dz}{dt}$	0	0.63	1.42	2.47		
Time interval, δt	10	10	10			
Increase in height, δz	0	6.3	14.2			

Table 14.2

You construct this table one column at a time. In column 1 the initial time (0 seconds) and height (0 km) are entered in rows 1 and 2. Copy the entry in row 3 (0 km s^{-1}) from Table 14.1, and enter the time-step (10 seconds) in row 4. Then find the number in row 5 by multiplying the entries in rows 3 and 4; this is only approximately the increase in height, based on the assumption of constant speed over the whole of the first time-step. It is clearly an underestimate, because the speed of the rocket is increasing.

When column 1 is complete, start column 2 by adding the increases in time and height from column 1 to the previous entries for time and height. Then repeat the procedure.

Some spaces in columns 4 and 5 have been left blank for you to fill in for yourself. You should arrive at a value of 85.1 km for the estimated height after 50 seconds.

You can use this step-by-step method to approximate to the solution of a differential equation. The only difference is that the third row is not determined by numerical data, but is calculated from the differential equation.

Starting from a given initial point (x_0, y_0) on the solution curve, you find a sequence of points (x_1, y_1), (x_2, y_2), ... whose x-coordinates form an arithmetic sequence with a suitable common difference δx. The y-coordinates are then calculated so that the points lie as close as possible to the solution curve.

Example 14.1.2

Use the step-by-step method to find an approximation to the solution of $\dfrac{dy}{dx} = \sqrt{x+y}$, with an initial value $y = 0.2$ when $x = 0$. Use 5 x-steps, each of size 0.2, to estimate values of y from $x = 0$ to $x = 1$.

The calculations are set out in Table 14.3, and illustrated by Fig. 14.4.

x_r	0	0.2	0.4	0.6	0.8	1.0
y_r		0.2	0.289 44	0.429 36	0.611 50		1.087 11
Gradient at (x_r, y_r)	0.447 21	0.699 60	0.910 69			
x-step	0.2	0.2	0.2			
Estimated y-step	0.089 44	0.139 92	0.182 14			

Table 14.3

In Table 14.3 x_r and y_r are the entries in rows 1 and 2 of any column. You then calculate the gradient g as $\sqrt{x_r + y_r}$ and enter it in row 3. Row 4 shows the chosen x-step, h (0.2 in this example), and you then calculate the y-step, $k = gh$. This completes the column. You then start the next column by calculating $x_{r+1} = x_r + h$, $y_{r+1} = y_r + k$.

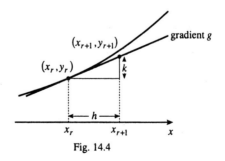

Fig. 14.4

Some spaces have been left in columns 4 and 5 for you to fill in for yourself. You should arrive at 1.087 11 as the estimated value of y when $x = 1$.

Fig. 14.4 shows what is happening. When you go from x_r to x_{r+1}, what you would like to find is the y-coordinate at x_{r+1} on the solution curve through (x_r, y_r). But you can't do this, because you don't know the equation of the curve. All you do know, from the differential equation, is the gradient of the tangent at (x_r, y_r). So the best guess you can make is to take the point on this tangent corresponding to $x = x_{r+1}$ as an approximation to the point on the solution curve.

The approximate step-by-step method illustrated in Example 11.4.2 is attributed to Euler, although the basic idea can be traced back to earlier mathematicians, including Fermat and Newton.

Euler's step-by-step algorithm

To find an approximate numerical solution of a first order differential equation:

Step 1 Choose an x-step.

Step 2 In column 1, enter the given initial values of x and y in rows 1 and 2. Denote these by x_0, y_0.

Step 3 In row 3 enter the gradient g, calculated from the differential equation for the values of x_r and y_r in rows 1 and 2.

Step 4 Enter the chosen x-step in row 4. Denote it by h.

Step 5 Calculate the y-step $k = gh$, and enter it in row 5.

Step 6 Calculate $x_{r+1} = x_r + h$, $y_{r+1} = y_r + k$ and enter these in rows 1 and 2 of the next column.

Step 7 If you want to go further, return to Step 3.

Exercise 14A

1   A racing car accelerates from 0 to 80 m s^{-1} (about 180 m.p.h.) in 12 seconds. Its speed after successive intervals of 2 seconds is given in the table. Estimate how far the car travels while accelerating.

Time (seconds)	0	2	4	6	8	10	12
Speed (m s^{-1})	0	8	20	40	58	74	80

Is your answer too large or too small?

2   The driver of a train travelling at 100 m s^{-1} applies the brakes and brings the train to rest in 25 seconds. The speed of the train after successive intervals of 5 seconds is given in the table. Approximately how far does the train travel in coming to rest?

Time (seconds)	0	5	10	15	20	25
Speed (m s^{-1})	100	88	60	30	12	0

Is your answer too large or too small?

3 For the differential equation and initial value in Example 14.1.2, carry out similar step-by-step calculations with

(a) 10 x-steps, each of 0.1,   (b) 20 x-steps, each of 0.05.

Keep your answers to Question 4 for use in Exercise 14B Questions 1 and 2.

4 Use Euler's step-by-step method to find points on the solution curves of the following differential equations.

(a) $\dfrac{dy}{dx} = \cos\frac{1}{2}(x+y)$; solution curve through $(0,0)$ over the interval $0 \le x \le 1$, taking

x-steps of   (i) $h = 0.5$,   (ii) $h = 0.25$;

(b) $\dfrac{dy}{dx} = \dfrac{1}{x+2y}$; solution curve through $(1,2)$ over the interval $1 \le x \le 5$, taking

x-steps of   (i) $h = 1$,   (ii) $h = 0.5$;

(c) $\dfrac{dy}{dx} = \sqrt{y} + e^{-x}$; solution curve through $(0,1)$ over the interval $0 \le x \le 2$, taking

x-steps of   (i) $h = 1$,   (ii) $h = 0.5$,   (iii) $h = 0.25$;

(d) $\dfrac{dy}{dx} = \dfrac{\sqrt{x}+\sqrt{y}}{2}$; solution curve through $(1,2)$ over the interval $0 \le x \le 2$, taking

x-steps of   (i) $h = \pm 0.5$,   (ii) $h = \pm 0.25$.

5 The speed v of an object falling from a height satisfies the equation $\dfrac{dv}{dt} = 10 - 0.01v^{\frac{3}{2}}$, and $v = 0$ when $t = 0$. Use a step-by-step method with t-steps of 4 and 2 to estimate v when $t = 20$.

6 The level, h metres, of water in a reservoir satisfies the differential equation $\dfrac{dh}{dt} = 0.5t - 0.1h$, where t is the time in weeks. When $t = 0$, the level is 10 metres.

Find the level when $t = 10$,

(a) by using Euler's step-by-step method with step lengths of 2 weeks and 1 week,

(b) by solving the differential equation exactly.

Calculate the errors in using the step-by-step method.

14.2 Slope fields

Another approach is to use numerical values of $\dfrac{dy}{dx}$ given by the differential equation to sketch approximate solution curves. You have already used this idea with homogeneous differential equations in Section 12.3. This method is especially effective if you want to know the nature of the general solution of the differential equation.

It is useful first to introduce some new notation. An expression like $\sqrt{x+y}$ is an example of a **function of two variables** x and y. Such a function is defined for a **domain** which is a set of number pairs (x,y). For $\sqrt{x+y}$ the natural domain is the set such that $x+y \ge 0$, represented in a coordinate plane by the points to the 'north-east' of the line $x+y=0$, shown by the shaded part of Fig. 14.5.

For each point of the domain the function defines a
unique value, denoted in general by $f(x, y)$. The set of
values taken by the function is its **range**; for $\sqrt{x+y}$ the
range is the set of non-negative real numbers.

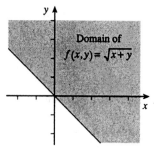

Fig. 14.5

A general first order differential equation can be written
as

$$\frac{dy}{dx} = f(x, y)$$

for some function f. This defines, at each point of the
domain of f, the gradient of the solution curve through
that point. These gradients constitute the **slope field**, or
tangent field, for the differential equation. It is
illustrated in Fig. 14.6, for the differential equation
$\frac{dy}{dx} = \sqrt{x+y}$, by the 'needles' drawn at the corners of
the grid. (You can't, of course, show it at more than a
few typical points. In Fig. 14.6 these are restricted to the
square $0 \le x \le 1$, $0 \le y \le 1$, but the slope field extends
throughout the domain of f.)

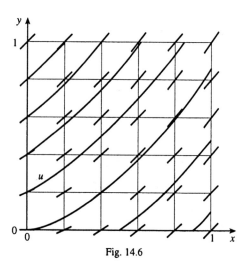

Fig. 14.6

There is a solution curve of the differential equation
through each point of the domain of f. Fig. 14.6 shows
a few such solution curves, and the needles help you to
imagine how others could be drawn starting at any point
of the domain. The curve labelled u is the one in
Example 14.1.2 with initial condition $y = 0.2$ when
$x = 0$.

14.3 Errors in Euler's method

The reason why Euler's method is only approximate is that it is based on the assumption that the value of
$\frac{dy}{dx}$ remains constant over an interval of values of x. This is obviously not true, but it suggests that the

method will be most accurate where $\frac{dy}{dx}$ is not changing very rapidly, that is where $\left|\frac{d^2 y}{dx^2}\right|$ is small.

The simplest way of improving the accuracy is to reduce the length of the x-steps. In this way you can
allow for the change in $\frac{dy}{dx}$ more frequently. The downside is that you have to use more intervals to reach
your destination. Halving the length of the x-steps doubles the number of intervals you need, and so
doubles the amount of arithmetic. But this may not matter if you are using a computer or calculator
program.

The purpose of this section is to investigate the effect on the accuracy of reducing the step length. This
will be done by comparing the results obtained for the differential equation in Example 14.1.2 with
different values for the x-step.

The differential equation in Example 14.1.2 can in fact be solved algebraically, but the solution

$$\sqrt{y+x} - \ln\left(1+\sqrt{y+x}\right) - \tfrac{1}{2}x = \sqrt{0.2} - \ln\left(1+\sqrt{0.2}\right)$$

is too complicated to be of much use. You cannot find from it an equation for y in terms of x, or for x in terms of y. The values described as 'exact' (correct to 5 decimal places) in row 2 of Table 14.7 have not been calculated from this equation, but by using a more advanced modification of Euler's method. However, if you like you can check for yourself that these values do satisfy the above equation.

When you use Euler's method you begin by choosing an x-step. Rows 3 to 5 of Table 14.7 show the results you get if you use x-steps of 0.2, 0.1 and 0.05 respectively. Of course, the shorter the x-step, the more steps you must take to get to a particular value of x. The entries in row 3 are the same as those found in Example 14.1.2, with 5 steps of 0.2.

The numbers of steps in rows 4 and 5 are 10 and 20, but only the values of y for $x = 0.2, 0.4, \ldots, 1$ are shown in the table. You calculated these in Exercise 14A Question 3.

Rows 6 to 8 of Table 14.7 are the errors in the values calculated in rows 3 to 5, found by subtraction from the exact entries in row 2.

	x	0	0.2	0.4	0.6	0.8	1.0
	y (exact)	0.2	0.318 05	0.484 61	0.692 67	0.938 41	1.219 38
	0.2	0.2	0.289 44	0.429 36	0.611 50	0.831 64	1.087 11
y (approx.) with $h =$	0.1	0.2	0.303 43	0.456 51	0.651 48	0.884 32	1.152 45
	0.05	0.2	0.310 68	0.470 46	0.671 95	0.911 22	1.185 75
	0.2	0	0.028 61	0.055 25	0.081 17	0.106 77	0.132 27
error with $h =$	0.1	0	0.014 62	0.028 10	0.041 19	0.054 09	0.066 93
	0.05	0	0.007 37	0.014 15	0.020 72	0.027 19	0.033 63

Table 14.7

Look first along rows 6 to 8 of the table. You can see that the error gets larger with each step taken, but according to a regular pattern. For example, the bottom row shows that after 4 steps of 0.05 the error is about 0.007; after 8 and 12 steps it is about 0.014 and 0.021, roughly twice and three times as much. You will find a similar pattern in rows 6 and 7.

Look down the columns in rows 6 to 8. Each time the x-step is halved, the error is roughly halved. So you can achieve greater accuracy by using a larger number of smaller steps.

Table 14.7 is typical of the results obtained when you use Euler's method. They can be summarised as the following error rules:

Error rules in Euler's method

For a given x-step, the error is approximately proportional to the number of steps taken.

For a given value of x, the error is approximately proportional to the size of the x-steps used.

Another way of improving the accuracy of numerical solutions is to modify the algorithm. For example, in Example 14.1.1 you might get a more accurate estimate of the height of the rocket by taking the time interval boundaries at 5, 15, 25, 35 and 45 seconds, so that the tabulated speeds are at the middle rather than the start of each interval. A number of ways of modifying Euler's method have been devised, some of which can produce very accurate numerical solutions. These are described in specialist books on numerical analysis.

14.4* A graphical explanation of the error rules

Fig. 14.8 illustrates the step-by-step process in Example 14.1.2. You begin at the point A(0,0.2). The basis of the Euler method is to suppose that, for the first x-step, the solution can be approximated by a line with gradient equal to the gradient at A. This takes you from A to P, which has coordinates $(0.2, 0.289\,44)$.

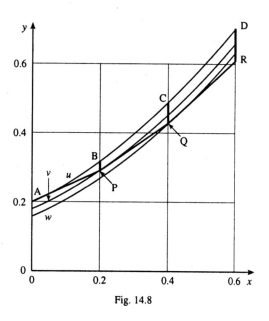

Now you would like P to be on the solution curve u, but in fact it is on a different solution curve, labelled v. The next step therefore takes you from P to Q, where the gradient of [PQ] is equal to that of the tangent to v at P. The coordinates of Q were calculated in Table 14.3 as $(0.4, 0.429\,36)$, and this lies on the curve labelled w. A further step takes you from Q to R, where R has coordinates $(0.6, 0.611\,50)$ and the gradient of [QR] is equal to that of the tangent to w at Q.

The exact values of y in row 2 of Table 14.7 correspond in the figure to the points A, B, C, D,... on u, and the step-by-step approximations correspond to A, P, Q, R,... , so the errors are represented by the lengths PB, QC, RD, ... You can see that the error increases by about the same amount at each step, so the total error is roughly proportional to the number of steps.

Fig. 14.8

The effect of halving the x-step is shown on a larger scale in Fig. 14.9. The points A, P, B and the curves u, v are the same as in Fig. 14.8, so that with $h = 0.2$ Euler's method takes you from A to P. But with an x-step of $h = 0.1$, the first step will go only as far as the mid-point S of [AP], and the next step will take you to T, where [ST] is the tangent to the solution curve through S. The error at $x = 0.2$ is therefore reduced from PB to TB. You can see that the effect of halving the step length is roughly to halve the error.

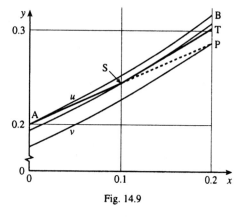

Fig. 14.9

Exercise 14B

1 For the differential equations in Exercise 14A Question 4, draw the slope fields and use these to make freehand sketches of the solution curves through the given points. On the same diagrams plot the points which you found from the step-by-step method, and compare these with the curves you have sketched.

2 The actual solution curves for the differential equations in Exercise 14A Question 4 pass through the points given in the table below. For each curve, find the errors in using the step-by-step method, and see whether these conform with the results summarised in the shaded box in Section 14.3.

(a)	$(0.5, 0.479\,91)$	$(1, 0.854\,59)$		
(b)	$(2, 2.176\,78)$	$(3, 2.320\,01)$	$(4, 2.441\,24)$	$(5, 2.546\,76)$
(c)	$(0.5, 2.003\,07)$	$(1, 3.033\,18)$	$(1.5, 4.121\,94)$	$(2, 5.292\,99)$
(d)	$(0, 1.060\,83)$	$(0.5, 1.457\,16)$	$(1.5, 2.659\,55)$	$(2, 3.425\,15)$

3* This question is designed to establish the error properties stated at the end of Section 14.3 for simple differential equations of the form $\dfrac{dy}{dx} = f(x)$. The notation for points and curves corresponds to that used in Fig. 14.8.

Let the solution curve have equation $y = F(x)$ passing through the point A with coordinates $(a, f(a))$. This satisfies the differential equation $F'(x) = f(x)$.

(a) Referring to Fig. 14.8. let the x-coordinate of B be $a + h$. Express the y-coordinates of B and P in terms of a, h and F. Use a Taylor polynomial (see Section 11.2) to show that the error in using Euler's method when $x = a + h$ is approximately $\frac{1}{2}h^2 f'(a)$.

(b) If the solution curve v through P has equation $y = F_1(x)$, explain why $F_1(x) = F(x) + k$, and show that $k = hf(a) + F(a) - F(a + h)$. Hence find the y-coordinate of Q, and deduce that the error when $x = a + 2h$ is approximately double that when $x = a + h$.

(c) Suppose that Euler's method is used with a single step of $2h$. State what the error would be when $x = a + 2h$, and show that doubling the step has the effect of approximately doubling the error.

Review exercise

1 If S_n denotes $\sum_{i=1}^{n} \frac{1}{i}$, prove that $S_{2n} - S_n > \frac{1}{2}$. Show that, if S_n tends to a limit S as $n \to \infty$, then $\lim_{n \to \infty} (S_{2n} - S_n)$ would equal 0.

What can you deduce about the infinite series $\sum \frac{1}{i}$?

2 (a) If $\lim_{n \to \infty} u_n = 0$, what is $\lim_{n \to \infty} \frac{1}{1 + u_n}$?

   (b) Use the limit comparison test to show that, if $u_i > 0$ for all i and $\sum u_i$ is convergent, then so is
   $$\sum \frac{u_i}{1 + u_i}.$$

3 (a) Use a calculator to find $\sum_{i=1}^{999} \frac{1}{i^3}$.

   (b) Prove that $\sum_{i=1000}^{9999} \frac{1}{i^3} < \frac{9}{1000^2}$, and find a similar inequality for $\sum_{i=10\,000}^{99\,999} \frac{1}{i^3}$.

   (c) Prove that $\sum_{i=1000}^{\infty} \frac{1}{i^3} < \frac{1}{110\,000}$. Hence give the value of $\sum_{i=1}^{\infty} \frac{1}{i^3}$ correct to as many decimal places as these calculations allow.

4 A sequence u_n of positive numbers has $\lim_{n \to \infty} u_n = L$.

   (a) If $L > 0$, use the identity $\left(\sqrt{u_n} - \sqrt{L}\right)\left(\sqrt{u_n} + \sqrt{L}\right) = u_n - L$ to prove that $\sqrt{u_n} - \sqrt{L} < \frac{u_n - L}{\sqrt{L}}$. Hence prove that $\lim_{n \to \infty} \sqrt{u_n} = \sqrt{L}$.

   (b) If $L = 0$, use the definition of limit to prove that $\lim_{n \to \infty} \sqrt{u_n} = 0$.

5 The Maclaurin polynomial of degree 6 is used to approximate to the value of e^x. Over what range of values of x can you be sure that the error is less than 0.001 in absolute value?

6 (a) Find an expression for $\sum_{i=1}^{n} \frac{1}{i(i + 2)}$ in terms of n.

   (b) For what values of x is the power series $\sum \frac{x^i}{i(i + 2)}$ convergent?

7 State the limits, as $n \to \infty$, of

   (a) $\frac{n^2}{2^n}$,
   (b) $n \tan \frac{1}{n}$,
   (c) $\frac{n(2n - 1)}{(3n - 2)(4n - 3)}$.

8 Use the integral test to prove that the value of $\sum_{i=1}^{\infty} \frac{1}{1 + i^2}$ is between $\frac{1}{4}\pi$ and $\frac{1}{4}\pi + \frac{1}{2}$.

9 By grouping the terms of the series in two different ways, prove that $1 + \dfrac{1}{2^p}G < \displaystyle\sum_{i=1}^{2^k}\dfrac{1}{i^p} < G + \dfrac{1}{2^{kp}}$,

where G is the sum of the geometric series $\displaystyle\sum_{j=1}^{k}\left(\dfrac{1}{2^{p-1}}\right)^{j-1}$.

Hence find lower and upper bounds for the value of $\displaystyle\sum_{i=1}^{\infty}\dfrac{1}{i^p}$ if $p > 1$.

10 (a) If the Maclaurin series for $\tan x$ begins $a + bx + cx^2 + dx^3 + \ldots$, use the identity $\tan x \times \cos x = \sin x$ to find a, b, c and d.

(b) Use a similar method to find the Maclaurin series for $\sec x$ as far as the term in x^4.

(c) Why is there no Maclaurin series for $\csc x$? Show that, when x is small, $\csc x \approx \dfrac{1}{x} + \dfrac{1}{6}x + \dfrac{7}{360}x^3$.

11 Prove that, if $f(x) = \cos^n x$, then $f''(x) = n(n-1)\cos^{n-2}x - n^2\cos^n x$. Hence expand $\sqrt{\cos x}$ as a Maclaurin series as far as the term in x^4.

Check by squaring your answer and showing that the resulting series agrees with the series for $\cos x$ as far as the term in x^4.

12 Find (a) $\displaystyle\lim_{x \to 1}\dfrac{\cos\frac{1}{2}\pi x}{1 - x^2}$,   (b) $\displaystyle\lim_{x \to 0}\dfrac{\left(e^x - 1\right)^2}{1 - \cos x}$.

13 A curve C passes through the origin and satisfies the differential equation $\dfrac{dy}{dx} + 2xy = x^3$.

(a) Use Euler's method to approximate to the value of y when $x = 1$ using x-steps of length

(i) 0.2,   (ii) 0.1.

(b) Solve the equation to find the value of y when $x = 1$ correct to 4 decimal places.

(c) If you make the assumption that the error in Euler's method is exactly halved when the length of the x-steps is halved, what value would your answers to part (a) suggest for the value of y when $x = 1$?

14 Find the implicit equation of the curve which passes through $(1,0)$ and satisfies the homogeneous differential equation $\dfrac{dy}{dx} = \dfrac{2x}{x+y}$. Check your answer by differentiation.

15 (a) Use Euler's method starting from $x = 0$ to find an approximation to the solution of the differential equation $\dfrac{dy}{dx} = y$ which passes through the point $(0,1)$. Take steps of length (i) 0.1 and (ii) 0.05 to find approximations to the value of y when $x = 1$. Compare your approximations with the exact value of y when $x = 1$.

(b) For the same equation, take a step length of $\dfrac{1}{n}$, giving n steps between $x = 0$ and $x = 1$. Denoting the value of y after the rth step by y_r, show that $y_{r+1} = \left(1 + \dfrac{1}{n}\right)y_r$, and deduce that the value of y when $x = 1$ is given by $\left(1 + \dfrac{1}{n}\right)^n$.

(c) Try calculating $\left(1 + \dfrac{1}{n}\right)^n$ for large values of n. (See Exercise 7 Question 3.)

Examination questions

1 For positive integers k and n let $u_k = \dfrac{1 + 2(-1)^k}{k+1}$ and $S_{2n} = \displaystyle\sum_{k=1}^{2n} u_k$.

(a) Show that $S_{2n} = \displaystyle\sum_{k=1}^{n} \dfrac{4k-1}{2k(2k+1)}$.

(b) Hence or otherwise, determine whether the series $\displaystyle\sum_{k=1}^{\infty} u_k$ is convergent or not, justifying your

answer.   (© IBO 2003)

2 (a) Describe how the integral test is used to show that a series is convergent. State all the necessary conditions.

(b) Test the series $\displaystyle\sum_{n=1}^{\infty} \dfrac{n}{e^{n^2}}$ for convergence.   (© IBO 2003)

3 (a) Find the first four non-zero terms of the Maclaurin series for

(i) $\sin x$,   (ii) e^{x^2}.

(b) Hence find the Maclaurin series for $e^{x^2} \sin x$, up to the term containing x^5.

(c) Use the result of part (b) to find $\displaystyle\lim_{x \to 0}\left(\dfrac{e^{x^2} \sin x - x}{x^3} \right)$ (© IBO 2003)

4 Find the Maclaurin series of the function $f(x) = \ln(1 + \sin x)$ up to and including the term in x^4.

(© IBO 2004)

5 Determine whether the following series is convergent or divergent.

$$\sum_{k=1}^{\infty} \cos\left(\frac{(k-1)\pi}{2k} \right)$$ (© IBO 2004)

6 Let $S_k = \displaystyle\sum_{k=1}^{n} \dfrac{\sin\left(\dfrac{k\pi}{2} \right)}{k + \sin\left(\dfrac{k\pi}{2} \right)}$.

(a) Show that, for $m \in \mathbb{Z}^+$, $S_{4m} = 0$.

(b) Show that $S_n \to 0$ as $n \to \infty$.

(c) Hence, or otherwise, show that the series converges as $n \to \infty$, and find its limit.

(© IBO 2004)

7 Find the range of values of x for which the following series is convergent.

$$\sum_{n=0}^{\infty} \frac{x^n}{n+1}$$ (© IBO 2004)

8 (a) Show that the series $\displaystyle\sum_{n=1}^{\infty} \sin\frac{2\pi}{n^2}$ is convergent.

Let $S = \displaystyle\sum_{n=1}^{\infty} \sin\frac{2\pi}{n^2}$.

(b) Show that for positive integers $n \geq 2$, $\dfrac{1}{n^2} < \dfrac{1}{n-1} - \dfrac{1}{n}$.

(c) Hence or otherwise show that $1 \leq S < 2\pi$.   (© IBO 2004)

9 (a) Show that the series $\displaystyle\sum_{k=1}^{\infty} \frac{k-1}{k!}$ is convergent.

(b) Find the sum of the series.   (© IBO 2005)

10 The function f is defined by $f(x) \equiv e^{-x} \cos 2x$.

(a) (i) Show that $f''(x) + 2f'(x) + 5f(x) = 0$.

(ii) Show that $f^{(n+2)}(0) + 2f^{(n+1)}(0) + 5f^{(n)}(0) = 0$, for $n \in \mathbb{Z}^+$.

(b) Find the Maclaurin series for $f(x)$ up to and including the term in x^4.   (© IBO 2005)

11 Given that $e^x \equiv 1 + x + \dfrac{x^2}{2!} + \dfrac{x^3}{3!} + \ldots$, and $\ln(1+x) = x - \dfrac{x^2}{2} + \dfrac{x^3}{3} - \dfrac{x^4}{4} + \ldots$, find the first four

non-zero terms of the Maclaurin series for $e^{-x} \ln(1+x)$.   (© IBO 2005)

12 Find the radius of convergence of the series $\displaystyle\sum_{k=1}^{\infty} \frac{(2k-2)!}{k!(k-1)!} x^k$.   (© IBO 2005)

Answers

1 Summing finite series

Exercise 1A (page 4)

2 (a) $\frac{1}{4}i(i+1)(i+2)(i+3)$;

$\frac{1}{4}n(n+1)(n+2)(n+3)$

(b) $-\dfrac{1}{2(i+1)(i+2)}$; $\dfrac{1}{4}\left(1-\dfrac{2}{(n+1)(n+2)}\right)$

3 $6i^5 + 2i^3$; $\frac{1}{12}n^2(n+1)^2(2n^2+2n-1)$

4 (a) $\ln(n+1)$ (b) $1-\dfrac{1}{n!}$

5 $(n+1)!-1$

6 $\dfrac{100}{201}$

7 $160i^4 + 80i^2 + 2$; 722 666

8 $\dfrac{1-(n+1)r^n + nr^{n+1}}{(1-r)^2}$

9 $\dfrac{\sin\left(n+\frac{1}{2}\right)\theta}{2\sin\frac{1}{2}\theta} - \dfrac{1}{2}$

Exercise 1B (page 8)

1 (a) $\dfrac{1}{x+5} + \dfrac{1}{x+3}$ (b) $\dfrac{3}{x-1} + \dfrac{7}{x+5}$

(c) $\dfrac{-4}{x-4} + \dfrac{5}{x-5}$ (d) $\dfrac{8}{2x-1} - \dfrac{4}{x+3}$

2 (a) $\dfrac{5}{x+2} + \dfrac{3}{x-1}$ (b) $\dfrac{5}{x-4} - \dfrac{5}{x+1}$

(c) $\dfrac{4}{x-3} + \dfrac{6}{x+3}$ (d) $\dfrac{3}{x} - \dfrac{6}{2x+1}$

3 (a) $\dfrac{3}{x+2} - \dfrac{5}{x-1} + \dfrac{2}{x-3}$

(b) $\dfrac{9}{x+3} - \dfrac{2}{x+1} + \dfrac{1}{x-1}$

(c) $\dfrac{3}{x} + \dfrac{5}{x-6} + \dfrac{7}{x+4}$

Exercise 1C (page 11)

1 (a) $\frac{1}{2}\left(1-\dfrac{1}{2n+1}\right)$ (b) $\frac{1}{3}\left(\dfrac{1}{2} - \dfrac{1}{3n+2}\right)$

(c) $\frac{1}{4}\left(\dfrac{1}{3} - \dfrac{1}{(2n+1)(2n+3)}\right)$

(d) $\frac{1}{15} - \dfrac{n+1}{(2n+3)(2n+5)}$

2 (a) $\dfrac{2^{n+1}}{n+2} - 1$ (b) $\dfrac{1}{2} - \dfrac{\left(\frac{1}{2}\right)^n}{n+2}$

(c) $\dfrac{1}{4}\left(1 - \dfrac{\left(\frac{1}{3}\right)^n}{2n+1}\right)$

2 Infinite series

Exercise 2A (page 14)

1 (a) 1 (b) $\frac{1}{4}$ (c) $\frac{1}{2}$

(d) $\frac{1}{6}$ (e) $\frac{1}{4}$ (f) $\frac{1}{12}$

2 (a) $\frac{1}{6}$ (b) $\frac{1}{4}$ (c) 2

3 (b) 1

Exercise 2B (page 18)

1 (a) $\displaystyle\lim_{i\to\infty} \dfrac{i}{2i-1} = \frac{1}{2} \neq 0$

(b) $\dfrac{1}{\sqrt[3]{i}} \geq \dfrac{1}{\sqrt{i}}$, and $\sum \dfrac{1}{\sqrt{i}}$ is divergent.

2 (a) $\dfrac{1}{i^{2.5}} \leq \dfrac{1}{i^2}$, and $\sum \dfrac{1}{i^2}$ is convergent.

(b) $\dfrac{1}{i^2+1} < \dfrac{1}{i^2}$, and $\sum \dfrac{1}{i^2}$ is convergent.

(c) $\dfrac{1}{2^i+1} < \dfrac{1}{2^i}$, and $\sum \left(\dfrac{1}{2}\right)^i$ is convergent.

3 (b) $\frac{1}{3}\pi^2 - 1 \approx 2.29$

(c) For example $S_{56} \approx 1.879\,853\,862$

4 (a) $\dfrac{1}{i^4} \leq \dfrac{1}{i^2}$, and $\sum\dfrac{1}{i^2}$ is convergent.

(b) E.g. $S_{999} \approx 1.082\,323\,233$. (c) 90

5 (a) $\dfrac{1}{i^3} \leq \dfrac{1}{i^2}$, and $\sum\dfrac{1}{i^2}$ is convergent.

(b) For example $S_{999} \approx 1.202\,056\,403$.

(d) $\sum\dfrac{1}{(i-1)i(i+1)}$ is not defined for $i=1$.

(e) $\displaystyle\sum_{i=2}^{\infty}\dfrac{1}{i^3} \leq \sum_{i=2}^{\infty}\dfrac{1}{(i-1)i(i+1)} = \dfrac{1}{4}$, so $\displaystyle\sum_{i=1}^{\infty}\dfrac{1}{i^3} \leq 1\frac{1}{4}$.

6 (a) $\sum\dfrac{1}{i}$ is divergent

(b) $S_{1000} > 5\frac{1}{2}$ (c) 7.485 471

7 (a) $i = 1, 2$; $S_\infty \leq 2$

(b) For $i > 2$, $i! \geq 2 \times 3^{i-2}$ (= when $i = 2, 3$);
$M = 8$
(Exact values of S_∞ are (a) $e - 1$, (b) $e^2 - 1$.)

8 (c) For example $S_{168} \approx 0.736\,399\,859$.

Exercise 2C (page 22)

2 (a) $\frac{3}{4}$

3 6

3 Tests for convergence

Exercise 3A (page 28)

1 (a) For example, $S_\infty \leq \frac{5}{16} = 0.3125$,
$S_{100} = 0.3017\ldots$

(b) For example, $S_\infty \leq \frac{4}{7} = 0.5714\ldots$,
$S_{15} = 0.5644\ldots$

(c) For example, $S_\infty \leq 7\frac{11}{56}$, $S_{100} = 6.000\ldots$

2 (a) $\lim\limits_{i \to \infty} \dfrac{u_i}{u_{i-1}} = \frac{1}{2}$ (b) $\lim\limits_{i \to \infty} \dfrac{u_i}{u_{i-1}} = \frac{1}{3}$

3 No; in fact it diverges.

4 (b) $\lim\limits_{i \to \infty} \dfrac{u_i}{u_{i-1}} = 1$

5 (a) $q < 1$ (b) all q (c) $q < 1$

Exercise 3B (page 31)

1 (a) 1   (b) $\frac{1}{2}$

3 (a),(b),(d),(f) convergent; (c),(e) divergent

4 Series and integrals

Exercise 4A (page 37)

1 (a) 3.5, 4.5; 3.9, 4.1; 3.99, 4.01; exact value 4
(b) 4.875, 9.375; 6.555, 7.455;
6.95505, 7.04505; exact value 7
(c) 4.146..., 5.146...; 4.616..., 4.716...;
4.661..., 4.671...; exact value $4\frac{2}{3}$
(d) 20, 43; 27.4375, 38.9375; exact value 33.75

2 (a) $50\left(1 - \dfrac{1}{n}\right)$, $50\left(1 + \dfrac{1}{n}\right)$; 50

(b) $\frac{1}{6}a^3\left(1 - \dfrac{1}{n}\right)\left(2 - \dfrac{1}{n}\right)$, $\frac{1}{6}a^3\left(1 + \dfrac{1}{n}\right)\left(2 + \dfrac{1}{n}\right)$;
$\frac{1}{3}a^3$

(c) $\dfrac{e - 1}{n\left(e^{\frac{1}{n}} - 1\right)}$, $\dfrac{e^{\frac{1}{n}}(e - 1)}{n\left(e^{\frac{1}{n}} - 1\right)}$; $e - 1$

3 (a) 0.2   (b) 0.01   (c) $\dfrac{1}{n}$

4 (a) 0.3   (b) 0.015   (c) $\dfrac{3}{2n}$

5 $S - s = \dfrac{\bigl(f(a) - f(b)\bigr)(b - a)}{n}$,
otherwise unchanged

Exercise 4B (page 43)

2 (a) 4246, 4243
(b) 30.69, 30.18
(c) 57.29, 56.29
(d) 0.007 854, 0.007 803

3 (a) $\dfrac{(n + m - 1)(n - m + 1)}{2(m - 1)^2 n^2}$, $\dfrac{(n + m + 1)(n - m + 1)}{2m^2(n + 1)^2}$

(b) $\frac{1}{2}\ln\dfrac{1 + n^2}{1 + (m - 1)^2}$, $\frac{1}{2}\ln\dfrac{1 + (n + 1)^2}{1 + m^2}$

(c) $\dfrac{(n + 1)^{n+1}}{(m + 1)^{m+1}}e^{-(n-m)}$, $\dfrac{n^n}{m^m}e^{-(n-m)}$

5 (b) $\frac{3}{4}\left(9^{\frac{4}{3}} - 1\right)$

(c) $\frac{3}{4}\left(201^{\frac{4}{3}} - 101^{\frac{4}{3}}\right)$; $\frac{3}{4}\left(200^{\frac{4}{3}} - 100^{\frac{4}{3}}\right)$

5 Infinite integrals and infinite series

Exercise 5A (page 46)

1 (a) 1   (c) 3   (d) 1   (f) 1
(b), (e) do not converge.

2 (a) $p < 0$ (b) $p < -1$

3 (a) $\frac{1}{2}$ (b) 1   (c) $\frac{1}{2}\pi$
(d) $\frac{1}{2}$ (e) $\frac{1}{4}$ (f) $2e^{-1}$

4 No, $f(x) = \dfrac{1}{x}$ is a counterexample.

Exercise 5B (page 52)

2 (a) $\ln 2$, $1 + \ln 2$; $S_{999} = 1.3857\ldots$
(b) $\frac{1}{6}\pi - \frac{1}{3}\arctan\frac{1}{3}$, $\frac{1}{10} + \frac{1}{6}\pi - \frac{1}{3}\arctan\frac{1}{3}$;
$S_{999} = 0.4670\ldots$
(c) $\ln\frac{3}{2}$, $1 + \ln\frac{3}{2}$; $S_{999} = 1.1683\ldots$
(d) $\sin 1$, $\cos 1 + \sin 1$; $S_{999} = 1.1437\ldots$
(e) 0.2, 0.208; $S_{999} = 0.2024\ldots$

4 $\dfrac{1}{\left(1+x^2\right)^{\frac{1}{2}}}$, $\dfrac{1}{\left(1+x^2\right)^{\frac{3}{2}}}$; $1-\dfrac{1}{\sqrt{2}}$, $1-\dfrac{1}{2\sqrt{2}}$

Exercise 5C (page 54)

1 (a) 1.644 933 567, 1.644 934 567
(b) 0.392 699 050, 0.392 699 112

2 (a) 1.386 29 (b) 0.468 043
(c) 1.168 524 (d) 1.144 79
(e) 0.203 41

6 Series with positive and negative terms

Exercise 6 (page 64)

1 (a) 21; 0.901 498, 0.901 593
(b) 5; 0.783 429, 0.783 451
(c) 7; 0.632 118, 0.632 143
(d) 10; 0.864 620, 0.864 673

2 (a) absolutely convergent
(b) conditionally convergent
(c) oscillates finitely
(d) conditionally convergent
(e) oscillates infinitely
(f) oscillates infinitely
(g) oscillates infinitely
(h) conditionally convergent
(i) absolutely convergent
(j) diverges to $+\infty$
(k) oscillates finitely
(l) oscillates infinitely

3 (a) $-\dfrac{1}{1440}\pi^4$ (b) $\dfrac{1}{96}\pi^4$ (c) $\dfrac{7}{720}\pi^4$

4 (a) $1-\dfrac{1}{2}-\dfrac{1}{4}+\dfrac{1}{3}-\dfrac{1}{6}-\dfrac{1}{8}+\dfrac{1}{5}-\dfrac{1}{10}+\dfrac{1}{7}-\dfrac{1}{12}$

(b) $1+\dfrac{1}{3}-\dfrac{1}{2}+\dfrac{1}{5}+\dfrac{1}{7}-\dfrac{1}{4}+\dfrac{1}{9}+\dfrac{1}{11}-\dfrac{1}{6}+\dfrac{1}{13}$

(c) $-\dfrac{1}{2}+1-\dfrac{1}{4}-\dfrac{1}{6}-\dfrac{1}{8}-\dfrac{1}{10}-\dfrac{1}{12}+\dfrac{1}{3}-\dfrac{1}{14}-\dfrac{1}{16}$

The series of positive terms diverges to $+\infty$ and the series of negative terms diverges to $-\infty$.

6 (a) $\sum\left(-\dfrac{1}{2}\right)^{i-1}i$ (b) 4
(c) $-\dfrac{16}{9}$ (d) $\dfrac{4}{9}$

7 The theory of limits

Exercise 7A (page 68)

1 (a) If $p<2$, $\dfrac{2n+3}{n+2}>p$ if $n>\dfrac{2p-3}{2-p}$.

(b) If $q>\dfrac{1}{2}$, $\dfrac{n}{2n-1}<q$ if $n>\dfrac{q}{2q-1}$.

2 (a) 300 (b) 3000 (c) $\dfrac{3}{q}$

3 (a) 30 (b) $\max\left(-\dfrac{1}{p},\dfrac{3}{q}\right)$

4 (a) $\dfrac{3}{2}$ (b) 1

6 1
8 1

Exercise 7B (page 72)

1 (a) 1 (b) $-\dfrac{1}{5}$ (c) $\dfrac{1}{3}$

2 (a) 0 (b) $\dfrac{1}{2}$ (c) $\dfrac{1}{2}$ (d) 1

3 For example, (a) $u_n=\dfrac{1}{n}$

(b) $u_n=-\dfrac{1}{n}$ (c) $u_n=\dfrac{(-1)^n}{n}$

Exercise 7C (page 78)

1 (a) $\dfrac{3}{5}$ (b) 4
2 (a) $\dfrac{1}{3}$ (b) 1 (c) 0 (d) 1
3 a, e^a; that if $\lim\limits_{n\to\infty} u_n=L$, then $\lim\limits_{n\to\infty} e^{u_n}=e^L$.
4 (a) $\dfrac{2}{3}$ (b) $\dfrac{4}{9}$ (c) $\ln 3$
5 (a) 0 (b) 0

8 Power series

Exercise 8 (page 84)

1 (a) $[-1,1]$ (b) $[-1,1[$ (c) $\mathbb{R}$
(d) $\left[-\dfrac{1}{2},\dfrac{1}{2}\right[$ (e) $x=0$ (f) $]-1,1[$
(g) $]-1,1[$ (h) $]-1,1[$ (i) $\left]-\dfrac{1}{4},\dfrac{1}{4}\right[$

2 (a) 1 (b) 1 (c) 2 (d) $\sqrt{2}$

9 Maclaurin series

Exercise 9A (page 90)

1 (a) $1+\dfrac{3}{2}x+\dfrac{3}{8}x^2-\dfrac{1}{16}x^3$
(b) $1+\dfrac{3}{2}x+\dfrac{15}{8}x^2+\dfrac{35}{16}x^3$

2 (a) $x-\dfrac{1}{6}x^3+\dfrac{1}{120}x^5$
(b) $2x-\dfrac{4}{3}x^3+\dfrac{4}{15}x^5$
(c) $1+x+\dfrac{1}{2}x^2+\dfrac{1}{6}x^3+\dfrac{1}{24}x^4$
(d) $1-3x+\dfrac{9}{2}x^2-\dfrac{9}{2}x^3+\dfrac{27}{8}x^4$
(e) x^2
(f) $1-x^2$
(g) $-x-\dfrac{1}{2}x^2-\dfrac{1}{3}x^3-\dfrac{1}{4}x^4$

(h) $1 + x + \frac{3}{2}x^2 + \frac{5}{2}x^3$

(i) $1 - \frac{1}{2}x^2 + \frac{1}{8}x^4$

(j) $x^2 - \frac{1}{2}x^4$

4 $1, \frac{1}{2}$

5 $1 + px + \dfrac{p(p-1)}{2}x^2 + \dfrac{p(p-1)(p-2)}{6}x^3$

$+ \dfrac{p(p-1)(p-2)(p-3)}{24}x^4$

Exercise 9B (page 93)

1 (a) 1.6487   (b) 0.8415
    (c) 0.9655   (d) 0.9397
    (e) −0.0513   (f) 0.8109
    (g) −0.9900

2 $2x + \frac{2}{3}x^3 + \frac{2}{5}x^5 + \ldots + \dfrac{2}{2i+1}x^{2i+1} + \ldots ,$

$-1 < x < 1; \ x = \frac{1}{2}, \ 1.099;$

$x = 2$ is outside interval of validity.

3 (a) $1 + \frac{1}{2}x^2 + \frac{5}{24}x^4, \ 8.5 \times 10^{-6}\%$

    (b) $x - \frac{1}{3}x^3, \ 2.0 \times 10^{-3}\%$

4 0.0433, 0.0063 too large; the second, which uses a value of x closer to 0

Exercise 9C (page 100)

1 (a) $1 + 3x + \frac{3}{2}x^2 - \frac{1}{2}x^3 + \frac{3}{8}x^4$

    (b) $1 - 2x + 2x^2 - \frac{4}{3}x^3 + \frac{2}{3}x^4$

    (c) x^3 (d) x^3

2 (a) $1 + 3x + \frac{9}{2}x^2 + \ldots + \dfrac{3^i}{i!}x^i + \ldots , \quad \mathbb{R}$

    (b) $1 - \frac{1}{8}x^2 + \frac{1}{384}x^4 - \ldots + \dfrac{(-1)^i}{2^{2i}(2i)!}x^{2i} + \ldots , \quad \mathbb{R}$

    (c) $x - \frac{1}{6}x^2 + \frac{1}{120}x^3 - \ldots + \dfrac{(-1)^{i-1}}{(2i-1)!}x^i + \ldots ,$

        positive $\mathbb{R}$

    (d) $-x - \frac{1}{2}x^2 - \frac{1}{3}x^3 - \ldots - \dfrac{1}{i}x^i - \ldots ,$

        $-1 \le x < 1$

    (e) $2x - 2x^2 + \frac{8}{3}x^3 - \ldots + \dfrac{(-1)^{i-1}2^i}{i}x^i + \ldots ,$

        $-\frac{1}{2} < x \le \frac{1}{2}$

    (f) $e + ex + \frac{1}{2}ex^2 + \ldots + \dfrac{e}{i!}x^i + \ldots , \quad \mathbb{R}$

    (g) $1 - x^2 + \frac{1}{3}x^4 + \ldots + \dfrac{(-1)^i 2^{2i-1}}{(2i)!}x^{2i} + \ldots , \quad \mathbb{R}$

    (h) $1 + \frac{1}{e}x - \dfrac{1}{2e^2}x^2 + \ldots + \dfrac{(-1)^{i-1}x^i}{ie^i} + \ldots ,$

        $-e < x \le e$

    (i) $\cos 1 - (\sin 1)x - \left(\frac{1}{2}\cos 1\right)x^2 + \ldots$

        $+ \dfrac{(-1)^i \cos 1}{(2i)!}x^{2i}$

        $+ \dfrac{(-1)^{i+1} \sin 1}{(2i+1)!}x^{2i+1} + \ldots , \quad \mathbb{R}$

3 (a) $x - x^2 + \frac{1}{3}x^3$

    (b) $1 - \frac{1}{2}x - \frac{5}{8}x^2 + \frac{3}{16}x^3 + \frac{25}{384}x^4$

    (c) $1 + \frac{1}{2}x^2 - \frac{1}{3}x^3 + \frac{3}{8}x^4$

    (d) $x + \frac{3}{2}x^2 + \frac{1}{3}x^3 - \frac{1}{12}x^4$

    (e) $3x - \frac{21}{2}x^2 + 24x^3 - \frac{205}{4}x^4$

    (f) $-6x^2 - 6x^3 + x^4$

4 (a) $1 - \frac{1}{2}x^2 + \frac{5}{24}x^4$

    (b) $\ln 2 + \frac{1}{2}x + \frac{1}{8}x^2 - \frac{1}{192}x^4$

5 $x + \frac{1}{6}x^3 + \frac{3}{40}x^5 + \ldots$

    $+ \dfrac{3 \times 5 \times 7 \times \ldots \times (2i-1)}{(2i+1)i!2^i}x^{2i+1} + \ldots ,$

    $\frac{1}{2}\pi - x - \frac{1}{6}x^3 - \frac{3}{40}x^5 - \ldots ; \ 3.1416$

6 $x - \frac{1}{18}x^3 + \frac{1}{600}x^5 - \ldots$

    $+ \dfrac{(-1)^i}{(2i+1)(2i+1)!}x^{2i+1} + \ldots$

7 $x + \frac{1}{4}x^2 + \frac{1}{18}x^3 + \ldots + \dfrac{1}{i(i)!}x^i + \ldots ; \ 0.570$

9 $-\frac{1}{3}x^3 + \frac{1}{30}x^5; \ -\frac{1}{3}$

10 (a) 2   (b) $\frac{1}{2}$

    (c) 1   (d) $-\frac{1}{2}$

11 $\frac{1}{3}\theta + \frac{2}{81}\theta^3; 0.82$ radians

10 The error term

Exercise 10 (page 113)

1 (a) 0.818 733 333
    (b) −0.000 002 580
    (c) $-\dfrac{e^c}{5!}(0.2)^5$ where $-0.2 < c < 0$,
        0.000 002 667
    (d) 0.000 002 667

2 (a) 0.479 427 083   (b) –0.000 001 545

(c) $R_5(0.5) = -\dfrac{\sin c}{6!}(0.5)^6$ where $0 < c < 0.5$,

0.000 021 701

(d) 0.000 001 550

(e) For the $\sin x$ series $p_5(x)$ and $p_6(x)$ are the same, so the error in part (c) could be found as $R_6(0.5)$ rather than $R_5(0.5)$; this is $-\dfrac{\cos c}{7!}(0.5)^7$ where $0 < c < 0.5$, with $\dfrac{(0.5)^7}{7!}$ as an upper bound for the magnitude of the error. This is the same as part (d).

3 (a) $\dfrac{(0.2)^6}{6} = 0.000\,010\,667$

(b) $(0.2)^5 = 0.000\,32$

(c) $\dfrac{(0.2)^6}{6} = 0.000\,010\,667$,

$\dfrac{(0.2)^6}{6 \times 0.8} = 0.000\,013\,333$

4 (a) $-2.62 < x < 2.62$

(b) $-0.517 < x < 0.664$

5 (a) 14   (b) 13

6 (a) $-\dfrac{1 \times 3 \times 5 \times \ldots \times (2i-3)}{2^i \times i!}$

(b) $-\dfrac{1 \times 3 \times 5 \times \ldots \times (2n-1)}{2^{n+1} \times (n+1)!} \times \dfrac{x^{n+1}}{(1-c)^{n+\frac{1}{2}}}$

(d) 5   (e) 1.56×10^{-6}

7 (a) $R_n(x) = (-1)^{n+1}\dfrac{(n+2)(n+3)x^{n+1}}{2(1+c)^{n+4}}$ where

$0 < c < x$, $|R_n(x)| < \dfrac{(n+2)(n+3)}{2}x^{n+1}$

(b)

$\displaystyle\int_0^x \dfrac{(n+1)(n+2)(n+3)}{2}(1-t)^{-(n+4)}(x-t)^n\,dt$

$\leq \dfrac{(n+1)(n+2)(n+3)}{6}x^n\left(\dfrac{1}{(1-x)^3}-1\right)$

8 $\left(1 + 3x + 6x^2 + \ldots + \dfrac{(n+1)(n+2)}{2}x^n\right)$

$\dfrac{(n+2)(n+3)x^{n+1} - 2(n+1)(n+3)x^{n+2}}{}$

$+\dfrac{+(n+1)(n+2)x^{n+3}}{2(1-x)^3}$

10 Expressions for successive derivatives soon become very complicated. 6 terms

11 Taylor series and l'Hôpital's rule

Exercise 11 (page 120)

1 $e^a\left(1 + (x-a) + \dfrac{(x-a)^2}{2!} + \ldots\right) = e^a \times e^{x-a}$;

$\displaystyle\int_a^x \dfrac{e^t}{n!}(x-t)^n\,dt$,

$\dfrac{e^c(x-a)^{n+1}}{(n+1)!}$ where c is between a and x.

2 $\dfrac{1}{\sqrt{2}}\left(1 + \left(x - \tfrac{1}{4}\pi\right) - \dfrac{\left(x - \tfrac{1}{4}\pi\right)^2}{2!} - \dfrac{\left(x - \tfrac{1}{4}\pi\right)^3}{3!}\right.$

$\left. + \dfrac{\left(x - \tfrac{1}{4}\pi\right)^4}{4!} + \dfrac{\left(x - \tfrac{1}{4}\pi\right)^5}{5!} - \dfrac{\left(x - \tfrac{1}{4}\pi\right)^6}{6!}\right)$;

$\displaystyle\int_{\frac{1}{4}\pi}^x \dfrac{-\cos t}{6!}(x-t)^6\,dt$;

$p_6(x) - \dfrac{1}{\sqrt{2}} \times \dfrac{\left(x - \tfrac{1}{4}\pi\right)^7}{7!},\ \displaystyle\int_{\frac{1}{4}\pi}^x \dfrac{\sin t}{7!}(x-t)^7\,dt$

3 $1 + \tfrac{1}{3}h - \tfrac{1}{9}h^2 + \tfrac{5}{81}h^3$,

$-\tfrac{10}{243}h^4(1+\theta h)^{-\frac{11}{3}}$, where $0 < \theta < 1$;

1.047 708, too large, 0.000 021

4 $(x-2)(x^2 + 2x - 1)$, $(x-2)(x^2 + x + 2)$; $\tfrac{7}{8}$

5 $(x-2)^2(x+1)$, $(x-2)^2(x+4)$; $\tfrac{1}{2}$

6 (a) 4   (b) –2   (c) $-\dfrac{2}{\sqrt{e}}$ (d) 2

7 (a) $\dfrac{8}{9\pi^2}$ (b) $\tfrac{25}{4}$ (c) –2   (d) $-\tfrac{1}{4}$

12 Homogeneous differential equations

Exercise 12A (page 128)

1 $y = \sqrt{x^2 + k}$

2 (a) $y = (\sqrt{x} + 2)^2$, $y = (\sqrt{x} + 1)^2$, $y = x$,

$y = \left(\sqrt{x} - 1\right)^2$ for $x > 1$,

$y = \left(\sqrt{x} - 2\right)^2$ for $x > 4$

(b) $y = \left(x\sqrt{x}+26\right)^{\frac{2}{3}}$, $y = \left(x\sqrt{x}+7\right)^{\frac{2}{3}}$, $y = x$,

$\quad y = \left(x\sqrt{x}-7\right)^{\frac{2}{3}}$ for $x > 7^{\frac{2}{3}}$,

$\quad y = \left(x\sqrt{x}-26\right)^{\frac{2}{3}}$ for $x > 26^{\frac{2}{3}}$

3 $y = x\sqrt{2\ln x + k}$

4 (a) $y = \sqrt{x^2+3x}$, $y = \sqrt{x^2+6x}$,

$\quad y = \sqrt{x^2+5x}$; all for $x > 0$

(b) $y = \sqrt{5x-x^2}$, $y = \sqrt{10x-x^2}$,

$\quad y = \sqrt{13x-x^2}$

5 $x = y\sqrt{1+2\ln y}$

6 $y = \dfrac{x}{\ln x + k}$

7 $\frac{1}{2}\ln\left(x^2+y^2\right) + \arctan\left(\dfrac{y}{x}\right) = k$

Exercise 12B (page 131)

1 $\sqrt{3}$

2 $y = (\sqrt{x}+2)^2$ is an enlargment of $y = (\sqrt{x}+1)^2$,

and $y = \left(\sqrt{x}-2\right)^2$ is an enlargement of

$y = \left(\sqrt{x}-1\right)^2$, both with a factor of 4.

3 (a) 2, $1\frac{2}{3}$ (b) 2, 2.6

4 Yes; $y = \dfrac{x}{\ln x}$ is transformed by an enlargement

of factor c to $y = \dfrac{x}{\ln x - \ln c}$, and $\ln c$ can take all

real values.

6 $y = 0$, $y = -x$. But in fact the solution is

$y = \dfrac{x}{k - \ln|x|}$ with stationary points at

$\left(\pm e^{k+1}, \mp e^{k+1}\right)$, so all stationary points are on

$y = -x$; there are no points on solution curves at

which $y = 0$, since the differential equation is

meaningless at $(0,0)$.

13 Linear differential equations

Exercise 13 (page 140)

1 (a) $y = \frac{1}{3}x^2 + \dfrac{k}{x}$ (b) $x = (t+k)\csc t$

(c) $y = -\dfrac{1}{2x} + kx$ (d) $u = (2x+k)e^{-x^2}$

2 (a) $y = \dfrac{x-1}{x^2}$ (b) $y = \csc x$

(c) $y = \dfrac{x^2+3}{4\sqrt{x}}$

3 (a) $u = \frac{1}{3}x + \dfrac{k}{x^2}$ (b) $y = k\sec x - \cos x$

(c) $x = ke^{4t} - \frac{1}{2}e^{2t}$ (d) $y = kx^3 - x^2$

(e) $y = (t+k)\cos t$ (f) $y = \cos x + k\cot x$

4 (a) $y = 3x - 1 + ke^{-3x}$ with $k = -1, 0, 1, 2, 3$

(b) $y = \frac{1}{4}x^2 + \dfrac{k}{x^2}$ with $k = -\frac{1}{4}, \frac{3}{4}, \frac{7}{4}, -4, 0, 4$

(c) $y = \sec x + k\cos x$ with $k = -3, -2, -1, 0, 1$

(d) $y = kx^3 - x$ with $k = 2, 1, 0, 0, 1, 2$

5 $y = x(1 - \ln x)$

6 $\dfrac{dx}{dt} = -0.1x$, $\dfrac{dy}{dt} = 0.1x - 0.2y$; $x = 50e^{-0.1t}$,

$y = 50\left(e^{-0.1t} - e^{-0.2t}\right)$; 12.5 litres, after 6.93 hours

7 $\dfrac{dx}{dt} = c(a + b\sin ct - x)$

9 $y = 2x + kx^2$; gradient positive within the acute angles between $y = x$ and the y-axis, negative within the obtuse angles

10 $y = \dfrac{k}{x} - \dfrac{1}{x^2}$; solution curves are concave up

above $y = \dfrac{2}{x^2}$, are concave down below.

14 Approximate methods

In this chapter your answers may differ from those given by 1 or 2 in the last decimal place. This will usually depend on whether or not you have rounded intermediate values in the calculations. Don't spend time trying to get an exact match between your answers and those given if they are close enough to indicate that you have used a correct procedure.

Exercise 14A (page 144)

1 400 m; too small

2 1450 m ; too large

3 Values at selected points are given in (a) line 4, (b) line 5 of Table 14.7 in Section 14.3.

4 (a) (i) $(0.5, 0.5)$, $\left(1, 0.938\,79\right)$

(ii) $\left(0.5, 0.492\,23\right)$, $\left(1, 0.898\,21\right)$

(b) (i) $(2, 2.2)$, $\left(3, 2.356\,25\right)$,

$\left(4, 2.485\,91\right)$, $\left(5, 2.597\,37\right)$

(ii) $\left(2, 2.187\,72\right)$, $\left(3, 2.337\,25\right)$,

$\left(4, 2.462\,60\right)$, $\left(5, 2.571\,05\right)$

(c) (i) $(1,3)$, $(2,5.099\ 93)$
   (ii) $(0.5,2)$, $(1,3.010\ 37)$,
        $(1.5,4.061\ 83)$, $(2,5.181\ 10)$
   (iii) $(0.5,2.000\ 89)$, $(1,3.020\ 01)$,
        $(1.5,4.088\ 86)$, $(2,5.232\ 72)$
(d) (i) $(0,0.924\ 24)$, $(0.5,1.396\ 45)$,
        $(1.5,2.603\ 55)$, $(2,3.313\ 13)$
   (ii) $(0,0.990\ 54)$, $(0.5,1.427\ 08)$,
        $(1.5,2.631\ 18)$, $(2,3.368\ 43)$

5 With t-step 4, 97.68; with t-step 2, 95.46

6 (a) 19.7 m, 20.9 m   (b) 22.07 m
   Errors 2.4 m, 1.2 m

Exercise 14B (page 149)

2 (a)

x	0.5	1.0
$h=0.5$	−0.020 09	−0.084 20
$h=0.25$	−0.012 32	−0.043 62

(b)

x	2	3
$h=1$	−0.023 22	−0.036 24
$h=0.5$	−0.010 94	−0.017 24

	4	5
	−0.044 67	−0.050 61
	−0.021 36	−0.024 29

(c)

x	0.5	1
$h=1$	−	0.033 18
$h=0.5$	0.003 07	0.022.81
$h=0.25$	0.002 18	0.013 17

	1.5	2.0
	−	0.193 06
	0.060 11	0.111 89
	0.033 08	0.060 27

(d)

x	0	0.5
$h=-0.5$	0.136 59	0.060 71
$h=-0.25$	0.070 29	0.030 08

	1.5	2.0
$h=+0.5$	0.056 00	0.112 02
$h=+0.25$	0.028 37	0.056 72

3 (a) $y_B = F(a+h)$, $y_P = F(a)+hf(a)$
   (b) $y_Q = F_1(a+h)+hf(a+h)$
   (c) $2h^2 f'(a)$

Review exercise

(page 150)

1 The series is divergent.

---

2 (a) 1

3 (a) 1.202 056 403   (b) $\displaystyle\sum_{i=10\ 000}^{99\ 999}\frac{1}{i^3} < \frac{9}{10\ 000^2}$
   (c) 1.2021 correct to 4 d.p.

5 $-1.26 < x < 1.08$

6 (a) $\frac{3}{4}-\frac{1}{2}\left(\dfrac{1}{n+1}+\dfrac{1}{n+2}\right)$ (b) $-1 \le x \le 1$

7 (a) 0 (b) 1 (c) $\frac{1}{6}$

9 $\dfrac{2^{p-1}-\frac{1}{2}}{2^{p-1}-1}$, $\dfrac{2^{p-1}}{2^{p-1}-1}$

10 (a) $0, 1, 0, \frac{1}{3}$ (b) $1+\frac{1}{2}x^2+\frac{5}{24}x^4$
   (c) If $f(x)=\csc x$, $f(0)$ doesn't exist.

11 $1-\frac{1}{4}x^2-\frac{1}{96}x^4$

12 (a) $\frac{1}{4}\pi$ (b) 2

13 (a) (i) 0.1391 (ii) 0.1624
   (b) 0.1839   (c) 0.1857

14 $(2x+y)(x-y)^2 = 2$

15 (a) 2.593 74, 2.653 30; e $\approx$ 2.718 28

Examination questions

1 (b) Not convergent
2 (b) Convergent
3 (a) (i) $x-\frac{1}{6}x^3+\frac{1}{120}x^5-\frac{1}{5040}x^7$
      (ii) $1+x^2+\frac{1}{2}x^4+\frac{1}{6}x^6$
   (b) $x+\frac{5}{6}x^3+\frac{41}{120}x^5$ (c) $\frac{5}{6}$

4 $x-\frac{1}{2}x^2+\frac{1}{6}x^3-\frac{1}{12}x^4$

5 Divergent
6 (c) 0
7 $-1 \le x < 1$
9 (b) 1
10 (b) $1-x-\frac{3}{2}x^2+\frac{11}{6}x^3-\frac{7}{24}x^4$

11 $x-\frac{3}{2}x^2+\frac{4}{3}x^3-x^4$

12 $\frac{1}{4}$

Index

The page numbers refer to the first mention of each term, or the shaded box if there is one.

absolute convergence, 60
agreement of functions, 87
alternating series, 55

binomial series, 85

comparison test, 18
conditional convergence, 60
convergence
    of integral, 45
    of series, 12

definite integral, 32
divergence, 15
domain (of $f(x,y)$), 145

error term, 102
    in Maclaurin series, 104, 106
    in Taylor series, 116
    integral form, 104, 116
    Lagrange's form, 106, 116
Euler's constant, 48
Euler's step-by-step method, 144
    error rules, 147

function of two variables, 145

harmonic series, 51
homogeneous differential equation, 121

improper integral, 45
infinite integral, 45
integral test, 49
integrating factor, 135
interval of convergence, 80
interval of validity, 91, 108

l'Hôpital's rule, 118, 119
limit, 67
    evaluation using series, 99
    forms a^n/n^k and $n^k b^n$, 20, 22
limit comparison test, 29

linear differential equation, 134
    general solution, 138
    standard form, 134
lower (Riemann) sum, 33

Maclaurin polynomial, 88
Maclaurin series, 90
method of differences, 2

oscillating series, 57

partial fractions, 5
partial sum, 12
power series, 79
p-series, 50

radius of convergence, 84
range (of $f(x,y)$), 146
ratio test, 24
    limit form, 26
relative error, 107
remainder
    in Maclaurin series, 104, 106
    in Taylor series, 116
Riemann's zeta-function, 51
Rolle's theorem, 104

slope field, 146
squeeze theorem, 76
Stirling's approximation, 84
summing series, 1
    using partial fractions, 9
sum sequence, 12
sum to infinity, 12

tangent field, 146
Taylor series, 116
    alternative form, 117
telescoping series, 2
term-by-term differentiation, 97
truncation error, 56

upper (Riemann) sum, 34

Topic 5
Discrete Mathematics

Stan Dolan, Hugh Neill and Douglas Quadling

Series Editor Hugh Neill

CAMBRIDGE
UNIVERSITY PRESS

Contents

Introduction   v

1   Integers   1

2   Linear diophantine equations   19

3   Modular arithmetic   25

4   Fermat's little theorem   41

5   Integers in different bases   45

6   Graphs   54

7   Isomorphic graphs   65

8   Minimum spanning trees   76

9   The shortest path   86

10   The Chinese Postman algorithm   92

11   The travelling salesperson problem   99

Review exercise   110

Answers   117

Index   123

Introduction

Discrete mathematics has been written especially for the International Baccalaureate Further Mathematics SL examination. This book covers the syllabus for Topic 5.

The book is in two parts: Chapters 1 to 5 on properties of integers, and Chapters 6 to 11 on graphs. These two parts can be studied independently. There is a small amount of material which extends a topic beyond the syllabus as printed, with the aim of enhancing students' appreciation of the subject. This is indicated by an asterisk (*) at the appropriate place in the text.

Occasionally within the text paragraphs appear in *this type style*. These paragraphs are usually outside the main stream of the mathematical argument, but may help to give insight, or suggest extra work or different approaches.

There are plenty of exercises throughout. At the end of the book there is a Review exercise which includes some questions from past International Baccalaureate examinations, but on a different syllabus. At the time of writing, there are few current versions of the Higher Level examinations, so there is no backlog of examination questions on the newer parts of the syllabus.

The authors thank OCR and IBO for permission to use some examination questions and Cambridge University Press for their help in producing this book. Particular thanks are due to Sharon Dunkley, for her help and advice, and to Linda Moore, who read the manuscript with great care and suggested many improvements. However, the responsibility for the text, and for any errors, remains with the authors.

1 Integers

This chapter develops the properties of integers which are concerned with division. When you have completed it, you should

- know the division algorithm
- be able to use the Euclidean algorithm to find the greatest common divisor of two integers
- be able to use the Euclidean algorithm in reverse
- be able to find the greatest common divisor of two integers
- know what prime numbers and relatively prime numbers are
- know the fundamental theorem of arithmetic
- be able to find the least common multiple of two integers.

1.1 Whole numbers

You have known about whole numbers from a very early age. You have learned to add, subtract, multiply and divide them, and to accept results sometimes without question.

For example, if you were asked to factor 12 into prime numbers, you would say without hesitation that $12 = 2^2 \times 3$. That is fine. But if you had to find the prime factors of 32123, you might hesitate a little more. You would probably think that it would be hard work, and if you really had to do it, you would probably start dividing by 2, 3, 5, 7 and so on to see what numbers divide into 32123.

But would you think that if you found a prime factorisation of 32123, and someone else found a prime factorisation of 32123, that you would be bound to get the same result? You probably would think that way because in early schooling you are encouraged to think that way, but if the numbers are really big, it is something that really does require proof.

And what answer would you give to the question, what is the result when you divide 11 by 4? Here are a number of possibilities.

4 doesn't divide into 11	$11 \div 4 = 2.75$
$11 \div 4 = 2\frac{3}{4}$	1, remainder 7
2, remainder 3	3, remainder -1

In some sense, these responses are all correct. But which one you give depends on the context, or on your sophistication as a student. It would help to know which number set, $\mathbb{R}$, $\mathbb{Q}$, $\mathbb{Z}$ or $\mathbb{N}$, you are working in.

In this chapter you will usually be working in $\mathbb{N} = \{0,1,2,3,\dots\}$, but sometimes you may be working in $\mathbb{Z} = \{\dots -3,-2,-1,0,1,2,3,\dots\}$.

A number of the laws of working with whole numbers will be assumed without proof or further comment. It is possible to go right back to first principles and to define numbers from the beginning, but it would make progress slow. So the following knowledge will be assumed.

You should be able to add, subtract and multiply integers, and you should be able to use inequalities.

Notice that division isn't included in that list.

There is one other property, which you may not have met explicitly before, but which you are probably happy to accept. It is called the **well-ordering** principle.

> Every non-empty set of positive integers has a least member.

1.2   Division

So what is division? It is the reverse of multiplication. So, for integers, define b divides a to mean that there is an integer q such that

$$a = qb,$$

or you might say that

$$a = qb \text{ for some } q \in \mathbb{Z}.$$

It is worth avoiding the case when $b = 0$ by removing it altogether. And it will also help with thinking to consider only those cases for which b is positive.

The statement b divides a is written symbolically as $b \,|\, a$.

> Let a and b be integers. Then b **divides** a if there is an integer q, called the **quotient**, such that $a = qb$.
>
> b divides a is denoted by $b \,|\, a$.

Notice two things here. First, nothing is said about whether a is positive or negative. And secondly the $b \,|\, a$ notation can easily be confused with the use of the vertical line in set notation. In this book, the two uses of this notation will be kept apart.

If b does not divide a, as 4 did not divide 11 in Section 1.1, there is a remainder, but how is the '1, remainder 7', '2, remainder 3' or '3, remainder -1' ambiguity mentioned in Section 1.1 resolved?

The answer is to limit the size of the remainder to ensure that the usual answer '2, remainder 3' is given, but to do that you need a definition of remainder.

Let a and b be integers with $b > 0$. Then consider the set

$$S = \{a - qb \text{ such that } q \in \mathbb{Z} \text{ and } a - qb \geq 0\}.$$

In the case when $a = 11$ and $b = 4$ this set is $\{3, 7, 11, 15, 19, \ldots\}$.

In the case when $a = -11$ and $b = 4$ this set is $\{1, 5, 9, 13, 17, \ldots\}$.

In both cases S is a non-empty set of positive integers and so, by the well-ordering principle in Section 1.1, has a least member, in one case 3 and in the other case 1. This least member is used to define the remainder.

First, it is important to show that in the general case the set

$$S = \{a - qb \text{ such that } q \in \mathbb{Z} \text{ and } a - qb \geq 0\},$$

where $b > 0$, is non-empty.

As $b > 0$, $a - qb$ can be made positive by choosing a negative integer q with a sufficiently large modulus. S is therefore non-empty.

Since S is non-empty it has a least member. Call this member r, and let Q be the particular value of q which gives r, so that $r = a - Qb$. Then $r - b = a - Qb - b = a - (Q+1)b$ is smaller than r, and so cannot be in S. (Remember r is the least member of S.) Therefore $r - b$ is negative, so $r < b$.

Now you can define the **remainder** as the least member of S.

But is this number uniquely determined, or could there be two different remainders? You won't be surprised that the remainder is uniquely determined by a and b. This result is proved in a theorem called the division algorithm.

Theorem 1.1   The division algorithm
Let a and b be integers with $b > 0$. Then there exist two integers q and r such that

$$a = qb + r \qquad \text{with } 0 \leq r < b,$$

and the integers q and r are uniquely determined by a and b.

Proof
Consider the set $S = \{a - qb \text{ such that } q \in \mathbb{Z} \text{ and } a - qb \geq 0\}$. S is non-empty, as shown above, so there are integers q and r such that $r = a - qb$, where $0 \leq r < b$.

Suppose now that there are two such pairs of integers, q_1, r_1 and q_2, r_2 which satisfy the conditions. Then $a = q_1 b + r_1 = q_2 b + r_2$.

Suppose that $r_2 \geq r_1$. Then

$$q_1 b + r_1 = q_2 b + r_2 \quad \Rightarrow \quad (q_1 - q_2)b = r_2 - r_1.$$

The right side is positive or zero since $r_2 \geq r_1$, and since $r_2 < b$ and $r_1 \geq 0$, $r_2 - r_1 < b$. Hence $0 \leq r_2 - r_1 < b$.

So $0 \leq (q_1 - q_2)b < b$.

But $(q_1 - q_2)b$ is a multiple of b. The only multiple of b which satisfies this is 0 so $q_1 = q_2$. It follows that $r_1 = r_2$. This concludes the theorem.

It's not surprising that teachers of small children assume, possibly without realising it, that this theorem is true.

1.3   Using a calculator

If you use a calculator to find a remainder when you divide one integer by another non-zero integer, you will find that it is more complicated than dividing to get an answer in decimal form.

For example, you find that $11 \div 4 = 2.75$. You must then deduce that the quotient is 2, and then calculate $11 - 2 \times 4 = 3$ to find the remainder. The process of going from 2.75 to 2 is called finding the **integer part** of 2.75.

If $x \in \mathbb{R}$, the function int x is defined to be the largest integer which is less than or equal to x. That is

$$\text{int } x \le x < \text{int } x + 1 \quad \text{or alternatively} \quad x - 1 < \text{int } x \le x.$$

Thus

$$\text{int}(11/4) = \text{int}(2.75) = 2 \quad \text{and} \quad \text{int}(-11/4) = \text{int}(-2.75) = -3.$$

Some calculators have variations of int. *Check your calculator with these examples so you know if* int *works the same way on your calculator.*

Using the int function, the remainder is given by

$$\begin{aligned} \text{remainder} &= 11 - \text{int}(11 \div 4) \times 4 \\ &= 11 - 2 \times 4 \\ &= 3. \end{aligned}$$

In general, when dividing a by b, where $b > 0$, the remainder r is given by

$$r = a - \text{int}(a \div b) \times b.$$

You may find it easier to separate the process of finding the remainder into two parts, and to find the integer part of the quotient manually.

Example 1.3.1

Find the remainders when
(a) $32\,123$ is divided by 37,   (b) $-43\,234$ is divided by 17.

(a) $32\,123 \div 37 = 868.18\ldots$ so the remainder is $32\,123 - 868 \times 37 = 7$.

Alternatively, $32\,123 - \text{int}(32\,123 \div 37) \times 37 = 7$.

(b) $-43\,234 \div 17 = -2543.17\ldots$, and $-43\,234 - (-2544 \times 17) = 14$ so the remainder is 14.

Alternatively, $-43\,234 - \text{int}(-43\,234 \div 17) \times 17 = 14$.

In part (b), notice that if you use the 'by hand' method, you must be sure that when you take the integer part of $-2543.17\ldots$, you take the greatest integer *less than* $-2543.17\ldots$. The integer -2543 is greater than $-2543.17\ldots$.

■■■■■■■■■■■■■■■■■■■■■■■ **Exercise 1A** ■■■■■■■■■■■■■■■■■

1 Find the remainders when a is divided by b in the following cases.

(a) $a = 435,\ b = 39$
(b) $a = 47\,435,\ b = 437$
(c) $a = 953\,357,\ b = 687$
(d) $a = -4\,836,\ b = 142$
(e) $a = -53\,185,\ b = 432$
(f) $a = -176\,472,\ b = 684$

2 Prove that if $m \mid a$ and $m \mid b$, then $m \mid a \pm b$.

3* In the proof of the division algorithm (Section 1.2) the condition $0 \le r < b$ was made. Show that you could prove that the new values of q and r are unique if the condition is changed to $-\frac{1}{2}b < r \le \frac{1}{2}b$.

1.4 Greatest common divisors

If you have ever tried to find the greatest common divisor (gcd) of two numbers such as 45 and 72, you have probably had to use a process like the one in Example 1.4.1. It should be emphasised that this process only works in practice because the numbers involved are small.

The term 'highest common factor' is often used in place of 'greatest common divisor'.

Example 1.4.1
Find the gcd of 102 and 18.

The divisors of 102 are 1, 2, 3, 6, 17, 34, 51 and 102.

The divisors of 18 are 1, 2, 3, 6, 9 and 18.

By inspection, the common divisors are 1, 2, 3, 6, so the gcd is 6.

This process is not practical if you are asked to find the gcd of two larger numbers, of the size of 1237 and 4569, for example, let alone really big numbers. This is because finding factors of big numbers is a really difficult process in practice.

In theory, finding factors of an integer n is easy. In succession, find the remainders on division of n by 2, 3, 4, 5, ... , or if you know about prime numbers (which have not yet been defined in this book) find the remainders on division of n by the prime numbers 2, 3, 5, 7, ... When you have a zero remainder, you can divide n by the current prime number, and then start again on the quotient. But the process takes too long. In fact modern codes for keeping information secret rely on the fact that the 'enemy' cannot find the factors of a large number, about 200 digits, in a time short enough for the information to be useful.

The next example shows another method you might use for finding the gcd.

Example 1.4.2
Find the gcd of 102 and 18.

Expressed in terms of their prime factors

$$102 = 2 \times 3 \times 17 \quad \text{and} \quad 18 = 2 \times 3^2.$$

The greatest power of 2 which divides both is 2^1; the greatest power of 3 which divides both is 3^1; the greatest power of 17 which divides both is $17^0 = 1$.

So the gcd is $2^1 \times 3^1 \times 17^0 = 6$.

This method, so far unjustified, is better theoretically, but suffers like Example 1.4.1 from the fact that finding factors is difficult, so you need a better method for finding the gcd of two integers.

First, Theorem 1.2 states an important result in the development of a better method for finding a gcd.

Theorem 1.2
If k, a and b are integers, and $k \mid a$ and $k \mid b$, then k divides every member of the set $S = \{am + bn \mid m, n \in \mathbb{Z}\}$.

Proof
If $k \mid a$, there exists $x \in \mathbb{Z}$ such that $a = kx$.

Similarly, if $k \mid b$, there exists $y \in \mathbb{Z}$ such that $b = ky$.

Then

$$\begin{aligned} am + bn &= (kx)m + (ky)n \\ &= k(xm) + k(yn) \\ &= k(mx + ny), \end{aligned}$$

so $k \mid am + bn$.

Hence k divides every member of the set $S = \{am + bn \mid m, n \in \mathbb{Z}\}$.

Note that $m, n \in \mathbb{Z}$, so m and n can be both positive or negative.

Here is the definition of the greatest common divisor:

Let a and b be two integers which are not both zero. Then if $k \mid a$ and $k \mid b$, k is called a **common divisor** of a and b.

An integer d is called the **greatest common divisor** of a and b if

- $d > 0$

- $d \mid a$ and $d \mid b$

- if $c \mid a$ and $c \mid b$, then $c \leq d$.

The greatest common divisor of a and b is denoted by $\gcd(a, b)$.

It is not obvious from this definition that there is always such a number d. But note that $c \le d$ in the third condition ensures that there is at most one such number d.

In the definition nothing is said about whether the integers a and b are positive, zero or negative, except that they are not both zero. But the definition of gcd, which is always positive, shows that, for example,

$$\gcd(57,95) = \gcd(-57,95) = \gcd(57,-95) = \gcd(-57,-95),$$

and in what follows, nothing is lost by assuming that the numbers involved are positive. If one of the integers, say a, is zero, then $\gcd(0,b) = b$.

One final comment: the third condition, if $c \mid a$ and $c \mid b$, then $c \le d$, is usually easiest to prove by showing that c divides d, and is therefore not greater than d.

Example 1.4.3 gives three examples of finding a gcd, at this stage without proof. The first uses fairly low numbers, but the second and third have numbers big enough to be difficult using the factor method. The justification for the method will be given afterwards in the Euclidean algorithm.

Example 1.4.3
(a) Find the gcd of 102 and 18.   (b) Find the gcd of $53\,059$ and $12\,028$.

(c) Find the gcd of $29\,303$ and $27\,066$.

(a)   Use the division algorithm (Theorem 1.1) to write

$$102 = 5 \times 18 + 12$$
$$18 = 1 \times 12 + 6$$
$$12 = 2 \times 6 + 0,$$

where at each stage the number at the right end is the remainder, which is then used to divide into the quotient on the same line. Eventually in this process you will end with 0. At that stage the previous remainder is the gcd. Then $\gcd(102,18) = 6$.

(b)   Use the division algorithm to write

$$53\,059 = 4 \times 12\,028 + 4947$$
$$12\,028 = 2 \times 4947 + 2134$$
$$4947 = 2 \times 2134 + 679$$
$$2134 = 3 \times 679 + 97$$
$$679 = 7 \times 97 + 0.$$

Then $\gcd(53\,059,12\,028) = 97$.

(c)   Use the division algorithm to write

$$29\,303 = 1 \times 27\,066 + 2237$$
$$27\,066 = 12 \times 2237 + 222$$
$$2237 = 10 \times 222 + 17$$
$$222 = 13 \times 17 + 1$$
$$17 = 17 \times 1 + 0.$$

Then $\gcd(29\,303,27\,066) = 1$.

> If the greatest common divisor of two numbers is 1, the two integers are said to be **relatively prime** (or **co-prime**).

Example 1.4.3(c) shows that $29\,303$ and $27\,066$ are relatively prime.

The next theorem shows not only that the gcd exists, but also how to find it.

Theorem 1.3   The Euclidean algorithm

Let a_0 and a_1 be two positive integers with $a_0 \geq a_1$. Then a_0 and a_1 have a unique gcd h which is found by the following process.

Using the division algorithm

$$a_0 = q_1 a_1 + a_2,$$

where a_2 is the remainder. If $a_2 = 0$, then $\gcd(a_0, a_1) = a_1$. If $a_2 \neq 0$, then, by the division algorithm

$$a_1 = q_2 a_2 + a_3,$$

where a_3 is the remainder. If $a_3 = 0$, then $\gcd(a_0, a_1) = a_2$. If $a_3 \neq 0$, then, continuing until the remainder is zero,

$$
\begin{aligned}
a_2 &= q_3 a_3 + a_4 \\
a_3 &= q_4 a_4 + a_5 \\
&\ \ \vdots \\
a_{n-2} &= q_{n-1} a_{n-1} + a_n \\
a_{n-1} &= q_n a_n.
\end{aligned}
$$

Then $\gcd(a_0, a_1) = a_n$.

Proof

First note that each remainder is positive and smaller than the one before, so, by the well-ordering principle, the process must stop.

To prove that a_n is the required gcd, show that it satisfies the three conditions in the shaded box.

Clearly, $a_n > 0$.

Also, from the last line of equations, $a_n \mid a_{n-1}$, and using Theorem 1.2 on each line in turn working upwards leads to $a_n \mid a_1$ and $a_n \mid a_0$, so the second condition holds.

To check the third condition, let $k \mid a_0$ and $k \mid a_1$. Then, from the equation $a_0 = q_1 a_1 + a_2$, $a_2 = a_0 - q_1 a_1$, so by Theorem 1.2 $k \mid a_2$. Proceeding down the equations one by one, $k \mid a_3$, $k \mid a_4$, $k \mid a_5$ and on arriving at the last but one equation, $k \mid a_n$. Since $k \mid a_n$, $k \leq a_n$.

So a_n satisfies all three conditions for the gcd. Therefore $a_n = \gcd(a_0, a_1)$.

Using the Euclidean algorithm in reverse enables you to express the gcd of two integers as the sum or difference of multiples of those integers.

Example 1.4.4

(a) Express the gcd of 102 and 18 in the form $x \times 102 + y \times 18$.

(b) Express the gcd of 29 303 and 27 066 in the form $x \times 29 303 + y \times 27 066$.

(a) Using the sequence, reproduced below, of equations from Example 1.4.3(a),

$$102 = 5 \times 18 + 12 \qquad \text{Line 1}$$
$$18 = 1 \times 12 + 6 \qquad \text{Line 2}$$
$$12 = 2 \times 6 + 0, \qquad \text{Line 3}$$

and reversing them, you find

$$6 = 18 - 1 \times 12 \qquad \text{(from Line 2)}$$
$$= 18 - 1 \times (102 - 5 \times 18) \qquad \text{(using Line 1)}$$
$$= 18 - 1 \times 102 + 5 \times 18 \qquad \text{(simplifying the line above)}$$
$$= 6 \times 18 - 102. \qquad \text{(simplifying the line above)}$$

(b) Using the sequence, reproduced below, of equations from Example 1.4.3(c),

$$29 303 = 1 \times 27 066 + 2237 \qquad \text{Line 1}$$
$$27 066 = 12 \times 2237 + 222 \qquad \text{Line 2}$$
$$2237 = 10 \times 222 + 17 \qquad \text{Line 3}$$
$$222 = 13 \times 17 + 1 \qquad \text{Line 4}$$
$$17 = 17 \times 1, \qquad \text{Line 5}$$

and reversing them, you find

$$1 = 222 - 13 \times 17 \qquad \text{(from Line 4)}$$
$$= 222 - 13 \times (2237 - 10 \times 222) \qquad \text{(using Line 3)}$$
$$= 131 \times 222 - 13 \times 2237 \qquad \text{(simplifying the line above)}$$
$$= 131 \times (27 066 - 12 \times 2237) - 13 \times 2237 \qquad \text{(using Line 2)}$$
$$= 131 \times 27 066 - 1585 \times 2237 \qquad \text{(simplifying the line above)}$$
$$= 131 \times 27 066 - 1585 \times (29 303 - 1 \times 27 066) \qquad \text{(using Line 1)}$$
$$= 1716 \times 27 066 - 1585 \times 29 303. \qquad \text{(simplifying the line above)}$$

Example 1.4.4 shows how to prove the first part of an important theorem, which is stated here without further proof, but a proof is given of the second part.

Theorem 1.4

Let a and b be two positive integers.

(a) Then $\gcd(a, b) = h$ can be expressed in the form $h = ax + by$ for some integers x and y.

(b) h is the smallest positive integer in the set $S = \{ax + by \text{ such that } x, y \text{ are integers}\}$.

Proof

(a) The proof follows exactly the lines of Example 1.4.4.

(b)   From part (a), h belongs to S.

Since $h \mid a$ and $h \mid b$, h divides every member of the set S.

Suppose that there is a positive integer, k, of S which is smaller than h.

Then since h divides every member of the set S, $h \mid k$, so $k \geq h$, which is a contradiction.

Therefore there is no positive integer, k, of S which is smaller than h.

Notice that Theorem 1.4 does not say that $\gcd(a,b) = h$ can be expressed *uniquely* in the form $h = ax + by$. For example, in the case of Example 1.4.4(a) where $a = 102$, $b = 18$ and $h = 6$,

$$6 = 6 \times 18 - 102 = 23 \times 18 - 4 \times 102.$$

This will be taken further in Chapter 2.

Example 1.4.5
Let a, b and c be positive integers.

(a) Prove that $\gcd(ca,cb) = c \gcd(a,b)$.

(b) Prove that $\gcd(a,b) = \gcd(a,a-b)$.

Both parts involve checking that a supposed gcd satisfies the three conditions.

(a)   Let $\gcd(a,b) = d$. Then you must check that cd is the gcd of ca and cb.

Since both c and d are positive, $cd > 0$.

As $d \mid a$, $cd \mid ca$ and as $d \mid b$, $cd \mid cb$.

By Theorem 1.4(a), $d = ax + by$ for some integers x and y, so

$$cd = c(ax + by) = (ca)x + (cb)y,$$

and is therefore divisible by any divisor of ca and cb.

Therefore if $k \mid ca$ and $k \mid cb$, then $k \mid cd$, so $k \leq cd$.

As the conditions are satisfied, $\gcd(ca,cb) = c \gcd(a,b)$.

(b)   Let $\gcd(a,b) = d$. Now check that d is also $\gcd(a,a-b)$.

First, as $\gcd(a,b) = d$ and the gcd is always positive, $d > 0$.

Secondly, as $\gcd(a,b) = d$, $d \mid a$ and $d \mid b$, so $d \mid a - b$.

Finally, suppose k is any divisor of a and of $a - b$.

Then writing b as $a - (a-b)$ shows that $k \mid a + (b-a)$, so $k \mid b$.

As $d = \gcd(a,b)$ and $k \mid a$ and $k \mid b$, it follows that $k \mid d$, so $k \leq d$.

As the conditions are satisfied, $\gcd(a,b) = \gcd(a,a-b)$.

1.5   Two important results

This section consists of two theoretical results which will be used many times in the following chapters, and also shows how the Euclidean algorithm is important in the development of results. Both results concern divisibility, and are actually very closely related.

Suppose that a number, say 312, is a product of two other numbers, $312 = 6 \times 52$, and that you know that another number, say 13, divides 312, but no part of the 13 cancels with the factor 6: then 13 must divide the factor 52.

For example, $13 \mid 312$, but 13 and 6 are relatively prime. Therefore $13 \mid 52$.

Put generally, if $m \mid ab$ and $\gcd(a, m) = 1$, then $m \mid b$.

Theorem 1.5

Let a, b and m be integers with $\gcd(a, m) = 1$. Then if $m \mid ab$, $m \mid b$.

Proof

The proof relies on a cunning use of the Euclidean algorithm.

Since $\gcd(a, m) = 1$, then, from Theorem 1.4, there exist integers x and y such that $1 = ax + my$.

Multiplying by b gives $b = bax + bmy$.

Look at both terms on the right side. By hypothesis, $m \mid ab$, so $m \mid abx$. And as $m \mid bmy$, m divides the right side, and so divides the left side.

Hence $m \mid b$.

The second result says that if two numbers m and n each divide another number a, and if m and n are relatively prime, that is, $\gcd(m, n) = 1$, then the product mn divides a.

For example, if 7 and 13 both divide a, then 91 divides a.

Theorem 1.6

Let a, m and n be integers with $\gcd(m, n) = 1$. Then if $m \mid a$ and $n \mid a$, $mn \mid a$.

Proof

If $m \mid a$, then $a = mx$ where x is an integer.

But $n \mid a$ and $\gcd(m, n) = 1$, so, by Theorem 1.5, $n \mid x$, so $x = ny$ where y is an integer.

Then $a = mny$, so $mn \mid a$.

In Exercise 1B, Questions 5 and 6 are to be answered in this way.

Exercise 1B

1   Use the Euclidean algorithm to find the gcd of each of the following pairs of integers.

   (a)   16 and 36   (b)   45 and 93   (c)   144 and 55
   (d)   1085 and 2345   (e)   198 and 2013   (f)   37 127 and 63 294

2 Use the Euclidean algorithm to find the gcd of each of the following pairs of integers, and then use it in reverse to write the gcd as the sum or difference of multiples of those integers, as in Example 1.4.4.

(a) 35 and 77

(b) 261 and 87

(c) 89 and 55

(d) 6177 and 2343

(e) 4553 and 9947

(f) 75 281 and 37 516

3 Determine which, if any, of the following pairs of integers are relatively prime. If the pair is relatively prime, express 1 as the sum of multiples of the original numbers.

(a) 317 and 742

(b) 1261 and 1385

(c) 12 389 and 55 421

4 Show that if $\gcd(a,b) = d$, and if $d = ax + by$ for some integers x and y, then

$$d = a\left(x + n\frac{b}{d}\right) + b\left(y - n\frac{a}{d}\right)$$ for any integer n. (This shows that the representation of d as the sum of multiples of a and b is not unique.)

5 Prove that if $a = bq + r$ and $r > 0$, $\gcd(a,b) = \gcd(b,r)$.

6 Prove that if $\gcd(a,b) = 1$ and $\gcd(b,c) = 1$, then $\gcd(a,bc) = 1$.

7 Prove that if $d = \gcd(a,b)$, then $\gcd\left(\dfrac{a}{d}, \dfrac{b}{d}\right) = 1$.

1.6   Unique factorisation

The fact that integers can be factored into primes in one way only, provided that the primes are written in order, is well-known to you. Proving it is more difficult, and at this stage the result will be assumed.

You probably know already what a prime number is, so the following definition will be familiar to you.

Let p be an integer. Then p is called a **prime** if

- $p > 1$

- the only divisors of p are ± 1 and $\pm p$.

Notice that 1 is *defined* not to be prime. The reason for this is that if 1 were a prime, then you could write any number as a product of primes in more than one way. For example, $6 = 2 \times 3$ and $6 = 1 \times 2 \times 3$ would be different products of primes both derived from the prime factors of 6.

Here is the **unique factorisation theorem**, also called the **fundamental theorem of arithmetic**.

Theorem 1.7   The fundamental theorem of arithmetic

Any positive integer a greater than 1 can be expressed in the form

$$a = p_1 p_2 \cdots p_m,$$

where the numbers p_i are primes, and this expression is unique, apart from the order of the primes.

A proof of this theorem is given at the end of the chapter (see Section 1.8).

In practice, many of these primes will be repeated. If you collect together the repeated primes, you get

$$n = p_1^{\alpha_1} p_2^{\alpha_2} \dots p_i^{\alpha_i},$$

where $p_1, p_2, \dots$ are distinct primes, $p_1 < p_2 < \dots < p_i$ and $\alpha_1, \alpha_2, \dots$ are positive integers.

So for example, $60 = 2^2 \times 3 \times 5$, where the primes 2, 3 and 5 are arranged in ascending order.

With this tool it is time to return to the gcd, and the method of Example 1.4.2.

Suppose a and b are two positive integers, and each of them has been expressed as a product of primes in the form

$$a = p_1^{\alpha_1} p_2^{\alpha_2} \dots p_i^{\alpha_i} \quad \text{and} \quad b = p_1^{\beta_1} p_2^{\beta_2} \dots p_i^{\beta_i},$$

where $p_1, p_2, \dots, p_i$ are the primes in order 2, 3, 5, ... , and p_i is the largest prime which occurs in either factorisation into primes. The exponents α_j and β_j are all positive integers or zero.

Thus

$$102 = 2^1 \times 3^1 \times 5^0 \times 7^0 \times 11^0 \times 13^0 \times 17^1$$

and

$$18 = 2^1 \times 3^2 \times 5^0 \times 7^0 \times 11^0 \times 13^0 \times 17^0.$$

The method of finding the gcd in Example 1.4.2 was to take the primes in turn, and to look for the minimum power of each prime.

So

$$\begin{aligned} \gcd(102, 18) &= 2^1 \times 3^1 \times 5^0 \times 7^0 \times 11^0 \times 13^0 \times 17^0 \\ &= 6. \end{aligned}$$

But to justify this, you need to show that the process does actually give you the gcd.

Theorem 1.8
Let a and b be two positive integers, and let $a = p_1^{\alpha_1} p_2^{\alpha_2} \dots p_i^{\alpha_i}$ and $b = p_1^{\beta_1} p_2^{\beta_2} \dots p_i^{\beta_i}$ be their factorisations into primes where $p_1, p_2, \dots, p_i$ are the primes in order 2, 3, 5, ... , and p_i is the largest prime which occurs in either factorisation into primes. The exponents α_j and β_j are all positive integers or zero.

Then $\gcd(a,b) = p_1^{\min(\alpha_1,\beta_1)} p_2^{\min(\alpha_2,\beta_2)} \dots p_i^{\min(\alpha_i,\beta_i)}$, where $\min(\alpha_1,\beta_1)$ denotes the smaller of the integers α_1 and β_1, etc.

Proof
You have to show that $p_1^{\min(\alpha_1,\beta_1)} p_2^{\min(\alpha_2,\beta_2)} \dots p_i^{\min(\alpha_i,\beta_i)}$ satisfies the conditions for a gcd.

It is certainly positive, since all the powers are positive integers or zero.

It divides both a and b, since for each prime p_j in the factorisation,

$$\min(\alpha_j, \beta_j) \le \alpha_j \quad \text{and} \quad \min(\alpha_j, \beta_j) \le \beta_j.$$

Suppose that k is a common divisor of a and b. Suppose that p_j is one of the primes in the factorisation of a and b, and its exponent is γ_j,

Then if $k \mid a$, $\gamma_j \le \alpha_j$ and if $k \mid b$, $\gamma_j \le \beta_j$.

Therefore $\gamma_j \le \min(\alpha_j, \beta_j)$.

This also holds for all the other primes $p_1, p_2, \ldots, p_i$.

As for each j, $\gamma_j \le \min(\alpha_j, \beta_j)$, $k \mid \gcd(a,b)$, so $k \le \gcd(a,b)$.

As $p_1^{\min(\alpha_1, \beta_1)} p_2^{\min(\alpha_2, \beta_2)} \ldots p_i^{\min(\alpha_i, \beta_i)}$ satisfies the three conditions, it is $\gcd(a,b)$.

Look back at Example 1.4.2 and see how this result was used.

1.7 Least common multiples

When adding fractions you are likely to have found and used the least common multiple (lcm) of two integers. However, you may be surprised that the best way of finding the lcm is to find the gcd first.

First, here is a method with which you are probably familiar.

Example 1.7.1
Find the lcm of 102 and 18.

The factors of 102 are 1, 2, 3, 6, 17, 34, 51 and 102.

The factors of 18 are 1, 2, 3, 6, 9 and 18.

When you find the gcd of 102 and 18, you can simply look at the factors and see that the gcd is 6. But you can't do that so easily for multiples; you might have to go as far as 102×18 to be certain of finding a common multiple.

In this case the multiples of 102 are 102, 204, 306, 408, ...

The multiples of 18 are 18, 36, 54, 72, 90, 108, ... , 198, 216, ... , 288, 306, ...

So $\text{lcm}(102,18) = 306$.

You should not find it hard to believe that you need a better method.

Example 1.7.2
Find the lcm of 102 and 18.

Expressed in terms of their prime factors

$$102 = 2 \times 3 \times 17 \quad \text{and} \quad 18 = 2 \times 3^2.$$

The greatest power of 2 which appears is 2^1;

the greatest power of 3 which appears is 3^2;

the greatest power of 17 which appears is $17^1 = 17$.

So the lcm is $2^1 \times 3^2 \times 17^1 = 306$.

But the remarkable thing is that using $\gcd(102,18) = 6$ and $\operatorname{lcm}(102,18) = 306$,

$$\gcd(102,18) \times \operatorname{lcm}(102,18) = 6 \times 306 = 1836 = 102 \times 18.$$

It is time for a definition of lcm. It shouldn't surprise you that it is very like that for gcd.

> Let a and b be two non-zero integers. Then if $a \mid k$ and $b \mid k$, k is called a **common multiple** of a and b.
>
> An integer l is called the **least common multiple** of a and b if
>
> - $l > 0$
> - $a \mid l$ and $b \mid l$
> - if $a \mid c$ and $b \mid c$, then $c \geq l$.
>
> The least common multiple of a and b is denoted by $\operatorname{lcm}(a,b)$.

You know already that you can split any positive integer into primes.

Theorem 1.8 says that if a and b are two positive integers, and each of them has been expressed as a product of primes in the form

$$a = p_1^{\alpha_1} p_2^{\alpha_2} \dots p_r^{\alpha_r} \quad \text{and} \quad b = p_1^{\beta_1} p_2^{\beta_2} \dots p_r^{\beta_r},$$

then $\gcd(a,b) = p_1^{\min(\alpha_1,\beta_1)} p_2^{\min(\alpha_2,\beta_2)} \dots p_r^{\min(\alpha_r,\beta_r)}$.

The equivalent theorem for lcm is

$$\operatorname{lcm}(a,b) = p_1^{\max(\alpha_1,\beta_1)} p_2^{\max(\alpha_2,\beta_2)} \dots p_r^{\max(\alpha_r,\beta_r)}.$$

Theorem 1.9
Let a and b be two positive integers, and let $a = p_1^{\alpha_1} p_2^{\alpha_2} \dots p_i^{\alpha_i}$ and $b = p_1^{\beta_1} p_2^{\beta_2} \dots p_i^{\beta_i}$ be their factorisations into primes where $p_1, p_2, \dots, p_i$ are the primes in order 2, 3, 5, $\dots$, and p_i is the largest prime which occurs in either factorisation into primes. The exponents α_j and β_j are all positive integers or zero.

Then $\operatorname{lcm}(a,b) = p_1^{\max(\alpha_1,\beta_1)} p_2^{\max(\alpha_2,\beta_2)} \dots p_i^{\max(\alpha_i,\beta_i)}$, where $\max(\alpha_1,\beta_1)$ denotes the larger of the integers α_1 and β_1, etc.

Proof
Show that $p_1^{\max(\alpha_1,\beta_1)} p_2^{\max(\alpha_2,\beta_2)} \dots p_i^{\max(\alpha_i,\beta_i)}$ satisfies the conditions for an lcm.

It is certainly positive, since all the powers are positive integers or zero.

It is a multiple of both a and b, since for each prime p_j in the factorisation,

$$\max\left(\alpha_j,\beta_j\right) \geq \alpha_j \quad \text{and} \quad \max\left(\alpha_j,\beta_j\right) \geq \beta_j$$

Suppose that k is a common multiple of a and b. Suppose that p_j is one of the primes in the factorisation of a and b.

Then if $a \mid k$, $\gamma_j \geq \alpha_j$ and if $b \mid k$, $\gamma_j \geq \beta_j$.

Therefore $\gamma_j \geq \max\left(\alpha_j,\beta_j\right)$.

This also holds for all the other primes $p_1, p_2, \ldots, p_i$.

As for each j, $\gamma_j \geq \max\left(\alpha_j,\beta_j\right)$, $\operatorname{lcm}(a,b) \mid k$, so $\operatorname{lcm}(a,b) \leq k$.

As $p_1{}^{\max(\alpha_1,\beta_1)} p_2{}^{\max(\alpha_2,\beta_2)} \ldots p_r{}^{\max(\alpha_r,\beta_r)}$ satisfies the three conditions, it is $\operatorname{lcm}(a,b)$.

After all that, it is now easy to prove that $\operatorname{lcm}(a,b) \times \gcd(a,b) = ab$.

Theorem 1.10
For any positive integers a and b, $\operatorname{lcm}(a,b) \times \gcd(a,b) = ab$.

Proof
The proof relies on a simple piece of arithmetic.

If m and n are two integers, $\max(m,n) + \min(m,n) = m + n$.

To prove this, note that if $m = n$, it is trivial.

If $m > n$, the left side is $m + n$, so the result is true.

And if $m < n$, the left side is $n + m$, and the result is true.

Now looking at the notation used in Theorems 1.8 and 1.9, for each prime p_j, the power of p_j in $\operatorname{lcm}(a,b) \times \gcd(a,b)$ is

$$\max\left(\alpha_j,\beta_j\right) + \min\left(\alpha_j,\beta_j\right).$$

The power of p_j in ab is $\alpha_j + \beta_j$.

The result at the start of the proof shows that $\max\left(\alpha_j,\beta_j\right) + \min\left(\alpha_j,\beta_j\right) = \alpha_j + \beta_j$.

This holds for each prime p_j in the factorisation, so $\operatorname{lcm}(a,b) \times \gcd(a,b) = ab$.

Example 1.7.3
Find the lcm of $53\,059$ and $12\,028$.

The gcd of $53\,059$ and $12\,028$ is 97. See Example 1.4.3(b).

Using the result from Theorem 1.10, $\operatorname{lcm}(a,b) \times \gcd(a,b) = ab$,

$$\text{lcm}(53\,059, 12\,028) = \frac{53\,059 \times 12\,028}{97} = 6\,579\,316.$$

Remember: there is no better way of finding the lcm of two large numbers than to find the gcd first and use the result $\text{lcm}(a,b) \times \text{gcd}(a,b) = ab$.

1.8* Proof of the fundamental theorem of arithmetic

The theorem states that:

Every integer $a > 1$ can be expressed in the form $p_1 p_2 p_3 \dots p_m$, where the numbers p_i are primes, and this expression is unique except for the order of the primes.

Proof

The proof consists of two parts, first showing that every integer can be written in such a form, and secondly showing that the expression is unique.

Part (i)

Let V be the set of integers $a > 1$ which *cannot* be expressed in the form $p_1 p_2 p_3 \dots p_m$. Suppose that V is not empty, so by the well-ordering principle (Section 1.1) V has a least member. Call this member v.

Since v is in V it cannot be prime. So there are integers x and y, with $1 < x < v$ and $1 < y < v$, such that $v = xy$.

Then x and y are less than v and so cannot be in V.

Therefore x and y can each be expressed as the product of primes and then v, their product, can also be so expressed.

This contradiction means that V must be empty.

Therefore every integer $a > 1$ can be expressed in the form $p_1 p_2 p_3 \dots p_m$.

Part (ii)

To prove the uniqueness, let U be the set of integers $a > 1$ which do *not* have a unique factorisation, and suppose that U is not empty, so by the well-ordering principle U has a least member. Call this member u.

So

$$u = p_1 p_2 p_3 \dots p_m = q_1 q_2 q_3 \dots q_n,$$

where the integers p_i and q_i are all primes.

Suppose that in each case, the primes are in order so that $p_1 \leq p_2 \leq p_3 \leq \dots \leq p_m$ and $q_1 \leq q_2 \leq q_3 \leq \dots \leq q_n$.

Then take the smaller of p_1 and q_1, and suppose that it is p_1.

Then $p_1 \mid u$, and so $p_1 \mid q_1 q_2 q_3 \dots q_n$.

If $p_1 \neq q_1$, then, from the definition of prime, $\gcd(p_1, q_1) = 1$ so, from Theorem 1.5, or rather, Exercise 1C Question 2, $p_1 = q_1$.

But p_1 is the smallest prime factor, so $p_1 = q_1$, so cancel p_1 and q_1 to get

$$p_2 p_3 \cdots p_m = q_2 q_3 \cdots q_n.$$

But the original factorisations of u were different, so these are different factorisations, and, moreover, the products $p_2 p_3 \cdots p_m = q_2 q_3 \cdots q_n$ are smaller than u.

But this is a contradiction, so the factorisations are identical.

Exercise 1C

1 Find the lcm of the following pairs of integers.

(a) 26 and 117   (b) 851 and 1012   (c) 136 and 221

(d) 243 and 729   (e) 7525 and 3675   (f) 4741 and 15 085

2 (a) Use Theorem 1.5 (see Section 1.5) to prove that if p is a prime which divides ab, then $p \mid a$ or $p \mid b$.

(b) Prove that if a prime p divides the product of two primes $q_1 q_2$, then either $p = q_1$ or $p = q_2$.

3 Prove that if two primes p_1 and p_2 both divide an integer a, then $p_1 p_2 \mid a$.

2 Linear diophantine equations

This chapter builds on the ideas of the previous chapter to show how to solve equations of the form $ax + by = c$, where a, b and c are integers, and the solutions required are all integers. When you have completed it, you should

- be able to decide whether a given equation of the form $ax + by = c$ has solutions
- be able to find a particular solution and the general solution of a given equations
- be able to find solutions to $ax + by = c$ which satisfy given conditions.

2.1 Some background

Suppose that you have a straight line of the form $ax + by = c$, where a, b and c are integers. To help to focus, think of the line $7x + 9y = 3$ (Fig. 2.1). If you draw the straight line with this equation, what points on an integer grid does it pass through, other than $(3, -2)$?

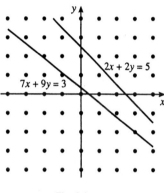

There are certainly some straight lines which don't pass through any points on an integer grid. For example $2x + 2y = 5$ has no integer points lying on it (Fig. 2.1), because whenever x and y are integers, the left side is even and the right side is odd. So what are the conditions on a, b and c for there to be points whose coordinates are integers to lie on $ax + by = c$?

Fig. 2.1

> Equations of the form $ax + by = c$ where a, b and c are integers are called **linear diophantine equations**.
>
> A diophantine equation is an equation in which only integer solutions are of interest.

Diophantus of Alexandria was a Greek mathematician who lived about AD 250.

To return to the equation $7x + 9y = 3$, how do you find solutions? You may see quite quickly that $x = 3$, $y = -2$ is a solution, but what other solutions are there? And if you have a system for calculating solutions, how can you be sure that you have *all* the solutions?

The first step in solving a linear diophantine equation is to find one solution. You can do this by inspection in a simple case, or, if you can't see a simple case, or the numbers are simply too big, use the method shown in Example 2.1.1.

In Chapter 1, you saw that $\gcd(a, b)$ can be expressed in the form $\gcd(a, b) = ax + by$ where x and y are integers. If $h = \gcd(a, b)$, then $ax + by = c$ can't be solved unless c is a multiple of h, for if h divides a and b, then h divides the left side, and so h must also divide the right side, c.

This shows that if $\gcd(a, b)$ does not divide c there are no solutions in integers to $ax + by = c$.

Example 2.1.1

Find a solution of the linear diophantine equation $7x + 9y = 3$.

Suppose that you can't see that $x = 3$, $y = -2$ is a solution. Then start by going through the process of finding $\gcd(7,9)$, using the method of Example 1.4.3.

$$9 = 1 \times 7 + 2$$
$$7 = 3 \times 2 + 1$$
$$2 = 2 \times 1 + 0.$$

This shows that 1 is the gcd of 7 and 9. Now use the method of Example 1.4.4 to write the gcd, in this case 1, in terms of 7 and 9.

$$\begin{aligned} 1 &= 7 - 3 \times 2 & \text{(from the second equation)} \\ &= 7 - 3 \times (9 - 1 \times 7) & \text{(from the first equation)} \\ &= 7 - 3 \times 9 + 3 \times 7 & \text{(simplifying the line above)} \\ &= 4 \times 7 - 3 \times 9. & \text{(simplifying the line above)} \end{aligned}$$

So $4 \times 7 - 3 \times 9 = 1$, and you can now multiply this equation by 3 to get $12 \times 7 - 9 \times 9 = 3$.

So $x = 12$, $y = -9$ is a solution of the equation $7x + 9y = 3$.

This is interesting, because the process hasn't given you the simplest solution, but it has given you a solution. If you examine the solutions $x = 3$, $y = -2$ and $x = 12$, $y = -9$, you will see that x has increased by 9 while y has decreased by 7, and a little reflection should convince you that $x = 12 + 9n$, $y = -9 - 7n$, where n is an integer, is also a solution.

You can see that $n = -1$ gives you the solution $x = 3$, $y = -2$, and when you allow n to take other integer values you have a set of solutions, in coordinate form,

$$\ldots, (-15, 12), (-6, 5), (3, -2), (12, -9), (21, -16), (30, -23), \ldots .$$

This does turn out to be all the solutions, as will be proved later.

A single solution such as $x = 12$, $y = -9$ will be called a **particular solution**; the solution $x = 12 + 9n$, $y = -9 - 7n$, where $n \in \mathbb{Z}$, is called the **general solution**.

Solving the linear diophantine equation $ax + by = c$

- If $\gcd(a,b)$ does not divide c, there is no solution.

- If $\gcd(a,b)$ divides c, divide a, b and c by $\gcd(a,b)$ to get a new equation $Ax + By = C$ with $\gcd(A,B) = 1$, see Exercise 1B, Question 7. So you need only consider equations of the form $ax + by = c$ with $\gcd(a,b) = 1$.

- Use the Euclidean algorithm to find integers x_1 and y_1 such that $ax_1 + by_1 = 1$.

- $x = cx_1$, $y = cy_1$ is a **particular solution** of $ax + by = c$.

  $x = cx_1 + nb$, $y = cy_1 - na$, where $n \in \mathbb{Z}$, is a **general solution** of $ax + by = c$.

Some of the statements in the shaded box need proof.

Theorem 2. 1

Using the notation in the shaded box:

(a) roots of $ax + by = c$ where $\gcd(a,b) = 1$ are given by $x = cx_1 + nb$, $y = cy_1 - na$, where n is an integer and $ax_1 + by_1 = 1$ is a particular solution of $ax + by = 1$.

(b) there are no other roots.

Proof

(a) Substituting $x = cx_1 + nb$, $y = cy_1 - na$ in $ax + by$ gives

$$ax + by = a(cx_1 + nb) + b(cy_1 - na)$$
$$= acx_1 + anb + bcy_1 - bna$$
$$= acx_1 + bcy_1$$
$$= (ax_1 + by_1)c$$
$$= c.$$

So $x = cx_1 + nb$, $y = cy_1 - na$ certainly gives roots of the equation $ax + by = c$.

(b) To show that there are no other solutions, let $x = cx_1 + nb$ and $y = cy_1 - na$ be the solution you already have and suppose that there is another, $x = cx_1 + nb + \lambda$, $y = cy_1 - na + \mu$. Then, substituting this into $ax + by$ gives c because it is a solution of $ax + by = c$.

So $c = a(cx_1 + nb + \lambda) + b(cy_1 - na + \mu)$
$$= a(cx_1 + nb) + a\lambda + b(cy_1 - na) + b\mu$$
$$= a(cx_1 + nb) + b(cy_1 - na) + a\lambda + +b\mu$$
$$= c + (a\lambda + b\mu),$$

giving

$$a\lambda + b\mu = 0$$

where $\gcd(a,b) = 1$.

Now since $a\lambda + b\mu = 0$ it follows that $b \mid a\lambda$.

But a, b and λ are integers with $\gcd(a,b) = 1$, so, using Theorem 1.5, $b \mid a\lambda$ implies $b \mid \lambda$.

Therefore $\lambda = Nb$ for some integer N, then $aNb + b\mu = 0$, giving $\mu = -Na$.

So the new solution is $x = cx_1 + nb + Nb$, $y = cy_1 - na - Na$, where n and N are integers.

But this is identical to $x = cx_1 + nb$, $y = cy_1 - na$, with another integer, $n + N$, in place of n.

So the solution $x = cx_1 + nb$, $y = cy_1 - na$ is the complete solution.

Example 2.1.2

Find the general solution of the linear diophantine equation $50x + 12y = 6$.

In this case you can see by inspection that $\gcd(50,12) = 2$, and $2 \mid 6$, so divide by 2 to get $25x + 6y = 3$.

Now use the Euclidean algorithm, as in Example 1.4.4, to find a solution of $25x + 6y = 1$.

$$25 = 4 \times 6 + 1, \quad \text{so} \quad 1 = 1 \times 25 - 4 \times 6.$$

So $x_1 = 1$, $y_1 = -4$ is a solution of $25x + 6y = 1$, and $x = 3 \times x_1 = 3$, $y = 3 \times y_1 = -12$ is a particular solution of $25x + 6y = 3$.

Using the shaded box, the general solution of $25x + 6y = 3$ is $x = 3 + 6n$, $y = -12 - 25n$, where $n \in \mathbb{Z}$. This is also the general solution of $50x + 12y = 6$.

Sometimes you may not be able to see by inspection that an equation has a common divisor.

Example 2.1.3

Find the general solution of the linear diophantine equation $1081x - 805y = 161$.

Start by using the Euclidean algorithm to find $\gcd(1081,805)$.

$$1081 = 1 \times 805 + 276$$
$$805 = 2 \times 276 + 253$$
$$276 = 1 \times 253 + 23$$
$$253 = 11 \times 23.$$

So $\gcd(1081,805) = 23$. Check that $23 \mid 161$: it does, since $161 = 7 \times 23$. The original equation is therefore equivalent to $47x - 35y = 7$.

Using Euclid's algorithm again,

$$47 = 1 \times 35 + 12$$
$$35 = 2 \times 12 + 11$$
$$12 = 1 \times 11 + 1,$$

which, in reverse gives

$$1 = 12 - 1 \times 11$$
$$= 12 - 1 \times (35 - 2 \times 12)$$
$$= 3 \times 12 - 1 \times 35$$
$$= 3 \times (47 - 1 \times 35) - 1 \times 35$$
$$= 3 \times 47 - 4 \times 35.$$

So $x_1 = 3$, $y_1 = 4$ is a solution of $47x + 35y = 1$, and $x = 7 \times x_1 = 21$, $y = 7 \times y_1 = 28$ is a particular solution of $47x - 35y = 7$.

Using the shaded box, the general solution of $47x - 35y = 7$ is $x = 21 + 35n$, $y = -28 + 47n$, where $n \in \mathbb{Z}$. This is also the general solution of $1081x - 805y = 161$.

The solution of a diophantine equation may need to satisfy certain conditions. For example, the solutions may need to be positive, or you may need the solution closest to a given point in the plane.

Example 2.1.4
Find the general solution of the linear diophantine equation $1591x + 3268y = 16168$. Find also the particular solutions

(a) with a y-value of least modulus,

(b) with the x-value lying between 1000 and 1100.

It is not possible to see gcd(1591,3268) by inspection, so use the Euclidean algorithm to find that $\gcd(1591,3268) = 43$. As $1591 = 37 \times 43$, $3268 = 76 \times 43$ and $16168 = 376 \times 43$, the original equation has solutions and is equivalent to $37x + 76y = 376$.

Using and then reversing the Euclidean algorithm to find a solution of $37x + 76y = 1$, you find that $x_1 = 37$, $y_1 = -18$.

The particular solution of $37x + 76y = 376$ is $x = 376 \times x_1 = 13912$, $y = 376 \times y_1 = -6768$.

The general solution of $37x + 76y = 376$ is

$$x = 13\,912 + 76n, \quad y = -6768 - 37n,$$

where $n \in \mathbb{Z}$.

(a) The value of n which makes y close to 0 is $-6768/37 \approx -183$.

Putting $n = -183$ gives $y = -6768 - 37 \times (-183) = 3$. This obviously gives the particular solution with a y-value of least modulus.

Therefore $x = 13912 - 76 \times 183 = 4$, $y = 3$ is the required solution.

(b) For $1000 < x < 1100$, $1000 < 13\,912 + 76n < 1100$, giving $n = -169$.

The particular values are then $x = 1068$, $y = -515$.

Exercise 2

1 Find the general solution to each of the following diophantine equations. Keep your answers for use in Question 2.

(a) $2x + 3y = 1$ (b) $5x - 7y = 1$ (c) $13x - 9y = 1$

(d) $248x - 121y = 1$ (e) $1568x - 23y = 1$ (f) $355x + 113y = 1$

2 Find the general solution to each of the following diophantine equations.

(a) $2x + 3y = 4$ (b) $5x - 7y = 3$ (c) $13x - 9y = 2$

(d) $248x - 121y = -1$ (e) $1568x - 23y = 3$ (f) $355x + 113y = -2$

3 Some of the following diophantine equations have solutions: others do not. Solve those that do have solutions.

(a) $4x + 6y = 12$ (b) $15x + 21y = 33$ (c) $15x + 25y = 32$

(d) $1720x + 559y = 817$ (e) $4182x - 1384y = 1072$ (f) $234x - 377y = 6188$

4 In each part of this question a diophantine equation is given, together with a condition. Find all the solutions, if any, which satisfy the given condition.

(a) $4x + 3y = 61$; all solutions in which both x and y are positive.

(b) $17x + 13y = 27$; the solution closest to the y-axis.

(c) $189x - 231y = 3024$; all solutions in the fourth quadrant.

(d) $322x + 667y = 1311$; all solutions which lie between $x = 100$ and $x = 200$.

5 A foreign country has stamps of just two denominations, 23 ruples and 31 ruples. How many different ways can they make up a total of 9800 ruples with these stamps?

3 Modular arithmetic

This chapter introduces modular arithmetic which is a generalised arithmetic based on remainders. When you have completed it, you should

- be able to carry out calculations in modular arithmetic
- be able to find solutions of congruences
- know how to find solutions to simultaneous equations involving modular arithmetic.

3.1 Calculations in modular arithmetic

When you work out that 3 o'clock in the afternoon is 5 hours after 10 o'clock in the morning, you are doing modular arithmetic. You are saying,

$$10 + 5 = 15 \quad \text{and} \quad 15 = 1 \times 12 + 3.$$

Similarly, if today is Thursday and you work out that in 37 days time it will be Saturday, recognising that the 37th day from now is the same day of the week as the 2nd day from now, you are doing modular arithmetic, saying

$$37 = 5 \times 7 + 2.$$

Modular arithmetic is an arithmetic using remainders. So if 3 and 15 give the same remainder when divided by 12, you would write

$$15 \equiv 3 \pmod{12},$$

which you would say as '15 is congruent to 3 mod 12'.

Similarly

$$37 \equiv 2 \pmod 7.$$

In both examples, the difference between the integers is divisible by the modulus; in the first case the modulus is 12 and in the second case the modulus is 7.

This leads to:

> Let m be a positive integer. Then two integers a and b are said to be **congruent modulo m** if, and only if,
>
> $$m \mid a - b.$$
>
> This is denoted by $a \equiv b \pmod m$.

This idea is useful because you can do arithmetic with these numbers, replacing each number by a simpler remainder.

For example,

$$37 \equiv 2\,(\text{mod } 7) \text{ and } 10 \equiv 3\,(\text{mod } 7).$$

Then

$$37 + 10 = 47$$
$$\equiv 5\,(\text{mod } 7), \qquad (\text{since 47 divided by 7 leaves a remainder of 5})$$

which is the same as $2 + 3 \equiv 5\,(\text{mod } 7)$.

Similarly,

$$37 \times 10 = 370$$
$$\equiv 6\,(\text{mod } 7), \qquad (\text{since 370 divided by 7 leaves a remainder of 6})$$

which is the same as $2 \times 3 \equiv 6\,(\text{mod } 7)$.

Theorem 3.1

If m is a positive integer, and a, b, c and d are integers such that $a \equiv b\,(\text{mod } m)$ and $c \equiv d\,(\text{mod } m)$, then $a + c \equiv b + d\,(\text{mod } m)$, $a - c \equiv b - d\,(\text{mod } m)$ and $ac \equiv bd\,(\text{mod } m)$.

Proof

If $a \equiv b\,(\text{mod } m)$ and $c \equiv d\,(\text{mod } m)$ then $m \mid a - b$ and $m \mid c - d$.

Then there exist integers x and y such that $a - b = mx$ and $c - d = my$.

So $a = b + mx$ and $c = d + my$.

Then

$$a + c = b + mx + d + my$$
$$= b + d + m(x + y),$$

and

$$(a + c) - (b + d) = m(x + y) \quad \Rightarrow \quad m \mid (a + c) - (b + d)$$
$$\Rightarrow \quad a + c \equiv b + d\,(\text{mod } m).$$

The proof that $a - c \equiv b - d\,(\text{mod } m)$ is left as an exercise.

To prove that $ac \equiv bd\,(\text{mod } m)$,

$$ac = (b + mx)(d + my)$$
$$= bd + bmy + dmx + m^2 xy$$
$$= bd + m(by + dx + mxy),$$

and

$$ac - bd = m(by + dx + mxy) \quad \Rightarrow \quad m \mid ac - bd$$
$$\Rightarrow \quad ac \equiv bd\,(\text{mod } m).$$

It is also clear that you can take powers of congruences. If n is a positive integer, then

$$a \equiv b(\bmod m) \quad \Rightarrow \quad \overbrace{aaa \ldots a}^{n \text{ times}} = \overbrace{bbb \ldots b}^{n \text{ times}} (\bmod m)$$
$$\Rightarrow \quad a^n \equiv b^n (\bmod m).$$

Summarising these results:

> If $a \equiv b(\bmod m)$ and $c \equiv d(\bmod m)$ where a, b, c, d, and m are integers, and $m > 0$, then
>
> $a + c \equiv b + d (\bmod m)$ and $a - c \equiv b - d (\bmod m)$,
>
> $ac \equiv bd (\bmod m)$,
>
> $a^n \equiv b^n (\bmod m)$, where n is a positive integer.

Also, by combining these results in various ways, you can show that any polynomial $p(x)$ has the property that if $a \equiv b(\bmod m)$ then $p(a) \equiv p(b)(\bmod m)$.

Here are some examples which show how these results can be used.

Example 3.1.1
Find the remainders when the following are divided by 7.

(a) 26×44 (b) 37^2 (c) $37^2 + 34^2$ (d) 23^{49}

(a) $26 \equiv 5(\bmod 7)$ and $44 \equiv 2(\bmod 7)$, so, by Theorem 3.1

$$26 \times 44 (\bmod 7) \equiv 5 \times 2 (\bmod 7) \equiv 10 (\bmod 7) \equiv 3(\bmod 7).$$

The remainder when 26×44 is divided by 7 is 3.

(b) $37 \equiv 2(\bmod 7)$, so, by Theorem 3.1, $37^2 \equiv 2^2 (\bmod 7) \equiv 4(\bmod 7)$.

The remainder when 37^2 is divided by 7 is 4.

(c)   From part (b), $37^2 \equiv 4(\bmod 7)$.

Also $34 \equiv -1(\bmod 7)$,
$$34^2 \equiv (-1)^2 \equiv 1(\bmod 7).$$

Therefore $37^2 + 34^2 \equiv 4 + 1(\bmod 7) \equiv 5(\bmod 7)$.

The remainder when $37^2 + 34^2$ is divided by 7 is 5.

(d) $23 \equiv 2(\bmod 7)$ and $2^6 \equiv 1(\bmod 7)$,   so $23^6 \equiv 1(\bmod 7)$.

As $49 = 6 \times 8 + 1$, $23^{49} \equiv (23^6)^8 \times 23 \equiv (1)^8 \times 23 (\bmod 7) \equiv 2(\bmod 7)$.

The remainder when 23^{49} is divided by 7 is 2.

Example 3.1.2

Find $x^{10} \pmod 8$, given that $7x \equiv 1 \pmod 8$.

It is often helpful to use numbers which are negative if they are numerically smaller. Thus

$$7x \equiv 1 \pmod 8 \quad \Rightarrow \quad -1 \times x \equiv 1 \pmod 8 \qquad (\text{as } 7 = -1 \pmod 8)$$
$$\Rightarrow \quad x \equiv -1 \pmod 8$$
$$\Rightarrow \quad x^{10} \equiv 1 \pmod 8.$$

Example 3.1.3

Prove that, for all positive values of n, $2^{n+2} + 3^{2n+1}$ is divisible by 7.

Using the rules for manipulating,

$$2^{n+2} = 4 \times 2^n \quad \Rightarrow \quad 2^{n+2} \equiv 4 \times 2^n \pmod 7,$$

and $\quad 3^{2n+1} = 3 \times 9^n \quad \Rightarrow \quad 3^{2n+1} \equiv 3 \times 2^n \pmod 7.$

Adding these equations

$$2^{n+2} + 3^{2n+1} \equiv 4 \times 2^n + 3 \times 2^n \pmod 7$$
$$\equiv 7 \times 2^n \pmod 7$$
$$\equiv 0 \pmod 7.$$

Therefore 7 divides $2^{n+2} + 3^{2n+1}$.

Example 3.1.4

By calculating the value of $3^{4n+2} + 5^{2n+1}$ for a few values of n, make a conjecture about a number which divides $3^{4n+2} + 5^{2n+1}$. Prove your conjecture.

The values of $3^{4n+2} + 5^{2n+1}$ for $n = 0$ and $n = 1$ are 14 and 854.

The conjecture is $14 \mid \left(3^{4n+2} + 5^{2n+1}\right)$.

$$3^{4n+2} + 5^{2n+1} \equiv \left(9 \times 81^n + 5 \times 25^n\right) \pmod{14}$$
$$\equiv \left(9 \times 11^n + 5 \times 11^n\right) \pmod{14}$$
$$\equiv 14 \times 11^n \pmod{14}$$
$$\equiv 0 \pmod{14},$$

so $14 \mid \left(3^{4n+2} + 5^{2n+1}\right)$.

You can sometimes do division in modular arithmetic. For example, if you know that $ac \equiv bc \pmod m$, under certain conditions you can divide by c to get $a \equiv b \pmod m$.

Example 3.1.5

Is it true that   (a) $3a \equiv 3b \pmod 7 \Rightarrow a \equiv b \pmod 7$,   (b) $3a \equiv 3b \pmod{12} \Rightarrow a \equiv b \pmod{12}$?
Justify your answers.

(a) $3a \equiv 3b \pmod 7 \Rightarrow 3a - 3b = 7x$ for an integer x

$\Rightarrow 7x = 3(a-b)$

$\Rightarrow 7 \mid a-b$ (from Theorem 1.5)

$\Rightarrow a \equiv b \pmod 7$.

(b) $3 \times 4 \equiv 3 \times 8 \pmod{12}$, but $4 \not\equiv 8 \pmod{12}$, so the result is false.

This suggests the following theorem.

Theorem 3.2

If $ac \equiv bc \pmod m$ and $\gcd(c,m) = 1$, then $a \equiv b \pmod m$.

The proof follows the method of Example 3.1.5.

Proof

$ac \equiv bc \pmod m \Rightarrow ac - bc = mx$ for some integer x

$\Rightarrow c(a-b) = mx$

$\Rightarrow mx \mid c(a-b)$.

But $\gcd(c,m) = 1$, so, by Theorem 1.5, m divides $a - b$.

So $a - b = mk$, where k is an integer, and hence $a \equiv b \pmod m$.

Exercise 3A

1 Calculate the remainders when the following are divided by 13.

(a) 62   (b) 17×53 (c) 7×2^{15} (d) $36^5 + 23^5$

2 Calculate the following.

(a) $31^{88} \pmod{13}$ (b) $88^{31} \pmod{13}$ (c) $1234^{2345} \pmod{11}$

3 Given that $5x \equiv -2 \pmod 8$, find $x^2 \pmod 8$.

4 Prove that 11 divides $2^{4n+1} + 3^{3n+2}$ for $n \in \mathbb{N}$.

5 Prove that, when n is a positive integer, $2^{n+1} + 9 \times 13^n \equiv 0 \pmod{11}$.

6 Let p and q be different primes, and let n be an integer. Prove that if $n \equiv 1 \pmod p$ and $n \equiv 1 \pmod q$, then $n \equiv 1 \pmod{pq}$.

7 Prove that, if p is prime, and if $ax \equiv bx \pmod p$ and $x \neq 0$ or a multiple of p, then $a \equiv b \pmod p$.

3.2 Congruences

How can you solve an equation like $7x \equiv 5 \pmod{16}$? Such an equation is called a **congruence**.

One way to solve it if the numbers are small is to check all the possibilities. This will be called the 'brute force' solution. Working modulo 16 you get

$7 \times 0 \equiv 0$	$7 \times 1 \equiv 7$	$7 \times 2 \equiv 14$	$7 \times 3 \equiv 5$
$7 \times 4 \equiv 12$	$7 \times 5 \equiv 3$	$7 \times 6 \equiv 10$	$7 \times 7 \equiv 1$
$7 \times 8 \equiv 8$	$7 \times 9 \equiv 15$	$7 \times 10 \equiv 6$	$7 \times 11 \equiv 13$
$7 \times 12 \equiv 4$	$7 \times 13 \equiv 11$	$7 \times 14 \equiv 2$	$7 \times 15 \equiv 9$

Then, going on, you find that results repeat.

$7 \times 16 \equiv 0$	$7 \times 17 \equiv 7$	$7 \times 18 \equiv 14$	$7 \times 19 \equiv 5$

until

$7 \times 28 \equiv 4$	$7 \times 29 \equiv 11$	$7 \times 30 \equiv 2$	$7 \times 31 \equiv 9$

and so on.

Looking at these results you can see that $x = 3$ and $x = 19$ are solutions, and you should notice that $19 \equiv 3 \pmod{16}$. You can also see that the products of 7 with 0, 1, 2, ... , 15 are all different. But will they always be so?

Note that, if the numbers are big, the brute force method is hopeless.

Now consider the congruence $9x \equiv 3 \pmod{12}$. Using brute force and working modulo 12 gives

$9 \times 1 \equiv 9$	$9 \times 2 \equiv 6$	$9 \times 3 \equiv 3$	$9 \times 4 \equiv 0$	$9 \times 5 \equiv 9$
$9 \times 6 \equiv 6$	$9 \times 7 \equiv 3$	$9 \times 8 \equiv 0$	$9 \times 9 \equiv 9$	$9 \times 10 \equiv 6$
$9 \times 11 \equiv 3$	$9 \times 12 \equiv 0$			

This time there are multiple solutions to $9x \equiv 3 \pmod{12}$, namely $x = 3$, $x = 7$ and $x = 11$. And you can see from the list that if the equation had been, for example, $9x \equiv 2 \pmod{12}$, there would have been no solutions.

So, this raises the question, if $ax \equiv b \pmod{m}$, where m is a positive integer and a and b are integers, what are the conditions on a, b and m for no roots for x, just one root for x, or multiple roots, and how do you find them?

First notice that $ax \equiv b \pmod{m}$ means that $m \mid ax - b$ so $ax - b = my$ for some integer y. Rearranging this equation gives

$$ax - my = b,$$

where you must find values of x and y which are integers.

You have seen this before. It is the linear diophantine equation $ax + by = c$ with $-m$ in place of b and b in place of c. So you can use all the theory that you have already seen for linear diophantine equations.

> Let m be a positive integer and let a and b be integers. Then the equation $ax \equiv b \pmod{m}$ is called a **congruence**.

Note that there are solutions of $ax \equiv b \pmod{m}$ if, and only if, $\gcd(a,m) \mid b$. (This is true, even in the case $a = 0$.) Here is an example.

Example 3.2.1
Solve for x the congruence $51x \equiv 66 \pmod{89}$.

This equation is equivalent to the diophantine equation $51x - 89y = 66$.

Using the Euclidean algorithm,

$$89 = 1 \times 51 + 38$$
$$51 = 1 \times 38 + 13$$
$$38 = 2 \times 13 + 12$$
$$13 = 1 \times 12 + 1$$
$$12 = 12 \times 1 + 0.$$

As $\gcd(51,89) = 1$ and $1 \mid 66$, there are solutions to the diophantine equation. Reversing the Euclidean algorithm gives

$$
\begin{aligned}
1 &= 13 - 1 \times 12 & &= 13 - 12 \\
&= 13 - (38 - 2 \times 13) & &= 3 \times 13 - 38 \\
&= 3 \times (51 - 1 \times 38) - 38 & &= 3 \times 51 - 4 \times 38 \\
&= 3 \times 51 - 4 \times (89 - 1 \times 51) & &= 7 \times 51 - 4 \times 89,
\end{aligned}
$$

so $7 \times 51 - 4 \times 89 = 1$.

Multiplying both sides by 66 gives

$$462 \times 51 - 264 \times 89 = 66.$$

So a particular solution of the diophantine equation $51x - 89y = 66$ is $x = 462$, $y = 264$.

The general solution (see Section 2.1) is $x = 462 + 89n$, $y = 264 - 51n$, where n is an integer.

Choosing n so that $0 \le 462 + 89n < 89$ gives

$$-5.19... \le n \quad \text{and} \quad n < -4.19... \;,$$

so $n = -5$ and $x = 462 - 5 \times 89 = 17$.

The solution of $51x \equiv 66 \pmod{89}$ is 17 and is unique.

Here is an example where the solution is not unique.

Example 3.2.2
Solve for x the congruence $51x \equiv 136 \,(\text{mod}\,833)$.

This equation is equivalent to the diophantine equation $51x - 833y = 136$.

Using the Euclidean algorithm,

$$833 = 16 \times 51 + 17$$
$$51 = 3 \times 17 + 0.$$

As $\gcd(51,833) = 17$ and $17\,|\,136$, there are solutions to the diophantine equation.

Dividing by 17 shows that the equation $51x - 833y = 136$ is equivalent to $3x - 49y = 8$.

It is now helpful to work in modulo 3 (note that $3\,|\,8 + 49y$) which shows that

$$8 + 49y \equiv 2 + y \,(\text{mod}\,3), \quad \text{or} \quad -y \equiv 2\,(\text{mod}\,3), \quad \text{which is the same as} \quad y \equiv 1\,(\text{mod}\,3).$$

So $y = 1 + 3n$, where n is an integer, and substituting this into the equation $3x - 49y = 8$ gives

$$3x = 49(1 + 3n) + 8 = 57 + 49 \times 3n,$$

so $x = 19 + 49n$.

If you write out the solutions which are numerically less than 833, you find that there are 17 of them:

19, 68, 117, 166, 215, 264, 313, 362, 411, 460, 509, 558, 607, 656, 705, 754, 803;

Is the fact that there are 17 roots and $\gcd(51,833) = 17$ a coincidence? Looking back at the brute force solution to $9x \equiv 3\,(\text{mod}\,12)$ shows that there are 3 roots, and $\gcd(9,12) = 3$. This suggests that, if $ax \equiv b\,(\text{mod}\,m)$ has roots, then there are $\gcd(a,m)$ of them.

Here is a proof of this statement.

Theorem 3.3
The congruence $ax \equiv b\,(\text{mod}\,m)$, where m is a positive integer and a and b are integers, has

(a) no roots if $\gcd(a,m)$ does not divide b,

(b) and $\gcd(a,m)$ distinct roots if $\gcd(a,m)\,|\,b$.

Proof
If $ax \equiv b\,(\text{mod}\,m)$, then, by definition, $m\,|\,ax - b$, so, for some integer y, $ax - b = my$, which is the same as the diophantine equation $ax - my = b$.

(a)   From the shaded box before Theorem 2.1, the equation $ax - my = b$ has no roots if $\gcd(a,m)$ does not divide b, so $ax \equiv b\,(\text{mod}\,m)$ also has no roots if $\gcd(a,m)$ does not divide b.

(b)   Suppose that $\gcd(a,m) = h$ and that $h\,|\,b$.

Then, from the shaded box before Theorem 2.1, the equation $ax - my = b$ can be solved.

Moreover, if x_1 is a particular solution of $ax - my = b$ for x, then the h numbers

$$x_1, \; x_1 + \frac{m}{h}, \; x_1 + 2\frac{m}{h}, \; \ldots, \; x_1 + (h-1)\frac{m}{h},$$

are all solutions.

Note that the next term of the sequence $x_1 + h\frac{m}{h} = x_1 + m \equiv x_1 \,(\mathrm{mod}\,m)$, so the sequence repeats. So there are $h = \gcd(a, m)$ distinct roots.

Sometimes you can use congruences to solve diophantine equations. Here are three more examples: in two of them it helps to use congruences, while in the other it does not.

Example 3.2.3
Solve the diophantine equations

(a) $14x - 53y = 37$,   (b) $12x - 53y = 37$,   (c) $29x - 53y = 37$.

(a)   The equation $14x - 53y = 37$ is equivalent to $14x \equiv 37 \,(\mathrm{mod}\,53)$.

So $14x \equiv 37 + 53 \equiv 90 \,(\mathrm{mod}\,53)$.

Dividing by 2 gives

$$7x \equiv 45 \,(\mathrm{mod}\,53).$$

Similarly, $7x \equiv 45 \equiv 98 \,(\mathrm{mod}\,53)$, so $x \equiv 14 \,(\mathrm{mod}\,53)$.

Therefore $x = 14 + 53n$, and substituting for x in $14x - 53y = 37$ gives

$$53y = 14(14 + 53n) - 37 = 196 - 37 + 14 \times 53n = 159 + 14 \times 53n$$

that is, $y = 3 + 14n$.

The solution is $x = 14 + 53n$, $y = 3 + 14n$.

(b)   The equation $12x - 53y = 37$ is equivalent to $12x \equiv 37 \,(\mathrm{mod}\,53)$.

So $12x \equiv 37 \equiv 90 \,(\mathrm{mod}\,53)$.

Dividing by 6 gives $2x \equiv 15 \,(\mathrm{mod}\,53)$.

Similarly $2x \equiv 15 \equiv 68 \,(\mathrm{mod}\,53)$ gives $x \equiv 34 \,(\mathrm{mod}\,53)$.

Therefore $x = 34 + 53n$, and substituting for x in $12x - 53y = 37$ gives

$$53y = 12(34 + 53n) - 37 = 408 + 12 \times 53n - 37 = 371 + 12 \times 53n$$

that is, $y = 7 + 12n$.

The solution is $x = 34 + 53n$, $y = 7 + 12n$.

(c)   The equation $29x - 53y = 37$ is equivalent to $29x \equiv 37 \pmod{53}$.

So $29x \equiv 37 \equiv 90 \equiv 143 \equiv 196 \equiv \ldots \pmod{53}$.

It is not easy to know how many times 53 needs to be added before it is possible to divide by 29, so in this example, it is easier to use the Euclidean algorithm, as in Chapter 2. You then find that $11 \times 29 - 6 \times 53 = 1$, and multiplying by 37 gives

$$29 \times (11 \times 37) - 53 \times (6 \times 37) = 37$$

leading to $x = 11 \times 37 = 407$, $y = 6 \times 37 = 222$ as a particular solution.

So a general solution is $x = 407 + 53n$, $y = 222 + 29n$, where $n \in \mathbb{Z}$.

But notice that $x \equiv 407 - 7 \times 53 \equiv 36 \pmod{53}$ and $y \equiv 222 - 7 \times 29 \equiv 19 \pmod{29}$, so an alternative solution is $x = 36 + 53n$, $y = 19 + 29n$, where $n \in \mathbb{Z}$.

Exercise 3B

1   Use brute force, or any other method, to solve the following congruences.
  (a) $5x \equiv 2 \pmod{7}$ (b) $8x \equiv 7 \pmod{13}$ (c) $29x \equiv 17 \pmod{97}$

2   Solve the following congruences; keep your answers for Question 3.
  (a) $13x \equiv 1 \pmod{47}$ (b) $23x \equiv 1 \pmod{83}$ (c) $43x \equiv 1 \pmod{101}$

3   Use your answers to Question 2 to solve the following congruences.
  (a) $13x \equiv 31 \pmod{47}$ (b) $23x \equiv 17 \pmod{83}$ (c) $43x \equiv 35 \pmod{101}$

4   Find all the solutions to the following congruences.
  (a) $9x \equiv 3 \pmod{87}$ (c) $15x \equiv 12 \pmod{33}$ (c) $13x \equiv 26 \pmod{117}$

5   Use congruences to solve the following diophantine equations.
  (a) $8x + 5y = 2$ (b) $6x + 11y = 4$ (c) $21x - 13y = 23$

3.3   Simultaneous congruences: the Chinese remainder theorem

The name Chinese remainder theorem was inspired by a problem posed in about AD 100 by the Chinese mathematician Sun-Tsu who wanted to find an integer which left a remainder of 2 when divided by 3, a remainder of 3 when divided by 5 and a remainder of 2 when divided by 7.

It is helpful to start with an easier problem: find a number x such that when it is divided by 5 it leaves a remainder of 3, and when it is divided by 17 it leaves a remainder of 7.

Example 3.3.1
Find all values of x which satisfy simultaneously the congruences $x \equiv 3 \pmod{5}$ and $x \equiv 7 \pmod{17}$.

Method 1
If $x \equiv 3 \pmod{5}$ then $x - 3 = 5y$ where y is an integer, and if $x \equiv 7 \pmod{17}$ then $x - 7 = 17z$ where z is an integer.

You can eliminate x and find that $5y + 3 = 17z + 7$, or

$$5y - 17z = 4.$$

This is a diophantine equation which you can solve using the Euclidean algorithm.

Using the Euclidean algorithm (see Section 2.1),

$$7 \times 5 - 2 \times 17 = 1, \quad \text{giving} \quad 28 \times 5 - 8 \times 17 = 4.$$

So $y = 28$ and $z = 8$ is a particular solution of the diophantine equation. You can use either of them to get $x = 143$.

The general solution of the diophantine equation is

$$y = 28 + 17n, \text{ where } n \in \mathbb{Z},$$

which gives

$$\begin{aligned} x &= 5(28 + 17n) + 3 \\ &= 143 + 85n. \end{aligned}$$

You can see that $x = 143$ is a solution and that solutions occur whenever

$$x \equiv 143 - 85 \,(\text{mod}\,85) \equiv 58 \,(\text{mod}\,85).$$

Method 2
If $x \equiv 3\,(\text{mod}\,5)$ then $x - 3 = 5y$ where y is an integer, so $3 + 5y \equiv 7\,(\text{mod}\,17)$, or $5y \equiv 4\,(\text{mod}\,17)$.

So $5y \equiv 4 \equiv 21 \equiv 38 \equiv 55\,(\text{mod}\,17)$, giving $y \equiv 11\,(\text{mod}\,17)$.

So $y = 11 + 17n$, where n is an integer, giving $x = 3 + 5y = 3 + 5(11 + 17n) = 58 + 85n$, or $x \equiv 58\,(\text{mod}\,85)$..

Example 3.3.2
Find all values of x which satisfy simultaneously the congruences $2x \equiv 7\,(\text{mod}\,11)$ and $5x \equiv 4\,(\text{mod}\,13)$.

If $2x \equiv 7\,(\text{mod}\,11)$, then $2x \equiv 7 \equiv 18\,(\text{mod}\,11)$, so $x \equiv 9\,(\text{mod}\,11)$, giving $x = 9 + 11n$, where $n \in \mathbb{Z}$.

Then substituting this value of x into $5x \equiv 4\,(\text{mod}\,13)$ gives $5(9 + 11n) \equiv 4\,(\text{mod}\,13)$, or $45 + 55n \equiv 4\,(\text{mod}\,13)$, which simplifies to $6 + 3n \equiv 4\,(\text{mod}\,13)$, or $3n \equiv -2 \equiv 11\,(\text{mod}\,13)$.

Then $3n \equiv 11 \equiv 24\,(\text{mod}\,13)$ gives $n \equiv 8\,(\text{mod}\,13)$, so $n = 8 + 13m$, where $m \in \mathbb{Z}$.

Substituting in $x = 9 + 11n$ gives $x = 9 + 11(8 + 13m)$, or $x = 97 + 143m$, that is, $x \equiv 97\,(\text{mod}\,143)$.

You can generalise the simultaneous equations above to solving the problem

$$x \equiv a\,(\text{mod}\,m_1) \text{ and } x \equiv b\,(\text{mod}\,m_2)$$

where a and b are integers, and m_1 and m_2 are positive integers.

By now it should not surprise you that

- if $\gcd(m_1, m_2)$ does not divide $b - a$ there are no solutions,
- if $\gcd(m_1, m_2) = 1$ the solution is unique modulo $m_1 m_2$.

Theorem 3.4

Let a and b be integers, m_1 and m_2 be positive integers, and let $\gcd(m_1, m_2) = 1$. Then the equations $x \equiv a \pmod{m_1}$ and $x \equiv b \pmod{m_2}$ have a unique solution for x modulo $m_1 m_2$.

Proof

If $x \equiv a \pmod{m_1}$ then $x - a = m_1 y$, where y is an integer.

If $x \equiv b \pmod{m_2}$, then $a + m_1 y \equiv b \pmod{m_2}$, so $a + m_1 y - b = m_2 z$ where z is an integer.

This leads to the diophantine equation

$$m_1 y - m_2 z = b - a.$$

Use the Euclidean algorithm to find integers k and l such that

$$km_1 + lm_2 = 1.$$

Then from Theorem 2.1, the general solution of this diophantine equation is

$$y = (b - a)k + nm_2, \quad z = (b - a)l + nm_1,$$

where n is an integer.

Using the y-value and the equation $x - a = m_1 y$,

$$x = a + \big(k(b - a)m_1 + nm_2\big)m_1 = a + km_1(b - a) + nm_1 m_2.$$

Working modulo $m_1 m_2$

$$x \equiv a + k(b - a)m_1 \pmod{m_1 m_2},$$

where n is an integer. So there is a solution.

Now suppose there are two solutions x_1 and x_2. Then as $x_1 \equiv a \pmod{m_1}$ and $x_2 \equiv a \pmod{m_1}$, $x_1 - x_2$ is divisible by m_1. Similarly $x_1 - x_2$ is divisible by m_2. Hence, by Theorem 1.6, it is divisible by $m_1 m_2$, since $\gcd(m_1, m_2) = 1$.

So the solution is unique, modulo $m_1 m_2$.

If $\gcd(m_1, m_2)$ is greater than 1 then there are conditions for solutions to exist. These are not explored in this book.

What happens then if there are more than two simultaneous congruences?

Example 3.3.3

Find an integer which leaves a remainder of 2 when divided by 3, a remainder of 3 when divided by 5 and a remainder of 2 when divided by 7. (This is Sun-Tsu's problem.)

Two solutions are given. The first is straightforward, while the second is probably quicker in practice and certainly extends better to three or more simultaneous congruences.

Method 1

In congruence notation, you have to solve

$$x \equiv 2 \pmod 3, \quad x \equiv 3 \pmod 5, \quad x \equiv 2 \pmod 7.$$

If you take the first two congruences, as $\gcd(3,5) = 1$, Theorem 3.4 applies, and you can solve the simultaneous congruences by the method of Examples 3.3.1 and 3.3.2 to get $x \equiv 8 \pmod{15}$.

Now you can use the same method for

$$x \equiv 8 \pmod{15} \quad \text{and} \quad x \equiv 2 \pmod 7.$$

Since $\gcd(15,7) = 1$, Theorem 3.4 again applies again. Using the same method as before, you find that $x \equiv 23 \pmod{105}$.

Method 2

Consider the products of the moduli, two at a time. These are

$$3 \times 5 = 15, \quad 3 \times 7 = 21 \quad \text{and} \quad 5 \times 7 = 35.$$

Then let $x = 15a + 21b + 35c$, where a, b and c are integers.

The equation $x \equiv 2 \pmod 3$ becomes, on substituting for x,

$$15a + 21b + 35c \equiv 2c \equiv 2 \pmod 3, \quad \text{or} \quad c \equiv 1 \pmod 3.$$

Similarly, the equation $x \equiv 3 \pmod 5$ becomes

$$15a + 21b + 35c \equiv b \equiv 3 \pmod 5,$$

and $x \equiv 2 \pmod 7$ becomes

$$15a + 21b + 35c \equiv a \equiv 2 \pmod 7.$$

So a solution is

$$x = 15a + 21b + 35c = 15 \times 2 + 21 \times 3 + 35 \times 1 = 128.$$

Working modulo $3 \times 5 \times 7 = 105$, this simplifies to $x \equiv 23 \pmod{105}$.

This suggests the following theorem which is called The Chinese remainder theorem.

Theorem 3.5   The Chinese remainder theorem

Let $m_1, m_2, \ldots, m_n$ be positive integers such that $\gcd(m_i, m_j) = 1$ if $i \neq j$. Then the congruences

$$x \equiv a_1 \pmod{m_1}, \quad x \equiv a_2 \pmod{m_2}, \quad \ldots, x \equiv a_n \pmod{m_n}$$

have a unique solution modulo $m_1 m_2 \ldots m_n$.

Proof

To make the notation easier put $M = m_1 m_2 \ldots m_n$ and $M_i = \dfrac{M}{m_i}$.

Then $M_1 = \dfrac{M}{m_1} = m_2 m_3 \dots m_n$, $M_2 = \dfrac{M}{m_2} = m_1 m_3 \dots m_n$ and so on.

Now let $x = x_1 M_1 + x_2 M_2 + \dots + x_n M_n$.

Working modulo m_1,

$$x \equiv a_1 \,(\mathrm{mod}\, m_1) \quad \Leftrightarrow \quad x_1 M_1 \equiv a_1 \,(\mathrm{mod}\, m_1),$$

and, by Theorem 3.4, this is solvable for x_1 since $\gcd(m_1, M_1) = 1$.

Similarly for $x_2, x_3, \dots, x_n$.

Hence the congruences have a solution.

Suppose that there are two solutions X_1 and X_2, then for each i, $X_1 \equiv a_i \equiv X_2 \,(\mathrm{mod}\, m_i)$. Hence for each i, $m_i \mid X_2 - X_1$, and so, as $\gcd(m_i, m_j) = 1$ if $i \neq j$, by Theorem 1.6,

$$m_1 m_2 \dots m_n \mid X_2 - X_1, \quad \text{that is,} \quad M \mid X_2 - X_1.$$

Hence $X_2 \equiv X_1 \,(\mathrm{mod}\, M)$, and the solution is unique.

Example 3.3.4

Solve the simultaneous congruences,

(a) $x \equiv 3 \,(\mathrm{mod}\, 5) \quad x \equiv 5 \,(\mathrm{mod}\, 7) \quad x \equiv 7 \,(\mathrm{mod}\, 11)$,

(b) $2x \equiv 5 \,(\mathrm{mod}\, 7) \quad 3x \equiv 4 \,(\mathrm{mod}\, 11) \quad 5x \equiv 9 \,(\mathrm{mod}\, 13)$.

(a) Using the notation of the Chinese remainder theorem,

$$a_1 = 3, \ a_2 = 5 \text{ and } a_3 = 7,$$

$$M = 5 \times 7 \times 11 = 385, \ M_1 = \frac{M}{5} = 77, \ M_2 = \frac{M}{7} = 55 \text{ and } M_3 = \frac{M}{11} = 35.$$

Let $x = 77x_1 + 55x_2 + 35x_3$.

The equation $x \equiv 3 \,(\mathrm{mod}\, 5)$ working modulo 5 gives $2x_1 \equiv 3 \,(\mathrm{mod}\, 5)$, or $x_1 \equiv 4 \,(\mathrm{mod}\, 5)$.

Similarly, $x \equiv 5 \,(\mathrm{mod}\, 7)$ in modulo 7 becomes $6x_2 \equiv 5 \,(\mathrm{mod}\, 7)$, or $x_2 \equiv 2 \,(\mathrm{mod}\, 7)$, and

$x \equiv 7 \,(\mathrm{mod}\, 11)$ in modulo 11 becomes $2x_3 \equiv 7 \,(\mathrm{mod}\, 11)$, or $x_3 \equiv 9 \,(\mathrm{mod}\, 11)$.

So $x = 77 \times 4 + 55 \times 2 + 35 \times 9 = 733$, and working modulo $M = 385$,

$$x = 733 - 385 = 348, \quad \text{or} \quad x \equiv 348 \,(\mathrm{mod}\, 385).$$

(b) In this case, $M = 7 \times 11 \times 13 = 1001$, $M_1 = \dfrac{M}{7} = 143$, $M_2 = \dfrac{M}{11} = 91$, $M_3 = \dfrac{M}{13} = 77$.

Start by making the coefficients of x in the equations $2x \equiv 5 \,(\mathrm{mod}\, 7)$, $3x \equiv 4 \,(\mathrm{mod}\, 11)$ and $5x \equiv 9 \,(\mathrm{mod}\, 13)$ equal to 1. (In this example you can use the brute force method of Section 3.2, but if the numbers are big, you may need the Euclidean algorithm to help.)

You now get the equations,

$$x \equiv 6 \pmod{7}, \quad x \equiv 5 \pmod{11}, \quad x \equiv 7 \pmod{13},$$

so that $a_1 = 6$, $a_2 = 5$, $a_3 = 7$, and the problem is now very similar to part (a).

Let $x = 143x_1 + 91x_2 + 77x_3$.

The equation $x \equiv 6 \pmod{7}$ gives $3x_1 \equiv 6 \pmod{7}$, that is, $x_1 \equiv 2 \pmod{7}$.

Similarly $x \equiv 5 \pmod{11}$ gives $3x_2 \equiv 5 \pmod{11}$, that is, $x_2 \equiv 9 \pmod{11}$.

Also $x \equiv 7 \pmod{13}$, gives $12x_3 \equiv 7 \pmod{13}$, that is, $x_3 \equiv 6 \pmod{13}$.

So $x = 143 \times 2 + 91 \times 9 + 77 \times 6 = 1567$, and, since this is working in modulo $M = 1001$,

$$x = 1567 - 1001 = 566, \quad \text{or} \quad x \equiv 566 \pmod{1001}.$$

Example 3.3.5

Solve the simultaneous congruences, $x \equiv 1 \pmod{5}$, $x \equiv 1 \pmod{7}$, $x \equiv 1 \pmod{11}$, $x \equiv 2 \pmod{13}$,

Using the notation of the Chinese remainder theorem, $M = 5 \times 7 \times 11 \times 13 = 5005$, and $M_1 = 1001$, $M_2 = 715$, $M_3 = 455$ and $M_4 = 385$.

Let $x = 1001x_1 + 715x_2 + 455x_3 + 385x_4$.

Then $x \equiv 1 \pmod{5}$ gives $x_1 \equiv 1 \pmod{5}$.

Similarly

$$x \equiv 1 \pmod{7} \text{ gives } x_2 \equiv 1 \pmod{7},$$

$$x \equiv 1 \pmod{11} \text{ gives } 4x_3 \equiv 1 \pmod{11}, \text{ or } x_3 \equiv 3 \pmod{11},$$

$$x \equiv 2 \pmod{13} \text{ gives } 8x_4 \equiv 2 \pmod{13}, \text{ or } x_4 \equiv 10 \pmod{13}.$$

So $x = 1001 \times 1 + 715 \times 1 + 455 \times 3 + 385 \times 10 = 6931$, and, since this is working in modulo $M = 5005$,

$$x = 6931 - 5005 = 1926, \quad \text{or} \quad x \equiv 1926 \pmod{5005}.$$

Exercise 3C

1 Find a number that leaves a remainder of 7 when divided by 9 and a remainder of 13 when divided by 19.

2 Solve the following simultaneous congruences.
   (a) $x \equiv 1 \pmod{17}$ and $x \equiv 5 \pmod{19}$
   (b) $x \equiv 5 \pmod{17}$ and $x \equiv 1 \pmod{19}$
   (c) $2x \equiv 5 \pmod{11}$ and $x \equiv 3 \pmod{13}$
   (d) $3x \equiv 5 \pmod{7}$ and $x \equiv 7 \pmod{11}$
   (e) $3x \equiv 5 \pmod{13}$ and $5x \equiv 2 \pmod{33}$
   (f) $4x \equiv 1 \pmod{17}$ and $5x \equiv 4 \pmod{21}$

3 Find an integer which leaves a remainder of 1 when divided by 2, a remainder of 2 when divided by 5 and a remainder of 6 when divided by 17.

4 Solve the following simultaneous congruences.

(a) $x \equiv 2 \pmod{5}$, $x \equiv 3 \pmod{7}$ and $x = 4 \pmod{11}$

(b) $x \equiv 1 \pmod{5}$, $x \equiv 6 \pmod{7}$ and $x \equiv 3 \pmod{9}$

(c) $2x \equiv 1 \pmod{3}$, $3x \equiv 2 \pmod{5}$ and $4x \equiv 1 \pmod{7}$

(d) $x \equiv 1 \pmod{2}$, $x \equiv 2 \pmod{5}$, $x \equiv 1 \pmod{7}$ and $x \equiv 2 \pmod{11}$

4 Fermat's little theorem

This chapter is about a remarkable theorem concerning congruences. When you have completed it, you should

- know and be able to use Fermat's little theorem.

4.1 Fermat's little theorem

Pierre de Fermat was a Frenchman who lived from 1601 to 1663. Fermat's theorem, as opposed to his little theorem, was only proved in the 1990s by Andrew Wiles. This states that the equation $x^n + y^n = z^n$ has solutions in integers for $n > 1$ only for $n = 2$.

Fermat's little theorem is about a^{p-1} when p is prime.

Example 4.1.1

Calculate the values of $2^6 \pmod 7$, $3^6 \pmod 7$, ... , $6^6 \pmod 7$.

$$2^6 \equiv 64 \equiv 1 \pmod 7.$$

$$3^6 \equiv 9^3 \equiv 2^3 \equiv 8 \equiv 1 \pmod 7.$$

$$4^6 \equiv \left(2^6\right)^2 \equiv 1^2 \equiv 1 \pmod 7.$$

$$5^6 \equiv 25^3 \equiv 4^3 \equiv 2^6 \equiv 1 \pmod 7.$$

$$6^6 \equiv (-1)^6 \equiv 1 \pmod 7.$$

There are many different ways to get these results.

Note also that $1^6 \pmod 7 \equiv 1 \pmod 7$. From this and Example 4.1.1 it appears that $a^{p-1} \equiv 1 \pmod p$, where p is a prime. Notice that this is not true for $a = 0$. This is Fermat's little theorem.

Theorem 4.1   Fermat's little theorem

Let p be a prime and a be a positive integer. If p does not divide a, then $a^{p-1} \equiv 1 \pmod p$.

Proof

Suppose that a is not divisible by p, where p is prime.

Consider the $p-1$ numbers $a, 2a, 3a, \dots, (p-1)a$ modulo p.

Suppose that two of them are equal, that is, $ai \equiv aj \pmod p$ with $i \neq j$.

Then $p \mid a(i-j)$, and since p does not divide a, by Theorem 1.5, $p \mid i - j$.

But $0 < i, j \leq p - 1$, so all the values of $i - j$ lie in the interval $-(p-1) \leq i - j \leq p - 1$.

But $p \mid (i - j)$, and the only value in the interval $-(p-1) \leq i - j \leq p - 1$ which is divisible by p is 0, so $i - j = 0$, that is $i \equiv j \pmod p$.

The supposition that $ai \equiv aj \,(\text{mod } p)$ is false, so $a, 2a, 3a, \ldots, (p-1)a$ are all different, modulo p.

Hence the $p-1$ numbers $a, 2a, 3a, \ldots, (p-1)a$ are, in some order, the same numbers as $1, 2, \ldots, p-1$, modulo p.

Multiplying them,

$$a \times 2a \times 3a \times \ldots \times (p-1)a \equiv 1 \times 2 \times 3 \times \ldots \times (p-1) \,(\text{mod } p),$$

which can be written as

$$1 \times 2 \times 3 \times \ldots \times (p-1) \times a^{p-1} \equiv 1 \times 2 \times 3 \times \ldots \times (p-1) \,(\text{mod } p).$$

It follows, on dividing by $1 \times 2 \times 3 \times \ldots \times (p-1)$, that $a^{p-1} \equiv 1 \,(\text{mod } p)$.

Fermat's little theorem is sometimes given in the equivalent form $a^p \equiv a \,(\text{mod } p)$.

> **Fermat's little theorem**
> Let p be a prime and a be a positive integer. If p does not divide a, then
> $a^{p-1} \equiv 1 \,(\text{mod } p)$ and $a^p \equiv a \,(\text{mod } p)$.

The following examples show Fermat's little theorem in action.

Example 4.1.1
Find the remainder when 100^{200} is divided by 7.

From Fermat's little theorem, since 7 does not divide 100, $100^6 \equiv 1 \,(\text{mod } 7)$.

It follows that since $200 = 6 \times 33 + 2$,

$$
\begin{aligned}
100^{200} &\equiv 100^{6 \times 33 + 2} \\
&\equiv 100^{6 \times 33} \times 100^2 \\
&\equiv 1^{33} \times 2^2 \equiv 4 \,(\text{mod } 7). \qquad \text{(as } 100 = 14 \times 7 + 2)
\end{aligned}
$$

The remainder when 100^{200} is divided by 7 is 4.

Example 4.1.2
Calculate $132^{75} \,(\text{mod } 37)$.

As 37 does not divide 132, using Fermat's little theorem, $132^{36} \equiv 1 \,(\text{mod } 37)$.

Since $75 = 2 \times 36 + 3$

$$
\begin{aligned}
132^{75} &\equiv \left(132^{36}\right)^2 \times 132^3 \,(\text{mod } 37) \\
&\equiv 1^2 \times 21^3 \,(\text{mod } 37) \qquad \text{(as } 132 = 3 \times 37 + 21) \\
&\equiv 11 \,(\text{mod } 37). \qquad \text{(as } 21^3 = 9261 = 250 \times 37 + 11)
\end{aligned}
$$

Fermat's little theorem sometimes gives you an alternative way of solving linear diophantine equations.

Example 4.1.3

(a) By calculating $18^{29} \pmod{31}$, find x such that $18x \equiv 1 \pmod{31}$.

(b) Use your answer to part (a) to find the general solution of the diophantine equation $18x - 31y = 1$.

$$18^{29} \equiv 18 \times \left(18^2\right)^{14} \pmod{31}$$

$\quad\quad\quad \equiv 18 \times 14^{14} \pmod{31} \quad\quad\quad\quad\text{(as } 18^2 = 324 = 10 \times 31 + 14)$

$\quad\quad\quad \equiv 18 \times 10^7 \pmod{31} \quad\quad\quad\quad\text{(as } 14^2 = 196 = 6 \times 31 + 10)$

$\quad\quad\quad \equiv 180 \times 10^6 \pmod{31}$

$\quad\quad\quad \equiv 25 \times 7^3 \pmod{31} \quad\quad\quad\quad\text{(as } 180 = 5 \times 31 + 25) \quad\text{and} \quad (10^2 = 100 = 3 \times 31 + 7)$

$\quad\quad\quad \equiv 25 \times 2 \pmod{31} \quad\quad\quad\quad\quad\text{(as } 7^3 = 343 = 11 \times 31 + 2)$

$\quad\quad\quad \equiv 19 \pmod{31}. \quad\quad\quad\quad\quad\quad\text{(as } 50 = 1 \times 31 + 19)$

Using Fermat's little theorem, since 31 does not divide 18 and 31 is prime,

$$18^{30} \equiv 1 \pmod{31}, \quad \text{and as } 18^{29} \equiv 19 \pmod{31}, \quad 18 \times 19 \equiv 1 \pmod{31}.$$

So $x = 19$.

(b) It follows that $18 \times 19 - 1 = 31y$ for some integer y, and, by direct calculation, $y = 11$.

So $x = 19 + 31n$, $y = 11 + 18n$, where $n \in \mathbb{Z}$, is the general solution of the diophantine equation.

Whether this is a better method for solving the diophantine equation than the Euclidean algorithm is for you to decide. It certainly is, if you have a solution to the equation $18x \equiv 1 \pmod{31}$. However, the best way to solve that equation is usually by the Euclidean algorithm.

Example 4.1.4

(a) Show that 13 divides $n^{13} - n$ for all $n \in \mathbb{Z}^+$.

(b) Show that 78 divides $n^{13} - n$ for all $n \in \mathbb{Z}^+$.

(a) If n is a multiple of 13, then as $n^{13} - n = n\left(n^{12} - 1\right)$, and $13 \mid n$, it follows that $13 \mid n^{13} - n$.

If n is not a multiple of 13, then by Fermat's little theorem $n^{12} \equiv 1 \pmod{13}$, so $13 \mid n^{12} - 1$.

So, either way, $13 \mid n\left(n^{12} - 1\right)$ and hence $13 \mid n^{13} - n$.

(b) First note that $78 = 6 \times 13 = 2 \times 3 \times 13$.

If n is a multiple of 2, then as $n^{13} - n = n\left(n^{12} - 1\right)$, and $2 \mid n$, it follows that $2 \mid n^{13} - n$.

If n is a multiple of 3, then as $n^{13} - n = n\left(n^{12} - 1\right)$, and $3 \mid n$, it follows that $3 \mid n^{13} - n$.

If n is not a multiple of 2, then by Fermat's little theorem, $n^{12} \equiv 1 \pmod{2}$, so $2 \mid n^{12} - 1$.

Then $2 \mid n\left(n^{12} - 1\right)$ and hence $2 \mid n^{13} - n$.

If n is not a multiple of 3, then by Fermat's little theorem $n^{12} \equiv 1 \pmod 3$, so $3 \mid n^{12} - 1$.

Then $3 \mid n(n^{12} - 1)$ and hence $3 \mid n^{13} - n$.

As $2 \mid n^{13} - n$, $3 \mid n^{13} - n$ and, from part (a), $13 \mid n^{13} - n$, it follows that $2 \times 3 \times 13 = 78 \mid n^{13} - n$ (see Exercise 1C Question 3.)

Exercise 4

1 Prove that, for all positive integers n, $\left(2^{10}\right)^n \equiv 1 \pmod{11}$ and $\left(2^{10}\right)^n \equiv 1 \pmod{31}$. Hence deduce that $\left(2^{10}\right)^n - 1$ is divisible by 341.

2 Given that $7 \times 13 \equiv 1 \pmod{15}$, solve the diophantine equation $7x + 15y = 2$.

3 (a) Use Fermat's little theorem to solve the equation $32x \equiv 1 \pmod{37}$.

   (b) Use your solution to find the complete solution of the diophantine equation $32x + 37y = 1$.

4 (a) State and prove Fermat's little theorem.

   (b) Prove that if $5 \mid x^5 + y^5$, where $x, y \in \mathbb{Z}^+$, then $5 \mid x + y$.

   (c) By considering $(x + y)^5$, deduce that if $5 \mid x^5 + y^5$ then $25 \mid x^5 + y^5$.

5 Prove that $30 \mid n^5 - n$ for $n \in \mathbb{Z}^+$.

5 Integers in different bases

In this chapter you will learn that integers can be represented in bases other than 10. When you have completed it, you should

- be able to express integers in bases other than 10
- know how to convert integers expressed in other bases to base 10
- be able to add, subtract and multiply in bases other than 10
- be able to prove some divisibility tests.

5.1 Some background

The reason we count in tens has much to do with the fact that we have ten fingers (and thumbs). We use only the ten digits 0 to 9, and talk about counting in base ten, called denary. But other counting systems have been and are being used.

Base 2, called binary, uses only the digits 0 and 1; binary is used in computers, to simulate situations in which current is, or is not, flowing.

Base 8, called octal, uses digits 0 to 7; this is used today in low-level programming.

Base 12, using the symbols 0 to 9 with T and E, or 0 to 9 with A and B, can still be seen in the Imperial system of measurements, where 12 inches is 1 foot. In fact a book of logarithm tables in base 12 was published in England early in the 20th century because the author was convinced that people would change to base 12.

Base 16, uses the symbols 0 to 9 with A to F, and is used in programming. One of the methods of describing colours uses base 16.

There is some evidence of base 20, with ideas of 'Three score years and ten, but this is now obsolete.

And finally base 60 was used by the Babylonians, and this is still used in 60 seconds in a minute and 60 minutes in an hour.

5.2 Counting and notation

Suppose that you are working in base 8, that is, the octal system.

Then when you count, after 7 you would write 10: the 10 means 1 eight plus 0. You would then proceed 11, 12, ... 17, 20, 21, ... 27, 30, 31, ... , 76, 77, 100, 101, ...

The number 100 means $1 \times 8^2 + 0 \times 8 + 0$, that is, $1 \times 8^2 + 0 \times 8^1 + 0 \times 8^0$.

To ensure that the number above does not get confused with the number 100 which is familiar to all, numbers in base 8 are denoted by a subscript $_8$, for example, 100_8. Thus

$$100_8 = 1 \times 8^2 + 0 \times 8 + 0 = 64,$$

where if there is no subscript on the other numbers they are understood to be in base 10.

Similarly,

$$FC8_{16} = F \times 16^2 + C \times 16 + 8,$$

and since $F = 15$ and $C = 12$,

$$FC8_{16} = 15 \times 16^2 + 12 \times 16 + 8$$
$$= 4040.$$

Example 5.2.1
Express the following numbers in denary notation.

(a) 11101_2 (b) 70402_8 (c) $ABC4_{16}$ (d) 121_n $(n > 2)$

(a) $11101_2 = 1 \times 2^4 + 1 \times 2^3 + 1 \times 2^2 + 0 \times 2 + 1$
$$= 16 + 8 + 4 + 0 + 1$$
$$= 29.$$

(b) $70402_8 = 7 \times 8^4 + 0 \times 8^3 + 4 \times 8^2 + 0 \times 8 + 2$
$$= 28672 + 0 + 256 + 0 + 2$$
$$= 28930.$$

(c) $ABC4_{16} = 10 \times 16^3 + 11 \times 16^2 + 12 \times 16 + 4$
$$= 40960 + 2816 + 192 + 4$$
$$= 43972.$$

(d) $121_n = 1 \times n^2 + 2 \times n + 1$
$$= n^2 + 2n + 1.$$

In part (d) the condition $n > 2$ is there to ensure that the digit 2 is less than the number base. Of course, in addition, n must be an integer.

It is interesting to note that part (d) shows that, in any number base greater than 2, the number 121 is always a perfect square. Why?

5.3 Changing out of the denary system

Changing out of denary is harder than changing into denary.

As an example, consider changing the denary number 343 to octal.

The problem amounts to finding a_n, a_{n-1}, a_{n-2}, ..., a_1 and a_0 so that

$$a_n \times 8^n + a_{n-1} \times 8^{n-1} + ... + a_1 \times 8^1 + a_0 = 343,$$

where all the values of a_i lie between 0 and 7 inclusive.

There are a number of ways to do this. Some people prefer a 'brute force' method, as in Example 5.2.1, because it relies very little on memory.

Example 5.2.1

Change 343 to octal.

As the powers of 8, in denary, are 1, 8, 64, 512, and so on, and 512 is greater than the given number 343,

$$343 = a_2 \times 8^2 + a_1 \times 8 + a_0$$
$$= 64a_2 + 8a_1 + a_0,$$

where $0 \le a_0, a_1, a_2 \le 7$.

If you now express 343 in the form $343 = 64q + r$, where r is the remainder and satisfies $0 \le r \le 63$, you find that

$$343 = 5 \times 64 + 23,$$

so $a_2 = 5$.

Now taking the remainder 23 and writing it in the form $23 = 8q_1 + r_1$ where $0 \le r_1 \le 7$, you find that

$$23 = 2 \times 8 + 7.$$

Then $343 = 5 \times 8^2 + 2 \times 8 + 7$, so $343 = 527_8$.

If you wish to learn an algorithm for this process, there is one. Here is the same example again to illustrate an algorithm for changing from base 10 to another base.

Example 5.2.2

Change 343 to octal.

Use the division algorithm to get

$$343 = 42 \times 8 + 7$$
$$42 = 5 \times 8 + 2$$
$$5 = 0 \times 8 + 5.$$

Then, reading up the remainders,

$$343 = 527_8.$$

Why does this work?

Suppose the integer N is expressed in base r and takes the form

$$N = a_n r^n + a_{n-1} r^{n-1} + \ldots + a_1 r + a_0,$$

where $r > 1$ and $0 \le a_n, a_{n-1}, \ldots a_1, a_0 \le r - 1$.

You need to find the coefficients $a_n, a_{n-1}, \ldots a_1, a_0$.

Using the division algorithm,

$$a_n r^n + a_{n-1} r^{n-1} + \ldots + a_1 r + a_0 = \left(a_n r^{n-1} + a_{n-1} r^{n-2} + \ldots + a_1 \right) r + a_0$$
$$a_n r^{n-1} + a_{n-1} r^{n-2} + \ldots + a_1 = \left(a_n r^{n-2} + a_{n-1} r^{n-3} + \ldots + a_2 \right) r + a_1$$
$$\vdots \qquad\qquad = \qquad\qquad \vdots$$
$$a_n r^2 + a_{n-1} r + a_{n-2} = \left(a_n r + a_{n-1} \right) r \qquad + a_{n-2}$$
$$a_n r + a_{n-1} = \qquad a_n r \qquad + a_{n-1}$$
$$a_n = \qquad 0 \times r \qquad + a_n.$$

You can now see that reading downwards gives you the coefficients $a_0, a_1, \ldots a_{n-1}, a_n$.

It is interesting to ask whether the expression

$$N = a_n r^n + a_{n-1} r^{n-1} + \ldots + a_1 r + a_0$$

is unique. That is, if one person uses the 'brute force' method of Example 5.2.1 and someone else uses the more systematic method of Example 5.2.2, are they bound to get the same answer?

Theorem 5.1
Every positive integer N has just one representation in base r, where $r > 1$.

Proof
Suppose that N has two distinct representations

$$N = a_n r^n + a_{n-1} r^{n-1} + \ldots + a_1 r + a_0 = b_m r^m + b_{m-1} r^{m-1} + \ldots + b_1 r + b_0.$$

Suppose that, starting from a_0, the first coefficients which are different from each other are a_i and b_i. Then

$$a_n r^n + a_{n-1} r^{n-1} + \ldots + a_{i+1} r^{i+1} + a_i r^i = b_m r^m + b_{m-1} r^{m-1} + \ldots + b_{i+1} r^{i+1} + b_i r^i.$$

Dividing by r^i gives

$$a_n r^{n-i} + a_{n-1} r^{n-1-i} + \ldots + a_{i+1} r + a_i = b_m r^{m-i} + b_{m-1} r^{m-1-i} + \ldots + b_{i+1} r + b_i.$$

Now work modulo r. The equation above becomes

$$a_i \equiv b_i \pmod{r}.$$

Since both $0 \le a_i < r$ and $0 \le b_i < r$, it follows that $a_i = b_i$, and the supposition was false.

There is no pair of coefficients which are different so the representations are identical.

5.3   Arithmetic in bases other than 10

Addition
Addition of two numbers in base n is very similar to addition in base 10, although you may find the language of the following algorithm a little unfamiliar.

The numbers which are written in base n as $a_k a_{k-1} \ldots a_1 a_0$ and $b_l b_{l-1} \ldots b_1 b_0$ are the numbers

$$a_k n^k + a_{k-1} n^{k-1} + \ldots + a_1 n + a_0 \quad \text{and} \quad b_l n^l + b_{l-1} n^{l-1} + \ldots + b_1 n + b_0.$$

These are polynomials in n whose sum is easy to calculate, except that they are written in descending powers of n, and there are the issues which arise when $a_i + b_i \geq n$, which lead to 'carrying'.

An algorithm for addition in base n

Suppose that the two numbers in base n are $a_k a_{k-1} \ldots a_1 a_0$ and $b_l b_{l-1} \ldots b_1 b_0$, and the sum is $c_m c_{m-1} \ldots c_1 c_0$.

Then the following algorithm computes $c_m c_{m-1} \ldots c_1 c_0$.

Addition in base n

Step 1 for $i = 0$ to $\max(k, l) + 1$ (i is a digit counter: $\max(k, l)$ is the greater of k and l)
Step 2 calculate in base 10, $a_i + b_i$
Step 3 if $a_i + b_i < n$
          then
$$c_i = a_i + b_i$$
          else
$$c_i = a_i + b_i - n$$
              add 1 to b_{i+1} (this 'carries' 1 to the next position)
          end if
Step 4 increase i by 1.

Example 5.3.1
Add 435 and 23 in base 6.

The algorithm proceeds as follows, where you work down and then across. Note that $\max(k, l) + 1 = 2 + 1 = 3$.

Step 1 $\quad i = 0$ $\qquad\qquad\qquad\qquad i = 1$ $\qquad\qquad\qquad\qquad i = 2$ $\qquad\qquad\qquad\qquad i = 3$

Step 2 $\quad a_0 + b_0 = 5 + 3 = 8$ $\qquad a_1 + b_1 = 3 + 3 = 6$ $\qquad a_2 + b_2 = 4 + 1 = 5$ $\qquad a_3 + b_3 = 0 + 0 = 0$

Step 3 $\quad$ as $8 \geq 6$, $\qquad\qquad\qquad$ as $6 \geq 6$ $\qquad\qquad\qquad$ as $5 < 6$ $\qquad\qquad\qquad$ as $0 < 6$
$\qquad\qquad c_0 = 8 - 6 = 2$ $\qquad\qquad c_1 = 6 - 6 = 0$ $\qquad\qquad c_2 = 5$ $\qquad\qquad\qquad c_3 = 0$
$\qquad\qquad b_{0+1} = b_1 = 2 + 1 = 3$ $\quad b_{1+1} = b_2 = 0 + 1 = 1$

Step 4 $\quad i = 1$ $\qquad\qquad\qquad\qquad i = 2$ $\qquad\qquad\qquad\qquad i = 3$ $\qquad\qquad\qquad\qquad i = 4$

As the value of $i = 4$ is now greater than $\max(k, l) + 1 = 2 + 1 = 3$, the process stops.

The answer is $c_3 c_2 c_1 c_0$ which is 0502, that is, 502 in base 6.

You are advised to practise this, especially in binary, where it can be very tricky.

Subtraction in base n
Most people have a favourite way to carry out subtractions. If you have one which works, stick to it, but always check your answer afterwards by using addition.

There is a method of subtraction called **complementary addition** which cuts out any notions of 'borrowing' or 'paying back' which you might have learnt as a child. Here is an example to show you the method.

Example 5.3.2
Subtract 435 from 502 in base 6.

Start by subtracting 435 from 555 (which is the equivalent of 999 in base 10), to get 120.

Then add 1 to get 121, so you now have the result of subtracting 435 from 1000 in base 6. This is the key idea. (121 is the complement of 435 since they add together to give 1000_6.)

Now add the 121 to 502 to get 1023.

Finally you need to subtract 1000 to get the answer, 23.

This is the same as Example 5.3.1 in reverse. There you saw that $435 + 23 = 502$ in base 6.

Why does it work?

Example 5.3.2 showed that in base 6,

$$\left(\left(555_6 - 435_6\right) + 1_6\right) + 502_6 - 1000_6 = 23_6.$$

If, in base n, $a = a_k a_{k-1} \ldots a_1 a_0$ and $c = c_m c_{m-1} \ldots c_1 c_0$ where $c > a$, and you need to calculate $c - a$, then first calculate a', the complement of a, which is given by

$$a' = n^{k+1} - a.$$

Then add a' to c, to give $c + a' = c + n^{k+1} - a$.

Finally, subtract n^{k+1} to get $c - a$.

Example 5.3.3
Calculate $1\,101\,101_2 - 101\,011_2$, giving your answer in base 2.

The complement of $101\,011$ in base 2 is $\left(111\,111 - 101\,011\right) + 1 = 10\,100 + 1 = 10\,101$. (This is the result of subtracting $101\,011$ from $1\,000\,000$.)

Now add $1\,101\,101$ to $10\,101$ to get $10\,000\,010$.

Now subtract $1\,000\,000$ to get the answer, $1\,000\,010_2$.

Example 5.3.4
Calculate $FE3 - 7FD$ in base 16.

The complement of $7FD$ in base 16 is $(FFF - 7FD) + 1 = 802 + 1 = 803$. (This is the result of subtracting $7FD$ from 1000.)

Now add 803 to $FE3$ to get $17E6$.

Now subtract 1000 to get the answer, $7E6_{16}$.

Multiplication in base n

Just as addition in base n is the same as the addition of polynomials in n, multiplication in base n is the same as multiplication of polynomials in n. Just as with addition, the problems come with carrying. Here are some examples.

Example 5.3.5
Calculate $36_7 \times 5_7$.

The layout of this process, sometimes called short multiplication, is probably familiar to you.

$$
\begin{array}{c}
3\,6 \\
\times\ \ 5 \\
\hline
{}_4 2 \\
\hline
\text{Step 1}
\end{array}
\qquad
\begin{array}{c}
3\,6 \\
\times\ \ 5 \\
\hline
{}_2 5{}_4 2 \\
\hline
\text{Step 2}
\end{array}
\qquad
\begin{array}{c}
3\,6 \\
\times\ \ 5 \\
\hline
2{}_2 5{}_4 2 \\
\hline
\text{Step 3}
\end{array}
$$

Step 1   In base 10, $6 \times 5 = 30$, and, translating into base 7, since $30 = 4 \times 7 + 2$,

$$30_{10} = 42_7.$$

At this stage, as in calculations in base 10, write down the 2, and carry the 4 into the next position.

Step 2   In base 10, $3 \times 5 + 4 = 15 + 4 = 19$, and, translating into base 7, since $19 = 2 \times 7 + 5$,

$$19_{10} = 25_7.$$

At this stage, as in calculations in base 10, write down the 5, and carry the 2 into the next position.

Step 3   There is no more to do, except add the 2 to 0, in base 7 and put it in the 7^2 position in the answer, giving $36_7 \times 5_7 = 252_7$.

Example 5.3.6
Calculate   (a) $36_7 \times 51_7$,   (b) $1011_2 \times 101_2$ (c) $7A_{12}{}^2$. (Recall that $A = 10$.)

In this example the calculations, long multiplications, are given without the commentary.

(a)
$$
\begin{array}{r}
3\,6 \\
\times\ \ 5\,2 \\
\hline
1{}_,0{}_,5 \\
2{}_,5{}_,2\,0 \\
\hline
2\,6\,2\,5 \\
\hline
\end{array}
$$

(b)
$$
\begin{array}{r}
1\,0\,1\,1 \\
\times\ \ \ \ 1\,0\,1 \\
\hline
1\,0\,1\,1 \\
0\,0\,0\,0 \\
1\,0\,1\,1\,0\,0 \\
\hline
1\,1{}_,0\,1\,1\,1 \\
\hline
\end{array}
$$

(c)
$$
\begin{array}{r}
7\,A \\
\times\ \ 7\,A \\
\hline
6{}_,6{}_,8 4 \\
4{}_,6{}_,5 A\,0 \\
\hline
5{}_,1{}_,1 4\,4 \\
\hline
\end{array}
$$

5.4 Divisibility tests

You probably know that in base 10 you can decide whether or not something is divisible by 9 by the method of 'casting out the nines'.

The number N in base 10 with digits a_n, a_{n-1}, ... , a_1, a_0 can be written as

$$N = a_n \times 10^n + a_{n-1} \times 10^{n-1} + ... + a_1 \times 10 + a_0,$$

where $0 \le a_0, a_1, ... , a_{n-1}, a_n < 10$.

Working modulo 9,

$$a_n \times 10^n + a_{n-1} \times 10^{n-1} + ... + a_1 \times 10 + a_0 \equiv a_n \times 1^n + a_{n-1} \times 1^{n-1} + ... + a_1 \times 1 + a_0$$
$$\equiv a_n + a_{n-1} + ... + a_1 + a_0 \pmod 9.$$

So if $9 \mid a_n + a_{n-1} + ... + a_1 + a_0$, that is, the sum of the digits is divisible by 9, then N is divisible by 9.

The same property is true in general for base r.

Theorem 5.2
When the number N is written in base r, the sum of its digits is divisible by $r-1$ if and only if N is divisible by $r-1$.

Let the representation of N be

$$N = a_n r^n + a_{n-1} r^{n-1} + ... + a_1 r + a_0$$

where $r > 1$ and $0 \le a_n, a_{n-1}, ... , a_1, a_0 < r$.

Now $r \equiv 1 \pmod{r-1}$, so $r^i \equiv 1 \pmod{r-1}$ for all i in $0 \le i \le n$, so

$$N = a_n r^n + a_{n-1} r^{n-1} + ... + a_1 r + a_0$$
$$\equiv a_n 1^n + a_{n-1} 1^{n-1} + ... + a_1 1 + a_0 \pmod{r-1}$$
$$\equiv a_n + a_{n-1} + ... + a_1 + a_0 \pmod{r-1}.$$

It now follows that if $r-1 \mid N$ then $r-1 \mid a_n + a_{n-1} + ... + a_1 + a_0$, and vice versa.

Exercise 5

1 Change the following numbers given in different bases into base 10.
   (a) 435_6,   (b) 1305_8 (c) 4321_{11} (d) $ABCD_{16}$
   (e) 1010101_2 (f) 123_8 (g) $147A_{12}$ (h) 11111_2

2 Change the following denary numbers into the base shown.
   (a) 125, base 7   (b) 431, base 2   (c) 876, base 16   (d) 512, base 8
   (e) 14 641, base 12   (f) 724, base 2   (g) 4097, base 16   (h) 4097, base 2

3 Carry out the following calculations in the bases shown.
   (a) $46_8 + 27_8$ (b) $576_9 + 647_9$ (c) $ABC_{15} + CBA_{15}$ (d) $1011_2 + 1101_2$
   (e) $45_8 - 16_8$ (f) $5219_{11} - 4736_{11}$ (g) $6321_9 - 1484_9$ (h) $11\,011_2 - 1101_2$
   (i) $37_8 \times 6_8$ (j) $314_{16} \times 227_{16}$ (k) $473_8{}^2$ (l) $1111_2{}^2$

4 It is possible to use a number base with negative coefficients. For example, in base 3, you could use the numbers 0, 1 and −1 as the coefficients instead of 0, 1 and 2.

Write out the numbers 1 to 13 in this system, using 0, + and − as the symbols for 0, 1 and −1 Show how your answers could be used to weigh any weight from 1 to 13 inclusive using a pair of scale pans and just three weights.

5 Show that, in all bases greater than 3, the number written as 1331 is a perfect cube.

6 Prove that if the positive integer N is divisible by 3, then the sum of the digits of its representation in base 10 is also divisible by 3.

7 Prove that in base 10, the number with digits $a_n a_{n-1} a_{n-2} \ldots a_2 a_1 a_0$ is divisible by 11 if and only if $a_0 - a_1 + a_2 - \ldots + (-1)^n a_n$ is divisible by 11.

6 Graphs

This chapter is about networks, which are given the name 'graphs'. When you have completed it, you should

- know the language associated with graphs
- know the meanings of simple, connected, complete, bipartite and planar as applied to graphs
- know and be able to use Euler's relation and simple deductions from it
- know what is meant by an Eulerian graph, and know a condition for a graph to be Eulerian.

6.1 What is a graph?

You are certainly familiar with graphs. Examples include the standard London Underground map and the maps of the New York and Paris metros which all show how the various stations are connected. They do not attempt to show other properties, such as distances, or whether or not the track is above or below ground.

A **graph** is a simple way of modelling connectedness. It consists of a set of **vertices** and a set of **edges**. An edge joins its endpoints (vertices). The graph shown in Fig. 6.1 has five vertices (the blobs) joined by four edges (the lines).

Fig. 6.1

The graph in Fig. 6.1 might represent one underground station which is linked directly to four other stations. It could just as easily represent the methane molecule CH_4, or a website with five pages, one of which has links to the other four. In each case the graph serves as a model highlighting the connectedness of the original real-world situation.

Note this quite different use of the word 'graph' from the conventional one. You should also be aware that many books which deal with graphs use different terminology from each other, so you need to check this when you pick up a book on graphs.

Two vertices are said to be **adjacent** if they are joined by an edge. Two edges are **adjacent** if they have a common vertex.

So, in Fig. 6.2a the vertex A is adjacent to all the other vertices, but B, C, D and E are only adjacent to A, while all the edges are adjacent because they all have the common vertex, A.

In Fig. 6.2b, A is adjacent to B; B is adjacent to A, C and D; C is adjacent to B and E; D is adjacent to B and E; and E is adjacent to C and D. The edges AB, BC and BD are adjacent; so are BC and CE, BD and DE, and DE and CE.

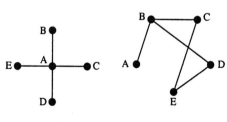

Fig. 6.2a   Fig. 6.2b

Note that in Fig. 6.2b the point where the line segment BD intersects the line segment CE is not a vertex, as there is no blob there. This graph could be redrawn so that the edges BD and CE do not cross: this would still represent the same graph because it has the same vertices and the same edges.

Graphs do not need to have edges which are straight. Indeed there can be more than one edge joining two vertices, as in Fig. 6.3a; the graph is then said to have **multiple edges**. There can be one or more edges whose endpoints are joined to the same vertex, as in Fig. 6.3b; these edges are called **loops**. Graphs which do not have multiple edges or loops are called **simple** graphs. Thus the graphs in Figs. 6.2a and 6.2b are simple, and the graphs in Figs. 6.3a and 6.3b are not simple.

In any graph the **degree of a vertex** is the number of edges which are joined to that vertex, counting a loop as two, one for each end.

Example 6.1.1

(a) How many edges in Fig. 6.3a are adjacent to BD? Write down the degree of each vertex of the graph in Fig. 6.3a.

(b) How many edges in Fig. 6.3b are adjacent to BD? Write down the degree of each vertex of the graph in Fig. 6.3b.

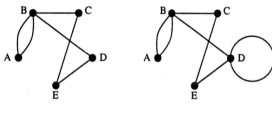

Fig. 6.3a   Fig. 6.3b

(a) There are four edges adjacent to BD. They are BC, DE and the two edges joining B to A. The degrees of the vertices A, B, C, D and E are respectively 2, 4, 2, 2 and 2.

(b) There are five edges adjacent to BD. They are BC, DE, the loop at D and the two edges joining B to A. The degrees of the vertices A, B, C, D and E are respectively 2, 4, 2, 4 and 2.

6.2 Types of graphs

Fig. 6.4 shows all the simple graphs with 1, 2 and 3 vertices. There is one with 1 vertex, and there are two with 2 vertices and eight with 3 vertices.

All eleven of the graphs in Fig. 6.4 can be thought of as being contained in the final graph, with 3 vertices and 3 edges.

In graph-theory terms you can say that each of the graphs in Fig. 6.4 is a subgraph of the graph shown in Fig. 6.5. A **subgraph** is a graph within a graph.

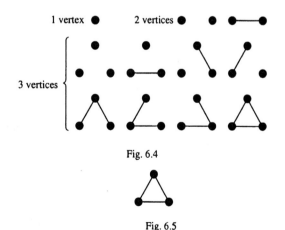

Fig. 6.4

Fig. 6.5

Now look at the eight graphs with 3 vertices in Fig. 6.4. In the lower row it is possible to move from any vertex to any other vertex by moving along adjacent edges. This is not true of the graphs in the upper row.

The graphs in the lower row are said to be connected, and those in the upper row are disconnected.

A **connected** graph is a graph in which a sequence of linked edges joins all the vertices. A graph which is not connected is **disconnected**; it has at least one vertex that is not joined in the sequence of linked edges.

A graph in which each of the vertices is connected by precisely one edge to every other vertex is called a **complete graph**. The notation K_n is used for the complete graph with n vertices. Fig. 6.6 shows K_2, K_3 and K_4.

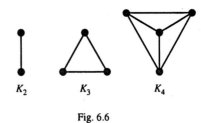

K_2 K_3 K_4

Fig. 6.6

Each simple graph is a subgraph of K_n for any sufficiently large n.

Example 6.2.1
Find a formula for the number of edges in the complete graph K_n.

Each vertex is connected to the other $n-1$ vertices and so it is at the end of $n-1$ edges. There are n vertices and so there are $n \times (n-1)$ ends of edges. As every edge has two ends, there are $\frac{1}{2}n(n-1)$ edges in total.

As a check, you can see that K_3 has $\frac{1}{2} \times 3 \times 2 = 3$ edges, and K_4 has $\frac{1}{2} \times 4 \times 3 = 6$ edges.

In addition to complete graphs, there is another important family of graphs, called **bipartite graphs**. Bipartite graphs have two sets of vertices. The edges only connect vertices from one set to the other, and do not connect vertices within a set. Fig. 6.7 shows a bipartite graph, with a set of 2 vertices in one oval, and a set of 3 vertices in another oval.

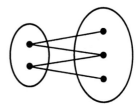

Fig. 6.7

Note that it is not necessary for every vertex in one set to be connected to every vertex in the other.

If, in a bipartite graph, every vertex in one set is connected to every vertex in the other set, the graph is called a **complete bipartite graph**. If there are r vertices in one set, and s vertices in the other, the complete bipartite graph is denoted by $K_{r,s}$. Fig. 6.8 shows $K_{2,3}$.

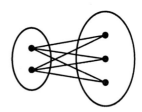

Fig. 6.8

Fig. 6.9 shows the bipartite graph $K_{3,3}$ which illustrates the classic problem about three houses being connected to three utilities, gas, electricity and water. The problem is to find whether this can be done without any of the edges crossing.

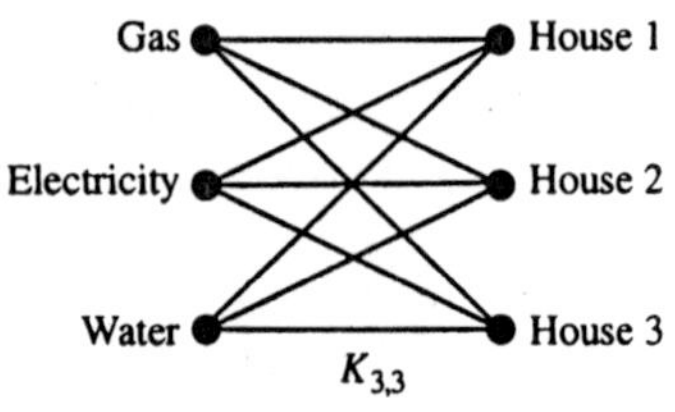

You will see the answer to this problem in Section 6.4.

Gas ●————————● House 1

Electricity ●————————● House 2

Water ●————————● House 3

$K_{3,3}$

Fig. 6.9

1 Draw connected graphs which have
   (a) 1 vertex of order 1 and 3 vertices of order 3,
   (b) 3 vertices of order 1 and 1 vertex of order 3.

2 What is the degree of each vertex of K_n?

3 Say whether the following statements are true or false. Justify your answers.
   (a) Every complete graph is connected.
   (b) Every connected graph is complete.
   (c) A complete graph is a subgraph of itself.
   (d) The complete graph K_5 has 25 edges.
   (e) The sum of the degrees of all the vertices of a graph is always even.

4 The Prime Minister is considering four Members of Parliament, Ann, Brian, Clare and David for four cabinet posts. Ann could be Foreign Secretary or Home Secretary, Brian could be Home Secretary or the Chancellor of the Exchequer, Clare could be Foreign Secretary or the Minister for Education and David could be the Chancellor or the Home Secretary.
   (a) Draw a bipartite graph to represent this situation.
   (b) How many options does the Prime Minister have?

5 Which of the following six graphs are bipartite?

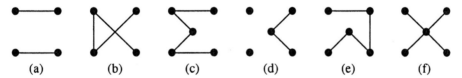

     (a)   (b)   (c)   (d)   (e)   (f)

6 Calculate the number of edges in the complete bipartite graph $K_{r,s}$.

6.3 Planar graphs

There are some connected graphs which you can draw in a plane in which no two edges intersect at a point which is not a vertex. These graphs are called **planar graphs**.

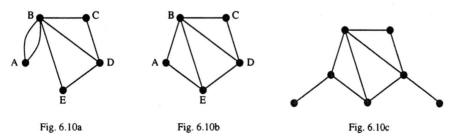

Fig. 6.10a   Fig. 6.10b   Fig. 6.10c

Figs. 6.10a, 6.10b and 6.10c are examples of planar graphs.

You might think that Fig. 6.11a is not a planar graph, but if you redraw it in the form of Fig. 6.11b you will see that it is actually planar.

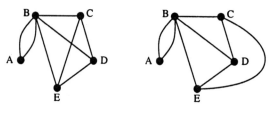

Fig. 6.11a   Fig. 6.11b

Table 6.12 shows the numbers of vertices, regions and edges in the diagrams in Figs. 6.10 and 6.11b.

	Vertices	Regions	Edges
Fig. 6.10a	5	4	7
Fig. 6.10b	5	4	7
Fig. 6.10c	7	4	9
Fig. 6.11b	5	5	8

Table 6.12

Let v be the number of vertices, f be the number of regions (faces) and e be the number of edges. In each case you can see that

$$v + f = e + 2.$$

This result is known as **Euler's relation**.

Notice that 'region' has not been defined, nor will it be. Your intuitive understanding of region won't let you down. Suffice it to say that two points in the plane are in different regions if to get from one to the other, you are forced to cross an edge.

Euler's relation
Let G be a connected planar graph, and let v be the number of vertices, f be the number of regions and e be the number of edges. Then $v + f = e + 2$.

Proof
The proof is by induction on the number of edges.

Proposition
Let $P(e)$ be the proposition that for any planar graph, $v + f = e + 2$.

Basis case
When $e = 0$, then, since G is connected, there is one vertex, so $v = 1$, and there is one region (the infinite region surrounding the vertex) so $f = 1$.

So the left side of $v + f = e + 2$ is $1 + 1 = 2$, and the right side is $0 + 2 = 2$.

Therefore $P(0)$ is true.

Inductive step

Suppose that $P(k)$ is true. Then $v + f = k + 2$ for all connected graphs with k edges. Now consider such a graph with $k + 1$ edges.

First case: the new edge is a loop.

This leaves the number v of vertices unchanged, and adds 1 to f, the number of regions.

Thus, since $v + f = k + 2$, it follows that $v + (f + 1) = (k + 1) + 2$.

Second case: the new edge joins two distinct vertices.

This leaves the number v of vertices unchanged, and adds 1 to f, the number of regions.

Thus, since $v + f = k + 2$, it follows that $v + (f + 1) = (k + 1) + 2$.

Third case: the third edge attaches a new vertex to an existing vertex.

This increases the number v of vertices by 1, and leaves the number f of regions unchanged.

Thus, since $v + f = k + 2$, it follows that $(v + 1) + f = (k + 1) + 2$.

In each case you have $P(e)$ with $e = k + 1$. Therefore, if $P(k)$ is true, then $P(k + 1)$ is true.

Completion

$P(0)$ is true and if $P(k)$ is true, then $P(k + 1)$ is true.

Using the principle of mathematical induction, $P(e)$ is true for zero and for all positive integers.

That is, $v + f = e + 2$ is true for $e = 0$ and all positive integers.

6.4 Deductions from Euler's relation

It is easy to check Euler's formula for a given planar connected graph G, but given a graph such as K_5, shown in Fig. 6.13, it is not easy to tell whether or not it is planar, because there are so many different ways of trying to draw it on a plane.

Fig. 6.13

However, no matter how it is drawn, the connected planar graph would have to be simple, that is, have no multiple edges or loops. Then every region would have to be bounded by at least three edges. This means that, if there are f regions, there will be at least $3f$ edges. But this would count each edge twice. Therefore $e \geq \frac{3}{2}f$, or $f \leq \frac{2}{3}e$. Since $v + f = e + 2$ is equivalent to $e + 2 - v = f$, this gives

$$e + 2 - v \leq \tfrac{2}{3}e,$$

which, when simplified becomes

$$e \leq 3v - 6.$$

Applying this general result to K_5 in Fig. 6.13, in which $e = 10$ and $v = 5$, the inequality $e \leq 3v - 6$ for simple, planar, connected graphs gives $10 \leq 3 \times 5 - 6 = 9$, which is a contradiction.

It follows that K_5 is not planar.

If the connected graph is a bipartite graph, such as $K_{3,3}$, shown in Fig. 6.14, you can apply Euler's relation in a different way.

In this case, every region is bounded by at least four edges. To see this, call the vertices in the two sets $\{v_1, v_2, \ldots, v_m\}$ and $\{w_1, w_2, \ldots, w_n\}$. In a bipartite graph, every edge has one vertex in $\{v_1, v_2, \ldots, v_m\}$ and the other in $\{w_1, w_2, \ldots, w_n\}$. If you trace a route which starts and ends at the same vertex and has no repeated edges, the route must take the form $v_i w_j v_k w_l \ldots$ with vertices from $\{v_1, v_2, \ldots, v_m\}$ and $\{w_1, w_2, \ldots, w_n\}$ appearing alternately. It follows that the shortest route consists of 4 edges, that is, there are no triangles. This means that, if there are f regions, there will be at least $4f$ edges. But this would count each edge twice. Therefore $e \geq 2f$, or $f \leq \frac{1}{2}e$.

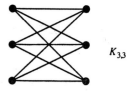

Fig. 6.14

So, in this case,

$$e + 2 - v \leq \tfrac{1}{2}e,$$

which leads to

$$e \leq 2v - 4.$$

For the complete bipartite graph $K_{3,3}$, $e = 9$ and $v = 6$. The inequality $e \leq 2v - 4$ for simple, planar, connected bipartite graphs gives $9 \leq 2 \times 6 - 4 = 8$, which is another contradiction.

It follows that $K_{3,3}$ is not planar.

Going back to the problem in Fig. 6.9, you can now see that, since $K_{3,3}$ is not planar, the three utilities cannot be connected to the three houses without the edges crossing.

> **Euler's relation**
> Let G be a connected planar graph, and let v be the number of vertices, f be the number of regions (faces) and e be the number of edges. Then
>
> $$v + f = e + 2.$$
>
> If in addition G is simple, then $e \leq 3v - 6$.
>
> If in addition G is bipartite, then $e \leq 2v - 4$.
>
> It follows from these inequalities that K_5 and $K_{3,3}$ are not planar.

Exercise 6B

1 Show that K_4 is planar.

2 Count the numbers of edges and vertices for each of the graphs in Exercise 6A Question 5, and verify that for each graph which is bipartite and planar $e \leq 2v - 4$. Show that the converse is not true, namely that if $e \leq 2v - 4$, the graph is not necessarily bipartite.

3 Say whether each of the following statements is true or false. Justify your answers.

    (a) A complete graph is not simple.

    (b) A bipartite graph has no regions with three edges.

    (c) Every simple graph is a subgraph of K_n, for some n.

6.5 The Königsberg bridges problem

Leonhard Euler is known as the father of graph theory. One of his main contributions is reputed to have arisen from a puzzle about the seven bridges over the river Pregel in the Prussian city of Königsberg, shown in Fig. 6.15. Can you find a 'round trip' which crosses each bridge precisely once?

Fig. 6.15

A suitable graphical representation of the Königsberg bridges problem has the four land-masses represented by vertices and the bridges represented by edges, as in Fig. 6.16.

Euler realised that, in any round trip, a land-mass is entered (via a bridge) the same number of times as it is left (via a bridge). For a round trip to exist, each land-mass would therefore need to be linked to the other land-masses by an even number of bridges. So a round

Fig. 6.16

trip would require each vertex of Fig. 6.16 to have an even number of edges coming out of it, that is, the degree of each vertex would have to be even. In fact, the degrees of the vertices are 3, 3, 3 and 5, and so a round trip is impossible.

Much of the description of the Königsberg bridges problem has been in informal language using words like 'round trip'. It is time to be clearer about what the words mean. Here is some more formal mathematical language which will add some precision.

- A **walk** is a sequence of linked edges. For example, in Fig. 6.17, ABC is a walk and so is EABCDBA .

- A **trail** is a walk in which no edge appears more than once. In Fig. 6.17, EABCDBA is not a trail, because the edge AB is repeated. However EABCDB is a trail, and so is ABC.

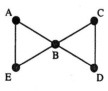

Fig. 6.17

- A **circuit** is a walk that begins and ends at the same vertex, and has no repeated edges. One example is ABEA, and another is ABCDBEA, but ABCDBA is not a circuit as AB is repeated. (A circuit can also be described as a trail that begins and ends at the same vertex.)

Be aware that different books use different definitions of these terms.

6.6   Eulerian trails and circuits

An **Eulerian trail** is a trail that contains every edge of a graph. That is, an Eulerian trail is a series of linked edges which contains every edge precisely once. An **Eulerian circuit** is a circuit that contains every edge of a graph precisely once, so the 'round trip' referred to in Section 6.5 is an Eulerian circuit. Fig. 6.18 shows one graph with an Eulerian trail, one with an Eulerian circuit and one which has neither.

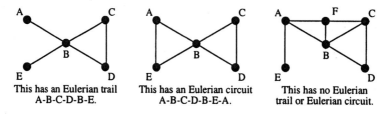

| This has an Eulerian trail A-B-C-D-B-E. | This has an Eulerian circuit A-B-C-D-B-E-A. | This has no Eulerian trail or Eulerian circuit. |

Fig. 6.18

It is a relatively easy task (see Exercise 5C Question 2) to prove that the degree of every vertex of an Eulerian circuit must be even. The converse is more difficult to prove.

Theorem 6.1

Suppose that G is a connected graph in which the degree of every vertex is even. Then G contains an Eulerian circuit.

Proof

First it is helpful to show that the theorem holds for a simple graph. So let G' be a simple connected graph in which the degree of every vertex is even.

If G' contains loops or multiple edges, then G' contains a circuit.

So suppose that G' contains n vertices, no loops and no multiple edges, that is, G' is simple. Visit one of the of the vertices, V_1. Start a trail which takes you to a new vertex, V_2. Since the degree of V_2 is even, you can continue this trail to V_3, and so on. But the number of vertices, n, of G' is finite, so at some stage this trail must contain a repeated vertex. Call this vertex V. Then the part of the trail which starts and finishes at V is a circuit. So G' contains a circuit.

Here is the main part of the theorem.

Suppose that G is a connected graph in which the degree of every vertex is even.

Now suppose that there are connected graphs in which the degree of every vertex is even but which do *not* contain an Eulerian circuit. Among all such graphs, by the well-ordering principle, there must be one in which there is a least number n of vertices. Call this graph G^*. Then all graphs with fewer than n vertices contain an Eulerian circuit.

Since G^* is connected, it must, by the previous result contain a circuit, C. Note that the degrees of all the vertices of C must be even.

Now consider the subgraph H of G^* which remains after removing from G^* the edges of C. Note that H may be disconnected into a finite number of subgraphs, H_1, H_2, etc. See Fig. 6.19.

The degrees of all the vertices of H are even, (why?) and H contains fewer edges than G^*, so, by hypothesis, each connected subgraph of H contains an Eulerian circuit.

Since G^* is connected, there must be at least one vertex, P, which is common to H and C.

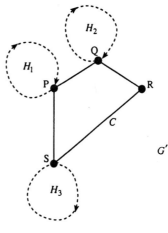

Now consider the path obtained by starting from P. Trace the Eulerian circuit of the subgraph of H until returning to P. Then trace C until reaching another subgraph of H, and then trace that subgraph. Then trace C again until another subgraph of H, until returning to C. At some point this procedure returns to P.

But this path is an Eulerian circuit, which is a contradiction. So if G^* is a connected graph in which the degree of every vertex is even, G^* contains an Eulerian circuit. It follows that G also contains an Eulerian circuit.

Fig. 6.19

A connected graph is an Eulerian graph if it contains a circuit that contains every edge precisely once.

A connected graph contains an Eulerian circuit if and only if the degree of every vertex is even.

Example 6.6.1
Explain why the graph in Fig. 6.20 contains no Eulerian circuit, but show that it has an Eulerian trail.

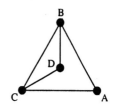

The degrees of the vertices B and C are both odd. Hence there is no Eulerian circuit.

BACBDC is an Eulerian trail.

Fig. 6.20

A well known modern puzzle is to trace the diagram shown in Fig. 6.21 without lifting the pen off the paper and without going over any lines twice.

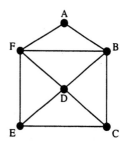

In graph theory terms the problem is therefore to find an Eulerian trail (not necessarily a circuit) which contains every edge precisely once. The degrees of the initial and final vertices, if different, will then be odd, whereas the degree of all the other vertices will be even.

Fig. 6.21

In Fig. 6.21 the only vertices with odd degree are C and E and therefore the trick is to make sure you start tracing from one or other of these two points. An example, is CBAFBDCEDFE.

A graph is called **semi-Eulerian** if it has a trail that contains every edge precisely once.

> A connected graph is semi-Eulerian if and only if the degrees of precisely two
> vertices are odd.

Exercise 6C

1 Which of the following graphs are Eulerian and which are semi-Eulerian?

(a)    (b) 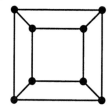   (c) 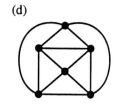   (d)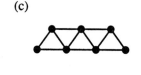

2 Explain carefully why a graph with an Eulerian circuit can only have vertices of even degree.

3 (a) For the system of islands and
bridges shown in the diagram, is
it possible to find a trail which
crosses every bridge precisely
once? Carefully explain your
reasoning.

  (b) Is it possible to find a circuit with
the same property?

4 In this diagram, is it possible to find a
route which passes through every door
precisely once?

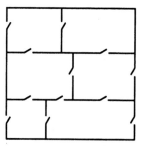

5 Think of one or two practical situations which it would be appropriate to model with a graph with
multiple edges.

6 For what value of n is K_n

  (a) Eulerian,   (b) semi-Eulerian?

7 (a) How many edges are there in the complete bipartite graph $K_{r,s}$?

  (b) Analyse $K_{r,s}$ in terms of containing an Eulerian circuit.

7 Isomorphic graphs

This chapter is about telling whether two graphs drawn by different people are the same as each other or not. When you have completed it, you should

- know the meaning of isomorphism
- know what is meant by isomorphic graphs and complements of graphs
- know how graphs can be represented using adjacency matrices
- be able to apply powers of adjacency matrices to numbers of walks.

7.1 Isomorphisms of simple graphs

Sometimes it can be hard to tell whether two graphs are the same or not. You may be able to recognise that the graphs in Fig. 7.1a and Fig. 7.1b are the same, but exactly why are they the same?

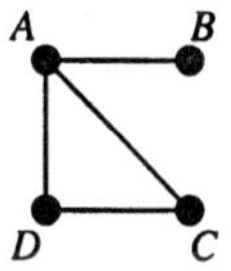

Fig. 7.1a 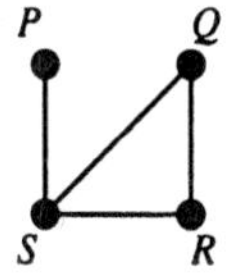   Fig. 7.1b

You can see that B on the left is essentially the same as P on the right, A corresponds to S, C corresponds to Q and D to R.

But this is the language of mappings or functions. What you really have is a function f, whose domain is $\{A,B,C,D\}$ and whose range is $\{P,Q,R,S\}$ such that an edge joins two of the vertices in the domain if and only if an edge joins the images of these vertices in the range.

In this case the function is defined by

$$f:\{A,B,C,D\} \to \{P,Q,R,S\} \text{ such that } A \mapsto S, \ B \mapsto P, \ C \mapsto Q \text{ and } D \mapsto R.$$

The edges on the left are $\{AB, AC, AD, CD\}$, and the corresponding edges are $\{SP, SQ, SR, QR\}$, which you can write as $\{f(A)f(B), f(A)f(C), f(A)f(D), f(C)f(D)\}$.

A mapping such as this is called an **isomorphism** and the graphs are said to be **isomorphic**.

An isomorphism between two graphs is only concerned with connectedness, and not with other features such as size or the precise location of the vertices.

> Two graphs G and H are **isomorphic** if and only if there is a function f which has as its domain the set of vertices $\{V_1, V_2, \ldots, V_n\}$ of G and as its range the set of vertices of H with the properties that
>
> - f is one-to-one (injective)
> - $V_i V_j$ is an edge in G if and only if $f(V_i)f(V_j)$ is an edge in H.

It is worth noting at this stage that two graphs can only be isomorphic if they have the same number of vertices. Why?

Note that for the graphs of Figs. 7.1a and 7.1b there is another isomorphism $g:\{A,B,C,D\} \to \{P,Q,R,S\}$. Can you see what it is?

The other isomorphism $g:\{A,B,C,D\} \rightarrow \{P,Q,R,S\}$ *is defined by* $(A) = S$, $g(B) = P$, $g(C) = R$ *and* $g(D) = Q$. *(In this case* R *is located above* Q, *but the connectedness is the same.)*

Example 7.1.1
Show that the graphs in Fig. 7.2 are isomorphic.

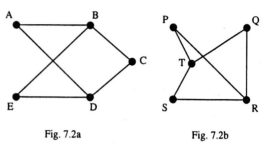

You need to find a function

$$f:\{A,B,C,D,E\} \rightarrow \{P,Q,R,S,T\}$$

so that the edges in the two graphs correspond.

Fig. 7.2a   Fig. 7.2b

It is quite helpful to note that in Fig. 7.2a B and D each have degree 3, while in Fig. 7.2b R and T have degree 3. So try $B \mapsto R$ and $D \mapsto T$.

The edges in Fig. 7.2a involving B are BA, BC and BE while the edges involving R in Fig. 7.2b are RP, RQ and RS. So try $A \mapsto P$ and $C \mapsto S$. This leaves $E \mapsto Q$. The sets of edges in the graphs are now

$$\{AB, AD, BC, BE, CD, DE\} \text{ and } \{PR, PT, RS, RQ, ST, TQ\}$$

which is the same as

$$\{AB, AD, BC, BE, CD, DE\} \text{ and }$$

$$\{f(A)f(B), f(A)f(D), f(B)f(C), f(B)f(E), f(C)f(D), f(D)f(E)\}.$$

So the graphs are isomorphic.

In Example 7.1.1, you might have worked alphabetically, and, in addition to $B \mapsto R$ and $D \mapsto T$, tried $A \mapsto P$, $C \mapsto Q$ and $E \mapsto S$. The sets of edges are then $\{AB, AD, BC, BE, CD, DE\}$ and $\{f(A)f(B), f(A)f(D), f(B)f(C), f(B)f(E), f(C)f(D), f(D)f(E)\}$, which you can check is $\{AB, AD, BC, BE, CD, DE\}$ and $\{PR, PT, RQ, RS, QT, TS\}$, which is the same as $\{PR, PT, RS, RQ, ST, TQ\}$. There are thus two different isomorphisms, but either of them would show that the graphs are isomorphic.

In Example 7.1.1 some useful properties of isomorphic graphs were used, so these should be proved.

Theorem 7.1
If two simple graphs G and H are isomorphic, then

(a) G and H have equal numbers of vertices

(b)   the degree of a vertex and the degree of the corresponding vertex are identical

(c)   the numbers of vertices in G and H with a given degree must be equal.

Proof
(a)   Let the isomorphism be f. The domain of f is the set of vertices in G, and the set of images is the set of vertices in H. So there is no vertex in H which is not the image under f of some vertex in G. Moreover, since f is one-to-one, no vertex in H is the image of two vertices in G. Hence the numbers of vertices in G and H are equal.

(b)   Suppose that there is a vertex P in G with image Q in H (so that $f(P) = Q$) such that the degree of P is different from that of Q.

Case 1   The degree of P is greater than that of Q.

Let the degree of P be k. Then there is a set $V = \{P_1, P_2, \ldots, P_k\}$ of k vertices in G, all distinct from P, such that PP_i $(i = 1, 2, \ldots, k)$ is an edge in G if and only if $f(P)f(P_i)$ is an edge in H.

Since f is an isomorphism, $f(P)f(P_i)$ is an edge in H for $(i = 1, 2, \ldots, k)$, so the degree of Q is at least that of P, which is a contradiction.

Case 2   The degree of P is less than that of Q.

Then there is an edge QY in H which does not correspond to an edge in G. Now let Y be the image of a point X in G, so $f(P) = Q$ and $f(X) = Y$. But since f is an isomorphism, if QY is an edge in H, then PX is an edge in G. This is a contradiction.

So the degree of P in G is the same as the degree of its image in H.

(c)   This follows immediately from part (a).

It can be quite hard to see that two graphs are isomorphic, but rather easier to show that they are not isomorphic. The theorem shows a useful way.

Example 7.1.2
Show that the graphs in Fig. 7.3 are not isomorphic.

In the graph in Fig. 7.3a, the degrees of the vertices K and Q are both 4 with all the other vertices having degree 3. In the graph in Fig. 7.3b all the vertices have degree 3.

So by Theorem 7.1, the graphs cannot be isomorphic.

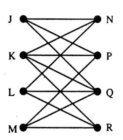

Fig. 7.3a

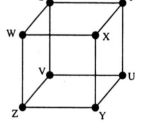

Fig. 7.3b

7.2 Complementary graphs

The two graphs in Fig. 7.4 have the property that they have the same set of vertices, but if there is an edge joining two vertices in one graph there is no corresponding edge in the other.

So the set of edges in the first graph is $\{AB, AD, BC, BE, CD, DE\}$, and in the second it is $\{AC, AE, BD, CE\}$.

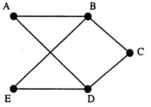

Fig. 7.4a

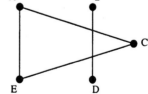

Fig. 7.4b

The graph in Fig. 7.4b is said to be the **complement** of the graph in Fig. 7.4a.

Two simple graphs G and H are said to be **complementary** if

- they have the same set of vertices $P_1, P_2, \ldots, P_n$

- $P_i P_j$ is an edge of G if and only if $P_i P_j$ is not an edge of H.

Example 7.2.1

Construct the graph H which is complementary to the graph G in Fig. 7.5.

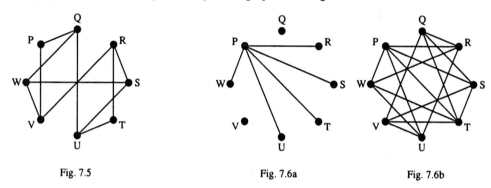

Fig. 7.5   Fig. 7.6a   Fig. 7.6b

As PQ and PV are edges in G, they are not edges in H. And as PR, PS, PT, PU and PW are not edges in G, they are edges in H.

So the graph of H has the edges from P shown in Fig. 7.6a. Continuing in this way for each vertex in turn gives the graph shown in Fig. 7.6b. This is the complement of G.

It is a useful check to ensure that the total number of edges from each vertex from the graph and the complementary graph is one less than the number of vertices because a graph plus its complement give a complete graph. So in Example 7.2.1, which has 8 vertices, P has $8 - 1 = 7$ edges, 2 in G and 5 in H.

Exercise 7A

1   Show that the following three graphs are isomorphic.

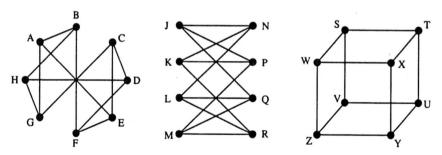

2   Show by means of an example using a graph with 5 vertices that a simple graph can be isomorphic to its complement.

3 Determine whether or not the graphs G and H are isomorphic.

4 Draw the complement of each of the graphs in Question 3.

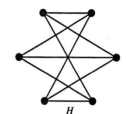
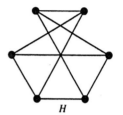

5 (a) Prove that two graphs are isomorphic if and only if their complements are isomorphic.

(b) Use part (a) to determine whether or not the graphs G and H shown in the diagram are isomorphic.

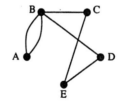
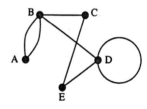

7.3 Representing graphs by matrices

It is important to have a way of representing a graph which does not rely on a diagram. In particular, computers cannot work with diagrams, so how can you tell a computer all the essential detail about a graph?

The answer is surprisingly simple. A matrix showing all the information about the vertices and the edges is all that you need. The rows and columns are labelled with the vertices of the graph, and the number in the row and column is the number of edges joining those two vertices. This is called an **adjacency matrix.**

Example 7.3.1
Write down the adjacency matrices for the graphs in Fig. 7.7a and Fig. 7.7b.

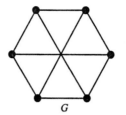
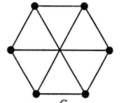

Fig. 7.7a   Fig. 7.7b

The adjacency matrices are respectively

$$
\begin{array}{c}
 & \begin{array}{ccccc} A & B & C & D & E \end{array} \\
\begin{array}{c} A \\ B \\ C \\ D \\ E \end{array} &
\left(\begin{array}{ccccc}
0 & 2 & 0 & 0 & 0 \\
2 & 0 & 1 & 1 & 0 \\
0 & 1 & 0 & 0 & 1 \\
0 & 1 & 0 & 0 & 1 \\
0 & 0 & 1 & 1 & 0
\end{array}\right)
\end{array}
\quad \text{and} \quad
\begin{array}{c}
 & \begin{array}{ccccc} A & B & C & D & E \end{array} \\
\begin{array}{c} A \\ B \\ C \\ D \\ E \end{array} &
\left(\begin{array}{ccccc}
0 & 2 & 0 & 0 & 0 \\
2 & 0 & 1 & 1 & 0 \\
0 & 1 & 0 & 0 & 1 \\
0 & 1 & 0 & 2 & 1 \\
0 & 0 & 1 & 1 & 0
\end{array}\right).
\end{array}
$$

Notice that the adjacency matrix is always symmetrical about its leading diagonal. Also the number of edges joined to a particular vertex is given by the *sum* of the numbers in the row or column for that matrix.

> The **adjacency matrix**, A_G, of a graph G with n vertices is the $n \times n$ matrix in which the entry in row i and column j is the number of edges joining the vertices i and j.
>
> A_G is symmetric about is leading diagonal.

Example 7.3.2

Draw a graph G which is represented by the matrix

$$A_G = \begin{array}{c} \\ A \\ B \\ C \\ D \end{array} \begin{array}{cccc} A & B & C & D \\ \left(\begin{array}{cccc} 2 & 1 & 0 & 1 \\ 1 & 0 & 2 & 1 \\ 0 & 2 & 2 & 2 \\ 1 & 1 & 2 & 2 \end{array} \right) \end{array}.$$

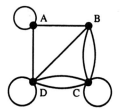

The graph G is shown in Fig. 7.8.

Fig. 7.8

Can you tell from their adjacency matrices whether or not two graphs are isomorphic? Obviously if the matrices are the same, then the graphs are isomorphic, but what if the rows and columns are mixed up.

Example 7.3.3

Graphs G and H have adjacency matrices $A_G = \begin{array}{c} \\ A \\ B \\ C \\ D \end{array} \begin{array}{cccc} A & B & C & D \\ \left(\begin{array}{cccc} 4 & 1 & 0 & 1 \\ 1 & 0 & 2 & 1 \\ 0 & 2 & 2 & 2 \\ 1 & 1 & 2 & 2 \end{array} \right) \end{array}$ and $A_H = \begin{array}{c} \\ P \\ Q \\ R \\ S \end{array} \begin{array}{cccc} P & Q & R & S \\ \left(\begin{array}{cccc} 2 & 2 & 1 & 1 \\ 2 & 2 & 0 & 2 \\ 1 & 0 & 4 & 1 \\ 1 & 2 & 1 & 0 \end{array} \right) \end{array}.$

Are G and H isomorphic?

Both matrices contain the same numbers of 0s, 1s, 2s and 4s. Also the row (and column) totals are 6, 6, 6, 4, which means that each graph has three vertices of degree 6 and one of degree 4, so they *might* be isomorphic.

Note that in G the number 4 at A shows that there are two loops at A. The only vertex in H with two loops is R, so define $f(A) = R$.

There is no edge connecting A to C in G: there is no edge from R to Q in H, so define $f(C) = Q$.

In G, the only vertex with no loop is B, while in H, the only such vertex is S, so define $f(B) = S$.

This leaves $f(D) = P$.

Now rearrange the rows and columns of A_H so that the order of the rows is $f(A)$, $f(B)$, $f(C)$, $f(D)$, that is, R, S, Q, P.

You then get $A_H = \begin{array}{c} \\ R \\ S \\ Q \\ P \end{array} \begin{array}{cccc} R & S & Q & P \\ \left(\begin{array}{cccc} 4 & 1 & 0 & 1 \\ 1 & 0 & 2 & 1 \\ 0 & 2 & 2 & 2 \\ 1 & 1 & 2 & 2 \end{array} \right) \end{array}$, which you can now see is identical to A_G, so graphs G and H are isomorphic.

Example 7.3.4

Determine whether or not the graphs G and H in Fig. 7.9 are isomorphic.

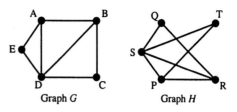

Graph G Graph H

Fig. 7.9

Start by finding the adjacency matrices A_G and A_H, for G and H, but find them by choosing vertices in a sensible order.

For G the vertex D has 4 adjacent edges, followed by A and B with 3 and C and E with 2. And for H, S has 4 adjacent edges, followed by P and R with 3 and Q and T with 2.

So, with the vertices in this order, the adjacency matrices are

$$
A_G = \begin{array}{c} \\ D \\ A \\ B \\ C \\ E \end{array}
\begin{array}{c} \begin{array}{ccccc} D & A & B & C & E \end{array} \\
\left(\begin{array}{ccccc}
0 & 1 & 1 & 1 & 1 \\
1 & 0 & 1 & 0 & 1 \\
1 & 1 & 0 & 1 & 0 \\
1 & 0 & 1 & 0 & 0 \\
1 & 1 & 0 & 0 & 0
\end{array}\right)\end{array}
\quad \text{and} \quad
A_H = \begin{array}{c} \\ S \\ P \\ R \\ Q \\ T \end{array}
\begin{array}{c} \begin{array}{ccccc} S & P & R & Q & T \end{array} \\
\left(\begin{array}{ccccc}
0 & 1 & 1 & 1 & 1 \\
1 & 0 & 1 & 0 & 1 \\
1 & 1 & 0 & 1 & 0 \\
1 & 0 & 1 & 0 & 0 \\
1 & 1 & 0 & 0 & 0
\end{array}\right)\end{array}.
$$

The matrices are identical so the graphs G and H are isomorphic.

Note that if you had taken the vertices in the order DABCE and SPRTQ, the adjacency matrices would be

$$
A_G = \begin{array}{c} \\ D \\ A \\ B \\ C \\ E \end{array}
\begin{array}{c} \begin{array}{ccccc} D & A & B & C & E \end{array} \\
\left(\begin{array}{ccccc}
0 & 1 & 1 & 1 & 1 \\
1 & 0 & 1 & 0 & 1 \\
1 & 1 & 0 & 1 & 0 \\
1 & 0 & 1 & 0 & 0 \\
1 & 1 & 0 & 0 & 0
\end{array}\right)\end{array}
\quad \text{and} \quad
A_H = \begin{array}{c} \\ S \\ P \\ R \\ T \\ Q \end{array}
\begin{array}{c} \begin{array}{ccccc} S & P & R & T & Q \end{array} \\
\left(\begin{array}{ccccc}
0 & 1 & 1 & 1 & 1 \\
1 & 0 & 1 & 1 & 0 \\
1 & 1 & 0 & 0 & 1 \\
1 & 1 & 0 & 0 & 0 \\
1 & 0 & 1 & 0 & 0
\end{array}\right)\end{array},
$$

and you could not yet tell that the graphs G and H were isomorphic. (But you would then continue with the vertices in a different order.)

Example 7.3.5

(a) Find the adjacency matrices for the graphs G and H in Fig. 7.10.

(b) Determine whether or not the graphs are isomorphic.

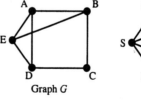

Graph G Graph H

Fig. 7.10

(a)   The matrices A_G and A_H are

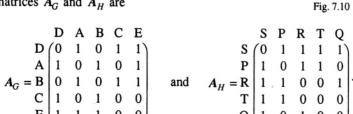

$$
A_G = \begin{array}{c} \\ D \\ A \\ B \\ C \\ E \end{array}
\begin{array}{c} \begin{array}{ccccc} D & A & B & C & E \end{array} \\
\left(\begin{array}{ccccc}
0 & 1 & 0 & 1 & 1 \\
1 & 0 & 1 & 0 & 1 \\
0 & 1 & 0 & 1 & 1 \\
1 & 0 & 1 & 0 & 0 \\
1 & 1 & 1 & 0 & 0
\end{array}\right)\end{array}
\quad \text{and} \quad
A_H = \begin{array}{c} \\ S \\ P \\ R \\ T \\ Q \end{array}
\begin{array}{c} \begin{array}{ccccc} S & P & R & T & Q \end{array} \\
\left(\begin{array}{ccccc}
0 & 1 & 1 & 1 & 1 \\
1 & 0 & 1 & 1 & 0 \\
1 & 1 & 0 & 0 & 1 \\
1 & 1 & 0 & 0 & 0 \\
1 & 0 & 1 & 0 & 0
\end{array}\right)\end{array}.
$$

(b)   You can see that there are 4 edges adjacent to vertex S in graph H, but there is no corresponding vertex in graph G, so the graphs are not isomorphic.

7.4   Walks and circuits

Suppose that you have a graph and that you wish to count the number of walks of length 2 edges between the different vertices, or the number of circuits of length 3 edges in the whole graph. How can you use the adjacency matrix to find this?

To keep things simple, look at graph G in Fig. 7.11, with adjacency matrix

$$A_G = \begin{array}{c} \\ A \\ B \\ C \\ D \\ E \end{array} \begin{array}{c} \begin{array}{ccccc} A & B & C & D & E \end{array} \\ \begin{pmatrix} 0 & 1 & 0 & 1 & 1 \\ 1 & 0 & 1 & 0 & 1 \\ 0 & 1 & 0 & 1 & 0 \\ 1 & 0 & 1 & 0 & 1 \\ 1 & 1 & 0 & 1 & 0 \end{pmatrix} \end{array}.$$

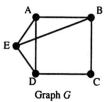

Graph G

Fig. 7.11

To find the number of two-edge walks from A to B using the matrix, note that there is a two-edge walk if there is a walk from A to another vertex, X, say and a walk from X to B. Suppose that X is in the ith row and column. If you think of the matrix as

$$\begin{array}{c} \\ \\ \\ \text{from} \\ \\ \end{array} \begin{array}{c} \\ A \\ B \\ C \\ D \\ E \end{array} \begin{array}{c} \text{to} \\ \begin{array}{ccccc} A & B & C & D & E \end{array} \\ \begin{pmatrix} 0 & 1 & 0 & 1 & 1 \\ 1 & 0 & 1 & 0 & 1 \\ 0 & 1 & 0 & 1 & 0 \\ 1 & 0 & 1 & 0 & 1 \\ 1 & 1 & 0 & 1 & 0 \end{pmatrix} \end{array}$$

then there will be a two-edge walk from A to B only if a 1 in the first row and ith column (a walk from A to X) coincides with a 1 in the ith row and second column (showing a walk from X to B).

Now, can you see what happens if you square A_G? A little reflection should convince you that when there is a 1 in the first row and ith column of the left matrix and a 1 in the ith row and second column of the right matrix, then you get a contribution of 1 to the first row and second column of the product, showing that there is a two-edge walk from A to B. There may of course be others.

$$A_G^2 = \begin{pmatrix} 0 & 1 & 0 & 1 & 1 \\ 1 & 0 & 1 & 0 & 1 \\ 0 & 1 & 0 & 1 & 0 \\ 1 & 0 & 1 & 0 & 1 \\ 1 & 1 & 0 & 1 & 0 \end{pmatrix} \begin{pmatrix} 0 & 1 & 0 & 1 & 1 \\ 1 & 0 & 1 & 0 & 1 \\ 0 & 1 & 0 & 1 & 0 \\ 1 & 0 & 1 & 0 & 1 \\ 1 & 1 & 0 & 1 & 0 \end{pmatrix} = \begin{pmatrix} 3 & 1 & 2 & 1 & 2 \\ 1 & 3 & 0 & 3 & 1 \\ 2 & 0 & 2 & 0 & 2 \\ 1 & 3 & 0 & 3 & 1 \\ 2 & 1 & 2 & 1 & 3 \end{pmatrix}.$$

Look at this final matrix closely. The number in the ith row and jth column is the number of two-edge walks from the vertex corresponding to the ith row and the vertex corresponding to the jth column.

For example, the 3 in the fourth row and second column tells you that there are 3 two-edge walks from D to B: these are DAB, DCB and DEB. Similarly, the 0 in the second row and third column tells you that there are no two-edge walks from B to C. And the number 2 in the third row and third column tells you that there are just 2 two-edge walks from C to C: these are CBC and CDC.

Similarly, if you calculate $A_G{}^3$ you will find the number of three-edge walks between various pairs of vertices.

$$A_G{}^3 = \begin{pmatrix} 0 & 1 & 0 & 1 & 1 \\ 1 & 0 & 1 & 0 & 1 \\ 0 & 1 & 0 & 1 & 0 \\ 1 & 0 & 1 & 0 & 1 \\ 1 & 1 & 0 & 1 & 0 \end{pmatrix} \begin{pmatrix} 3 & 1 & 2 & 1 & 2 \\ 1 & 3 & 0 & 3 & 1 \\ 2 & 0 & 2 & 0 & 2 \\ 1 & 3 & 0 & 3 & 1 \\ 2 & 1 & 2 & 1 & 3 \end{pmatrix} = \begin{pmatrix} 4 & 7 & 2 & 7 & 5 \\ 7 & 2 & 6 & 2 & 7 \\ 2 & 6 & 0 & 6 & 2 \\ 7 & 2 & 6 & 2 & 7 \\ 5 & 7 & 2 & 7 & 4 \end{pmatrix}.$$

The number 4 in the first row and first column tells you the number of three-edge walks from A to A. These are ABEA, ADEA, AEBA and AEDA. You might say here that each walk can be reversed, so in some sense there are only really 2 distinct three-edge walks from A to A. But note that the adjacency matrix counts all possible walks.

The number 7 in the fifth row and second column is the number of three-edge walks from E to B. These are EAEB, EBAB, EBCB, EBEB, EDAB, EDCB and EDEB. Again, all possible walks must be counted, including those with repeated edges.

Calculating the nth power of the adjacency matrix gives you information about the number of walks of edge length n.

The procedure for calculating the number of different walks between any two vertices can be shown to be true by induction.

Theorem 7.2
Let $\{v_1, v_2, \ldots, v_p\}$ be the vertices of a graph G which has adjacency matrix A_G. Then the number of different walks with n edges beginning at vertex v_i and ending at vertex v_j is the element in the ith row and jth column of the matrix $A_G{}^n$.

Proof
Proposition
Let $P(n)$ be the proposition that the element in the ith row and jth column of $A_G{}^n$ is the number of different walks with n edges beginning at vertex v_i and ending at vertex v_j.

Basis case
$P(1)$ is true, by definition.

Inductive step
Suppose that $P(k)$ is true. Then the numbers of different walks with k edges from v_i to $v_1, v_2, \ldots v_p$ respectively are the elements in the ith row of $A_G{}^k$. Suppose that these elements are $b_{i1}, b_{i2}, \ldots, b_{ip}$.

Let the jth column of A_G be $a_{1j}, a_{2j}, \ldots, a_{pj}$.

Consider the last edge before v_j in the walk with $k+1$ edges beginning at vertex v_i and ending at vertex v_j.

If this last vertex before v_j is v_1, then the number of walks from v_i to v_j is

$$b_{i1} \times a_{1j}.$$

Similarly, if the last vertex before v_j is v_2, the number of walks is $b_{i2} \times a_{2j}$; and so on , so that if the last vertex on the walk before v_j is v_p, the number of walks is $b_{ip} \times a_{pj}$.

So the total number of different walks with $k+1$ edges beginning at vertex v_i and ending at vertex v_j is

$$b_{i1} \times a_{1j} + b_{i2} \times a_{2j} + ... + b_{ip} \times a_{pj}.$$

But this is the element in the ith row and jth column of $A_G{}^{k+1}$.

This is $P(n)$ with $n = k+1$. Therefore, if $P(k)$ is true, then $P(k+1)$ is true.

Completion
$P(1)$ is true and if $P(k)$ is true, then $P(k+1)$ is true.

Using the principle of mathematical induction, $P(n)$ is true for all positive integers.

Example 7.4.1
Write down the adjacency matrix for the graph G in Fig. 7.12, and
hence find the number of three-edge walks from B to itself.

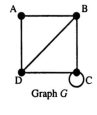

Graph G

Fig. 7.12

$$\text{The adjacency matrix is } A_G = \begin{array}{c} \\ A \\ B \\ C \\ D \end{array} \begin{array}{cccc} A & B & C & D \\ \begin{pmatrix} 0 & 1 & 0 & 1 \\ 1 & 0 & 1 & 1 \\ 0 & 1 & 2 & 1 \\ 1 & 1 & 1 & 0 \end{pmatrix} \end{array},$$

$$A_G{}^2 = \begin{pmatrix} 0 & 1 & 0 & 1 \\ 1 & 0 & 1 & 1 \\ 0 & 1 & 2 & 1 \\ 1 & 1 & 1 & 0 \end{pmatrix}\begin{pmatrix} 0 & 1 & 0 & 1 \\ 1 & 0 & 1 & 1 \\ 0 & 1 & 2 & 1 \\ 1 & 1 & 1 & 0 \end{pmatrix} = \begin{pmatrix} 2 & 1 & 2 & 1 \\ 1 & 3 & 3 & 2 \\ 2 & 3 & 6 & 3 \\ 1 & 2 & 3 & 3 \end{pmatrix}$$

$$\text{and } A_G{}^3 = \begin{pmatrix} 0 & 1 & 0 & 1 \\ 1 & 0 & 1 & 1 \\ 0 & 1 & 2 & 1 \\ 1 & 1 & 1 & 0 \end{pmatrix}\begin{pmatrix} 2 & 1 & 2 & 1 \\ 1 & 3 & 3 & 2 \\ 2 & 3 & 6 & 3 \\ 1 & 2 & 3 & 3 \end{pmatrix} = \begin{pmatrix} 2 & 5 & 6 & 5 \\ 5 & 6 & 11 & 7 \\ 6 & 11 & 18 & 11 \\ 5 & 7 & 11 & 6 \end{pmatrix}.$$

The number of three-edge walks from B to itself is the element in the second row and second
column of $A_G{}^3$, namely 6. (These walks are BADB, BCCB, BCCB, BCDB, BDAB and BDCB,
where BCCB is counted twice, once for each way round the loop at C.)

1 Write down the adjacency matrices for the following graphs. In each case use powers of the adjacency matrix to find the number of three-edge walks from C to D. In how many of these three-edge walks from C to D is a vertex repeated?

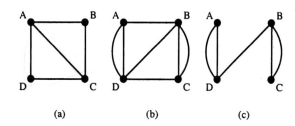

(a)   (b)   (c)

2 (a) In Example 7.4.1, write down the number of two-edge walks from D to C, and list these walks.

   (b) In Example 7.4.1, write down the number of three-edge walks from C to C, and list them.

3 Draw graphs for each of the following adjacency matrices. They all refer to a graph with vertices A, B, C and D.

(a) $\begin{pmatrix} 0 & 1 & 0 & 1 \\ 1 & 0 & 0 & 0 \\ 0 & 0 & 0 & 1 \\ 1 & 0 & 1 & 0 \end{pmatrix}$ (b) $\begin{pmatrix} 0 & 0 & 1 & 0 \\ 0 & 1 & 1 & 0 \\ 1 & 1 & 1 & 1 \\ 0 & 0 & 1 & 0 \end{pmatrix}$ (c) $\begin{pmatrix} 1 & 0 & 1 & 1 \\ 0 & 0 & 1 & 0 \\ 1 & 1 & 1 & 0 \\ 1 & 0 & 0 & 0 \end{pmatrix}$

Are any two of the graphs isomorphic?

8 Minimum spanning trees

This chapter introduces two algorithms about connecting all the vertices of a graph in the most effective way. When you have completed it, you should

- know what a spanning tree for a connected graph is
- know the term 'greedy algorithm', and the steps of the greedy algorithms called Prim's and Kruskal's algorithms
- be able to find a spanning tree of minimum weight by using either Prim's algorithm or Kruskal's algorithm.

8.1 Introduction

Suppose that you are creating an internal computer network in a school, and have to lay cable between the five main computer areas in the school. These five areas and the costs of the various alternative runs of cables are shown in Fig. 8.1.

To connect all of the areas together just four runs of cable are needed. Three of the many possibilities are shown in Fig. 8.2.

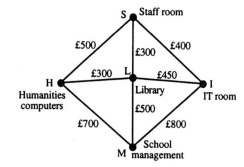

Fig. 8.1

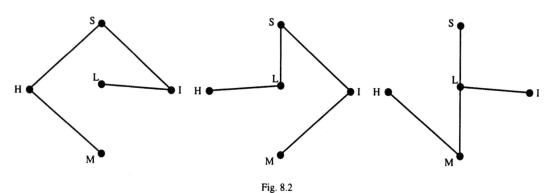

Fig. 8.2

Find the costs of each of these three possibilities. Can you find a cheaper way of laying the cable? (See Section 8.3 and Exercise 8 Question 3.)

You may have been able to spot the solution to the simple problem posed above. However, for problems such as connecting cable TV to all the main areas of a town, linking up houses to the national electricity grid, or joining up soldering points on a printed circuit, the number of possible connections is so large that you have to use an algorithm that can be performed by a computer. The purpose of this chapter is to study such algorithms.

8.2   Spanning trees

Compare the graph shown in Fig. 8.1 with those in Fig. 8.2, and you will see important differences. In Fig. 8.1 it is possible to walk from M to M via to the vertices MILM (or many other possibilities) but that is not possible in any of the graphs in Fig. 8.2 without repeating a vertex. A path such as MILM is an example of a cycle. A **cycle** is a walk that begins and ends at the same vertex, and has no other repeated vertices.

Each of the possible runs of cable considered in Section 8.1 is a connected graph with no cycles. Such a graph is called a **tree**. All of the graphs in Fig. 8.3 are trees.

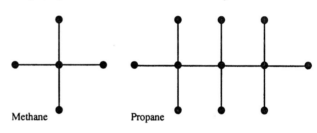

Fig. 8.3

Trees were important in the early history of graph theory because they were used by the 19th-century English mathematician, Sir Arthur Cayley, to study the possible structure of saturated hydrocarbons. Fig. 8.4, in which vertices of degree 4 represent carbon atoms and vertices of degree 1 represent hydrogen atoms, shows methane, CH_4, and propane, C_3H_8.

Trees are also important in the study of connected graphs.

Methane   Propane

Fig. 8.4

Any connected graph contains at least one subgraph which is a tree connecting every vertex of the original graph. The complete graph with four vertices, K_4, has many such trees. Fig. 8.5 shows one example obtained by removing successive edges.

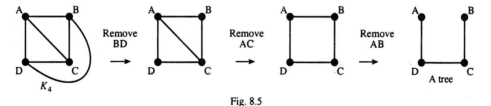

Fig. 8.5

Example 8.2.1
The number of vertices in a connected planar graph is one greater than the number of edges. Prove that the graph is a tree.

According to Euler's relation, $v + f = e + 2$.

You are given that $v = e + 1$, so, substituting this in $v + f = e + 2$ gives $f = 1$.

The graph has only one region and therefore has no cycles, so it is a tree.

Any tree which connects all the vertices of a graph is called a **spanning tree** for that graph.

Notice that each of the spanning trees for a particular graph contains the same number of edges, and that this number is one less than the number of vertices of the graph. This is illustrated in Fig. 8.6.

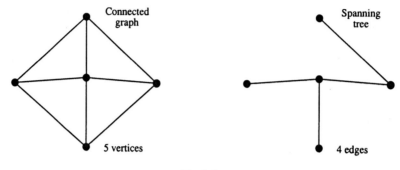

Fig. 8.6

This relationship between the number of vertices of the connected graph and the number of edges of the spanning tree is always true.

> For a connected graph with n vertices, each spanning tree has precisely $n-1$ edges.

Example 8.2.2

Find the number of spanning trees of the graph in Fig. 8.7.

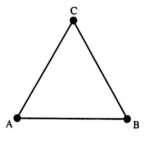

The graph has three vertices, so each spanning tree has two edges. There are three different ways of deleting an edge from the original graph, so the spanning trees are the three shown in Fig. 8.8.

Fig. 8.7

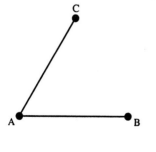 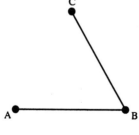 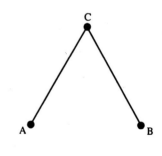

Fig. 8.8

Remember that a 'complete' graph is one which has every possible edge. The number of possible spanning trees for a complete graph increases very rapidly as the number of vertices increases (see Table 8.9).

Number of vertices	Number of spanning trees
3	3
4	16
...	...
20	2.6×10^{23}
...	...

Table 8.9

Fig. 8.10 shows the complete graph with four vertices.
Fig. 8.11 shows the 16 possible spanning trees.

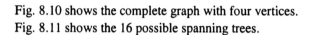

Fig. 8.10

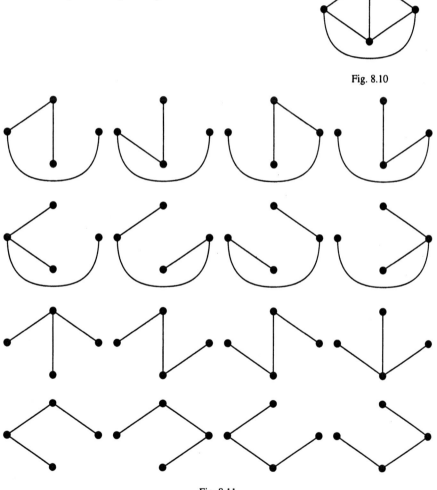

Fig. 8.11

For graphs with a reasonably large number of vertices, it is not possible for even the most powerful computer to scan all the possible spanning trees to find the best one for problems like those in Section 8.1. To do it in a reasonable amount of time, you need an efficient algorithm.

8.3   Prim's algorithm

In the introduction to this chapter in Fig. 8.1, which is reproduced here (with the vertices relabelled) as Fig. 8.12, each of the edges of the graph had a cost in £ attached to it. This cost is called the **weight** of the edge, and a graph in which each edge is allocated a number or weight, is known as a **weighted graph**. The weight of an edge might be measured in terms of money or distance or time or number of joints or many other quantities.

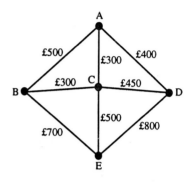

Fig. 8.12

A convenient way of describing the weights in a graph is to use a matrix, called a cost adjacency matrix.

> The **cost adjacency matrix**, C_G, of a graph G with n vertices is the $n \times n$ matrix in which the entry in row i and column j is the weight of the edge joining vertex i to vertex j.

So the cost adjacency matrix, C, for the graph in Fig. 8.12 is

$$
C = \begin{array}{c} \\ A \\ B \\ C \\ D \\ E \end{array}
\begin{array}{c} \\ \left(\begin{array}{ccccc}
A & B & C & D & E \\
- & 500 & 300 & 400 & - \\
500 & - & 300 & - & 700 \\
300 & 300 & - & 450 & 500 \\
400 & - & 450 & - & 800 \\
- & 700 & 500 & 800 & -
\end{array} \right) \end{array},
$$

where vertices with no connection are shown by a dash.

The spanning tree of minimum weight is called the **minimum spanning tree**, or the **minimum connector**. For a given connected graph, Prim's algorithm is a quick method of finding the minimum spanning tree. The algorithm was first discovered by Jamik in 1933 and later independently by Robert Prim in 1957. The sequence of steps to be followed is shown below.

> **Prim's algorithm**   To find a minimum spanning tree T:
>
> **Step 1**   Select any vertex to be the first vertex of T.
>
> **Step 2**   Consider the edges which connect vertices in T to vertices outside T. Pick the one with minimum weight. Add this edge and the extra vertex to T. (If there are two or more edges of minimum weight, choose any one of them.)
>
> **Step 3**   Repeat Step 2 until T contains every vertex of the graph.

Example 8.3.1

Use Prim's algorithm to obtain a minimum spanning tree for the graph in Fig. 8.13.

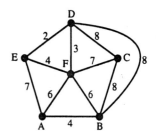

The successive stages, starting from C, are shown in Fig. 8.14.

At the fourth stage, either FA *or* FB *could have been chosen.*
Although EF *is of lower weight than* FA *it cannot be selected to add to the tree because the vertex* E *is already part of the spanning tree and a cycle would be formed.*

Fig. 8.13

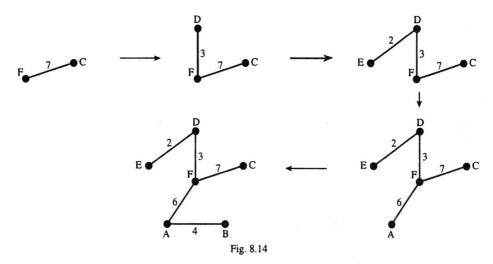

Fig. 8.14

The minimum spanning tree has weight $7+3+2+6+4 = 22$ units.

When you apply Prim's algorithm, you are simply choosing the edge which is immediately 'best' without being concerned about the long-term consequences of your choice. An algorithm of this type is called **greedy**. This 'greedy' approach to the problem of finding a minimum spanning tree always leads to the best solution.

Sometimes you are given a cost adjacency matrix and you need to find a minimum spanning tree. In that case, you might find it helpful first to draw a graph from the cost adjacency matrix.

Example 8.3.2

The cost adjacency matrix M for a graph G is given by

$$
\begin{array}{c}
\begin{array}{ccccc} & A & B & C & D & E \end{array} \\
\begin{array}{c} A \\ B \\ C \\ D \\ E \end{array}
\left(
\begin{array}{ccccc}
- & 10 & 20 & 40 & 30 \\
10 & - & 30 & 50 & 15 \\
20 & 30 & - & 40 & 20 \\
40 & 50 & 40 & - & 10 \\
30 & 15 & 20 & 10 & -
\end{array}
\right).
\end{array}
$$

Use Prim's algorithm, starting from B, to find a minimum spanning tree for G.

Fig. 8.15 shows a graph, with the vertices A, B, C, D and E drawn at the vertices of a regular pentagon, corresponding to the adjacency matrix M.

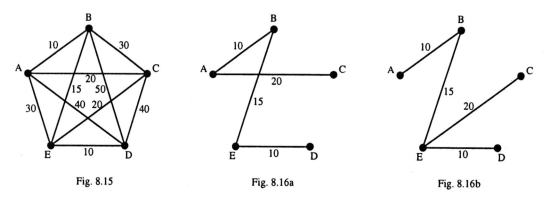

Fig. 8.15   Fig. 8.16a   Fig. 8.16b

Starting from B, the edges are added in the order BA, BE, ED, and either AC or EC. Fig 8.16 shows two possible spanning trees. They each have weight $10 + 15 + 10 + 20 = 55$ units.

8.4   Kruskal's algorithm

Another algorithm for finding the minimum spanning tree was invented by an American mathematician, Martin Kruskal, who died in 2006.

> **Kruskal's algorithm**   To find a minimum spanning tree for a connected graph with n vertices:
>
> **Step 1**   Choose the edge of least weight.
>
> **Step 2**   Choose from those edges remaining the edge of least weight which does *not* form a cycle with already chosen edges. (If there are several such edges, choose one arbitrarily.)
>
> **Step 3**   Repeat Step 2 until $n - 1$ edges have been chosen.

Example 8.4.1
Apply Kruskal's algorithm to the graph in Fig. 8.17.

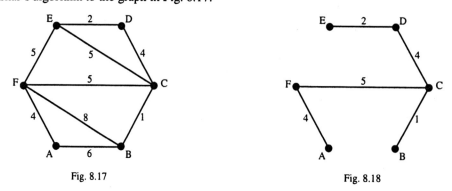

Fig. 8.17   Fig. 8.18

Starting with the edge of least weight, BC of weight 1, Kruskal's algorithm gives the results in Table 8.19, leading to the minimum spanning tree in Fig. 8.18. Table 8.19 shows which edges were part of the minimum spanning tree, and when they were added to the tree.

Edge	Weight	Choice
BC	1	1st
DE	2	2nd
AF	4	3rd
CD	4	4th
CE	5	Not chosen
CF	5	5th
EF	5	–
AB	6	–
BF	8	–

Table 8.19

Kruskal's algorithm, which is also a greedy algorithm, is very easy to apply to a small graph. The need to spot whether or not a cycle has been produced makes it less useful for more involved questions and also harder to program for a computer.

Exercise 8

1 Find all the possible spanning trees for the graph in the diagram.

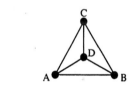

2 (a) Draw all possible spanning trees for this graph.

   (b) Which of the spanning trees has minimum weight?

   (c) Use Prim's algorithm, starting with vertex A, to find the minimum spanning tree.

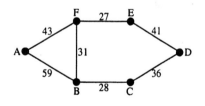

3 Find the cheapest way of laying the cable for the problem posed at the beginning of Section 8.1, whose diagram is reproduced here.

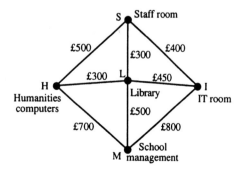

4 Consider the graph of Question 2. Show that Kruskal's algorithm produces the same minimum spanning tree as Prim's algorithm.

5 Apply Kruskal's algorithm to the graph shown here.
Draw a diagram showing the minimum spanning tree,
state the order in which you added edges and work
out the total weight of the minimum spanning tree.

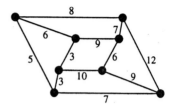

6 The costs in £ sterling of tickets for direct flights between six cities are shown in the table.

	A	B	C	D	E	F
A	–	45	60	50	90	145
B	45	–	70	25	80	110
C	60	70	–	55	70	320
D	50	25	55	–	35	175
E	90	80	70	35	–	80
F	145	110	320	175	80	–

(a) Use Prim's algorithm to construct a minimum spanning tree and work out its total weight. Show
all your working clearly and state the order in which you add edges or vertices.

(b) Suppose that, in addition to the cost of tickets, an airport tax of 10% must be paid on leaving
any airport. What effect will this have on the minimum spanning tree?

(c) Suppose that airport taxes are actually £15 for any flight involving airports D, E or F and £5
otherwise, so the tax for the flight from A to D is £15 + £5 = £20. find the new minimum
spanning tree and work out its total weight.

7 The road distances in kilometres between eight towns are shown in the table. Boxes with thick
borders refer to motorway routes.

	A	B	C	D	E	F	G	H
A	–	20	45	50	60	50	40	50
B	20	–	50	60	50	65	30	30
C	45	50	–	30	10	80	80	75
D	50	60	30	–	55	70	85	100
E	60	50	10	55	–	85	75	55
F	50	65	80	70	85	–	70	100
G	40	30	80	85	75	70	–	45
H	50	30	75	100	55	100	45	–

(a) Use Prim's algorithm, starting with A, to find the minimum spanning tree for the towns. Draw a
diagram showing the minimum spanning tree, state the order in which you added edges, and
work out the total weight of the minimum spanning tree.

(b) The time for journeys can be estimated by assuming an average speed of 100 km h^{-1} for the motorway routes and 60 km h^{-1} for the other roads. Complete a table of times, in minutes, between the towns. Find the minimum spanning tree for the times, and write down the total of all the times on the minimum spanning tree.

(c) Explain why the answer for part (b) is not the total time for the minimum spanning tree found in part (a).

8 The table shows the distances in miles between six US cities.

	C	Da	De	LA	NY	W
Chicago	–	800	900	1800	700	650
Dallas	800	–	650	1300	1350	1200
Denver	900	650	–	850	1650	1500
Los Angeles	1800	1300	850	–	2500	2350
New York	700	1350	1650	2500	–	200
Washington DC	650	1200	1500	2350	200	–

Use Kruskal's algorithm to find the minimum spanning tree. Draw the minimum spanning tree and find its total length.

9 Define the term 'tree'. Prove that if the number of vertices in a planar graph G is one greater than the number of edges, then the graph is a tree.

10 The figure shows the distances in kilometres along recommended motoring routes between ten French towns.

Dijon									
296	Grenoble								
462	714	Le Mans							
507	282	926	Marseille						
662	334	1081	188	Nice					
297	549	138	761	916	Orléans				
313	565	203	776	931	130	Paris			
515	560	182	733	888	212	330	Poitiers		
244	139	507	309	464	392	513	421	St-Etienne	
415	534	82	745	900	112	234	100	425	Tours

(a) Use Prim's algorithm, starting with Paris, to find the minimum spanning tree. Show all your working clearly, and work out the minimum spanning tree's total length.

(b) The distances from Geneva (in Switzerland) to the ten French towns are as follows.

D	G	L	M	N	O	Pa	Po	S	T
199	144	634	434	477	496	537	501	164	528

What is the total length of the minimum spanning tree when Geneva is included?

9 The shortest path

This chapter looks at the problem of finding the shortest path between two given vertices. When you have completed it, you should

- know the steps of the greedy algorithm called Dijkstra's algorithm
- be able to apply Dijkstra's algorithm to obtain the path of minimum weight between two vertices.

9.1 What is 'shortest'?

It is now relatively inexpensive to buy a route planner for a private car. With this you can find the route to your destination which has the shortest distance, or which takes the least time based upon the latest traffic information and expected speeds on different roads. The same algorithm will solve both of these problems; in one case you must consider the graph of distances, and in the other case you must consider the graph of times. This type of problem is generally known as a 'shortest path' problem but it is better thought of as a problem of finding the path of minimum weight. The weights of edges may be distances or times, as above, or they could be something entirely different, such as depreciation costs or petrol charges.

A **path** is defined as a walk which has no repeated vertices.

The map in Fig. 9.1 shows the main routes between six towns. Single lines are A-roads, and double lines are motorways.

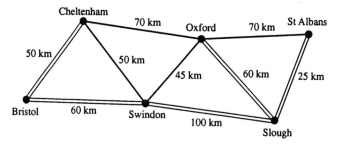

Fig. 9.1

Try to solve the following problems by inspection before looking at the solutions (page 119).

1 What is the shortest path from St Albans to Bristol?

2 Suppose the average speed on the A-roads to be 80 km h^{-1} and on the motorways to be 110 km h^{-1}. What is the quickest route from St Albans to Cheltenham?

3 Suppose further that there is a 15 minute delay on the M25 from St Albans to Slough. What now is the quickest route from St Albans to Bristol?

As shortest path questions become more complicated it soon becomes necessary to develop a systematic approach to solving them. One of the most commonly used methods for the shortest path problem is an algorithm invented by Edsger Dijkstra, who died in 2002.

9.2 Dijkstra's algorithm

This algorithm is based upon the idea of labelling each vertex with the length of the shortest path from the start vertex found so far. This temporary label is replaced whenever a shorter path is found. When you can be certain that there is no shorter route you 'box' the label to show that it is now a **permanent label**.

> **Dijkstra's algorithm**
>
> **Step 1** Label the start vertex with zero and box this label.
>
> **Step 2** Consider the vertex with the most recently boxed label. Suppose this vertex to be X and let D be its permanent label. Then, in turn, consider each vertex directly joined to X but not yet permanently boxed. For each such vertex, Y say, temporarily label it with the lesser of D + (the weight of edge XY) and its existing label (if any).
>
> **Step 3** Choose the least of all temporary labels on the graph. Make this label permanent by boxing it.
>
> **Step 4** Repeat Steps 2 and 3 until the destination vertex has a permanent label.
>
> **Step 5** Go backwards through the graph, retracing the path of minimum weight from the destination vertex to the start vertex.

Example 9.2.1

Find the shortest path from A to G in Fig. 9.2.

Fig. 9.3a shows the situation after Step 1, in which A was labelled 0 and boxed, and the first pass through Step 2, where B, C and D have temporary labels.

In Step 3, the least of the temporary labels is at B, so this is made permanent by boxing it, as shown in Fig. 9.3b.

Fig. 9.3c shows the situation after the next pass through Step 2, where the temporary label 5 on E comes from adding the most recently boxed label, 3 at B, and the length 2 from B to E. Similarly, the temporary label at C comes from adding the permanent label 3 at B and the length 4 from B to C to make a total of 7. As 7 is less than the existing temporary label 8 at C, the 8 is crossed out and replaced with 7.

Fig. 9.3d shows the label at E boxed, as it is the least of the temporary labels. This provides the starting point for the next pass through Step 2.

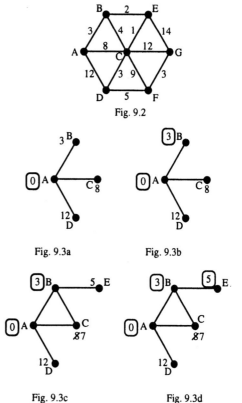

Fig. 9.2

Fig. 9.3a

Fig. 9.3b

Fig. 9.3c

Fig. 9.3d

Continuing in this way, you eventually get to the point at which all the labels are permanently boxed. This is shown in Fig. 9.4.

You are now ready for Step 5.

Retracing the path backwards through the network, you can see that

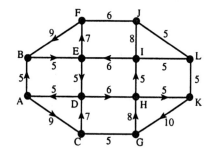

17_G was produced by $14_F + 3$.

14_F was produced by $9_D + 5$, and so on.

The shortest path is ABECDFG, which has length 17.

Note that a bonus of Dijkstra's algorithm is that once the algorithm has been carried out you know the shortest paths to all permanently labelled vertices.

If you are required to show the order of permanent labelling, it can be useful to put your working at each vertex in a box, as shown in Fig. 9.5.

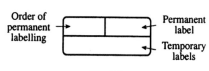

Fig. 9.5

The box in Fig. 9.6 shows that the relevant vertex had received an initial temporary label of 8, then one of 7, and finally one of 5. This became its permanent label, and it was the 6th vertex to be permanently labelled.

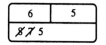

Fig. 9.6

Example 9.2.2

The graph shown in Fig. 9.7 represents part of a road system in a city. Some of the roads are one-way (as shown by the arrows), and the weights on the edges represent estimated travel times, in minutes. What is the quickest route from A to K?

Fig. 9.8 shows the result of applying Dijkstra's algorithm.

Retracing the steps you find that the quickest route is ABEDHK, taking a total time of 26 minutes.

Notice that you need not draw a new diagram for each pass through Dijkstra's algorithm.

Fig. 9.7

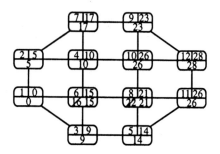

Fig. 9.8

9.3   A drawback of Dijkstra's algorithm

One drawback of Dijkstra's algorithm is that it cannot be used if any weights are negative. (The cost of a route might be negative if, for example, a firm could achieve a profit by making a delivery along that route.)

Example 9.3.1

(a)   What is the shortest route from A to C in the graph of Fig. 9.9?

(b)   What is the result of applying Dijkstra's algorithm?

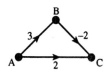

Fig. 9.9

    (a)   You can see by inspection that the shortest route is ABC, which has weight 1.

    (b)   Fig. 9.10 shows the effect of applying Dijkstra's algorithm. The problem is that vertex C is permanently labelled before the route ABC is considered.

Similarly, Dijkstra's algorithm cannot be used for longest path problems.

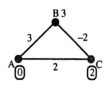

Fig. 9.10

Exercise 9

1   Use Dijkstra's algorithm to find the shortest path from A to G for the graph shown in the diagram. Show how you arrive at your result.

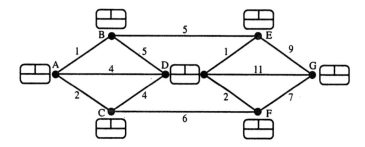

2   Use Dijkstra's algorithm to find the shortest path from A to J for the graph in the diagram.

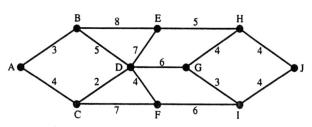

3   Each move of a counter is one square horizontally or vertically on the board shown here. The counter cannot move across the thick lines.

Apply Dijkstra's algorithm to find the smallest number of moves from the square marked with a counter to each other square.

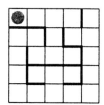

4 The table shows the cost in £ of direct routes between six towns. Draw a graph and use Dijkstra's algorithm to find the minimum cost from A to F.

	A	B	C	D	E	F
A	–	11	12	–	–	–
B	11	–	–	15	18	–
C	12	–	–	8	21	–
D	–	15	8	–	–	20
E	–	18	21	–	–	15
F	–	–	–	20	15	–

5 Moore's algorithm for a connected graph with two specified vertices, m and n, is as follows.

Step 1   Let $i = 0$.

Step 2   Label m with 0.

Step 3   Find all unlabelled vertices that are adjacent to a vertex labelled i, and label them $i+1$.

Step 4   Replace i by $i+1$.

Step 5   Repeat Steps 3 and 4 until vertex n is labelled.

(a) Apply Moore's algorithm to the graph in the figure.

(b) What is Moore's algorithm designed to accomplish?

(c) What is the connection between Moore's algorithm and Dijkstra's algorithm?

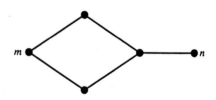

6 The numbers on the diagram represent the times in minutes of the journeys between railway stations.

(a) What is the quickest route from A to D?

(b) How could you adjust the numbers to model the fact that there is a delay of 20 minutes on all journeys passing through station O?

What is now the quickest route from A to D?

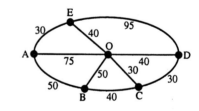

7 (a) Use Dijkstra's algorithm to find the shortest path from A to F. Show all necessary working.

(b) A directed edge from C to D is now added, with weight -4. What is the shortest path from A to F now? Explain why Dijkstra's algorithm cannot be used to find this path.

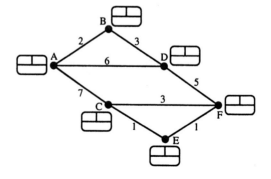

8 It is required to find the shortest paths from each of A, B and C to N.

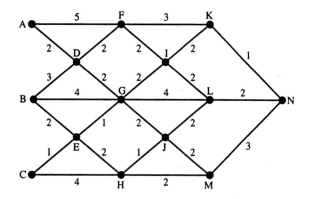

(a) How can these paths be determined by applying Dijkstra's algorithm just once?

(b) Obtain the three shortest paths. Which of A, B and C is nearest to N?

9 Fares (in £) for direct flights between five cities are shown in the table.

	A	B	C	D	E
A	–	90	70	35	30
B	90	–	40	150	55
C	70	40	–	20	50
D	35	150	20	–	100
E	30	55	50	100	–

(a) Draw a graph and use Dijkstra's algorithm to find the cheapest routes from A to each other city.

(b) Suppose each change of flight is estimated to cost an extra £10 of sundry expenses. Find the cheapest routes now.

10 The Chinese Postman algorithm

This chapter looks at the problem of finding a route covering every edge of a graph. When you have completed it, you should

- be aware of a wide range of route inspection problems
- be able to apply the Chinese Postman algorithm to obtain the route of minimum weight.

10.1 Traversability

Consider the task of a village police officer who must traverse each of the streets shown in Fig. 10.1.

Replacing roads by edges and junctions by vertices, you obtain the graph shown in Fig. 10.2.

Since the degree of each vertex is even, the graph has an Eulerian circuit (see Section 6.6). The police officer can therefore choose a route which contains every edge precisely once, as shown in Fig. 10.3.

The length of the police officer's route is then precisely the same as the length of all the streets, and that is clearly the best that can be achieved. However, for most graphs the situation will not be so simple.

For example, consider Fig. 10.4.

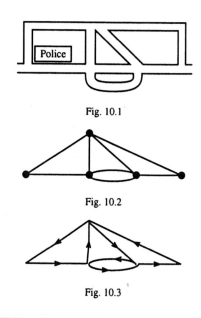

Fig. 10.1

Fig. 10.2

Fig. 10.3

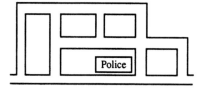

Fig. 10.4

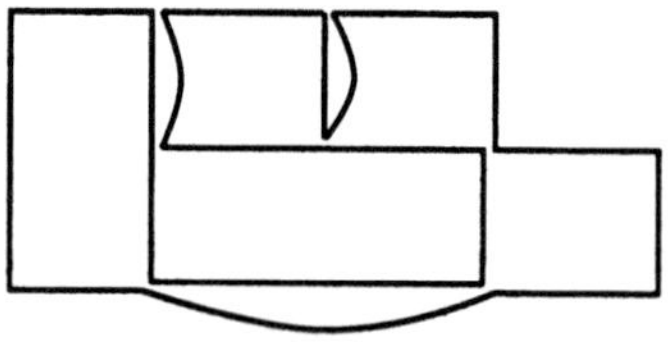

Fig. 10.5

Here, the underlying graph includes six vertices of odd degree. The only way that a route can traverse *every* edge is if some edges are repeated. For example, Fig. 10.5 shows that three edges are traversed twice.

The length of the police officer's route can now be thought of as

the length of all the streets + the lengths of repeated streets.

The police patrol is an example of a practical situation which requires the solution of a **route inspection problem**, that is, the finding of a route containing every edge at least once. Other examples include repairing track, delivering mail, seeding fields and clearing snow.

A further application of route inspection is checking every link on a website. Websites can have hundreds of pages and thousands of links, and checking these links requires the involvement of both computers and humans. Computer software is used to check simple links and to keep track of the whole checking process, whereas human input is especially required for checking the more descriptive links.

10.2 The Chinese Postman (route inspection) algorithm

Route inspection problems can involve large graphs with weighted edges. There is therefore a need for a systematic procedure to obtain the minimum-weight route.

The following well known procedure for finding the minimum-weight route which starts and ends at the same vertex and traverses every edge (as required by a postman) was invented by a Chinese mathematician, Kuan Mei-Ko, in 1962.

> **Chinese Postman algorithm**
>
> **Step 1** Find all vertices of odd degree.
>
> **Step 2** For each pair of odd vertices find the connecting path of minimum weight.
>
> **Step 3** Pair up all the odd vertices so that the sum of the weights of the connecting paths from Step 2 is minimised.
>
> **Step 4** In the original graph, duplicate the minimum-weight paths found in Step 3.
>
> **Step 5** Find a route containing every edge for the new (Eulerian) graph.

Example 10.2.1
Find the minimum-weight route containing all edges for the graph in Fig. 10.6.

The odd vertices are A, B, C and D (Step 1).

The minimum weights of the connecting paths are

AB 8,   BC 8,   AC 7,   BD 7,   AD 6,   CD 5 (Step 2).

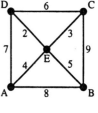

Fig. 10.6

The possible pairs, in which all the odd vertices are connected, are

AB, CD $8 + 5 = 13$,   AC, BD $7 + 7 = 14$,   AD, BC $6 + 8 = 14$.

So the odd vertices should be paired up as AB and CD (Step 3).

Add in the duplicated edges AB and CED (Step 4).

Step 5 gives a route of minimum weight: for example, ABAEBCECDEDA.

Its weight is

the weight of all the edges + the weights of repeated edges $= 44 + 13 = 57$.

The Chinese Postman algorithm assumes that the original graph has an even number of vertices of odd degree. This is actually true for *all* graphs. Note that each edge of a graph contributes 1 to the degrees of two vertices, and so the sum of the degrees of all the vertices is twice the number of edges. The number of vertices of odd degree must therefore be even, as required.

When the number of vertices of odd degree is relatively large, it can be very time-consuming to check all the possibilities, as in the next example.

Example 10.2.2*

The graph in Fig. 10.7 gives the times (in minutes) that it takes to drive along a number of streets in central London.

(a) List the vertices of odd degree.

(b) Draw up a table showing the least times between the vertices of odd degree.

(c) What would be the minimum time needed to complete a route inspection of every one of these streets? Write down such a route.

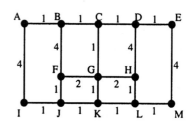

Fig. 10.7

(a)   B, C, D, F, H, J, K, L.

(b)

	B	C	D	F	H	J	K	L
B	–	1	2	4	4	4	3	4
C	1	–	1	3	3	3	2	3
D	2	1	–	4	4	4	3	4
F	4	3	4	–	4	1	2	3
H	4	3	4	4	–	3	2	1
J	4	3	4	1	3	–	1	2
K	3	2	3	2	2	1	–	1
L	4	3	4	3	1	2	1	–

Table 10.8

(c)   The total weight of all streets is 32.

For Step 3, one good possibility for pairing off the vertices is

BD, CK, FJ, HL.

These paths have total length $2 + 2 + 1 + 1 = 6$.

For this to be beaten or even equalled, no edge of length 4 can be used, since $1 + 1 + 1 + 4 > 6$. Thus the extra path from B *must* start BC and the extra path from D *must* start DC. It should now be clear that the extra 6 minutes cannot be beaten and so the minimum time is $32 + 6 = 38$ minutes. An example of a minimum-time route is

AIJFJ KLHLM EDHGF BCDCG KGCBA.

1   A person delivering leaflets has to walk along each of the
    roads shown on the map. All the measurements are metres,
    and, except for at the crescent, all the angles are right
    angles.

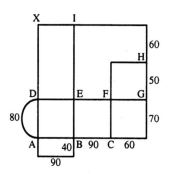

   (a) Explain the relevance of those intersections where an
        odd number of roads meet.

   (b) Find the shortest possible distance the person has to
        walk, starting and finishing at X. Show the results of
        each possible pairing of odd vertices.

   (c) For each of the nine road intersections, find the number of times that the delivery person will
        pass through that intersection.

   (d) What is the shortest possible distance the delivery person would have to walk if they started and
        finished at C? Explain your answer.

2   (In this question ignore the widths of the roads.)

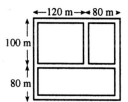

   (a) Model this road system as a graph in an appropriate way
        for

       (i)   a delivery man who only needs to walk along each
             road once,

       (ii) a postwoman who walks along both sides of each
             road,

       (iii) a street cleaner who travels along both sides of each road in the correct direction.

   (b) What is the total length of the roads in the graph?

   (c) In each case considered in part (a), find the total distance that will need to be travelled.

3   An electronic game takes place in an arena consisting of a 4×4
    block of connected rooms.

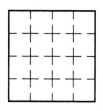

    To complete the game, it is necessary to travel through each of
    the 24 doorways. Convert this problem into a route inspection
    problem, and find the least number of doorways that will have to
    be gone through twice.

4* (a) Consider the problem in Question 3, but with an $n \times n$ block of rooms, where n is even. The
        rooms are connected as in Question 3. Copy and complete the table.

Degree	2	3	4
Number of vertices of that degree			

        How many edges (doorways) will need to be repeated?

   (b) How many edges must be repeated if n is odd?

10.3 Pairing odd vertices

You have seen that the version of the Chinese Postman algorithm given in this chapter depends upon your performing the following operations.

- Consider all possible pairings of the vertices of odd degree.
- Find the shortest distance between each pair of vertices of odd degree.

The second operation can be performed by Dijkstra's algorithm. The important question is how many times must this algorithm be performed, that is, how many pairings are there of the vertices of odd degree.

For two odd vertices A and B, the only edge is AB, so there is 1 pairing.

For four odd vertices, A, B, C and D, the possible choices are AB with CD, AC with BD and AD with BC, so there are 3 pairings.

For six odd vertices, A, B, C, D, E and F,

> you can choose AB along with each of the three pairings of C, D, E and F;
> you can choose AC along with each of the three pairings of B, D, E and F;
> you can choose AD along with each of the three pairings of B, C, E and F;
> you can choose AE along with each of the three pairings of B, C, D and F;
> you can choose AF along with each of the three pairings of B, C, D and E.

There are therefore 15 pairings in total.

Table 10.9 shows the results for various numbers of vertices of odd degree.

Number of odd vertices	Number of ways of pairing
2	1
4	3
6	15
8	105
10	945
12	10 395
14	135 135

Table 10.9

For more than six vertices of odd degree it is clearly impractical to apply the Chinese Postman algorithm by hand. Even using a computer is problematical if the number of odd vertices is large, because the number of pairings is so large.

======== **Exercise 10B** ========

1 A child's toy consists of a number of pegs around which elastic bands are wrapped.

Which of (a) and (b) can be made with a single, continuous elastic band? Explain your answer.

(a)    (b)

2 A snow-plough must drive along all the main roads shown, starting and finishing at the garage at A. The distances in kilometres are marked.

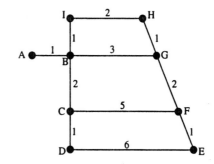

(a) Explain why 25 km is a lower bound for the distance the snow plough must travel.

(b) Find the least distance it must actually travel, showing your method clearly.

3 The matrix form for a weighted graph is shown in the table below.

	A	B	C	D	E	F	G	H
A	–	23	17	–	18	–	15	–
B	23	–	9	10	12	16	–	14
C	17	9	–	9	20	–	27	–
D	–	10	9	–	–	–	–	16
E	18	12	20	–	–	7	20	–
F	–	16	–	–	7	–	24	17
G	15	–	27	–	20	24	–	–
H	–	14	–	16	–	17	–	–

(a) Use Dijkstra's algorithm to find the shortest paths from H to C, D and E.

(b) Draw a weighted graph with vertices C, D, E, H and with each edge having the weight of the corresponding shortest path.

(c) Apply the Chinese Postman algorithm to the original graph. Which edges should be duplicated?

4 The table shows distances (in metres) measured along the paths connecting features in the gardens of a stately home.

	A	B	C	D	E	F	G
A	–	250	200	–	500	300	–
B	250	–	400	200	–	70	–
C	200	400	–	300	400	–	300
D	–	200	300	–	–	–	350
E	500	–	400	–	–	–	500
F	300	70	–	–	–	–	–
G	–	–	300	350	500	–	–

(a) What is the total length of all the paths?

(b) What distance must be covered if each path is to be inspected?

5 Apply the Chinese Postman algorithm to the graph of distances, in kilometres, shown below. Which roads should be repeated?

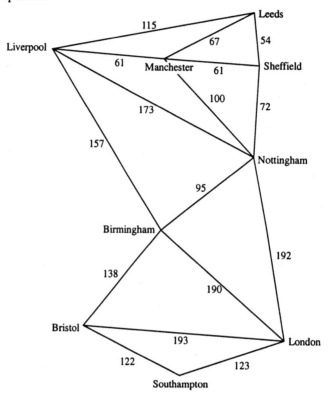

6 A network of pipelines is as shown, with distances in metres. A fault has to be located. What is the shortest route which will cover every length of pipeline at least once? Show your method fully.

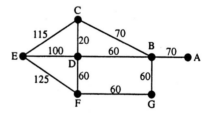

11 The travelling salesperson problem

This chapter is about finding a tour that visits every vertex of a graph. When you have completed it, you should

- appreciate that evaluating all tours is not practical for large scale problems
- be able to apply an algorithm to find a solution (not necessarily the best)
- know how to obtain bounds within which the best solution must lie.

11.1 The classical problem

A travelling salesperson needs to visit each place (vertex of a graph) and must plan how to do so in a way that minimises travelling time.

You have seen that the problem of finding a route traversing every edge (the route inspection problem) depended upon the earlier work of the mathematician Euler. Similarly, the problem of finding a tour visiting every vertex was studied in the 19th century by the Irish mathematician Sir William Hamilton.

A **Hamiltonian path** is defined to be a walk which contains every vertex precisely once. A **Hamiltonian cycle** is a cycle which contains every vertex precisely once. In a simple case, such as that of the graph in Fig. 11.1, it is easy to list all the Hamiltonian cycles.

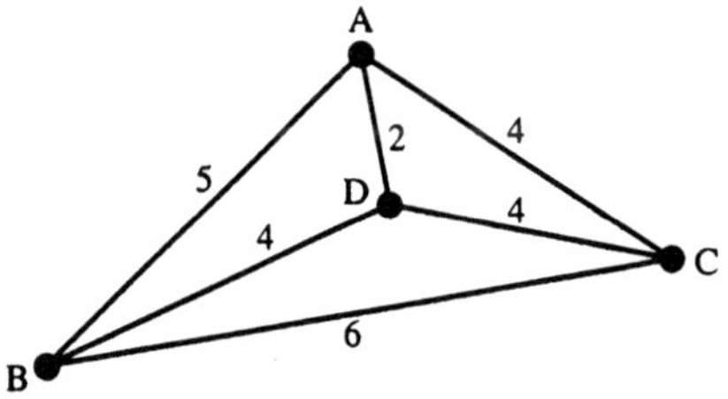

There are just three essentially different Hamiltonian cycles:

    ACBDA with weight 16,
    ABCDA with weight 17,
    ABDCA with weight 17.

Fig. 11.1

Note, for example, that the cycle ADBCA is just the first cycle reversed and so is not essentially different from it.

The classical **travelling salesperson problem** is to find the Hamiltonian cycle of minimum weight. In the above case this is the cycle ACBDA.

However, not all graphs have Hamiltonian cycles. For example, the graph in Fig. 11.2 does not have any cycles passing through A.

Nevertheless, a salesperson living, say, in town B might still need to find the shortest round trip visiting every town. To enable you to use this chapter's methods for finding Hamiltonian cycles, you can replace any graph like Fig. 11.2 by the complete graph of shortest distances. The shortest distance between A and C is 33, via D. If you add the direct edge AC, of weight 33, you have not changed the problem.

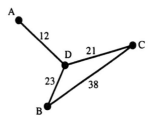

Fig. 11.2

Adding all such edges, you get Fig. 11.3.

For the remainder of this chapter it is therefore assumed that the problem is always the classical one of finding a Hamiltonian cycle of minimum weight, with no repetition of vertices.

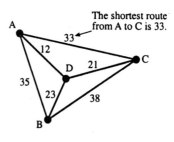

Fig. 11.3

11.2 A difficult problem

In Section 11.1 you saw how to find the minimum Hamiltonian cycle for a graph with four vertices by listing all three possible cycles.

Unfortunately, as the number of vertices increases, the number of possible Hamiltonian cycles tends to increase very rapidly. For complete graphs, where all vertices are directly linked to each other, Table 11.4 shows the numbers of Hamiltonian cycles for small values of n.

Number of vertices, n	Number of Hamiltonian cycles
3	1
4	3
5	12
6	60
7	360

Table 11.4

To see how to calculate these numbers, consider the case $n = 5$ and suppose the vertices are A, B, C, D and E. Vertex A must be on each cycle, and so you may as well always start from A. There are then four possibilities for the next vertex, three for the one after, two for the one after that, and just one possibility for the final vertex before returning to A.

This gives $4 \times 3 \times 2 \times 1 = 24$ sequences. However, each Hamiltonian cycle corresponds to two sequences, since, for example, ABCDEA and its reverse AEDCBA are taken to be the same Hamiltonian cycle. So if $n = 5$, there are $\frac{1}{2} \times 24$, or 12, Hamiltonian cycles.

In general, for n vertices, the number of Hamiltonian cycles is

$$\tfrac{1}{2} \times (n-1) \times (n-2) \times \ldots \times 3 \times 2 \times 1 = \tfrac{1}{2}(n-1)!$$

The method of evaluating all Hamiltonian cycles therefore requires consideration of $\frac{1}{2}(n-1)!$ cycles. To see what this means for computer time, consider a 3 GHz processor (that is, one capable of performing 3×10^9 simple operations per second). If there were 20 vertices, there would be $\frac{1}{2} \times 19!$, or 6×10^{16}, Hamiltonian cycles. Even with the assumption that the computer could check an entire tour in a single operation, a problem with just 20 vertices would require about 2×10^7 seconds, which is about 8 months, of computer time!

All methods discovered to date for solving the travelling salesperson problem take a similar time and so attention has been focused on finding not the optimal solution, but simply a reasonably good solution.

11.3 The Nearest Neighbour algorithm

A simple way of trying to find a reasonably good Hamiltonian cycle is to try a greedy algorithm, such as the Nearest Neighbour algorithm. At each stage it visits the nearest vertex which has not already been visited.

> **The Nearest Neighbour algorithm**
>
> **Step 1** Choose any starting vertex.
>
> **Step 2** Consider the edges which join the previously chosen vertex to not-yet-chosen vertices. From these edges pick one that has minimum weight. Choose this edge, and the new vertex on the end of it, to be part of the cycle.
>
> **Step 3** Repeat Step 2 until all vertices have been chosen.
>
> **Step 4** Then add the edge that joins the last-chosen vertex to the first-chosen vertex.

Example 11.3.1
A small chemical plant can be used to produce any one of five chemicals, A, B, C, D and E. The times (in hours) required for cleaning the equipment, and setting it up again for making the next chemical, are as shown in Fig. 11.5. Use the Nearest Neighbour algorithm to find a small total changeover time for production of all five chemicals, starting and finishing with chemical A.

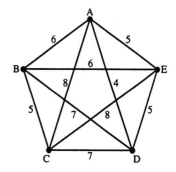

Fig. 11.5

Starting from A, the first edge is AD, as 4 is the least of 6, 8, 4 and 5.

From D, DE is chosen as 5 is the least of 7, 7 and 5.

This is followed by EB, with weight 6 as the lesser of 6 and 8.

Finally, you are forced to choose BC and CA.

The cycle is ADEBCA, which has weight 28 hours.

The Nearest Neighbour algorithm is 'greedy' because at each stage the immediately best route is chosen, without a look ahead to possible future problems. The next example shows how this greed can sometimes lead to a poor solution.

Example 11.3.2

A warehouse in Toulouse supplies goods to retail outlets in Bordeaux, Calais, Dijon, Lyons, Marseille, Orléans, Poitiers and St-Etienne. The distances (in kilometres) are shown in Fig. 11.6. Use the Nearest Neighbour algorithm, starting and ending at Toulouse, to find a single delivery route to all the towns.

Bordeaux								
870	Calais							
641	543	Dijon						
550	751	192	Lyons					
649	1067	507	316	Marseille				
457	421	297	445	761	Orléans			
247	625	515	431	733	212	Poitiers		
519	803	244	59	309	392	421	St-Etienne	
244	996	726	535	405	582	435	528	Toulouse

Fig. 11.6

The solution is

Toulouse $\xrightarrow{244}$ Bordeaux $\xrightarrow{247}$ Poitiers $\xrightarrow{212}$ Orléans $\xrightarrow{297}$ Dijon

$\Big\downarrow 192$

Toulouse $\xleftarrow{996}$ Calais $\xleftarrow{1067}$ Marseille $\xleftarrow{309}$ St-Etienne $\xleftarrow{59}$ Lyons

You should notice that because it was greedy early on, the algorithm has had to include two extremely large distances at the end. A glance at a map of France shows that Calais should have been included somewhere near the Poitiers–Orléans–Dijon stretch of the tour. Sometimes, a different choice of initial vertex avoids this type of problem (see Exercise 11A Question 3).

Another possible problem with the Nearest Neighbour algorithm is that it may lead to an incomplete tour, as you will see in the next example.

Example 11.3.3

A holidaymaker on Guernsey hires a bicycle at St Peter Port and wants to complete a tour of the nine places marked on the map of Fig. 11.7. What happens if the Nearest Neighbour algorithm is applied, starting at St Peter Port?

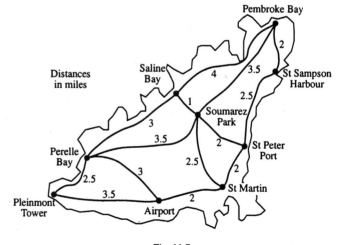

Fig. 11.7

Depending upon the first choice of edge from St Peter Port, the algorithm starts by giving either

> St Peter Port–Soumarez Park–Saline Bay–...

or

> St Peter Port–St Martin–Airport–Perelle Bay–... .

In both cases, you have crossed from one side of the island to the other. If you now go south, you cannot complete the tour by visiting the places in the north without re-visiting one of the places on the route which crosses the island. Similarly, if you go north, you also have to re-visit one of the places on the route which crosses the island to get to the south of the island.

In conclusion, you should treat the Nearest Neighbour algorithm as only a rough and ready attempt to obtain a good tour. Do not worry about the fact that it does not always lead to a good solution.

Exercise 11A

1 (a) Write down all the Hamiltonian paths starting from A in the graph.

  (b) Which of these paths can be made into a Hamiltonian cycle by simply adding the vertex A to the end of the path?

2 (a) List the Hamiltonian paths for the graph in Fig. 11.3. Which is the shortest?

  (b) List the three possible Hamiltonian cycles for the graph in Fig. 11.3.

  (c) What route should the salesperson take for the graph in Fig. 11.2?

3 Apply the Nearest Neighbour algorithm to Example 11.3.2, but this time starting from Calais.

4 Delete the road from Perelle Bay to the Airport on the map given in Fig. 11.7. Show how the Nearest Neighbour algorithm, starting at Pembroke Bay, can now lead to a Hamiltonian cycle for this graph. What is its length?

5 A delivery firm's costs (in £) for travelling between five towns are as shown in the table.

	A	B	C	D	E
A	–	60	50	40	70
B	60	–	90	–	80
C	50	90	–	80	–
D	40	–	80	–	90
E	70	80	–	90	–

  (a) Find the cost for a round trip through all the towns by using the Nearest Neighbour algorithm starting from A.

  (b) Find an improved route by using the Nearest Neighbour algorithm starting from a different town.

  (c) From which town does the Nearest Neighbour algorithm not work?

11.4 A lower bound

You have seen that even when the Nearest Neighbour algorithm does lead to a Hamiltonian cycle, this may well not have the minimum possible weight. How, therefore, do you know whether a cycle that you have found is close to being the best possible, or whether you should continue searching for a much better one? Fortunately, there is a clever method for showing that there is a limit to how low the total weight of a Hamiltonian cycle can be.

In Example 11.3.1, a Hamiltonian cycle of total weight 28 was found for the graph shown in Fig. 11.8. Consider this Hamiltonian cycle as drawn in Fig. 11.9.

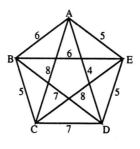

Fig. 11.8

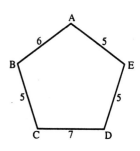

Fig. 11.9

You should be able to see that *any* Hamiltonian cycle for the original graph will consist of

- two edges from vertex A, and
- three edges linking the vertices B, C, D and E.

Note that the two edges from vertex A must have a total weight at least $4+5$ (taking the two smallest weights of edges incident at A). Furthermore, by applying Prim's algorithm to the graph on just the vertices B, C, D and E, you can see that the three edges linking the vertices B, C, D and E must have total weight at least $5+5+6$ (the weight of a minimum spanning tree for B, C, D and E).

So it is *impossible* for any Hamiltonian cycle to have total weight less than $4+5+5+5+6 = 25$.

You now know that the minimum possible weight for a Hamiltonian cycle for this graph lies between 25 hours and the value found in Example 11.3.1, 28 hours.

The upper bound of 28 hours was found by simply finding a tour with that weight. The lower bound of 25 hours was found by considering the edges linking B, C, D and E separately from the edges incident at A.

Either by finding a different cycle or by splitting the graph up differently, or both, it may be possible to further 'improve' these bounds. That is, it may be possible to narrow the range within which the weight of the minimum Hamiltonian cycle must lie.

The method for finding a lower bound can be described in general as an algorithm.

> **The Lower Bound algorithm**
>
> **Step 1**   Choose an arbitrary vertex, say X. Find the total of the two smallest weights of edges incident at X.
>
> **Step 2**   Consider the graph obtained by ignoring X and all edges incident to X. Find the total weight of the minimum spanning tree for this graph .
>
> **Step 3**   The sum of the two totals is a lower bound.

Example 11.4.1

Consider the graph shown in Fig. 11.8.

(a) Apply the Nearest Neighbour algorithm starting from B.

(b) Apply the Lower Bound algorithm with C as the starting vertex.

(c) What can you say about the minimum weight Hamiltonian cycle?

(a) The algorithm gives $B \xrightarrow{5} C \xrightarrow{7} D \xrightarrow{4} A \xrightarrow{5} E \xrightarrow{6} B$, with weight 27.

(b) For C, the sum of the two smallest edges is $5 + 7 = 12$. For the remainder, the minimum spanning tree has weight $4 + 5 + 6 = 15$.

The total is therefore $12 + 15 = 27$.

(c) The solutions to (a) and (b) show that $27 \le$ minimum weight ≤ 27. So in this case the Nearest Neighbour algorithm has found the Hamiltonian cycle of minimum weight.

11.5 Tour improvement

In cases where there is a large gap between the upper and lower bounds for a tour, it may be worth trying to improve the best tour obtained so far, rather than looking for a completely different tour. A number of algorithms have been developed to attempt this improvement. In this section you will learn to use one of them.

Consider, for example, the graph shown in Fig. 11.10 with the weight on each edge being the distance on the page between the two points.

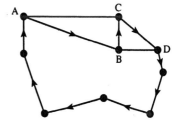

Fig. 11.10

Applying the Nearest Neighbour algorithm from the vertex B would lead to the tour shown in Fig. 11.10. However, the part of the tour ABCD can be replaced by ACBD. This gives a reduction in distance, because

$$d(A,C) + d(B,D) < d(A,B) + d(C,D),$$

where $d(V,W)$ means the weight of the edge between vertices V and W.

You can use this idea as the basis for a general attempt to improve tours. Let V_1, V_2, ... , V_n be the successive vertices of a Hamiltonian cycle, and let $V_{n+1} = V_1$, $V_{n+2} = V_2$ and $V_{n+3} = V_3$.

> **Tour Improvement algorithm**
>
> **Step 1**   Let $i = 1$.
>
> **Step 2**   If $d(V_i, V_{i+2}) + d(V_{i+1}, V_{i+3}) < d(V_i, V_{i+1}) + d(V_{i+2}, V_{i+3})$, then swap V_{i+1} and V_{i+2}.
>
> **Step 3**   Replace i by $i + 1$.
>
> **Step 4**   If $i \le n$ then go back to Step 2.

To apply an algorithm such as this one to a large tour may be time-consuming. However, it can easily be programmed for a computer.

When using a computer program to improve tours it can be useful to start with an initial tour, even a very inefficient one. One possibility is to travel along each edge of a minimum spanning tree twice, as in the next example. Note that this will give you a walk that starts and ends at the same vertex but not a cycle; a Hamiltonian cycle can then be obtained by finding shortcuts.

Example 11.5.1
Consider the graph in Fig. 11.11, which is a copy of Fig. 11.1.

(a) Find a minimum spanning tree, and hence find a walk containing all the vertices, starting and ending at the same vertex with total weight twice that of the minimum spanning tree.

(b) Obtain a Hamiltonian cycle by finding shortcuts, and then apply the Tour Improvement algorithm to obtain a cycle of weight 16.

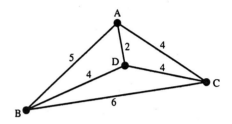

Fig. 11.11

(a)   Fig. 11.12 shows a minimum spanning tree, and Fig. 11.13 shows a walk ADCDBDA whose weight is twice that of the minimum spanning tree.

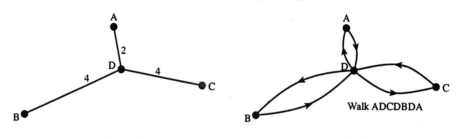

Fig. 11.12   Fig. 11.13

(b)   The walk can be reduced by going from A to C directly instead of via D, and by going from B to A directly instead of via D. This gives the Hamiltonian cycle ACDBA, which has weight 17.

When you do Step 2 of the Tour Improvement algorithm on this cycle with $i = 2$, you find that

$$\text{weight(CB)} + \text{weight(DA)} = 6 + 2 = 8,$$

whereas

$$\text{weight(CD)} + \text{weight(BA)} = 4 + 5 = 9.$$

So swap D and B. This gives the better Hamiltonian cycle ACBDA, with weight 16.

Exercise 11B

1 Consider the travelling salesperson problem for the graph in the diagram.

(a) Apply the Lower Bound algorithm with A, B, C or D as the starting vertex. What do you notice?

(b) Apply the Lower Bound algorithm with E as the starting vertex.

(c) Explain why the bound of part (b) cannot be attained.

(d) What is the optimum solution?

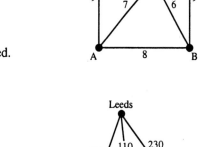

2 The distances shown on the graph are in kilometres.

(a) Apply the Nearest Neighbour algorithm from Birmingham.

(b) Improve the tour of part (a) by using the Tour Improvement algorithm.

(c) Apply the Lower Bound algorithm with Leeds as the starting vertex. What can you now say about the optimum solution to the travelling salesperson problem for this graph?

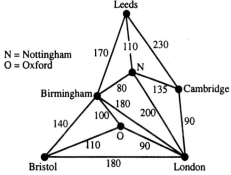

3 A firm uses certain specified routes between cities for its deliveries. The distances between cities in the table are in miles.

	Bi	Br	Ld	Le	Li	Lo	M	N	Sh	So
Birmingham	–	138	–	68	157	190	–	95	–	–
Bristol	138	–	–	–	–	193	–	–	–	122
Leeds	–	–	–	–	115	–	67	–	54	–
Leicester	68	–	–	–	–	150	–	40	–	–
Liverpool	157	–	115	–	–	–	61	173	–	–
London	190	193	–	150	–	–	–	–	–	123
Manchester	–	–	67	–	61	–	–	100	61	–
Nottingham	95	–	–	40	173	–	100	–	72	–
Sheffield	–	–	54	–	–	–	61	72	–	–
Southampton	–	122	–	–	–	123	–	–	–	–

(a) Apply the Nearest Neighbour algorithm starting from Leicester.

(b) Find the weight of a minimum spanning tree for the graph with Southampton deleted.

(c) Make a deduction about the optimum solution to the travelling salesperson problem.

4 Draw three simple graphs, with Hamiltonian paths, such that the optimum solutions to the travelling salesperson problem have weights

(a) less than twice,   (b) exactly twice,   (c) more than twice

the weight of the minimum spanning tree.

5 A ring main consists of cable running from the electricity meter M to five double sockets in turn and then back to the meter. The estimated cost in £ of each possible stretch of cable is as shown in the table.

	M	A	B	C	D	E
M	–	13	14	13	16	12
A	13	–	12	–	–	11
B	14	12	–	16	–	–
C	13	–	16	–	14	–
D	16	–	–	14	–	13
E	12	11	–	–	13	–

(a) Apply the Nearest Neighbour algorithm from M, then A, and finally E.

(b) Apply the Lower Bound algorithm from M. What can you deduce about the least cost of laying the ring main cable?

(c) Fitting each double socket costs £25. What effect does this have on the optimum path for laying the cable?

6 A modification of the Nearest Neighbour algorithm for use with the *practical* travelling salesperson problem is as follows.

Step 1   Choose any starting vertex.

Step 2   Choose a vertex which is at a minimal distance from the previously chosen vertex.

Step 3   Repeat Step 2 until all vertices have been chosen.

Apply this algorithm to Question 5(a), starting from A. What is the total cost

7 An assembly line is used to produce five items, A, B, C, D and E. The times (in minutes) needed for each possible changeover are shown in the table.

	To A	B	C	D	E
From A	–	30	50	70	40
B	20	–	30	80	50
C	60	50	–	20	30
D	40	70	40	–	40
E	80	20	30	40	–

All five items need to be produced, and the assembly line must be returned to its initial state. The factory manager wishes to minimise the changeover time.

(a) What is the result of applying the Nearest Neighbour algorithm from A?

(b) Apply the Lower Bound algorithm with A as the starting vertex.

(c) Improve the upper bound of part (a).

8 Find a Hamiltonian cycle in this graph of the dodecahedron. (This was the problem initially considered by Hamilton.)

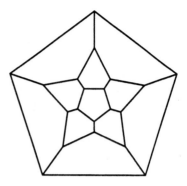

9 Pirate Pete is hunting for buried treasure. He knows that the treasure is buried at one of the places marked on his map, shown in the figure, but he cannot solve the clues to find out where he should dig.

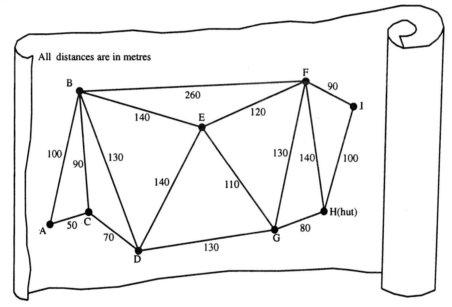

Pirate Pete decides to dig at each of the places marked on his map.

(a) Demonstrate, clearly, the use of a greedy algorithm, starting from the hut, H, to construct a minimum spanning tree for the graph.

(b) Explain, briefly, why twice the length of the minimum spanning tree gives an upper bound to the length of the route which is the solution to the travelling salesperson problem for the graph.

(c) Write down a route that gives a better upper bound than that found in part (b), and state the length of this route.

(OCR)

Review exercise

1 The diagram shows a set of holes drilled
   through a printed circuit board which has a
   1 cm grid drawn on it. These need to be joined
   together using the shortest possible length of
   conductor. The conductor can only be laid
   parallel to the sides of the printed circuit board.

   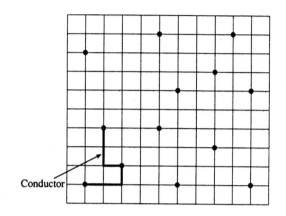

   (a) Find the least possible length of
        conductor, given that two lengths of
        conductor may only meet at the drilled
        holes; that is, no new vertices can be
        created. (Part of the conductor is shown
        drawn in.)

   (b) By how much can the length of conductor be reduced if new vertices may be created?

2 Calculate the remainder when 6543^{4567} is divided by 19.

3 Use an appropriate algorithm to find a path of
   least weight from A to B in the graph shown. To
   demonstrate your application of the algorithm,
   show all temporary labels.

   Give the least weight path and its total weight.

   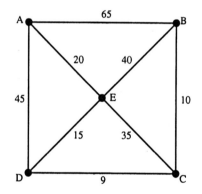

4 (a) For a connected graph with n vertices, state the number of edges in a minimum spanning tree.

   The following table shows the distances, in miles, between six towns.

	A	B	C	D	E	F
A	–	11	19	15	16	22
B	11	–	21	8	12	9
C	19	21	–	15	13	14
D	15	8	15	–	21	11
E	16	12	13	21	–	14
F	22	9	14	11	14	–

   (b) Use an algorithm to find the minimum spanning tree and its length. Show your working in full,
        and draw the spanning tree. State the order in which edges are chosen.

5 A company has offices in six towns. The costs, in £, of travelling between these towns are shown in the table below.

	A	B	C	D	E	F
A	–	15	26	13	14	25
B	15	–	16	16	25	13
C	26	16	–	38	16	15
D	13	16	38	–	15	19
E	14	25	16	15	–	14
F	25	13	15	19	14	–

(a) Use Prim's algorithm, starting from A, to find the cheapest way of visiting the six towns. You should indicate the order in which the towns were included.

The travel times, in minutes, between the six towns are given in the table below.

	A	B	C	D	E	F
A	–	20	30	20	10	30
B	20	–	20	30	20	10
C	30	20	–	30	30	30
D	20	30	30	–	10	30
E	10	20	30	10	–	10
F	30	10	30	30	10	–

(b) The company wants it to be possible to travel from any town to any other town in under an hour. Show that this is not possible if they just use the edges from the solution to part (a).

(c) Construct the minimum spanning tree for the travel times. Work out how much it would cost to travel from A to C, using just these edges, and how long it would take.   (OCR)

6 (a) The Fibonacci sequence $u_1, u_2, \ldots u_n, \ldots$ is defined inductively by $u_1 = 1$, $u_2 = 1$ and $u_{n+2} = u_{n+1} + u_n$ for $n \geq 1$. Calculate the value of u_7.

(b) Prove by induction that, if n is even, $u_{n+2}u_{n-1} - u_{n+1}u_n = 1$ and that if n is odd $u_{n+2}u_{n-1} - u_{n+1}u_n = -1$. Deduce that the gcd of two consecutive numbers in the Fibonacci sequence is 1.

7 Use the Euclidean algorithm to prove that if $a \mid m$ and $b \mid m$ and $\gcd(a,b) = 1$, then $ab \mid m$.

8 Solve the linear congruences

(a) $47x \equiv 31 \pmod{53}$,   (b) $31x \equiv 47 \pmod{53}$.

9 Find the solutions to the simultaneous congruences

(a) $x \equiv 7 \pmod{15}$ and $x \equiv 23 \pmod{29}$,

(b) $x \equiv 2 \pmod{7}$, $2x \equiv 5 \pmod{9}$ and $x = 9 \pmod{13}$.

10 Dina Mite has set up a fireworks display involving eight different fireworks, A, B, ... , H. She had wanted to ignite the eight fireworks simultaneously. However, due to a lack of fuse wire, she has to sprint from one firework to another until she has ignited all eight, and then sprint back to safety.

It takes Dina 10 seconds to sprint from safety to any one of the fireworks, or to sprint from a firework back to safety. It takes her 2 seconds to ignite each firework, and the times in seconds taken to sprint between the fireworks are given in the table.

	A	B	C	D	E	F	G	H
A	–	2	9	7	9	6	9	6
B	2	–	8	5	8	5	8	4
C	9	8	–	2	5	6	8	8
D	7	5	2	–	4	5	6	2
E	9	8	5	4	–	3	4	6
F	6	5	6	5	3	–	3	5
G	9	8	8	6	4	3	–	5
H	6	4	8	2	6	5	5	–

(a)   Use Prim's algorithm, starting from A, to find the minimum spanning tree for the eight fireworks. Draw a diagram showing the minimum spanning tree, and write down its total length, T..

Let θ be the time that it takes Dina to get from safety, to ignite all eight fireworks and return to safety.

(b)   Explain why $\theta \geq 36 + T$.

(c)   Explain why $\theta \leq 36 + 2T$.

Dina has 45 seconds from when she has ignited the first firework to when she reaches safety.

(d)   Find a route that enables Dina to ignite all eight fireworks and get back to safety in time.

(OCR)

11 (a)   The number $a_5 a_4 a_3 a_2 a_1 a_0$ in base n is written in the form $b_2 b_1 b_0$ in the base n^2. Find b_0, b_1 and b_2 in terms of $a_0, a_1, \ldots, a_5$.

(b)   Genaralise your answer to the case when the number $a_5 a_4 a_3 a_2 a_1 a_0$ is written in base n^3 as $c_1 c_0$.

(c)   Convert the number $101\,011_2$ to base 8, and calculate the square of your result in base 8.

(d)   Convert your answer to base 2.

12 (a)   Prove that if the numbers $a_k a_{k-1} \ldots a_1 a_0$ and $b_k b_{k-1} \ldots b_1 b_0$ in base n are equal, where $0 \leq a_i < n$ and $0 \leq b_i < n$ for $0 \leq i < k$, then $a_i = b_i$ for $0 \leq i < k$.

(b)   Change the number 2890 in base 10 to base 16, using the symbols A, B, ... , F for 10, 11, ... 15, and then subtract $A6C_{16}$ from it, leaving your answer in base 16.

13 The distances, in kilometres, between four towns are as shown.

	A	B	C	D
A	–	110	90	70
B	110	–	80	90
C	90	80	–	60
D	70	90	60	–

(a) Use Prim's algorithm, starting from A, to find the length of the minimum spanning tree for the four towns. Show all your working clearly and draw the minimum spanning tree. State the order in which edges are chosen.

A politician's constituency, H, is at distances 80, 90, 50 and 70 km from A, B, C and D respectively. The politician has to start from H and visit each town before returning to H.

(b) Apply the Nearest Neighbour algorithm from H to find a solution to this travelling salesperson problem.

(c) Find an improvement upon the solution of part (b) and explain why your new solution is an upper bound for the optimal solution.

(d) Use your answer to part (a) to find a lower bound for the optimal solution. Explain your answer.

14 Say whether each of the following is true or false and justify your answers.

(a) The complement of a bipartite graph can be connected.

(b) The complement of a complete bipartite graph is disconnected.

(c) The complement of a disconnected graph is a complete bipartite graph.

15 (a) Prove that, in a simple graph, at least two vertices have the same degree.

(b) Prove Euler's relation about the numbers of vertices, regions and edges of a connected planar graph.

(c) Use Euler's relation to show that it is not possible for the degree of every vertex to be 6 or greater.

Examination questions

1 The following diagram shows a weighted graph.

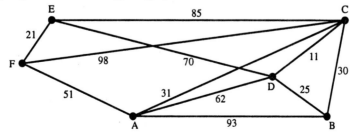

(a) Use Kruskal's algorithm to find a minimal spanning tree for the graph.

(b) Draw the minimal spanning tree and find its weight.   (© IBO 2004)

2 (a) Define the following terms.

   (i) A bipartite graph.

   (ii) An isomorphism between two graphs, M and N.

 (b) Prove that an isomorphism between two graphs maps a cycle of one graph into a cycle of the other graph.

 (c) The graphs G, H and J are drawn below.

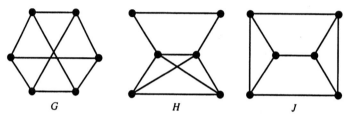

   (i) Giving a reason, determine whether or not G is a bipartite graph.

   (ii) Giving a reason, determine whether or not there exists an isomorphism between graphs G and H.

   (iii) Using the result in part (b), or otherwise, determine whether or not graph H is isomorphic to graph J.

   (© IBO 2004)

3 (a) Define the isomorphism of two graphs G and H.

 (b) Determine whether the two graphs G and H are isomorphic. Give a reason for your answer.

 (c) Find an Eulerian trail for the graph G starting with vertex B.

 (d) State a result which shows that the graph H has an Eulerian circuit.

   (© IBO 2002)

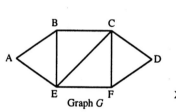

Graph G

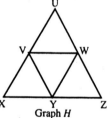

Graph H

4 The diagram below shows a weighted graph.

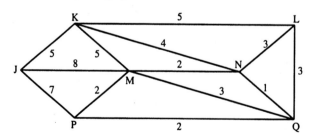

Use Prim's algorithm to find a minimal spanning tree, starting at J. Draw the tree, and find its total weight.

   (© IBO 2002)

5 (a)   Using Euclid's algorithm, find integers x and y such that $17x + 31y = 1$.

(b)   Given that $17p + 31q = 1$, where $p, q \in \mathbb{Z}$ show that $|p| \geq 11$ and $|q| \geq 6$.   (© IBO 2003)

6 Consider the following matrix M.

$$
\begin{array}{cc}
 & \begin{array}{ccccc} A & B & C & D & E \end{array} \\
\begin{array}{c} A \\ B \\ C \\ D \\ E \end{array} &
\begin{pmatrix}
0 & 1 & 1 & 1 & 1 \\
1 & 0 & 0 & 2 & 1 \\
1 & 0 & 0 & 2 & 1 \\
1 & 2 & 2 & 0 & 1 \\
1 & 1 & 1 & 1 & 0
\end{pmatrix}
\end{array}
$$

(a)   Draw a planar graph G with 5 vertices A, B, C, D, E such that M is its adjacency matrix.

(b)   Give a reason why G has an Eulerian circuit.

(c)   Find an Eulerian circuit for G.

(d)   Find a spanning tree for G.   (© IBO 2003)

7 (a)   Explain how to use Euclid's algorithm to obtain the greatest common divisor (gcd) of two positive integers a, b with $b < a$.

(b)   Let d be the gcd of 364 and 154. Use Euclid's algorithm to find d, and hence find integers x and y such that $d = 364x + 154y$.   (© IBO 2002)

8 The floor plan of a certain building is shown below. There are four rooms A, B, C, D and doorways are indicated between the rooms and to the exterior O.

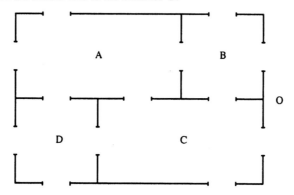

(a)   Draw a graph by associating a vertex with each room using the letters A, B, C, D, and O. If there is a door between the two rooms, draw an edge joining the corresponding two vertices.

(b)   Does the graph in part (a) possess an Eulerian trail? Give a reason for your answer. What does your answer mean about the floor plan?

(c)   Does the graph in part (a) possess a Hamiltonian cycle? Give a reason for your answer. What does your answer mean about the floor plan?   (© IBO 2002)

9 (a)   If k, $(0 \leq k < 8)$ is a solution of the congruence $5x \equiv 3 \pmod 8$ find the value of k.

(b)   Show that all solutions of $5x \equiv 3 \pmod 8$ are congruent to k.   (© IBO 2003)

10 Let p, q and $r \in \mathbb{Z}^+$ with p and q relatively prime.

Show that $r \equiv p \pmod{q}$ *and* $r \equiv q \pmod{p}$ if and only if $r \equiv p + q \pmod{pq}$.

(© IBO 2004)

11 The following diagram shows a weighted graph.

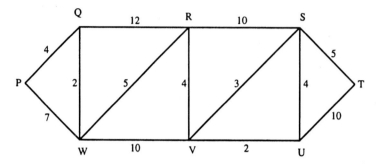

Use Dijkstra's algorithm to find the length of the shortest path between the vertices P and T. Show all the steps used by the algorithm and write down the shortest path.   (© IBO 2005)

Answers

1 Integers

Exercise 1A (page 5)

1. (a) 6   (b) 239   (c) 488
   (d) 134   (e) 383   (f) 0

Exercise 1B (page 11)

1. (a) 4   (b) 3   (c) 1
   (d) 35   (e) 33   (f) 137

2. (a) $7, \; 7 = 77 - 2 \times 35$
   (b) $87, \; 87 = 0 \times 261 + 1 \times 87$
   (c) $1, \; 1 = 34 \times 55 - 21 \times 89$
   (d) $213, \; 213 = 8 \times 2343 - 3 \times 6177$
   (e) $29, \; 29 = 65 \times 9947 - 142 \times 4553$
   (f) $83, \; 83 = 151 \times 75\,281 - 303 \times 37\,516$

3. All three pairs are relatively prime.
   (a) $1 = -213 \times 317 + 91 \times 742$
   (b) $1 = -659 \times 1261 + 600 \times 1385$
   (c) $1 = 841 \times 12\,389 - 188 \times 55\,421$

Exercise 1C (page 18)

1. (a) 234   (b) 37 444   (c) 1768
   (d) 729   (e) 158 025   (f) 165 935

2 Linear diophantine equations

Exercise 2 (page 23)

1. (a) $x = 2 + 3n, \; y = -1 - 2n, \; n \in \mathbb{Z}$
   (b) $x = 3 + 7n, \; y = 2 + 5n, \; n \in \mathbb{Z}$
   (c) $x = -2 + 9n, \; y = -3 + 13n, \; n \in \mathbb{Z}$
   (d) $x = -20 + 121n, \; y = -41 + 248n, \; n \in \mathbb{Z}$
   (e) $x = 6 + 23n, \; y = 409 + 1568n, \; n \in \mathbb{Z}$
   (f) $x = -7 + 113n, \; y = 22 - 355n, \; n \in \mathbb{Z}$

2. (a) $x = 8 + 3n, \; y = -4 - 2n, \; n \in \mathbb{Z}$
   (b) $x = 9 + 7n, \; y = 6 + 5n, \; n \in \mathbb{Z}$
   (c) $x = -4 + 9n, \; y = -6 + 13n, \; n \in \mathbb{Z}$
   (d) $x = 20 + 121n, \; y = 41 + 248n, \; n \in \mathbb{Z}$
   (e) $x = 18 + 23n, \; y = 1227 + 1568n, \; n \in \mathbb{Z}$
   (f) $x = 14 + 113n, \; y = -44 - 355n, \; n \in \mathbb{Z}$

3. (a) $x = 6 + 3n, \; y = -6 - 2n, \; n \in \mathbb{Z}$
   (b) $x = 33 + 7n, \; y = -22 - 5n, \; n \in \mathbb{Z}$
   (c) No solution
   (d) $x = 19 + 13n, \; y = -57 - 40n, \; n \in \mathbb{Z}$

(e) $x = 173\,128 + 692n, \; y = 523\,136 + 2091n, \; n \in \mathbb{Z}$

(f) $x = -3808 + 29n, \; y = 2380 + 18n, \; n \in \mathbb{Z}$

4. (a) $(13, 3), (10, 7), (7, 11), (4, 15), (1, 19)$
   (b) $(-3, 6)$
   (c) One solution, $(5, -9)$
   (d) Three solutions: $(118, -55), (147, -69), (176, -83)$

5. 14

3 Modular arithmetic

Exercise 3A (page 29)

1. (a) 10 (b) 4 (c) 4 (d) 8
2. (a) 12 (b) 10 (c) 10
3. 1

Exercise 3B (page 34)

1. (a) 6 (b) 9 (c) 24
2. (a) 29 (b) 65 (c) 47
3. (a) 6 (b) 26 (c) 29
4. (a) 10, 39, 68
   (b) 3, 14, 25
   (c) 2, 11, 20, 29, 38, 47, 56, 65 , 74, 83, 92, 101, 110
5. (a) $x = 4 + 5n, \; y = -6 - 8n, \; n \in \mathbb{Z}$
   (b) $x = 8 - 11n, \; y = -4 + 6n, \; n \in \mathbb{Z}$
   (c) $x = 11 + 13n, \; y = 16 - 21n, \; n \in \mathbb{Z}$

Exercise 3C (page 38)

1. 70
2. (a) 290   (b) 39   (c) 107
   (d) 18   (e) 57   (f) 47
3. 57
4. (a) 367   (b) 426   (c) 44   (d) 827

4 Fermat's little theorem

Exercise 4 (page 44)

2. $x = 26 + 15n, \; y = -12 - 7n, \; n \in \mathbb{Z}$

3 (a) 22
(b) $x = 22 + 37n$, $y = -19 - 32n$, $n \in \mathbb{Z}$

5 Integers in different bases

Exercise 5 (page 52)

1 (a) 167 (b) 709 (c) 5710
(d) 43 981 (e) 85 (f) 83
(g) 2398 (h) 31

2 (a) 236 (b) 110 101 111
(c) 36C (d) 1000
(e) 8581 (f) 1011 010 100
(g) 1001 (h) 1000 000 000 001

3 (a) 75_8 (b) 1334_9
(c) 1887_{15} (d) $11\,000_2$
(e) 27_8 (f) 593_{11}
(g) 4726_9 (h) 1110_2
(i) 272_8 (j) $6A\,00C_{16}$
(k) $301\,631_8$ (l) $11\,100\,001_2$

4 +, +−, +0, ++, +−−, +−0, +−+, +0−, +00, +0+, ++−, ++0, +++

Use weights of 1, 3 and 9. To weigh 2 for example, which is + −, put the 3 in one pan, the 1 in the other and leave out the 9; To weigh 6, which is + − 0, use the 9 in one pan, the 3 in the other and leave out the 1.

6 Graphs

Exercise 6A (page 57)

Your graphs may appear different to those drawn in these answers.

1 (a) (b)

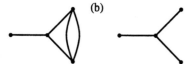

2 $n - 1$

3 (a) T (b) F (c) T (d) F (e) T

4 (a)
A → FS
B → HS
C → CE
D → ME

(b) 2, Brian/David → Home Sec./Chancellor

5 (a), (c) are bipartite.

6 rs

Exercise 6B (page 60)

3 (a) F (b) T (c) T

Exercise 6C (page 64)

1 (a) Eulerian
(b) Not Eulerian or semi -Eulerian
(c) Semi-Eulerian
(d) Eulerian

3 (a) No (b) No

4 Yes. Start or finish in the top left room or the bottom left room.

5 Two towns linked by a motorway and by one or more local roads.

6 (a) For n odd (b) For $n = 1$

7 (a) rs
(b) $K_{r,s}$ is Eulerian if and only if r and s are both even. It is semi-Eulerian either if $r = 1$ and $s = 1$, or if $r = 2$ and s is odd, or if $s = 2$ and r is odd.

7 Isomorphic graphs

Exercise 7A (page 68)

2 If you arrange the vertices in the form of a regular pentagon, and your subgraph of K_5 is the pentagon ABCDE, then the complement is isomorphic to the original graph.

3 These graphs are isomorphic.

4

5 The graphs are not isomorphic.

Exercise 7B (page 75)

1 (a) $\begin{pmatrix} 0 & 1 & 1 & 1 \\ 1 & 0 & 1 & 0 \\ 1 & 1 & 0 & 1 \\ 1 & 0 & 1 & 0 \end{pmatrix}$; 5, 4

(b) $\begin{pmatrix} 0 & 1 & 0 & 2 \\ 1 & 0 & 2 & 1 \\ 0 & 2 & 0 & 1 \\ 2 & 1 & 1 & 0 \end{pmatrix}$; 14, 9

(c) $\begin{pmatrix} 0 & 0 & 0 & 2 \\ 0 & 0 & 2 & 1 \\ 0 & 2 & 0 & 0 \\ 2 & 1 & 0 & 0 \end{pmatrix}$; 0, 0

2 (a) 2; DBC, DCC
(b) 7; CBCC, CBDC, CCBC, CCCC, CCDC, CDBC, CDCC

3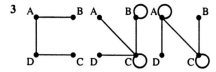

No two are isomorphic.

8 Minimum spanning trees

Exercise 8 (page 83)

1 You should find 16 spanning trees.

2 (a) There are 14 spanning trees.
   (b) The minimum spanning tree contains the edges with weights 27, 28, 31, 36, 43. The weight is 165.
   (c) The order of choice is 43, 27, 31, 28, 36.

3 The cheapest way costs £1500, and consists of the edges HL, ML, LS, and SI.

5 The edges used are two of weight 3, one each of weight 5 and 6, two of weight 7 and one of weight 8. The total weight is 39.

6 (a) Starting from A, the minimum spanning tree consists of the following edges, added in this order: AB, BD, DE, DC, EF. The total cost is £240.
   (b) This has no effect. The total cost of every spanning tree is increased by 10%.
   (c) It is now better to connect C to A, rather than to D. The total cost is £345.

7 (a) AB, BH, BG, AC, CE, CD, AF in that order. Total length 215 km.
   (b)

	A	B	C	D	E	F	G	H
A	–	20	27	50	60	30	24	50
B	20	–	50	60	50	65	30	30
C	27	50	–	30	10	80	80	75
D	50	60	30	–	33	70	85	100
E	60	50	10	33	–	85	75	55
F	30	65	80	70	85	–	70	100
G	24	30	80	85	75	70	–	45
H	50	30	75	100	55	100	45	–

The minimum spanning tree consists of the edges AB, AG, AC, CE, BH, AF, CD and takes 171 minutes.
   (c) The two minimum spanning trees are different. The route of least length connecting G to other points is 30 km from G to B which takes 30 minutes. The connection of shortest time is the motorway route of 40 km from G to A which takes 24 minutes.

8 New York – Washington – Chicago – Dallas – Denver – Los Angeles; 3150 miles

10 (a) The minimum spanning tree is, in order: Paris – Orléans – Tours – Le Mans – Poitiers – Dijon – St-Etienne – Grenoble – Marseilles – Nice. The length is 1574 km.
   (b) The length is increased by only 99 km. Geneva is linked to Grenoble and Dijon, and the Dijon – St-Etienne link is dropped.

9 The shortest path

Questions (page 86)

1 St. Albans – Oxford – Swindon – Bristol, 175 km

2 St. Albans – Slough – Oxford – Cheltenham, 1 hour 39 minutes

3 St. Albans – Slough – Swindon – Bristol, 1 hour 56 minutes

Exercise 9 (page 89)

1 ADFG, length 13. The labels on G are successively 15, 14, 13.

2 ACDGIJ, length 19

3

0	1	2	3	6
7	6	3	4	5
8	5	4	5	6
9	12	11	12	7
10	11	10	9	8

4 ACDF, £40

5 (a)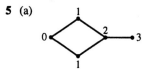

   (b) It finds the minimum number of edges needed to link vertex m to vertex n.
   (c) Moore's algorithm is a special case of Dijkstra's algorithm when all edges have weight 1.

6 (a) AEOD, 110 minutes
   (b) Add 10 to the numbers on each edge at O. ABCD, 120 minutes

7 (a) ACEF, length 9
   (b) ACDF, length 8. D is permanently labelled before ACD is considered.

8 (a) By applying the algorithm from N.
   (b) ADFKN, length 8; BEGIKN, length 8, CEGIKN, length 7. C is nearest.

9 (a) AD costs £35; AE costs £30;
ADC costs £55; AEB costs £85

(b) AB (£90) is now better than AEB (£95).

10 The Chinese postman algorithm

Exercise 10A (page 95)

1 (a) A route containing every road enters each
intersection the same number of times as it
leaves the intersection and therefore
contributes an even number to the degree of
each intersection. Each intersection of odd
degree must therefore be made even by
duplicating some roads.

(b) Total of original roads is 1690 metres.
IH + GC = 340 m; IG + HC = 440 m;
IC + HG = 320 m which is least, so shortest
distance is $(1690 + 320)$ m $= 2010$ m.

(c) All twice, except for E and either B or F
which are passed through three times.

(d) 2010 m; the original route passes
through all the intersections and is therefore
the shortest route for any starting point.

2 (a) (i)

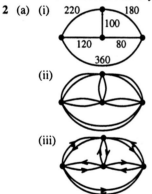

(ii)

(iii)

(b) 1060 m

(c) (i) 1360 m   (ii) 2120 m
(iii) 2120 m

3 Represent rooms by vertices and doorways as
edges. Four edges need to be repeated.

4 (a) The row is 4, $4n - 8$, $(n - 2)^2$.
$2n - 4$ need to be repeated.

(b) $2n - 2$

Exercise 10B (page 96)

1 (a) Cannot be done as it has two odd vertices.
(b) Can be done as all the vertices are even.

2 (a) 25 km is the sum of the lengths of the roads.
(b) The pairings AC, FG give 5 km; AF, CG
give 11 km; AG, CF give 9 km. 5 km is
lowest, so distance is $(25 + 5)$ km $= 30$ km.

3 (a) HBC, length 23; HD, length 16;
HFE, length 24

(b)

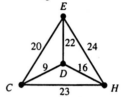

(c) EF, FH, CD; additional weight $24 + 9 = 33$

4 (a) 3770 m   (b) 4520 m

5 Leeds - Sheffield, Nottingham - Birmingham,
Birmingham - Bristol

6 EF and ABC must be repeated.
One path is ABCEFEDFGBDCBA.

11 The travelling salesperson problem

Exercise 11A (page 103)

1 (a) ABCD, ABDC, ACBD, ACDB are
Hamiltonian paths.

(b) ABDCA and ACDBA are Hamiltonian
cycles. (One is the reverse of the other.)

2 (a) ABCD, ABDC, ACBD, ACDB, ADBC,
ADCB; shortest is ADCB = 71.

(b) ABCDA, ABDCA, ACBDA

(c) ADCBDA

3 Calais – Orléans – Poitiers – Bordeaux –
Toulouse – Marseille – St-Etienne – Lyons –
Dijon – Calais; total 2632 km

4 Pembroke Bay – St Sampson Harbour – St Peter
Port – St Martin – Airport – Pleinmont Tower –
Perelle Bay – Saline Bay – Soumarez Park –
Pembroke Bay; total 22 miles

5 (a) £360; ADCBEA
(b) From C or D, the total is £350; CADEBC or
DACBED.
(c) B

Exercise 11B (page 107)

1 (a) In each case the lower bound is 30.
(b) 34
(c) 34 is only possible if the edges have weights
4, 5, 8, 8, 9. But the edges of weight 4 and 5
form a cycle with one of the edges of weight
8.
(d) $4 + 5 + 9 + 8 + 9 = 35$

2 The units are kilometres.
(a) $80 + 110 + 230 + 90 + 90 + 110 + 140 = 850$
(b) $170 + 110 + 135 + 90 + 90 + 110 + 140 = 845$

(c) $(170 + 110)$

$\qquad +(80 + 90 + 90 + 100 + 110) = 750$

$\qquad 750 \leq$ optimum ≤ 845

3 (a) $\left(\begin{array}{l} 40 + 72 + 54 + 67 + \\ 61 + 157 + 138 + \\ 122 + 123 + 150 \end{array}\right)$ miles = 984 miles

   (b) $\left(\begin{array}{l} 40 + 54 + 61 + \\ 61 + 68 + 72 + \\ 138 + 150 \end{array}\right)$ miles = 644 miles

   (c)   The optimum solution has length between $(122 + 123 + 644)$ miles = 889 miles and 984 miles.

4 (a)   For example:

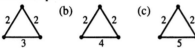

   (b)   (c)

5 (a)   MEABCDM giving a cost of £81;
         AEMCD – not possible;
         EABMCDE giving a cost of £77

   (b) $£(12 + 13) + £(11 + 12 + 13 + 14) = £75$
         $£75 \leq$ cost $\leq £77$

   (c)   No effect on the path. The cost of each possible path will be increased by £125.

6   AEMCD(via M or C)BA ,
     $£(11 + 12 + 13 + 14 + 30 + 12) = £92$

7 (a)   ABCDEA , 200 minutes

   (b)   Smallest pair of in and out edges is
         $B \rightarrow A \rightarrow E$ taking 60 minutes.
         Minimum spanning tree for B, C, D, E is
         $20 + 20 + 30$ minutes.
         Total is 130 minutes.

   (c)   EBCDAE , 150 minutes

8

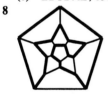

9 (a)   Starting from H, Prim's algorithm chooses, in order, HG, HI, IF, GE, GD, DC, CA, CB. The length of this route is 720 metres.

   (b)   The worst situation occurs when you have to follow the minimum spanning tree out and back to visit all vertices. This, an upper bound, is twice the length of the minimum spanning tree , namely 1440 metres.

   (c)   A better route is HGDCABEFIH, of length 880 metres.

Review exercise

(page 110)

1 (a)   42 cm   (b) By 7 cm to 35 cm

2   7

3   AEDCB, 54

4 (a) $n - 1$

   (b)

   D•

   A •——┼——• C
      B   E
   F•

   53 miles;   BD, BF, AB, BC, CE

5 (a)   The order is AD, AE, EF, FB, FC, with a total cost of £69.

   (b)   The furthest towns on the minimum spanning tree are D and C. The route is DAEFC with a time of 70 minutes, so it is not possible, even with B omitted.

   (c)   The minimum spanning tree is now, in order from A, AE, ED, EF, FB, BC, so the route from A to C is AEFBC with a total time of 50 minutes, and a cost of £57.

6 (a)   13

8 (a)   39   (b) 34

9 (a)   52   (b) 646

10 (a)   The minimum spanning tree is, AB, BH, HD, DC, DE, EF, FG; $T = 20$ seconds.

   (b)   The time to sprint to the fireworks and back, and light all the fireworks is 36 seconds. The route between the first and last firework takes at least T seconds, so $\theta \geq 36 + T$.

   (c)   The route between the first and last firework takes at most $2T$ seconds, so $\theta \leq 36 + 2T$.

   (d)   The route ABHDCEFG takes 21 seconds. She has 7 more fireworks to light, taking 14 seconds and a sprint lasting 10 seconds, total 45 seconds.

11 (a) $b_0 = a_1 n + a_0$, $b_1 = a_3 n + a_2$, $b_2 = a_5 n + a_4$

   (b) $c_0 = a_2 n^2 + a_1 n + a_0$, $c_1 = a_5 n^2 + a_5 n + a_3$

   (c) 53_8, 3471_8

   (d) 11100111001_2

12 (b) $B4A_{16}$, DE_{16}

13 (a) $B \bullet \overset{80}{} \underset{C}{} \overset{60}{} \underset{D}{} \overset{70}{} \bullet A$

         210 km, AD, CD, BC

   (b)   HCDABH, 380 km

   (c)   HADBCH, 370 km

   (d) $50 + 70 + 210 = 330$ km

14 (a)   True   (b) True   (c) False

Examination questions

1 (b) The minimal spanning tree contains the edges CD, DB, CA, AF, FE. Weight 139.

2 (c) (i) It is bipartite, with alternate vertices in different sets.

(ii) They are not isomorphic because the degree of every vertex of *G* is 3, and there are two vertices of *H* of degree 2.

(iii) They are not isomorphic because the degree of every vertex of *J* is 3, and there are two vertices of *H* of degree 2.

3 (b) They are not isomorphic: There are two vertices of degree 2 in *G* and 3 in *H*.

(c) BAEBCEFDCF

(d) There exists an Eulerian circuit if every vertex has even degree.

4 Use edges JK, KN, NQ, QP, PM, QL (or NL) Weight 17.

5 (a) 11, −6

6 (a)

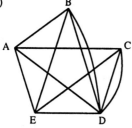

(b) All vertices have even degree.

(c) For example, ABDBEDCDAECA

(d) For example, AB, BD, DC, DE

7 (b) 14; 3, −7

8 (a)

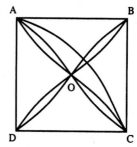

(b) Yes; there are just two vertices, A and C, of odd degree. It means that provided you start at A and finish at C, or vice versa, you can pass through each door precisely once.

(c) Yes; ABOCDA. You can visit each room and the outside, without visiting a room twice.

9 (a) 7

11 23; PQWRVST

Index

The page numbers refer to the first mention of each term, or the shaded box if there is one.

addition in different bases, 49

adjacency matrix, 70

adjacent edges, 54

adjacent vertices, 54

algorithm

    Chinese Postman, 93

    Dijkstra's, 87

    Euclidean, 8

    greedy, 81

    Kruskal's, 82

    Lower Bound, 104

    Nearest Neighbour, 101

    Prim's, 80

    Tour Improvement, 105

base, 45

binary, 45

bipartite graph, 56

Chinese Postman algorithm, 93

Chinese remainder theorem, 37

circuit, 61

common divisor, 6

common multiple, 15

complementary addition, 49

complementary graphs, 68

complete bipartite graph, 56

complete graph, 56

congruence, 31

    simultaneous, 34

congruent modulo m, 25

connected graph, 56

co-prime integers, 8

cost adjacency matrix, 80

cycle, 77

degree, of a vertex, 55

denary, 45

Dijkstra's algorithm, 87

diophantine equation, 19

disconnected graph, 56

divisibility tests, 51

division, 2

division algorithm, 3

edge(s), 54

    weight of, 80

Euclidean algorithm, 8

Eulerian

    circuit, 62

    graph, 63

    trail, 62

Euler's relation, 60

Fermat's Little theorem, 42

fundamental theorem of arithmetic, 12, 17

gcd, 6

general solution, 20

graph, 54

    bipartite, 56

    complementary, 67

    complete, 56

    connected, 56

    disconnected, 56

    Eulerian, 63

    matrix of, 69

    planar, 57

    semi-Eulerian, 63

    simple, 55

    weighted, 80

greatest common divisor, *see* gcd

greedy algorithm, 81

Hamiltonian cycle, 99

Hamiltonian path, 99

int, 4
integer part, 4
isomorphic graphs, 65
isomorphism, 65

Königsberg bridges problem, 61
Kruskal's algorithm, 82

lcm, 15
least common multiple, *see* lcm
linear diophantine equation, 19
    solution of, 20
loop, 55
Lower Bound algorithm, 104

matrix representation of a graph, 69
minimum connector, 80
minimum spanning tree, 80
modular arithmetic, 25
multiple edges, 55
multiplication in different bases, 51

Nearest Neighbour algorithm, 101

octal, 45

particular solution, 20
path, 86
permanent label, 87
planar graph, 57
powers of adjacency matrix, 73
prime, 12
Prim's algorithm, 80

quotient, 2

region of a graph, 58
relatively prime integers, 8
remainder, 3
    using a calculator, 4
route inspection problem, 92

semi-Eulerian graph, 64
shortest path, 86
simple graph, 55
simultaneous congruences, 34
spanning tree, 78
subgraph, 55
subtraction in different bases, 49

Tour Improvement algorithm, 105
trail, 61
travelling salesperson's problem, 99
tree, 77

unique factorisation, 12, 17

vertex (vertices), 54
    degree of, 55

walk, 61
weight, 80
weighted graph, 80
well-ordering principle, 2

Lightning Source UK Ltd.
Milton Keynes UK
177693UK00002B/57/P